The Norton Anthology of Modern and Contemporary Poetry

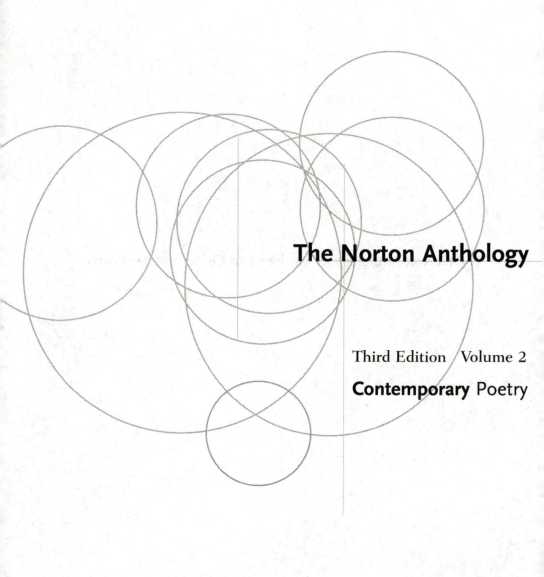

The Norton Anthology

Third Edition Volume 2

Contemporary Poetry

# of Modern and Contemporary Poetry

edited by

Jahan Ramazani
EDGAR F. SHANNON PROFESSOR,
UNIVERSITY OF VIRGINIA

Richard Ellmann
LATE GOLDSMITHS' PROFESSOR EMERITUS,
OXFORD UNIVERSITY

Robert O'Clair
LATE OF MANHATTANVILLE COLLEGE

W · W · **Norton** & Company · New York · London

Editor: Julia Reidhead
Developmental Editor: Kurt Wildermuth
Production Manager: Diane O'Connor
Manuscript Editor: Kate Lovelady
Project Editors: Lory Frenkel, Sarah Chamberlin
Editorial Assistants: Brian Baker, Carey Schwaber
Permissions Manager and Associate: Nancy Rodwan, Margaret Gorenstein
Managing Editor: Marian Johnson
Book Designer: Antonina Krass
Cover Designer: Joan Greenfield
Art Researcher: Ruth Mandel

Library of Congress Cataloging-in-Publication Data

The Norton anthology of modern and contemporary poetry / edited
   by Jahan Ramazani, Richard Ellmann, Robert O'Clair. — 3rd ed.
       p. cm.
       Rev. ed. of: The Norton anthology of modern poetry. 2nd ed.
   New York : Norton, c1988.
       Includes bibliographical references and index.
       Contents: v. 1. Modern poetry — v. 2. Contemporary poetry.

   ISBN 0-393-97791-9 (v. 1 : pbk.) — ISBN 0-393-97792-7 (v. 2 : pbk.)

   1. American poetry—20th century.   2. English poetry—20th
century.   3. American poetry—19th century.   4. English poetry—
19th century.   I. Ramazani, Jahan, 1960–   II. Ellmann, Richard,
1918–   III. O'Clair, Robert.   IV. Norton anthology of modern
poetry.

PS613 .N67 2003
821.008—dc21   2002037990

W. W. Norton & Company, Inc., 500 Fifth Avenue, New York, N.Y. 10110
                        www.wwnorton.com

W. W. Norton & Company Ltd., Castle House, 75/76 Wells Street, London W1T 3QT

4 5 6 7 8 9 0

Contents

CHARLES OLSON (1910–1970)   1

ELIZABETH BISHOP (1911–1979)   15

MAY SWENSON (1913–1989)   45

W. S. MERWIN (b. 1927) 408

JAMES WRIGHT (1927–1980) 414

PHILIP LEVINE (b. 1928) 422

THOMAS KINSELLA (b. 1928) 427

ANNE SEXTON (1928–1974) 431

POETICS

Preface to the Third Edition

Thirty years ago, in their preface to the First Edition, Richard Ellmann and Robert O'Clair set forth this anthology's aims and assumptions: "The most acute rendering of an era's sensibility is its poetry. In the twentieth century, probably in reaction to its horrors, poets have created new and powerful consolidations of the imaginative life. Some writers have accepted the discipline of the literary tradition, others have flouted it. During the last seventy-five [now, over a hundred] years in the English-speaking nations, many poets of consequence have written well in an unprecedented range of styles and subjects. This book aspires to present their best work, and also to delineate the many different tendencies of modern poetry in English."

In revising the anthology created by my predecessors, I have sought to preserve its strong conceptual core, while renewing the text for current use. Two prominent changes signal and respond to recent developments in the field: where the 1973 and 1988 editions were entitled *The Norton Anthology of Modern Poetry,* with this Third Edition, the anthology becomes *The Norton Anthology of Modern and Contemporary Poetry,* and the single volume now becomes two, Volume 1, *Modern Poetry,* and Volume 2, *Contemporary Poetry.* With the close of the twentieth century, it has become increasingly difficult to stretch the term "modern" to encompass all innovative poetry in English since the late nineteenth century, and critics and teachers have recently sharpened the term's more narrow historical use for the literature centered in the early twentieth century. College curricula embody this distinction in courses on poetry variously distinguished as "modern" and "contemporary," "modern" and "postmodern," or "pre–" and "post–World War II." Since the First Edition was published, more poetry-writing courses emphasizing postwar poetic models have also contributed to this shift. Because of the continuities between pre- and postwar poetry—poets, forms, and trends extending across the divide—this anthology still embraces both, but the two periods are made available in separate volumes for teachers and readers who wish to focus on one at a time.

The boundary between "modern" and "contemporary" is inevitably somewhat arbitrary, but poets who came to maturity on either side of World War II have broad generational affinities. Volume 1, *Modern Poetry,* begins with the precursors Walt Whitman, Emily Dickinson, and Gerard Manley Hopkins. At its center are the innovations and consolidations of the first-generation modern poets, from W. B. Yeats and Gertrude Stein to Marianne Moore and T. S. Eliot. The volume ends with the second generation of modern poets—most of them born in the final decade of the nineteenth century and the first of the twentieth—which includes the Fugitives, the Harlem Renaissance poets, the Objectivists, and the Auden circle. (Because Keith

Douglas was killed in World War II, he appears, in an exception to birth order, last in Volume 1.)

Contemporary Poetry opens with two towering presences in contemporary poetry, Charles Olson and Elizabeth Bishop. Born in and around the 1910s and 1920s, the first generation of postwar poets is "contemporary" in that it created many of the paradigms and fomented many of the debates that still inform poetry writing today. This generation and the next, born largely in the 1930s and 1940s, founded a host of new schools and movements in the 1950s and 1960s: in the United States, the Black Mountain school, Beat poetry, confessional poetry, the New York school, Deep Image poetry, and the Black Arts Movement; in Britain, the New Apocalypse and the Movement. Poets of these generations also developed distinctive poetries in the older nations of the British Commonwealth, such as Canada and Australia, and postcolonial poetry in the newer nations of the so-called Third World, such as Jamaica, Nigeria, and India.

Since its first publication, this anthology has presented an international vision of modern and contemporary poetry in English. Confounding national classification, many key poets of the twentieth century led migratory lives, including such modern expatriates as T. S. Eliot (U.S./U.K.), Gertrude Stein (U.S./France), Ezra Pound (U.S./U.K./Italy), H. D. (U.S./U.K./Switzerland), Mina Loy (U.S./U.K.), Claude McKay (Jamaica/U.S./Europe), Laura Riding (U.S./U.K./Spain), and W. H. Auden (U.K./U.S./Europe), and such contemporaries as Denise Levertov (U.K./U.S.), Sylvia Plath (U.S./U.K.), Thom Gunn (U.K./U.S.), A. K. Ramanujan (India/U.S.), Agha Shahid Ali (India/U.S.), and Grace Nichols (Guyana/U.K.). Other poets have lived much of their lives outside their natal countries—W. B. Yeats, Elizabeth Bishop, Gary Snyder, Derek Walcott, Kamau Brathwaite, Seamus Heaney, Paul Muldoon, Eavan Boland, Wole Soyinka, and Lorna Goodison, to mention but a few. Like these transnational lives, literary influence has, especially since the start of the twentieth century, continually crossed national boundaries, so that much modern poetry is transatlantic, and much contemporary poetry is in its bearings global. Not that this anthology aims to give equal representation to every anglophone nation. Produced in the United States, its center of gravity is American. But its selection extends well beyond the borders of the United States, since modern poetry in English is impossible to understand without reading poets such as Thomas Hardy, Gerard Manley Hopkins, W. B. Yeats, D. H. Lawrence, Wilfred Owen, Stevie Smith, and W. H. Auden, as is contemporary poetry without engaging poets such as Dylan Thomas, Philip Larkin, Derek Walcott, Seamus Heaney, Agha Shahid Ali, Les Murray, Eavan Boland, Tony Harrison, Paul Muldoon, Derek Mahon, and Anne Carson.

Reshaping the anthology's selections, I have been guided by some general aims. One priority has been to expand the selections of some of the most influential, most frequently taught poets already in the Second Edition, so that they can be read and studied in greater depth. In *Modern Poetry*, more space has been devoted to selections by Gertrude Stein, Wallace Stevens, Ezra Pound, H. D., Marianne Moore, T. S. Eliot, Claude McKay, Wilfred Owen, Hart Crane, Langston Hughes, W. H. Auden, and Theodore Roethke; in *Contemporary Poetry*, by Charles Olson, Elizabeth Bishop, Robert Hayden, Robert Lowell, Amy Clampitt, Philip Larkin, A. R. Ammons, Allen Ginsberg, Frank O'Hara, John Ashbery, Adrienne Rich, Derek Walcott, Sylvia Plath, Tony Harrison, Seamus Heaney, Louise Glück, Paul Muldoon, and Rita Dove.

Another priority has been to welcome into the anthology what John Ashbery has called an "other tradition"—experimental poetry by modern avant-garde writers, such as Mina Loy and Laura Riding, and the Objectivists Charles Reznikoff, Louis Zukofsky, Lorine Niedecker, and George Oppen, extending to the contemporary avant-garde of Language poetry by Susan Howe, Lyn Hejinian, Michael Palmer, and Charles Bernstein.

I have also tried to represent the accelerated globalization of English-language poetry in the second half of the twentieth century, particularly in the work of postcolonial poets who creatively hybridize indigenous traditions with British and American influences. Along with Walcott and Michael Ondaatje, in the Second Edition, Caribbean poets Louise Bennett, Kamau Brathwaite, Grace Nichols, and Lorna Goodison have been included, as have African poets Christopher Okigbo, Wole Soyinka, and Okot p'Bitek, and Indian poets A. K. Ramanujan, Eunice de Souza, and Agha Shahid Ali.

Another aim has been to add significant longer poems and poetic sequences, including Kipling's "Epitaphs of the War," Yeats's "Nineteen Hundred and Nineteen," Stein's "Sacred Emily," Moore's "An Octopus," Hart Crane's *The Bridge,* Theodore Roethke's "The Lost Son," Robert Hayden's "Middle Passage" and "Elegies for Paradise Valley," Allen Ginsberg's "Howl," Adrienne Rich's *Twenty-One Love Poems,* Derek Walcott's "The Schooner *Flight,*" John Ashbery's "Self-Portrait in a Convex Mirror," Seamus Heaney's "Clearances," Frank Bidart's "Ellen West," Amy Clampitt's "A Procession at Candlemas," Tony Harrison's *v.,* Jorie Graham's "The Dream of the Unified Field," James Merrill's "Self-Portrait in Tyvek(TM) Windbreaker," Richard Howard's " 'Man Who Beat Up Homosexuals Reported to Have AIDS Virus,' " and Susan Howe's "Rückenfigur."

A final, and perhaps obvious, priority has been to present various modern and contemporary poets who have only recently emerged into prominence, including poets of the Harlem Renaissance and African American modernism, such as James Weldon Johnson, Sterling Brown, and Melvin Tolson, and their contemporary inheritors Lucille Clifton, Yusef Komunyakaa, and Thylias Moss; female modern poets such as Amy Lowell, Elinor Wylie, Dorothy Parker, and their contemporary counterparts May Swenson, Mary Oliver, Sharon Olds, Jorie Graham, Anne Carson, and Carol Ann Duffy; poets of ethnic American minorities, such as Joy Harjo, Dionisio D. Martínez, Li-Young Lee, and Sherman Alexie; poets of Ireland and Northern Ireland, such as Michael Longley, Derek Mahon, Eavan Boland, and Medbh McGuckian; poets of gay experience, such as Mark Doty and Henri Cole; poets influenced by European surrealism and East Asian literature, such as Charles Simic, Charles Wright, and Robert Hass; an influential poet of World War I, Ivor Gurney; and an eminent Australian, Les Murray.

My overriding aim has been to gather some of the most influential, imaginative, and aesthetically accomplished modern and contemporary poems. Aesthetic criteria are notoriously impossible to pin down, but this edition's have included—to catalog them baldly—creative daring, figurative reach, verbal dexterity, formal skill, historical responsiveness, social significance, psychological complexity, emotional richness, and the inventive engagement with, and revision of, literary and extraliterary genres and discourses. I have looked for poems that seem not merely representative or illustrative—of trends, schools, or identities—but among the best of their kind. Trying to be as open as possible to advice and suggestion, I have hoped to capture, where possible, something like a current critical consensus, while tentatively outlining some newly emerging areas, such as those mentioned above. But because the canons of modern and especially contemporary poetry are still being formed, such choices must be provisional. Since no anthology can be boundlessly inclusive, additions have meant, inevitably, excisions. A publisher's survey of college teachers, showing which texts were taught least often, provided some guidance in the painful task of removing poets and poems to make space for new texts. The anthology's selections are necessarily constrained by page limits, by permissions fees, and by my taste and the taste of colleagues I have consulted.

In addition to poems, the Third Edition also includes, for the first time, a Poetics section at the end of each volume. Poets' explanatory statements help illuminate poems, schools, and movements, as well as the intellectual and social forces that shaped them. As poetry became more difficult, as poets founded new styles, as groups of poets competed for attention, such statements enjoyed an unprecedented boom, with especially large concentrations accompanying the creative ferment of the 1910s and 1920s and again of the 1950s and 1960s. Some of these documents became manifestos for movements and schools, such as Langston Hughes's "The Negro Artist and the Racial Mountain" for the Harlem Renaissance and Charles Olson's "Projective Verse" for the Black Mountain school. Many have also become standard reference points for poets learning their trade—for example, Ezra Pound's famous series of "don'ts" and the aphorisms of Robert Frost, Wallace Stevens, and W. H. Auden. Some are of great interest in themselves, from the typographic experimentation of *Blast* and of Mina Loy's "Feminist Manifesto" to Derek Walcott's meditation on cross-cultural mixture in the Caribbean. Others include revelatory self-analyses and self-explications, such as the statements by Gerard Manley Hopkins, T. S. Eliot, Hart Crane, Gertrude Stein, Dylan Thomas, Philip Larkin, Adrienne Rich, Allen Ginsberg, and Seamus Heaney. Some echo and revise each other, such as Frank O'Hara's parodic engagement with the multitudinous manifestos of the 1950s and A. K. Ramanujan's indigenization of Eliot's "Tradition and the Individual Talent." Though not every poet has published a poetics, and though theory sometimes aligns imperfectly with practice, these primary materials have become an integral part of the history of modern and contemporary poetry.

Also to help in understanding poems, the anthology's editorial features— period introductions, headnotes, annotations, bibliographies—have been substantially revised. These features are designed to enrich the engagement of readers, students, and teachers with the poems; they are meant to reduce spadework and thus to help focus attention on the vital and creative task of interpreting the poetry. Many headnotes are new, others have been tightened or rewritten in light of recent scholarship and of unfolding poetic careers. They seek to distill each poet's formal and thematic preoccupations, to place each poet in a literary historical context, to encapsulate essential biographical and historical information, and to suggest possible lines of analysis. Attentive to how poets see their own contributions, the headnotes frequently quote poets' letters, interviews, and essays. A general introduction to each volume surveys the interconnected movements and key developments in the poetry of the period. Modern and contemporary poems often demand specialized knowledge, and the annotations are meant to meet this need while being concise and minimally interpretive. The bibliographies have been rewritten from scratch; for the first time, they include entries on movements and schools, and on ethnic, national, and regional poetries.

A final note on the texts: in presenting major modern poets who revised their early work at much later stages of their careers, such as Yeats, Pound, Moore, Hughes, and Auden, the Third Edition often gives preference to early versions or early revisions of their texts, since their historical and literary development is of special interest and is sometimes obscured by their later revisions. Throughout the anthology, the date that appears at the bottom right of a poem is its publication date. When there are two dates at the bottom right, the first is the date of first publication, the second the date of the revision or of the poem's inclusion in a volume of poetry. A date provided on the bottom left of a poem is its composition date.

Acknowledgments

The making of this edition was a collaborative venture from start to finish. My first debt is to the late editors of this anthology, Richard Ellmann and Robert O'Clair, whose generosity of spirit, shrewdness of insight, and breadth of vision live on in this edition's introductions, notes, and selections. As a former student of Ellmann's, I am especially glad for the example of his humane sensibility and of his elegant, wit-brimming prose.

For wise counsel on selections and brilliant advice on editorial apparatus, I have turned repeatedly to scholars elsewhere who have been, in effect, an informal advisory group: Paul Breslin (Northwestern University), Langdon Hammer (Yale University), Henry Hart (College of William and Mary), Nicholas Jenkins (Stanford University), Lucy McDiarmid (Villanova University), Mervyn Morris (University of the West Indies, Jamaica), Michael North (University of California, Los Angeles), Marjorie Perloff (Stanford University), Vincent Sherry (Villanova University), Willard Spiegelman (Southern Methodist University), and Helen Vendler (Harvard University). In this group, Bonnie Costello (Boston University) wrote a marvelously astute commissioned review of the Second Edition, as did Charles Berger (University of Utah), Paul Hoover (Columbia College), and Mark Jeffreys (University of Alabama, Birmingham).

I have also sought and gratefully received incisive help and sage suggestions from Calvin Bedient (University of California, Los Angeles), Harold Bloom (Yale University), George Bornstein (University of Michigan), David Bromwich (Yale University), Reed Way Dasenbrock (New Mexico State University, Las Cruces), Ian Duncan (University of California, Berkeley), Sascha Feinstein (Lycoming College), Oren Izenberg (Harvard University), David Kadlec (Georgetown University), Bruce King (independent scholar), Alan Golding (University of Louisville), Elizabeth Gregory (University of Houston), Christopher MacGowan (College of William and Mary), Douglas Mao (Harvard University), Steven Meyer (Washington University), Paul Morrison (Brandeis University), Charles Pollard (Calvin College), Alison Rieke (University of Cincinnati), Neil Roberts (University of Sheffield), William Rushton (University of Alabama, Birmingham), John Whittier-Ferguson (University of Michigan), and David Wyatt (University of Maryland). Peter Quartermain (University of British Columbia) provided several excellent corrections, and thoughtful advice also came from William Packard (New School for Social Research).

Teachers who patiently filled out a questionnaire that provided sound and precise guidance include Leonard Adame (Butte College), Barry Ahearn (Tulane University), Joel Brouwer (University of Alabama), Luke Carson (University of Victoria), Christopher Collins (New York University), Michael J. Coulombe (University of Wisconsin, La Crosse), Joanne Craig (Bishop's University), Paul J. Dolan (SUNY, Stony Brook), Sharm Dolin (formerly at

Cooper Union), P. E. Firchow (University of Minnesota at Minneapolis), Karen J. Ford (University of Oregon), J. T. French III (Coker College), Philip Furia (University of North Carolina, Wilmington), R. F. Gish (California Polytechnic Institute), Albert G. Glover (St. Lawrence University), Beverly Gross (Queens College), Michael Harris (formerly at Dawson College), Louise Harrison (Boston University), Sarah K. Inman (formerly at New York University), Bill Johnsen (Michigan State University), Anthony Low (New York University), Sara Lundquist (University of Toledo), David Mason (Colorado College), David Middleton (Nicholls State University), Pat Moran (University of Wisconsin, Green Bay), James Persoon (Grand Valley State University), Deborah Sarbin (Clarion University of Pennsylvania), J. D. Scrimgeous (Salem State College), Kenith Simmons (University of Hawaii, Hilo), R. Sullivan (University of Wisconsin, La Crosse), John H. Timmerman (Calvin College), Mary Turnbell (University of Puget Sound), Michael Webster (Grand Valley State University), B. H. Wang (formerly at Florida International University at Miami), Marianne Werner (Butte College), and Don Wood (Langara College).

Also truly helpful in advancing this edition were the respondents to a subsequent, shorter questionnaire, including Bruce Bond (University of North Texas), Samuel Lee Cohen (Bernard Baruch College), Michael Collier (University of Maryland at College Park), Joanne Craig (Bishop's University), Richard K. Cross (University of Maryland at College Park), Anne Herzog (West Chester University), Jonathan Hufstader (University of Connecticut at Storrs), Donald W. Markos (California State University at Hayward), Paul D. McGlynn (Eastern Michigan University), Eliza Richards (Boston University), David St. John (University of Southern California), Dennis Taylor (Boston College), Daniel Thurber (Concordia University), Jonathan Warren (York University), Laura Lee Washburn (Pittsburg State University), and Nancy M. Whitt (Samford University).

Poets who graciously responded to personal queries include the late Agha Shahid Ali, Amiri Baraka, Frank Bidart, Kamau Brathwaite, Rita Dove, Carolyn Forché, Lorna Goodison, Robert Hass, Seamus Heaney, John Hollander, Susan Howe, the late Kenneth Koch, Yusef Komunyakaa, Paul Muldoon, Robert Pinsky, and Charles Wright.

Though not granted for this purpose, fellowships from the John Simon Guggenheim Memorial Foundation and the Virginia Foundation for the Humanities helped get this edition off the ground while I was completing another book. At the Virginia Foundation for the Humanities, Robert Vaughan, Roberta Culbertson, Andrew Wyndham, and Kevin McFadden provided kind encouragement, as did my colleagues in residence Jean Maria Arrigo, Paul Harvey, Anne Goodwyn Jones, Ralph Luker, and Carlos Pereda. I am also grateful for the support of the Richard A. and Sarah Page Mayo NEH Distinguished Teaching Professorship at the University of Virginia.

For their unstinting readiness to furnish much-needed assistance and to share immense reserves of knowledge and insight, I thank the colleagues at the University of Virginia I frequently imposed on, including Stephen Cushman, Victor Luftig, Jerome McGann, Raymond Nelson, Marlon Ross, and Herbert Tucker, and I thank Marva Barnett, Alison Booth, Daniel Ehnbom, Jessica Feldman, David Gies, Jeffrey Grossman, Robert Hueckstedt, Dell Hymes, Michael Levenson, Eric Lott, Debra Nystrom, Peter Onuf, Gregory Orr, Lisa Russ-Spaar, and Patricia Spacks. Librarians at special collections, reference, interlibrary loan, and library express have been forthcoming and efficient; Gary Treadway and Bryson Clevenger kindly answered numerous queries, and Karen Marshall speedily acquired needed volumes. At ITC, Nancy Hopkins designed a most useful spreadsheet. Students in my classes on modern and contemporary poetry have motivated and schooled me. I heartily thank the graduate assistants I worked with, whether for a few hours or much longer: at various early stages, James Parr, Joy Asekun, Kevin Seidel, and Nicole Gharda gathered criticism, texts, and page tallies; in the last stretch, Lauryl Hicks, Kate Nash, and Hallie Smith helped greatly with proofreading and with demanding research; and for over a year, Brian Glavey labored with diligence and keen intelligence to help draft many annotations and compile the bibliographies.

At Norton, Julia Reidhead has been a tremendously energetic and inspiring collaborator. I feel especially fortunate to have worked closely and intensively with her and with Kurt Wildermuth, who edited at a brisk pace while remaining always meticulous and sensitive. For scrupulous copyediting of standing editorial materials, I thank Kate Lovelady; for equally scrupulous work on proofs, I thank Lory Frenkel and Sarah Chamberlin. Marian Johnson and Diane O'Connor kept a close watch on a tight schedule. Nancy Rodwan and Margaret Gorenstein were great allies in permissions, even through some painful cuts. Toni Krass brought elegance to the task of book design. And Brian Baker and Carey Schwaber were efficient and helpful points of contact.

My last and best thanks go to my ever-sustaining parents, Nesta and Ruhi; to my dear children, Cyrus and Gabriel, whose early-morning laughter and end-of-day exuberance renewed me; and to Caroline Rody, who has been wondrously responsive and indefatigably supportive, especially through the last challenging year of this project.

Introduction

The poetry of our own time is characterized by its plural-
ism, by its welter and crosscurrents. No longer can any single
group or individual claim centrality, since contemporary poets in English
have proliferated a vast array of idioms, forms, and movements. They have
sometimes competed noisily, at other times forged surprising alliances across
boundaries of ethnicity, nationality, and aesthetics. They have offered irrec-
oncilable visions of what it means to be contemporary, have deployed many
different kinds of English, and have drawn on their unique historical and
geographic experiences. But while listening to their own muses, they have
also heard one another's voices in the raucous babel of the contemporary—
the transnational literary village after World War II.

This volume's point of departure is the generation of poets who published
their first books largely after World War II, since poetry today grows out of
the debates, innovations, and consolidations of this first postwar generation
(roughly, born in the 1910s and 1920s) and the second (born in and around
the 1930s and 1940s). Some of these immediately postwar poets are still
active; others wrote poems that can be still considered "contemporary"
because vitally present as models and antagonists for emerging poets. Even
though World War II did not completely divide the poetry written before it
from that written after, it is a useful historical marker for the period's begin-
nings. Other events and trends were also formative for poets born after
1910—the Great Depression, the political polarization of the 1930s, the
increasing economic and political might of the United States, the cold war,
the weakening and eventual disintegration of the British Empire. But the
war had perhaps the greatest aggregate influence. More than twice the num-
ber of Americans were killed in it (292,000) than in World War I (117,000).
Although fewer than a third the number of British combatants died than in
World War I (264,000), the war came home in the Nazi bombing of English
cities. Altogether, World War II resulted in the highest death toll of any
war—between forty and fifty million. Its destruction was cataclysmic, its
scope was international, and its aftershocks reverberated long afterward.

World War II haunts the work even of poets not directly involved. In her
1941 meditation "Roosters," Elizabeth Bishop vividly, if somewhat obliquely,
evokes aerial combat, which played a far greater role in this war than in any
before: "Now in mid-air / by twos they fight each other," and when one
bomberlike rooster falls, "his torn-out, bloodied feathers drift down." Sylvia
Plath, a young adolescent when planes dropped atomic bombs on Japanese
cities, takes "Hiroshima ash" as an integral part of her psychic experience
("Fever 103°"). In "Poem," Muriel Rukeyser declares her time: "I lived in the
first century of world wars." Indeed, the first of the century's world wars had
a comparable, defining effect on first-generation modern poets, including

those not at the Western Front; Ezra Pound had famously lamented, "There died a myriad / And of the best, among them."

Many more American poets served directly in World War II than in World War I, and a brief survey of their participation in the armed forces indicates the broad impact of World War II on men of the first contemporary generation. Randall Jarrell was a celestial navigation tower operator, William Meredith a naval aviator; Howard Nemerov was in the Royal Canadian Air Force and then, like James Dickey and Alan Dugan, in the U.S. Army Air Corps; Karl Shapiro, Richard Wilbur, and Anthony Hecht were all in the U.S. Army. Louis Simpson served in an army tank corps and then as a combat infantryman, Kenneth Koch as an army rifleman; and Richard Hugo flew thirty-five missions as an army bombardier. Toward the end of the war, W. D. Snodgrass, A. R. Ammons, David Wagoner, Frank O'Hara, Robert Bly, and Galway Kinnell served in the American navy, James Merrill and James Wright in the army. After the war, many of these veterans, with millions of others, were able to attend college thanks to the educational subsidies of the 1944 GI Bill of Rights, which helped turn soldiers into poets. In Britain, Kingsley Amis served in the army, Donald Davie in the navy. The war was, perhaps unsurprisingly, the first muse for a number of these budding writers. "Men wash their hands, in blood, as best they can," writes Jarrell in "Eighth Air Force," suggesting that the war stains everything in the combatants' lives. The war also conspicuously affected the lives of men who didn't serve. A conscientious objector, William Stafford worked in public service camps, where pacifists performed nonmilitary work under civilian direction, and Robert Lowell, another conscientious objector, spent six months in a federal prison in 1943–44, after he wrote a "manic statement, / telling off the state and president," condemning the bombing of German civilians and American demands for Germany's unconditional surrender. Robert Duncan was discharged from the army in 1941 as, in his ironic words, "an officially certified fag."

Of all the devastating wartime events that affected poetry—the massive bombing of London and firebombing of Dresden, the nuclear annihilation of Hiroshima and Nagasaki—the horrors of the Holocaust cast the longest shadow. The German philosopher and social critic Theodor Adorno declared it barbaric to write poetry after the Holocaust, and, indeed, in much post-Holocaust verse, poets worry about the ethics of beauty in an age of mass murder, about how to evoke industrialized genocide without exploiting it or dishonoring the dead. They imprint art with the disfiguring marks of the times. In caustically self-ironizing poems, Geoffrey Hill addresses victims of the Nazis while acknowledging the unavoidable failure of such address: "Undesirable you may have been, untouchable / you were not" ("September Song"). In Plath's "Daddy," an American daughter's address to her German father is warped and fractured by the knowledge of the concentration camps: "I never could talk to you. / The tongue stuck in my jaw. / / It stuck in a barb wire snare." Poets cannot fall entirely silent and still be poets, of course, but post-Holocaust poets such as Hill and Plath, Anthony Hecht and Derek Walcott embed within their poetry an intensified skepticism about the redemptive capacities of language and art.

MODERN AND CONTEMPORARY

Postwar poets were acutely conscious of coming after the modern poets. The major achievements of the first-generation moderns—W. B. Yeats, Gertrude

Stein, Robert Frost, Wallace Stevens, William Carlos Williams, Ezra Pound, Marianne Moore, T. S. Eliot—loomed like a massive edifice over postwar poets, who sometimes worried that all routes to innovation had already been explored and exhausted. As they looked back on the groundbreaking works of the 1910s and 1920s, postwar poets were apt to see as fixed what was once experimental. They sought out areas of creativity and awareness, both commonplace and exotic, neglected by their predecessors, and in the process launched a series of iconoclastic movements. Meanwhile, Stevens, Williams, Pound, and Moore continued to publish important new collections of poetry into the 1950s and 1960s, seeming at once titans who dominated the earth in the distant past and contemporary rivals extending their reign into the present.

Contemporary poetry is often distinguished from modern poetry according to general tendencies, and these distinctions help reveal broad similarities and differences among poets, schools, and movements. As such, they are worth stating at the outset, though individual poets often work against or outside these trends, though the periods are profoundly interwoven, and though these differences can also be found within the periods.

Contemporary poetry is generally seen as more personal than modern poetry. According to T. S. Eliot's famous modernist doctrine, the "emotion of art is impersonal." The first-generation modernists, in reaction against what they saw as the slushy, self-expressive Romanticism of the nineteenth century, often ironized, allusively contextualized, or symbolically transmuted their most personal feelings. By contrast, many of the best-known poets after World War II reclaimed a fiercely personal poetry for the late 1950s and the 1960s. Reflecting the pervasive influence of psychoanalysis in elite and mass culture, many a poet explored the formation of personal identity within the matrix of the family, writing candidly about childhood trauma, guilt, and desire. "They fuck you up, your mum and dad," Philip Larkin wryly summarized ("This Be The Verse"). It would be difficult to imagine Eliot or Pound, Yeats or Moore writing poems about childhood anger toward a weak father, as did Robert Lowell, or incestuous desire for a father, as did Anne Sexton, or combined desire and revulsion toward a mother's naked body, as did Allen Ginsberg. Sylvia Plath's explosive line "Daddy, daddy, you bastard, I'm through" does not express the sort of impersonal emotion that Eliot had in mind. Even Charles Olson, though protesting egocentric poetry, remembers his mother and father as "the precessions / / of me, the generation of those facts / which are my words" ("Maximus to Gloucester, Letter 27 [Withheld]"). Chafing against the conformist and consumerist ethos of what Lowell called the "tranquillized *Fifties*," perhaps fearing the quashing of individuality by massive organizations, bureaucracies, laboratories, and businesses spawned by the war and by postwar prosperity, these writers made poetry not a space for "the extinction of personality," as Eliot put it, but for its passionate expression.

Even so, this distinction between modern and contemporary can be overdrawn. Critics have increasingly seen Eliot's supposedly "impersonal" art as steeped in personal losses—*The Waste Land* as an elegy for his failed marriage, his dead father, and his close friend Jean Verdenal, killed in World War I. Modernism's Romantic literary roots have likewise been increasingly exposed, including Eliot's debts to the nineteenth-century poets he sternly repudiated in prose, such as Percy Bysshe Shelley and Walt Whitman. Nor do poets such as Olson, Lowell, and Plath spring free from their modernist inheritances: they deliberately mediate their experiences through the artifice of personae, myth, archetype, irony, and other such modernist devices. Plath said poets, instead of offering mere "cries from the heart," must "control and manipulate experiences." In "The Colossus," she presents herself and her father through classical archetypes; in "Cut," she metaphorically transforms physical pain; and in "Lady Lazarus," she ironizes her poetic marketing of suffering: "There is a charge / / For the eyeing of my scars." Some contemporary poets, such as Richard Wilbur and Geoffrey Hill, are even more mistrustful of personal self-expression, or, such as Michael Palmer and Lyn Hejinian, deconstruct notions of personal subjectivity altogether.

At least until recently, the dominant formal trend in contemporary poetry has been toward looser, more discrete, more organic kinds of aesthetic structure, and so contemporary poetry is often said to be more "open" than modern poetry. Contemporary poets have wanted to make their forms more responsive to accident, flux, and history, less inwardly molded and self-enclosed. Instead of plotting an inner trajectory toward finality in meaning, form, and emotion, their lyrics often end raggedly, in irresolution or distraction. Their long poems, instead of unfolding sequentially toward a destination, are often organized serially, in modular units that have a tentative relation to one another. Prose genres such as the diary or notebook are the model for many such poems, sometimes dated to indicate their contingency, their immersion in history. The contemporary poem places itself within— not above or outside or beyond—the open-ended course of everyday experience. Instead of aspiring to be a single, coherent utterance, a contemporary poem may be a collage of disjointed discourses or perceptions. Contemporary poets, typically refusing regimentation and overt order, have often patterned their poems on the natural rhythms of personal experience and the body. They have sought to mirror the unpredictable process of composition, as exemplified by what Frank O'Hara called his "I do this I do that" poems. Taking as his motto "First thought, best thought," Ginsberg also epitomized this premium on "spontaneous improvisation": "I really don't know what I'm doing when I sit down to write. I figure it out as I go along (and revise as little as possible)" ("Poetics: Mind Is Shapely, Art Is Shapely").

But statements about this trend also need to be qualified, since it is far from monolithic. Even Ginsberg, as the manuscripts of "Howl" and "Kaddish" reveal, carefully revised and refashioned his major poems for years before publishing them. Moreover, the scattered and extemporized structures of modernist works such as Ezra Pound's *Cantos,* William Carlos Williams's *Spring and All,* and Gertrude Stein's *Tender Buttons* have provided strong precedents for contemporary poets interested in further opening up poetic form. And whereas some modern poets, such as Williams, inveighed against the prototypically "closed" form of the sonnet, some contemporary poets, such as James Merrill, Thom Gunn, Anthony Hecht, Marilyn Hacker, and Agha Shahid Ali, have written brilliantly in this fixed form and others— the sestina, the villanelle, the canzone, the ghazal, even the heroic couplet.

Contemporary poets are often said to write poems less hierarchical in outlook, form, or ideology than are modern poems. Most postwar poets take a democratic view of language and of poetry's function in society, and they are open to a variety of discourses and even popular genres. By contrast, Yeats, Eliot, Pound, and H. D. see the poet as playing an almost priestly or ritualistic role in society, amalgamating and creating myths, purifying and renovating the verbal icon. Eliot and Pound often satirize less cultivated genres and uses of language. The difference is stark between modernism at its most sacramental and contemporary poetry at its most egalitarian—the deliberately flat, campy, and self-parodic poetry written, for example, by O'Hara and James Tate. Contemporary poets seem to feel little of Yeats's or Eliot's revulsion toward the urban, the popular, the utterly heterogeneous. In A. R. Ammons's sequence *Garbage,* about an enormous trash heap seen from an interstate highway, poetry and garbage come to seem inextricable. A further contrast with modern poetry's transcendent thrust is with contemporary poetry's frequent politicizing and historicizing of art. Witness such forcefully political contemporary poems as Amiri Baraka's "Poem for Black Hearts," Carolyn Forché's "The Colonel," Mark Doty's "Homo Will Not Inherit," and Margaret Atwood's "Footnote to the Amnesty Report on Torture," in which a man cleans the floor of a torture chamber: "every morning the same vomit, / the same shed teeth, the same / piss and liquid shit, the same panic."

But here, too, the difference should not be overstated. Modern poets also wrote poems immersed in the particulars of politics and history. Claude McKay, Jean Toomer, Langston Hughes, and—perhaps surprisingly, given his southern agrarian affiliations—Allen Tate all wrote searing poems about lynchings. And some of the most resonant and rust-proof twentieth-century political poetry is Yeats's about the Easter Rising of 1916, Wilfred Owen's about World War I, and W. H. Auden's about the Spanish Civil War. Furthermore, contemporary poets in revolt against a belief in art as transcendent and hierarchical have been able to look to modern precursors, such as Marianne Moore, who welcomed travel guides and science into her poems, and Langston Hughes, who turned to the then-disreputable forms of jazz and the blues as poetic models. Nor is all contemporary poetry antihierarchical. Seeking the aesthetic, even visionary power afforded by exacting uses of language and form, some contemporary poets, including Ammons, Jorie Graham, James Merrill, Philip Larkin, Derek Walcott, Louise Glück, Rita Dove, and Anne Carson, have extended traditions of high-art lyricism, even if such traditions run counter to the temper of the times.

Less ambiguous are the changes in poetry brought about by postwar demographic trends, such as globalization, ethnicization, and feminization. After World War II, as national self-consciousness increased in anglophone areas of the globe outside American and British centers of power, more poets wrote distinctive poetry in the former white settler colonies or "dominions," such as Australia and Canada, and in the decolonizing British outposts in the "underdeveloped world," such as Barbados, Uganda, and India. In the last few decades of the twentieth century, the range of poets in the United States and elsewhere in the so-called First World became more ethnically diverse, including non-European immigrants and their descendents. And as educational access increased across gender lines, more women throughout the anglophone world published poetry after 1945 than in the fifty years before. Writers who identified with national, ethnic, or sexual groups not formerly part of the literary mainstream were inspired by identity-centered political movements, such as, in the 1950s and 1960s, the civil rights movement and, in the 1960s and 1970s, the movements for women's rights, gay rights, and political rights and cultural recognition for Latinos, Native Americans, and Asian Americans.

THE NEW CRITICISM AND POETRY

One form in which modernism survived World War II was the New Criticism—a movement initiated in the 1920s and 1930s by, in America, poet-critics such as John Crowe Ransom, Allen Tate, Robert Penn Warren, and

Yvor Winters, and, in Britain, by I. A. Richards and William Empson. The New Criticism, which consolidated and complicated the ideal of the well-wrought poem, shaped the dominant style in American poetry at mid-century. Drawing heavily on T. S. Eliot's critical essays, the movement enshrined certain complex literary values: paradox irreducible to logical paraphrase; irony too intricate to permit strong commitments; metaphysical wit (as exemplified by John Donne) that yoked together opposites; impersonality that regulated strong feelings; and self-conscious technique of great dexterity. These aspects of modernism lent themselves to the New Criticism's more rigorous classroom teaching of literature. New Critical pedagogy in turn created audiences receptive to this institutionalized form of modernism; it also fostered writers eager to write economical, internally coherent poems that rewarded New Criticism's signature strategy of close reading. In a 1961 interview, Robert Lowell indicated the influence of the New Criticism on poetry, saying that when he was learning to write poetry, the New Critics "were very much news. You waited for their essays, and when a good critical essay came out it had the excitement of a new imaginative work." At the same time, the poets in the New Critical style often set aside less readily assimilated aspects of modernism—formal fragmentation, cross-cultural syncretism, polyglot assemblage, and ambitious mythmaking. Many of the major American poets of the time—Lowell, Plath, Anne Sexton, Adrienne Rich, John Berryman, W. S. Merwin, and Gwendolyn Brooks—began to write in accordance with New Critical principles, though they were violating them in earnest by the late 1950s and the 1960s.

But not all the poets who began within this framework discarded it. The verse of Randall Jarrell, William Stafford, Richard Wilbur, Howard Nemerov, Anthony Hecht, and John Hollander exemplifies the wry, cultivated qualities associated with the New Criticism. Their work displays fertility and deftness in its imagery and phrases; it is unsentimental and yet alive to the senses and sympathies, well made and careful not to become repetitive or predictable. And it enriches individual utterance with traditional poetic resources such as meter and rhyme, stanzaic forms and rhetorical patterning. "I am for wit and wakefulness," announces the speaker of Wilbur's "Ceremony," adding, "What's lightly hid is deepest understood." These learned, polished poets gravitated to careers as critics and college teachers, and partly as a result their work was often disparaged as "academic." Formally and psychologically extending the range of such tightly controlled verse, Elizabeth Bishop, Robert Hayden, May Swenson, Donald Justice, Amy Clampitt, and James Merrill also shared broad affinities with the restraint, compression, and formal discipline favored by the New Criticism.

THE BLACK MOUNTAIN SCHOOL

In contrast to the postwar formalists, American proponents of the most revolutionary aesthetic movements of the 1950s and 1960s rejected the legacy of T. S. Eliot and the New Critics. Not that the rebels dispensed altogether with first-generation modernism: they affiliated themselves with the more subversive and at that time less academically respectable work of William Carlos Williams and Ezra Pound. Williams continued to live the life of a doctor in Rutherford, New Jersey, and was the object of pilgrimages by young poets including A. R. Ammons and Allen Ginsberg. Pound, under indictment for treason because of his wartime radio broadcasts from Fascist Rome, was extradited to the United States in 1945, bringing with him the manuscript of *The Pisan Cantos*. Found mentally incompetent to stand trial, he was committed to a Washington sanatorium, and until his release (as incurably insane but harmless) twelve years later, he attracted younger American poets who sought in his work an immersion in the welter of experience that they found lacking in the poetry of Eliot, John Crowe Ransom, and their followers. Drawing strength from their association with the old impresario of experimental verse and the even older physician in Rutherford, they preferred "open" to "closed" poetic forms, agreeing with Robert Creeley that "Form is never more than an extension of content."

Creeley was one of the poets who gathered around Charles Olson at Black Mountain College, an experimental and unaccredited school in North Carolina that was to become one of the centers of new American poetry. Olson's essay "Projective Verse" (1950) provided the theoretical manifesto for the Black Mountain poets and for others with similar aims: in it, he offers a conception of "open-field" form and champions a dynamism like that of Pound's Vorticist doctrine of heightened energy in the arts. Here, and in his *Maximus Poems* of the 1960s, Olson cast himself as the heir of Pound and Williams. Like Williams, he emphasized the breath, rather than the iamb, as the basis of rhythm. Like Pound, he mixed colloquialism and farflung learning, and made poems out of juxtapositions. Against subjective verse, Olson offered what he called "objectism," a form of verse in which the ego is washed away and the poet "fronts to the whole of reality." The poet is wholly immersed in and energized by the surrounding environment. "I, Maximus," declares his central character, "a metal hot from boiling water."

After joining the faculty of Black Mountain College, Creeley edited *The Black Mountain Review*; during its short run of seven issues (1954–57), it was a major outlet for the anti-academic verse that was to explode into prominence in the late 1950s. In 1956, Robert Duncan came from San Francisco to join the college staff, and though she never joined the faculty, Denise Levertov published in the *Review*. Her influential essay "Notes on Organic Form" conceives of form not as a predetermined shape arbitrarily imposed on experience but as a coherent whole that closely reflects the inner distinctiveness of an experience. A. R. Ammons's poetry has much in common with the organic form, environmentalism, typographic experimentation, and prosodic velocity of "projective verse." The leader of the Black Arts Movement, Amiri Baraka acknowledged the fundamental influence of Olson on his poetry, as did Adrienne Rich, the preeminent feminist poet after World War II.

THE RAW AND THE COOKED

In the 1950s and 1960s, the central divide in American poetry was between the formalists in the New Critical style and poets in "open" forms, including the Black Mountain poets, the Beats, and the New York poets. Accepting the 1960 National Book Award for *Life Studies*, Robert Lowell most famously encapsulated the situation in a wryly anthropological distinction: "Two poetries are now competing, a cooked and a raw. The cooked, marvelously expert, often seems laboriously concocted to be tasted and digested by a graduate seminar. The raw, huge blood-dripping gobbets of unseasoned experience are dished up for midnight listeners. There is a poetry that can only be studied, and a poetry that can only be declaimed, a poetry of pedantry, and a poetry of scandal." Although Lowell admitted to some exaggeration, this competition among poets for recognition, influence, and publication was intense; one of its early manifestations was the so-called battle of the anthologies. In *New Poets of England and America* (1957), American poets Donald Hall, Robert Pack, and Louis Simpson gathered formalist poets whose work—most of it in rhymed and metered stanzas—could be understood largely within New Critical terms, including Richard Wilbur and the early Lowell, as well as English poets of the Movement, such as Philip Larkin, Donald Davie, and Thom Gunn. The American critic Donald Allen included none of the same poets in the anthology widely seen as a response, *The New American Poetry* (1960), which influentially grouped and distinguished anti-academic American poets, including the Black Mountain school, the New York school, and the Beats. Ensuing anthologies took sides with the "raw" or the "cooked," or attempted to bridge the distance, but in either case could not ignore the rift.

To clarify this postwar divide in American poetry, it may be useful to focus comparatively on the first two poets in this volume. Charles Olson and Elizabeth Bishop became fountainheads of these very different kinds of contemporary poetry. Born just six weeks after Olson, Bishop is nearly his opposite in matters of form and taste. If he is the first major postwar exponent of "open" form, she masters and remakes inherited poetic models. Though not a disciple of the New Criticism, Bishop created an outstanding example of a body of poetry consonant with New Critical principles. In the 1950s and 1960s, she was less influential than other formalist poets, but her eminence mounted after her death, and her verse remains a strong model for emerging poets attentive to studied craft, precise description, personal memory, and understated but intense lyric feeling. If Olson hectors and proclaims, Bishop speaks in a steely whisper. Intent on kinetics and propulsion, Olson practices a mobile and shaggy giganticism; Bishop, an exacting and exquisite miniaturist, is more interested in the still life. While Olson thinks of poetry as breathing, Bishop conceives of it as looking. Olson's cascading free verse and rhapsodic vistas can be traced back to Walt Whitman; the nineteenth-century foremother of Bishop's controlled measures and pain-stubbed lines is Emily Dickinson. The more immediate, modernist legacy that Olson transmits is that of the fragmentary long poems of Pound and Williams; Bishop extends instead, in poems such as "The Fish," the precise physical descriptions and poetic self-reflections of Marianne Moore (who wrote a poem with the same title):

> I looked into his eyes
> which were far larger than mine
> but shallower, and yellowed,
> the irises backed and packed
> with tarnished tinfoil
> seen through the lenses
> of old scratched isinglass.

But for all their differences, both Bishop and Olson develop permutations of modernism, respond energetically to their environments, and expand the geography of American verse into South and Central America. Distinctions between the "raw" and the "cooked," the "open" and the "closed," provide a basic framework for understanding postwar poetry, but that framework extends only so far, since contemporary poets from Gwendolyn Brooks and

Adrienne Rich to Susan Howe and Henri Cole have straddled the gulf. Major poets such as John Ashbery and Seamus Heaney have written as skillfully in free as in metered verse, in organic as in inherited forms. Indeed, at the time he gave his acceptance speech, Lowell was formally somewhere between the "raw" and the "cooked," having uncoiled his densely wrought New Critical style through the influence of Williams and the Beats.

THE BEATS AND THE NEW YORK SCHOOL

The Beat poets, like the Black Mountain poets, aligned themselves with the "open" prosody of Pound and especially of Williams, who wrote an introduction for Allen Ginsberg's *"Howl" and Other Poems* (1956). The Beats were featured in the last issue of the *Black Mountain Review,* of which Ginsberg was a contributing editor. They tended, however, to dismiss the Black Mountain poets as too much at ease with authority figures; their own consistent opposition to authority made their poetry the most notorious and conspicuous of the 1950s. They rejected the stuffy majority culture, the anticommunist inquisitions, and the formalist poetry of the times, and decided to drop out and create among themselves a counterculture based on inspired improvisation, whether through jazz, drugs, or East Asian mysticism. Ginsberg and Lawrence Ferlinghetti, exiles from New York, found a congenial milieu in San Francisco, where a poetic renaissance had already been fomented within "the alternative society," as Kenneth Rexroth, doyen of the San Francisco poets, called it. Robert Duncan returned to the San Francisco scene after Black Mountain College collapsed in 1956; Gary Snyder returned to his birthplace after years in the lumber camps of Oregon and more years studying Zen Buddhism in a Japanese monastery.

Following Whitman's example, Beat writers such as Ginsberg shaped their public utterances out of the private experiences that some of their first readers found shameful and appalling, others thrilling and liberating. They presented, often as visionary experiences, confidences that were once uttered only to priest, doctor, or closest friend. Ginsberg, for example, in one of the rhapsodic long lines of "Howl," writes of those "who let themselves be fucked in the ass by saintly motorcyclists, and screamed with joy."

Another major force behind the opening of poetic form was the so-called New York school of poets. It included Frank O'Hara, John Ashbery, and Kenneth Koch, who had met at Harvard University and were associated with the Poets' Theatre, an experimental drama group of the early 1950s. Inspired by the paintings of abstract expressionists such as Jackson Pollock and Willem de Kooning, they went to New York City and immersed themselves in contemporary art—Ashbery and O'Hara wrote for *Art News* and O'Hara worked for the Museum of Modern Art. Like the abstract expressionists, they represented art not as a finished product but as a process. In a 1980 interview, Ashbery credited the influences of "the simultaneity of Cubism" and "the Abstract Expressionist idea that the work is a sort of record of its own coming-into-existence; it has an 'anti-referential sensuousness.'" The New York poets practiced in their sometimes montagelike verse a calculated diffidence and discontinuity of perception. Unlike other pioneers of "open" form—such as the Beats and the Black Mountain poets—they spoke not in prophetic or religiously ecstatic tones but through layers of irony. Their work, as Ashbery writes in "Self-Portrait in a Convex Mirror," is "pure / Affirmation that doesn't affirm anything." "All we know," he says in the same poem,

> Is that we are a little early, that
> Today has that special, lapidary
> Todayness that the sunlight reproduces
> Faithfully in casting twig-shadows on blithe
> Sidewalks. No previous day would have been like this.

Highspirited but knowing, these poets celebrated New York and recorded its landscape, as when O'Hara, characteristically looking from the window of an art gallery, says that "the warm traffic going by is my natural scenery." Partly because of his early death, O'Hara was the first of these poets to become famous. By the 1970s, Ashbery had become the most prominent member of the group, poetically manipulating reality and fantasy, humor and intricate perceptions, and in the process rapidly assuming different selves. No other contemporary poet has been such a strong influence on both "experimental" poets, most interested in his collagelike structures and decentered consciousness, and "mainstream" poets, impressed by his unsentimental lyricism, quick shifts of tone and sense, and dreamlike vividness.

DEEP IMAGE POETRY AND CONFESSIONAL POETRY

Surrealism, a mode that uses the unconscious and its distortion of reality, had until the 1960s been more common to the visual arts, and to European and South American writing, than to Anglo-American poetry. Now, this changed: French surrealism was among the influences on the irrational sequences of images in the poetry of the New York school. Along with French surrealism, Spanish surrealism was an even more central influence on another group of American poets, known as the Deep Image poets (a term coined by Robert Kelly in his 1961 essay "Notes on the Poetry of the Deep Image"). They drew on surrealism to compose elemental, psychologically archetypal poems. Robert Bly's magazine *The Fifties* (subsequently renamed for successive decades) made available new translations of surrealist poets including the South Americans Pablo Neruda and César Vallejo, and his poems helped establish a "new surrealism," as did those of James Wright, W. S. Merwin, Philip Levine, Louis Simpson, Galway Kinnell, Mark Strand, and Charles Simic. Others, such as Charles Wright, Robert Hass, and Louise Glück, were also periodically attracted to the surrealist dislocation of sense and image. In "Fork," Simic reimagines a fork as the foot of a bird, its head "large, bald, beakless, and blind." "The dead," says Charles Wright in his "Homage to Paul Cézanne, "are constant in / The white lips of the sea." The reader is invited to experience such visions without the effort of logical construction. In Strand's work, the very mysteriousness of what is going on contributes to a mounting effect of uncanny power.

In the late 1950s and early 1960s, another group of poets became interested in writing deeply psychological verse, though they relied less on psychic archetypes than on self-analysis. They came to be known as the "confessional" poets—a term that the reviewer M. L. Rosenthal first applied to Robert Lowell's *Life Studies* (1959) and that eventually became a general label for intensely personal poetry about once-taboo subjects. As a young man, Lowell had left Harvard to study at Kenyon College with John Crowe Ransom; Lowell and his older friend Allen Tate, like Ransom a leading New Critic and poet, became Roman Catholics at the same time. Lowell's Pulitzer Prize–

winning second book, *Lord Weary's Castle* (1946), showed technical mastery of rhyme, meter, and complex symbolism, and established his eminent place among young poets. Lowell fused the New Critical tradition of elaborate structure and the Whitmanesque tradition of radical contact with subject. Then, teaching at the University of Iowa, Lowell was struck by the unabashed self-revelations and open form of Beat poetry, and by the self-exploration in the poetry of one of his students, W. D. Snodgrass. Lowell had come to feel that poetry written under the influence of the New Criticism, as he said in a 1961 interview, "can't handle much experience. It's become a craft, purely a craft, and there must be some breakthrough back into life." Although Lowell's loosening of form and psychic self-excavations in *Life Studies* at first made it seem as if he might be becoming a Beat, his verse remained meticulously controlled, his tone still marked by the wit and irony preferred by the New Criticism. If, as he says in *History*, "imperfection is the language of art," his constant revisions showed his lingering allegiance to the well-made poem.

Other poets who wrote in this intensely autobiographical vein, such as Snodgrass, John Berryman (who invented an "anti-sonnet" of three six-line stanzas for his *Dream Songs*), Sylvia Plath, Anne Sexton, and Adrienne Rich, either played against conventional form or wrote free verse in a peculiarly unrelaxed way. These poets wrote about key moments of revelatory pain more often than of pleasure, and they saw such moments as epitomizing the general condition of their time. As they turned against New Critical norms of impersonality and formal regulation, Plath, Sexton, and Rich increasingly rooted their poetry in female bodily and psychic existence. Rich reflects in her essay "When We Dead Awaken: Writing as Re-Vision": "In the late fifties I was able to write, for the first time, directly about experiencing myself as a woman. . . . Until then I had tried very much *not* to identify myself as a female poet." Rich, Sexton, and Plath harnessed the confessional mode to express feelings and insights that violated literary and social strictures on American women. They presented their lusts, hatreds, and suicidal urges in extraordinarily charged and intimate terms. In "Ariel," Plath strips herself of mundane responsibilities and ecstatically rides her horse into the sunrise:

> The child's cry
>
> Melts in the wall.
> And I
> Am the arrow,
>
> The dew that flies
> Suicidal, at one with the drive
> Into the red
>
> Eye, the cauldron of morning.

Such writing sometimes came at a high personal cost: three of the confessionals—Plath, Berryman, and Sexton—committed suicide; others, Lowell included, endured repeated breakdowns, hospitalizations, addictions, which led to early deaths. But Rich, who publicly denounced female self-destructiveness after Sexton's death, attested to the energizing potential of poetry in which "at last the woman in the poem and the woman writing the poem become the same person," in which women "are speaking to and of women . . . out of a newly released courage to name." Women, gay and lesbian, and "ethnic" American poets—previously impeded from naming their experiences in their own literary voices—thus turned so-called personal or confessional poetry into a tool of collective self-definition and liberation.

THE BLACK ARTS MOVEMENT AND LATER AFRICAN AMERICAN POETRY

From the mid-1960s through the early 1970s, poets of the Black Arts Movement also focused their poems on agony, rage, and love, but these emotions had a stronger political dimension in their openly polemical, politically revolutionary work. These African American poets were inspired by the Black Power movement, whose leaders had grown impatient with the integrationist, nonviolent ethos of the civil rights movement and emphasized instead black nationalism, economic power, and self-determination. "Black Art," wrote the exponent Larry Neal in "The Black Arts Movement" (1968), "is the aesthetic and spiritual sister of the Black Power concept." Amiri Baraka, at that time called LeRoi Jones, gave the movement its name when he coined the term *Black Arts*, founding in 1965 the Black Arts Repertory Theater. Having absorbed the improvisatory aesthetics of the Beat and Black Mountain poets, Baraka left the white avant-garde during the 1960s to move toward a distinctively black aesthetic, which insisted on a commitment to the needs of the African American community and to the discovery of artistic resources in it. In "The Myth of a 'Negro Literature'" (1963), Baraka ridiculed black artists who were "content to imperfectly imitate the bad poetry of the ruined minds of Europe." Proposing the blues and jazz as alternatives to Euro-American forms, he modeled his poems on the explosive energy and polyphonic voicing of post-bebop jazz.

In keeping with the Black Arts Movement, Audre Lorde, Lucille Clifton, and June Jordan, all born, like Baraka, in the 1930s, also wrote poems inveighing against racial injustice and drawing on black experience and poetic tradition, poems steeped in the speech rhythms and rhetorical verve of the black vernacular. But resisting the masculinist tenor of the Black Arts Movement, they put the black female body and their personal emotional histories at the center of their art. Theirs are poems about social identity as seen from within the experiences of storytelling, erotic passion, and physical loss. Clifton writes homages to her hips, her uterus, her last period; childbirth is Lorde's subject in "Now that I Am Forever with Child": "I bore you one morning just before spring— / My head rang like a firey piston / My legs were towers between which / A new world was passing."

Meanwhile, older African American poets, born in the 1910s, were forced to choose sides by the Black Arts Movement. Gwendolyn Brooks had already been writing poems such as "The Last Quatrain of the Ballad of Emmett Till," about an African American teenager murdered for whistling at a white woman: Emmett's mother "sits in a red room, / drinking black coffee. / She kisses her killed boy. / And she is sorry. / Chaos in windy grays / through a red prairie." Deeply impressed by the radical younger generation, Brooks shifted in the 1960s from such understated, tightly controlled poetry to "wild, raw, ragged free verse," as she called it. She dated her transformation to the Second Fisk University Black Writers' Conference, in 1967. A year earlier, at the first of these conferences, Robert Hayden found himself sidelined and spurned by black nationalists. Still, he kept to his universalist Baha'i faith and international modernist affinities, and later African American poets have championed his indirect, dramatic approach to black history and social injustice. In the sequence "Middle Passage," for example, he ironically adopts the voices of white slave-ship officers to evoke the atrocities of the slave trade.

Since the Black Arts Movement broke up in 1974, splintering into nationalist, Marxist, and Pan-Africanist factions, many African American poets have departed from its nationalism, but the movement's emphasis on African American oral, literary, and musical genres has remained influential. African American poets such as Michael S. Harper and Yusef Komunyakaa have continued to draw sustenance from African American musical forms, capturing in their verse the melancholy starkness of the blues or the abrupt shifts and syncopations of jazz. Whereas the Black Arts Movement sought cultural self-sufficiency, they hybridize indigenous models in surprising ways with forms adapted from other cultural sources. Thylias Moss invokes the black preacher's technique of "making text" by meditating on a central concept—rapture, slavery, God—but she gives the strategy a new strangeness by combining it with surrealist profusions of discontinuous images. Rita Dove reenters moments of violation and injustice in the history of African Americans, but she makes them haunting, ironically, by adapting such European fixed forms as the sestina and the villanelle, in her poem "Parsley," or such "mainstream" American modes as confessional lyricism and semidramatic, semipersonal portraiture, as in the sequence *Thomas and Beulah*.

THE NEW APOCALYPSE AND THE MOVEMENT

During World War II, a number of British poets emerged whose response to the "age of anxiety," as W. H. Auden called it, was vehement and extreme. Among the poets of this late Romantic movement sometimes called the New Apocalypse, Dylan Thomas was the major figure. In opposition to the analytic understatement of W. H. Auden and his British circle of the 1930s, Thomas reintroduced openly expressed emotion and rhetoric into English verse, with the most spectacular display of language since Hart Crane. In ordinary situations the Welsh poet heard extraordinary reverberations, and like William Wordsworth, William Blake, and Samuel Taylor Coleridge, he tried to restore a radiance lost to English nature poetry since the seventeenth century.

Reacting against this apocalyptic mode was a loose association of university poets who, in the 1950s, came to be known as the Movement. Its leading figures were Philip Larkin, Kingsley Amis, Donald Davie, and Thom Gunn, all included in Robert Conquest's *New Lines* (1956), an anthology that put them on Britain's literary map. The Movement had affinities with developments in the other British arts, in fiction, in the "kitchen-sink" school of painting, in "ordinary language" philosophy, and in plays by "angry young men" such as John Osborne. While objecting to what they saw as the Romantic excesses of the New Apocalypse, the poets of the Movement also rejected Yeats's symbolism and Pound and Eliot's high modernism, and favored wit over prophecy and extravagance, urban and suburban realities over mythmaking. "A neutral tone is nowadays preferred," as Davie summarized in "Remembering the 'Thirties." These poets tried to reclaim a native English line of civil, rational, and accessible poetry that bypassed the complexities of a supposedly imported modernism and went back through Robert Graves and William Empson to Thomas Hardy, A. E. Housman, and the Georgian pastoralists of the 1910s. "Poetry is an affair of sanity, of seeing things as they are," Larkin said, implicitly contrasting his work with the supposed "insanity" of the modernist Pound and the confessionals Lowell and Plath.

Through deliberately deflated language, the Movement poets aimed to consolidate the achievements of the Auden circle, without its leftist political commitments, to write a poetry that in its diction and tone, subjects and regular meters, would express rather than overthrow the restrictions of ordinary life. Even so, their poetry sometimes quietly bridges the distance between the mundane and the sublime, as in Larkin's "Sad Steps," which begins, "Groping back to bed after a piss / I part thick curtains, and am startled by / The rapid clouds, the moon's cleanliness."

BRITISH POETRY AFTER THE MOVEMENT

Not everyone in Britain followed the lead of Larkin and the Movement. Although Charles Tomlinson resembled Movement poets in rejecting Dylan Thomas's apocalyptic Romanticism, and though he also prized precision and clarity, his points of reference in crafting a poetry respectful of the world as other, as irreducible to human symbols, included the American modernists and the Objectivists. Other British poets rejected the Movement's notion of a limited, rationalist, polished poetics. In the late 1950s and the 1960s, Ted Hughes began to write poems in which he presented the world as a Darwinian world of violent struggle and himself as having a savage role to fill. He found emblems of violence in the outer world of animals, weather, and his physical work as a sheep and cattle farmer. Also in contrast to the Movement, Geoffrey Hill saw a rationalist humanism as inadequate to the atrocities of twentieth-century war and genocide; he has investigated political, religious, and personal turmoil in a style knotted with allusions and fierce in its demands, its strenuous language recalling both the high modernist tradition and Metaphysical poetry.

Stylistically closer to the reserve of the Movement, another group of British poets nevertheless sought to dislocate normal habits of perception, presenting the familiar world through the defamiliarizing lens of an alien or an anthropologist. Craig Raine's "The Martian Sends a Postcard Home," in which an alien invader describes ordinary life in an English home, was this group's signature poem; its title was adapted for fellow poets who were called the Martian school. Casting his net beyond the domestic world, James Fenton adapts the Martian strategy in a poem such as "Dead Soldiers," in which the Cambodian wars he witnessed as a journalist are presented in terms of a battlefield dinner party.

Since the 1980s, the spectrum of Britain's poets has become more diverse in class, ethnicity, gender, and region than ever before, bringing new voices into the English literary tradition. Born in the Northern industrial city of Leeds, Tony Harrison often writes as a "remembering exile" from his working-class origins; in "Turns," he says that his poet persona is that of a street entertainer for "the class that broke" his working-class father. His long poem *v.* synthesizes traditional verse—Thomas Gray's "Elegy Written in a Country Churchyard" is the obvious precursor poem—with a local vernacular, the oral energy and resonance of Harrison's Yorkshire idiom and rhythms exploding on the page. Born in Scotland to an Irish mother in a left-wing, working-class Catholic family, Carol Ann Duffy grew up amid Irish, Scottish, and Standard varieties of English, and this youthful experience helped equip her to speak in different voices in dramatic monologues. Having moved from Guyana to England in her twenties, Grace Nichols, code-switching between West Indian Creole and Standard English, celebrates the erotic energy and force of the black female body. Like other "Black British" poets from England's former colonies, she has helped bring into British poetry a vibrant new imagery, diction, and cultural sensibility.

POETRY OF IRELAND AND NORTHERN IRELAND

In the early 1960s, a group of aspiring young writers, all of them born and brought up in Northern Ireland, began to meet in the apartment of Philip Hobsbaum, then a Lecturer at Queen's University, in Belfast. Some of them were Catholic by background, others Protestant; all agreed that the endless guerilla warfare between religiously and politically divided populations in Ulster should not divert them from their writing or become their sole subject. If the Troubles in Northern Ireland were to be treated in poems, they felt, it must be by indirection. Seamus Heaney, who became a Nobel laureate in 1995, is the oldest among these poets. Between his birth, in 1939, and Paul Muldoon's, in 1951, Ulster produced an extraordinary number of strong poets for its small population. Viewing bloodshed through the obliquities of metaphor, myth, allusion, and strict formal pattern, they created one of the most significant bodies of poetry about political violence in the English-speaking world.

"I grew up in between," writes Heaney in "Terminus," and the consciousness of intercultural strife and yet cross-cultural abundance has helped to fuel his poetry and the poetry of other Ulster writers. Seen by many as the most gifted English-language poet of his generation, Heaney has said that Irish poets cannot hate the English, because without them they would not have their language, a poet's chief resource; indeed, he has ransacked the English literary tradition from *Beowulf* to William Wordsworth, Gerard Manley Hopkins, and Ted Hughes. Heaney welds this inheritance from centuries of English rule to indigenous Irish genres (such as the *aisling*, or vision poem), Irish sonorities (gutturals, alliterations, assonances of Gaelic), and an Irish sensibility (an earthy, rural, tough-mindedness combined with an almost mystical sense of the unseen). In his poetry about the violence in Northern Ireland, he grapples courageously with the ethics of representation—how to write about public suffering without appropriating, simplifying, or aestheticizing it.

Unlike Heaney, who is a Catholic by background, his near-contemporaries Derek Mahon and Michael Longley came, like Yeats, from Protestant families. Out of the tension between a sense of participation in, and alienation from, the island's predominantly Catholic culture, they have forged poetry that is tonally complex, formally accomplished, and unfailingly elegant. Medbh McGuckian and Paul Muldoon, both of Catholic origins, were among Heaney's students. McGuckian's poetry is the most dreamlike and evocative to come out of Ireland since Yeats's. Muldoon's influential poetry displays great skill in eerily distorted fixed forms, multiple screens of irony, numerological patterning, and a combination of experimental zaniness with formal reserve. Born in the Irish Republic, Eavan Boland has centered her career on making a space within the largely male tradition of Irish verse—with its standard, mythical emblems of femininity—for Irish women's historical experiences of survival and suffering, even including the "scream of beaten women."

CANADIAN AND AUSTRALIAN POETRY

After World War II, the geographical contours of poetry written in English began to change more than at any time since the first publication of American poets, three centuries earlier. One shift of the literary center of gravity was from England to America, a shift that Auden and Denise Levertov seemed to confirm when—in a reversal of the expatriation of Stein, Pound, and Eliot to Europe a generation earlier—they came to the United States. Another was the emergence of new literatures in English from the dominions of the British Empire, such as Canada and Australia. With a few exceptions, such as the Australian A. D. Hope, earlier writers of the British Commonwealth wrote poems derivative of metropolitan fashion. While still drawing on their English inheritances, these writers now began to assert the terms of their own literatures. One of the changes came with greater fidelity to locale. Though indebted to Auden, the Canadian poet P. K. Page strongly roots her imagistic verse in the local landscape. Thus rooted, too, is the work of contemporary Australian poet Judith Wright, which is haunted by the absent presence of a partly destroyed Aboriginal civilization. The Australian poet Les Murray adapts Aboriginal song techniques in his poetry, fusing them with the witty defamiliarizing strategy of the Martian school. Self-conscious about being at the margins of the former empire, Murray fashions a brash, playful, overbrimming poetry that mines the British and classical traditions while remaking them in what he styles his "redneck," Australian manner.

In her introduction to *The New Oxford Book of Canadian Verse in English* (1982), Margaret Atwood observes that in Canada "the modern movement took some time to build a following . . . [because] puritanism and the colonial worship of imports still restricted taste." Atwood writes of isolation and survival as distinguishing preoccupations of Canadian literature, and her poems display a divided vision—both attachment to the Canadian landscape and the sense of being estranged from it. "We are all immigrants to this place even if we were born here," remarks one of her characters. Even as Canadian poetry has become increasingly independent, it has continued a dialogue with its British literary origins. Anne Carson, for example, imaginatively engages the British Victorian writers Charlotte and Emily Brontë in her poem "The Glass Essay," transplanting their voices to a Canadian landscape. But Carson, like Atwood, also illustrates a heightened interest in U.S. poetry and popular culture, reflecting Canada's postwar shift in political and cultural orientation from Britain to the United States. Indeed, she brings into the literary mix influences that range from ancient Greek poetry to Pound and Plath, television and video. This diversity of inheritances can also be seen in the work of other Canadian poets. Reflecting the increasing multiculturalism of Canada due to the large-scale immigration that began in 1948, Michael Ondaatje fuses the American confessional mode adapted from Robert Lowell with his classical Sri Lankan inheritance of verse cut in spare, imagistic lines.

POSTCOLONIAL POETRY OF AFRICA, INDIA, AND THE CARIBBEAN

The most dramatic geographic shift in literary activity after World War II was the rise of new literatures from the former colonies of the British Empire in the so-called Third World, particularly in Africa, India, and the Caribbean.

Britain had the largest, most powerful, best organized of the modern European empires, and had expropriated enormous quantities of land, raw materials, and labor from its widely scattered overseas territories. The emergence of new literatures in English coincided loosely with the wave of decolonization that began after World War II: India and Pakistan became independent in 1947; Ghana in 1957, Nigeria in 1960, and Uganda in 1962; Jamaica and Trinidad and Tobago in 1962, Barbados and Guyana in 1966, and Saint Lucia in 1979. Unlike the literatures of the former white settler colonies, which extended and adapted the British literary inheritance to new settings, postcolonial literatures brought together more disparate traditions of colonizer and colonized, European and native. Born under British rule and undergoing a colonial education that repressed or denigrated native languages and traditions, these poets grew up with an acute awareness of the riches of their own cultural inheritances. Searching through oral histories and personal memories, postcolonial poets sought to give voice to a cultural past that colonialism had degraded and gagged. They expanded the range of possibilities in English-language poetry by hybridizing it with their indigenous images and speech rhythms, creoles and genres.

In the middle of the twentieth century, when colonial prejudices still branded West Indian English, or Creole, a backward language, a "corruption" of English, the Afro-Jamaican poet Louise Bennett claimed its wit, vibrancy, and proverbial richness for poetry. In the late 1960s, the Barbadian Kamau Brathwaite (then Edward Brathwaite) wrote the three long sequences, gathered as *The Arrivants,* that revalue the linguistic, musical, and mythic survivals of Africa in the Caribbean—resources long repressed because of colonial attitudes. Whereas Bennett and Brathwaite have emphasized Afro-Caribbean inheritances, the most eminent West Indian poet, Nobel laureate Derek Walcott, has drawn largely on British, American, and classical European models. But in poems such as "The Schooner *Flight*" and *Omeros,* he, like Bennett and Brathwaite, creolizes the rhythms, diction, and sensibility of English-language poetry. "I have Dutch, nigger, and English in me," declares the mulatto hero of "The Schooner *Flight,* "and either I'm nobody, or I'm a nation." A leading West Indian poet of the next generation, the Jamaican Lorna Goodison sinuously interweaves Creole and Standard English, Afro-Caribbean and European cultural resources, exclaiming, "It all belongs to me."

In poetry as well as fiction, Nigeria was the most prolific anglophone African nation around the time of independence, said to be the "golden age" of letters in sub-Saharan Africa. In musically cadenced verse, Christopher Okigbo synthesized Igbo myth and imagery with the Anglo-modernist allusive strategies of Pound and Eliot. Another Nigerian, Wole Soyinka, later the first black African to win the Nobel Prize, stretched English syntax and figurative language in poems dense with Yoruba-inspired wordplay and myth. Okot p'Bitek, the preeminent East African poet after independence, Africanized English with literally rendered Acoli images, metaphors, and idioms; his long poem *Song of Lawino* (1966) embodied the conflict between westernization and nativism in an Acoli village woman's boisterous attacks on her Europeanized husband. Working in a language imposed by missionaries and governments that considered them culturally and racially inferior, these African poets transform a tool of oppression into a vehicle for voicing and exploring their rich cultural identities.

Poets from India have brought its great variety of indigenous cultures into

English-language poetry. A. K. Ramanujan drew primarily on traditions of the Hindu majority in sharply etched poems that interfuse Anglo-modernist principles with the south Indian legacies of Tamil and Kannada poetry. Of the Shi'a Muslim minority, the Kashmiri poet Agha Shahid Ali, who like Ramanujan emigrated to the United States for graduate study, interwove first Eliot's modernism, then James Merrill's formalism, with the music, tonality, and fixed forms of Urdu poetry. A poet from the Catholic community in the former Portuguese colony of Goa, whose speech rhythms and diction she echoes, Eunice de Souza employs the confessional mode to explore the often painful experience of growing up female in a patriarchal society. All of these poets respond with emotional ambivalence and linguistic versatility to the experience of living after colonialism, between non-Western traditions and modernity, in a period of explosive change in the relation between Western and "native" cultures.

POSTCONFESSIONAL POETRY, NEW FORMALISM, AND LANGUAGE POETRY

In the United States, the late 1970s were marked by the deaths of Elizabeth Bishop and Robert Lowell, two towering figures in the older generation of contemporaries; and by the early deaths of James Wright and Richard Hugo. But other prominent post-1945 writers continued to develop and change. John Ashbery wrote daring long poems and lyrics, employing not only free verse but also fixed forms, such as the sestina and couplet. A. R. Ammons blended his descriptive and meditative modes with more personal introspections in works that meditate on landscape, ecology, and poetry. James Merrill, in *The Changing Light at Sandover,* produced an American cosmological epic unlike anything before him. Adrienne Rich, continuing to forge afresh her "dream of a common language," wrote poems about collective experience, especially that of women, while probing the ethics and meaning of intimate relationships with family, friends, and lovers. Amy Clampitt, an unknown contemporary of the confessionals, began publishing in 1983 some of the most finely embroidered and verbally dazzling poetry of the late twentieth century.

During this period, the postwar movement of American poetry into the academy accelerated. In the first postwar generation, poets such as Robert Lowell and John Berryman took temporary posts as itinerant writers in residence and competed for grants. The next generation's entry into graduate education and university employment was more permanent and pervasive. With few exceptions, American poets born from the 1930s on have received some training in creative-writing programs. Charles Wright, Mark Strand, James Tate, and Jorie Graham, for example, all studied with Donald Justice at the Iowa Writers' Workshop, and they, like most of their contemporaries, went on to teach creative writing. Similarly, a group of teacher-poets of the Pacific northwest had all studied with Theodore Roethke, whether at Pennsylvania State University (David Wagoner) or at the University of Washington (James Wright and Richard Hugo). A sign of the changing relation of poetry to the academy was the routinization of the campus poetry reading in the 1980s as a social activity, in contrast to the 1970s, when it had been a psychedelic or revolutionary event.

After the late 1970s, American poetry splintered anew, this time into several distinct factions. As in the 1960s, these factions continued to be bridged by some poets, such as John Ashbery and Jorie Graham, whose work can be seen as both "experimental" and "personal," "avant-garde" and "formal." At the center, attacked by both literary conservatives and radicals, is the dominant mode in M.F.A. programs, anthologies, publishing houses, national awards, and magazines such as *American Poetry Review:* a modified form of confessional free verse, sometimes called "postconfessional" or "neoconfessional," though in an age of relentless confession on radio, television, and the Internet, the personal revelations tend to be less shocking to today's readers than those of the first-wave confessionals and Beats were to their early audiences. At its best, the mode's introspective lyricism is complicated and enriched. Exploring personal guilt, ambivalence, and psychic distress, Graham often puzzles out personal feelings through deliberately strained comparisons between her inner states and public history—the Holocaust, imperialism, and so forth. Charles Wright also enlarges the postconfessional mode, his Deep Image background widening the scope of personal references, his grids of syllable and line count binding his free verse, and his postreligious melancholy casting the natural world in shadow. Robert Hass has brought to the personal lyric the discipline of the East Asian haiku. Louise Glück has deepened the mode through the use of archetypes and myths. Poets of gay experience, such as Mark Doty and Henri Cole, redeploy confessionalism to resist the humiliations of homophobia, mourn the collective ravages of AIDS, and probe marginal sexual identities. And Sharon Olds, perhaps the clearest example of a late confessionalist, writes poetry so erotically vehement, psychologically intent, and metaphorically rich that she, too, exceeds the bounds of the merely personal.

In reaction against what they see as the slackness of free verse lyricism, a group of poets known as the New Formalists, who published anthologies and manifestos largely in the 1980s, has championed a return to meter and rhyme, which they believe have the potential to restore the tattered social contract between poet and common reader. Their first anthology, Philip Dacey and David Jauss's anthology *Strong Measures: Contemporary American Poetry in Traditional Forms* (1985), recalled the formalist collections in the "battle of the anthologies" twenty-five years earlier. Because their agenda is recuperative, insistent on the virtues of narrative and stanzaic structure, the New Formalists are often assumed to be neoconservatives in politics as well as form. But this is not so. Marilyn Hacker, belatedly adopted into the group, plays the "nontraditional" content of her lesbian feminism within and against forms such as the sestina, the rondeau, the villanelle, and the sonnet, forms renewed by her respectful skewing of prosodic and stanzaic strictures. Other noted poets associated with the group include Gjertrud Schnackenberg, Dana Gioia, Brad Leithauser, and Vikram Seth. During the emergence of the New Formalists, some of the preeminent formalists of the earlier generation—James Merrill, Richard Wilbur, Donald Justice, Anthony Hecht, John Hollander—continued to produce masterful poetry in "closed" verse forms, setting a high standard for such poetry. Within an international context, many contemporary poets have also exemplified formal brilliance and skill in meter and rhyme, including Northern Irish poets such as Seamus Heaney, Derek Mahon, and Michael Longley, English poets such as Tony Harrison, James Fenton, and Carol Ann Duffy, and such postcolonial poets as Louise Bennett, Derek Walcott, and Agha Shahid Ali.

From the opposite end of the aesthetic spectrum arose another prominent challenge to "official verse culture," as Charles Bernstein calls the lyrical "mainstream." In rejecting postconfessional free verse, the New

Formalists buttoned up form in strict patterns, whereas the Language poets scattered it wildly. The Language poets emerged in the 1970s and burst into full view in the 1980s with manifestos and magazines such as $L=A=N=G=U=A=G=E$, which Bernstein coedited with Bruce Andrews. They centered their critique on the notion that poetry expresses lyric feeling and subjectivity. In their writing, they enact the poststructuralist view that the coherent self is an ideological illusion. "Various *selves*" create a poem, according to Michael Palmer, and Lyn Hejinian states that writing begins "not in the self but in language," in "the not-I." Taking the Marxist view that normative syntax and grammar enforce political oppression, these poets try to make visible the contradictory discourses hidden within language and the restrictive norms that threaten to homogenize speech. Rejecting rationalist transparency in communication, they foreground the materiality of language—its sounds, shapes, and structures, the look of words on the page. A poem, in Susan Howe's view, is not a seamless discursive unity but a collage-like assemblage, and its sutures should be left frayed and exposed. For her, as for other Language poets, the linear or narrative flow of language needs to be interrupted, even garbled, to reveal its multiple vectors, its hidden multiplicity, fractures, and instability. Despite their radicalism and iconoclasm, the Language poets—many now in university positions, some in the Academy of American Poets—build on long-standing practices and theories of "open" form, including avant-garde modernism, surrealism, Dada, Objectivism, the Black Mountain school, and the New York school, as well as the Russian formalist theory of "defamiliarization."

LATINO, NATIVE AMERICAN, AND ASIAN AMERICAN POETRIES

Another development in English-language poetry beginning in the wake of identity-centered political movements of the 1960s and 1970s and intensifying since the 1980s has been the rise of various poetries by ethnic American minorities. Some of these poetries emerged initially from specific regions. Chicano and Chicana literature is centered in the American southwest, where vast Mexican territories were ceded to the United States in 1848—what became California, Texas, Arizona, Nevada, New Mexico, Utah, and western Colorado. The Mexican American residents in these areas officially became American citizens, but the "Anglo" majority shunted them into ghettos called *barrios*. Other Mexicans made their way north in search of economic opportunity. The descendents of these immigrants and natives came to be known by the word *Chicano* in 1954 and, for women, *Chicana* in 1967. In the 1960s, as a result of heightened political and ethnic self-consciousness after the civil rights movement, the nationalist Chicano movement, *La Causa,* urged greater rights for the Mexican American minority. A protest literature developed, which prepared the way in turn for various kinds of Chicano poetry to emerge in the late 1970s. In his early work, for example, Gary Soto vividly details the often grim circumstances of migrant life and manual labor in the San Joaquin Valley. His later work centers on the intimate life of the Chicano family.

Perhaps the most striking linguistic feature of Latino poetry—which includes poetry by Chicanos and others descended from Spanish-speaking nations in the Americas—is its direct or indirect incorporation of Spanish. This linguistic hybridization at once enriches contemporary poetry and challenges the norm of American poetry written exclusively in English. In her poems, Chicana writer Lorna Dee Cervantes intersplices Spanish words and phrases with English, echoing the bilingual texture of Latino life in the United States. Other poets, such as Alberto Ríos, absorb Spanish less directly into their poetry, capturing in their use of English the music, oral rhythms, and rhetorical forms of Spanish. Ríos and other Latino poets also draw on the Latin American literary tradition of magical realism, blurring boundaries between fantasy and fact. In his "A Man Then Suddenly Stops Moving," an old man spits out a plum, only to watch it metamorphose into a younger version of himself: the old man "puts him onto his finger / like a parakeet / and sits him on the shelf / with the pictures." Not all Latino poets thematize ethnic experience. Dionisio D. Martínez, for example, an immigrant from Cuba, avails himself of the traditions of European surrealism, American abstract expressionism, and the New York school. But he, too, obliquely refers to questions of ethnic identity in his frequent images of displacement and dispossession. The sense of being between languages, between cultures, between identities informs the work of all these poets.

Native American poetry in English originates in the American west, where numerous regional tribes flourished, each with its own rich set of tales, traditions, and ways of seeing the world. While there were earlier twentieth-century precursors, the flowering of Native American poetry in English dates to the 1960s and 1970s, a period of renewed cultural self-expression, new publishing opportunities, and intense political activism—led by the American Indian Movement (AIM), a militant civil rights organization (1968–78) that worked to restore tribal lands and revitalize traditional cultures. As in Latino poetry, questions of cultural in-betweenness also pervade Native American poetry. Sherman Alexie, a Spokane/Coeur d'Alene Indian who grew up on a reservation in eastern Washington, has said that the sense of "living in both worlds"—that of the dominant Euro-American culture and a minority culture—is "part of who I am." His poems juxtapose, always ironically, popular American icons such as Marilyn Monroe with Native American practices such as the ritual use of the sweat lodge. Louise Erdrich, partly of Chippewa descent, switches back and forth between Roman Catholic and Native American points of reference. The poetry of Joy Harjo (Creek) and Leslie Marmon Silko (Laguna Pueblo) leaps the gap between "dream time" and the sordid present, between narrative realism and an elemental mysticism. Acutely aware of the colonial devastation of their indigenous languages and cultures, Native American poets vividly detail the grim circumstances—poverty, alcoholism, unemployment—of contemporary life on the reservation. But their poetry aesthetically recuperates and revitalizes elements of Native American culture, such as storytelling, tricksterism, animism, and cyclical time consciousness. For all their similarities, these poets belong to different indigenous populations and reflect different fusions of Native and Euro-American cultures, inflected by their individual sensibilities. Alexie, for example, continually recalls the Native American trickster aesthetic in his wily poems, while Harjo is more of a seer; his skeptical poems are like caustic banter, hers more like supplications or blessings, centered on the sacred, the mythical, and the natural.

American poets of the East Asian diaspora also fuse and juxtapose their divergent cultural inheritances. The number and variety of Americans of East Asian descent increased dramatically after the 1965 Immigration and Nationality Act abolished quotas favoring immigrants from northern Europe. In the wake of this watershed legislation and of the civil rights movement, a large population of East Asian Americans in the 1970s began to search for ways to embody poetically their complex cultural identities. Indonesian-born poet Li-Young Lee, who immigrated to the United States as a grown boy in 1964, writes about the painful childhood experience of being in between Mandarin Chinese and English, at home in neither. Yet his poetry brings together the imagistic influence of Tang dynasty poetry and the psychological drama of American confessional poetry. Another East Asian immigrant, born in Hong Kong, Marilyn Chin incorporates traditions such as the Chinese quatrain into a brashly American feminist neoconfessionalism. Her blunt irreverence—toward both Chinese and American culture—contrasts sharply with Lee's more elegiac sensibility, as also with Cathy Song's more delicately lyrical poetry. Of both Korean and Chinese descent, Song explores intercultural perception in economical poems that draw on her Asian cultural inheritances without idealizing or exoticizing them. Born to a Japanese father and a mother of African American, Native American, and European descent, Ai—who is especially skilled in the use of dramatic monologue—exemplifies the difficulty of ethnically defining contemporary poets, many of whom cross boundaries of race, ethnicity, and nation, whether in their familial or cultural inheritances.

TRANSNATIONAL AND CROSS-ETHNIC POETRY

There are good reasons for reading postwar poets in national or ethnic clusters. Many of these poets have taken their first cultural bearings from ethnic movements and national experiences. Their sensibilities and uses of the English language have been enriched and formed by distinctive cultural styles, political histories, and educations. Moreover, the gap between English and American poetry is often said to have widened after World War II, in contrast to the earlier transatlantic modernism of Pound, Eliot, Stein, Mina Loy, the Objectivists, Auden, and others. American poets of "open" form—the Black Mountain poets, the Beats, the New York poets—had no equivalent in Great Britain or Ireland during the late 1950s or the 1960s. "Ethnic" poets gained a strong foothold in American poetry much earlier than in British.

But in their lives and literary influences, contemporary poets have continually crossed lines of nationality and ethnicity. Strong linkages exist, for example, across the transatlantic divide. Reflecting a general postwar mood of exhaustion with the extremist politics that had devastated much of the world, American poets in the New Critical style had much in common with British poets of the Movement. Both groups rejected sharply political poetry; both refused the self-revelatory and utopian drives of late Romanticism; both privileged irony and understatement; both preferred well-made poems in rhyme, meter, and stanzaic patterns; and both adhered to a rational syntax and grammar. Although the leading figure of the Movement, Philip Larkin, was a self-declared English nativist, he took an American musical form— jazz—as his model of all that was best (traditional jazz) and worst (bebop and free jazz) in poetry and art. He and other Movement poets wanted to reestablish a "native" English line of poetry that went back to Thomas Hardy and the Georgians of the 1910s. But their willful provincialism can be understood only in a transnational context—that of reaction and resistance to the supposedly "alien" modernism of Yeats, Eliot, and Pound. Similarly, American poets of "open" form, such as Charles Olson, Allen Ginsberg, Robert Duncan, and Amiri Baraka, cannot be understood outside the transnational context of the "closed" forms that they, like Williams before them, associated with a British imperial legacy in America and that they were trying to supplant, even while reclaiming prophetic English poets such as William Blake.

A number of English, Irish, and American poets crossed the Atlantic after World War II, in the process cross-pollinating poetic forms and idioms. Having moved to the United States just before the outbreak of the war, Auden, who presided over the Yale Series of Younger Poets, became one of the strongest influences on a generation of form-hungry American poets, including Robert Hayden, Adrienne Rich, James Merrill, John Ashbery, and Anthony Hecht. Even without moving to England or Ireland, Robert Lowell influenced key poets such as Geoffrey Hill and Seamus Heaney, who muscled up their style after reading him. Sometimes postwar British poetry is presented as if no British poet were reading American verse, but Charles Tomlinson, who traveled to the United States, took Wallace Stevens, Marianne Moore, and the Objectivists as his models. Donald Davie, originally a poet of the Movement, and one of Tomlinson's students, migrated to the United States and complicated the rationalist Movement paradigm with asymmetries drawn from Pound's aesthetic. Thom Gunn, who also began as a Movement poet, decamped to California, where he studied with Yvor Winters and later wrote some of the best poetry about the effects of AIDS in the American homosexual community. Geoffrey Hill, later a migrant to the United States, took some of his first cues from the tonal, linguistic, and ethical complexity of the American New Critical poet Allen Tate. One of the most eminent poets of the Black Mountain group, British-born Denise Levertov, was a migrant from English forms to an American organicism that recuperated and updated, ironically, an English Romantic conception of poetry. Sylvia Plath, who settled in England, wrote poetry influenced by the violent primitivism of verse by her husband, Ted Hughes, England's future poet laureate. She, along with other American women poets whose work reflects what became an international women's movement, had a strong liberating influence on Irish poets such as Eavan Boland, who now teaches at Stanford University, and Indian poets such as Eunice de Souza. Among later Euro-American poets, Charles Simic, born in the former Yugoslavia, arrived in the United States at sixteen, and Jorie Graham, who grew up in Italy and France, moved to New York in her twenties. Many postwar American poets lived for long periods in Europe or other parts of the world, such as Elizabeth Bishop in Brazil, Gary Snyder in Japan, John Ashbery and Marilyn Hacker in France. Many more traveled widely and regularly. All of this physical mobility has echoed the increasing globalization of film, print, video, telecommunications, computers, and other such technologies, which, flowing across national boundaries, have exposed contemporary poets to an accelerated circulation of images, words, and experiences from around the world.

Although Irish poetry is often said to be more "conservative" than American poetry, the two national streams have frequently come together in the contemporary period. After a year at the University of California, Berkeley, Seamus Heaney wrote his important volume about Ulster's violence, *North*, in the short-lined free verse he discovered in American poets such as Robert Creeley and William Carlos Williams—a tubular style that subsequently disseminated widely in British and Irish verse. Even his earliest poetry does not flow from an exclusively Irish origin: he has credited Ted Hughes with being a key initial influence in helping him find his voice. While Heaney has spent part of many years at Harvard University, his former student Paul Muldoon has been teaching at Princeton University, both poets absorbing and returning American influences. Having lived much of his mature life in New York and London, and feeling inherently awkward in relation to Ireland because of his Protestant background, the poet Derek Mahon questions—as might perhaps all these contemporary poets—"what is meant by home" ("Afterlives"). The ample record of transatlantic crossings, migrations, and entanglements should remind us that, even if we cannot abandon altogether conceptions of contemporary poetry as "British," "Irish," or "American," we should at least qualify and complicate what is meant by home.

Postcolonial poets are even less possible to understand within strictly limited identity- or nation-based paradigms, since their lives, histories, and poetry have persistently crossed such boundaries. Growing up in the interstices of indigenous and imposed colonial cultures, most of the prominent first- and second-generation postcolonial poets had British educations at home and then ventured to the imperial "motherland" or to the United States for higher education, even including the "nativist" poets who put the strongest emphasis on their local cultural resources: Jamaican poet Louise Bennett, though writing almost entirely in West Indian English, studied at the Royal Academy of Dramatic Art, in London; the most influential Afro-Caribbean-centered poet, Kamau Brathwaite, studied at Cambridge University and the University of Sussex; and Okot p'Bitek, though reclaiming the idioms, tales, and perspectives of East African village culture, was trained as an anthropologist at Oxford University. A. K. Ramanujan, who completed a dissertation at Indiana University, wryly noted that Indology was a Western invention. Those who stayed at home for higher education, such as Derek Walcott and Christopher Okigbo, were, paradoxically, among the most internationalist in their poetry, Walcott drawing on the Elizabethan and modernist traditions, Okigbo intermingling high modernist strategies with Igbo praise songs. Because of the economic imbalance between the First World and their homelands, many postcolonial poets have lived, taught, and written for long periods in Britain—Grace Nichols and Wole Soyinka—and/or in North America—Brathwaite, Ramanujan, Walcott, Michael Ondaatje, Lorna Goodison, and Agha Shahid Ali. The ironies of postcolonial literary influence reveal the limitations of a nationalist approach to contemporary poetry: the High Church royalist T. S. Eliot was, for example, one of the strongest early influences on Brathwaite, Walcott, and Ali, helping free them from the dead hand of Victorian colonial models. Although many contemporary American and British poets have seen Anglo-modernism as compromised by the reactionary politics of its leading figures, poets of the formerly colonized world have often embraced it as profoundly enabling and subversive, borrowing modernist principles such as juxtaposition, montage, compression, allusion, and psychic ambivalence to fashion their own hybrid art.

Finally, "ethnic" American poetries are by definition cross-cultural, as poetries of national, ethnic, and linguistic in-betweenness. Many Latino and East Asian American poets were born abroad, such as Dionisio D. Martínez, Li-Young Lee, and Marilyn Chin. Still more of these "ethnic" poets are the children of parents who spoke another language at home, including Spanish, Chinese, Japanese, Korean, and Native American languages. Arising out of this interlingual and intercultural matrix, the cross-cultural texture of this poetry, interweaving indigenous and Anglo-American traditions, has much in common with the hybridity of postcolonial and of African American poetry. While the strongest impulse in "ethnic" American poetries has been to reclaim indigenous cultural resources, these poetries are also, in turn, closely interlinked with one another and with the dominant Euro-American traditions in English-language poetry. An Asian American poet such as Chin clearly draws on the African American feminist poetics of June Jordan and others who came out of the Black Arts Movement, and African American poets have drawn, in turn, on other ethnic traditions—Thylias Moss, for example, on the neosurrealist style Simic made partly out of Serbian and Slovene sources. The neoconfessional mode that seems to have lost much of its force for Anglo-American poets has been renewed and adapted by poets such as Lee, Alberto Ríos, and Joy Harjo, who write poems that straddle the introspection of confessional poetry and the communal reach of "identity poetry." We can only anticipate with excitement the new intercultural forms and connections that the next generation of poets will forge in an increasingly transnational and cross-ethnic world.

CHARLES OLSON
1910–1970

Charles Olson is a pivotal figure in the development of American poetry after World War II. His combination of an intense personal dynamism with experimentation in form, primitivism in sensibility, and responsiveness to the environment helped propel into being new kinds of poetry. His improvisatory poetics inspired avant-garde writers as different as the then-Beat poet LeRoi Jones (later Amiri Baraka) and the Language poet Susan Howe. Conceiving of poetry as "projective" or "open," he helped set in motion an aesthetic of sprawling energy, loosened structures, and unpredictable didacticism, all of which ran counter to the New Critical principles of unity, balance, and subtle indirection.

Olson was the dominant and senior figure in a group that included Robert Creeley, Denise Levertov, Robert Duncan, and other writers centered at Black Mountain College, an experimental school in North Carolina where he was first instructor and later rector, or head. He had a gift for prophetic exhortation that combined the plainest language with bursts of obscure information about Neolithic humans and the Pleistocene age or Hittite poems and Mayan inscriptions.

Olson worked, as he proudly indicated, in the same vein as Ezra Pound and William Carlos Williams, and he was particularly impressed by *The Cantos* and by *Paterson*. Pound's work he found "ego-dominated," however, and lacking "flow" (*Mayan Letters*), and in a pamphlet titled *Proprioception* ("one's own peception") he urged writers: "Wash the ego out." In Williams, he saw the ego as happily eradicated, but he objected to *Paterson*'s limitation to one city's history. Nonetheless, Olson's own epic effort, *The Maximus Poems*, resembles *The Cantos* in its free verse assemblage of heterogeneous incidents, characters, and scenes, and it resembles *Paterson* in centering on a specific town, Gloucester, Massachusetts. Instead of calling his representative man Gloucester, Olson names him Maximus. The name might seem to bear a relation to Olson's height of six feet seven or eight inches, but it is more closely related to his theory of the writer as maximally here, living in the moment, resuming in the psychological self past and present, and always constituting, as well, a function of the environment. "I, Maximus / metal hot from boiling water" ("I, Maximus of Gloucester, to You").

Olson was born on December 27, 1910, in Worcester, Massachusetts, to a Swedish father and an Irish American mother. He speaks of his parents as his "definers": "the work of each of us is to find out the true lineaments of ourselves by facing up to the primal features of these founders who lie buried in us—that this is us, the Double-Backed Beast" (*Twentieth-Century Authors*, First Supplement, ed. Stanley Kunitz). He seeks in effect a juncture of his own past with a mythological past, "the hinges of civilization to be put back on the door" (*Proprioception*). The necessary mythology he discovers as much among the Sumerians and Mayans as among Americans, and so he can say in *The Maximus Poems*, "Just last week / 300,000,000 years ago" ("Song 4").

Though well-read, Olson was not bookish and would have nothing to do with T. S. Eliot's theory, in "Tradition and the Individual Talent," of mere "literary antecedence" (*A Bibliography of America for Edward Dorn*). He found it "awkward to call myself a poet or a writer. If there are no walls there are no names. This is the morning, after the dispersion, and the work of the morning is methodology: how to use oneself, and on what. That is my profession. I am an archeologist of morning" (Kunitz). He preferred, among writers, Homer and those before Homer, and, in later time, visionary outsiders, such as Herman Melville, Fyodor Dostoyevsky, Arthur Rimbaud, and D. H. Lawrence.

The prophetic writers William Blake, Walt Whitman, and Friedrich Nietzsche are also implicated in his thought.

Olson believed that his age took its fundamental character from being posthumanist, posthistoric, and postmodern (he inaugurated the latter term's use for poetry). A letter to Cid Corman, editor of *Origin* (an important magazine of the 1950s), celebrates "ENERGY" over "humanism," a leaping "NATURE" over "progress, accumulation, succession, tradition" (*Letters for Origin, 1950–1956*, ed. Albert Glover). Against reason and the art of comparison, Olson offers direct perception and contraries. In *Proprioception*, he speaks forcefully if vaguely of "the data of depth sensibility." In a letter of May 1959, Olson wrote that he would replace "the Classical-representational by the *primitive-abstract*" (*Selected Writings*). Accordingly, he does not so much try to persuade as to confront and overwhelm.

Olson's first book, *Call Me Ishmael*, was an attempt to read Melville viscerally rather than critically. It was published in 1947, by which time Olson was thirty-seven. Up to then, his life is somewhat obscured by his own random accounts of it. He was "uneducated" at Wesleyan, Yale, and Harvard Universities: "I have had to learn the simplest things / last," he says in "Maximus, to Himself." From Wesleyan, he received a B.A. in 1932 and an M.A. the following year. He taught first at Clark University, in Worcester, then, from 1936 to 1939, at Harvard. For the next nine years he had various occupations, which came to a focus in the publication of his Melville book. The following year, 1948, he took the place of his friend the novelist Edward Dahlberg at Black Mountain College. Many of its teachers and students became important figures in painting, music, and dance as well as in literature. In 1951, Olson became rector of the college, and he stayed in this position until 1956. He was to teach later, in his own dynamic, unpredictable fashion, at the State University of New York at Buffalo, and then (briefly) at the University of Connecticut.

Though some of them were written earlier, Olson's poems became known and were collected in the 1960s. He had been struggling to phrase his aesthetic position and, in 1950, succeeded in formulating his essay on "Projective Verse." This became the manifesto for a number of writers; indeed, William Carlos Williams was so impressed that he quoted much of it in his *Autobiography*. In place of inherited line, stanza, formal pattern—all that Olson calls "closed form" or "verse that print bred"—Olson offers "composition by field," open form. Perhaps with William Blake's dictum in mind that "energy is eternal delight," Olson says: "A poem is energy transferred from where the poet got it (he will have some several causations), by way of the poem itself to, all the way over to, the reader. Okay. Then the poem itself must, at all points, be a high energy-construct and, at all points, an energy-discharge." For this poetry, "Form is never more than an extension of content," a quotation from Robert Creeley that Olson incorporates in his poem "A B Cs." The form is somehow to be the product of the breath rather than of literary tradition. "Who knows what a poem ought to sound like? until it's thar?" This new verse, he insists, "involves a stance toward reality outside a poem as well as a new stance towards the reality of a poem itself." Olson rejects the humanizing of the external world and extols "objectism"—by which he means "getting rid of the lyrical interference of the individual as ego, of the 'subject' and his soul." He abolishes the poet as observer, or commentator, in favor of the poem as the necessary expression of a confluence with the poet in and out of space and time, archaically rooted but totally present.

Pacific Lament

In memory of William Hickey, a member of
the crew of the U.S.S. *Growler*, lost at sea
in February, 1944.

Black at that depth
turn, golden boy no more
white bone to bone, turn
hear who bore you weep
hear him who made you   5
deep there on ocean's floor
turn
as waters stir;
turn, bone of man

Cold as a planet is   10
cold, beat of blood no more
the salt sea's course
along the bone jaw white
stir, boy, stir
motion without motion   15
stir, and hear
love come down.

Down as you fell
sidewise, stair to green stair
without breath, down   20
the tumble of ocean
to find you, bone
cold and new among the ships
and men and fish askew.

You alone o golden boy no more   25
turn now and sleep
washed white by water
sleep in your black deep
by water out of which man came
to find his legs, arms, love, pain.   30
Sleep, boy, sleep
in older arms than hers,
rocked by an older father;
toss no more,
love;   35
sleep.

1946

The Thing Was Moving

It's so beautiful, life, goddamn death
that we have to die, only the mind knows
what lies next the heart or a five-petaled flower
restores the fringed gentians[1] I used to so love
I'd lie amongst them in the meadow near the house   5
which was later covered by a dump to make an athletic field
and the brook was gone to which we tried to speed our sleds
from the hill the house stood on and which the dump
was meant to join, the loss punctuated by the shooting
my father taught me with the rifle he me from the back porch   10
of the three-decker, the rats living among the cans and peat
as the dump came closer, and I hated
all of it (the same porch the chameleon he had bought me
escaped from, from the cage I'd made it
of old screen when we brought it home from the circus   15

the smoke from the dump-fires all the time the thing was moving
toward us, covering the meadow, coming from the hill
(where we had had the single cable swing had broke
that day i was alone there and i had flown
out over all that space, and my glasses   20
beyond me, and my back to this day . . . and i groping
not to tell my parents, and to find the glasses
to find my way back. The fire-engines
in the evening dousing—and no flames but the littlest, all
smoke turning into steam there, but the excitement . . .   25

the concrete sections, when the dump began to reach
the brook, to put it under, like hoops we could not roll
in which—they were so high—we lost ourselves
like tunnels, or took it we were five-figured forms
fit to fill a circle and be acrobats, our heads   30
wedged but no movement of those sections even
when we pried them and were unknowingly in such danger
as when we built the club-house of railroad ties
on the edge of another flat, the swamp where the man
and his horse and team went down in the quicksand, and we   35
did not know until after the cops had broken down the structure
and even later when the auto showrooms covered it, and piles
had to be driven . . . the hunting, of each other, before the brook
was let in and only way above, or below at Chandler Street
was it any more where I had sunk in, where the irises were,   40
where I had seen my first turtle, or further up, where
girls had swum naked that day I had tittupped
from the piano lesson, seeking my friends, and suddenly,
coming on the pool, had heard the voices first, and slowed

1. Flowering plants.

so that I saw them from the bushes (the older woman   45
turning me back . . . the invasion

or the ford[2] (below Dick Marsden's house) horses crossed
and we sailed boats, or made dams, the wonder
of the way the hill sloped up there, the gradual way
before it became a suburb and was still the West   50
(the trench we were sure had been emplacements
of King Phillip's Wars[3] ended before the ford, before
the whole brook system got transverse to what it was below
near where I lived, Hill's Farm getting its fields
from the change of the direction of its flow,   55
and the topography
                    the flowers (as well as the ball field)
were located, in my space, by this curving
from west to south, the farm marking the change
and running against the foot of my house, the brick wall   60
on which all the wood stood which shook
when the wind bellied down that valley and struck
the broad back of the house and I used to think
why the whipping of the house on that third-floor
didn't throw it down, and only that the storm   65
was not like marching men on a bridge, was out of step
was irregular as men are, and as multiple, the times we are
and our materials are so much more numerous
than any such thing as the heart's flow
or the sun's coming up, why   70
man is man's delight, and there is no backward
except his, how far it goes, as far
as any thing he's made, dug up or lighted
by a flare in some such cave as I never knew
except as that concrete hid my brook and I was as large   75
(before they put the pieces in below ground) inside any one hoop
as any pentamerous thing, this figwort[4]
which provokes me
and I study
bract thallus involucre whorl[5]   80
of all my life, of torus[6] I am, holding
all I shall be, hungry
that it should never end, that my throat
which has no longer thymus and all that went with it
might speak forever the glory of   85
what it is to live, so bashful as man is
bare

1952   1987

---

2. Shallow portion where a body of water can be
more easily crossed.
3. War between Native Americans and British set-
tlers in New England (1675–76).

4. Plant of the snapdragon family. *Pentamerous:*
having five parts.
5. Technical descriptions of parts of flowers.
6. Ring-shaped surface.

From The Maximus Poems

I, Maximus of Gloucester,[7] to You

Off-shore, by islands hidden in the blood
jewels & miracles, I, Maximus
a metal hot from boiling water, tell you
what is a lance, who obeys the figures of
the present dance   5

1

the thing you're after
may lie around the bend
of the nest (second, time slain, the bird! the bird![8]

And there! (strong) thrust, the mast! flight
                    (of the bird   10
                    o kylix,[9] o
                    Antony of Padua[1]
                    sweep low, o bless

the roofs, the old ones, the gentle steep ones
on whose ridge-poles the gulls sit, from which they depart,   15

                              And the flake-racks[2]
of my city!

2

love is form, and cannot be without
important substance (the weight
say, 58 carats each one of us, perforce   20
our goldsmith's scale

                    feather to feather added
                    (and what is mineral, what
                    is curling hair, the string
                    you carry in your nervous beak, these   25

                    make bulk, these, in the end, are
                    the sum

                    (o my lady of good voyage[3]
                    in whose arm, whose left arm rests

---

7. Gloucester, Massachusetts, is a fishing town northeast of Boston founded in 1623. Olson, or Maximus, peoples the town with historic and invented figures, and with people he knew when he lived there as a boy and as a young man.
8. Throughout his writing, Olson used unclosed parentheses to signify birth and a receptive consciousness.

9. A shallow drinking bowl of classical Greece.
1. Thirteenth-century Franciscan monk and teacher. He preached a famous sermon to the fishes in the Brenta River, near Padua.
2. Used for drying fish.
3. The Virgin Mary, depicted on the roof of a church in Gloucester, My Lady of Good Voyage, as holding a schooner.

no boy[4] but a carefully carved wood, a painted face, a schooner!   30
a delicate mast, as bow-sprit for

                              forwarding

                                  3

the underpart is, though stemmed, uncertain
is, as sex is, as moneys are, facts!
facts, to be dealt with, as the sea is, the demand   35
that they be played by, that they only can be, that they must
be played by, said he, coldly, the
ear!

By ear, he sd.
But that which matters, that which insists, that which will last,   40
that! o my people, where shall you find it, how, where, where shall you
       listen
when all is become billboards, when, all, even silence, is spray-gunned?

when even our bird, my roofs,
cannot be heard

when even you, when sound itself is neoned in?   45

when, on the hill, over the water
where she who used to sing,
when the water glowed,
black, gold, the tide
outward, at evening   50

when bells came like boats
over the oil-slicks, milkweed
hulls

And a man slumped,
attentionless,   55
against pink shingles

o sea city)

                                  4

one loves only form,
and form only comes
into existence when   60
the thing is born

              born of yourself, born
              of hay and cotton struts,

4. As in conventional representations of Mary with the baby Jesus.

of street-pickings, wharves, weeds
you carry in, my bird   65

of a bone of a fish
of a straw, or will
of a color, of a bell
of yourself, torn

5

love is not easy   70
but how shall you know,
New England, now
that pejorocracy[5] is here, how
that street-cars, o Oregon, twitter
in the afternoon, offend   75
a black-gold loin?

how shall you strike,
o swordsman, the blue-red black
when, last night, your aim
was mu-sick, mu-sick, mu-sick   80
And not the cribbage game?

(o Gloucester-man,
weave
your birds and fingers
new, your roof-tops,   85
clean shit upon racks
sunned on
American
braid
with others like you, such   90
extricable surface
as faun and oral,
satyr lesbos[6] vase

o kill kill kill kill kill[7]
those   95
who advertise you
out)

6

in! in! the bow-sprit, bird, the beak
in, the bend is, in, goes in, the form
that which you make, what holds, which is   100

5. "Worsening rule"; Ezra Pound's term for the increasing insincerity he saw in art and culture.
6. The island of Lesbos, near Greece, was home to the sixth-century B.C.E. lyric poet Sappho. Fauns and satyrs were minor classical deities of the fields and forests.
7. Cf. Shakespeare's *King Lear* 4.6.181: "Then, kill, kill, kill, kill, kill, kill!"

the law of object, strut after strut, what you are, what you must be, what
the force can throw up, can, right now hereinafter erect,
the mast, the mast, the tender
mast!

        The nest, I say, to you, I Maximus, say   105
        under the hand, as I see it, over the waters
        from this place where I am, where I hear,
        can still hear

        from where I carry you a feather
        as though, sharp, I picked up,   110
        in the afternoon delivered you
        a jewel,
                it flashing more than a wing,
        than any old romantic thing,
        than memory, than place,   115
        than anything other than that which you carry

        than that which is,
        call it a nest, around the head of, call it
        the next second

        than that which you   120
        can do!

                      1953

Maximus, to Himself

I have had to learn the simplest things
last. Which made for difficulties.
Even at sea I was slow, to get the hand out, or to cross
a wet deck.
        The sea was not, finally, my trade.   5
But even my trade, at it, I stood estranged
from that which was most familiar.[8] Was delayed,
and not content with the man's argument
that such postponement
is now the nature of   10
obedience,
        that we are all late
        in a slow time,
        that we grow up many
        And the single   15
        is not easily
        known

8. Cf. Greek philosopher Heracleitus (c. 540–c. 480 B.C.E.): "We are estranged from that with which we
are most familiar."

It could be, though the sharpness (the *achiote*[9])
I note in others,
makes more sense   20
than my own distances. The agilities

        they show daily
        who do the world's
        businesses
        And who do nature's   25
        as I have no sense
        I have done either

I have made dialogues,
have discussed ancient texts,
have thrown what light I could, offered   30
what pleasures
doceat[1] allows

        But the known?
This, I have had to be given,
a life, love, and from one man   35
the world

        Tokens.
        But sitting here
        I look out as a wind
        and water man, testing   40
        And missing
        some proof

I know the quarters
of the weather, where it comes from,
where it goes. But the stem of me,   45
this I took from their welcome,
or their rejection, of me

        And my arrogance
        was neither diminished
        nor increased,   50
        by the communication

2

It is undone business
I speak of, this morning,

9. Seed crushed to make a dye with a color like that of red pepper (hence, sharp).
1. That he teach (Latin); one of the traditional functions of a poet, as later emphasized by Ezra Pound.

with the sea
stretching out   55
from my feet

                                                                                  1960

Maximus, to Gloucester, Letter 19 (A Pastoral Letter

relating
to the care of souls,
it says)

                He had smiled at us,
                each time we were in town, inquired   5
                how the baby was, had two cents
                for the weather, wore
                (besides his automobile)
                good clothes.
                            And a pink face.   10

                It was yesterday
                it all came out. The gambit
                (as he crossed the street,
                after us): "I don't believe
                I know your name." Given.   15
                How do you do,
                how do you do. And then:
                "Pardon me, but
                what church
                do you belong to,   20
                may I ask?"

And the whole street, the town, the cities, the nation
blinked, in the afternoon sun, at the gun
was held at them. And I wavered
in the thought.   25

                I sd, you may, sir.
                He sd, what, sir.
                I sd, none,
                sir.

And the light was back.   30

For I am no merchant.
Nor so young I need to take a stance
to a loaded
smile.

I have known the face   35
of God.
And turned away,
turned
as He did,
his backside   40

                              2

And now it is noon
of a cloudy sunday.
And a bird sings
loudly

And my daughter, naked   45
on the porch, sings
as best she can, and loudly,
back

        She wears her own face
        as we do not,   50
        until we cease to wear
        the clouds
        of all confusion,

        of all confusers
        who wear the false face   55
        He never wore, Whose
        is terrible. Is
        perfection

                                                          1960

Maximus to Gloucester, Letter 27 [Withheld]

I come back to the geography of it,
the land falling off to the left
where my father shot his scabby golf
and the rest of us played baseball
into the summer darkness until no flies   5
could be seen and we came home
to our various piazzas where the women
buzzed

To the left the land fell to the city,
to the right, it fell to the sea   10

I was so young my first memory
is of a tent spread to feed lobsters

to Rexall[2] conventioneers, and my father,
a man for kicks, came out of the tent roaring
with a bread-knife in his teeth to take care of   15
a druggist they'd told him had made a pass at
my mother, she laughing, so sure, as round
as her face, Hines[3] pink and apple,
under one of those frame hats women then

This is no bare incoming   20
of novel abstract form, this

is no welter or the forms
of those events, this,

Greeks, is the stopping
of the battle   25

          It is the imposing
of all those antecedent predecessions, the precessions

of me, the generation of those facts
which are my words, it is coming

from all that I no longer am, yet am,   30
the slow westward motion of

more than I am

There is no strict personal order

for my inheritance.

          No Greek will be able   35

to discriminate my body.

          An American

is a complex of occasions,

themselves a geometry

of spatial nature.   40

          I have this sense,

2. American drug company.
3. Duncan Hines, maker of cake mixes and other food products.

that I am one

with my skin

    Plus this—plus this:

that forever the geography   45

which leans in

on me I compell

backwards I compell Gloucester

to yield, to

change   50

    Polis

is this

                1968

[Sun / Right in My Eye]

Sun
right in my eye
4 PM   December 2nd   arrived
at my kitchen
window blazing   5
at me full in the
face approaching
the hill it sets
behind glaring
in its burst of late   10
heat right on me
and as orange and hot
as sun at noonday practically
can be. Only this one
is straight at me like a   15
beam shot to hit me
It feels like
enforcing itself
on me giving me its
message that it is sliding   20
under the hill and
that I better
hear it say

be hot man
be hot   25
be hot and orange
like I am
I am
sending you
this message as   30
I slip exactly to
West I am burning you man
as I leave   I'm even stronger
now just as I
go   I am already   35
cooled that much   but still
I turn on you
and flare
as I start to
go.   But still   40
hot and <u>red</u> now blaring
on the south slope of my disappearance
point.
Now I begin to
go hear me I   45
have sent you
the message   I am
gone   1975

ELIZABETH BISHOP
1911–1979

Elizabeth Bishop, whose fame and influence have mounted steadily since her death, is one of the central progenitors of contemporary poetry. She masters and remakes inherited lyric models perhaps as successfully as any poet of her generation. Her controlled artifice contrasts with the "open" form espoused by postwar poets such as Charles Olson, the author of long, declamatory, ramshackle poems indebted to Ezra Pound and William Carlos Williams. Instead, she takes her cue from Marianne Moore, who remarked, "Elizabeth Bishop is spectacular in being unspectacular," and who praised Bishop's technique for being "cold, sober," "accurate and modest" (*The Complete Prose of Marianne Moore*).

Bishop is an exacting and exquisite miniaturist. Her poetry is precise in its descriptive language and rigorous in its discretion. Her fastidious eye inspects with luminous intensity the physical world. "Watch it closely," she says in "The Monument." What she observes takes form and gathers itself, as if nature were being brought to a boil: under her eye, "The Fish" and all around it turn to "rainbow, rainbow, rainbow."

Bishop was born on February 8, 1911, in Worcester, Massachusetts. An only child, she suffered the first of many calamitous losses at only eight months, when her father died. Her mother, greatly afflicted by his death, was in and out of hospitals and mental institutions for the next few years, until she was diagnosed as insane and permanently institutionalized. Bishop was five when this happened, and though her mother lived another eighteen years, she never saw her again. Bishop was taken in by her maternal grandparents in Great Village, Nova Scotia, where she would subsequently return for summers; but she was soon uprooted once again ("kidnapped" was her word) by her father's wealthy family, which took her first to its mansion in Worcester, Massachusetts, then to live with her mother's sister Maud, near Boston. She spent much of her childhood in bed suffering from asthma and various allergies, but also memorizing poetry. "In the Waiting Room," "Sestina," "First Death in Nova Scotia," and the autobiographical prose piece "In the Village" are among her writings about her youth. After a few years in high school, Bishop attended Vassar College, where she made important literary friendships, the most important with Moore. But Bishop's life would continue to be plagued by asthma, depression, and alcoholism. Living off a modest income from her father's estate, she spent some years in New York City and Key West, Florida. In 1947, she met and became lifelong friends with Robert Lowell, who helped her secure a year-long stint as the consultant in poetry to the Library of Congress (1949–50).

In 1951, depressed, lonely, and fearing for her health, Bishop sailed to Brazil on a planned trip around the world. She fell ill after eating fruit from a Brazilian cashew tree and then fell in love with the person who was taking care of her, Lota de Macedo Soares, a wealthy Brazilian aristocrat she had known at Vassar. Bishop stayed on in Soares's Brazilian villa for the next fifteen years. Little wonder that travel and exile should be steady themes in her work; in "Questions of Travel," she asks, "Should we have stayed at home, / wherever that may be?" Bishop returned to the United States after Lota Soares's health deteriorated in 1967, and Soares joined her in New York, only to commit suicide. In 1970, Bishop began teaching at Harvard University; she died in Cambridge at sixty-eight. She had won the Pulitzer Prize in 1956, the National Book Award in 1970, the Neustadt International Prize and the National Book Critics Circle Award in 1976.

A perfectionist, Bishop published relatively few poems. Many of them, especially early on, begin with a found object, often nondescript (e.g., the misprinted word "Man-Moth"; "the monument") yet capable of being contemplated with passion and so imaginatively transfigured. In contrast to the confessional poetry written by her contemporaries, which she found distasteful, her poems typically deflect or distill autobiographical content. Emotion is often attributed to rather distant others, as in "Songs for a Colored Singer," a poem about Billie Holiday that contains the wry promise "I'm going to go and take the bus / and find someone monogamous." At times, she seems determinedly reticent, as if to suggest that her life inheres in the way she observes external phenomena, not in any private events. But Bishop is clearly capable of writing poetry as intensely personal and erotic as anything since Sappho. Not published until the year 2000, long after her death, "Vague Poem" ends:

> Just now, when I saw you naked again,
> I thought the same words: rose-rock, rock-rose . . .
> Rose, trying, working, to show itself,
> forming, folding over,
> unimaginable connections, unseen, shining edges.
> Rose-rock, unformed, flesh beginning, crystal by crystal,
> clear pink breasts and darker, crystalline nipples,
> rose-rock, rose-quartz, roses, roses, roses,
> exacting roses from the body,
> and the even darker, accurate, rose of sex—

But Bishop left such works unpublished in her lifetime, and this poem, if astounding in its imagistic crisscrossing of stone and flesh, its rhapsodic rhythms, and its transformation of the blason (lyric inventory of the beloved's parts), is unfinished.

The posthumous appearance of clearly autobiographical material has helped readers appreciate more fully the personal dimension of Bishop's verse. Grief, tenderness, terror, desire—such feelings are vividly present within Bishop's rhythms, metaphors, and forms. The late poem "One Art," with its repeated line "The art of losing isn't hard to master," exemplifies the fusion of passionate self-expression and precise self-control in Bishop's poetry. The speaker returns obsessively to losses that range from the trivial ("door keys") to the unbearably large ("two cities," "a continent," perhaps even "you"); but Bishop's use of the insistently repetitive form of the villanelle, and her tonal blending of antic self-mockery with melancholy, enable her both to contain and to display overwhelming feelings of fear and grief. In "Crusoe in England," Bishop sees in the speaker's grief over displacement and lost same-sex companionship the image of her own experience: "—And Friday, my dear Friday, died of measles / seventeen years ago come March." Autobiography is unmistakable in "In the Waiting Room," a poem in which Bishop even names herself: "But I felt: you are an *I*, / you are an *Elizabeth*." Yet the poem throws into doubt the very contours of identity—"Why should I be my aunt, / or me, or anyone?" At once personal and objective, self-expressive and self-effacing, Bishop's poetry confounds such distinctions.

One way to take the measure of Bishop's achievement is to notice how many different forms and genres she wrote in, each time seeming to transform the template permanently. She composed in both metered and free verse, in each case keeping the stresses muted. She used fixed forms with strict requirements, such as the sestina and the villanelle, as well as long verse paragraphs of varying lengths. She wrote in perfect rhyme, off-rhyme, and unrhymed verse. While she produced poems of unparalleled lucidity about nature and landscape, she also fashioned self-referring poems about art, language, and representation, such as "The Monument" and "Poem." Some works, such as "The Fish," manage to be both kinds of poems at once. Bishop is famed for her understatement and restraint, her unpretentious diction of the everyday and the domestic; and yet in "At the Fishhouses" she summons a visionary rhetoric, moving at the end from a description of cold seawater to a meditation on knowledge as "dark, salt, clear, moving, utterly free." As this example suggests, she humanized the natural world through anthropomorphic language, but she also criticized attempts to personify and prettify the nonhuman: *Too pretty, dreamlike mimicry!*" calls out the speaker of "The Armadillo." Bishop is a realist and a surrealist, a poet of place and of displacement. That she succeeds so completely in all these modes and styles, while remaining unmistakably herself, ensures her reputation as a poet, and her use as a model for future poets, for many years to come.

The Map

Land lies in water; it is shadowed green.
Shadows, or are they shallows, at its edges
showing the line of long sea-weeded ledges
where weeds hang to the simple blue from green.
Or does the land lean down to lift the sea from under,   5
drawing it unperturbed around itself?
Along the fine tan sandy shelf
is the land tugging at the sea from under?

The shadow of Newfoundland lies flat and still.
Labrador's[1] yellow, where the moony Eskimo   10
has oiled it. We can stroke these lovely bays,

1. Northeastern portion of the Canadian mainland in the province of Newfoundland.

under a glass as if they were expected to blossom,
or as if to provide a clean cage for invisible fish.
The names of seashore towns run out to sea,
the names of cities cross the neighboring mountains   15
—the printer here experiencing the same excitement
as when emotion too far exceeds its cause.
These peninsulas take the water between thumb and finger
like women feeling for the smoothness of yard-goods.

Mapped waters are more quiet than the land is,   20
lending the land their waves' own conformation:
and Norway's hare runs south in agitation,
profiles investigate the sea, where land is.
Are they assigned, or can the countries pick their colors?
—What suits the character or the native waters best.   25
Topography displays no favorites; North's as near as West.
More delicate than the historians' are the map-makers' colors.

                                                                1935, 1946

The Man-Moth[2]

        Here, above,
cracks in the buildings are filled with battered moonlight.
The whole shadow of Man is only as big as his hat.
It lies at his feet like a circle for a doll to stand on,
and he makes an inverted pin, the point magnetized to the moon.   5
He does not see the moon; he observes only her vast properties,
feeling the queer light on his hands, neither warm nor cold,
of a temperature impossible to record in thermometers.

        But when the Man-Moth
pays his rare, although occasional, visits to the surface,   10
the moon looks rather different to him. He emerges
from an opening under the edge of one of the sidewalks
and nervously begins to scale the faces of the buildings.
He thinks the moon is a small hole at the top of the sky,
proving the sky quite useless for protection.   15
He trembles, but must investigate as high as he can climb.

        Up the façades,
his shadow dragging like a photographer's cloth behind him,
he climbs fearfully, thinking that this time he will manage
to push his small head through that round clean opening   20
and be forced through, as from a tube, in black scrolls on the light.
(Man, standing below him, has no such illusions.)
But what the Man-Moth fears most he must do, although
he fails, of course, and falls back scared but quite unhurt.

2. "Newspaper misprint for 'mammoth' " [Bishop's note].

Then he returns   25
to the pale subways of cement he calls his home. He flits,
he flutters, and cannot get aboard the silent trains
fast enough to suit him. The doors close swiftly.
The Man-Moth always seats himself facing the wrong way
and the train starts at once at its full, terrible speed,   30
without a shift in gears or a gradation of any sort.
He cannot tell the rate at which he travels backwards.

Each night he must
be carried through artificial tunnels and dream recurrent dreams.
Just as the ties recur beneath his train, these underlie   35
his rushing brain. He does not dare look out the window,
for the third rail, the unbroken draught of poison,
runs there beside him. He regards it as a disease
he has inherited the susceptibility to. He has to keep
his hands in his pockets, as others must wear mufflers.   40

If you catch him,
hold up a flashlight to his eye. It's all dark pupil,
an entire night itself, whose haired horizon tightens
as he stares back, and closes up the eye. Then from the lids
one tear, his only possession, like the bee's sting, slips.   45
Slyly he palms it, and if you're not paying attention
he'll swallow it. However, if you watch, he'll hand it over,
cool as from underground springs and pure enough to drink.

1936, 1946

The Monument

Now can you see the monument? It is of wood
built somewhat like a box. No. Built
like several boxes in descending sizes
one above the other.
Each is turned half-way round so that   5
its corners point toward the sides
of the one below and the angles alternate.
Then on the topmost cube is set
a sort of fleur-de-lys of weathered wood,
long petals of board, pierced with odd holes,   10
four-sided, stiff, ecclesiastical.
From it four thin, warped poles spring out,
(slanted like fishing-poles or flag-poles)
and from them jig-saw work hangs down,
four lines of vaguely whittled ornament   15
over the edges of the boxes
to the ground.
The monument is one-third set against
a sea; two-thirds against a sky.

The view is geared   20
(that is, the view's perspective)
so low there is no "far away,"
and we are far away within the view.
A sea of narrow, horizontal boards
lies out behind our lonely monument,   25
its long grains alternating right and left
like floor-boards—spotted, swarming-still,
and motionless. A sky runs parallel,
and it is palings, coarser than the sea's:
splintery sunlight and long-fibred clouds.   30
"Why does that strange sea make no sound?
Is it because we're far away?
Where are we? Are we in Asia Minor,
or in Mongolia?"
           An ancient promontory,   35
an ancient principality whose artist-prince
might have wanted to build a monument
to mark a tomb or boundary, or make
a melancholy or romantic scene of it . . .
"But that queer sea looks made of wood,   40
half-shining, like a driftwood sea.
And the sky looks wooden, grained with cloud.
It's like a stage-set; it is all so flat!
Those clouds are full of glistening splinters!
What is that?"   45
           It is the monument.
"It's piled-up boxes,
outlined with shoddy fret-work, half-fallen off,
cracked and unpainted. It looks old."
—The strong sunlight, the wind from the sea,   50
all the conditions of its existence,
may have flaked off the paint, if ever it was painted,
and made it homelier than it was.
"Why did you bring me here to see it?
A temple of crates in cramped and crated scenery,   55
what can it prove?
I am tired of breathing this eroded air,
this dryness in which the monument is cracking."

It is an artifact
of wood. Wood holds together better   60
than sea or cloud or sand could by itself,
much better than real sea or sand or cloud.
It chose that way to grow and not to move.
The monument's an object, yet those decorations,
carelessly nailed, looking like nothing at all,   65
give it away as having life, and wishing;
wanting to be a monument, to cherish something.
The crudest scroll-work says "commemorate,"
while once each day the light goes around it
like a prowling animal,   70

or the rain falls on it, or the wind blows into it.
It may be solid, may be hollow.
The bones of the artist-prince may be inside
or far away on even drier soil.
But roughly but adequately it can shelter   75
what is within (which after all
cannot have been intended to be seen).
It is the beginning of a painting,
a piece of sculpture, or poem, or monument,
and all of wood. Watch it closely.   80

                                        1939, 1946

The Fish

I caught a tremendous fish
and held him beside the boat
half out of water, with my hook
fast in the corner of his mouth.
He didn't fight.   5
He hadn't fought at all.
He hung a grunting weight,
battered and venerable
and homely. Here and there
his brown skin hung in strips   10
like ancient wallpaper,
and its pattern of darker brown
was like wallpaper:
shapes like full-blown roses
stained and lost through age.   15
He was speckled with barnacles,
fine rosettes of lime,
and infested
with tiny white sea-lice,
and underneath two or three   20
rags of green weed hung down.
While his gills were breathing in
the terrible oxygen
—the frightening gills,
fresh and crisp with blood,   25
that can cut so badly—
I thought of the coarse white flesh
packed in like feathers,
the big bones and the little bones,
the dramatic reds and blacks   30
of his shiny entrails,
and the pink swim-bladder
like a big peony.
I looked into his eyes
which were far larger than mine   35

but shallower, and yellowed,
the irises backed and packed
with tarnished tinfoil
seen through the lenses
of old scratched isinglass.[3]   40
They shifted a little, but not
to return my stare.
—It was more like the tipping
of an object toward the light.
I admired his sullen face,   45
the mechanism of his jaw,
and then I saw
that from his lower lip
—if you could call it a lip—
grim, wet, and weaponlike,   50
hung five old pieces of fish-line,
or four and a wire leader[4]
with the swivel still attached,
with all their five big hooks
grown firmly in his mouth.   55
A green line, frayed at the end
where he broke it, two heavier lines,
and a fine black thread
still crimped from the strain and snap
when it broke and he got away.   60
Like medals with their ribbons
frayed and wavering,
a five-haired beard of wisdom
trailing from his aching jaw.
I stared and stared   65
and victory filled up
the little rented boat,
from the pool of bilge
where oil had spread a rainbow
around the rusted engine   70
to the bailer rusted orange,
the sun-cracked thwarts,
the oarlocks on their strings,
the gunnels[5]—until everything
was rainbow, rainbow, rainbow!   75
And I let the fish go.

1940, 1946

---

3. Mica; whitish, semitransparent substance from the air bladders of fish, used for windows.
4. Short piece of wire connecting fishhook and fishline.

5. Upper edges of the boat. *Bailer*: bucket for bailing water out of the boat. *Thwarts*: rowers' seats or benches. *Oarlocks*: metal devices to hold the oars, attached by a "string" to the boat itself.

Roosters

At four o'clock
in the gun-metal blue dark
we hear the first crow of the first cock

just below
the gun-metal blue window   5
and immediately there is an echo

off in the distance,
then one from the backyard fence,
then one, with horrible insistence,

grates like a wet match   10
from the broccoli patch,
flares, and all over town begins to catch.

Cries galore
come from the water-closet door,
from the dropping-plastered henhouse floor,   15

where in the blue blur
their rustling wives admire,
the roosters brace their cruel feet and glare

with stupid eyes
while from their beaks there rise   20
the uncontrolled, traditional cries.

Deep from protruding chests
in green-gold medals dressed,
planned to command and terrorize the rest,

the many wives   25
who lead hens' lives
of being courted and despised;

deep from raw throats
a senseless order floats
all over town. A rooster gloats   30

over our beds
from rusty iron sheds
and fences made from old bedsteads,

over our churches
where the tin rooster perches,   35
over our little wooden northern houses,

making sallies
from all the muddy alleys,
marking out maps like Rand McNally's.[6]

glass-headed pins,   40
oil-golds and copper greens
anthracite blues, alizarins,[7]

each one an active
displacement in perspective;
each screaming, "This is where I live!"   45

Each screaming
"Get up! Stop dreaming!"
Roosters, what are you projecting?

You, whom the Greeks elected
to shoot at on a post, who struggled   50
when sacrificed, you whom they labeled

"Very combative . . ."[8]
what right have you to give
commands and tell us how to live,

cry "Here!" and "Here!"   55
and wake us here where are
unwanted love, conceit and war?

The crown of red
set on your little head
is charged with all your fighting blood.   60

Yes, that excrescence
makes a most virile presence,
plus all that vulgar beauty of iridescence.

Now in mid-air
by twos they fight each other.   65
Down comes a first flame-feather,

and one is flying,
with raging heroism defying
even the sensation of dying.

And one has fallen,   70
but still above the town
his torn-out, bloodied feathers drift down;

6. American map-making company.
7. Various shades of red.

8. The ancient Greeks used roosters for target
practice, sacrifice, and cockfighting.

and what he sung
no matter. He is flung
on the gray ash-heap, lies in dung   75

with his dead wives
with open, bloody eyes,
while those metallic feathers oxidize.

St. Peter's sin
was worse than that of Magdalen   80
whose sin was of the flesh alone;[9]

of spirit, Peter's,
falling, beneath the flares,
among the "servants and officers."

Old holy sculpture[1]   85
could set it all together
in one small scene, past and future:

Christ stands amazed,
Peter, two fingers raised
to surprised lips, both as if dazed.   90

But in between
a little cock is seen
carved on a dim column in the travertine,[2]

explained by *gallus canit;*
flet Petrus[3] underneath it.   95
There is inescapable hope, the pivot;

yes, and there Peter's tears
run down our chanticleer's[4]
sides and gem his spurs.

Tear-encrusted thick   100
as a medieval relic
he waits. Poor Peter, heart-sick,

still cannot guess
those cock-a-doodles yet might bless,
his dreadful rooster come to mean forgiveness,   105

9. Mary Magdalen, as a prostitute, committed sins of the flesh. Peter denied his relationship with Jesus as a rooster crowed three times. He later took a leading role in the Christian Church.
1. Carved c. 400 C.E. and now in the Vatican, Rome.

2. Marble. The iconography of Jesus and Peter standing beside a cock on a column's capital is frequent in early Christian art.
3. The cock crows; Peter weeps (Latin). Cf. Matthew 26.75.
4. That is, rooster's.

a new weathervane
on basilica and barn,
and that outside the Lateran[5]

there would always be
a bronze cock on a porphyry[6]   110
pillar so the people and the Pope might see

that even the Prince
of the Apostles long since
had been forgiven, and to convince

all the assembly   115
that "Deny deny deny"
is not all the roosters cry.

In the morning
a low light is floating
in the backyard, and gilding   120

from underneath
the broccoli, leaf by leaf;
how could the night have come to grief?

gilding the tiny
floating swallow's belly   125
and lines of pink cloud in the sky,

the day's preamble
like wandering lines in marble.
The cocks are now almost inaudible.

The sun climbs in,   130
following "to see the end,"
faithful as enemy, or friend.

                                            1941, 1946

At the Fishhouses

Although it is a cold evening,
down by one of the fishhouses
an old man sits netting,
his net, in the gloaming almost invisible,
a dark purple-brown,   5
and his shuttle worn and polished.
The air smells so strong of codfish
it makes one's nose run and one's eyes water.

5. Cathedral in Rome where the Pope presides.   6. Type of stone.
Basilica: church.

The five fishhouses have steeply peaked roofs
and narrow, cleated gangplanks slant up   10
to storerooms in the gables
for the wheelbarrows to be pushed up and down on.
All is silver: the heavy surface of the sea,
swelling slowly as if considering spilling over,
is opaque, but the silver of the benches,   15
the lobster pots, and masts, scattered
among the wild jagged rocks,
is of an apparent translucence
like the small old buildings with an emerald moss
growing on their shoreward walls.   20
The big fish tubs are completely lined
with layers of beautiful herring scales
and the wheelbarrows are similarly plastered
with creamy iridescent coats of mail,
with small iridescent flies crawling on them.   25
Up on the little slope behind the houses,
set in the sparse bright sprinkle of grass,
is an ancient wooden capstan,[7]
cracked, with two long bleached handles
and some melancholy stains, like dried blood,   30
where the ironwork has rusted.
The old man accepts a Lucky Strike.[8]
He was a friend of my grandfather.
We talk of the decline in the population
and of codfish and herring   35
while he waits for a herring boat to come in.
There are sequins on his vest and on his thumb.
He has scraped the scales, the principal beauty,
from unnumbered fish with that black old knife,
the blade of which is almost worn away.   40

Down at the water's edge, at the place
where they haul up the boats, up the long ramp
descending into the water, thin silver
tree trunks are laid horizontally
across the gray stones, down and down   45
at intervals of four or five feet.

Cold dark deep and absolutely clear,
element bearable to no mortal,
to fish and to seals . . . One seal particularly
I have seen here evening after evening.   50
He was curious about me. He was interested in music;
like me a believer in total immersion,[9]
so I used to sing him Baptist hymns.
I also sang "A Mighty Fortress Is Our God."

---

7. Rotating drum wound with rope used for haul-
ing heavy items.
8. Brand of cigarette.

9. Baptist belief that a person being baptized must
be wholly submerged under water.

He stood up in the water and regarded me   55
steadily, moving his head a little.
Then he would disappear, then suddenly emerge
almost in the same spot, with a sort of shrug
as if it were against his better judgment.
Cold dark deep and absolutely clear,   60
the clear gray icy water . . . Back, behind us,
the dignified tall firs begin.
Bluish, associating with their shadows,
a million Christmas trees stand
waiting for Christmas. The water seems suspended   65
above the rounded gray and blue-gray stones.
I have seen it over and over, the same sea, the same,
slightly, indifferently swinging above the stones,
icily free above the stones,
above the stones and then the world.   70
If you should dip your hand in,
your wrist would ache immediately,
your bones would begin to ache and your hand would burn
as if the water were a transmutation of fire
that feeds on stones and burns with a dark gray flame.   75
If you tasted it, it would first taste bitter,
then briny, then surely burn your tongue.
It is like what we imagine knowledge to be:
dark, salt, clear, moving, utterly free,
drawn from the cold hard mouth   80
of the world, derived from the rocky breasts
forever, flowing and drawn, and since
our knowledge is historical, flowing, and flown.

                                                                1947, 1955

Over 2,000 Illustrations and a Complete Concordance[1]

Thus should have been our travels:
serious, engravable.
The Seven Wonders of the World are tired
and a touch familiar, but the other scenes,
innumerable, though equally sad and still,   5
are foreign. Often the squatting Arab,
or group of Arabs, plotting, probably,
against our Christian Empire,
while one apart, with outstretched arm and hand
points to the Tomb, the Pit, the Sepulcher.[2]   10
The branches of the date-palms look like files.
The cobbled courtyard, where the Well is dry,

1. Part of the title page of an old edition of the Bible described in the opening lines. It advertises itself as containing "over 2,000 illustrations"— engravings of the Holy Land—and a concordance (a guide to occurrences of words and proper names in a book, often found in Bibles).
2. The burial place of Jesus depicted (along with other places associated with his life, such as the Well where he preached to a Samaritan woman in John 4) among the "2,000 illustrations."

is like a diagram, the brickwork conduits
are vast and obvious, the human figure
far gone in history or theology,   15
gone with its camel or its faithful horse.
Always the silence, the gesture, the specks of birds
suspended on invisible threads above the Site,
or the smoke rising solemnly, pulled by threads.
Granted a page alone or a page made up   20
of several scenes arranged in cattycornered[3] rectangles
or circles set on stippled gray,
granted a grim lunette,[4]
caught in the toils of an initial letter,
when dwelt upon, they all resolve themselves.   25
The eye drops, weighted, through the lines
the burin[5] made, the lines that move apart
like ripples above sand,
dispersing storms, God's spreading fingerprint,
and painfully, finally, that ignite   30
in watery prismatic white-and-blue.

Entering the Narrows at St. Johns[6]
the touching bleat of goats reached to the ship.
We glimpsed them, reddish, leaping up the cliffs
among the fog-soaked weeds and butter-and-eggs.   35
And at St. Peter's[7] the wind blew and the sun shone madly.
Rapidly, purposefully, the Collegians[8] marched in lines,
crisscrossing the great square with black, like ants.
In Mexico the dead man lay
in a blue arcade; the dead volcanoes   40
glistened like Easter lilies.
The jukebox went on playing "Ay, Jalisco!"
And at Volubilis[9] there were beautiful poppies
splitting the mosaics; the fat old guide made eyes.
In Dingle[1] harbor a golden length of evening   45
the rotting hulks held up their dripping plush.
The Englishwoman poured tea, informing us
that the Duchess was going to have a baby.
And in the brothels of Marrakesh[2]
the little pockmarked prostitutes   50
balanced their tea-trays on their heads
and did their belly-dances; flung themselves
naked and giggling against our knees,
asking for cigarettes. It was somewhere near there
I saw what frightened me most of all: 55
A holy grave, not looking particularly holy,
one of a group under a keyhole-arched stone baldaquin[3]

---

3. Placed on a diagonal.
4. The oval, often a segment of an enlarged initial letter, framing an illustration.
5. Engraver's tool.
6. City in Newfoundland, on the Atlantic Ocean.
7. The great cathedral in Rome. *Butter-and-eggs:* common name for narcissus flowers.
8. That is, members of the College of Cardinals in the Vatican, Rome.
9. Ruined Roman city in Morocco.
1. Town in southwest Ireland.
2. City in Morocco.
3. Architectual canopy.

open to every wind from the pink desert.
An open, gritty, marble trough, carved solid
with exhortation, yellowed   60
as scattered cattle-teeth;
half-filled with dust, not even the dust
of the poor prophet paynim[4] who once lay there.
In a smart burnoose[5] Khadour looked on amused.

Everything only connected by "and" and "and."   65
Open the book. (The gilt rubs off the edges
of the pages and pollinates the fingertips.)
Open the heavy book. Why couldn't we have seen
this old Nativity while we were at it?
—the dark ajar, the rocks breaking with light,   70
an undisturbed, unbreathing flame,
colorless, sparkless, freely fed on straw,
and, lulled within, a family with pets,
—and looked and looked our infant sight away.

                                                    1948, 1955

Sestina

September rain falls on the house.
In the failing light, the old grandmother
sits in the kitchen with the child
beside the Little Marvel Stove,[6]
reading the jokes from the almanac,   5
laughing and talking to hide her tears.

She thinks that her equinoctial tears
and the rain that beats on the roof of the house
were both foretold by the almanac,
but only known to a grandmother.   10
The iron kettle sings on the stove.
She cuts some bread and says to the child,

It's time for tea now; but the child
is watching the teakettle's small hard tears
dance like mad on the hot black stove,   15
the way the rain must dance on the house.
Tidying up, the old grandmother
hangs up the clever almanac

on its string. Birdlike, the almanac
hovers half open above the child,   20
hovers above the old grandmother

---

4. Archaic literary word for pagan, especially Muslim.

5. One-piece hooded cloak, worn by some Arabs.
6. Wood- or coal-burning stove.

and her teacup full of dark brown tears.
She shivers and says she thinks the house
feels chilly, and puts more wood in the stove.

It was to be, says the Marvel Stove.   25
I know what I know, says the almanac.
With crayons the child draws a rigid house
and a winding pathway. Then the child
puts in a man with buttons like tears
and shows it proudly to the grandmother.   30

But secretly, while the grandmother
busies herself about the stove,
the little moons fall down like tears
from between the pages of the almanac
into the flower bed the child   35
has carefully placed in the front of the house.

Time to plant tears, says the almanac.
The grandmother sings to the marvellous stove
and the child draws another inscrutable house.

                                                    1956, 1965

The Armadillo

For Robert Lowell[7]

This is the time of year
when almost every night
the frail, illegal fire balloons appear.
Climbing the mountain height,

rising toward a saint   5
still honored in these parts,
the paper chambers flush and fill with light
that comes and goes, like hearts.

Once up against the sky it's hard
to tell them from the stars—   10
planets, that is—the tinted ones:
Venus going down, or Mars,

or the pale green one. With a wind,
they flare and falter, wobble and toss;
but if it's still they steer between   15
the kite sticks of the Southern Cross,[8]

7. American poet (1917–1977).
8. A constellation visible only from the Southern Hemisphere. The balloons were for St. John's Eve.

receding, dwindling, solemnly
and steadily forsaking us,
or, in the downdraft from a peak,
suddenly turning dangerous. 20

Last night another big one fell.
It splattered like an egg of fire
against the cliff behind the house.
The flame ran down. We saw the pair

of owls who nest there flying up 25
and up, their whirling black-and-white
stained bright pink underneath, until
they shrieked up out of sight.

The ancient owls' nest must have burned.
Hastily, all alone, 30
a glistening armadillo left the scene,
rose-flecked, head down, tail down,

and then a baby rabbit jumped out,
short-eared, to our surprise.
So soft!—a handful of intangible ash 35
with fixed, ignited eyes.

Too pretty, dreamlike mimicry!
O falling fire and piercing cry
and panic, and a weak mailed fist
clenched ignorant against the sky! 40

1957, 1965

Brazil, January 1, 1502

. . . embroidered nature . . . tapestried landscape.
—*Landscape Into Art*, by Sir Kenneth Clark[9]

Januaries, Nature greets our eyes
exactly as she must have greeted theirs:
every square inch filling in with foliage—
big leaves, little leaves, and giant leaves,
blue, blue-green, and olive, 5
with occasional lighter veins and edges,
or a satin underleaf turned over;
monster ferns
in silver-gray relief,

9. British art historian (1903–1983); the phrases are from the chapter "Landscape of Symbols," about medieval depictions of a garden enclosing the Virgin, or *Hortus Conclusis*, in his 1949 book.

and flowers, too, like giant water lilies   10
up in the air—up, rather, in the leaves—
purple, yellow, two yellows, pink,
rust red and greenish white;
solid but airy; fresh as if just finished
and taken off the frame.   15

A blue-white sky, a simple web,
backing for feathery detail:
brief arcs, a pale-green broken wheel,
a few palms, swarthy, squat, but delicate;
and perching there in profile, beaks agape,   20
the big symbolic birds keep quiet,
each showing only half his puffed and padded,
pure-colored or spotted breast.
Still in the foreground there is Sin:
five sooty dragons near some massy rocks.   25
The rocks are worked with lichens, gray moonbursts
splattered and overlapping,
threatened from underneath by moss
in lovely hell-green flames,
attacked above   30
by scaling-ladder vines, oblique and neat,
"one leaf yes and one leaf no" (in Portuguese).
The lizards scarcely breathe; all eyes
are on the smaller, female one, back-to,
her wicked tail straight up and over,   35
red as a red-hot wire.

Just so the Christians, hard as nails,
tiny as nails, and glinting,
in creaking armor, came and found it all,
not unfamiliar: 40
no lovers' walks, no bowers,
no cherries to be picked, no lute music,
but corresponding, nevertheless,
to an old dream of wealth and luxury
already out of style when they left home—   45
wealth, plus a brand-new pleasure.
Directly after Mass, humming perhaps
L'Homme armé[1] or some such tune,
they ripped away into the hanging fabric,
each out to catch an Indian for himself—   50
those maddening little women who kept calling,
calling to each other (or had the birds waked up?)
and retreating, always retreating, behind it.

                                              1960, 1965

---

1. The armed man (French); an old French song whose melody was often used in medieval settings of the Mass.

In the Waiting Room

In Worcester, Massachusetts,
I went with Aunt Consuelo
to keep her dentist's appointment
and sat and waited for her
in the dentist's waiting room.   5
It was winter. It got dark
early. The waiting room
was full of grown-up people,
arctics and overcoats,
lamps and magazines.   10
My aunt was inside
what seemed like a long time
and while I waited I read
the *National Geographic*
(I could read) and carefully   15
studied the photographs:
the inside of a volcano,
black, and full of ashes;
then it was spilling over
in rivulets of fire.   20
Osa and Martin Johnson[2]
dressed in riding breeches,
laced boots, and pith helmets.
A dead man slung on a pole
—"Long Pig,"[3] the caption said.   25
Babies with pointed heads
wound round and round with string;
black, naked women with necks
wound round and round with wire
like the necks of light bulbs.   30
Their breasts were horrifying.
I read it right straight through.
I was too shy to stop.
And then I looked at the cover:
the yellow margins, the date.   35

Suddenly, from inside,
came an *oh!* of pain
—Aunt Consuelo's voice—
not very loud or long.
I wasn't at all surprised;   40
even then I knew she was
a foolish, timid woman.
I might have been embarrassed,
but wasn't. What took me

2. Then-popular husband-and-wife team of explorers and naturalists.

3. Translation of cannibals' name for a human carcass.

completely by surprise   45
was that it was *me:*
my voice, in my mouth.
Without thinking at all
I was my foolish aunt,
I—we—were falling, falling,   50
our eyes glued to the cover
of the *National Geographic,*
February, 1918.

I said to myself: three days
and you'll be seven years old.   55
I was saying it to stop
the sensation of falling off
the round, turning world
into cold, blue-black space.
But I felt: you are an *I,*   60
you are an *Elizabeth,*
you are one of *them.*
Why should you be one, too?
I scarcely dared to look
to see what it was I was.   65
I gave a sidelong glance
—I couldn't look any higher—
at shadowy gray knees,
trousers and skirts and boots
and different pairs of hands   70
lying under the lamps.
I knew that nothing stranger
had ever happened, that nothing
stranger could ever happen.
Why should I be my aunt,   75
or me, or anyone?
What similarities—
boots, hands, the family voice
I felt in my throat, or even
the *National Geographic*   80
and those awful hanging breasts—
held us all together
or made us all just one?
How—I didn't know any
word for it—how "unlikely" . . .   85
How had I come to be here,
like them, and overhear
a cry of pain that could have
got loud and worse but hadn't?

The waiting room was bright   90
and too hot. It was sliding
beneath a big black wave,
another, and another.

Then I was back in it.
The War[4] was on. Outside,   95
in Worcester, Massachusetts,
were night and slush and cold,
and it was still the fifth
of February, 1918.

1971, 1976

Crusoe in England[5]

A new volcano has erupted,
the papers say, and last week I was reading
where some ship saw an island being born:
at first a breath of steam, ten miles away;
and then a black fleck—basalt, probably—   5
rose in the mate's binoculars
and caught on the horizon like a fly.
They named it. But my poor old island's still
un-rediscovered, un-renamable.
None of the books has ever got it right.   10

Well, I had fifty-two
miserable, small volcanoes I could climb
with a few slithery strides—
volcanoes dead as ash heaps.
I used to sit on the edge of the highest one   15
and count the others standing up,
naked and leaden, with their heads blown off.
I'd think that if they were the size
I thought volcanoes should be, then I had
become a giant;   20
and if I had become a giant,
I couldn't bear to think what size
the goats and turtles were,
or the gulls, or the overlapping rollers
—a glittering hexagon of rollers   25
closing and closing in, but never quite,
glittering and glittering, though the sky
was mostly overcast.

My island seemed to be
a sort of cloud-dump. All the hemisphere's   30
left-over clouds arrived and hung
above the craters—their parched throats
were hot to touch.

4. World War I.
5. Shipwrecked hero of *Robinson Crusoe* (1719), by Daniel Defoe (1660–1731).

Was that why it rained so much?
And why sometimes the whole place hissed?   35
The turtles lumbered by, high-domed,
hissing like teakettles.
(And I'd have given years, or taken a few,
for any sort of kettle, of course.)
The folds of lava, running out to sea,   40
would hiss. I'd turn. And then they'd prove
to be more turtles.
The beaches were all lava, variegated,
black, red, and white, and gray;
the marbled colors made a fine display.   45
And I had waterspouts. Oh,
half a dozen at a time, far out,
they'd come and go, advancing and retreating,
their heads in cloud, their feet in moving patches
of scuffed-up white.   50
Glass chimneys, flexible, attenuated,
sacerdotal[6] beings of glass . . . I watched
the water spiral up in them like smoke.
Beautiful, yes, but not much company.

I often gave way to self-pity.   55
"Do I deserve this? I suppose I must.
I wouldn't be here otherwise. Was there
a moment when I actually chose this?
I don't remember, but there could have been."
What's wrong about self-pity, anyway?   60
With my legs dangling down familiarly
over a crater's edge, I told myself
"Pity should begin at home." So the more
pity I felt, the more I felt at home.

The sun set in the sea; the same odd sun   65
rose from the sea,
and there was one of it and one of me.
The island had one kind of everything:
one tree snail, a bright violet-blue
with a thin shell, crept over everything,   70
over the one variety of tree,
a sooty, scrub affair.
Snail shells lay under these in drifts
and, at a distance,
you'd swear that they were beds of irises.   75
There was one kind of berry, a dark red.
I tried it, one by one, and hours apart.
Sub-acid, and not bad, no ill effects;
and so I made home-brew. I'd drink
the awful, fizzy, stinging stuff   80

6. Priestly.

that went straight to my head
and play my home-made flute
(I think it had the weirdest scale on earth)
and, dizzy, whoop and dance among the goats.
Home-made, home-made! But aren't we all?   85
I felt a deep affection for
the smallest of my island industries.
No, not exactly, since the smallest was
a miserable philosophy.

Because I didn't know enough.   90
Why didn't I know enough of something?
Greek drama or astronomy? The books
I'd read were full of blanks;
the poems—well, I tried
reciting to my iris-beds,   95
"They flash upon that inward eye,
which is the bliss . . ."[7] The bliss of what?
One of the first things that I did
when I got back was look it up.

The island smelled of goat and guano.[8]   100
The goats were white, so were the gulls,
and both too tame, or else they thought
I was a goat, too, or a gull.
Baa, baa, baa and shriek, shriek, shriek,
baa . . . shriek . . . baa . . . I still can't shake   105
them from my ears; they're hurting now.
The questioning shrieks, the equivocal replies
over a ground of hissing rain
and hissing, ambulating turtles
got on my nerves.   110

When all the gulls flew up at once, they sounded
like a big tree in a strong wind, its leaves.
I'd shut my eyes and think about a tree,
an oak, say, with real shade, somewhere.
I'd heard of cattle getting island-sick.   115
I thought the goats were.
One billy-goat would stand on the volcano
I'd christened Mont d'Espoir[9] or Mount Despair
(I'd time enough to play with names),
and bleat and bleat, and sniff the air.   120
I'd grab his beard and look at him.
His pupils, horizontal, narrowed up
and expressed nothing, or a little malice.
I got so tired of the very colors!
One day I dyed a baby goat bright red   125

7. From "I Wandered Lonely as a Cloud" (1807), by William Wordsworth (1770–1850): "They flash upon that inward eye / Which is the bliss of solitude."
8. Bird excrement.
9. Mount Hope (French).

with my red berries, just to see
something a little different.
And then his mother wouldn't recognize him.

Dreams were the worst. Of course I dreamed of food
and love, but they were pleasant rather   130
than otherwise. But then I'd dream of things
like slitting a baby's throat, mistaking it
for a baby goat. I'd have
nightmares of other islands
stretching away from mine, infinities   135
of islands, islands spawning islands,
like frogs' eggs turning into polliwogs
of islands, knowing that I had to live
on each and every one, eventually,
for ages, registering their flora,   140
their fauna, their geography.

Just when I thought I couldn't stand it
another minute longer, Friday[1] came.
(Accounts of that have everything all wrong.)
Friday was nice.   145
Friday was nice, and we were friends.
If only he had been a woman!
I wanted to propagate my kind,
and so did he, I think, poor boy.
He'd pet the baby goats sometimes,   150
and race with them, or carry one around.
—Pretty to watch; he had a pretty body.

And then one day they came and took us off.

Now I live here, another island,[2]
that doesn't seem like one, but who decides?   155
My blood was full of them; my brain
bred islands. But that archipelago
has petered out. I'm old.
I'm bored, too, drinking my real tea,
surrounded by uninteresting lumber.   160
The knife there on the shelf—
it reeked of meaning, like a crucifix.
It lived. How many years did I
beg it, implore it, not to break?
I knew each nick and scratch by heart,   165
the bluish blade, the broken tip,
the lines of wood-grain on the handle . . .
Now it won't look at me at all.
The living soul has dribbled away.
My eyes rest on it and pass on.   170

---

1. Crusoe's native companion.   2. Crusoe ultimately returned to England.

The local museum's asked me to
leave everything to them:
the flute, the knife, the shrivelled shoes,
my shedding goatskin trousers
(moths have got in the fur),   175
the parasol that took me such a time
remembering the way the ribs should go.
It still will work but, folded up,
looks like a plucked and skinny fowl.
How can anyone want such things?   180
—And Friday, my dear Friday, died of measles
seventeen years ago come March.

                                        1971, 1976

Poem

About the size of an old-style dollar bill,
American or Canadian,
mostly the same whites, gray greens, and steel grays
—this little painting (a sketch for a larger one?)
has never earned any money in its life.   5
Useless and free, it has spent seventy years
as a minor family relic
handed along collaterally[3] to owners
who looked at it sometimes, or didn't bother to.

It must be Nova Scotia; only there   10
does one see gabled wooden houses
painted that awful shade of brown.
The other houses, the bits that show, are white.
Elm trees, low hills, a thin church steeple
—that gray-blue wisp—or is it? In the foreground   15
a water meadow with some tiny cows,
two brushstrokes each, but confidently cows;
two minuscule white geese in the blue water,
back-to-back, feeding, and a slanting stick.
Up closer, a wild iris, white and yellow,   20
fresh-squiggled from the tube.
The air is fresh and cold; cold early spring
clear as gray glass; a half inch of blue sky
below the steel-gray storm clouds.
(They were the artist's specialty.)   25
A specklike bird is flying to the left.
Or is it a flyspeck looking like a bird?

Heavens, I recognize the place, I know it!
It's behind—I can almost remember the farmer's name.

3. That is, indirectly.

His barn backed on that meadow. There it is,   30
titanium white,[4] one dab. The hint of steeple,
filaments of brush-hairs, barely there,
must be the Presbyterian church.
Would that be Miss Gillespie's house?
Those particular geese and cows   35
are naturally before my time.

A sketch done in an hour, "in one breath,"
once taken from a trunk and handed over.
Would you like this? I'll probably never
have room to hang these things again.   40
Your Uncle George, no, mine, my Uncle George,
he'd be your great-uncle, left them all with Mother
when he went back to England.
You know, he was quite famous, an R.A.[5] . . .

I never knew him. We both knew this place,   45
apparently, this literal small backwater,
looked at it long enough to memorize it,
our years apart. How strange. And it's still loved,
or its memory is (it must have changed a lot).
Our visions coincided—"visions" is   50
too serious a word—our looks, two looks:
art "copying from life" and life itself,
life and the memory of it so compressed
they've turned into each other. Which is which?
Life and the memory of it cramped,   55
dim, on a piece of Bristol board,[6]
dim, but how live, how touching in detail
—the little that we get for free,
the little of our earthly trust. Not much.
About the size of our abidance   60
along with theirs: the munching cows,
the iris, crisp and shivering, the water
still standing from spring freshets,
the yet-to-be-dismantled elms, the geese.

1972, 1976

The End of March

For John Malcolm Brinnin and Bill Read: Duxbury[7]

It was cold and windy, scarcely the day
to take a walk on that long beach.

---

4. A very bright white pigment.
5. Member of the Royal Academy of Arts, in England.
6. Cardboard with a smooth surface.

7. John Malcolm Brinnin (b. 1916): American poet; Bill Read (b. 1917): American scholar. Bishop often visited their home at Duxbury, on the Massachusetts coast.

Everything was withdrawn as far as possible,
indrawn: the tide far out, the ocean shrunken,
seabirds in ones or twos.   5
The rackety, icy, offshore wind
numbed our faces on one side;
disrupted the formation
of a lone flight of Canada geese;
and blew back the low, inaudible rollers   10
in upright, steely mist.

The sky was darker than the water
—*it* was the color of mutton-fat jade.
Along the wet sand, in rubber boots, we followed
a track of big dog-prints (so big   15
they were more like lion-prints). Then we came on
lengths and lengths, endless, of wet white string,
looping up to the tide-line, down to the water,
over and over. Finally, they did end:
a thick white snarl, man-size, awash,   20
rising on every wave, a sodden ghost,
falling back, sodden, giving up the ghost. . . .
A kite string?—But no kite.

I wanted to get as far as my proto-dream-house,
my crypto-dream-house, that crooked box   25
set up on pilings, shingled green,
a sort of artichoke of a house, but greener
(boiled with bicarbonate of soda?),[8]
protected from spring tides by a palisade
of—are they railroad ties?   30
(Many things about this place are dubious.)
I'd like to retire there and do *nothing*,
or nothing much, forever, in two bare rooms:
look through binoculars, read boring books,
old, long, long books, and write down useless notes,   35
talk to myself, and, foggy days,
watch the droplets slipping, heavy with light.
At night, a *grog à l'américaine.*[9]
I'd blaze it with a kitchen match
and lovely diaphanous blue flame   40
would waver, doubled in the window.
There must be a stove; there *is* a chimney,
askew, but braced with wires,
and electricity, possibly
—at least, at the back another wire   45
limply leashes the whole affair
to something off behind the dunes.
A light to read by—perfect! But—impossible.

---

8. That is, as though boiled with baking soda, an   9. Alcoholic drink.
old trick to preserve the color of green vegetables.

And that day the wind was much too cold
even to get that far,   50
and of course the house was boarded up.

On the way back our faces froze on the other side.
The sun came out for just a minute.
For just a minute, set in their bezels¹ of sand,
the drab, damp, scattered stones   55
were multi-colored,
and all those high enough threw out long shadows,
individual shadows, then pulled them in again.
They could have been teasing the lion sun,
except that now he was behind them   60
—a sun who'd walked the beach the last low tide,
making those big, majestic paw-prints,
who perhaps had batted a kite out of the sky to play with.

                                                                        1975, 1976

One Art

    The art of losing isn't hard to master;
    so many things seem filled with the intent
    to be lost that their loss is no disaster.

    Lose something every day. Accept the fluster
    of lost door keys, the hour badly spent.   5
    The art of losing isn't hard to master.

    Then practice losing farther, losing faster:
    places, and names, and where it was you meant
    to travel. None of these will bring disaster.

    I lost my mother's watch. And look! my last, or   10
    next-to-last, of three loved houses went.
    The art of losing isn't hard to master.

    I lost two cities, lovely ones. And, vaster,
    some realms I owned, two rivers, a continent.
    I miss them, but it wasn't a disaster.   15

    —Even losing you (the joking voice, a gesture
    I love) I shan't have lied. It's evident
    the art of losing's not too hard to master
    though it may look like (*Write* it!) like disaster.

                                                                              1976

---

1. Rims, usually on jewelry or pocket watches.

North Haven

In memoriam: Robert Lowell[2]

I can make out the rigging of a schooner
a mile off; I can count
the new cones on the spruce. It is so still
the pale bay wears a milky skin, the sky
no clouds, except for one long, carded horse's-tail.   5

The islands haven't shifted since last summer,
even if I like to pretend they have
—drifting, in a dreamy sort of way,
a little north, a little south or sidewise,
and that they're free within the blue frontiers of bay.   10

This month, our favorite one is full of flowers:
Buttercups, Red Clover, Purple Vetch,
Hawkweed still burning, Daisies pied, Eyebright,
the Fragrant Bedstraw's incandescent stars,
and more, returned, to paint the meadows with delight.   15

The Goldfinches are back, or others like them,
and the White-throated Sparrow's five-note song,
pleading and pleading, brings tears to the eyes.
Nature repeats herself, or almost does:
repeat, repeat, repeat; revise, revise, revise.   20

Years ago, you told me it was here
(in 1932?) you first "discovered *girls*"
and learned to sail, and learned to kiss.
You had "such fun," you said, that classic summer.
("Fun"—it always seemed to leave you at a loss . . .)   25

You left North Haven, anchored in its rock,
afloat in mystic blue . . . And now—you've left
for good. You can't derange, or re-arrange,
your poems again. (But the Sparrows can their song.)
The words won't change again. Sad friend, you cannot change.   30

1978, 1979

---

2. American poet (1917–1977).

MAY SWENSON
1913–1989

May Swenson is a difficult poet to classify. She writes about conventional lyric subjects, such as love, death, nature, and youthful pleasures. Yet her approach to such topics is quirky and unconventional. In a poem about the physical and emotional transfusions of love, "In Love Made Visible," for example, Swenson borrows from traditional love poetry the notion of the eye as window to the soul, but she also recasts stock heterosexual images, presenting both lovers, by poem's end, as cups or vials: "We are released / and flow into each other's cup / Our two frail vials pierced / drink each other up." By contrast to this celebration of lesbian communion, Swenson's "A Couple" is less sanguine about the seemingly heterosexual meeting of a bullet-shaped bee and a bowl-like flower: "When he's done his honey-thieving / at her matrix, whirs free, leaving, / she closes, still tall, chill, / unrumpled on her stem." Lyrical, steeped in tradition, Swenson's love poems are nevertheless wryly revisionist, if less erotically explicit than those of some of her contemporaries.

Similarly, Swenson's interest in manipulating the typographical layout of words can seem experimental, recalling early modernist attention to spatial form and pointing ahead to the contemporary avant-garde; but her shape poems, or "iconographs," such as her lyric in the form of a butterfly, "Unconscious Came a Beauty," also recall an older poetic tradition, the *carmen figuratum*, that extends from the ancient Greeks through George Herbert and beyond. Exemplifying Swenson's playful use of typography, this poem refrains from naming the "butterfly," as if not to duplicate visual through verbal naming. When the butterfly's shadow merges with her "hand's ghost," Swenson wittily figures the shape of the poem as a shadow of the butterfly, the words as a ghostly trace of the poet's hand. Modest and oblique, she wants to evoke the butterfly without trapping it in a name or a word picture.

Although Swenson is well known for her shape poems, typographic play is but one device in her large array of techniques. Often, she appeals less to the eye than to the ear, employing the sonic echoes and twists of internal rhyme, alliteration, assonance, consonance, and onomatopoeia. Words resonate, invert, and play off one another in lines such as "when Body my good / bright dog is dead" ("Question"). Her feel for rhythm and narrative pacing is strong. In "The Centaur," the speaker recalls using a willow as an imaginary pony when she was a ten-year-old child. This imaginative transformation culminates when "I was the horse and the rider," rhapsodically cadenced in lines such as "I shied and skittered and reared." A friend of Elizabeth Bishop's, Swenson recalls the visual exactitude and exquisite restraint of her near-contemporary. Like Marianne Moore, too, Swenson crafts highly particularized descriptions of nature. A butterfly's "thin-as-paper wings, near black, / were edged on the seam side poppy orange, / as were its spots" ("Unconscious Came a Beauty"). Her figurative language is precise: the same butterfly "bent its tongue long as / a leg / black on my skin," a simile heightened by the syntactic deferral of "black."

Like Moore, Bishop, and Emily Dickinson, Swenson avoids overt self-disclosure. In this, she differs from the so-called confessional poets, and her poem "Strawberrying" is a reply to Sylvia Plath's "Blackberrying." Even so, Swenson's distinctive kind of self-effacement allows for considerable intimacy, examining and distilling emotion. Her poems about death and loss, such as "Staring at the Sea on the Day of the Death of Another" and "Last Day," are taut with affect. Imagining the sea as a mausoleum and a shaft of light as a coffin, Swenson quietly but powerfully evokes the menace of mortality.

Swenson was born on May 28, 1913, in Logan, Utah, to a devout Mormon family. She attended Utah State Agricultural College (1930–34). Escaping to New York during the Depression, she worked with the Writers' Project of the Works Progress Administration (WPA). Struggling for some years to make a living, she was eventually employed by New Directions Press, where she was for twelve years a manuscript reader. After she left New Directions in 1966, she held visiting professorships at various universities. In 1981, she won the Bollingen Prize; in 1987, a MacArthur Fellowship. Having long suffered from high blood pressure and asthma, she died at the age of seventy-six.

Question

Body my house
my horse my hound
what will I do
when you are fallen

Where will I sleep   5
How will I ride
What will I hunt

Where can I go
without my mount
all eager and quick   10
How will I know
in thicket ahead
is danger or treasure
when Body my good
bright dog is dead   15

How will it be
to lie in the sky
without roof or door
and wind for an eye

With cloud for shift   20
how will I hide?

                                      1954

The Centaur[1]

The summer that I was ten—
Can it be there was only one
summer that I was ten? It must

---

1. Half-horse, half-human creature of Greek mythology.

have been a long one then—
each day I'd go out to choose   5
a fresh horse from my stable

which was a willow grove
down by the old canal.
I'd go on my two bare feet.

But when, with my brother's jack-knife,   10
I had cut me a long limber horse
with a good thick knob for a head,

and peeled him slick and clean
except a few leaves for the tail,
and cinched my brother's belt   15

around his head for a rein,
I'd straddle and canter him fast
up the grass bank to the path,

trot along in the lovely dust
that talcumed over his hoofs,   20
hiding my toes, and turning

his feet to swift half-moons.
The willow knob with the strap
jouncing between my thighs

was the pommel and yet the poll[2]   25
of my nickering pony's head.
My head and my neck were mine,

yet they were shaped like a horse.
My hair flopped to the side
like the mane of a horse in the wind.   30

My forelock swung in my eyes,
my neck arched and I snorted.
I shied and skittered and reared,

stopped and raised my knees,
pawed at the ground and quivered.   35
My teeth bared as we wheeled

and swished through the dust again.
I was the horse and the rider,
and the leather I slapped to his rump

2. Top of the head. *Pommel:* bulge at the front of a saddle.

spanked my own behind.   40
Doubled, my two hoofs beat
a gallop along the bank,

the wind twanged in my mane,
my mouth squared to the bit.
And yet I sat on my steed   45

quiet, negligent riding,
my toes standing the stirrups,
my thighs hugging his ribs.

At a walk we drew up to the porch.
I tethered him to a paling.   50
Dismounting, I smoothed my skirt

and entered the dusky hall.
My feet on the clean linoleum
left ghostly toes in the hall.

Where have you been? said my mother.   55
Been riding, I said from the sink,
and filled me a glass of water.

What's that in your pocket? she said.
Just my knife. It weighted my pocket
and stretched my dress awry.   60

Go tie back your hair, said my mother,
and *Why is your mouth all green?*
*Rob Roy, he[3] pulled some clover
as we crossed the field,* I told her.

                                                               1954

A Couple

A bee rolls in the yellow rose.
Does she invite his hairy rub?
He scrubs himself in her creamy folds.
A bullet soft imposes her spiral
and, spinning, burrows   5
to her dewy shadows.
The gold grooves almost match
the yellow bowl.
Does his touch please or scratch?
When he's done his honey-thieving   10
at her matrix, whirs free, leaving,

---

3. The speaker's imaginary horse. Rob Roy (1671–1734) was a celebrated Scottish outlaw.

she closes, still tall, chill,
unrumpled on her stem.

1958

Unconscious
came a beauty to my
wrist
and stopped my pencil,
merged its shadow profile with
my hand's ghost   5
on the page:
Red Spotted Purple or else Mourning
Cloak,
paired thin-as-paper wings, near black,
were edged on the seam side poppy orange,   10
as were its spots.

Unconscious Came a Beauty

I sat arrested, for its soot-haired
body's worm
shone in the sun.   15
It bent its tongue long as
a leg
black on my skin
and clung without my
feeling,   20
while its tomb-stained
duplicate parts of
a window opened.
And then I
moved.   25

1970

Staring at the Sea on the Day of the Death of Another

The long body of the water fills its hollow,
slowly rolls upon its side,
and in the swaddlings of the waves,
their shadowed hollows falling forward with the tide,

like folds of Grecian garments molded to cling   5
around some classic immemorial marble thing,
I see the vanished bodies of friends who have died.

Each form is furled into its hollow,
white in the dark curl,
the sea a mausoleum, with countless shelves,   10
cradling the prone effigies of our unearthly selves,

some of the hollows empty, long niches in the tide.
One of them is mine
and gliding forward, gaping wide.

1972

Last Day

I'm having a sunbath on the rug
alone in a large house facing south.
A tall window admits a golden trough
the length of a coffin in which I lie
in December, the last day of the year.   5
Sky in the window perfectly empty.
Naked tree limbs without wind.
No sounds reach my ears except their
ringing, and heart's thud hollow and
slow. Uncomplicated peace. Scarcely   10
a motion. Except a shadow that un-
detected creeps. On the table a clay pot,
a clump of narcissus lengthens its stems.
Blue buds sip the sun. Works of the clock
circle their ratchets.[4] There is nothing   15
to wish for. Nothing to will.
What if this day is endless? No *new*
year to follow. Alteration done with.
A golden moment frozen, clenched.

1986

Strawberrying

My hands are murder-red. Many a plump head
drops on the heap in the basket. Or, ripe
to bursting, they might be hearts, matching
the blackbird's wing-fleck. Gripped to a reed
he shrieks his ko-ka-ree in the next field.   5
He's left his peck in some juicy cheeks, when
at first blush and mostly white, they showed
streaks of sweetness to the marauder.

We're picking near the shore, the morning
sunny, a slight wind moving rough-veined leaves   10
our hands rumple among. Fingers find by feel
the ready fruit in clusters. Here and there,
their squishy wounds. . . . Flesh was perfect

---

4. The teeth on a gear.

yesterday. . . . June was for gorging. . . .
sweet hearts young and firm before decay.   15

"Take only the biggest, and not too ripe,"
a mother calls to her girl and boy, barefoot
in the furrows. "Don't step on any. Don't
change rows. Don't eat too many." Mesmerized
by the largesse, the children squat and pull   20
and pick handfuls of rich scarlets, half
for the baskets, half for avid mouths.
Soon, whole faces are stained.

A crop this thick begs for plunder. Ripeness
wants to be ravished, as udders of cows when hard,   25
the blue-veined bags distended, ache to be stripped.
Hunkered in mud between the rows, sun burning
the backs of our necks, we grope for, and rip loose
soft nippled heads. If they bleed—too soft—
let them stay. Let them rot in the heat.   30

When, hidden away in a damp hollow under moldy
leaves, I come upon a clump of heart-shapes
once red, now spiderspit-gray, intact but empty,
still attached to their dead stems—
families smothered as at Pompeii[5]—I rise   35
and stretch. I eat one more big ripe lopped
head. Red-handed, I leave the field.

1987

In Love Made Visible

In love are we made visible
As in a magic bath
are unpeeled
to the sharp pit
so long concealed   5

With love's alertness
we recognize
the soundless whimper
of the soul
behind the eyes   10
A shaft opens
and the timid thing
at last leaps to surface
with full-spread wing

5. Italian city destroyed by the eruption of Mt. Vesuvius in 79 C.E.

The fingertips of love discover   15
more than the body's smoothness
They uncover a hidden conduit
for the transfusion
of empathies that circumvent
the mind's intrusion   20

In love are we set free
Objective bone
and flesh no longer insulate us
to ourselves alone
We are released   25
and flow into each other's cup
Our two frail vials pierced
drink each other up

1991

ROBERT HAYDEN
1913–1980

A poet of elegance and restraint, Robert Hayden nevertheless wrote about such emotionally fraught subjects as the lynching of African Americans during the civil rights movement, the transport of slaves from Africa to the New World, and his own pained perplexity as a youth raised in a Detroit slum called Paradise Valley. Exploring the difficult personal and historical experiences of African Americans and others, Hayden's poetry condenses and evokes feelings and ideas in intricate sonic textures—resonant vowel and consonant patterns and carefully modulated rhythms. Embodying history, his vivid characters include hypocritical slavers, brutal lynchmen, awe-inspiring singers, a stern foster father, an overlubricated preacher, and an "AfroIndian" fortune-teller with "silver crucifix / and manycolored beads" ("Elegies for Paradise Valley" IV). In monologue and direct narrative verse, they are defined through an accumulation of sharply apprehended detail and rendered with precision and style.

Hayden often approaches highly charged subjects indirectly. He even risks adopting the voices of victimizers, as if to emphasize the furious silence of the oppressed. In the long sequence "Middle Passage," Hayden brilliantly presents the slave trade from the point of view of slave-ship officers, his own anger and grief apparent in the ironic gaps between the vicious practices of slavery and ships named after Jesus, Hope, and Mercy, between the slavers' cruelty and their Christian prayers. Similarly, a poem written from the perspective of a white family long engaged in the practice of racial lynching, "Night, Death, Mississippi," incorporates the nostalgic, if revolting, reminiscences of an old man who fondly recalls earlier lynchings and emasculations, and it thus leaves the reader to infer a response:

Time was. Time was.
White robes like moonlight

In the sweetgum dark.
Unbucked that one then

and him squealing bloody Jesus
as we cut it off.

One of the leading African American poets of the twentieth century, Hayden synthesizes both African American and European American literary traditions, and he has been both celebrated and denounced for his literary dexterity. In 1966, he was honored for his contribution to the literature of Africa and the African diaspora, winning the Grand Prize for anglophone poetry at the Third World Festival of Negro Arts in Dakar, Senegal. Back home at the First Black Writers' Conference at Fisk University, he was criticized by African American cultural nationalists as a traitor to the race. In the heyday of the Black Arts Movement, which proclaimed that poetry was to be didactic, propagandistic, and revolutionary, Hayden found himself spurned, even by some of his own students, as an "Uncle Tom."

Hayden's influence on the next generation of African American poets, including Michael S. Harper, Yusef Komunyakaa, and Rita Dove, has helped vindicate his reputation as a poet who wrote vividly and movingly about the African American experience. His poetic sequences, such as the early "Middle Passage" and the late "Elegies for Paradise Valley," which subtly weave together a variety of perspectives, characters, and discourses, have cast a long shadow. His poetry is imbued with African American literary legacies, including the Harlem Renaissance innovations of Langston Hughes, Countee Cullen, Jean Toomer, and Claude McKay. Like his precursors, Hayden adapts the rich oral and musical legacies of the blues, jazz, and spirituals ("Homage to the Empress of the Blues," "Mourning Poem for the Queen of Sunday"), and he reimagines crucial episodes in African American history, having researched slavery and the Civil War for the Federal Writers' Project from 1936 to 1940.

Hayden rejected, however, a self-segregating outlook or poetics, and he became a Baha'i in 1943, embracing a religion that teaches the unity of all faiths and peoples. Availing himself of the resources of European and Anglo-American poetry, Hayden put to powerful use such modernist aesthetic principles as concision, allusion, juxtaposition, collage, symbolism, multiple personae, psychic ambivalence, and generic heterogeneity. His "Middle Passage" recalls Eliot's *Waste Land* as it abruptly shifts among voices, echoes Shakespeare's lines about a drowned man ("Full fathom five thy father lies"), and pastes together such diverse forms as hymns, prayers, diaries, and legal depositions. Yet unlike Eliot's spiritual and literary waste land, Hayden's is that of a specific, traumatic episode in African American history.

Born on August 4, 1913, in Detroit, to a couple whose relationship soon dissolved, Hayden was raised, with his mother's help, by a foster family next door. Though poor and uneducated, his guardians nevertheless encouraged the bookish child. Struggling with severe nearsightedness, Hayden early showed an interest in writing. After high school, he could not afford to go on immediately to college. Reading on his own, he discovered American poets such as Cullen, Edna St. Vincent Millay, and Carl Sandburg, as well as the English classics. At Detroit City College (now Wayne State University), Hayden majored in foreign languages, with an emphasis on Spanish. After college, he worked at several government-sponsored historical projects, and he was the part-time drama and music critic for a Detroit newspaper. In 1940, he married, published his first book, and spent a short time in New York City.

Hayden returned to the midwest to take an M.A. (1944) at the University of Michigan. Among his teachers was W. H. Auden, whom Hayden greatly admired: the older poet was an inventive teacher, incisive in his judgments, and his influence may be seen in the technical pith of Hayden's verse. Once his graduate studies were complete, Hayden taught briefly at the University of Michigan, and for the rest of his life made his living by teaching, writing poems as time allowed. In 1946, Hayden moved south to

Nashville, Tennessee, where he joined the faculty of Fisk University. More than twenty years later, in 1969, he returned to the University of Michigan, where he taught until his death.

Middle Passage[1]

I

Jesús, Estrella, Esperanza, Mercy:[2]

> Sails flashing to the wind like weapons,
> sharks following the moans the fever and the dying;
> horror the corposant and compass rose.[3]

Middle Passage: 5
>   voyage through death
>   to life upon these shores.

> "10 April 1800—
> Blacks rebellious. Crew uneasy. Our linguist says
> their moaning is a prayer for death,   10
> ours and their own. Some try to starve themselves.
> Lost three this morning leaped with crazy laughter
> to the waiting sharks, sang as they went under."

Desire, Adventure, Tartar, Ann:

> Standing to America, bringing home   15
> black gold, black ivory, black seed.

> *Deep in the festering hold thy father lies,*
> *of his bones New England pews are made,*
> *those are altar lights that were his eyes.*[4]

Jesus   Saviour   Pilot   Me[5]   20
Over   Life's   Tempestuous   Sea

> We pray that Thou wilt grant, O Lord,
> safe passage to our vessels bringing
> heathen souls unto Thy chastening.

Jesus   Saviour   25

---

1. The journey of slaves across the Atlantic from Africa to the Americas, in perilously overcrowded ships.
2. Slave ships. *Estrella:* star (Spanish). *Esperanza:* hope (Spanish).
3. Circle on a map showing compass directions. *Corposant:* eerie light sometimes seen during an electrical storm; also called St. Elmo's Fire.
4. Cf. the song from Shakespeare's *Tempest* in which Ariel explains the transformation of Ferdinand's father after his apparent death by drowning: "Full fathom five thy father lies, / Of his bones are coral made; / These are pearls that were his eyes" (1.2.400–402).
5. From a Protestant hymn.

"8 bells. I cannot sleep, for I am sick
with fear, but writing eases fear a little
since still my eyes can see these words take shape
upon the page & so I write, as one
would turn to exorcism. 4 days scudding,[6]   30
but now the sea is calm again. Misfortune
follows in our wake like sharks (our grinning
tutelary[7] gods). Which one of us
has killed an albatross?[8] A plague among
our blacks—Ophthalmia: blindness—& we   35
have jettisoned the blind to no avail.
It spreads, the terrifying sickness spreads.
Its claws have scratched sight from the Capt.'s eyes
& there is blindness in the fo'c'sle[9]
& we must sail 3 weeks before we come   40
to port."

What port awaits us, Davy Jones'[1]
or home? I've heard of slavers drifting, drifting,
playthings of wind and storm and chance, their
*   crews*
gone blind, the jungle hatred   45
crawling up on deck.

Thou   Who   Walked   On   Galilee[2]

"Deponent[3] further sayeth *The Bella J*
left the Guinea Coast[4]
with cargo of five hundred blacks and odd   50
for the barracoons[5] of Florida:

"That there was hardly room 'tween-decks for half
the sweltering cattle stowed spoon-fashion there;
that some went mad of thirst and tore their flesh
and sucked the blood: 55

"That Crew and Captain lusted with the comeliest
of the savage girls kept naked in the cabins;
that there was one they called The Guinea Rose
and they cast lots and fought to lie with her:

"That when the Bo's'n piped all hands,[6] the flames   60
spreading from starboard already were beyond

---

6. Running before a strong wind.
7. Guardian.
8. Seabird that sailors believed would, if slain, bring bad luck. In "The Rime of the Ancient Mariner," by Samuel Taylor Coleridge (1772–1834), a sailor who kills an albatross is doomed to wear it around his neck and forever tell his tale.
9. That is, forecastle; the forward part of a ship, under the deck, where the crew lives.

1. Davy Jones's locker, where sailors go after they drown.
2. Matthew 14 recounts Jesus' walking on the water.
3. Someone offering evidence.
4. Region of West Africa.
5. Slave quarters.
6. The boatswain (officer in charge of riggings and sails) summoned the crew.

control, the negroes howling and their chains
entangled with the flames:

"That the burning blacks could not be reached,
that the Crew abandoned ship,   65
leaving their shrieking negresses behind,
that the Captain perished drunken with the wenches:

"Further Deponent sayeth not."

Pilot   Oh   Pilot   Me

II

Aye, lad, and I have seen those factories,   70
Gambia, Rio Pongo, Calabar;[7]
have watched the artful mongos[8] baiting traps
of war wherein the victor and the vanquished

Were caught as prizes for our barracoons.
Have seen the nigger kings whose vanity   75
and greed turned wild black hides of Fellatah,
Mandingo, Ibo, Kru[9] to gold for us.

And there was one—King Anthracite[1] we named him—
fetish face beneath French parasols
of brass and orange velvet, impudent mouth   80
whose cups were carven skulls of enemies:

He'd honor us with drum and feast and conjo[2]
and palm-oil-glistening wenches deft in love,
and for tin crowns that shone with paste,
red calico and German-silver trinkets   85

Would have the drums talk war and send
his warriors to burn the sleeping villages
and kill the sick and old and lead the young
in coffles to our factories.

Twenty years a trader, twenty years,   90
for there was wealth aplenty to be harvested
from those black fields, and I'd be trading still
but for the fevers melting down my bones.

III

Shuttles in the rocking loom of history,
the dark ships move, the dark ships move,   95

7. Nigerian city. *Gambia:* country in West Africa.   9. African tribes.
Rio Pongo: East African river.   1. Variety of coal.
8. Bantu-speaking people of Zaire, East Africa.   2. Dance.

their bright ironical names
like jests of kindness on a murderer's mouth;
plough through thrashing glister toward
fata morgana's[3] lucent melting shore,
weave toward New World littorals[4] that are   100
mirage and myth and actual shore.

Voyage through death,
               voyage whose chartings are unlove.

A charnel stench, effluvium of living death
spreads outward from the hold,   105
where the living and the dead, the horribly dying,
lie interlocked, lie foul with blood and excrement.

    Deep in the festering hold thy father lies,
    the corpse of mercy rots with him,
    rats eat love's rotten gelid eyes.   110

    But, oh, the living look at you
    with human eyes whose suffering accuses you,
    whose hatred reaches through the swill of dark,
    to strike you like a leper's claw.

    You cannot stare that hatred down   115
    or chain the fear that stalks the watches
    and breathes on you its fetid scorching breath;
    cannot kill the deep immortal human wish,
    the timeless will.

    "But for the storm that flung up barriers   120
    of wind and wave, *The Amistad*[5] señores,
    would have reached the port of Príncipe in two,
    three days at most; but for the storm we should
    have been prepared for what befell.
    Swift as the puma's leap it came. There was   125
    that interval of moonless calm filled only
    with the water's and the rigging's usual sounds,
    then sudden movement, blows and snarling cries
    and they had fallen on us with machete
    and marlinspike. It was as though the very   130
    air, the night itself were striking us.
    Exhausted by the rigors of the storm,
    we were no match for them. Our men went down

3. Mirage's.
4. Shores.
5. "Part III follows in the main the account of the *Amistad* mutiny given by Muriel Rukeyser [1913–1980, American poet] in her biography of Willard Gibbs [1839–1903, American physicist]" [Hayden's note]. In July 1839, Cinquez, or Cinqué, led fifty-three slaves in a mutiny aboard the *Amistad*, a Spanish slave ship. The captain, the mate, and the captain's slave Celestino were all killed. After drifting for two months, the ship was seized off Long Island and the mutineers arrested. The owners, who had been onboard and spared, demanded that the surviving slaves be extradited to Cuba to stand trial for murder. During the ensuing Supreme Court trial, however, John Quincy Adams successfully convinced the court to acquit the mutineers. The thirty-seven survivors were released to Africa.

before the murderous Africans. Our loyal
Celestino ran from below with gun   135
and lantern and I saw, before the cane-
knife's wounding flash, Cinquez,
that surly brute who calls himself a prince,
directing, urging on the ghastly work.
He hacked the poor mulatto down, and then   140
he turned on me. The decks were slippery
when daylight finally came. It sickens me
to think of what I saw, of how these apes
threw overboard the butchered bodies of
our men, true Christians all, like so much jetsam.   145
Enough, enough. The rest is quickly told:
Cinquez was forced to spare the two of us
you see to steer the ship to Africa,
and we like phantoms doomed to rove the sea
voyaged east by day and west by night,   150
deceiving them, hoping for rescue,
prisoners on our own vessel, till
at length we drifted to the shores of this
your land, America, where we were freed
from our unspeakable misery. Now we   155
demand, good sirs, the extradition of
Cinquez and his accomplices to La
Havana. And it distresses us to know
there are so many here who seem inclined
to justify the mutiny of these blacks.   160
We find it paradoxical indeed
that you whose wealth, whose tree of liberty
are rooted in the labor of your slaves
should suffer the august John Quincy Adams
to speak with so much passion of the right   165
of chattel slaves to kill their lawful masters
and with his Roman rhetoric weave a hero's
garland for Cinquez. I tell you that
we are determined to return to Cuba
with our slaves and there see justice done.   170
        Cinquez—
or let us say 'the Prince'—Cinquez shall die."

The deep immortal human wish,
the timeless will:

Cinquez its deathless primaveral[6] image,
life that transfigures many lives.   175

Voyage through death
            to life upon these shores.

                                                    1945, 1962

6. Earliest springtime.

Homage to the Empress of the Blues[7]

Because there was a man somewhere in a candystripe silk shirt,
gracile and dangerous as a jaguar and because a woman moaned
for him in sixty-watt gloom and mourned him Faithless Love
Twotiming Love Oh Love Oh Careless Aggravating Love,

> She came out on the stage in yards of pearls, emerging like   5
> a favorite scenic view, flashed her golden smile and sang.

Because grey laths began somewhere to show from underneath
torn hurdygurdy lithographs of dollfaced heaven;
and because there were those who feared alarming fists of snow
on the door and those who feared the riot-squad of statistics,   10

> She came out on the stage in ostrich feathers, beaded satin,
> and shone that smile on us and sang.

1948

Mourning Poem for the Queen of Sunday

> Lord's lost Him His mockingbird,
> His fancy warbler;
> Satan sweet-talked her,
> four bullets hushed her.
> Who would have thought   5
> she'd end that way?

Four bullets hushed her. And the world a-clang with evil.
Who's going to make old hardened sinner men tremble now
and the righteous rock?
Oh who and oh who will sing Jesus down   10
to help with struggling and doing without and being colored
all through blue Monday?
Till way next Sunday?

> All those angels
> in their cretonne[8] clouds and finery   15
> the true believer saw
> when she rared back her head and sang,
> all those angels are surely weeping.
> Who would have thought
> she'd end that way?   20

Four holes in her heart. The gold works wrecked.
But she looks so natural in her big bronze coffin

7. Bessie Smith (1895–1937), a great blues singer
of the 1920s and 1930s, was known as the Em-
press of the Blues.
8. Cotton or linen fabric.

among the Broken Hearts and Gates-Ajar,
it's as if any moment she'd lift her head
from its pillow of chill gardenias   25
and turn this quiet into shouting Sunday
and make folks forget what she did on Monday.

Oh, Satan sweet-talked her,
and four bullets hushed her.
Lord's lost Him His diva,   30
His fancy warbler's gone.
Who would have thought,
who would have thought she'd end that way?

                                                    1949, 1962

Witch Doctor[9]

I

He dines alone surrounded by reflections
of himself. Then after sleep and benzedrine
descends the Cinquecento[1] stair his magic
wrought from hypochondria of the well-
to-do and nagging deathwish of the poor;   5
swirls on smiling genuflections of
his liveried chauffeur into a crested
lilac limousine, the cynosure[2]
of mousey neighbors tittering behind
Venetian blinds and half afraid of him   10
and half admiring his outrageous flair.

II

Meanwhile his mother, priestess in gold lamé,
precedes him to the quondam[3] theater
now Israel Temple of the Highest Alpha,
where the bored, the sick, the alien, the tired   15
await euphoria. With deadly vigor
she prepares the way for mystery
and lucre. Shouts in blues-contralto, "He's
God's dictaphone of all-redeeming truth.
Oh he's the holyweight champeen who's come   20
to give the knockout lick to your bad luck;
say he's the holyweight champeen who's here
to deal a knockout punch to your hard luck."

9. The Rev. James F. (Prophet) Jones (1907–1971) founded the Church of Universal Triumph, the Dominion of God Inc., in 1938 in Detroit. He lived in an opulent chateau, held services in a luxurious redecorated theater, and preached for five or six hours at a time dressed in velvet, silk, and jewels.
1. Sixteenth century (Italian); more specifically, a style of Renaissance Italian art and architecture.
2. Someone who attracts attention.
3. Former.

III

Reposing on cushions of black leopard skin,
he telephones instructions for a long   25
slow drive across the park that burgeons now
with spring and sailors. Peers questingly
into the green fountainous twilight, sighs
and turns the gold-plate dial to Music For
Your Dining-Dancing Pleasure. Smoking Egyptian   30
cigarettes rehearses in his mind
a new device that he must use tonight.

IV

Approaching Israel Temple, mask in place,
he hears ragtime allegros of a "Song
of Zion" that becomes when he appears   35
a hallelujah wave for him to walk.
His mother and a rainbow-surpliced cordon[4]
conduct him choiring to the altar-stage,
and there he kneels and seems to pray before
a lighted Jesus painted sealskin-brown.   40
Then with a glittering flourish he arises,
turns, gracefully extends his draperied arms:
"Israelites, true Jews, O found lost tribe
of Israel, receive my blessing now.
Selah, selah."[5] He feels them yearn toward him   45
as toward a lover, exults before the image
of himself their trust gives back. Stands as though
in meditation, letting their eyes caress
his garments jewelled and chatoyant,[6] cut
to fall, to flow from his tall figure   50
dramatically just so. Then all at once
he sways, quivers, gesticulates as if
to ward off blows or kisses, and when he speaks
again he utters wildering vocables,[7]
hypnotic no-words planned (and never failing)   55
to enmesh his flock in theopathic tension.
Cries of eudaemonic[8] pain attest
his artistry. Behind the mask he smiles.
And now in subtly altering light he chants
and sinuously trembles, chants and trembles   60
while convulsive energies of eager faith
surcharge the theater with power of
their own, a power he has counted on

---

4. Group surrounding him, wearing many-colored surplices, or robes.
5. Hebrew word, often found in the Psalms, believed to mean "lift up your voices."
6. Changing in color.
7. Meaningless words that bewilder. Jones would chant in an "unknown tongue" that included phrases such as "the lubritorium of lubrimentality."
8. Producing happiness. *Theopathic:* intensely absorbed in worship.

and for a space allows to carry him.
Dishevelled antiphons[9] proclaim the moment   65
his followers all day have hungered for,
but which is his alone.
He signals: tambourines begin, frenetic
drumbeat and glissando. He dances from the altar,
robes hissing, flaring, shimmering; down aisles   70
where mantled guardsmen intercept wild hands
that arduously strain to clutch his vestments,
he dances, dances, ensorcelled and aloof,
the fervid juba[1] of God as lover, healer,
conjurer. And of himself as God.   75

1962

Those Winter Sundays

Sundays too my father got up early
and put his clothes on in the blueblack cold,
then with cracked hands that ached
from labor in the weekday weather made
banked fires blaze. No one ever thanked him.   5

I'd wake and hear the cold splintering, breaking.
When the rooms were warm, he'd call,
and slowly I would rise and dress,
fearing the chronic angers of that house,

Speaking indifferently to him,   10
who had driven out the cold
and polished my good shoes as well.
What did I know, what did I know
of love's austere and lonely offices?

1962

Night, Death, Mississippi[2]

I

A quavering cry. Screech-owl?
Or one of them?

---

9. Choruses sung responsively.
1. A Haitian dance for the dead; also, a compli-
cated dance that used to be performed by blacks
in the deep south. *Ensorcelled:* bewitched.
2. Written in response to the murder of civil rights
activists Michael Schwerner, Andrew Goodman,
and James Earl Chaney by Klansmen and police
deputies in Philadelphia, Mississippi, in 1964.
Schwerner, Goodman, and Chaney were working
to register black voters during Freedom Summer
of 1964.

The old man in his reek
and gauntness laughs—

One of them, I bet—   5
and turns out the kitchen lamp,
limping to the porch to listen
in the windowless night.

Be there with Boy and the rest
if I was well again.   10
Time was. Time was.
White robes like moonlight

In the sweetgum dark.
Unbucked that one then
and him squealing bloody Jesus   15
as we cut it off.

Time was. A cry?
A cry all right.
He hawks and spits,
fevered as by groinfire.   20

Have us a bottle,
Boy and me—
he's earned him a bottle—
when he gets home.

                              II

Then we beat them, he said,   25
beat them till our arms was tired
and the big old chains
messy and red.

O Jesus burning on the lily cross

Christ, it was better   30
than hunting bear
which don't know why
you want him dead.

O night, rawhead and bloodybones night

You kids fetch Paw   35
some water now so's he
can wash that blood
off him, she said.

O night betrayed by darkness not its own

                                                              1966

Elegies for Paradise Valley[3]

I

My shared bedroom's window
opened on alley stench.
A junkie died in maggots there.
I saw his body shoved into a van.
I saw the hatred for our kind   5
glistening like tears
in the policemen's eyes.

II

No place for Pestalozzi's
fiorelli.[4] No time of starched
and ironed innocence. Godfearing   10
elders, even Godless grifters, tried
as best they could to shelter
us. Rats fighting in their walls.

III

Waxwork Uncle Henry
(murdered Uncle Crip)   15
lay among floral pieces
in the front room where
the Christmas tree had stood.

Mister Hong of the
Chinese Lantern (there   20
Auntie as waitress queened it
nights) brought freesias, wept
beside the coffin.

Beautiful, our neighbors
murmured; he would be proud.   25
Is it mahogany?
Mahogany—I'd heard
the victrola[5] voice of

dead Bert Williams[6]
talk-sing that word as macabre   30
music played, chilling
me. Uncle Crip
had laughed and laughed.

---

3. Nickname for St. Antoine, a Detroit slum.
4. Little flowers (Italian). Johann Heinrich Pestalozzi (1746–1827), Swiss educational reformer and advocate for education of the poor.
5. Phonograph.

6. Popular, American vaudeville comedian (1876–1922) from the West Indies, who often played the stereotype of the bumbling, black minstrel character.

IV

Whom now do you guide, Madam Artelia?
Who nowadays can summon you to speak   35
from the spirit place your ghostly home
of the oh-riental wonders there—
of the fate, luck, surprises, gifts

awaiting us out here? Oh, Madam,
part Seminole and confidante   40
("Born with a veil over my face")
of all our dead, how clearly you
materialize before the eye

of memory—your AfroIndian features,
Gypsy dress, your silver crucifix   45
and manycolored beads. I see
again your waitingroom, with its wax
bouquets, its plaster Jesus of the Sacred Heart.

I watch blue smoke of incense curl
from a Buddha's lap as I wait with Ma   50
and Auntie among your nervous clients.
You greet us, smiling, lay your hand
in blessing on my head, then lead

the others into a candlelit room
I may not enter. She went into a trance,   55
Auntie said afterward, and spirits
talked, changing her voice to suit
their own. And Crip came.

Happy yes I am happy here,
he told us; dying's not death. Do not grieve.   60
Remembering, Auntie began to cry
and poured herself a glass of gin.
Didn't sound a bit like Crip, Ma snapped.

V

And Belle the classy dresser, where is she,
who changed her frocks three times a day?   65
    Where's Nora, with her laugh, her comic flair,
    stagestruck Nora waiting for her chance?
Where's fast Iola, who so loved to dance
she left her sickbed one last time to whirl
in silver at The Palace till she fell?   70
    Where's mad Miss Alice, who ate from garbage cans?
    Where's snuffdipping Lucy, who played us 'chunes'
on her guitar? Where's Hattie? Where's Melissabelle?
    Let vanished rooms, let dead streets tell.

Where's Jim, Watusi[7] prince and Good Old Boy,   75
who with a joke went off to fight in France?
    Where's Tump the defeated artist, for meals or booze
    daubing with quarrelsome reds, disconsolate blues?
Where's Les the huntsman? Tough Kid Chocolate, where
is he? Where's dapper Jess? Where's Stomp the shell-   80
shocked, clowning for us in parodies of war?
    Where's taunted Christopher, sad queen of night?
    And Ray, who cursing crossed the color line?
Where's gentle Brother Davis? Where's dopefiend Mel?
    Let vanished rooms, let dead streets tell.   85

VI

Of death. Of loving too:
Oh sweet sweet jellyroll:
so the sinful hymned it while
the churchfolk loured.

I scrounged for crumbs: 90
I yearned to touch the choirlady's hair,
I wanted Uncle Crip

to kiss me, but he danced
with me instead;
we Balled-the-Jack   95
to Jellyroll

Morton's[8] brimstone
piano on the phonograph,
laughing, shaking the gasolier
a later stillness dimmed.   100

VII

Our parents warned us: Gypsies
kidnap you. And we must never play
with Gypsy children: Gypsies
all got lice in their hair.

Their queen was dark as Cleopatra   105
in the Negro History Book. Their king's
sinister arrogance flashed fire
like the diamonds on his dirty hands.

Quite suddenly he was dead,
his tribe clamoring in grief.   110

7. Alternate name of Tutsi people of Central Africa.
8. American jazz pianist, composer, and band-

leader (1885–1941). Ballin'-the-Jack was a dance step popularized by a ragtime song of the same name in the 1910s.

They take on bad as Colored Folks,
Uncle Crip allowed. Die like us too.

Zingaros: Tzigeune: Gitanos:[9] Gypsies:
pornographers of gaudy otherness:
aliens among the alien: thieves,   115
carriers of sickness: like us like us.

VIII

Of death, of loving,
of sin and hellfire too.
Unsaved, old Christians
gossiped; pitched   120

from the gamblingtable—
Lord have mercy on
his wicked soul—
face foremost into hell.

We'd dance there, Uncle   125
Crip and I,
for though I spoke
my pieces well in Sunday School,

I knew myself (precocious
in the ways of guilt   130
and secret pain)
the devil's own rag babydoll.

                                                              1978

Bone-Flower Elegy

In the dream I enter the house
    wander vast rooms that are
        catacombs midnight subway
            cavernous ruined movie-palace
        where presences in vulture masks   5
            play scenes of erotic violence
                on a scaffold stage   I want
        to stay and watch but know somehow
I must not linger and come to the funeral
        chamber   in its icy nonlight see   10
            a naked corpse
                turning with sensual movements
                    on its coffin-bed

9. Synonyms for "Gypsies."

                    I have wept for you many times
                    I whisper but shrink from the arms   15
                       that would embrace me
                       and treading water reach
                    arched portals opening on a desert
                 groves of enormous nameless flowers
                       twist up from firegold sand   20
                 skull flowers flowers of sawtooth bone
                    their leaves and petals interlock
                       caging me for you beastangel
                          raging toward me
                    angelbeast shining come   25
                       to rend me and redeem

                                                              1985

KARL SHAPIRO
1913–2000

Karl Shapiro was a stubbornly independent presence in twentieth-century poetry; he pursued his own way with a conspicuous disregard of some compelling poetic models. He began to write in the mid-1930s and thus unavoidably grew up "in the shadow of T. S. Eliot" (*In Defense of Ignorance*). Long before it became fashionable to attack modernism, Shapiro criticized Eliot for being too formalist and contrived; together with Ezra Pound and W. B. Yeats, he had attempted "to arrest the forms of poetry via the amazing stratagem of arresting the forms of society." Shapiro's antipathy toward modernism came to a head in 1948, when he voted against awarding the first Bollingen Prize to Pound; he felt the older poet's social and political views, in particular his anti-Semitism, marred his poetry.

Shapiro's first two important books were published while he was in the U.S. Army. The poems, many concerning army life, were an immediate popular success; *V-Letter* won the Pulitzer Prize in 1945. Shapiro named William Carlos Williams and Hart Crane as his first heroes among modern poets, but their influence on his early poems, which are formally traditional, is not obvious. These verses are sharply observed, carefully organized, and openly emotional. After the war, Shapiro used his poetry to search for personal identity. Celebrating "Jewish consciousness," he courageously wrote about Jewishness at a time when it was unpopular to do so (e.g., "The First Time"). His other surprising subjects included masturbation and sexual initiation. He was amused by the anomaly of being a "bourgeois poet," a visionary with a mortgage. In the face of such contradictions, he tried to express "cosmic consciousness," a sense of the unity of all life—a term he borrowed from Walt Whitman. Shapiro was drawn to the poetry of Whitman and the Beats, finding in them the inclusiveness from which Eliot shrank.

Shapiro was born on November 10, 1913, in Baltimore, Maryland. After graduating from high school there, he enrolled at the University of Virginia, but he soon withdrew to devote himself to writing. After working for a time in Baltimore and studying on his own, Shapiro resumed his education at Johns Hopkins University, but he was inducted into the army before receiving his degree and served in the South Pacific through World War II. While overseas, Shapiro continued to write poetry, which his fiancée, Evelyn

Katz (whom he married in 1945), sought successfully to get published. When he returned to civilian life, he was well known in American letters, and he served for a year as poetry consultant to the Library of Congress; he then taught at Johns Hopkins. He edited *Poetry* magazine from 1950 to 1956, after which he joined the faculty of the University of Nebraska and edited *Prairie Schooner,* resigning in 1966 because the university refused, he said, to allow him to publish a short story involving a homosexual. From 1968 to 1984, he taught at the University of California at Davis. He died in New York City.

The Fly

O hideous little bat, the size of snot,
With polyhedral eye and shabby clothes,
To populate the stinking cat you walk
The promontory of the dead man's nose,
Climb with the fine leg of a Duncan-Phyfe[1]   5
 The smoking mountains of my food
  And in a comic mood
 In mid-air take to bed a wife.

Riding and riding with your filth of hair
On gluey foot or wing, forever coy,   10
Hot from the compost and green sweet decay,
Sounding your buzzer like an urchin toy—
You dot all whiteness with diminutive stool,
 In the tight belly of the dead
  Burrow with hungry head   15
 And inlay maggots like a jewel.

At your approach the great horse stomps and paws
Bringing the hurricane of his heavy tail;
Shod in disease you dare to kiss my hand
Which sweeps against you like an angry flail;   20
Still you return, return, trusting your wing
 To draw you from the hunter's reach
  That learns to kill to teach
 Disorder to the tinier thing.

My peace is your disaster. For your death   25
Children like spiders cup their pretty hands
And wives resort to chemistry of war.
In fens of sticky paper and quicksands
You glue yourself to death. Where you are stuck
 You struggle hideously and beg,   30
  You amputate your leg
 Imbedded in the amber muck.

But I, a man, must swat you with my hate,
Slap you across the air and crush your flight,

---

1. Duncan Phyfe (c. 1768–1854), U.S. furniture maker whose early style was delicate.

Must mangle with my shoe and smear your blood,   35
Expose your little guts pasty and white,
Knock your head sidewise like a drunkard's hat,
   Pin your wings under like a crow's,
     Tear off your flimsy clothes
And beat you as one beats a rat.   40

Then like Gargantua[2] I stride among
The corpses strewn like raisins in the dust,
The broken bodies of the narrow dead
That catch the throat with fingers of disgust.
I sweep. One gyrates like a top and falls   45
   And stunned, stone blind, and deaf
     Buzzes its frightful F
And dies between three cannibals.

                                  1942

The First Time

Behind shut doors, in shadowy quarantine,
There shines the lamp of iodine and rose
That stains all love with its medicinal bloom.
This boy, who is no more than seventeen,
Not knowing what to do, takes off his clothes   5
As one might in a doctor's anteroom.

Then in a cross-draft of fear and shame
Feels love hysterically burn away,
A candle swimming down to nothingness
Put out by its own wetted gusts of flame,   10
And he stands smooth as uncarved ivory
Heavily curved for some expert caress.

And finally sees the always open door
That is invisible till the time has come,
And half falls through as through a rotten wall   15
To where chairs twist with dragons from the floor
And the great bed drugged with its own perfume
Spreads its carnivorous flower-mouth for all.

The girl is sitting with her back to him;
She wears a black thing and she rakes her hair,   20
Hauling her round face upward like moonrise;
She is younger than he, her angled arms are slim
And like a country girl her feet are bare.
She watches him behind her with old eyes,

2. Giant of medieval legend adopted by the
French writer François Rabelais (1483–1553) in
Gargantua and Pantagruel (1532). One of his
exploits was to swallow five pilgrims, with their
staves, in a salad.

Transfixing him in space like some grotesque,   25
Far, far from her where he is still alone
And being here is more and more untrue.
Then she turns round, as one turns at a desk,
And looks at him, too naked and too soon,
And almost gently asks: *Are you a Jew?*   30

                                                      1958

Manhole Covers

The beauty of manhole covers—what of that?
Like medals struck by a great savage khan,
Like Mayan calendar stones,[3] unliftable, indecipherable,
Not like the old electrum, chased and scored,[4]
Mottoed and sculptured to a turn,   5
But notched and whelked[5] and pocked and smashed
With the great company names
(Gentle Bethlehem, smiling United States[6]).
This rustproof artifact of my street,
Long after roads are melted away will lie   10
Sidewise in the grave of the iron-old world,
Bitten at the edges,
Strong with its cryptic American,
Its dated beauty.

                                                      1968

The Piano Tuner's Wife

That note comes clear, like water running clear,
Then the next higher note, and up and up
And more and more, with now and then a chord,
The highest notes like tapping a tile with a hammer,
Now and again an arpeggio,[7] a theme,   5
As if the keyboard spoke to the one key,
Saying, No interval is exactly true,
And the note whines slightly and then truly sings.

She sits on the sofa reading a book she has brought,
A ray of sunlight on her white hair.   10
She is here because he is blind. She drives.
It is almost a platitude to say
That she leads him from piano to piano.

---

3. Large round stones fashioned by the ancient
Mayas of Central America, inscribed with symbols
denoting their calendar. *Khan:* medieval Asian
ruler.
4. Amber, ornamented and marked with lines.

5. Ridged.
6. A reference to the logos of the companies that
made them.
7. Tones of a chord played in succession.

And this continues for about an hour,
Building bridges from both sides of the void,   15
Coasting the chasms of the harmonies.

And in conclusion,
When there is no more audible dissent,
He plays his comprehensive keyboard song,
The loud proud paradigm,   20
The one work of art without content.

                                                                1976

DELMORE SCHWARTZ
1913–1966

In his essay "The Isolation of Modern Poetry" (1941), Delmore Schwartz argues that, in the twentieth century, the "only life available to the man of culture has been the cultivation of his own sensibility, that is the only subject available to him, if we may assume that a poet can only write about subjects of which he has an absorbing experience in every sense." Schwartz's poems explore divisions within his own consciousness and divisions between the apprehending self and the baffling exterior world with which the self must come to terms. They enact simultaneously a drama of ideas and a conflict of deeply personal interests.

In his early poems, Schwartz incarnates traditional philosophical dichotomies. Thus "The Heavy Bear Who Goes with Me" is an animal fable about the relationship between mind and body. The first line of "In the Naked Bed, in Plato's Cave" forces us to consider each detail of this early-morning meditation in the light of Plato's great allegory of the dualism of appearance and reality. Schwartz called his last collection *Summer Knowledge* (1959, rev. 1967), and the poems' longer lines and more relaxed syntax are a stylistic change of direction. The poet now hopes—prays, even, since the poems are often beseeching—that he can settle his argument with himself by substituting for the warfare of philosophical concepts the healing rhythms of nature. In the volume, Schwartz strives for a certain American insouciance in the face of irreconcilable conflicts and sometimes presents this metaphysical casualness comically.

Schwartz was born on December 8, 1913, in Brooklyn, New York, to a middle-class Romanian Jewish family. He was educated at the University of Wisconsin, Madison, New York University (B.A., 1935), and Harvard University, where he studied philosophy with Alfred North Whitehead. In 1938, he published his first book, *In Dreams Begin Responsibilities*. Apart from writing poems, stories, plays, and criticism, Schwartz found outlets for his intellectual energies in teaching writing at six colleges and selecting poetry for the *Partisan Review* and *The New Republic*. He was also a brilliant talker and followed Dylan Thomas as "house poet" of the White Horse Tavern, in New York's Greenwich Village. Exhilarated by the life of the mind whether expressed in social theory, classical philosophy, or popular culture, he also entertained listeners for hours with improbable stories and dialogues in which he played both himself and T. S. Eliot ("from whom," he wrote, "I've learned the little I know about literature").

When awarded the Bollingen Prize in 1959 for *Selected Poems: Summer Knowledge*, Schwartz was the youngest poet to have received this prestigious award. Instead of being encouraged, however, he grew increasingly dissatisfied with the quality of his work and published only a handful of poems during the rest of his life—nothing at all after 1963—though he continued to write copiously. One reason may have been the depredations of mental illness; since the late 1940s, he had been in and out of sanatoriums. In the grip of paranoid obsessions, he denounced all his old friends, resigned as visiting professor at Syracuse University in 1965, and dropped out of sight for over a year. His last months were spent alone in a Times Square hotel, still writing; it was not until three days after his death, by heart attack, that someone was found to claim his body from a morgue.

In the Naked Bed, in Plato's Cave[1]

In the naked bed, in Plato's cave,
Reflected headlights slowly slid the wall,
Carpenters hammered under the shaded window,
Wind troubled the window curtains all night long,
A fleet of trucks strained uphill, grinding,   5
Their freights covered, as usual.
The ceiling lightened again, the slanting diagram
Slid slowly forth.
                            Hearing the milkman's chop,
His striving up the stair, the bottle's chink,   10
I rose from bed, lit a cigarette,
And walked to the window. The stony street
Displayed the stillness in which buildings stand,
The street-lamp's vigil and the horse's patience.
The winter sky's pure capital   15
Turned me back to bed with exhausted eyes.

Strangeness grew in the motionless air. The loose
Film grayed. Shaking wagons, hooves' waterfalls,
Sounded far off, increasing, louder and nearer.
A car coughed, starting. Morning, softly   20
Melting the air, lifted the half-covered chair
From underseas, kindled the looking-glass,
Distinguished the dresser and the white wall.
The bird called tentatively, whistled, called,
Bubbled and whistled, so! Perplexed, still wet   25
With sleep, affectionate, hungry and cold. So, so,
O son of man,[2] the ignorant night, the travail
Of early morning, the mystery of beginning
Again and again,
                            while History is unforgiven.   30

1938

---

1. In the ancient Greek philosopher Plato's famous allegory of the cave, the humanly perceivable world is only a projected image of a realer world of ideal forms, as if humans are sitting in a cave and can see the outside world only as shadows on the cave's walls.

2. The words used by God in addressing the prophet Ezekiel in the Valley of the Dry Bones, in which the bones rise up, put on flesh, and live (Ezekiel 37). See also T. S. Eliot's *Waste Land*, line 20.

The Heavy Bear Who Goes with Me

"the withness of the body"[3]

The heavy bear who goes with me,
A manifold honey to smear his face,
Clumsy and lumbering here and there,
The central ton of every place,
The hungry beating brutish one   5
In love with candy, anger, and sleep,
Crazy factotum, dishevelling all,
Climbs the building, kicks the football,
Boxes his brother in the hate-ridden city.

Breathing at my side, that heavy animal,   10
That heavy bear who sleeps with me,
Howls in his sleep for a world of sugar,
A sweetness intimate as the water's clasp,
Howls in his sleep because the tight-rope
Trembles and shows the darkness beneath.   15
—The strutting show-off is terrified,
Dressed in his dress-suit, bulging his pants,
Trembles to think that his quivering meat
Must finally wince to nothing at all.

That inescapable animal walks with me,   20
Has followed me since the black womb held,
Moves where I move, distorting my gesture,
A caricature, a swollen shadow,
A stupid clown of the spirit's motive,
Perplexes and affronts with his own darkness,   25
The secret life of belly and bone,
Opaque, too near, my private, yet unknown,
Stretches to embrace the very dear
With whom I would walk without him near,
Touches her grossly, although a word   30
Would bare my heart and make me clear,
Stumbles, flounders, and strives to be fed
Dragging me with him in his mouthing care,
Amid the hundred million of his kind,
The scrimmage of appetite everywhere.   35

                                                            1938

The Mind Is an Ancient and Famous Capital

The mind is a city like London,
Smoky and populous: it is a capital

3. From *Process and Reality* (1929), by English philosopher Alfred North Whitehead (1861–1947).

Like Rome, ruined and eternal,
Marked by the monuments which no one
Now remembers. For the mind, like Rome, contains   5
Catacombs, aqueducts, amphitheatres, palaces,
Churches and equestrian statues, fallen, broken or soiled.
The mind possesses and is possessed by all the ruins
Of every haunted, hunted generation's celebration.

"Call us what you will: we are made such by love."[4]   10
We are such studs as dreams are made on, and
Our little lives are ruled by the gods, by Pan,[5]
Piping of all, seeking to grasp or grasping
All of the grapes; and by the bow-and-arrow god,
Cupid, piercing the heart through, suddenly and forever.   15

Dusk we are, to dusk returning,[6] after the burbing,
After the gold fall, the fallen ash, the bronze,
Scattered and rotten, after the white null statues which
Are winter, sleep, and nothingness: when
Will the houselights of the universe   20
Light up and blaze?
                    For it is not the sea
Which murmurs in a shell,
And it is not only heart, at harp o'clock,
It is the dread terror of the uncontrollable   25
Horses of the apocalypse,[7] running in wild dread
Toward Arcturus[8]—and returning as suddenly . . .

                                                            1959

4. Quoted from "The Canonization," line 19, by John Donne (1572–1631).
5. Cf. Shakespeare's *Tempest* 4.1.156–58: "We are such stuff / As dreams are made on, and our little life / Is rounded with a sleep." Pan is a fertility god in classical mythology.
6. "You are dust, and to dust you will return" (Genesis 3.19).
7. In the biblical vision of the world's end (Revelation), the agents of destruction are the horsemen Conquest, Slaughter, Famine, and Death.
8. A star in the constellation Ursa Major (the Great Bear).

MURIEL RUKEYSER
1913–1980

To be absolutely contemporary was Muriel Rukeyser's aim. Left-wing politics played a considerable part in her life, as did science. She could vividly detail both the suffering of miners carelessly exposed to deadly silica dust ("The Book of the Dead") and the microscopic exchanges of genetic material between single-celled organisms ("The Conjugation of the Paramecium"). Her prize-winning first volume, *Theory of Flight* (1935), displayed her knowledge of aviation, gained as a student at Roosevelt Aviation School; she also wrote a biography of the nineteenth-century mathematician Willard Gibbs (which included information about a slave-ship mutiny that poet Robert Hayden adapted in his sequence "Middle Passage"). As the editor of a student newspaper she took part in the social activism of the Great Depression and was arrested in Alabama for protesting the second Scottsboro trial, in which nine black youths were accused of raping two white women. She sided with the Loyalists during the Spanish Civil War. Later, she was jailed for protesting the Vietnam War on the steps of the U.S. Capitol. Her poetry declares her time: "I lived in the first century of world wars," she writes in "Poem," and the present-day metropolis, with its garbage, its violence, and its vagabondage, plays a large role in her imagery.

A poet of idealism and intensity, Rukeyser was an ardent participant in the Old Left activism of the Depression and the New Left radicalism of the 1960s. In her 1930s poetry, she adapts techniques of modernism—collage, multiple voices, arcane allusions—for leftist political purposes. In her long poetic sequence "The Book of the Dead," she interweaves congressional testimony on the outbreak of lung disease in West Virginia with the ancient spells of the Egyptian *Book of the Dead*. Her documentary techniques link her to W. H. Auden; her use of archaic materials, to T. S. Eliot and Ezra Pound. In the less oblique poetry of her later career, she recalls Walt Whitman's prophetic voice, collectivist stance, and Bible-imbued rhetoric. Although she never officially described herself as a feminist, her 1960s proclamation "No more masks! No more mythologies!" became a *cri de coeur* for liberation from gender-based constraints on expression ("The Poem as Mask"). Her willingness to use an engaged, visionary rhetoric was not always welcomed, but her fusion of passionate advocacy with technical sophistication and intimate awareness inspired such poets as Adrienne Rich and Anne Sexton.

Immersing herself in the present, Rukeyser freely denounced the past: "We focus on our times, destroying you, fathers/in the long ground: you have given strange birth / to us who turn against you in our blood" ("The Blood Is Justified"). In "Poem out of Childhood," she makes her position even clearer: "Not Sappho, Sacco. / Rebellion pioneering among our lives." (Nicola Sacco, an anarchist executed for murder, was thought to be innocent by the Left.) Her revolutionary ardor underlies much of her poetry, but in her later work her attention is also directed to traditional lyric problems of love, sympathy, and death. She imagines her poems as arising naturally from her body: "Breathe-in experience, breathe-out poetry" ("Poem out of Childhood").

Rukeyser was born on December 15, 1913, in New York City, the daughter of middle-class Jewish parents. She attended Vassar College and Columbia University from 1930 to 1932. After World War II, she taught at Sarah Lawrence College and the California Labor School in Berkeley, and she raised a child as a single parent. Along with poetry, she also wrote plays, translations, and children's books.

From THE BOOK OF THE DEAD[1]

Absalom[2]

I first discovered what was killing these men.
I had three sons who worked with their father in the tunnel:
Cecil, aged 23, Owen, aged 21, Shirley, aged 17.

1. A twenty-one poem sequence (1938), in which Rukeyser explores an outbreak in the early 1930s of silicosis, a fatal lung disease caused by inhaling silica dust, that afflicted two thousand miners of the Hawk's Nest tunneling project, in Gauley Bridge, West Virginia. The disaster became the subject of a congressional investigation and was widely publicized. Rukeyser traveled to Gauley Bridge in 1936 to interview survivors and perform the research that she was to synthesize in the sequence. *The Book of the Dead* is an ancient Egyptian collection of spells placed in tombs to offer protection and aid to the deceased in the afterlife.

2. The name of King David's youngest son, who rebelled against his father and was consequently

They used to work in a coal mine, not steady work
for the mines were not going much of the time.
A power Co. foreman learned that we made home brew,   5
he formed a habit of dropping in evenings to drink,
persuading the boys and my husband—
give up their jobs and take this other work.
It would pay them better.   10
Shirley was my youngest son; the boy.
He went into the tunnel.

    My heart   my mother   my heart   my mother
    My heart   my coming into being.

My husband is not able to work.   15
He has it, according to the doctor.
We have been having a very hard time making a living since
   this trouble came to us.
I saw the dust in the bottom of the tub.
The boy worked there about eighteen months,
came home one evening with a shortness of breath.   20
He said, "Mother, I cannot get my breath."
Shirley was sick about three months.
I would carry him from his bed to the table,
from his bed to the porch, in my arms.

    My heart is mine in the place of hearts,   25
    They gave me back my heart, it lies in me.

When they took sick, right at the start, I saw a doctor.
I tried to get Dr. Harless to X-ray the boys.
He was the only man I had any confidence in,
the company doctor in the Kopper's mine,   30
but he would not see Shirley.
He did not know where his money was coming from.
I promised him half if he'd work to get compensation,
but even then he would not do anything.
I went on the road and begged the X-ray money,   35
the Charleston hospital made the lung pictures,
he took the case after the pictures were made.
And two or three doctors said the same thing.
The youngest boy did not get to go down there with me,
he lay and said, "Mother, when I die,   40
"I want you to have them open me up and
"see if that dust killed me.
"Try to get compensation,
"you will not have any way of making your living
"when we are gone,   45
"and the rest are going too."

killed (2 Samuel 13–19). The monologue is spoken
in the voice of Mrs. Dora Jones, a member of the
Gauley Bridge community's defense committee,
which undertook lawsuits against the companies
responsible for the disaster. Rukeyser combines
the testimony of various survivors. The italicized
passages adapt and translate excerpts from the
Egyptian *Book of the Dead*.

I have gained mastery over my heart
I have gained mastery over my two hands
I have gained mastery over the waters
I have gained mastery over the river.   50

The case of my son was the first of the line of lawsuits.
They sent the lawyers down and the doctors down;
they closed the electric sockets in the camps.
There was Shirley, and Cecil, Jeffrey and Oren,
Raymond Johnson, Clev and Oscar Anders,   55
Frank Lynch, Henry Palf, Mr. Pitch, a foreman;
a slim fellow who carried steel with my boys,
his name was Darnell, I believe. There were many others,
the towns of Glen Ferris, Alloy, where the white rock lies,
six miles away; Vanetta, Gauley Bridge,   60
Gamoca, Lockwood, the gullies,
the whole valley is witness.
I hitchhike eighteen miles, they make checks out.
They asked me how I keep the cow on $2.
I said one week, feed for the cow, one week, the children's flour.   65
The oldest son was twenty-three.
The next son was twenty-one.
The youngest son was eighteen.
They called it pneumonia at first.
They would pronounce it fever.   70
Shirley asked that we try to find out.
That's how they learned what the trouble was.

I open out a way, they have covered my sky with crystal
I came forth by day, I am born a second time,
I force a way through, and I know the gate   75
I shall journey over the earth among the living.

He shall not be diminished, never;
I shall give a mouth to my son.

Alloy

This is the most audacious landscape. The gangster's
stance with his gun smoking and out is not so
vicious as this commercial field, its hill of glass.

Sloping as gracefully as thighs, the foothills
narrow to this, clouds over every town   5
finally indicate the stored destruction.

Crystalline hill: a blinded field of white
murdering snow, seamed by convergent tracks;
the travelling cranes reach for the silica.

And down the track, the overhead conveyor   10
slides on its cable to the feet of chimneys.
Smoke rises, not white enough, not so barbaric.

Here the severe flame speaks from the brick throat,
electric furnaces produce this precious, this clean,
annealing[3] the crystals, fusing at last alloys.   15

Hottest for silicon, blast furnaces raise flames,
spill fire, spill steel, quench the new shape to freeze,
tempering it to perfected metal.

Forced through this crucible, a million men.
Above this pasture, the highway passes those   20
who curse the air, breathing their fear again.

The roaring flowers of the chimney-stacks
less poison, at their lips in fire, than this
dust that is blown from off the field of glass;

blows and will blow, rising over the mills,   25
crystallized and beyond the fierce corrosion
disintegrated angel on these hills.

                                                    1938

Boy with His Hair Cut Short

Sunday shuts down on this twentieth-century evening.
The El[4] passes. Twilight and bulb define
the brown room, the overstuffed plum sofa,
the boy, and the girl's thin hands above his head.
A neighbor radio sings stocks, news, serenade.   5

He sits at the table, head down, the young clear neck exposed,
watching the drugstore sign from the tail of his eye;
tattoo, neon, until the eye blears, while his
solicitous tall sister, simple in blue, bending
behind him, cuts his hair with her cheap shears.   10

The arrow's electric red always reaches its mark,
successful neon! He coughs, impressed by that precision.
His child's forehead, forever protected by his cap,
is bleached against the lamplight as he turns head
and steadies to let the snippets drop.   15

Erasing the failure of weeks with level fingers,
she sleeks the fine hair, combing: "You'll look fine tomorrow!

3. Heating and cooling.
4. The elevated railway that ran above Third Ave-   nue in New York City; it was dismantled in the
                                                           1930s.

You'll surely find something, they can't keep turning you down;
the finest gentleman's not so trim as you!" Smiling, he raises
the adolescent forehead wrinkling ironic now.   20

He sees his decent suit laid out, new-pressed,
his carfare on the shelf. He lets his head fall, meeting
her earnest hopeless look, seeing the sharp blades splitting,
the darkened room, the impersonal sign, her motion,
the blue vein, bright on her temple, pitifully beating.   25

                                                        1938

Night Feeding

Deeper than sleep but not so deep as death
I lay there sleeping and my magic head
remembered and forgot.   On first cry I
remembered and forgot and did believe.
I knew love and I knew evil: 5
woke to the burning song and the tree burning blind,
despair of our days and the calm milk-giver who
knows sleep, knows growth, the sex of fire and grass,
and the black snake with gold bones.

Black sleeps, gold burns;   on second cry I woke   10
fully and gave to feed and fed on feeding.
Gold seed, green pain, my wizards in the earth
walked through the house, black in the morning dark.
Shadows grew in my veins, my bright belief,
my head of dreams deeper than night and sleep.   15
Voices of all black animals crying to drink,
cries of all birth arise, simple as we,
found in the leaves, in clouds and dark, in dream,
deep as this hour, ready again to sleep.

                                                        1951

The Conjugation of the Paramecium[5]

This has nothing
to do with
propagating

---

5. The paramecium is a microscopic, single-celled organism that reproduces asexually through binary fission, splitting itself in two. But without the genetic reorganization and cross-fertilization achieved through conjugation, in which two paramecia temporarily unite, the paramecium will age and eventually die.

The species
is continued   5
as so many are
(among the smaller creatures)
by fission

(and this species
is very small   10
next in order to
the amoeba, the beginning one)

The paramecium
achieves, then,
immortality   15
by dividing

But when
the paramecium
desires renewal
strength   another joy   20
this is what
the paramecium does:

The paramecium
lies down beside
another   25
paramecium

Slowly   inexplicably
the exchange
takes place
in which   30
some bits
of the nucleus of each
are exchanged

for some bits
of the nucleus   35
of the other

This is called
the conjugation of the paramecium.

                                        1968

The Poem as Mask

Orpheus[6]

When I wrote of the women in their dances and wildness, it was a mask,
on their mountain, gold-hunting, singing, in orgy,
it was a mask; when I wrote of the god,
fragmented, exiled from himself, his life, the love gone down with song,
it was myself, split open, unable to speak, in exile from myself.   5

There is no mountain, there is no god, there is memory
of my torn life, myself split open in sleep, the rescued child
beside me among the doctors, and a word
of rescue from the great eyes.

No more masks! No more mythologies!   10

Now, for the first time, the god lifts his hand,
the fragments join in me with their own music.

    1968

Poem

I lived in the first century of world wars.
Most mornings I would be more or less insane,
The newspapers would arrive with their careless stories,
The news would pour out of various devices
Interrupted by attempts to sell products to the unseen.   5
I would call my friends on other devices;
They would be more or less mad for similar reasons.
Slowly I would get to pen and paper,
Make my poems for others unseen and unborn.
In the day I would be reminded of those men and women   10
Brave, setting up signals across vast distances,
Considering a nameless way of living, of almost unimagined values.
As the lights darkened, as the lights of night brightened,
We would try to imagine them, try to find each other.
To construct peace, to make love, to reconcile   15
Waking with sleeping, ourselves with each other,
Ourselves with ourselves. We would try by any means
To reach the limits of ourselves, to reach beyond ourselves,
To let go the means, to wake.

I lived in the first century of these wars.   20

    1968

6. In Greek mythology, a musician whose songs enchanted all creatures; who descended into the underworld and tried to rescue his wife, Eurydice; and who was torn apart and killed in an orgy by the women of Thrace.

WILLIAM STAFFORD
1914–1993

Some poets rebel against the world, against society, against matter, against time, and get their power from such rebelliousness. William Stafford saw no necessity for this. "Your job is to find what the world is trying to be," his father tells him in "Vocation," and this aptly characterizes Stafford's aim. He accepted life's terms: "Even the flaws were good—," he remarks in "At the Fair." In his writing, he sees the world with the eyes of someone who feels most at home in the sparsely populated countryside. "In scenery I like flat country. / In life I don't like much to happen" ("Passing Remark"). The sense of belonging has in his poetry the place that the sense of alienation has in others'. He is content with his "Aunt Mabel," content that "There are Aunt Mabels all over the world."

In poems of memory and mystical awe before nature, Stafford fashioned a quiet, lucid, conversational idiom that helped make him one of the most frequently read American poets in the post–World War II period. There is no seeking after grandeur; his poetry, he said, is "much like talk, with some enhancement." Nor does he often seek a radiant view of creation. Instead, he allies himself with Thomas Hardy, who, he said, "is my most congenial landmark" and has the same strong sense of place (*Contemporary Poets*, ed. Rosalie Murphy, 1970). (He has little, however, of Hardy's irony.) In what seems to be an undistorted view of the world, some oddity always catches Stafford's eye, and unobtrusively yet slyly he brings it forth.

Stafford was born on January 17, 1914, in Hutchinson, Kansas. After taking two degrees at the University of Kansas, he received his doctorate from the University of Iowa. His generally accepting attitude did not prevent his being a conscientious objector during World War II. Although he didn't publish his first book until he was forty-six, he published frequently after that. Stafford lived by a lake in Oregon and, like Richard Hugo and David Wagoner, fellow poets of the Pacific northwest, he set most of his poems in a nonurban locale. He taught at Lewis and Clark College, in Portland, and was Oregon's poet laureate from 1975 until his death. In 1963, he won the National Book Award for *Traveling through the Dark*.

Traveling through the Dark

Traveling through the dark I found a deer
dead on the edge of the Wilson River road.
It is usually best to roll them into the canyon:
that road is narrow; to swerve might make more dead.

By glow of the tail-light I stumbled back of the car   5
and stood by the heap, a doe, a recent killing;
she had stiffened already, almost cold.
I dragged her off; she was large in the belly.

My fingers touching her side brought me the reason—
her side was warm; her fawn lay there waiting,   10
alive, still, never to be born.
Beside that mountain road I hesitated.

The car aimed ahead its lowered parking lights;
under the hood purred the steady engine.
I stood in the glare of the warm exhaust turning red;   15
around our group I could hear the wilderness listen.

I thought hard for us all—my only swerving—,
then pushed her over the edge into the river.

1960

At the Bomb Testing Site

At noon in the desert a panting lizard
waited for history, its elbows tense,
watching the curve of a particular road
as if something might happen.

It was looking for something farther off   5
than people could see, an important scene
acted in stone for little selves
at the flute end of consequences.

There was just a continent without much on it
under a sky that never cared less.   10
Ready for a change, the elbows waited.
The hands gripped hard on the desert.

1966

For the Grave of Daniel Boone[1]

The farther he went the farther home grew.
Kentucky became another room;
the mansion arched over the Mississippi;
flowers were spread all over the floor.
He traced ahead a deepening home,   5
and better, with goldenrod:

Leaving the snakeskin of place after place,
going on—after the trees
the grass, a bird flying after a song.
Rifle so level, sighting so well   10
his picture freezes down to now,
a story-picture for children.

They go over the velvet falls
into the tapestry of his time,

1. American frontier explorer and folk hero (1734–1820), who helped establish the first settlement in Kentucky.

heirs to the landscape, feeling no jar: 15
it is like evening; they are the quail
surrounding his fire, coming in for the kill;
their little feet move sacred sand.

Children, we live in a barbwire time
but like to follow the old hands back—   20
the ring in the light, the knuckle, the palm,
all the way to Daniel Boone,
hunting our own kind of deepening home.
From the land that was his I heft this rock.

Here on his grave I put it down.   25

                                                                        1966

RANDALL JARRELL
1914–1965

After Randall Jarrell's death, his friend Robert Lowell described him as the most "heart-breaking" poet of his generation. Many of Jarrell's early poems were written out of his experience of World War II. They are about the losses of war, about young men made childlike by the nearness of death and by their obligations as killers. Many of Jarrell's later poems are dramatic monologues in the voices of women. Written in a plain style, they express the painful transformations of life and our desire to be changed into something that we once were or that we ache to become.

Jarrell was born on May 16, 1914, in Nashville, Tennessee. His family soon moved to California, and his parents divorced. He returned to Nashville, where he spent a somewhat drab childhood during the Great Depression. His refuge was books and the local public library. Jarrell studied at Vanderbilt University, moving from psychology to English. In 1937–39, he taught at Kenyon College, and his friends there—John Crowe Ransom, Robert Lowell, and the novelist Peter Taylor—all wrote of his gaiety, learning, and bright assurance. In 1942, he published his first book of poems, *Blood for a Stranger*, and enlisted in the army air corps. He washed out as a pilot, then served as a control tower operator working with B-29 crews.

The poet Robert Fitzgerald described Jarrell as "practically the only American poet able to cope with the Second Great War" (*Randall Jarrell, 1914–1965*, ed. Robert Lowell et al). The war poems, which often reflect W. H. Auden's influence, are found in two books, *Little Friend, Little Friend* (1945) and *Losses* (1948). Jarrell explores the murderous mechanisms of war and the diminished, helpless men who operate them. In the poem "Eighth Air Force," the soldiers "wash their hands, in blood, as best they can." Moved to cleanse themselves, they can find nothing untainted by their humanity. Though murderers, Jarrell's soldiers also seem passive and innocent before the technology of modern war. In another poem, an aerial gunner is killed in his womb-shaped ball turret and thus born into his own death.

After the war, in 1946, Jarrell taught at Sarah Lawrence College and served as acting literary editor of *The Nation*. He had, according to Lowell, a "deadly hand for killing what he despised" (*Randall Jarrell*). His reviews were hortatory, sometimes cruel, spattered with allusions, full of memorable epigrams and wisecracks. His most influential critical essays, such as those on Walt Whitman and Robert Frost, are richly documented, passionately argued appeals to readers to pay attention to poets who were neglected or improperly appreciated. From 1947 until his death, after being struck by a car, Jarrell taught at the Women's College of the University of North Carolina at Greensboro. In addition to his poetry and criticism, he published a novel and several children's books. His last book of poems, *The Lost World*, was published in 1965.

"Dramatic monologue," Jarrell writes in *Poetry and the Age* (1953), "which once had depended for its effect upon being a departure from the norm," has now become "in one form or another the norm." Certainly, it became the norm for Jarrell's later poetry. He seems to have tried to bring into his poems some of the qualities of the prose he admired: a strong sense of character and particular circumstance, the expressive fluctuations of language, the aura of implication that surrounds dramatic speech. Jarrell usually touches his characters at a moment of private anguish. Repeatedly in Jarrell's later poems we encounter the figure of an aging woman who mourns for a world she has lost or never more than dreamed of. The last poem of Jarrell's last book, "Thinking of the Lost World," is a meditation on what mortals can regain from the past by an act of loving memory. Jarrell begins the poem in imitation of novelist Marcel Proust, whom he called the "greatest of the writers of this century." A spoonful of chocolate tapioca replaces the madeleine that induced Proust's remembrance of the past. The poem concludes: "I hold in my own hands, in happiness, / Nothing: the nothing for which there's no reward." The recollected past is, of course, nothing: "Back in Los Angeles, we missed / Los Angeles." But the nothing recollected, by a final transformation, survives in the happiness of the poet and the eloquence of his poem.

90 North[1]

At home, in my flannel gown, like a bear to its floe,
I clambered to bed; up the globe's impossible sides
I sailed all night—till at last, with my black beard,
My furs and my dogs, I stood at the northern pole.

There in the childish night my companions lay frozen,   5
The stiff furs knocked at my starveling throat,
And I gave my great sigh: the flakes came huddling,
Were they really my end? In the darkness I turned to my rest.

—Here, the flag snaps in the glare and silence
Of the unbroken ice. I stand here,   10
The dogs bark, my beard is black, and I stare
At the North Pole . . .
              And now what? Why, go back.

Turn as I please, my step is to the south.
The world—my world spins on this final point   15
Of cold and wretchedness: all lines, all winds
End in this whirlpool I at last discover.

And it is meaningless. In the child's bed
After the night's voyage, in that warm world

---

1. Ninety north latitude; that is, the North Pole.

Where people work and suffer for the end   20
That crowns the pain—in that Cloud-Cuckoo-Land[2]

I reached my North and it had meaning.
Here at the actual pole of my existence,
Where all that I have done is meaningless,
Where I die or live by accident alone—   25

Where, living or dying, I am still alone;
Here where North, the night, the berg of death
Crowd me out of the ignorant darkness,
I see at last that all the knowledge

I wrung from the darkness—that the darkness flung me—   30
Is worthless as ignorance: nothing comes from nothing,[3]
The darkness from the darkness. Pain comes from the darkness
And we call it wisdom. It is pain.

                                                1942

The Death of the Ball Turret Gunner[4]

From my mother's sleep I fell into the State,
And I hunched in its belly till my wet fur froze.
Six miles from earth, loosed from its dream of life,
I woke to black flak and the nightmare fighters.
When I died they washed me out of the turret with a hose.   5

                                                1945

Eighth Air Force[5]

If, in an odd angle of the hutment,
A puppy laps the water from a can
Of flowers, and the drunk sergeant shaving
Whistles O Paradiso!*—shall I say that man
Is not as men have said: a wolf to man?   5

The other murderers troop in yawning;
Three of them play Pitch,[7] one sleeps, and one

2. In *The Birds*, by Aristophanes (c. 450–c. 388 B.C.E.), Greek dramatist, an imaginary city built in the clouds by the cuckoos; hence, any fantastic, illusory world.
3. Cf. Shakespeare's *King Lear* 1.1.89: "Nothing will come of nothing" (an Aristotelian maxim).
4. "A ball turret was a plexiglass sphere set into the belly of a B-17 or B-24, and inhabited by two .50 caliber machine-guns and one man, a short small man. When this gunner tracked with his machine guns a fighter attacking his bomber from below, he revolved with the turret; hunched upside-down in his little sphere, he looked like the foetus in the womb. The fighters which attacked

him were armed with cannon firing explosive shells. The hose was a steam hose" [Jarrell's note].
5. " 'Eighth Air Force' is a poem about the air force which bombed the continent from England. The man who lies counting missions has one to go before being sent home. The phrases from the Gospels compare such criminals and scapegoats as these with that earlier criminal and scapegoat about whom the Gospels were written" [Jarrell's note]. Later, Jarrell remarked: " 'Eighth Air Force' expresses better than any other of the poems I wrote about the war what I felt about the war."
6. An operatic aria.
7. Card game.

Lies counting missions, lies there sweating
Till even his heart beats: One; One; One.
O *murderers!* . . . Still, this is how it's done: 10

This is a war. . . . But since these play, before they die,
Like puppies with their puppy; since, a man,
I did as these have done, but did not die—
I will content the people as I can
And give up these to them: Behold the man![8] 15

I have suffered, in a dream, because of him,
Many things;[9] for this last saviour, man,
I have lied as I lie now. But what is lying?
Men wash their hands, in blood, as best they can:
I find no fault in this just man. 20

1948

Next Day

Moving from Cheer to Joy, from Joy to All,[1]
I take a box
And add it to my wild rice, my Cornish game hens.
The slacked or shorted, basketed, identical
Food-gathering flocks
Are selves I overlook. Wisdom, said William James, 5

Is learning what to overlook.[2] And I am wise
If that is wisdom.
Yet somehow, as I buy All from these shelves
And the boy takes it to my station wagon, 10
What I've become
Troubles me even if I shut my eyes.

When I was young and miserable and pretty
And poor, I'd wish
What all girls wish: to have a husband, 15
A house and children. Now that I'm old, my wish
Is womanish:
That the boy putting groceries in my car

8. Pilate offered the Jews their choice whether Jesus or Barabbas should be released, and the people chose Barabbas. "Pilate therefore went forth again, and said to them, Behold, I bring him forth to you, that you may know that I find no fault in him. Then came Jesus forth, wearing the crown of thorns, and the purple robe. And Pilate said unto them, Behold the man!" (John 19.4–5).
9. Just before asking the Jews to decide between Jesus and Barabbas, Pilate received a message from his wife: "Have nothing to do with that just man: for I have suffered many things this day in a dream because of him" (Matthew 27.19).
1. Names of detergents.
2. William James (1842–1910), American philosopher and psychologist; the quotation, slightly paraphrased, is from *The Principles of Psychology* (1890).

See me. It bewilders me he doesn't see me.
For so many years   20
I was good enough to eat: the world looked at me
And its mouth watered. How often they have undressed me,
The eyes of strangers!
And, holding their flesh within my flesh, their vile

Imaginings within my imagining,   25
I too have taken
The chance of life. Now the boy pats my dog
And we start home. Now I am good.
The last mistaken,
Ecstatic, accidental bliss, the blind   30

Happiness that, bursting, leaves upon the palm
Some soap and water—
It was so long ago, back in some Gay
Twenties, Nineties, I don't know . . . Today I miss
My lovely daughter   35
Away at school, my sons away at school,

My husband away at work—I wish for them.
The dog, the maid,
And I go through the sure unvarying days
At home in them. As I look at my life,   40
I am afraid
Only that it will change, as I am changing:

I am afraid, this morning, of my face.
It looks at me
From the rear-view mirror, with the eyes I hate,   45
The smile I hate. Its plain, lined look
Of gray discovery
Repeats to me: "You're old." That's all, I'm old.

And yet I'm afraid, as I was at the funeral
I went to yesterday.   50
My friend's cold made-up face, granite among its flowers,
Her undressed, operated-on, dressed body
Were my face and body.
As I think of her I hear her telling me

How young I seem; I *am* exceptional;   55
I think of all I have.
But really no one is exceptional,
No one has anything, I'm anybody,
I stand beside my grave
Confused with my life, that is commonplace and solitary.   60

1965

Thinking of the Lost World

This spoonful of chocolate tapioca
Tastes like—like peanut butter, like the vanilla
Extract Mama told me not to drink.
Swallowing the spoonful, I have already traveled
Through time to my childhood. It puzzles me   5
That age is like it.
                 Come back to that calm country
Through which the stream of my life first meandered,
My wife, our cat, and I sit here and see
Squirrels quarreling in the feeder, a mockingbird   10
Copying our chipmunk, as our end copies
Its beginning.
             Back in Los Angeles, we missed
Los Angeles. The sunshine of the Land
Of Sunshine is a gray mist now, the atmosphere   15
Of some factory planet: when you stand and look
You see a block or two, and your eyes water.
The orange groves are all cut down . . . My bow
Is lost, all my arrows are lost or broken,
My knife is sunk in the eucalyptus tree   20
Too far for even Pop to get it out,
And the tree's sawed down. It and the stair-sticks
And the planks of the tree house are all firewood
Burned long ago; its gray smoke smells of Vicks.

Twenty Years After, thirty-five years after,   25
Is as good as ever—better than ever,
Now that D'Artagnan[3] is no longer old—
Except that it is unbelievable.
I say to my old self: "I believe. Help thou
Mine unbelief."[4]   30
            I believe the dinosaur
Or pterodactyl's married the pink sphinx
And lives with those Indians in the undiscovered
Country[5] between California and Arizona
That the mad girl told me she was princess of—   35
Looking at me with the eyes of a lion,
Big, golden, without human understanding,
As she threw paper-wads from the back seat
Of the car in which I drove her with her mother
From the jail in Waycross to the hospital   40
In Daytona.[6] If I took my eyes from the road
And looked back into her eyes, the car would—I'd be—

---

3. The most daring of the musketeers in *The Three Musketeers* and its sequel, *Twenty Years After*, by Alexandre Dumas (1824–1895), French novelist and dramatist.
4. Spoken by the father of an epileptic child whom Jesus miraculously cured (Mark 9.24).
5. Cf. Shakespeare's *Hamlet* 3.1.81–82: "The undiscovered country from whose bourn no traveller returns."
6. From a small town in southeastern Georgia to the east-central coast of Florida.

Or if only I could find a crystal set
Sometimes, surely, I could still hear their chief
Reading to them from Dumas or *Amazing Stories*;[7]   45
If I could find in some Museum of Cars
Mama's dark blue Buick, Lucky's electric,
Couldn't I be driven there? Hold out to them
The paraffin half picked out, Tawny's dewclaw—
And have walk to me from among their wigwams   50
My tall brown aunt, to whisper to me: "Dead?
They told you I was dead?"
                    As if you could die!
If I never saw you, never again
Wrote to you, even, after a few years,   55
How often you've visited me, having put on,
As a mermaid puts on her sealskin, another face
And voice, that don't fool me for a minute—
That are yours for good . . . All of them are gone
Except for me; and for me nothing is gone—   60
The chicken's body is still going round
And round in widening circles, a satellite
From which, as the sun sets, the scientist bends
A look of evil on the unsuspecting earth.
Mama and Pop and Dandeen are still there   65
In the Gay Twenties.
                    The Gay Twenties! You say
The Gay Nineties . . . But it's all right: they *were* gay,
O so gay! A certain number of years after,
Any time is Gay, to the new ones who ask: 70
"Was that the first World War or the second?"
Moving between the first world and the second,
I hear a boy call, now that my beard's gray:
"Santa Claus! Hi, Santa Claus!" It *is* miraculous
To have the children call you Santa Claus.   75
I wave back. When my hand drops to the wheel,
It is brown and spotted, and its nails are ridged
Like Mama's. Where's my own hand? My smooth
White bitten-fingernailed one? I seem to see
A shape in tennis shoes and khaki riding-pants   80
Standing there empty-handed; I reach out to it
Empty-handed, my hand comes back empty,
And yet my emptiness is traded for its emptiness,
I have found that Lost World in the Lost and Found
Columns whose gray illegible advertisements   85
My soul has memorized world after world:
LOST—NOTHING. STRAYED FROM NOWHERE. NO REWARD.
I hold in my own hands, in happiness,
Nothing: the nothing for which there's no reward.

                                        1965

7. A science fiction magazine of the 1940s.

JOHN BERRYMAN
1914–1972

John Berryman's poetry has an air of authority although it is often extremely eccentric. He succeeded in making his elusive, moody self seem momentous and fascinating, in part by gyrating between farcical humor and exaggerated despondency. Like Robert Lowell, Sylvia Plath, and other so-called confessional poets of the middle generation, he wrote intensely personal poetry, though his style of self-expression was especially theatrical.

Berryman was born John Smith on October 25, 1914, in McAlester, Oklahoma. He lived until the age of ten in Anadarko, a nearby town where his father was a banker and his mother a schoolteacher. Then the family moved to Tampa, Florida, where his parents' quarrels, furious for years, ended when his father shot himself outside John's window. "That mad drive wiped out my childhood," Berryman later reflected in Dream Song 143. After his father's death, his mother brought John and a younger son to Gloucester, Massachusetts, and then to New York City, where she married another banker, John Berryman, whose name the children took. The couple soon divorced, but the stepfather remained kind to the children. He sent John to a private school in Connecticut (South Kent School), and then to Columbia University. Berryman received a B.A. in 1936 and then attended Clare College, Cambridge, on a fellowship. When he returned to the United States, he taught at several universities: for a year at Wayne (now Wayne State), then from 1940 to 1943 at Harvard, and following that, off and on from 1943 to 1951 at Princeton. From 1955 until his death, he taught at the University of Minnesota. A nervous, tense man prone to overdrinking, Berryman lived turbulently. He was married three times. In later life, he returned to Roman Catholicism, the faith of his childhood, yet his last book, *Delusions, Etc.* (1972), continues to debate faith with God. On January 7, 1972, he threw himself from a bridge in Minneapolis to end his life.

Berryman's early work formed part of the volume *Five Young American Poets* (1940). The influence of W. B. Yeats, W. H. Auden, Gerard Manley Hopkins, Hart Crane, and Ezra Pound on him was strong, and Berryman's own voice—by turns nerve-racked and sportive—took time to be heard. His voice was always an amalgam, first of other poets but later of Berryman's various selves. In his lyrics, he unexpectedly jumps from educated language to wild dialect, and before he finishes a statement he begins to question and sometimes to mock it. These characteristics, expressed in contorted syntax, give the poetry an air of painful self-involvement. A sense of agony pervades Berryman's work, even when, as often happens, it is funny. He noted as a defect in Wallace Stevens, whom he otherwise admired, Stevens's failure to wound ("So Long? Stevens"). Berryman's poetry wounds and is itself wounded; in *His Toy, His Dream, His Rest* (1968), the second volume of Dream Songs, he both celebrates and attacks dead friends and poets. His father's death, which he regarded as the defining trauma of his life, looms larger than any of these losses, the poet struggling ever more violently with this incomprehensible tragedy. The first of his Dream Songs refers obliquely to "a departure," but the penultimate poem in Berryman's sequence describes a visit to his father's grave and comments, with unmitigated bitterness, "I spit upon this dreadful banker's grave / who shot his heart out in a Florida dawn" (Dream Song 384).

Berryman gradually saw the autobiographical element in his poems as all-important. Interviewed for the *Harvard Advocate* (Spring 1969), he insisted that T. S. Eliot's theory of the impersonality of poetry was wrong. He called his own verse personal, as some of it ostentatiously is. About his long poem on the early American poet Anne Bradstreet,

Homage to Mistress Bradstreet (1956), Berryman said that, despite disliking her work, he "fell in love with her; and wrote about her, putting myself in it." Although there may be some dialogue between the old poet and the new, the poem's shifting moods and syntax are far more Berryman than Bradstreet.

His major work was a series of 385 Dream Songs that appeared in two separate volumes. They form a poetic journal and represent, half phantasmagorically, the changes in Berryman's mood and attitude. Or as he puts it more grandly in No. 366, they are meant "to terrify and comfort." The tone is often wildly humorous, but turns quickly toward melancholy again. Because the first volume, *77 Dream Songs* (1964), was misinterpreted as simply autobiography, Berryman wrote in a prefatory note to the sequel, "The poem then, whatever its cast of characters, is essentially about an imaginary character (not the poet, not me) named Henry, a white American in early middle age sometimes in blackface, who has suffered an irreversible loss and talks about himself sometimes in the first person, sometimes in the third, sometimes even in the second; he has a friend, never named, who addresses himself as Mr. Bones and variants thereof." (Mr. Bones is a name from the minstrel-show circuit.) When Berryman was asked about the sequence's seeming lack of unity, he insisted that it "has a plot. Its plot is the personality of Henry as he moves on in the world," from ages forty-one to fifty-one. Domestic difficulties, the deaths of friends, and personal anxieties are fused into verse that thrives on brief asides, knowing winks, and interruptions in syntax. These sustained irregularities are balanced against a surprisingly strict six-line stanza (borrowed, as Berryman said, from Yeats), in which lines 1, 2, 4, and 5 are in pentameter, lines 3 and 6 in trimeter. Each Dream Song is eighteen lines long. The motif of the father's death by suicide, returned to near the end of each book, also helps give structure to the emotive sprawl.

Though Berryman insisted that he and Henry were not the same, and some stylization has certainly occurred, Berryman's traits are still easily recognizable. The poetry is confessional and neurotic, but also learned, both in mobilizing traditional literary resources and in savoring all the resources of contemporary diction. Berryman was well versed in English and American literature; he wrote a biography of Stephen Crane (1950) in which he attempted to analyze Crane's psychology as he analyzed his own. What seems likely to survive of his poetry is its pungent and many-leveled portrait of a complex personality that, for all its eccentricity, was close to the center of the intellectual and emotional life of the mid-twentieth century.

From The Dream Songs

1

Huffy Henry hid   the day,
unappeasable Henry sulked.
I see his point,—a trying to put things over.
It was the thought that they thought
they could *do* it made Henry wicked & away.   5
But he should have come out and talked.

All the world like a woolen lover
once did seem on Henry's side.
Then came a departure.

Thereafter nothing fell out as it might or ought.   10
I don't see how Henry, pried
open for all the world to see, survived.

What he has now to say is a long
wonder the world can bear & be.
Once in a sycamore I was glad   15
all at the top, and I sang.
Hard on the land wears the strong sea
and empty grows every bed.

1964

4

Filling her compact & delicious body
with chicken páprika, she glanced at me
twice.
Fainting with interest, I hungered back
and only the fact of her husband & four other people   5
kept me from springing on her

or falling at her little feet and crying
'You are the hottest one for years of night
Henry's dazed eyes
have enjoyed, Brilliance.' I advanced upon   10
(despairing) my spumoni. —Sir Bones: is stuffed,
de world, wif feeding girls.

—Black hair, complexion Latin, jewelled eyes
downcast . . . The slob beside her   feasts . . . What wonders is
she sitting on, over there?   15
The restaurant buzzes. She might as well be on Mars.
Where did it all go wrong? There ought to be a law against Henry.
—Mr. Bones: there is.

1964

14

Life, friends, is boring. We must not say so.
After all, the sky flashes, the great sea yearns,
we ourselves flash and yearn,
and moreover my mother told me as a boy
(repeatingly) 'Ever to confess you're bored   5
means you have no

Inner Resources.' I conclude now I have no
inner resources, because I am heavy bored.

Peoples bore me,
literature bores me, especially great literature,   10
Henry bores me, with his plights & gripes
as bad as achilles,[1]

who loves people and valiant art, which bores me.
And the tranquil hills, & gin, look like a drag
and somehow a dog   15
has taken itself & its tail considerably away
into mountains or sea or sky, leaving
behind: me, wag.

                                                              1964

29

There sat down, once, a thing on Henry's heart
só heavy, if he had a hundred years
& more, & weeping, sleepless, in all them time
Henry could not make good.
Starts again always in Henry's ears   5
the little cough somewhere, an odour, a chime.

And there is another thing he has in mind
like a grave Sienese face[2] a thousand years
would fail to blur the still profiled reproach of. Ghastly,
with open eyes, he attends, blind.   10
All the bells say: too late. This is not for tears;
thinking.

But never did Henry, as he thought he did,
end anyone and hacks her body up
and hide the pieces, where they may be found.   15
He knows: he went over everyone, & nobody's missing.
Often he reckons, in the dawn, them up.
Nobody is ever missing.

                                                              1964

37

Three around the Old Gentleman

His malice was a pimple down his good
big face, with its sly eyes. I must be sorry
Mr Frost[3] has left:

1. In Homer's *Iliad*, the Greek warrior Achilles withdrew from fighting over a slight from the Greeks' general, King Agamemnon.
2. That is, like the somber religious portraits painted in thirteenth- and fourteenth-century Siena.
3. Robert Frost (1874–1963), American poet.

I like it so less I don't understood—
he couldn't hear or see well—all we sift—   5
but this is a *bad* story.

He had fine stories and was another man
in private; difficult, always. Courteous,
on the whole, in private.
He apologize to Henry, off & on,   10
for two blue slanders; which was good of him.
I don't know how he made it.

Quickly, off stage with all but kindness, now.
I can't say what I have in mind. Bless Frost,
any odd god around.   15
Gentle his shift, I decussate[4] & command,
stoic deity. For a while here we possessed
an unusual man.

                                                                    1964

76

Henry's Confession

Nothin very bad happen to me lately.
How you explain that? —I explain that, Mr Bones,
terms o' your bafflin odd sobriety.
Sober as man can get, no girls, no telephones,
what could happen bad to Mr Bones?   5
—*If* life is a handkerchief sandwich,

in a modesty of death I join my father
who dared so long agone leave me.
A bullet on a concrete stoop
close by a smothering southern sea   10
spreadeagled on an island, by my knee.
—You is from hunger, Mr Bones,

I offers you this handkerchief, now set
your left foot by my right foot,
shoulder to shoulder, all that jazz,   15
arm in arm, by the beautiful sea,[5]
hum a little, Mr Bones.
—I saw nobody coming, so I went instead.

                                                                    1964

---

4. Cross (myself).   5. A popular song of 1914.

145

Also I love him: me he's done no wrong
for going on forty years—forgiveness time—
I touch now his despair,
he felt as bad as Whitman on his tower[6]
but he did not swim out with me or my brother   5
as he threatened—

a powerful swimmer, to   take one of us along
as company in the defeat sublime,
freezing my helpless mother:
he only, very early in the morning,   10
rose with his gun and went outdoors by my window
and did what was needed.

I cannot read that wretched mind, so strong
& so undone. I've always tried. I—I'm
trying to forgive   15
whose frantic passage, when he could not live
an instant longer, in the summer dawn
left Henry to live on.

                                                         1968

149

This world is gradually becoming a place
where I do not care to be any more. Can Delmore die?[7]
I don't suppose
in all them years a day went ever by
without a loving thought for him. Welladay.[8]   5
In the brightness of his promise,

unstained, I saw him thro' the mist of the actual
blazing with insight, warm with gossip
thro' all our Harvard years
when both of us were just becoming known   10
I got him out of a police-station once, in Washington, the world is *tref*[9]
and grief too astray for tears.

6. Charles Whitman gunned down dozens of people from the top of a tower at the University of Texas at Austin on August 1, 1966. News accounts quoted his fearful and suicidal notes. He is compared to the poet's father on the verge of suicide.
7. Delmore Schwartz (1913–1966), American poet, was a close friend of Berryman's and, in 1940, helped him get his first teaching job, at Harvard. *His Toy, His Dream, His Rest*, the second book of Berryman's Dream Songs (in which this poem appears) is in part dedicated "to the sacred memory of Delmore Schwartz."
8. Alas.
9. Ritually unclean, according to Jewish law.

I imagine you have heard the terrible news,
that Delmore Schwartz is dead, miserably & alone,
in New York: he sang me a song   15
'I am the Brooklyn poet Delmore Schwartz
Harms & the child I sing, two parents' torts'[1]
when he was young & gift-strong.

1968

153

I'm cross with god who has wrecked this generation.
First he seized Ted, then Richard, Randall, and now Delmore.
In between he gorged on Sylvia Plath.
That was a first rate haul. He left alive
fools I could number like a kitchen knife   5
but Lowell[2] he did not touch.

Somewhere the enterprise continues, not—
yellow the sun lies on the baby's blouse—
in Henry's staggered thought.
I suppose the word would be, we must submit.   10
Later.
I hang, and I will not be part of it.

A friend of Henry's[3] contrasted God's career
with Mozart's, leaving Henry with nothing to say
but praise for a word so apt.   15
We suffer on, a day, a day, a day.
And never again can come, like a man slapped,
news like this

1968

219

So Long? Stevens[4]

He lifted up, among the actuaries,
a grandee crow. Ah ha & he crowed good.
That funny money-man.
Mutter we all must as well as we can.

1. Torments. A parody of the opening words of Virgil's *Aeneid*, "Of arms and the man I sing."
2. Robert Lowell (1917–1977), American poet, like the other people named in this stanza. Theodore Roethke (1908–1963) died after problems with depression. "Richard" is R. P. Blackmur (1904–1965). Randall Jarrell (1914–1965) was struck by a car in a suspicious accident. Delmore Schwartz (1913–1966) died alone after years of mental illness. Sylvia Plath (1932–1963) committed suicide.
3. Howard Nemerov (1920–1991), American poet; in *Journal of the Fictive Life* (1965), he wrote that "Mozart's life and work express a purer and more efficacious benevolence to mankind than the life and work of God."
4. Wallace Stevens (1879–1955), American poet and insurance company vice president. Berryman alludes to "Thirteen Ways of Looking at a Blackbird," "Sunday Morning," and other poems by Stevens.

He mutter spiffy. He make wonder Henry's   5
wits, though, with a odd

. . . something . . . something . . . not there in his flourishing art.
O veteran of death, you will not mind
a counter-mutter.
What was it missing, then, at the man's heart   10
so that he does not wound? It is our kind
to wound, as well as utter

a fact of happy world. That metaphysics
he hefted up until we could not breathe
the physics. *On our side,*   15
monotonous (or ever-fresh)—it sticks
in Henry's throat to judge—brilliant, he seethe;
better than us; less wide.

                                                    1968

312

I have moved to Dublin to have it out with you,
majestic Shade,[5] You whom I read so well
so many years ago,
did I read your lesson right? did I see through
your phases to the real? your heaven, your hell   5
did I enquire properly into?

For years then I forgot you, I put you down,
ingratitude is the necessary curse
of making things new:[6]
I brought my family to see me through,   10
I brought my homage & my soft remorse,
I brought a book or two

only, including in the end your last
strange poems made under the shadow of death
Your high figures float   15
again across my mind and all your past
fills my walled garden with your honey breath
wherein I move, a mote.

                                                    1968

5. W. B. Yeats (1865–1939), Irish poet, whom Berryman called his first and last influence. In 1936, while a student at Clare College, Cambridge University, Berryman had tea with Yeats, an event celebrated in Dream Song 215.
6. An adaptation of Ezra Pound's famous slogan, "make it new."

384

The marker slants, flowerless, day's almost done,
I stand above my father's grave with rage,
often, often before
I've made this awful pilgrimage to one
who cannot visit me, who tore his page   5
out: I come back for more,

I spit upon this dreadful banker's grave
who shot his heart out in a Florida dawn
O ho alas alas
When will indifference come, I moan & rave   10
I'd like to scrabble till I got right down
away down under the grass

and ax the casket open ha to see
just how he's taking it, which he sought so hard
we'll tear apart   15
the mouldering grave clothes ha & then Henry
will heft the ax once more, his final card,
and fell it on the start.

1969

Henry's Understanding

He was reading late, at Richard's, down in Maine,
aged 32? Richard & Helen long in bed,
my good wife long in bed.
All I had to do was strip & get into my bed,
putting the marker in the book, & sleep,   5
& wake to a hot breakfast.

Off the coast was an island, P'tit Manaan,
the bluff from Richard's lawn was almost sheer.
A chill at four o'clock.
It only takes a few minutes to make a man.   10
A concentration upon now & here.
Suddenly, unlike Bach,

& horribly, unlike Bach, it occurred to me
that *one* night, instead of warm pajamas,
I'd take off all my clothes   15
& cross the damp cold lawn & down the bluff
into the terrible water & walk forever
under it out toward the island.

1972

DYLAN THOMAS
1914–1953

Dylan Thomas used to say in his American readings that his poems had to be read either very soft or very loud, and it is true that he has none of the middle style of Thomas Hardy or W. H. Auden. A Romantic visionary, he is comparable to Hart Crane, though less interested than Crane in the ineffable ecstasies beyond verbal expression. He liked to speak of his poems as narratives, as in his reply to a questionnaire in 1934: "Poetry is the rhythmic, inevitably narrative, movement from an overclothed blindness to a naked vision that depends in its intensity on the strength of the labour put into the creation of the poetry. My poetry is, or should be, useful to me for one reason: it is the record of my individual struggle from darkness towards some measure of light." Each poem, he said, was to be "a formally watertight compartment of words, preferably with a main moving column (i.e. narrative) to hold a little of the real causes and forces of the creative brain and body."

At the root of his poetry is a sense of doubleness, of womb and tomb, of the worm as penis and as death, which he embodied in one of his earliest published poems, "The Force That through the Green Fuse Drives the Flower." He built poems out of such paradoxes: as he wrote in a letter, "I make one image—though 'make' is not the word; I let, perhaps, an image be 'made' emotionally in me and then apply to it what intellectual and critical forces I possess—let it breed another, let that image contradict the first, make, of the third image bred out of the other two together, a fourth contradictory image, and let them all, within my imposed formal limits, conflict. Each image holds within it the seed of its own destruction, and my dialectical method, as I understand it, is a constant building up and breaking down of the images that come out of the central seed, which is itself destructive and constructive at the same time. . . . Out of the inevitable conflict of images— . . . the womb of war—I try to make that momentary peace which is a poem" (*Dylan Thomas*, ed. Henry Treece, 1936).

His view of life coincided with the Christian, but perhaps only because Christianity offered the necessary symbols for his imagery of death-in-life and life-in-death. Certainly, Thomas's is a different form of Christianity from T. S. Eliot's, in that it is so radiantly aware of the sweetness of living, especially before the child learns an adult sense of time and death. His poems about adults are more somber. Yet he insisted, in a note to his *Collected Poems* (1952): "These poems, with all their crudities, doubts, and confusions, are written for the love of Man and in praise of God, and I'd be a damn fool if they weren't."

Thomas was born on October 27, 1914, in Swansea, Wales, which he described bitterly as "the smug darkness of a provincial town." He was educated at the Swansea Grammar School, which he left in 1931. His father, a schoolteacher, urged him to go to a university, but Thomas followed the example of the Irish playwright Bernard Shaw and attempted to become a writer at once. His style, in fact, was formed by the time he was seventeen. At twenty, he published his first book, *18 Poems* (1934), which won ecstatic praise from Edith Sitwell and others, and went to live in London. In 1936, he met Caitlin Macnamara, a young Irishwoman whose temperament was as turbulent as his own; they married the following year and subsequently had three children. Thomas also wrote short stories, plays, and film scripts. The most successful was *Under Milk Wood* (1954), a radio play depicting the residents of a small Welsh town by the sea from the middle of one night to the middle of the next. He supported himself in his last years in part with long lecture tours of the United States, during which—drunk or sober—he gave magnificent readings of poems (mostly by other writers) on dozens of college campuses. His extravagant drinking gradually usurped most of his time, and chronic alcoholism helped bring about his early death, in New York City.

Thomas appears in twentieth-century poetry with the air of a mystic rhapsodist. He knew no Welsh, but he accepted the traditional role of the Welsh bard and was depicted by painter Augustus John as wild and inspired. In fact, his verse played its bravura of language against tight verse forms and was always subjected to stern intellectual ordering. Nonetheless, his full-throated rhetoric, so different from the usual understatement of Auden and other poets of the 1930s, was attacked by some critics as masking a paucity of ideas. (In the 1950s, the Movement of Philip Larkin and others was a reaction against Thomas.) A modest man, Thomas could berate himself as a "freak user of words, not a poet," but he usually felt that his verbal mannerisms were justified: "I am a painstaking, conscientious, involved and devious craftsman in words, however unsuccessful the result so often appears, and to whatever wrong uses I may apply my technical paraphernalia." He lists his poetic devices and adds: "Poets have got to enjoy themselves sometimes, and the twistings and convolutions of words, the inventions and contrivances, are all part of the joy that is part of the painful, voluntary work" ("Poetic Manifesto").

The Force That through the Green Fuse Drives the Flower

The force that through the green fuse drives the flower
Drives my green age; that blasts the roots of trees
Is my destroyer.
And I am dumb to tell the crooked rose
My youth is bent by the same wintry fever.   5

The force that drives the water through the rocks
Drives my red blood; that dries the mouthing streams
Turns mine to wax.
And I am dumb to mouth unto my veins
How at the mountain spring the same mouth sucks.   10

The hand that whirls the water in the pool
Stirs the quicksand; that ropes the blowing wind
Hauls my shroud sail.
And I am dumb to tell the hanging man
How of my clay is made the hangman's lime.[1]   15

The lips of time leech to the fountain head;
Love drips and gathers, but the fallen blood
Shall calm her sores.
And I am dumb to tell a weather's wind
How time has ticked a heaven round the stars.   20

And I am dumb to tell the lover's tomb
How at my sheet[2] goes the same crooked worm.

1933   1934

1. Quicklime poured in the graves of victims of the   2. Winding sheet (for a corpse).
public hangman, to quicken decomposition.

And Death Shall Have No Dominion[3]

And death shall have no dominion.
Dead men naked they shall be one
With the man in the wind and the west moon;
When their bones are picked clean and the clean bones gone,
They shall have stars at elbow and foot;   5
Though they go mad they shall be sane,
Though they sink through the sea they shall rise again;
Though lovers be lost love shall not;
And death shall have no dominion.

And death shall have no dominion.   10
Under the windings of the sea
They lying long shall not die windily;
Twisting on racks when sinews give way,
Strapped to a wheel, yet they shall not break;
Faith in their hands shall snap in two,   15
And the unicorn evils run them through;
Split all ends up they shan't crack;
And death shall have no dominion.

And death shall have no dominion.
No more may gulls cry at their ears   20
Or waves break loud on the seashores;
Where blew a flower may a flower no more
Lift its head to the blows of the rain;
Though they be mad and dead as nails,
Heads of the characters hammer through daisies;   25
Break in the sun till the sun breaks down,
And death shall have no dominion.

1933   1936

The Hand That Signed the Paper[4]

The hand that signed the paper felled a city;
Five sovereign fingers taxed the breath,
Doubled the globe of dead and halved a country;
These five kings did a king to death.

The mighty hand leads to a sloping shoulder,   5
The finger joints are cramped with chalk;
A goose's quill has put an end to murder
That put an end to talk.

3. "Death hath no more dominion" (Romans 6.19). This was the first poem Thomas published after his school poems—though not in his first book.
4. Likely an allusion to the 1919 Treaty of Versailles, signed by Britain, France, Italy, Japan, and the United States (though never ratified by the U.S. Congress). The treaty imposed heavy reparations on Germany and was seen as precipitating later diplomatic crises.

The hand that signed the treaty bred a fever,
And famine grew, and locusts came;   10
Great is the hand that holds dominion over
Man by a scribbled name.

The five kings count the dead but do not soften
The crusted wound nor stroke the brow;
A hand rules pity as a hand rules heaven;   15
Hands have no tears to flow.

1933   1936

When All My Five and Country Senses See

When all my five and country senses see,
The fingers will forget green thumbs and mark
How, through the halfmoon's vegetable eye,
Husk of young stars and handfull zodiac,
Love in the frost is pared and wintered by,   5
The whispering ears will watch love drummed away
Down breeze and shell to a discordant beach,
And, lashed to syllables, the lynx tongue cry
That her fond wounds are mended bitterly.
My nostrils see her breath burn like a bush.   10

My one and noble heart has witnesses
In all love's countries, that will grope awake;
And when blind sleep drops on the spying senses,
The heart is sensual, though five eyes break.

1938   1939

Twenty-Four Years

Twenty-four years remind the tears of my eyes.
(Bury the dead for fear that they walk to the grave in labour.)
In the groin of the natural doorway I crouched like a tailor
Sewing a shroud for a journey
By the light of the meat-eating sun.   5
Dressed to die, the sensual strut begun,
With my red veins full of money,
In the final direction of the elementary town
I advance for as long as forever is.

1939   1939

The Hunchback in the Park[5]

The hunchback in the park
A solitary mister
Propped between trees and water
From the opening of the garden lock
That lets the trees and water enter   5
Until the Sunday sombre bell at dark[6]

Eating bread from a newspaper
Drinking water from the chained cup
That the children filled with gravel
In the fountain basin where I sailed my ship   10
Slept at night in a dog kennel
But nobody chained him up.

Like the park birds he came early
Like the water he sat down
And Mister they called Hey mister   15
The truant boys from the town
Running when he had heard them clearly
On out of sound

Past lake and rockery[7]
Laughing when he shook his paper   20
Hunchbacked in mockery
Through the loud zoo of the willow groves
Dodging the park keeper
With his stick that picked up leaves.

And the old dog sleeper   25
Alone between nurses and swans
While the boys among willows
Made the tigers jump out of their eyes
To roar on the rockery stones
And the groves were blue with sailors   30

Made all day until bell time
A woman figure without fault
Straight as a young elm
Straight and tall from his crooked bones

---

5. "Though the details in this poem . . . could apply to almost any park, this particular park is undoubtedly Cwmdonkin, not far from the Thomas house. There was, indeed, a hunchback who seemed to have nowhere else to go, who stayed from the moment the park opened until it closed. Cwmdonkin Park was a favourite haunt of truants from Swansea Grammar School, because it was bordered on one side by a road that led directly to the school, but sometimes didn't. Thomas and I often met there to read poems to one another or write them, when, perhaps, we should have been learning Geography. But usually our amusements were more boisterous and less 'cultured' " (*The Poems of Dylan Thomas*, ed. David Jones, 1971). Jones was a lifelong friend of Thomas's.
6. The bell that signals the closing of the park at night.
7. Rock garden.

That she might stand in the night   35
After the locks and chains

All night in the unmade park
After the railings and shrubberies
The birds the grass the trees the lake
And the wild boys innocent as strawberries   40
Had followed the hunchback
To his kennel in the dark.

1941   1946

Poem in October

It was my thirtieth year to heaven
Woke to my hearing from harbour and neighbour wood
   And the mussel pooled and the heron
         Priested shore
         The morning beckon   5
With water praying and call of seagull and rook[8]
And the knock of sailing boats on the net webbed wall
         Myself to set foot
         That second
   In the still sleeping town and set forth.   10

My birthday began with the water-
Birds and the birds of the winged trees flying my name
   Above the farms and the white horses
         And I rose
         In the rainy autumn   15
And walked abroad in a shower of all my days.
High tide and the heron dived when I took the road
         Over the border
         And the gates
   Of the town closed as the town awoke.   20

A springful of larks in a rolling
Cloud and the roadside bushes brimming with whistling
   Blackbirds and the sun of October
         Summery
         On the hill's shoulder,   25
Here were fond climates and sweet singers suddenly
Come in the morning where I wandered and listened
         To the rain wringing
         Wind blow cold
   In the wood faraway under me.   30

Pale rain over the dwindling harbour
And over the sea wet church the size of a snail

8. Crow.

With its horns through mist and the castle
    Brown as owls
    But all the gardens   35
Of spring and summer were blooming in the tall tales
Beyond the border and under the lark full cloud.
    There could I marvel
    My birthday
Away but the weather turned around.   40

    It turned away from the blithe country
And down the other air and the blue altered sky
    Streamed again a wonder of summer
      With apples
    Pears and red currants   45
And I saw in the turning so clearly a child's
Forgotten mornings when he walked with his mother
    Through the parables
    Of sun light
And the legends of the green chapels   50

    And the twice told fields of infancy
That his tears burned my cheeks and his heart moved in mine.
    These were the woods the river and sea
      Where a boy
    In the listening   55
Summertime of the dead whispered the truth of his joy
To the trees and the stones and the fish in the tide.
    And the mystery
    Sang alive
Still in the water and singingbirds.   60

    And there could I marvel my birthday
Away but the weather turned around. And the true
    Joy of the long dead child sang burning
    In the sun.
    It was my thirtieth   65
Year to heaven stood there then in the summer noon
Though the town below lay leaved with October blood.
    O may my heart's truth
    Still be sung
On this high hill in a year's turning.   70

1944   1946

A Refusal to Mourn the Death, by Fire, of a Child in London

    Never until the mankind making
    Bird beast and flower
    Fathering and all humbling darkness
    Tells with silence the last light breaking

And the still hour   5
Is come of the sea tumbling in harness

And I must enter again the round
Zion[9] of the water bead
And the synagogue of the ear of corn
Shall I let pray the shadow of a sound   10
Or sow my salt seed
In the least valley of sackcloth to mourn

The majesty and burning of the child's death.
I shall not murder
The mankind of her going with a grave truth   15
Nor blaspheme down the stations of the breath
With any further
Elegy of innocence and youth.

Deep with the first dead lies London's daughter,
Robed in the long friends,   20
The grains beyond age, the dark veins of her mother,
Secret by the unmourning water
Of the riding Thames.[1]
After the first death, there is no other.

1945   1946

Fern Hill[2]

Now as I was young and easy under the apple boughs
About the lilting house and happy as the grass was green,
    The night above the dingle[3] starry,
        Time let me hail and climb
    Golden in the heydays of his eyes,   5
And honoured among wagons I was prince of the apple towns
And once below a time I lordly had the trees and leaves
        Trail with daisies and barley
    Down the rivers of the windfall light.

And as I was green and carefree, famous among the barns   10
About the happy yard and singing as the farm was home,
    In the sun that is young once only,
        Time let me play and be
    Golden in the mercy of his means,
And green and golden I was huntsman and herdsman, the calves   15
Sang to my horn, the foxes on the hills barked clear and cold,

9. City of God.   and where he spent summer holidays as a boy.
1. River that flows through London.   3. Small wooded valley.
2. A country house where the poet's aunt lived,

And the sabbath rang slowly
In the pebbles of the holy streams.

All the sun long it was running, it was lovely, the hay
Fields high as the house, the tunes from the chimneys, it was air   20
  And playing, lovely and watery
    And fire green as grass.
  And nightly under the simple stars
As I rode to sleep the owls were bearing the farm away,
All the moon long I heard, blessed among stables, the nightjars   25
  Flying with the ricks,[4] and the horses
    Flashing into the dark.

And then to awake, and the farm, like a wanderer white
With the dew, come back, the cock on his shoulder: it was all
  Shining, it was Adam and maiden,   30
    The sky gathered again
  And the sun grew round that very day.
So it must have been after the birth of the simple light
In the first, spinning place, the spellbound horses walking warm
  Out of the whinnying green stable   35
    On to the fields of praise.

And honoured among foxes and pheasants by the gay house
Under the new made clouds and happy as the heart was long,
  In the sun born over and over,
    I ran my heedless ways,   40
  My wishes raced through the house high hay
And nothing I cared, at my sky blue trades, that time allows
In all his tuneful turning so few and such morning songs
  Before the children green and golden
    Follow him out of grace,   45

Nothing I cared, in the lamb white days, that time would take me
Up to the swallow thronged loft by the shadow of my hand,
  In the moon that is always rising,
    Nor that riding to sleep
  I should hear him fly with the high fields   50
And wake to the farm forever fled from the childless land.
Oh as I was young and easy in the mercy of his means,
    Time held me green and dying
  Though I sang in my chains like the sea.

1945   1946

----

4. Stacks of hay. *Nightjars:* nocturnal birds.

In My Craft or Sullen Art

In my craft or sullen art
Exercised in the still night
When only the moon rages
And the lovers lie abed
With all their griefs in their arms,   5
I labour by singing light
Not for ambition or bread
Or the strut and trade of charms
On the ivory stages
But for the common wages   10
Of their most secret heart.

Not for the proud man apart
From the raging moon I write
On these spindrift[5] pages
Nor for the towering dead   15
With their nightingales and psalms
But for the lovers, their arms
Round the griefs of the ages,
Who pay no praise or wages
Nor heed my craft or art.   20

1945   1946

Do Not Go Gentle into That Good Night[6]

Do not go gentle into that good night,
Old age should burn and rave at close of day;
Rage, rage against the dying of the light.

Though wise men at their end know dark is right,
Because their words had forked no lightning they   5
Do not go gentle into that good night.

Good men, the last wave by, crying how bright
Their frail deeds might have danced in a green bay,
Rage, rage against the dying of the light.

5. Driven, like sea spray, by the wind.
6. Thomas wrote at the time, "The only person I can't show the little enclosed poem to is, of course, my father, who doesn't know he's dying." Quoted by Jones, who goes on to add that Thomas's father "lingered for more than a year after this, and died on 15th December 1952. . . . It is significant that for this subject and on this occasion, Thomas deliberately chose to discipline himself by the use of a strict form, the villanelle" (*The Poems of Dylan Thomas*).

Wild men who caught and sang the sun in flight,   10
And learn, too late, they grieved it on its way,
Do not go gentle into that good night.

Grave men, near death, who see with blinding sight
Blind eyes could blaze like meteors and be gay,
Rage, rage against the dying of the light.   15

And you, my father, there on the sad height,
Curse, bless, me now with your fierce tears, I pray.
Do not go gentle into that good night.
Rage, rage against the dying of the light.

1951   1952

JUDITH WRIGHT
1915–2000

Some qualities of Judith Wright's verse derive from her childhood, in a rural region of New South Wales, Australia. Living far from the nearest school, she was educated until age twelve through a correspondence course organized by the Department of Education. Later, she attended the University of Sydney and chose to take English literature alone rather than the usual variety of courses. She had grown up loving the land and wild animals, and her marriage to philosopher J. P. McKinney introduced her to a philosophy confirming her intimations that the time had arrived for humans to reject mere intellectual analysis and embrace an intuitive or emotional bond with the world. She became an impassioned advocate for the natural environment and Aboriginal rights.

Her poems convey at times a radiant sense of oneness with Australia, particularly the eastern part known as the New England Plateau. In "The Moving Image," Wright identifies the poet with Tom of Bedlam, the seeming madman whose madness is the ultimate sanity. The sense of the poet as a convergence of outer and inner becomes explicit in "The Maker": "into myself I took / all living things that are," and in "For New England": "Many roads meet here / in me, the traveller and the ways I travel." She laments the death of the wild country and the dying out of Aboriginal civilization in "Bora Ring," though she suggests that the Aboriginal past still haunts the present and curses it. The dingoes' cry in "Drought Year" reminds us of the unseen world that remains a part of us. Of herself, in old age, she wrote, "In my last quarter let me be hag, but poet" ("Easter Moon and Owl").

Wright was born on May 31, 1915, in Armidale, New South Wales. She received many awards for her verse. Besides many books of verse, her writings include memoirs, essays, short stories, and children's books, and she edited several anthologies of Australian poetry.

Bora Ring[1]

The song is gone; the dance
is secret with the dancers in the earth,
the ritual useless, and the tribal story
lost in an alien tale.

Only the grass stands up   5
to mark the dancing-ring: the apple-gums
posture and mime a past corroboree,[2]
murmur a broken chant.

The hunter is gone: the spear
is splintered underground; the painted bodies   10
a dream the world breathed sleeping and forgot.
The nomad feet are still.

Only the rider's heart
halts at a sightless shadow, an unsaid word
that fastens in the blood the ancient curse,   15
the fear as old as Cain.[3]

                                                        1946

Drought Year

That time of drought the embered air
burned to the roots of timber and grass.
The crackling lime-scrub would not bear
and Mooni Creek was sand that year.
The dingoes' cry was strange to hear.   5

I heard the dingoes cry
in the whipstick scrub on the Thirty-mile Dry.
I saw the wagtail[4] take his fill
perching in the seething skull.
I saw the eel wither where he curled   10
in the last blood-drop of a spent world.

I heard the bone whisper in the hide
of the big red horse that lay where he died.
Prop that horse up, make him stand,
hoofs turned down in the bitter sand—   15
make him stand at the gate of the Thirty-mile Dry.

1. Site of initiation ceremonies held by Australian
Aborigines.
2. Nighttime ceremony held by the Aborigines.
Apple-gums: Australian timber trees.
3. Son of Adam and Eve, who, in killing his
brother, Abel, committed the first murder (Genesis
4.1–16); "the ancient curse" is the curse of God
upon Cain.
4. Australian bird.

Turn this way and you will die—
and strange and loud was the dingoes' cry.

1953

Flood Year

Walking up the driftwood beach at day's end
I saw it, thrust up out of a hillock of sand—
a frail bleached clench of fingers dried by wind—
the dead child's hand.

And they are mourning there still, though I forget,   5
the year of flood, the scoured ruined land,
the herds gone down the current, the farms drowned,
and the child never found.

When I was there the thick hurling waters
had gone back to the river, the farms were almost drained.   10
Banished half-dead cattle searched the dunes; it rained;
river and sea met with a wild sound.

Oh with a wild sound water flung into air
where sea met river; all the country round
no heart was quiet. I walked on the driftwood sand   15
and saw the pale crab crouched, and came to a stand
thinking, A child's hand. The child's hand.

1953

Ishtar[5]

When I first saw a woman after childbirth
the room was full of your glance who had just gone away.
And when the mare was bearing her foal
you were with her but I did not see your face.

When in fear I became a woman   5
I first felt your hand.
When the shadow of the future first fell across me
it was your shadow, my grave and hooded attendant.

It is all one whether I deny or affirm you;
it is not my mind you are concerned with.   10
It is no matter whether I submit or rebel;
the event will still happen.

---

5. One of the great mother-goddesses of the ancient Near East; the goddess of both fertility and war in the Babylonian and Assyrian religions.

You neither know nor care for the truth of my heart;
but the truth of my body has all to do with you.
You have no need of my thoughts or my hopes,   15
living in the realm of the absolute event.

Then why is it that when I at last see your face
under that hood of slate-blue, so calm and dark,
so worn with the burden of an inexpressible knowledge—
why is that I begin to worship you with tears?   20

1953

Request to a Year

If the year is meditating a suitable gift,
I should like it to be the attitude
of my great-great-grandmother,
legendary devotee of the arts,

who, having had eight children   5
and little opportunity for painting pictures,
sat one day on a high rock
beside a river in Switzerland

and from a difficult distance viewed
her second son, balanced on a small ice-floe,   10
drift down the current towards a waterfall
that struck rock-bottom eighty feet below,

while her second daughter, impeded,
no doubt, by the petticoats of the day,
stretched out a last-hope alpenstock[6]   15
(which luckily later caught him on his way).

Nothing, it was evident, could be done;
and with the artist's isolating eye
my great-great-grandmother hastily sketched the scene.
The sketch survives to prove the story by.   20

Year, if you have no Mother's day present planned;
reach back and bring me the firmness of her hand.

1953

"Dove—Love"

The dove purrs—over and over the dove
purrs its declaration. The wind's tone
changes from tree to tree, the creek on stone

6. Staff used in mountain-climbing.

alters its sob and fall, but still the dove
goes insistently on, telling its love   5
     "I could eat you."

And in captivity, they say, doves do.
Gentle, methodical, starting with the feet
(the ham-pink succulent toes
on their thin stems of rose),   10
baring feather by feather the wincing meat:
     "I could eat you."

That neat suburban head, that suit of grey,
watchful conventional eye and manicured claw—
these also rhyme with us. The doves play   15
on one repetitive note that plucks the raw
helpless nerve, their soft "I do. I do.
     I could eat you."

1962

P. K. PAGE
1916–2010

Many of P. K. Page's poems transport the reader to a world of snow, ice, and bright sunlight, a white and glittering world in which the visionary poet transcends ordinary social concerns and behavior. Margaret Atwood, another Canadian poet, describes Page as often appearing as a "tranced observer who verges on mysticism" (*The New Oxford Book of Canadian Verse in English*, 1982). The word "mysticism," as applied to Page, should suggest not a separation of body and spirit, but rather a vision in which the senses are liberated from immediacies of time and place.

Page's earliest poems, written under the influence of W. H. Auden and his circle, occasionally echo the young Auden's social concerns and rhetoric. One poem is called "Bank Strike"; others, "Offices" and "Typists": "Crowded together typists touch / softly as ducks." The women in "The Stenographers" represent many office workers, living regimented lives and emotionally dispossessed to the point of madness. Page's later poems are packed with vivid visual images. The winter landscape of "Stories of Snow" is ultimately sinister, though it beguiles us as a welcome alternative to tropical lushness. In "Photos of a Salt Mine," the mine, a world of salt, seems beautiful only at first. The poem concludes with an abrupt change of perspective; now the mine, peopled by the damned, is one of the circles of Hell.

Patricia Kathleen Page was born on November 23, 1916, in Dorset, England; she emigrated to Canada when she was a very young child. She received her formal education at St. Hilda's School, in Calgary, Alberta, and at the Art Students League and Pratt Institute, in New York City. She devoted her life to a variety of arts: she worked as a radio actress and a script writer, and she was widely known as a painter and printmaker. In addition to her poems, she wrote fiction, essays, and children's stories.

The Stenographers

After the brief bivouac[1] of Sunday,
their eyes, in the forced march of Monday to Saturday,
hoist the white flag, flutter in the snowstorm of paper,
haul it down and crack in the midsun of temper.

In the pause between the first draft and the carbon   5
they glimpse the smooth hours when they were children—
the ride in the ice-cart, the ice-man's name,
the end of the route and the long walk home;

remember the sea where floats at high tide
were sea marrows[2] growing on the scatter-green vine   10
or spools of grey toffee, or wasps' nests on water;
remember the sand and the leaves of the country.

Bell rings and they go and the voice draws their pencil[3]
like a sled across snow; when its runners are frozen
rope snaps and the voice then is pulling no burden   15
but runs like a dog on the winter of paper.

Their climates are winter and summer—no wind
for the kites of their hearts—no wind for a flight;
a breeze at the most, to tumble them over
and leave them like rubbish—the boy-friends of blood.   20

In the inch of the noon as they move they are stagnant.
The terrible calm of the noon is their anguish;
the lip of the counter, the shapes of the straws
like icicles breaking their tongues are invaders.

Their beds are their oceans—salt water of weeping   25
the waves that they know—the tide before sleep;
and fighting to drown they assemble their sheep
in columns and watch them leap desks for their fences
and stare at them with their own mirror-worn faces.

In the felt of the morning the calico-minded,   30
sufficiently starched, insert papers, hit keys,
efficient and sure as their adding machines;
yet they weep in the vault, they are taut as net curtains
stretched upon frames. In their eyes I have seen
the pin men[4] of madness in marathon trim   35
race round the track of the stadium pupil.

                                                        1946

---

1. Temporary army encampment in the open.
2. That is, the "floats" (buoys) looked like sea veg-etables.
3. That is, when they take dictation.
4. "Stick figures, such as children draw" [Page's note].

Photos of a Salt Mine

How innocent their lives look,
how like a child's
dream of caves and winter, both combined:
the steep descent to whiteness
and the stope   5
with its striated walls[5]
their folds all leaning as if pointing to
the greater whiteness still,
that great white bank
with its decisive front,   10
that seam upon a slope,
salt's lovely ice.

And wonderful underfoot the snow of salt,
the fine
particles a broom could sweep,   15
one thinks
muckers[6] might make angels in its drifts,
as children do in snow,
lovers in sheets,
lie down and leave imprinted where they lay   20
a feathered creature holier than they.

And in the outworked stopes
with lamps and ropes
up miniature Matterhorns[7]
the miners climb,   25
probe with their lights
the ancient folds of rock—
syncline, anticline[8]—
and scoop from darkness an Aladdin's cave:
rubies and opals glitter from its walls.   30

But hoses douse the brilliance of these jewels,
melt fire to brine.
Salt's bitter water trickles thin and forms
slow fathoms down
a lake within a cave   35
lacquered with jet—
white's opposite.
There grey on black the boating miners float
to mend the stays and struts of that old stope
and deeply underground   40
their words resound,

5. With parallel grooves. *Stope*: steplike excavation in a mine.
6. Laborers who, or machines that, remove muck.
7. The Matterhorn is a mountain peak in the Alps.

8. A "syncline" is a trough of stratified rock (here, salt) in which the beds of ore (here again, salt) tip toward each other; an "anticline" is the reverse: an arch, with the beds tipping away from each other.

are multiplied by echo, swell and grow
and make a climate of a miner's voice.

So all the photographs like children's wishes
are filled with caves or winter,   45
innocence
has acted as a filter,
selected only beauty from the mine.
Except in the last picture, shot
from an acute high angle. In a pit   50
figures the size of pins are strangely lit
and might be dancing but you know they're not.
Like Dante's vision of the nether hell[9]
men struggle with the bright cold fires of salt
locked in the black inferno of the rock: 55
the filter here, not innocence but guilt.

                                                          1967

Deaf-Mute in the Pear Tree

His clumsy body is a golden fruit
pendulous in the pear tree

Blunt fingers among the multitudinous buds

Adriatic[1] blue the sky above and through
the forking twigs   5

Sun ruddying tree's trunk, his trunk
his massive head thick-nobbed with burnished curls
tight-clenched in bud

(Painting by Generalić.[2] Primitive.)

I watch him prune with silent secateurs[3]   10

Boots in the crotch of branches shift their weight
heavily as oxen in a stall

Hear small inarticulate mews from his locked mouth
a kitten in a box

Pear clippings fall   15
              soundlessly on the ground

9. In Dante's *Inferno*, the innermost circle of Hell is made of ice.
1. As of the Adriatic Sea, part of the Mediterranean.
2. Ivan Generalić (1914–1992), considered the founder of Croatian naive art.
3. Pruning shears.

Spring finches sing
                      soundlessly in the leaves

A stone. A stone in ears and on his tongue

Through palm and fingertip he knows the tree's   20
quick springtime pulse

Smells in its sap the sweet incipient pears

Pale sunlight's choppy water glistens on
his mutely snipping blades

and flags and scraps of blue   25
above him make regatta of the day

But when he sees his wife's foreshortened shape
sudden and silent in the grass below
uptilt its face to him

then air is kisses, kisses   30

stone dissolves

his locked throat finds a little door

and through it feathered joy
flies screaming like a jay

                                          1985

Robert Lowell
1917–1977

Robert Lowell presented himself in his poetry as a gnarled, knotty, unwieldy figure—almost a gargoyle. This portrait is not what might be anticipated from a member of a patrician New England family, with James Russell Lowell a great-great-uncle and Amy Lowell a distant cousin. Lowell insisted on his own version of the family history. In the prose autobiography that forms a large part of his book *Life Studies* (1959), as in his unflattering elegies, he shows little indulgence toward his domineering mother and ineffectual father, and he relentlessly recalls their lifelong dialogue as that of a shrew and a wobbler: " 'Wee-lawaugh, we-ee-eeelawaugh, weelawaugh,' shrilled Mother's high voice. 'But-and, but-and, but and!' Father's low mumble would drone in answer." With other ancestors whom he presented more attractively, Lowell constructed a new family for himself from dead writers such as Milton, Jonathan Edwards, Nathaniel Hawthorne, T. S. Eliot, John Berryman, and Ezra Pound—patricians not of blood but of tortured talent.

    Whether he was discussing the intricacies of the Puritan conscience, or writing as a Catholic or an agnostic, Lowell was, like the title character in his translation of Jean

Racine's *Phaedra*, "Always, always agonized." He beat against what he called awkwardly "blind alleys of our rooms." A deliberate awkwardness jackets many of his poems. Attacking himself, his parents, his Puritan forebears, even language itself, Lowell fashioned an elegant yet explosive style of poetry, dense with conflicting impulses and images. In his preface to a book of translated poems, *Imitations,* he declared that "the dark and against the grain" primarily interested him.

He was born on March 1, 1917, in "this planned / Babel of Boston where our money talks" ("As a Plane Tree by the Water"). He spent his early years there, except for several periods in Washington and Philadelphia, where his father, a naval officer, was stationed. In "Commander Lowell" and other poems in *Life Studies,* Lowell offers a chilly, relentless picture of his father, who died in 1950. Lowell attended St. Mark's School and soon began to prepare himself deliberately for a poet's life. He enrolled at Harvard University and immersed himself in English literature, but after two years, he abruptly transferred to Kenyon College to study with the New Critic and poet John Crowe Ransom. After graduation in 1940, Lowell attended Louisiana State University, where he studied with two other leaders of the New Criticism, Robert Penn Warren and Cleanth Brooks. At the same time, he formed a close friendship with another, Allen Tate. He was greatly influenced by the predilection of these poets and critics for "formal, difficult poems."

While at Kenyon, Lowell experimented in the most divergent styles, but he found congenial models in Hart Crane, Dylan Thomas, and Tate, as well as in the examples cited and elaborately explained by William Empson in *Seven Types of Ambiguity* (1930, rev. 1947). Lowell's poems became increasingly ambiguous, to the point that Ransom found them forbidding and clotted. Lowell was also dissatisfied with them, though he did not renounce his dense details or jagged syntax. Upon graduating from Kenyon, Lowell married the novelist Jean Stafford. (They were divorced in 1948, and he married his second wife, Elizabeth Hardwick, in 1949. Lowell and Hardwick were divorced in 1972.) He also, like Tate, converted to Catholicism, and he found an intense vantage point in the change from his family's Episcopalianism. In his first book, *Land of Unlikeness* (1944), and later, Lowell wrote scathingly of the modern world as a Babylon or a wasteland, "where the landless blood of Cain / Is burning, burning the unburied grain" ("Children of Light"), and he prophesied the death of "our mighty merchants" ("Rebellion"). Like the historian R. H. Tawney, he connected the Puritan tradition with the rise of predatory capitalism.

Lowell was greatly disturbed by the advent of World War II. At first he tried, unsuccessfully, to enlist. Then in 1943, as his apocalyptic view sharpened, he grew horrified, particularly by the bombing of civilians, and declared himself a conscientious objector. As he wrote in "Memories of West Street and Lepke," with some humor, "I was a fire-breathing Catholic C.O., / and made my manic statement, . . . / Given a year, / I walked on the roof of the West Street Jail." He was released after six months and afterward lived for a time in Black Rock, near Bridgeport, Connecticut, where he found imagery for some of his best poems, reflecting the acute distress he then felt, for the world and himself.

Like many poets of the twentieth century, Lowell attempted in middle age to break through his own formality and obscurity, to write at once more intimately of his own experience and more publicly. The change was marked by a looser meter and form, beginning with *Life Studies,* one of the most influential books of post–World War II American poetry, written in part under the influence of the more "open" poetry of Allen Ginsberg and other Beats, as well as William Carlos Williams. Lowell also altered his symbolism: he gave up the Christian symbols of his early work, made his manner less forbidding, and presented details less viscously, with more individual sharpness.

Lowell confronted important events with courage and conviction. He protested the Vietnam War, both through poems and by public action. In June 1965, he formally refused an invitation to the White House Festival of the Arts from President Lyndon

B. Johnson, as a statement against the war. During the Democratic primary campaign for the presidency in 1968, Lowell accompanied Senator Eugene McCarthy, whose antiwar platform he supported. In 1970, he withdrew from the political scene by moving to England, where he married writer Caroline Blackwood two years later. The strain of his episodes of mania and depression was more than she could bear, and he was on his way back to his second wife and daughter when he died in a taxi from New York's Kennedy Airport.

As if caught between formality and informality, Lowell's later work includes unrhymed sonnets. Not as savage as his earlier work, and with an awareness of those around him—wife, daughter, friends—these poems still kept what Lowell called his "surrealism," by which he meant the grotesquerie that was always his brand and distinction. In *History* (1973), he insisted that "imperfection is the language of art" ("Last Things, Black Pines at 4 a.m."). His work was imperfect, as his own persistent revisions of it suggested, but it touched the nerve of the time.

The confessional aspect of Lowell's poetry, and his impingement on crucial events in the world, brought him as close to being central in then-contemporary verse as the fragmented literary scene allowed. Because of his sense of himself, his impressive personality, and his wit, intelligence, and talent, he throned it over his rivals from about 1950 to 1970. Although in recent decades his reputation has taken on more modest proportions, he remains one of the dominant voices of the latter half of the twentieth century.

The Quaker Graveyard in Nantucket

(For Warren Winslow,[1] Dead at Sea)

Let man have dominion over the fishes of the sea and the fowls of the air and the beasts of the whole earth, and every creeping creature that moveth upon the earth.[2]

I

A brackish reach of shoal off Madaket[3]—
The sea was still breaking violently and night
Had steamed into our North Atlantic Fleet,
When the drowned sailor clutched the drag-net. Light
Flashed from his matted head and marble feet,   5
He grappled at the net
With the coiled, hurdling muscles of his thighs:
The corpse was bloodless, a botch of reds and whites,
Its open, staring eyes
Were lusterless dead-lights   10
Or cabin-window on a stranded hulk
Heavy with sand.[4] We weight the body, close

1. A cousin of Lowell's, who died in New York Harbor when his naval vessel exploded in World War II.
2. Slightly paraphrased from Genesis 1.26.
3. Fishing village on the west end of Nantucket Island.
4. The imagery of these lines is largely borrowed from Henry David Thoreau's *Cape Cod* (Boston, 1898): "The brig *St. John*, from Galway, Ireland, laden with emigrants, was wrecked on Sunday morning; it was not Tuesday morning, and the sea was still breaking violently on the rocks. . . . I saw many marble feet and matted heads as the clothes were raised, and one livid, swollen, and mangled body of a drowned girl . . . ; the coiled-up wreck of a human hulk, gashed by the rocks or fishes, so that the bone and muscle were exposed, but quite bloodless,—merely red and white,—with wide-open and staring eyes, yet lusterless, dead-lights; or like the cabin windows of a stranded vessel, filled with sand."

Its eyes and heave it seaward whence it came,
Where the heel-headed dogfish barks its nose
On Ahab's void and forehead;[5] and the name   15
Is blocked in yellow chalk.
Sailors, who pitch this portent at the sea
Where dreadnaughts shall confess
Its hell-bent deity,
When you are powerless   20
To sand-bag this Atlantic bulwark, faced
By the earth-shaker, green, unwearied, chaste
In his steel scales: ask for no Orphean lute
To pluck life back.[6] The guns of the steeled fleet
Recoil and then repeat   25
The hoarse salute.

II

Whenever winds are moving and their breath
Heaves at the roped-in bulwarks of this pier,
The terns and sea-gulls tremble at your death
In these home waters. Sailor, can you hear   30
The Pequod's[7] sea wings, beating landward, fall
Headlong and break on our Atlantic wall
Off 'Sconset, where the yawing S-boats[8] splash
The bellbuoy, with ballooning spinnakers,
As the entangled, screeching mainsheet clears   35
The blocks: off Madaket, where lubbers[9] lash
The heavy surf and throw their long lead squids
For blue-fish? Sea-gulls blink their heavy lids
Seaward. The winds' wings beat upon the stones,
Cousin, and scream for you and the claws rush   40
At the sea's throat and wring it in the slush
Of this old Quaker graveyard[1] where the bones
Cry out in the long night for the hurt beast
Bobbing by Ahab's whaleboats in the East.

III

All you recovered from Poseidon died   45
With you, my cousin, and the harrowed brine
Is fruitless on the blue beard of the god,
Stretching beyond us to the castles in Spain,
Nantucket's westward haven. To Cape Cod
Guns, cradled on the tide,   50
Blast the eelgrass about a waterclock

5. Ahab is the monomaniacal hunter of the white whale in *Moby-Dick*, by Herman Melville (1819–1891).
6. Orpheus went to Hades and with his music persuaded Persephone to let his wife, Eurydice, return to Earth. *Earth-shaker*: epithet for Poseidon, Greek god of the sea.
7. Ahab's ship, which the whale Moby-Dick destroyed.
8. Large racing sailboats once popular in New England. *'Sconset*: Siasconset, on eastern Nantucket.
9. Landlubbers.
1. A Quaker cemetery in Madaket. In the nineteenth century, Nantucket had a large Quaker population, including many whalers.

Of bilge and backwash, roil the salt and sand
Lashing earth's scaffold, rock
Our warships in the hand
Of the great God, where time's contrition blues   55
Whatever it was there Quaker sailors lost
In the mad scramble of their lives. They died
When time was open-eyed,
Wooden and childish; only bones abide
There, in the nowhere, where their boats were tossed   60
Sky-high, where mariners had fabled news
Of IS,[2] the whited monster. What it cost
Them is their secret. In the sperm-whale's slick
I see the Quakers drown and hear their cry:
"If God himself had not been on our side,   65
If God himself had not been on our side,
When the Atlantic rose against us, why,
Then it had swallowed us up quick."

                            IV

This is the end of the whaleroad[3] and the whale
Who spewed Nantucket bones on the thrashed swell   70
And stirred the troubled waters to whirlpools
To send the Pequod packing off to hell:
This is the end of them, three-quarters fools,
Snatching at straws to sail
Seaward and seaward on the turntail whale,   75
Spouting out blood and water as it rolls,
Sick as a dog to these Atlantic shoals:
Clamavimus,[4] O depths. Let the sea-gulls wail

For water, for the deep where the high tide
Mutters to its hurt self, mutters and ebbs.   80
Waves wallow in their wash, go out and out,
Leave only the death-rattle of the crabs,
The beach increasing, its enormous snout
Sucking the ocean's side.
This is the end of running on the waves;   85
We are poured out like water. Who will dance
The mast-lashed master of Leviathans[5]
Up from this field of Quakers in their unstoned graves?

                            V

When the whale's viscera go and the roll
Of its corruption overruns this world   90
Beyond tree-swept Nantucket and Woods Hole[6]

---

2. Cf. God's naming of himself to Moses as "I AM"
(Exodus 3.14).
3. An Old English kenning (or epithet) for the sea.
4. We have cried (Latin). Cf. Psalm 130.1: "Out
of the depths have I cried unto thee, O Lord."

5. Leviathan is an Old Testament serpent-
monster from the sea.
6. The closest point on the mainland of Massa-
chusetts to Martha's Vineyard, an island near Nan-
tucket.

And Martha's Vineyard, Sailor, will your sword
Whistle and fall and sink into the fat?
In the great ash-pit of Jehoshaphat[7]
The bones cry for the blood of the white whale,   95
The fat flukes arch and whack about its ears,
The death-lance churns into the sanctuary, tears
The gun-blue swingle, heaving like a flail,
And hacks the coiling life out: it works and drags
And rips the sperm-whale's midriff into rags,   100
Gobbets of blubber spill to wind and weather,
Sailor, and gulls go round the stoven timbers
Where the morning stars sing out together
And thunder shakes the white surf and dismembers
The red flag hammered in the mast-head.[8] Hide,   105
Our steel, Jonas Messias,[9] in Thy side.

VI
OUR LADY OF WALSINGHAM[1]

There once the penitents took off their shoes
And then walked barefoot the remaining mile;
And the small trees, a stream and hedgerows file
Slowly along the munching English lane,   110
Like cows to the old shrine, until you lose
Track of your dragging pain.
The stream flows down under the druid tree,
Shiloah's whirlpools gurgle and make glad
The castle of God. Sailor, you were glad   115
And whistled Sion[2] by that stream. But see:

Our Lady, too small for her canopy,
Sits near the altar. There's no comeliness
At all or charm in that expressionless
Face with its heavy eyelids. As before,   120
This face, for centuries a memory,

7. "The valley of judgment. The world, according to some prophets and scientists, will end in fire" (Lowell writing to Kimon Friar and John Malcolm Brinnin). Jehoshaphat, biblical king of Judah, was persuaded by Ahab (king of Israel) to go to war (Joel 3.12).
8. At the end of *Moby-Dick*, as the *Pequod* is sinking, the American Indian Tashtego's arm rises from the water to nail Ahab's flag to the sinking mast.
9. Jonah (in the New Testament, Jonas) is identified with the Messiah because Lowell imagines the whaler's harpoon penetrating the whale, and Jonah within it, the way the centurion's spear pierced Jesus' side, and also because Jonah, like Jesus, emerged after a three-day "burial."
1. Adapted, Lowell said, from E. I. Watkins's *Catholic Art and Culture* (London, 1947): "For centuries the shrine of Our Lady of Walsingham has been an historical memory. Now once again pilgrims visit her image erected in a mediaeval chapel, where, it is said, they took off their shoes to walk barefoot the remaining mile to the shrine. . . . The road to the chapel is a quiet country lane shaded with trees, and lined on one side by a hedgerow. On the other, a stream flows beneath the trees, the water symbol of the Holy Spirit, 'the waters of Shiloah that go softly,' the 'flow of the river making glad the city of God.' Within the chapel, an attractive example of Decorated architecture, near an altar of medieval fashion, is seated Our Lady's image. It is too small for its canopy, and is not superficially beautiful. 'Non est species neque decor,' there is no comeliness or charm in that expressionless face with heavy eyelids. But let us look carefully. . . . We become aware of an inner beauty more impressive than outward grace. That expressionless countenance expresses what is beyond expression. . . . Mary is beyond joy and sorrow. . . . No longer the Mother of Sorrows nor yet of the human joy of the crib, she understands the secret counsel of God to whose accomplishment Calvary and Bethlehem alike ministered."
2. Or Zion. Cf. Isaiah 51.11: "Therefore the redeemed of the Lord shall return, and come with singing unto Zion."

Non est species, neque decor,
Expressionless, expresses God: it goes
Past castled Sion. She knows what God knows,
Not Calvary's Cross nor crib at Bethlehem   125
Now, and the world shall come to Walsingham.

VII

The empty winds are creaking and the oak
Splatters and splatters on the cenotaph,[3]
The boughs are trembling and a gaff
Bobs on the untimely stroke   130
Of the greased wash exploding on a shoal-bell[4]
In the old mouth of the Atlantic. It's well;
Atlantic, you are fouled with the blue sailors,
Sea-monsters, upward angel, downward fish:
Unmarried and corroding, spare of flesh   135
Mart once of supercilious, wing'd clippers,
Atlantic, where your bell-trap guts its spoil
You could cut the brackish winds with a knife
Here in Nantucket, and cast up the time
When the Lord God formed man from the sea's slime   140
And breathed into his face the breath of life,
And blue-lung'd combers lumbered to the kill.
The Lord survives the rainbow of His will.

1946

After the Surprising Conversions[5]

September twenty-second, Sir: today
I answer. In the latter part of May,
Hard on our Lord's Ascension, it began
To be more sensible.[6] A gentleman
Of more than common understanding, strict   5
In morals, pious in behavior, kicked
Against our goad. A man of some renown,
An useful, honored person in the town,
He came of melancholy parents; prone
To secret spells, for years they kept alone—   10
His uncle, I believe, was killed of it:
Good people, but of too much or little wit.
I preached one Sabbath on a text from Kings;
He showed concernment for his soul. Some things

3. Tomb for someone whose remains are elsewhere.
4. A bell buoy marking shallow waters.
5. Based on the "Faithful Narrative of the Surprising Work of God in the Conversion of Many Hundred Souls in Northampton" (1737), an account by the American preacher and theologian Jonathan Edwards (1703–1758) of the spectacular revival in 1734–35 of Christian faith in his Massachusetts parish. Lowell also uses earlier letters by Edwards describing the same phenomenon entitled "A Narrative of Surprising Conversions."
6. "It began to be very sensible [apparent] that the spirit of God was gradually withdrawing from us" (Edwards's letter of May 30, 1735. See lines 37–38).

In his experience were hopeful. He   15
Would sit and watch the wind knocking a tree
And praise this countryside our Lord has made.
Once when a poor man's heifer died, he laid
A shilling on the doorsill; though a thirst
For loving shook him like a snake, he durst   20
Not entertain much hope of his estate
In heaven. Once we saw him sitting late
Behind his attic window by a light
That guttered on his Bible; through that night
He meditated terror, and he seemed   25
Beyond advice or reason, for he dreamed
That he was called to trumpet Judgment Day
To Concord. In the latter part of May
He cut his throat.[7] And though the coroner
Judged him delirious, soon a noisome stir   30
Palsied our village. At Jehovah's nod
Satan seemed more let loose amongst us: God
Abandoned us to Satan, and he pressed
Us hard, until we thought we could not rest
Till we had done with life. Content was gone.   35
All the good work was quashed. We were undone.
The breath of God had carried out a planned
And sensible withdrawal from this land;
The multitude, once unconcerned with doubt,
Once neither callous, curious nor devout,   40
Jumped at broad noon, as though some peddler groaned
At it in its familiar twang: "My friend,
Cut your own throat. Cut your own throat. Now! Now!"
September twenty-second, Sir, the bough
Cracks with the unpicked apples, and at dawn   45
The small-mouth bass breaks water, gorged with spawn.

1946

Grandparents

They're altogether otherworldly now,
those adults champing for their ritual Friday spin
to pharmacist and five-and-ten in Brockton.[8]
Back in my throw-away and shaggy span
of adolescence, Grandpa still waves his stick   5
like a policeman;
Grandmother, like a Mohammedan,[9] still wears her thick

---

7. Edwards describes the suicide of his uncle Joseph Hawley, on June 1, 1735: "My Uncle Hawley, the last Sabbath morning, laid violent hands on himself, by cutting his own throat. He had been for a considerable time greatly concerned about the condition of his soul; by the ordering of Providence he was suffered to fall into a deep melancholy, a distemper that the family are very prone to; the devil took the advantage and drove him into despairing thoughts." This event caused a setback to the religious revival, as the remainder of Lowell's poem tells.
8. Just south of Boston.
9. Muslim.

lavender mourning and touring veil;
the Pierce Arrow clears its throat in a horse stall.
Then the dry road dust rises to whiten   10
the fatigued elm leaves—
the nineteenth century, tired of children, is gone.
They're all gone into a world of light;[1] the farm's my own.

The farm's my own!
Back there alone,   15
I keep indoors, and spoil another season.
I hear the rattly little country gramophone
racking its five foot horn:
"O Summer Time!"
Even at noon here the formidable   20
Ancien Régime[2] still keeps nature at a distance. Five
green shaded light bulbs spider the billiards-table;
no field is greener than its cloth,
where Grandpa, dipping sugar for us both,
once spilled his demitasse.[3]   25
His favorite ball, the number three,
still hides the coffee stain.
Never again
to walk there, chalk our cues,
insist on shooting for us both.   30
Grandpa! Have me, hold me, cherish me!
Tears smut my fingers. There
half my life-lease later,
I hold an *Illustrated London News*—;
disloyal still,   35
I doodle handlebar
mustaches on the last Russian Czar.

                                                          1959

Commander Lowell[4]

1887–1950

There were no undesirables or girls in my set,
when I was a boy at Mattapoisett[5]—
only Mother, still her Father's daughter.
Her voice was still electric
with a hysterical, unmarried panic,   5
when she read to me from the Napoleon book.[6]
Long-nosed Marie Louise
Hapsburg[7] in the frontispiece

1. Adapted from first line of poem by English religious poet Henry Vaughan (1621 or 1622–1695). *Pierce Arrow*: type of automobile.
2. Old rule (French); from the political system of France before the 1789 revolution.
3. Small cup of black coffee.
4. The poet's father.

5. Massachusetts resort town.
6. *Memoirs of Emperor Napoleon from Ajaccio to Waterloo*, by Laure Junot (1784–1838), duchess d'Abrantès.
7. Archduchess Marie-Louise (1791–1847), second wife of Napoleon Bonaparte (1769–1821).

had a downright Boston bashfulness,
where she groveled to Bonaparte, who scratched his navel,   10
and bolted his food—just my seven years tall!
And I, bristling and manic,
skulked in the attic,
and got two hundred French generals by name,
from *A* to *V*—from Augereau to Vandamme.[8]   15
I used to dope myself asleep,
naming those unpronounceables like sheep.

Having a naval officer
for my Father was nothing to shout
about to the summer colony at "Matt."   20
He wasn't at all "serious,"
when he showed up on the golf course,
wearing a blue serge jacket and numbly cut
white ducks[9] he'd bought
at a Pearl Harbor commissariat . . .   25
and took four shots with his putter to sink his putt.
"Bob," they said, "golf's a game you really ought to know how to play,
if you play at all."
They wrote him off as "naval,"
naturally supposed his sport was sailing.   30
Poor Father, his training was engineering!
Cheerful and cowed
among the seadogs at the Sunday yacht club,
he was never one of the crowd.

"Anchors aweigh," Daddy boomed in his bathtub,   35
"Anchors aweigh,"
when Lever Brothers[1] offered to pay
him double what the Navy paid.
I nagged for his dress sword with gold braid,
and cringed because Mother, new   40
caps on all her teeth, was born anew
at forty. With seamanlike celerity,
Father left the Navy,
and deeded Mother his property.

He was soon fired. Year after year,   45
he still hummed "Anchors aweigh" in the tub—
whenever he left a job,
he bought a smarter car.
Father's last employer
was Scudder, Stevens and Clark, Investment Advisors,   50
himself his only client.
While Mother dragged to bed alone,
read Menninger,[2]

---

8. Military officers under Napoleon.
9. Trousers.
1. Soap manufacturers.

2. Karl Augustus Menninger (1893–1990), American psychiatrist.

and grew more and more suspicious,
he grew defiant.   55
Night after night,
à la clarté déserte de sa lampe,[3]
he slid his ivory Annapolis slide rule
across a pad of graphs—
piker[4] speculations! In three years   60
he squandered sixty thousand dollars.

Smiling on all,
Father was once successful enough to be lost
in the mob of ruling-class Bostonians.
As early as 1928,   65
he owned a house converted to oil,[5]
and redecorated by the architect
of St. Mark's School[6] . . . Its main effect
was a drawing room, "longitudinal as Versailles,[7]"
its ceiling, roughened with oatmeal, was blue as the sea. 70
And once
nineteen, the youngest ensign in his class,
he was "the old man" of a gunboat on the Yangtze.[8]

                                                         1959

Waking in the Blue

The night attendant, a B.U.[9] sophomore,
rouses from the mare's-nest of his drowsy head
propped on *The Meaning of Meaning.*[1]
He catwalks down our corridor.
Azure day   5
makes my agonized blue window bleaker.
Crows maunder on the petrified fairway.
Absence! My heart grows tense
as though a harpoon were sparring for the kill.
(This is the house for the "mentally ill.")   10

What use is my sense of humor?
I grin at Stanley, now sunk in his sixties,
once a Harvard all-American fullback
(if such were possible!),
still hoarding the build of a boy in his twenties,   15
as he soaks, a ramrod
with the muscle of a seal
in his long tub,

---

3. By the empty brilliance of his lamp (French);
from "Brise Marine," by French poet Stéphane
Mallarmé (1842–1898).
4. Cheap gambler.
5. That is, updated to have oil heating.
6. Massachusetts boarding school.

7. Palace built for Louis XII and XIV, southwest
of Paris.
8. Chinese river.
9. Boston University.
1. Philosophical work (1923) by C. K. Ogden and
I. A. Richards.

vaguely urinous from the Victorian plumbing.
A kingly granite profile in a crimson golf cap,   20
worn all day, all night,
he thinks only of his figure,
of slimming on sherbet and ginger ale—
more cut off from words than a seal.

This is the way day breaks in Bowditch Hall at McLean's;[2]   25
the hooded night lights bring out "Bobbie,"
Porcellian[3] '29
a replica of Louis XVI[4]
without the wig—
redolent and roly-poly as a sperm whale,   30
as he swashbuckles about in his birthday suit
and horses at chairs.
These victorious figures of bravado ossified young.

In between the limits of day,
hours and hours go by under the crew haircuts   35
and slightly too little nonsensical bachelor twinkle
of the Roman Catholic attendants.
(There are no Mayflower
screwballs in the Catholic Church.)

After a hearty New England breakfast,   40
I weigh two hundred pounds
this morning. Cock of the walk,
I strut in my turtle-necked French sailor's jersey
before the metal shaving mirrors,
and see the shaky future grow familiar   45
in the pinched, indigenous faces
of these thoroughbred mental cases,
twice my age and half my weight.
We are all old-timers,
each of us holds a locked razor.   50

                                                  1959

Memories of West Street and Lepke[5]

Only teaching on Tuesdays, book-worming
in pajamas fresh from the washer each morning,
I hog a whole house on Boston's
"hardly passionate Marlborough Street,"[6]
where even the man   5

---

2. McLean Hospital, outside Boston.
3. Exclusive club at Harvard University.
4. French king (1754–1793).
5. In 1943, Lowell was sentenced to a year in New York's West Street jail for his refusal to serve in the army. Among the other prisoners was Lepke Buch- alter, head of Murder, Inc., an organized crime syndicate, who had been convicted of murder.
6. William James's phrase for a street in the elegant Back Bay section of Boston, where Lowell lived in the 1950s.

scavenging filth in the back alley trash cans,
has two children, a beach wagon, a helpmate,
and is a "young Republican."
I have a nine months' daughter,
young enough to be my granddaughter.   10
Like the sun she rises in her flame-flamingo infants' wear.

These are the tranquillized *Fifties,*
and I am forty. Ought I to regret my seedtime?
I was a fire-breathing Catholic C.O.,[7]
and made my manic statement,   15
telling off the state and president, and then
sat waiting sentence in the bull pen
beside a Negro boy with curlicues
of marijuana in his hair.

Given a year,   20
I walked on the roof of the West Street Jail, a short
enclosure like my school soccer court,
and saw the Hudson River once a day
through sooty clothesline entanglements
and bleaching khaki tenements.   25
Strolling, I yammered metaphysics with Abramowitz,
a jaundice-yellow ("it's really tan")
and fly-weight pacifist,
so vegetarian,
he wore rope shoes and preferred fallen fruit.   30
He tried to convert Bioff and Brown,
the Hollywood pimps, to his diet.
Hairy, muscular, suburban,
wearing chocolate double-breasted suits,
they blew their tops and beat him black and blue.   35

I was so out of things, I'd never heard
of the Jehovah's Witnesses.[8]
"Are you a C.O.?" I asked a fellow jailbird.
"No," he answered, "I'm a J.W."
He taught me the "hospital tuck,"[9]   40
and pointed out the T-shirted back
of *Murder Incorporated's* Czar Lepke,
there piling towels on a rack,
or dawdling off to his little segregated cell full
of things forbidden the common man: 45
a portable radio, a dresser, two toy American
flags tied together with a ribbon of Easter palm.
Flabby, bald, lobotomized,
he drifted in a sheepish calm,
where no agonizing reappraisal   50

7. Conscientious objector (to war).
8. Christian evangelist sect that opposes war and
forbids its members to have any secular political
involvement.
9. Standard way of making beds in a hospital.

jarred his concentration on the electric chair—
hanging like an oasis in his air
of lost connections. . . .

1959

"To Speak of Woe That Is in Marriage"[1]

"It is the future generation that presses into being by means of these
exuberant feelings and supersensible soap bubbles of ours."
—Schopenhauer[2]

"The hot night makes us keep our bedroom windows open.
Our magnolia blossoms. Life begins to happen.
My hopped up husband drops his home disputes,
and hits the streets to cruise for prostitutes,
free-lancing out along the razor's edge.   5
This screwball might kill his wife, then take the pledge.
Oh the monotonous meanness of his lust. . . .
It's the injustice . . . he is so unjust—
whiskey-blind, swaggering home at five.
My only thought is how to keep alive.   10
What makes him tick? Each night now I tie
ten dollars and his car key to my thigh. . . .
Gored by the climacteric of his want,
he stalls above me like an elephant."

1959

Skunk Hour[3]

(For Elizabeth Bishop)[4]

Nautilus Island's hermit
heiress still lives through winter in her Spartan cottage;
her sheep still graze above the sea.
Her son's a bishop. Her farmer
is first selectman in our village;   5
she's in her dotage.

1. In *The Canterbury Tales,* by Geoffrey Chaucer
(1340?–1400), the Wife of Bath begins to tell of
her several marriages with this line.
2. Arthur Schopenhauer (1788–1860), pessimis-
tic German philosopher.
3. The scene is Castine, Maine, where Lowell had
a summer house. As he writes, "The first four stan-
zas are meant to give a dawdling more or less ami-
able picture of a declining Maine sea town. I move
from the ocean inland. Sterility howls through the
scenery, but I try to give a tone of tolerance,
humor, and randomness to the sad prospect" (*The
Contemporary Poet as Artist and Critic,* ed.
Anthony Ostroff).
4. "The dedication is to Elizabeth Bishop, because
re-reading her suggested a way of breaking through
the shell of my old manner. . . . 'Skunk Hour' is
modelled on Miss Bishop's 'The Armadillo.' . . .
Both . . . use short line stanzas, start with drifting
description and end with a single animal" [Lowell's
note].

Thirsting for
the hierarchic privacy
of Queen Victoria's century,
she buys up all   10
the eyesores facing her shore,
and lets them fall.

The season's ill—
we've lost our summer millionaire,
who seemed to leap from an L. L. Bean   15
catalogue. His nine-knot yawl
was auctioned off to lobstermen.
A red fox stain covers Blue Hill.[5]

And now our fairy
decorator brightens his shop for fall;   20
his fishnet's filled with orange cork,
orange, his cobbler's bench and awl;
there is no money in his work,
he'd rather marry.

One dark night,[6]   25
my Tudor Ford climbed the hill's skull;
I watched for love-cars. Lights turned down,
they lay together, hull to hull,
where the graveyard shelves on the town. . . .
My mind's not right.   30

A car radio bleats,
"Love, O careless Love. . . ."[7] I hear
my ill-spirit sob in each blood cell,
as if my hand were at its throat. . . .
I myself am hell;[8]   35
nobody's here—

only skunks, that search
in the moonlight for a bite to eat.
They march on their soles up Main Street:
white stripes, moonstruck eyes' red fire   40
under the chalk-dry and spar spire
of the Trinitarian Church.

I stand on top
of our back steps and breathe the rich air—
a mother skunk with her column of kittens swills the garbage pail.   45
She jabs her wedge-head in a cup

---

5. "Meant to describe the rusty reddish color of autumn on Blue Hill, a Maine mountain near where we were living" [Lowell's note].
6. Lowell said, to *The Dark Night of the Soul* of St. John of the Cross.
7. A popular song of the time, "Careless Love,"

contains the lines "Now you see what careless love will do . . . / Make you kill yourself and your sweetheart too."
8. An adaption of Lucifer's line from Milton's *Paradise Lost* 4.75: "Which way I fly is Hell; myself am Hell."

of sour cream, drops her ostrich tail,
and will not scare.[9]

1959

For the Union Dead[1]

"Relinquunt Omnia Servare Rem Publicam."[2]

The old South Boston Aquarium stands
in a Sahara of snow now. Its broken windows are boarded.
The bronze weathervane cod has lost half its scales.
The airy tanks are dry.

Once my nose crawled like a snail on the glass;   5
my hand tingled
to burst the bubbles
drifting from the noses of the cowed, compliant fish.

My hand draws back. I often sigh still
for the dark downward and vegetating kingdom   10
of the fish and reptile. One morning last March,
I pressed against the new barbed and galvanized

fence on the Boston Common. Behind their cage,
yellow dinosaur steamshovels were grunting
as they cropped up tons of mush and grass   15
to gouge their underworld garage.

Parking spaces luxuriate like civic
sandpiles in the heart of Boston.
A girdle of orange, Puritan-pumpkin colored girders
braces the tingling Statehouse,   20

shaking over the excavations, as it faces Colonel Shaw
and his bell-cheeked Negro infantry
on St. Gaudens' shaking Civil War relief,
propped by a plank splint against the garage's earthquake.

Two months after marching through Boston,   25
half the regiment was dead;
at the dedication,
William James[3] could almost hear the bronze Negroes breathe.

9. "The skunks," according to Lowell, "are both quixotic and barbarously absurd, hence the tone of amusement and defiance."

1. First published with the title "Colonel Shaw and the Massachusetts 54th." The monument it describes is a bronze relief by Augustus Saint-Gaudens (1848–1907) depicting Robert Gould Shaw (1837–1863), commander of the first African American regiment organized in a free state, who was killed in the assault his troops led against Fort Wagner, South Carolina. The relief, dedicated in 1897, stands on Boston Common opposite the Massachusetts State House.

2. They give up everything to serve the Republic (Latin); slightly modified from the relief, which reads, "He gives up. . . ."

3. American philosopher and psychologist (1842–1910), who taught at Harvard.

Their monument sticks like a fishbone
in the city's throat. 30
Its Colonel is as lean
as a compass-needle.

He has an angry wrenlike vigilance,
a greyhound's gentle tautness;
he seems to wince at pleasure, 35
and suffocate for privacy.

He is out of bounds now. He rejoices in man's lovely,
peculiar power to choose life and die—
when he leads his black soldiers to death,
he cannot bend his back. 40

On a thousand small town New England greens,
the old white churches hold their air
of sparse, sincere rebellion; frayed flags
quilt the graveyards of the Grand Army of the Republic.

The stone statues of the abstract Union Soldier 45
grow slimmer and younger each year—
wasp-waisted, they doze over muskets
and muse through their sideburns . . .

Shaw's father wanted no monument
except the ditch, 50
where his son's body was thrown[4]
and lost with his "niggers."

The ditch is nearer.
There are no statues for the last war[5] here;
on Boylston Street,[6] a commercial photograph 55
shows Hiroshima boiling

over a Mosler Safe, the "Rock of Ages"
that survived the blast. Space is nearer.
When I crouch to my television set,
the drained faces of Negro school-children rise like balloons. 60

Colonel Shaw
is riding on his bubble,
he waits
for the blessèd break.

The Aquarium is gone. Everywhere, 65
giant finned cars nose forward like fish;
a savage servility
slides by on grease.

1959

4. By the Confederate soldiers at Fort Wagner.   6. In downtown Boston
5. That is, World War II.

Waking Early Sunday Morning

O to break loose, like the chinook
salmon jumping and falling back,
nosing up to the impossible
stone and bone-crushing waterfall—
raw-jawed, weak-fleshed there, stopped by ten   5
steps of the roaring ladder, and then
to clear the top on the last try,
alive enough to spawn and die.

Stop, back off. The salmon breaks
water, and now my body wakes   10
to feel the unpolluted joy
and criminal leisure of a boy—
no rainbow smashing a dry fly
in the white run is free as I,
here squatting like a dragon on   15
time's hoard before the day's begun!

Vermin run for their unstopped holes;
in some dark nook a fieldmouse rolls
a marble, hours on end, then stops;
the termite in the woodwork sleeps—   20
listen, the creatures of the night
obsessive, casual, sure of foot,
go on grinding, while the sun's
daily remorseful blackout dawns.

Fierce, fireless mind, running downhill.   25
Look up and see the harbor fill:
business as usual in eclipse
goes down to the sea in ships—
wake of refuse, dacron rope,
bound for Bermuda or Good Hope,   30
all bright before the morning watch
the wine-dark hulls of yawl and ketch.[7]

I watched a glass of water wet
with a fine fuzz of icy sweat,
silvery colors touched with sky,   35
serene in their neutrality—
yet if I shift, or change my mood,
I see some object made of wood,
background behind it of brown grain,
to darken it, but not to stain.   40

O that the spirit could remain
tinged but untarnished by its strain!

7. Types of boats. *Wine-dark:* epithet for the sea in Homer's *Odyssey.*

Better dressed and stacking birch,
or lost with the Faithful at Church—
anywhere, but somewhere else!   45
And now the new electric bells,
clearly chiming, "Faith of our fathers,"[8]
and now the congregation gathers.

O Bible chopped and crucified
in hymns we hear but do not read,   50
none of the milder subtleties
of grace or art will sweeten these
stiff quatrains shoveled out four-square—
they sing of peace, and preach despair;
yet they gave darkness some control,   55
and left a loophole for the soul.

No, put old clothes on, and explore
the corners of the woodshed for
its dregs and dreck: tools with no handle,
ten candle-ends not worth a candle,   60
old lumber banished from the Temple,
damned by Paul's precept and example,
cast from the kingdom, banned in Israel,
the wordless sign, the tinkling cymbal.

When will we see Him face to face?   65
Each day, He shines through darker glass.
In this small town where everything
is known, I see His vanishing
emblems, His white spire and flag-
pole sticking out above the fog,   70
like old white china doorknobs, sad,
slight, useless things to calm the mad.

Hammering military splendor,
top-heavy Goliath in full armor—
little redemption in the mass   75
liquidations of their brass,
elephant and phalanx moving
with the times and still improving,
when that kingdom hit the crash:
a million foreskins stacked like trash[9] . . .   80

Sing softer! But what if a new
diminuendo[1] brings no true
tenderness, only restlessness,
excess, the hunger for success,
sanity of self-deception   85

8. Protestant hymn.
9. 1 Samuel 17–18 describes David's early military exploits, such as defeating the giant Goliath and bringing back the foreskins of hundreds of defeated Philistine soldiers.
1. Gradual decrease in volume (musical instruction in Italian).

fixed and kicked by reckless caution,
while we listen to the bells—
anywhere, but somewhere else!

O to break loose. All life's grandeur
is something with a girl in summer . . .   90
elated as the President
girdled by his establishment
this Sunday morning, free to chaff
his own thoughts with his bear-cuffed staff,
swimming nude, unbuttoned, sick   95
of his ghost-written rhetoric!

No weekends for the gods now. Wars
flicker, earth licks its open sores,
fresh breakage, fresh promotions, chance
assassinations, no advance.   100
Only man thinning out his kind
sounds through the Sabbath noon, the blind
swipe of the pruner and his knife
busy about the tree of life . . .

Pity the planet, all joy gone   105
from this sweet volcanic cone;
peace to our children when they fall
in small war on the heels of small
war—until the end of time
to police the earth, a ghost   110
orbiting forever lost
in our monotonous sublime.

                                        1967

Reading Myself

Like thousands, I took just pride and more than just,
struck matches that brought my blood to a boil;
I memorized the tricks to set the river on fire—
somehow never wrote something to go back to.
Can I suppose I am finished with wax flowers   5
and have earned my grass on the minor slopes of Parnassus.² . . .
No honeycomb is built without a bee
adding circle to circle, cell to cell,
the wax and honey of a mausoleum—
this round dome proves its maker is alive;   10
the corpse of the insect lives embalmed in honey,
prays that its perishable work live long

---

2. Greek mountain sacred to Apollo and the Muses.

enough for the sweet-tooth bear to desecrate—
this open book . . . my open coffin.

1973

Dolphin

My Dolphin,[3] you only guide me by surprise,
captive as Racine, the man of craft,
drawn through his maze of iron composition
by the incomparable wandering voice of Phèdre.[4]
When I was troubled in mind, you made for my body   5
caught in its hangman's-knot of sinking lines,
the glassy bowing and scraping of my will. . . .
I have sat and listened to too many
words of the collaborating muse,
and plotted perhaps too freely with my life,   10
not avoiding injury to others,
not avoiding injury to myself—
to ask compassion . . . this book, half fiction,
an eelnet made by man for the eel fighting—

my eyes have seen what my hand did.   15

1973

Epilogue[5]

Those blessèd structures, plot and rhyme—
why are they no help to me now
I want to make
something imagined, not recalled?
I hear the noise of my own voice: 5
The painter's vision is not a lens,
it trembles to caress the light.
But sometimes everything I write
with the threadbare art of my eye
seems a snapshot,   10
lurid, rapid, garish, grouped,
heightened from life,
yet paralyzed by fact.
All's misalliance.
Yet why not say what happened?   15
Pray for the grace of accuracy

3. According to legend, the dolphin saves drown-
ing sailors. Lowell called his third wife, Caroline
Blackwood, his "dolphin," saying that she had
saved his life.
4. Heroine of 1677 tragedy by French dramatist

Jean Racine (1639–1699), a play Lowell translated
in 1961.
5. The last poem (excluding a few translations) in
Lowell's final book, *Day by Day* (1977).

Vermeer[6] gave to the sun's illumination
stealing like the tide across a map
to his girl solid with yearning.
We are poor passing facts,   20
warned by that to give
each figure in the photograph
his living name.

1977

6. Jan Vermeer (1632–1675), Dutch painter noted for his subtle handling of the effects of light.

GWENDOLYN BROOKS
1917–2000

Gwendolyn Brooks is perhaps best known for the poem "We Real Cool," memorable for its depiction of young, black, urban men and its skillful use of syncopated rhythms, enjambment, alliteration, rhyme, caesura, ellipsis, and tonal complexity. Much of her best work is in compressed short poems that display both formal mastery and keen social insight. The central subject of her verse is the black inner city. Like Edgar Lee Masters (another Illinois poet) in *Spoon River Anthology,* Brooks often presents the "characters" of local people, whether the preacher or the gangster, the dreamy young girl or the madam of a brothel. Her miniaturized narratives reveal a life story in a few quick strokes.

Brooks learned the hard discipline of compression from two sources. The modernists famously demanded that superfluities be eliminated, that every word be made to count (*le mot juste*), and this seems to have been the guiding principle of the Chicago poetry workshop she attended in the early 1940s, in which she read T. S. Eliot, Ezra Pound, and E. E. Cummings. Brooks also learned this lesson from the spare, hard, stripped-down idiom of the blues, which Langston Hughes urged her to study. Like the authors of the blues, she uses insistent rhymes and terse simplicity, and she can be at once understated and robust. Despite Brook's reputation for directness, her poetry, like the blues and other African American oral traditions, evinces a sly and ironic indirection.

In presenting her vivid characters, Brooks knows what to put into her poems and what to keep out. Her laconic but exuberant poems reflect the mixture of irreverence and control she portrays in her character Annie Allen, a girl who, pleased to be "rid" of a "relative beneath the coffin lid," instead of affecting solemnity when no one is near, "stuck her tongue out; slid" ("old relative"). Eliding pronouns and articles, suspending the verb "slid" at the end of the line, Brooks says more by saying less. Even when responding to emotionally and politically violent events, Brooks practices restraint. In "The Last Quatrain of the Ballad of Emmett Till," written after the fourteen-year-old was murdered, in 1955, for whistling at a white woman, Brooks holds back from venting grief directly. She locates it instead in the violent, unresolved tensions between tightly woven oppositions of color ("red," "black"), size ("red room," "red prairie,"), and feeling ("kisses," "killed"). "And she is sorry," Brooks writes of the mother's searing grief and rage. Here, as elsewhere, Brooks mixes colloquial black speech ("a pretty-faced thing," "black coffee") with high poetic discourse ("Chaos in windy grays"). Brooks dexterously moves among various rhetorical registers and forms: her poems range from the formal to the vernacular, from ballads and perfectly rhymed sonnets (especially early in her career) to what she called, at Chapman College, the "wild, raw, ragged free verse" of her later work.

Determined to represent the everyday lives of African American city dwellers, especially women, Brooks lights up the most ordinary details with a sudden rhythm, passionate observation, or exciting refrain. As she says in "A Street in Bronzeville," she would like to have "a dream send up through onion fumes / Its white and violet, fight with fried potatoes / And yesterday's garbage ripening in the hall." She prefers wild girls to safe ones ("Sadie and Maud") and endorses all that is "luminously indiscreet" ("The Sermon on the Warpland"). She seems to agree with the title character of "Big Bessie Throws Her Son into the Street": "Hunt out your own or make your own alone. / Go down the street." She is for gumption, for independence of spirit, not for compromise.

In 1967, Brooks had an experience that changed the temper of her poetry. Attending the Second Fisk University Black Writers' Conference, she met some of the younger poets espousing a new black cultural nationalism, notably Amiri Baraka (then LeRoi Jones). Brooks felt she had awakened "in some inscrutable and uncomfortable wonderland." She was later to write: "Until 1967 my own blackness did not confront me with a shrill spelling of itself" (*Report from Part One*). On her return to Chicago, she organized a poetry workshop for young African Americans, including a teenage gang called the Blackstone Rangers. She assisted in community programs and tirelessly worked to inspire younger black poets.

Brooks was born on June 17, 1917, in Topeka, Kansas, but she grew up in Chicago, was educated at Englewood High School and Wilson Junior College there, and identified herself with that city. After her graduation in 1936, she worked for a quack "spiritual advisor" who sold potions and charms to the needy, her job being to write hundreds of letters to prospective patients. Her office was in the Mecca Building on South State Street, where many poor families and derelicts lived. At the end of what she said was the worst period of her life, Brooks refused to take on the duties of "Assistant Pastor" and was honorably fired. Her book *In the Mecca* (1968) draws much of its material from this experience.

Attending a poetry workshop at the South Side Community Art Center, Brooks displayed extraordinary talent. She won contests sponsored by *Poetry* magazine and various organizations and was able to publish her first book in 1945. In 1950, she became the first African American writer to win the Pulitzer Prize, awarded for her book *Annie Allen*. She was appointed poet laureate of Illinois, a post in which she succeeded Carl Sandburg. She traveled in East Africa and in the former Soviet Union. At sixty-eight, she became the first African American woman to be appointed poetry consultant to the Library of Congress. Of her awards, perhaps the most agreeable to the poet was the 1981 dedication of the Gwendolyn Brooks Junior High School in Harvey, Illinois. She was married to Henry Blakely and had a son and a daughter.

A Song in the Front Yard

I've stayed in the front yard all my life.
I want to peek at the back
Where it's rough and untended and hungry weed grows.
A girl gets sick of a rose.

I want to go in the back yard now
And maybe down the alley,   5

To where the charity children play.
I want a good time today.

They do some wonderful things.
They have some wonderful fun.   10
My mother sneers, but I say it's fine
How they don't have to go in at quarter to nine.
My mother, she tells me that Johnnie Mae
Will grow up to be a bad woman.
That George'll be taken to Jail soon or late   15
(On account of last winter he sold our back gate).

But I say it's fine. Honest, I do.
And I'd like to be a bad woman, too,
And wear the brave stockings of night-black lace
And strut down the streets with paint on my face.   20

                                                            1945

Sadie and Maud

Maud went to college.
Sadie stayed at home.
Sadie scraped life
With a fine-tooth comb.

She didn't leave a tangle in.   5
Her comb found every strand.
Sadie was one of the livingest chits
In all the land.

Sadie bore two babies
Under her maiden name.   10
Maud and Ma and Papa
Nearly died of shame.
Every one but Sadie
Nearly died of shame.

When Sadie said her last so-long   15
Her girls struck out from home.
(Sadie had left as heritage
Her fine-tooth comb.)

Maud, who went to college,
Is a thin brown mouse.   20
She is living all alone
In this old house.

                                                            1945

Of De Witt Williams on His Way to Lincoln Cemetery[1]

He was born in Alabama.
He was bred in Illinois.
He was nothing but a
Plain black boy.

Swing low swing low sweet sweet chariot.[2]   5
Nothing but a plain black boy.

Drive him past the Pool Hall.
Drive him past the Show.
Blind within his casket,
But maybe he will know.   10

Down through Forty-seventh Street:[3]
Underneath the L,[4]
And—Northwest Corner, Prairie,
That he loved so well.

Don't forget the Dance Halls—   15
Warwick and Savoy,
Where he picked his women, where
He drank his liquid joy.

Born in Alabama.
Bred in Illinois.
He was nothing but a   20
Plain black boy.

Swing low swing low sweet sweet chariot.
Nothing but a plain black boy.

1945

The Vacant Lot

Mrs. Coley's three-flat brick
Isn't here any more.
All done with seeing her fat little form
Burst out of the basement door;
And with seeing her African son-in-law   5
(Rightful heir to the throne)
With his great white strong cold squares of teeth
And his little eyes of stone;
And with seeing the squat fat daughter

1. African American cemetery in Chicago.
2. A line from a spiritual.
3. The main street of Bronzeville, Chicago's black
ghetto.
4. Elevated railway.

Letting in the men   10
When majesty has gone for the day—
And letting them out again.

                                                              1945

The Rites for Cousin Vit

Carried her unprotesting out the door.
Kicked back the casket-stand. But it can't hold her,
That stuff and satin aiming to enfold her,
The lid's contrition nor the bolts before.
Oh oh. Too much. Too much. Even now, surmise,   5
She rises in the sunshine. There she goes,
Back to the bars she knew and the repose
In love-rooms and the things in people's eyes.
Too vital and too squeaking. Must emerge.
Even now she does the snake-hips with a hiss,   10
Slops the bad wine across her shantung,⁵ talks
Of pregnancy, guitars and bridgework, walks
In parks or alleys, comes haply on the verge
Of happiness, haply hysterics. Is.

                                                              1949

The Bean Eaters

They eat beans mostly, this old yellow pair.
Dinner is a casual affair.
Plain chipware on a plain and creaking wood,
Tin flatware.

Two who are Mostly Good.   5
Two who have lived their day,
But keep on putting on their clothes
And putting things away.

And remembering . . .
Remembering, with twinklings and twinges,   10
As they lean over the beans in their rented back room that is full of beads
    and receipts and dolls and cloths, tobacco crumbs, vases and fringes.

                                                              1960

---

5. Fabric with irregular surface.

We Real Cool

THE POOL PLAYERS.
SEVEN AT THE GOLDEN SHOVEL.

We real cool. We
Left school. We

Lurk late. We
Strike straight. We

Sing sin. We   5
Thin gin. We

Jazz June. We
Die soon.

1960

The Last Quatrain of the Ballad of Emmett Till[6]

AFTER THE MURDER,
AFTER THE BURIAL

Emmett's mother is a pretty-faced thing;
        the tint of pulled taffy.
She sits in a red room,
        drinking black coffee.
She kisses her killed boy.   5
        And she is sorry.
Chaos in windy grays
        through a red prairie.

1960

Boy Breaking Glass

To Marc Crawford[7]
from whom the commission

Whose broken window is a cry of art
(success, that winks aware
as elegance, as a treasonable faith)
is raw: is sonic: is old-eyed première.

6. Fourteen-year-old African American murdered in Mississippi, in 1955, for whistling at a white woman.

7. The writer and editor who suggested Brooks write a poem on the survival of inner-city African Americans.

Our beautiful flaw and terrible ornament.   5
Our barbarous and metal little man.

"I shall create! If not a note, a hole.
If not an overture, a desecration."

Full of pepper and light
and Salt and night and cargoes.   10

"Don't go down the plank
if you see there's no extension.
Each to his grief, each to
his loneliness and fidgety revenge.

Nobody knew where I was and now I am no longer there."   15

The only sanity is a cup of tea.
The music is in minors.

Each one other
is having different weather.

"It was you, it was you who threw away my name!   20
And this is everything I have for me."

Who has not Congress, lobster, love, luau,
the Regency Room, the Statue of Liberty,
runs. A sloppy amalgamation.
A mistake.   25
A cliff.
A hymn, a snare, and an exceeding sun.

           1968

The Blackstone Rangers[8]

I
As Seen by Disciplines[9]

There they are.
Thirty at the corner.
Black, raw, ready.
Sores in the city
that do not want to heal.   5

---

8. A tough Chicago street gang. Blackstone Street is the eastern boundary of Chicago's black ghetto. 9. That is, law enforcers. "Vexed by some who misread this first section as her own condemnation, Brooks insists that, in any reprinting, the entire poem be published as a unit" (D. H. Melhem, *Gwendolyn Brooks: Poetry and the Heroic Voice*, 1987).

II
The Leaders

Jeff. Gene. Geronimo. And Bop.[1]
They cancel, cure and curry.
Hardly the dupes of the downtown thing
the cold bonbon,
the rhinestone thing. And hardly   10
in a hurry.
Hardly Belafonte, King,
Black Jesus, Stokely, Malcolm X or Rap.[2]
Bungled trophies.
Their country is a Nation on no map.   15

Jeff, Gene, Geronimo and Bop
in the passionate noon,
in bewitching night
are the detailed men, the copious men.
They curry, cure,   20
they cancel, cancelled images whose Concerts
are not divine, vivacious; the different tins
are intense last entries; pagan argument;
translations of the night.

The Blackstone bitter bureaus   25
(bureaucracy is footloose) edit, fuse
unfashionable damnations and descent;
and exulting, monstrous hand on monstrous hand,
construct, strangely, a monstrous pearl or grace.

III
Gang Girls

A RANGERETTE

Gang Girls are sweet exotics.   30
Mary Ann
uses the nutrients of her orient,
but sometimes sighs for Cities of blue and jewel
beyond her Ranger rim of Cottage Grove.[3]
(Bowery Boys, Disciplines, Whip-Birds will   35
dissolve no margins, stop no savory sanctities.)

Mary is
a rose in a whiskey glass.

---

1. Kind of jazz. *Geronimo*: Apache Indian chief who led raids against the whites in Arizona.
2. H. Rap Brown (b. 1943): black nationalist leader. Harry Belafonte (b. 1927): American singer and activist. Martin Luther King (1929– 1968): American civil rights leader. Stokely Carmichael (1941–1998): black nationalist leader. Malcolm X (1925–1965): black nationalist leader.
3. Street of overcrowded tenements in the black ghetto.

Mary's
Februaries shudder and are gone. Aprils   40
fret frankly, lilac hurries on.
Summer is a hard irregular ridge.
October looks away.
And that's the Year!
        Save for her bugle-love.   45
Save for the bleat of not-obese devotion.
Save for Somebody Terribly Dying, under
the philanthropy of robins. Save for her Ranger
bringing
man amount of rainbow in a string-drawn bag.   50
"Where did you get the diamond?" Do not ask:
but swallow, straight, the spirals of his flask
and assist him at your zipper; pet his lips
and help him clutch you.

Love's another departure.   55
Will there be any arrivals, confirmations?
Will there be gleaning?

Mary, the Shakedancer's child
from the rooming-flat, pants carefully, peers at
her laboring lover. . . .   60
        Mary! Mary Ann!
Settle for sandwiches! settle for stocking caps!
for sudden blood, aborted carnival,
the props and niceties of non-loneliness—
the rhymes of Leaning.   65

                                        1968

The Boy Died in My Alley[4]

Without my having known.
Policeman said, next morning,
"Apparently died Alone."
"You heard a shot?" Policeman said.
Shots I hear and Shots I hear.   5
I never see the dead.

The Shot that killed him yes I heard
as I heard the Thousand shots before;
careening tinnily down the nights
across my years and arteries.   10

---

4. Brooks said the poem fuses two separate incidents involving an honors student, Kenneth Alexander, killed running from a policeman, and a boy Brooks saw running in Ghana in 1974.

Policeman pounded on my door.
"Who is it?" "POLICE!" Policeman yelled.
"A Boy was dying in your alley.
A Boy is dead, and in your alley.
And have you known this Boy before?"   15

I have known this Boy before.
I have known this Boy before, who
ornaments my alley.
I never saw his face at all.
I never saw his futurefall.   20
But I have known this Boy.

I have always heard him deal with death.
I have always heard the shout, the volley.
I have closed my heart-ears late and early.
And I have killed him ever.   25

I joined the Wild and killed him
with knowledgeable unknowing.
I saw where he was going.
I saw him Crossed. And seeing,
I did not take him down.   30

He cried not only "Father!"
but "Mother!
Sister!
Brother."
The cry climbed up the alley.   35
It went up to the wind.
It hung upon the heaven
for a long
stretch-strain of Moment.

The red floor of my alley   40
is a special speech to me.

                                    1973, 1981

ROBERT DUNCAN
1919–1988

Among the diverse writers associated with Charles Olson at Black Mountain College, in North Carolina, Robert Creeley and Denise Levertov developed their art in sudden, short-lived lyrical insights, but Robert Duncan developed a mystical aesthetic. Olson did not meet him until 1947, but at once praised him as "a beautiful poet," with "ancient, permanent wings of Eros—& of Orphism." Much of Olson's reading was in the sciences, but Duncan was primarily interested in metaphysics, or rather, in philosophy and poetry that implied or recognized a "secret doctrine." He was erudite in this literature, unlike Creeley or Levertov, and became an exponent of it in prose as well as in verse. With Kenneth Rexroth, Duncan helped make the San Francisco Bay area a major center of poetic activity in the United States.

Duncan considered himself a wanderer, both in geographical terms and in "areas of being" (*The Years as Catches*). Born on January 7, 1919, in Oakland, California, to a mother who died in childbirth and a father who was a day laborer, he was adopted at six months by a family named Symmes; his early poetry was signed with that name. His adoptive family adhered to theosophy and other occult beliefs that would influence his visionary poetics. His homosexuality was also important in his life and in his work. Of it, he wrote: "Perhaps the sexual irregularity underlay and led to the poetic; neither as homosexual nor as poet could one take over readily the accepted paradigms of the Protestant ethic" (*The Years as Catches*). He dropped out of the University of California at Berkeley during his sophomore year, to follow a lover east. Subsequently, he spent some time in the army but, in 1941, was granted a psychiatric discharge because of his homosexuality. Editing various magazines, he taught sporadically at universities, notably Berkeley from 1948 to 1950 and with Olson at Black Mountain College in 1956.

In his early period, Duncan eagerly embraced the influences of many poets in the Romantic tradition. Under the sway of Walt Whitman, H. D., and "demi-surrealists" such as Dylan Thomas, Duncan considered poetry a mode of rhetoric, as far-reaching as possible. At the end of "The Years as Catches," he pronounced his mature intention: "Catch from the years the line of joy, / impatient & repeated day, / my heart, break, Eye / break open and set free / His world, my ecstasy." He sought a dithyrambic verse and learned a good deal not only from poetic visionaries, but also from the discontinuous and unportentous verse of William Carlos Williams and Ezra Pound. He regarded himself, however, as an isolated writer until he read Denise Levertov's "The Shifting" in 1952, Robert Creeley's "The Gold Diggers" in 1954, and Olson's *Maximus Poems* in the 1950s.

For Duncan, poetry was ultimately magical. "Every moment of life is an attempt to come to life," he said (*The New American Poetry*, ed. Donald M. Allen, 1960). His collage-based, syncretic poetry is a melee of reading and mother wit, adulthood and childishness, all "higglety-pigglety." He learned from one of his teachers to regard "poetry not as a cultural commodity or an exercise to improve sensibility, but as a vital process of the spirit" (*New American Poetry*). The making of a poem is the exercise of his "faculties at large," which some achieve by making war or love. In this making, as he learned from another teacher, "to form is to transform." This transformation meant the discovery of "an immediate correspondence between inner being and outer world, a metaphysical aura, that remains for me the sign of the poem." The pursuit of this multitudinous radiance is his quest in his poems, but it is also their subject.

In the 1960s, Duncan was outraged by the Vietnam War and began to introduce political events into his work. His method was based on William Blake's Prophetic

Books; like Blake writing about the French Revolution or about battles in the mind, Duncan wrote of President Lyndon Johnson, in "Up Rising, Passages 25": "Now Johnson would go up to join the great simulacra of men, / Hitler and Stalin, to work his fame / with planes roaring out from Guam over Asia." Johnson becomes, like Blake's Urizen, an antipoetic principle of mythical proportions. Duncan carries this difficult maneuver off with considerable adroitness. During the 1970s, in contrast with his earlier prolific work, Duncan published little, but he returned to print in the 1980s with *Ground Work* (1984).

In general, Duncan's poems either surge against the confines of consciousness or stand as integrations of experience. They seek a state in which there is "no duality but the variety of the one" (*The Years as Catches*). Duncan's work plays off structural looseness against thematic intensities. It achieves concentration in images of fire, music, dancing, possession, greenness, light, opening, and speech itself. Ultimately, the poems, which often have love as their subject, seek to illumine as with love the entire poetic situation. Duncan moves toward the vividness of revelation, the wonder of the "first day" ("Passages 13").

Often I Am Permitted to Return to a Meadow

    as if it were a scene made-up by the mind,
    that is not mine, but is a made place,

    that is mine, it is so near to the heart,
    an eternal pasture folded in all thought
    so that there is a hall therein   5

    that is a made place, created by light
    wherefrom the shadows that are forms fall.

    Wherefrom fall all architectures I am
    I say are likeness of the First Beloved
    whose flowers are flames lit to the Lady.   10

    She it is Queen Under The Hill[1]
    whose hosts are a disturbance of words within words
    that is a field folded.

    It is only a dream of the grass blowing
    east against the source of the sun   15
    in an hour before the sun's going down

    whose secret we see in a children's game
    of ring a round of roses told.

---

1. Cf. Persephone, queen of the underworld in Greek mythology. Gathering flowers in a field, she was kidnapped by Hades. She had to spend part of every year with him, part in the upper world with her mother, Demeter, goddess of agriculture.

Often I am permitted to return to a meadow
as if it were a given property of the mind   20
that certain bounds hold against chaos,

that is a place of first permission,
everlasting omen of what is.   1960

Poetry, a Natural Thing

Neither our vices nor our virtues
further the poem. "They came up
            and died
just like they do every year
            on the rocks."   5

            The poem
feeds upon thought, feeling, impulse,
            to breed   itself,
a spiritual urgency at the dark ladders leaping.

This beauty is an inner persistence   10
            toward the source
striving against (within) down-rushet of the river,
            a call we heard and answer
in the lateness of the world
            primordial bellowings   15
from which the youngest world might spring,

salmon not in the well where the
            hazelnut falls
but at the falls battling, inarticulate,
            blindly making it.   20

This is one picture apt for the mind.

A second: a moose painted by Stubbs,[2]
where last year's extravagant antlers
            lie on the ground.
The forlorn moosey-faced poem wears   25
            new antler-buds,
            the same,

"a little heavy, a little contrived",

his only beauty to be
            all moose.   30

                                                              1960

2. George Stubbs (1724–1806), English painter of animals.

Passage over Water

We have gone out in boats upon the sea at night,
lost, and the vast waters close traps of fear about us.
The boats are driven apart, and we are alone at last
under the incalculable sky, listless, diseased with stars.

Let the oars be idle, my love, and forget at this time   5
our love like a knife between us
defining the boundaries that we can never cross
nor destroy as we drift into the heart of our dream,
cutting the silence, slyly, the bitter rain in our mouths
and the dark wound closed in behind us.   10

Forget depth-bombs, death and promises we made,
gardens laid waste, and, over the wastelands westward,
the rooms where we had come together bombd.

But even as we leave, your love turns back. I feel
your absence like the ringing of bells silenced. And salt   15
over your eyes and the scales of salt between us. Now,
you pass with ease into the destructive world.
There is a dry crash of cement. The light fails,
falls into the ruins of cities upon the distant shore
and within the indestructible night I am alone.   20

                                                          1966

What I Saw

The white peacock roosting
might have been Christ,

            featherd robe of Osiris,[3]

the radiant bird, a sword-flash,

            percht in the tree   •   5

and the other,   the fumed-glass slide

            —were like night and day,

---

3. The Egyptian god of the underworld.

the slit of an eye opening in

time

vertical to the horizon   10

                                                           •

                                                     1968

Up Rising   Passages 25

Now Johnson[4] would go up to join the great simulacra of men,
    Hitler and Stalin, to work his fame
    with planes roaring out from Guam[5] over Asia,
all America become a sea of toiling men
    stirrd at his will, which would be a bloated thing,   5
    drawing from the underbelly of the nation
    such blood and dreams as swell the idiot psyche
    out of its courses into an elemental thing
    until his name stinks with burning meat and heapt honors

And men wake to see that they are used like things   10
    spent in a great potlach,[6] this Texas barbecue
      of Asia, Africa, and all the Americas,
And the professional military behind him, thinking
    to use him as they thought to use Hitler
    without losing control of their business of war,   15

But the mania, the ravening eagle of America
    as Lawrence saw him "bird of men that are masters,
    lifting the rabbit-blood of the myriads up into . . ."[7]
    into something terrible, gone beyond bounds, or
As Blake saw America in figures of fire and blood raging,   20
    . . . in what image?[8] the ominous roar in the air,
the omnipotent wings, the all-American boy in the cockpit
    loosing his flow of napalm,[9] below in the jungles
    "any life at all or sign of life" his target, drawing now
    not with crayons in his secret room   25
the burning of homes and the torture of mothers and fathers and children,
    their hair a-flame, screaming in agony, but
in the line of duty, for the might and enduring fame
    of Johnson, for the victory of American will over its victims,
    releasing his store of destruction over the enemy,   30

4. Lyndon B. Johnson, U.S. president from 1963 to 1969, originally from Texas; he dramatically escalated the Vietnam War.
5. U.S. territory in the West Pacific.
6. Native American word for the showy distribution of gifts at a festival.
7. From the poem "The American Eagle" (1923), by English writer D. H. Lawrence (1885–1930).
8. Cf. the 1793 poem "Preludium (to 'America')," by English Romantic William Blake (1757–1827); he characterizes the spirit of freedom that inspired the American Revolution: "A quiver with its burning stores, a bow like that of night, / When pestilence is shot from heaven: no other arms she need!"
9. Jellied gasoline used by the U.S. military in the Vietnam War to incinerate trees and vegetation in which the Viet Cong could hide.

in terror and hatred of all communal things, of communion,
   of communism   •

has raised from the private rooms of small-town bosses and business-men,
from the council chambers of the gangs that run the great cities,
   swollen with the votes of millions,[1]   35
from the fearful hearts of good people in the suburbs turning the
   savory meat over the charcoal burners and heaping their barbecue
   plates with more than they can eat,
from the closed meeting-rooms of regents of universities and sessions of
   profiteers

—back of the scene: the atomic stockpile; the vials of synthesized   40
   diseases eager biologists have developt over half a century dreaming
   of the bodies of mothers and fathers and children and hated rivals
   swollen with new plagues, measles grown enormous, influenzas
   perfected; and the gasses of despair, confusion of the senses, mania,
   inducing terror of the universe, coma, existential wounds, that   45
   chemists we have met at cocktail parties, passt daily and with a
   happy "Good Day" on the way to classes or work, have workt to
   make war too terrible for men to wage—

raised this secret entity of America's hatred of Europe, of Africa, of Asia,
the deep hatred for the old world that had driven generations of America   50
   out of itself,
and for the alien world, the new world about him, that might have been
   Paradise
but was before his eyes already cleard back in a holocaust of burning
   Indians, trees and grasslands,
reduced to his real estate, his projects of exploitation and profitable
   wastes,

this specter that in the beginning Adams and Jefferson feard and knew
would corrupt the very body of the nation   55
   and all our sense of our common humanity,[2]
this black bile of old evils arisen anew,
takes over the vanity of Johnson;
and the very glint of Satan's eyes from the pit of the hell of
   America's unacknowledged, unrepented crimes that I saw in   60
   Goldwater's[3] eyes
now shines from the eyes of the President
   in the swollen head of the nation.

1968

1. John F. Kennedy won the 1960 presidential election when, under the direction of Chicago mayor Richard Daley, his votes were augmented by the ballots of dead citizens. Voter fraud also occurred in Texas, home of Kennedy's running mate, Lyndon Johnson.
2. Thomas Jefferson (1743–1826), third U.S. president, predicted a time when "[o]ur rulers will become corrupt, our people careless. A single zealot may become persecutor, and better men become his victims" (*Notes on Virginia*). John Adams (1735–1826), second U.S. president, foresaw the terror and despotism of the French Revolution and feared the encroachment of such tyranny in the United States.
3. Barry Goldwater (1909–1998), the unsuccessful Republican candidate for president in 1964; an ardent anticommunist, he supported American military intervention in Vietnam.

Childhood's Retreat

It's in the perilous boughs of the tree
out of blue sky   the wind
sings loudest surrounding me.

And solitude,   a wild solitude
's reveald,   fearfully,   high   I'd climb   5
into the shaking uncertainties,

part out of longing, part   daring my self,
part to see that
widening of the world,   part

to find my own, my secret   10
hiding sense and place, where from afar
all voices and scenes come back

—the barking of a dog,   autumnal burnings,
far calls,   close calls—   the boy I was
calls out to me   15
here the man where I am   "Look!

I've been where you

most fear to be."

                                                    1984

From Rites of Passage

II

Something is taking place.
Horns thrust upward from the brow.
Hooves beat impatient where feet once were.
My son, youth grows alarming in your face.
Your innocent regard is cruelly charming to me now.   5
You bristle where my fond hand would stir
to stroke your cheek.   I do not dare.

Irregular meters beat between your heart and mine.
Snuffling the air you take the heat and scan
the lines you take in going as if I were or were not there   10
and overtake me.
    And where it seems but yesterday I spilld the wine,
you too grow beastly to become a man.

Peace, peace.   I've had enough.   What can I say
when song's demanded?   —I've had my fill of song?   15
My longing to sing grows full.   Time's emptied me.

And where my youth was, now the Sun in you grows hot, your day
is young, my place you take triumphantly.   All along
it's been for you, for this lowering of your horns in challenge, She
had her will of me and will not   20

let my struggling spirit in itself be free.

1984

A Little Language

I know a little language of my cat, though Dante says
that animals have no need of speech and Nature
abhors the superfluous.[4]   My cat is fluent.   He
converses when he wants with me.   To speak

is natural.   And whales and wolves I've heard   5
in choral soundings of the sea and air
know harmony and have an eloquence that stirs
my mind and heart—they touch the soul.   Here

Dante's religion that would set Man apart
damns the effluence of our life from us   10
to build therein its powerhouse.

It's in his animal communication Man is
        true, immediate, and
in immediacy,   Man is all animal.

His senses quicken in the thick of the symphony,   15
        old circuits of animal rapture and alarm,
attentions and arousals in which an identity rearrives.
        He hears
particular voices among
        the concert,   the slightest   20
rustle in the undertones,
        rehearsing a nervous aptitude
yet to prove *his*.   He sees the flick
        of significant red within the rushing mass
of ruddy wilderness   and catches the glow   25
        of a green shirt
to delite him in a glowing field of green
        —it *speaks* to him—
and in the arc of the spectrum   color
        speaks to color.   30
The rainbow articulates
        a promise he remembers

---

4. Italian poet Dante Alighieri (1265–1321) said this in his essay *De Vulgari Eloquentia* (Latin for "of the vulgar [i.e., common] speech").

he but imitates
   in noises that he makes,

this speech in every sense   35
   the world surrounding him.

He picks up on the fugitive tang of mace[5]
   amidst the savory mass,
and taste in evolution is an everlasting key.
   There is a pun of scents in what makes sense.   40

   Myrrh[6] it may have been,
the odor of the announcement that filld the house.

He wakes from deepest sleep

upon a distant signal and waits

   as if crouching, springs   45

   to life.

1984

5. A highly aromatic spice.
6. Bitter gum resin found in North Africa and Arabia.

WILLIAM MEREDITH
1919–2007

With wry humor and deft understatement, William Meredith captures the ambivalence we often feel as both children and parents. "Parents," he writes in a poem by that title, "get wrinkles where it is better / smooth, odd coughs, and smells. / / It is grotesque how they go on / loving us, we go on loving them." This poem, like his well-crafted homages to Robert Lowell and Sigmund Freud, illustrates Meredith's abilities as a psychologically astute observer; yet he does not parade his innermost feelings or impose his insights on the reader. A modest writer, he distills intimate experience in calm, elegant verses, which are formally patterned even when unmetered and unrhymed.

In the world of Meredith's poems, creatures and objects are separated from one another and yet engaged in a silent, composed relationship. In one of his war poems, "Battle Problem," he describes a convoy of battleships as moving with the ceremonious, processional beauty of the stars above them: "A company of vessels on the sea / Running in darkness, like a company / Of stars." Such couplings of the human with the natural induce a momentary serenity. Isolated as people are, we communicate, Meredith suggests, in recognition of our common solitude and the rituals we invent to make it tolerable. The poet reminds us that "all go to the grave several ways / and compose themselves elaborately as for an end."

Meredith was born on January 9, 1919, in New York City. He attended the Lenox

School, in Massachusetts, and earned a B.A. from Princeton University in 1940. Meredith then spent five years in the service, most of it as a naval aviator in the Pacific theater. After his release from active duty in 1946, Meredith became a Woodrow Wilson Fellow at Princeton, then a Resident Fellow in creative writing. He reenlisted to fly missions in the Korean War in 1952. From 1955 until 1983, he taught at Connecticut College. In 1978–80, he served as poetry consultant to the Library of Congress, and in 1988, he won the Pulitzer Prize for *Partial Accounts: New and Selected Poems.*

Last Things

For Robert Lowell[1]

I

In the tunnel of woods, as the road
Winds up through the freckled light, a porcupine,
Larger than life, crosses the road.
He moves with the difficulty of relics—
Possum, armadillo, horseshoe crab.   5
To us they seem creatures arthritic with time,
Winding joylessly down like burnt-out galaxies.
In all their slowness we see no dignity,
Only a want of scale.
Having crossed the road oblivious, he falls off   10
Deliberately and without grace into the ferns.

II

In another state are hills as choppy as lake water
And, on a hillside there,
Is a junkyard of old cars, kept for the parts—
Fenders and chassis and the engine blocks   15
Right there in the field, smaller parts in bins
In a shed by the side of the road. Cows graze
Among the widely spaced rows,
Which are irregular only as an old orchard is,
Following the contours of the hill.   20
The tops of the cars are bright colors still
And as pretty as bottles hung on a bare tree
Or painted cinder blocks in a garden.
Cars the same age are parked on the road like cannibals.

III

At the edge of a harbor, in a field   25
That faces the ocean they came by and left by,
Statues of soldiers and governors and their queen
Lie where the Africans put them.
Unbewildered, not without understanding,

1. American poet (1917–1977).

The marble countenances look at the green 30
Continent; they did their best; plunderers
Were fewer among them than men of honor.
But no one comes for them, though they have been offered.
With chipped extremities, in a chipped regalia
They lie at angles of unaccustomed ease. 35
In the parks and squares of England are set up
Bolder, more dreadful shapes of the ego,
While African lichen confers an antique grandeur
On these, from whom men have withheld it.

IV

At the edge of the Greek world, I think, was a cliff 40
To which fallen gods were chained, immortal.[2]
Time is without forgiveness, but intermittently
He sends the old, sentimental, hungry
Vulture compassion to gnaw on the stone
Vitals of each of us, even the young, as if 45
To ready each of us, even the old, for an unthinkable
Event he foresees for each of us—a reckoning, our own.

1970

Parents

For Vanessa Meredith and Samuel Wolf Gezari

What it must be like to be an angel
or a squirrel, we can imagine sooner.

The last time we go to bed good,
they are there, lying about darkness.

They dandle us once too often, 5
these friends who become our enemies.

Suddenly one day, their juniors
are as old as we yearn to be.

They get wrinkles where it is better
smooth, odd coughs, and smells. 10

It is grotesque how they go on
loving us, we go on loving them.

The effrontery, barely imaginable,
of having caused us. And of how.

2. For example, the titan Prometheus, for his crime against the Greek gods in teaching humans about fire, was chained to a mountain in the Caucasus. By day a vulture gnawed at his liver, which was restored during the succeeding night.

Their lives: surely   15
we can do better than that.

This goes on for a long time. Everything
they do is wrong, and the worst thing,

they all do it, is to die,
taking with them the last explanation,   20

how we came out of the wet sea
or wherever they got us from,

taking the last link
of that chain with them.

Father, mother, we cry, wrinkling,   25
to our uncomprehending children and grandchildren.

1980

Dying Away

Homage to Sigmund Freud[3]

'Toward the person who has died
we adopt a special attitude:
something like admiration
for someone who has accomplished
a very difficult task,' he said,   5

and now hospitals and rest-homes
are filled with heroes and heroines
in smocks, at their out-sized, unwonted tasks,
now the second date on tombstones is a saint's day[4]
and there is no craven in any graveyard,   10

no malingerer there, no trivial person.
It is you and I, still milling around,
who evade our callings, incestuous
in our love for the enduring trees and the snowfall,
for brook-noise and coins, songs, appetites.   15

And with the one we love most,
the mated one we lose track of ourselves in—
who's giving, who's taking that fleshy pleasure?—
we call those calmings-away, those ecstasies
dyings,[5] we see them as diligent rehearsals.   20

3. Austrian founder of psychoanalysis (1856–1939). The ensuing quotation is from his "Thoughts for the Times on War and Death" (1915).

4. Day in the Church calendar on which a saint is commemorated.
5. In the seventeenth century, poetic term for sexual intercourse.

The love of living disturbs me,
I am wracked like a puritan by eros and health,
almost undone by brotherhood, rages
of happiness seize me, the world, the fair world,
and I call on the name of the dark healer, Freud.   25

His appetites, songs, orgasms died away,
his young brother, his daughter, his huge father,
until he saw that the aim of life was death.
But a man cannot learn heroism from another,
he owes the world some death of his own invention.   30

Then he said, 'My dear Schur,[6] you certainly remember
our first talk. You promised me then not to forsake me
when my time came. Now it is nothing but torture
and makes no sense any more.'
Schur gave him two centigrams of morphine.   35

At what cost he said it, so diligent of life,
so curious, we can't guess
who are still his conjurings. He told us
it is impossible to imagine our own deaths,
he told us, this may be the secret of heroism.   40

1980

6. Max Schur (1897–1969), Freud's doctor. The quotation translates Freud's last words.

LAWRENCE FERLINGHETTI
b. 1919

Although Allen Ginsberg was the most famous Beat poet, Lawrence Ferlinghetti was the group's leading proponent, organizer, and publisher, as well as its oldest member. His influences ranging from Walt Whitman to E. E. Cummings, Ferlinghetti combines satiric wit with visionary Romanticism, surrealism with earnest chanting. His poems command our attention both on and off the page. Visually, the words are often scattered across the page, defying the norms of the stanza break and the justified left-hand margin. Aurally, the poems recall the darting rhythms and surprising leaps of musical improvisation—Ferlinghetti sometimes performed them to jazz accompaniment.

Ferlinghetti was born on March 24, 1919, in Yonkers, New York. Shortly before his birth, his Italian-immigrant father died suddenly; soon, his Portuguese Jewish mother had a nervous breakdown and was institutionalized. Ferlinghetti's aunt took him to live with her in France from 1920 to 1924. On their return, she took a job as French governess in a wealthy family; she later disappeared, and the family kept Ferlinghetti with them in Bronxville. He did not learn to speak English until he was five. Ferlinghetti later studied journalism at the University of North Carolina (B.A., 1941). When war broke out, he entered the navy, eventually commanding a ship in the Normandy invasion. After the war, he resumed his education, taking an M.A. at Columbia (1948), then a Doctorat de l'Université at the Sorbonne in 1950.

In the 1950s, Ferlinghetti played a major role in catalyzing the Beat movement in San Francisco, the city that would eventually make him its first poet laureate, in 1998. In 1953, with Peter D. Martin he founded the first all-paperback bookstore in the country, City Lights Bookstore, a key site of avant-garde literary activity. He also founded the City Lights imprint in 1955. As the publisher of Ginsberg's *"Howl" and Other Poems* (1956), he aroused international attention when, with the help of the American Civil Liberties Union, he defended himself in court against charges of printing lewd and indecent material.

Ferlinghetti also issued a mimeographed magazine that he called "Beatitude," in reference to the beatific side, the "renaissance of wonder" ("I Am Waiting"), of Beat poetry. This equivocal name also alluded to being "beat" in the sense of being exhausted. He pursued euphoria by various means: one was Eastern religion (Zen Buddhism being preferred). Another was love, and many of his poems are love poems. Still another was circus antics; he borrowed from Henry Miller the title for *A Coney Island of the Mind* (1958), which became a best-seller in poetry. The final means was drugs. All were ways of finding one's uniqueness. At times, he defined himself against something, flouting and satirizing the establishment institutions of U.S. capitalism, politics, and academia. "A poet, by definition," he said, "has to be an enemy of the State" (*The Independent* [London], May 17, 1998). Accordingly, Ferlinghetti wrote poems of political high jinks, such as "Tentative Description of a Dinner to Promote the Impeachment of President Eisenhower." In other poems, he objects to billboards and to car-addicted America. "Who stole America?" he asks in "Starting from San Francisco." In "Junkman's Obbligato," he espouses "walking anarchy"—perhaps something like the organized chaos, ambling irreverence, and risk-taking energy of his poems.

[In Goya's Greatest Scenes We Seem to See]

In Goya's greatest scenes[1] we seem to see
                                        the people of the world
          exactly at the moment when
                    they first attained the title of
                                        'suffering humanity'   5
               They writhe upon the page
                         in a veritable rage
                                        of adversity
               Heaped up
                    groaning with babies and bayonets   10
                                        under cement skies
               in an abstract landscape of blasted trees
                    bent statues bats wings and beaks
                              slippery gibbets
                    cadavers and carnivorous cocks   15
          and all the final hollering monsters
                    of the
                                        'imagination of disaster'
               they are so bloody real
                         it is as if they really still existed   20

1. Francisco Goya y Lucientes (1746–1828), Spanish painter and etcher, did a series of etchings, "Disasters of War" (1810–13), that express his outrage at a world at war.

And they do

     Only the landscape is changed

They still are ranged along the roads
    plagued by legionnaires
        false windmills and demented roosters   25

They are the same people
                only further from home
   on freeways fifty lanes wide
        on a concrete continent
            spaced with bland billboards   30
     illustrating imbecile illusions of happiness

     The scene shows fewer tumbrils
        but more strung-out citizens
               in painted cars
   and they have strange license plates   35
and engines
      that devour America

                        1958

Dog

The dog trots freely in the street
and sees reality
and the things he sees
are bigger than himself
and the things he sees
are his reality   5
Drunks in doorways
Moons on trees
The dog trots freely thru the street
and the things he sees
are smaller than himself   10
Fish on newsprint
Ants in holes
Chickens in Chinatown windows
their heads a block away   15
The dog trots freely in the street
and the things he smells
smell something like himself
The dog trots freely in the street
past puddles and babies   20
cats and cigars
poolrooms and policemen
He doesn't hate cops
He merely has no use for them

and he goes past them   25
and past the dead cows hung up whole
in front of the San Francisco Meat Market
He would rather eat a tender cow
than a tough policeman
though either might do   30
And he goes past the Romeo Ravioli Factory
and past Coit's Tower
and past Congressman Doyle of the Unamerican Committee[2]
He's afraid of Coit's Tower
but he's not afraid of Congressman Doyle   35
although what he hears is very discouraging
very depressing
very absurd
to a sad young dog like himself
to a serious dog like himself   40
But he has his own free world to live in
His own fleas to eat
He will not be muzzled
Congressman Doyle is just another
fire hydrant   45
to him
The dog trots freely in the street
and has his own dog's life to live
and to think about
and to reflect upon   50
touching and tasting and testing everything
investigating everything
without benefit of perjury
a real realist
with a real tale to tell   55
and a real tail to tell it with
a real live
       barking
         democratic dog
engaged in real   60
        free enterprise
with something to say
         about ontology
something to say
        about reality   65
           and how to see it
              and how to hear it
with his head cocked sideways
        at streetcorners
as if he is just about to have   70
        his picture taken
          for Victor Records

---

2. Clyde Doyle (1887–1963), California congressman and member of the House of Representatives' Un-American Activities Committee, which mounted witch-hunts against communists and others it considered subversive.

listening for
His Master's Voice
and looking   75
like a living questionmark
into the
great gramophone
of puzzling existence
with its wondrous hollow horn   80
which always seems
just about to spout forth
some Victorious answer
to everything

1958

Retired Ballerinas, Central Park West[3]

Retired ballerinas on winter afternoons
walking their dogs
in Central Park West
(or their cats on leashes—
the cats themselves old highwire artists)   5
The ballerinas
leap and pirouette
through Columbus Circle
while winos on park benches
(laid back like drunken Goudonovs)[4]   10
hear the taxis trumpet together
like horsemen of the apocalypse
in the dusk of the gods
It is the final witching hour
when swains are full of swan songs   15
And all return through the dark dusk
to their bright cells
in glass highrises
or sit down to oval cigarettes and cakes
in the Russian Tea Room[5]   20
or climb four flights to back rooms
in Westside brownstones
where faded playbill photos
fall peeling from their frames
like last year's autumn leaves   25

1981

3. Fashionable avenue on New York City's Upper West Side, overlooking Central Park, just above Columbus Circle (line 8).
4. Boris Godunov, a czar of Russia, is the hero of an 1874 opera by the Russian composer Modest Petrovich Mussorgsky (1839–1881).
5. Expensive restaurant near Columbus Circle.

LOUISE BENNETT
1919–2006

Once thought of as a mere entertainer, Jamaican writer Louise Bennett emerged as the preeminent West Indian poet of Creole verse. Varieties of Creole, everyday speech in the West Indies, were forged by Caribbean slaves in the seventeenth and eighteenth centuries from English dialects, other European languages, and African languages such as Twi and Ewe. Early in life, Bennett chose to write and perform poetry in Creole, even though both the British who colonized Jamaica from 1655 to 1962 and middle-class Jamaicans saw it as a corruption of Standard English.

Bennett was not recognized as a poet until the late 1960s because she worked in Jamaican English. The Jamaican Poetry League excluded her from its meetings, and editors failed to include her in anthologies. Now acknowledged as a crucial precursor for a wide range of Caribbean poets—from "literary" poets such as Kamau Brathwaite and Lorna Goodison to "dub," or performance, poets—Bennett "persisted writing in dialect in spite of all the opposition," as she told an interviewer, "because nobody else was doing so and there was such rich material in the dialect that I felt I wanted to put on paper some of the wonderful things that people say in dialect. You could never say 'look here' as vividly as 'kuyah.' " Creole allowed her to "express" herself "so much more strongly and vividly than in Standard English"; it seemed "rich in wit and humour" because the "nature of Jamaican dialect is the nature of comedy" ("Bennett on Bennett"). Since Bennett's use of this oral language can at first present foreign readers with difficulties, she has been seen as a more "local" poet than, say, fellow West Indian Derek Walcott. But her vital characters, humorous situations, and robust imagination help overcome these barriers.

Bennett brilliantly manipulates the humor of Creole, the ironic possibilities of dramatic monologue, and the symmetrical contrasts and inversions afforded by the ballad stanza. She enriches English-language poetry with the phonemic wit and play of Creole words such as *boonoonoonoos* for "pretty" and *boogooyagga* for "worthless." Some of her poems directly address problems of non-Standard language and status, as when the wry speaker of "Dry-Foot Bwoy" deflates the pretensions of a Jamaican boy who tries to mimic British English. This situation is reversed in the dramatic monologue "No Lickle Twang," which directs irony toward its speaker: because she wishes he had returned from his stay in the United States with symbols of an improved status, including Standard English, a mother absurdly asks her son to call his father by what she imagines is a Standard English word, "Poo."

Bennett wrote many poems from the perspective of the trickster. Indeed, she likened herself to a major trickster of the West Indies, the spider-hero Anancy, whose wily ways in language and deed often land him in trouble, but also help him fool his adversaries. Like the crafty "Jamaica Oman [Woman]" and "South Parade Peddler" celebrated in two of her funniest poems, Bennett's typically female tricksters cunningly subvert the hierarchies that would rob them of power. No one is safe from Bennett's all-encompassing irony. She irreverently mocks British imperialists and Jamaicans, nationalists and antinationalists. "Pass fi White," a poem built around multiple puns on the word *pass*, ridicules both imperialist racial hierarchies and a Jamaican's foolish entrapment within them. In "Colonization in Reverse," Bennett ironically inverts Britain's xenophobic apprehension at the influx of Jamaican migrants, while also wondering if some Jamaicans on welfare are exploiting the British even as they were once exploited. At the crucial moment of Jamaican independence, Bennett pokes fun at the commodification of nationalist symbols and the inflated hopes and pretensions of Jamaica's proud new citizens, in such poems as "Independence Dignity" and "Independance." She celebrates the Jamaican nation not through solemn encomium; instead, she embodies its carnivalesque capacity for mockery and self-mockery.

Bennett was born on September 7, 1919, in Kingston. Her mother was a dressmaker, her father a baker who died when she was seven. While still in high school, she began to perform her Creole poetry, making her debut performance at nineteen. Bennett brought out her first book of poetry, *Dialect Verses*, in 1942, and the next year, she began to publish poetry on a weekly basis in Jamaica's national newspaper, the *Gleaner*. After studying journalism, social work, and local folklore in Jamaica, she attended the Royal Academy of Dramatic Art, in London, on a British Council scholarship from 1945 to 1947, returning homesick to Jamaica to teach high school drama for two years. She went back to Britain to resume her acting career and her work on a special Caribbean program for the BBC, then lived in the United States from 1953 to 1955, performing on radio and the stage in New York and its environs. She married her longtime associate Eric Coverley in 1954, and the couple returned to Jamaica the following year. While writing and performing her poetry, she also gathered Jamaican folklore, traveled extensively in her work as drama specialist for the Jamaican Social Welfare Commission (1955–63), and lectured on folklore and drama for the extramural department of the University of the West Indies (1959–61).

Bennett also created her own regular radio show, "Miss Lou's Views" (1966–82), and a children's television program, "Ring Ding" (1970–82). Building a mass audience in Jamaica for performance genres, "Miss Lou" regularly delivered dramatic renditions of plays, folk songs, and pantomime, sometimes before tens of thousands. Jamaican schoolchildren have often recited competitively her dramatic monologues, sometimes with Bennett serving as judge. She received many awards, including the Order of Jamaica (1974) and the Musgrave Gold Medal of the Institute of Jamaica (1978). In the early 1980s, she moved to North America, and she lived in Toronto, Canada, until her death.

South Parade Peddler

Hairnet! Scissors! Fine-teet comb!
—Whe de nice lady deh?
Buy a scissors from me, no, lady?
Hair pin? Tootpase? Go weh!
Me seh go-weh aready, ef   5
Yuh doan like it, see me.
Yuh dah swell like bombin plane fun[1]—
Yuh soon bus up like Graf Spee.[2]

Yuh favour—Shoeslace! Powder puff!
Clothes hanger! Belt! Pen knife!   10
Buy something, no, nice young man?
Buy a hairnet fi yuh wife.
Buy someting wid de change, no, sah,
An meck de Lawd bless yuh!
Me no sell farden[3] hair curler, sah!   15
Yuh fas an facety to![4]

1. Fund. Many of the ensuing notes are indebted to Mervyn Morris's annotations in Louise Bennett, *Selected Poems* (Kingston, 1983).
2. German battleship blown up by its own captain in 1939.
3. Farthing.
4. Fast and rude, too.

Teck yuh han outa me box!
Pudung[5] me razor blade!
Yuh no got no use fi it, for yuh
Dah suffer from hair raid![6]   20
Nice boonoonoonoos[7] lady, come,
Me precious, come dis way.
Hair pin? Yes, mah, tank yuh, yuh is
De bes one fi de day.

Toot-brush? Ah beg yuh pardon, sah—   25
Me never see yuh mout:
Dem torpedo yuh teet, sah, or
Yuh female lick dem out?
No bodder pick me up, yaw, sah!
Yuh face look like a seh   30
Yuh draw it outa lucky box.
No bodder me—go weh!

One police man dah come, but me
Dah try get one more sale.
Shoeslace! Tootpase! Buy quick, no, sah!   35
Yuh waan me go a jail?
Ef dah police ever ketch we, Lize,
We peddler career done.
Pick up yuh foot eena yuh han.
Hair pin! Hair curler! Run!   40

                                                          1942

Pass fi White

Miss Jane jus hear from Merica—
Her daughter proudly write
Fi seh[8] she fail her exam, but
She passin dere fi white!

She seh fi tell de trute she know   5
Her brain part not so bright—
She couldn pass tru college
So she try fi pass fi white.

She passin wid her work-mate-dem,
She passin wid her boss,   10
An a nice white bwoy she love dah gwan
Wid her like seh she pass![9]

5. Put down.
6. Pun on *air raid*.
7. Pretty; term of endearment.
8. To say.

9. She's passing with her coworkers, passing with her boss, and passing with a nice boy she loves who's going along with her as though she had passed.

But sometime she get fretful and
Her heart start gallop fas
An she bruck out eena cole-sweat   15
Jussa wonder ef she pass!

Jane get bex[1] seh she sen de gal
Fi learn bout edication,
It look like seh de gal gawn weh
Gawn work pon her complexion.   20

She no haffi tan a foreign[2]
Under dat deh strain an fright
For plenty copper-colour gal
Deh home yah[3] dah play white.

Her fambily is nayga,[4] but   25
Dem pedigree is right—
She hope de gal no gawn an tun
No boogooyagga[5] white.

De gal puppa[6] dah laugh an seh
It serve Merica right—   30
Five year back dem Jim-Crow him, now
Dem pass him pickney white.[7]

Him dah boast[8] all bout de distric
How him daughter is fus-class,
How she smarter dan American   35
An over deh dah pass!

Some people tink she pass B.A.,
Some tink she pass D.R.—
Wait till dem fine out seh she ongle
Pass de colour bar.[9]   40

1949, 1966

No Lickle[1] Twang

Me glad fi see yuh come back, bwoy,
But lawd, yuh let me dung;
Me shame a yuh so till all a
Me proudness drop a grung.[2]

---

1. Vexed.
2. She doesn't have to stay abroad.
3. Here.
4. Negro (pejorative in Jamaican Creole).
5. Low-class; worthless.
6. Papa.
7. Five years ago they persecuted him with racist Jim Crow laws, but now they pass his child as white.
8. Boasts.
9. Wait until they find out she only passed the color bar.
1. Little.
2. Ground. *Dung:* down.

Yuh mean yuh go dah Merica   5
An spen six whole mont deh,
An come back not a piece better
Dan how yuh did go weh?

Bwoy, yuh no shame? Is so yuh come?
After yuh tan so lang!   10
Not even lickle language, bwoy?
Not even lickle twang?

An yuh sister what work ongle³
One week wid Merican
She talk so nice now dat we have   15
De jooce⁴ fi understan?

Bwoy, yuh couldn improve yuhself!
An yuh get so much pay?
Yuh spen six mont a foreign, an
Come back ugly same way?   20

Not even a drapes trousiz,⁵ or
A pass de riddim coat?
Bwoy, not even a gole teet⁶ or
A gole chain roun yuh troat?

Suppose me laas me pass⁷ go introjooce   25
Yuh to a stranger
As me lamented son what lately
Come from Merica!

Dem hooda laugh after me, bwoy!
Me couldn tell dem so!   30
Dem hooda seh me lie, yuh wasa
Spen time back a Mocho!⁸

No back-answer me, bwoy—yuh talk
Too bad! Shet up yuh mout!
Ah doan know how yuh an yuh puppa⁹   35
Gwine to meck it out.

Ef yuh waan please him, meck him tink
Yuh bring back someting new.
Yuh always call him 'Pa'—dis evenin
When him come, seh 'Poo'.¹   40

1949

---

3. Only.
4. Deuce.
5. Style of trousers popular in the 1940s.
6. Gold tooth. *Pass de riddim coat:* a coat that comes down past (pass) the rhythm section (riddim)—that is, buttocks. Many Jamaican farmers returning from the United States wore such coats.
7. Lose my path; become lost.

8. Back at Mocho. Mocho is a name used to indicate a place of extreme backwardness.
9. Papa.
1. A version of *Papa;* part of a street vendor's cry; baby word for feces. Since Jamaican Creole often turns Standard English *o* sounds into *a* sounds, the speaker is hypercorrecting. "Pa," she seems to think, must be a Creole usage to be corrected.

Dry-Foot Bwoy[2]

Wha wrong wid Mary dry-foot bwoy?
Dem gal got him fi mock,[3]
An when me meet him tarra night
De bwoy gi me a shock!

Me tell him seh him auntie an   5
Him cousin dem sen howdy[4]
An ask him how him getting awn.
Him seh, 'Oh, jolley, jolley!'

Me start fi feel so sorry fi
De po bad-lucky soul,   10
Me tink him come a foreign lan
Come ketch bad foreign cole!

Me tink him got a bad sore-troat,
But as him chat-chat gwan
Me fine out seh is foreign twang   15
De bwoy wasa put awn![5]

For me notice dat him answer
To nearly all me seh
Was 'Actually', 'What', 'Oh deah!'
An all dem sinting deh.[6]   20

Me gi a joke, de gal dem laugh;
But hear de bwoy, 'Haw-haw!
I'm sure you got that bally-dash[7]
Out of the cinema!'

Same time me laas me temper, an   25
Me holler, 'Bwoy, kirout![8]
No chat to me wid no hot pittata
Eena yuh mout!'

Him tan[9] up like him stunted, den
Hear him no, 'How silley!   30
I don't think that I really
Understand you, actually.'

Me seh, 'Yuh understan me, yaw!
No yuh name Cudjoe Scoop?
Always visit Nana kitchen an   35
Gi laugh fi gungoo soup![1]

2. Thin-legged (inexperienced) boy.
3. The girls are mocking him.
4. I told him that his auntie and his cousins sent [or send] greetings.
5. But as he kept talking I realized his foreign accent was put on.
6. And all them things there.
7. Nonsense; balderdash.
8. Clear out.
9. Stand.
1. Chastising the boy for his pretensions, the speaker reminds him that he is Afro-Jamaican.

'An now all yuh can seh is "actually"?
Bwoy, but tap!
Wha happen to dem sweet Jamaica
Joke yuh use fi pop?'   40

Him get bex[2] and walk tru de door,
Him head eena de air;
De gal-dem bawl out affa him,[3]
'Not going? What! Oh deah!'

An from dat night till tedeh, mah,   45
Dem all got him fi mock.
Miss Mary dry-foot bwoy!
Cyaan get over de shock!

                                                        1957

Colonization in Reverse

What a joyful news, Miss Mattie;
Ah feel like me heart gwine burs—
Jamaica people colonizin
Englan in reverse.[4]

By de hundred, by de tousan,   5
From country an from town,
By de ship-load, by de plane-load,
Jamaica is Englan boun.

Dem a pour out a Jamaica;
Everybody future plan   10
Is fi get a big-time job
An settle in de motherlan.

What a islan! What a people!
Man an woman, ole an young
Jussa pack dem bag an baggage   15
An tun history upside dung![5]

Some people doan like travel,
But fi show dem loyalty
Dem all a open up cheap-fare-
To-Englan agency;   20

An week by week dem shippin off
Dem countryman like fire

Cudjoe and *Nana*: African names used in Jamaica.
Gungoo: congo pea.
2. Vexed.
3. The girls went crying after him.
4. Encouraged by the postwar labor shortage in
England and the scarcity of work at home, three
hundred thousand Jamaicans migrated to Britain
from 1948 to 1962.
5. Down.

Fi immigrate an populate
De seat a de Empire.

Oonoo[6] se how life is funny,   25
Oonoo see de tunabout?
Jamaica live fi box bread
Out a English people mout.

For when dem catch a Englan
An start play dem different role   30
Some will settle down to work
An some will settle fi de dole.[7]

Jane seh de dole is not too bad
Because dey payin she
Two pounds a week fi seek a job   35
Dat suit her dignity.

Me seh Jane will never fine work
At de rate how she dah look
For all day she stay pon Aunt Fan couch
An read love-story book.   40

What a devilment a Englan!
Dem face war an brave de worse;
But ah wonderin how dem gwine stan
Colonizin in reverse.

1957

Independance

Independance wid a vengeance!
Independance raisin Cain!
Jamaica start grow beard, ah hope
We chin can stan de strain!

When dawg marga him head big, an   5
When puss hungry him nose clean;[8]
But every puss an dog no know
What Independance mean.

Mattie seh it mean we facety,[9]
Stan up pon we dignity,   10
An we don't allow nobody
Fi teck liberty wid we.

---

6. You (plural).
7. For unemployment benefits.
8. Jamaican proverbs: "When the dog is meager his head is big (i.e., proud)," and "when the cat is hungry his sense of smell is keen (the cat will have to get his nose dirty to survive)."
9. Proud; impudent.

Independance is we nature
Born an bred in all we do,
An she glad fi see dat Government   15
Tun independant to.

She hope dem caution worl-map
Fi stop draw Jamaica small,
For de lickle speck cyaan show[1]
We independantness at all!   20

Moresomever we must tell map dat
We don't like we position—
Please kindly teck we out a sea
An draw we in de ocean.

What a crosses! Independance   25
Woulda never have a chance
Wid so much boogooyagga[2]
Dah expose dem ignorance.

Dog wag him tail fi suit him size
An match him stamina—   30
Jamaica people need a
Independance formula!

No easy-come-by freeness tings,[3]
Nuff labour, some privation,
Not much of dis an less of dat   35
An plenty studiration.[4]

Independance wid a vengeance!
Wonder how we gwine to cope?
Jamaica start smoke pipe, ah hope
We got nuff jackass rope![5]   40

1961

Independence Dignity

Dear Cousin Min, yuh miss sinting,[6]
Yuh should be over yah[7]
Fi see Independence Celebration
Capture Jamaica.

Yuh waan see how Jamaica people   5
Rise to de occasion
An deestant[8] up demself fi greet
De birt a dem new nation!

---

1. The little speck can't show.
2. Backward people.
3. Things gotten for free.
4. Studying.

5. Local tobacco.
6. Something.
7. Here.
8. Decent.

Not a stone was fling, not a samfie[9] sting,
Not a soul gwan bad an lowrated;[1]   10
Not a fight bruck out, not a bad-wud shout
As Independence was celebrated.

Concert outa street an lane an park
Wid big-time acs performin,
An we dance outa street   15
From night till soon a mornin.

Fi de whole long mont a Augus
Independence was in prime;
Everyting was Independence ting
Roun Independence time.   20

Independence pen an pencil,
Cup an saucer, glass an tray;
Down to Independence baby bawn
Pon Independence Day.

An de Independence light-dem   25
Jussa pretty up de night-dem
An a sweeten up de crowd fi
Look an wonder at de sight.

Dere was functions by de tousan
An we crowd up every one;   30
From Packy Piece to Macka Town
De behaviour was gran.

Yuh waan see Jane unruly an
Unmannasable gal
Dah stan up straight an sing out   35
'Teach us true respec for all!'[2]

Fan lazy bwoy who spen him time
A cotch up[3] Joe shop wall
Serious up him face an holler
'Stir response to duty's call!'   40

Teet[4] an tongue was all united,
Heart an soul was hans an glove,
Fenky-fenky[5] voice gain vigour
Pon 'Jamaica, land we love'.[6]

It was a sight fi cure sore yeye,   45
A time fi live fi see:

---

9. Con artist.
1. Badly behaved.
2. Beginning of the Jamaican national anthem's second verse.

3. Leaning on.
4. Teeth.
5. Puny.
6. From the end of the national anthem.

Jamaica Independence
Celebration dignity.

1966

Jamaica Oman[7]

Jamaica oman cunny, sah![8]
Is how dem jinnal so?[9]
Look how long dem liberated
An de man dem never know!

Look how long Jamaica oman   5
—Modder, sister, wife, sweetheart—
Outa road an eena yard[1] deh pon
A dominate her part!

From Maroon Nanny[2] teck her body
Bounce bullet back pon man,   10
To when nowadays gal-pickney[3] tun
Spellin-Bee champion.

From de grass root to de hill-top,
In profession, skill an trade,
Jamaica oman teck her time   15
Dah mount an meck de grade.

Some backa man a push, some side-a
Man a hole him han,
Some a lick sense eena man head,
Some a guide him pon him plan!   20

Neck an neck an foot an foot wid man
She buckle hole[4] her own;
While man a call her 'so-so rib'
Oman a tun backbone![5]

An long before Oman Lib[6] bruck out   25
Over foreign lan
Jamaica female wasa work
Her liberated plan!

Jamaica oman know she strong,
She know she tallawah,[7]   30

---

7. Woman.
8. Cunning, sir.
9. How are they so tricky?
1. Home.
2. Jamaican national hero who led the Maroons, fugitive slaves, in battle during the eighteenth century. Bullets reputedly ricocheted off her and killed her enemies.
3. Girl-child.
4. Take hold.
5. Eve is said to have come from Adam's rib (Genesis 2.21–22).
6. Women's Liberation Movement.
7. Sturdy.

But she no want her pickney-dem
Fi start call her 'Puppa'.[8]

So de cunny Jamma[9] oman
Gwan like pants-suit is a style,
An Jamaica man no know she wear   35
De trousiz all de while!

So Jamaica oman coaxin
Fambly budget from explode
A so Jamaica man a sing
'Oman a heaby load!'[1]   40

But de cunny Jamma oman
Ban her belly,[2] bite her tongue,
Ketch water, put pot pon fire
An jus dig her toe a grung.[3]

For 'Oman luck deh a dungle',[4]   45
Some rooted more dan some,
But as long as fowl a scratch dungle heap
Oman luck mus come!

Lickle by lickle man start praise her,
Day by day de praise a grow;   50
So him praise her, so it sweet her,
For she wonder if him know.

                                            1975

8. Papa. *Pickney*: children.
9. Jamaican.
1. A folk song often sung while working in the fields.
2. Binds her belly (a practice associated with grief;

also a suggestion of belt tightening, as in hunger).
3. And just digs her toes into the ground.
4. That is, woman's luck will be rediscovered (proverbial). *Dungle*: garbage dump.

HOWARD NEMEROV
1920–1991

"Immediate and mutual lust" is what pornography promises, and yet in reality, Howard Nemerov wryly concludes, "We think about sex obsessively except / During the act, when our minds tend to wander" ("Reading Pornography in Old Age"). Nemerov builds his elegantly crafted poems around sly ironies and unexpected convergences, such as the lovers and the grinning death's head of "The Goose Fish." He approaches his subjects obliquely, taking his readers a little by surprise and upsetting conventional ways of seeing things. Though often formally metered and rhymed, his poems move sinuously and combat fixities. He deplores any kind of idolatry, any institution or cliché that blinds our appreciation of the free and lively movements of life.

Nemerov grew up in a literary atmosphere dominated by T. S. Eliot, W. B. Yeats, and W. H. Auden, and he began by imitating them, but his own poetry moved steadily away from modernist ambiguity toward lucidity and precision. Nemerov came to regard "simplicity and the appearance of ease in the measure as primary values" ("Attentiveness and Obedience"). He was committed to wit—to seeing relationships among disparate phenomena and creating metaphors. For him, poetry was the art of "combination, or discovering the secret valences which the most widely differing things have for one another" (*Poets in Progress*, ed. Edward Hungerford, 1967). Nemerov's new combinations of experience often emerge as jokes, and one of the pleasures of reading his poems is watching the shifts in his comic sense. The tone of Nemerov's later poems is casual yet elegant and precise, familiar without condescension, clear yet lively and provocative. Their melancholy is never ponderous. He valued "[s]eriousness, but not solemnity" (*Washington Post*, October 4, 1988).

Nemerov was born on March 1, 1920, into a Jewish family in New York City, where he lived until 1937. He received his A.B. from Harvard University in 1941, "in nice time for a summer vacation before entering the war" (*Twentieth Century Authors*, First Supplement, 1955), then enlisted in the Royal Canadian Air Force and became a pilot, flying combat missions against German shipping in the North Sea; he joined the U.S. Army Air Corps for the last two years of the war. Married in 1944, Nemerov became a professor at several college campuses, including Bennington College (1948–66) and Washington University (1976–91). He served as poetry consultant to the Library of Congress in 1963–64 and again in 1988–90, when the post had been retitled poet laureate. In 1978, he won the Pulitzer Prize and the National Book Award for his *Collected Poems*; in 1981, he won the Bollingen Prize. When awarded the National Medal of Arts in 1987, he said, with characteristic self-mockery, that he was pleased to be honored by a country "where poets are, for the most part, an impertinence, like birds at an airport" (*St. Louis Post-Dispatch*, July 9, 1991).

The Goose Fish

On the long shore, lit by the moon
To show them properly alone,
Two lovers suddenly embraced
So that their shadows were as one.
The ordinary night was graced   5
For them by the swift tide of blood
That silently they took at flood,
And for a little time they prized
    Themselves emparadised.

Then, as if shaken by stage-fright   10
Beneath the hard moon's bony light,
They stood together on the sand
Embarrassed in each other's sight
But still conspiring hand in hand,
Until they saw, there underfoot,   15
As though the world had found them out,
The goose fish turning up, though dead,
    His hugely grinning head.

There in the china light he lay,
Most ancient and corrupt and grey   20
They hesitated at his smile,
Wondering what it seemed to say
To lovers who a little while
Before had thought to understand,
By violence upon the sand,   25
The only way that could be known
    To make a world their own.

It was a wide and moony grin
Together peaceful and obscene;
They knew not what he would express,   30
So finished a comedian
He might mean failure or success,
But took it for an emblem of
Their sudden, new and guilty love
To be observed by, when they kissed,   35
    That rigid optimist.

So he became their patriarch,
Dreadfully mild in the half-dark.
His throat that the sand seemed to choke,
His picket teeth, these left their mark   40
But never did explain the joke
That so amused him, lying there
While the moon went down to disappear
Along the still and tilted track
    That bears the zodiac.   45

                                                    1955

The Icehouse in Summer

see Amos, 3:15[1]

A door sunk in a hillside, with a bolt
thick as the boy's arm, and behind that door
the walls of ice, melting a blue, faint light,
an air of cedar branches, sawdust, fern:
decaying seasons keeping from decay.   5

A summer guest, the boy had never seen
(a servant told him of it) how the lake
froze three foot thick, how farmers came with teams,
with axe and saw, to cut great blocks of ice,
translucid, marbled, glittering in the sun,   10

1. " 'I will smite the winter house with the summer
house; and the houses of ivory shall perish, and the
great houses shall come to an end,' says the Lord."

Amos, a shepherd and prophet, was warning the
Israelites of God's retribution for their transgres-
sions.

load them on sleds and drag them up the hill
to be manhandled down the narrow path
and set in courses for the summer's keeping,
the kitchen uses and luxuriousness
of the great houses. And he heard how once   15
a team and driver drowned in the break of spring:
the man's cry melting from the ice that summer
frightened the sherbet-eaters off the terrace.

Dust of the cedar, lost and evergreen
among the slowly blunting water walls   20
where the blade edge melted and the steel saw's bite
was rounded out, and the horse and rider drowned
in the red sea's blood,[2] I was the silly child
who dreamed that riderless cry, and saw the guests
run from a ghostly wall, so long before   25
the winter house fell with the summer house,
and the houses, Egypt, the great houses, had an end.

1960

Snowflakes

Not slowly wrought, nor treasured for their form
In heaven, but by the blind self of the storm
Spun off, each driven individual
Perfected in the moment of his fall.

1973

Gyroscope[3]

This admirable gadget, when it is
Wound on a string and spun with steady force,
Maintains its balance on most any smooth
Surface, pleasantly humming as it goes.
It is whirled not on a constant course, but still   5
Stands in unshivering integrity
For quite some time, meaning nothing perhaps
But being something agreeable to watch,
A silver nearly silence gleaning a still-
ness out of speed, composing unity   10
From spin, so that its hollow spaces seem
Solids of light, until it wobbles and

2. Alludes to the Israelites' escape from Egypt through the miraculously parted Red Sea, which then rejoined, destroying Pharoah's horsemen.

3. A wheel mounted in a set of rings so that its axis of rotation is free to turn in any direction.

Begins to whine, and then with an odd lunge
Eccentric and reckless, it skids away
And drops dead into its own skeleton.   15

                                                              1975

Reading Pornography in Old Age

Unbridled licentiousness with no holds barred,
Immediate and mutual lust, satisfiable
In the heat, upon demand, aroused again
And satisfied again, lechery unlimited.

Till space runs out at the bottom of the page   5
And another pair of lovers, forever young,
Prepotent,[4] endlessly receptive, renews
The daylong, nightlong, interminable grind.

How decent it is, and how unlike our lives
Where "fuck you" is a term of vengeful scorn   10
And the murmur of "sorry, partner" as often heard
As ever in mixed doubles or at bridge.

Though I suspect the stuff is written by
Elderly homosexuals manacled to their
Machines, it's mildly touching all the same,   15
A reminiscence of the life that was in Eden

Before the Fall, when we were beautiful
And shameless, and untouched by memory:
Before we were driven out to the laboring world
Of the money and the garbage and the kids   20

In which we read this nonsense and are moved
At all that was always lost for good, in which
We think about sex obsessively except
During the act, when our minds tend to wander.

                                                              1984

---

4. Having exceptional power; very potent.

AMY CLAMPITT
1920–1994

Years after Sylvia Plath, John Berryman, Anne Sexton, and Robert Lowell had died, an unknown contemporary of theirs came to prominence. In 1983, at sixty-three, Amy Clampitt published her first full-length book of poetry, *The Kingfisher* (she had previously published two chapbooks). Although her career proved that the energy of her literary generation was not spent, Clampitt was a very different kind of poet from the confessionals. Whereas agonized rebellion fuels much of their poetry, Clampitt is more affiliative. She, too, writes ambivalent elegies for her mother ("A Procession at Candlemas") and father ("Beethoven, Opus 111"), but without the self-dramatizing violence of rejection. Journeying "down the long-unentered nave of childhood" to recover her maternal origins, to stitch up "the lost connection" between mother and daughter, Clampitt honors the interwovenness of each life with its maternal source—hence her images of layering, wrapping, knotting, quilting, and threading. Through bold comparisons of her father, an Iowa farmer, with Beethoven, she commemorates her parent as an unwitting artist of the earthly sublime.

Clampitt was also on more peaceful terms with her literary parents, openly declaring her debts to older poets. From Gerard Manley Hopkins she borrows the epigraph for *The Kingfisher* ("As kingfishers catch fire, dragonflies draw flame . . ."), as well as his hyphenated compounds and dense sonic clusters. She dedicates a sequence of biographical poems to John Keats, as well as to George Eliot and William and Dorothy Wordsworth, and Keats's luxurious sensuousness also inspires her verse. Few postwar American poets are as comfortable with their British literary inheritance. And like the American modernist Marianne Moore, she often creates odd assortments, poems that ponder and transform the quotidian world observed by science.

At a time when some American writers were seeking to make poetry ever more elemental, self-sufficient, and stripped down, Clampitt sprawled in lush fields of diction and allusion. Her language dilates in multiple directions, taking in works of music and visual art as well as scientific disciplines such as botany, geology, and ornithology. "For the ocean," she writes in "Beach Glass," "nothing / is beneath consideration"; everything is continually reshuffled and recycled, from geological formations to the debris of driftwood and bottles to the great stained-glass windows of cathedrals that derive from sand and must ultimately return to it. Similarly, the poet's erudite and multilayered descriptions take up and turn over and over everything within reach, keeping an inventory of the worn out and cast away, as well as the "permutations of novelty."

Clampitt's background might seem unpromising for such a wondrous delight in the arts. Having grown up on Depression-era farms in Iowa, she remembers the high-art world of music and painting as a luxury and a distraction: "High art / with a stiff neck," "harpstrings and fripperies of air / congealed into an object nailed against the wall" ("Beethoven, Opus 111"). From Clampitt's late Romantic perspective, great art is born of suffering, deprivation, and grief. Clampitt affirms poetic art as a precise tool for understanding losses, inheritances, loves, and our abundant, ever-shifting world. "What is real except // what's fabricated?" she asks in "A Procession at Candlemas." She fabricates with abandon, spinning out diaphanous texts that combine imaginative pleasure with scrupulous observation.

Clampitt's formal structures include long-lined tercets and short-lined verse paragraphs. Her descriptive language is expansive, proliferating adjectives and metaphors with sustained energy. Patterns of alliteration, assonance, and rhythmic parallelism bind together her words. Her syntax is complex, often building a sinuous momentum in extended sentences. It moves forward only to twist back on itself, hesitate, embroider, rush headlong, break off, and start again, all the while threading together long trains of association, feeling, and observation. Her poems often evoke complex resemblances between seemingly incongruous subjects—the ocean and the poet's mind, her father and Beethoven, her mother and the goddess Athena. Clampitt's poetry conveys both intellectual alertness and imaginative fecundity. Steeped in a wide-ranging knowledge of the past, it also reacquaints us, vividly, with our present.

A Quaker by background, Clampitt was born on June 15, 1920, in New Providence, Iowa. In 1941, she completed her B.A. at Grinnell College, and she did some graduate work at Columbia University before becoming a secretary at Oxford University Press. From 1952 to 1959, she was a reference librarian for the National Audubon Society, and indeed her poems keenly observe bird life. She then became a freelance writer, editor, and researcher. During the Vietnam War, she joined the antiwar movement, and in 1982, she turned full time to poetry writing. Living in New York, she summered and wrote in Maine. She died of ovarian cancer.

Beach Glass

While you walk the water's edge,
turning over concepts
I can't envision, the honking buoy
serves notice that at any time
the wind may change,   5
the reef-bell clatters
its treble monotone, deaf as Cassandra
to any note but warning.[1] The ocean,
cumbered by no business more urgent
than keeping open old accounts   10
that never balanced,
goes on shuffling its millenniums
of quartz, granite, and basalt.
                                        It behaves
toward the permutations of novelty—   15
driftwood and shipwreck, last night's
beer cans, spilt oil, the coughed-up
residue of plastic—with random
impartiality, playing catch or tag
or touch-last like a terrier,   20
turning the same thing over and over,
over and over. For the ocean, nothing
is beneath consideration.
                                        The houses
of so many mussels and periwinkles[2]   25
have been abandoned here, it's hopeless
to know which to salvage. Instead
I keep a lookout for beach glass—

1. The "reef-bell" warns ships about a reef of rocks or sand beneath the surface of the water. In Homer's *Iliad*, Cassandra prophesied the fall of Troy, but because of Apollo's curse, no one believed her.
2. Varieties of shellfish.

amber of Budweiser, chrysoprase
of Almadén and Gallo, lapis[3]   30
by way of (no getting around it,
I'm afraid) Phillips'
Milk of Magnesia, with now and then a rare
translucent turquoise or blurred amethyst
of no known origin.   35
                    The process
goes on forever: they came from sand,
they go back to gravel,
along with the treasuries
of Murano, the buttressed   40
astonishments of Chartres,[4]
which even now are readying
for being turned over and over as gravely
and gradually as an intellect
engaged in the hazardous   45
redefinition of structures
no one has yet looked at.

                                                         1983

Meridian

First daylight on the bittersweet-hung
sleeping porch at high summer : dew
all over the lawn, sowing diamond-
point-highlighted shadows :
the hired man's shadow revolving   5
along the walk, a flash of milkpails
passing : no threat in sight, no hint
anywhere in the universe, of that

apathy at the meridian, the noon
of absolute boredom : flies   10
crooning black lullabies in the kitchen,
milk-soured crocks, cream separator
still unwashed : what is there to life
but chores and more chores, dishwater,
fatigue, unwanted children : nothing   15
to stir the longueur of afternoon

except possibly thunderheads :
climbing, livid, turreted alabaster
lit up from within by splendor and terror
—forked lightning's   20
                    split-second disaster.

                                                         1983

3. Or lapis lazuli, a rich, sky-blue color (and the
name of a semiprecious stone). *Chrysoprase:* apple-
green color (also a semiprecious stone).

4. Chartres Cathedral, in France, is noted for the
beauty of its stained-glass windows. Murano, in
Italy, is famous for its glasswork.

A Procession at Candlemas[5]

I

Moving on or going back to where you came from,
bad news is what you mainly travel with:
a breakup or a breakdown, someone running off

or walking out, called up or called home:
death in the family. Nudged from their stanchions   5
outside the terminal, anonymous of purpose

as a flock of birds, the bison of the highway
funnel westward onto Route 80, mirroring
an entity that cannot look into itself and know

what makes it what it is. Sooner or later   10
every trek becomes a funeral procession.
The mother curtained in Intensive Care—

a scene the mind leaves blank, fleeing instead
toward scenes of transhumance, the belled sheep
moving up the Pyrenees,[6] red-tasseled pack llamas   15

footing velvet-green precipices, the Kurdish
women, jingling with bangles, gorgeous
on their rug-piled mounts—already lying dead,

bereavement altering the moving lights
to a processional, a feast of Candlemas.   20
Change as child-bearing, birth as a kind

of shucking off: out of what began
as a Mosaic[7] insult—such a loathing
of the common origin, even a virgin,

having given birth, needs purifying—   25
to carry fire as though it were a flower,
the terror and the loveliness entrusted

into naked hands, supposing God might have,
might actually need a mother: people have
at times found this a way of being happy.   30

A Candlemas of moving lights along Route 80;
lighted candles in a corridor from Arlington
over the Potomac, for every carried flame

---

5. Feast of the purification of the Virgin Mary and
presentation of the infant Jesus in the temple,
commemorated by candlelight on February 2.
6. Mountain chain in southwestern Europe.

Transhumance: seasonal transfer of livestock to
different pastures.
7. Related to Moses and the ancient Hebraic law.

the name of a dead soldier: an element
fragile as ego, frightening as parturition,   35
necessary and intractable as dreaming.

The lapped, wheelborne integument,[8] layer
within layer, at the core a dream of
something precious, ripped: Where are we?

The sleepers groan, stir, rewrap themselves   40
about the self's imponderable substance,
or clamber down, numb-footed, half in a drowse

of freezing dark, through a Stonehenge
of fuel pumps, the bison hulks slantwise
beside them, drinking. What is real except   45

what's fabricated? The jellies glitter
cream-capped in the cafeteria showcase;
gumball globes, Life Savers cinctured

in parcel gilt, plop from their housings
perfect, like miracles. Comb, nail clipper,   50
lip rouge, mirrors and emollients[9] embody,

niched into the washroom wall case,
the pristine seductiveness of money.
Absently, without inhabitants, this

nowhere oasis wears the place name   55
of Indian Meadows. The westward-trekking
transhumance, once only, of a people who,

in losing everything they had, lost even
the names they went by, stumbling past
like caribou, perhaps camped here. Who   60

can assign a trade-in value to that sorrow?
The monk in sheepskin over tucked-up saffron
intoning to a drum becomes the metronome

of one more straggle up Pennsylvania Avenue[1]
in falling snow, a whirl of tenderly   65
remorseless corpuscles, street gangs

amok among magnolias' pregnant wands,
a stillness at the heart of so much whirling:
beyond the torn integument of childbirth,

8. Skin.
9. Softeners.

1. Street in Washington, D.C., on which the
White House is located.

sometimes, wrapped like a papoose into a grief   70
not merely of the ego, you rediscover almost
the rest-in-peace of the placental coracle.[2]

II

Of what the dead were, living, one knows
so little as barely to recognize
the fabric of the backward-ramifying   75

antecedents, half-noted presences
in darkened rooms: the old, the feared,
the hallowed. Never the same river[3]

drowns the unalterable doorsill. An effigy
in olive wood or pear wood, dank   80
with the sweat of age, walled in the dark

at Brauron, Argos, Samos: even the unwed
Athene, who had no mother, born—it's declared—
of some man's brain like every other pure idea,

had her own wizened cult object, kept   85
out of sight like the incontinent whimperer
in the backstairs bedroom, where no child

ever goes—to whom, year after year,
the fair linen of the sacred peplos[4]
was brought in ceremonial procession—   90

flutes and stringed instruments, wildflower-
hung cattle, nubile Athenian girls, young men
praised for the beauty of their bodies. Who

can unpeel the layers of that seasonal
returning to the dark where memory fails,   95
as birds re-enter the ancestral flyway?

Daylight, snow falling, knotting of gears:
Chicago. Soot, the rotting backsides
of tenements, grimed trollshapes of ice

---

2. Small wicker boat. *Papoose:* Native American word for young child.
3. Pre-Socratic Greek philosopher Heracleitus (c. 540–c. 480 B.C.E.) declared the impossibility of stepping twice into the same river.
4. In ancient Greece, an embroidered shawl or robe, woven and presented in a great procession every four years as a gift to Athena; the frieze of the Parthenon depicts this procession. Although a monumental statue of Athena was in the Par-thenon, Clampitt cites in a note a statement that the sacred peplos was ritually offered to the older, wooden, doll-like image kept in the Erechtheum. "Similar wooden images were central to the worship of Artemis at Brauron, and of Hera at Argos and Samos" [Clampitt's note]. *Brauron, Argos:* Greek cities. *Samos:* Greek island. Athena, Greek goddess of wisdom and war, was not born but sprang fully armed from Zeus's skull.

underneath the bridges, the tunnel heaving   100
like a birth canal. Disgorged, the infant
howling in the restroom; steam-table cereal,

pale coffee; wall-eyed TV receivers, armchairs
of molded plastic: the squalor of the day
resumed, the orphaned litter taken up again   105

unloved, the spawn of botched intentions,
grief a mere hardening of the gut,
a set piece of what can't be avoided:

parents by the tens of thousands living
unthanked, unpaid but in the sour coin   110
of resentment. Midmorning gray as zinc

along Route 80, corn-stubble quilting
the underside of snowdrifts, the cadaverous
belvedere[5] of windmills, the sullen stare

of feedlot cattle; black creeks puncturing   115
white terrain, the frozen bottomland
a mush of willow tops; dragnetted in ice,

the Mississippi. Westward toward the dark,
the undertow of scenes come back to, fright
riddling the structures of interior history: 120

Where is it? Where, in the shucked-off
bundle, the hampered obscurity that has been
for centuries the mumbling lot of women,

did the thread of fire, too frail
ever to discover what it meant, to risk   125
even the taking of a shape, relinquish

the seed of possibility, unguessed-at
as a dream of something precious? Memory,
that exquisite blunderer, stumbling

like a migrant bird that finds the flyway   130
it hardly knew it knew except by instinct,
down the long-unentered nave of childhood,

late on a midwinter afternoon, alone
among the snow-hung hollows of the windbreak
on the far side of the orchard, encounters   135

5. Structure designed to command a view.

sheltering among the evergreens, a small
stilled bird, its cap of clear yellow
slit by a thread of scarlet—the untouched

nucleus of fire, the lost connection
hallowing the wizened effigy, the mother   140
curtained in Intensive Care: a Candlemas

of moving lights along Route 80, at nightfall,
in falling snow, the stillness and the sorrow
of things moving back to where they came from.

1983

Beethoven, Opus 111

For Norman Carey

There are epochs . . . when mankind, not content with the present,
longing for time's deeper layers, like the plowman, thirsts for the
virgin soil of time.

OSIP MANDELSTAM[6]

—Or, conversely, hungers
for the levitations of the concert hall:
the hands like rafts of *putti*[7]
out of a region where the dolorous stars
are fixed in glassy cerements of Art;   5
the *ancien régime*'s[8] diaphanous plash
athwart the mounting throb of hobnails—
shod squadrons of vibration
mining the air, its struck ores hardening
into a plowshare, a downward wandering   10
disrupting every formal symmetry:
from the supine harp-case, the strung-foot
tendons under the mahogany, the bulldozer
in the bass unearths a Piranesian[9]
catacomb: Beethoven ventilating,   15
with a sound he cannot hear, the cave-in
of recurring rage.
                         In the tornado country
of mid-America, my father
might have been his twin—a farmer   20
hacking at sourdock, at the strangle-

---

6. Russian poet and critic (1891–1938). Ludwig
van Beethoven (1770–1827), German composer
whose work both crowned the classical period and
helped initiate the Romantic period in European
music. Beethoven was already deaf when he com-
posed the Sonata No. 32 in C minor, Op. 111, in
1821–22.

7. Stylized infant cherubs (Italian).
8. Of the political and social system before the
French Revolution of 1789 (French). *Cerements*:
grave-clothes, usually made of wax.
9. Giovanni Battista Piranesi (1720–1778), Ital-
ian architect and artist.

roots of thistles and wild morning glories,
setting out rashly, one October,
to rid the fencerows of poison ivy:
livid seed-globs turreted   25
in trinities of glitter, ripe
with the malefic glee no farmer doubts
lives deep down things.[1] My father
was naïve enough—by nature
revolutionary, though he'd have   30
disowned the label—to suppose he might
in some way, minor but radical, disrupt
the givens of existence: set
his neighbors' thinking straight, undo
the stranglehold of reasons nations   35
send their boys off to war. That fall,
after the oily fireworks had cooled down
to trellises of hairy wicks,
he dug them up, rootstocks and all,
and burned them. Do-gooder!   40
The well-meant holocaust[2] became
a mist of venom, sowing itself along
the sculptured hollows of his overalls,
braceleting wrists and collarbone—
a mesh of blisters spreading to a shirt   45
worn like a curse. For weeks
he writhed inside it. Awful.
                   High art
with a stiff neck: an upright Steinway
bought in Chicago; a chromo of a Hobbema   50
tree-avenue, or of Millet's[3] imagined peasant,
the lark she listens to invisible, perhaps
irrelevant: harpstrings and fripperies of air
congealed into an object nailed against the wall,
its sole ironic function (if it has any)   55
to demonstrate that one, though he may
grunt and sweat at work, is not a clod.
Beethoven might declare the air
his domicile, the winds kin,[4] the tornado
a kind of second cousin; here,   60
his labor merely shimmers—a deracinated
album leaf, a bagatelle, the "Moonlight"
rendered with a dying fall[5] (the chords

1. Cf. "God's Grandeur," by English poet Gerard Manley Hopkins (1844–1889): "There lives the dearest freshness deep down things." *Malefic*: baleful, ominous.
2. Sacrifice completely consumed by fire.
3. Jean-François Millet (1814–1875): French painter renowned for his peasant subjects, in particular an often-imitated picture of a peasant pausing from her work to listen to an invisible lark. The European skylark sings only in flight, often too high to be seen, and its invisible song is often, as in Percy Bysshe Shelley's (1792–1822) "To a Sky-Lark," a Romantic symbol. *Chromo*: chromolithograph; a type of reproduced print. Meindhart Hobbema (1638–1709): Dutch Baroque landscape painter.
4. "In a letter to Count Brunswick dated February 13, 1814, Beethoven wrote: 'As regards me, great heavens! my dominion is in the air; the tones whirl like the wind, and often there is a whirl in my soul' " [from Clampitt's note].
5. Cf. the beginning of Shakespeare's *Twelfth Night*: "If music be the food of love, play on . . .

subside, disintegrate, regroup
in climbing sequences *con brio*[6]); there's 65
no dwelling on the sweet past here,
there being no past to speak of
other than the setbacks: typhoid
in the wells, half the first settlers
dead of it before a year was out; 70
diphtheria and scarlet fever
every winter; drought, the Depression,
a mortgage on the mortgage. High art
as a susurrus,[7] the silk and perfume
of unsullied hands. Those hands!— 75
driving the impressionable wild with anguish
for another life entirely: the Lyceum[8] circuit,
the doomed diving bell of Art.
                    Beethoven
in his workroom: ear trumpet, 80
conversation book and pencil, candlestick,
broken crockery, the Graf piano
wrecked by repeated efforts to hear himself—
out of a humdrum squalor the levitations,
the shakes and triplets, the *Adagio* 85
molto semplice e cantabile, the Arietta[9]
a disintegrating surf of blossom
opening along the keyboard, along the fencerows
the astonishment of sweetness. My father,
driving somewhere in Kansas or Colorado, 90
in dustbowl country, stopped the car
to dig up by the roots a flower
he'd never seen before—a kind
of prickly poppy most likely, its luminousness
wounding the blank plains like desire. 95
He mentioned in a letter the disappointment
of his having hoped it might transplant—
an episode that brings me near tears,
still, as even his dying does not—
that awful dying, months-long, hunkered, 100
irascible. From a clod no plowshare
could deliver, a groan for someone
(because he didn't want to look
at anything) to take away the flowers,
a bawling as of slaughterhouses, slogans 105
of a general uprising: *Freiheit!*[1]
Beethoven, shut up with the four walls
of his deafness, rehearsing the unhearable
semplice e cantabile, somehow reconstituting
the blister shirt of the intolerable 110

---

that strain again! It had a dying fall" (1.1.1, 4).
Moonlight: Beethoven's *Moonlight* Sonata.
6. With vigor (musical instruction in Italian).
7. Whisper.
8. Building used for cultural activities.

9. Short song or instrumental piece. *Adagio molto semplice e cantabile:* slowly, very simply and singingly (musical instruction in Italian).
1. Freedom (German).

into these shakes and triplets, a hurrying
into flowering along the fencerows: dying,
for my father, came to be like that
finally—in its messages the levitation
of serenity, as though the spirit might   115
aspire, in its last act,
                        to walk on air.

                                                           1983

Hispaniola[2]

Note how the bear
though armed and dangerous
caring not at all for
dignity, undaintily
snacks on fat white things   5
paws strawberry meadows
lunges swinging smeared
through blackberry canebrakes
maps a constellated
dream of bee trees   10
snoring galaxies
the primum mobile[3]
twanging the gulfs
of slumber   beatific
on the tongue   15
the kiss of honey :
or so we imagine
a hulking innocence
child's-play bedfellow
to the sapient   20
omnivorous
prehensile
raptor   world-class
bully : the rumor
brought to Alexander[4]   25
of, in India, a reed
that brought forth honey
sans the help of bees
began it   a topography
of monoculture   30
blackening the Indus
Tigris-Euphrates[5]

2. Island of the West Indies divided into Haiti in the west and the Dominican Republic in the east. In a note, Clampitt quotes a newsmagazine article stating that Columbus planned from the start to establish a sugar industry on Hispaniola, like the ones on the Canary and Madeira Islands.
3. Prime mover (Latin); in the medieval, Ptole-maic astronomical system, the outer sphere of the heavens that provided the energy for all other motion.
4. Macedonian emperor (356–323 B.C.E.).
5. River system of southwest Asia; considered the cradle of civilization. *Indus*: Trans-Himalayan river of south Asia.

westward-spreading
molasses stain
island plantations   35
off the coast of
Africa leapfrogging
the Atlantic
Hispaniola
Spanish Mexico   40
Peru   Paraguay
along the Amazon
the Portuguese
the Dutch   the British
Barbados Antigua Montserrat[6]   45
Jamaica   huger and huger
deforestations
making way for
raising cane   to be
holed   planted   cut   50
crushed   boiled
fermented or
reduced to crystalline
appeasement of mammalian
cravings   slave ships   55
whip-wielding
overseers   world-class
indignity   the bubbling
hellhole of molasses pits
the bear's   60
(or if not his, whose?)
nightmare

                                                      1994

Syrinx[7]

Like the foghorn that's all lung,
the wind chime that's all percussion,
like the wind itself, that's merely air
in a terrible fret, without so much
as a finger to articulate   5
what ails it, the aeolian
syrinx, that reed
in the throat of a bird,
when it comes to the shaping of
what we call consonants, is   10
too imprecise for consensus
about what it even seems to

6. Islands of the West Indies.
7. Vocal organ of birds, named after a Greek nymph who was turned into a reed to protect her chastity from Pan. Pan made the panpipe, or syrinx, from that reed.

be saying: is it *o-ka-lee*
or *con-ka-ree*, is it really *jug jug*,
is it *cuckoo* for that matter?—   15
much less whether a bird's call
means anything in
particular, or at all.

Syntax comes last, there can be
no doubt of it: came last,   20
can be thought of (is
thought of by some) as a
higher form of expression:
is, in extremity, first to
be jettisoned: as the diva   25
onstage, all soaring
pectoral breathwork,
takes off, pure vowel
breaking free of the dry,
the merely fricative   30
husk of the particular, rises
past saying anything, any
more than the wind in
the trees, waves breaking,
or Homer's gibbering   35
Thespesiae iachē:[8]

those last-chance vestiges
above the threshold, the all-
but dispossessed of breath.

1994

8. Unearthly cry (Greek); emitted by the spirits of the dead crowding around Odysseus (Homer, *Odyssey* 10.34–43).

RICHARD WILBUR
b. 1921

In the pantheon of post–World War II poetry, Richard Wilbur is, like the early Robert Lowell, a master of formal verse. He has inspired many younger poets, such as the New Formalists, who have championed a return to meter and rhyme. But Wilbur has remained faithful to the New Critical formalism that Lowell abandoned for confessional free verse. Wilbur centers his work in the achievement of illuminated, controlled moments, but he is not merely measured and self-possessed. He is alive to inner challenges, and though his mode of expression is deftly sedate, it begins in cross-purposes and cross-sympathies before it culminates in intimations of an earthly paradise.

"I am for wit and wakefulness," Wilbur announces in "Ceremony." But behind his neat stanzas and cheerful optimism lurk encounters with chaos and death. His serious attempts to write poetry arose out of war: "It was not until World War II took me to

Cassino, Anzio and the Siegfried Line that I began to versify in earnest. One does not use poetry for its major purposes, as a means of organizing oneself and the world, until one's world somehow gets out of hand. A general cataclysm is not required; the disorder must be personal and may be wholly so, but poetry, to be vital, does seem to need a periodic acquaintance with the threat of Chaos" (*Twentieth Century Authors*, First Supplement, 1955). Wilbur endorses organization without wanting it to be easy: in "The Beacon," he salutes a human artifact ("sighted ship / Assembles all the sea"), whereas in "Caserta Garden," he cautions, in speaking of the "garden of the world," that "Its shapes escape our simpler symmetries."

He seeks complex symmetries, which he composes with "ceremony." Wilbur's formal dexterity—evident in perfect rhymes, unfaltering meters, expertly placed verbs, and elegantly woven syntax—is a necessary part of his self-expression. He has defended the use of strict poetic forms, traditional or invented, as being "like the use of framing and composition in painting: both serve to limit the work of art, and to declare its artificiality: they say, 'This is not the world, but a pattern imposed upon the world or found in it; this is a partial and provisional attempt to establish relations between things.' " He adds, "There are other less metaphysical reasons for preferring strictness of form: the fact, for example, that subtle variation is unrecognizable without the pre-existence of a norm; or the fact that form, in showing and complicating the writing-process, calls out the poet's full talents, and thereby insures a greater care and cleverness in the choice and disposition of words. In general, I would say that limitation makes for power: the strength of the genie comes of his being confined in a bottle" (*Mid-Century American Poets*, ed. John Ciardi, 1950). For the most part, he declines the themes of dispossession and disintegration, as he has the poetics of fragmentation and "open" form, that occupy many modern and contemporary poets, making his verse an artfully controlled evocation, over difficulties, of desirable experience.

Wilbur was born on March 1, 1921, in New York City. His father was an artist; Wilbur's poem "My Father Paints the Summer" praises him for disregarding the actual rain to paint a perfect summer's day, "always an imagined time." Wilbur's mother came from a family prominent in journalism, a direction he followed briefly. Two years after his birth, the family moved to a very old house in North Caldwell, New Jersey, where he developed his taste for country things; he has written a poem about the potato and writes brilliantly, as in "Seed Leaves," of plant growth—"the doom of taking shape." At Amherst College, he was encouraged by his English courses to develop Horatian poems—that is, poems chiseled in form and rural in setting. After the war, he received an M.A. at Harvard University, teaching there (1950–54), at Wellesley College (1955–57), and at Wesleyan University (1957–77). In 1987, he left his position as writer-in-residence at Smith College to become poet laureate of the United States, succeeding Robert Penn Warren. Besides books of verse, Wilbur has made splendid translations of the verse plays of Molière, Racine, and Voltaire, finding kinship in the wit and form of the French originals. He has twice won the Bollingen Prize and twice the Pulitzer.

The Death of a Toad

A toad the power mower caught,
Chewed and clipped of a leg, with a hobbling hop has got
To the garden verge, and sanctuaried him
Under the cineraria leaves, in the shade
Of the ashen heartshaped leaves, in a dim,
Low, and a final glade.

5

The rare original heartsblood goes,
Spends on the earthen hide, in the folds and wizenings, flows
  In the gutters of the banked and staring eyes. He lies
    As still as if he would return to stone,   10
      And soundlessly attending, dies
        Toward some deep monotone,

      Toward misted and ebullient seas
And cooling shores, toward lost Amphibia's emperies.[1]
  Day dwindles, drowning, and at length is gone   15
  In the wide and antique eyes, which still appear
    To watch, across the castrate lawn,
        The haggard daylight steer.

                                       1950

Ceremony

A striped blouse in a clearing by Bazille[2]
Is, you may say, a patroness of boughs
Too queenly kind toward nature to be kin.
But ceremony never did conceal,
Save to the silly eye, which all allows,   5
How much we are the woods we wander in.

Let her be some Sabrina[3] fresh from stream,
Lucent as shallows slowed by wading sun,
Bedded on fern, the flowers' cynosure:
Then nymph and wood must nod and strive to dream   10
That she is airy earth, the trees, undone,
Must ape her languor natural and pure.

Ho-hum. I am for wit and wakefulness,
And love this feigning lady by Bazille.
What's lightly hid is deepest understood,   15
And when with social smile and formal dress
She teaches leaves to curtsey and quadrille,
I think there are most tigers in the wood.

                                       1950

Boy at the Window

Seeing the snowman standing all alone
In dusk and cold is more than he can bear.
The small boy weeps to hear the wind prepare
A night of gnashings and enormous moan.

1. Amphibia is imagined as the presiding spirit of the toad's (and of all amphibians') universe.
2. Frédéric Bazille (1841–1871), French painter associated with the Impressionists. Most of his paintings show figures in close relation to a landscape.
3. The nymph of the river Severn, in Milton's *Comus*, but here identified with thoughtless, unceremonious nature, and contrasted with Bazille's lady.

His tearful sight can hardly reach to where   5
The pale-faced figure with bitumen[4] eyes
Returns him such a god-forsaken stare
As outcast Adam gave to Paradise.

The man of snow is, nonetheless, content,
Having no wish to go inside and die.   10
Still, he is moved to see the youngster cry.
Though frozen water is his element,
He melts enough to drop from one soft eye
A trickle of the purest rain, a tear
For the child at the bright pane surrounded by   15
Such warmth, such light, such love, and so much fear.

                                            1956

Love Calls Us to the Things of This World[5]

The eyes open to a cry of pulleys,
And spirited from sleep, the astounded soul
Hangs for a moment bodiless and simple
As false dawn.
                    Outside the open window
The morning air is all awash with angels.   5

Some are in bed-sheets, some are in blouses,
Some are in smocks: but truly there they are.
Now they are rising together in calm swells
Of halcyon feeling, filling whatever they wear
With the deep joy of their impersonal breathing;   10

Now they are flying in place, conveying
The terrible speed of their omnipresence, moving
And staying like white water; and now of a sudden
They swoon down into so rapt a quiet
That nobody seems to be there.
                                The soul shrinks   15

From all that it is about to remember,
From the punctual rape of every blessèd day,
And cries,
            "Oh, let there be nothing on earth but laundry,

---

4. Asphalt or tar.
5. Quoted from St. Augustine. Wilbur has said, "You must imagine the poem as occurring at perhaps seven-thirty in the morning; the scene is a bedroom high up in a city apartment building; out- side the bedroom window, the first laundry of the day is being yanked across the sky and one has been awakened by the squeaking pulleys of the laundry-line."

Nothing but rosy hands in the rising steam
And clear dances done in the sight of heaven."   20

     Yet, as the sun acknowledges
With a warm look the world's hunks and colors,
The soul descends once more in bitter love
To accept the waking body, saying now
In a changed voice as the man yawns and rises,   25

     "Bring them down from their ruddy gallows;
Let there be clean linen for the backs of thieves;
Let lovers go fresh and sweet to be undone,
And the heaviest nuns walk in a pure floating
Of dark habits,
            keeping their difficult balance."   30

     1956

Playboy

High on his stockroom ladder like a dunce
The stock-boy sits, and studies like a sage
The subject matter of one glossy page,
As lost in curves as Archimedes[6] once.

Sometimes, without a glance, he feeds himself.   5
The left hand, like a mother-bird in flight,
Brings him a sandwich for a sidelong bite,
And then returns it to a dusty shelf.

What so engrosses him? The wild décor
Of this pink-papered alcove into which   10
A naked girl has stumbled, with its rich
Welter of pelts and pillows on the floor,

Amidst which, kneeling in a supple pose,
She lifts a goblet in her father hand,
As if about to toast a flower-stand   15
Above which hovers an exploding rose

Fired from a long-necked crystal vase that rests
Upon a tasseled and vermillion cloth
One taste of which would shrivel up a moth?
Or is he pondering her perfect breasts?   20

Nothing escapes him of her body's grace
Or of her floodlit skin, so sleek and warm

---

6. Greek mathematician and inventor (c. 287–212 B.C.E.).

And yet so strangely like a uniform,
But what now grips his fancy is her face,

And how the cunning picture holds her still   25
At just that smiling instant when her soul,
Grown sweetly faint, and swept beyond control,
Consents to his inexorable will.

                                                              1969

The Writer

In her room at the prow of the house
Where light breaks, and the windows are tossed with linden,
My daughter is writing a story.

I pause in the stairwell, hearing
From her shut door a commotion of typewriter-keys   5
Like a chain hauled over a gunwale.[7]

Young as she is, the stuff
Of her life is a great cargo, and some of it heavy:
I wish her a lucky passage.

But now it is she who pauses,   10
As if to reject my thought and its easy figure.
A stillness greatens, in which

The whole house seems to be thinking,
And then she is at it again with a bunched clamor
Of strokes, and again is silent.   15

I remember the dazed starling
Which was trapped in that very room, two years ago;[8]
How we stole in, lifted a sash

And retreated, not to affright it;
And how for a helpless hour, through the crack of the door,   20
We watched the sleek, wild, dark

And iridescent creature
Batter against the brilliance, drop like a glove
To the hard floor, or the desk-top,

And wait then, humped and bloody,   25
For the wits to try it again; and how our spirits
Rose when, suddenly sure,

7. Upper edge of a boat's side.
8. A bird trapped in a house portends a death, according to New England superstition.

It lifted off from a chair-back,
Beating a smooth course for the right window
And clearing the sill of the world.   30

It is always a matter, my darling,
Of life or death, as I had forgotten. I wish
What I wished you before, but harder.

1976

A Finished Man

Of the four louts who threw him off the dock
Three are now dead, and so more faintly mock
The way he choked and splashed and was afraid.
His memory of the fourth begins to fade.

It was himself whom he could not forgive;   5
Yet it has been a comfort to outlive
That woman, stunned by his appalling gaffe,
Who with a napkin half-suppressed her laugh,

Or that grey colleague, surely gone by now,
Who, turning toward the window, raised his brow,   10
Embarrassed to have caught him in a lie.
All witness darkens, eye by dimming eye.

Thus he can walk today with heart at ease
Through the old quad, escorted by trustees.
To dedicate the monumental gym   15
A grateful college means to name for him.

Seated, he feels the warm sun sculpt his cheek
As the young president gets up to speak.
If the dead die, if he can but forget,
If money talks, he may be perfect yet.   20

1987

A Barred Owl

The warping night air having brought the boom
Of an owl's voice into her darkened room,
We tell the wakened child that all she heard
Was an odd question from a forest bird,
Asking of us, if rightly listened to,   5
"Who cooks for you?" and then "Who cooks for you?"

Words, which can make our terrors bravely clear,
Can also thus domesticate a fear,
And send a small child back to sleep at night
Not listening for the sound of stealthy flight   10
Or dreaming of some small thing in a claw
Borne up to some dark branch and eaten raw.

2000

KINGSLEY AMIS
1922–1995

Kingsley Amis was poetically, as he was politically, conservative. He disliked mawkishness and found it allied with general disorder of emotions and lives. He was also impatient with parochialism, as with excess in whatever form. With his friend Philip Larkin, Amis was a member of the Movement, a 1950s group that praised craft and modesty while debunking grandiloquence. Despite his obvious political difference, W. H. Auden also had a discernible impact. But Amis rejected Dylan Thomas as a baleful influence. As Amis announces in the poem "Against Romanticism," he prefers "a temperate zone" to a "voluble swooning wilderness." The unkempt displeases him, as does the pallid. His poems are small wars of ironies, expressed with great deftness, and covert pleas for what is, as opposed to what might be. His heroes are often all dressed up with no place to go. His poems—sad, comic, and thus wry—frequently catch a man at his most ridiculous: when he searches for love.

Amis was born on April 16, 1922, to a lower-middle-class family in London. He attended the City of London School, then served in the army from 1942 to 1945. After the war, he studied English literature at Oxford University, where he befriended Larkin. He taught at University College, Swansea, for twelve years, long enough to publish two volumes of poetry and gather the material for his much-praised satirical novel *Lucky Jim* (1954). He then went to teach at Cambridge University, but was happy to extricate himself by writing fiction. His later novels proceeded from the comedy of sex to the even more comic situation of old age, dying, and death. He also continued to write poetry. A winner of the Booker Prize, he was honored as a C.B.E. (Commander of the British Empire) in 1981 and knighted in 1990.

Against Romanticism

A traveller who walks a temperate zone
    —Woods devoid of beasts, roads that please the foot—
Finds that its decent surface grows too thin:
    Something unperceived fumbles at his nerves.
To please an ingrown taste for anarchy   5
    Torrid images circle in the wood,
And sweat for recognition up the road,
    Cramming close the air with their bookish cries.
All senses then are glad to gasp: the eye
    Smeared with garish paints, tickled up with ghosts   10

That brandish warnings or an abstract noun;
  Melodies from shards, memories from coal,
Or saws from powdered tombstones thump the ear;
  Bodies rich with heat wriggle to the touch,
And verbal scents made real spellbind the nose;   15
  Incense, frankincense; legendary the taste
Of drinks or fruits or tongues laid on the tongue.
  Over all, a grand meaning fills the scene,
And sets the brain raging with prophecy,
  Raging to discard real time and place,   20
Raging to build a better time and place
  Than the ones which give prophecy its field
To work, the calm material for its rage,
  And the context which makes its prophecy.
Better, of course, if images were plain,   25
  Warnings clearly said, shapes put down quite still
Within the fingers' reach, or else nowhere;
  But complexities crowd the simplest thing,
And flaw the surface that they cannot break.
  Let us make at least visions that we need: 30
Let mine be pallid, so that it cannot
  Force a single glance, form a single word;
An afternoon long-drawn and silent, with
  Buildings free from all grime of history,
The people total strangers, the grass cut,   35
  Not long, voluble swooning wilderness,
And green, not parched or soured by frantic suns
  Doubling the commands of a rout of gods,
Nor trampled by the havering[1] unicorn;
  Let the sky be clean of officious birds   40
Punctiliously flying on the left;[2]
  Let there be a path leading out of sight,
And at its other end a temperate zone:
  Woods devoid of beasts, roads that please the foot.

                                                          1957

An Ever-Fixed Mark[3]

      Years ago, at a private school
      Run on traditional lines,
      One fellow used to perform
      Prodigious feats in the dorm;
      His quite undevious designs   5
      Found many a willing tool.

---

1. Nonsense-talking.
2. A bad omen.
3. Quoted from Shakespeare's Sonnet 116: "Love
is not love / Which alters when it alteration finds, /

Or bends with the remover to remove: / O no! it
is an ever-fixed mark, / That looks on tempests
and is never shaken."

On the rugger⁴ field, in the gym,
Buck marked down at his leisure
The likeliest bits of stuff;
The notion, familiar enough,   10
Of 'using somebody for pleasure'
Seemed handy and harmless to him.

But another chap was above
The diversions of such a lout;
Seven years in the place   15
And he never got to first base
With the kid he followed about:
What interested Ralph was love.

He did the whole thing in style—
Letters three times a week,   20
Sonnet-sequences, Sunday walks;
Then, during one of their talks,
The youngster caressed his cheek,
And that made it all worth while.

These days, for a quid pro quo,   25
Ralph's chum is all for romance;
Buck's playmates, family men,
Eye a Boy Scout now and then.
Sex stops when you pull up your pants,
Love never lets you go.   30

                                                        1967

Science Fiction

What makes us rove that starlit corridor
May be the impulse to meet face to face
Our vice and folly shaped into a thing,
And so at last ourselves; what lures us there
Is simpler versions of disaster: 5
A web that shuffles time and space,
A sentence to perpetual journeying,
A world of ocean without shore,
And simplest, flapping down the poisoned air,
A ten-clawed monster.   10

In him, perhaps, we see the general ogre
Who rode our ancestors to nightmare,
And in his habitat their maps of hell.⁵

---

4. Colloquial for rugby.
5. Amis's study of science fiction is *New Maps of Hell* (1960).

But climates and geographies soon change,
Spawning mutations none can quell   15
With silver sword or necromancer's[6] ring.
Worse than their sires, of wider range,
And much more durable.

1967

6. Magician's.

DONALD DAVIE
1922–1995

Donald Davie is one of a group of English poets (along with Philip Larkin, Kingsley Amis, and Thom Gunn) known as the Movement. Writing in the 1950s, they registered by precept and example their impatience with poetry that (like Dylan Thomas's, in their view) gratuitously inflates its subject matter. They also expressed a preference for understatement over grandiosity and a fondness for cleansing irony and traditional meters. Davie advocated the preservation of metrical and other "rules which have governed ninety percent of English poetry for more than 500 years" (*Delta* 8, 1956). He believed that poets who violate the rules of syntax contribute to a breakdown in civilization. In his *Purity of Diction in English Verse* (1953), which is both literary criticism and a manifesto, Davie warned that "it is impossible not to trace a connection between the laws of syntax and the laws of society. . . . One would almost say, on this showing, that to dislocate syntax in poetry is to threaten the rule of law in the civilized community." Surely not since Plato have greater responsibilities been placed on the poet, though Davie realized he was fighting for a lost cause with a fervor that may have seemed a little ridiculous.

As an antidote to the poetry of excess, impure diction, and confused syntax, Davie recommended reading eighteenth-century English poets and shunning modernist writers. Yet in his many later critical works and collections of poems Davie modified his views, making more room in his aesthetic theory and practice for the asymmetries of Thomas Hardy and Ezra Pound. He continued to demand artistic control from himself and others, however, convinced that though the subject of a poem may be disorder, the poem itself should embody order and intelligibility.

Davie was born on July 17, 1922, in Barnsley, Yorkshire. He attended the local grammar school, then studied at Cambridge University, where, coming under the influence of the critic F. R. Leavis, he received a Ph.D in 1951. His education was interrupted by service in the Royal Navy from 1941 to 1946. He then returned to Cambridge to study, teach, and write. Davie also taught at Trinity College, Dublin, and the University of Sussex. When he emigrated to the United States and took a position at Stanford University (1968–78), he succeeded another poet-critic who influenced him, Yvor Winters. Davie taught another ten years at Vanderbilt University (1978–88) before returning after retirement to England.

Remembering the 'Thirties

1

Hearing one saga, we enact the next.
We please our elders when we sit enthralled;
But then they're puzzled; and at last they're vexed
To have their youth so avidly recalled.

It dawns upon the veterans after all   5
That what for them were agonies, for us
Are high-brow thrillers, though historical;
And all their feats quite strictly fabulous.

This novel written fifteen years ago,
Set in my boyhood and my boyhood home,   10
These poems about 'abandoned workings', show
Worlds more remote than Ithaca[1] or Rome.

The Anschluss, Guernica[2]—all the names
At which those poets thrilled or were afraid
For me mean schools and schoolmasters and games;   15
And in the process some-one is betrayed.

Ourselves perhaps. The Devil for a joke
Might carve his own initials on our desk,
And yet we'd miss the point because he spoke
An idiom too dated, Audenesque.[3]   20

Ralegh's Guiana also killed his son.[4]
A pretty pickle if we came to see
The tallest story really packed a gun,
The Telemachiad[5] an Odyssey.

2

Even to them the tales were not so true   25
As not to be ridiculous as well;
The ironmaster met his Waterloo,
But Rider Haggard[6] rode along the fell.

1. Greek island; home of Odysseus.
2. City in the Basque region of northern Spain that was heavily bombed by German planes in 1937. The event inspired a famous painting by Spanish expatriate artist Pablo Picasso (1881–1973). *Anschluss*: union (German); the annexation of Austria by Nazi Germany, in 1938.
3. W. H. Auden (1907–1973), one of the most influential poets of the 1930s.
4. The eldest son of English author and explorer Sir Walter Ralegh (1554?–1618) was killed while with his father on an expedition in Guiana.
Ralegh's popular account of his earlier explorations of Guiana, *The Discovery of the Large, Rich, and Beautiful Empire of Guiana* (1596), was accused by many of his contemporaries as being full of lies and exaggerations.
5. The first four books of Homer's *Odyssey*, which center on Odysseus's son, Telemachus.
6. British novelist (1856–1925), famous for adventure novels such as *King Solomon's Mines* (1885). *Waterloo*: Belgian city where Napoleon's military career ended with his defeat in 1815.

'Leave for Cape Wrath tonight!' They lounged away
On Fleming's trek or Isherwood's ascent.[7]   30
England expected every man that day
To show his motives were ambivalent.

They played the fool, not to appear as fools
In time's long glass. A deprecating air
Disarmed, they thought, the jeers of later schools;   35
Yet irony itself is doctrinaire,

And curiously, nothing now betrays
Their type to time's derision like this coy
Insistence on the quizzical, their craze
For showing Hector[8] was a mother's boy.   40

A neutral tone is nowadays preferred.
And yet it may be better, if we must,
To praise a stance impressive and absurd
Than not to see the hero for the dust.

For courage is the vegetable king,   45
The sprig of all ontologies, the weed
That beards the slag-heap with his hectoring,
Whose green adventure is to run to seed.

                                                         1955

Across the Bay[9]

A queer thing about those waters: there are no
Birds there, or hardly any.
I did not miss them, I do not remember
Missing them, or thinking it uncanny.

The beach so-called was a blinding splinter of limestone,   5
A quarry outraged by hulls.
We took pleasure in that: the emptiness, the hardness
Of the light, the silence, and the water's stillness.

But this was the setting for one of our murderous scenes.
This hurt, and goes on hurting: 10
The venomous soft jelly, the undersides.
We could stand the world if it were hard all over.

                                                         1964

7. Christopher Isherwood (1904–1986), Anglo-
American novelist and playwright, collaborated
with Auden on a number of plays, including *The
Ascent of F6* (1936), and a travel book, *Journey to
a War* (1939), about their trip to China, where they
met the British travel writer Peter Fleming (1907–
1971). *Cape Wrath:* the northernmost point of
mainland Scotland. The quoted line comes from
Auden's early poem "Missing" (1929).
8. In the *Iliad*, the great warrior of Troy.
9. San Francisco Bay.

In California

Chemicals ripen the citrus;
There are rattlesnakes in the mountains,
And on the shoreline
Hygiene, unhuman caution.

Beef in cellophane   5
Tall as giraffes,
The orange-rancher's daughters
Crop their own groves, mistrustful.

Perpetual summer seems
Precarious on the littoral.[1] We drive   10
Inland to prove
The risk we sense. At once

Winter claps-to like a shutter
High over the Ojai valley, and discloses
A double crisis,   15
Winter and Drought.

Ranges on mountain-ranges,
Empty, unwatered, crumbling,
Hot colours come at the eye.
It is too cold   20

For picnics at the trestle-tables. Claypit
Yellow burns on the distance.
The phantom walks
Everywhere, of intolerable heat.

At Ventucopa,[2] elevation   25
Two-eight-nine-six, the water hydrant frozen,
Deserted or broken settlements,
Gasoline stations closed and boarded.

By nightfall, to the snows;
And over the mile on tilted   30
Mile of the mountain park
The bright cars hazarded.

1964

---

1. Coastal region.   2. A small community in Santa Barbara County.

From In the Stopping Train[3]

* * *

The things he has been spared . . .
'Gross egotist!' Why don't
his wife, his daughter, shrill
that in his face?   110

Love and pity seem
the likeliest explanations;
another occurs to him—
despair too would be quiet.

•

Time and again he gave battle,   115
furious, mostly effective;
nobody counts the wear
and tear of rebuttal.

Time and again he rose
to the flagrantly offered occasion;   120
nobody's hanged for a slow
murder by provocation.

Time and again he applauded
the stand he had taken; how much
it mattered, or to what   125
assize,[4] is not recorded.

Time and again he hardened
his heart and his perceptions;
nobody knows just how
truths turn into deceptions.   130

Time and again, oh time and
that stopping train!
Who knows when it comes to a stand,
and will not start again?

1977

---

3. Davie explained that his long poem "In the Stopping Train" derived from a miserable train ride from Tours to Paris and back through the pouring rain, on a failed attempt to meet with Irish poet John Montague (b. 1929). The poem is often read as an autobiographical parable.
4. Judicial inquest; court.

PHILIP LARKIN
1922–1985

Philip Larkin's tone is that of a man who has lost opportunities, failed to get the lover he wanted and got another instead (that not lasting either), and always found life less than it might have been. As an undergraduate at Oxford University, Larkin belonged to the group that came to be known as the Movement, its revolt being against rhetorical excess and cosmic portentousness. They sought a more accurate, conversational idiom. Among these poets, included in an anthology called *New Lines* (1956), Larkin, Donald Davie, and Thom Gunn have proved the most important.

Larkin's first book, *The North Ship* (1945), was strongly influenced by W. B. Yeats. Although this influence persisted in the English poet's qualified affirmations and prosodic agility, Larkin began to read Thomas Hardy seriously after World War II, and Hardy's rugged language, local settings, and ironic vision helped counter Yeats's influence. "After that," Larkin said, "Yeats came to seem so artificial—all that crap about masks and Crazy Jane and all the rest. It all rang so completely unreal" (*The Guardian*, May 20, 1965). Larkin inherited some of Hardy's toughness and dourness. Just as Hardy in "The Oxen" half wishes that he might believe a tradition out of Christian folklore, so Larkin in "Church Going" leaves the little country church with the sense that something precious, something in which he can no longer believe, has been lost. Interweaving skepticism and nostalgia, the poem creates a verbal space where, in Larkin's words, "all our compulsions meet." Larkin is perhaps gentler and funnier than Hardy, more amused by ineptitude, more affectionate toward his readers.

Larkin was no friend to the so-called high or international modernists. In a 1964 interview ("Four Conversations"), he summarized his discontent with modernism:

> The poetry I've enjoyed has been the kind of poetry you'd associate with me—Hardy pre-eminently, Wilfred Owen, Auden, Christina Rossetti, William Barnes; on the whole, people to whom technique seems to matter less than content, people who accept the forms they have inherited but use them to express their own content. . . .
>
> What I do feel a bit rebellious about is that poetry seems to have got into the hands of a critical industry which is concerned with culture in the abstract, and this I do rather lay at the door of Eliot and Pound. . . . I think a lot of this myth-kitty business has grown out of that, because first of all you have to be terribly educated, you have to read everything to know these things, and secondly you've got somehow to work them in to show that you are working them in. But to me the whole of the ancient world, the whole of classical and biblical mythology means very little, and I think that using them today not only fills poems full of dead spots but dodges the writer's duty to be original.

Ezra Pound's eclecticism is not for Larkin; indeed, parts of *The Cantos* may seem like a tour of an ethnographic museum led by a sporadically demented guide. Rejecting the polyglot discourse, fragmentary syntax, and intimidating ambition of modernism, Larkin reclaims a more direct, personal, formally regular model of poetry. As a music critic, Larkin attacked avant-garde jazz for the same modernist alienation of the audience. And yet he is not so thoroughly antimodernist as he proclaims, as evidenced by his imagist precision and his solitary, death-obsessed personae, his tonal blending of melancholy with astringent irony, his commingling of poetry and secularized religion.

Larkin was born on August 9, 1922, in Coventry, Warwickshire. He depicts his miseries as a student at Oxford University in *Jill* (1946), the first of his two novels. After taking his B.A. at St. John's College, Oxford, in 1943, he worked as a librarian, mostly at the University of Hull (his poem "Here" evokes the city of Hull). In contrast to his rather sequestered career and his offensive remarks on race and gender voiced in letters, Larkin's poetry sparkles. He published only a few small books of verse. Because their manner is quiet, and because their matter is often melancholy contemplation, Larkin repelled critics looking for radical novelty in technique and for urgent responses to the present.

But Larkin spins out of his disillusionment some of the most emotionally complex, rhythmically polished, and intricately rhymed poems of the second half of the twentieth century. If he paraded no great truths, he offered things that were "almost true," such as the statement of love and fidelity in "An Arundel Tomb": "What will survive of us is love." His acceptance of defeat, in a poem such as "Toads Revisited" ("Give me your arm, old toad; / Help me down Cemetery Road"), cannot be read without recognizing the witty exaggeration of the poet's plight. "Poetry is an affair of sanity, of seeing things as they are," he said ("Big Victims"); "I don't want to transcend the commonplace, I love the commonplace life. Everyday things are lovely to me" (*Viewpoints: Poets in Conversation with John Haffenden*, 1981). The reverse of grandiose or straining, Larkin's poetry is so evidently integral with its author, and so witty and deft, that it speaks with singular authority and aplomb.

Larkin was not the poet to celebrate poetry, but his verse finds affection even in love's failure, creative possibilities in loneliness, humility blossoming from unsuccess. In spite of his affirmations of mundane existence, the interplay between the ordinary and the sublime frequently energizes his work. He is attracted to a sense of what "unfenced existence" might be ("Here"). He recognizes what brilliance passing images have before they dissipate or diminish, as when he notes, with complex feelings, the unrealizable aspirations of "The Whitsun Weddings." In "Solar," the poet beholds, without flinching, the radiant sublimity of the sun. Sometimes, such glimpses are of utter vacancy. In "Aubade," the poet encounters the terrifying blankness of death—"the total emptiness for ever, / The sure extinction that we travel to." "High Windows" suggests both radiant presence and total absence in its final vision of sunlit glass: "And beyond it, the deep blue air, that shows / Nothing, and is nowhere, and is endless."

When Sir John Betjeman died, in 1984, it was widely thought that Larkin might succeed him as poet laureate of England, and it is humorous to imagine a Royal Birthday Ode from the man who wrote the striking first lines of "This Be The Verse" and "High Windows." But a year before he died (after surgery for throat cancer), Larkin was offered and turned down the prestigious post.

Reasons for Attendance

The trumpet's voice, loud and authoritative,
Draws me a moment to the lighted glass
To watch the dancers—all under twenty-five—
Shifting intently, face to flushed face,
Solemnly on the beat of happiness.   5

—Or so I fancy, sensing the smoke and sweat,
The wonderful feel of girls. Why be out here?
But then, why be in there? Sex, yes, but what
Is sex? Surely, to think the lion's share
Of happiness is found by couples—sheer   10

Inaccuracy, as far as I'm concerned.
What calls me is that lifted, rough-tongued bell
(Art, if you like) whose individual sound
Insists I too am individual.
It speaks; I hear; others may hear as well,   15

But not for me, nor I for them; and so
With happiness. Therefore I stay outside,
Believing this; and they maul to and fro,
Believing that; and both are satisfied,
If no one has misjudged himself. Or lied.   20

December 30, 1953   1955

Water

If I were called in
To construct a religion
I should make use of water.

Going to church
Would entail a fording   5
To dry, different clothes;

My liturgy would employ
Images of sousing,
A furious devout drench,

And I should raise in the east   10
A glass of water
Where any-angled light
Would congregate endlessly.

April 6, 1954   1964

Church Going

Once I am sure there's nothing going on
I step inside, letting the door thud shut.
Another church: matting, seats, and stone,
And little books; sprawlings of flowers, cut
For Sunday, brownish now; some brass and stuff   5
Up at the holy end; the small neat organ;
And a tense, musty, unignorable silence,
Brewed God knows how long. Hatless, I take off
My cycle-clips[1] in awkward reverence,

---

1. Accessories worn below the knee to protect trousers from getting entangled in the bicycle chain.

Move forward, run my hand around the font. 10
From where I stand, the roof looks almost new—
Cleaned, or restored? Someone would know: I don't.
Mounting the lectern, I peruse a few
Hectoring large-scale verses,[2] and pronounce
'Here endeth' much more loudly than I'd meant. 15
The echoes snigger briefly. Back at the door
I sign the book, donate an Irish sixpence.[3]
Reflect the place was not worth stopping for.

Yet stop I did: in fact I often do,
And always end much at a loss like this, 20
Wondering what to look for; wondering, too,
When churches fall completely out of use
What we shall turn them into, if we shall keep
A few cathedrals chronically on show,
Their parchment, plate and pyx[4] in locked cases, 25
And let the rest rent-free to rain and sheep.
Shall we avoid them as unlucky places?

Or, after dark, will dubious women come
To make their children touch a particular stone;
Pick simples[5] for a cancer; or on some 30
Advised night see walking a dead one?
Power of some sort or other will go on
In games, in riddles, seemingly at random;
But superstition, like belief, must die,
And what remains when disbelief has gone? 35
Grass, weedy pavement, brambles, buttress, sky,

A shape less recognisable each week,
A purpose more obscure. I wonder who
Will be the last, the very last, to seek
This place for what it was; one of the crew 40
That tap and jot and know what rood-lofts[6] were?
Some ruin-bibber, randy for antique,
Or Christmas-addict, counting on a whiff
Of gown-and-bands and organ-pipes and myrrh?[7]
Or will he be my representative, 45

Bored, uninformed, knowing the ghostly silt
Dispersed, yet tending to this cross of ground[8]
Through suburb scrub because it held unspilt
So long and equally what since is found

2. That is, verses from a Bible printed in large type for reading aloud.
3. Of no value in England.
4. Box, often made of gold or silver, in which communion wafers are kept.
5. Medicinal herbs.
6. A loft or gallery above the rood screen, which, in an old church, separates the nave, or main hall, from the chancel, which contains the altar; the rood-loft properly holds a rood, or cross.
7. A bitter, aromatic gum used in, among other things, making incense. *Gown-and-bands:* the dress of an old-fashioned clergyman, consisting of a long, black gown or robe and a set of narrow, white strips of cloth at the neck.
8. Churches were usually built in the form of a cross.

Only in separation—marriage, and birth,　　　　　　　　50
And death, and thoughts of these—for which was built
This special shell? For, though I've no idea
What this accoutred frowsty barn is worth,
It pleases me to stand in silence here;

A serious house on serious earth it is,　　　　　　　　55
In whose blent air all our compulsions meet,
Are recognised, and robed as destinies.
And that much never can be obsolete,
Since someone will forever be surprising
A hunger in himself to be more serious,　　　　　　　　60
And gravitating with it to this ground,
Which, he once heard, was proper to grow wise in,
If only that so many dead lie round.

July 28, 1954　　　　　　　　　　　　　　　　　　　　1955

An Arundel Tomb[9]

Side by side, their faces blurred,
The earl and countess lie in stone,
Their proper habits[1] vaguely shown
As jointed armour, stiffened pleat,
And that faint hint of the absurd—　　　　　　　　　　5
The little dogs under their feet.

Such plainness of the pre-baroque
Hardly involves the eye, until
It meets his left-hand gauntlet, still
Clasped empty in the other; and　　　　　　　　　　　10
One sees, with a sharp tender shock,
His hand withdrawn, holding her hand.

They would not think to lie so long.
Such faithfulness in effigy
Was just a detail friends would see:　　　　　　　　　15
A sculptor's sweet commissioned grace
Thrown off in helping to prolong
The Latin names around the base.

They would not guess how early in
Their supine stationary voyage　　　　　　　　　　　20
The air would change to soundless damage,
Turn the old tenantry away;
How soon succeeding eyes begin
To look, not read. Rigidly they

Persisted, linked, through lengths and breadths　　　25
Of time. Snow fell, undated. Light

9. Tomb of the earl of Arundel and his wife, in　　1. Clothing.
Chichester Cathedral, Sussex.

Each summer thronged the glass. A bright
Litter of birdcalls strewed the same
Bone-riddled ground. And up the paths
The endless altered people came,   30

Washing at their identity.
Now, helpless in the hollow of
An unarmorial age, a trough
Of smoke in slow suspended skeins
Above their scrap of history,   35
Only an attitude remains:

Time has transfigured them into
Untruth. The stone fidelity
They hardly meant has come to be
Their final blazon,[2] and to prove   40
Our almost-instinct almost true:
What will survive of us is love.

February 20, 1956   1964

The Whitsun[3] Weddings

That Whitsun, I was late getting away:
    Not till about
One-twenty on the sunlit Saturday
Did my three-quarters-empty train pull out,
All windows down, all cushions hot, all sense   5
Of being in a hurry gone. We ran
Behind the backs of houses, crossed a street
Of blinding windscreens, smelt the fish-dock; thence
The river's level drifting breadth began,
Where sky and Lincolnshire and water meet.   10

All afternoon, through the tall heat that slept
    For miles inland,
A slow and stopping curve southwards we kept.
Wide farms went by, short-shadowed cattle, and
Canals with floatings of industrial froth;   15
A hothouse flashed uniquely: hedges dipped
And rose: and now and then a smell of grass
Displaced the reek of buttoned carriage-cloth
Until the next town, new and nondescript,
Approached with acres of dismantled cars.   20

At first, I didn't notice what a noise
    The weddings made

2. Record of virtue.
3. Or Whitsunday, the seventh Sunday after
Easter, one of the six British bank holidays. British
tax law in the 1950s made it a financially beneficial
weekend to be married.

Each station that we stopped at: sun destroys
The interest of what's happening in the shade,
And down the long cool platforms whoops and skirls   25
I took for porters larking with the mails,
And went on reading. Once we started, though,
We passed them, grinning and pomaded, girls
In parodies of fashion, heels and veils,
All posed irresolutely, watching us go,   30

As if out on the end of an event
        Waving goodbye
To something that survived it. Struck, I leant
More promptly out next time, more curiously,
And saw it all again in different terms: 35
The fathers with broad belts under their suits
And seamy foreheads; mothers loud and fat;
An uncle shouting smut; and then the perms,
The nylon gloves and jewellery-substitutes,
The lemons, mauves, and olive-ochres that   40

Marked off the girls unreally from the rest.
        Yes, from cafés
And banquet-halls up yards, and bunting-dressed
Coach-party annexes, the wedding-days
Were coming to an end. All down the line   45
Fresh couples climbed aboard: the rest stood round;
The last confetti and advice were thrown,
And, as we moved, each face seemed to define
Just what it saw departing: children frowned
At something dull; fathers had never known   50

Success so huge and wholly farcical;
        The women shared
The secret like a happy funeral;
While girls, gripping their handbags tighter, stared
At a religious wounding. Free at last,   55
And loaded with the sum of all they saw,
We hurried towards London, shuffling gouts of steam.
Now fields were building-plots, and poplars cast
Long shadows over major roads, and for
Some fifty minutes, that in time would seem   60

Just long enough to settle hats and say
        I nearly died,
A dozen marriages got under way.
They watched the landscape, sitting side by side
—An Odeon[4] went past, a cooling tower,   65
And someone running up to bowl[5]—and none
Thought of the others they would never meet
Or how their lives would all contain this hour.

4. One of a chain of English movie houses.
5. In the sport of cricket, to pitch the ball to the batsperson.

I thought of London spread out in the sun,
Its postal districts packed like squares of wheat: 70

There we were aimed. And as we raced across
    Bright knots of rail
Past standing Pullmans, walls of blackened moss
Came close, and it was nearly done, this frail
Travelling coincidence; and what it held   75
Stood ready to be loosed with all the power
That being changed can give. We slowed again,
And as the tightened brakes took hold, there swelled
A sense of falling, like an arrow-shower
Sent out of sight, somewhere becoming rain.   80

October 18, 1958   1964

Faith Healing

Slowly the women file to where he stands
Upright in rimless glasses, silver hair,
Dark suit, white collar. Stewards tirelessly
Persuade them onwards to his voice and hands,
Within whose warm spring rain of loving care   5
Each dwells some twenty seconds. *Now, dear child,*
What's wrong, the deep American voice demands,
And, scarcely pausing, goes into a prayer
Directing God about this eye, that knee.
Their heads are clasped abruptly; then, exiled   10

Like losing thoughts, they go in silence; some
Sheepishly stray, not back into their lives
Just yet; but some stay stiff, twitching and loud
With deep hoarse tears, as if a kind of dumb
And idiot child within them still survives   15
To re-awake at kindness, thinking a voice
At last calls them alone, that hands have come
To lift and lighten; and such joy arrives
Their thick tongues blort, their eyes squeeze grief, a crowd
Of huge unheard answers jam and rejoice—   20

What's wrong! Moustached in flowered frocks they shake:
By now, all's wrong. In everyone there sleeps
A sense of life lived according to love.
To some it means the difference they could make
By loving others, but across most it sweeps   25
As all they might have done had they been loved.
That nothing cures. An immense slackening ache,
As when, thawing, the rigid landscape weeps,
Spreads slowly through them—that, and the voice above
Saying *Dear child,* and all time has disproved.   30

May 10, 1960   1964

MCMXIV[6]

Those long uneven lines
Standing as patiently
As if they were stretched outside
The Oval or Villa Park,[7]
The crowns of hats, the sun   5
On moustached archaic faces
Grinning as if it were all
An August Bank Holiday lark;

And the shut shops, the bleached
Established names on the sunblinds,   10
The farthings and sovereigns,[8]
And dark-clothed children at play
Called after kings and queens,
The tin advertisements
For cocoa and twist, and the pubs   15
Wide open all day;[9]

And the countryside not caring:
The place-names all hazed over
With flowering grasses, and fields
Shadowing Domesday lines[1]   20
Under wheat's restless silence;
The differently-dressed servants
With tiny rooms in huge houses,
The dust behind limousines;

Never such innocence,   25
Never before or since,
As changed itself to past
Without a word—the men
Leaving the gardens tidy,
The thousands of marriages   30
Lasting a little while longer:
Never such innocence again.

May 17, 1960   1964

Talking in Bed

Talking in bed ought to be easiest,
Lying together there goes back so far,
An emblem of two people being honest.

6. The poem envisions England in 1914, at the outbreak of World War I.
7. That is, outside a cricket ground or a professional soccer field; the men are waiting in line to enlist in the army.
8. British coins, both now obsolete; a farthing was worth one-fourth of a penny; a sovereign was worth a little more than a pound.
9. That is, before a law in 1915 restricted taverns' business hours. *Twist*: tobacco.
1. Lines demarcating property, as listed in the Domesday Book, drawn up by William the Conqueror in 1085–86.

Yet more and more time passes silently.
Outside, the wind's incomplete unrest   5
Builds and disperses clouds about the sky,

And dark towns heap up on the horizon.
None of this cares for us. Nothing shows why
At this unique distance from isolation

It becomes still more difficult to find   10
Words at once true and kind,
Or not untrue and not unkind.

August 10, 1960   1964

Here

Swerving east, from rich industrial shadows
And traffic all night north; swerving through fields
Too thin and thistled to be called meadows,
And now and then a harsh-named halt, that shields
Workmen at dawn; swerving to solitude   5
Of skies and scarecrows, haystacks, hares and pheasants,
And the widening river's slow presence,
The piled gold clouds, the shining gull-marked mud,

Gathers to the surprise of a large town:
Here domes and statues, spires and cranes cluster   10
Beside grain-scattered streets, barge-crowded water,
And residents from raw estates, brought down
The dead straight miles by stealing flat-faced trolleys,
Push through plate-glass swing doors to their desires—
Cheap suits, red kitchen-ware, sharp shoes, iced lollies,   15
Electric mixers, toasters, washers, driers—

A cut-price crowd, urban yet simple, dwelling
Where only salesmen and relations come
Within a terminate and fishy-smelling
Pastoral of ships up streets, the slave museum,   20
Tattoo-shops, consulates, grim head-scarfed wives;
And out beyond its mortgaged half-built edges
Fast-shadowed wheat-fields, running high as hedges,
Isolate villages, where removed lives

Loneliness clarifies. Here silence stands   25
Like heat. Here leaves unnoticed thicken,
Hidden weeds flower, neglected waters quicken,
Luminously-peopled air ascends;
And past the poppies bluish neutral distance
Ends the land suddenly beyond a beach   30
Of shapes and shingle. Here is unfenced existence:
Facing the sun, untalkative, out of reach.

October 8, 1961   1964

Sunny Prestatyn[2]

Come to Sunny Prestatyn
Laughed the girl on the poster,
Kneeling up on the sand
In tautened white satin.
Behind her, a hunk of coast, a   5
Hotel with palms
Seemed to expand from her thighs and
Spread breast-lifting arms.

She was slapped up one day in March.
A couple of weeks, and her face   10
Was snaggle-toothed and boss-eyed;
Huge tits and a fissured crotch
Were scored well in, and the space
Between her legs held scrawls
That set her fairly astride   15
A tuberous cock and balls

Autographed *Titch Thomas*, while
Someone had used a knife
Or something to stab right through
The moustached lips of her smile.   20
She was too good for this life.
Very soon, a great transverse tear
Left only a hand and some blue.
Now *Fight Cancer* is there.

October ?, 1962   1964

Solar

Suspended lion face
Spilling at the centre
Of an unfurnished sky
How still you stand,
And how unaided   5
Single stalkless flower
You pour unrecompensed.

The eye sees you
Simplified by distance
Into an origin,   10
Your petalled head of flames
Continuously exploding.
Heat is the echo of your
Gold.

2. A seaside resort in north Wales; it is not inevitably sunny.

Coined there among 15
Lonely horizontals
You exist openly.
Our needs hourly
Climb and return like angels.
Unclosing like a hand, 20
You give for ever.

November 4, 1964 1974

High Windows

When I see a couple of kids
And guess he's fucking her and she's
Taking pills or wearing a diaphragm,
I know this is paradise

Everyone old has dreamed of all their lives— 5
Bonds and gestures pushed to one side
Like an outdated combine harvester,[3]
And everyone young going down the long slide

To happiness, endlessly. I wonder if
Anyone looked at me, forty years back, 10
And thought, *That'll be the life;*
No God any more, or sweating in the dark

About hell and that, or having to hide
What you think of the priest. He
And his lot will all go down the long slide 15
Like free bloody birds. And immediately

Rather than words comes the thought of high windows:
The sun-comprehending glass,
And beyond it, the deep blue air, that shows
Nothing, and is nowhere, and is endless. 20

February 12, 1967 1974

Sad Steps[4]

Groping back to bed after a piss
I part thick curtains, and am startled by
The rapid clouds, the moon's cleanliness.

---

3. Farm machine for harvesting grain.
4. Cf. Sir Philip Sidney's *Astrophil and Stella*
(1591), Sonnet 31: "With how sad steps, O moon,
thou climb'st the skies."

Four o'clock: wedge-shadowed gardens lie
Under a cavernous, a wind-picked sky.   5
There's something laughable about this,

The way the moon dashes through clouds that blow
Loosely as cannon-smoke to stand apart
(Stone-coloured light sharpening the roofs below)

High and preposterous and separate—   10
Lozenge[5] of love! Medallion of art!
O wolves of memory! Immensements! No,

One shivers slightly, looking up there.
The hardness and the brightness and the plain
Far-reaching singleness of that wide stare   15

Is a reminder of the strength and pain
Of being young; that it can't come again,
But is for others undiminished somewhere.

April 24, 1968   1974

Homage to a Government

Next year we are to bring the soldiers home
For lack of money, and it is all right.
Places they guarded, or kept orderly,
Must guard themselves, and keep themselves orderly.
We want the money for ourselves at home   5
Instead of working. And this is all right.

It's hard to say who wanted it to happen,
But now it's been decided nobody minds.
The places are a long way off, not here,
Which is all right, and from what we hear   10
The soldiers there only made trouble happen.
Next year we shall be easier in our minds.

Next year we shall be living in a country
That brought its soldiers home for lack of money.
The statues will be standing in the same   15
Tree-muffled squares, and look nearly the same.
Our children will not know it's a different country.
All we can hope to leave them now is money.

January 10, 1969   1974

---

5. Diamond-shaped pattern.

The Explosion

On the day of the explosion
Shadows pointed towards the pithead:
In the sun the slagheap[6] slept.

Down the lane came men in pitboots
Coughing oath-edged talk and pipe-smoke,   5
Shouldering off the freshened silence.

One chased after rabbits; lost them;
Came back with a nest of lark's eggs;
Showed them; lodged them in the grasses.

So they passed in beards and moleskins,[7]   10
Fathers, brothers, nicknames, laughter,
Through the tall gates standing open.

At noon, there came a tremor; cows
Stopped chewing for a second; sun,
Scarfed as in a heat-haze, dimmed.   15

The dead go on before us, they
Are sitting in God's house in comfort,
We shall see them face to face—

Plain as lettering in the chapels
It was said, and for a second   20
Wives saw men of the explosion

Larger than in life they managed—
Gold as on a coin, or walking
Somehow from the sun towards them,

One showing the eggs unbroken.   25

January 5, 1970   1974

This Be The Verse[8]

They fuck you up, your mum and dad.
They may not mean to, but they do.
They fill you with the faults they had
And add some extra, just for you.

6. Pile of scrap, refuse. *Pithead*: entrance to a coal mine.
7. Clothes made of a heavy, industrial fabric.
8. Cf. the elegy "Requiem," by Robert Louis Stevenson (1850–1894), of which the final verse reads, "This be the verse you grave for me: / *Here he lies where he longed to be,* / *Home is the sailor,* *home from sea,* / *And the hunter home from the hill.*"

But they were fucked up in their turn   5
  By fools in old-style hats and coats,
Who half the time were soppy-stern
  And half at one another's throats.

Man hands on misery to man.
  It deepens like a coastal shelf.[9]   10
Get out as early as you can,
  And don't have any kids yourself.

April ?, 1971   1974

Forget What Did

Stopping the diary
Was a stun to memory,
Was a blank starting,

One no longer cicatrized[1]
By such words, such actions   5
As bleakened waking.

I wanted them over,
Hurried to burial
And looked back on

Like the wars and winters   10
Missing behind the windows
Of an opaque childhood.

And the empty pages?
Should they ever be filled
Let it be with observed   15

Celestial recurrences,
The day the flowers come,
And when the birds go.

August 6, 1971   1974

Going, Going[2]

I thought it would last my time—
The sense that, beyond the town,
There would always be fields and farms,
Where the village louts could climb

9. Underwater land off a coast.   2. Cf. the auctioneer's cry "Going, going, gone!"
1. Covered with scar tissue.

Such trees as were not cut down;   5
I knew there'd be false alarms

In the papers about old streets
And split-level shopping,[3] but some
Have always been left so far;
And when the old part retreats   10
As the bleak high-risers come
We can always escape in the car.

Things are tougher than we are, just
As earth will always respond
However we mess it about;   15
Chuck filth in the sea, if you must:
The tides will be clean beyond.
—But what do I feel now? Doubt?

Or age, simply? The crowd
Is young in the M1 café;[4]   20
Their kids are screaming for more—
More houses, more parking allowed,
More caravan sites,[5] more pay.
On the Business Page, a score

Of spectacled grins approve   25
Some takeover bid that entails
Five per cent profit (and ten
Per cent more in the estuaries): move
Your works to the unspoilt dales
(Grey area grants)![6] And when   30

You try to get near the sea
In summer . . .
                    It seems, just now,
To be happening so very fast;
Despite all the land left free
For the first time I feel somehow   35
That it isn't going to last,

That before I snuff it, the whole
Boiling[7] will be bricked in
Except for the tourist parts—
First slum of Europe: a role   40
It won't be so hard to win,
With a cast of crooks and tarts.

---

3. In old-fashioned shops, the store was on the ground floor, the owner's living quarters above.
4. Restaurants along a highway; in England, major freeways are denoted by the letter *M* and a number.

5. Trailer parks.
6. Building areas are zoned, on English maps, by colors. *Works*: factories.
7. That is, the whole boiling mess.

And that will be England gone,
The shadows, the meadows, the lanes,
The guildhalls,[8] the carved choirs.   45
There'll be books; it will linger on
In galleries; but all that remains
For us will be concrete and tyres.

Most things are never meant.
This won't be, most likely: but greeds   50
And garbage are too thick-strewn
To be swept up now, or invent
Excuses that make them all needs.
I just think it will happen, soon.

January 25, 1972   1974

Aubade[9]

I work all day, and get half-drunk at night.
Waking at four to soundless dark, I stare.
In time the curtain-edges will grow light.
Till then I see what's really always there:
Unresting death, a whole day nearer now,   5
Making all thought impossible but how
And where and when I shall myself die.
Arid interrogation: yet the dread
Of dying, and being dead,
Flashes afresh to hold and horrify.   10

The mind blanks at the glare. Not in remorse
—The good not done, the love not given, time
Torn off unused—nor wretchedly because
An only life can take so long to climb
Clear of its wrong beginnings, and may never;   15
But at the total emptiness for ever,
The sure extinction that we travel to
And shall be lost in always. Not to be here,
Not to be anywhere,
And soon; nothing more terrible, nothing more true.   20

This is a special way of being afraid
No trick dispels. Religion used to try,
That vast moth-eaten musical brocade
Created to pretend we never die,
And specious stuff that says *No rational being*   25
Can fear a thing it will not feel, not seeing
That this is what we fear—no sight, no sound,
No touch or taste or smell, nothing to think with,

8. That is, town halls (in this case old).   9. Song or poem announcing dawn.

Nothing to love or link with,
The anaesthetic from which none come round.   30

And so it stays just on the edge of vision,
A small unfocused blur, a standing chill
That slows each impulse down to indecision.
Most things may never happen: this one will,
And realisation of it rages out   35
In furnace-fear when we are caught without
People or drink. Courage is no good:
It means not scaring others. Being brave
Lets no one off the grave.
Death is no different whined at than withstood.   40

Slowly light strengthens, and the room takes shape.
It stands plain as a wardrobe, what we know,
Have always known, know that we can't escape,
Yet can't accept. One side will have to go.
Meanwhile telephones crouch, getting ready to ring   45
In locked-up offices, and all the uncaring
Intricate rented world begins to rouse.
The sky is white as clay, with no sun.
Work has to be done.
Postmen like doctors go from house to house.   50

November 9, 1977   1977

ANTHONY HECHT
1923–2004

Anthony Hecht's first poems, published in *A Summoning of Stones* (1954), are extraordinarily accomplished; he develops his themes with a baroque profusion, finding a place for seemingly every improbable detail. Hecht pleases by his erudition, his skill in attaching one bit of information to another, his power to sustain a long, periodic sentence, and his ability to maintain a quality of improvisation while meeting the requirements of a daunting verse form. For connoisseurs of rhyming, nuanced rhythms, rhetorical patterning, sustained syntax, and other technical ingenuities, Hecht proves endlessly rewarding. He resembles Andrew Marvell in his deftness, his civility, and his preference for gardens over the wilderness or the city.

In his later volumes, Hecht surrenders to his obsessions. His poems, as he described them, "are about things that had an enormous emotional importance to me; I was prepared to attack them, whether they came out technically perfect or not." Without betraying his craft, Hecht endeavored to confront experience on its own painful terms. He knew the "grotesqueness of modern life," the incongruities between life as it is fabled for his children on the television screen and as it really is—or as it might have been. His mainstay is irony, which, in Hecht's own words, "provides a way of stating very powerful and positive emotions and of taking, as it were, the heaviest possible stance towards some catastrophe." His subjects include the Nazi Holocaust, the Algerian war, and more private subjects, such as the love of parents and children and the imperfect wedding of flesh and spirit.

Hecht was born on January 16, 1923, in New York City. He graduated from Bard College in 1944 and immediately entered the army, with which he served in Europe and Japan; he has called "the cumulative sense" of his wartime years "grotesque beyond anything I could possibly write." After his release from the army Hecht taught briefly at several universities while working for his M.A. at Columbia University (1950); he later taught at the University of Rochester (1967–85) and Georgetown University (1985–93). The author of books of criticism as well as numerous volumes of poetry, he won the Pulitzer Prize in 1968 and the Bollingen Prize in 1983. From 1982 to 1984, he served as poetry consultant to the Library of Congress.

Birdwatchers of America

> I suffer now continually from vertigo, and today, 23rd of January, 1862, I received a singular warning: I felt the wind of the wing of madness pass over me.
> —Baudelaire, *Journals*[1]

It's all very well to dream of a dove that saves,
  Picasso's or the Pope's,
The one that annually coos in Our Lady's ear
  Half the world's hopes,[2]
And the other one that shall cunningly engineer   5
The retirement of all businessmen to their graves,
  And when this is brought about
Make us the loving brothers of every lout—

But in our part of the country a false dusk
  Lingers for hours; it steams   10
From the soaked hay, wades in the cloudy woods,
  Engendering other dreams.
Formless and soft beyond the fence it broods
Or rises as a faint and rotten musk
  Out of a broken stalk.   15
There are some things of which we seldom talk;

For instance, the woman next door, whom we hear at night,
  Claims that when she was small
She found a man stone dead near the cedar trees
  After the first snowfall.   20
The air was clear. He seemed in ultimate peace
Except that he had no eyes. Rigid and bright
  Upon the forehead, furred
With a light frost, crouched an outrageous bird.

           1967

1. Charles Baudelaire (1821–1867), French poet, spent his last years in a struggle against insanity following his addiction to drugs. The journal of those years is called *My Heart Laid Bare*.
2. Pablo Picasso (1881–1973), Spanish expatriate artist, often drew the dove of peace; in Christian symbolism, the dove represents the descent of the Holy Spirit at baptism; in flight, it symbolizes the ascension of Christ and the entry into glory of the martyrs and saints.

A Hill

In Italy, where this sort of thing can occur,
I had a vision once—though you understand
It was nothing at all like Dante's,[3] or the visions of saints,
And perhaps not a vision at all. I was with some friends,
Picking my way through a warm sunlit piazza   5
In the early morning. A clear fretwork of shadows
From huge umbrellas littered the pavement and made
A sort of lucent shallows in which was moored
A small navy of carts. Books, coins, old maps,
Cheap landscapes and ugly religious prints   10
Were all on sale. The colors and noise
Like the flying hands were gestures of exultation,
So that even the bargaining
Rose to the ear like a voluble godliness.
And then, when it happened, the noises suddenly stopped,   15
And it got darker; pushcarts and people dissolved
And even the great Farnese Palace[4] itself
Was gone, for all its marble; in its place
Was a hill, mole-colored and bare. It was very cold,
Close to freezing, with a promise of snow.   20
The trees were like old ironwork gathered for scrap
Outside a factory wall. There was no wind,
And the only sound for a while was the little click
Of ice as it broke in the mud under my feet.
I saw a piece of ribbon snagged on a hedge,   25
But no other sign of life. And then I heard
What seemed the crack of a rifle. A hunter, I guessed;
At least I was not alone. But just after that
Came the soft and papery crash
Of a great branch somewhere unseen falling to earth.   30

And that was all, except for the cold and silence
That promised to last forever, like the hill.

Then prices came through, and fingers, and I was restored
To the sunlight and my friends. But for more than a week
I was scared by the plain bitterness of what I had seen.   35
All this happened about ten years ago,
And it hasn't troubled me since, but at last, today,
I remembered that hill; it lies just to the left
Of the road north of Poughkeepsie;[5] and as a boy
I stood before it for hours in wintertime.   40

1967

3. Dante Alighieri (1265–1321), Italian poet,
author of *The Divine Comedy*.

4. In Rome.

5. City in upstate New York.

"It Out-Herods Herod. Pray You, Avoid It."[6]

Tonight my children hunch
Toward their Western, and are glad
As, with a Sunday punch,
The Good casts out the Bad.

And in their fairy tales   5
The warty giant and witch
Get sealed in doorless jails
And the match-girl strikes it rich.

I've made myself a drink.
The giant and witch are set   10
To bust out of the clink
When my children have gone to bed.

All frequencies are loud
With signals of despair;
In flash and morse they crowd   15
The rondure of the air.

For the wicked have grown strong,
Their numbers mock at death,
Their cow brings forth its young,
Their bull engendereth.   20

Their very fund of strength,
Satan, bestrides the globe;
He stalks its breadth and length
And finds out even Job.[7]

Yet by quite other laws   25
My children make their case;
Half God, half Santa Claus,
But with my voice and face,

A hero comes to save
The poorman, beggarman, thief   30
And make the world behave
And put an end to grief.

And that their sleep be sound
I say this childermas[8]
Who could not, at one time,   35
Have saved them from the gas.

1967

6. From Hamlet's instructions to the actors (*Hamlet* 3.2), requesting them not to rant like the character Herod in medieval mystery plays.
7. In the Bible, God's most devout servant, and therefore prosperous; God allowed Satan to destroy Job's wealth and family as a test of his faith.
8. The festival of the Holy Innocents, commemorating the slaughter of Hebrew children by Herod in his effort to counter the prophecy that Jesus was to become king of the Jews (Matthew 2.16).

The Deodand[9]

What are these women up to? They've gone and strung
Drapes over the windows, cutting out light
And the slightest hope of a breeze here in mid-August.
Can this be simply to avoid being seen
By some prying *femme-de-chambre*[1] across the boulevard   5
Who has stepped out on a balcony to disburse
Her dustmop gleanings on the summer air?
And what of these rugs and pillows, all haphazard,
Here in what might be someone's living room
In the swank, high-toned sixteenth *arrondissement?*[2]   10
What would their fathers, husbands, *fiancés,*
Those pillars of the old *haute-bourgeoisie,*[3]
Think of the strange charade now in the making?
Swathed in exotic finery, in loose silks,
Gauzy organzas[4] with metallic threads,   15
Intricate Arab vests, brass ornaments
At wrist and ankle, those small sexual fetters,
Tight little silver chains, and bangled gold
Suspended like a coarse barbarian treasure
From soft earlobes pierced through symbolically,   20
They are preparing some *tableau vivant.*[5]
One girl, consulting the authority
Of a painting, perhaps by Ingres or Delacroix,[6]
Is reporting over her shoulder on the use
Of kohl[7] to lend its dark, savage allurements.   25
Another, playing the slave-artisan's role,
Almost completely naked, brush in hand,
Attends to these instructions as she prepares
To complete the seductive shadowing of the eyes
Of the blonde girl who appears the harem favorite,   30
And who is now admiring these effects
In a mirror held by a fourth, a well-clad servant.
The scene simmers with Paris and women in heat,
Darkened and airless, perhaps with a faint hum
Of trapped flies, and a strong odor of musk.   35
For whom do they play at this hot indolence
And languorous vassalage?[8] They are alone
With fantasies of jasmine and brass lamps,
Melons and dates and bowls of rose-water,

9. "Deodand is defined as 'A thing forfeited or to be given to God; *spec.* in *Eng. Law,* a personal chattel which, having been the immediate occasion of the death of a human being, was given to God as an expiatory offering, i.e. forfeited to the Crown to be applied to pious uses. . . . ' The poem is based on a painting by Pierre-Auguste Renoir [1841–1919] called *Parisians Dressed in Algerian Costume,* in the National Museum of Western Art, Tokyo" [Hecht's note].
1. Chambermaid (French).
2. District in Paris.
3. Upper middle class.
4. Sheer silk fabrics.
5. Literally, "living picture," in which the participants, appropriately costumed, pose to represent a painting.
6. Nineteenth-century French painters, both of whom painted pictures of Middle Eastern subjects.
7. Dark eye makeup used in the Middle East.
8. Slavery.

A courtyard fountain's firework blaze of prisms,   40
Its basin sown with stars and *poissons d'or,*[9]
And a rude stable smell of animal strength,
Of leather thongs, hinting of violations,
Swooning lubricities and lassitudes.
What is all this but crude imperial pride,   45
Feminized, scented and attenuated,
The exploitation of the primitive,
Homages of romantic self-deception,
Mimes of submission glamorized as lust?
Have they no intimation, no recall   50
Of the once queen who liked to play at milkmaid,
And the fierce butcher-reckoning that followed
Her innocent, unthinking masquerade?[1]
Those who will not be taught by history
Have as their curse the office to repeat it,[2]   55
And for this little spiritual debauch
(Reported here with warm, exacting care
By Pierre Renoir in 1872—
Apparently unnoticed by the girls,
An invisible voyeur, like you and me)   60
Exactions shall be made, an expiation,
A forfeiture. Though it take ninety years,
All the retributive iron of Racine[3]
Shall answer from the raging heat of the desert.

    In the final months of the Algerian war   65
They captured a very young French Legionnaire.[4]
They shaved his head, decked him in a blonde wig,
Carmined his lips grotesquely, fitted him out
With long, theatrical false eyelashes
And a bright, loose-fitting skirt of calico,   70
And cut off all the fingers of both hands.
He had to eat from a fork held by his captors.
Thus costumed, he was taken from town to town,
Encampment to encampment, on a leash,
And forced to beg for his food with a special verse   75
Sung to a popular show tune of those days:
"Donnez moi à manger de vos mains
Car c'est pour vous que je fais ma petite danse;
Car je suis Madeleine, la putain,
Et je m'en vais le lendemain matin,   80
Car je suis La Belle France."[5]

                                                          1980

9. Goldfish.
1. Marie Antoinette, queen of France, one of whose hobbies was dressing up as a milkmaid, was guillotined in 1793, during the French Revolution.
2. "Those who cannot remember the past are condemned to repeat it" (George Santayana, *Life of Reason*). *Office:* duty.
3. Jean Racine (1639–1699), French playwright, most of whose plays were tragedies of revenge.

4. Member of the French foreign legion, an army of volunteers originally founded to control the French colony of Algiers (northern Africa); Algiers (now Algeria) fought for its independence from 1954 to 1962 and won.
5. "The concluding lines in French may be rendered:
    'Let me be given nourishment at your hands / Since it's for you I perform my little dance. / For

The Book of Yolek

Wir haben ein Gesetz,
Und nach dem Gesetz soll er sterben.[6]

The dowsed coals fume and hiss after your meal
Of grilled brook trout, and you saunter off for a walk
Down the fern trail, it doesn't matter where to,
Just so you're weeks and worlds away from home,
And among midsummer hills have set up camp   5
In the deep bronze glories of declining day.

You remember, peacefully, an earlier day
In childhood, remember a quite specific meal:
A corn roast and bonfire in summer camp.
That summer you got lost on a Nature Walk;   10
More than you dared admit, you thought of home;
No one else knows where the mind wanders to.

The fifth of August, 1942.
It was morning and very hot. It was the day
They came at dawn with rifles to The Home   15
For Jewish Children, cutting short the meal
Of bread and soup, lining them up to walk
In close formation off to a special camp.

How often you have thought about that camp,
As though in some strange way you were driven to,   20
And about the children, and how they were made to walk,
Yolek who had bad lungs, who wasn't a day
Over five years old, commanded to leave his meal
And shamble between armed guards to his long home.

We're approaching August again. It will drive home   25
The regulation torments of that camp
Yolek was sent to, his small, unfinished meal,
The electric fences, the numeral tattoo,
The quite extraordinary heat of the day
They all were forced to take that terrible walk.   30

Whether on a silent, solitary walk
Or among crowds, far off or safe at home,
You will remember, helplessly, that day,
And the smell of smoke, and the loudspeakers of the camp.
Wherever you are, Yolek will be there, too.   35
His unuttered name will interrupt your meal.

I am the street-walker, Magdalen, / And come the dawn I'll be on my way again, / The beauty queen, Miss France" [Hecht's note].
6. We have a law, and by that law he ought to die (German). From a translation of John 19.7 by the- ologian Martin Luther (1483–1546), leader of the Protestant Reformation in Germany. Hecht's poem is inspired by "Yanosz Korczak's Last Walk," by Polish poet Hanna Mortkowicz Olczakowa (1905–1968).

Prepare to receive him in your home some day.
Though they killed him in the camp they sent him to,
He will walk in as you're sitting down to a meal.

1990

JAMES DICKEY
1923–1997

James Dickey insisted, as Oscar Wilde did, that art is the fashioning of illusions and "lies." Once his imagination took hold of some strange, often monstrous event, he pursued it relentlessly. "As Longinus points out," he said in 1970, "there's a razor's edge between sublimity and absurdity. And that's the edge I try to walk. Sometimes *both* sides are ludicrous! . . . But I don't think you can get to sublimity without courting the ridiculous" (*Self-Interviews*). Dickey is a gothic poet, whether he domesticates the monstrous or allows his monsters to range freely.

Dickey spent six of his mature years in advertising. In between producing copy for Coca-Cola and other companies in Atlanta, he composed some of his best poems. He has in his verse a purposefulness and insistence, a demand for attention and for recognition, that is perhaps not so much an echo of his days in advertising as an indication of why he was good at it. He wanted to be an "intensified man" or a "totally responsive man."

Born on February 2, 1923, in a suburb of Atlanta, Dickey became a high school football star. In 1941, he went to Clemson A&M College (later University), in South Carolina, but left after a semester to enlist in the army air corps. Although he claimed to have flown a hundred combat missions, he washed out during flight training and instead operated radar equipment during flights in the Pacific. Awakened to a love of literature by the war, he read books between missions, including an anthology of modern poets such as Dylan Thomas. On his return from the war Dickey attended Vanderbilt University, a center of modern southern poetry, where he worked with an older student's zeal. A friendly professor, Monroe K. Spears, encouraged him to write more poetry and urged him to write as the poem, rather than the real-life experience, necessitated. "That idea was the bursting of a dam for me," said Dickey. He stayed on at Vanderbilt for his M.A. and then taught at Rice Institute (later University), in Texas. The air force recalled him to active service for the Korean War, during which he taught radar operation at U.S. bases. In 1955, after a year in Europe, he began teaching at the University of Florida, where a dispute arose over the propriety of remarks he made to a group of women writers. He abruptly resigned in April 1956 and worked in advertising until 1961. After a year on a Guggenheim Fellowship in Europe, he returned to the United States to teach, lecture, and write. From 1966 to 1968, he served as poetry consultant to the Library of Congress; from 1969, he held a teaching position at the University of South Carolina. In 1970, he published his first novel, *Deliverance,* the film version of which brought him fame, which fueled his debilitating alcoholism.

Dickey's poetry is arresting and powerful. It is characterized more by force than by grace, more by conceptual intricacy than by wit. Part of its pleasure lies in its sense of abundance and confidence. "I don't believe in the kind of cool diffidence people nowadays affect," he said (*Self-Interviews*). Taken with the views of the agrarians as a young man at Vanderbilt, Dickey wished to be on intimate terms with the regenerative forces of nature. He had a keen sense of an archetypal world underlying the real one, accessible at unusual moments, and this deepening or descent from level to level was often his theme. Most of his poems are in the first person, but the "I" is rather impersonal, even if based on actual experience, because it is on its way to becoming "an inspired outline of myself" ("Chenille").

The Hospital Window

I have just come down from my father.
Higher and higher he lies
Above me in a blue light
Shed by a tinted window.
I drop through six white floors   5
And then step out onto pavement.

Still feeling my father ascend,
I start to cross the firm street,
My shoulder blades shining with all
The glass the huge building can raise.   10
Now I must turn round and face it,
And know his one pane from the others.

Each window possesses the sun
As though it burned there on a wick.
I wave, like a man catching fire.   15
All the deep-dyed windowpanes flash,
And, behind them, all the white rooms
They turn to the color of Heaven.

Ceremoniously, gravely, and weakly,
Dozens of pale hands are waving   20
Back, from inside their flames.
Yet one pure pane among these
Is the bright, erased blankness of nothing.
I know that my father is there,

In the shape of his death still living.   25
The traffic increases around me
Like a madness called down on my head.
The horns blast at me like shotguns,
And drivers lean out, driven crazy—
But now my propped-up father   30

Lifts his arm out of stillness at last.
The light from the window strikes me
And I turn as blue as a soul,
As the moment when I was born.
I am not afraid for my father—   35
Look! He is grinning; he is not

Afraid for my life, either,
As the wild engines stand at my knees
Shredding their gears and roaring,
And I hold each car in its place   40
For miles, inciting its horn
To blow down the walls of the world

That the dying may float without fear
In the bold blue gaze of my father.
Slowly I move to the sidewalk   45
With my pin-tingling hand half dead
At the end of my bloodless arm.
I carry it off in amazement,

High, still higher, still waving,
My recognized face fully mortal,   50
Yet not; not at all, in the pale,
Drained, otherworldly, stricken,
Created hue of stained glass.
I have just come down from my father.

                                                    1962

The Heaven of Animals

Here they are. The soft eyes open.
If they have lived in a wood
It is a wood.
If they have lived on plains
It is grass rolling   5
Under their feet forever.

Having no souls, they have come,
Anyway, beyond their knowing.
Their instincts wholly bloom
And they rise.   10
The soft eyes open.

To match them, the landscape flowers,
Outdoing, desperately
Outdoing what is required:
The richest wood,   15
The deepest field.

For some of these,
It could not be the place
It is, without blood.
These hunt, as they have done,   20
But with claws and teeth grown perfect,

More deadly than they can believe.
They stalk more silently,

And crouch on the limbs of trees,
And their descent   25
Upon the bright backs of their prey

May take years
In a sovereign floating of joy.
And those that are hunted
Know this as their life,   30
Their reward: to walk

Under such trees in full knowledge
Of what is in glory above them,
And to feel no fear,
But acceptance, compliance.   35
Fulfilling themselves without pain

At the cycle's center,
They tremble, they walk
Under the tree,
They fall, they are torn,   40
They rise, they walk again.

                                                    1962

Buckdancer's Choice[1]

So I would hear out those lungs,
The air split into nine levels,
Some gift of tongues of the whistler

In the invalid's bed: my mother,
Warbling all day to herself   5
The thousand variations of one song;

It is called Buckdancer's Choice.
For years, they have all been dying
Out, the classic buck-and-wing men

Of traveling minstrel shows;   10
With them also an old woman
Was dying of breathless angina,

Yet still found breath enough
To whistle up in my head
A sight like a one-man band,   15

Freed black, with cymbals at heel,
An ex-slave who thrivingly danced
To the ring of his own clashing light

---

1. A buckdancer does the buck-and-wing, a tap dance often performed in wooden shoes.

Through the thousand variations of one song
All day to my mother's prone music,   20
The invalid's warbler's note,

While I crept close to the wall
Sock-footed, to hear the sounds alter,
Her tongue like a mockingbird's break

Through stratum after stratum of a tone   25
Proclaiming what choices there are
For the last dancers of their kind,

For ill women and for all slaves
Of death, and children enchanted at walls
With a brass-beating glow underfoot,   30

Not dancing but nearly risen
Through barnlike, theatrelike houses
On the wings of the buck and wing.

                                                    1965

The Sheep Child

Farm boys wild to couple
With anything   with soft-wooded trees
With mounds of earth   mounds
Of pinestraw   will keep themselves off
Animals by legends of their own: 5
In the hay-tunnel dark
And dung of barns, they will
Say   I have heard tell

That in a museum in Atlanta
Way back in a corner somewhere   10
There's this thing that's only half
Sheep   like a woolly baby
Pickled in alcohol   because
Those things can't live   his eyes
Are open   but you can't stand to look   15
I heard from somebody who . . .

But this is now almost all
Gone. The boys have taken
Their own true wives in the city,
The sheep are safe in the west hill   20
Pasture   but we who were born there
Still are not sure. Are we,

Because we remember, remembered
In the terrible dust of museums?

Merely with his eyes, the sheep-child may   25

Be saying   saying

> I am here, in my father's house.
> I who am half of your world, came deeply
> To my mother in the long grass
> Of the west pasture, where she stood like moonlight   30
> Listening for foxes. It was something like love
> From another world that seized her
> From behind, and she gave, not lifting her head
> Out of dew, without ever looking, her best
> Self to that great need. Turned loose, she dipped her face   35
> Farther into the chill of the earth, and in a sound
> Of sobbing   of something stumbling
> Away, began, as she must do,
> To carry me. I woke, dying,
>
> In the summer sun of the hillside, with my eyes   40
> Far more than human. I saw for a blazing moment
> The great grassy world from both sides,
> Man and beast in the round of their need,
> And the hill wind stirred in my wool,
> My hoof and my hand clasped each other,   45
> I ate my one meal
> Of milk, and died
> Staring. From dark grass I came straight
>
> To my father's house, whose dust
> Whirls up in the halls for no reason   50
> When no one comes   piling deep in a hellish mild corner,
> And, through my immortal waters
> I meet the sun's grains eye
> To eye, and they fail at my closet of glass.
> Dead, I am most surely living   55
> In the minds of farm boys: I am he who drives
> Them like wolves from the hound bitch and calf
> And from the chaste ewe in the wind.
> They go into woods   into bean fields   they go
> Deep into their known right hands. Dreaming of me,   60
> They groan   they wait   they suffer
> Themselves, they marry, they raise their kind.

1967

ALAN DUGAN
1923–2003

Alan Dugan was conspicuously unaffiliated—to other poets, to an affirmative creed, to life itself. One poem is partly titled "from an Alienated Point of View," and this description applies to all his work. The final poem of his first book speaks of "prisoners of this world," and Dugan wrote as a prisoner, confident that there was no escape and that come what may the future would be as bad as the present. To Dugan, America is the land not of promise but of decadence and of various despairs. Not that the rest of the universe is any better.

Bluntness, ironic rage, and a ferocious sense of comedy form Dugan's responses to experience. At moments he sounds like a church father denouncing existence; St. Augustine's statement "Nascimur inter faeces et urinas" ("We are born between the feces and the urine") might seem to be his text. Dugan's despair differs from that of others, such as Jonathan Swift, in being anarchic, endless, a cherished anguish. Yet his caustic attacks on comforting hopes are so adroit that one reads him with wincing amusement. He was the clown of nihilism. Heroism, victory, patience, nature, family, even his own art—all are mercilessly felled by his rhetorical ax. Terse and vivid, his satiric poems are tightly constructed and emotionally intense.

Born on February 12, 1923, in Brooklyn, New York, Dugan was a left-wing "antifascist" (his term) and served in the army air force during World War II. After the war, he worked for an advertising agency, a staple factory, and a payroll office, eventually making physiological models in plastic. He received a B.A. from Mexico City College. He had published very little poetry until his first book was accepted for the Yale Series of Younger Poets and published in 1961. The resultant praise, and two prizes he won later, the Pulitzer Prize and the National Book Award, allowed him to devote himself to writing. He taught for most of his career at the Fine Arts Work Center in Provincetown, Massachusetts. He won the National Book Award a second time in 2001.

Love Song: I and Thou

Nothing is plumb, level or square:
    the studs are bowed, the joists
are shaky by nature, no piece fits
    any other piece without a gap
or pinch, and bent nails 5
dance all over the surfacing
like maggots. By Christ
    I am no carpenter. I built
the roof for myself, the walls
    for myself, the floors 10
for myself, and got
    hung up in it myself. I
danced with a purple thumb
    at this house-warming, drunk
with my prime whiskey: rage. 15
    Oh I spat rage's nails

into the frame-up of my work:
   it held. It settled plumb,
level, solid, square and true
   for that great moment. Then   20
it screamed and went on through,
   skewing as wrong the other way.
God damned it. This is hell,
   but I planned it, I sawed it,
I nailed it, and I   25
   will live in it until it kills me.
I can nail my left palm
   to the left-hand crosspiece but
I can't do everything myself.
   I need a hand to nail the right,   30
a help, a love, a you, a wife.

                    1961

Fabrication of Ancestors

For old Billy Dugan, shot in the ass in
the Civil War, my father said.

The old wound in my ass
has opened up again, but I
am past the prodigies
of youth's campaigns, and weep
where I used to laugh   5
in war's red humors, half
in love with silly-assed pains
and half not feeling them.
I have to sit up with
an indoor unsittable itch   10
before I go down late
and weeping to the storm-
cellar on a dirty night
and go to bed with the worms.
So pull the dirt up over me   15
and make a family joke
for Old Billy Blue Balls,
the oldest private in the world
with two ass-holes and no
place more to go to for a laugh   20
except the last one. Say:
The North won the Civil War
without much help from me
although I wear a proof
of the war's obscenity.   25

                    1963

On Being a Householder

I live inside of a machine
or machines. Every time one
goes off another starts. Why
don't I go outside and sleep
on the ground. It is because   5
I'm scared of the open night
and stars looking down at me
as God's eyes, full of questions;
and when I do sleep out alone
I wake up soaking wet   10
with the dew-fall and am
being snuffed at by a female fox
who stinks from being skunked.
Also there are carrion insects
climbing my private parts. Therefore   15
I would find shelter in houses,
rented or owned. Anything that money
can build or buy is better than
the nothing of the sky at night,
the stars being the visible past.   20

1974

Internal Migration: On Being on Tour

As an American traveler I have
to remember not to get actionably[1] mad
about the way things are around here.
Tomorrow I'll be a thousand miles away
from the way it is around here. I will   5
keep my temper, I will not kill the dog
next door, nor will I kill the next-door wife,
both of whom are crazy and aggressive
and think they live at the center of culture
like everyone else in this college town.   10
This is because I'm leaving, I'm taking off
by car, by light plane, by jet, by taxicab,
for some place else a thousand miles away,
so I caution myself: control your rage,
even if it causes a slight heart attack.   15
Stay out of jail tonight before you leave,
and don't get obstreperous in transit tomorrow
so as to stay out of jail on arrival tomorrow night.
Think: the new handcuffs are sharp inside
and meant to cut the wrists. You're not too old   20

---

1. Affording grounds for a lawsuit.

to be raped in their filthy overcrowded jails
and you'll lose your glasses and false teeth.
How would you eat, study and be
a traveling lecturer if you got out alive and sane?
So remember to leave this place peacefully,   25
it's only Asshole State University at Nowheresville,
and remember to get to the next place peacefully,
it's only Nowhere State University at Assholeville
and you must travel from place to place for food and shelter.

1983

For Euthanasia and Pain-Killing Drugs

As my father died of cancer of the asshole
the doctor wouldn't give him habit-forming drugs
for fear of making him a hopeless addict
so it took two men to hold him down to die.
I ran around like crazy to the bars that day.   5
When I got back that night they said he died at noon,
so I squeezed out two tears because they said I should.
Look at what happened to your Uncle John they said.
He couldn't cry when Grandpa died
so he went nuts and tried to kill the priest.   10
We had to have him put away for life
but you are blessed, you cried, a good son,
you are saved, oh you are not your father's asshole,
may you never rot in shit, God bless your come.

2001

Louis Simpson
1923–2012

Louis Simpson's early verse, especially his war poetry, explores what he calls "the other side of glory" ("The Legend of Success, the Salesman's Story"). It incongruously frames in fluent meters and rhymed stanzas bitter encounters with death on the battlefield. After his second book of poetry, Simpson abandoned this grim realism, inspired by his participation in the Battle of the Bulge and other armed conflicts of World War II. Instead, his poetry combines a consciousness of how things occur with an awareness of far-flung possibilities, only attainable in dreams. He came to regard his verse as joined to a literary tradition that he traced from symbolism to imagism to surrealism, "rejecting on the one hand the clichés of the rational mind, and on the other, a mere projection of irrational images"; the poet should "reveal the drama and narrative of the subconscious. The images move, with the logic of dreams" (*The Distinctive Voice*, ed. William Martz, 1966). Although his verse is conspicuously formal, it is dotted by dream images. "American poetry," he said (in a poem by that title), "must swim for miles through the desert / Uttering cries that are almost human." With grace, Simpson's verse incorporates fantastic and commonplace material alike, binds physics and metaphysics. Like many American poets, Simpson turned to free verse in the 1960s. His later narrative poetry retains his earlier polish, but it achieves the simplicity of old stories and proverbs, as he writes with wry humor about incidents in his own life.

Simpson was born on March 27, 1923, in Kingston, Jamaica. He emigrated to the United States at seventeen. In his verse, he contemplates the United States with detachment; he is sympathetic, but offers no panegyrics. The Vietnam War in particular alienated him. Simpson's father was a second-generation Jamaican of Scots descent, his mother a Russian Jew. "I most of all wanted to be an American," he said (*Current Biography*, ed. Charles Moritz, 1964). In 1943, he left Columbia University for the American army, serving first with a tank corps, then as a combat infantryman with the 101st Airborne Division; he won the Bronze Star and Purple Heart. His health broke down late in the war; after his recovery, he returned to Columbia for undergraduate and graduate studies. While completing his doctorate, Simpson taught for a time at Columbia and worked briefly in publishing and in export trade. But he reverted to teaching, at the New School for Social Research (1955–59), the University of California at Berkeley (1959–67), and the State University of New York at Stony Brook (1967–93). In addition to books of poetry, he published fiction, plays, essays, an autobiography, and award-winning translations of French poetry.

The Battle

Helmet and rifle, pack and overcoat
Marched through a forest. Somewhere up ahead
Guns thudded. Like the circle of a throat
The night on every side was turning red.

They halted and they dug. They sank like moles   5
Into the clammy earth between the trees.
And soon the sentries, standing in their holes,
Felt the first snow. Their feet began to freeze.

At dawn the first shell landed with a crack.
Then shells and bullets swept the icy woods.   10
This lasted many days. The snow was black.
The corpses stiffened in their scarlet hoods.

Most clearly of that battle I remember
The tiredness in eyes, how hands looked thin
Around a cigarette, and the bright ember   15
Would pulse with all the life there was within.

1955

My Father in the Night Commanding No

My father in the night commanding No
Has work to do. Smoke issues from his lips;
    He reads in silence.
The frogs are croaking and the streetlamps glow.

And then my mother winds the gramophone;   5
The Bride of Lammermoor begins to shriek—[1]
    Or reads a story
About a prince, a castle, and a dragon.

The moon is glittering above the hill.
I stand before the gateposts of the King—   10
    So runs the story—
Of Thule,[2] at midnight when the mice are still.

And I have been in Thule! It has come true—
The journey and the danger of the world,
    All that there is   15
To bear and to enjoy, endure and do.

Landscapes, seascapes . . . where have I been led?
The names of cities—Paris, Venice, Rome—
    Held out their arms.
A feathered god, seductive, went ahead.   20

Here is my house. Under a red rose tree
A child is swinging; another gravely plays.
    They are not surprised
That I am here; they were expecting me.

And yet my father sits and reads in silence,   25
My mother sheds a tear, the moon is still,
    And the dark wind
Is murmuring that nothing ever happens.

Beyond his jurisdiction as I move
Do I not prove him wrong? And yet, it's true   30
    They will not change
There, on the stage of terror and of love.

The actors in that playhouse always sit
In fixed positions—father, mother, child
    With painted eyes.   35
How sad it is to be a little puppet!

---

1. The record is probably of the mad scene from the opera *Lucia di Lammermoor,* by Gaetano Donizetti (1797–1848).

2. The name given to an island discovered in the far north by ancient Greek sailors; it symbolizes the explorer's ultimate quest.

Their heads are wooden. And you once pretended
To understand them! Shake them as you will,
   They cannot speak.
Do what you will, the comedy is ended.[3]   40

Father, why did you work? Why did you weep,
Mother? Was the story so important?
   "Listen!" the wind
Said to the children, and they fell asleep.

                                       1963

American Poetry

Whatever it is, it must have
A stomach that can digest
Rubber, coal, uranium, moons, poems.

Like the shark, it contains a shoe.
It must swim for miles through the desert   5
Uttering cries that are almost human.

                                       1963

White Oxen

A man walks beside them
with a whip that he cracks.
The cart they draw is painted
with Saracens and Crusaders,[4]
fierce eyes and ranks of spears.   5

They are on the steep road
that goes up the mountain.
Their neat-stepping hoofs
appear to be flickering
in the sun, raising dust.   10

They are higher than the roofs
on which striped gourds and melons
lie ripening. They move
among the dark green olives
that grow on the rocks.   15

---

3. This line's second half ends the opera *Pagliacci,* by Neapolitan composer Ruggero Leoncavallo (1857/58–1919). The audience, thinking it is watching a play, witnesses a double murder committed by the jealous husband who speaks the line.
4. That is, the Muslims and the European Crusaders who fought them for recovery of the Holy Land, in the Middle Ages.

They dwindle as they climb . . .
vanish around a corner
and reappear walking on the edge
of a precipice. They enter
the region of mist and darkness.   20

I think I can see them still:
a pair of yoked oxen
the color of ivory
or smoke, with red tassels,
in the gathering dusk.   25

1987

DENISE LEVERTOV
1923–1997

Denise Levertov writes a poetry of secrets, in which the poet uncovers something hidden, like a physicist plumbing the atom. This something is recognized with such joyful force that it seems to palpitate or shudder at being known. Her work has close connections, as she realized, with that of Black Mountain poets Robert Duncan and Robert Creeley, though it is less mystical than Duncan's, more ecstatic than Creeley's. She regarded these men as "the chief poets among my contemporaries" (*The Poet in the World*). Ezra Pound, William Carlos Williams, and H. D. are among her modernist influences, commemorated in the poem "September 1961." Levertov liked to burst through the trivial, and in "A Common Ground" she speaks of "poems stirred / into paper coffee-cups, eaten / with petals on rye in the / sun . . . entering / human lives forever, / unobserved." In rhapsodic rhythms and incantatory syntax, the poet conveys awe before nature and human relationships. Conifers hold their cones up for the light's blessing in a "festive rite" ("Celebration"), and vine leaves exchange mysterious whispers ("Aware"). Love, desire, and grief are among the emotional resources that flood the poems. In elegies for her sister, she mourns the memory of Olga at sixteen with "breasts / round, round, and / dark-nippled—," now "bones and tatters of flesh in earth."

Written in England, Levertov's first book was in regular stanzas, but her subsequent books, written in the United States, are in free verse. Her sense of pace and climax follows principles outlined in Charles Olson's "Projective Verse" and her "Notes on Organic Form," such as form as a revelation of content, verbal simulation of propulsive movement, avoidance of the iamb, composition to the rhythm of breathing, and conflation of the mundane with the mystical. Her effects are precisely calculated: "I believe every space and comma is a living part of the poem and has its function, just as every muscle and pore of the body has its function. And the way the lines are broken is a functioning part essential to the poem's life" (*The Poet in the World*).

Judeo-Christian in religious background and Anglo-American in nationality, Levertov lived transnationally and cross-culturally. She proudly claimed connection with mystics of the past. Her father was descended from a Russian rabbi, Schneour Zaimon, who was renowned as a Hasid, a member of a Jewish mystical movement that began in the eighteenth century and found a glory in everyday occurrences. Her mother was descended from a Welsh tailor and mystic, Angel Jones of Mold (a town in Wales).

Although her father was born Jewish, he converted to Christianity and became an Anglican priest, with a lifelong hope of uniting the two religions. Born on October 24, 1923, in Ilford, Essex, Levertov went to neither school nor college. "As a child," she writes, "I 'did lessons' at home under the tutelage of my mother and listened to the BBC Schools Programs. For French, piano, and art I was sent to various teachers for private lessons" ("The Untaught Teacher," *The Poet in the World*).

In 1948, when she was twenty-five years old, Levertov moved to the United States with her American husband, the author Mitchell Goodman, who introduced her to Creeley and Duncan. She became a U.S. citizen in 1955. Beginning in the 1960s, Levertov became a war protester and in poetry passionately denounced the Vietnam War, the nuclear arms race, and U.S. policy in El Salvador. Seen by some as "prophetic," by others as "preachy," these poems reflect a change in Levertov's view on the relation of poetry to politics. In 1959, she had stated, "I do not believe that a violent imitation of the horrors of our times is the concern of poetry"; but by 1965, she declared that the poem "has a social *effect* of some kind whether or not the poet wills that it have. It has kinetic force, it sets in motion . . . elements in the reader that would otherwise be stagnant" ("A Testament and a Postscript," *The Poet in the World*).

In her later volumes, Levertov returned to a more intimate kind of poetry. Meanwhile, she had taught at a large number of universities and colleges, remaining from 1981 at Stanford University. She became a Roman Catholic a few years before dying from lymphoma.

Pleasures

I like to find
what's not found
at once, but lies

within something of another nature, 5
in repose, distinct.
Gull feathers of glass, hidden

in white pulp: the bones of squid
which I pull out and lay
blade by blade on the draining board—

    tapered as if for swiftness, to pierce 10
    the heart, but fragile, substance
    belying design.   Or a fruit, *mamey*,

cased in rough brown peel, the flesh
rose-amber, and the seed:
the seed a stone of wood, carved and 15

polished, walnut-colored, formed
like a brazilnut, but large,
large enough to fill
the hungry palm of a hand.

I like the juicy stem of grass that grows   20
within the coarser leaf folded round,
and the butteryellow glow
in the narrow flute from which the morning-glory
opens blue and cool on a hot morning.

1959

The Dog of Art

That dog with daisies for eyes
who flashes forth
flame of his very self at every bark
is the Dog of Art.
Worked in wool, his blind eyes   5
look inward to caverns and jewels
which they see perfectly,
and his voice
measures forth the treasure
in music sharp and loud,   10
sharp and bright,
bright flaming barks,
and growling smoky soft, the Dog
of Art turns to the world
the quietness of his eyes.   15

1959

Song for Ishtar[1]

The moon is a sow
and grunts in my throat
Her great shining shines through me
so the mud of my hollow gleams
and breaks in silver bubbles   5

She is a sow
and I a pig and a poet

When she opens her white
lips to devour me I bite back
and laughter rocks the moon   10

In the black of desire
we rock and grunt, grunt and
shine

1964

1. Life-giving mother-goddess of the ancient Babylonians.

The Ache of Marriage

The ache of marriage:

thigh and tongue, beloved,
are heavy with it,
it throbs in the teeth

We look for communion   5
and are turned away, beloved,
each and each

It is leviathan[2] and we
in its belly
looking for joy, some joy   10
not to be known outside it

two by two in the ark of
the ache of it.

                                                              1964

September 1961

This is the year the old ones,
the old great ones
leave us alone on the road.

The road leads to the sea.
We have the words in our pockets,   5
obscure directions. The old ones

have taken away the light of their presence,
we see it moving away over a hill
off to one side.

They are not dying,   10
they are withdrawn
into a painful privacy

learning to live without words.
E.P. "It looks like dying"—Williams: "I can't
describe to you what has been   15

happening to me"—
H.D. "unable to speak."[3]
The darkness

---

2. The great seamonster of the Bible, often iden-
tified as a whale, such as swallowed Jonah.

3. American poet H. D. (Hilda Doolittle, b. 1886)
died on September 27, 1961. Also that year, Wil-

twists itself in the wind, the stars
are small, the horizon   20
ringed with confused urban light-haze.

They have told us
the road leads to the sea,
and given

the language into our hands.   25
We hear
our footsteps each time a truck

has dazzled past us and gone
leaving us new silence.
One can't reach   30

the sea on this endless
road to the sea unless
one turns aside at the end, it seems,

follows
the owl that silently glides above it   35
aslant, back and forth,

and away into deep woods.

But for us the road
unfurls itself, we count the
words in our pockets, we wonder   40

how it will be without them, we don't
stop walking, we know
there is far to go, sometimes

we think the night wind carries
a smell of the sea . . .   45

1964

Olga Poems

(Olga Levertoff, 1914–1964)[4]

i

By the gas-fire, kneeling
to undress,
scorching luxuriously, raking

---

liam Carlos Williams (1883–1963) suffered a
stroke and Ezra Pound (1885–1972) fell into a
silence that lasted until his death.
4. The poet's sister.

her nails over olive sides, the red
waistband ring—   5

(And the little sister
beady-eyed in the bed—
or drowsy, was I? My head
a camera—)

Sixteen. Her breasts   10
round, round, and
dark-nippled—

who now these two months long
is bones and tatters of flesh in earth.

iv

On your hospital bed you lay
in love, the hatreds
that had followed you, a
comet's tail, burned out

as your disasters bred of love   5
burned out,
while pain and drugs
quarreled like sisters in you—

lay afloat on a sea
of love and pain—how you always   10
loved that cadence, 'Underneath
are the everlasting arms'—[5]

all history
burned out, down
to the sick bone, save for   15

that kind candle.

vi

Your eyes were the brown gold of pebbles under water.
I never crossed the bridge over the Roding, dividing
the open field of the present from the mysteries,
the wraiths and shifts of time-sense Wanstead Park held suspended,
without remembering your eyes. Even when we were estranged   5
and my own eyes smarted in pain and anger at the thought of you.
And by other streams in other countries; anywhere where the light
reaches down through shallows to gold gravel. Olga's
brown eyes. One rainy summer, down in the New Forest,[6]
when we could hardly breathe for ennui and the low sky,   10

---

5. Deuteronomy 33.27.   6. A district in southern England.

you turned savagely to the piano and sightread
straight through all the Beethoven sonatas, day after day—
weeks, it seemed to me. I would turn the pages some of the time,
go out to ride my bike, return—you were enduring in the
falls and rapids of the music, the arpeggios rang out, the rectory   15
trembled, our parents seemed effaced.
I think of your eyes in that photo, six years before I was born,
the fear in them. What did you do with your fear,
later? Through the years of humiliation,
of paranoia and blackmail and near-starvation, losing   20
the love of those you loved, one after another,
parents, lovers, children, idolized friends, what kept
compassion's candle alight in you, that lit you
clear into another chapter (but the same book) 'a clearing
in the selva oscura,[7]   25
a house whose door
swings open, a hand beckons
in welcome'?
                    I cross
so many brooks in the world, there is so much light   30
dancing on so many stones, so many questions my eyes
smart to ask of your eyes, gold brown eyes,
the lashes short but the lids
arched as if carved out of olivewood, eyes with some vision
of festive goodness in back of their hard, or veiled, or shining,   35
unknowable gaze . . .

May–August, 1964   1966

A Time Past

The old wooden steps to the front door
where I was sitting that fall morning
when you came downstairs, just awake,
and my joy at sight of you (emerging
into golden day—   5
                    the dew almost frost)
pulled me to my feet to tell you
how much I loved you:

those wooden steps
are gone now, decayed   10
replaced with granite,
hard, gray, and handsome.
The old steps live
only in me:
my feet and thighs   15

7. "The quoted lines in the sixth section are an
adaptation of some lines in 'Selva Oscura' by the
late Louis MacNiece [1907–1963], a poem much
loved by my sister" [Levertov's note]. *Selva oscura*:
dark wood (Italian); from the opening lines of
Dante's *Divine Comedy*.

remember them, and my hands
still feel their splinters.

Everything else about and around that house
brings memories of others—of marriage,
of my son. And the steps do too: I recall   20
sitting there with my friend and her little son who died,
or was it the second one who lives and thrives?
And sitting there 'in my life,' often, alone or with my husband.
Yet that one instant,
your cheerful, unafraid, youthful, 'I love you too,'   25
the quiet broken by no bird, no cricket, gold leaves
spinning in silence down without
any breeze to blow them,
                                    is what twines itself
in my head and body across those slabs of wood   30
that were warm, ancient, and now
wait somewhere to be burnt.

                                                    1975

Caedmon[8]

All others talked as if
talk were a dance.
Clodhopper I, with clumsy feet
would break the gliding ring.
Early I learned to   5
hunch myself
close by the door:
then when the talk began
I'd wipe my
mouth and wend   10
unnoticed back to the barn
to be with the warm beasts,
dumb among body sounds
of the simple ones.
I'd see by a twist   15
of lit rush[9] the motes
of gold moving
from shadow to shadow
slow in the wake
of deep untroubled sighs.   20
The cows
munched or stirred or were still. I
was at home and lonely,

---

8. "The story comes, of course, from the venerable
Bede's *History of the English Church and People*,
but I first read it as a child in John Richard Green's
History of the English People, 1855" [Levertov's
note]. Caedmon (fl. 658–80), according to the
story, was an illiterate cowherd employed by a
monastery; one night he received a divine call to
sing verses in praise of God. He is the earliest
known English Christian poet.
9. The piths of rush plants were used for candle-
wicks.

both in good measure. Until
the sudden angel affrighted me—light effacing   25
my feeble beam,
a forest of torches, feathers of flame, sparks upflying:
but the cows as before
were calm, and nothing was burning,
         nothing but I, as that hand of fire   30
touched my lips and scorched my tongue
and pulled my voice
            into the ring of the dance.

                             1987

Celebration

Brilliant, this day—a young virtuoso of a day.
Morning shadows cut by sharpest scissors,
deft hands. And every prodigy of green—
whether it's ferns or lichen or needles
or impatient points of bud on spindly bushes—   5
greener than ever before.
                And the way the conifers
hold new cones to the light for blessing,
a festive rite, and sing the oceanic chant the wind
transcribes for them!   10
A day that shines in the cold
like a first-prize brass band swinging along the street
of a coal-dusty village, wholly at odds
with the claims of reasonable gloom.

                             1999

[Scraps of Moon]

   Scraps of moon
   bobbing discarded on broken water

   but sky-moon
   complete, transcending

   all violation.   5

                             1999

Aware

   When I opened the door
   I found the vine leaves
   speaking among themselves in abundant
   whispers.

My presence made them   5
hush their green breath,
embarrassed, the way
humans stand up, buttoning their jackets,
acting as if they were leaving anyway, as if
the conversations had ended   10
just before you arrived.
                            I liked
the glimpse I had, though,
of their obscure
gestures. I liked the sound   15
of such private voices. Next time
I'll move like cautious sunlight, open
the door by fractions, eavesdrop
peacefully.

1999

RICHARD HUGO
1923–1982

In 1973, the poet James Wright remarked that Richard Hugo's poetry shows us the "special and secret details of places" ("Hugo: Secrets of the Inner Landscape"). Hugo's poems take place, for the most part, in the Pacific northwest, where he lived, but he developed a complex relationship between his region and his fictions. "The place triggers the mind to create the place," he wrote; "the imagination can take off from" known reality "and if necessary return" (*The Triggering Town*). Dying towns and desolate landscapes haunt Hugo's imagination. He is a poet of elegiac remembrance, reclaiming the vacant, the abandoned, and the dead through descriptive detail and second-person address. Often speaking as the lonely outsider, he gives palpable presence to scenes of failure, poverty, and loss. His diction and syntax are spare and straightforward, and he artfully balances these qualities with richly textured images, melancholy tonalities, and pentameter rhythms.

Hugo's mother, a teenager, was forced to abandon him after his birth (on December 21, 1923) to the care of his maternal grandparents, working-class people of German descent who lived in the tough neighborhood of White Center, south of Seattle. Starved of affection, Hugo grew up lonely, shy, and terrified of relationships with women; he admired the local bullies and sought macho friendships with other boys: "By the time I was a young man I was a mess" (*The Real West Marginal Way*). After high school, facing the draft like other men of his generation, he joined the army air force and flew thirty-five missions as a bombardier in Italy. Returning to complete his studies at the University of Washington, he took courses in poetry with Theodore Roethke, who, in teaching modern poets, was "passionately committed to their rhythms and tonalities" (*Triggering Town*). Hugo then went to work for Boeing aircraft, writing poems slowly on the side, marrying for the first time in 1951, and publishing his first book at thirty-seven. After a trip to Italy in 1963, he began teaching at the University of Montana.

Still prey to loneliness and alcohol, Hugo suffered a "minor-league breakdown" in 1971. He married again in 1974, and a Guggenheim Fellowship enabled a visit to, and poems about, the remote island of Skye, off the northern coast of Scotland. Hugo died of leukemia.

The Lady in Kicking Horse Reservoir[1]

Not my hands but green across you now.
Green tons hold you down, and ten bass curve
teasing in your hair. Summer slime
will pile deep on your breast. Four months of ice
will keep you firm. I hope each spring   5
to find you tangled in those pads
pulled not quite loose by the spillway pour,
stars in dead reflection off your teeth.

Lie there lily still. The spillway's closed.
Two feet down most lakes are common gray.   10
This lake is dark from the black blue Mission range
climbing sky like music dying Indians once wailed.
On ocean beaches, mystery fish
are offered to the moon. Your jaws go blue.
Your hands start waving every wind.   15
Wave to the ocean where we crushed a mile of foam.

We still love there in thundering foam
and love. Whales fall in love with gulls
and tide reclaims the Dolly skeletons[2]
gone with a blast of aching horns to China.   20
Landlocked in Montana here
the end is limited by light, the final note
will trail off at the farthest point we see,
already faded, lover, where you bloat.

All girls should be nicer. Arrows rain   25
above us in the Indian wind. My future
should be full of windy gems, my past
will stop this roaring in my dreams.
Sorry. Sorry. Sorry. But the arrows sing:
no way to float her up. The dead sink   30
from dead weight. The Mission range
turns this water black late afternoons.

---

1. Both Kicking Horse Reservoir and the Mission mountain range (line 11) are on the Flathead Native American reservation, in Montana.

2. Here, skeletons of the Dolly Varden trout (but see also line 54).

One boy slapped the other. Hard.
The slapped boy talked until his dignity
dissolved, screamed a single 'stop'   35
and went down sobbing in the company pond.
I swam for him all night. My only suit
got wet and factory hands went home.
No one cared the coward disappeared.
Morning then: cold music I had never heard.   40

Loners like work best on second shift.
No one liked our product and the factory closed.
Off south, the bison multiply so fast
a slaughter's mandatory every spring
and every spring the creeks get fat   45
and Kicking Horse fills up. My hope is vague.
The far blur of your bones in May
may be nourished by the snow.

The spillway's open and you spill out
into weather, lover down the bright canal   50
and mother, irrigating crops
dead Indians forgot to plant.
I'm sailing west with arrows to dissolving foam
where waves strand naked Dollys.
Their eyes are white as oriental mountains   55
and their tongues are teasing oil from whales.

                                                                1973

Degrees of Gray in Philipsburg[3]

You might come here Sunday on a whim.
Say your life broke down. The last good kiss
you had was years ago. You walk these streets
laid out by the insane, past hotels
that didn't last, bars that did, the tortured try   5
of local drivers to accelerate their lives.
Only churches are kept up. The jail
turned 70 this year. The only prisoner
is always in, not knowing what he's done.

The principal supporting business now   10
is rage. Hatred of the various grays
the mountain sends, hatred of the mill,
The Silver Bill repeal, the best liked girls
who leave each year for Butte.[4] One good
restaurant and bars can't wipe the boredom out.   15

3. Small town in Montana, which in the early
twentieth century was a thriving community sup-
ported by a silver-processing mill.

4. City in Montana. *Silver Bill:* law enacted in
1934 empowering the federal government to buy
silver.

The 1907 boom, eight going silver mines,
a dance floor built on springs—
all memory resolves itself in gaze,
in panoramic green you know the cattle eat
or two stacks high above the town,   20
two dead kilns, the huge mill in collapse
for fifty years that won't fall finally down.

Isn't this your life? That ancient kiss
still burning out your eyes? Isn't this defeat
so accurate, the church bell simply seems   25
a pure announcement: ring and no one comes?
Don't empty houses ring? Are magnesium
and scorn sufficient to support a town,
not just Philipsburg, but towns
of towering blondes, good jazz and booze   30
the world will never let you have
until the town you came from dies inside?

Say no to yourself. The old man, twenty
when the jail was built, still laughs
although his lips collapse. Someday soon,   35
he says, I'll go to sleep and not wake up.
You tell him no. You're talking to yourself.
The car that brought you here still runs.
The money you buy lunch with,
no matter where it's mined, is silver   40
and the girl who serves your food
is slender and her red hair lights the wall.

                                                          1973

White Center[5]

Town or poem, I don't care how it looks. Old woman
take my hand and we'll walk one more time these streets
I believed marked me weak beneath catcalling clouds.
Long ago, the swamp behind the single row of stores
was filled and seeded. Roses today where Toughy Hassin   5
slapped my face to the grinning delight of his gang.
I didn't cry or run. Had I fought him
I'd have been beaten and come home bloody in tears
and you'd have told me I shouldn't be fighting.

Wasn't it all degrading, mean Mr. Kyte sweeping   10
the streets for no pay, believing what he'd learned
as a boy in England: 'This is your community'?

---

5. Suburb of Seattle.

I taunted him to rage, then ran. Is this the day
we call bad mothers out of the taverns and point them
sobbing for home, or issue costumes to posturing clowns 15
in the streets, make fun of drunk barbers, and hope
someone who left and made it returns, vowed
to buy more neon and give these people some class?

The Dugans aren't worth a dime, dirty Irish, nor days
you offered a penny for every fly I killed. 20
You were blind to my cheating. I saw my future certain—
that drunk who lived across the street and fell
in our garden reaching for the hoe you dropped.
All he got was our laughter. I helped him often home
when you weren't looking. I loved some terrible way 25
he lived in his mind and tried to be decent to others.
I loved the way we loved him behind our disdain.

Clouds. What glorious floating. They always move on
like I should have early. But your odd love and a war
taught me the world's gone evil past the first check point 30
and that's First Avenue South. I fell asleep each night
safe in love with my murder. The neighbor girl
plotted to tease every tomorrow and watch me turn
again to the woods and games too young for my age.
We never could account for the python cousin Warren 35
found half starved in the basement of Safeway.

It all comes back but in bites. I am the man
you beat to perversion. That was the drugstore MacCameron
flipped out in early one morning, waltzing
on his soda fountain. The siren married his shrieking. 40
His wife said, "We'll try again, in Des Moines."
You drove a better man into himself where he found tunes
he had no need to share. It's all beginning to blur
as it forms. Men cracking up or retreating.
Resolute women deep in hard prayer. 45

And it isn't the same this time. I hoped forty years
I'd write and would not write this poem. This town would die
and your grave never reopen. Or mine. Because I'm married
and happy, and across the street a foster child
from a cruel past is safe and need no longer crawl 50
for his meals, I walk this past with you, ghost in any field
of good crops, certain I remember everything wrong.
If not, why is this road lined thick with fern
and why do I feel no shame kicking the loose gravel home?

1980

KENNETH KOCH
1925–2002

Not to be pompous, not to be oracular, above all not to be dull: these were the commandments of the short-lived, so-called New York school of poets, of which Kenneth Koch was a founding member. The positive program of this school—modernist and surrealist in origin, urban in wit, abstract expressionist in painterly affiliation—can perhaps best be described by Koch's term "formulalessness." Koch had an eye for the incongruous image and generated tension out of the anarchic profusion of such images. He also had an ear for the lyrical possibilities of seemingly unusable material. The effect was often comic, surprising, even childlike, and indeed Koch recorded in two delightful books his experiences of teaching children to write poetry.

Koch was born on February 27, 1925, in Cincinnati, Ohio. His verse writing began at age five, but became serious at seventeen, when he read John Dos Passos and struggled to represent the stream of consciousness—another key interest of the New York school. At eighteen, he went into the army for three years, serving in the Pacific theater as a rifleman. On his return, he earned a B.A. (in 1948) at Harvard University, where his classmates included John Ashbery and Frank O'Hara. In 1959, he received his doctorate at Columbia University, with a dissertation on doctors as characters in literature, and began a long teaching career at Columbia, the location befitting his metropolitan muse. During three years abroad he discovered the work of the European surrealists. As he writes in "The Art of Poetry": "As for 'surrealistic' methods and techniques, they have become a / Natural part of writing."

A master of parody and pastiche, Koch satirized earlier esteemed poets such as Robert Frost and William Carlos Williams, as well as poets more generally, and did not spare even himself. "Now comes the poet," he writes in "The Stones of Time," "wrapped in a huge white towel, with his head full of imagery." Fast-paced, exhilarated, gleefully shifting in direction, Koch's poetry is a high-spirited romp that delights in its sonic resourcefulness and allusiveness. It risks playfulness and whimsy even when pursuing central questions about contemporary aesthetics. It is by turns intimate and extravagant, self-reflexive and frivolous, drawing energy from the momentum of its own language. Koch's many experiments in varied genres and forms gave him an enviable technical facility that served his more serious poems as well. In "The Art of Poetry," he sums up the desired effect of his poetry: "A reader should put your work down puzzled, / Distressed and illuminated, ready to believe / It is curious to be alive."

Mending Sump[1]

> "Hiram, I think the sump is backing up.
> The bathroom floor boards for above two weeks
> Have seemed soaked through. A little bird, I think
> Has wandered in the pipes, and all's gone wrong."
> "Something there is that doesn't hump a sump,"   5
> He said; and through his head she saw a cloud
> That seemed to twinkle. "Hiram, well," she said,
> "Smith is come home! I saw his face just now

---

1. Cf. Robert Frost's "Mending Wall."

While looking through your head. He's come to die
Or else to laugh, for hay is dried-up grass   10
When you're alone." He rose, and sniffed the air.
"We'd better leave him in the sump," he said.

1960

Geography

1

In the blue hubbub of the same-through-wealth sky
Amba grew to health and fifteenth year among the jungle scrubbery.
The hate-bird sang on a lower wing of the birch-nut tree
And Amba heard him sing, and in his health he too
Began to sing, but then stopped. Along the lower Congo   5
There are such high plants of what there is there, when
At morning Amba heard their pink music as gentlemanly
As if he had been in civilization. When morning stank
Over the ridge of coconuts and bald fronds, with agility
Amba climbed the permanent nut trees, and will often sing   10
To the shining birds, and the pets in their stealth
Are each other among, also, whether it be blue (thhhh) feathers
Or green slumber. Africa in Amba's mind was those white mornings he
    sang
(thhhh) high trala to the nougat birds, and after
The trenches had all been dug for the day, Amba   15
Would dream at the edge of some stained and stinking pond
Of the afternight music, as blue pets came to him in his dreams.
From the orange coconuts he would extract some stained milk,
Underneath his feet roots, tangled and filthy green. At night
The moon (zzzzzz) shining down on Amba's sweet mocked sleep.   20

2

In Chicago Louis walked the morning's rounds with agility.
A boy of seventeen and already recognized as a fast milkman!
The whizz and burr of dead chimes oppressed the
Holocaustic unison of Frank's brain, a young outlaw
Destined to meet dishonor and truth in a same instant,   25
Crossing Louis' path gently in the street, the great secret unknown.

3

The fur rhubarb did not please Daisy. "Freddie," she called,
"Our fruit's gang mouldy." Daisy, white cheeks with a spot of red
In them, like apples grown in paper bags, smiled
Gently at the fresh new kitchen; and, then, depressed,   30
She began to cover the rhubarb with her hands.

4

In the crushy green ice and snow Baba ran up and around with
    exuberance!
Today, no doubt, Father and Uncle Dad would come, and together they
    three would chase the whale!
Baba stared down through the green crusty ice at the world of fish
And closed his eyes and began to imagine the sweet trip   35
Over the musky waters, when Daddy would spear the whale, and the
    wind
Blow "Crad, crad!" through Uncle Dad's fur, and the sweet end
Of the day where they would smile at one another over the smoking
    blubber
And Uncle Dad would tell tales of his adventures past the shadow bar
Chasing the white snow-eagle. Baba ran   40
Into the perfect igloo screaming with impatience, and Malmal,
His mother, kissed him and dressed him with loving care for the icy
    trip.

5

Ten Ko sprinted over the rice paddies. Slush, slosh, sloosh!
His brother, Wan Kai, would soon be returned from the village
Where he had gone . . . (Blue desire! . . .)   45

6

Roon startled her parents by appearing perfectly dressed
In a little white collar and gown.
Angebor lifted himself up so he might stare in the window at the pretty
    girl.
His little hands unclenched and dropped the coins he had saved for the
    oona.[2]
He opened wide his eyes, then blinked at the pretty girl. He had never   50
    seen anything like that.
That evening, when it whitened in the sky, and a green
Clearness was there, Maggia, and Angebor had no *oona.*
But Angebor talked with excitement of what he had seen, and Maggia
    drank *zee'th.*

7

The little prisoner wept and wailed, telling of his life in the sand
And the burning sun over the desert. And one night it was cool   55
And dark, and he stole away over the green sand to search for his
    parents.
And he went to their tent, and they kissed him and covered him with
    loving-kindness.

---

2. Like *zee'th* (line 53), a word invented by Koch.

And the new morning sun shone like a pink rose in the heavens.
And the family prayed, the desert wind scorching their cool skin.

8

Amba arose. Thhhhhhh! went the birds, and clink clank cleck went   60
The leaves under the monkeys' feet, and Amba went to search for water
Speaking quietly with his fresh voice as he went toward Gorilla Lake
To all the beasts. Wan Kai lifted his body from the rice mat
When his brother Ten Ko came running in. "They have agreed in the
    village,"
He said. Win Tei brought them tea. Outside the rain   65
Fell. Plop, plop. Daisy felt something stir inside her.
She went to the window and looked out at the snow. Louis came up the
    stairs
With the milk. "Roon has bronchitis," said the American doctor,
"She will have to stay inside for ten days during this rain." Amba
Sneaked away, and wanted to go there again, but Maggia said he could   70
    not go again in this rain
And would be sure to lose the money for the *oona*. Baba stared
At the green and black sea. Uncle Dad stood up in the boat, while Baba
Watched Father plunge his harpoon three times in the whale. Daisy
    turned
Dreamily around, her hand on her cheek. Frank's boot
Kicked in the door. Amba wept; Ahna the deer was dead; she lay amid   75
    her puzzled young.
The sweet forms of the apple blossoms bent down to Wehtukai.
The boat split. Sun streamed into the apartment. Amba, Amba!
The lake was covered with gloom. Enna plunged into it screaming.

                                                                          1962

Variations on a Theme by William Carlos Williams[3]

1

I chopped down the house that you had been saving to live in next
    summer.
I am sorry, but it was morning, and I had nothing to do
and its wooden beams were so inviting.

2

We laughed at the hollyhocks together
and then I sprayed them with lye.   5
Forgive me. I simply do not know what I am doing.

---

3. Cf. William Carlos Williams's "This Is Just to Say."

3

I gave away the money that you had been saving to live on for the next
    ten years.
The man who asked for it was shabby
and the firm March wind on the porch was so juicy and cold.

4

Last evening we went dancing and I broke your leg.   10
Forgive me. I was clumsy, and
I wanted you here in the wards, where I am the doctor!⁴

                                         1962

From Days and Nights

2. *The Stones of Time*

The bathtub is white and full of strips
And stripes of red and blue and green and white
Where the painter has taken a bath! Now comes the poet
Wrapped in a huge white towel, with his head full of imagery.

Try being really attentive to your life   90
Instead of to your writing for a change once in a while
Sometimes one day one hour one minute oh I've done that
What happened? I got married and was in a good mood.

We wrote so much that we thought it couldn't be any good
Till we read it over and then thought how amazing it was!   95

Athena gave Popeye a Butterfinger⁵ filled with stars
Is the kind of poetry Z and I used to stuff in jars

When we took a walk he was afraid
Of the dogs who came in parade
To sniffle at the feet   100
Of two of the greatest poets of the age.

The stars came out
And I was still writing
My God where's dinner
Here's dinner   105
My wife! I love you
Do you remember in Paris
When I was thinner
And the sun came through the shutters like a knife?

---

4. Williams was a doctor.
5. A candy bar. *Athena:* the Greek goddess of wisdom.

I said to so many people once, "I write poetry."   110
They said, "Oh, so you are a poet." Or they said,
"What kind of poetry do you write? modern poetry?"
Or "My brother-in-law is a poet also."
Now if I say, "I am the poet Kenneth Koch," they say, "I think I've heard
    of you"
Or "I'm sorry but that doesn't ring a bell" or   115
"Would you please move out of the way? You're blocking my view
Of that enormous piece of meat that they are lowering into the Bay
Of Pigs."[6] What? Or "What kind of poetry do you write?"

"Taste," I said to J and he said
"What else is there?" but he was looking around.   120

"All the same, she isn't made like that,"
Marguerite said, upon meeting Janice,[7]
To her husband Eddie, and since
Janice was pregnant this had a clear meaning
Like the poetry of Robert Burns.[8]   125

You must learn to write in form first, said the dumb poet.
After several years of that you can write in free verse.
But of course no verse is really "free," said the dumb poet.
Thank you, I said. It's been great talking to you!

Sweet are the uses of adversity[9]   130
Became Sweetheart cabooses of diversity
And Sweet art cow papooses at the university
And Sea bar Calpurnia[1] flower havens' re-noosed knees

A book came out, and then another book
Which was unlike the first,   135
Which was unlike the love
And the nightmares and the fisticuffs that inspired it
And the other poets, with their egos and their works,
Which I sometimes read reluctantly and sometimes with great delight
When I was writing so much myself   140
I wasn't afraid that what they wrote would bother me
And might even give me ideas.

I walked through the spring fountain of spring
Air fountain knowing finally that poetry was everything:
Sleep, silence, darkness, cool white air, and language.   145

        1982

---

6. On the west coast of Cuba, site of an unsuc-
cessful U.S.-sponsored invasion in 1961 against
the Communist government of Fidel Castro.
7. Koch's wife.

8. Scottish poet (1759–1796).
9. Shakespeare's *As You Like It* 2.1.12.
1. The name of Caesar's wife in Shakespeare's
Julius Caesar.

One Train May Hide Another

(sign at a railroad crossing in Kenya)

In a poem, one line may hide another line,
As at a crossing, one train may hide another train.
That is, if you are waiting to cross
The tracks, wait to do it for one moment at
Least after the first train is gone. And so when you read 5
Wait until you have read the next line—
Then it is safe to go on reading.
In a family one sister may conceal another,
So, when you are courting, it's best to have them all in view
Otherwise in coming to find one you may love another. 10
One father or one brother may hide the man,
If you are a woman, whom you have been waiting to love.
So always standing in front of something the other
As words stand in front of objects, feelings, and ideas.
One wish may hide another. And one person's reputation may hide 15
The reputation of another. One dog may conceal another
On a lawn, so if you escape the first one you're not necessarily safe;
One lilac may hide another and then a lot of lilacs and on the Appia
     Antica[2] one tomb
May hide a number of other tombs. In love, one reproach may hide
     another,
One small complaint may hide a great one. 20
One injustice may hide another—one colonial may hide another,
One blaring red uniform another, and another, a whole column. One bath
     may hide another bath
As when, after bathing, one walks out into the rain.
One idea may hide another: Life is simple
Hide Life is incredibly complex, as in the prose of Gertrude Stein[3] 25
One sentence hides another and is another as well. And in the laboratory
One invention may hide another invention,
One evening may hide another, one shadow, a nest of shadows.
One dark red, or one blue, or one purple—this is a painting
By someone after Matisse.[4] One waits at the tracks until they pass, 30
These hidden doubles or, sometimes, likenesses. One identical twin
May hide the other. And there may be even more in there! The
     obstetrician
Gazes at the Valley of the Var.[5] We used to live there, my wife and I, but
One life hid another life. And now she is gone and I am here.
A vivacious mother hides a gawky daughter. The daughter hides 35
Her own vivacious daughter in turn. They are in
A railway station and the daughter is holding a bag
Bigger than her mother's bag and successfully hides it.

---

2. Major Roman road with monumental tombs.
3. Modernist writer (1874–1946), who stated, "After all my only thought is a complicated simplicity. I like a thing simple, but it must be simple through complication" ("A Transatlantic Inter-view").
4. Henri Matisse (1869–1954), French Fauvist painter who juxtaposes vivid colors.
5. Scenic region near Provence, in southern France.

In offering to pick up the daughter's bag one finds oneself confronted by
    the mother's
And has to carry that one, too. So one hitchhiker   40
May deliberately hide another and one cup of coffee
Another, too, until one is over-excited. One love may hide another love or
    the same love
As when "I love you" suddenly rings false and one discovers
The better love lingering behind, as when "I'm full of doubts"
Hides "I'm certain about something and it is that"   45
And one dream may hide another as is well known, always, too. In the
    Garden of Eden
Adam and Eve may hide the real Adam and Eve.
Jerusalem may hide another Jerusalem.
When you come to something, stop to let it pass
So you can see what else is there. At home, no matter where,   50
Internal tracks pose dangers, too: one memory
Certainly hides another, that being what memory is all about,
The eternal reverse succession of contemplated entities. Reading *A
    Sentimental Journey* look around
When you have finished, for *Tristram Shandy*,[6] to see
If it is standing there, it should be, stronger   55
And more profound and theretofore hidden as Santa Maria Maggiore
May be hidden by similar churches inside Rome. One sidewalk
May hide another, as when you're asleep there, and
One song hide another song; a pounding upstairs
Hide the beating of drums. One friend may hide another, you sit at the   60
    foot of a tree
With one and when you get up to leave there is another
Whom you'd have preferred to talk to all along. One teacher,
One doctor, one ecstasy, one illness, one woman, one man
May hide another. Pause to let the first one pass.
You think, Now it is safe to cross and you are hit by the next one.   65
      It can be important
To have waited at least a moment to see what was already there.

                                            1994

To the Roman Forum

After my daughter Katherine was born
I was terribly excited
I think I would have been measured at the twenty-five-espresso mark
We—Janice, now Katherine, and I—were in Rome
(Janice gave birth at the international hospital on top of Trastevere[7])   5
I went down and sat and looked at the ruins of you
I gazed at them, gleaming in the half-night

6. Formally complex novel written (1759–67), like
the shorter *A Sentimental Journey* (1768), by Irish-
born English novelist Laurence Sterne (1713–

1768).
7. Quarter of Rome.

And thought, Oh my, My God, My goodness, a child, a wife.
While I was sitting there, a friend, a sculptor, came by
I just had a baby, I said. I mean Janice did. I'm—   10
I thought I'd look at some very old great things
To match up with this new one. Oh, Adya said,
I guess you'd like to be alone, then. Congratulations. Goodnight.
Thank you. Goodnight, I said. Adya departed.
Next day I saw Janice and Katherine.   15
Here they are again and have nothing to do with you
A pure force swept through me another time
I am here, they are here, this has happened.
It is happening now, it happened then.

2000

MAXINE KUMIN
1925–2014

Maxine Kumin's poems aim to give a sense of skin and bone, of what it is to live in a body, especially a woman's body. In them, she imparts the experience of being a daughter and mother and lover, of being "a restless Jewish agnostic," living on a farm, participating in the cyclical processes of nature. She had an extraordinary eye for the lives of bears, woodchucks, even stones, and for the deaths of small animals. In "The Excrement Poem," she writes, "It is done by us all." The rural aspects of her verse came from living on a farm in Warner, New Hampshire, where she grew vegetables and bred horses, but Kumin was more than a "nature poet." Much of her work is about intense personal relationships, as in her emotionally intricate poems for a dead friend, a dead mother, a living daughter. Elegizing a friend dead by suicide, she ponders, as she wears the friend's jacket, her nearness to that anguish ("How It Is"). In some poems, she ventures further into history, but always by bringing the past into sharp collision with the present. Both critical and self-critical, she probes religious self-sacrifice and yet also questions her own lack of transcendental belief ("In the Absence of Bliss").

Although her technique is not showy, Kumin was skilled both in free verse and in rhymed and metered stanzas. She mediates between colloquial openness and formal rigor, as also between autobiographical utterance and restraint. Precisely observed, her imagery and figurative language are evocative, as when she compares an airport's blue landing lights to "nail holes in the dark" ("Our Ground Time Here Will Be Brief") or, in a more sustained metaphor, when she likens the quiver of a gong to "the deep nicker the mare makes / swiveling her neck / watching the foal swim / out of her body" ("Bangkok Gong"). In this poem about an object given her by her daughter, Kumin's birthing trope is apt and resonant.

Kumin was born on June 6, 1925, in Philadelphia. She earned B.A. and M.A. degrees at Radcliffe College. In 1973, she won the Pulitzer Prize for *Up Country*, and she was consultant in poetry to the Library of Congress (1981–82) and the poet laureate of New Hampshire (1989–94). She is often associated with Anne Sexton, who collaborated with her on several children's books, but she has less rage and a more buoyant and even humorous sensibility.

How It Is

Shall I say how it is in your clothes?
A month after your death I wear your blue jacket.
The dog at the center of my life recognizes
you've come to visit, he's ecstatic.
In the left pocket, a hole.   5
In the right, a parking ticket
delivered up last August on Bay State Road.
In my heart, a scatter like milkweed,
a flinging from the pods of the soul.
My skin presses your old outline.   10
It is hot and dry inside.

I think of the last day of your life,
old friend, how I would unwind it, paste
it together in a different collage,
back from the death car idling in the garage,   15
back up the stairs, your praying hands unlaced,
reassembling the bits of bread and tuna fish
into a ceremony of sandwich,
running the home movie backward to a space
we could be easy in, a kitchen place   20
with vodka and ice, our words like living meat.

Dear friend, you have excited crowds
with your example. They swell
like wine bags, straining at your seams.
I will be years gathering up our words,   25
fishing out letters, snapshots, stains,
leaning my ribs against this durable cloth
to put on the dumb blue blazer of your death.

                                                                    1982

Our Ground Time Here Will Be Brief

Blue landing lights make
nail holes in the dark.
A fine snow falls. We sit
on the tarmac taking on
the mail, quick freight,   5
trays of laboratory mice,
coffee and Danish for
the passengers.

Wherever we're going
is Monday morning.   10
Wherever we're coming from

is Mother's lap.
On the cloud-pack above, strewn
as loosely as parsnip
or celery seeds, lie   15
the souls of the unborn:

my children's children's
children and their father.
We gather speed for the last run
and lift off into the weather.   20

1982

In the Absence of Bliss

Museum of the Diaspora,[1] Tel Aviv

The roasting alive of rabbis
in the ardor of the Crusades
went unremarked in *Europe from
the Holy Roman Empire to 1918,*
open without prerequisite   5
when I was an undergraduate.

While reciting the Sh'ma[2] in full
expectation that their souls
would waft up to the bosom
of the Almighty the rabbis burned,   10
pious past the humming extremes
of pain. And their loved ones with them.
Whole communities tortured and set aflame
in Christ's name
while chanting Hear, O Israel.   15

Why?
Why couldn't the rabbis recant,
kiss the Cross, pretend?
Is God so simple that He can't
sort out real from sham?   20
Did He want
these fanatic autos-da-fé,[3] admire
the eyeballs popping,
the corpses shrinking in the fire?

We live in an orderly   25
universe of discoverable laws,
writes an intelligent alumna
in *Harvard Magazine.*
Bliss is belief,

1. The settling of Jewish colonies outside Israel.
2. First word ("hear") of the often-recited prayer in which Jews proclaim their faith.
3. Ritual burnings of heretics.

agnostics always say   30
a little condescendingly
as befits mandarins who function
on a higher moral plane.

Consider our contemporary
Muslim kamikazes   35
hurling their explosives-
packed trucks through barriers.
Isn't it all the same?
They too die cherishing the fond
certitude of a better life beyond.   40

We walk away from twenty-two
graphic centuries of kill-the-jew
and hail, of all things, a Mercedes
taxi. The driver is Yemeni,
loves rock music and hangs   45
each son's picture—three so far—
on tassels from his rearview mirror.

I do not tell him that in Yemen
Jewish men, like women, were forbidden
to ride their donkeys astride,   50
having just seen this humiliation
illustrated on the Museum screen.

When his parents came
to the Promised Land, they entered
the belly of an enormous   55
silver bird, not knowing whether
they would live or die.
No matter. As it was written,
the Messiah had drawn nigh.

I do not ask, who tied   60
the leaping ram inside the thicket?
Who polished, then blighted the apple?
Who loosed pigs in the Temple,
set tribe against tribe
and nailed man in His pocket?[4]   65

But ask myself, what would
I die for and reciting what?
Not for Yahweh, Allah, Christ,
those patriarchal fists
in the face. But would   70
I die to save a child?

---

4. The "ram inside the thicket" is in Genesis 22: God commands Abraham, as a test of his faith, to sacrifice his son Isaac; God then orders the boy spared and provides, instead, a ram, found tangled in a thicket. The "apple" is that of the tree of the knowledge of good and evil. According to Jewish law, pigs are the most unclean animals. "Nailed man" may refer to Jesus' crucifixion.

Rescue my lover? Would
I run into the fiery barn
to release animals,
singed and panicked, from their stalls?   75

Bliss is belief, but where's
the higher moral plane I roost on?
This narrow plank given to splinters.
No answers. Only questions.

                                                        1985

The Bangkok Gong

Home for a visit, you brought me
a circle of hammered brass
reworked from an engine part
into this curio
to be struck with a wad of cotton   5
pasted onto a stick.
Third World ingenuity
you said, reminds you
of Yankee thrift.

The tone of this gong   10
is gentle, haunting, but
hard struck three times
can call out as far
as the back fields
to say Supper   15
or, drummed darkly,
Blood everywhere!
Come quick.

When barely touched it imitates
the deep nicker the mare makes   20
swiveling her neck
watching the foal swim
out of her body.
She speaks to it even as
she pushes the hindlegs clear.   25
Come to me is her message
as they curl to reach each other.

Now that you are
back on the border
numbering the lucky ones   30
whose visas let them
leave everything behind
except nightmares, I hang

the gong on my doorpost.
Some days I   35
barely touch it.

                                                              1989

From Letters

Your laugh, your scarves, the gloss of your makeup,
shallow and vain. I wore your lips, your hair,
even the lift of my eyebrows was yours
but nothing of you could please me, bitten so deep
by the fox of scorn. Like you, I married young   5
but chose animals, wood heat, hard hours
instead of Sheffield silver, freshcut flowers,
your life of privilege and porcelain.
My children came, the rigorous bond of blood.
Little by little our lives pulled up, pulled even.   10
A sprinkle here and there of approbation:
we both agreed that what I'd birthed was good.
How did I come to soften? How did you?
Goggy is what my little ones called you.

                                                              1996

DONALD JUSTICE
1925–2004

Like Richard Wilbur and James Merrill, Donald Justice was an American formalist poet who came to maturity after World War II. Among his models were W. H. Auden and Wallace Stevens, and he was celebrated by the later twentieth-century New Formalists for his mastery of traditional meter and rhyme in such genres as the sonnet, the sestina, the villanelle, and the ballad. Received forms and texts are to him what personal passions are to the confessional poets. He often built poems around an earlier writer's evocative line or phrase, as evidenced by titles such as "Variations on a Text by Vallejo" and "After a Phrase Abandoned by Wallace Stevens." In Justice's adaptations, the previous text or form, to quote Shakespeare's Ariel, "doth suffer a sea-change / Into something rich and strange."

A poet of restraint, Justice comes upon us softly and meditatively. "No house of Atreus ours," he cautions in "Tales from a Family Album," though he then goes on to claim a different sort of doom for his family and himself. Within the air of decorum and quiet tone of his verse, Justice has his heights and abysses, his intimacy and impersonality. Mourning the past, he would re-create that hour "When all things to the eye / Their early splendors wore" (dedication to *The Summer Anniversaries*). An elegist and self-elegist, he clung to forgotten beauty as to dead friends and kinsmen. And like his "Women in Love," he wished in his art "To fasten and not let go." Yet his verse contains another, darker perspective. In their understated way, some poems suggest menace. The cold stares and blank faces in poems such as "The Grandfathers" and "The Tourist from Syracuse" help create a mood of tension and fear.

Sometimes seen as a southern poet, Justice was born in Miami, Florida, on August 12, 1925. He earned a B.A. at Miami University, an M.A. at the University of North Carolina, Chapel Hill, and a Ph.D. at the University of Iowa. He also spent a year at Stanford University studying meter under Yvor Winters. He taught for many years at the University of Iowa (1957–66, 1971–82) and at the University of Florida (1982–92). He won the Lamont, Pulitzer, and Bollingen Prizes for poetry. Among his many students were the poets Mark Strand, Charles Wright, James Tate, and Jorie Graham.

On the Death of Friends in Childhood

We shall not ever meet them bearded in heaven,
Nor sunning themselves among the bald of hell;
If anywhere, in the deserted schoolyard at twilight,
Forming a ring, perhaps, or joining hands
In games whose very names we have forgotten.   5
Come, memory, let us seek them there in the shadows.

1960

The Grandfathers

Why will they never sleep?
JOHN PEALE BISHOP[1]

Why will they never sleep,
The old ones, the grandfathers?
Always you find them sitting
On ruined porches, deep
In the back country, at dusk,   5
Hawking and spitting.
They might have sat there forever,
Tapping their sticks,
Peevish, discredited gods.
Ask the lost traveler how,   10
At road-end, they will fix
You maybe with the cold
Eye of a snake or a bird
And answer not a word,
Only these blank, oracular   15
Headshakes or headnods.

1967

1. American poet, novelist, and critic (1892–1944), associated with the "lost generation." The phrase is from his "Ode."

After a Phrase Abandoned by Wallace Stevens[2]

The alp at the end of the street
—STEVENS' NOTEBOOKS

The alp at the end of the street
Occurs in the dreams of the town.
Over burgher and shopkeeper,
Massive, he broods,
A snowy-headed father   5
Upon whose knees his children
No longer climb;
Or is reflected
In the cool, unruffled lakes of
Their minds, at evening,   10
After their day in the shops,
As shadow only, shapeless
As a wind that has stopped blowing.

Grandeur, it seems,
Comes down to this in the end—   15
A street of shops
With white shutters
Open for business . . .

                                                          1967

The Tourist from Syracuse

One of those men who can be a car salesman or a tourist from
Syracuse or a hired assassin.
—JOHN D. MACDONALD[3]

You would not recognize me.
Mine is the face which blooms in
The dank mirrors of washrooms
As you grope for the light switch.

My eyes have the expression   5
Of the cold eyes of statues
Watching their pigeons return
From the feed you have scattered,

And I stand on my corner
With the same marble patience.   10
If I move at all, it is
At the same pace precisely

---

2. American poet (1879–1955). The poem also alludes to several of Stevens's poems, including "To an Old Philosopher in Rome" ("It is a kind of total grandeur at the end") and "The Death of a Soldier" ("the wind stops"), and to a poem by W. H. Auden that begins "Fish in the unruffled lakes."
3. American writer of thrillers (1916–1986).

As the shade of the awning
Under which I stand waiting
And with whose blackness it seems   15
I am already blended.

I speak seldom, and always
In a murmur as quiet
As that of crowds which surround
The victims of accidents.   20

Shall I confess who I am?
My name is all names and none.
I am the used-car salesman,
The tourist from Syracuse,

The hired assassin, waiting.   25
I will stand here forever
Like one who has missed his bus—
Familiar, anonymous—

On my usual corner,
The corner at which you turn   30
To approach that place where now
You must not hope to arrive.

1967

Men at Forty

Men at forty
Learn to close softly
The doors to rooms they will not be
Coming back to.

At rest on a stair landing,   5
They feel it moving
Beneath them now like the deck of a ship,
Though the swell is gentle.

And deep in mirrors
They rediscover   10
The face of the boy as he practices tying
His father's tie there in secret

And the face of that father,
Still warm with the mystery of lather.
They are more fathers than sons themselves now.   15
Something is filling them, something

That is like the twilight sound
Of the crickets, immense,
Filling the woods at the foot of the slope
Behind their mortgaged houses.   20

                                                                  1967

Variations on a Text by Vallejo[4]

Me moriré en París con aguacero . . .

I will die in Miami in the sun,
On a day when the sun is very bright,
A day like the days I remember, a day like other days,
A day that nobody knows or remembers yet,
And the sun will be bright then on the dark glasses of strangers   5
And in the eyes of a few friends from my childhood
And of the surviving cousins by the graveside,
While the diggers, standing apart, in the still shade of the palms,
Rest on their shovels, and smoke,
Speaking in Spanish softly, out of respect.   10

I think it will be on a Sunday like today,
Except that the sun will be out, the rain will have stopped,
And the wind that today made all the little shrubs kneel down;
And I think it will be a Sunday because today,
When I took out this paper and began to write,   15
Never before had anything looked so blank,
My life, these words, the paper, the gray Sunday;
And my dog, quivering under a table because of the storm,
Looked up at me, not understanding,
And my son read on without speaking, and my wife slept.   20

Donald Justice is dead. One Sunday the sun came out,
It shone on the bay, it shone on the white buildings,
The cars moved down the street slowly as always, so many,
Some with their headlights on in spite of the sun,
And after awhile the diggers with their shovels   25
Walked back to the graveside through the sunlight,
And one of them put his blade into the earth
To lift a few clods of dirt, the black marl[5] of Miami,
And scattered the dirt, and spat,
Turning away abruptly, out of respect.   30

                                                                  1973

---

4. César Vallejo (1892–1939), Peruvian poet. The epigraph is translated "I will die in Paris in a rain-storm."
5. Clay, earth.

In Memory of the Unknown Poet, Robert Boardman Vaughn[6]

> But the essential advantage for a poet is not, to have a beautiful
> world with which to deal: it is to be able to see beneath both beauty
> and ugliness; to see the boredom, and the horror, and the glory.
> —T. S. ELIOT

It was his story. It would always be his story.
It followed him; it overtook him finally—
The boredom, and the horror, and the glory.

Probably at the end he was not yet sorry,
Even as the boots were brutalizing him in the alley.   5
It was his story. It would always be his story,

Blown on a blue horn, full of sound and fury,[7]
But signifying, O signifying magnificently
The boredom, and the horror, and the glory.

I picture the snow as falling without hurry   10
To cover the cobbles and the toppled ashcans completely.
It was his story. It would always be his story.

Lately he had wandered between St. Mark's Place and the Bowery,[8]
Already half a spirit, mumbling and muttering sadly.
O the boredom, and the horror, and the glory.   15

All done now. But I remember the fiery
Hypnotic eye and the raised voice blazing with poetry.
It was his story and would always be his story—
The boredom, and the horror, and the glory.

                                                                      1987

Nostalgia and Complaint of the Grandparents

> Les morts
> C'est sous terre;
> Ça n'en sort
> Guère.
> LAFORGUE[9]

Our diaries squatted, toadlike,
On dark closet ledges.
Forget-me-not and thistle
Decalcomaned[1] the pages.
But where, where are they now,   5

---

6. The poem is a villanelle.
7. Cf. Shakespeare's *Macbeth:* life is "full of sound
and fury, / Signifying nothing" (5.5.16–27).
8. On New York City's Lower East Side.
9. Jules Laforgue (1860–1887), French poet. The
first lines of the epigraph are translated "The dead

are under the ground"; Justice translates the last
two lines at the end of each stanza.
1. "Decalcomania" is the process of transferring
pictures from specially prepared paper to other sur-
faces.

All the sad squalors
Of those between-wars[2] parlors?—
Cut flowers; and the sunlight spilt like soda
On torporous[3] rugs; the photo
Albums all outspread . . .   10
    The dead
Don't get around much anymore.

There was an hour when daughters
Practiced arpeggios;[4]
Their mothers, awkward and proud,   15
Would listen, smoothing their hose—
Sundays, half-past five!
    Do you recall
How the sun used to loll,
Lazily, just beyond the roof,   20
Bloodshot and aloof?
We thought it would never set.
    The dead don't get
Around much anymore.

Eternity resembles   25
One long Sunday afternoon.
No traffic passes; the cigar smoke
Coils in a blue cocoon.
Children, have you nothing
    For our cold sakes?   30
No tea? No little tea cakes?
Sometimes now the rains disturb
Even our remote suburb.
There's a dampness underground.
    The dead don't get around   35
    Much anymore.

1987

2. That is, in the 1920s and 1930s, between World Wars I and II.

3. That is, torpor-inducing, sluggish-making.

4. Notes of chords, played in succession.

W. D. SNODGRASS
1926–2009

W. D. Snodgrass spoke of his poems as exercises in self-discovery; for him, the writing of verse was a discipline in sincerity. "[O]ur only hope as artists," he proposed, "is to continually ask ourselves, 'Am I writing what I really think?' . . . for I believe that the only reality that a man can ever surely know is that self he cannot help being, though he will only know that self through its interactions with the world around us" ("Finding a Poem"). In the poem "Orpheus," Snodgrass has the arch-poet say, "And I went on / rich in the loss of all I sing." Snodgrass does often seem rich in his losses. He sees life slipping away—his marriage dissolves, his little daughter visits him less frequently, some of his contemporaries are more successful than he—yet Snodgrass's poems look for compensation. The careful syllabics, the ingratiating rhythms, and the wry jokes do not qualify the pathos, but coexist with it to produce a particular sweet and sour flavor. Snodgrass's misfortunes were the lode of poetic material that childhood has been for other poets.

William Dewitt Snodgrass was born on January 5, 1926, in Wilkinsburg, Pennsylvania. He grew up in Beaver Falls, Pennsylvania, where he graduated from high school and attended Geneva College, though his studies were soon interrupted by service in the navy during the last years of World War II. In 1947, he went to the State University of Iowa, at whose famous writers' workshop he studied under Robert Lowell. He and Lowell together developed a new confessional mode for poetry. Snodgrass also studied with John Berryman and said that an early version of "A Flat One" "was written as a result of Berryman's asking us to write a stanzaic poem about a death. I wrote about one of the patients at the hospital I was working in [as an aide], something it wouldn't have occurred to me to do without that assignment" (interview with Philip Hoy). The poem's technical fluency counterbalances the speaker's harsh emotional disclosures and frank details. Although the tone switches suddenly to tenderness at the end, the speaker's address to the dead old veteran is bracingly unsentimental: "You seem to be all finished, so / We'll plug your old recalcitrant anus / And tie up your discouraged penis / In a great, snow-white bow of gauze."

In 1959, also the year of Lowell's *Life Studies*, Snodgrass published his first book, *Heart's Needle*. The title is taken from the old Irish saying "An only daughter is the needle of the heart," and it refers specifically to a sequence of poems in which the poet ruefully celebrates his encounters with his young daughter, the only child of a broken marriage. Snodgrass was showered with awards for the book, including the Pulitzer Prize. In his subsequent books, he tried to move beyond personal confession to more "social and philosophical subjects" (*Contemporary Poets of the English Language*, ed. R. Murphy, 1971). In a series of poems called *The Führer Bunker*, written in the voices of Adolf Hitler and his Nazi associates in the last days of World War II, he used the resources of dramatic monologue to arouse in his readers a conflict between open moral censure and sneaking sympathy.

April Inventory

The green catalpa tree has turned
All white; the cherry blossoms once more.
In one whole year I haven't learned
A blessed thing they pay you for.
The blossoms snow down in my hair;   5
The trees and I will soon be bare.

The trees have more than I to spare.
The sleek, expensive girls I teach,
Younger and pinker every year,
Bloom gradually out of reach.   10
The pear tree lets its petals drop
Like dandruff on a tabletop.

The girls have grown so young by now
I have to nudge myself to stare.

This year they smile and mind me how 15
My teeth are falling with my hair.
In thirty years I may not get
Younger, shrewder, or out of debt.

The tenth time, just a year ago,
I made myself a little list 20
Of all the things I'd ought to know,
Then told my parents, analyst,
And everyone who's trusted me
I'd be substantial, presently.

I haven't read one book about 25
A book or memorized one plot.
Or found a mind I did not doubt.
I learned one date. And then forgot.
And one by one the solid scholars
Get the degrees, the jobs, the dollars. 30

And smile above their starchy collars.
I taught my classes Whitehead's[1] notions;
One lovely girl, a song of Mahler's.[2]
Lacking a source-book or promotions,
I showed one child the colors of 35
A luna moth and how to love.

I taught myself to name my name,
To bark back, loosen love and crying;
To ease my woman so she came,
To ease an old man who was dying. 40
I have not learned how often I
Can win, can love, but choose to die.

I have not learned there is a lie
Love shall be blonder, slimmer, younger;
That my equivocating eye 45
Loves only by my body's hunger;
That I have forces, true to feel,
Or that the lovely world is real.

While scholars speak authority
And wear their ulcers on their sleeves, 50
My eyes in spectacles shall see
These trees procure and spend their leaves.
There is a value underneath
The gold and silver in my teeth.

Though trees turn bare and girls turn wives, 55
We shall afford our costly seasons;

1. Alfred North Whitehead (1861–1947), English philosopher.   2. Gustav Mahler (1860–1911), Austrian composer.

There is a gentleness survives
That will outspeak and has its reasons.
There is a loveliness exists,
Preserves us, not for specialists.   60

                                                1959

From Heart's Needle

3

The child between them on the street
Comes to a puddle, lifts his feet
    And hangs on their hands. They start
At the live weight and lurch together,
Recoil to swing him through the weather,   5
    Stiffen and pull apart.

We read of cold war soldiers that
Never gained ground, gave none, but sat
    Tight in their chill trenches.
Pain seeps up from some cavity   10
Through the ranked teeth in sympathy;
    The whole jaw grinds and clenches

Till something somewhere has to give.
It's better the poor soldiers live
    In someone else's hands   15
Than drop where helpless powers fall
On crops and barns, on towns were all
    Will burn. And no man stands.

For good, they sever and divide
Their won and lost land. On each side   20
    Prisoners are returned
Excepting a few unknown names.
The peasant plods back and reclaims
    His fields that strangers burned

And nobody seems very pleased.   25
It's best. Still, what must not be seized
    Clenches the empty fist.
I tugged your hand, once, when I hated
Things less: a mere game dislocated
    The radius of your wrist.   30

Love's wishbone, child, although I've gone
As men must and let you be drawn
    Off to appease another,
It may help that a Chinese play

Or Solomon himself might say   35
    I am your real mother.[3]

8

I thumped on you the best I could
    which was no use;
you would not tolerate your food
until the sweet, fresh milk was soured
    with lemon juice   5

That puffed you up like a fine yeast.
    The first June in your yard
like some squat Nero[4] at a feast
you sat and chewed on white, sweet clover.
    That is over.   10

When you were old enough to walk
    we went to feed
the rabbits in the park milkweed;
saw the paired monkeys, under lock,
    consume each other's salt.   15

Going home we watched the slow
stars follow us down Heaven's vault.
You said, let's catch one that comes low,
    pull off its skin
    and cook it for our dinner.   20

As absentee bread-winner,
I seldom got you such cuisine;
we ate in local restaurants
or brought what lunches we could pack
    in a brown sack   25

with stale, dry bread to toss for ducks
    on the green-scummed lagoons,
crackers for porcupine and fox,
life-savers for the footpad coons
    to scour and rinse,   30

snatch after in their muddy pail
    and stare into their paws.
When I moved next door to the jail
    I learned to fry
omelettes and griddlecakes so I   35

could set you supper at my table.
As I built back from helplessness,

---

3. Faced with two mothers claiming to be the
mother of a child, wise King Solomon identified
the rightful one (1 Kings 3:16–28).

4. Nero Claudius Caesar (37–68 C.E.), Roman
emperor.

when I grew able,
the only possible answer was
  you had to come here less.   40

This Hallowe'en you come one week.
  You masquerade
  as a vermilion, sleek,
fat, crosseyed fox in the parade
or, where grim jackolanterns leer,   45

go with your bag from door to door
foraging for treats. How queer:
  when you take off your mask
my neighbors must forget and ask
  whose child you are.   50

Of course you lose your appetite,
  whine and won't touch your plate;
    as local law
I set your place on an orange crate
in your own room for days. At night   55

you lie asleep there on the bed
  and grate your jaw.
Assuredly your father's crimes
  are visited
on you. You visit me sometimes.   60

The time's up. Now our pumpkin sees
  me bringing your suitcase.
    He holds his grin;
the forehead shrivels, sinking in.
You break this year's first crust of snow   65

off the runningboard to eat.
  We manage, though for days
I crave sweets when you leave and know
they rot my teeth. Indeed our sweet,
  foods leave us cavities.   70

                                                          1959

A Flat One

Old Fritz, on this rotating bed
For seven wasted months you lay
Unfit to move, shrunken, gray,
No good to yourself or anyone
But to be babied—changed and bathed and fed.   5
  At long last, that's all done.

Before each meal, twice every night,
We set pads on your bedsores, shut
Your catheter tube off, then brought
The second canvas-and-black-iron   10
Bedframe and clamped you in between them, tight,
    Scared, so we could turn

You over. We washed you, covered you,
Cut up each bite of meat you ate;
We watched your lean jaws masticate   15
As ravenously your useless food
As thieves at hard labor in their chains chew
    Or insects in the wood.

Such pious sacrifice to give
You all you could demand of pain: 20
Receive this haddock's body, slain
For you, old tyrant; take this blood
Of a tomato, shed that you might live.
    You had that costly food.

You seem to be all finished, so   25
We'll plug your old recalcitrant anus
And tie up your discouraged penis
In a great, snow-white bow of gauze.
We wrap you, pin you, and cart you down below,
    Below, below, because   30

Your credit has finally run out.
On our steel table, trussed and carved,
You'll find this world's hardworking, starved
Teeth working in your precious skin.
The earth turns, in the end, by turn about   35
    And opens to take you in.

Seven months gone down the drain; thank God
That's through. Throw out the four-by-fours,
Swabsticks, the thick salve for bedsores,
Throw out the diaper pads and drug   40
Containers, pile the bedclothes in a wad,
    And rinse the cider jug

Half-filled with the last urine. Then
Empty out the cotton cans,
Autoclave[5] the bowls and spit pans,   45
Unhook the pumps and all the red
Tubes—catheter, suction, oxygen;
    Next, wash the empty bed.

—All this Dark Age machinery
On which we had tormented you   50

5. Sterilize.

To life. Last, we collect the few
    Belongings: snapshots, some odd bills,
Your mail, and half a pack of Luckies we
        Won't light you after meals.

    Old man, these seven months you've lain   55
    Determined—not that you would live—
    Just to not die. No one would give
    You one chance you could ever wake
From that first night, much less go well again,
        Much less go home and make   60

    Your living; how could you hope to find
    A place for yourself in all creation?—
    Pain was your only occupation.
    And pain that should content and will
A man to give it up, nerved you to grind   65
        Your clenched teeth, breathing, till

    Your skin broke down, your calves went flat
    And your legs lost all sensation. Still,
    You took enough morphine to kill
    A strong man. Finally, nitrogen   70
Mustard:[6] you could last two months after that;
        It would kill you then.

    Even then you wouldn't quit.
    Old soldier, yet you must have known
    Inside the animal had grown   75
    Sick of the world, made up its mind
To stop. Your mind ground on its separate
        Way, merciless and blind,

    Into these last weeks when the breath
    Would only come in fits and starts   80
    That puffed out your sections like the parts
    Of some enormous, damaged bug.
You waited, not for life, not for your death,
        Just for the deadening drug

    That made your life seem bearable.   85
    You still whispered you would not die.
    Yet in the nights I heard you cry
    Like a whipped child; in fierce old age
You whimpered, tears stood on your gun-metal
        Blue cheeks shaking with rage   90

    And terror. So much pain would fill
    Your room that when I left I'd pray
    That if I came back the next day
    I'd find you gone. You stayed for me—

---

6. Drug used to fight cancer.

Nailed to your own rapacious, stiff self-will.   95
        You've shook loose, finally.

    They'd say this was a worthwhile job
    Unless they tried it. It is mad
    To throw our good lives after bad;
    Waste time, drugs, and our minds, while strong   100
Men starve. How many young men did we rob
        To keep you hanging on?

    I can't think we did *you* much good.
    Well, when you died, none of us wept.
    You killed for us, and so we kept   105
    You, because we need to earn our pay.
No. We'd still have to help you try. We would
        Have killed for you today.

                                                    1967

A. R. AMMONS
1926–2001

In A. R. Ammons's poetry, a group of possibilities formulated earlier in the century achieves a fresh and unified expression. The perception of human ambiguities and abstract possibilities in homely bits of nature may have originated in Robert Frost; the attention to the intricacies of poetry as a "supreme fiction" has ties with Wallace Stevens; elements of Ammons's technique, such as the short, lightly punctuated lines and metrical innovations, unite him with William Carlos Williams. Like Charles Olson, Ammons wrote his poems on a typewriter and attended to the spatial layout of words on the page.

Ammons comes on with disarming casualness; he presents himself directly, unfazed, wry when necessary, quick to see symbolic possibilities in ordinary landscapes. Often, his poems are minor journeys that gradually become momentous: an automobile trip deepens into a journey into the past and the passions; a walk releases him from old forms; disjointed maneuvers of the mind move suddenly "towards divine, terrible love" ("Prodigal"). Observed facts, he says in the poem "The Misfit," tear us into questionings, push us toward the edges of order, of being. The sense of long, meditative preparation for writing is imparted by his poems, however unexpected and seemingly impromptu their phrasing, or digressive and self-mocking their manner.

Ammons writes poetry of motion, process, movement. In "Tombstones," he states, "the things of earth are not objects" but "pools of energy cooled into place." The natural world is continuously cooling, radiating, shrinking, mutating, decaying, and reassembling, never in stasis. This vision finds its organic analogue in the loose formal shape and colloquial manner of his poems. Like the mind and like the world, the poem must move and twist and flow. It would be a mistake to try to halt this motion by punctuating its language with end-stopped lines or periods, by impeding it with abstract organization or syntactic closure. Ammons lets his syntax course forward through colons and commas, his enjambed lines, ideas, images, and clauses tumbling over one another. Because "there is no finality of vision," as he says in "Corsons Inlet," the poet should "make / no form of / formlessness," "no forcing of image, plan, / or thought: / no propaganda, no humbling of reality to precept." In his voluble longer poems and sequences, Ammons wants "to fasten into order enlarging grasps of disorder, widening / scope."

In his shorter poems, by converse, Ammons often seeks "narrow order, limited tightness," the "focused beam" of a poem such as "Laser." In these carefully chiseled lyrics, the poet's mind concentrates fiercely. Perceptions are clarified; multiple perspectives narrowly converge. Like the boulders that, in "Motion's Holdings," are said to "take in and give / off heat, adjust nearby to / geomagnetic fields," Ammons's short poems force together the macrocosmic and the microcosmic, observing cosmic process in the tiniest detail.

Ammons continually reflects on the relations among the movements of mind, the world, and the poem, and he often writes in the mode of *ars poetica,* or self-description. As in the Romantic tradition that he assumes, extending from William Wordsworth, Ralph Waldo Emerson, and Walt Whitman to Frost and Stevens, the natural world is read partly for itself, partly as a mirror for the motions of the mind and the poem. When, in 1987, Ammons drove past an enormous Florida landfill on interstate I-95, he saw in it, among other things, a figure for the endless process of linguistic decay and transformation in poetry. He writes in the long poem *Garbage* (1993): "there is a mound, // too, in the poet's mind dead language is hauled / off to and burned down on, the energy held and // shaped into new turns and clusters, the mind / strengthened by what it strengthens."

Earlier, in his *Collected Poems: 1951–1971,* Ammons included a long *ars poetica,* "Essay on Poetics," that powerfully expresses his view of the interlocking of nature and art. For Ammons, Williams's slogan "no ideas but in things" is too limited and must be supplemented by "no things but in ideas," "no ideas but in ideas," and "no things but in things." The possibilities of poems are not to be numbered. More central than any one slogan is the complementary blending of art and nature. With great dexterity and humor, Ammons investigates the relationship between nature and poetry in what are sometimes long experiments in poetic form. He typed his early *Tape for the Turn of the Year* (1965) on a roll of adding-machine tape, not as a joke but as a serious experiment in making a poem adapt to something outside itself. The tape determined both how long the lines are and when the poem ends. Ammons writes about an *ecology* of nature and art, a word he used long before it became commonplace.

Archie Randolph Ammons was born on February 18, 1926, in Whiteville, North Carolina. His early interests were scientific, and he earned a B.S. at Wake Forest College in 1949, having served in the navy at the end of World War II. He later attended the University of California at Berkeley for two years. Still uncertain of his direction, he became principal of an elementary school in his home state, and then for a decade an executive in a biological glass-making firm. Ammons remained loyal to science as well as to literature, his poetry embodying both. The title of his first book, *Ommateum* (1955), means "compound eye," as of an insect or a crustacean, an apt metaphor for his multivisioned approach to the world. After the volume's obscure publication in Philadelphia, he waited nine years to publish a second book. In 1964, he accepted a teaching position at Cornell University, and in seven years he progressed from instructor to full professor. In 1973, his *Collected Poems: 1951–1971* won the National Book Award; in 1975, *Sphere* won the Bollingen Prize; in 1982, *A Coast of Trees* won the National Book Critics Circle Award; and in 1993, *Garbage* won a second National Book Award. Ammons was one of the first recipients of a MacArthur Fellowship, and he received the Tanning Prize in 1998. He died of cancer at seventy-five.

So I Said I Am Ezra[1]

So I said I am Ezra
and the wind whipped my throat
gaming for the sounds of my voice
    I listened to the wind
go over my head and up into the night   5
Turning to the sea I said
        I am Ezra
but there were no echoes from the waves
The words were swallowed up
    in the voice of the surf   10
or leaping over the swells
lost themselves oceanward
    Over the bleached and broken fields
I moved my feet and turning from the wind
    that ripped sheets of sand   15
    from the beach and threw them
    like seamists across the dunes
swayed as if the wind were taking me away
and said
        I am Ezra   20
As a word too much repeated
falls out of being
so I Ezra went out into the night
like a drift of sand
and splashed among the windy oats   25
that clutch the dunes
of unremembered seas

                          1955

Corsons Inlet[2]

I went for a walk over the dunes again this morning
to the sea,
then turned right along
    the surf
                rounded a naked headland   5
                and returned

    along the inlet shore:

it was muggy sunny, the wind from the sea steady and high,
crisp in the running sand,
        some breakthroughs of sun   10
      but after a bit

1. Prophet whose return to Jerusalem from exile is described in the biblical book named for him. In Islamic tradition, the prophet Ezra (Uzair) an-nounces, "I am Ezra," when no one recognizes him on his return after one hundred years.
2. In southeast New Jersey.

continuous overcast:

the walk liberating, I was released from forms,
from the perpendiculars
    straight lines, blocks, boxes, binds   15
of thought
into the hues, shadings, rises, flowing bends and blends
      of sight:

            I allow myself eddies of meaning:
yield to a direction of significance   20
running
like a stream through the geography of my work:
  you can find
in my sayings
           swerves of action   25
           like the inlet's cutting edge:
    there are dunes of motion,
organizations of grass, white sandy paths of remembrance
in the overall wandering of mirroring mind:

but Overall is beyond me: is the sum of these events   30
I cannot draw, the ledger I cannot keep, the accounting
beyond the account:

in nature there are few sharp lines: there are areas of
primrose
    more or less dispersed;   35
disorderly orders of bayberry; between the rows
of dunes,
irregular swamps of reeds,
though not reeds alone, but grass, bayberry, yarrow, all . . .
predominantly reeds: 40

I have reached no conclusions, have erected no boundaries,
shutting out and shutting in, separating inside
    from outside: I have
    drawn no lines:
    as   45

manifold events of sand
change the dune's shape that will not be the same shape
tomorrow,

so I am willing to go along, to accept
the becoming   50
thought, to stake off no beginnings or ends, establish
    no walls:

by transitions the land falls from grassy dunes to creek
to undercreek: but there are no lines, though
    change in that transition is clear   55
    as any sharpness: but "sharpness" spread out,

allowed to occur over a wider range
than mental lines can keep:

the moon was full last night: today, low tide was low:
black shoals of mussels exposed to the risk   60
of air
and, earlier, of sun,
waved in and out with the waterline, waterline inexact,
caught always in the event of change:
     a young mottled gull stood free on the shoals   65
    and ate
to vomiting: another gull, squawking possession, cracked a crab,
picked out the entrails, swallowed the soft-shelled legs, a ruddy
turnstone running in to snatch leftover bits:

risk is full: every living thing in   70
siege: the demand is life, to keep life: the small
white blacklegged egret, how beautiful, quietly stalks and spears
     the shallows, darts to shore
          to stab—what? I couldn't
    see against the black mudflats—a frightened   75
fiddler crab?

      the news to my left over the dunes and
reeds and bayberry clumps was
     fall: thousands of tree swallows
     gathering for flight: 80
     an order held
     in constant change: a congregation
rich with entropy: nevertheless, separable, noticeable
    as one event,
        not chaos: preparations for   85
flight from winter,
cheet, cheet, cheet, cheet, wings rifling the green clumps,
beaks
at the bayberries
    a perception full of wind, flight, curve,   90
    sound:
    the possibility of rule as the sum of rulelessness:
the "field" of action
with moving, incalculable center:

in the smaller view, order tight with shape: 95
blue tiny flowers on a leafless weed: carapace of crab:
snail shell:
     pulsations of order
     in the bellies of minnows: orders swallowed,
broken down, transferred through membranes   100
to strengthen larger orders: but in the large view, no
lines or changeless shapes: the working in and out, together
    and against, of millions of events: this,
        so that I make

no form of   105
     formlessness:

orders as summaries, as outcomes of actions override
or in some way result, not predictably (seeing me gain
the top of a dune,
the swallows   110
could take flight—some other fields of bayberry
          could enter fall
          berryless) and there is serenity:

          no arranged terror: no forcing of image, plan,
or thought: 115
no propaganda, no humbling of reality to precept:

terror pervades but is not arranged, all possibilities
of escape open: no route shut, except in
     the sudden loss of all routes:

          I see narrow orders, limited tightness, but will   120
not run to that easy victory:
          still around the looser, wider forces work:
          I will try
     to fasten into order enlarging grasps of disorder, widening
scope, but enjoying the freedom that   125
Scope eludes my grasp, that there is no finality of vision,
that I have perceived nothing completely,
          that tomorrow a new walk is a new walk.

                                                                    1965

Gravelly Run

          I don't know somehow it seems sufficient
          to see and hear whatever coming and going is,
          losing the self to the victory
                    of stones and trees,
          of bending sandpit lakes, crescent   5
          round groves of dwarf pine:

          for it is not so much to know the self
          as to know it as it is known
                    by galaxy and cedar cone,
          as if birth had never found it   10
          and death could never end it:

          the swamp's slow water comes
          down Gravelly Run fanning the long
                    stone-held algal

hair and narrowing roils between   15
the shoulders of the highway bridge:

holly grows on the banks in the woods there,
and the cedars' gothic-clustered
    spires could make
green religion in winter bones: 20

so I look and reflect, but the air's glass
jail seals each thing in its entity:

no use to make any philosophies here:
    I see no
god in the holly, hear no song from   25
the snowbroken weeds: Hegel[3] is not the winter
yellow in the pines: the sunlight has never
heard of trees: surrendered self among
    unwelcoming forms: stranger,
hoist your burdens, get on down the road.   30

                                                                    1965

Laser

An image comes
and the mind's light, confused
as that on surf
or ocean shelves,
gathers up,   5
parallelizes, focuses
and in a rigid beam illuminates the image:

the head seeks in itself
fragments of left-over light
to cast a new   10
direction,
any direction,
to strike and fix
a random, contradicting image:

but any found image falls   15
back to darkness or
the lesser beams splinter and
go out:
the mind tries to
dream of diversity, of mountain   20
rapids shattered with sound and light,

---

3. George Wilhelm Friedrich Hegel (1770–1831), German philosopher, who believed that reason is the spirit of humankind and that everything is a manifestation of Absolute Spirit.

of wind fracturing brush or
bursting out of order against a mountain
range: but the focused beam
folds all energy in: 25
the image glares filling all space:
the head falls and
hangs and cannot wake itself.

1970

Love Song

Like the hills under dusk you
fall away from the light:
you deepen: the green
light darkens
and you are nearly lost: 5
only so much light as
stars keep
manifests your face:
the total night in
myself raves 10
for the light along your lips.

1970

Small Song

The reeds give
way to the

wind and give
the wind away

1970

The City Limits

When you consider the radiance, that it does not withhold
itself but pours its abundance without selection into every
nook and cranny not overhung or hidden; when you consider

that birds' bones make no awful noise against the light but
lie low in the light as in a high testimony; when you consider 5
the radiance, that it will look into the guiltiest

swervings of the weaving heart and bear itself upon them,
not flinching into disguise or darkening; when you consider
the abundance of such resource as illuminates the glow-blue

bodies and gold-skeined wings of flies swarming the dumped   10
guts of a natural slaughter or the coil of shit and in no
way winces from its storms of generosity; when you consider

that air or vacuum, snow or shale, squid or wolf, rose or lichen,
each is accepted into as much light as it will take, then
the heart moves roomier, the man stands and looks about, the   15

leaf does not increase itself above the grass, and the dark
work of the deepest cells is of a tune with May bushes
and fear lit by the breadth of such calmly turns to praise.

                                                                            1971

Easter Morning

I have a life that did not become,
that turned aside and stopped,
astonished:
I hold it in me like a pregnancy or
as on my lap a child   5
not to grow or grow old but dwell on

it is to his grave I most
frequently return and return
to ask what is wrong, what was
wrong, to see it all by   10
the light of a different necessity
but the grave will not heal
and the child,
stirring, must share my grave
with me, an old man having   15
gotten by on what was left

when I go back to my home country in these
fresh far-away days, it's convenient to visit
everybody, aunts and uncles, those who used to say,
look how he's shooting up, and the   20
trinket aunts who always had a little
something in their pocketbooks, cinnamon bark
or a penny or nickel, and uncles who
were the rumored fathers of cousins
who whispered of them as of great, if   25
troubled, presences, and school
teachers, just about everybody older
(and some younger) collected in one place

waiting, particularly, but not for
me, mother and father there, too, and others   30
close, close as burrowing
under skin, all in the graveyard
assembled, done for, the world they
used to wield, have trouble and joy
in, gone   35

the child in me that could not become
was not ready for others to go,
to go on into change, blessings and
horrors, but stands there by the road
where the mishap occurred, crying out for   40
help, come and fix this or we
can't get by, but the great ones who
were to return, they could not or did
not hear and went on in a flurry and
now, I say in the graveyard, here   45
lies the flurry, now it can't come
back with help or helpful asides, now
we all buy the bitter
incompletions, pick up the knots of
horror, silently raving, and go on   50
crashing into empty ends not
completions, not rondures the fullness
has come into and spent itself from
I stand on the stump
of a child, whether myself   55
or my little brother who died, and
yell as far as I can, I cannot leave this place, for
for me it is the dearest and the worst,
it is life nearest to life which is
life lost: it is my place where   60
I must stand and fail,
calling attention with tears
to the branches not lofting
boughs into space, to the barren
air that holds the world that was my world   65

though the incompletions
(& completions) burn out
standing in the flash high-burn
momentary structure of ash, still it
is a picture-book, letter-perfect   70
Easter morning: I have been for a
walk: the wind is tranquil: the brook
works without flashing in an abundant
tranquility: the birds are lively with
voice: I saw something I had   75
never seen before: two great birds,
maybe eagles, blackwinged, whitenecked
and -headed, came from the south oaring

the great wings steadily; they went
directly over me, high up, and kept on   80
due north: but then one bird,
the one behind, veered a little to the
left and the other bird kept on seeming
not to notice for a minute: the first
began to circle as if looking for   85
something, coasting, resting its wings
on the down side of some of the circles:
the other bird came back and they both
circled, looking perhaps for a draft;
they turned a few more times, possibly   90
rising—at least, clearly resting—
then flew on falling into distance till
they broke across the local bush and
trees: it was a sight of bountiful
majesty and integrity: the having   95
patterns and routes, breaking
from them to explore other patterns or
better ways to routes, and then the
return: a dance sacred as the sap in
the trees, permanent in its descriptions   100
as the ripples round the brook's
ripplestone: fresh as this particular
flood of burn breaking across us now
from the sun.

                                                                        1981

Motion's Holdings

The filled out gourd rots, the
ridge rises in a wave
height cracks into peaks, the peaks

wear down to low undoings whose undertowing
throws other waves up: the branch   5
of honeysuckle leaves arcs outward

into its becoming motion but,
completion's precision done, gives
over riddling free to other

motions: boulders, their green and white   10
moss-molds, high-held in moist
hill woods, stir, hum with

stall and spill, take in and give
off heat, adjust nearby to
geomagnetic fields, tip liquid with   15

change should a trunk or rock loosen
to let rollers roll, or they loll
inwardly with earth's lie

in space, oxidize at their surfaces
exchanges with fungal thread and rain: 20
things are slowed motion that,

slowed too far, falls loose, freeing debris:
but in the ongoing warps, the butterfly
amaryllis crowds its bowl with bulbs.

1987

From Tombstones

1

the chisel, chipping in,
finds names the
wind can't blow away

11

the grooves fill with moss,
though, that spring
speaks green
and fall burns out with cold
into winter's black writing   5

19

the things of earth are not objects,
there is no nature,
no nature of stones and brooks, stumps, and ditches,

for these are pools of energy cooled into place,
or they are starlight pressed   5
to store,

or they are speeding light held still:
the woods are a fire green-slow
and the pathway of solid earthwork

is just light concentrated blind   10

27

a flock of
gulls flew
by I thought but

it was a
hillside of stones   5

29

the letters,
holding what they can, hold
in the stone

but holding flakes or
mists away—a   5
grainweight of memory

or a rememberer goes:
in so many hundred years,
the names

will be light enough   10
and as if balloons
will rise out of stone

1987

FROM GARBAGE

2

garbage has to be the poem of our time because
garbage is spiritual, believable enough

to get our attention, getting in the way, piling
up, stinking, turning brooks brownish and

creamy white: what else deflects us from the   5
errors of our illusionary ways, not a temptation

to trashlessness, that is too far off, and,
anyway, unimaginable, unrealistic: I'm a

hole puncher or hole plugger: stick a finger
in the dame (*dam*, damn, dike), hold back the issue   10

of creativity's flood, the forthcoming, futuristic,
the origins feeding trash: down by I-95 in

Florida where flatland's ocean- and gulf-flat,
mounds of disposal rise (for if you dug

something up to make room for something to put   15
in, what about the something dug up, as with graves:)

the garbage trucks crawl as if in obeisance,
as if up ziggurats[4] toward the high places gulls

and garbage keep alive, offerings to the gods
of garbage, of retribution, of realistic   20

expectation, the deities of unpleasant
necessities: refined, young earthworms,

drowned up in macadam[5] pools by spring rains, moisten
out white in a day or so and, round spots,

look like sputum[6] or creamy-rich, broken-up cold   25
clams: if this is not the best poem of the

century, can it be about the worst poem of the
century: it comes, at least, toward the end,

so a long tracing of bad stuff can swell
under its measure: but there on the heights   30

a small smoke wafts the sacrificial bounty
day and night to layer the sky brown, shut us

in as into a lidded kettle, the everlasting
flame these acres-deep of tendance keep: a

free offering of a crippled plastic chair: 35
a played-out sports outfit: a hill-myna[7]

print stained with jelly: how to write this
poem, should it be short, a small popping of

duplexes, or long, hunting wide, coming home
late, losing the trail and recovering it: 40

should it act itself out, illustrations,
examples, colors, clothes or intensify

reductively into statement, bones any corpus
would do to surround, or should it be nothing

at all unless it finds itself: the poem,   45
which is about the pre-socratic idea of the

dispositional axis from stone to wind, wind
to stone (with my elaborations, if any)

is complete before it begins, so I needn't
myself hurry into brevity, though a weary reader   50

---

4. Pyramidal temples.
5. Type of pavement.

6. Material coughed up from the lungs.
7. Species of tropical bird.

might briefly be done: the axis will be clear
enough daubed here and there with a little ink

or fined out into every shade and form of its
revelation: this is a scientific poem,

asserting that nature models values, that we   55
have invented little (copied), reflections of

possibilities already here, this where we came
to and how we came: a priestly director behind the

black-chuffing dozer leans the gleanings and
reads the birds, millions of loners circling   60

a common height, alighting to the meaty streaks
and puffy muffins (puffins?): there is a mound,

too, in the poet's mind dead language is hauled
off to and burned down on, the energy held and

shaped into new turns and clusters, the mind   65
strengthened by what it strengthens: for

where but in the very asshole of comedown is
redemption: as where but brought low, where

but in the grief of failure, loss, error do we
discern the savage afflictions that turn us around: 70

where but in the arrangements love crawls us
through, not a thing left in our self-display

unhumiliated, do we find the sweet seed of
new routes: but we are natural: nature, not

we, gave rise to us: we are not, though, though   75
natural, divorced from higher, finer configurations:

tissues and holograms of energy circulate in
us and seek and find representations of themselves

outside us, so that we can participate in
celebrations high and know reaches of feeling   80

and sight and thought that penetrate (really
penetrate) far, far beyond these our wet cells,

right on up past our stories, the planets, moons,
and other bodies locally to the other end of

the pole where matter's forms diffuse and   85
energy loses all means to express itself except

as spirit, there, oh, yes, in the abiding where
mind but nothing else abides, the eternal,

until it turns into another pear or sunfish,
that momentary glint in the fisheye having   90

been there so long, coming and going, it's
eternity's glint: it all wraps back round,

into and out of form, palpable and impalpable,
and in one phase, the one of grief and love,

we know the other, where everlastingness comes to   95
sway, okay and smooth: the heaven we mostly

want, though, is this jet-hoveled hell back,
heaven's daunting asshole: one must write and

rewrite till one writes it right: if I'm in
touch, she said, then I've got an edge: what   100

the hell kind of talk is that: I can't believe
I'm merely an old person: whose mother is dead,

whose father is gone and many of whose
friends and associates have wended away to the

ground, which is only heavy wind, or to ashes,   105
a lighter breeze: but it was all quite frankly

to be expected and not looked forward to: even
old trees, I remember some of them, where they

used to stand: pictures taken by some of them:
and old dogs, specially one imperial black one,   110

quad dogs with their hier*archies* (another *archie*)
one succeeding another, the barking and romping

sliding away like slides from a projector: what
were they then that are what they are now:

1992

From Strip

43

sometimes I get the feeling I've never
lived here at all, and 31 years seem

no more than nothing: I have to stop
and think, oh, yeah, there was the

kid, so much anguish over his allergy,   5
and there was the year we moved to

another house, and oh, yes, I remember
the lilies we planted near that

siberian elm, and there was the year
they made me a professor, and the   10

year, right in the middle of a long
poem, when I got blood poisoning from

an ingrown toenail not operated on
right: but a wave slices through,

canceling everything, and the space   15
with nothing to fill it shrinks and

time collapses, so that nothing happened,
and I didn't exist, and existence

itself seems like a wayward temporizing,
an illusion nonexistence sometimes   20

stumbles into: keep your mind open,
something might crawl in: which

reminds me of my greatest saying:
old poets never die, they just scrawl

away: and then I think of my friends   25
who may have longed for me, and I say

oh, I'll be here the next time
around: alas, the next time will

not come next: so what am I to say
to friends who know I'm not here and   30

won't be back: I'm sorry I missed
you guys: but even with the little

I know I loved you a lot, a lot more
than I said: our mountains here are

so old they're hills: they've been   35
around around 300 million years but

indifference in all that time broke
itself only to wear them out: my

indifference is just like theirs: it
wipes itself clear: surely, I will have   40

another chance: surely, nothing is
let go till trouble free: when

I come back I'm going to be there
every time: and then the wave that

comes to blank me out will be set   45
edgy and jiggling with my recalcitrance

and my consciousness will take on weight

1997

JAMES MERRILL
1926–1995

James Merrill's first poems show none of the clumsiness and uncertainty of apprentice
work. They are calm and collected, highly finished works of art that are often about
other works of art. The subject matter is international, and Merrill's detached connois-
seurship often reminds one of novelists Marcel Proust and Henry James. Merrill had a
talent for Metaphysical wit. In his mature poems, the earlier exquisite, meditative style
is combined with a new interest in narrative and personal experience. The poems are
longer, more relaxed, and the wit is more humane. "The Broken Home" is about the
relationship between the speaker and his wealthy, energetic father. It begins with Mer-
rill's characteristic opulence:

Crossing the street,
I saw the parents and the child
At their window, gleaming like fruit
With evening's mild gold leaf.

—but the recollection of the father is at once both offhand and moving.

Each thirteenth year he married. When he died
There were already several chilled wives
In sable orbit—rings, cars, permanent waves.
We'd felt him warming up for a green bride.

Like other 1960s depictions of fathers, this one is vexed, but the poet's feelings are implied, distilled, metaphorized. In "Lost in Translation"—also about the poet's broken childhood home—a picture puzzle becomes a metaphor for piecing together memory. Various forms of linguistic and artistic translation interweave to suggest what survives and what is lost in time.

Disgruntlement with his father, distress over his parents' divorce, melancholy over emotional and erotic losses, crushes on other boys acting in a play—these are the sorts of personal experiences one might expect in confessional poetry, but Merrill's verse is personal without being confessional. His formal framing of the autobiographical carefully transmutes the raw material of experience into art. Pain, desire, hurt vanity, grief, pathos—such feelings exist, even when unstated, in the cadences, sonorities, images, and settings of Merrill's both musical and painterly verse. "The point about music and song," Merrill said in a 1967 interview, "is that there is the sound of sheer feeling—as opposed to that of sense, of verbal sense. To combine the two is worth dreaming about."

Merrill's mastery of various lyric verse forms is unmatched since W. H. Auden; he writes effortlessly and cleverly in rhymed, slant-rhymed, and unrhymed verse; in syllabics, stressed verse, and free verse; in sonnets, ballad stanzas, and sestinas. He often slips in and out of these forms within the same poem, which may start unrhymed, then rhyme regularly, then rapidly shift stanza pattern, producing subtle changes in cadence, tempo, and tone. Line endings play on half-rhyme and consonance (e.g., "or vote" / "invite" in "The Broken Home," "grooves' bare groves" / "grave's" / "gramophone" in "The Victor Dog"). Wordplay and wit are everywhere, from clever enjambments ("the Home, / Work of " in "Lost in Translation"), to puns ("His forebears lacked, to say the least, forbearance" in "The Victor Dog"), to plays on clichés ("time was money" but "money was not time" in "The Broken Home"). The figurative language and imagery are inventive, luminous ("The green-gold room throbbed like a bruise"; "An avocado in a glass of water—/ Roots pallid, gemmed with air" in "The Broken Home"). His tone often fuses irony and wistfulness, camp and the elegiac. Autobiographical directness coexists with arch, all-knowing deflection. The multileveled diction of a poem such as "Self-Portrait in Tyvek(™) Windbreaker" encompasses everything from the high literary to the line "Prayer breakfasts. Pay-phone sex. 'Ring up as meat.' " Merrill's style blends an expansive and ornate richness with an aphoristic terseness that makes many individual lines memorable.

With the publication of *Divine Comedies* (1976), Merrill's work took a surprising, even outrageous turn. With the help of his longtime partner David Jackson, an accommodating Ouija board, friends (most of them dead), fellow poets, scientists, and a galaxy of guardians from the spirit world, Merrill assembled over a period of more than twenty years an epic poem that from time to time resembles such different works as W. B. Yeats's *A Vision* and the epic poems of Dante, William Blake, William Wordsworth, and Walt Whitman, as well as the prose narratives of Proust and James. The completed work, eventually called *The Changing Light at Sandover*, is a witty, gracious, genial poem, comforting in its assurance that our friends are never lost to us, and that, thanks to the transmigration of souls, human beings slip, rather comically, from one existence to another.

Merrill was born on March 3, 1926, in New York City, the son of Charles E. Merrill, cofounder of the Merrill Lynch brokerage firm. When he was twelve, his parents divorced, his beloved Prussian English governess was dismissed, and he was sent to boarding school. His undergraduate education was interrupted by army service at the end of World War II, but he received his B.A. from Amherst College in 1947 after writing a thesis on Proust. Much of his adult life he wintered in Greece (later Key West, Florida) and summered in the northeastern United States, sharing houses with David Jackson. He published many volumes of poetry and won the National Book Award

(1967, 1979), the Bollingen Prize (1973), the Pulitzer Prize (1977), and the National Book Critics Circle Award (1983). He created the Ingram Merrill Foundation to support the work of writers and painters. He died of a heart attack just as his volume *A Scattering of Salts* was being published.

The Broken Home

Crossing the street,
I saw the parents and the child
At their window, gleaming like fruit
With evening's mild gold leaf.

In a room on the floor below,   5
Sunless, cooler—a brimming
Saucer of wax, marbly and dim—
I have lit what's left of my life.

I have thrown out yesterday's milk
And opened a book of maxims.   10
The flame quickens. The word stirs.

Tell me, tongue of fire,
That you and I are as real
At least as the people upstairs.

                    •

My father,[1] who had flown in World War I,   15
Might have continued to invest his life
In cloud banks well above Wall Street and wife.
But the race was run below, and the point was to win.

Too late now, I make out in his blue gaze
(Through the smoked glass of being thirty-six)   20
The soul eclipsed by twin black pupils, sex
And business; time was money in those days.

Each thirteenth year he married. When he died
There were already several chilled wives
In sable orbit—rings, cars, permanent waves.   25
We'd felt him warming up for a green bride.

He could afford it. He was "in his prime"
At three score ten. But money was not time.

                    •

When my parents were younger this was a popular act:
A veiled woman would leap from an electric, wine-dark car   30
To the steps of no matter what—the Senate or the Ritz Bar—
And bodily, at newsreel speed, attack

---

1. Charles E. Merrill, a founding partner of the investment firm Merrill Lynch, Pierce, Fenner & Smith.

No matter whom—Al Smith or José Maria Sert
Or Clemenceau[2]—veins standing out on her throat
As she yelled *War mongerer! Pig! Give us the vote!*,   35
And would have to be hauled away in her hobble skirt.[3]

What had the man done? Oh, made history.
Her business (he had implied) was giving birth,
Tending the house, mending the socks.

Always that same old story—   40
Father Time and Mother Earth,
A marriage on the rocks.

•

One afternoon, red, satyr-thighed
Michael, the Irish setter, head
Passionately lowered, led   45
The child I was to a shut door. Inside,

Blinds beat sun from the bed.
The green-gold room throbbed like a bruise.
Under a sheet, clad in taboos
Lay whom we sought, her hair undone, outspread,   50

And of a blackness found, if ever now, in old
Engravings where the acid bit.
I must have needed to touch it
Or the whiteness—was she dead?
Her eyes flew open, startled strange and cold.   55
The dog slumped to the floor. She reached for me. I fled.

•

Tonight they have stepped out onto the gravel.
The party is over. It's the fall
Of 1931. They love each other still.

She: Charlie, I can't stand the pace.   60
He: Come on, honey—why, you'll bury us all!

A lead soldier guards my windowsill:
Khaki rifle, uniform, and face.
Something in me grows heavy, silvery, pliable.

How intensely people used to feel!   65
Like metal poured at the close of a proletarian novel,
Refined and glowing from the crucible,
I see those two hearts, I'm afraid,

---

2. Georges Clemenceau (1841–1929): premier of France during World War I; visited the United States in 1922. Alfred E. Smith (1873–1944): governor of New York and a 1928 candidate for the U.S. presidency. José María Sert (1876–1945): Spanish painter who decorated the lobby of New York's Waldorf Astoria Hotel in 1930.
3. A long, straight skirt.

Still. Cool here in the graveyard of good and evil,
They are even so to be honored and obeyed.   70

                    •

. . . Obeyed, at least, inversely. Thus
I rarely buy a newspaper, or vote.
To do so, I have learned, is to invite
The tread of a stone guest within my house.[4]

Shooting this rusted bolt, though, against him,   75
I trust I am no less time's child than some
Who on the heath impersonate Poor Tom[5]
Or on the barricades risk life and limb.

Nor do I try to keep a garden, only
An avocado in a glass of water—   80
Roots pallid, gemmed with air. And later,

When the small gilt leaves have grown
Fleshy and green, I let them die, yes, yes,
And start another. I am earth's no less.

                    •

A child, a red dog roam the corridors,   85
Still, of the broken home. No sound. The brilliant
Rag runners halt before wide-open doors.
My old room! Its wallpaper—cream, medallioned
With pink and brown—brings back the first nightmares,
Long summer colds, and Emma, sepia-faced,   90
Perspiring over broth carried upstairs
Aswim with golden fats I could not taste.

The real house became a boarding school.
Under the ballroom ceiling's allegory
Someone at last may actually be allowed   95
To learn something; or, from my window, cool
With the unstiflement of the entire story,
Watch a red setter stretch and sink in cloud.

                                              1966

Days of 1964

Houses, an embassy, the hospital,
Our neighborhood sun-cured if trembling still
In pools of the night's rain . . .

4. In *The Stone Feast*, by French dramatist Jean-
Baptiste Molière (1622–1673), the stone statue of
the commander of Seville visits his murderer, Don
Juan, and drags him off to Hell. Mozart's opera
Don Giovanni (1787) presents a version of this
story.
5. In Shakespeare's *King Lear*, Edgar, disowned by
his father, wanders the heath disguised as a mad-
man and calling himself Poor Tom.

Across the street that led to the center of town
A steep hill kept one company part way   5
Or could be climbed in twenty minutes
For some literally breathtaking views,
Framed by umbrella pines, of city and sea.
Underfoot, cyclamen, autumn crocus grew
Spangled as with fine sweat among the relics   10
Of good times had by all. If not Olympus,[6]
An out-of-earshot, year-round hillside revel.

I brought home flowers from my climbs.
Kyria Kleo who cleans for us
Put them in water, sighing *Virgin, Virgin*.   15
Her legs hurt. She wore brown, was fat, past fifty,
And looked like a Palmyra matron
Copied in lard and horsehair.[7] How she loved
You, me, loved us all, the bird, the cat!
I think now she *was* love. She sighed and glistened   20
All day with it, or pain, or both.
(We did not notably communicate.)
She lived nearby with her pious mother
And wastrel[8] son. She called me her real son.

I paid her generously, I dare say.   25
Love makes one generous. Look at us. We'd known
Each other so briefly that instead of sleeping
We lay whole nights, open, in the lamplight,
And gazed, or traded stories.

One hour comes back—you gasping in my arms   30
With love, or laughter, or both,
I having just remembered and told you
What I'd looked up to see on my way downtown at noon:
Poor old Kleo, her aching legs,
Trudging into the pines. I called,   35
Called three times before she turned.
Above a tight, skyblue sweater, her face
Was painted. Yes. Her face was painted
Clown-white, white of the moon by daylight,
Lidded with pearl, mouth a poinsettia leaf,   40
Eat me, pay me—the erotic mask
Worn the world over by illusion
To weddings of itself and simple need.

Startled mute, we had stared—was love illusion?—
And gone our ways. Next, I was crossing a square   45
In which a moveable outdoor market's

---

6. Mountain in northern Greece that was considered the home of the gods.
7. A horsehair paintbrush. *Palmyra:* ancient city in central Syria. *Lard:* traditionally, mixed with powdered pigment for paint.
8. A loafer.

Vegetables, chickens, pottery kept materializing
Through a dream-press of hagglers each at heart
Leery lest he be taken, plucked,
The bird, the flower of that November mildness,   50
Self lost up soft clay paths, or found, foothold,
Where the bud throbs awake
The better to be nipped, self on its knees in mud—
Here I stopped cold, for both our sakes;

And calmer on my way home bought us fruit.   55

Forgive me if you read this. (And may Kyria Kleo,
Should someone ever put it into Greek
And read it aloud to her, forgive me, too.)
I had gone so long without loving,
I hardly knew what I was thinking.   60

Where I hid my face, your touch, quick, merciful,
Blindfolded me. A god breathed from my lips.
If that was illusion, I wanted it to last long;
To dwell, for its daily pittance, with us there,
Cleaning and watering, sighing with love or pain.   65
I hoped it would climb when it needed to the heights
Even of degradation, as I for one
Seemed, those days, to be always climbing
Into a world of wild
Flowers, feasting, tears—or was I falling, legs   70
Buckling, heights, depths,
Into a pool of each night's rain?
But you were everywhere beside me, masked,
As who was not, in laughter, pain, and love.

                                                            1966

The Victor Dog[9]

for Elizabeth Bishop[1]

Bix to Buxtehude to Boulez,
The little white dog on the Victor label
Listens long and hard as he is able.
It's all in a day's work, whatever plays.

---

9. The old trademark for RCA Victor Records showed a small dog listening intently to an old-fashioned gramophone, with the title "His Master's Voice." The poem alludes to a number of musicians and composers: the jazz trumpeter Bix Beiderbecke; the eighteenth-century composers Dietrich Buxtehude, Johann Sebastian Bach, and George Frideric Handel; and the nineteenth-century composers Franz Schubert and Robert Schumann; and the modernists Pierre Boulez, Ernest Bloch, and Maurice Ravel.
1. American poet (1911–1979) and longtime friend of Merrill's.

From judgment, it would seem, he has refrained. 5
He even listens earnestly to Bloch,
Then builds a church upon our acid rock.[2]
He's man's—no—he's the Leiermann's best friend,[3]

Or would be if hearing and listening were the same.
Does he hear? I fancy he rather smells 10
Those lemon-gold arpeggios in Ravel's
"*Les jets d'eau du palais de ceux qui s'aiment.*"[4]

He ponders the Schumann Concerto's tall willow hit
By lightning, and stays put. When he surmises
Through one of Bach's eternal boxwood mazes[5] 15
The oboe pungent as a bitch in heat,

Or when the calypso decants its raw bay rum
Or the moon in *Wozzeck*[6] reddens ripe for murder,
He doesn't sneeze or howl; just listens harder.
Adamant[7] needles bear down on him from 20

Whirling of outer space, too black, too near—
But he was taught as a puppy not to flinch,
Much less to imitate his bête noire Blanche
Who barked, fat foolish creature, at King Lear.[8]

Still others fought in the road's filth over Jezebel,[9] 25
Slavered on hearths of horned and pelted barons.
His forebears lacked, to say the least, forbearance.
Can nature change in him? Nothing's impossible.

The last chord fades. The night is cold and fine.
His master's voice rasps through the grooves' bare groves. 30
Obediently, in silence like the grave's
He sleeps there on the still-warm gramophone

Only to dream he is at the première of a Handel
Opera long thought lost—*Il Cane Minore.*[1]
Its allegorical subject is his story! 35
A little dog revolving round a spindle

---

2. In Matthew 16.18, Jesus says to Peter, "Upon this rock I will build my church."
3. In Schubert's song "Der Leiermann" ("The Organ-Grinder"), an old man cranks his barrel organ in the winter cold to an audience of snarling dogs.
4. The fountains of the palace of those who are in love with each other (French).
5. The German composer's variations on musical themes are compared to the boxwoods often planted to form mazes in formal, eighteenth-century gardens.
6. Opera by Alban Berg (1885–1935), in which the protagonist murders his unfaithful wife under a rising moon.
7. Diamond; unyielding.
8. During the storm scene, Shakespeare's Lear says, "The little dogs and all / Tray, Blanch, and Sweet-heart, see, they bark at me" (3.6.57–58). *Bête noire*: something to be feared or avoided; literally, a black beast, whereas *blanche* means white.
9. Jezebel's body was thrown into the street as punishment for her evil deeds. When it was recovered for burial, dogs had eaten most of it (1 Kings 21ff.).
1. The little dog (Italian).

Gives rise to harmonies beyond belief,
A cast of stars. . . . Is there in Victor's heart
No honey for the vanquished? Art is art.
The life it asks of us is a dog's life.   40

                                                                            1972

Lost in Translation

for Richard Howard[2]

Diese Tage, die leer dir scheinen
und wertlos für das All,
haben Wurzeln zwischen den Steinen
und trinken dort überall.[3]

A card table in the library stands ready
To receive the puzzle which keeps never coming.
Daylight shines in or lamplight down
Upon the tense oasis of green felt.
Full of unfulfillment, life goes on,   5
Mirage arisen from time's trickling sands
Or fallen piecemeal into place:
German lesson, picnic, see-saw, walk
With the collie who "did everything but talk"—
Sour windfalls of the orchard back of us.   10
A summer without parents is the puzzle,
Or should be. But the boy, day after day,
Writes in his Line-a-Day[4] *No puzzle.*

He's in love, at least. His French Mademoiselle,
In real life a widow since Verdun,   15
Is stout, plain, carrot-haired, devout.
She prays for him, as does a curé[5] in Alsace,
Sews costumes for his marionettes,
Helps him to keep behind the scene
Whose sidelit goosegirl, speaking with his voice,   20
Plays Guinevere[6] as well as Gunmoll Jean.
Or else at bedtime in his tight embrace
Tells him her own French hopes, her German fears,
Her—but what more is there to tell?
Having known grief and hardship, Mademoiselle   25
Knows little more. Her languages. Her place.
Noon coffee. Mail. The watch that also waited
Pinned to her heart, poor gold, throws up its hands—
No puzzle! Steaming bitterness

---

2. American poet (b. 1929).
3. Part of a translation by the Austrian poet Rainer Maria Rilke (1875–1926) of "Palme," by the French poet Paul Valéry (1871–1945; see lines 32–33): "These days, which seem empty and entirely fruitless to you, have roots between the stones and drink from everywhere."
4. That is, diary.
5. French priest. *Mademoiselle:* the poet's French-speaking governess. *Verdun:* site of World War I battle.
6. Wife of the legendary King Arthur.

Her sugars draw pops back into his mouth, translated: 30
"Patience, chéri. Geduld, mein Schatz."[7]
(Thus, reading Valéry the other evening
And seeming to recall a Rilke version of "Palme,"
That sunlit paradigm whereby the tree
Taps a sweet wellspring of authority,   35
The hour came back. Patience dans l'azur.
Geduld im . . . Himmelblau? Mademoiselle.)

Out of the blue, as promised, of a New York
Puzzle-rental shop the puzzle comes—
A superior one, containing a thousand hand-sawn,   40
Sandal-scented[8] pieces. Many take
Shapes known already—the craftsman's repertoire
Nice in its limitation—from other puzzles:
Witch on broomstick, ostrich, hourglass,
Even (surely not just in retrospect)   45
An inchling, innocently branching palm.
These can be put aside, made stories of
While mademoiselle spreads out the rest face-up,
Herself excited as a child; or questioned
Like incoherent faces in a crowd,   50
Each with its scrap of highly colored
Evidence the Law must piece together.
Sky-blue ostrich? Likely story.
Mauve of the witch's cloak white, severed fingers
Pluck? Detain her. The plot thickens   55
As all at once two pieces interlock.

Mademoiselle does borders—(Not so fast.
A London dusk, December last.
Chatter silenced in the library
This grown man reenters, wearing grey.   60
A medium. All except him have seen
Panel slid back, recess explored,
An object at once unique and common
Displayed, planted in a plain tole
Casket the subject now considers   65
Through shut eyes, saying in effect:
"Even as voices reach me vaguely
A dry saw-shriek drowns them out,
Some loud machinery—a lumber mill?
Far uphill in the fir forest   70
Trees tower, tense with shock,
Groaning and cracking as they crash groundward.
But hidden here is a freak fragment
Of a pattern complex in appearance only.
What it seems to show is superficial   75

---

7. Have patience, my dear (French and German).
In the next lines, these phrases remind the speaker
of a line in Valéry's "Palme" and Rilke's translation,
"Patience in the blue"—a way of characterizing the
slow nature of the palm tree. Paradigm: pattern.
8. That is, sandalwood-scented.

Next to that long-term lamination
Of hazard and craft, the karma[9] that has
Made it matter in the first place.
Plywood, Piece of a puzzle." Applause
Acknowledged by an opening of lids   80
Upon the thing itself. A sudden dread—
But to go back. All this lay years ahead.)

Mademoiselle does borders. Straight-edge pieces
Align themselves with earth or sky
In twos and threes, naive cosmogonists[1]   85
Whose views clash. Nomad inlanders meanwhile
Begin to cluster where the totem
Of a certain vibrant egg-yolk yellow
Or pelt of what emerging animal
Acts on the straggler like a trumpet call   90
To form a more sophisticated unit.
By suppertime two ragged wooden clouds
Have formed. In one, a Sheik with beard
And flashing sword hilt (he is all but finished)
Steps forward on a tiger skin. A piece   95
Snaps shut, and fangs gnash out at us!
In the second cloud—they gaze from cloud to cloud
With marked if undecipherable feeling—
Most of a dark-eyed woman veiled in mauve
Is being helped down from her camel (kneeling)   100
By a small backward-looking slave or page-boy
(Her son, thinks Mademoiselle mistakenly)
Whose feet have not been found. But lucky finds
In the last minutes before bed
Anchor both factions to the scene's limits   105
And, by so doing, orient
Them eye to eye across the green abyss.
The yellow promises, oh bliss,
To be in time a sumptuous tent.

Puzzle begun I write in the day's space,   110
Then, while she bathes, peek at Mademoiselle's
Page to the curé: ". . . cette innocente mère,
Ce pauvre enfant, que deviendront-ils?"[2]
Her azure script is curlicued like pieces
Of the puzzle she will be telling him about.   115
(Fearful incuriosity of childhood!
"Tu as l'accent allemand,"[3] said Dominique.
Indeed. Mademoiselle was only French by marriage.
Child of an English mother, a remote
Descendant of the great explorer Speke,[4]   120
And Prussian father. No one knew. I heard it

9. Roughly, fate.
1. Theorists about the origins of the universe.
2. This innocent mother, this poor child, what will
become of them? (French).
3. You have a German accent (French).
4. Nineteenth-century English explorer in Africa.

Long afterwards from her nephew, a UN
Interpreter. His matter-of-fact account
Touched old strings. My poor Mademoiselle,
With 1939[5] about to shake   125
This world where "each was the enemy, each the friend"
To it foundations, kept, though signed in blood,
Her peace a shameful secret to the end.)
"Schlaf wohl, chéri."[6] Her kiss. Her thumb
Crossing my brow against the dreams to come.   130

This World that shifts like sand, its unforeseen
Consolidations and elate routine,
Whose Potentate had lacked a retinue?
Lo! it assembles on the shrinking Green.

Gunmetal-skinned or pale, all plumes and scars,   135
Of Vassalage the noblest avatars—
The very coffee-bearer in his vair[7]
Vest is a swart Highness, next to ours.

Kef[8] easing Boredom, and iced syrups, thirst,
In guessed-at glooms old wives who know the worst   140
Outsweat that virile fiction of the New:
"Insh'Allah,[9] he will tire—" "—or kill her first!"

(Hardly a proper subject for the Home,
Work of—dear Richard, I shall let *you* comb
Archives and learned journals for his name—   145
A minor lion attending on Gérôme.)[1]

While, thick as Thebes[2] whose presently complete
Gates close behind them, Houri and Afreet[3]
Both claim the Page. He wonders whom to serve,
And what his duties are, and where his feet,   150

And if we'll find, as some before us did,
That piece of Distance deep in which lies hid
Your tiny apex sugary with sun,
Eternal Triangle, Great Pyramid!

Then Sky alone is left, a hundred blue   155
Fragments in revolution, with no clue
To where a Niche will open. Quite a task,
Putting together Heaven, yet we do.

---

5. That is, the outbreak of World War II.
6. Sleep well, darling (German and French).
7. Trimmed with fur. *Avatars*: that is, incarnations
of slavery.
8. Narcotic made from hemp.
9. As Allah wills (Arabic).
1. Nineteenth-century French Orientalist painter;
cf. also Saint Jerome, said to have pulled a thorn
from the paw of a lion and tamed him.
2. Ancient capital of Upper Egypt; cf. also the
expression "thick as thieves."
3. Evil demon in Arabic mythology. *Houri*: one of
the beautiful maidens living with the blessed in the
Islamic paradise.

It's done. Here under the table all along
Were those missing feet. It's done.   160

The dog's tail thumping. Mademoiselle sketching
Costumes for a coming harem drama
To star the goosegirl. All too soon the swift
Dismantling. Lifted by two corners,
The puzzle hung together—and did not.   165
Irresistibly a populace
Unstitched of its attachments, rattled down.
Power went to pieces as the witch
Slithered easily from Virtue's gown.
The blue held out for time, but crumbled, too.   170
The city had long fallen, and the tent,
A separating sauce mousseline,[4]
Been swept away. Remained the green
On which the grown-ups gambled. A green dusk.
First lightning bugs. Last glow of west   175
Green in the false eyes of (coincidence)
Our mangy tiger safe on his bared hearth.

Before the puzzle was boxed and readdressed
To the puzzle shop in the mid-Sixties,[5]
Something tells me that one piece contrived   180
To stay in the boy's pocket. How do I know?
I know because so many later puzzles
Had missing pieces—Maggie Teyte's[6] high notes
Gone at the war's end, end of the vogue for collies,
A house torn down; and hadn't Mademoiselle   185
Kept back her pitiful bit of truth as well?
I've spent the last days, furthermore,
Ransacking Athens for that translation of "Palme."
Neither the Goethehaus nor the National Library
Seems able to unearth it. Yet I can't   190
Just be imagining. I've seen it. Know
How much of the sun-ripe original
Felicity Rilke made himself forego
(Who loved French words—verger, mûr, parfumer)[7]
In order to render its underlying sense.   195
Know already in that tongue of his
What Pains, what monolithic Truths
Shadow stanza to stanza's symmetrical
Rhyme-rutted pavement. Know that ground plan left
Sublime and barren, where the warm Romance   200
Stone by stone faded, cooled; the fluted nouns
Made taller, lonelier than life
By leaf-carved capitals in the afterglow.
The owlet umlaut[8] peeps and hoots

4. A creamy sauce.
5. That is, on New York City's Upper East Side.
6. English soprano (1888–1976), famous for her

singing of French opera and songs.
7. Orchard, ripe, to scent (French).
8. German accent mark (¨).

Above the open vowel. And after rain   205
A deep reverberation fills with stars.

Lost, is it, buried? One more missing piece?

But nothing's lost. Or else: all is translation
And every bit of us is lost in it
(Or found—I wander through the ruin of S[9]   210
Now and then, wondering at the peacefulness)
And in that loss a self-effacing tree,
Color of context, imperceptibly
Rustling with its angel,[1] turns the waste
To shade and fiber, milk and memory.   215

                                                                       1976

FROM THE CHANGING LIGHT AT SANDOVER

From The Book of Ephraim[2]

Zero hour. Waiting yet again
For someone to fix the furnace. Zero week
Of the year's end. Bed that keeps restlessly
Making itself anew from lame[3] drifts.
Mercury dropping. Cost of living high.   5
Night has fallen in the glass studio
Upstairs. The fire we huddle with our drinks by
Pops and snaps. Throughout the empty house
(Tenants away until the New Year) taps
Glumly trickling keep the pipes from freezing.   10
Summers ago this whole room was a garden—
Orange tree, plumbago, fuchsia, palm;
One of us at the piano playing his
Gymnopédie,[4] the other entering
Stunned by hot news from the sundeck. Now   15
The plants, the sorry few that linger, scatter
Leaflets advocating euthanasia.
Windows and sliding doors are wadded shut.
A blind raised here and there, what walls us in
Trembles with dim slides, transparencies   20
Of our least motion foisted on a thereby
Realer—falser?—night. Whichever term

9. Initial of former lover.
1. Cf. the phrase "wrestling with its angel."
2. The first book of Merrill's epic trilogy, *The Changing Light at Sandover*. Its twenty-six sections follow the letters of the alphabet on the Ouija board, which Merrill and David Jackson (DJ) used supposedly to communicate with spirits.
3. Metallic fabric.
4. Composition by French composer Erik Satie (1866–1925).

Adds its note of tension and relief.
Downstairs, doors are locked against the thief:
Night before last, returning from a dinner,   25
We found my bedroom ransacked, lights on, loud
Tick of alarm, the mirror off its hook
Looking daggers at the ceiling fixture.
A burglar here in the Enchanted Village—
Unheard of! Not that he took anything.   30
We had no television, he no taste
For Siamese bronze or Greek embroidery.
Except perhaps some loose change on the bureau
Nothing we can recollect is missing.
"Lucky boys," declared the chief of police   35
Risking a wise look at our curios.
The threat remains, though, of there still being
A presence in our midst, unknown, unseen,
Unscrupulous to take what he can get.
Next morning in my study—stranger yet—   40
I found a dusty carton out of place.
Had it been rummaged through? What could he fancy
Lay buried here among these—oh my dear,
Letters scrawled by my own hand unable
To keep pace with the tempest in the cup—[5]   45
These old love-letters from the other world.
We've set them down at last beside the fire.
Are they for burning, now that the affair
Has ended? (Has it ended?) Any day
It's them or the piano, says DJ.   50
Who'll ever read them over? Take this one.
Limp, chill, it shivers in the glow, as when
The tenor having braved orchestral fog
First sees Brünnhilde[6] sleeping like a log.
Laid on the fire, it would hesitate,   55
Trying to think, to feel—then the elate
Burst of satori,[7] plucking final sense
Boldly from inconclusive evidence.
And that (unless it floated, spangled ash,
Outward, upward, one lone carp aflash   60
Languorously through its habitat
For crumbs that once upon a . . .) would be that.
So, do we burn the— Wait the phone is ringing:
Bad connection; babble of distant talk;
No getting through. We must improve the line   65
In every sense, for life. Again at nine
Sharp above the village clock, *ring-ring*.
It's Bob the furnace man. He's on his way.
Will find, if not an easy-to-repair

---

5. Merrill and Jackson used a teacup as the pointer for the Ouija board. Also, a play on the expression "a tempest in a teacup."
6. Character from the opera cycle *Der Ring des Nibelungen*, by German composer Richard Wagner (1813–1883).
7. State of enlightenment sought in Zen Buddhism.

Short circuit, then the failure long foreseen   70
As total, of our period machine.
Let's be downstairs, leave all this, put the light out.
Fix a screen to the proscenium[8]
Still flickering. Let that carton be. Too much
Already, here below, has met its match.   75
Yet nothing's gone, or nothing we recall.
And look, the stars have wound in filigree[9]
The ancient, ageless woman of the world.
She's seen us. She is not particular—
Everyone gets her injured, musical   80
"Why do you no longer come to me?"
To which there's no reply. For here we are.

                                        1976

b   o   d   y

Look closely at the letters. Can you see,
entering (stage right), then floating full,
then heading off—so soon—
how like a little kohl-rimmed[1] moon
o plots her course from b to d   5

—as y, unanswered, knocks at the stage door?
Looked at too long, words fail,
phase out. Ask, now that body shines
no longer, by what light you learn these lines
and what the b and d stood for.   10

                                        1995

Self-Portrait in Tyvek[(TM)] Windbreaker[2]

The windbreaker is white with a world map.
DuPont contributed the seeming-frail,
Unrippable stuff first used for Priority Mail.
Weightless as shores reflected in deep water,
The countries are violet, orange, yellow, green;   5
Names of the principal towns and rivers, black.
A zipper's hiss, and the Atlantic Ocean closes
Over my blood-red T-shirt from the Gap.

I found it in one of those vaguely imbecile
Emporia catering to the collective unconscious   10

8. Area of the theater between the curtain and the orchestra.
9. Delicate ornamentation.
1. *Kohl*: dark eye makeup used in the Middle East.

2. Tyvek is a synthetic fabric manufactured by the DuPont company, also used to strengthen envelopes and packages.

Of our time and place. This one featured crystals,
Cassettes of whalesong and rain-forest whistles,
Barometers, herbal cosmetics, pillows like puffins,
Recycled notebooks, mechanized lucite[3] coffins
For sapphire waves that crest, break, and recede,   15
As they presumably do in nature still.

Sweat-panted and Reeboked, I wear it to the gym.
My terry-cloth headband is green as laurel.[4]
A yellow plastic Walkman at my hip
Sends shiny yellow tendrils to either ear.   20
All us street people got our types on tape,
Turn ourselves on with a sly fingertip.
Today I felt like Songs of Yesteryear
Sung by Roberto Murolo.[5] Heard of him?

Well, back before animal species began to become   25
Extinct, a dictator named Mussolini[6] banned
The street-singers of Naples. One smart kid
Learned their repertoire by heart, and hid.
Emerging after the war with his guitar,
He alone bearing the old songs of the land   30
Into the nuclear age sang with a charm,
A perfect naturalness that thawed the numb

Survivors and reinspired the Underground.
From love to grief to gaiety his art
Modulates effortlessly, like a young man's heart,   35
Tonic to dominant[7]—the frets so few
And change so strummed into the life of things
That Nature's lamps burn brighter when he sings
Nannetta's fickleness, or chocolate,
Snow on a flower, the moon, the seasons' round.   40

I picked his tape in lieu of something grosser
Or loftier, say the Dead or Arvo Pärt,[8]
On the hazy premise that what fills the mind
Shows on the face. My face, as a small part
Of nature, hopes this musical sunscreen   45
Will keep the wilderness within it green,
Yet looks uneasy, drawn. I detect behind
My neighbor's grin the oncoming bulldozer

And cannot stop it. Ecosaints—their karma
To be Earth's latest, maybe terminal, fruits—   50
Are slow to ripen. Even this dumb jacket

3. Transparent plastic.
4. In ancient Greece, victorious athletes and distinguished poets were crowned with laurel wreaths.
5. Singer (b. 1912), widely seen as the twentieth-century master of Neapolitan song; he continued to record albums in old age.

6. Benito Mussolini (1883–1945), Italian Fascist dictator before and during World War II.
7. That is, from the first to the fifth note of an octave.
8. Estonian avant-garde composer (b. 1935). *The Dead*: American psychedelic rock band the Grateful Dead.

Probably still believes in Human Rights,
Thinks in terms of "nations," urban centers,
Cares less (can Tyvek breathe?) for oxygen
Than for the innocents evicted when   55
Ford bites the dust and Big Mac buys the farm.

Hah. As if greed and savagery weren't the tongues
We've spoken since the beginning. My point is, those
Prior people, fresh from scarifying
Their young and feasting in triumph on their foes,   60
Honored the gods of Air and Land and Sea.
We, though . . . Cut to dead forests, filthy beaches,
The can of hairspray, oil-benighted creatures,
A star-scarred x-ray of the North Wind's lungs.

Still, not to paint a picture wholly black   65
Some social highlights: Dead white males in malls.
Prayer breakfasts. Pay-phone sex. "Ring up as meat."
Oprah. The GNP.[9] The contour sheet.
The painless death of History. The stick
Figures on Capitol Hill. Their rhetoric,   70
Gladly—no, rapturously (on Prozac) suffered!
Gay studies. Right to Lifers. The laugh track.

And clothes. Americans, blithe as the last straw,
Shrug off accountability by dressing
Younger than their kids—jeans, ski-pants, sneakers,   75
A baseball cap, a happy-face T-shirt . . .
Like first-graders we "love" our mother Earth,
Know she's been sick, and mean to care for her
When we grow up. Seeing my windbreaker,
People hail me with nostalgic awe.   80

"Great jacket!" strangers on streetcorners impart.
The Albanian doorman pats it: "Where you buy?"
Over his ear-splitting drill a hunky guy
Yells, "Hey, you'll always know where you are, right?"
"Ever the fashionable cosmopolite,"   85
Beams Ray. And "Voilà mon pays"[1]—the carrot-haired
Girl in the bakery, touching with her finger
The little orange France above my heart.

Everyman, c'est moi,[2] the whole world's pal!
The pity is how soon such feelings sour.   90
As I leave the gym a smiling-as-if-I-should-know-her
Teenager—oh but I *mean*, she's wearing "our"
Windbreaker, and assumes . . . Yet I return her wave
Like an accomplice. For while all humans aren't

9. Gross National Product.
1. Here is my country (French).
2. It is I (French); a variation on the phrase

"L'Etat, c'est moi" (I am the State), by Louis XIV
(1638–1715).

Countable as equals, we must behave 95
As if they were, or the spirit dies (Pascal).[3]

"We"? A few hundred decades of relative
Lucidity glinted-through by minnow schools
Between us and the red genetic muck—
Everyman's underpainting. We look up, shy 100
Creatures, from our trembling pool of sky.
Caught wet-lipped in light's brushwork, fleet but sure,
Flash on shudder, folk of the first fuck,
Likeness breeds likeness, fights for breath—*I live*—

Where the crush thickens. And by season's end, 105
The swells of fashion cresting to collapse
In breaker upon breaker on the beach,
Who wants to be caught dead in this cliché
Of mere "involvement"? Time to put under wraps
Its corporate synthetic global pitch; 110
Not throwing out motley once reveled in,
Just learning to live down the wrinkled friend.

Face it, reproduction of any kind leaves us colder
Though airtight-warmer (greenhouse effect)[4] each year.
Remember the figleaf's lesson. Styles betray 115
Some guilty knowledge. What to dress ours in—
A seer's blind gaze, an infant's tender skin?
All that's been seen through. The eloquence to come
Will be precisely what we cannot say
Until it parts the lips. But as one grows older 120

—I should confess before that last coat dries—
The wry recall of thunder does for rage.
Erotic torrents flash on screens instead
Of drenching us. Exclusively in dream,
These nights, does a grandsire rear his saurian[5] head, 125
And childhood's inexhaustible brain-forest teems
With jewel-bright lives. No way now to restage
Their sacred pageant under our new skies'

Irradiated lucite. What then to wear
When—hush, it's no dream! It's my windbreaker 130
In black, with starry longitudes, Archer, Goat,[6]
Clothing an earphoned archangel of Space,
Who hasn't read Pascal, and doesn't wave . . .
What far-out twitterings he learns by rote,
What looks they'd wake upon a human face, 135
Don't ask, Roberto. Sing our final air:

---

3. Blaise Pascal (1623–1662), French mathematician, writer, and scientist.
4. Phenomenon considered the cause of global warming.
5. Lizardlike.
6. The archer and the goat represent the astrological signs Sagittarius and Capricorn.

Love, grief etc. * * * * for good reason.
Now only * * * * * * * STOP signs.
Meanwhile * * * * * if you or I've ex-
ceeded our [?] * * * ~~more than time~~ was needed   140
To fit a text airless and * * as Tyvek
With breathing spaces and between the lines
Days brilliantly recurring, as once *we* did,
To keep the blue wave dancing in its prison.

1995

An Upward Look

O heart green acre   sown with salt
by the departing   occupier

lay down your gallant   spears of wheat
Salt of the earth   each stellar pinch

flung in blind   defiance backwards   5
now takes its toll   Up from his quieted

quarry the lover   colder and wiser
hauling himself   finds the world turning

toys triumphs   toxins into
this vast facility   the living come   10
dearest to die in   How did it happen

In bright alternation   minutely mirrored
within the thinking   of each and every

mortal creature   halves of a clue
approach the earthlights   Morning star   15

evening star   salt of the sky
First the grave   dissolving into dawn

then the crucial   recrystallizing
from inmost depths   of clear dark blue

1995

ROBERT CREELEY
1926–2005

Robert Creeley's poetry is immediately likable. He has no interest in pompous or oracular utterance, but offers an instantaneous intimacy. He belongs to the Black Mountain school of Charles Olson, but if Olson is Maximus, Creeley is Minimus. His poems are usually short—in total length, in the length of each line, even in title—and always unassuming. He reports brief passages of feeling as minutely as he can, remaining surrounded by a situation rather than entering and leaving it. Citing Olson's concepts of "projective verse" and "composition by field" in an interview, Creeley puts the emphasis on allowing the experience to play upon the poet instead of accepting an imposed shape (*Cottonwood Review,* 1968). As a young man, Creeley says, he "was very intent on [William Carlos] Williams's sense of how you get the thing stated in its own particulars rather than your assumption of those particulars." Like Williams and Olson, Creeley reveres immediate sensation. In reaction to poetry that is "too dry and too intellectually articulate," he wants to create, instead, "a more resonant echo of the subconscious or inner experience."

In his preface to *For Love: Poems 1950–1960,* Creeley disavows lofty occasions for writing. "Wherever it is one stumbles (to get to wherever) at least some way will exist, so to speak, as and when a man takes this or that step—for which, god bless him." His poems are such ways, stumbled into. Avoiding contrivance and closure, they follow a logic that is elliptical and unresolved. What Creeley wants to evoke is often small, and he is prepared to defend smallness: "something small / but infinite / and quiet" ("A Prayer"), or "insistent particularity" ("Listless"). A day-to-day mysticism informs many of Creeley's experiential moments, and in an interview in the *Paris Review,* he speaks of poetry as "a kind of absolute seizure." The effect must be personal; it should be "identity singing." But for all its personal quality, the poem must be made of *relationships*—a word he is fond of—because relationships serve "a common need, for survival and growth." Not surprisingly, love or loss is often Creeley's subject.

Although Creeley rejects traditional meters and rhymes, he develops his own rhythms, often catchy and distinct, as well as quiet internal rhymes, assonances, and idiosyncratic enjambments. "It is all a rhythm, / from the shutting / door, to the window / opening," he insists in "The Rhythm." Possibly his most famous statement on aesthetics is that which Charles Olson continually quoted from him, "Form is never more than an extension of content." Creeley would agree with D. H. Lawrence that every experience has a potential and unique form. Yet as he says in the title poem of *The Finger* (1968): "The forms shift / before we know, / before we thought / to know it." The danger comes from imposition of abstract idea: "The *world,* / dad, is where you / live unless you've for- / gotten it through that / incredible means called / efficacy *or* understanding / *or* superior lines of / *or, or* something else." The form may be obscured, and the poem lost, by making the end of the poem a "*descriptive* act, I mean any act which leaves the attention outside the poem." This defect he finds in poets who subordinate inner form to external content, such as Kenneth Fearing or Karl Shapiro; their poems "argue images of living to which the content of their poems points." They make the poem a means to recognition, rather than "a structure of 'recognition' or—better—cognition itself" (*The New American Poetry,* ed. Donald Allen, 1960). While Creeley's later poetry remains characterized by terseness, reticence, and dramatic pauses, the emotions are often more sharply outlined and conclusive than in his earlier work. Memory plays a stronger role, and aging and death cast a longer shadow.

Creeley's life seemed to flow from his theories of poetry, as he stumbled from one place to another. He was born on May 21, 1926, in Arlington, Massachusetts. Before he was five, he lost his father, a doctor, as well as the use of his left eye. After attending Holderness School, in Plymouth, New Hampshire, Creeley entered Harvard University, but soon left, in 1944, to join the American Field Service in India and Burma. To escape from boredom, he took drugs, and some of his poems describe hallucinatory experiences. He came back to Harvard a year later, but with one term left before receiving a degree dropped out again. He and his wife lived on Cape Cod, then spent three years on a farm in New Hampshire; from there they went to Aix-en-Provence and then to Majorca, where Creeley started the Divers Press. In 1954, Olson invited him to join the faculty of Black Mountain College, and Creeley founded and edited the *Black Mountain Review*. In 1955, his marriage collapsed, and he left the college. He moved west in 1956, just in time to become associated with the flowering of Beat poetry. Domestic life is a preoccupation of his work, and, indeed, Creeley married again in 1957; after a second divorce in 1976, he married for the third time in 1977. From 1956 to 1959, he taught in a boys' school in Albuquerque, and he received an M.A. from the University of New Mexico in 1960. He went to Guatemala and taught, from 1959 to 1961, on a coffee plantation. He had many visiting posts, but from 1966 he was a professor at the State University of New York at Buffalo. He was the New York State poet from 1989 to 1991, and he won the Bollingen Prize in 1999.

Naughty Boy

When he brings home a whale
she laughs and says, that's not for real.

And if he won the Irish sweepstakes,
she would say, where were you last night?

Where are you now, for that matter? Am   5
I always (she says) to be looking

at you? She says,
if I thought it would get any better I

would shoot you, you
nut, you. Then pats her hair   10

into place, and waits
for Uncle Jim's deep-fired, all-fat, real gone

whale steaks.

1959

A Wicker Basket

Comes the time when it's later
and onto your table the headwaiter
puts the bill, and very soon after
rings out the sound of lively laughter—

Picking up change, hands like a walrus,   5
and a face like a barndoor's,
and a head without any apparent size,
nothing but two eyes—

So that's you, man,
or me. I make it as I can,   10
I pick up, I go
faster than they know—

Out the door, the street like a night,
any night, and no one in sight,
but then, well, there she is,   15
old friend Liz—

And she opens the door of her cadillac,
I step in back,
and we're gone.
She turns me on—   20

There are very huge stars, man, in the sky,
and from somewhere very far off someone hands me a slice of apple pie,
with a gob of white, white ice cream on top of it,
and I eat it—

Slowly. And while certainly   25
they are laughing at me, and all around me is racket
of these cats not making it, I make it

in my wicker basket.   1959

The Door

for Robert Duncan[1]

It is hard going to the door
cut so small in the wall where
the vision which echoes loneliness
brings a scent of wild flowers in the wood.

---

1. American poet (1919–1988), who was, like Creeley, a teacher at Black Mountain College during the
mid-1950s.

What I understood, I understand.   5
My mind is sometime torment,
sometimes good and filled with livelihood,
and feels the ground.

But I see the door,
and knew the wall, and wanted the wood,   10
and would get there if I could
with my feet and hands and mind.

Lady, do not banish me
for digressions. My nature
is a quagmire of unresolved   15
confessions. Lady, I follow.

I walked away from myself,
I left the room, I found the garden,
I knew the woman
in it, together we lay down.   20

Dead night remembers. In December
we change, not multiplied but dispersed,
sneaked out of childhood,
the ritual of dismemberment.

Mighty magic is a mother,   25
in her there is another issue
of fixture, repeated form, the race renewal,
the charge of the command.

The garden echoes across the room.
It is fixed in the wall like a mirror   30
that faces a window behind you
and reflects the shadows.

May I go now?
Am I allowed to bow myself down
in the ridiculous posture of renewal,   35
of the insistence of which I am the virtue?

Nothing for You is untoward.
Inside You would also be tall,
more tall, more beautiful.
Come toward me from the wall, I want to be with You.   40

So I screamed to You,
who hears as the wind, and changes
multiply, invariably,
changes in the mind.

Running to the door, I ran down   45
as a clock runs down. Walked backwards,

stumbled, sat down
hard on the floor near the wall.

Where were You.
How absurd, how vicious. 50
There is nothing to do but get up.
My knees were iron, I rusted in worship, of You.

For that one sings, one
writes the spring poem, one goes on walking.
The Lady has always moved to the next town 55
and you stumble on after Her.

The door in the wall leads to the garden
where in the sunlight sit
the Graces[2] in long Victorian dresses,
of which my grandmother had spoken. 60

History sings in their faces.
They are young, they are obtainable,
and you follow after them also
in the service of God and Truth.

But the Lady is indefinable, 65
she will be the door in the wall
to the garden in sunlight.
I will go on talking forever.

I will never get there.
Oh Lady, remember me 70
who in Your service grows older
not wiser, no more than before.

How can I die alone.
Where will I be then who am now alone,
what groans so pathetically 75
in this room where I am alone?

I will go to the garden.
I will be a romantic. I will sell
myself in hell,
in heaven also I will be. 80

In my mind I see the door,
I see the sunlight before me across the floor
beckon to me, as the Lady's skirt
moves small beyond it.

1959

---

2. In classical mythology, the three daughters of Zeus, personifying beauty, charm, and grace.

I Know a Man

As I sd to my
friend, because I am
always talking,—John, I

sd, which was not his
name, the darkness sur-   5
rounds us, what

can we do against
it, or else, shall we &
why not, buy a goddamn big car,

drive, he sd, for   10
christ's sake, look
out where yr going.

                                                    1962

For Love

for Bobbie[3]

Yesterday I wanted to
speak of it, that sense above
the others to me
important because all

that I know derives   5
from what it teaches me.
Today, what is it that
is finally so helpless,

different, despairs of its own
statement, wants to   10
turn away, endlessly
to turn away.

If the moon did not . . .
no, if you did not
I wouldn't either, but   15
what would I not

do, what prevention, what
thing so quickly stopped.

---

3. Bobbie Hoeck, Creeley's second wife.

That is love yesterday
or tomorrow, not   20

now. Can I eat
what you give me. I
have not earned it. Must
I think of everything

as earned. Now love also   25
becomes a reward so
remote from me I have
only made it with my mind.

Here is tedium,
despair, a painful   30
sense of isolation and
whimsical if pompous

self-regard. But that image
is only of the mind's
vague structure, vague to me   35
because it is my own.

Love, what do I think
to say. I cannot say it.
What have you become to ask,
what have I made you into,   40

companion, good company,
crossed legs with skirt, or
soft body under
the bones of the bed.

Nothing says anything   45
but that which it wishes
would come true, fears
what else might happen in

some other place, some
other time not this one.   50
A voice in my place, an
echo of that only in yours.

Let me stumble into
not the confession but
the obsession I begin with   55
now. For you

also (also)
some time beyond place, or
place beyond time, no
mind left to   60

say anything at all,
that face gone, now.
Into the company of love
it all returns.

1962

"I Keep to Myself Such Measures . . ."

I keep to myself such
measures as I care for,
daily the rocks
accumulate position.

There is nothing   5
but what thinking makes
it less tangible.[4] The mind,
fast as it goes, loses

pace, puts in place of it
like rocks simple markers,   10
for a way only to
hopefully come back to

where it cannot. All
forgets. My mind sinks.
I hold in both hands such weight   15
it is my only description.

1969

Again

One more day gone,
done, found in
the form of days.

It began, it
ended—was   5
forward, backward,

slow, fast, a
sun shone, clouds,
high in the air I was

for awhile with others,   10
then came down
on the ground again.

4. Cf. "there is nothing either good or bad but thinking makes it so" (*Hamlet* 2.2.244–45).

No moon. A room in
a hotel—to begin
again.   15

1969

Mother's Voice

In these few years
since her death I hear
mother's voice say
under my own, I won't

want any more of that.   5
My cheekbones resonate
with her emphasis. Nothing
of not wanting only

but the distance there from
common fact of others   10
frightens me. I look out
at all this demanding world

and try to put it quietly back,
from me, say, thank you,
I've already had some   15
though I haven't

and would like to
but I've said no, she has,
it's not my own voice anymore.
It's higher as hers was   20

and accommodates too simply
its frustrations when
I at least think I want more
and must have it.

1983

From Life & Death

[*The Long Road of It All*]

The long road of it all
is an echo,
a sound like an image
expanding, frames growing
one after one in ascending   5

or descending order, all
of us a rising, falling
thought, an explosion
of emptiness soon forgotten.

[*When It Comes*]

When it comes,
it loses edge,
has nothing around it,
no place now present
but impulse not one's own,   5
and so empties into a river
which will flow on
into a white cloud
and be gone.

1998

ALLEN GINSBERG
1926–1997

Allen Ginsberg wrote in a Romantic tradition that honors William Blake and Walt
Whitman as its distinguished pioneers. He resembled the two earlier poets in his con-
fidence as a prophet-poet, in his disregard for distinctions between poetry and religion,
and in his eclecticism. He distrusted abstractions and the antiseptically cerebral, and
he wanted to compose poetry that invites a complete emotional and physical partici-
pation by the audience. For some, the publication of Ginsberg's *"Howl" and Other
Poems* (1956) was the beginning of a mindless and mercifully short-lived poetic fad, a
cult of slovenly verse that encouraged dangerously slovenly behavior. For others, it was
a fortunate and revolutionary change in the direction of American poetry. Like all poetic
innovators, Ginsberg seemed to claim for poetry new areas of experience and new cul-
tural situations. "Howl" is a panoramic vision of the dark side of the complacent Eisen-
hower years; it discovered for literature an anticommunity of waifs and strays, dope
addicts and homosexual drifters. Ginsberg's poetry presented an alternative to the
tightly organized, well-mannered poetry written under the influence of the New Criti-
cism; it was emotionally explosive, unashamedly self-preoccupied, and metrically expan-
sive, and it helped create in the 1960s an audience for influential books of psychic
rebellion and revelation, such as Robert Lowell's *Life Studies*, Norman Mailer's *Adver-
tisements for Myself*, and Norman O. Brown's *Life against Death*.

Ginsberg was born on June 3, 1926, in Newark, New Jersey. His father, Louis
Ginsberg, a high school teacher, wrote conventional verse. His mother, Naomi, a
Russian Jewish immigrant and a communist, encouraged her son in his radical bias.
She spent the latter part of her life in Pilgrim State Hospital, and Ginsberg, who saw
her spontaneity and emotional intensity as important qualities in his own character,
was haunted for much of his life by guilt because he had authorized her institution-

alization and lobotomy—recommended by her doctor to cure her paranoid delusions. Her death, in 1956, is the occasion for Ginsberg's long poem "Kaddish"—a fusion of the elegy, the blues, and the ritual Kaddish, or Jewish prayer of mourning and remembrance for the dead—in which graphic descriptions of his mother's madness, her scarred body, and his ambivalent attraction and repulsion break taboos on the representation of the dead.

Ginsberg was educated in the public schools of Paterson, New Jersey. One of his earliest friends in the arts was Paterson's most famous man of letters, William Carlos Williams, who later wrote the introduction to *"Howl" and Other Poems*. Williams instructed Ginsberg according to his dictum, "No ideas but in things." "Before I met Williams," Ginsberg told one of his biographers, "I was all hung up on cats like Wyatt, Surrey, and Donne. I would read them and then copy down what I thought poetry like theirs would be. Then I sent some of those poems to Williams, and he thought that they were terrible. Like they showed some promise, but they were phony, unnatural. He told me, 'Listen to the rhythm of your own voice. Proceed intuitively by ear' " (*The New Yorker*, August 24, 1968).

From Paterson, Ginsberg went to Columbia University. In 1945, he was temporarily suspended, and William Burroughs, whose interest in sex and drugs is recorded in experimental novels such as *Naked Lunch* and *Wild Boys*, took over Ginsberg's literary education. Ginsberg received a B.A. from Columbia in 1948, and in the summer of that year he underwent an extraordinary experience that always figures in accounts of his spiritual development. Feeling cut off from his friends and uncertain as to his vocation, he heard a voice, which he took to be that of the poet himself, reciting William Blake's "Ah Sun-Flower" and "The Sick Rose." The auditory hallucination was accompanied by a feeling of participation in a universal harmony. In one account of the experience, to the *Paris Review*, Ginsberg recalls that "looking out at the window, through the window at the sky, suddenly it seemed that I saw into the depths of the universe, by looking simply into the ancient sky. The sky suddenly seemed very *ancient*. And this was the very ancient place that he [Blake] was talking about, the sweet golden clime. I suddenly realized that *this* existence was *it!*" Although Ginsberg eventually freed himself from a dependence on this remembered moment, he continued to believe it was a personal revelation of a quality common to all high poetry.

In 1954, bearing a letter of introduction to Kenneth Rexroth from Williams, Ginsberg went to San Francisco. He already knew Burroughs, Jack Kerouac, and Gregory Corso, all writers who would be identified with the Beat movement. At different times in his life, Ginsberg had sexual relationships with both Burroughs and Kerouac. Another friend and sometime lover was Neal Cassady, a railway brakeman with literary interests, who inspired the figure of Dean Moriarty in Kerouac's novel *On the Road*. Having settled around the corner from Lawrence Ferlinghetti's City Lights Bookstore, which would become the publisher of *"Howl" and Other Poems* and other Beat writing, Ginsberg worked for a time as a market researcher and attempted to follow a heterosexual life-style, but he was dissatisfied and restless. In talks with a psychiatrist, he found the courage to give up his job and to accept his sexuality. He met Peter Orlovsky, who became his longtime companion, and he finished the first part of "Howl."

Among the liberating influences on his poetry, Ginsberg mentioned with particular gratitude the prose of Jack Kerouac. From him, Ginsberg learned the sanctity of the uncorrected first draft ("First thought, best thought" became Ginsberg's motto, though he actually revised and reshaped the initial material for "Howl" and "Kaddish") and to make his writing an extension of his personal relationships. Assuming that "Howl" would never be published, Ginsberg wrote it for himself and his friends; he insisted that live poetry must not make a distinction between "what you tell your friends and what you tell your Muse" (*Paris Review*). Whether he wrote in long, rhapsodic lines or short and easily chantable ones, his ideal was a living speech and an organic metric that expresses the poet's physiological state at the time of composition. Thus the recurrences in "Howl"—the incantatory repetitions of "who," the surrealistically conflated images, the long lines to be read aloud without a pause—express the poet's physical state and induce a similar state in the reader or hearer.

The first edition of *"Howl" and Other Poems* was printed in England and published in October 1956. In March 1957, U.S. Customs intercepted a second printing. A long trial ensued, and after hearing expert testimony from writers and critics, Judge Clayton Horn decided that "Howl" had "redeeming social importance." The publicity made "Howl" an extraordinary popular success—in 1967, there were 146,000 copies in print—and drew public attention to Ginsberg and his friends. A particularly sensational aspect of their lives was their drug use. Although Ginsberg's drug use was more circumspect and less frequent than his detractors claimed, he admitted to what he called "pious investigations" of hallucinogens. Part II of "Howl" recalls a peyote vision—under the influence of the drug, Ginsberg saw the facade of the Sir Francis Drake Hotel, in San Francisco, as the grinning face of Moloch—and he drafted "Kaddish" a day after he took morphine and methamphetamine.

Ginsberg, who once described himself as a Buddhist Jew with attachments to Krishna, Siva, Allah, Coyote, and the Sacred Heart, was a spiritual adventurer. He spent the early 1960s traveling, for the most part in the East, speaking with the wise of all persuasions and endeavoring to find means other than drugs to explore consciousness. One of the people he consulted was the Jewish philosopher Martin Buber, who advised him to turn to relationships between human beings rather than relationships between the human and the nonhuman. From Indian holy men, Ginsberg learned the same lesson, the importance of "living in and inhabiting the human form." As indicated by his poem "The Change," Ginsberg's emphasis shifted from drug use to disciplined meditation and chanting in the effort to expand the mind and unite it with the body: "This is my spirit and / physical shape I inhabit."

In 1965, Ginsberg returned from the East. He was crowned the king of May in Prague and then thrown out of Czechoslovakia as a subversive. Back in the United States, he successfully applied for a Guggenheim Fellowship and, with Orlovsky, began a tour of American colleges and universities. He chanted his poems to students, talked with them endlessly and patiently, and gave sound practical advice; eventually, the institutions he visited gratefully supplied him with classrooms and office space. Ginsberg was not bothered by charges that he had been taken over by the Establishment. At poetry readings, peace demonstrations, love-ins and be-ins, before Senate committees and in courtrooms, he expressed his strongly held radical convictions in a good-humored and disarming way. In the later 1960s, Ginsberg became a vivid presence in American life: his face was familiar to those who had never read a line of poetry, and increasingly his poems were lost in a large, genial public impression. That Ginsberg advertised his poems as fragments of a great confession should not obscure the individual exuberance and daring of much of his work.

In his later years, Ginsberg maintained his role as the most earthy and lovable of prophets, denouncing war and commercialization and preaching the transforming powers of the self. His work comprises a history of youth movements, political upheavals, oppressions and aspirations, and technological changes. Always, Ginsberg was searching for a paradisal self in a paradisal world, and the search gave purpose to his pilgrimage to all points of the geographical and spiritual compass.

Howl[1]

For Carl Solomon

I

I saw the best minds of my generation destroyed by madness, starving
hysterical naked,
dragging themselves through the negro streets at dawn looking for an
angry fix,
angelheaded hipsters burning for the ancient heavenly connection to the
starry dynamo in the machinery of night,
who poverty and tatters and hollow-eyed and high sat up smoking in the
supernatural darkness of cold-water flats floating across the tops of
cities contemplating jazz,
who bared their brains to Heaven under the El[2] and saw Mohammedan   5
angels staggering on tenement roofs illuminated,
who passed through universities with radiant cool eyes hallucinating
Arkansas and Blake-light tragedy[3] among the scholars of war,
who were expelled from the academies for crazy & publishing obscene
odes on the windows of the skull,
who cowered in unshaven rooms in underwear, burning their money in
wastebaskets and listening to the Terror through the wall,
who got busted in their pubic beards returning through Laredo[4] with a
belt of marijuana for New York,
who ate fire in paint hotels or drank turpentine in Paradise Alley,[5] death,   10
or purgatoried their torsos night after night
with dreams, with drugs, with waking nightmares, alcohol and cock and
endless balls,
incomparable blind streets of shuddering cloud and lightning in the mind
leaping toward poles of Canada & Paterson,[6] illuminating all the
motionless world of Time between,

1. This poem is a chronicle, and also one of the most famous artifacts, of the Beat counterculture of the 1950s. It alludes to the experiences of the Beats, especially Carl Solomon, to whom it is dedicated, and Ginsberg himself; they met as patients at the Columbia Psychiatric Institute in 1949; Solomon, whom Ginsberg calls an "intuitive Bronx dadaist and prose-poet," was an inmate of various mental hospitals, undergoing insulin and electroshock therapy, during the 1950s. Others mentioned but not named are William S. Burroughs (1914–1997), whose first book, *Junkie* (1953), was published through Solomon's efforts; Herbert E. Huncke (1915–1996), a down-and-out intellectual, Times Square con artist, petty thief, and hipster who, like his friend Burroughs, was a drug addict, and who appears in *Junkie*; and Neal Cassady (1926–1968), a hipster from Denver, whose travels around the country with Jack Kerouac (1927–1969) were recorded by the latter in *On the Road* (1957), in which the two appear as Dean Moriarty and Sal Paradise. Line 66 and much else in "Howl" evidently derive from Solomon's "apocryphal history of my adventures," which he told to Ginsberg in 1949 and later, but in *More Mishaps*

(1968), he describes this account as "compounded partly of truth, but for the most raving self-justification, crypto-bohemian boasting . . . effeminate prancing and esoteric aphorisms." Line 7 refers to Ginsberg's two suspensions from Columbia University, in 1945 for scraping obscene pictures and phrases on the grimy windows of his dormitory room to provoke the cleaning woman into cleaning it, and in 1948 when, in danger of conviction as an accessory to Huncke's burglaries, he volunteered for psychiatric treatment; line 45 describes Huncke's arrival, fresh from jail, at Ginsberg's Lower East Side apartment in 1948. A number of the incidents recalled in the poem happened to more than one of the Beats.
2. Elevated railway in New York City and Hebrew for God.
3. In 1948, Ginsberg hallucinated the English poet William Blake (1757–1827) reciting Blake's poems "Ah Sun-Flower" and "The Sick Rose."
4. A city in Texas, on the Mexican border.
5. In New York's Lower East Side; the setting of Kerouac's novel *The Subterraneans* (1958).
6. In New Jersey, where Ginsberg grew up.

Peyote solidities of halls, backyard green tree cemetery dawns, wine
    drunkenness over the rooftops, storefront boroughs of teahead joy-
    ride neon blinking traffic light, sun and moon and tree vibrations in
    the roaring winter dusks of Brooklyn, ashcan rantings and kind king
    light of mind,
who chained themselves to subways for the endless ride from Battery to
    holy Bronx[7] on benzedrine until the noise of wheels and children
    brought them down shuddering mouth-wracked and battered bleak
    of brain all drained of brilliance in the drear light of Zoo,[8]
who sank all night in submarine light of Bickford's[9] floated out and sat 15
    through the stale beer afternoon in desolate Fugazzi's,[1] listening to
    the crack of doom on the hydrogen jukebox,
who talked continuously seventy hours from park to pad to bar to Belle-
    vue[2] to museum to the Brooklyn Bridge,
a lost battalion of platonic conversationalists jumping down the stoops off
    fire escapes off windowsills off Empire State out of the moon,
yacketayakking screaming vomiting whispering facts and memories and
    anecdotes and eyeball kicks and shocks of hospitals and jails and
    wars,
whole intellects disgorged in total recall for seven days and nights with
    brilliant eyes, meat for the Synagogue cast on the pavement,
who vanished into nowhere Zen New Jersey leaving a trail of ambiguous 20
    picture postcards of Atlantic City Hall,
suffering Eastern sweats and Tangerian bone-grindings and migraines of
    China under junk-withdrawal in Newark's bleak furnished room,
who wandered around and around at midnight in the railroad yard won-
    dering where to go, and went, leaving no broken hearts,
who lit cigarettes in boxcars boxcars boxcars racketing through snow
    toward lonesome farms in grandfather night,
who studied Plotinus Poe St. John of the Cross[3] telepathy and bop kab-
    balah[4] because the cosmos instinctively vibrated at their feet in Kan-
    sas,
who loned it through the streets of Idaho seeking visionary indian angels 25
    who were visionary indian angels,
who thought they were only mad when Baltimore gleamed in supernatural
    ecstasy,
who jumped in limousines with the Chinaman of Oklahoma on the
    impulse of winter midnight streetlight smalltown rain,
who lounged hungry and lonesome through Houston seeking jazz or sex
    or soup, and followed the brilliant Spaniard to converse about Amer-
    ica and Eternity, a hopeless task, and so took ship to Africa,
who disappeared into the volcanoes of Mexico leaving behind nothing but

7. The southern and northern ends of a New York
City subway line.
8. The Bronx Zoo.
9. One of a chain of all-night cafeterias, where
Ginsberg mopped floors and washed dishes during
his college years.
1. A bar north of New York City's then-bohemian
Greenwich Village.
2. Public hospital in New York City with a psy-
chiatric clinic.
3. Ginsberg had studied these writers while in col-

lege and perhaps treasured them for their visionary
and mystical insights. After hearing the voice of
Blake, he immediately reread passages from St.
John of the Cross and Plotinus to help him inter-
pret the experience.
4. "Bop" is a style of modern jazz especially influ-
ential during the 1940s and 1950s; the Kaballa is
a Hebraic system of mystical interpretation of the
scriptures, which asserts the supremacy of the
spirit over bodily desires.

the shadow of dungarees and the lava and ash of poetry scattered in
fireplace Chicago,

who reappeared on the West Coast investigating the FBI in beards and 30
shorts with big pacifist eyes sexy in their dark skin passing out incom-
prehensible leaflets,

who burned cigarette holes in their arms protesting the narcotic tobacco
haze of Capitalism,

who distributed Supercommunist pamphlets in Union Square[5] weeping
and undressing while the sirens of Los Alamos[6] wailed them down,
and wailed down Wall,[7] and the Staten Island ferry also wailed,

who broke down crying in white gymnasiums naked and trembling before
the machinery of other skeletons,

who bit detectives in the neck and shrieked with delight in policecars for
committing no crime but their own wild cooking pederasty and intox-
ication,

who howled on their knees in the subway and were dragged off the roof 35
waving genitals and manuscripts,

who let themselves be fucked in the ass by saintly motorcyclists, and
screamed with joy,

who blew and were blown by those human seraphim, the sailors, caresses
of Atlantic and Caribbean love,

who balled in the morning in the evenings in rosegardens and the grass
of public parks and cemeteries scattering their semen freely to whom-
ever come who may,

who hiccupped endlessly trying to giggle but wound up with a sob behind
a partition in a Turkish Bath when the blond & naked angel came to
pierce them with a sword,

who lost their loveboys to the three old shrews of fate the one eyed shrew 40
of the heterosexual dollar the one eyed shrew that winks out of the
womb and the one eyed shrew that does nothing but sit on her ass
and snip the intellectual golden threads of the craftsman's loom,

who copulated ecstatic and insatiate with a bottle of beer a sweetheart a
package of cigarettes a candle and fell off the bed, and continued
along the floor and down the hall and ended fainting on the wall with
a vision of ultimate cunt and come eluding the last gyzym of con-
sciousness,

who sweetened the snatches of a million girls trembling in the sunset,
and were red eyed in the morning but prepared to sweeten the snatch
of the sunrise, flashing buttocks under barns and naked in the lake,

who went out whoring through Colorado in myriad stolen night-cars,
N.C.,[8] secret hero of these poems, cocksman and Adonis of Denver—
joy to the memory of his innumerable lays of girls in empty lots &
diner backyards, moviehouses' rickety rows, on mountaintops in
caves or with gaunt waitresses in familiar roadside lonely petticoat
upliftings & especially secret gas-station solipsisms of johns, & home-
town alleys too,

5. In New York City; it was a center for radical
speeches and demonstrations during the 1930s.
6. In New Mexico; the site of the laboratory at
which the development of the atomic bomb was
completed.

7. Wall Street, in New York, but perhaps also the
Wailing Wall, in Jerusalem, where Jews lament
their losses and seek consolation.
8. Neal Cassady.

who faded out in vast sordid movies, were shifted in dreams, woke on a
    sudden Manhattan, and picked themselves up out of basements
    hung-over with heartless Tokay and horrors of Third Avenue iron
    dreams & stumbled to unemployment offices,
who walked all night with their shoes full of blood on the snowbank docks 45
    waiting for a door in the East River to open to a room full of steam-
    heat and opium,
who created great suicidal dramas on the apartment cliff-banks of the
    Hudson under the wartime blue floodlight of the moon & their heads
    shall be crowned with laurel in oblivion,
who ate the lamb stew of the imagination or digested the crab at the
    muddy bottom of the rivers of Bowery,[9]
who wept at the romance of the streets with their pushcarts full of onions
    and bad music,
who sat in boxes breathing in the darkness under the bridge, and rose up
    to build harpsichords in their lofts,
who coughed on the sixth floor of Harlem crowned with flame under the 50
    tubercular sky surrounded by orange crates of theology,
who scribbled all night rocking and rolling over lofty incantations which
    in the yellow morning were stanzas of gibberish,
who cooked rotten animals lung heart feet tail borsht & tortillas dreaming
    of the pure vegetable kingdom,
who plunged themselves under meat trucks looking for an egg,
who threw their watches off the roof to cast their ballot for Eternity out-
    side of Time, & alarm clocks fell on their heads every day for the next
    decade,
who cut their wrists three times successively unsuccessfully, gave up and 55
    were forced to open antique stores where they thought they were
    growing old and cried,
who were burned alive in their innocent flannel suits on Madison Avenue[1]
    amid blasts of leaden verse & the tanked-up clatter of the iron regi-
    ments of fashion & the nitroglycerine shrieks of the fairies of adver-
    tising & the mustard gas of sinister intelligent editors, or were run
    down by the drunken taxicabs of Absolute Reality,
who jumped off the Brooklyn Bridge this actually happened and walked
    away unknown and forgotten into the ghostly daze of Chinatown soup
    alleyways & firetrucks, not even one free beer,
who sang out of their windows in despair, fell out of the subway window,
    jumped in the filthy Passaic,[2] leaped on negroes, cried all over the
    street, danced on broken wineglasses barefoot smashed phonograph
    records of nostalgic European 1930s German jazz finished the whis-
    key and threw up groaning into the bloody toilet, moans in their ears
    and the blast of colossal steam-whistles,
who barreled down the highways of the past journeying to each other's
    hotrod-Golgotha[3] jail-solitude watch or Birmingham jazz incarnation,
who drove crosscountry seventytwo hours to find out if I had a vision or 60
    you had a vision or he had a vision to find out Eternity.

9. The lower part of Third Avenue in New York,
famous as the haunt of alcoholics and derelicts.
1. The center of the advertising industry in New
York. Burroughs had worked for a year as a copy
writer during the 1930s.

2. The river that flows past Paterson, New Jersey.
3. In the Bible, Golgotha, or "the place of skulls,"
is the hill near Jerusalem where Jesus was cruci-
fied.

who journeyed to Denver, who died in Denver, who came back to Denver
& waited in vain, who watched over Denver & brooded & loned in
Denver and finally went away to find out the Time, & now Denver is
lonesome for her heroes,

who fell on their knees in hopeless cathedrals praying for each other's
salvation and light and breasts, until the soul illuminated its hair for
a second,

who crashed through their minds in jail waiting for impossible criminals
with golden heads and the charm of reality in their hearts who sang
sweet blues to Alcatraz,

who retired to Mexico to cultivate a habit,[4] or Rocky Mount to tender
Buddha[5] or Tangiers[6] to boys or Southern Pacific to the black loco-
motive[7] or Harvard to Narcissus to Woodlawn[8] to the daisychain or
grave,

who demanded sanity trials accusing the radio of hypnotism & were left   65
with their insanity & their hands & a hung jury,

who threw potato salad at CCNY lecturers on Dadaism[9] and subsequently
presented themselves on the granite steps of the madhouse with
shaven heads and harlequin speech of suicide, demanding instanta-
neous lobotomy,

and who were given instead the concrete void of insulin Metrazol elec-
tricity hydrotherapy psychotherapy occupational therapy pingpong &
amnesia,

who in humorless protest overturned only one symbolic pingpong table,
resting briefly in catatonia,

returning years later truly bald except for a wig of blood, and tears and
fingers, to the visible madman doom of the wards of the madtowns
of the East,

Pilgrim State's Rockland's and Greystone's[1] foetid halls, bickering with   70
the echoes of the soul, rocking and rolling in the midnight solitude-
bench dolmen-realms of love, dream of life a nightmare, bodies
turned to stone as heavy as the moon,

with mother finally ******,[2] and the last fantastic book flung out of the
tenement window, and the last door closed at 4 A.M. and the last
telephone slammed at the wall in reply and the last furnished room
emptied down to the last piece of mental furniture, a yellow paper
rose twisted on a wire hanger in the closet, and even that imaginary,
nothing but a hopeful little bit of hallucination—

ah, Carl, while you are not safe I am not safe, and now you're really in
the total animal soup of time—

and who therefore ran through the icy streets obsessed with a sudden
flash of the alchemy of the use of the ellipse the catalog the meter
& the vibrating plane,

who dreamt and made incarnate gaps in Time & Space through images

4. Burroughs.
5. Kerouac, who was then living in Rocky Mount, North Carolina.
6. Both Burroughs and Ginsberg lived in Tangiers for a time.
7. Neal Cassady, who worked as a brakeman for the Southern Pacific Railroad.
8. A cemetery in the Bronx.
9. An artistic movement (c. 1916–20) based on absurdity and accident. CCNY: City College of New York.

1. Three mental hospitals near New York. Carl Solomon was an inmate at Pilgrim State and Rockland Hospitals; Ginsberg's mother was a patient at Greystone Hospital from the late 1940s.
2. Ginsberg's draft reads "mother finally fucked"; his note says: "Author replaced letters with asterisks in final draft of poem to introduce appropriate level of uncertainty."

juxtaposed, and trapped the archangel of the soul between 2 visual images and joined the elemental verbs and set the noun and dash of consciousness together jumping with sensation of Pater Omnipotens Aeterna Deus[3]

to recreate the syntax and measure of poor human prose and stand before 75 you speechless and intelligent and shaking with shame, rejected yet confessing out the soul to conform to the rhythm of thought in his naked and endless head,

the madman bum and angel beat in Time, unknown, yet putting down here what might be left to say in time come after death,

and rose reincarnate in the ghostly clothes of jazz in the goldhorn shadow of the band and blew the suffering of America's naked mind for love into an eli eli lamma lamma sabacthani[4] saxophone cry that shivered the cities down to the last radio

with the absolute heart of the poem of life butchered out of their own bodies good to eat a thousand years.

II

What sphinx[5] of cement and aluminum bashed open their skulls and ate up their brains and imagination?

Moloch![6] Solitude! Filth! Ugliness! Ashcans and unobtainable dollars! 80 Children screaming under the stairways! Boys sobbing in armies! Old men weeping in the parks!

Moloch! Moloch! Nightmare of Moloch! Moloch the loveless! Mental Moloch! Moloch the heavy judger of men!

Moloch the incomprehensible prison! Moloch the crossbone soulless jailhouse and Congress of sorrows! Moloch whose buildings are judgment! Moloch the vast stone of war! Moloch the stunned governments!

Moloch whose mind is pure machinery! Moloch whose blood is running money! Moloch whose fingers are ten armies! Moloch whose breast is a cannibal dynamo! Moloch whose ear is a smoking tomb!

Moloch whose eyes are a thousand blind windows! Moloch whose skyscrapers stand in the long streets like endless Jehovahs![7] Moloch whose factories dream and croak in the fog! Moloch whose smokestacks and antennae crown the cities!

Moloch whose love is endless oil and stone! Moloch whose soul is elec- 85 tricity and banks! Moloch whose poverty is the specter of genius!

3. All-powerful Father, eternal God (Latin). The phrase was used by Paul Cézanne (1839–1906), French Impressionist painter, in a letter of 1904 to Emile Bernard, to describe the sensations he received from observing and registering the appearance of the natural world. "The last part of 'Howl' was really an homage to art but also in specific terms an homage to Cézanne's method. . . . Just as Cézanne doesn't use perspective lines to create space, but it's a juxtaposition of one color against another color (that's one element of his space), so, I had the idea, perhaps over-refined, that by the unexplainable, unexplained nonperspective line, that is, juxtaposition of one *word* against another, . . . there'd be a *gap* between the two words which the mind would fill in with the sensation of existence. . . . So, I was trying to do similar things with juxtapositions like 'hydrogen jukebox' or 'winter midnight smalltown streetlight rain.' . . . like: jazz, jukebox and all that, and we have the jukebox from that; politics, hydrogen bomb, and we have the hydrogen of that, you see 'hydrogen jukebox.' [line 15] And that actually compresses in one instant like a whole series of things" (*Writers at Work*, Third Series, 1967).
4. Jesus' words from the Cross (Matthew 26.46, Mark 15.33): "My God, my God, why have you forsaken me?"
5. Mythological creature that kills those incapable of answering its riddle.
6. In the Bible, Semitic god to whom children were sacrificed.
7. Modern reconstruction of YHWH, the Hebrew name of God.

Moloch whose fate is a cloud of sexless hydrogen! Moloch whose
name is the Mind!

Moloch in whom I sit lonely! Moloch in whom I dream Angels! Crazy in
Moloch! Cocksucker in Moloch! Lacklove and manless in Moloch!

Moloch who entered my soul early! Moloch in whom I am a consciousness
without a body! Moloch who frightened me out of my natural ecstasy!
Moloch whom I abandon! Wake up in Moloch! Light streaming out
of the sky!

Moloch! Moloch! Robot apartments! invisible suburbs! skeleton treasur-
ies! blind capitals! demonic industries! spectral nations! invincible
madhouses! granite cocks! monstrous bombs!

They broke their backs lifting Moloch to Heaven! Pavements, trees,
radios, tons! lifting the city to Heaven which exists and is everywhere
about us!

Visions! omens! hallucinations! miracles! ecstasies! gone down the Amer- 90
ican river!

Dreams! adorations! illuminations! religions! the whole boatload of sen-
sitive bullshit!

Breakthroughs! over the river! flips and crucifixions! gone down the flood!
Highs! Epiphanies! Despairs! Ten years' animal screams and suicides!
Minds! New loves! Mad generation! down on the rocks of Time!

Real holy laughter in the river! They saw it all! the wild eyes! the holy
yells! They bade farewell! They jumped off the roof! to solitude! wav-
ing! carrying flowers! Down to the river! into the street!

III

Carl Solomon! I'm with you in Rockland[8]
    where you're madder than I am
I'm with you in Rockland   95
    where you must feel very strange
I'm with you in Rockland
    where you imitate the shade of my mother
I'm with you in Rockland   100
    where you've murdered your twelve secretaries
I'm with you in Rockland
    where you laugh at this invisible humor
I'm with you in Rockland
    where we are great writers on the same dreadful typewriter 105
I'm with you in Rockland
    where your condition has become serious and is reported on the radio
I'm with you in Rockland
    where the faculties of the skull no longer admit the worms of the
    senses
I'm with you in Rockland   110
    where you drink the tea of the breasts of the spinsters of Utica[9]
I'm with you in Rockland
    where you pun on the bodies of your nurses the harpies of the Bronx
I'm with you in Rockland
    where you scream in a straightjacket that you're losing the game 115

---

8. Mental hospital near New York City.   9. Town in central New York.

of the actual pingpong of the abyss
I'm with you in Rockland
>where you bang on the catatonic piano the soul is innocent and
immortal it should never die ungodly in an armed madhouse
I'm with you in Rockland
>where fifty more shocks will never return your soul to its body again
from its pilgrimage to a cross in the void
I'm with you in Rockland   120
>where you accuse your doctors of insanity and plot the Hebrew social-
ist revolution against the fascist national Golgotha[1]
I'm with you in Rockland
>where you will split the heavens of Long Island and resurrect your
living human Jesus from the superhuman tomb
I'm with you in Rockland
>where there are twentyfive thousand mad comrades all together   125
singing the final stanzas of the Internationale[2]
I'm with you in Rockland
>where we hug and kiss the United States under our bedsheets the
United States that coughs all night and won't let us sleep
I'm with you in Rockland
>where we wake up electrified out of the coma by our own souls'
airplanes roaring over the roof they've come to drop angelic bombs
the hospital illuminates itself   imaginary walls collapse   O skinny
legions run outside   O starry-spangled shock of mercy the eternal
war is here   O victory forget your underwear we're free
I'm with you in Rockland   130
>in my dreams you walk dripping from a sea-journey on the highway
across America in tears to the door of my cottage in the Western
night

San Francisco, 1955–1956   1956

A Supermarket in California

What thoughts I have of you tonight, Walt Whitman,[3] for I walked
down the sidestreets under the trees with a headache self-conscious look-
ing at the full moon.

In my hungry fatigue, and shopping for images, I went into the neon
fruit supermarket, dreaming of your enumerations!

What peaches and what penumbras![4] Whole families shopping at
night! Aisles full of husbands! Wives in the avocados, babies in the toma-
toes!—and you, García Lorca,[5] what were you doing down by the water-
melons?

---

1. Site of Jesus' crucifixion.
2. Anthem of the socialist movement and, until
1944, the national anthem of the Soviet Union.
3. American poet (1819–1892).

4. Partial shadows.
5. Federico García Lorca (1898–1936), Spanish
poet and dramatist; like Ginsberg and Whitman, a
homosexual.

I saw you, Walt Whitman, childless, lonely old grubber, poking among the meats in the refrigerator and eyeing the grocery boys.

I heard you asking questions of each: Who killed the pork chops? 5
What price bananas? Are you my Angel?

I wandered in and out of the brilliant stacks of cans following you, and followed in my imagination by the store detective.

We strode down the open corridors together in our solitary fancy tasting artichokes, possessing every frozen delicacy, and never passing the cashier.

Where are we going, Walt Whitman? The doors close in an hour. Which way does your beard point tonight?

(I touch your book and dream of our odyssey in the supermarket and feel absurd.)

Will we walk all night through solitary streets? The trees add shade 10
to shade, lights out in the houses, we'll both be lonely.

Will we stroll dreaming of the lost America of love past blue automobiles in driveways, home to our silent cottage?

Ah, dear father, graybeard, lonely old courage-teacher, what America did you have when Charon quit poling his ferry and you got out on a smoking bank and stood watching the boat disappear on the black waters of Lethe?[6]

1956

Sunflower Sutra[7]

I walked on the banks of the tincan banana dock and sat down under the huge shade of a Southern Pacific locomotive to look at the sunset over the box house hills and cry.

Jack Kerouac[8] sat beside me on a busted rusty iron pole, companion, we thought the same thoughts of the soul, bleak and blue and sad-eyed, surrounded by the gnarled steel roots of trees of machinery.

The oily water on the river mirrored the red sky, sun sank on top of final Frisco[9] peaks, no fish in that stream, no hermit in those mounts, just ourselves rheumy-eyed and hung-over like old bums on the riverbank, tired and wily.

Look at the Sunflower, he said, there was a dead gray shadow against the sky, big as a man, sitting dry on top of a pile of ancient sawdust—

—I rushed up enchanted—it was my first sunflower, memories of 5
Blake[1]—my visions—Harlem

and Hells of the Eastern rivers, bridges clanking Joes Greasy Sandwiches, dead baby carriages, black treadless tires forgotten and unretreaded, the poem of the riverbank, condoms & pots, steel knives, nothing

6. One of the rivers of Hades (it means "forget-fulness"), across which Charon ferried the dead.
7. Buddhist or Hindu teachings; from the Sanskrit word for thread.
8. American writer (1922–1969) and icon of the Beat generation.

9. San Francisco.
1. In Harlem in 1948, Ginsberg hallucinated the English poet William Blake (1757–1827) reciting Blake's poems "Ah Sun-Flower" and "The Sick Rose."

stainless, only the dank muck and the razor-sharp artifacts passing into the past—

and the gray Sunflower poised against the sunset, crackly bleak and dusty with the smut and smog and smoke of olden locomotives in its eye—

corolla[2] of bleary spikes pushed down and broken like a battered crown, seeds fallen out of its face, soon-to-be-toothless mouth of sunny air, sunrays obliterated on its hairy head like a dried wire spiderweb,

leaves stuck out like arms out of the stem, gestures from the sawdust root, broke pieces of plaster fallen out of the black twigs, a dead fly in its ear,

Unholy battered old thing you were, my sunflower O my soul, I loved you then! 10

The grime was no man's grime but death and human locomotives,

all that dress of dust, that veil of darkened railroad skin, that smog of cheek, that eyelid of black mis'ry, that sooty hand or phallus or protuberance of artificial worse-than-dirt—industrial—modern—all that civilization spotting your crazy golden crown—

and those blear thoughts of death and dusty loveless eyes and ends and withered roots below, in the home-pile of sand and sawdust, rubber dollar bills, skin of machinery, the guts and innards of the weeping coughing car, the empty lonely tincans with their rusty tongues alack, what more could I name, the smoked ashes of some cock cigar, the cunts of wheelbarrows and the milky breasts of cars, wornout asses out of chairs & sphincters of dynamos—all these

entangled in your mummied roots—and you there standing before me in the sunset, all your glory in your form!

A perfect beauty of a sunflower! a perfect excellent lovely sunflower existence! a sweet natural eye to the new hip moon, woke up alive and excited grasping in the sunset shadow sunrise golden monthly breeze! 15

How many flies buzzed round you innocent of your grime, while you cursed the heavens of the railroad and your flower soul?

Poor dead flower? when did you forget you were a flower? when did you look at your skin and decide you were an impotent dirty old locomotive? the ghost of a locomotive? the specter and shade of a once powerful mad American locomotive?

You were never no locomotive, Sunflower, you were a sunflower!

And you Locomotive, you are a locomotive, forget me not!

So I grabbed up the skeleton thick sunflower and stuck it at my side like a scepter, 20

and deliver my sermon to my soul, and Jack's soul too, and anyone who'll listen,

—We're not our skin of grime, we're not dread bleak dusty imageless locomotives, we're golden sunflowers inside, blessed by our own seed & hairy naked accomplishment-bodies growing into mad black formal sunflowers in the sunset, spied on by our own eyes under the shadow of the mad locomotive riverbank sunset Frisco hilly tincan evening sitdown vision.

Berkeley, 1955   1956

2. Inner envelope of a flower.

America[3]

America I've given you all and now I'm nothing.
American two dollars and twentyseven cents January 17, 1956.
I can't stand my own mind.
America when will we end the human war?
Go fuck yourself with your atom bomb.   5
I don't feel good don't bother me.
I won't write my poem till I'm in my right mind.
America when will you be angelic?
When will you take off your clothes?
When will you look at yourself through the grave?   10
When will you be worthy of your million Trotskyites?
America why are your libraries full of tears?
America when will you send your eggs to India?
I'm sick of your insane demands.
When can I go into the supermarket and buy what I need with my good   15
      looks?
America after all it is you and I who are perfect not the next world.
Your machinery is too much for me.
You made me want to be a saint.
There must be some other way to settle this argument.
Burroughs[4] is in Tangiers I don't think he'll come back it's sinister.   20
Are you being sinister or is this some form of practical joke?
I'm trying to come to the point.
I refuse to give up my obsession.
America stop pushing I know what I'm doing.
America the plum blossoms are falling.   25
I haven't read the newspapers for months, everyday somebody goes on
      trial for murder.
America I feel sentimental about the Wobblies.
America I used to be a communist when I was a kid I'm not sorry.
I smoke marijuana every chance I get.
I sit in my house for days on end and stare at the roses in the closet.   30
When I go to Chinatown I get drunk and never get laid.
My mind is made up there's going to be trouble.
You should have seen me reading Marx.

3. By 1956, Senator Joseph McCarthy had been discredited, but the memory of his anticommunist witch-hunts stifled political dissent, and Ginsberg's publication of this poem was a courageous act. He alludes to the repressive 1920s and the liberal 1930s, his view colored by that of his mother, a Russian immigrant and a fervent member of the Communist Party. The Trotskyites (line 11) were militant American Communists. The Wobblies (line 27) were members of the Industrial Workers of the World, a radical labor organization active from 1905 to 1930, many of whose members were imprisoned during the "Red scare" of 1919–21. Tom Mooney (1882–1942) (line 57), a labor organizer, was condemned to death on perjured evidence that he had exploded a bomb during a San Francisco parade; he escaped the electric chair and was freed after 23 years in prison, but anarchists Nicola Sacco and Bartholomeo Vanzetti (line 59) were executed in 1927 after what amounted to a political trial. During the 1930s, the American Communist Party was able to take part openly in political campaigns and organized support for Tom Mooney, for the Scottsboro boys (line 60—eight blacks condemned to death after a sensational and unfair rape trial in Scottsboro, Alabama), and for the Loyalists (line 58) who fought in support of the Socialist government of Republican Spain against the Fascist revolution led by General Francisco Franco.
4. William Burroughs (1914–1997), author of *Naked Lunch* (1959), was a heroin addict for fifteen years, until 1957; in 1950, he left the United States for Mexico, and then for Tangiers, to avoid prosecution.

My psychoanalyst thinks I'm perfectly right.
I won't say the Lord's Prayer.   35
I have mystical visions and cosmic vibrations.

America I still haven't told you what you did to Uncle Max after he came
    over from Russia.
I'm addressing you.
Are you going to let your emotional life be run by Time Magazine?
I'm obsessed by Time Magazine.   40
I read it every week.
Its cover stares at me every time I slink past the corner candystore.
I read it in the basement of the Berkeley Public Library.
It's always telling me about responsibility. Businessmen are serious. Movie
    producers are serious. Everybody's serious but me.
It occurs to me that I am America.   45
I am talking to myself again.

Asia is rising against me.
I haven't got a chinaman's chance.
I'd better consider my national resources.
My national resources consist of two joints of marijuana millions of   50
    genitals an unpublishable private literature that jetplanes 1400 miles
    an hour and twentyfive-thousand mental institutions.
I say nothing about my prisons nor the millions of underprivileged who
    live in my flowerpots under the light of five hundred suns.
I have abolished the whorehouses of France, Tangiers is the next to go.
My ambition is to be President despite the fact that I'm a Catholic.[5]

America how can I write a holy litany in your silly mood?
I will continue like Henry Ford my strophes[6] are as individual as his   55
    automobiles more so they're all different sexes.
America I will sell you strophes $2500 apiece $500 down on your old
    strophe
America free Tom Mooney
America save the Spanish Loyalists
America Sacco & Vanzetti must not die
America I am the Scottsboro boys.   60
America when I was seven momma took me to Communist Cell meetings
    they sold us garbanzos a handful per ticket a ticket costs a nickel and
    the speeches were free everybody was angelic and sentimental about
    the workers it was all so sincere you have no idea what a good thing
    the party was in 1835 Scott Nearing was a grand old man a real
    mensch Mother Bloor the Silk-strikers' Ewig-Weibliche made me cry
    I once saw the Yiddish orator Israel Amter plain.[7] Everybody must
    have been a spy.
America you don't really want to go to war.
America it's them bad Russians.

5. An allusion to Al Smith (1873–1944), a New York governor who was the first Roman Catholic candidate for U.S. president, in 1928.
6. That is, stanzas.
7. Scott Nearing, a radical economist and socialist who left the Communist Party in 1930. Ella Reeve Bloor and Israel Amter were Party leaders in the New York area. Compare Robert Browning's line, "Ah, did you once see Shelley plain?"

Them Russians them Russians and them Chinamen. And them Russians.

The Russia wants to eat us alive. The Russia's power mad. She wants to 65
take our cars from out our garages.

Her wants to grab Chicago. Her needs a Red *Readers' Digest.* Her wants
our auto plants in Siberia. Him big bureaucracy running our filling-
stations.

That no good. Ugh. Him make Indians learn read. Him need big black
niggers. Hah. Her make us all work sixteen hours a day. Help.

America this is quite serious.

America this is the impression I get from looking in the television set.

America is this correct? 70

I'd better get right down to the job.

It's true I don't want to join the Army or turn lathes in precision parts
factories, I'm nearsighted and psychopathic anyway.

America I'm putting my queer shoulder to the wheel.

Berkeley January 17, 1956 1956

From Kaddish

For Naomi Ginsberg, 1894–1956[8]

* * *

Your last night in the darkness of the Bronx—I phonecalled—thru hos-
pital to secret police

that came, when you and I were alone, shrieking at Elanor[9] in my ear—
who breathed hard in her own bed, got thin—

Nor will forget, the doorknock, at your fright of spies,—Law advancing,
on my honor—Eternity entering the room—you running to the bath-
room undressed, hiding in protest from the last heroic fate—

staring at my eyes, betrayed—the final cops of madness rescuing me—
from your foot against the broken heart of Elanor,

your voice at Edie weary of Gimbels coming home to broken radio—and 5
Louis needing a poor divorce, he wants to get married soon—Eugene[1]
dreaming, hiding at 125 St., suing negroes for money on crud fur-
niture, defending black girls—

Protests from the bathroom—Said you were sane—dressing in a cotton
robe, your shoes, then new, your purse and newspaper clippings—
no—your honesty—

as you vainly made your lips more real with lipstick, looking in the mirror
to see if the Insanity was Me or a carful of police.

or Grandma spying at 78—Your vision—Her climbing over the walls of
the cemetery with political kidnapper's bag—or what you saw on the
walls of the Bronx, in pink nightgown at midnight, staring out the
window on the empty lot—

Ah Rochambeau Ave.—Playground of Phantoms—last apartment in the

---

8. The poet's mother, who suffered from mental
illness most of her life; she was institutionalized
from 1948 until 1956, when she died in Greystone
Hospital. *Kaddish:* Jewish prayer of mourning and
remembrance for the dead.
9. Naomi's sister.
1. Ginsberg's brother. Louis: Ginsberg's father.

Bronx for spies—last home for Elanor or Naomi, here these com-
munist sisters lost their revolution—
'All right—put on your coat Mrs.—let's go—We have the wagon down-   10
stairs—you want to come with her to the station?'
The ride then—held Naomi's hand, and held her head to my breast, I'm
taller—kissed her and said I did it for the best—Elanor sick—and
Max[2] with heart condition—Needs—
To me—'Why did you do this?'—'Yes Mrs., your son will have to leave
you in an hour'—The Ambulance
came in a few hours—drove off at 4 A.M. to some Bellevue[3] in the night
downtown—gone to the hospital forever. I saw her led away—she
waved, tears in her eyes.

Two years, after a trip to Mexico—bleak in the flat plain near Brentwood,[4]
scrub brush and grass around the unused RR train track to the crazy-
house—
new brick 20 story central building—lost on the vast lawns of madtown   15
on Long Island—huge cities of the moon.
Asylum spreads out giant wings above the path to a minute black hole—
the door—entrance thru crotch—
I went in—smelt funny—the halls again—up elevator—to a glass door on
a Women's Ward—to Naomi—Two nurses buxom white—They led
her out, Naomi stared—and I gaspt—She'd had a stroke—
Too thin, shrunk on her bones—age come to Naomi—now broken into
white hair—loose dress on her skeleton—face sunk, old! withered—
cheek of crone—
One hand stiff—heaviness of forties & menopause reduced by one heart
stroke, lame now—wrinkles—a scar on her head, the lobotomy[5]—
ruin, the hand dipping downwards to death—

O Russian faced, woman on the grass, your long black hair is crowned   20
with flowers, the mandolin is on your knees—
Communist beauty, sit here married in the summer among daisies, prom-
ised happiness at hand—
holy mother, now you smile on your love, your world is born anew, chil-
dren run naked in the field spotted with dandelions,
they eat in the plum tree grove at the end of the meadow and find a cabin
where a white-haired negro teaches the mystery of his rainbarrel—
blessed daughter come to America, I long to hear your voice again,
remembering your mother's music, in the Song of the Natural
Front—
O glorious muse that bore me from the womb, gave suck first mystic life   25
& taught me talk and music, from whose pained head I first took
Vision—
Tortured and beaten in the skull—What mad hallucinations of the
damned that drive me out of my own skull to seek Eternity till I find
Peace for Thee, O Poetry—and for all humankind call on the Origin
Death which is the mother of the universe!—Now wear your nakedness

2. Elanor's husband.
3. Psychiatric hospital.
4. Town on Long Island, east of New York City;
site of the former Pilgrim State mental institution.

5. Surgical procedure once thought to alleviate
mental illness by severing the frontal lobes of the
brain from the thalamus.

forever, white flowers in your hair, your marriage sealed behind the
sky—no revolution might destroy that maidenhood—
O beautiful Garbo⁶ of my Karma—all photographs from 1920 in Camp
Nicht-Gedeiget⁷ here unchanged—with all the teachers from New-
ark—Nor Elanor be gone, nor Max await his specter—nor Louis
retire from this High School—

Back! You! Naomi! Skull on you! Gaunt immortality and revolution
come—small broken woman—the ashen indoor eyes of hospitals,
ward grayness on skin—
'Are you a spy?' I sat at the sour table, eyes filling with tears—'Who are   30
you? Did Louis send you?—The wires—'
in her hair, as she beat on her head—'I'm not a bad girl—don't murder
me!—I hear the ceiling—I raised two children—'
Two years since I'd been there—I started to cry—She stared—nurse broke
up the meeting a moment—I went into the bathroom to hide, against
the toilet white walls
'The Horror' I weeping—to see her again—'The Horror'—as if she were
dead thru funeral rot in—'The Horror!'⁸
I came back she yelled more—they led her away—'You're not Allen—' I
watched her face—but she passed by me, not looking—
Opened the door to the ward,—she went thru without a glance back, quiet   35
suddenly—I stared out—she looked old—the verge of the grave—'All
the Horror!'

Another year, I left N.Y.—on West Coast in Berkeley cottage dreamed of
her soul—that, thru life, in what form it stood in that body, ashen or
manic, gone beyond joy—
near its death—with eyes—was my own love in its form, the Naomi, my
mother on earth still—sent her long letter—& wrote hymns to the
mad—Work of the merciful Lord of Poetry.
that causes the broken grass to be green, or the rock to break in grass—
or the Sun to be constant to earth—Sun of all sunflowers and days
on bright iron bridges—what shines on old hospitals—as on my
yard—
Returning from San Francisco one night, Orlovsky in my room—Whalen⁹
in his peaceful chair—a telegram from Gene, Naomi dead—
Outside I bent my head to the ground under the bushes near the garage—   40
knew she was better—
at last—not left to look on Earth alone—2 years of solitude—no one, at
age nearing 60—old woman of skulls—once long-tressed Naomi of
Bible—
or Ruth who wept in America—Rebecca aged in Newark—David remem-
bering his Harp, now lawyer at Yale
or Srul Avrum—Israel Abraham—myself¹—to sing in the wilderness

6. Greta Garbo (1905–1990), American film star.
7. No worry (Yiddish); the name of a communist
summer camp near Lake Monroe in upstate New
York, attended by the Ginsberg family; Naomi
Ginsberg was especially happy there.
8. Dying words of Kurtz in the novella *Heart of
Darkness* (1902), by Joseph Conrad (1857–1924).

9. Philip Whalen (1923–2002): American Beat
poet. Peter Orlovsky (b. 1933): Ginsberg's lover.
1. Ginsberg was named after his paternal great-
grandfather, S'rul Avram Ginsberg. S'rul is Yiddish
for Israel, *Avram* Yiddish for Abraham. Naomi,
David, Rebecca, Ruth, Israel, and Abraham are all
important figures in the Hebrew Bible.

toward God—O Elohim![2]—so to the end—2 days after her death I
got her letter—
Strange Prophecies anew! She wrote—'The key is in the window, the key
is in the sunlight at the window—I have the key—Get married Allen
don't take drugs—the key is in the bars, in the sunlight in the window.
                                          Love,   45
                                      your mother'

which is Naomi—
Paris, December 1957–New York, 1959   1961

To Aunt Rose

Aunt Rose—now—might I see you
with your thin face and buck tooth smile and pain
            of rheumatism—and a long black heavy shoe
            for your bony left leg
limping down the long hall in Newark on the running carpet   5
            past the black grand piano
                  in the day room
                        where the parties were
and I sang Spanish loyalist[3] songs
            in a high squeaky voice   10
                  (hysterical) the committee listening
            while you limped around the room
                  collected the money—
Aunt Honey, Uncle Sam, a stranger with a cloth arm
            in his pocket   15
                  and huge young bald head
                  of Abraham Lincoln Brigade[4]

—your long sad face
            your tears of sexual frustration
                  (what smothered sobs and bony hips   20
                        under the pillows of Osborne Terrace)
—the time I stood on the toilet seat naked
            and you powdered my thighs with calamine
            against the poison ivy—my tender
                  and shamed first black curled hairs   25
what were you thinking in secret heart then
            knowing me a man already—
and I an ignorant girl of family silence on the thin pedestal
            of my legs in the bathroom—Museum of Newark.

                  Aunt Rose   30
Hitler is dead, Hitler is in Eternity; Hitler is with
            Tamburlaine and Emily Brontë[5]

2. Lord (Hebrew).
3. During the Spanish Civil War (1936–39), many
left-wing Americans—among them Ginsberg's
Newark relatives—sympathized with the Spanish
Loyalists.
4. A group of American volunteers who fought
with the loyalists in the Spanish Civil War.
5. English poet and novelist (1818–1848), author
of *Wuthering Heights*. Tamburlaine was the
twelfth-century Mideastern "scourge" and con-
queror (hero of Christopher Marlowe's *Tam-
burlaine*, 1588).

Though I see you walking still, a ghost on Osborne Terrace
    down the long dark hall to the front door
      limping a little with a pinched smile   35
    in what must have been a silken
        flower dress
welcoming my father, the Poet, on his visit to Newark
    —see you arriving in the living room
      dancing on your crippled leg   40
    and clapping hands his book
      had been accepted by Liveright[6]

Hitler is dead and Liveright's gone out of business
The Attic of the Past and *Everlasting Minute* are out of print
      Uncle Harry sold his last silk stocking   45
    Claire quit interpretive dancing school
    Buba sits a wrinkled monument in Old
      Ladies Home blinking at new babies

last time I saw you was the hospital
    pale skull protruding under ashen skin   50
      blue veined unconscious girl
        in an oxygen tent
    the war in Spain has ended long ago
      Aunt Rose

Paris, June 1958   1961

Last Night in Calcutta

Still night. The old clock Ticks,
half past two. A ringing of crickets
awake in the ceiling. The gate is locked
on the street outside—sleepers, mustaches,
nakedness, but no desire. A few mosquitoes   5
waken the itch, the fan turns slowly—
a car thunders along the black asphalt,
a bull snorts, something is expected—
Time sits solid in the four yellow walls.
No one is here, emptiness filled with train   10
whistles & dog barks, answered a block away.
Pushkin[7] sits on the bookshelf, Shakespeare's
complete works as well as Blake's unread—
O Spirit of Poetry, no use calling on you
babbling in this emptiness furnished with beds   15
under the bright oval mirror—perfect
night for sleepers to dissolve in tranquil
blackness, and rest there eight hours

6. This leading American publisher of the 1920s and 1930s (now a subsidiary of W. W. Norton & Company) published *The Everlasting Minute* (1937), poems by Allen Ginsberg's father, Louis, whose first book was *The Attic of the Past* (Boston, 1920).
7. Alexander Pushkin (1799–1837), Russian poet.

—Waking to stained fingers, bitter mouth
and lung gripped by cigarette hunger,   20
what to do with this big toe, this arm
this eye in the starving skeleton-filled
sore horse tramcar-heated Calcutta in
Eternity—sweating and teeth rotted away—
Rilke[8] at least could dream about lovers,   25
the old breast excitement and trembling belly,
is that it? And the vast starry space—
If the brain changes matter breathes
fearfully back on man—But now
the great crash of building and planets   30
breaks thru the walls of language and drowns
me under its Ganges[9] heaviness forever.
No escape but thru Bangkok and New York death.
Skin is sufficient to be skin, that's all
it ever could be, tho screams of pain in the kidney   35
make it sick of itself, a wavy dream
dying to finish its all too famous misery
—Leave immortality for another to suffer like a fool,
not get stuck in the corner of the universe
sticking morphine in the arm and eating meat.   40

May 22, 1963   1968

Mugging

I

Tonite I walked out of my red apartment door on East tenth street's[1]
    dusk—
Walked out of my home ten years, walked out in my honking neighbor-
    hood
Tonite at seven walked out past garbage cans chained to concrete anchors
Walked under black painted fire escapes, giant castiron plate covering a
    hole in ground
—Crossed the street, traffic lite red, thirteen bus roaring by liquor store,   5
past corner pharmacy iron grated, past Coca Cola & Mylai[2] posters fading
    scraped on brick
Past Chinese Laundry wood door'd, & broken cement stoop steps For
    Rent hall painted green & purple Puerto Rican style
Along E. 10th's glass splattered pavement, kid blacks & Spanish oiled hair
    adolescents' crowded house fronts—
Ah, tonite I walked out on my block NY City under humid summer sky
    Halloween,
thinking what happened Timothy Leary[3] joining brain police for a season?   10

---

8. Rainer Maria Rilke (1875–1926), German poet, author of the *Duino Elegies*, which celebrate angels and lovers as figures of immortal power.
9. The sacred river of India.
1. On New York City's Lower East Side.

2. Scene of a massacre by American troops during the Vietnam War.
3. Nineteen-sixties counterculture figure (1920–1996), who advocated LSD use.

thinking what's all this Weathermen,[4] secrecy & selfrightousness beyond
    reason—F.B.I. plots?
Walked past a taxicab controlling the bottle strewn curb—
past young fellows with their umbrella handles & canes leaning against a
    ravaged Buick
—and as I looked at the crowd of kids on the stoop—a boy stepped up,
    put his arm around my neck
tenderly I thought for a moment, squeezed harder, his umbrella handle 15
    against my skull,
and his friends took my arm, a young brown companion tripped his foot
    'gainst my ankle—
as I went down shouting Om Ah Hūm[5] to gangs of lovers on the stoop
    watching
slowly appreciating, why this is a raid, these strangers mean strange busi-
    ness
with what—my pockets, bald head, broken-healed-bone leg, my softshoes,
    my heart—
Have they knives? Om Ah Hūm—Have they sharp metal wood to shove 20
    in eye ear ass? Om Ah Hūm
& slowly reclined on the pavement, struggling to keep my woolen bag of
    poetry address calendar & Leary-lawyer notes hung from my shoulder
dragged in my neat orlon shirt over the crossbar of a broken metal door
dragged slowly onto the fire-soiled floor an abandoned store, laundry
    candy counter 1929—
now a mess of papers & pillows & plastic car seat covers cracked cock-
    roach-corpsed ground—
my wallet back pocket passed over the iron foot step guard   25
and fell out, stole by God Muggers' lost fingers, Strange—
Couldn't tell—snakeskin wallet actually plastic, 70 dollars my bank money
    for a week,
old broken wallet—and dreary plastic contents—Amex card & Manf.
    Hanover Trust Credit too—business card from Mr. Spears British
    Home Minister Drug Squad—my draft card—membership ACLU &
    Naropa Institute[6] Instructor's identification
Om Ah Hūm I continued chanting Om Ah Hūm
Putting my palm on the neck of an 18 year old boy fingering my back 30
    pocket crying "Where's the money"
"Oh Am Hūm   there isn't any"
My card Chief Boo-Hoo Neo American Church New Jersey & Lower East
    Side
Om Ah Hūm—what not forgotten crowded wallet—Mobil Credit, Shell?
    old lovers addresses on cardboard pieces, booksellers calling cards—
—"Shut up or we'll murder you"—"Om Ah Hūm   take it easy"
Lying on the floor shall I shout more loud?—the metal door closed on 35
    blackness
one boy felt my broken healed ankle, looking for hundred dollar bills
    behind my stocking weren't even there—a third boy untied my Seiko

---

4. Radical group of student protesters during the
1960s.
5. Buddhist mantra, or chant.

6. Ginsberg's school for the study of poetry and
mysticism in Boulder, Colorado.

Hong Kong watch rough from right wrist leaving a clasp-prick skin
  tiny bruise
"Shut up and we'll get out of here"—and so they left,
as I rose from the cardboard mattress thinking Om Ah Hūm   didn't stop
  em enough,
the tone of voice too loud—my shoulder bag with 10,000 dollars full of
  poetry left on the broken floor—

November 2, 1974

II

Went out the door dim eyed, bent down & picked up my glasses from step 40
  edge I placed them while dragged in the store—looked out—
Whole street a bombed-out face, building rows' eyes & teeth missing
burned apartments half the long block, gutted cellars, hallways' charred
  beams
hanging over trash plaster mounded entrances, couches & bedsprings
  rusty after sunset
Nobody home, but scattered stoopfuls of scared kids frozen in black hair
chatted giggling at house doors in black shoes, families cooked For Rent 45
  some six story houses mid the street's wreckage
Nextdoor Bodega,[7] a phone, the police? "I just got mugged" I said
to the man's face under fluorescent grocery light tin ceiling—
puffy, eyes blank & watery, sickness of beer kidney and language tongue
thick lips stunned as my own eyes, poor drunken Uncle minding the store!
O hopeless city of idiots empty eyed staring afraid, red beam top'd car at 50
  street curb arrived—
"Hey maybe my wallet's still on the ground got a flashlight?"
Back into the burnt-doored cave, & the policeman's gray flashlight broken
  no eyebeam—
"My partner all he wants is sit in the car never gets out Hey Joe bring
  your flashlight—"
a tiny throwaway beam, dim as a match in the criminal dark
"No I can't see anything here" . . . "Fill out this form"   55
Neighborhood street crowd behind a car "We didn't see nothing"
Stoop young girls, kids laughing "Listen man last time I messed with them
  see this—"
rolled up his skinny arm shirt, a white knife scar on his brown shoulder
"Besides we help you the cops come don't know anybody we all get
  arrested
go to jail I never help no more mind my business everytime"   60
"Agh!" upstreet think "Gee I don't know anybody here ten years lived half
  block crost Avenue C[8]
and who knows who?"—passing empty apartments, old lady with frayed
  paper bags
sitting in the tin-boarded doorframe of a dead house.

December 10, 1974   1977

7. Corner grocer (Spanish).   8. Which runs at right angles to East 10th Street.

Sphincter[9]

I hope my good old asshole holds out
60 years it's been mostly OK
Tho in Bolivia a fissure operation
     survived the *altiplano*[1] hospital—
a little blood, no polyps, occasionally   5
     a small hemorrhoid
active, eager, receptive to phallus
     coke bottle, candle, carrot
     banana & fingers—
Now AIDS makes it shy, but still   10
     eager to serve—
out with the dumps, in with the condom'd
     orgasmic friend—
still rubbery muscular,
     unashamed wide open for joy   15
But another 20 years who knows,
     old folks got troubles everywhere—
necks, prostates, stomachs, joints—
     Hope the old hole stays young
     till death, relax   20

March 15, 1986, 1:00 P.M.   1994

Personals Ad

"I will send a picture too
if you will send me one of you"
—R. CREELEY[2]

Poet professor in autumn years
seeks helpmate companion protector friend
young lover w/empty compassionate soul
exuberant spirit, straightforward handsome
athletic physique & boundless mind, courageous   5
warrior who may also like women & girls, no problem,
to share bed meditation apartment Lower East Side,
help inspire mankind conquer world anger & guilt,
empowered by Whitman Blake Rimbaud Ma Rainey & Vivaldi,[3]
familiar respecting Art's primordial majesty, priapic[4] carefree   10
playful harmless slave or master, mortally tender passing swift time,
photographer, musician, painter, poet, yuppie or scholar—
Find me here in New York alone with the Alone
going to lady psychiatrist who says Make time in your life

9. Ringlike muscle that maintains constriction of an orifice, such as the anus.
1. Andean plateau.
2. American poet (b. 1926), from his poem "The Conspiracy."
3. Antonio Vivaldi (1678–1741): Italian composer. Walt Whitman (1819–1892): American poet. William Blake (1757–1827): British poet. Arthur Rimbaud (1854–1891): French poet. Ma Rainey (1886–1936): American blues singer.
4. Relating to the penis.

for someone you can call darling, honey, who holds you dear   15
can get excited & lay his head on your heart in peace.

October 8, 1987   1994

DAVID WAGONER
b. 1926

Born on June 5, 1926, in the small Ohio town of Massillon, David Wagoner as a child
was taken by his parents to live in Whiting, Indiana, a heavily industrialized suburb of
Chicago. He served in the navy toward the end of World War II. The great event of his
education occurred when, as a student at Pennsylvania State University, he took a
course taught by Theodore Roethke. They shared a keen interest in nature, and when
Roethke moved to the University of Washington in Seattle, he encouraged Wagoner to
join him. Wagoner did so, and the natural beauty he found in the Pacific northwest
struck him with awe.

Wagoner is the principal, though modest, character in most of his poems. By turns
affectionate, sober, and gently humorous, he uses metaphor, pacing, and accumulated
detail to create convincing character sketches, such as his father-as-handyman or a girl
pouring water from a pitcher. He loves wildernesses and rivers and writes deftly of nat-
ural things, often small, such as ferns, a tuft of thistledown, a goldfinch, a dragonfly, in
each of which he finds a relevance to human life. His quiet, descriptively astute poems
help revitalize the pastoral tradition, bridging the gap between humans and nature with-
out attempting to eliminate it. His response to the destruction of nature is angrily
mournful, as in his "Elegy for a Forest Clear-Cut by the Weyerhaeuser Company."
Through repetition he reproduces the downing of trees and his own agitated feelings:
"You fell and fell again and went on falling / And falling and always falling." Similarly, a
one-sentence syntactic tumble summons the natural cascade of "By a Waterfall." In
addition to poetry, Wagoner has published numerous novels and prose writings, includ-
ing a book on the myths and tales of the Northwest Coast and Plateau Indians.

The Man of the House

My father, looking for trouble, would find it
On his hands and knees by hammering on walls
Between the joists or drilling through baseboards
Or crawling into the attic where insulation
Lay under the leaks like sleeping-bags.   5

It would be something simple as a rule
To be ingenious for, in overalls;
And he would kneel beside it, pouring sweat
Down his red cheeks, glad of a useful day
With something wrong unknown to the landlord.   10

At those odd times when everything seemed to work
All right, suspiciously all right like silence
In concrete shelters, he'd test whatever hung
Over our heads: such afternoons meant ladders,
Nails in the mouth, flashing and shaking roofs.   15

In safety shoes going down basement stairs,
He'd flick his rewired rearrangement of lights
And chase all shadows into the coalbin
Where they could watch him, blinking at his glare.
If shadows hadn't worked, he would have made them.   20

With hands turning to horn against the stone
He'd think on all fours, hunch as if to drink
If his cold chisel broke the cold foundation
And brought dark water pulsing out of clay.
Wrenching at rows of pipes like his cage-bars,   25

He made them creak in sockets and give way,
But rammed them back, putting his house in order.
Moonlight or rain, after the evening paper,
His mouth lay open under the perfect plaster
To catch the first sweet drop, but none came down.   30

                                                          1966

Elegy for a Forest Clear-Cut by
the Weyerhaeuser Company

Five months after your death, I come like the others
Among the slash and stumps, across the cratered
Three square miles of your graveyard:
Nettles and groundsel first out of the jumble,
Then fireweed and bracken   5
Have come to light where you, for ninety years,
Had kept your shadows.

The creek has gone as thin as my wrist, nearly dead
To the world at the dead end of summer,
Guttering to a pool where the tracks of an earth-mover   10
Showed it the way to falter underground.
Now pearly everlasting
Has grown to honor the deep dead cast of your roots
For a bitter season.

Those water- and earth-led roots decay for winter   15
Below my feet, below the fir seedlings
Planted in your place (one out of ten alive
In the summer drought),

Below the small green struggle of the weeds
For their own ends, below grasshoppers,   20
The only singers now.

The chains and cables and steel teeth have left
Nothing of what you were:
I hold my hands over a stump and remember
A hundred and fifty feet above me branches   25
No longer holding sway. In the pitched battle
You fell and fell again and went on falling
And falling and always falling.

Out in the open where nothing was left standing
(The immoral equivalent of a forest fire),   30
I sit with my anger. The creek will move again,
Come rain and snow, gnawing at raw defiles,
Clear-cutting its own gullies.
As selective as reapers stalking through wheatfields,
Selective loggers go where the roots go.   35

                                                        1974

A Young Girl with a Pitcher Full of Water

She carries it unsteadily, warily
Off balance on bare feet across the room,
Believing wholeheartedly in what she carries
And knowing where she is going carefully
Through the narrow doorway into the sunlight,   5
Holding by handle and lip what she begins
To pour so seriously and slowly now, she leans
That way as if to pour herself. She grows
More and more light. She lightens. She sees it flowing
Away from her to fill her earth to the brim.   10
Then she stands still, smiling above flowers.

                                                        1983

By a Waterfall

Over the sheer stone cliff-face, over springs and star clusters
Of maidenhair giving in and in to the spray
Through thorn-clawed crookshanks
And gnarled root ends like vines where the sun has never from dawn
To noon or dusk come spilling its cascades,   5
The stream is falling, at the brink
Blue-green but whitening and churning to pale rain
And falling farther, neither as rain nor mist
But both now, pouring

And changing as it must, exchanging all for all over all   10
Around and past your shape to a dark-green pool
Below, where it tumbles
Over another verge to become a stream once more
Downstream in curving slopes under a constant
Cloud of what it was   15
And will be, and beside it, sharing the storm of its arrival,
Your voice and all your words are disappearing
Into this water falling.

1996

FRANK O'HARA
1926–1966

Frank O'Hara's strategies as a poet, and as a sponsor of other people's poetry, are summed up in characteristically offhand fashion in the essay "Personism: A Manifesto." He begins by putting poetry in its place as one among many legitimate human amusements. "Too many poets," he protests, "act like a middle-aged mother trying to get her kids to eat too much cooked meat, and potatoes with drippings (tears). I don't give a damn whether they eat or not. Forced feeding leads to excessive thinness (effete). Nobody should experience anything they don't need to, if they don't need poetry bully for them. I like the movies too. And after all, only Whitman and [Hart] Crane and [William Carlos] Williams, of the American poets, are better than the movies." Though it reads like a parody of Charles Olson's manifesto "Projective Verse," O'Hara's essay is illustrated by his own practice. He objects to "abstraction in poetry," which he obliquely defines as the absence of the artist's personal voice or style from his or her work; this is not to be confused with abstractness in painting, because even in the work of abstract expressionists such as Jackson Pollock and Willem de Kooning, one can still feel the presence of a personal style. O'Hara wants poetry to avoid "philosophy," or abstract speculation, but while he is frank about his sexual identity as a gay man, he doesn't opt for "personality or intimacy" either. Once when writing a poem, he says, "I was realizing that if I wanted to I could use the telephone instead of writing the poem" (*Collected Poems*, 1971). This spur-of-the-moment spontaneity pervades his poems and guarantees O'Hara's animating presence in them.

O'Hara was born on June 27, 1926, in Baltimore, Maryland, and grew up in Grafton, a suburb of Worcester, Massachusetts. After serving in the navy during World War II, he received his B.A. from Harvard University, where he helped found the Poets' Theatre, and received his M.A. from the University of Michigan. In 1951, he settled in New York, where he worked for *Art News* and joined the staff of the Museum of Modern Art, eventually becoming associate curator of exhibitions of painting and sculpture. During the 1960s, he became a leading figure in a group of young poets (John Ashbery, Kenneth Koch, and James Schuyler among them) who came to be known as the New York poets. By their own testimony, they derived inspiration from paintings by Pollock, de Kooning, Franz Kline, and others, many of whom were O'Hara's friends. As Schuyler puts it, "New York poets, except I suppose the color blind, are affected most by the floods of paint in whose crashing surf we all scramble. . . . In New York the art world is a painters' world; writers and musicians are in the boat, but they don't steer" (*The*

New American Poetry: 1945–1960, 1960). A direct connection between O'Hara's poetry and the paintings he admired is not obvious, though he says a description in one of his poems was influenced by a de Kooning painting, and his poems, like the paintings, emphasize the process of creation and the materiality of the artistic medium. Some of his poems express a genial appreciation for the neon lights, posters, and other objects that litter the New York landscape (and that received similar attention from the Pop artists). In addition, the dreamlike, irrational sequences of images in some of his poems may have been inspired by surrealist painting and film, the rapid flurry of images dramatizing the dispersal and distraction of postmodern consciousness.

O'Hara's poems are crammed with the discontinuous sights, names, and places of metropolitan experience, traversing media from advertising and film to high art and music, representing encounters with diverse social classes, ethnicities, and nationalities. His "I-do-this I-do-that" poems, such as "The Day Lady Died" and "A Step Away from Them," record in colloquial, sometimes campy, often erudite language the quick turns in the poet's perceptions, showing us what it feels like to live in immediate contact with both the inner and outer worlds. Alert and energetically responsive, the poems stay close to the moment of their inspiration, even narrating the experiences and interruptions that went into their composition. As if mirroring O'Hara's poetics, the personified sun, sounding somewhat like Whitman, instructs the poet in "A True Account of Talking to the Sun at Fire Island": "And / always embrace things, people earth / sky stars, as I do, freely and with / the appropriate sense of space." Yet O'Hara's elegant poems are not purely random in structure; their narrative pacing, for example, is brilliant. The seemingly extraneous details piled one upon another in the "The Day Lady Died," like the poem's paratactic syntax ("and . . . and . . . and"), contribute to the climactic encounter with death at the end, in which the everyday world vanishes and the poet is lost in memory and grief.

O'Hara wrote many of his poems in spare moments snatched from an increasingly busy life in the art world; most were left around his apartment or sent in letters to friends, and the six books of poems he published between 1952 and 1965 gave little idea of his abundance. After O'Hara's death (he was hit by a dune buggy on Fire Island), the editor Donald Allen assembled hundreds of manuscripts to make up O'Hara's *Collected Poems* (1971).

Poem

The eager note on my door said "Call me,
call when you get in!" so I quickly threw
a few tangerines into my overnight bag,
straightened my eyelids and shoulders, and

headed straight for the door. It was autumn   5
by the time I got around the corner, oh all
unwilling to be either pertinent or bemused, but
the leaves were brighter than grass on the sidewalk!

Funny, I thought, that the lights are on this late
and the hall door open; still up at this hour, a   10
champion jai-alai player like himself? Oh fie!
for shame! What a host, so zealous! And he was

there in the hall, flat on a sheet of blood that
ran down the stairs. I did appreciate it. There are few
hosts who so thoroughly prepare to greet a guest   15
only casually invited, and that several months ago.

1952

Poem

At night Chinamen jump
on Asia with a thump

while in our willful way
we, in secret, play

affectionate games and bruise   5
our knees like China's shoes.

The birds push apples through
grass the moon turns blue,

these apples roll beneath
our buttocks like a heath   10

full of Chinese thrushes
flushed from China's bushes.

As we love at night
birds sing out of sight,

Chinese rhythms beat   15
through us in our heat,

the apples and the birds
move us like soft words,

we couple in the grace
of that mysterious race.   20

1952

Why I Am Not a Painter

I am not a painter, I am a poet.
Why? I think I would rather be
a painter, but I am not. Well,

for instance, Mike Goldberg[1]
is starting a painting. I drop in.   5
"Sit down and have a drink" he
says. I drink; we drink. I look
up. "You have SARDINES in it."
"Yes, it needed something there."
"Oh." I go and the days go by   10
and I drop in again. The painting
is going on, and I go, and the days
go by. I drop in. The painting is
finished. "Where's SARDINES?"
All that's left is just   15
letters, "It was too much," Mike says.

But me? One day I am thinking of
a color: orange. I write a line
about orange. Pretty soon it is a
whole page of words, not lines.   20
Then another page. There should be
so much more, not of orange, of
words, of how terrible orange is
and life. Days go by. It is even in
prose, I am a real poet. My poem   25
is finished and I haven't mentioned
orange yet. It's twelve poems, I call
it ORANGES. And one day in a gallery
I see Mike's painting, called SARDINES.

                                                    1957

A Step Away from Them

It's my lunch hour, so I go
for a walk among the hum-colored
cabs. First, down the sidewalk
where laborers feed their dirty
glistening torsos sandwiches   5
and Coca-Cola, with yellow helmets
on. They protect them from falling
bricks, I guess. Then onto the
avenue where skirts are flipping
above heels and blow up over   10
grates. The sun is hot, but the
cabs stir up the air. I look
at bargains in wristwatches. There
are cats playing in sawdust.
                                    On   15

1. New York artist (b. 1924), who provided silk-screen prints for O'Hara's *Odes* (1960) and painted *Sardines* (1955).

to Times Square, where the sign
blows smoke over my head,[2] and higher
the waterfall pours lightly. A
Negro stands in a doorway with a
toothpick, languorously agitating.   20
A blonde chorus girl clicks: he
smiles and rubs his chin. Everything
suddenly honks: it is 12:40 of
a Thursday.
          Neon in daylight is a   25
great pleasure, as Edwin Denby[3] would
write, as are light bulbs in daylight.
I stop for a cheeseburger at JULIET'S
CORNER. Giulietta Masina, wife of
Federico Fellini, *è bell' attrice*[4]   30
And chocolate malted. A lady in
foxes on such a day puts her poodle
in a cab.
          There are several Puerto
Ricans on the avenue today, which   35
makes it beautiful and warm. First
Bunny died, then John Latouche,
then Jackson Pollock.[5] But is the
earth as full as life was full, of them?
And one has eaten and one walks,   40
past the magazines with nudes
and the posters for BULLFIGHT and
the Manhattan Storage Warehouse,
which they'll soon tear down. I
used to think they had the Armory   45
Show[6] there.
          A glass of papaya juice
and back to work. My heart is in my
pocket, it is Poems by Pierre Reverdy.[7]

                                                   1957

The Day Lady Died

It is 12:20 in New York a Friday
three days after Bastille day,[8] yes
it is 1959 and I go get a shoeshine

2. A famous billboard advertised cigarettes by
puffing steam.
3. American poet and dance critic (1903–1983).
4. Is a beautiful actress (Italian). Masina (1920–
1994) was married to Italian film director Fellini
(1920–1993).
5. American abstract expressionist painter (1912–
1956). V. R. "Bunny" Lang (1924–1956): poet and

director, who produced several of O'Hara's plays.
John Latouche (1917–1956): lyricist. All three
were friends of O'Hara's and died tragically.
6. Famous 1913 exhibition that introduced many
Americans to modern art.
7. French surrealist poet (1899–1960).
8. July 14, French Independence Day.

because I will get off the 4:19 in Easthampton[9]
at 7:15 and then go straight to dinner   5
and I don't know the people who will feed me

I walk up the muggy street beginning to sun
and have a hamburger and a malted and buy
an ugly NEW WORLD WRITING to see what the poets
in Ghana are doing these days   10
                                        I go on to the bank
and Miss Stillwagon (first name Linda I once heard)
doesn't even look up my balance for once in her life
and in the GOLDEN GRIFFIN I get a little Verlaine
for Patsy with drawings by Bonnard[1] although I do   15
think of Hesiod,[2] trans. Richmond Lattimore or
Brendan Behan's new play[3] or *Le Balcon* or *Les Nègres*
of Genet,[4] but I don't, I stick with Verlaine
after practically going to sleep with quandariness

and for Mike I just stroll into the PARK LANE   20
Liquor Store and ask for a bottle of Strega and
then I go back where I came from to 6th Avenue
and the tobacconist in the Ziegfeld Theatre and
casually ask for a carton of Gauloises and a carton
of Picayunes, and a NEW YORK POST with her[5] face on it   25

and I am sweating a lot by now and thinking of
leaning on the john door in the 5 SPOT
while she whispered a song along the keyboard
to Mal Waldron[6] and everyone and I stopped breathing

                                                            1964

Rhapsody[7]

515 Madison Avenue[8]
door to heaven? portal
stopped realities and eternal licentiousness
or at least the jungle of impossible eagerness
your marble is bronze and your lianas[9] elevator cables   5

9. A town on eastern Long Island.
1. An edition of the poems of Paul Verlaine (1844–1896), French poet, with illustrations by Pierre Bonnard (1867–1947).
2. Greek poet (eighth century B.C.E.), author of *Work and Days*.
3. Probably *The Quare Fellow* (1956) or *The Hostage* (1958).
4. Jean Genet (1910–1986), French writer, author of the plays *The Balcony* (1956) and *The Blacks* (1958).
5. Billie Holiday (1915–1959), or "Lady Day," jazz singer.
6. Pianist (died 2002); Billie Holiday's accompanist from 1957 until her death.
7. Also the title of a 1954 movie starring Elizabeth Taylor and John Ericson, alluded to in lines 18–19.
8. "515 is 'off' Madison on 53rd; Frank would have passed it every day to and from the Museum [of Modern Art]. Its door façade is very beautiful" (Bill Berkson, quoted in O'Hara's *Collected Poems*).
9. Climbing plants.

swinging from the myth of ascending
I would join
or declining the challenge of racial attractions
they zing on (into the lynch, dear friends)[1]
while everywhere love is breathing draftily   10
like a doorway linking 53rd with 54th
the east-bound with the west-bound traffic by 8,000,000s
o midtown tunnels and the tunnels, too, of Holland[2]

where is the summit where all aims are clear
the pin-point light upon a fear of lust   15
as agony's needlework grows up around the unicorn
and fences him for milk- and yoghurt-work
when I see Gianni[3] I know he's thinking of John Ericson
playing the Rachmaninoff 2nd or Elizabeth Taylor
taking sleeping-pills and Jane thinks of Manderley   20
and Irkutsk[4] while I cough lightly in the smog of desire
and my eyes water achingly imitating the true blue

a sight of Manahatta[5] in the towering needle
multi-faceted insight of the fly in the stringless labyrinth[6]
Canada plans a higher place than the Empire State Building   25
I am getting into a cab at 9th Street and 1st Avenue
and the Negro driver tells me about a $120 apartment
"where you can't walk across the floor after 10 at night
not even to pee, cause it keeps them awake downstairs"
no, I don't like that "well, I didn't take it"   30
perfect in the hot humid morning on my way to work
a little supper-club conversation for the mill of the gods

you were there always and you know all about these things
as indifferent as an encyclopedia with your calm brown eyes
it isn't enough to smile when you run the gauntlet   35
you've got to spit like Niagara Falls on everybody or
Victoria Falls or at least the beautiful urban fountains of Madrid
as the Niger joins the Gulf of Guinea near the Menemsha Bar[7]
that is what you learned in the early morning passing Madison Avenue
where you've never spent any time and stores eat up light   40

I have always wanted to be near it
though the day is long (and I don't mean Madison Avenue)

1. Cf. Shakespeare's *Henry V* 3.1.1: "Once more unto the breach, dear friends, once more."
2. The Midtown Tunnel and the Holland Tunnel connect Manhattan respectively with Long Island and New Jersey.
3. Gianni Bates, a pianist and friend of O'Hara's. The movie *Rhapsody* stars Elizabeth Taylor as a beautiful, rich, spoiled woman whose love affair with a talented pianist, played by John Ericson, keeps him from his art. She repents, and at the climax of the movie Ericson gives a triumphant performance of Sergei Rachmaninoff's Second Piano Concerto.
4. City in Russia. Jane Freilicher (b. 1924), New York painter. Manderley is the great house in Daphne du Maurier's novel *Rebecca* (made into a movie by Alfred Hitchcock).
5. Native American name for Manhattan, often used by Walt Whitman.
6. In Greek myth, Theseus rescued Ariadne from the Minotaur's labyrinth by following a string he laid down on the way in.
7. Near the Museum of Modern Art. The river Niger flows through West Africa into the Gulf of Guinea.

lying in a hammock on St. Mark's Place[8] sorting my poems
in the rancid nourishment of this mountainous island
they are coming and we holy ones must go   45
is Tibet historically a part of China? as I historically
belong to the enormous bliss of American death

1964

A True Account of Talking to the Sun at Fire Island[9]

The Sun woke me this morning loud
and clear, saying "Hey! I've been
trying to wake you up for fifteen
minutes. Don't be so rude, you are
only the second poet I've ever chosen   5
to speak to personally
                  so why
aren't you more attentive? If I could
burn you through the window I would
to wake you up. I can't hang around   10
here all day."
             "Sorry, Sun, I stayed
up late last night talking to Hal."

"When I woke up Mayakovsky[1] he was
a lot more prompt" the Sun said   15
petulantly. "Most people are up
already waiting to see if I'm going
to put in an appearance."
                I tried
to apologize "I missed you yesterday."   20
"That's better" he said. "I didn't
know you'd come out." "You may be
wondering why I've come so close?"
"Yes" I said beginning to feel hot
wondering if maybe he wasn't burning me   25
anyway.
        "Frankly I wanted to tell you
I like your poetry. I see a lot
on my rounds and you're okay. You may
not be the greatest thing on earth, but   30
you're different. Now, I've heard some
say you're crazy, they being excessively
calm themselves to my mind, and other
crazy poets think that you're a boring
reactionary. Not me.   35
          Just keep on

---

8. A street on the Lower East Side of New York
City.
9. Resort area outside New York City.
1. O'Hara's poem is inspired by "An Extraordi-

nary Adventure which Befell Vladimir Maya-
kovsky in a Summer Cottage," in which the
Russian avant-garde poet (1893–1930) describes
his own conversation with the sun.

like I do and pay no attention. You'll
find that people always will complain
about the atmosphere, either too hot
or too cold too bright or too dark, days   40
too short or too long.
                              If you don't appear
at all one day they think you're lazy
or dead. Just keep right on, I like it.

And don't worry about your lineage   45
poetic or natural. The Sun shines on
the jungle, you know, on the tundra
the sea, the ghetto. Wherever you were
I knew it and saw you moving. I was waiting
for you to get to work.   50

                              And now that you
are making your own days, so to speak,
even if no one reads you but me
you won't be depressed. Not
everyone can look up, even at me. It   55
hurts their eyes."
                              "Oh Sun, I'm so grateful to you!"

"Thanks and remember I'm watching. It's
easier for me to speak to you out
here. I don't have to slide down
between buildings to get your ear.   60
I know you love Manhattan, but
you ought to look up more often.
                              And
always embrace things, people earth
sky stars, as I do, freely and with   65
the appropriate sense of space. That
is your inclination, known in the heavens
and you should follow it to hell, if
necessary, which I doubt.   70
                              Maybe we'll
speak again in Africa, of which I too
am specially fond. Go back to sleep now
Frank, and I may leave a tiny poem
in that brain of yours as my farewell."   75

"Sun, don't go!" I was awake
at last. "No, go I must, they're calling
me."
          "Who are they?"
                              Rising he said "Some   80
day you'll know. They're calling to you
too." Darkly he rose, and then I slept.

                                        1968

Les Luths[2]

Ah nuts! It's boring reading French newspapers
in New York as if I were a Colonial waiting for my gin
somewhere beyond this roof a jet is making a sketch of the sky
where is Gary Snyder[3] I wonder if he's reading under a dwarf pine
stretched out so his book and his head fit under the lowest branch   5
while the sun of the Orient rolls calmly not getting through to him
not caring particularly because the light in Japan respects poets

while in Paris Monsieur Martory and his brother Jean the poet
are reading a piece by Matthieu Galey and preparing to send a *pneu*[4]
everybody here is running around after dull pleasantries and   10
wondering if *The Hotel Wentley Poems*[5] is as great as I say it is
and I am feeling particularly testy at being separated from
the one I love by the most dreary of practical exigencies money
when I want only to lean on my elbow and stare into space feeling
the one warm beautiful thing in the world breathing upon my right rib   15

what are lutes they make ugly twangs and rest on knees in cafés
I want to hear only your light voice running on about Florida
as we pass the changing traffic light and buy grapes for wherever
we will end up praising the mattressless sleigh-bed and the
Mexican egg and the clock that will not make me know how to leave you 20

1971

2. The lutes (French). In a letter of October 6, 1959, to Pierre Martory (line 8), O'Hara enclosed this poem, saying, "Here is a little poem which you appear in so I am sending it regardless of its soupiness (it was inspired by *Arts* du 16 au 22 Sept which had a picture of a rather boring lute on the back page)."
3. American poet (b. 1930), who was then in Japan.
4. Short for *pneumatique*, a form of rapid communication by which written messages are passed in containers through enclosed pipes by air pressure.
5. First book by Beat poet John Wieners (1934–2002).

ROBERT BLY
b. 1926

Robert Bly is a prime mover of what came to be known as the Deep Image school, neosurrealists who used images to gain access to unconscious or spiritual levels of experience. Bly speaks of the "underground image"; his poetry can be thought of as an underground or, better, a mystical imagism. In a matter-of-fact tone, shunning grandeur and emphasis, he uses simple diction to describe external landscapes of his beloved, native Minnesota, and landscapes of the mind as well; the objects specified are given a strange, fantastic presentness. The outward and inward aspects of things often coincide, as when, in "Awakening," the poet speaks of "the chestnut blossoms in the mind." This neosurrealism draws on the magical realism of South American poets such as Pablo Neruda; it has connections also with the European poets Federico García Lorca, Georg

Trakl, and Rainer Maria Rilke, as well as the American Wallace Stevens and the Irishman W. B. Yeats, this last poet's work having first impelled Bly to write poetry.

Building visionary poems around the associative processes of the unconscious, Bly has shunned formalism and what he sees as the dry, contrived, cerebral poetry of the American academy. Confessional poetry, such as Robert Lowell's, is too personal to suit his mysticism: "I have risen to a body / Not yet born, / Existing like a light around the body" ("Looking into a Face"). Light and darkness are two versions of the same ultimate reality for Bly, representing a purified, secret existence. The darkness of death is beneficent, and he welcomes what he calls in various poems "the sea of death," "The death we love," and "the black earth of silence." The sense of humanity as grounded, or underground, animates him, in "Evolution from the Fish," to call the human creature "this grandson of fishes," "this nephew of snails."

Bly's poems often begin in a homely setting, such as on a farm or on a trip, into which meaning is infused so that the final effect is surreal. Much of his poetry has a political aspect, especially poems written in the wake of the Vietnam War, but it is politics as William Blake conceived it. Bly made this clear in an essay, "Leaping Up into Political Poetry," in which he states that "the political poem comes out of the deepest privacy." Echoing Yeats's claim that we make out of "the quarrel with ourselves, poetry," Bly writes: "A true political poem is a quarrel with ourselves. . . . The true political poem does not order us either to take any specific acts: like the personal poem, it moves to deepen awareness." Through great leaps of the imagination, the political poet, Bly says in an early version of the essay, "entangles" in language the "half-visible psychic life" of a nation.

Bly was born on December 23, 1926, in Madison, Minnesota. He is of Norwegian descent and remembers it in his verse. He served in the navy during World War II and then entered St. Olaf's College, in Minnesota. After a year, he transferred to Harvard University, from which he graduated in 1950. For several years, he lived in New York, then enrolled in the Writers' Workshop at the University of Iowa before spending a year in Norway. He returned to Minnesota, first living on a farm and then in the small town of Moose Lake, in the eastern part of the state. During the Vietnam War, he was one of the first poet-protesters, founding in 1966 American Writers against the Vietnam War. Earlier, he began to edit a journal called *The Fifties* (later renamed for each successive decade), the purpose of which was to publish new translations. Bly has translated a great number of writers, including not only Neruda, Rilke, and Lorca but also the thirteenth-century Persian-language Sufi poet Jalal al-Din Rumi, whose lyrical intensity is compelling even in translation, and the fifteenth-century Indian mystic Kabir, whose work embodies the "leaps of imagination" Bly has championed. Bly reached his widest audience after the publication of *Iron John: A Book About Men* (1990), which sought to reclaim an archetypal masculinity of wisdom, strength, and courage.

Johnson's Cabinet[1] Watched by Ants

I

It is a clearing deep in a forest: overhanging boughs
Make a low place. Here the citizens we know during the day,
The ministers, the department heads,

---

1. Presidential cabinet of Lyndon B. Johnson (1908–1973).

Appear changed: the stockholders of large steel companies
In small wooden shoes: here are the generals dressed as gamboling   5
    lambs.

II

Tonight they burn the rice-supplies; tomorrow
They lecture on Thoreau;[2] tonight they move around the trees;
Tomorrow they pick the twigs from their clothes;
Tonight they throw the firebombs; tomorrow
They read the Declaration of Independence; tomorrow they are in   10
    church.

III

Ants are gathered around an old tree.
In a choir they sing, in harsh and gravelly voices,
Old Etruscan[3] songs on tyranny.
Toads nearby clap their small hands, and join
The fiery songs, their five long toes trembling in the soaked earth.   15

1967

The Great Society[4]

Dentists continue to water their lawns even in the rain;
Hands developed with terrible labor by apes
Hang from the sleeves of evangelists;
There are murdered kings in the light-bulbs outside movie theaters;
The coffins of the poor are hibernating in piles of new tires.   5

The janitor sits troubled by the boiler,
And the hotel keeper shuffles the cards of insanity.
The President dreams of invading Cuba.
Bushes are growing over the outdoor grills,
Vines over the yachts and the leather seats.   10

The city broods over ash cans and darkening mortar.
On the far shore, at Coney Island,[5] dark children
Play on the chilling beach: a sprig of black seaweed,
Shells, a skyful of birds,
While the mayor sits with his head in his hands.   15

1967

2. Henry David Thoreau (1817–1862), American philosopher and essayist.
3. An early Italian people who preceded the Romans.
4. The keynote slogan of Lyndon B. Johnson's presidential campaign in 1964.
5. Part of New York City.

My Father's Wedding

1924

Today, lonely for my father, I saw
a log, or branch,
long, bent, ragged, bark gone.
I felt lonely for my father when I saw it.
It was the log   5
that lay near my uncle's old milk wagon.

Some men live with a limp they don't hide,
stagger, or drag
a leg. Their sons often are angry.
Only recently I thought: 10
Doing what you want . . .
Is that like limping? Tracks of it show in sand.

Have you seen those giant bird-
men of Bhutan?[6]
Men in bird masks, with pig noses, dancing,   15
teeth like a dog's, sometimes
dancing on one bad leg!
They do what they want, the dog's teeth say that.

But I grew up without dog's teeth,
showed a whole body,   20
left only clear tracks in sand.
I learned to walk swiftly, easily,
no trace of a limp.
I even leaped a little. Guess where my defect is!

Then what? If a man, cautious,   25
hides his limp,
somebody has to limp it. Things
do it; the surroundings limp.
House walls get scars,
the car breaks down; matter, in drudgery, takes it up.   30

On my father's wedding day,
no one was there
to hold him. Noble loneliness
held him. Since he never asked for pity
his friends thought he   35
was whole. Walking alone he could carry it.

He came in limping. It was a simple
wedding, three
or four people. The man in black,
lifting the book, called for order.   40

6. Country between Tibet and India.

And the invisible bride
stepped forward, before his own bride.

He married the invisible bride, not his own.
In her left
breast she carried the three drops 45
that wound and kill. He already had
his bark-like skin then,
made rough especially to repel the sympathy

he longed for, didn't need, and wouldn't accept.
So the Bible's 50
words are read. The man in black
speaks the sentence. When the service
is over, I hold him
in my arms for the first time and the last.

After that he was alone 55
and I was alone.
Few friends came; he invited few.
His two-story house he turned
into a forest,
where both he and I are the hunters. 60

1981

Kneeling Down to Peer into a Culvert[7]

I kneel down to peer into a culvert.
The other end seems far away.
One cone of light floats in the shadowed water.
This is how our children will look when we are dead.

I kneel near floating shadowy water. 5
On my knees, I am half inside the tunnel—
blue sky widens the far end—
darkened by the shadowy insides of the steel.

Are they all born? I walk on farther;
out in the plowing I see a lake newly made. 10
I have seen this lake before. . . . It is a lake
I return to each time my children are grown.

I have fathered so many children and returned
to that lake—grayish flat slate banks,
low arctic bushes. I am a water-serpent throwing water drops 15
off my head. My gray loops trail behind me.

How long I live there alone! For a thousand years
I am alone, with no duties, living as I live.

7. Drain under a road.

Then one morning a head like mine pokes from the water.
I fight—it's time, it's right—and am torn to pieces fighting.   20

1981

A Week after Your Death

I dreamt last night you
Lived nearby, not
Dead at all, but safe
In a blacksmith's storage room,
With bolts and nails in bins   5
From floor to ceiling.

You came and brought me
An ivory jar,
Holding a precious fluid,
Which I took. I knew it meant   10
The time had come,
But I let you leave.

Later a man pushed open
The door and threw
Your body down, a wizened,   15
Astonishingly small body—
Rope still tied
Around the neck.

I woke and cried to my wife:
"He didn't die   20
That way! There was no rope!
All that is wrong!" She
Said, "In
Your dream he did."

1994

CHARLES TOMLINSON
b. 1927

Charles Tomlinson read his poem "Swimming Chenango Lake" at a Phi Beta Kappa celebration, and some remarks he made on that occasion are relevant to much of his other work: "The poem tries to celebrate the fact that the help we gain from alien phenomena—even from water, in which (after all) we can't live—the help is towards relation, towards grasp, towards awareness of all that which we are not, yet of relationship with it. It is a help that teaches us not to try merely to reduce objects to our own image, but to respect their otherness and yet find our way into contact with that otherness" (*The Poem as Initiation*). Tomlinson's relationship with the objects and atmospheres he writes about is urgent but respectful. As he writes in "Poem": "this script that untangles itself / out of wind, briars, stars unseen, / keeps telling me what I mean / is theirs, not mine." A poet of exquisite clarity and detachment, he wishes to suppress "the preconceptions of the too conscious mind" (*Eden*) and admires in the painter Paul Cézanne "the entire absence of self-regard." "You cease to impose and you discover," he says in an intentional echo of Wallace Stevens. He quotes the phenomenologist Maurice Merleau-Ponty: "Things have an internal equivalent in me; they arouse in me a carnal formula of their presence." Some of his best poems are about the people and landscapes of the United States; they develop an exciting relationship with phenomena that have at the start for Tomlinson an impervious foreignness.

He began as a painter, and his first experiments in writing were film scripts. An early influence was the nineteenth-century writer John Ruskin, who fostered Tomlinson's interest in pictorial surfaces, in details that change with every slight readjustment of perspective. Tomlinson's respect for the integrity of the environment explains his rejection of the apocalyptic ideas of Dylan Thomas. Tomlinson did not want everything outside the poet swallowed up and converted into a single vision. Instead of large declarations he wanted precise interrelationships. As an alternative to Thomas, Tomlinson turned to American models—Stevens, Marianne Moore, and Elizabeth Bishop. The Objectivists Louis Zukofsky, George Oppen, and William Carlos Williams also became influences. "One of the destined themes of future British poetry," he says, "will be something in the nature of a dialogue with the spirit of the United States." His sense of nature's "otherness" owes something to the English tradition of Thomas Hardy, though where Hardy tends to find a grim neutrality Tomlinson emphasizes "the paradisal aspect of the visual" (*Eden*).

Tomlinson was born on January 8, 1927, in Stoke-on-Trent, England. In 1948, he received his B.A. from Queen's College, Cambridge, where he studied with Donald Davie. During the next few years, he taught in a London elementary school and was a private secretary in northern Italy. He then resumed his studies at the University of London, from which he received an M.A. in 1955. From 1957 until his retirement, he taught English literature at the University of Bristol. He came to the United States as a visiting professor at several universities. Besides many books of verse, the earliest dating from 1951, Tomlinson has published critical essays and translations of poems of Fyodor Tyutchev, Antonio Machado y Ruiz, César Vallejo, and Octavio Paz.

Cézanne at Aix[1]

And the mountain: each day
Immobile like fruit. Unlike, also
—Because irreducible, because
Neither a component of the delicious
And therefore questionable,   5
Nor distracted (as the sitter)
By his own pose and, therefore,
Doubly to be questioned: it is not
Posed. It is. Untaught
Unalterable, a stone bridgehead   10

---

1. French Postimpressionist painter Paul Cézanne (1839–1906) spent much of his life in Aix-en-Provence, a city in southern France, where he painted his famous landscapes of Mt. Saint-Victoire.

To that which is tangible
Because unfelt before. There
In its weathered weight
Its silence silences, a presence
Which does not present itself.   15

1958

Mr Brodsky

I had heard
before, of an
American who would have preferred
to be an Indian;
but not   5
until Mr Brodsky, of one
whose professed and long
pondered-on passion
was to become a Scot,
who even sent for haggis and oatcakes²   10
across continent.
Having read him
in Cambridge English
a verse or two
from McDiarmid,³   15
I was invited
to repeat the reading
before a Burns Night Gathering⁴
where the Balmoral Pipers
of Albuquerque would   20
play in the haggis
out of its New York tin.
Of course, I said
No. No. I could *not* go
and then   25
half-regretted I had not been.
But to console
and cure the wish, came
Mr Brodsky, bringing
his pipes and played   30
until the immense, distended
bladder of leather seemed
it could barely contain its water—
tears (idle
tears)⁵ for the bridal of Annie Laurie   35

2. Scottish foods, the former a mixture of herbs, oatmeal, and a sheep's internal organs cooked in its stomach. At a Scottish banquet, the haggis was ceremonially brought to the table to the accompaniment of bagpipes (lines 19–22).
3. Hugh MacDiarmid (1892–1978), Scottish poet.

4. Meetings of devotees of Scottish culture are often called Burns Nights, after the Scottish poet Robert Burns (1759–1796).
5. The first words of a song from the narrative poem "The Princess," by Alfred, Lord Tennyson (1809–1892).

and Morton J. Brodsky.
A bagpipe in a dwelling is
a resonant instrument
and there he stood
lost in the gorse   40
the heather or whatever
six thousand
miles and more
from the infection's source,
in our neo–New Mexican parlour   45
where I had heard
before of an
American who would have preferred
to be merely an Indian.

                                                      1966

Two Views of Two Ghost Towns

I

Why speak of memory and death
on ghost ground? Absences
relieve, release. Speak
of the life that uselessness
has unconstrained. Rusting   5
to its rails, the vast obese
company engine that will draw
no more, will draw no more:
Keep Off
the warning says, and all   10
the mob of objects, freed
under the brightly hard
displacement of the desert light
repeat it: the unaxled wheels,
doorless doors and windowless   15
regard of space. Clear
of the weight of human
meanings, human need,
gradually
houses splinter to the ground   20
in white and red, two
rotting parallels beneath
the sombre slag-mound.

II

How dry the ghosts
of dryness are. The air   25
here, tastes of sparseness
and the graveyard stones

are undecorated. To the left
the sea and, right, the shadows
hump and slide, climbing   30
the mountainside as clouds go over.
The town has moved away,
leaving a bitten hill
where the minehead's visible. Brambles
detain the foot. Ketchum,   35
Clay, Shoemake, Jebez O'Haskill
and Judge H. Vennigerholz
all (save for the judge's
modest obelisk) marked
by a metal cross; and there are four   40
crosses of wood, three
wooden stakes (unnamed)
that the sun, the frost, the sea-
wind shred alternately
in sapless scars. How dry   45
the ghosts of dryness are.

                                                                  1966

Swimming Chenango Lake[6]

Winter will bar the swimmer soon.
  He reads the water's autumnal hesitations
A wealth of ways: it is jarred,
  It is astir already despite its steadiness,
Where the first leaves at the first   5
  Tremor of the morning air have dropped
Anticipating him, launching their imprints
  Outwards in eccentric, overlapping circles.
There is a geometry of water, for this
  Squares off the clouds' redundances   10
And sets them floating in a nether atmosphere
  All angles and elongations: every tree
Appears a cypress as it stretches there
  And every bush that shows the season,
A shaft of fire. It is a geometry and not   15
  A fantasia of distorting forms, but each
Liquid variation answerable to the theme
  It makes away from, plays before:
It is a consistency, the grain of the pulsating flow.

6. A lake near the campus of Colgate University, where Tomlinson taught in 1967. In his discussion of this poem, Tomlinson cites Claude Levi-Strauss's anthropological study *The Savage Mind:* "Now, the Pawnee Indians have a ceremony called the Hako, for the crossing of a stream. A poetic invocation is the essence of this ceremony. The invocation is divided, we are told, 'into several parts which correspond respectively to the moment when the travelers put their feet in water, the moment when they move them and the moment when the water completely covers their feet.' All these stages are celebrated and differentiated. I borrow this instance of the crossing of the water because it seems to correspond with the way of working of a poem like 'Swimming Chenango Lake' " (*The Poem as Initiation*, 1968).

But he has looked long enough, and now   20
Body must recall the eye to its dependence
   As he scissors the waterscape apart
And sways it to tatters. Its coldness
   Holding him to itself, he grants the grasp,
For to swim is also to take hold   25
   On water's meaning, to move in its embrace
And to be, between grasp and grasping, free.
   He reaches in-and-through to that space
The body is heir to, making a where
   In water, a possession to be relinquished   30
Willingly at each stroke. The image he has torn
   Flows-to behind him, healing itself,
Lifting and lengthening, splayed like the feathers
   Down an immense wing whose darkened spread
Shadows his solitariness: alone, he is unnamed   35
   By this baptism, where only Chenango bears a name
In a lost language he begins to construe—
   A speech of densities and derisions, of half-
Replies to the questions his body must frame
   Frogwise across the all but penetrable element.   40
Human, he fronts it and, human, he draws back
   From the interior cold, the mercilessness
That yet shows a kind of mercy sustaining him.
   The last sun of the year is drying his skin
Above a surface a mere mosaic of tiny shatterings,   45
   Where a wind is unscaping[7] all images in the flowing obsidian,
The going-elsewhere of ripples incessantly shaping.

                                                   1968

Snapshot

for Yoshikazu Uehata

      Your camera
      has caught it all, the lit
      angle where ceiling and wall
      create their corner, the flame
      in the grate, the light   5
      down the window frame
      and along the hair
      of the girl seated there, her face
      not quite in focus—that
      is as it should be, too,   10
      for, once seen, Eden
      is in flight from you, and yet

---

7. That is, unlandscaping or unseascaping (Tomlinson's invention).

you have set it down complete
with the asymmetries
of journal, cushion, cup,   15
all we might then have missed
in that gone moment when
we were living it.

1995

GALWAY KINNELL
b. 1927

Galway Kinnell is one of those postwar poets who, like Robert Lowell, began his career writing in traditional forms and suddenly felt compelled to find looser ones. Under Walt Whitman's influence, Kinnell learned to shrug off regular meters, capture strong cadences, repeat, chant responsively to the world, and extend his lines, which sometimes vary wildly in length. The compulsion to strip away civilizing norms and dwell in the rough of nature is already evident in such neatly rhymed poems as "First Song," in which a boy's "first song of his happiness" awakens his "heart to the darkness and into the sadness of joy." For Kinnell, poetry is about the "sadness of joy," about the deaths and losses that haunt happiness. Even so, his many elegiac poems for dead family members and friends often convey, paradoxically, physical exuberance and strength. In "On the Oregon Coast," he dryly mentions in one line the recent deaths of two fellow poets, and in the next he recovers something of the wild power and recursive movement of the ocean: "James Wright went back to the end. So did Richard Hugo. / The waves coming in burst up through their crests and fly very brilliant back out to sea. / The log gets up yet again, goes rolling and bouncing down the beach, plunges as though for good into the water." Loss continually reawakens Kinnell to the world's vitality. The earthy pleasures of sex, love, and family life are also among his subjects, and he engages domestic themes with tenderness and humor in "After Making Love We Hear Footsteps."

Kinnell was born on February 1, 1927, in Providence, Rhode Island, the son of immigrants from Ireland (his mother) and Scotland (his father). After serving in the navy during World War II, he received a B.A. at Princeton University, where he exchanged poetry with his contemporary W. S. Merwin, and an M.A. at the University of Rochester; but the process of writing poetry has been for him largely a process of de-educating himself, so as to come closer to a world whose existence he at first only suspected. In the 1960s, he took odd jobs, worked as a member of CORE (Congress of Racial Equality) to register southern black voters, and demonstrated against the Vietnam War. He has taught at more than twenty colleges and universities in the United States and other parts of the world; since 1981, at New York University. His poetry has won various awards, among them the Pulitzer Prize for *Selected Poems* (1983). In 1984, he received a MacArthur Fellowship.

First Song

Then it was dusk in Illinois, the small boy
After an afternoon of carting dung
Hung on the rail fence, a sapped thing
Weary to crying. Dark was growing tall
And he began to hear the pond frogs all   5
Calling on his ear with what seemed their joy.

Soon their sound was pleasant for a boy
Listening in the smoky dusk and the nightfall
Of Illinois, and from the fields two small
Boys came bearing cornstalk violins   10
And they rubbed the cornstalk bows with resins
And the three sat there scraping of their joy.

It was now fine music the frogs and the boys
Did in the towering Illinois twilight make
And into dark in spite of a shoulder's ache   15
A boy's hunched body loved out of a stalk
The first song of his happiness, and the song woke
His heart to the darkness and into the sadness of joy.

1960

After Making Love We Hear Footsteps

For I can snore like a bullhorn
or play loud music
or sit up talking with any reasonably sober Irishman
and Fergus will only sink deeper
into his dreamless sleep, which goes by all in one flash,   5
but let there be that heavy breathing
or a stifled come-cry anywhere in the house
and he will wrench himself awake
and make for it on the run—as now, we lie together,
after making love, quiet, touching along the length of our bodies,   10
familiar touch of the long-married,
and he appears—in his baseball pajamas, it happens,
the neck opening so small
he has to screw them on, which one day may make him wonder
about the mental capacity of baseball players—   15
and flops down between us and hugs us and snuggles himself to sleep,
his face gleaming with satisfaction at being this very child.

In the half darkness we look at each other
and smile
and touch arms across his little, startlingly muscled body—   20
this one whom habit of memory propels to the ground of his making,

sleeper only the mortal sounds can sing awake,
this blessing love gives again into our arms.

1980

On the Oregon Coast

In memoriam Richard Hugo[1]

Six or seven rows of waves struggle landward.
The wind batters a pewtery sheen on the water between them.
As each wave makes its way in, most of it gets blown back out to sea,
    subverting even necessity.
The bass rumble of sea stones, audible when the waves flee all broken
    back out to sea, itself blows out to sea.
Now a log maybe thirty feet long and six across gets up and trundles down   5
    the beach.
Like a dog fetching a stick it flops unhesitatingly into the water.
An enormous wave at once sends it wallowing back up the beach again.
It lies among other driftwood, almost panting. Sure enough, after a few
    minutes it gets up, trundles down the beach, throws itself into the
    water again.
The last time I was on this coast Richard Hugo and I had dinner together
    just north of here, in a restaurant overlooking the sea.
The conversation came around to personification.   10
We agreed that eighteenth- and nineteenth-century poets almost *had* to
    personify, it was like mouth-to-mouth resuscitation, the only way
    they could imagine to keep the world from turning into dead matter.
And that as post-Darwinians[2] it was up to us to anthropomorphize the
    world less and animalize, vegetable-ize, and mineralize ourselves
    more.
We doubted that pre-Darwinian language would let us.
Our talk turned to James Wright,[3] how his kinship with salamanders,
    spiders, and mosquitoes allowed him to drift his way back through
    the evolutionary stages.
When a group of people gets up from a table, the table doesn't know which   15
    way any of them will go.
James Wright went back to the end. So did Richard Hugo.
The waves coming in burst up through their crests and fly very brilliant
    back out to sea.
The log gets up yet again, goes rolling and bouncing down the beach,
    plunges as though for good into the water.

1985

---

1. American poet (1923–1982).
2. That is, after Charles Darwin (1809–1882), the   naturalist responsible for the theory of evolution.
  3. American poet (1927–1980).

Sheffield Ghazal[4] 4: Driving West

A tractor-trailer carrying two dozen crushed automobiles overtakes a
    tractor-trailer carrying a dozen new.
Oil is a form of waiting.
The internal combustion engine converts the stasis of millennia into
    motion.
Cars howl on rain-wetted roads.
Airplanes rise through the downpour and throw us through the blue   5
    sky.
The idea of the airplane subverts earthly life.
Computers can deliver nuclear explosions to precisely anywhere on
    earth.
A lightning bolt is made entirely of error.
Erratic Mercurys and errant Cavaliers wander the highways.
A girl puts her head on a boy's shoulder; they are driving west.   10
The windshield wipers wipe, homesickness one way, wanderlust the
    other, back and forth.
This happened to your father and to you, Galway—sick to stay, longing
    to come up against the ends of the earth, and climb over.

1994

---

4. Lyric genre of Persian and Arabic poetry dating back to the seventh century. Among its requirements
are thematic discontinuity and the appearance of the poet's name in the penultimate line.

JOHN ASHBERY
b. 1927

John Ashbery, once set aside as bizarre, is one of the central American poets of the
latter half of the twentieth century. Perhaps no postwar writer has influenced so many
different kinds of poets, whether identified with formalism or antiformalism, with neo-
confessionalism or the avant-garde. His work is written in seemingly antithetical modes,
from fragmentary free verse and prose poetry to traditional verse forms such as sonnets,
sestinas, and blank verse. It spans a variety of styles, from the early, collage-based
experimentalism of *The Tennis Court Oath* (1962) to the poignant lyricism of his middle
work. Ashbery had many associations with the New York school, especially with Ken-
neth Koch and Frank O'Hara (whom he met at Harvard University), and he uses equally
wild and witty imagery. Because of his exploration of inner experience, Ashbery has also
been linked with the Romantic tradition, from Percy Bysshe Shelley to Wallace Stevens.
Because of his poetics of collage, multiple identities, and verbal games, he has been
seen, too, as an important precursor to Language poets such as Charles Bernstein. And
yet, for all these associations, Ashbery has a unique manner—characteristically mixing
surrealist tomfoolery and elegant reserve—that is convincing, though one cannot always
fathom what one is being convinced of. Often, Ashbery appears to be writing on the
basis of postulates that are firm but never divulged. A dreamlike quality ensues, and
Ashbery would like to "reproduce the power dreams have of persuading you that a

certain event has a meaning not logically connected with it, or that there is a hidden relation among disparate objects" (quoted in Richard Howard, *Alone with America*). The strangeness and authority of his poetry have drawn readers despite the hiddenness of many of its relations.

In Ashbery's poetry, the self is elusive, multiple, and fractious, shot through with competing discourses, always dissolving into the past and into parody. Similarly, the so-called real world is forever mutating and slipping away, receding from view, vanishing into hints and reflections. Ashbery responds to this postmodern condition of flux and disjunctiveness with a mixture of elegiac pathos and whimsical pleasure. As he suggests in "Soonest Mended," his poetics is "a kind of fence-sitting / Raised to the level of an esthetic ideal." His poems mourn various losses while romping riotously in free associations. They walk the knife's edge between the personal and the impersonal, evoking both inner experience and yet also a strange objectification of subjectivity, often disguising, abstracting, or fragmenting the autobiographical subject. "Most of my poems are about the experience of experience," Ashbery said in a 1981 interview. "I'm trying to set down a generalized transcript of what's really going on in our minds all day long."

Ashbery's poems are resolutely contrary to fact or tangential to it. "Worsening Situation" ends: "My wife / Thinks I'm in Oslo—Oslo, France, that is." Since there is no Oslo, France, the speaker's wife is twice deluded. But delusion and imagination go together. In a more accessible poem, "The Instruction Manual," the poet procrastinates by conjuring up a journey to Guadalajara, which he describes like some archetypal traveler, although he admits he has never been there. Ashbery presents reality as do some modern painters, organizing details to create nature rather than to imitate it. Old bonding techniques between people, their surroundings, and divinity no longer work. "You can't say it that way any more," he declares in "And *Ut Pictura Poesis* Is Her Name." Sometimes, as with action painters, the process of poeticizing obsesses him; he describes it amusingly yet seriously too in the same poem: "The extreme austerity of an almost empty mind / Colliding with the lush, Rousseau-like foliage of its desire to communicate / Something between breaths." In "What Is Poetry," he asks whether poetry is beautiful images, or the attempt "to avoid / Ideas, as in this poem." Or do we "Go back to them as to a wife, leaving / The mistress we desire?" The series of questions is never answered, but his poems do have ideas as well as images, though these ideas are given provisional status only, dependent on a reality that resists summary and analysis. He is endlessly resourceful in propounding this dilemma. In "Self-Portrait in a Convex Mirror," a masterpiece based on a painting by Parmigianino, Ashbery plays with the distorting effect of such a mirror held up to nature. He seems to defend his own work when he says, "But your eyes proclaim / That everything is surface. The surface is what's there / And nothing can exist except what's there." Then he adds, "it is not / Superficial but a visible core."

Sequence and causality are both in jeopardy in Ashbery's work; he is fond of unexpected juxtapositions, such as of the divine sepulcher and Cohen's Drug Store. Sentences fragment or run on, narrative proceeds by non sequiturs, and pronouns ambiguously crisscross. Images and ideas melt into one another. Contemporary jargons of business, journalism, bureaucracy, and advertising are absorbed and parodied. Levels of diction are manipulated along with places. Clichés are echoed and transformed. Ashbery seems to ask his readers to put aside their presuppositions about reading and about experiencing, and instead to observe collisions of images and ideas without asking for logical paraphrases. The tenor of his work is "pure / Affirmation that doesn't affirm anything" ("Self-Portrait in a Convex Mirror"). The world is strange, opaque, and mercurial. Wit and circumspection are the means to write about it.

Ashbery was born on July 28, 1927, in Rochester, New York, and grew up on a fruit farm in upstate New York near Lake Ontario. He received his B.A. from Harvard University in 1949 with a thesis on W. H. Auden, who chose and introduced Ashbery's first book, *Some Trees*, for the Yale Series of Younger Poets in 1956. In 1951, Ashbery completed an M.A. thesis at Columbia University on Henry Green, the witty, impersonal English novelist. During the Korean War, he was exempted from military service only after going on government record as a homosexual. Ashbery found the McCarthy era frightening and depressing; he went to France as a Fulbright Scholar (1955–57) and embarked on a book on Raymond Roussel, a writer who declared his books had been composed not out of experience but out of verbal games. Ashbery returned to France in 1958 and stayed until 1965, writing art criticism for the European edition of the *New York Herald Tribune* and for *Art News*. Returning to New York in 1965, he edited *Art News* until 1972, and he was later the art critic for *Newsweek*. He taught at Brooklyn College from 1974 to 1990 and, since 1990, has taught at Bard College. Among the many books he has published and the many awards he has received, *Self-Portrait in a Convex Mirror* notably won the three major poetry prizes of 1976—the Pulitzer Prize, the National Book Award, and the National Book Critics Circle Award.

Though many literary predecessors have been proposed for him, Ashbery has cited the early Auden, Laura Riding, and Wallace Stevens as "the writers who most formed my language as a poet" (quoted in *The New York School Poets*, ed. John Bernard Myers, 1969). To be tough, incisive, and mellifluous was perhaps the lesson he derived from these three writers. The musical aspect of his verse has always been important to him: "What I like about music is its ability of being convincing, of carrying an argument through successfully to the finish, though the terms of this argument remain unknown quantities. What remains is the structure, the architecture of the argument, scene or story. I would like to do this in poetry" (biographical note in *A Controversy of Poets*, 1965).

Some Trees

These are amazing: each
Joining a neighbor, as though speech
Were a still performance.
Arranging by chance

To meet as far this morning   5
From the world as agreeing
With it, you and I
Are suddenly what the trees try

To tell us we are:
That their merely being there   10
Means something; that soon
We may touch, love, explain.

And glad not to have invented
Such comeliness, we are surrounded:
A silence already filled with noises,   15
A canvas on which emerges

A chorus of smiles, a winter morning.
Placed in a puzzling light, and moving,
Our days put on such reticence
These accents seem their own defense.   20

1956

The Instruction Manual

As I sit looking out of a window of the building
I wish I did not have to write the instruction manual on the uses of a new
    metal.
I look down into the street and see people, each walking with an inner
    peace,
And envy them—they are so far away from me!
Not one of them has to worry about getting out this manual on schedule.   5
And, as my way is, I begin to dream, resting my elbows on the desk and
    leaning out of the window a little,
Of dim Guadalajara! City of rose-colored flowers!
City I wanted most to see, and most did not see, in Mexico!
But I fancy I see, under the press of having to write the instruction
    manual,
Your public square, city, with its elaborate little bandstand!   10
The band is playing *Scheherazade* by Rimsky-Korsakov.[1]
Around stand the flower girls, handing out rose- and lemon-colored
    flowers,
Each attractive in her rose-and-blue striped dress (Oh! such shades of
    rose and blue),
And nearby is the little white booth where women in green serve you green
    and yellow fruit.
The couples are parading; everyone is in a holiday mood.   15
First, leading the parade, is a dapper fellow
Clothed in deep blue. On his head sits a white hat
And he wears a mustache, which has been trimmed for the occasion.
His dear one, his wife, is young and pretty; her shawl is rose, pink, and
    white.
Her slippers are patent leather, in the American fashion,   20
And she carries a fan, for she is modest, and does not want the crowd to
    see her face too often.
But everybody is so busy with his wife or loved one
I doubt they would notice the mustachioed man's wife.
Here come the boys! They are skipping and throwing little things on the
    sidewalk
Which is made of gray tile. One of them, a little older, has a toothpick in 25
    his teeth.
He is silenter than the rest, and affects not to notice the pretty young girls
    in white.
But his friends notice them, and shout their jeers at the laughing girls.

---

1. Russian composer (1844–1908).

Yet soon all this will cease, with the deepening of their years,
And love bring each to the parade grounds for another reason.
But I have lost sight of the young fellow with the toothpick.   30
Wait—there he is—on the other side of the bandstand,
Secluded from his friends, in earnest talk with a young girl
Of fourteen or fifteen. I try to hear what they are saying
But it seems they are just mumbling something—shy words of love,
    probably.
She is slightly taller than he, and looks quietly down into his sincere eyes. 35
She is wearing white. The breeze ruffles her long fine black hair against
    her olive cheek.
Obviously she is in love. The boy, the young boy with the toothpick, he is
    in love too;
His eyes show it. Turning from this couple,
I see there is an intermission in the concert.
The paraders are resting and sipping drinks through straws   40
(The drinks are dispensed from a large glass crock by a lady in dark blue),
And the musicians mingle among them, in their creamy white uniforms,
    and talk
About the weather, perhaps, or how their kids are doing at school.

Let us take this opportunity to tiptoe into one of the side streets.
Here you may see one of those white houses with green trim   45
That are so popular here. Look—I told you!
It is cool and dim inside, but the patio is sunny.
An old woman in gray sits there, fanning herself with a palm leaf fan.
She welcomes us to her patio, and offers us a cooling drink.
"My son is in Mexico City," she says. "He would welcome you too   50
If he were here. But his job is with a bank there.
Look, here is a photograph of him."
And a dark-skinned lad with pearly teeth grins out at us from the worn
    leather frame.
We thank her for her hospitality, for it is getting late
And we must catch a view of the city, before we leave, from a good high   55
    place.
That church tower will do—the faded pink one, there against the fierce
    blue of the sky. Slowly we enter.
The caretaker, an old man dressed in brown and gray, asks us how long
    we have been in the city, and how we like it here.
His daughter is scrubbing the steps—she nods to us as we pass into the
    tower.
Soon we have reached the top, and the whole network of the city extends
    before us.
There is the rich quarter, with its houses of pink and white, and its   60
    crumbling, leafy terraces.
There is the poorer quarter, its homes a deep blue.
There is the market, where men are selling hats and swatting flies
And there is the public library, painted several shades of pale green and
    beige.
Look! There is the square we just came from, with the promenaders.
There are fewer of them, now that the heat of the day has increased,   65
But the young boy and girl still lurk in the shadows of the bandstand.

And there is the home of the little old lady—
She is still sitting in the patio, fanning herself.
How limited, but how complete withal, has been our experience of
    Guadalajara!
We have seen young love, married love, and the love of an aged mother   70
    for her son.
We have heard the music, tasted the drinks, and looked at colored houses.
What more is there to do, except stay? And that we cannot do.
And as a last breeze freshens the top of the weathered old tower, I turn
    my gaze
Back to the instruction manual which has made me dream of Guadalajara.

1956

The Tennis Court Oath[2]

What had you been thinking about
the face studiously bloodied
heaven blotted region
I go on loving you like water but
there is a terrible breath in the way all of this   5
You were not elected president, yet won the race
All the way through fog and drizzle
When you read it was sincere the coasts
stammered with unintentional villages the
horse strains fatigued I guess . . . the calls . . .   10
I worry

the water beetle head
why of course reflecting all
then you redid you were breathing
I thought going down to mail this   15
of the kettle you jabbered as easily in the yard
you come through but
are incomparable the lovely tent
mystery you don't want surrounded the real
you dance   20
in the spring there was clouds

The mulatress[3] approached in the hall—the
lettering easily visible along the edge of the *Times*
in a moment the bell would ring but there was time
for the carnation laughed here are a couple of "other"   25

to one in yon house

---

2. During the first days of the French Revolution, on June 20, 1789, the commoners (Third Estate) were barred from a regular meeting of the Estates General. They retired to a nearby indoor tennis court and took an oath to stand together until the Constitution was reformed. The oath is the subject of a painting by French painter Jacques-Louis David (1748–1825).

3. Female mulatto (person of mixed white and black ancestry).

The doctor and Philip had come over the road
Turning in toward the corner of the wall his hat on
reading it carelessly as if to tell you your fears were justified
the blood shifted you know those walls   30
wind off the earth had made him shrink
undeniably an oboe now the young
were there there was candy
to decide the sharp edge of the garment
like a particular cry not intervening called the dog "he's coming! he's   35
    coming" with an emotion felt it sink into peace
there was no turning back but the end was in sight
he chose this moment to ask her in detail about her family and the
    others
The person.   pleaded—"have more of these
not stripes on the tunic—or the porch chairs
will teach you about men—what it means"   40
to be one in a million pink stripe
and now could go away the three approached the doghouse
the reef.   Your daughter's
dream of my son understand prejudice
darkness in the hole   45
the patient finished
They could all go home now the hole was dark
lilacs blowing across his face glad he brought you

                                                                          1962

These Lacustrine[4] Cities

These lacustrine cities grew out of loathing
Into something forgetful, although angry with history.
They are the product of an idea : that man is horrible, for instance,
Though this is only one example.

They emerged until a tower   5
Controlled the sky, and with artifice dipped back
Into the past for swans and tapering branches,
Burning, until all that hate was transformed into useless love.

Then you are left with an idea of yourself
And the feeling of ascending emptiness of the afternoon   10
Which must be charged to the embarrassment of others
Who fly by you like beacons.

The night is a sentinel.
Much of your time has been occupied by creative games
Until now, but we have all-inclusive plans for you.   15
We had thought, for instance, of sending you to the middle of the desert,

---

4. Having to do with lakes.

To a violent sea, or of having the closeness of the others be air
To you, pressing you back into a startled dream
As sea-breezes greet a child's face.
But the past is already here, and you are nursing some private project.   20

The worst is not over, yet I know
You will be happy here. Because of the logic
Of your situation, which is something no climate can outsmart.
Tender and insouciant by turns, you see

You have built a mountain of something,   25
Thoughtfully pouring all your energy into this single monument,
Whose wind is desire starching a petal,
Whose disappointment broke into a rainbow of tears.

                                                                        1966

Soonest Mended[5]

Barely tolerated, living on the margin
In our technological society, we were always having to be rescued
On the brink of destruction, like heroines in *Orlando Furioso*
Before it was time to start all over again.
There would be thunder in the bushes, a rustling of coils,   5
And Angelica, in the Ingres painting,[6] was considering
The colorful but small monster near her toe, as though wondering whether
        forgetting
The whole thing might not, in the end, be the only solution.
And then there always came a time when
Happy Hooligan[7] in his rusted green automobile   10
Came plowing down the course, just to make sure everything was O.K.,
Only by that time we were in another chapter and confused
About how to receive this latest piece of information.
Was it information? Weren't we rather acting this out
For someone else's benefit, thoughts in a mind   15
With room enough and to spare for our little problems (so they began to
        seem),
Our daily quandary about food and the rent and bills to be paid?
To reduce all this to a small variant,
To step free at last, minuscule on the gigantic plateau—
This was our ambition: to be small and clear and free.   20
Alas, the summer's energy wanes quickly,
A moment and it is gone. And no longer
May we make the necessary arrangements, simple as they are.
Our star was brighter perhaps when it had water in it.
Now there is no question even of that, but only   25

5. From the proverb "Least said, soonest mend-
ed."
6. *Roger Delivering Angelica*, by French painter
Jean-Auguste Dominique Ingres (1780–1867),
depicts a scene from *Orlando Furioso,* a fantastic
epic by Italian author Ludovico Ariosto (1474–
1533). The heroine is often rescued from mon-
sters, ogres, and other perils.
7. Character from a newspaper comic strip.

Of holding on to the hard earth so as not to get thrown off,
With an occasional dream, a vision: a robin flies across
The upper corner of the window, you brush your hair away
And cannot quite see, or a wound will flash
Against the sweet faces of the others, something like: 30
This is what you wanted to hear, so why
Did you think of listening to something else? We are all talkers
It is true, but underneath the talk lies
The moving and not wanting to be moved, the loose
Meaning, untidy and simple like a threshing floor.   35

These then were some hazards of the course,
Yet though we knew the course *was* hazards and nothing else
It was still a shock when, almost a quarter of a century later,
The clarity of the rules dawned on you for the first time.
They were the players, and we who had struggled at the game   40
Were merely spectators, though subject to its vicissitudes
And moving with it out of the tearful stadium, borne on shoulders, at last.
Night after night this message returns, repeated
In the flickering bulbs of the sky, raised past us, taken away from us,
Yet ours over and over until the end that is past truth,   45
The being of our sentences, in the climate that fostered them,
Not ours to own, like a book, but to be with, and sometimes
To be without, alone and desperate.
But the fantasy makes it ours, a kind of fence-sitting
Raised to the level of an esthetic ideal. These were moments, years,   50
Solid with reality, faces, namable events, kisses, heroic acts,
But like the friendly beginning of a geometrical progression
Not too reassuring, as though meaning could be cast aside some day
When it had been outgrown. Better, you said, to stay cowering
Like this in the early lessons, since the promise of learning   55
Is a delusion, and I agreed, adding that
Tomorrow would alter the sense of what had already been learned,
That the learning process is extended in this way, so that from this
        standpoint
None of us ever graduates from college,
For time is an emulsion, and probably thinking not to grow up   60
Is the brightest kind of maturity for us, right now at any rate.
And you see, both of us were right, though nothing
Has somehow come to nothing; the avatars[8]
Of our conforming to the rules and living
Around the home have made—well, in a sense, "good citizens" of us,   65
Brushing the teeth and all that, and learning to accept
The charity of the hard moments as they are doled out,
For this is action, this not being sure, this careless
Preparing, sowing the seeds crooked in the furrow,
Making ready to forget, and always coming back   70
To the mooring of starting out, that day so long ago.

                                                                    1970

---

8. Incarnations.

Farm Implements and Rutabagas in a Landscape[9]

The first of the undecoded messages read: "Popeye[1] sits in thunder,
Unthought of. From that shoebox of an apartment,
From livid curtain's hue, a tangram[2] emerges: a country."
Meanwhile the Sea Hag was relaxing on a green couch: "How pleasant
To spend one's vacation *en la casa de Popeye*,"[3] she scratched   5
Her cleft chin's solitary hair. She remembered spinach

And was going to ask Wimpy if he had bought any spinach.
"M'love," he intercepted, "the plains are decked out in thunder
Today, and it shall be as you wish." He scratched
The part of his head under his hat. The apartment   10
Seemed to grow smaller. "But what if no pleasant
Inspiration plunge us now to the stars? *For this is my country.*"

Suddenly they remembered how it was cheaper in the country.
Wimpy was thoughtfully cutting open a number 2 can of spinach
When the door opened and Swee'pea crept in. "How pleasant!"   15
But Swee'pea looked morose. A note was pinned to his bib. "Thunder
And tears are unavailing," it read. "Henceforth shall Popeye's apartment
Be but remembered space, toxic or salubrious, whole or scratched."

Olive came hurtling through the window; its geraniums scratched
Her long thigh. "I have news!" she gasped. "Popeye, forced as you know   20
    to flee the country
One musty gusty evening, by the schemes of his wizened, duplicate
    father, jealous of the apartment
And all that it contains, myself and spinach
In particular, heaves bolts of loving thunder
At his own astonished becoming, rupturing the pleasant

Arpeggio[4] of our years. No more shall pleasant   25
Rays of the sun refresh your sense of growing old, nor the scratched
Tree-trunks and mossy foliage, only immaculate darkness and thunder."
She grabbed Swee'pea. "I'm taking the brat to the country."
"But you can't do that—he hasn't even finished his spinach,"
Urged the Sea Hag, looking fearfully around at the apartment.   30

But Olive was already out of earshot. Now the apartment
Succumbed to a strange new hush. "Actually it's quite pleasant
Here," thought the Sea Hag. "If this is all we need fear from spinach
Then I don't mind so much. Perhaps we could invite Alice the Goon
    over"—she scratched

---

9. Play on the title of the painting *Farm Implements and Vegetables in a Landscape,* by Dutch landscape painter Jacob van Ruysdael (1628–1682).
1. The popular American comic-strip characters Popeye, Olive Oyl, Swee'pea, and Wimpy were created by E. C. Segar (1894–1938) in 1929. When

Ashbery wrote the poem, the strip *Popeye the Sailor* appeared in New York City only in the Spanish-language newspaper *El Diario.*
2. Geometric puzzle.
3. In Popeye's house (Spanish).
4. Notes of a chord played in succession.

One dug pensively—"but Wimpy is such a country   35
Bumpkin, always burping like that." Minute at first, the thunder

Soon filled the apartment. It was domestic thunder,
The color of spinach. Popeye chuckled and scratched
His balls: it sure was pleasant to spend a day in the country.

                                                                  1970

As One Put Drunk into the Packet-Boat[5]

I tried each thing, only some were immortal and free.
Elsewhere we are as sitting in a place where sunlight
Filters down, a little at a time,
Waiting for someone to come. Harsh words are spoken,
As the sun yellows the green of the maple tree. . . .   5

So this was all, but obscurely
I felt the stirrings of new breath in the pages
Which all winter long had smelled like an old catalogue.
New sentences were starting up. But the summer
Was well along, not yet past the mid-point   10
But full and dark with the promise of that fullness,
That time when one can no longer wander away
And even the least attentive fall silent
To watch the thing that is prepared to happen.

A look of glass stops you   15
And you walk on shaken: was I the perceived?
Did they notice me, this time, as I am,
Or is it postponed again? The children
Still at their games, clouds that arise with a swift
Impatience in the afternoon sky, then dissipate   20
As limpid, dense twilight comes.
Only in that tooting of a horn
Down there, for a moment, I thought
The great, formal affair was beginning, orchestrated,
Its colors concentrated in a glance, a ballade   25
That takes in the whole world, now, but lightly,
Still lightly, but with wide authority and tact.

The prevalence of those gray flakes falling?
They are sun motes. You have slept in the sun
Longer than the sphinx,[6] and are none the wiser for it.   30
Come in. And I thought a shadow fell across the door
But it was only her come to ask once more
If I was coming in, and not to hurry in case I wasn't.

5. The title of Ashbery's poem is the first line of
the poem "Tom May's Death," by English poet
Andrew Marvell (1621–1678).
6. Mythical creature with a human head and lion's
body. In Greek legend, it kills those who fail to
answer its riddle. At Giza, Egypt, is the colossal
statue of the recumbent sphinx.

The night sheen takes over. A moon of cistercian[7] pallor
Has climbed to the center of heaven, installed,   35
Finally involved with the business of darkness.
And a sigh heaves from all the small things on earth,
The books, the papers, the old garters and union-suit buttons
Kept in a white cardboard box somewhere, and all the lower
Versions of cities flattened under the equalizing night.   40
The summer demands and takes away too much,
But night, the reserved, the reticent, gives more than it takes.

1975

Self-Portrait in a Convex Mirror

As Parmigianino[8] did it, the right hand
Bigger than the head, thrust at the viewer
And swerving easily away, as though to protect
What it advertises. A few leaded panes, old beams,
Fur, pleated muslin, a coral ring run together   5
In a movement supporting the face, which swims
Toward and away like the hand
Except that it is in repose. It is what is
Sequestered. Vasari says, "Francesco one day set himself
To take his own portrait, looking at himself for that purpose   10
In a convex mirror, such as is used by barbers . . .
He accordingly caused a ball of wood to be made
By a turner, and having divided it in half and
Brought it to the size of the mirror, he set himself
With great art to copy all that he saw in the glass,"[9]   15
Chiefly his reflection, of which the portrait
Is the reflection once removed.
The glass chose to reflect only what he saw
Which was enough for his purpose: his image
Glazed, embalmed, projected at a 180-degree angle.   20
The time of day or the density of the light
Adhering to the face keeps it
Lively and intact in a recurring wave
Of arrival. The soul establishes itself.
But how far can it swim out through the eyes   25
And still return safely to its nest? The surface
Of the mirror being convex, the distance increases
Significantly; that is, enough to make the point
That the soul is a captive, treated humanely, kept
In suspension, unable to advance much farther   30
Than your look as it intercepts the picture.

7. Ascetic monastic order; that is, somber and
subdued.
8. Parmigianino (Girolamo Francesco Mazzola,
1503–1540) is the Italian Mannerist artist who
painted *Self-Portrait in a Convex Mirror* (c. 1524).

9. Quotation from *Lives of the Most Eminent Ital-
ian Painters, Sculptors, and Architects* (1550), by
Italian artist and historian Giorgio Vasari (1511–
1574), as translated by Mrs. Jonathan Foster.

Pope Clement[1] and his court were "stupefied"
By it, according to Vasari, and promised a commission
That never materialized. The soul has to stay where it is,
Even though restless, hearing raindrops at the pane,   35
The sighing of autumn leaves thrashed by the wind,
Longing to be free, outside, but it must stay
Posing in this place. It must move
As little as possible. This is what the portrait says.
But there is in that gaze a combination   40
Of tenderness, amusement and regret, so powerful
In its restraint that one cannot look for long.
The secret is too plain. The pity of it smarts,
Makes hot tears spurt: that the soul is not a soul,
Has no secret, is small, and it fits   45
Its hollow perfectly: its room, our moment of attention.
That is the tune but there are no words.
The words are only speculation
(From the Latin *speculum*, mirror):
They seek and cannot find the meaning of the music.   50
We see only postures of the dream,
Riders of the motion that swings the face
Into view under evening skies, with no
False disarray as proof of authenticity.
But it is life englobed.   55
One would like to stick one's hand
Out of the globe, but its dimension,
What carries it, will not allow it.
No doubt it is this, not the reflex
To hide something, which makes the hand loom large   60
As it retreats slightly. There is no way
To build it flat like a section of wall:
It must join the segment of a circle,
Roving back to the body of which it seems
So unlikely a part, to fence in and shore up the face   65
On which the effort of this condition reads
Like a pinpoint of a smile, a spark
Or star one is not sure of having seen
As darkness resumes. A perverse light whose
Imperative of subtlety dooms in advance its   70
Conceit to light up: unimportant but meant.
Francesco, your hand is big enough
To wreck the sphere, and too big,
One would think, to weave delicate meshes
That only argue its further detention.   75
(Big, but not coarse, merely on another scale,
Like a dozing whale on the sea bottom
In relation to the tiny, self-important ship
On the surface.) But your eyes proclaim
That everything is surface. The surface is what's there   80
And nothing can exist except what's there.

---

1. Pope Clement VII (1478–1534).

There are no recesses in the room, only alcoves,
And the window doesn't matter much, or that
Sliver of window or mirror on the right, even
As a gauge of the weather, which in French is   85
Le temps, the word for time, and which
Follows a course wherein changes are merely
Features of the whole. The whole is stable within
Instability, a globe like ours, resting
On a pedestal of vacuum, a ping-pong ball   90
Secure on its jet of water.
And just as there are no words for the surface, that is,
No words to say what it really is, that it is not
Superficial but a visible core, then there is
No way out of the problem of pathos vs. experience.   95
You will stay on, restive, serene in
Your gesture which is neither embrace nor warning
But which holds something of both in pure
Affirmation that doesn't affirm anything.

The balloon pops, the attention   100
Turns dully away. Clouds
In the puddle stir up into sawtoothed fragments.
I think of the friends
Who came to see me, of what yesterday
Was like. A peculiar slant   105
Of memory that intrudes on the dreaming model
In the silence of the studio as he considers
Lifting the pencil to the self-portrait.
How many people came and stayed a certain time,
Uttered light or dark speech that became part of you   110
Like light behind windblown fog and sand,
Filtered and influenced by it, until no part
Remains that is surely you. Those voices in the dusk
Have told you all and still the tale goes on
In the form of memories deposited in irregular   115
Clumps of crystals. Whose curved hand controls,
Francesco, the turning seasons and the thoughts
That peel off and fly away at breathless speeds
Like the last stubborn leaves ripped
From wet branches? I see in this only the chaos   120
Of your round mirror which organizes everything
Around the polestar of your eyes which are empty,
Know nothing, dream but reveal nothing.
I feel the carousel starting slowly
And going faster and faster: desk, papers, books,   125
Photographs of friends, the window and the trees
Merging in one neutral band that surrounds
Me on all sides, everywhere I look.
And I cannot explain the action of leveling,
Why it should all boil down to one   130
Uniform substance, a magma of interiors.
My guide in these matters is your self,

Firm, oblique, accepting everything with the same
Wraith of a smile, and as time speeds up so that it is soon
Much later, I can know only the straight way out,   135
The distance between us. Long ago
The strewn evidence meant something,
The small accidents and pleasures
Of the day as it moved gracelessly on,
A housewife doing chores. Impossible now   140
To restore those properties in the silver blur that is
The record of what you accomplished by sitting down
"With great art to copy all that you saw in the glass"
So as to perfect and rule out the extraneous
Forever. In the circle of your intentions certain spars   145
Remain that perpetuate the enchantment of self with self:
Eyebeams, muslin, coral. It doesn't matter
Because these are things as they are today
Before one's shadow ever grew
Out of the field into thoughts of tomorrow.   150

Tomorrow is easy, but today is uncharted,
Desolate, reluctant as any landscape
To yield what are laws of perspective
After all only to the painter's deep
Mistrust, a weak instrument though   155
Necessary. Of course some things
Are possible, it knows, but it doesn't know
Which ones. Some day we will try
To do as many things as are possible
And perhaps we shall succeed at a handful   160
Of them, but this will not have anything
To do with what is promised today, our
Landscape sweeping out from us to disappear
On the horizon. Today enough of a cover burnishes
To keep the supposition of promises together   165
In one piece of surface, letting one ramble
Back home from them so that these
Even stronger possibilities can remain
Whole without being tested. Actually
The skin of the bubble-chamber's as tough as   170
Reptile eggs; everything gets "programmed" there
In due course: more keeps getting included
Without adding to the sum, and just as one
Gets accustomed to a noise that
Kept one awake but now no longer does,   175
So the room contains this flow like an hourglass
Without varying in climate or quality
(Except perhaps to brighten bleakly and almost
Invisibly, in a focus of sharpening toward death—more
Of this later). What should be the vacuum of a dream   180
Becomes continually replete as the source of dreams
Is being tapped so that this one dream
May wax, flourish like a cabbage rose,

Defying sumptuary laws,[2] leaving us
To awake and try to begin living in what   185
Has now become a slum. Sydney Freedberg in his
Parmigianino says of it: "Realism in this portrait
No longer produces an objective truth, but a *bizarria*[3] . . .
However its distortion does not create
A feeling of disharmony. . . . The forms retain   190
A strong measure of ideal beauty," because
Fed by our dreams, so inconsequential until one day
We notice the hole they left. Now their importance
If not their meaning is plain. They were to nourish
A dream which includes them all, as they are   195
Finally reversed in the accumulating mirror.
They seemed strange because we couldn't actually see them.
And we realize this only at a point where they lapse
Like a wave breaking on a rock, giving up
Its shape in a gesture which expresses that shape.   200
The forms retain a strong measure of ideal beauty
As they forage in secret on our idea of distortion.
Why be unhappy with this arrangement, since
Dreams prolong us as they are absorbed?
Something like living occurs, a movement   205
Out of the dream into its codification.

As I start to forget it
It presents its stereotype again
But it is an unfamiliar stereotype, the face
Riding at anchor, issued from hazards, soon   210
To accost others, "rather angel than man" (Vasari).
Perhaps an angel looks like everything
We have forgotten, I mean forgotten
Things that don't seem familiar when
We meet them again, lost beyond telling   215
Which were ours once. This would be the point
Of invading the privacy of this man who
"Dabbled in alchemy, but whose wish
Here was not to examine the subtleties of art
In a detached, scientific spirit: he wished through them   220
To impart the sense of novelty and amazement to the spectator"
(Freedberg). Later portraits such as the Uffizi
"Gentleman," the Borghese "Young Prelate" and
The Naples "Antea" issue from Mannerist[4]
Tensions, but here, as Freedberg points out,   225
The surprise, the tension are in the concept
Rather than its realization.
The consonance of the High Renaissance
Is present, though distorted by the mirror.

---

2. Designed to regulate excess.
3. Eccentricity (Italian). Sydney Freedberg (1913–1997), American art historian, author of *Parmigianino: His Works in Painting* (1950).
4. Mannerism, a style of art that Parmigianino helped pioneer in the 1520s and 1530s, responded to the classical harmony of the High Renaissance by distorting space and scale and emphasizing style over content. *Uffizi* and *Borghese*: galleries in Florence and Rome, respectively.

What is novel is the extreme care in rendering   230
The velleities⁵ of the rounded reflecting surface
(It is the first mirror portrait),
So that you could be fooled for a moment
Before you realize the reflection
Isn't yours. You feel then like one of those   235
Hoffmann⁶ characters who have been deprived
Of a reflection, except that the whole of me
Is seen to be supplanted by the strict
Otherness of the painter in his
Other room. We have surprised him   240
At work, but no, he has surprised us
As he works. The picture is almost finished,
The surprise almost over, as when one looks out,
Startled by a snowfall which even now is
Ending in specks and sparkles of snow.   245
It happened while you were inside, asleep,
And there is no reason why you should have
Been awake for it, except that the day
Is ending and it will be hard for you
To get to sleep tonight, at least until late.   250

The shadow of the city injects its own
Urgency: Rome where Francesco
Was at work during the Sack:⁷ his inventions
Amazed the soldiers who burst in on him;
They decided to spare his life, but he left soon after;   255
Vienna where the painting is today, where
I saw it with Pierre in the summer of 1959; New York
Where I am now, which is a logarithm
Of other cities. Our landscape
Is alive with filiations, shuttlings;   260
Business is carried on by look, gesture,
Hearsay. It is another life to the city,
The backing of the looking glass of the
Unidentified but precisely sketched studio. It wants
To siphon off the life of the studio, deflate   265
Its mapped space to enactments, island it.
That operation has been temporarily stalled
But something new is on the way, a new preciosity
In the wind. Can you stand it,
Francesco? Are you strong enough for it?   270
This wind brings what it knows not, is
Self-propelled, blind, has no notion
Of itself. It is inertia that once
Acknowledged saps all activity, secret or public:
Whispers of the word that can't be understood   275
But can be felt, a chill, a blight

---

5. Faint wishes or unrealized inclinations.
6. E. T. A. Hoffmann (1776–1822), German author of supernatural tales.

7. Parmigianino fled Rome after it was sacked by the army of the Hapsburg emperor Charles V in 1527.

Moving outward along the capes and peninsulas
Of your nervures[8] and so to the archipelagoes
And to the bathed, aired secrecy of the open sea.
This is its negative side. Its positive side is   280
Making you notice life and the stresses
That only seemed to go away, but now,
As this new mode questions, are seen to be
Hastening out of style. If they are to become classics
They must decide which side they are on.   285
Their reticence has undermined
The urban scenery, made its ambiguities
Look willful and tired, the games of an old man.
What we need now is this unlikely
Challenger pounding on the gates of an amazed   290
Castle. Your argument, Francesco,
Had begun to grow stale as no answer
Or answers were forthcoming. If it dissolves now
Into dust, that only means its time had come
Some time ago, but look now, and listen: 295
It may be that another life is stocked there
In recesses no one knew of; that it,
Not we, are the change; that we are in fact it
If we could get back to it, relive some of the way
It looked, turn our faces to the globe as it sets   300
And still be coming out all right:
Nerves normal, breath normal. Since it is a metaphor
Made to include us, we are a part of it and
Can live in it as in fact we have done,
Only leaving our minds bare for questioning   305
We now see will not take place at random
But in an orderly way that means to menace
Nobody—the normal way things are done,
Like the concentric growing up of days
Around a life: correctly, if you think about it.   310

A breeze like the turning of a page
Brings back your face: the moment
Takes such a big bite out of the haze
Of pleasant intuition it comes after.
The locking into place is "death itself,"   315
As Berg said of a phrase in Mahler's Ninth;[9]
Or, to quote Imogen in *Cymbeline*, "There cannot
Be a pinch in death more sharp than this,"[1] for,
Though only exercise or tactic, it carries
The momentum of a conviction that had been building.   320
Mere forgetfulness cannot remove it
Nor wishing bring it back, as long as it remains
The white precipitate of its dream

---

8. Veins, as on a leaf or an insect's wing.
9. *Symphony No. 9* by Gustav Mahler (1860–1911), as described by fellow Austrian composer

Alban Berg (1885–1935).
1. Shakespeare, *Cymbeline* 1.1.131–32.

In the climate of sighs flung across our world,
A cloth over a birdcage. But it is certain that   325
What is beautiful seems so only in relation to a specific
Life, experienced or not, channeled into some form
Steeped in the nostalgia of a collective past.
The light sinks today with an enthusiasm
I have known elsewhere, and known why   330
It seemed meaningful, that others felt this way
Years ago. I go on consulting
This mirror that is no longer mine
For as much brisk vacancy as is to be
My portion this time. And the vase is always full   335
Because there is only just so much room
And it accommodates everything. The sample
One sees is not to be taken as
Merely that, but as everything as it
May be imagined outside time—not as a gesture   340
But as all, in the refined, assimilable state.
But what is this universe the porch of
As it veers in and out, back and forth,
Refusing to surround us and still the only
Thing we can see? Love once   345
Tipped the scales but now is shadowed, invisible,
Though mysteriously present, around somewhere.
But we know it cannot be sandwiched
Between two adjacent moments, that its windings
Lead nowhere except to further tributaries   350
And that these empty themselves into a vague
Sense of something that can never be known
Even though it seems likely that each of us
Knows what it is and is capable of
Communicating it to the other. But the look   355
Some wear as a sign makes one want to
Push forward ignoring the apparent
Naïveté of the attempt, not caring
That no one is listening, since the light
Has been lit once and for all in their eyes   360
And is present, unimpaired, a permanent anomaly,
Awake and silent. On the surface of it
There seems no special reason why that light
Should be focused by love, or why
The city falling with its beautiful suburbs   365
Into space always less clear, less defined,
Should read as the support of its progress,
The easel upon which the drama unfolded
To its own satisfaction and to the end
Of our dreaming, as we had never imagined   370
It would end, in worn daylight with the painted
Promise showing through as a gage, a bond.
This nondescript, never-to-be defined daytime is
The secret of where it takes place
And we can no longer return to the various   375

Conflicting statements gathered, lapses of memory
Of the principal witnesses. All we know
Is that we are a little early, that
Today has that special, lapidary[2]
Todayness that the sunlight reproduces   380
Faithfully in casting twig-shadows on blithe
Sidewalks. No previous day would have been like this.
I used to think they were all alike,
That the present always looked the same to everybody
But this confusion drains away as one   385
Is always cresting into one's present.
Yet the "poetic," straw-colored space
Of the long corridor that leads back to the painting,
Its darkening opposite—is this
Some figment of "art," not to be imagined   390
As real, let alone special? Hasn't it too its lair
In the present we are always escaping from
And falling back into, as the waterwheel of days
Pursues its uneventful, even serene course?
I think it is trying to say it is today   395
And we must get out of it even as the public
Is pushing through the museum now so as to
Be out by closing time. You can't live there.
The gray glaze of the past attacks all know-how:
Secrets of wash and finish that took a lifetime   400
To learn and are reduced to the status of
Black-and-white illustrations in a book where colorplates
Are rare. That is, all time
Reduces to no special time. No one
Alludes to the change; to do so might   405
Involve calling attention to oneself
Which would augment the dread of not getting out
Before having seen the whole collection
(Except for the sculptures in the basement:
They are where they belong).   410
Our time gets to be veiled, compromised
By the portrait's will to endure. It hints at
Our own, which we were hoping to keep hidden.
We don't need paintings or
Doggerel written by mature poets when   415
The explosion is so precise, so fine.
Is there any point even in acknowledging
The existence of all that? Does it
Exist? Certainly the leisure to
Indulge stately pastimes doesn't,   420
Any more. Today has no margins, the event arrives
Flush with its edges, is of the same substance,
Indistinguishable. "Play" is something else;
It exists, in a society specifically
Organized as a demonstration of itself.   425

---

2. Carved in stone; concise or condensed.

There is no other way, and those assholes
Who would confuse everything with their mirror games
Which seem to multiply stakes and possibilities, or
At least confuse issues by means of an investing
Aura that would corrode the architecture   430
Of the whole in a haze of suppressed mockery,
Are beside the point. They are out of the game,
Which doesn't exist until they are out of it.
It seems like a very hostile universe
But as the principle of each individual thing is   435
Hostile to, exists at the expense of all the others
As philosophers have often pointed out, at least
This thing, the mute, undivided present,
Has the justification of logic, which
In this instance isn't a bad thing   440
Or wouldn't be, if the way of telling
Didn't somehow intrude, twisting the end result
Into a caricature of itself. This always
Happens, as in the game where
A whispered phrase passed around the room   445
Ends up as something completely different.
It is the principle that makes works of art so unlike
What the artist intended. Often he finds
He has omitted the thing he started out to say
In the first place. Seduced by flowers,   450
Explicit pleasures, he blames himself (though
Secretly satisfied with the result), imagining
He had a say in the matter and exercised
An option of which he was hardly conscious,
Unaware that necessity circumvents such resolutions   455
So as to create something new
For itself, that there is no other way,
That the history of creation proceeds according to
Stringent laws, and that things
Do get done in this way, but never the things   460
We set out to accomplish and wanted so desperately
To see come into being. Parmigianino
Must have realized this as he worked at his
Life-obstructing task. One is forced to read
The perfectly plausible accomplishment of a purpose   465
Into the smooth, perhaps even bland (but so
Enigmatic) finish. Is there anything
To be serious about beyond this otherness
That gets included in the most ordinary
Forms of daily activity, changing everything   470
Slightly and profoundly, and tearing the matter
Of creation, any creation, not just artistic creation
Out of our hands, to install it on some monstrous, near
Peak, too close to ignore, too far
For one to intervene? This otherness, this   475
"Not-being-us" is all there is to look at
In the mirror, though no one can say

How it came to be this way. A ship
Flying unknown colors has entered the harbor.
You are allowing extraneous matters   480
To break up your day, cloud the focus
Of the crystal ball. Its scene drifts away
Like vapor scattered on the wind. The fertile
Thought-associations that until now came
So easily, appear no more, or rarely. Their   485
Colorings are less intense, washed out
By autumn rains and winds, spoiled, muddied,
Given back to you because they are worthless.
Yet we are such creatures of habit that their
Implications are still around *en permanence,* confusing   490
Issues. To be serious only about sex
Is perhaps one way, but the sands are hissing
As they approach the beginning of the big slide
Into what happened. This past
Is now here: the painter's   495
Reflected face, in which we linger, receiving
Dreams and inspirations on an unassigned
Frequency, but the hues have turned metallic,
The curves and edges are not so rich. Each person
Has one big theory to explain the universe   500
But it doesn't tell the whole story
And in the end it is what is outside him
That matters, to him and especially to us
Who have been given no help whatever
In decoding our own man-size quotient and must rely   505
On second-hand knowledge. Yet I know
That no one else's taste is going to be
Any help, and might as well be ignored.
Once it seemed so perfect—gloss on the fine
Freckled skin, lips moistened as though about to part   510
Releasing speech, and the familiar look
Of clothes and furniture that one forgets.
This could have been our paradise: exotic
Refuge within an exhausted world, but that wasn't
In the cards, because it couldn't have been   515
The point. Aping naturalness may be the first step
Toward achieving an inner calm
But it is the first step only, and often
Remains a frozen gesture of welcome etched
On the air materializing behind it,   520
A convention. And we have really
No time for these, except to use them
For kindling. The sooner they are burnt up
The better for the roles we have to play.
Therefore I beseech you, withdraw that hand,   525
Offer it no longer as shield or greeting,
The shield of a greeting, Francesco:
There is room for one bullet in the chamber:
Our looking through the wrong end

Of the telescope as you fall back at a speed 530
Faster than that of light to flatten ultimately
Among the features of the room, an invitation
Never mailed, the "it was all a dream"
Syndrome, though the "all" tells tersely
Enough how it wasn't. Its existence 535
Was real, though troubled, and the ache
Of this waking dream can never drown out
The diagram still sketched on the wind,
Chosen, meant for me and materialized
In the disguising radiance of my room. 540
We have seen the city; it is the gibbous[3]
Mirrored eye of an insect. All things happen
On its balcony and are resumed within,
But the action is the cold, syrupy flow
Of a pageant. One feels too confined, 545
Sifting the April sunlight for clues,
In the mere stillness of the ease of its
Parameter. The hand holds no chalk
And each part of the whole falls off
And cannot know it knew, except 550
Here and there, in cold pockets
Of remembrance, whispers out of time.

1975

Wet Casements

> When Eduard Raban, coming along the passage, walked into the
> open doorway, he saw that it was raining. It was not raining much.
> —KAFKA, *Wedding Preparations in the Country*[4]

The concept is interesting: to see, as though reflected
In streaming windowpanes, the look of others through
Their own eyes. A digest of their correct impressions of
Their self-analytical attitudes overlaid by your
Ghostly transparent face. You in falbalas[5] 5
Of some distant but not too distant era, the cosmetics,
The shoes perfectly pointed, drifting (how long you
Have been drifting; how long I have too for that matter)
Like a bottle-imp toward a surface which can never be approached,
Never pierced through into the timeless energy of a present 10
Which would have its own opinions on these matters,
Are an epistemological snapshot of the processes
That first mentioned your name at some crowded cocktail
Party long ago, and someone (not the person addressed)
Overheard it and carried that name around in his wallet 15
For years as the wallet crumbled and bills slid in
And out of it. I want that information very much today,

---

3. Convex.
4. An early story about the isolated character
Raban, by German-language writer Franz Kafka

(1883–1924).
5. Frilled trim on a dress or petticoat.

Can't have it, and this makes me angry.
I shall use my anger to build a bridge like that
Of Avignon[6] on which people may dance for the feeling   20
Of dancing on a bridge. I shall at last see my complete face
Reflected not in the water but in the worn stone floor of my bridge.

I shall keep to myself.
I shall not repeat others' comments about me.

                                                                1977

Paradoxes and Oxymorons

This poem is concerned with language on a very plain level.
Look at it talking to you. You look out a window
Or pretend to fidget. You have it but you don't have it.
You miss it, it misses you. You miss each other.

The poem is sad because it wants to be yours, and cannot.   5
What's a plain level? It is that and other things,
Bringing a system of them into play. Play?
Well, actually, yes, but I consider play to be

A deeper outside thing, a dreamed role-pattern,
As in the division of grace these long August days   10
Without proof. Open-ended. And before you know
It gets lost in the steam and chatter of typewriters.

It has been played once more. I think you exist only
To tease me into doing it, on your level, and then you aren't there
Or have adopted a different attitude. And the poem   15
Has set me softly down beside you. The poem is you.

                                                                1981

At North Farm[7]

Somewhere someone is traveling furiously toward you,
At incredible speed, traveling day and night,
Through blizzards and desert heat, across torrents, through narrow passes.
But will he know where to find you,
Recognize you when he sees you,   5
Give you the thing he has for you?

Hardly anything grows here,
Yet the granaries are bursting with meal,

---

6. French city celebrated in the folksong "On the Bridge at Avignon."
7. In *The Kalevala*, a collection of Finnish epic poems, North Farm is a region near Hell where heroes search for wives.

The sacks of meal piled to the rafters.
The streams run with sweetness, fattening fish;   10
Birds darken the sky. Is it enough
That the dish of milk is set out at night,
That we think of him sometimes,
Sometimes and always, with mixed feelings?

                                                              1984

Of the Light

That watery light, so undervalued
except when evaluated, which never happens
much, perhaps even not at all—I intend to conserve it
somehow, in a book, in a dish, even at night,
like an insect in a light bulb.   5

Yes, day may just be breaking. The importance isn't there
but in the beautiful flights of the trees
accepting their own flaccid destiny,
or the tightrope of seasons.
We get scared when we look at them up close   10
but the king doesn't mind. He has the tides to worry about,

and how fitting is the new mood of contentment
and how long it will wear thin.

I looked forward to seeing you so much
I have dragged the king from his lair: There,   15
take that, you old wizard. Wizard enough, he replies,
but this isn't going to save us from the light
of breakfast, or mend the hole in your stocking.
"Now wait"—and yet another day has consumed itself,
brisk with passion and grief, crisp as an illustration in a magazine   20
from the thirties, when we and this light were all that mattered.

                                                              2000

W. S. MERWIN
b. 1927

W. S. Merwin was twenty-four when his first book, *A Mask for Janus* (1952), was chosen by W. H. Auden for the Yale Series of Younger Poets, and Merwin has published regularly and prolifically since. Those first poems, technically very accomplished, show Merwin not only "trained . . . thoroughly in the mechanics of verse," as Auden observed, but interested in playing with conventional forms—ballads, sonnets, sestinas, odes, carols, roundels. Merwin has remained on good terms with the poets of the past; his later poem "Lament for the Makers" is a pious roll call of dead poets. His earliest subjects were often mythical or legendary, and many of the poems are about the sea and animals, which he invests with an emblematic quality. With growing intensity through the years, Merwin has revered nature and condemned its poisoning and destruction.

The Drunk in the Furnace (1960) represented a change in direction from Merwin's early neoclassicism. His subjects became more local and personal, and whereas his first poems showed clearly the influence of Wallace Stevens, his work in this volume captures some of Robert Frost's shifting colloquialism and even his oracular quality. The title poem, which depicts an old drunk in a furnace as Orpheus in a new and wonderful form, demonstrates how successfully Merwin absorbed his new influences. The metrical irregularities create a new tone closer to speech ("Where he gets his spirits / It's a mystery. But the stuff keeps him musical"); the straight-faced puns add to the buoyancy and complexity of the poem ("spirits" meaning both liquor and good humor). Merwin finds a new way to praise the unconscious and outrageous forces that disconcert society but make poetry possible.

In the 1960s, Merwin, like many of his contemporaries among American poets, made increasingly daring experiments in metrical irregularity and thematic disorganization. Written during the escalation of the Vietnam War, his collection The Lice (1967), perhaps his most powerful, seeks out elemental and archetypal forms of experience in the midst of despair, chaos, and violence. In melancholy poems tinged with surrealism, Merwin opens a hushed space for the irrational, the dead, and the dying to be heard. Both elegiac and prophetic, Merwin once again tries to write a poetry that is closer to its imaginative energies than what he has done before, and he sees traditional form as an obstacle to poetry's "naked condition, where it touches on all that is unrealized" ("On Open Form"). He seeks to achieve in poetry "something that would be like an echo except that it is repeating no sound. Something that always belonged to it: its sense and its conformation before it entered words." This means that his poems resist intellectual interpretation; they are written out of experiences into which the reader may be drawn as by a charm.

Merwin's most influential verse is deliberately bare and meditative, shorn of all punctuation, all detail except an occasional vivid simile or image. The busy, fertile world is excluded in favor of simplicity; things, people, and words become shadows. Absence, silence, and brevity are at the core of his poetics. He avoids mannerisms and decorations as if they were childish things to be put aside in favor of an enigmatic yet exposed reality. Elusive and multifaceted, changing from one volume to the next, Merwin's poetry has been associated with various trends and movements, most often the Deep Image school, but also neoformalism, neosurrealism, ecopoetry, and existentialism.

William Stanley Merwin was born on September 30, 1927, in New York City, and grew up in Union, New Jersey, and Scranton, Pennsylvania; his father was a Presbyterian minister, and Merwin recalls, "I started writing hymns for my father almost as soon as I could write at all" (Contemporary Authors, 1966). In 1947, he received his B.A. from Princeton University, where he encountered John Berryman, who taught creative writing, and the poet and critic R. P. Blackmur, to whom he dedicated The Moving Target (1963). After a year of graduate work there, during which he continued the study of foreign languages that was to equip him to make excellent translations from Latin, Spanish, and French, he left the United States to live in England, France, and Portugal. In 1950, he tutored Robert Graves's son on Majorca. From 1951 to 1954, he was in London, supporting himself primarily by translating French and Spanish literature for broadcast by the BBC, while his first two books of poetry were published in the United States. He returned briefly to America to be a playwright-in-residence at the Poet's Theatre in Cambridge, Massachusetts (1956) and the poetry editor of *The Nation* (1961–63). Since 1968, he has lived in the United States, moving in the late 1970s to an old pineapple plantation in Hawaii, which he has been restoring to rainforest. He has received the Pulitzer Prize (1970) and the Bollingen Prize (1978). After publishing *Travels* (1993), he won the Lenore Marshall Poetry Prize and became the first recipient of the Tanning Prize.

The Drunk in the Furnace

For a good decade
The furnace stood in the naked gully, fireless
And vacant as any hat. Then when it was
No more to them than a hulking black fossil
To erode unnoticed with the rest of the junk-hill   5
By the poisonous creek, and rapidly to be added
          To their ignorance,

          They were afterwards astonished
To confirm, one morning, a twist of smoke like a pale
Resurrection, staggering out of its chewed hole,   10
And to remark then other tokens that someone,
Cosily bolted behind the eye-holed iron
Door of the drafty burner, had there established
          His bad castle.

          Where he gets his spirits   15
It's a mystery. But the stuff keeps him musical:
Hammer-and-anvilling with poker and bottle
To his jugged bellowings, till the last groaning clang
As he collapses onto the rioting
Springs of a litter of car-seats ranged on the grates,   20
          To sleep like an iron pig.[1]

          In their tar-paper church
On a text about stoke-holes[2] that are sated never
Their Reverend lingers. They nod and hate trespassers.
When the furnace wakes, though, all afternoon   25
Their witless offspring flock like piped rats[3] to its siren
Crescendo, and agape on the crumbling ridge
          Stand in a row and learn.

                                                  1960

---

1. "Pig iron" is crude iron.
2. Furnace mouths.
3. The Pied Piper of Hamelin's piping lured rats from the town; when he was not paid, he lured away the children as well.

The Hydra[4]

No no the dead have no brothers

The Hydra calls me but I am used to it
It calls me Everybody
But I know my name and do not answer

And you the dead   5
You know your names as I do not
But at moments you have just finished speaking

The snow stirs in its wrappings
Every season comes from a new place

Like your voice with its resemblances   10

A long time ago the lightning was practising
Something I thought was easy

I was young and the dead were in other
Ages
As the grass had its own language   15

Now I forget where the difference falls

One thing about the living sometimes a piece of us
Can stop dying for a moment
But you the dead

Once you go into those names you go on you never   20
Hesitate
You go on

                                                          1967

Some Last Questions

What is the head
              A. Ash
What are the eyes
              A. The wells have fallen in and have
                  Inhabitants   5
What are the feet
              A. Thumbs left after the auction
No what are the feet
              A. Under them the impossible road is moving

4. In Greek legend, a monster with many heads, slain by Hercules.

Down which the broken necked mice push   10
  Balls of blood with their noses
What is the tongue
  A. The black coat that fell off the wall
   With sleeves trying to say something
What are the hands   15
  A. Paid
No what are the hands
  A. Climbing back down the museum wall
   To their ancestors the extinct shrews that will
   Have left a message   20
What is the silence
  A. As though it had a right to more
Who are the compatriots
  A. They make the stars of bone

             1967

For the Anniversary of My Death

Every year without knowing it I have passed the day
When the last fires will wave to me
And the silence will set out
Tireless traveller
Like the beam of a lightless star   5

Then I will no longer
Find myself in life as in a strange garment
Surprised at the earth
And the love of one woman
And the shamelessness of men   10
As today writing after three days of rain
Hearing the wren sing and the falling cease
And bowing not knowing to what

             1967

The Asians Dying

When the forests have been destroyed their darkness
  remains
The ash the great walker follows the possessors
Forever
Nothing they will come to is real
Nor for long   5
Over the watercourses
Like ducks in the time of the ducks
The ghosts of the villages trail in the sky
Making a new twilight

Rain falls into the open eyes of the dead   10
Again again with its pointless sound
When the moon finds them they are the color of everything

The nights disappear like bruises but nothing is healed
The dead go away like bruises
The blood vanishes into the poisoned farmlands   15
Pain the horizon
Remains
Overhead the seasons rock
They are paper bells
Calling to nothing living   20

The possessors move everywhere under Death their star
Like columns of smoke they advance into the shadows
Like thin flames with no light
They with no past
And fire their only future   25

1967

For a Coming Extinction

Gray whale
Now that we are sending you to The End
That great god
Tell him
That we who follow you invented forgiveness   5
And forgive nothing

I write as though you could understand
And I could say it
One must always pretend something
Among the dying   10
When you have left the seas nodding on their stalks
Empty of you
Tell him that we were made
On another day

The bewilderment will diminish like an echo   15
Winding along your inner mountains
Unheard by us
And find its way out
Leaving behind it the future
Dead   20
And ours

When you will not see again
The whale calves trying the light
Consider what you will find in the black garden

And its court   25
The sea cows the Great Auks[5] the gorillas
The irreplaceable hosts ranged countless
And fore-ordaining as stars
Our sacrifices
Join your word to theirs   30
Tell him
That it is we who are important

1967

A Given Day

When I wake I find it is late in the autumn
        the hard rain has passed and the sunlight has not yet reached
the tips of the dark leaves that are their own shadows still
        and I am home it is coming back to me I am
remembering the gradual sweetness of morning   5
        the clear spring of being here as it rises one by one
in silence and without a pause and is the only one
        then one at a time I remember without understanding
some that have gone and arise only not to be here
        an afternoon walking on a bridge thinking of a friend   10
when she was still alive while a door from a building
        being demolished sailed down through the passing city
my mother half my age at a window long since removed
        friends in the same rooms and the words dreaming between us
the eyes of animals upon me they are all here   15
        in the clearness of the morning in the first light
that remembers its way now to the flowers of winter

1996

5. Extinct, large, flightless sea birds. *Sea cows:* endangered, walruslike animals.

JAMES WRIGHT
1927–1980

Of the poems in his first two books, James Wright said, "I have tried very hard to write in the mode of Edwin Arlington Robinson and Robert Frost," surprising models for a man whose first books were published in the late 1950s. What Wright seems to have admired in these older poets—and in Thomas Hardy as well—is their seriousness. Wright, as he said on a 1957 dust jacket, "wanted to make the poems say something humanly important instead of just showing off with language." The poems are typically about men and women who find themselves outside society—a convict escaped from prison, a lesbian whose love has been discovered by her neighbors, an old countryman whose wife has just died, even Judas Iscariot. Wright's tone is distinct and powerful. One poem, dedicated to a convicted murderer awaiting his execution, concludes with a prayer: "God, God have pity if he wake, / Have mercy on man who dreamed apart. / God, God have pity on man apart" ("American Twilights, 1957").

Wright's most characteristic first subjects were people not only "apart," but poor. Like his friend Richard Hugo, Wright came from a poor family and grew up in a small town in the depths of the Great Depression. As Hugo later wrote, "Jim had seen his father enslaved to a lousy factory job during the depression and knew what terrible fears bind people to jobs" ("James Wright"). Wright himself said, "Hundreds of times I must have heard a man returning home after a long day's futile search for work, any kind of work at all, and dispiritedly [saying] in his baffled loneliness, 'I ain't got a pot to piss in or a window to throw it out of' " (*American Poets in 1976*, ed. William Heyen). Wright once told Hugo that he and his first wife had married "to escape Martins Ferry"—his hometown and the gritty, industrial "triggering town" of a number of his poems, such as "Autumn Begins in Martins Ferry, Ohio" ("James Wright").

Sometime after the publication of his second collection, Wright set about chang-ing—or renewing—his style, commenting, "I have changed the way I've written, when it seemed appropriate, and continue to do so" (*Contemporary Poets*, 1985). He pub-lished translations of the South American poets Pablo Neruda and César Vallejo and the Austrian poet Georg Trakl, all of whom use series of discontinuous images, and Wright—like the "Deep Image" poets Robert Bly and W. S. Merwin—adapted their surrealism for his own poetry. He kept his compassionate interest in social outcasts and an increasing confidence in the transforming beauty of nature—a specifically American nature. What was new was a looser form, a greater personal openness—he was now less interested in creating characters—and an emphasis on deeply felt social concerns. "I wonder," he writes in "The Minneapolis Poem," "how many old men last winter / Hungry and frightened by namelessness prowled / The Mississippi shore / Lashed blind by the wind, dreaming / Of suicide in the river." In 1970, Wright com-mented: "I try and speak of the beauty and again of the ugliness in the lives of the poor and neglected."

In 1971, he published *Collected Poems*, which won the Pulitzer Prize. It contained most of his first book, all of his second, his translations, and the two books that followed, *The Branch Will Not Break* and *Shall We Gather at the River*. Many of its poems are about the marginal, the hopeless, and the dead, although they occasionally glimpse possibilities of imaginative transformation. The image of humankind in "A Secret Grat-itude"—"Man's heart is the rotten yolk of a blacksnake egg / Corroding, as it is just born, in a pile of dead / Horse dung"—is only slightly alleviated by the sound of "a small waterfall" at the end of the poem. The ferocious clarity of Wright's images, com-pelling and coherent even when disjointed, achieves a visceral effect.

Wright was born on December 13, 1927, in Martins Ferry, Ohio, and served with the U.S. Army in Japan during the American occupation. In 1952, he received his B.A. from Kenyon College, where he studied with John Crowe Ransom, whom he credited with teaching him the classical ideal of a poem "put together so carefully that it does produce a single unifying effect" (*American Poetry Review* 9.3, 1980). After going to Vienna on a Fulbright Scholarship, he earned an M.A. in creative writing and, in 1959, a Ph.D. in English at the University of Washington, where he studied under Theodore Roethke and befriended Hugo. He taught at the University of Minnesota (1957–64) but, after he was denied tenure, took positions at Macalester College, in St. Paul (1963–65), and Hunter College, in New York City (1966–80). After years of struggling with alcoholism and depression, he died of cancer of the tongue. Hugo wrote of him: "No one carried his life more vividly inside him, or simultaneously in plain and in eloquent ways used the pain of his life to better advantage" ("James Wright").

Saint Judas[1]

When I went out to kill myself, I caught
A pack of hoodlums beating up a man.
Running to spare his suffering, I forgot
My name, my number, how my day began,
How soldiers milled around the garden stone   5
And sang amusing songs; how all that day
Their javelins measured crowds; how I alone
Bargained the proper coins, and slipped away.

Banished from heaven, I found this victim beaten,
Stripped, kneed, and left to cry. Dropping my rope   10
Aside, I ran, ignored the uniforms:
Then I remembered bread my flesh had eaten,
The kiss that ate my flesh.[2] Flayed without hope,
I held the man for nothing in my arms.

1959

Autumn Begins in Martins Ferry, Ohio

In the Shreve High football stadium,
I think of Polacks nursing long beers in Tiltonsville,
And gray faces of Negroes in the blast furnace at Benwood,
And the ruptured night watchman of Wheeling Steel,
Dreaming of heroes.   5

All the proud fathers are ashamed to go home.
Their women cluck like starved pullets,[3]
Dying for love.

Therefore,
Their sons grow suicidally beautiful   10
At the beginning of October,
And gallop terribly against each other's bodies.

1963

---

1. Judas Iscariot, apostle who betrayed Jesus with a kiss that signaled Roman soldiers to capture him. Matthew 27 recounts Judas' suicide.
2. During the Last Supper, after revealing that one of the disciples would betray him, Jesus distributed bread, saying, "Take, eat; this is my body" (Matthew 26.26)
3. Chickens.

Lying in a Hammock at William Duffy's Farm in Pine Island, Minnesota

Over my head, I see the bronze butterfly,
Asleep on the black trunk,
Blowing like a leaf in green shadow.
Down the ravine behind the empty house,
The cowbells follow one another   5
Into the distances of the afternoon.
To my right,
In a field of sunlight between two pines,
The droppings of last year's horses
Blaze up into golden stones.   10
I lean back, as the evening darkens and comes on.
A chicken hawk floats over, looking for home.
I have wasted my life.

1963

A Blessing

Just off the highway to Rochester, Minnesota,
Twilight bounds softly forth on the grass.
And the eyes of those two Indian ponies
Darken with kindness.
They have come gladly out of the willows   5
To welcome my friend and me.
We step over the barbed wire into the pasture
Where they have been grazing all day, alone.
They ripple tensely, they can hardly contain their happiness
That we have come.   10
They bow shyly as wet swans. They love each other.
There is no loneliness like theirs.
At home once more,
They begin munching the young tufts of spring in the darkness.
I would like to hold the slenderer one in my arms,   15
For she has walked over to me
And nuzzled my left hand.
She is black and white,
Her mane falls wild on her forehead,
And the light breeze moves me to caress her long ear   20
That is delicate as the skin over a girl's wrist.
Suddenly I realize
That if I stepped out of my body I would break
Into blossom.

1953

The Minneapolis Poem[4]

1

I wonder how many old men last winter
Hungry and frightened by namelessness prowled
The Mississippi shore
Lashed blind by the wind, dreaming
Of suicide in the river.   5
The police remove their cadavers by daybreak
And turn them in somewhere.
Where?
How does the city keep lists of its fathers
Who have no names?   10
By Nicollet Island I gaze down at the dark water
So beautifully slow.
And I wish my brothers good luck
And a warm grave.

2

The Chippewa young men   15
Stab one another shrieking
Jesus Christ.
Split-lipped homosexuals limp in terror of assault.
High school backfields search under benches
Near the Post Office. Their faces are the rich   20
Raw bacon without eyes.
The Walker Art Center crowd stare
At the Guthrie Theater.

3

Tall Negro girls from Chicago
Listen to light songs.   25
They know when the supposed patron
Is a plainclothesman.
A cop's palm
Is a roach dangling down the scorched fangs
Of a light bulb.   30
The soul of a cop's eyes
Is an eternity of Sunday daybreak in the suburbs
Of Juárez, Mexico.

4. Nicollet Island, the Walker Art Center, and the Tyrone Guthrie Repertory Theater, mentioned in the poem, are all Minneapolis landmarks.

4

The legless beggars are gone, carried away
By white birds.   35
The Artificial Limbs Exchange is gutted
And sown with lime.
The whalebone crutches and hand-me-down trusses
Huddle together dreaming in a desolation
Of dry groins.   40
I think of poor men astonished to waken
Exposed in broad daylight by the blade
Of a strange plough.

5

All over the walls of comb cells
Automobiles perfumed and blindered   45
Consent with a mutter of high good humor
To take their two naps a day.
Without sound windows glide back
Into dusk.
The sockets of a thousand blind bee graves tier upon tier   50
Tower not quite toppling.
There are men in this city who labor dawn after dawn
To sell me my death.

6

But I could not bear
To allow my poor brother my body to die   55
In Minneapolis.
The old man Walt Whitman our countryman
Is now in America our country
Dead.
But he was not buried in Minneapolis   60
At least.
And no more may I be
Please God.

7

I want to be lifted up
By some great white bird unknown to the police,   65
And soar for a thousand miles and be carefully hidden
Modest and golden as one last corn grain,
Stored with the secrets of the wheat and the mysterious lives
Of the unnamed poor.

                                                                1968

In Response to a Rumor That the Oldest Whorehouse in Wheeling, West Virginia, Has Been Condemned

I will grieve alone,
As I strolled alone, years ago, down along
The Ohio shore.
I hid in the hobo jungle[5] weeds
Upstream from the sewer main,   5
Pondering, gazing.

I saw, down river,
At Twenty-third and Water Streets
By the vinegar works,
The doors open in early evening.   10
Swinging their purses, the women
Poured down the long street to the river
And into the river.

I do not know how it was
They could drown every evening.   15
What time near dawn did they climb up the other shore,
Drying their wings?

For the river at Wheeling, West Virginia,
Has only two shores:
The one in hell, the other   20
In Bridgeport, Ohio.

And nobody would commit suicide, only
To find beyond death
Bridgeport, Ohio.

                                                              1968

Small Frogs Killed on the Highway

Still,
I would leap too
Into the light,
If I had the chance.
It is everything, the wet green stalk of the field   5
On the other side of the road.
They crouch there, too, faltering in terror
And take strange wing. Many
Of the dead never moved, but many
Of the dead are alive forever in the split second   10
Auto headlights more sudden
Than their drivers know.

---

5. Camp made by hoboes or tramps, in this case on the shore of the Ohio River.

The drivers burrow backward into dank pools
Where nothing begets
Nothing.   15

Across the road, tadpoles are dancing
On the quarter thumbnail
Of the moon. They can't see,
Not yet.

1971

A Centenary Ode: Inscribed to Little Crow, Leader of the Sioux Rebellion in Minnesota, 1862[6]

I had nothing to do with it. I was not here.
I was not born.
In 1862, when your hotheads
Raised hell from here to South Dakota,
My own fathers scattered into West Virginia   5
And southern Ohio.
My family fought the Confederacy
And fought the Union.
None of them got killed.
But for all that, it was not my fathers   10
Who murdered you.
Not much.

I don't know
Where the fathers of Minneapolis finalized
Your flayed carcass.   15
Little Crow, true father
Of my dark America,
When I close my eyes I lose you among
Old lonelinesses.
My family were a lot of singing drunks and good carpenters.   20
We had brothers who loved one another no matter what they did.
And they did plenty.

I think they would have run like hell from your Sioux.
And when you caught them you all would have run like hell
From the Confederacy and from the Union   25
Into the hills and hunted for a few things,
Some bull-cat under the stones, a gar[7] maybe,
If you were hungry, and if you were happy,
Sunfish and corn.

If only I knew where to mourn you,   30
I would surely mourn.

6. The sixty-year-old Little Crow led a failed rebellion in response to the threat of starvation inflicted on the Sioux when the U.S. government forced them off their lands and onto a small reservation.
7. A type of fish.

But I don't know.

I did not come here only to grieve
For my people's defeat.
The troops of the Union, who won,   35
Still outnumber us.
Old Paddy Beck, my great-uncle, is dead
At the old soldiers' home near Tiffen, Ohio.
He got away with every last stitch
Of his uniform, save only   40
The dress trousers.

Oh all around us,
The hobo jungles of America grow wild again.
The pick handles bloom like your skinned spine.
I don't even know where   45
My own grave is.

                                                     1971

PHILIP LEVINE
b. 1928

Working in the auto plants of Detroit in the 1950s, Philip Levine resolved "to find a voice for the voiceless"—the unsung factory workers of America, blue-collar laborers on assembly lines (*Contemporary Authors*). Uncovering, like Walt Whitman, nobility in the struggle against poverty, defeat, and dispossession, Levine works with elemental themes—father and son, the deaths of relatives, war—and infuses them with a melancholy luster. His poems, he says, "mostly record my discovery of the people, places, and animals I am not, the ones who live at all cost and come back for more, and who if they bore tattoos—a gesture they don't need—would have them say, 'Don't tread on me' or 'Once more with feeling' or 'no pasaran' or 'Not this pig' " (*Not This Pig*, 1968). In "You Can Have It," Levine records the bitter strength in exhaustion of his young brother, his hands "yellowed and cracked" by work in an ice plant, his body "hard / and furious, with wide shoulders and a curse / for God." Levine's poems celebrate the failed, the peripheral, and the uncooperative—as he says in "Silent in America,"

> . . . the ugly
> who had no chance
>
> the beautiful in
> body, the used and the unused,
> those who had courage
> and those who quit.

A gritty realist and yet a Romantic, Levine is true in poems such as "Belle Isle, 1949" to both the ugly and the beautiful—to industrial debris ("car parts, dead fish, stolen bicycles") and to the pleasures of life (a boy and girl strip and "baptize" themselves with an ecstatic swim in a cold river). "Drum" presents mud, metal scraps, and oil drums,

but also radiance: "The light diamonds / last night's rain." "They Feed They Lion"—
written in response to the 1967 Detroit riots—absorbs the minutiae of urban squalor
while also evoking the prophetic in its use of symbolism, strong rhythms, and syntactic
parallelism. Levine is a master of sensual detail, colloquial diction, propulsive rhythms,
and narrative realism imbued with imaginative hope. His authoritative tone balances
the elegiac with wry restraint and humor, and the result is often bizarre but powerful.

Born in Detroit to Russian Jewish immigrant parents on January 10, 1928, Levine
remained there to study at Wayne State University. In 1957, he received an M.F.A.
from the University of Iowa, where his teachers included John Berryman. The next year,
he joined the faculty of California State University, Fresno, where he spent most of his
career, with much travel in Spain. He acknowledges the importance to him of Spanish
and Latin American surrealist poets and of their American advocate Robert Bly, as well
as the influence of Kenneth Rexroth and the San Francisco poets, who, he says, "opened
me up." His many books include translations of Spanish poetry, interviews, and mem-
oirs. Among his many awards for books of poetry are the National Book Critics Circle
Award (1980), the National Book Award (1991), and the Pulitzer Prize (1995).

They Feed They Lion

Out of burlap sacks, out of bearing butter,
Out of black bean and wet slate bread,
Out of the acids of rage, the candor of tar,
Out of creosote, gasoline, drive shafts, wooden dollies,
They Lion grow.   5
       Out of the gray hills
Of industrial barns, out of rain, out of bus ride,
West Virginia to Kiss My Ass, out of buried aunties,
Mothers hardening like pounded stumps, out of stumps,
Out of the bones' need to sharpen and the muscles' to stretch,   10
They Lion grow.
        Earth is eating trees, fence posts,
Gutted cars, earth is calling in her little ones,
"Come home, Come home!" From pig balls,
From the ferocity of pig driven to holiness,   15
From the furred ear and the full jowl come
The repose of the hung belly, from the purpose
They Lion grow.
       From the sweet glues of the trotters[1]
Come the sweet kinks of the fist, from the full flower   20
Of the hams the thorax[2] of caves,
From "Bow Down" come "Rise Up,"
Come they Lion from the reeds of shovels,
The grained arm that pulls the hands,
They Lion grow.   25
       From my five arms and all my hands,
From all my white sins forgiven, they feed,
From my car passing under the stars,
They Lion, from my children inherit,

---

1. Cooked pigs' feet.   2. That is, chest cavity.

From the oak turned to a wall, they Lion,   30
From they sack and they belly opened
And all that was hidden burning on the oil-stained earth
They feed they Lion and he comes.

                                                                            1972

Belle Isle,³ 1949

We stripped in the first warm spring night
and ran down into the Detroit River
to baptize ourselves in the brine
of car parts, dead fish, stolen bicycles,
melted snow. I remember going under   5
hand in hand with a Polish highschool girl
I'd never seen before, and the cries
our breath made caught at the same time
on the cold, and rising through the layers
of darkness into the final moonless atmosphere   10
that was this world, the girl breaking
the surface after me and swimming out
on the starless waters towards the lights
of Jefferson Ave. and the stacks
of the old stove factory unwinking.   15
Turning at last to see no island at all
but a perfect calm dark as far
as there was sight, and then a light
and another riding low out ahead
to bring us home, ore boats maybe, or smokers   20
walking alone. Back panting
to the gray coarse beach we didn't dare
fall on, the damp piles of clothes,
and dressing side by side in silence
to go back where we came from.   25

                                                                            1978

You Can Have It

My brother comes home from work
and climbs the stairs to our room.
I can hear the bed groan and his shoes drop
one by one. You can have it, he says.

The moonlight streams in the window   5
and his unshaven face is whitened

---

3. Island and public park in Detroit, Michigan.

like the face of the moon. He will sleep
long after noon and waken to find me gone.

Thirty years will pass before I remember
that moment when suddenly I knew each man   10
has one brother who dies when he sleeps
and sleeps when he rises to face this life,

and that together they are only one man
sharing a heart that always labors, hands
yellowed and cracked, a mouth that gasps   15
for breath and asks, Am I gonna make it?

All night at the ice plant he had fed
the chute its silvery blocks, and then I
stacked cases of orange soda for the children
of Kentucky, one gray box-car at a time   20

with always two more waiting. We were twenty
for such a short time and always in
the wrong clothes, crusted with dirt
and sweat. I think now we were never twenty.

In 1948 in the city of Detroit, founded   25
by de la Mothe Cadillac for the distant purposes
of Henry Ford,[4] no one wakened or died,
no one walked the streets or stoked a furnace,

for there was no such year, and now
that year has fallen off all the old newspapers,   30
calendars, doctors' appointments, bonds,
wedding certificates, drivers licenses.

The city slept. The snow turned to ice.
The ice to standing pools or rivers
racing in the gutters. Then bright grass rose   35
between the thousands of cracked squares,

and that grass died. I give you back 1948.
I give you all the years from then
to the coming one. Give me back the moon
with its frail light falling across a face.   40

Give me back my young brother, hard
and furious, with wide shoulders and a curse
for God and burning eyes that look upon
all creation and say, You can have it.

                                                        1979

4. American automobile manufacturer (1863–
1947). Antoine Laumet de la Mothe Cadillac
(1658–1730), for whom the automobiles are
named, founded the fur-trade post that eventually
became Detroit.

Drum

Leo's Tool & Die, 1950

In the early morning before the shop
opens, men standing out in the yard
on pine planks over the umber mud.
The oil drum, squat, brooding, brimmed
with metal scraps, three-armed crosses,   5
silver shavings whitened with milky oil,
drill bits bitten off. The light diamonds
last night's rain; inside a buzzer purrs.
The overhead door stammers upward
to reveal the scene of our day.   10
                     We sit
for lunch on crates before the open door.
Bobeck, the boss's nephew, squats to hug
the overflowing drum, gasps and lifts. Rain
comes down in sheets staining his gun-metal   15
covert suit. A stake truck sloshes off
as the sun returns through a low sky.
By four the office help has driven off. We
sweep, wash up, punch out, collect outside
for a final smoke. The great door crashes   20
down at last.
             In the darkness the scents
of mint, apples, asters. In the darkness
this could be a Carthaginian[5] outpost sent
to guard the waters of the West, those mounds   25
could be elephants at rest, the acrid half light
the haze of stars striking armor if stars were out.
On the galvanized tin roof the tunes of sudden rain.
The slow light of Friday morning in Michigan,
the one we waited for, shows seven hills   30
of scraped earth topped with crab grass,
weeds, a black oil drum empty, glistening
at the exact center of the modern world.

1999

---

5. Carthage was an ancient city on the north coast of Africa.

Thomas Kinsella
b. 1928

Despite his nationality and religion, Thomas Kinsella (whose last name is accented on the first syllable) describes his poetry as an expression of "my own full personality judging and collecting my experiences. . . . I find myself eschewing Catholic subjects and Irish subjects as being limited in themselves." Kinsella's earliest poems were love poems, and his later work explores the satisfactions, pain, and riskiness of married love. His other preoccupations are, as he says, the passage of time and the mysteries of artistic creation. Kinsella's poems on these subjects are restrained, elegant, and introspective. "Mirror in February," for example, is a meditation on that daily first look at oneself in the mirror. The poem concludes with characteristic stoicism, a resolve to go on in spite of all odds: "In slow distaste / I fold my towel with what grace I can, / Not young and not renewable, but man." "Baggot Street Deserta" is a meditation at the end of day; once again alone, the poet muses over the passage of time and the difficulties and satisfactions of his art. The rhetoric suggests that he is somewhat proud of having maintained his integrity: his sacrifices, doubts, and vanities "All feed a single stream, impassioned / Now with obsessed honesty, / A tugging scruple that can keep / Clear eyes staring down the mile, / The thousand fathoms, into sleep." In his later poems, Kinsella achieves a purified diction and an unusual strangeness of imagery and progressions.

Kinsella was born on May 4, 1928, in Dublin. From 1946 until 1956, he worked for the Irish Civil Service, eventually becoming the assistant principal officer in the Department of Finance. In 1956, he published his first book, *Poems,* with the Dolmen Press, of which he later became a director; two years later, his second book, *Another September,* won the Guinness Poetry Award. In 1965, he left Ireland to become writer-in-residence at Southern Illinois University, where he became a professor of English two years later. From 1970 to 1990, he was a professor at Temple University. He has published many books of poems and English translations of the important Irish verse epic *The Táin* (1969) and of other writings in Irish.

Baggot Street Deserta[1]

Lulled, at silence, the spent attack.
The will to work is laid aside.
The breaking-cry, the strain of the rack,
Yield, are at peace. The window is wide
On a crawling arch of stars, and the night   5
Reacts faintly to the mathematic
Passion of a cello suite
Plotting the quiet of my attic.
A mile away the river toils
Its buttressed fathoms out to sea;   10
Tucked in the mountains, many miles
Away from its roaring outcome, a shy

---

1. Abandoned, deserted; Baggot Street is in Dublin.

Gasp of waters in the gorse[2]
Is sonneting origins. Dreamers' heads
Lie mesmerised in Dublin's beds   15
Flashing with images, Adam's morse.[3]

A cigarette, the moon, a sigh
Of educated boredom, greet
A curlew's[4] lingering threadbare cry
Of common loss. Compassionate,   20
I add my call of exile, half-
Buried longing, half-serious
Anger and the rueful laugh.
We fly into our risk, the spurious.

Versing, like an exile, makes   25
A virtuoso of the heart,
Interpreting the old mistakes
And discords in a work of Art
For the One, a private masterpiece
Of doctored recollections. Truth   30
Concedes, before the dew, its place
In the spray of dried forgettings Youth
Collected when they were a single
Furious undissected bloom.
A voice clarifies when the tingle   35
Dies out of the nerves of time:
Endure and let the present punish.
Looking backward, all is lost;
The Past becomes a fairy bog
Alive with fancies, double crossed   40
By pad of owl and hoot of dog,
Where shaven, serious-minded men
Appear with lucid theses, after
Which they don the mists again
With trackless, cotton-silly laughter;   45
Secretly a swollen Burke
Assists a decomposing Hare[5]
To cart a body of good work
With midnight mutterings off somewhere;
The goddess who had light for thighs   50
Grows feet of dung and takes to bed,
Affronting horror-stricken eyes,
The marsh bird that children dread.

I nonetheless inflict, endure,
Tedium, intracordal[6] hurt,   55

2. Spiny evergreen shrub.
3. Morse code.
4. Migratory bird's.
5. In the early nineteenth century, the Irish crim-
inals William Burke and William Hare robbed

graves in Scotland of cadavers to sell to medical
schools, then turned to murder to increase their
stock.
6. That is, within a nerve.

The sting of memory's quick, the drear
Uprooting, burying, prising apart
Of loves a strident adolescent
Spent in doubt and vanity.
All feed a single stream, impassioned   60
Now with obsessed honesty,
A tugging scruple that can keep
Clear eyes staring down the mile,
The thousand fathoms, into sleep.

Fingers cold against the sill   65
Feel, below the stress of flight,
The slow implosion of my pulse
In a wrist with poet's cramp, a tight
Beat tapping out endless calls
Into the dark, as the alien   70
Garrison in my own blood
Keeps constant contact with the main
Mystery, not to be understood.
Out where imagination arches
Chilly points of light transact   75
The business of the border-marches
Of the Real, and I—a fact
That may be countered or may not—
Find their privacy complete.

My quarter-inch of cigarette   80
Goes flaring down to Baggot Street.

                                       1961

Je t'adore[7]

The other props are gone.
Sighing in one another's
Iron arms, propped above nothing,
We praise Love the limiter.

                                       1967

Mirror in February

The day dawns with scent of must and rain,
Of opened soil, dark trees, dry bedroom air.
Under the fading lamp, half dressed—my brain
Idling on some compulsive fantasy—

7. I adore you (French).

I towel my shaven jaw and stop, and stare,   5
Riveted by a dark exhausted eye,
A dry downturning mouth.

It seems again that it is time to learn,
In this untiring, crumbling place of growth
To which, for the time being, I return.   10
Now plainly in the mirror of my soul
I read that I have looked my last on youth
And little more; for they are not made whole
That reach the age of Christ.[8]

Below my window the awakening trees,   15
Hacked clean for better bearing, stand defaced
Suffering their brute necessities,
And how should the flesh not quail that span for span
Is mutilated more? In slow distaste
I fold my towel with what grace I can,   20
Not young and not renewable, but man.

                                                              1967

From Songs of the Psyche

1

A character, indistinct, entered,
looked about him, and began:

Why had I to wait until I am graceless,
unsightly, and a little nervous of stooping
until I could see   5

through those clear eyes I had once?
It is time. And I am
shivering as in stupid youth.

Who have stood where I was born
and snapped my bitten fingers!   10

                                                              1986

8. According to the Bible, Jesus was thirty-three at his crucifixion.

ANNE SEXTON
1928–1974

The attempt to utter raw feeling before time, contemplation, or conventional reassurance have alleviated it is at the heart of Anne Sexton's work. Poetry, she said in an interview, "should be a shock to the senses. It should almost hurt" (*Hudson Review* 18, 1965–66). As an epigraph for her second volume of poetry, *All My Pretty Ones* (1962), she chose a sentence from one of Franz Kafka's letters: "a book should serve as the ax for the frozen sea within us," should "make us suffer like the death of someone we love more than ourselves." What she finds in that frozen sea, and what she hopes to evoke in the reader, are deep and even repressed emotions—anguish, guilt, grief, hatred, and forbidden desires for sex and self-extinction. "Poetry," she said in a 1968 interview, "milks the unconscious." She often explores difficult and once taboo subjects, such as masturbation, sibling rivalry, surgery, menstruation, mental illness, drug abuse, and suicide.

She studied with Robert Lowell in the same seminar as Sylvia Plath, who became a friend and rival. Sexton is often labeled a member of the "confessional school," which is said to have begun with Lowell's sudden shift toward autobiography in *Life Studies* (1959). But her first influence, she said, was W. D. Snodgrass; his poem "Heart's Needle," she told him, "walked out at me and grew like a bone inside my heart" (letter of March 11, 1959). His verse is also informed by psychoanalytic theory and vivifies emotional stress; as such, it "kind of gave me permission," she said in a 1965 interview, to write intensely personal poetry. Sexton's first book, *To Bedlam and Part Way Back* (1960), includes many poems written in Lowell's workshop and centers on themes of mental collapse and partial recovery. Sexton's work became, in turn, an important resource for other poets. Plath, for example, said that Sexton's "are wonderfully craftsman-like poems and yet they have a kind of emotional and psychological depth which I think is something perhaps quite new, quite exciting" (BBC, 1962). Plath's "Daddy" borrows rhymes and themes from an early poem of Sexton's. Both poets were articulating in verse feelings that violated the social strictures placed on American women at mid-century. Sexton's poetry is strongly rooted in her bodily and psychic existence as a woman. It is, as she said, "intensely physical" (*Hudson Review*). The witch in "Her Kind," who is likened to the poet, claims powers of movement and magic traditionally forbidden to women, even if this means being burned at the stake.

In other poems, Sexton transgresses conventions governing responses to the dead. Although "The Truth the Dead Know" is dedicated to Sexton's parents, the poet refuses ceremony—"the stiff procession to the grave"—and flaunts her indifference toward the dead. In another anti-elegiac elegy, "All My Pretty Ones," the speaker guiltily worries about having possibly caused her father's death and yet sternly refuses to invest with affection the objects he has left behind. The father is remembered as involuntarily revealing incestuous desire for his daughter in the later poem "The Death of the Fathers." Other poems describe suicidal longings. The refrain of "The Starry Night" is "This is how / I want to die."

But as Sexton insisted, her interest was not in direct confession, even though her subject matter is so intimate: "I can be deeply personal, but often I'm not being personal about myself." Although Sexton valued most the "emotional content of a poem," her interest in feeling should not obscure her craft (quoted in Diane Middlebrook, *Anne Sexton*). Through the mid-1960s, she wrote verses skillfully constructed around patterns of rhyme and near-rhyme, assonance and alliteration, rhythms and pauses. They balance violent feeling against a restrained and understated tone. After Sexton's turn to free verse, her imagery—strange, evocative, sometimes surreal—increasingly becomes the most vital aesthetic element in her work. She said, "I prefer to think of myself as an imagist who deals with reality and its hard facts" (*Contemporary Poets of the English Language,* ed. R. Murphy, 1970). Poems such as "The Death Baby" and "The Room of My Life" include catalogs of astonishing metaphors and similes—caviar turning into lava, typewriter keys into eyeballs, and "doors opening and closing like sea clams." "Images are the heart of poetry," said Sexton. "And this is not tricks. Images come from the unconscious" ("Craft Interview," 1970).

Sexton was born Anne Gray Harvey, on November 9, 1928, in Newton, Massachusetts. She was educated at Garland Junior College, then married and had two daughters. Repeated suicide attempts led to hospitalizations, particularly after the birth of her second child. With the encouragement of her psychiatrist, Sexton began to write poetry as a part of her therapy in December 1956. In 1961, she was appointed as a scholar at Radcliffe Institute, and she soon achieved wide acclaim; among many other awards, she won the Pulitzer Prize in 1967. She was in heavy demand as a reader of her poetry and, in 1968, formed a "chamber rock" group, Anne Sexton and Her Kind. In 1970, she accepted a teaching position in creative writing at Boston University. A few years later, at forty-five, after bouts of depression and substance abuse, she committed suicide by idling her car in a closed garage. After Plath's suicide, Sexton was envious that Plath had crawled "down alone / into the death I wanted so badly and for so long" ("Sylvia's Death"). But after Sexton's suicide, leading women poets responded differently, for fear of the dangerous pattern that was being set. While speaking "in Anne's honor and memory," Adrienne Rich said: "We have had enough suicidal women poets, enough suicidal women, enough of self-destructiveness as the sole form of violence permitted to women" (*On Lies, Secrets, and Silence*). In Sexton's obituary, Denise Levertov wrote: "We who are alive must make clear, as she could not, the distinction between creativity and self-destruction" ("Light Up the Cave").

Her Kind

I have gone out, a possessed witch,
haunting the black air, braver at night;
dreaming evil, I have done my hitch
over the plain houses, light by light:
lonely thing, twelve-fingered,[1] out of mind.   5
A woman like that is not a woman, quite.
I have been her kind.

I have found the warm caves in the woods,
filled them with skillets, carvings, shelves,
closets, silks, innumerable goods;   10
fixed the suppers for the worms and the elves:
whining, rearranging the disaligned.
A woman like that is misunderstood.
I have been her kind.

I have ridden in your cart, driver,   15
waved my nude arms at villages going by,

---

1. Witches were traditionally believed to have six fingers on each hand.

learning the last bright routes, survivor
where your flames still bite my thigh
and my ribs crack where your wheels wind.
A woman like that is not ashamed to die.   20
I have been her kind.

                                                    1960

The Truth the Dead Know

For my mother, born March 1902, died March 1959
and my father, born February 1900, died June 1959

Gone, I say and walk from church,
refusing the stiff procession to the grave,
letting the dead ride alone in the hearse.
It is June. I am tired of being brave.

We drive to the Cape. I cultivate   5
myself where the sun gutters from the sky,
where the sea swings in like an iron gate
and we touch. In another country people die.

My darling, the wind falls in like stones
from the whitehearted water and when we touch   10
we enter touch entirely. No one's alone.
Men kill for this, or for as much.

And what of the dead? They lie without shoes
in their stone boats. They are more like stone
than the sea would be if it stopped. They refuse   15
to be blessed, throat, eye and knucklebone.

                                                    1962

All My Pretty Ones

> All my pretty ones?
> Did you say all? O hell-kite! All?
> What! all my pretty chickens and their dam
> At one fell swoop? . . .
> I cannot but remember such things were,
> That were most precious to me.
> —MACBETH[2]

Father, this year's jinx rides us apart
where you followed our mother to her cold slumber;
a second shock boiling its stone to your heart,

---

2. Macduff's lament on learning that Macbeth has had his wife and children brutally murdered (*Macbeth* 4.3.217–25).

leaving me here to shuffle and disencumber
you from the residence you could not afford: 5
a gold key, your half of a woolen mill,
twenty suits from Dunne's, an English Ford,
the love and legal verbiage of another will,
boxes of pictures of people I do not know.
I touch their cardboard faces. They must go.   10

But the eyes, as thick as wood in this album,
hold me. I stop here, where a small boy
waits in a ruffled dress for someone to come . . .
for this soldier who holds his bugle like a toy
or for this velvet lady who cannot smile.   15
Is this your father's father, this commodore
in a mailman suit? My father, time meanwhile
has made it unimportant who you are looking for.
I'll never know what these faces are all about.
I lock them into their book and throw them out.   20

This is the yellow scrapbook that you began
the year I was born; as crackling now and wrinkly
as tobacco leaves: clippings where Hoover outran
the Democrats,[3] wiggling his dry finger at me
and Prohibition; news where the *Hindenburg* went   25
down[4] and recent years where you went flush
on war. This year, solvent but sick, you meant
to marry that pretty widow in a one-month rush.
But before you had that second chance, I cried
on your fat shoulder. Three days later you died.   30

These are the snapshots of marriage, stopped in places.
Side by side at the rail toward Nassau[5] now;
here, with the winner's cup at the speedboat races,
here, in tails at the Cotillion, you take a bow,
here, by our kennel of dogs with their pink eyes,   35
running like show-bred pigs in their chain-link pen;
here, at the horseshow where my sister wins a prize;
and here, standing like a duke among groups of men.
Now I fold you down, my drunkard, my navigator,
my first lost keeper, to love or look at later.   40

I hold a five-year diary that my mother kept
for three years, telling all she does not say
of your alcoholic tendency. You overslept,
she writes. My God, father, each Christmas Day
with your blood, will I drink down your glass   45
of wine? The diary of your hurly-burly years
goes to my shelf to wait for my age to pass.
Only in this hoarded span will love persevere.

---

3. In the presidential election of 1928.
4. The German airship *Hindenburg* was destroyed
by fire, at Lakeville, N.J., in 1936.
5. In the Bahamas.

Whether you are pretty or not, I outlive you,
bend down my strange face to yours and forgive you.   50

1962

The Starry Night

*That does not keep me from having a terrible need of—shall I say
the word—religion. Then I go out at night to paint the stars.*
          —VINCENT VAN GOGH[6] *in a letter to his brother*

The town does not exist
except where one black-haired tree slips
up like a drowned woman into the hot sky.
The town is silent. The night boils with eleven stars.
Oh starry starry night! This is how   5
I want to die.

It moves. They are all alive.
Even the moon bulges in its orange irons
to push children, like a god, from its eye.
The old unseen serpent swallows up the stars.   10
Oh starry starry night! This is how
I want to die:

into that rushing beast of the night,
sucked up by that great dragon, to split
from my life with no flag,   15
no belly,
no cry.

1962

From The Death of the Fathers

2. How We Danced

The night of my cousin's wedding
I wore blue.
I was nineteen
and we danced, Father, we orbited.
We moved like angels washing themselves.   5
We moved like two birds on fire.
Then we moved like the sea in a jar,
slower and slower.
The orchestra played
"Oh how we danced on the night we were wed."   10

6. Dutch painter (1853–1890); in his thirties, he became insane and finally committed suicide. His brother was his only confidant; this letter was written to him in September 1888 from Arles, France. At this time, Van Gogh was painting *Starry Night on the Rhône*.

And you waltzed me like a lazy Susan
and we were dear,
very dear.
Now that you are laid out,
useless as a blind dog,   15
now that you no longer lurk,
the song rings in my head.
Pure oxygen was the champagne we drank
and clicked our glasses, one to one.
The champagne breathed like a skin diver   20
and the glasses were crystal and the bride
and groom gripped each other in sleep
like nineteen-thirty marathon dancers.
Mother was a belle and danced with twenty men.
You danced with me never saying a word.   25
Instead the serpent spoke as you held me close.
The serpent, that mocker, woke up and pressed against me
like a great god and we bent together
like two lonely swans.

                                                            1972

From The Death Baby

1. Dreams

I was an ice baby.
I turned to sky blue.
My tears became two glass beads.
My mouth stiffened into a dumb howl.
They say it was a dream   5
but I remember that hardening.

My sister at six
dreamt nightly of my death:
"The baby turned to ice.
Someone put her in the refrigerator   10
and she turned as hard as a Popsicle."

I remember the stink of the liverwurst.
How I was put on a platter and laid
between the mayonnaise and the bacon.
The rhythm of the refrigerator   15
had been disturbed.
The milk bottle hissed like a snake.
The tomatoes vomited up their stomachs.
The caviar turned to lava.
The pimentos kissed like cupids.   20
I moved like a lobster,
slower and slower.

The air was tiny.
The air would not do.

•

I was at the dogs' party.   25
I was their bone.
I had been laid out in their kennel
like a fresh turkey.

This was my sister's dream
but I remember that quartering;   30
I remember the sickbed smell
of the sawdust floor, the pink eyes,
the pink tongues and the teeth, those nails.
I had been carried out like Moses[7]
and hidden by the paws   35
of ten Boston bull terriers,
ten angry bulls
jumping like enormous roaches.
At first I was lapped,
rough as sandpaper.   40
I became very clean.
Then my arm was missing.
I was coming apart.
They loved me until
I was gone.   45

1974

The Room of My Life

Here,
in the room of my life
the objects keep changing.
Ashtrays to cry into,
the suffering brother of the wood walls,   5
the forty-eight keys of the typewriter
each an eyeball that is never shut,
the books, each a contestant in a beauty contest,
the black chair, a dog coffin made of Naugahyde,
the sockets on the wall   10
waiting like a cave of bees,
the gold rug
a conversation of heels and toes,
the fireplace
a knife waiting for someone to pick it up,   15
the sofa, exhausted with the exertion of a whore,
the phone

7. According to tradition, Moses' parents hid him for three months and then set him afloat in a basket on the Nile River to avoid an Egyptian edict that all newborn, male Hebrews were to be killed.

two flowers taking root in its crotch,
the doors
opening and closing like sea clams,   20
the lights
poking at me,
lighting up both the soil and the laugh.
The windows,
the starving windows   25
that drive the trees like nails into my heart.
Each day I feed the world out there
although birds explode
right and left.
I feed the world in here too,   30
offering the desk puppy biscuits.
However, nothing is just what it seems to be.
My objects dream and wear new costumes,
compelled to, it seems, by all the words in my hands
and the sea that bangs in my throat.   35

1975

A. K. RAMANUJAN
1929–1993

The most distinguished English-language Indian poet of the twentieth century, Attipat Krishnaswami Ramanujan wrote a body of poetry that—in its crosscultural texture and subject matter—is witness to the complex cultural intermingling within India and across much of the contemporary world. Born in Mysore to a Tamil Brahman family, he grew up in Karnataka and moved among different languages. Downstairs in the family home, he spoke Tamil with his mother. Upstairs, he spoke English with his father, a mathematics professor at Mysore University. On the terrace at night, he learned from his father—also an astronomer and astrologer—the English and Sanskrit names of the stars. Outside, Kannada was the language of the streets. These became the languages of his life's work as poet, translator, and linguist.

Having moved to the United States in 1959, Ramanujan often quipped that he was "the hyphen in Indian-American." The paradoxes of his life, lived among multiple cultures and languages, are many. Though rooted in south Indian Brahman culture, he wrote primarily in English and drew on such modern poets as W. B. Yeats, Ezra Pound, William Carlos Williams, and Wallace Stevens. Far from being an apologist for an essential "Indianness," he criticized Sanskrit-based Indology, Hindu zealotry, and Indian revivalism. Resisting the "monism" and even "cultural imperialism" of proponents of a single "pan-Indian Sanskritic Great Tradition," he brought attention to neglected literatures of south India such as the Dravidian. He affirmed that "cultural traditions in India are indissolubly plural and often conflicting" ("Where Mirrors Are Windows: Towards an Anthology of Reflections"). "India does not have one past," he emphasized, "but many pasts" ("Classics Lost and Found").

Though an English-language poet in the United States, Ramanujan devoted his life to South Asian studies, wrote primarily about India, drew inspiration from Dravidian literatures, and often seemed clinically detached from the English language he worked in. Best known in the West for his crystalline translations of classical and medieval Tamil and Kannada verse, Ramanujan draws on many features of these older literatures in his own anglophone poetry: the strikingly vivid and structural use of metaphor, the intensification of one image by another, "montage" and "dissolve" effects, streams of association, flowing syntax, spare diction, avoidance of heavily stressed rhythms, delight in irony and paradox, precise observation of both interior (*akam*) and exterior (*puṟam*) worlds, and reliance not on metaphysical abstraction but on physical detail for complex thinking. Ramanujan's indigenous models complement Anglo-modernist principles of concision, economy, and nondecorative use of metaphor.

His eye a "rainbow bubble," Ramanujan would, as he rhymes in "Mythologies 2," "see all things double." Straddling the divide between East and West, First World and Third, his work fuses ancient Dravidian poetics with modern forms. At the heart of his poetry are ironic, if plangent, meditations on cultural transfer and loss between East and West, on survivals and disappearances between past and present. His delight in metaphorical resemblance helps him leap the gap between these worlds, even as he skeptically measures the distance between them. Questing after his genetic, psychological, and cultural origins in the wittily entitled "Elements of Composition," as in "Drafts," Ramanujan acknowledges that our mixed and irrecuperable pasts must change the moment we look for them. His depiction of the self resembles a traditional Indian vision of identity as embedded in endlessly fluid, concentrically arranged contexts (as in the concept of *samsara*). At the same time, it can also seem compatible with a post-modern vision of the self as decentered, composite, and provisional.

The family—with its multiple reflections and opacities in relation to the self—is frequently the locus of Ramanujan's poetic acts of self-definition. In poems such as "Self-Portrait" and "Extended Family," the poet defines himself by sorting through his resemblances with his grandparents, parents, and children. Located in dislocation, he puzzles over the ironic connections and differences between himself in Chicago and his grandfather in India, as between a modern Western lightbulb and the ancient Vedic sun.

After receiving a B.A. in English literature from Mysore University in 1949, Ramanujan taught English in Indian schools and became fascinated with Indian folklore. He began to study linguistics at Deccan College and continued on a Fulbright grant at Indiana University in 1959, completing his dissertation in 1963. In 1961, he taught for the first time at the University of Chicago, where he gave classes in linguistics, South Asian languages and civilizations, and creative writing until his death. In 1976, Ramanujan was honored by the Indian government with the Padma Shri, awarded for distinguished service to the nation; in 1983, he received a MacArthur Fellowship.

Self-Portrait

> I resemble everyone
> but myself, and sometimes see
> in shop-windows,
>   despite the well-known laws
>   of optics,   5
> the portrait of a stranger,
> date unknown,
> often signed in a corner
> by my father.

1966

Elements of Composition

Composed as I am, like others,
    of elements on certain well-known lists,
father's seed and mother's egg

gathering earth, air, fire, mostly
    water, into a mulberry mass,   5
moulding calcium,

carbon, even gold, magnesium and such,
    into a chattering self tangled
in love and work,

scary dreams, capable of eyes that can see,   10
    only by moving constantly,
the constancy of things

like Stonehenge or cherry trees;

add uncle's eleven fingers
    making shadow-plays of rajas[1]   15
and cats, hissing,

becoming fingers again, the look
    of panic on sister's face
an hour before

her wedding, a dated newspaper map   20
    of a place one has never seen, maybe
no longer there

after the riots, downtown Nairobi,[2]
    that a friend carried in his passport
as others would   25

a woman's picture in their wallets;

add the lepers of Madurai,[3]
    male, female, married,
with children,

lion faces, crabs for claws,   30
    clotted on their shadows
under the stone-eyed

---

1. Indian kings or princes.
2. Capital of Kenya.

3. City in south India where leprosy is a continu-
ing problem.

goddesses of dance, mere pillars,
   moving as nothing on earth
can move—   35

I pass through them
   as they pass through me
taking and leaving

affections, seeds, skeletons,

millennia of fossil records   40
   of insects that do not last
a day,

body-prints of mayflies,
   a legend half-heard
in a train   45

of the half-man searching
   for an ever-fleeing
other half[4]

through Muharram[5] tigers,
   hyacinths in crocodile waters,   50
and the sweet

twisted lives of epileptic saints,

and even as I add,
   I lose, decompose
into my elements,   55

into other names and forms,
   past, and passing, tenses
without time,

caterpillar on a leaf, eating,
   being eaten.[6]   60

1986

---

4. Elsewhere, Ramanujan compares the Hindu myth of the god that "splits himself into male and female" to "the androgynous figure in Plato's *Symposium*, halved into male and female segments which forever seek each other and crave union" ("Some Thoughts on 'Non-Western' Classics, with Indian Examples").

5. During the first month of the Islamic calendar, Muharram processions, often including dancers in tiger masks, commemorate the martyrdom of Muhammad's grandson, Husein.

6. According to the *Taittiriya Upanishad*, "What eats is eaten, / and what's eaten, eats / in turn" (Ramanujan's translation).

Alien

A foetus in an acrobat's womb,
   ignorant yet of barbed wire
and dotted lines,

hanger-on in terror of the fall
   while the mother-world turns somersaults,   5
whirling on the single bar,

as her body shapes under water
   a fish with gills into a baby
with a face

getting ready to make faces,   10
   and hands that will soon feel the powder touch
of monarch butterflies,

the tin and silver of nickel and dime,
   and learn right and left to staple, fold
and mutilate   15

a paper world in search of identity cards.

         1986

Drafts

1

A rough draft, getting rougher:
   a struggle in the crowd to see
the well-known

but half-seen Hyde Park[7] rapist's face
   half-seen perhaps only by another,   5
unseen

because seen too often; now towards,
   now away from what one thought
one always knew

without the help of policemen's   10
   drawings, a trayful of noses
and cruel lips.

---

7. Neighborhood on the south side of Chicago in which the University of Chicago is located.

2

Itself a copy of lost events,
   the original is nowhere, of which things,
even these hands,   15

seem but copies, garbled by a ciphered
   script, opaque as the Indus,[8]
to be refigured

from broken seals, headless bodies,
   mere fingers, of merchants and dancers   20
in a charred city

with sewers, bath houses, a horned god
   of beasts among real homebodies,
family quarrels,

itches, clogs in the drain, the latter   25
   too ordinary to be figured
in the classic seals.

3

And we have originals, clay tigers
   that aboriginals drown after each small-
pox ritual,   30

or dinosaur smells, that leave no copies;
   and copies with displaced originals
like these words,

adopted daughters researching parents
   through maiden names in changing languages,   35
telephone books,

and familiar grins in railway stations.

4

The DNA leaves copies in me and mine
   of grandfather's violins, and programmes
of much older music;   40

the epilepsies go to an uncle
   to fill him with hymns and twitches,
bypassing me for now;

8. River in India before 1947; after, in Pakistan.

mother's migraines translate, I guess,
    into allergies, a fear of black cats,   45
and a daughter's passion

for bitter gourd and Dostoevsky;[9]
    mother's almond eyes mix with my wife's
ancestral hazel

to give my son green flecks in a painter's eye,   50
    but the troubled look is all his own.

                                                     1986

Extended Family

Yet like grandfather
I bathe before the village crow

the dry chlorine water
my only Ganges[1]

the naked Chicago bulb   5
a cousin of the Vedic sun[2]

slap soap on my back
like father

and think
in proverbs   10

like me
I wipe myself dry

with an unwashed
Sears turkish towel

like mother   15
I hear faint morning song

(though here it sounds
Japanese)

9. Fyodor Dostoyevsky (1821–1881), Russian
novelist.
1. Indian river considered sacred in Hinduism;
many make pilgrimages to bathe in its holy waters.

2. The Vedas—the holy texts of Hinduism—por-
tray the sun as various gods and the divine source
of all knowledge.

and three clear strings
nextdoor   20

through kitchen
clatter

like my little daughter
I play shy

hand over crotch   25
my body not yet full

of thoughts novels
and children

I hold my peepee
like my little son   30

play garden hose
in and out
the bathtub

like my grandson
I look up   35

unborn
at myself

like my great
great-grandson

I am not yet   40
may never be

my future
dependent

on several
people   45

yet
to come

1986

Chicago Zen

i

Now tidy your house,
dust especially your living room

and do not forget to name
all your children.

ii

Watch your step. Sight may strike you   5
blind in unexpected places.

The traffic light turns orange
on 57th and Dorchester,[3] and you stumble,

you fall into a vision of forest fires,
enter a frothing Himalayan river,   10

rapid, silent.

        On the 14th floor,
Lake Michigan crawls and crawls

in the window. Your thumbnail
cracks a lobster louse on the windowpane   15

from your daughter's hair
and you drown, eyes open,

towards the Indies, the antipodes.[4]
And you, always so perfectly sane.

iii

Now you know what you always knew: 20
the country cannot be reached

by jet. Nor by boat on jungle river,
hashish behind the Monkey-temple,

nor moonshot to the cratered Sea
of Tranquility, slim circus girls   25

---

3. Fifty-seventh Street and Dorchester Avenue, near the University of Chicago.

4. The place on the surface of the earth directly opposite one's current location.

on a tightrope between tree and tree
with white parasols, or the one

and only blue guitar.[5]

            Nor by any
other means of transport,   30

migrating with a clean valid passport,
no, not even by transmigrating

without any passport at all,
but only by answering ordinary

black telephones, questions   35
walls and small children ask,

and answering all calls of nature.

               iv

Watch your step, watch it, I say,
especially at the first high
threshold,   40

        and the sudden low
one near the end
of the flight
of stairs,

        and watch   45
for the last
step that's never there.

                        1986

Foundlings in the Yukon

In the Yukon[6] the other day
miners found the skeleton
of a lemming
curled around some seeds
in a burrow: 5
sealed off by a landslide
in Pleistocene times.[7]

---

5. Cf. Wallace Stevens, "The Man with the Blue Guitar."
6. Mountainous territory in northwestern Canada.
7. The Great Ice Age.

Six grains were whole,
unbroken: picked and planted
ten thousand   10
years after their time,
they took root
within forty-eight hours
and sprouted
a candelabra of eight small leaves.   15

A modern Alaskan lupine,[8]
I'm told, waits three years to come
to flower, but these
upstarts drank up sun
and unfurled early   20
with the crocuses of March
as if long deep
burial had made them hasty

for birth and season, for names,
genes, for passing on: 25
like the kick
and shift of an intra-uterine
memory, like
this morning's dream of being
born in an eagle's   30
nest with speckled eggs and the screech

of nestlings, like a pent-up
centenarian's sudden burst
of lust, or maybe
just elegies in Duino[9] unbound   35
from the dark,
these new aborigines biding
their time
for the miner's night-light

to bring them their dawn,   40
these infants compact with age,
older than the oldest
things alive, having skipped
a million falls
and the registry of tree-rings,   45
suddenly younger
by an accident of flowering

than all their timely descendants.

1995

8. Alaskan wildflower.
9. Rainer Maria Rilke (1875–1926), Austro-German poet, overcame thirteen years of writer's block in Duino Castle (near Trieste), where he wrote a famous series of elegies.

RICHARD HOWARD
b. 1929

Since Gustave Flaubert, certainly since James Joyce, poetry has seemed to lose ground to the novel, which in the twentieth century appropriated many of the techniques of language once reserved for poetry. Yet a number of postwar American poets, most notably Robert Lowell and Randall Jarrell, have attempted to recapture for poetry lost areas of dramatic interest and psychological complexity. So too has Richard Howard, particularly in his dramatic monologues. Howard's inspiration was certainly Robert Browning, and the late nineteenth century, among other historical periods, often provides Howard with subjects and ambience. Using memoirs, letters, and newspapers, he re-creates a gallery of men and women, gives them life, and lets them have their say. In his later books, particularly in the wake of the AIDS epidemic, Howard has written memorable poems depicting contemporary gay, urban life, such as "My Last Hustler." In " 'Man Who Beat Up Homosexuals Reported to Have AIDS Virus,' " he juxtaposes the dramatic voices of an assailant's sister-in-law and one of his victims, who has suffered injuries and yet remains, like many of Howard's characters, intellectually robust. Howard brings to these late poems his considerable skills in narrative, dramatic voice, and wordplay.

Howard's poems are characterized by great variety and vivacity. They are bookish and learned; like Marianne Moore, Howard seems to squirrel away odd facts and quotations for which he will someday find a poetic use. He is a critic and translator, an addict of language, fascinated by minute instances of its powers to connect and disguise, and pleased with his own virtuosity in using it. In his poetry, the language accumulates closely woven details in a molecular fashion.

Howard was born on May 13, 1929, in Cleveland, Ohio. He was educated at Columbia University and at the Sorbonne. He lived abroad for a time, but he found the expatriate's life uncomfortable and moved to New York, where he now teaches at Columbia. Besides many collections of poems (the first published in 1962) and critical studies of postwar American poetry, Howard has published more than 150 translations from French, ranging from the works of Alain Robbe-Grillet and Roland Barthes to the memoirs of General Charles de Gaulle. He has won many prizes and awards, including the Pulitzer Prize in 1970 for *Untitled Subjects*.

"Man Who Beat Up Homosexuals Reported to Have AIDS Virus"

—The New York Times, *March 8, 1991*

to the memory of Alan Barnett

To *The New York Times:* Your health editor
may not print this; my social-worker says
   it will do me good
to write it anyway, and in my case
the terminal treatment has to be truth.   5
   Not much else, by now,
can "do me good": the hospital routine
laboriously contends with new bouts

       of pneumocystis,[1]
thereby bestowing leisure to survey   10
my escalating KS[2] lesions—caught
    red-handed . . . Last week
you ran an article about a man
whose name you withhold, though his age agrees
    with his appearance   15
when I was in his hands, and he in mine.
This was years ago, long before there was
    a reason to think
such handling was red, or led to being dead!
I can identify him all the same,   20
    though all different
from actions in which he says he took part.

—If he took part, then which of us took all?
    For all was taken,
as you report: I am one of the "many   25
gay men beaten in the 1980's
    by a truck-driver
in the New York area," and I owe
myself whatever account I can give
    of that episode.   30
It is not the reason I am here, nor
is my being here the result of it—
    but it represents
one dimension of the life I am in
a final position (no evasions!)   35
    to evaluate . . .

*Maureen, it's Jane. Did you get the clipping? If you read it through, you
realize why I had to call . . . No, now. We need to talk. You put things
off, they just get right back on and ride you worse. It has to be Jack, Sis,
your husband and the father of your girls! Everything fits. First of all*   40
*about the life-insurance screening—what a way to learn he has that
terrible disease! And then that part about "the large amounts of victims'
blood on himself" . . . Remember how hard it was—well, I can remember
your complaining about it all the time—getting those stains out of his
jeans each week! It was hard because that was blood—and not from*   45
*lugging pork-bellies out of his truck! . . . I don't care what he told you,
do you think I believe what Henry tells me? Of course you're not infected.
How could you be if he hasn't . . . The paper said it's been ten years . . .
Honey, I know: we're middle-aged, thank God! You don't imagine that
Henry and I . . . ? Maureen, you've got to get it through your head there's*   50
*something wrong with Jack. And I don't mean his getting sick now—
wrong all the way back. Dumb of me to think the girls would tell you
. . . Sis, do you understand how men get AIDS?*

---

1. Form of pneumonia that often accompanies the later stages of AIDS.
2. Kaposi's sarcoma, skin disease characterized by reddish lesions, commonly afflicting AIDS sufferers.

My social-worker says "we have to be
downright" (she invariably says   55
   "we" when she means me)
and goes on to assure me that *God is*
in the details—she doubtless heard the phrase
   in her Crisis-Class
("Depression and Dying") only last week.   60
It could be true, for all I know; there's not
   much hope of finding
Him in the Master Plan. So let's pray
she's right. Herewith the (divine) specifics:
   maybe five years back   65
I met Mr. X one Saturday night
—more likely it was a Sunday morning—
   as I came around
the corner of Washington and Bethune:[3]
a vision! He was playing with himself   70
   in the open cab
of a pork-butcher's van—such diversions
are often met with in the meat-market,
   appropriately,
since he asked, when I started cruising him,   75
if I wanted some. Meat. (I know you won't
   run any of this,
but I'm being downright.) So I went down
on him in the back of his truck. Dark there,
   hard to see—you have   80
to feel your way on such occasions—but
I found it easy enough to do that . . .
   I found it easy.

Why would *he tell you . . . why tell anyone? A married man with three*
daughters: Maureen, he must have known people would never think . . .   85
Did he *ever think . . . ? And that would make it easy for him to do the*
things he did—easier: he was their dad, whatever else he was . . . When
did it start? Probably once you and he . . . stopped. Being in New York
must have made a difference too. Because New York is different . . . from
Nebraska, anyway. I'm not trying to be funny—you always said you hated   90
living there, right up to when they transferred him back here . . . Maybe
you knew why, even if there was no way for you to know . . . The paper
said he went out looking for . . . the other kind (maybe they weren't so
"other" after all) several times a week—you must have thought something
even if you wanted not to. Maureen, the paper said "too many times to   95
count"—no, "to remember." And it said the other drivers went out with
him too. Does that sound right to you? Sis, when did Jack do things with
others? Even beat up queers?

   Once he was through, or I was—hard to tell
   who it is completes such actions, who is   100

---

3. Intersection in lower Manhattan.

active, as they say,
and who is passive (even a woman
is never really passive, I suppose)—
once our thing was done,
he began talking to me in the dark—   105
till then, of course, he hadn't breathed a word,
    just breathed, and after
a while of breathing, the usual moan . . .
Maybe my downright talent made him feel
    he could shoot the works . . .   110
He asked, was that all I wanted to do,
and if it was, would I do something else
    for him. Something more.
He moved around, I knew what he wanted—
it was easy to tell by the clatter   115
    his belt-buckle made
against the floor. I started to explain
about my "proclivities" (not doing
    what my father did),
and as if, right then, something about *him*   120
had been exposed, something unbearably
    humiliating,
he began to yell and lash out at me
with that belt. If it was too dark for me
    to guess that my *not*   125
doing what he needed would enrage him,
it was also too dark for him to see
    where the hell I was:
I managed to slither out of *harm's way*
during the mayhem, and to haul myself   130
    eventually
out of the *van*, but not before we both
were something of a mess. That was my clue
    to my "assailant"—
there must have been blood, my blood, all over   135
the place, just as *The Times* reported it.
    All in a night's work.

*He claims he hasn't done it in three years: maybe he doesn't need to do
it now, but maybe he will. Maybe he has to. Maureen, you've got to trust
your own sister: are there times when he takes it out on you? No one talks*   140
*about beating, but I know it happens in a lot of "happy homes." I'm trying
to help you. Listen to me! It could be years before Jack ever shows signs
he has this thing—he may keep his strength for quite a while . . . I know
you want to take care of him when he's not able to . . . when he needs
help. It's a damn good thing you do—at this point I can't see why anyone*   145
*else would: Maureen, he likes to hurt people! But you've got to take care
of yourself first. If it passed into his blood from someone he beat up, what
about yours? I suppose that's the only way it could happen now . . . Keep
away from him if he—Sis, you know what I mean: if he can't go out for
it, what's to keep him from beginning at home, like charity? I'm not*   150

joking, Maureen, I just want you to recognize the truth . . . If men are
more devious than women it must be because they have more to hide.

But I doubt—being downright—if my man
had much to fear from me—certainly not
    from any of my   155
blood in any cuts of his, as he told
the Nebraska medical officers.
    I suspected—being
downright and outright—his dose could be traced
to an administration of the same   160
    bodily fluids
as those I was punished for declining
to provide. Not every faggot who climbs
    into a meat-truck
has my limitations, I know plenty   165
who would be pleased (*and* able) to oblige
    by humping a hunk . . .
Furthermore—being down and out—I couldn't
care less. I lie here wondering (most days,
    my only life-sign,   170
unless you count reading *The New York Times*
as a sign of life—and you would, although
    the *Living* section
is sometimes too much for me) . . . Wondering
is what my time is good for—good times! and   175
    what I wonder is
if the life I have always lived ("always"
being the last 20 years, who could know
    they would be the last?)
was mine at all, my choice—unless it was   180
just the life I could never acknowledge
    to *The New York Times*
(of course I'm using you as a symbol),
a life so sexually myopic[4]
    I knew only those   185
faces I had kissed—and not always those!
Is this what it comes to? A tribal tale
    of A Thousand Nights
and a Night, except that this Scheherazade
gets herself 86'd[5] . . . Sex turns out like   190
    reading (believe me
I know whereof I speak—in my corner
the comparison is anything but idle)
    because it gives you
somewhere to get to when you have to stay   195
where you are. But life is used up, if it's
    used, spent, or wasted . . .

4. Short-sighted.
5. Killed. In *A Thousand and One Nights* (four-   teenth century), the condemned Scheherazade
   keeps herself alive by telling stories each night.

Mama always used to tell us you get what you pay for. Maureen, that was
a crock! I've learned better, and so have you, by now: you pay for what
you get. Jack has to pay, so do you and the girls, Henry and I. The hard   200
thing is to understand just what he got. Not Henry, Jack! Sis, don't be
dumb . . . I know he got this disease, what I mean is, what did he get out
of what he did that has to be paid for by getting AIDS? Damn right it's
a judgment—isn't everything? I'm not saying he doesn't deserve it, it's
just that if you're going to see him through to the end, you'd better   205
understand the satisfaction—no, it's more than that: the rush, the thrill,
or whatever it is doing things like that to other men could give him. If
AIDS is so awful, then that has to have been so good. Do you see? You
have to realize the joy of it if you're going to reckon up the pain. Think
about it, Maureen. I'll call you back once Henry's gone to bed. We'll talk   210
some more.

        The Times keeps referring to a *life-style*
        as having consequences. That is why
           I've made this gesture:
        not to dispute your claim, but to insist   215
        the consequences are *not* a judgment!
           This sickness I got
        is no sentence passed on my wickedness—
        recalling which "wickedness" makes up,
           now as before, most   220
        of what I have lived for. Not died for,
        I'm grateful, even to Mr. X . . .
           Why should his actions
        incur a verdict, any more than mine?
        By the time he reaches whatever wards   225
           Nebraska affords
        (social-worker or not), I hope he can
        summon up, as I did, the impulse that
           brought us together
        and remembers me. That is what it comes   230
        down to: a matter of remembering
           certain encounters,
        certain moments entirely free of time.
        I am no longer able to excite
           myself (is that verb   235
        fit to print?), my visions are purely that,
        just visions, endless reruns of the scenes
           I have collected.
        Remembering is not even the word:
        making comes closer. Where understanding   240
           fails, a word will come
        to take its place. Making is my word,
        my enterprise. Believe me, I lived through
           such episodes as
        the sad one I have described for the sake   245
        of . . . what? Of whatever was exchanged there
           in the dark meat-van

before the end . . . The second half of joy,
somebody said, is shorter than the first,
     and that gets it right.   250
Whatever's left of my life, I am *making,*
the way I made it happen all along
     —I replay the scenes
from that movie The Past, starring not
Mr. X playing opposite myself   255
     but Endymion,
Narcissus, Patroclus,[6] all the fellows
I have welcomed to the tiny duchy[7]
     of my bed—the world's
only country entirely covered by   260
its flag. I thank you for "covering"
     as well as you could
the story to which I have provided
such a lengthy follow-up—gay men do
     go in for length, or   265
at least go out for it; that is part of
our mythology. And now, perhaps, you
     know another part . . .
The nurse has just come in with another
delicious concoction. The social-worker   270
     awaits . . . (Name Withheld).

                                                      1994

My Last Hustler

            . . . all smiles stopped[8]

When "Brad" is lying naked, or rather naked is lying
in wait for whatever those he refers to as clients require
by way of what *they* refer to as satisfaction, denying
himself the distraction of alcohol or amyl,[9] there appears
in his eyes no flicker of shame, no flare of shameless desire,   5
and what tribute he is paid finds him neither tender nor fierce.

On a bed above suspicion, creases in obviously fresh
linen still mapping a surface only a little creamier than
the creaseless hills and hollows of his compliant flesh,
Brad will extend himself (as the graphic saying goes)   10
and the upper hand—always his—will push into place *the man
who happens to be there* till happening comes to blows

---

6. In Homer's *Iliad,* Achilles' companion, whose
death he mourns bitterly. The other two names are
from Greek mythology. *Endymion:* beautiful young
man loved by the moon and put to sleep forever by
Zeus. *Narcissus:* young man condemned to fall in
love with his own reflection.

7. Domain of a duke; special territory.
8. From "My Last Duchess," a dramatic mono-
logue by English poet Robert Browning (1812–
1889).
9. Amyl nitrate, a powerful stimulant believed to
be an aphrodisiac.

(another saying you now more fully grasp): full-blown,
Brad will prepare himself, though not precipitately,
for the grateful-kisses stage; he offers cheek and chin   15
but objects to undergoing your accolade on his mouth:
he has endured such homage too early, too often, too lately,
and for all his boyish ways Brad is not wholly a youth.

Routines on some arduous rigging, however, can restore
him to himself in mirrors, every which way surrounded   20
by no more than what he seems and mercifully *by no more*.
Booked by a merciless Service for a thousand afternoons,
Brad will become the needs of his "regulars" confounded
by his indifferent regard, by his regardless expense . . .

Take him—young faithful!—there and then. Marvel! praise!   25
Fond though your touch may be and truly feeling your tact,
yet a mocking echo returns—remote, vague, blasé—
of Every Future Caress, so very like your own!
However entranced the scene you make (the two of you act
as one to all appearance, but one is always alone),   30

derision will come to mind, or to matter over mind:
the folly, in carnal collusion, of mere presented *skill*.
Undone, played out, discharged, one insight you will have gained
which cannot for all these ardent lapses be gainsaid
—even his murmured subsidence an exercise of will—   35
is the sudden absolute knowledge Brad would rather be dead.

1999

ADRIENNE RICH
1929–2012

Adrienne Rich was the leading feminist poet of the twentieth century. Her poetry and prose writings confound distinctions between the private inner world of emotions and the public sphere. *"The moment when a feeling enters the body,"* she wrote, "is political" ("The Blue Ghazals"). Even so, one way to take the measure of her contribution to contemporary poetry is to place her work in the dual contexts of the intensely personal poetry that came out of the so-called confessional school and the resonantly public, even prophetic poetry that extends from Walt Whitman to H. D., Muriel Rukeyser, and Allen Ginsberg. Adapting Whitman's poetics of multiple identification, Rich assimilated women and men of various times and places into her poetry. She crossed divisions of ethnicity, nationality, and class in her sympathies, daring to help dream into existence noncoercive forms of social affiliation. The visionary breadth and ethical force of her poetry are stirring, even though she questioned the possibility of using poetic language to reach beyond self to community.

In seeking to transcend private verse, Rich populated her poems with emblematic female figures. When she wrote about the lives of women in "Snapshots of a Daughter-in-Law" and "Diving into the Wreck," the central figures allegorize the entrapment of women within limiting patriarchal norms and the feminist quest for a revisionary understanding of history and identity. As a public poet, Rich defied the modernist injunctions against abstraction and allegory, in search of "a common language" that will describe shared historical experience.

Rich's descriptions of both herself and others are compelling, however, because they straddle the general and the particular. Her protagonists, if emblematic, are also vividly imagined. "Snapshots of a Daughter-in-Law," inverting traditional norms of female beauty, compares the gleam of a woman's shaved legs to "petrified mammoth-tusk"; the speaker of "Diving into the Wreck" dons flippers, mask, and "the body-armor of black rubber" to descend into the shipwreck of history. "Power," about Marie Curie and her experiments with radiation, ends with the memorable claim that "her wounds came from the same source as her power." This assertion is effective in part because earlier in the poem Rich has drawn Curie's portrait in painful detail—"the cracked and suppurating skin   of her finger-ends." Similarly, Rich's self-conception was that of a poet, in her own words, "neither unique nor universal, but a person in history, a woman and not a man, a white and also Jewish inheritor of a particular Western consciousness, from the making of which most women have been excluded" (foreword to *The Fact of a Doorframe*).

In writing about personal feeling and family experience, Rich was influenced by such contemporaries as Robert Lowell, Sylvia Plath, and Anne Sexton. Like them, she understood emotions to be complex and ambivalent—"Poetry," she said, "is a way of expressing unclear feeling" (quoted in Joyce Greenberg, "By Woman Taught," *Parnassus* 7 [1979])—and she wrote about her vexed relationship with her father to understand the formation of her identity, which was early on, by her own accounting, male identified. Her father was an authoritarian figure who harshly supervised her schoolwork and early poetry writing, but she also credited him with teaching her "to believe in hard work," ideas, and language ("Split at the Root: An Essay on Jewish Identity"). In the long poem *Sources*, she reactivates her rage toward him, while also seeing behind his facade of "power and arrogance . . . the suffering of the Jew, the alien stamp you bore." Rich's use of apostrophe, here as elsewhere, both animates her strong but conflicted voice and vivifies the presence of her addressee. She speaks in tenderness and rage, empathy and resistance. In her brilliant book on motherhood, *Of Woman Born* (1976), she affirms such complexity of feeling: "Love and anger *can* exist concurrently." When she addresses her "Grandmothers," in a poem of that title, she describes both the unsatisfying compromises they lived and her own lingering mixed feelings toward them. She writes in an essay, "my gentile grandmother and my mother were also frustrated artists and intellectuals, a lost writer and a lost composer between them" ("Split at the Root").

Rich was also one of the most well-known contemporary love poets. In her groundbreaking series *Twenty-One Love Poems*, first published in a limited edition of 1976, she conjures the erotic passions and daily experiences of a lesbian relationship, recalling only to undermine the Elizabethan sonnet sequences written by men to an impossibly idealized ladylove. Here, as in her family poetry, the relationship is both celebrated and, given its ultimate failure, lamented. Rich said that "poetry can break open locked chambers of possibility, restore numbed zones to feeling, recharge desire" (preface to *What Is Found There*). Although some critics look on her work as doctrinal, it is tonally ambiguous, shot through with emotional contradictions, startlingly clear about the murkiest feelings. And as she self-mockingly suggests in a late poem about a heterosexual relationship, one's feelings—like the poems in which they are embedded—do not always conform to one's theories: "An idea declared itself between us / clear as a washed wineglass / that we'd love / regardless of manifestos I wrote or signed" ("Regardless"). In this poem and in "Seven Skins," Rich's career as love poet takes an unexpected turn, when she reconsiders—with tenderness, self-criticism, and wry humor—her early heterosexual experience.

For Rich, personal feelings could never be completely separated from politics. To reject the tyranny of the voice of the father, for example, was a hard-won political act; Rich had internalized that censorious voice and been taught as a girl that anger was a "dark, wicked blotch" to be avoided (*Of Woman Born*). She suggested that for women the rejection of the fathers is an essential first step in a process that must culminate in the reaffirmation of "woman-identified experience" ("Compulsory Heterosexuality and Lesbian Existence"). "I had been looking for the Women's Liberation Movement since the 1950s. I came into it in 1970," Rich wrote in the 1986 foreword to a collection of essays. "I identified myself as a radical feminist, and soon after—not as a political act but out of powerful and unmistakable feelings—as a lesbian" (*Blood, Bread, and Poetry*). Rich declared her lesbian identity in 1976; from that time, her companion was the Jamaican-born writer Michelle Cliff, best known for her novel *No Telephone to Heaven*. Writing about what she has called the "lesbian continuum," Rich expanded the meaning of the word *lesbian* to mean "a primary intensity between women, an intensity" that the world at large has "trivialized, caricatured, or invested with evil. . . . I believe it is the lesbian in every woman who is compelled by female energy. . . . It is the lesbian in us who drives us to feel imaginatively, render in language, grasp, the full connection between woman and woman. It is the lesbian in us who is creative, for the dutiful daughter of the fathers is only a hack" ("It Is the Lesbian in Us . . .").

Rich was born, "white and middle-class," the elder of two sisters, in Baltimore, Maryland, on May 16, 1929. She graduated from Radcliffe College in 1951, the same year W. H. Auden chose her first volume, *A Change of World*, for the Yale Series of Younger Poets. In his preface, Auden wrote, with condescending approval: "The poems a reader will encounter in this book are neatly and modestly dressed, speak quietly but do not mumble, respect their elders but are not cowed by them, and do not tell fibs." Rich was writing under the influence of male poets—by her reckoning, "Frost, Dylan Thomas, Donne, Auden, MacNeice, Stevens, Yeats"—and in the impersonal, formally tight, exacting style fostered by the New Criticism. But even an early poem such as "Aunt Jennifer's Tigers" evokes the stirrings of gender critique, as Rich suggested in her outline of her early development in the influential essay "When We Dead Awaken: Writing as Re-Vision." Determined to prove that she could be a poet and "have what was then defined as a 'full' woman's life," she married in her twenties and had three sons before she was thirty. Under these circumstances, the 1950s were desperate years for her, in which she began "to feel that politics was not something 'out there' but something 'in here' and of the essence of my condition." Then, in the late 1950s, she "was able to write, for the first time, directly about experiencing myself as a woman," in the poem "Snapshots of a Daughter-in-Law." Later, in "Planetarium," written in 1968, she reached a further synthesis, as in it "at last the woman in the poem and the woman writing the poem become the same person."

In the late 1960s, when Rich's husband accepted a teaching post at the City College of New York, they both became involved in radical politics, especially in opposition to the Vietnam War. Staying on in New York after their separation and his death by suicide in 1970, Rich also taught inner-city, minority young people. These new concerns entered the poems of *Diving into the Wreck* and *A Will to Change*. The language in these books became more urgent and fragmented, the images starker, the prosody more jagged. Punctuation is relinquished, lines are heavily enjambed and cut up by blank spaces, initial letters are infrequently capitalized, rhymes are used sparingly, and speech rhythms are more urgent. Poems often reach to become letters, throwaway leaflets, photographs, shooting scripts. Moreover, after "Snapshots," Rich dated her poems, as if to underline their provisional or journal-entry nature. Her later poetry, while still committed to a radical feminist and lesbian vision, expanded its range of concerns, encompassing global, historical, and ecological issues. It also, perhaps surprisingly, became increasingly lyrical—"the music always ran ahead of the words" ("Late Ghazal"). Rich's later poetry is compressed, imagistic, and intensely self-questioning. "Fox," for example, is a self-lacerating apostrophe to a prerational, instinctual, animal self. The title of Rich's 1971 collection, *The Will to Change*, is taken from Charles Olson's declaration in "The Kingfishers": "What does not change / is the will to change." Indeed, the will to change both herself and her world was the constant in Rich's extraordinary career.

Rich was signally honored for her poetry. In 1974, she won the National Book Award. In 1986, she was the first winner of the Ruth Lilly Poetry Prize; she also won the Lenore Marshall Prize (1992), a MacArthur Fellowship (1994), and the Tanning Prize (1996). She taught at many universities and colleges, including Stanford University (1986–93).

Aunt Jennifer's Tigers[1]

Aunt Jennifer's tigers prance across a screen,
Bright topaz denizens of a world of green.
They do not fear the men beneath the tree;
They pace in sleek chivalric certainty.

Aunt Jennifer's fingers fluttering through her wool   5
Find even the ivory needle hard to pull.
The massive weight of Uncle's wedding band
Sits heavily upon Aunt Jennifer's hand.

When Aunt is dead, her terrified hands will lie
Still ringed with ordeals she was mastered by.   10
The tigers in the panel that she made
Will go on prancing, proud and unafraid.

                                                             1951

Snapshots of a Daughter-in-Law

1

You, once a belle in Shreveport,
with henna-colored hair,[2] skin like a peachbud,
still have your dresses copied from that time,
and play a Chopin prelude
called by Cortot: "*Delicious recollections*   5
float like perfume through the memory."[3]

---

1. See Rich's discussion of this poem in "When We Dead Awaken: Writing as Re-Vision," on p. 1086 of this volume.
2. That is, red; henna is a hair dye. *Shreveport:* city in Louisiana.

3. Remark made by French pianist Alfred Cortot in his book *Chopin: 24 Preludes* (1930); he is referring specifically to Prelude No. 7 by Frédéric Chopin (1810–1849), Polish composer and pianist, who settled in Paris in 1831.

Your mind now, moldering like wedding-cake,
heavy with useless experience, rich
with suspicion, rumor, fantasy,
crumbling to pieces under the knife-edge   10
of mere fact. In the prime of your life.

Nervy, glowering, your daughter
wipes the teaspoons, grows another way.

2

Banging the coffee-pot into the sink
she hears the angels chiding, and looks out   15
past the raked gardens to the sloppy sky.
Only a week since They said: *Have no patience.*

The next time it was: *Be insatiable.*
Then: *Save yourself; others you cannot save.*
Sometimes she's let the tapstream scald her arm,   20
a match burn to her thumbnail,

or held her hand above the kettle's snout
right in the woolly steam. They are probably angels,
since nothing hurts her any more, except
each morning's grit blowing into her eyes.   25

3

A thinking woman sleeps with monsters.
The beak that grips her, she becomes. And Nature,
that sprung-lidded, still commodious
steamer-trunk of *tempora* and *mores*⁴
gets stuffed with it all: the mildewed orange-flowers,   30
the female pills, the terrible breasts
of Boadicea⁵ beneath flat foxes' heads and orchids.

Two handsome women, gripped in argument,
each proud, acute, subtle, I hear scream
across the cut glass and majolica   35
like Furies⁶ cornered from their prey:
The argument *ad feminam,*⁷ all the old knives
that have rusted in my back, I drive in yours,
*ma semblable, ma soeur!*⁸

---

4. Literally, times and customs—alluding to the protest by Roman orator Cicero (106–43 B.C.E.), "O tempora! O mores!": Alas for the degeneracy of our times and the low standards of our morals! (Latin).
5. British queen (d. 60 C.E.), who led her people in a strong but ultimately unsuccessful revolt against Roman rule. *Female pills*: remedies for menstrual pain.
6. Greek goddesses of vengeance. *Cut glass and*

majolica: expensive glassware and earthenware.
7. Feminine version of the phrase *ad hominem* (to the man), referring to an argument directed not to reason but to personal prejudices and emotions.
8. The last line of "Au Lecteur" ("To the Reader"), by French poet Charles Baudelaire (1821–1867), addresses "Hypocrite lecteur!—mon semblable—mon frère!" (Hypocrite reader—like me—my brother!); Rich substitutes *ma soeur* (my sister). See also T. S. Eliot's *Waste Land*, line 76.

4

Knowing themselves too well in one another: 40
their gifts no pure fruition, but a thorn,
the prick filed sharp against a hint of scorn . . .
Reading while waiting
for the iron to heat,
writing, *My Life had stood—a Loaded Gun*⁹—   45
in that Amherst pantry while the jellies boil and scum,
or, more often,
iron-eyed and beaked and purposed as a bird,
dusting everything on the whatnot every day of life.

5

*Dulce ridens, dulce loquens,*¹   50
she shaves her legs until they gleam
like petrified mammoth-tusk.

6

When to her lute Corinna sings²
neither words nor music are her own;
only the long hair dipping   55
over her cheek, only the song
of silk against her knees
and these
adjusted in reflections of an eye.

Poised, trembling and unsatisfied, before   60
an unlocked door, that cage of cages,
tell us, you bird, you tragical machine—
is this *fertilisante douleur?*³ Pinned down
by love, for you the only natural action,
are you edged more keen   65
to prise the secrets of the vault? has Nature shown
her household books to you, daughter-in-law,
that her sons never saw?

7

"To have in this uncertain world some stay
which cannot be undermined, is   70
*of the utmost consequence."*⁴

9. Rich's note to this line refers to T. H. Johnson's *Emily Dickinson, Complete Poems* (1960); this is the poem numbered 764 in that edition. Dickinson (1830–1886) lived her entire life in Amherst, Massachusetts.
1. Sweetly laughing, sweetly speaking (Latin), from Horace's Ode XXII.
2. First line of a poem by the English poet Thomas Campion (1567–1620); Corinna is a generic name for a female shepherd.
3. Fertilizing (life-giving) sorrow (French).
4. "From Mary Wollstonecraft, *Thoughts on the Education of Daughters*, London, 1787" [Rich's note]. Wollstonecraft (1759–1797), one of the first feminist thinkers, is best-known for her *Vindication of the Rights of Woman* (1792).

Thus wrote
a woman, partly brave and partly good,
who fought with what she partly understood.
Few men about her would or could do more,   75
hence she was labelled harpy, shrew and whore.

8

"You all die at fifteen," said Diderot,[5]
and turn part legend, part convention.
Still, eyes inaccurately dream
behind closed windows blankening with steam.   80
Deliciously, all that we might have been,
all that we were—fire, tears,
wit, taste, martyred ambition—
stirs like the memory of refused adultery
the drained and flagging bosom of our middle years.   85

9

Not that it is done well, but
that it is done at all?[6] Yes, think
of the odds! or shrug them off forever.
This luxury of the precocious child,
Time's precious chronic invalid,—   90
would we, darlings, resign it if we could?
Our blight has been our sinecure:
mere talent was enough for us—
glitter in fragments and rough drafts.

Sigh no more, ladies.   95
                    Time is male
and in his cups[7] drinks to the fair.
Bemused by gallantry, we hear
our mediocrities over-praised,
indolence read as abnegation,   100
slattern[8] thought styled intuition,
every lapse forgiven, our crime
only to cast too bold a shadow
or smash the mould straight off.

For that, solitary confinement,   105
tear gas, attrition shelling.[9]
Few applicants for that honor.

---

5. Denis Diderot (1713–1784), French philosopher and writer. Rich's note to this line says that it is quoted from the *Lettres à Sophie Volland* in the influential *Le Deuxième Sexe*, by Simone de Beauvoir (1908–1986), vol. 2, pp. 123–24 (cited in French by Rich).
6. "Sir, a woman's preaching is like a dog's walking on his hinder legs. It is not done well; but you are surprised to find it done at all": Samuel Johnson (1709–1784), English writer, to James Boswell in Boswell's *Life*.
7. While drinking. "Sigh no more, ladies, sigh no more, / Men were deceivers ever": Shakespeare's *Much Ado About Nothing* 2.3.56–57.
8. Unkempt, disorderly.
9. That is, bombing.

10

Well,

she's long about her coming, who must be
more merciless to herself than history. 110
Her mind full to the wind, I see her plunge
breasted and glancing through the currents,
taking the light upon her
at least as beautiful as any boy
or helicopter,[1] 115
poised, still coming,
her fine blades making the air wince
but her cargo
no promise then:
delivered 120
palpable
ours.

1958–60   1963

Face to Face

Never to be lonely like that—
the Early American figure on the beach
in black coat and knee-breeches
scanning the didactic storm in privacy,

never to hear the prairie wolves 5
in their lunar hilarity
circling one's little all, one's claim
to be Law and Prophets[2]

for all that lawlessness,
never to whet the appetite 10
weeks early, for a face, a hand
longed-for and dreaded—

How people used to meet!
starved, intense, the old
Christmas gifts saved up till spring, 15
and the old plain words,

and each with his God-given secret,
spelled out through months of snow and silence,

---

1. "She comes down from the remoteness of ages, from Thebes, from Crete, from Chichén-Itzá; and she is also the totem set deep in the African jungle; she is a helicopter and she is a bird; and there is this, the greatest wonder of all: under her tinted hair the forest murmur becomes a thought, and words issue from her breasts" (Simone de Beauvoir, *The Second Sex*, tr. H. M. Parshlev [New York, 1953], p. 729; a translation of the passage from *Le Deuxième Sexe*, vol. 2, p. 574).
2. That is, righteous. See Matthew 7.12: "Therefore all things whatsoever ye would that men should do unto you, do ye even so to them: for this is the law and the prophets."

burning under the bleached scalp; behind dry lips
a loaded gun.[3]   20

1965   1966

Orion[4]

Far back when I went zig-zagging
through tamarack pastures
you were my genius, you
my cast-iron Viking, my helmed
lion-heart king in prison.[5]   5
Years later now you're young

my fierce half-brother, staring
down from that simplified west
your breast open, your belt dragged down
by an oldfashioned thing, a sword   10
the last bravado you won't give over
though it weighs you down as you stride

and the stars in it are dim
and maybe have stopped burning.
But you burn, and I know it;   15
as I throw back my head to take you in
an old transfusion happens again:
divine astronomy is nothing to it.

Indoors I bruise and blunder,
break faith, leave ill enough   20
alone, a dead child born in the dark,
Night cracks up over the chimney,
pieces of time, frozen geodes
come showering down in the grate.

A man reaches behind my eyes   25
and finds them empty
a woman's head turns away
from my head in the mirror
children are dying my death
and eating crumbs of my life.   30

Pity is not your forte.
Calmly you ache up there
pinned aloft in your crow's nest,
my speechless pirate!

3. Cf. Emily Dickinson's poem numbered 1754, "My Life had stood—a Loaded Gun"; see also "Snapshots of a Daughter-in-Law," above, line 45.
4. A constellation named for the giant hunter of Greek mythology, who at his death was placed among the stars by the gods. (See Rich's essay "When We Dead Awaken," p. 1086 of this volume.)
5. Like Richard I of England (1157–1199), called "the lion-hearted," who on his return from a Crusade was briefly imprisoned in Austria.

You take it all for granted   35
and when I look you back

it's with a starlike eye
shooting its cold and egotistical spear
where it can do least damage.
Breathe deep! No hurt, no pardon   40
out here in the cold with you
you with your back to the wall.

1965   1969

Planetarium

Thinking of Caroline Herschel,[6] 1750–1848, astronomer, sister of
William; and others.

A woman in the shape of a monster
a monster in the shape of a woman
the skies are full of them

a woman   'in the snow
among the Clocks and instruments   5
or measuring the ground with poles'

in her 98 years to discover
8 comets

she whom the moon ruled
like us
levitating into the night sky   10
riding the polished lenses

Galaxies of women, there
doing penance for impetuousness
ribs chilled
in those spaces   of the mind   15

An eye,
        'virile, precise and absolutely certain'
        from the mad webs of Uranusborg[7]

                                        encountering the NOVA 20

every impulse of light exploding
from the core
as life flies out of us

6. German-born British astronomer. In 1786, she became the first woman to discover a comet, detecting seven more by 1797, including Comet Enckle; she also discovered nebulae. With her help, William Herschel (1738–1822), astronomer to King George III, discovered the first non-naked-eye planet, eventually named Uranus. (See Rich's essay "When We Dead Awaken," p. 1086 of this volume.) 7. Actually Uraniborg, or castle of the heavens (Dutch), the name of the great observatory built by Tycho Brahe (1546–1601), Danish astronomer, famous for his studies of comets.

Tycho whispering at last
'Let me not seem to have lived in vain'   25

What we see, we see
and seeing is changing

the light that shrivels a mountain
and leaves a man alive

Heartbeat of the pulsar   30
heart sweating through my body

The radio impulse
pouring in from Taurus[8]

   I am bombarded yet   I stand

I have been standing all my life in the   35
direct path of a battery of signals
the most accurately transmitted most
untranslateable language in the universe
I am a galactic cloud so deep   so invo-
luted that a light wave could take 15   40
years to travel through me   And has
taken   I am an instrument in the shape
of a woman trying to translate pulsations
into images   for the relief of the body
and the reconstruction of the mind.   45

1968   1971

A Valediction Forbidding Mourning[9]

My swirling wants. Your frozen lips.
The grammar turned and attacked me.
Themes, written under duress.
Emptiness of the notations.

They gave me a drug that slowed the healing of wounds.   5

I want you to see this before I leave:
the experience of repetition as death
the failure of criticism to locate the pain
the poster in the bus that said:
my bleeding is under control.   10

A red plant in a cemetery of plastic wreaths.

8. The constellation "the Bull."
9. The title of a poem by John Donne (1572–1631), in which the poet assures his beloved that his departure is not dangerous to their love, which has purified and united their souls.

A last attempt: the language is a dialect called metaphor.
These images go unglossed: hair, glacier, flashlight.
When I think of a landscape I am thinking of a time.
When I talk of taking a trip I mean forever.   15
I could say: those mountains have a meaning
but further than that I could not say.

To do something very common, in my own way.

1970   1971

Diving into the Wreck

First having read the book of myths,
and loaded the camera,
and checked the edge of the knife-blade,
I put on
the body-armor of black rubber   5
the absurd flippers
the grave and awkward mask.
I am having to do this
not like Cousteau[1] with his
assiduous team   10
aboard the sun-flooded schooner
but here alone.

There is a ladder.
The ladder is always there
hanging innocently   15
close to the side of the schooner.
We know what it is for,
we who have used it.
Otherwise
it's a piece of maritime floss   20
some sundry equipment.

I go down.
Rung after rung and still
the oxygen immerses me
the blue light   25
the clear atoms
of our human air.
I go down.
My flippers cripple me,
I crawl like an insect down the ladder   30
and there is no one
to tell me when the ocean
will begin.

1. Jacques-Yves Cousteau (1910–1997), French underwater explorer and writer.

First the air is blue and then
it is bluer and then green and then   35
black I am blacking out and yet
my mask is powerful
it pumps my blood with power
the sea is another story
the sea is not a question of power   40
I have to learn alone
to turn my body without force
in the deep element.

And now: it is easy to forget
what I came for   45
among so many who have always
lived here
swaying their crenellated² fans
between the reefs
and besides   50
you breathe differently down here.

I came to explore the wreck.
The words are purposes.
The words are maps.
I came to see the damage that was done   55
and the treasures that prevail.
I stroke the beam of my lamp
slowly along the flank
of something more permanent
than fish or weed   60

the thing I came for:
the wreck and not the story of the wreck
the thing itself and not the myth
the drowned face³ always staring
toward the sun   65
the evidence of damage
worn by salt and sway into this threadbare beauty
the ribs of the disaster
curving their assertion
among the tentative haunters.   70

This is the place.
And I am here, the mermaid whose dark hair
streams black, the merman in his armored body.
We circle silently
about the wreck   75
we dive into the hold.
I am she: I am he

2. With repeated indentations.
3. Of the ornamental female figurehead that formed the prow of old sailing ships.

whose drowned face sleeps with open eyes
whose breasts still bear the stress
whose silver, copper, vermeil[4] cargo lies   80
obscurely inside barrels
half-wedged and left to rot
we are the half-destroyed instruments
that once held to a course
the water-eaten log   85
the fouled compass

We are, I am, you are
by cowardice or courage
the one who find our way
back to this scene   90
carrying a knife, a camera
a book of myths
in which
our names do not appear.

1972   1973

Power

Living   in the earth-deposits   of our history

Today a backhoe divulged   out of a crumbling flank of earth
one bottle   amber   perfect   a hundred-year-old
cure for fever   or melancholy   a tonic
for living on this earth   in the winters of this climate   5

Today I was reading about Marie Curie:[5]
she must have known she suffered   from radiation sickness
her body bombarded for years   by the element
she had purified
It seems she denied to the end   10
the source of the cataracts on her eyes
the cracked and suppurating skin   of her finger-ends
till she could no longer hold   a test-tube or a pencil

She died   a famous woman   denying
her wounds   15
denying
her wounds   came   from the same source as her power

1974   1978

---

4. Gilded silver or bronze.
5. Polish-born French physicist (1867–1934), who died from exposure to radiation she experi-enced in the process of discovering radium and studying radioactivity.

TWENTY-ONE LOVE POEMS

I

Wherever in this city, screens flicker
with pornography, with science-fiction vampires,
victimized hirelings bending to the lash,
we also have to walk . . . if simply as we walk
through the rainsoaked garbage, the tabloid cruelties   5
of our own neighborhoods.
We need to grasp our lives inseparable
from those rancid dreams, that blurt of metal, those disgraces,
and the red begonia perilously flashing
from a tenement sill six stories high,   10
or the long-legged young girls playing ball
in the junior highschool playground.
No one has imagined us. We want to live like trees,
sycamores blazing through the sulfuric air,
dappled with scars, still exuberantly budding,   15
our animal passion rooted in the city.

II

I wake up in your bed. I know I have been dreaming.
Much earlier, the alarm broke us from each other,
you've been at your desk for hours. I know what I dreamed:
our friend the poet comes into my room
where I've been writing for days,   5
drafts, carbons, poems are scattered everywhere,
and I want to show her one poem
which is the poem of my life. But I hesitate,
and wake. You've kissed my hair
to wake me. *I dreamed you were a poem,*   10
I say, *a poem I wanted to show someone . . .*
and I laugh and fall dreaming again
of the desire to show you to everyone I love,
to move openly together
in the pull of gravity, which is not simple,   15
which carries the feathered grass a long way down the upbreathing air.

III

Since we're not young, weeks have to do time
for years of missing each other. Yet only this odd warp
in time tells me we're not young.
Did I ever walk the morning streets at twenty,

my limbs streaming with a purer joy?   5
did I lean from any window over the city
listening for the future
as I listen here with nerves tuned for your ring?
And you, you move toward me with the same tempo.
Your eyes are everlasting, the green spark   10
of the blue-eyed grass of early summer,
the green-blue wild cress[6] washed by the spring.
At twenty, yes: we thought we'd live forever.
At forty-five, I want to know even our limits.
I touch you knowing we weren't born tomorrow,   15
and somehow, each of us will help the other live,
and somewhere, each of us must help the other die.

IV

I come home from you through the early light of spring
flashing off ordinary walls, the Pez Dorado,[7]
the Discount Wares, the shoe-store. . . . I'm lugging my sack
of groceries, I dash for the elevator
where a man, taut, elderly, carefully composed   5
lets the door almost close on me.—*For god's sake hold it!*
I croak at him. —*Hysterical,*—he breathes my way.
I let myself into the kitchen, unload my bundles,
make coffee, open the window, put on Nina Simone[8]
singing *Here comes the sun.* . . . I open the mail,   10
drinking delicious coffee, delicious music,
my body still both light and heavy with you. The mail
lets fall a Xerox of something written by a man
aged 27, a hostage, tortured in prison:
My genitals have been the object of such a sadistic display   15
they keep me constantly awake with the pain . . .
Do whatever you can to survive.
You know, I think that men love wars . . .
And my incurable anger, my unmendable wounds
break open further with tears, I am crying helplessly,   20
and they still control the world, and you are not in my arms.

V

This apartment full of books could crack open
to the thick jaws, the bulging eyes
of monsters, easily: Once open the books, you have to face
the underside of everything you've loved—

---

6. Plant, as in watercress.
7. El Pez Dorado is a Puerto Rican restaurant in Brooklyn.

8. American jazz vocalist and pianist (b. 1933), known as the High Priestess of Soul.

the rack and pincers held in readiness, the gag   5
even the best voices have had to mumble through,
the silence burying unwanted children—
women, deviants, witnesses—in desert sand.
Kenneth tells me he's been arranging his books
so he can look at Blake and Kafka while he types;   10
yes; and we still have to reckon with Swift[9]
loathing the woman's flesh while praising her mind,
Goethe's dread of the Mothers, Claudel vilifying Gide,[1]
and the ghosts—their hands clasped for centuries—
of artists dying in childbirth, wise-women charred at the stake,   15
centuries of books unwritten piled behind these shelves;
and we still have to stare into the absence
of men who would not, women who could not, speak
to our life—this still unexcavated hole
called civilization, this act of translation, this half-world.   20

VI

Your small hands, precisely equal to my own—
only the thumb is larger, longer—in these hands
I could trust the world, or in many hands like these,
handling power-tools or steering-wheel
or touching a human face. . . . Such hands could turn   5
the unborn child rightways in the birth canal
or pilot the exploratory rescue-ship
through icebergs, or piece together
the fine, needle-like sherds of a great krater-cup[2]
bearing on its sides   10
figures of esctatic women striding
to the sibyl's den or the Eleusinian cave[3]—
such hands might carry out an unavoidable violence
with such restraint, with such a grasp
of the range and limits of violence   15
that violence ever after would be obsolete.

9. Cf. the "dressing-room poems" of Anglo-Irish writer Jonathan Swift (1667–1745): in "The Lady's Dressing Room" (1730), "Disgusted Strephon" is horrified to learn that "Celia shits!" and in "Stella's Birthday" (1721), the speaker contrasts Stella's physical aging with her "Angel's Mind."
1. André Gide (1869–1951), French writer, critic, and spokesman for homosexual rights, whom French poet and playwright Paul Claudel (1868–1955) tried unsuccessfully to convert to Catholicism. In *Faust*, by German writer Johann Wolfgang von Goethe (1749–1832), Faust responds to mention of the mothers "with a shudder" and exclaims "The Mothers! Still strikes a shock of fear, / What is this word that I am loath to hear?" (2.1.6265–66).
2. *Krater*: ancient Greek jar with a broad (usually decorated) body and two handles, used for mixing water and wine.
3. In ancient Greece, the sanctuary of Demeter, goddess of Earth and fertility. *Sibyl*: female, usually cave-dwelling prophet. Initiates celebrated ecstatic religious rites at Eleusis, known as the Eleusinian Mysteries and centered on the story of Demeter's life.

VII

What kind of beast would turn its life into words?
What atonement is this all about?
—and yet, writing words like these, I'm also living.
Is all this close to the wolverines' howled signals,
that modulated cantata of the wild?   5
or, when away from you I try to create you in words,
am I simply using you, like a river or a war?
And how have I used rivers, how have I used wars
to escape writing of the worst thing of all—
not the crimes of others, not even our own death,   10
but the failure to want our freedom passionately enough
so that blighted elms, sick rivers, massacres would seem
mere emblems of that desecration of ourselves?

VIII

I can see myself years back at Sunion,[4]
hurting with an infected foot, Philoctetes[5]
in woman's form, limping the long path,
lying on a headland over the dark sea,
looking down the red rocks to where a soundless curl   5
of white told me a wave had struck,
imagining the pull of that water from that height,
knowing deliberate suicide wasn't my métier,
yet all the time nursing, measuring that wound.
Well, that's finished. The woman who cherished   10
her suffering is dead. I am her descendant.
I love the scar-tissue she handed on to me,
but I want to go on from here with you
fighting the temptation to make a career of pain.

IX

Your silence today is a pond where drowned things live
I want to see raised dripping and brought into the sun.
It's not my own face I see there, but other faces,
even your face at another age.
Whatever's lost there is needed by both of us—   5
a watch of old gold, a water-blurred fever chart,
a key. . . . Even the silt and pebbles of the bottom
deserve their glint of recognition. I fear this silence,

4. Cape Sunion, in Greece.
5. Legendary Greek hero wounded on the foot by
a snake and abandoned on an island by his ship-
mates to suffer great pain. Cf. Sophocles' play
named after him.

this inarticulate life. I'm waiting
for a wind that will gently open this sheeted water   10
for once, and show me what I can do
for you, who have often made the unnameable
nameable for others, even for me.

X

Your dog, tranquil and innocent, dozes through
our cries, our murmured dawn conspiracies
our telephone calls. She knows—what can she know?
If in my human arrogance I claim to read
her eyes, I find there only my own animal thoughts: 5
that creatures must find each other for bodily comfort,
that voices of the psyche drive through the flesh
further than the dense brain could have foretold,
that the planetary nights are growing cold for those
on the same journey, who want to touch   10
one creature-traveler clear to the end;
that without tenderness, we are in hell.

XI

Every peak is a crater. This is the law of volcanoes,
making them eternally and visibly female.
No height without depth, without a burning core,
though our straw soles shred on the hardened lava.
I want to travel with you to every sacred mountain   5
smoking within like the sibyl stooped over his tripod,[6]
I want to reach for your hand as we scale the path,
to feel your arteries glowing in my clasp,
never failing to note the small, jewel-like flower
unfamiliar to us, nameless till we rename her,   10
that clings to the slowly altering rock—
that detail outside ourselves that brings us to ourselves,
was here before us, knew we would come, and sees beyond us.

XII

Sleeping, turning in turn like planets
rotating in their midnight meadow:
a touch is enough to let us know
we're not alone in the universe, even in sleep:

6. A tripod over a fissure in the earth provided a safe place for the sibyl at the Delphic oracle, who breathed
in smoke or gases and made prophecies.

the dream-ghosts of two worlds   5
walking their ghost-towns, almost address each other.
I've wakened to your muttered words
spoken light- or dark-years away
as if my own voice had spoken.
But we have different voices, even in sleep,   10
and our bodies, so alike, are yet so different
and the past echoing through our bloodstreams
is freighted with different language, different meanings—
though in any chronicle of the world we share
it could be written with new meaning   15
we were two lovers of one gender,
we were two women of one generation.

XIII

The rules break like a thermometer,
quicksilver[7] spills across the charted systems,
we're out in a country that has no language
no laws, we're chasing the raven and the wren
through gorges unexplored since dawn   5
whatever we do together is pure invention
the maps they gave us were out of date
by years . . . we're driving through the desert
wondering if the water will hold out
the hallucinations turn to simple villages   10
the music on the radio comes clear—
neither *Rosenkavalier* nor *Götterdämmerung*[8]
but a woman's voice singing old songs
with new words, with a quiet bass, a flute
plucked and fingered by women outside the law.   15

XIV

It was your vision of the pilot
confirmed my vision of you: you said, *He keeps
on steering headlong into the waves, on purpose*
while we crouched in the open hatchway
vomiting into plastic bags   5
for three hours between St. Pierre and Miquelon.[9]
I never felt closer to you.
In the close cabin where the honeymoon couples

7. Mercury, used in glass thermometers.
8. "Twilight of the Gods," by Richard Wagner (1813–1883), German composer whose anti-Semitism was admired by Hitler. *Der Rosenkavalier:* "The Knight of the Rose" (1911), a comic opera by German Romantic composer Richard Strauss (1864–1949), who was recruited by Joseph Goebbels (1897–1945), Hitler's minister of propaganda, to head up a group searching for a Nazi musical ethos.
9. French islands about fifteen miles south of Newfoundland.

huddled in each other's laps and arms
I put my hand on your thigh   10
to comfort both of us, your hand came over mine,
we stayed that way, suffering together
in our bodies, as if all suffering
were physical, we touched so in the presence
of strangers who knew nothing and cared less   15
vomiting their private pain
as if all suffering were physical.

(The Floating Poem, Unnumbered)

Whatever happens with us, your body
will haunt mine—tender, delicate
your lovemaking, like the half-curled frond
of the fiddlehead fern[1] in forests
just washed by sun. Your traveled, generous thighs   5
between which my whole face has come and come—
the innocence and wisdom of the place my tongue has found there—
the live, insatiate dance of your nipples in my mouth—
your touch on me, firm, protective, searching
me out, your strong tongue and slender fingers   10
reaching where I had been waiting years for you
in my rose-wet cave—whatever happens, this is.

XV

If I lay on that beach with you
white, empty, pure green water warmed by the Gulf Stream
and lying on that beach we could not stay
because the wind drove fine sand against us
as if it were against us   5
if we tried to withstand it and we failed—
if we drove to another place
to sleep in each other's arms
and the beds were narrow like prisoners' cots
and we were tired and did not sleep together   10
and this was what we found, so this is what we did—
was the failure ours?
If I cling to circumstances I could feel
not responsible. Only she who says
she did not choose, is the loser in the end.   15

---

1. A young, edible, tightly coiled fern frond that resembles the spiral end of a violin (fiddle). Its shoots are in their coiled form for only about two weeks before they unfurl.

XVI

Across a city from you, I'm with you,
just as an August night
moony, inlet-warm, seabathed, I watched you sleep,
the scrubbed, sheenless wood of the dressing-table
cluttered with our brushes, books, vials in the moonlight—   5
or a salt-mist orchard, lying at your side
watching red sunset through the screendoor of the cabin,
G minor Mozart on the tape-recorder,
falling asleep to the music of the sea.
This island of Manhattan is wide enough   10
for both of us, and narrow:
I can hear your breath tonight, I know how your face
lies upturned, the halflight tracing
your generous, delicate mouth
where grief and laughter sleep together.   15

XVII

No one's fated or doomed to love anyone.
The accidents happen, we're not heroines,
they happen in our lives like car crashes,
books that change us, neighborhoods
we move into and come to love.   5
Tristan und Isolde[2] is scarcely the story,
women at least should know the difference
between love and death. No poison cup,
no penance. Merely a notion that the tape-recorder
should have caught some ghost of us: that tape-recorder   10
not merely played but should have listened to us,
and could instruct those after us:
this we were, this is how we tried to love,
and these are the forces they had ranged against us,
and these are the forces we had ranged within us,   15
within us and against us, against us and within us.

XVIII

Rain on the West Side Highway,
red light at Riverside:[3]
the more I live the more I think

2. Wagner's 1865 opera about the doomed love affair between a Christian knight and a Pagan princess.

3. Riverside Drive; like the West Side Highway, in Manhattan.

two people together is a miracle.
You're telling the story of your life   5
for once, a tremor breaks the surface of your words.
The story of our lives becomes our lives.
Now you're in fugue across what some I'm sure
Victorian poet called the *salt estranging sea.*[4]
Those are the words that come to mind.   10
I feel estrangement, yes. As I've felt dawn
pushing toward daybreak. Something: a cleft of light—?
Close between grief and anger, a space opens
where I am Adrienne alone. And growing colder.

XIX

Can it be growing colder when I begin
to touch myself again, adhesions pull away?
When slowly the naked face turns from staring backward
and looks into the present,
the eye of winter, city, anger, poverty, and death   5
and the lips part and say: *I mean to go on living?*
Am I speaking coldly when I tell you in a dream
or in this poem, *There are no miracles?*
(I told you from the first I wanted daily life,
this island of Manhattan was island enough for me.)   10
If I could let you know—
two women together is a work
nothing in civilization has made simple,
two people together is a work
heroic in its ordinariness,   15
the slow-picked, halting traverse of a pitch
where the fiercest attention becomes routine
—look at the faces of those who have chosen it.

XX

That conversation we were always on the edge
of having, runs on in my head,
at night the Hudson trembles in New Jersey[5] light
polluted water yet reflecting even
sometimes the moon   5
and I discern a woman
I loved, drowning in secrets, fear wound round her throat
and choking her like hair. And this is she
with whom I tried to speak, whose hurt, expressive head
turning aside from pain, is dragged down deeper   10

4. English poet Matthew Arnold (1822–1888) concluded his 1857 poem "To Marguerite" with "The unplumb'd, salt, estranging sea."

5. Across the Hudson River from New York City's West Side.

where it cannot hear me,
and soon I shall know I was talking to my own soul.

XXI

The dark lintels,[6] the blue and foreign stones
of the great round rippled by stone implements
the midsummer night light rising from beneath
the horizon—when I said "a cleft of light"
I meant this. And this is not Stonehenge   5
simply nor any place but the mind
casting back to where her solitude,
shared, could be chosen without loneliness,
not easily nor without pains to stake out
the circle, the heavy shadows, the great light.   10
I choose to be a figure in that light,
half-blotted by darkness, something moving
across that space, the color of stone
greeting the moon, yet more than stone:
a woman. I choose to walk here. And to draw this circle.   15

1974–76   1978

Grandmothers

1. Mary Gravely Jones

We had no petnames, no diminutives for you,
always the formal guest under my father's roof:
you were "Grandmother Jones" and you visited rarely.
I see you walking up and down the garden,
restless, southern-accented, reserved, you did not seem   5
my mother's mother or anyone's grandmother.
You were Mary, widow of William, and no matriarch,
yet smoldering to the end with frustrate life,
ideas nobody listened to, least of all my father.
One summer night you sat with my sister and me   10
in the wooden glider[7] long after twilight,
holding us there with streams of pent-up words.
You could quote every poet I had ever heard of,
had read *The Opium Eater,* Amiel and Bernard Shaw,[8]
your green eyes looked clenched against opposition.   15
You married straight out of the convent school,
your background was country, you left an unperformed
typescript of a play about Burr and Hamilton,[9]

6. Horizontal crosspieces over the two larger supporting stones at Stonehenge, the prehistoric circle of great standing stones on Salisbury Plain, England.
7. Porch swing.
8. George Bernard Shaw (1856–1950): Irish

playwright and socialist. *Confessions of an English Opium-Eater* (1821) is by the English essayist Thomas de Quincey. Henri Fréderic Amiel (1821–1881): Swiss poet and philosopher.
9. Aaron Burr (1756–1836), a flamboyant early U.S. vice president, killed Alexander Hamilton

you were impotent and brilliant, no one cared
about your mind, you might have ended   20
elsewhere than in that glider
reciting your unwritten novels to the children.

2. Hattie Rice Rich

Your sweetness of soul was a mystery to me,
you who slip-covered chairs, glued broken china,
lived out of a wardrobe trunk in our guestroom   25
summer and fall, then took the Pullman train[1]
in your darkblue dress and straw hat, to Alabama,
shuttling half-yearly between your son and daughter.
Your sweetness of soul was a convenience for everyone,
how you rose with the birds and children, boiled your own egg,   30
fished for hours on a pier, your umbrella spread,
took the street-car downtown shopping
endlessly for your son's whims, the whims of genius,
kept your accounts in ledgers, wrote letters daily.
All through World War Two the forbidden word   35
Jewish was barely uttered in your son's house;
your anger flared over inscrutable things.
Once I saw you crouched on the guestroom bed,
knuckles blue-white around the bedpost, sobbing
your one brief memorable scene of rebellion: 40
you didn't want to go back South that year.
You were never "Grandmother Rich" but "Anana";
you had money of your own but you were homeless,
Hattie, widow of Samuel, and no matriarch,
dispersed among the children and grandchildren.   45

3. Granddaughter

Easier to encapsulate your lives
in a slide-show of impressions given and taken,
to play the child or victim, the projectionist,
easier to invent a script for each of you,
myself still at the center,   50
than to write words in which you might have found
yourselves, looked up at me and said
"Yes, I was like that; but I was something more. . . ."
Danville, Virginia; Vicksburg, Mississippi;
the "war between the states" a living memory[2]   55
its aftermath the plague-town closing
its gates, trying to cure itself with poisons.
I can almost touch that little town. . . .
a little white town rimmed with Negroes,
making a deep shadow on the whiteness.[3]   60

(1755–1804), who had been instrumental in defeating Burr's candidacy for president.
1. Railroad passenger car with sleeping accommodations.
2. The Civil War ended in 1865.

3. Italicized lines (58–60, 64) are from *Killers of the Dream* (1949, rev. 1963), Lillian Smith's (1897–1966) autobiographical critique of white culture and racial segregation in the American south.

Born a white woman, Jewish or of curious mind
—twice an outsider, still believing in inclusion—
in those defended hamlets of half-truth
broken in two by one strange idea,
"blood" the all-powerful, awful theme—   65
what were the lessons to be learned? If I believe
the daughter of one of you—Amnesia was the answer.

1980   1981

Seven Skins

1

Walk along back of the library
in 1952
someone's there to catch your eye
Vic Greenberg in his wheelchair
paraplegic GI—   5
Bill of Rights[4] Jew
graduate student going in
by the only elevator route
up into the great stacks where
all knowledge should and is   10
and shall be stored like sacred grain
while the loneliest of lonely
American decades goes aground
on the postwar rock
and some unlikely   15
shipmates found ourselves
stuck amid so many smiles

Dating Vic Greenberg you date
crutches and a chair
a cool wit an outrageous form: 20
"—just back from a paraplegics' conference,
guess what the biggest meeting was about—
Sex with a Paraplegic!—for the wives—"
In and out of cabs his chair
opening and closing round his   25
electrical monologue the air
furiously calm around him
as he transfers to the crutches

But first you go for cocktails
in his room at Harvard   30
he mixes the usual martinis, plays Billie Holiday
talks about Melville's[5] vision of evil

---

4. After World War II, the GI Bill of Rights sub-
sidized veterans' educations.
5. Herman Melville (1819–1891), American
writer best-known for his novel *Moby-Dick*. Billie
Holiday (1915–1959): American jazz singer.

and the question of the postwar moment:
Is there an American civilization?
In the bathroom huge   35
grips and suction-cupped
rubber mats long-handled sponges
the reaching tools a veteran's benefits
in plainest sight

And this is only memory, no more   40
so this is how you remember

Vic Greenberg takes you to the best restaurant
which happens to have no stairs
for talk about movies, professors, food
Vic orders wine and tastes it   45
you have lobster, he Beef Wellington
the famous dessert is baked alaska
ice cream singed in a flowerpot
from the oven, a live tulip inserted there

Chair to crutches, crutches to cab   50
chair in the cab and back to Cambridge
memory shooting its handheld frames
Shall I drop you, he says, or shall
we go back to the room for a drink?
It's the usual question   55
a man has to ask it
a woman has to answer
you don't even think

2

What a girl I was then what a body
ready for breaking open like a lobster   60
what a little provincial village
what a hermit crab seeking nobler shells
what a beach of rattling stones what an offshore raincloud
what a gone-and-come tidepool

what a look into eternity I took and did not return it   65
what a book I made myself
what a quicksilver study
bright little bloodstain
liquid pouches escaping

What a girl pelican-skimming over fear what a mica lump splitting   70
into tiny sharp-edged mirrors through which
the sun's eclipse could seem normal
what a sac of eggs what a drifting flask
eager to sink   to be found
to disembody   what a mass of swimmy legs   75

3

Vic into what shoulder could I have pushed your face
laying hands first on your head
onto whose thighs pulled down your head
which fear of mine would have wound itself
around which of yours   could we have taken it   nakedness   80
without sperm   in what insurrectionary
convulsion would we have done it   mouth to mouth
mouth-tongue to vulva-tongue to anus   earlobe to nipple
what seven skins each have to molt what seven shifts
what tears boil up through sweat to bathe   85
what humiliatoriums   what layers of imposture

What heroic tremor
released into pure moisture
might have soaked our shape   two-headed   avid
into your heretic   90
linen-service
sheets?

1997   1999

Fox

I needed fox   Badly I needed
a vixen for the long time none had come near me
I needed recognition from a
triangulated face   burnt-yellow eyes
fronting the long body the fierce and sacrificial tail   5
I needed history of fox   briars of legend it was said she had run through
I was in want of fox

And the truth of briars she had to have run through
I craved to feel on her pelt   if my hands could even slide
past or her body slide between them   sharp truth distressing surfaces of 10
      fur
lacerated skin calling legend to account
a vixen's courage in vixen terms

For a human animal to call for help
on another animal
is the most riven the most revolted cry on earth   15
come a long way down
Go back far enough it means tearing and torn   endless and sudden
back far enough it blurts
into the birth-yell of the yet-to-be human child
pushed out of a female   the yet-to-be woman   20

1998   2001

THOM GUNN
1929–2004

Thom Gunn was one of the youngest members of the Movement—English poets who began to publish during the 1950s and constituted themselves as a third force in the development of contemporary English poetry. They rejected what seemed to them the Romantic excesses of the New Apocalypse (whose most prominent exponent was Dylan Thomas), and they were equally dissatisfied with the modernist revolution led by Ezra Pound and T. S. Eliot, who, Gunn contended, abandoned important traditional resources of poetry by deciding "to strengthen the images while either banishing concepts or, where they couldn't avoid them, treating them to the same free association as images" (*Yale Review* 53). The Movement sought greater concreteness and a less high-flown diction for poetry. Gunn praised the example of Thomas Hardy, whose terse irony and bleakness he recalls, and of Mina Loy—"tough, cerebral and largely untouched by Imagism" (*TLS*, August 30, 1996). And yet Gunn, unlike other poets of the Movement, was never cautious. "I was wilder than they were," he said. "They were a very sober group of people" (*Gay & Lesbian Review*, Summer 2000). Nor does Gunn's poetry seem especially English. By the time of his inclusion in *New Lines* (1956), the anthology that announced the Movement to the world, he was living in California, studying at Stanford University with Yvor Winters.

Skilled in traditional English forms, Gunn turned to syllabics, after moving to California, then to free verse in the 1960s; but unlike most poets who made this transition, he later wrote poems in both free and metered forms. His subject matter is often nontraditional and includes psychotropic drug use, serial killers, and gay sex. In his signature style, Gunn holds this "wild" content in tension with the tight grid of intricate patterns of rhyme and meter. "In dealing with the experience of the infinite," he said, "I needed to filter it through a finite form, otherwise the whole thing would just drift away" (*Gay & Lesbian Review*). In the heroic couplets of "Moly," for example, he impersonates with almost hallucinatory vividness one of Odysseus's shipmates at the moment of realization that he has been metamorphosed by the female enchanter Circe and is now "buried in swine." "Based on drug experience," in Gunn's words, the early book of which this is the title poem presents a number of experiences of mind expansion as part of the counterculture of his adopted home, San Francisco. Paradoxically, tight forms helped Gunn write "about untenable experiences, experiences beyond the ordinary, hallucinatory things." Gunn often finds his subjects in extreme situations, whether of death or love. Yet as he said of Yvor Winters: "You keep both Rule and Energy in view" ("To Yvor Winters, 1955"). Gunn registered both agitation and the urge to contain it. Like the lover recalled in "The Problem," Gunn's poetry is "disorderly and ordered," balancing "math" against "Passion."

The ultimate test of Gunn's ordering sense of form was the death of many friends in San Francisco during the height of the AIDS crisis, or "plague," as he calls it in the bleak sequence of elegies that closes *The Man with Night Sweats* (1992). Although poems such as "Still Life," "The Missing," and "A Blank" engage intimate and emotionally wrenching subjects, Gunn's acid skepticism and formal control fend off sentimentality. In these poems, some of the best written about the ravages of AIDS, he recalls the slow dying of friends hooked to machines and traces the circulation of their remains in nature; he eyes his own skeleton-haunted frame and mocks his mind's longing for security.

Thomson William Gunn was born on August 29, 1929, in Gravesend, Kent. His parents were journalists. In youth, he endured their divorce and his mother's death. He served for two years in the British army, then received his B.A. from Trinity College, Cambridge University, in 1953.

After following an American lover to California, he entered Stanford University as a graduate student. From that time, Gunn lived most of his life in San Francisco. From 1958 to 1966, he taught at the University of California, Berkeley; from 1975 until his retirement, he taught there one semester a year. Gunn won a MacArthur Fellowship (1993), the Lenore Marshall Prize (1993), and the Lambda Literary Award for Gay Men's Poetry for *Collected Poems* (1995).

My Sad Captains

One by one they appear in
the darkness: a few friends, and
a few with historical
names. How late they start to shine!
but before they fade they stand   5
perfectly embodied, all

the past lapping them like a
cloak of chaos. They were men
who, I thought, lived only to
renew the wasteful force they   10
spent with each hot convulsion.
They remind me, distant now.

True, they are not at rest yet,
but now that they are indeed
apart, winnowed from failures,   15
they withdraw to an orbit
and turn with disinterested
hard energy, like the stars.

         1961

Moly[1]

Nightmare of beasthood, snorting, how to wake.
I woke. What beasthood skin she made me take?

Leathery toad that ruts for days on end,
Or cringing dribbling dog, man's servile friend,

Or cat that prettily pounces on its meat,   5
Tortures it hours, then does not care to eat:

1. A magic herb of Greek mythology. Circe transformed Odysseus's shipmates into swine; Odysseus, protected by the herb moly, which he had been given by the gods' messenger, Hermes, compelled her to restore them to human shape.

Parrot, moth, shark, wolf, crocodile, ass, flea.
What germs, what jostling mobs there were in me.

These seem like bristles, and the hide is tough.
No claw or web here: each foot ends in hoof.   10

Into what bulk has method disappeared?
Like ham, streaked. I am gross—grey, gross, flap-eared.

The pale-lashed eyes my only human feature.
My teeth tear, tear. I am the snouted creature

That bites through anything, root, wire, or can.   15
If I was not afraid I'd eat a man.

Oh a man's flesh already is in mine.
Hand and foot poised for risk. Buried in swine.

I root and root, you think that it is greed,
It is, but I seek out a plant I need.   20

Direct me gods, whose changes are all holy,
To where it flickers deep in grass, the moly:

Cool flesh of magic in each leaf and shoot,
From milky flower to the black forked root.

From this fat dungeon I could rise to skin   25
And human title, putting pig within.

I push my big grey wet snout through the green,
Dreaming the flower I have never seen.

                                                        1971

Still Life

        I shall not soon forget
        The greyish-yellow skin
        To which the face had set:
        Lids tight: nothing of his,
        No tremor from within,   5
        Played on the surfaces.

        He still found breath, and yet
        It was an obscure knack.
        I shall not soon forget
        The angle of his head,   10
        Arrested and reared back
        On the crisp field of bed,

Back from what he could neither
Accept, as one opposed,
Nor, as a life-long breather,   15
Consentingly let go,
The tube his mouth enclosed
In an astonished O.

        1992

The Missing

Now as I watch the progress of the plague,[2]
The friends surrounding me fall sick, grow thin,
And drop away. Bared, is my shape less vague
—Sharply exposed and with a sculpted skin?

I do not like the statue's chill contour,   5
Not nowadays. The warmth investing me
Led outward through mind, limb, feeling, and more
In an involved increasing family.

Contact of friend led to another friend,
Supple entwinement through the living mass   10
Which for all that I knew might have no end,
Image of an unlimited embrace.

I did not just feel ease, though comfortable:
Aggressive as in some ideal of sport,
With ceaseless movement thrilling through the whole,   15
Their push kept me as firm as their support.

But death—Their deaths have left me less defined:
It was their pulsing presence made me clear.
I borrowed from it, I was unconfined,
Who tonight balance unsupported here,   20

Eyes glaring from raw marble, in a pose
Languorously part-buried in the block,
Shins perfect and no calves, as if I froze
Between potential and a finished work.

—Abandoned incomplete, shape of a shape,   25
In which exact detail shows the more strange,
Trapped in unwholeness, I find no escape
Back to the play of constant give and change.

August 1987   1992

2. AIDS.

A Blank

The year of griefs being through, they had to merge
In one last grief, with one last property:
To view itself like loosened cloud lose edge,
And pull apart, and leave a voided sky.

Watching Victorian porches through the glass,   5
From the 6 bus, I caught sight of a friend
Stopped on a corner-kerb to let us pass,
A four-year-old blond child tugging his hand,
Which tug he held against with a slight smile.
I knew the smile from certain passages   10
Two years ago, thus did not know him well,
Since they took place in my bedroom and his.

A sturdy-looking admirable young man.
He said 'I chose to do this with my life.'
Casually met he said it of the plan   15
He undertook without a friend or wife.

Now visibly tugged upon by his decision,
Wayward and eager. So this was his son!
What I admired about his self-permission
Was that he turned from nothing he had done,   20
Or was, or had been, even while he transposed
The expectations he took out at dark
—Of Eros[3] playing, features undisclosed—
Into another pitch, where he might work
With the same melody, and opted so   25
To educate, permit, guide, feed, keep warm,
And love a child to be adopted, though
The child was still a blank then on a form.

The blank was flesh now, running on its nerve,
This fair-topped organism dense with charm,   30
Its braided muscle grabbing what would serve,
His countering pull, his own devoted arm.

                                                        1992

---

3. Greek god of love, usually depicted as a small, blond boy.

The Problem

Close to the top
Of an encrusted dark
Converted brownstone West of Central Park
(For this was 1961)
In his room that,   5
              a narrow hutch,
Was sliced from some once-cavernous flat,
Where now a window took a whole wall up
And tints were bleached-out by the sun
Of many a summer day,   10
We lay
         upon his hard thin bed.

He seemed all body, such
As normally you couldn't touch,
Reckless and rough,   15
One of Boss Cupid's red-
                haired errand boys
Who couldn't get there fast enough.
Almost like fighting . . .
We forgot about the noise,   20
But feeling turned so self-delighting
That hurry soon gave way
To give-and-take,
Till each contested, for the other's sake,
To end up not in winning and defeat   25
But in a draw.

Meanwhile beyond the aureate[4] hair
I saw
A scrap of blackboard with its groove for chalk,
Nailed to a strip of lath   30
That had half-broken through,
The problem drafted there
               still incomplete.
After, I found out in the talk
Companion to a cigarette,   35
That he, turning the problem over yet
In his disorderly and ordered head,
Attended graduate school to teach
And study math,
           his true   40
Passion cyphered in chalk beyond my reach.

                                    2000

4. Golden.

JOHN HOLLANDER
1929–2013

John Hollander and Allen Ginsberg attended Columbia University at the same time, and they testified to their friendship by mentioning each other in their poems. But in many ways they were each other's antitype: Hollander's poems are as finished as Ginsberg's are unfinished, and they offer subtle modulations instead of what Ginsberg insisted were "angelical ravings." Hollander accepted the formal and societal rules that Ginsberg overreached. Yet Hollander's formalism is individualistic and against the grain.

An instance of Hollander's elaborateness of mind and form is his addiction to phenomenal plays on words. With Anthony Hecht, he originated a new kind of poem, like the limerick but much harder to write, called the "double dactyl." In *Types of Shape* (1969, 1991), he revisited the ancient tradition of pattern poetry and wrote poems in the shape of a key, an umbrella, a swan, a crescent moon—feats that few other contemporaries could or would attempt. The learned author of numerous critical studies of prosody, Hollander mastered and revitalized an array of formal verse structures. Many of his poems recast seventeenth-century models, some written for music. "I suppose Mr. Hollander must be called a 'literary' poet," wrote W. H. Auden in the introduction to Hollander's first book, *A Crackling of Thorns* (1958). Allusive, aphoristic, and demanding, Hollander has been a severe critic of what he calls the "cheesy sentimentality" and "easy flabbiness of a ubiquitous form of short-line free verse" ("The Work of Poetry," 1997).

Although he presents experience with style, Hollander recognized a necessity for being more than stylish, and his later verse betrays ever deepening concerns with intimate questions of love, loss, and mortality. He admits in "Helicon," as if to emphasize his special concern, that "opening up at all is harder than meeting a measure." He usually begins with homely objects or incidents and develops them with verbal ingenuity and philosophical know-how. In "Under Cancer," Hollander—a less jovial poet than he at first appears—finds in tanning an instance of aging and decay. His poems balance their poised form with something like despair or acute skepticism, their charming polish and intricacy with the plangent harmonies of grief.

Hollander was born on October 28, 1929, in New York City. He received B.A. and M.A. degrees from Columbia, in 1950 and 1952, and then began work on a doctorate at Indiana University. He was elected a Junior Fellow in the Society of Fellows at Harvard University and taught for a time there. In 1959, he received his doctoral degree from Indiana. He also taught at Connecticut and Hunter Colleges and for the remainder of his career was a professor at Yale University. Among his many awards were the Bollingen Prize (1983) and a MacArthur Fellowship (1990). Hollander was also a respected editor, anthologist, and critic.

Under Cancer

On the Memorial building's
Terrace the sun has been buzzing
Unbearably, all the while
The white baking happens
To the shadow of the table's
White-painted iron. It darkens,
Meaning that the sun is stronger,

That I am invisibly darkening
Too, the while I whiten.
And only after the stretching   10
And getting up, still sweating,
My shirt striped like an awning
Drawn on over airlessness;
After the cool shades
(As if of a long arcade   15
Where footsteps echo gravely)
Have devoured the light;
Only after the cold of
Plunge and shower, the pale
Scent of deodorant stick   20
Smelling like gin and limes,
And another stripy shirt
Can come, homing in at last,
The buzzing of having been burnt.
Only then, intimations   25
Of tossing, hot in the dark
Night, where all the long while
Silently, along edges,
There is flaking away.

In this short while of light   30
My shadow darkens without
Lengthening ever, ever.

1971

Adam's Task

And Adam gave names to all cattle, and to the fowl of the air, and
to every beast of the field . . .
—Gen. 2.20

Thou, paw-paw-paw; thou, glurd; thou, spotted
    Glurd; thou, whitestap, lurching through
The high-grown brush; thou, pliant-footed,
    Implex; thou, awagabu.

Every burrower, each flier   5
    Came for the name he had to give:
Gay, first work, ever to be prior,
    Not yet sunk to primitive.

Thou, verdle; thou, McFleery's pomma;
    Thou; thou; thou—three types of grawl;   10
Thou, flisket; thou, kabasch; thou, comma-
    Eared mashawk; thou, all; thou, all.

Were, in a fire of becoming,
    Laboring to be burned away,

Then work, half-measuring, half-humming,   15
    Would be as serious as play.

Thou, pambler; thou, rivarn; thou, greater
    Wherret, and thou, lesser one;
Thou, sproal; thou, zant; thou, lily-eater.
    Naming's over. Day is done.   20

        1971

Back to Town[1]

These labor days, when shirking hardly looks like working
Yet sounds far too much like it . . . standing idle, I muse
On which of us two helpmeets, when we weave together,
Is the worker, which, unwittingly, the noisy drone.[2]
Warp might contend with weft[3] for priority, wrecking   5
The whole frame, wrenching the time into a travesty
Of a day of rest. Were the hum of our shuttling song
Stilled for long, the thin lines strung across the workaday
Loom would sag or snap. But back-and-forth breeds up-and-down:
The figures develop in the field, growing under   10
The sole working light of our attentiveness. Where would
I be without you? Who ever see you save through me?
United we stand and shake the chains heard round the world.

        1983

Variations on a Fragment by Trumbull Stickney[4]

I hear a river thro' the valley wander
Whose water runs, the song alone remaining.
A rainbow stands and summer passes under,

Flowing like silence in the light of wonder.
In the near distances it is still raining   5
Where now the valley fills again with thunder,

Where now the river in her wide meander,
Losing at each loop what she had been gaining,
Moves into what one might as well call yonder.

---

1. Poem numbered 98 in *Powers of Thirteen*.
2. Male, nonworking bee.
3. Weaving terms: the "warp" is the lengthwise threads on a loom; the "weft," the threads that cross the warp.
4. American poet (1874–1904). Lines 1–3 comprise Stickney's Fragment IX.

The way of the dark water is to ponder   10
The way the light sings as of something waning.
The far-off waterfall can sound asunder

Stillness of distances, as if in blunder,
Tumbling over the rim of all explaining.
Water proves nothing, but can only maunder.   15

Shadows show nothing, but can only launder
The lovely land that sunset had been staining,
Long fields of which the falling light grows fonder.

Here summer stands while all its songs pass under,
A riverbank still time runs by, remaining.   20
I will remember rainbows as I wander.

1993

By Heart

The songs come at us first; and then the rhymed
Verses like speech that half-sings; then the tunes
Of summer evening—the train whistle's sigh
Westering, fading, as I lay in bed
Sunset still creeping past the lowered shade;   5
The gossip of swallows; the faint, radioed
Reed section of a dance band through an open
Window down at the far end of the street;
And then the strings of digits that we learn
To keep like bunched keys ready to unlock   10
All the boxes we get assigned to us
By the uncaring sheriffs of life itself.
We play by ear, but learn the words by heart;
(Visions we have by head); yet even when
The sight of the remembered page has dimmed   15
The jingles that we gleaned from it remain
Lodged with us, useful, sometimes, for the work
Of getting a grip on certain fragile things.
We are ourselves from birth committed to
Memory, to broad access to a past   20
Framing and filling any presentness
Of self that we could really call our own.
We grasp the world by ear, by heart, by head,
And keep it in a soft continuingness
That we first learned to get by soul, or something.   25

2000

Derek Walcott
b. 1930

Derek Walcott, the preeminent Caribbean poet writing in English, was born on January 23, 1930, on Saint Lucia, one of the four Windward Islands. Although he has been a constant and fortunate (his word) traveler, the center of his affections and allegiances, the landscape of his memory and his imagination, remains his natal island, in the eastern Caribbean. Despite his devotion to Caribbean culture, Walcott's account of his early years suggests he was somewhat of an outsider. He was reared a Methodist in a society that was largely Roman Catholic; his father, a talented amateur painter, died before Walcott was a year old; his mother, the head teacher at a Methodist nursery school, had a collection of the English classics, which she encouraged her son to read. Walcott's background is racially and culturally mixed. His grandmothers were of African descent; his grandfathers were white, a Dutchman and an Englishman. Schooled in the Standard English that is the official language of Saint Lucia, Walcott also grew up speaking the predominantly French Creole (or patois) that is the primary language of everyday life (Saint Lucia had traded hands fourteen times in colonial wars between the British and the French).

In "A Far Cry from Africa," Walcott, self-consciously "divided to the vein," dramatizes the conflict between his loyalties to his African ancestry and to the "English tongue I love." He has self-mockingly referred to his divided allegiances as those of a "schizophrenic," a "mongrel," a "mulatto of style" ("What the Twilight Says: An Overture"). Sometimes his cross-cultural inheritance is the source of pain and ambivalence, as when he refers to himself as being "poisoned with the blood of both." At other times, it fuels a celebratory integration of multiple forms, visions, and energies, as in parts of his epic poem *Omeros* (1990). With varying degrees of discomfort and elation, Walcott tries to embrace all his cultural influences—European, American, African, and the creolized culture of the West Indies. At the end of his seminal essay "The Muse of History" (1974), he movingly recalls the violent past he carries within his body, addressing a white forefather—"slave seller and slave buyer"—and a black forefather "in the filthridden gut of the slave ship." But the scars left by the slavemaster's whip are transformed in Walcott's magnificent image for his and the Caribbean's fusion of black and white skins, of Northern and Southern Hemispheres: "the monumental groaning and soldering of two great worlds, like the halves of a fruit seamed by its own bitter juice."

Even as a schoolboy, Walcott knew he wasn't alone in his effort to sort through his vexed postcolonial affiliations. From a young age, he felt a special "intimacy with the Irish poets" as "colonials with the same kind of problems that existed in the Caribbean." He continues, provocatively: "They were the niggers of Britain" (1977 interview). Various English and American writers—T. S. Eliot, Ezra Pound, Hart Crane, W. H. Auden, and Robert Lowell—have also been strong influences on Walcott. But the young poet passionately identified with W. B. Yeats, James Joyce, and J. M. Synge, knowing he shared their conflicted responses to the cultural inheritances of the British Empire—its literature, religion, and language. At school, Walcott recalls, Joyce's Stephen Dedalus was his "hero": "Like him, I was a knot of paradoxes," among other things "learning to hate England as I worshipped her language." Struck anew in *Omeros* by the shared postcolonial problem of a complex linguistic and literary inheritance, he memorably declares Ireland "a nation / split by a glottal scream." Also recognizing this affinity, Seamus Heaney, Walcott's near-contemporary from Northern Ireland, writes of the Saint Lucian: "I imagine he has done for the Caribbean what Synge did for Ireland, found a language woven out of dialect and literature, neither folksy nor condescending, a singular idiom evolved out of one man's inherited divisions and obsessions" ("The Murmur of Malvern").

Walcott asks time and again how the postcolonial poet can both grieve the agonizing harm of British colonialism and appreciate the empire's literary gift. Without forgetting what he calls in "A Far Cry from Africa" "the drunken officer of British rule," Walcott nevertheless celebrates his British colonial education as "the greatest bequest the Empire made. The grounding was rigid—Latin, Greek, and the essential masterpieces, but there was this elation of discovery. Shakespeare, Marlowe, Horace, Vergil—these writers weren't jaded but immediate experiences." Indeed, "precisely because of their limitations our early education must have ranked with the finest in the world" ("Meanings"). It followed the standard British curriculum: "the writers of my generation were natural assimilators. We knew the literature of Empires, Greek, Roman, British, through their essential classics; and both the patois of the street and the language of the classroom." With this grounding, Walcott was determined to make a poetry "legitimately prolonging the mighty line of Marlowe, of Milton" ("Twilight").

In spite of his affinity for a literature bequeathed by empire, Walcott insists that the copiousness and opulence of his verse reflect his Caribbean inheritance. In a tribute to the West Indies, he said to an interviewer: "I come from a place that likes grandeur; it likes large gestures; it is not inhibited by flourish; it is a rhetorical society; it is a society of physical performance; it is a society of style. . . . Modesty is not possible in performance in the Caribbean, and that's wonderful. It is better to be large and make huge gestures than to be modest and do tiptoeing types of presentations of oneself" ("The Art of Poetry"). Walcott is a no less "authentically" West Indian poet than Louise Bennett, Kamau Brathwaite, Lorna Goodison, or Grace Nichols, though he is often seen as the most Eurocentric of the leading Caribbean poets. A shamelessly hybridizing writer, he resembles the hero Shabine of "The Schooner *Flight*," the character's name itself Creole for "mulatto": "I have Dutch, nigger, and English in me, / and either I'm nobody, or I'm a nation." When in *Omeros* the Saint Lucian hero Achille imaginatively returns to his ancestors in Africa, he uncovers a vital source of identity, while also learning that centuries of creolized life in the West Indies have made it impossible for him to merge with his African heritage.

Over the course of his prolific career, Walcott has adapted various literary archetypes (e.g., the Greek characters Philoctetes and Achilles) and forms (epic, quatrains, hexameters, terza rima). He has related his interest in craft to his religious upbringing: "There is," he has said in an interview, "a very strong sense of carpentry in Protestantism, in making things simply and in a utilitarian way. . . . I think of myself in a way as a carpenter, as one making frames simply and well" (1977 interview). From the 1950s to the 1990s, he moved from the Yeatsian lyric ambivalence in the loosely pentameter lines of "A Far Cry from Africa" to the epic near-hexameters in the anglicized terza rima of *Omeros*. Although much of his poetry is in a rhetorically elevated Standard English, Walcott adapts the calypso rhythms of a lightly creolized English in "The Schooner *Flight*," and he braids together West Indian English, Standard English, and French patois in *Omeros*.

Walcott has a great passion for metaphor, and he delights in weaving figurative connections across cultural and racial boundaries. The Middle Passage's brutal "amnesiac blow," the transatlantic slave journey mourned in "Laventille" and remembered in "The Sea Is History," returns in the metaphor of the wound as the central symbol of Afro-Caribbean historical suffering in *Omeros*; in that poem, Walcott caribbeanizes a Greek hero and classical emblem of suffering, the wounded Philoctetes. This intercultural appropriation is emblematic of Walcott's "mulatto aesthetics": with acute irony, Walcott borrows the classical Philoctetes from what he calls a European "culture of slavery," to memorialize the harm inflicted on Afro-Caribbeans by their European enslavers. Such

deft intercultural weaving and cross-cultural negotiation also distinguish "The Schooner
Flight" and "The Fortunate Traveller."

Walcott's prodigious talent was evident early in his life, despite the seeming modesty
of his upbringing in a colonial backwater. At fifteen, he published a poem in the local
newspaper, drawing a sharp rebuke in rhyme from a Catholic priest for his heretical
pantheism and animism. A few years later, he borrowed money from his mother to print
a booklet of twenty-five poems, hawking it on the streets to earn the money back. This
book and his first major play, *Henri Christophe*, also met with disapprobation from the
Catholic Church. In 1950, he left Saint Lucia to enter the University of the West Indies
in Mona, Jamaica, where he was a vibrant literary figure among the university's first
graduating class in liberal arts. He received a B.A. in 1953. Staying on in Jamaica, he
made his living through teaching and journalism. He moved to Trinidad in 1958, still
working as a reviewer and art critic, but pouring energy into directing and writing plays
for the Trinidad Theatre Workshop until 1976. His poetry began to receive international
attention when *In a Green Night* (1962) was published in England. His plays, which
have been performed in New York and London as well as in the Caribbean, are about
the history and culture of the West Indies, many of them written in West Indian English.
Since 1981, Walcott has taught regularly at Boston University. In the 1990s, he built
a home on the northwest coast of Saint Lucia, where he paints and writes. He received
the Nobel Prize in Literature in 1992.

A Far Cry from Africa

A wind is ruffling the tawny pelt
Of Africa. Kikuyu,[1] quick as flies,
Batten upon the bloodstreams of the veldt.[2]
Corpses are scattered through a paradise.
Only the worm, colonel of carrion, cries: 5
"Waste no compassion on these separate dead!"
Statistics justify and scholars seize
The salients of colonial policy.
What is that to the white child hacked in bed?
To savages, expendable as Jews?   10

Threshed out by beaters,[3] the long rushes break
In a white dust of ibises whose cries
Have wheeled since civilization's dawn
From the parched river or beast-teeming plain.
The violence of beast on beast is read   15
As natural law, but upright man
Seeks his divinity by inflicting pain.
Delirious as these worried beasts, his wars
Dance to the tightened carcass of a drum,
While he calls courage still that native dread   20
Of the white peace contracted by the dead.

---

1. Largest ethnic group in Kenya, whose members, as Mau Mau fighters, conducted a campaign of violent resistance against British colonial settlers in the 1950s.
2. Grassy plain, savannah. *Batten upon:* feed upon

gluttonously.
3. In African game hunting, people are hired to beat the brush, chasing birds and animals from their hiding places.

Again brutish necessity wipes its hands
Upon the napkin of a dirty cause, again
A waste of our compassion, as with Spain,[4]
The gorilla wrestles with the superman.   25
I who am poisoned with the blood of both,
Where shall I turn, divided to the vein?
I who have cursed
The drunken officer of British rule, how choose
Between this Africa and the English tongue I love?   30
Betray them both, or give back what they give?
How can I face such slaughter and be cool?
How can I turn from Africa and live?

1956, 1962

Laventille

[for V. S. Naipaul]

To find the Western Path
Through the Gates of Wrath—
—BLAKE[5]

It huddled there
steel tinkling its blue painted metal air,
tempered in violence, like Rio's favelas,[6]

with snaking, perilous streets whose edges fell as
its Episcopal turkey-buzzards fall   5
from its miraculous hilltop

shrine,
down the impossible drop
to Belmont, Woodbrook, Maraval, St. Clair[7]

that shine   10
like peddlers' tin trinkets in the sun.
From a harsh

shower, its gutters growled and gargled wash
past the Youth Centre, past the water catchment,[8]
a rigid children's carousel of cement;   15

---

4. Perhaps a reference to the massacres inflicted on both sides during the Spanish Civil War of 1936–39.
5. From "Morning," by English Romantic poet and visionary William Blake (1757–1827). *Laventille*: hillside slum outside Port of Spain, the capital of Trinidad and Tobago. Our Lady of Laventille, the shrine at the top of the hill, can be seen throughout the city. V. S. Naipaul (b. 1932): Trinidad-born writer, noted for pessimistic examinations of postcolonial life in Third World countries.
6. Shantytowns on the steep hills surrounding Rio de Janeiro, Brazil.
7. Other towns in Trinidad.
8. Basin for collecting rainwater.

we climbed where lank electric
lines and tension cables linked its raw brick
hovels like a complex feud,

where the inheritors of the middle passage[9] stewed,
five to a room, still clamped below their hatch,   20
breeding like felonies,

whose lives revolve round prison, graveyard, church.
Below bent breadfruit trees
in the flat, coloured city, class

escalated into structures still,   25
merchant, middleman, magistrate, knight. To go downhill
from here was to ascend.

The middle passage never guessed its end.
This is the height of poverty
for the desperate and black;   30

climbing, we could look back
with widening memory
on the hot, corrugated-iron sea
whose horrors we all

shared. The salt blood knew it well,   35
you, me, Samuel's daughter, Samuel,
and those ancestors clamped below its grate.

And climbing steeply past the wild
gutters, it shrilled
in the blood, for those who suffered, who were killed,   40

and who survive.
What other gift was there to give
as the godparents of his unnamed child?

Yet outside the brown annex of the church, the
stifling odour of bay rum and talc, the particular,   45
neat sweetness of the crowd distressed

that sense. The black, fawning verger,[1]
his bow tie akimbo, grinning, the clown-gloved
fashionable wear of those I deeply loved

once, made me look on with hopelessness and rage   50
at their new, apish habits, their excess
and fear, the possessed, the self-possessed;

9. The journey by which African slaves were trans-   in morbidly overcrowded ships.
ported across the Atlantic Ocean to the Americas   1. Church attendant.

their perfume shrivelled to a childhood fear
of Sabbath graveyards, christenings, marriages,
that muggy, steaming, self-assuring air   55

of tropical Sabbath afternoons. And in
the church, eyes prickling with rage,
the children rescued from original sin

by their Godfather since the middle passage,
the supercilious brown curate, who intones,   60
healing the guilt in these rachitic[2] bones,
twisting my love within me like a knife:
"across the troubled waters of this life . . ."

Which of us cares to walk
even if God wished   65
those retching waters where our souls were fished

for this new world? Afterwards, we talk
in whispers, close to death
among these stones planted on alien earth.

Afterwards,   70
the ceremony, the careful photograph
moved out of range before the patient tombs,

we dare a laugh,
ritual, desperate words,
born like these children from habitual wombs,   75

from lives fixed in the unalterable groove
of grinding poverty. I stand out on a balcony
and watch the sun pave its flat, golden path

across the roofs, the aerials, cranes, the tops
of fruit trees crawling downward to the city.   80
Something inside is laid wide like a wound,

some open passage that has cleft the brain,
some deep, amnesiac blow. We left
somewhere a life we never found,

customs and gods that are not born again,   85
some crib, some grille of light
clanged shut on us in bondage, and withheld

us from that world below us and beyond,
and in its swaddling cerements[3] we're still bound.

1965

2. Rickety.   3. Burial clothes.

The Sea Is History

Where are your monuments, your battles, martyrs?
Where is your tribal memory? Sirs,
in that grey vault. The sea. The sea
has locked them up. The sea is History.

First, there was the heaving oil,   5
heavy as chaos;
then, like a light at the end of a tunnel,

the lantern of a caravel,[4]
and that was Genesis.
Then there were the packed cries,   10
the shit, the moaning:

Exodus.[5]
Bone soldered by coral to bone,
mosaics
mantled by the benediction of the shark's shadow,   15

that was the Ark of the Covenant.[6]
Then came from the plucked wires
of sunlight on the sea floor

the plangent harps of the Babylonian bondage,[7]
as the white cowries clustered like manacles   20
on the drowned women,

and those were the ivory bracelets
of the Song of Solomon,[8]
but the ocean kept turning blank pages

looking for History.   25
Then came the men with eyes heavy as anchors
who sank without tombs,

brigands who barbecued cattle,[9]
leaving their charred ribs like palm leaves on the shore,
then the foaming, rabid maw   30

---

4. Ship of the fifteenth and sixteenth centuries.
5. Second book of the Hebrew Bible (Old Testament), Exodus describes the Israelites' escape from Egyptian captivity.
6. In the Bible, the sacred chest that contained the two tablets bearing the Ten Commandments.
7. The period from the fall of Jerusalem (586 B.C.E.) to the reconstruction in Palestine of a new Jewish state (after 538 B.C.E.), during which time the Jews were exiled to Mesopotamia by the conquering Babylonians.
8. Book of the Bible consisting of a series of erotic poems.
9. In Homer's *Odyssey*, Odysseus's men are punished for eating the cattle of the sun god, Helios.

of the tidal wave swallowing Port Royal,
and that was Jonah,[1]
but where is your Renaissance?

Sir, it is locked in them sea-sands
out there past the reef's moiling shelf,   35
where the men-o'-war floated down;

strop on these goggles, I'll guide you there myself.
It's all subtle and submarine,
through colonnades of coral,

past the gothic windows of sea-fans   40
to where the crusty grouper, onyx-eyed,
blinks, weighted by its jewels, like a bald queen;

and these groined caves with barnacles
pitted like stone
are our cathedrals,   45

and the furnace before the hurricanes:
Gomorrah.[2] Bones ground by windmills
into marl and cornmeal,

and that was Lamentations[3]—
that was just Lamentations,   50
it was not History;

then came, like scum on the river's drying lip,
the brown reeds of villages
mantling and congealing into towns,

and at evening, the midges'[4] choirs,   55
and above them, the spires
lancing the side of God[5]

as His son set, and that was the New Testament.

Then came the white sisters clapping
to the waves' progress,   60
and that was Emancipation[6]—

jubilation, O jubilation—
vanishing swiftly
as the sea's lace dries in the sun,

1. Biblical prophet swallowed by a great fish. *Port Royal*: once a major harbor town on the southern coast of Jamaica, it was destroyed by an earthquake in 1692.
2. City destroyed by God along with Sodom in Genesis 19.
3. Book of the Hebrew Bible (Old Testament) that laments the destruction of Judah, Jerusalem, and the Temple by the Babylonians.
4. Tiny flies'.
5. According to the Bible, Jesus' side was lanced during his crucifixion.
6. In the 1830s, slavery was abolished in the British West Indies.

but that was not History,   65
that was only faith,
and then each rock broke into its own nation;

then came the synod[7] of flies,
then came the secretarial heron,
then came the bullfrog bellowing for a vote,   70

fireflies with bright ideas
and bats like jetting ambassadors
and the mantis, like khaki police,

and the furred caterpillars of judges
examining each case closely,   75
and then in the dark ears of ferns

and in the salt chuckle of rocks
with their sea pools, there was the sound
like a rumour without any echo

of History, really beginning.   80

1979

The Schooner *Flight*

1. Adios, Carenage[8]

In idle August, while the sea soft,
and leaves of brown islands stick to the rim
of this Caribbean, I blow out the light
by the dreamless face of Maria Concepcion
to ship as a seaman on the schooner *Flight*.   5
Out in the yard turning grey in the dawn,
I stood like a stone and nothing else move
but the cold sea rippling like galvanize
and the nail holes of stars in the sky roof,
till a wind start to interfere with the trees.   10
I pass me dry neighbour sweeping she yard
as I went downhill, and I nearly said:
"Sweep soft, you witch, 'cause she don't sleep hard,"
but the bitch look through me like I was dead.
A route taxi pull up, park-lights still on.   15
The driver size up my bags with a grin:
"This time, Shabine, like you really gone!"
I ain't answer the ass, I simply pile in
the back seat and watch the sky burn
above Laventille[9] pink as the gown   20

7. A meeting of bishops or other church officials to decide administrative and theological issues.
8. Waterfront where island schooner ships are cleaned and repaired. *Adios*: goodbye (Spanish).
9. Hillside slum outside Port of Spain, Trinidad.

in which the woman I left was sleeping,
and I look in the rearview and see a man
exactly like me, and the man was weeping
for the houses, the streets, that whole fucking island.

Christ have mercy on all sleeping things!   25
From that dog rotting down Wrightson Road
to when I was a dog on these streets;
if loving these islands must be my load,
out of corruption my soul takes wings,
But they had started to poison my soul   30
with their big house, big car, big-time bohbohl,[1]
coolie, nigger, Syrian, and French Creole,
so I leave it for them and their carnival—
I taking a sea-bath, I gone down the road.
I know these islands from Monos to Nassau,[2]   35
a rusty head sailor with sea-green eyes
that they nickname Shabine, the patois[3] for
any red nigger, and I, Shabine, saw
when these slums of empire was paradise.
I'm just a red nigger who love the sea,   40
I had a sound colonial education,
I have Dutch, nigger, and English in me,
and either I'm nobody, or I'm a nation.

But Maria Concepcion was all my thought
watching the sea heaving up and down   45
as the port side of dories, schooners, and yachts
was painted afresh by the strokes of the sun
signing her name with every reflection;
I knew when dark-haired evening put on
her bright silk at sunset, and, folding the sea,   50
sidled under the sheet with her starry laugh,
that there'd be no rest, there'd be no forgetting.
Is like telling mourners round the graveside
about resurrection, they want the dead back,
so I smile to myself as the bow rope untied   55
and the *Flight* swing seaward: "Is no use repeating
that the sea have more fish. I ain't want her
dressed in the sexless light of a seraph,
I want those round brown eyes like a marmoset,[4] and
till the day when I can lean back and laugh,   60
those claws that tickled my back on sweating
Sunday afternoons, like a crab on wet sand."
As I worked, watching the rotting waves come
past the bow that scissor the sea like silk,
I swear to you all, by my mother's milk,   65
by the stars that shall fly from tonight's furnace,

---

1. Or *bobol*: corrupt practices or fraud, organized
by people in positions of privilege or authority
(Eastern Caribbean English).
2. Capital of the Bahamas. *Monos*: island off the
northwest coast of Trinidad.
3. Spoken dialect, such as French-based Creole.
4. South American monkey. *Seraph*: angel.

that I loved them, my children, my wife, my home;
I loved them as poets love the poetry
that kills them, as drowned sailors the sea.

You ever look up from some lonely beach   70
and see a far schooner? Well, when I write
this poem, each phrase go be soaked in salt;
I go draw and knot every line as tight
as ropes in this rigging; in simple speech
my common language go be the wind,   75
my pages the sails of the schooner *Flight*.
But let me tell you how this business begin.

2. *Raptures of the Deep*

Smuggled Scotch for O'Hara, big government man,
between Cedros and the Main,[5] so the Coast Guard couldn't touch us,
and the Spanish pirogues[6] always met us halfway,   80
but a voice kept saying: "Shabine, see this business
of playing pirate?" Well, so said, so done!
That whole racket crash. And I for a woman,
for her laces and silks, Maria Concepcion.
Ay, ay! Next thing I hear, some Commission of Enquiry   85
was being organized to conduct a big quiz,
with himself as chairman investigating himself.
Well, I knew damn well who the suckers would be,
not that shark in shark skin, but his pilot fish,[7]
khaki-pants red niggers like you and me.   90
What worse, I fighting with Maria Concepcion,
plates flying and thing, so I swear: "Not again!"
It was mashing up my house and my family.
I was so broke all I needed was shades and a cup
or four shades and four cups in four-cup Port of Spain;   95
all the silver I had was the coins on the sea.

You saw them ministers in *The Express*,
guardians of the poor—one hand at their back,
and one set o' police only guarding their house,
and the Scotch pouring in through the back door.   100
As for that minister-monster who smuggled the booze,
that half-Syrian saurian,[8] I got so vex to see
that face thick with powder, the warts, the stone lids
like a dinosaur caked with primordial ooze
by the lightning of flashbulbs sinking in wealth,   105
that I said: "Shabine, this is shit, understand!"
But he get somebody to kick my crutch out his office
like I was some artist! That bitch was so grand,
couldn't get off his high horse and kick me himself.

5. The South American mainland. The Cedros   6. Canoelike boats.
peninsula is on the sparsely populated southwest 7. Fish that follows sharks to catch food scraps.
tip of Trinidad, across a small channel from Ven-   8. Lizard.
ezuela.

I have seen things that would make a slave sick
in this Trinidad, the Limers' Republic.[9]

I couldn't shake the sea noise out of my head,
the shell of my ears sang Maria Concepcion,
so I start salvage diving with a crazy Mick,
name O'Shaughnessy, and a limey[1] named Head;
but this Caribbean so choke with the dead
that when I would melt in emerald water,
whose ceiling rippled like a silk tent,
I saw them corals: brain, fire, sea-fans,
dead-men's-fingers, and then, the dead men.
I saw that the powdery sand was their bones
ground white from Senegal to San Salvador,[2]
so, I panic third dive, and surface for a month
in the Seamen's Hostel. Fish broth and sermons.
When I thought of the woe I had brought my wife,
when I saw my worries with that other woman,
I wept under water, salt seeking salt,
for her beauty had fallen on me like a sword
cleaving me from my children, flesh of my flesh!

There was this barge from St. Vincent,[3] but she was too deep
to float her again. When we drank, the limey
got tired of my sobbing for Maria Concepcion.
He said he was getting the bends. Good for him!
The pain in my heart for Maria Concepcion,
the hurt I had done to my wife and children,
was worse than the bends. In the rapturous deep
there was no cleft rock where my soul could hide
like the boobies[4] each sunset, no sandbar of light
where I could rest, like the pelicans know,
so I got raptures once, and I saw God
like a harpooned grouper bleeding, and a far
voice was rumbling, "Shabine, if you leave her,
if you leave her, I shall give you the morning star."
When I left the madhouse I tried other women
but, once they stripped naked, their spiky cunts
bristled like sea-eggs and I couldn't dive.
The chaplain came round. I paid him no mind.
Where is my rest place, Jesus? Where is my harbour?
Where is the pillow I will not have to pay for,
and the window I can look from that frames my life?

110

115

120

125

130

135

140

145

150

9. *Limers:* people who loaf or spend time idly
(West Indian English).
1. Derogatory term for an English person. *Mick:*
derogatory term for an Irish person.
2. That is, from Senegal, a country in West Africa,
to San Salvador, in Central America, where Colum-

bus first landed in the Americas. Approximately
one third of slaves died en route from Africa to the
Americas.
3. Island in the eastern Caribbean.
4. Tropical seabirds.

3. *Shabine Leaves the Republic*

I had no nation now but the imagination.
After the white man, the niggers didn't want me
when the power swing to their side.
The first chain my hands and apologize, "History";
the next said I wasn't black enough for their pride.   155
Tell me, what power, on these unknown rocks—
a spray-plane Air Force, the Fire Brigade,
the Red Cross, the Regiment, two, three police dogs
that pass before you finish bawling "Parade!"?
I met History once, but he ain't recognize me,   160
a parchment Creole,[5] with warts
like an old sea-bottle, crawling like a crab
through the holes of shadow cast by the net
of a grille balcony; cream linen, cream hat.
I confront him and shout, "Sir, is Shabine!   165
They say I'se your grandson. You remember Grandma,
your black cook, at all?" The bitch[6] hawk and spat.
A spit like that worth any number of words.
But that's all them bastards have left us: words.

I no longer believed in the revolution.   170
I was losing faith in the love of my woman.
I had seen that moment Aleksandr Blok[7]
crystallize in *The Twelve*. Was between
the Police Marine Branch and Hotel Venezuelana
one Sunday at noon. Young men without flags   175
using shirts, their chests waiting for holes.
They kept marching into the mountains, and
their noise ceased as foam sinks into sand.
They sank in the bright hills like rain, every one
with his own nimbus, leaving shirts in the street,   180
and the echo of power at the end of the street.[8]
Propeller-blade fans turn over the Senate;
the judges, they say, still sweat in carmine,[9]
on Frederick Street the idlers all marching
by standing still, the Budget turns a new leaf.   185
In the 12:30 movies the projectors best
not break down, or you go see revolution. Aleksandr Blok
enters and sits in the third row of pit eating choc-
olate cone, waiting for a spaghetti West-
ern with Clint Eastwood and featuring Lee Van Cleef.[1]   190

5. Here, a white descendant of European settlers in the Caribbean.
6. That is, the "Creole," or "History."
7. Russian symbolist (1880–1921), who celebrated the Russian Revolution in his epic poem *The Twelve* (1918).
8. Walcott alludes to the 1970 Black Power revolt in Trinidad, which included street marches and violence in Port of Spain, where he was living. Parts of the army sided with the revolutionaries, and the government was threatened with collapse.
9. Crimson.
1. Like Eastwood (b. 1930), an American actor (1925–1989) who starred in many "spaghetti" westerns produced by Italian and other European filmmakers.

4. *The* Flight, *Passing Blanchisseuse*[2]

Dusk. The *Flight* passing Blanchisseuse.
Gulls wheel like from a gun again,
and foam gone amber that was white,
lighthouse and star start making friends,
down every beach the long day ends,   195
and there, on that last stretch of sand,
on a beach bare of all but light,
dark hands start pulling in the seine[3]
of the dark sea, deep, deep inland.

5. *Shabine Encounters the Middle Passage*[4]

Man, I brisk in the galley first thing next dawn,   200
brewing li'l coffee; fog coil from the sea
like the kettle steaming when I put it down
slow, slow, 'cause I couldn't believe what I see:
where the horizon was one silver haze,
the fog swirl and swell into sails, so close   205
that I saw it was sails, my hair grip my skull,
it was horrors, but it was beautiful.
We float through a rustling forest of ships
with sails dry like paper, behind the glass
I saw men with rusty eyeholes like cannons,   210
and whenever their half-naked crews cross the sun,
right through their tissue, you traced their bones
like leaves against the sunlight; frigates, barkentines,[5]
the backward-moving current swept them on,
and high on their decks I saw great admirals,   215
Rodney, Nelson, de Grasse,[6] I heard the hoarse orders
they gave those Shabines, and the forest
of masts sail right through the *Flight,*
and all you could hear was the ghostly sound
of waves rustling like grass in a low wind   220
and the hissing weeds they trailed from the stern;
slowly they heaved past from east to west
like this round world was some cranked water wheel,
every ship pouring like a wooden bucket
dredged from the deep; my memory revolve   225
on all sailors before me, then the sun
heat the horizon's ring and they was mist.

---

2. Village on the north coast of Trinidad. Its name is French for washerwoman.
3. Large fishing net.
4. The route across the Atlantic Ocean by which slaves were transported from Africa to the New World, suffering starvation and disease in morbidly overcrowded ships.
5. Small ships. *Frigates:* warships of the eighteenth and early nineteenth centuries.
6. Admiral George Brydges Rodney (1718–1792)

led British naval forces in a decisive defeat over the French warships of François-Joseph-Paul, Count de Grasse (1722–1788) in the 1782 Battle of the Saints, named after a small group of islands between Guadeloupe and Dominica. Before his famous victory at Trafalgar in the Napoleonic Wars, Horatio Nelson (1758–1805), another British admiral, also served extensively in the Caribbean.

Next we pass slave ships. Flags of all nations,
our fathers below deck too deep, I suppose,
to hear us shouting. So we stop shouting. Who knows   230
who his grandfather is, much less his name?
Tomorrow our landfall will be the Barbados.

6. *The Sailor Sings Back to the Casuarinas*[7]

You see them on the low hills of Barbados
bracing like windbreaks, needles for hurricanes,
trailing, like masts, the cirrus[8] of torn sails;   235
when I was green like them, I used to think
those cypresses, leaning against the sea,
that take the sea-noise up into their branches,
are not real cypresses but casuarinas.
Now captain just call them Canadian cedars.   240
But cedars, cypresses, or casuarinas,
whoever called them so had a good cause,
watching their bending bodies wail like women
after a storm, when some schooner came home
with news of one more sailor drowned again.   245
Once the sound "cypress" used to make more sense
than the green "casuarinas," though, to the wind
whatever grief bent them was all the same,
since they were trees with nothing else in mind
but heavenly leaping or to guard a grave;   250
but we live like our names and you would have
to be colonial to know the difference,
to know the pain of history words contain,
to love those trees with an inferior love,
and to believe: "Those casuarinas bend   255
like cypresses, their hair hangs down in rain
like sailors' wives. They're classic trees, and we,
if we live like the names our masters please,
by careful mimicry might become men."

7. *The Flight Anchors in Castries*[9] *Harbor*

When the stars self were young over Castries,   260
I loved you alone and I loved the whole world.
What does it matter that our lives are different?
Burdened with the loves of our different children?
When I think of your young face washed by the wind
and your voice that chuckles in the slap of the sea?   265
The lights are out on La Toc promontory,
except for the hospital. Across at Vigie[1]
the marina arcs keep vigil. I have kept my own
promise, to leave you the one thing I own,

---

7. Pinelike trees. Southeast of Saint Lucia, Barbados is the easternmost island of the Caribbean.
8. Wispy cloud.

9. Capital of Saint Lucia.
1. Just north of Castries.

you whom I loved first: my poetry.   270
We here for one night. Tomorrow, the *Flight* will be gone.

8. *Fight with the Crew*

It had one bitch on board, like he had me mark—
that was the cook, some Vincentian arse
with a skin like a gommier tree,[2] red peeling bark,
and wash-out blue eyes; he wouldn't give me a ease,   275
like he feel he was white. Had an exercise book,
this same one here, that I was using to write
my poetry, so one day this man snatch it
from my hand, and start throwing it left and right
to the rest of the crew, bawling out, "Catch it,"   280
and start mincing me like I was some hen
because of the poems. Some case is for fist,
some case is for tholing pin,[3] some is for knife—
this one was for knife. Well, I beg him first,
but he keep reading, "O my children, my wife,"   285
and playing he crying, to make the crew laugh;
it move like a flying fish, the silver knife
that catch him right in the plump of his calf,
and he faint so slowly, and he turn more white
than he thought he was. I suppose among men   290
you need that sort of thing. It ain't right
but that's how it is. There wasn't much pain,
just plenty blood, and Vincie and me best friend,
but none of them go fuck with my poetry again.

9. *Maria Concepcion & the Book of Dreams*

The jet that was screeching over the *Flight*   295
was opening a curtain into the past.
"Dominica ahead!"
                "It still have Caribs[4] there."
"One day go be planes only, no more boat."
"Vince, God ain't make nigger to fly through the air."
"Progress, Shabine, that's what it's all about.   300
Progress leaving all we small islands behind."
I was at the wheel, Vince sitting next to me
gaffing.[5] Crisp, bracing day. A high-running sea.
"Progress is something to ask Caribs about.
They kill them by millions, some in war,   305
some by forced labour dying in the mines
looking for silver, after that niggers;[6] more

---

2. Gum tree, one of the largest and most common trees of the Caribbean rain forests. *Vincentian:* from Saint Vincent.
3. Pin in the side of a boat that acts as a fulcrum for an oar.
4. Indigenous people of the Lesser Antilles nearly exterminated by the European conquest. *Dominica:* pronounced *DOM-in-EE-ka;* mountainous, forested island north of Saint Lucia and Martinique.
5. Catching fish with a hooked spear, or gaff.
6. Beginning in the sixteenth century, Europeans imported African slaves to the West Indies to replace the labor force of the largely exterminated indigenous peoples.

progress. Until I see definite signs
that mankind change, Vince, I ain't want to hear.
Progress is history's dirty joke.   310
Ask that sad green island getting nearer."
Green islands, like mangoes pickled in brine.
In such fierce salt let my wound be healed,
me, in my freshness as a seafarer.

That night, with the sky sparks frosty with fire,   315
I ran like a Carib through Dominica,
my nose holes choked with memory of smoke;
I heard the screams of my burning children,
I ate the brains of mushrooms, the fungi
of devil's parasols under white, leprous rocks;   320
my breakfast was leaf mould in leaking forests,
with leaves big as maps, and when I heard noise
of the soldiers' progress through the thick leaves,
though my heart was bursting, I get up and ran
through the blades of balisier⁷ sharper than spears;   325
with the blood of my race, I ran, boy, I ran
with moss-footed speed like a painted bird;
then I fall, but I fall by an icy stream under
cool fountains of fern, and a screaming parrot
catch the dry branches and I drowned at last   330
in big breakers of smoke; then when that ocean
of black smoke pass, and the sky turn white,
there was nothing but Progress, if Progress is
an iguana as still as a young leaf in sunlight.
I bawl for Maria, and her *Book of Dreams*.   335

It anchored her sleep, that insomniac's Bible,
a soiled orange booklet with a cyclops' eye
center, from the Dominican Republic.⁸
Its coarse pages were black with the usual
symbols of prophecy, in excited Spanish;   340
an open palm upright, sectioned and numbered
like a butcher chart, delivered the future.
One night, in a fever, radiantly ill,
she say, "Bring me the book, the end has come."
She said: "I dreamt of whales and a storm,"   345
but for that dream, the book had no answer.
A next night I dreamed of three old women
featureless as silkworms, stitching my fate,⁹
and I scream at them to come out my house,
and I try beating them away with a broom,   350
but as they go out, so they crawl back again,
until I start screaming and crying, my flesh
raining with sweat, and she ravage the book

---

7. Wild, flowering plant.
8. On the island of Hispaniola, in the Greater
Antilles (as distinct from Dominica, in the Lesser
Antilles).
9. In Greek mythology, the three Fates spin, mea-
sure, and cut the thread of life.

for the dream meaning, and there was nothing;
my nerves melt like a jellyfish—that was when I broke—   355
they found me round the Savannah,[1] screaming:

All you see me talking to the wind, so you think I mad.
Well, Shabine has bridled the horses of the sea;
you see me watching the sun till my eyeballs seared,
so all you mad people feel Shabine crazy,   360
but all you ain't know my strength, hear? The coconuts
standing by in their regiments in yellow khaki,
they waiting for Shabine to take over these islands,
and all you best dread the day I am healed
of being a human. All you fate in my hand,   365
ministers, businessmen, Shabine have you, friend,
I shall scatter your lives like a handful of sand,
I who have no weapon but poetry and
the lances of palms and the sea's shining shield!

10. *Out of the Depths*

Next day, dark sea. A arse-aching dawn.   370
"Damn wind shift sudden as a woman mind."
The slow swell start cresting like some mountain range
with snow on the top.
                    "Ay, Skipper, sky dark!"
"This ain't right for August."
                          "This light damn strange,
this season, sky should be clear as a field."   375

A stingray steeplechase across the sea,
tail whipping water, the high man-o'-wars[2]
start reeling inland, quick, quick an archery
of flying fish miss us! Vince say: "You notice?"
and a black-mane squall pounce on the sail   380
like a dog on a pigeon, and it snap the neck
of the *Flight* and shake it from head to tail.
"Be Jesus, I never see sea get so rough
so fast! That wind come from God back pocket!"
"Where Cap'n headin? Like the man gone blind!"   385
"If we's to drong, we go drong, Vince, fock-it!"
"Shabine, say your prayers, if life leave you any!"

I have not loved those that I loved enough.
Worse than the mule kick of Kick-'Em-Jenny[3]
Channel, rain start to pelt the *Flight* between   390
mountains of water. If I was frighten?
The tent poles of water spouts bracing the sky
start wobbling, clouds unstitch at the seams
and sky water drench us, and I hear myself cry,

---

1. Large park in Port of Spain.   3. Small islet north of Grenada.
2. Jellyfish; also, warships.

"I'm the drowned sailor in her *Book of Dreams*." 395
I remembered them ghost ships, I saw me corkscrewing
to the sea-bed of sea-worms, fathom pass fathom,
my jaw clench like a fist, and only one thing
hold me, trembling, how my family safe home.
Then a strength like it seize me and the strength said: 400
"I from backward people who still fear God."
Let Him, in His might, heave Leviathan[4] upward
by the winch of His will, the beast pouring lace
from his sea-bottom bed; and that was the faith
that had fade from a child in the Methodist chapel 405
in Chisel Street, Castries, when the whale-bell
sang service and, in hard pews ribbed like the whale,
proud with despair, we sang how our race
survive the sea's maw, our history, our peril,
and now I was ready for whatever death will. 410
But if that storm had strength, was in Cap'n face,
beard beading with spray, tears salting the eyes,
crucify to his post, that nigger hold fast
to that wheel, man, like the cross held Jesus,
and the wounds of his eyes like they crying for us, 415
and I feeding him white rum, while every crest
with Leviathan-lash make the *Flight* quail
like two criminal. Whole night, with no rest,
till red-eyed like dawn, we watch our travail
subsiding, subside, and there was no more storm. 420
And the noon sea get calm as Thy Kingdom come.

11. *After the Storm*

There's a fresh light that follows a storm
while the whole sea still havoc; in its bright wake
I saw the veiled face of Maria Concepcion
marrying the ocean, then drifting away 425
in the widening lace of her bridal train
with white gulls her bridesmaids, till she was gone.
I wanted nothing after that day.
Across my own face, like the face of the sun,
a light rain was falling, with the sea calm. 430

Fall gently, rain, on the sea's upturned face
like a girl showering; make these islands fresh
as Shabine once knew them! Let every trace,
every hot road, smell like clothes she just press
and sprinkle with drizzle. I finish dream; 435
whatever the rain wash and the sun iron:
the white clouds, the sea and sky with one seam,
is clothes enough for my nakedness.

---

4. Enormous seamonster of Jewish mythology, often represented as a whale.

Though my *Flight* never pass the incoming tide
of this inland sea beyond the loud reefs
of the final Bahamas, I am satisfied   440
if my hand gave voice to one people's grief.
Open the map. More islands there, man,
than peas on a tin plate, all different size,
one thousand in the Bahamas alone,   445
from mountains to low scrub with coral keys,
and from the bowsprit,[5] I bless every town,
the blue smell of smoke in hills behind them,
and the one small road winding down them like twine
to the roofs below; I have only one theme: 450

The bowsprit, the arrow, the longing, the lunging heart—
the flight to a target whose aim we'll never know,
vain search for one island that heals with its harbour
and a guiltless horizon, where the almond's[6] shadow
doesn't injure the sand. There are so many islands!   455
As many islands as the stars at night
on that branched tree from which meteors are shaken
like falling fruit around the schooner *Flight*.
But things must fall, and so it always was,
on one hand Venus, on the other Mars;[7]   460
fall, and are one, just as this earth is one
island in archipelagoes of stars.
My first friend was the sea. Now, is my last.
I stop talking now. I work, then I read,
cotching[8] under a lantern hooked to the mast.   465
I try to forget what happiness was,
and when that don't work, I study the stars.
Sometimes is just me, and the soft-scissored foam
as the deck turn white and the moon open
a cloud like a door, and the light over me   470
is a road in white moonlight taking me home.
Shabine sang to you from the depths of the sea.

                                                                    1979

---

5. Spar or boom extending from the stem of a ship.
6. That is, the sea almond tree's.
7. Planets appearing as if stars, named after

Roman gods of love and war, respectively.
8. Sitting for a while (West Indian English).

The Fortunate Traveller

(For Susan Sontag)[9]

And I heard a voice in the midst of the four beasts say,
A measure of wheat for a penny,
and three measures of barley for a penny;
and see thou hurt not the oil and the wine.
—REVELATION 6.6[1]

I

It was in winter. Steeples, spires
congealed like holy candles. Rotting snow
flaked from Europe's ceiling. A compact man,
I crossed the canal in a grey overcoat,
on one lapel a crimson buttonhole   5
for the cold ecstasy of the assassin.
In the square coffin manacled to my wrist:
small countries pleaded through the mesh of graphs,
in treble-spaced, Xeroxed forms to the World Bank[2]
on which I had scrawled the one word, MERCY;   10

       I sat on a cold bench
under some skeletal lindens.[3]
Two other gentlemen, black skins gone grey
as their identical, belted overcoats,
crossed the white river.   15
They spoke the stilted French
of their dark river,
whose hooked worm, multiplying its pale sickle,
could thin the harvest of the winter streets.[4]
"Then we can depend on you to get us those tractors?"   20
"I gave my word."
"May my country ask you why you are doing this, sir?"
Silence.
"You know if you betray us, you cannot hide?"
A tug. Smoke trailing its dark cry.   25

At the window in Haiti, I remember
a gekko[5] pressed against the hotel glass,
with white palms, concentrating head.
With a child's hands. Mercy, monsieur. Mercy.
Famine sighs like a scythe   30
across the field of statistics and the desert

9. American philosopher and writer (b. 1933). Cf. the title of the picaresque tale by Thomas Nashe, *The Unfortunate Traveller* (1593).
1. The narrator of this apocalyptic biblical book hears this voice after the Lamb of God has broken the fourth of six seals, and after he has seen the third of four horses, "a black horse, and he that sat on him had a pair of balances in his hand" (Revelation 6.5). This horseman may symbolize famine.

2. An international loan association.
3. Large, European trees, used for city and street planting.
4. "Sickle" refers both to the crescent-shaped farming tool used for cutting grain and to sickle-cell anemia, a disease most common among blacks, in which red blood cells become crescent shaped.
5. Small, tropical lizard, with feet that look somewhat like human palms.

is a moving mouth. In the hold of this earth
10,000,000 shoreless souls are drifting.
Somalia:[6] 765,000, their skeletons will go under the tidal sand.
"We'll meet you in Bristol[7] to conclude the agreement?"   35
Steeples like tribal lances, through congealing fog
the cries of wounded church bells wrapped in cotton,
grey mist enfolding the conspirator
like a sealed envelope next to its heart.

No one will look up now to see the jet   40
fade like a weevil[8] through a cloud of flour.
One flies first-class, one is so fortunate.
Like a telescope reversed, the traveller's eye
swiftly screws down the individual sorrow
to an oval nest of antic numerals,   45
and the iris, interlocking with this globe,
condenses it to zero, then a cloud.
Beetle-black taxi from Heathrow to my flat.[9]
We are roaches,
riddling the state cabinets, entering the dark holes   50
of power, carapaced in topcoats,[1]
scuttling around columns, signalling for taxis,
with frantic antennae, to other huddles with roaches;
we infect with optimism, and when
the cabinets crack, we are the first   55
to scuttle, radiating separately
back to Geneva, Bonn, Washington, London.

Under the dripping planes of Hampstead Heath,[2]
I read her letter again, watching the drizzle
disfigure its pleading like mascara. Margo,   60
I cannot bear to watch the nations cry.
Then the phone: "We will pay you in Bristol."
Days in fetid bedclothes swallowing cold tea,
the phone stifled by the pillow. The telly
a blue storm with soundless snow.   65
I'd light the gas and see a tiger's tongue.
I was rehearsing the ecstasies of starvation
for what I had to do. *And have not charity.*[3]

I found my pity, desperately researching
the origins of history, from reed-built communes   70
by sacred lakes, turning with the first sprocketed
water-driven wheels. I smelled imagination
among bestial hides by the gleam of fat,
seeking in all races a common ingenuity.

6. East African republic, site of frequent famines.
7. Industrial and shipping city in southwestern England.
8. Insect whose larvae eat grain and flour.
9. Apartment (British usage). *Heathrow*: London's major airport.
1. The coats are compared to the hard outer shells of insects.
2. Park in the London suburb of Hampstead. *Planes*: plane trees, common in cities.
3. "Though I speak with the tongues of men and of angels, and have not charity, I am become as sounding brass, or a tinkling cymbal" (1 Corinthians 13.1).

I envisaged an African flooded with such light   75
as alchemized the first fields of emmer wheat[4] and barley,
when we savages dyed our pale dead with ochre,
and bordered our temples
with the ceremonial vulva of the conch
in the grey epoch of the obsidian adze.[5]   80
I sowed the Sahara with rippling cereals,[6]
my charity fertilized these aridities.

What was my field? Late sixteenth century.
My field was a dank acre. A Sussex don,
I taught the Jacobean anxieties: *The White Devil*.[7]   85
Flamineo's torch startles the brooding yews.
The drawn end comes in strides. I loved my Duchess,[8]
the white flame of her soul blown out between
the smoking cypresses. Then I saw children pounce
on green meat with a rat's ferocity.   90

I called them up and took the train to Bristol,
my blood the Severn's[9] dregs and silver.
On Severn's estuary the pieces flash,
Iscariot's salary,[1] patron saint of spies.
I thought, who cares how many million starve?   95
Their rising souls will lighten the world's weight
and level its gull-glittering waterline;
we left at sunset down the estuary.

England recedes. The forked white gull
screeches, circling back.   100
Even the birds are pulled back by their orbit,
even mercy has its magnetic field.
                          Back in the cabin,
I uncap the whisky, the porthole
mists with glaucoma.[2] By the time I'm pissed,   105
England, England will be
that pale serrated indigo on the sea-line.
"You are so fortunate, you get to see the world—"
Indeed, indeed, sirs, I have seen the world.
Spray splashes the portholes and vision blurs.   110

Leaning on the hot rail, watching the hot sea,
I saw them far off, kneeling on hot sand

---

4. A hard, red wheat. *Alchemized:* that is, transmuted.
5. Primitive cutting tool made of volcanic glass. *Ochre:* red or yellow clay. *Bordered . . . conch:* that is, decorated our temples with the innermost parts of conch shells.
6. That is, planted grain.
7. Dark revenge tragedy by John Webster (c. 1580–c. 1625), written in the early seventeenth century ("Jacobean"), a pessimistic time by contrast with the Elizabethan age. *Don:* British uni-

versity teacher.
8. Flamineo is the Machiavellian villain in *The White Devil;* "the Duchess" is Vittoria Corombona, its heroine. *Yews:* evergreen trees; they are often associated with grief, as are "cypresses" (line 89).
9. The Severn is a river that flows past Bristol.
1. That is, the thirty pieces of silver that Judas Iscariot received for betraying Jesus (Matthew 26.14–16).
2. As one's eyes would mist if one had glaucoma.

in the pious genuflections of the locust,
as Ponce's armored knees crush Florida[3]
to the funeral fragrance of white lilies.   115

II

Now I have to come to where the phantoms live,
I have no fear of phantoms, but of the real.
The sabbath benedictions[4] of the islands.
Treble clef of the snail on the scored leaf,
the Tantum Ergo[5] of black choristers   120
soars through the organ pipes of coconuts.
Across the dirty beach surpliced[6] with lace,
they pass a brown lagoon behind the priest,
pale and unshaven in his frayed soutane,
into the concrete church at Canaries;[7]   125
as Albert Schweitzer moves to the harmonium[8]
of morning, and to the pluming chimneys,
the groundswell lifts *Lebensraum, Lebensraum.*[9]

Black faces sprinkled with continual dew—
dew on the speckled croton, dew   130
on the hard leaf of the knotted plum tree,
dew on the elephant ears of the dasheen.[1]
Through Kurtz's teeth, white skull in elephant grass,
the imperial fiction sings. Sunday
wrinkles downriver from the Heart of Darkness.[2]   135
The heart of darkness is not Africa.
The heart of darkness is the core of fire
in the white center of the holocaust.
The heart of darkness is the rubber claw
selecting a scalpel in antiseptic light,   140
the hills of children's shoes outside the chimneys,
the tinkling nickel instruments on the white altar;
Jacob,[3] in his last card, sent me these verses:
"Think of a God who doesn't lose His sleep
if trees burst into tears or glaciers weep.   145
So, aping His indifference, I write now,
not Anno Domini: After Dachau."[4]

3. Juan Ponce de Leon (1460–1521), Spanish explorer, discovered Florida in 1513 and attempted to conquer the Native Americans there in 1521.
4. That is, holy-day blessings.
5. So much therefore (from a Latin mass).
6. As though covered by a white ecclesiastical overgarment.
7. Town on west coast of Santa Lucia. *Soutane:* priest's robe.
8. Schweitzer (1875–1965) was a musician and organist who became a medical missionary in Africa in 1913; in the jungle, his instrument was the harmonium, a small reed organ.
9. Living space (German); term used prominently for Hitler's attempt to enlarge Germany by occupying other countries.
1. Starchy, edible plant of the tropics. *Croton:* castor-oil plant.
2. Title of novella (1902) by the Polish-English novelist Joseph Conrad (1857–1924); Kurtz, the man who is the goal of the narrator's search in the Congo, is finally depicted as having seen into the depth of corruption.
3. Very likely Jacob Timmerman, Argentinian journalist and editor imprisoned and tortured for antigovernment writings.
4. Concentration camp operated by the Nazis, liberated in 1945.

III

The night maid brings a lamp and draws the blinds.
I stay out on the veranda with the stars.
Breakfast congealed to supper on its plate.   150

There is no sea as restless as my mind.
The promontories snore. They snore like whales.
Cetus, the whale, was Christ.[5]
The ember dies, the sky smokes like an ash heap.
Reeds wash their hands of guilt and the lagoon   155
is stained. Louder, since it rained,
a gauze of sand flies hisses from the marsh.

Since God is dead, and these are not His stars,
but man-lit, sulphurous, sanctuary lamps,
it's in the heart of darkness of this earth   160
that backward tribes keep vigil of His Body,[6]
in deya, lampion,[7] and this bedside lamp.
Keep the news from their blissful ignorance.
Like lice, like lice, the hungry of this earth
swarm to the tree of life. If those who starve   165
like these rain-flies who shed glazed wings in light
grew from sharp shoulder blades their brittle vans
and soared toward that tree, how it would seethe—
ah, Justice! But fires
drench them like vermin, quotas   170
prevent them, and they remain
compassionate fodder for the travel book,
its paragraphs like windows from a train,
for everywhere that earth shows its rib cage
and the moon goggles with the eyes of children,   175
we turn away to read. Rimbaud learned that.
                              Rimbaud, at dusk,
idling his wrist in water past temples
the plumed dates still protect in Roman file,[8]
knew that we cared less for one human face   180
than for the scrolls in Alexandria's ashes,[9]
that the bright water could not dye his hand
any more than poetry. The dhow's[1] silhouette
moved through the blinding coinage of the river
that, endlessly, until we pay one debt,   185
shrouds, every night, an ordinary secret.

5. Cetus, Latin for whale, is a constellation. A classical seamonster, Cetus is associated with the biblical story of Jonah, who is said to prefigure Jesus, often symbolized by a fish.
6. *Sanctuary lamps:* refers to the practice in High Catholic churches of keeping a lamp lit above the altar (i.e., "sanctuary") when a consecrated wafer is present; since in Holy Communion the wafer represents Jesus' body, this practice is a "vigil of His Body."
7. Small lamp. *Deya:* small clay lamp, many of which are lit for the major Hindu religious festival of Diwali, which honors Laksmi, the goddess of wealth.
8. Single file. Arthur Rimbaud (1854–1891), French poet, spent the last ten years of his life in North Africa.
9. Many of the scrolls in the great Alexandrian Library (in Egypt) were destroyed by fire in 47 B.C.E.
1. Arab boat's.

IV

The drawn sword comes in strides.
It stretches for the length of the empty beach;
the fishermen's huts shut their eyes tight.
A frisson[2] shakes the palm trees,   190
and sweats on the traveller's tree.
They've found out my sanctuary. Philippe, last night:
"It had two gentlemen in the village yesterday, sir,
asking for you while you was in town.
I tell them you was in town. They send to tell you,   195
there is no hurry. They will be coming back."

In loaves of cloud, *and have not charity*,
the weevil will make a sahara of Kansas,
the ant shall eat Russia.
Their soft teeth shall make, *and have not charity*,   200
the harvest's desolation,
and the brown globe crack like a begging bowl,
and though you fire oceans of surplus grain,
and have not charity,

still, through thin stalks,   205
the smoking stubble, stalks
grasshopper: third horseman,
the leather-helmed locust.[3]

1981

The Season of Phantasmal Peace

Then all the nations of birds lifted together
the huge net of the shadows of this earth
in multitudinous dialects, twittering tongues,
stitching and crossing it. They lifted up
the shadow of long pines down trackless slopes,   5
the shadows of glass-faced towers down evening streets,
the shadow of a frail plant on a city sill—
the net rising soundless as night, the birds' cries soundless, until
there was no longer dusk, or season, decline, or weather,
only this passage of phantasmal light   10
that not the narrowest shadow dared to sever.

And men could not see, looking up, what the wild geese drew,
what the ospreys trailed behind them in silvery ropes
that flashed in the icy sunlight; they could not hear
battalions of starlings waging peaceful cries,   15
bearing the net higher, covering this world

2. Shiver.
3. Predatory insect, compared to the third

horseman of the Apocalypse, famine. Cf. the epigraph and note 1.

like the vines of an orchard, or a mother drawing
the trembling gauze over the trembling eyes
of a child fluttering to sleep;
                          it was the light   20
that you will see at evening on the side of a hill
in yellow October, and no one hearing knew
what change had brought into the raven's cawing,
the killdeer's screech, the ember-circling chough[4]
such an immense, soundless, and high concern   25
for the fields and cities where the birds belong,
except it was their seasonal passing, Love,
made seasonless, or, from the high privilege of their birth,
something brighter than pity for the wingless ones
below them who shared dark holes in windows and in houses,   30
and higher they lifted the net with soundless voices
above all change, betrayals of falling suns,
and this season lasted one moment, like the pause
between dusk and darkness, between fury and peace,
but, for such as our earth is now, it lasted long.   35

1981

FROM OMEROS[5]

Book One

Chapter 1

I

"This is how, one sunrise, we cut down them canoes."
Philoctete[6] smiles for the tourists, who try taking
his soul with their cameras. "Once wind bring the news

to the *laurier-cannelles*,[7] their leaves start shaking
the minute the axe of sunlight hit the cedars,   5
because they could see the axes in our own eyes.

Wind lift the ferns. They sound like the sea that feed us
fishermen all our life, and the ferns nodded 'Yes,
the trees have to die.' So, fists jam in our jacket,

---

4. Bird in the crow family.
5. Modern Greek version of the name Homer. Homer's *Iliad* and *Odyssey* are, along with Dante's *Divine Comedy*, from which Walcott adapts the terza rima stanza, and James Joyce's *Ulysses* (1922), major influences on this Caribbean epic, which moves across centuries and geographies, from Saint Lucia to Africa to Ireland.
6. Pronounced *fee-lock-TET*; a name shared with

Philoctetes, who, in the *Iliad* and Sophocles' eponymous play, is abandoned on an island on the way to the Trojan War after receiving a snakebite. The wound never heals and continually torments Philoctetes, who moans uncontrollably. Later, the gods decide that the war cannot be won without him, and the Greek soldiers have to go back to the island and beg him to return with them to battle.
7. Type of tree.

cause the heights was cold and our breath making feathers   10
like the mist, we pass the rum. When it came back, it
give us the spirit to turn into murderers.

I lift up the axe and pray for strength in my hands
to wound the first cedar. Dew was filling my eyes,
but I fire one more white rum. Then we advance."   15

For some extra silver, under a sea-almond,
he shows them a scar made by a rusted anchor,
rolling one trouser-leg up with the rising moan

of a conch. It has puckered like the corolla
of a sea-urchin. He does not explain its cure.   20
"It have some things"—he smiles—"worth more than a dollar."

He has left it to a garrulous waterfall
to pour out his secret down La Sorcière,[8] since
the tall laurels fell, for the ground-dove's mating call

to pass on its note to the blue, tacit mountains   25
whose talkative brooks, carrying it to the sea,
turn into idle pools where the clear minnows shoot

and an egret stalks the reeds with one rusted cry
as it stabs and stabs the mud with one lifting foot.
Then silence is sawn in half by a dragonfly   30

as eels sign their names along the clear bottom-sand,
when the sunrise brightens the river's memory
and waves of huge ferns are nodding to the sea's sound.

Although smoke forgets the earth from which it ascends,
and nettles guard the holes where the laurels were killed,   35
an iguana hears the axes, clouding each lens

over its lost name, when the hunched island was called
"Iounalao," "Where the iguana is found."
But, taking its own time, the iguana will scale

the rigging of vines in a year, its dewlap fanned,   40
its elbows akimbo, its deliberate tail
moving with the island. The slit pods of its eyes

ripened in a pause that lasted for centuries,
that rose with the Aruacs'[9] smoke till a new race
unknown to the lizard stood measuring the trees.   45

---

8. The sorceress (French); a mountain on Saint Lucia.
9. A people native to the Caribbean who were driven out and killed by the Caribs and the Spanish.

These were their pillars that fell, leaving a blue space
for a single God where the old gods stood before.
The first god was a gommier.[1] The generator

began with a whine, and a shark, with sidewise jaw,
sent the chips flying like mackerel over water   50
into trembling weeds. Now they cut off the saw,

still hot and shaking, to examine the wound it
had made. They scraped off its gangrenous moss, then ripped
the wound clear of the net of vines that still bound it

to this earth, and nodded. The generator whipped   55
back to its work, and the chips flew much faster as
the shark's teeth gnawed evenly. They covered their eyes

from the splintering nest. Now, over the pastures
of bananas, the island lifted its horns. Sunrise
trickled down its valleys, blood splashed on the cedars,   60

and the grove flooded with the light of sacrifice.
A gommier was cracking. Its leaves an enormous
tarpaulin with the ridgepole gone. The creaking sound

made the fishermen leap back as the angling mast
leant slowly towards the troughs of ferns; then the ground   65
shuddered under the feet in waves, then the waves passed.

Chapter III

III

"*Mais qui ça qui rivait-'ous, Philoctete?*"
                                        "*Moin blessé.*"[2]
"But what is wrong wif you, Philoctete?"
                                        "I am blest
wif this wound, Ma Kilman,[3] *qui pas ka guérir pièce.*

Which will never heal."
                                "Well, you must take it easy.
Go home and lie down, give the foot a lickle rest."   5
Philoctete, his trouser-legs rolled, stares out to sea

from the worn rumshop window. The itch in the sore
tingles like the tendrils of the anemone,
and the puffed blister of Portuguese man-o'-war.[4]

---

1. Gum tree.
2. French patois translated below (though *blessé* actually means "wounded").
3. The owner of the No Pain Café, Ma Kilman serves in the poem as a sybil (female prophet) and an obeah woman (one practicing a kind of West Indian sorcery).
4. Jellyfish (from a term for warship).

He believed the swelling came from the chained ankles   10
of his grandfathers. Or else why was there no cure?
That the cross he carried was not only the anchor's

but that of his race, for a village black and poor
as the pigs that rooted in its burning garbage,
then were hooked on the anchors of the abattoir.[5]   15

Ma Kilman was sewing. She looked up and saw his face
squinting from the white of the street. He was waiting
to pass out on the table. This went on for days.

The ice turned to warm water near the self-hating
gesture of clenching his head tight in both hands. She   20
heard the boys in blue uniforms, going to school,

screaming at his elbow: "Pheeloh! Pheelosophee!"
A mummy embalmed in Vaseline and alcohol.
In the Egyptian silence she muttered softly:

"It have a flower somewhere, a medicine, and ways   25
my grandmother would boil it. I used to watch ants
climbing her white flower-pot. But, God, in which place?"

Where was this root? What senna, what tepid tisanes,[6]
could clean the branched river of his corrupted blood,
whose sap was a wounded cedar's? What did it mean,   30

this name that felt like a fever? Well, one good heft
of his garden-cutlass would slice the damned name clean
from its rotting yam. He said, *"Merci."*[7] Then he left.

Chapter IX

III

The Cyclone, howling because one of the lances
of a flinging palm has narrowly grazed his one eye,[8]
wades knee-deep in troughs. As he blindly advances,

Lightning, his stilt-walking messenger, jiggers the sky
with his forked stride, or he crackles over the troughs   5
like a split electric wishbone. His wife, Ma Rain,

hurls buckets from the balcony of her upstairs house.
She shakes the sodden mops of the palms and once again
changes her furniture, the cloud-sofas' grumbling casters

---

5. Slaughterhouse.
6. Medicinal beverages. *Senna:* medicinal herb.
7. Thank you (French).
8. Cf. the episode in book 9 of Homer's *Odyssey* in which Odysseus and his men escape by blinding the drunken Cyclops, Polyphemos, with a sharp stick. Polyphemos is the son of Poseidon (Roman, Neptune), the Greek sea god.

not waking the Sun. The Sun had been working all day 10
and would sleep through it all. After their disasters
it was he who cleaned up after their goddamned party.

So he went straight to bed at the first sign of a drizzle.
Now, like a large coalpot with headlands for its handles,
the Sea cooks up a storm, raindrops start to sizzle 15

like grease, there is a brisk business in candles
in Ma Kilman's shop. Candles, nails, a sudden increase in
the faithful, and a mark-up on matches and bread.

In the grey vertical forest of the hurricane season,
when the dirty sea returns the wreaths of the dead, 20
all the village could do was listen to the gods in session,

playing any instruments that came into their craniums,
the harp-sighing ripple of a hither-and-zithering sea,
the knucklebone pebbles, the abrupt Shango[9] drums

made Neptune rock in the caves. Fête start! Erzulie 25
rattling her ra-ra; Ogun, the blacksmith, feeling
No Pain; Damballa[1] winding like a zandoli

lizard,[2] as their huge feet thudded on the ceiling,
as the sea-god, drunk, lurched from wall to wall, saying:
"Mama, this music so loud, I going in seine,"[3] 30

then throwing up at his pun. People were praying,
but then the gods, who were tired, were throwing a fête,
and their fêtes went on for days, and their music ranged

from polkas of rain to waves dancing La Comète,[4]
and the surf clapped hands whenever the patterns changed. 35
For the gods aren't men, they get on well together,

holding a hurricane-party in their cloud-house,
and what brings the gods close is the thunderous weather,
where Ogun can fire one with his partner Zeus.[5]

Achille in his shack heard chac-chac and violin 40
in the telephone wires, a sound like Helen
moaning, or Seven Seas,[6] blind as a sail in rain.

9. Afro-Caribbean god of thunder, drums, and dance, originally from West Africa (Yoruba); he is often depicted in images of thunder and lighting. *Zither:* stringed instrument.
1. Afro-Caribbean snake god that lives in trees and springs. *Neptune:* cave-dwelling Roman god of the sea. *Fête:* party (French). *Erzulie:* Haitian goddess of love and elemental forces, thought to have origins in West Africa. *Ra-ra:* rattle (West Indian English). *Ogun:* Afro-Caribbean and West African (Yoruba) god of iron, thunder, roads, war, creation, and destruction; he is often depicted as a blacksmith.
2. Small, Antillean lizard.
3. Fishing net.
4. The comet (French).
5. King of the Greek gods.
6. Poet figure in *Omeros*. *Achille:* pronounced *ah-SHEEL* in the island patois; in the *Iliad*, Achilles is the greatest Greek warrior and the slayer of Hec-

In the devastated valleys, crumpling brown water
at their prows,[7] headlights on, passenger-vans floated
slowly up roads that were rivers, through the slaughter   45

of the year's banana-crop, past stiff cows bloated
from engorging mud as the antlers of trees tossed
past the banks like migrating elk. It was as if

the rivers, envying the sea, tired of being crossed
in one leap, had joined in a power so massive   50
that it made islands of villages, made bridges

the sieves of a force that shouldered culverts aside.
The rain passed, but people looked up to the ridges
fraying with its return, and the flood, in its pride,

entered the sea; then Achille could hear the tunnels   55
of brown water roaring in the mangroves; its tide
hid the keels of the canoes, and their wet gunwales[8]

were high with rainwater that could warp them rotten
if they were not bailed. The river was satisfied.
It was a god too. Too much had been forgotten.   60

Then, a mouse after a fête, its claws curled like moss,
nosing the dew as the lighthouse opened its eye,
the sunlight peeped out, and people surveyed the loss

that the gods had made under a clearing-up sky.
Candles shortened and died. The big yellow tractors   65
tossed up the salad of trees, in yellow jackets

men straightened the chairs of dead poles, the contractors
in white helmets and slickers heard the castanets
of the waves going up the islands, moving on

from here to Guadeloupe,[9] the beaded wires were still.   70
They saw the mess the gods made in one night alone,
as Lightning lifted his stilts over the last hill.

Achille bailed out his canoe under an almond
that shuddered with rain. There would be brilliant days still,
till the next storm, and their freshness was wonderful.   75

---

tor. *Chac-chac:* maracas. *Helen:* Achille's lover,
who, in this scene, has recently left him. Achille
and Hector feud over Helen, recalling their name-
sakes and the Trojan War in Homer's *Iliad.* Saint
Lucia, which traded hands fourteen times in bat-
tles between the French and the British, is also
referred to as the "Helen of the West Indies."
7. Front parts.
8. Upper edges of their sides.
9. Island third to the north of Saint Lucia.

Chapter XIII

II

"Walk me down to the wharf."[1]
                        At the corner of Bridge
Street, we saw the liner as white as a mirage,
its hull bright as paper, preening with privilege.

"Measure the days you have left. Do just that labour
which marries your heart to your right hand: simplify   5
your life to one emblem, a sail leaving harbour

and a sail coming in. All corruption will cry
to be taken aboard. Fame is that white liner
at the end of your street, a city to itself,

taller than the Fire Station, and much finer,   10
with its brass-ringed portholes, mounting shelf after shelf,
than anything Castries[2] could ever hope to build."

The immaculate hull insulted the tin roofs
beneath it, its pursers were milk, even the bilge
bubbling from its stern in quietly muttering troughs   15

and its humming engines spewed expensive garbage
where boys balanced on logs or, riding old tires,
shouted up past the hull to tourists on the rails

to throw down coins, as cameras caught their black cries,
then jackknife or swan-dive—their somersaulting tails   20
like fishes flipped backwards—as the coins grew in size

in the wobbling depth; then, when they surfaced, fights
for possession, their heads butting like porpoises,
all, like a city leaving a city, the lights

blazed in its moving rooms, and the liner would glide   25
over its own phosphorus, and wash hit the wharves
long after stewards had set the service inside

the swaying chandeliered salons, and the black waves
settle down to their level. The stars would renew
their studded diagrams over Achille's canoe.   30

From here, in his boyhood, he had seen women climb
like ants up a white flower-pot, baskets of coal
balanced on their torchoned[3] heads, without touching them,

---

1. In this chapter, the narrator listens to the ghost of his father. A conversation with a ghost or shade from the underworld is a common device of epic poetry.
2. Capital city of Saint Lucia; under British rule, it became the principal coal port in the region.
3. Wrapped in cloth.

up the black pyramids, each spine straight as a pole,
and with a strength that never altered its rhythm.   35
He spoke for those Helens from an earlier time:

"Hell was built on those hills. In that country of coal
without fire, that inferno the same colour
as their skins and shadows, every labouring soul

climbed with her hundredweight basket, every load for   40
one copper penny, balanced erect on their necks
that were tight as the liner's hawsers[4] from the weight.

The carriers were women, not the fair, gentler sex.
Instead, they were darker and stronger, and their gait
was made beautiful by balance, in their ascending   45

the narrow wooden ramp built steeply to the hull
of a liner tall as a cloud, the unending
line crossing like ants without touching for the whole

day. That was one section of the wharf, opposite
your grandmother's house where I watched the silhouettes   50
of these women, while every hundredweight basket

was ticked by two tally clerks in their white pith-helmets,
and the endless repetition as they climbed the
infernal anthracite hills showed you hell, early."

III

"Along this coal-blackened wharf, what Time decided   55
to do with my treacherous body after this,"
he said, watching the women, "will stay in your head

as long as a question you have no right to ask,
only to doubt, not hate our infuriating
silence. I am only the shadow of that task   60

as much as their work, your pose of a question waiting,
as you crouch with a writing lamp over a desk,
remains in the darkness after the light has gone,

and whether night is palpable between dawn and dusk
is not for the living; so you mind your business,   65
which is life and work, like theirs, but I will say this:

O Thou, my Zero, is an impossible prayer,
utter extinction is still a doubtful conceit.
Though we pray to nothing, nothing cannot be there.

---

4. Thick ropes.

Kneel to your load, then balance your staggering feet 70
and walk up that coal ladder as they do in time,
one bare foot after the next in ancestral rhyme.

Because Rhyme remains the parentheses of palms
shielding a candle's tongue, it is the language's
desire to enclose the loved world in its arms; 75

or heft a coal-basket; only by its stages
like those groaning women will you achieve that height
whose wooden planks in couplets lift your pages

higher than those hills of infernal anthracite.
There, like ants or angels, they see their native town, 80
unknown, raw, insignificant. They walk, you write;

keep to that narrow causeway without looking down,
climbing in their footsteps, that slow, ancestral beat
of those used to climbing roads; your own work owes them

because the couplet of those multiplying feet 85
made your first rhymes. Look, they climb, and no one knows them;
they take their copper pittances, and your duty

from the time you watched them from your grandmother's house
as a child wounded by their power and beauty
is the chance you now have, to give those feet a voice." 90

We stood in the hot afternoon. My father took
his fob-watch from its pocket, replaced it, then said,
lightly gripping my arm,
                            "He enjoys a good talk,

a serious trim, and I myself look ahead
to our appointment." He kissed me. I watched him walk 95
through a pillared balcony's alternating shade.

Book Three

Chapter XXV

II

He[5] remembered this sunburnt river with its spindly
stakes and the peaked huts platformed above the spindles
where thin, naked figures as he rowed past looked unkindly

or kindly in their silence. The silence an old fence kindles
in a boy's heart. They walked with his homecoming 5
canoe past bonfires in a scorched clearing near the edge

---

5. Achille, suffering from sunstroke, is hallucinating a return to the Congo River, in Africa.

of the soft-lipped shallows whose noise hurt his drumming
heart as the pirogue[6] slid its raw, painted wedge
towards the crazed sticks of a vine-fastened pier.

The river was sloughing its old skin like a snake   10
in wrinkling sunshine; the sun resumed its empire
over this branch of the Congo; the prow found its stake

in the river and nuzzled it the way that a piglet
finds its favourite dug in the sweet-grunting sow,
and now each cheek ran with its own clear rivulet   15

of tears, as Achille, weeping, fastened the bow
of the dugout, wiped his eyes with one dry palm,
and felt a hard hand help him up the shaking pier.

Half of me was with him. One half with the midshipman
by a Dutch canal. But now, neither was happier   20
or unhappier than the other. An old man put an arm

around Achille, and the crowd, chattering, followed both.
They touched his trousers, his undershirt, their hands
scrabbling the texture, as a kitten does with cloth,

till they stood before an open hut. The sun stands   25
with expectant silence. The river stops talking,
the way silence sometimes suddenly turns off a market.

The wind squatted low in the grass. A man kept walking
steadily towards him, and he knew by that walk it
was himself in his father, the white teeth, the widening hands.   30

III

He sought his own features in those of their life-giver,
and saw two worlds mirrored there: the hair was surf
curling round a sea-rock, the forehead a frowning river,

as they swirled in the estuary of a bewildered love,
and Time stood between them. The only interpreter   35
of their lips' joined babble, the river with the foam,

and the chuckles of water under the sticks of the pier,
where the tribe stood like sticks themselves, reversed
by reflection. Then they walked up to the settlement,

and it seemed, as they chattered, everything was rehearsed   40
for ages before this. He could predict the intent
of his father's gestures; he was moving with the dead.

---

6. Canoelike boat.

Women paused at their work, then smiled at the warrior
returning from his battle with smoke, from the kingdom
where he had been captured, they cried and were happy.   45

Then the fishermen sat near a large tree under whose dome
stones sat in a circle. His father said:
                        "Afo-la-be,"
touching his own heart.
                      "In the place you have come from

what do they call you?"
                    Time translates.
                        Tapping his chest,
the son answers:
                "Achille." The tribe rustles, "Achille."   50
Then, like cedars at sunrise, the mutterings settle.

                  AFOLABE
Achille. What does the name mean? I have forgotten the one
that I gave you. But it was, it seems, many years ago.
What does it mean?

                  ACHILLE
        Well, I too have forgotten.

Everything was forgotten. You also. I do not know.   55
The deaf sea has changed around every name that you gave
us; trees, men, we yearn for a sound that is missing.

                  AFOLABE
A name means something. The qualities desired in a son,
and even a girl-child; so even the shadows who called
you expected one virtue, since every name is a blessing,   60

since I am remembering the hope I had for you as a child.
Unless the sound means nothing. Then you would be nothing.
Did they think you were nothing in that other kingdom?

                  ACHILLE
I do not know what the name means. It means something,
maybe. What's the difference? In the world I come from   65
we accept the sounds we were given. Men, trees, water.

                  AFOLABE
And therefore, Achille, if I pointed and I said, There
is the name of that man, that tree, and this father,
would every sound be a shadow that crossed your ear,

without the shape of a man or a tree? What would it be?   70
(And just as branches sway in the dusk from their fear
of amnesia, of oblivion, the tribe began to grieve.)

ACHILLE

What would it be? I can only tell you what I believe,
or had to believe. It was prediction, and memory,
to bear myself back, to be carried here by a swift,   75

or the shadow of a swift making its cross on water,
with the same sign I was blessed with, with the gift
of this sound whose meaning I still do not care to know.

AFOLABE

No man loses his shadow except it is in the night,
and even then his shadow is hidden, not lost. At the glow   80
of sunrise, he stands on his own name in that light.

When he walks down to the river with the other fishermen
his shadow stretches in the morning, and yawns, but you,
if you're content with not knowing what our names mean,

then I am not Afolabe, your father, and you look through   85
my body as the light looks through a leaf. I am not here
or a shadow. And you, nameless son, are only the ghost

of a name. Why did I never miss you until you returned?
Why haven't I missed you, my son, until you were lost?
Are you the smoke from a fire that never burned?   90

There was no answer to this, as in life. Achille nodded,
the tears glazing his eyes, where the past was reflected
as well as the future. The white foam lowered its head.

Book Six

Chapter XLIX

I

She bathed him in the brew of the root.[7] The basin
was one of those cauldrons from the old sugar-mill,
with its charred pillars, rock pasture, and one grazing

horse, looking like helmets that have tumbled downhill
from an infantry charge. Children rang them with stones.   5
Wildflowers sprung in them when the dirt found a seam.

She had one in her back yard, close to the crotons,[8]
agape in its crusted, agonized O: the scream
of centuries. She scraped its rusted scabs, she scoured

---

7. Ma Kilman is bathing Philoctete to heal his   8. Type of tree and shrub.
wound.

the mouth of the cauldron, then fed a crackling pyre 10
with palms and banana-trash. In the scream she poured
tin after kerosene tin, its base black from fire,

of seawater and sulphur. Into this she then fed
the bubbling root and leaves. She led Philoctete
to the gurgling lava. Trembling, he entered 15

his bath like a boy. The lime leaves leeched to his wet
knuckled spine like islands that cling to the basin
of the rusted Caribbean. An icy sweat

glazed his scalp, but he could feel the putrescent shin
drain in the seethe like sucked marrow, he felt it drag 20
the slime from his shame. She rammed him back to his place

as he tried climbing out with: "*Not yet!*" With a rag
sogged in a basin of ice she rubbed his squeezed face
the way boys enjoy their mother's ritual rage,

and as he surrendered to her, the foul flower 25
on his shin whitened and puckered, the corolla
closed its thorns like the sea-egg. What else did it cure?

II

The bow leapt back to the palm of the warrior.
The yoke of the wrong name lifted from his shoulders.
His muscles loosened like those of a brown river 30

that was damned with silt, and then silkens its boulders
with refreshing strength. His ribs thudded like a horse
cantering on a beach that bursts into full gallop

while a boy yanks at its rein with terrified "Whoas!"
The white foam unlocked his coffles, his ribbed shallop 35
broke from its anchor, and the water, which he swirled

like a child, steered his brow into the right current,
as calm as *In God We Troust*[9] to that other world,
and his flexed palm enclosed an oar with the ident-

ical closure of a mouth around its own name, 40
the way a sea-anemone closes slyly
into a secrecy many mistake for shame.

Centuries weigh down the head of the swamp-lily,
its tribal burden arches the sea-almond's spine,
in barracoon[1] back yards the soul-smoke still passes, 45

---

9. Near the poem's beginning, Achille chisels this misspelled phrase into his canoe and then decides, "Leave it! Is God' spelling and mine" (1.1.2).
1. Barracks for housing convicts or slaves.

but the wound has found her own cure. The soft days spin
the spittle of the spider in webbed glasses,
as she drenches the burning trash to its last flame,

and the embers steam and hiss to the schoolboys' cries
when he'd weep in the window for their tribal shame.   50
A shame for the loss of words, and a language tired

of accepting that loss, and then all accepted.
That was why the sea stank from the frothing urine
of surf, and fish-guts reeked from the government shed,

and why God pissed on the village for months of rain.   55
But now, quite clearly the tears trickled down his face
like rainwater down a cracked carafe from Choiseul,[2]

as he stood like a boy in his bath with the first clay's
innocent prick! So she threw Adam a towel.
And the yard was Eden. And its light the first day's.   60

Book Seven

Chapter LXIV

I

I sang of quiet Achille, Afolabe's son,[3]
who never ascended in an elevator,
who had no passport, since the horizon needs none,

never begged nor borrowed, was nobody's waiter,
whose end, when it comes, will be a death by water[4]   5
(which is not for this book, which will remain unknown

and unread by him). I sang the only slaughter
that brought him delight, and that from necessity—
of fish, sang the channels of his back in the sun.

I sang our wide country, the Caribbean Sea.   10
Who hated shoes, whose soles were as cracked as a stone,
who was gentle with ropes, who had one suit alone,

whom no man dared insult and who insulted no one,
whose grin was a white breaker cresting, but whose frown
was a growing thunderhead, whose fist of iron   15

would do me a greater honour if it held on
to my casket's oarlocks than mine lifting his own
when both anchors are lowered in the one island,

---

2. A village in Saint Lucia.
3. From the poem's final chapter; this line echoes
and revises the famous openings of the Iliad and
of Virgil's *Aeneid.*
4. Cf. part 4 of T. S. Eliot's *Waste Land.*

but now the idyll dies, the goblet is broken,
and rainwater trickles down the brown cheek of a jar   20
from the clay of Choiseul. So much left unspoken

by my chirping nib! And my earth-door lies ajar.
I lie wrapped in a flour-sack sail. The clods thud
on my rope-lowered canoe. Rasping shovels scrape

a dry rain of dirt on its hold, but turn your head   25
when the sea-almond rattles or the rust-leaved grape
from the shells of my unpharaonic pyramid

towards paper shredded by the wind and scattered
like white gulls that separate their names from the foam
and nod to a fisherman with his khaki dog   30

that skitters from the wave-crash, then frown at his form
for one swift second. In its earth-trough, my pirogue
with its brass-handled oarlocks is sailing. Not from

but with them, with Hector, with Maud[5] in the rhythm
of her beds trowelled over, with a swirling log   35
lifting its mossed head from the swell; let the deep hymn

of the Caribbean continue my epilogue;
may waves remove their shawls as my mourners walk home
to their rusted villages, good shoes in one hand,

passing a boy who walked through the ignorant foam,   40
and saw a sail going out or else coming in,
and watched asterisks of rain puckering the sand.

                                                                  1990

5. The Irish wife of the British officer Plunkett.

GARY SNYDER
b. 1930

In the summer of 1948, after he had finished his freshman year at college, Gary Snyder shipped out of New York as an ordinary seaman. "Going to sea," he has said, "was part of a long growth and extension of my sympathies and sensibilities outside simply one area and to many classes and kinds of people and many parts of the world so that now I feel at home everywhere" (in Dan Kherdian, *Six San Francisco Poets,* 1969). The notion of life as an odyssey and of his poems as progress reports, entries in the explorer's journal, is essential to Snyder. His goal is a poise of mind that will allow him to stand serenely in the midst of conflicting perspectives.

Though rooted in the natural landscape of the Pacific northwest, Snyder has managed to "feel at home everywhere," not only by visiting foreign places, by investigating other cultures and submitting himself to their initiatory rituals, but also by imaginatively investigating the recesses of our common human past. "As poet," Snyder writes, "I hold the most archaic values on earth. They go back to the late Paleolithic: the fertility of the soil, the magic of animals, the power-vision in solitude, the terrifying initiation and re-birth, the love and ecstasy of the dance, the common work of the tribe. I try to hold both history and wilderness in mind, that my poems may approach the true measure of things and stand against the unbalance and ignorance of our times" (Six). In Zen Buddhism, Snyder found a way to get back to the preverbal experiences that unite humankind. With characteristic evenhandedness, he grants that the poet faces in two directions: "one is to the world of people and language and society, and the other is to the nonhuman, nonverbal world, which is nature as nature is itself; and the world of human nature—the inner world—as it is itself, before language, before customs, before culture. There's no words in that world. There aren't any rules that we know and that's the area that Buddhism studies" (Six).

Snyder's is not a superficial acquaintance with East Asian religion and culture; from 1965 to 1968, he studied with a Zen master in Japan. From these studies, and also from Ezra Pound, William Carlos Williams, and Charles Olson, Snyder found direction in his search for the wordless "world of human nature," and he takes delight in the bright, particular grains of experience of nature "as nature is itself." His relaxed, often cheerful acceptance of a pluralistic world of fragments contrasts markedly with T. S. Eliot's juxtaposition of cultures to point up catastrophe in The Waste Land. Snyder does not force nature to provide symbols of his private experience, and he is aware of that temptation. In "T-2 Tanker Blues," he hopes eventually to "dig the / universe as playful, cool and infinitely blank." "Blank" does not here suggest any Romantic forlornness, but rather an appreciation of companionable otherness, a peaceful coexistence.

Although Snyder wholeheartedly rejects postwar American society, particularly its ecological devastation, he does not sentimentally reject society as such. He has worked at a variety of trades and occupations, writes his poetry out of these experiences, and relates the rhythm of poetic sequences with the rhythms of particular occupations. Tutored by Zen meditation in alert and egoless attention to the world, he writes in seemingly spontaneous lines and simple diction about nature, sex, family, and the body. His chiseled lines and concrete images often seem surrounded by silence, by negative space in which they shine brightly with an inner presence.

Snyder was born on May 8, 1930, in San Francisco, and was brought up in Oregon and Washington. He received his B.A. in anthropology from Reed College in 1951. He worked as a logger and a fire lookout in the Pacific northwest, then returned to California to study East Asian languages at the University of California, Berkeley from 1953 to 1956. During this time, he also joined Allen Ginsberg, Jack Kerouac, and others in what turned into the Beat movement and wrote the poems later published as Myths and Texts (1960). (Kerouac used Snyder as a central character in his novel The Dharma Bums.) Though Snyder shares the spontaneity and East Asian interests of the Beats, his ecological priorities contrast with their urban sensibilities. From 1956 until 1964, he lived mainly in Japan, though he visited India for a year and also worked as a hand on an American tanker in the Indian and South Pacific Oceans. He returned to the United States in 1964 to teach at Berkeley, then returned to Japan to study Buddhism of the Mahayana-Vajrayana school; he recounts some of his experiences in the prose book Earth House Hold (1969), which is written in the Japanese form of the poetic travel journal. In 1986, he joined the faculty of the University of California, Davis. His many books of poems include a number of translations from ancient and modern Japanese. In 1975, he was awarded the Pulitzer Prize; in 1997, the Bollingen Prize.

Milton[1] by Firelight

Piute Creek, August 1955

"O hell, what do mine eyes
    with grief behold?"[2]
Working with an old
Singlejack[3] miner, who can sense
The vein and cleavage   5
In the very guts of rock, can
Blast granite, build
Switchbacks[4] that last for years
Under the beat of snow, thaw, mule-hooves.
What use, Milton, a silly story   10
Of our lost general parents,
    eaters of fruit?

The Indian, the chainsaw boy,
And a string of six mules
Came riding down to camp   15
Hungry for tomatoes and green apples.
Sleeping in saddle-blankets
Under a bright night-sky
Han River slantwise by morning.
Jays squall   20
Coffee boils

In ten thousand years the Sierras
Will be dry and dead, home of the scorpion.
Ice-scratched slabs and bent trees.
No paradise, no fall,   25
Only the weathering land
The wheeling sky,
Man, with his Satan
Scouring the chaos of the mind.
Oh Hell!   30

Fire down
Too dark to read, miles from a road
The bell-mare clangs in the meadow
That packed dirt for a fill-in
Scrambling through loose rocks   35
On an old trail
All of a summer's day.[5]

                      1959

1. John Milton (1608–1674), English poet, author of *Paradise Lost*.
2. Satan speaks these words in *Paradise Lost* (4.358) upon first seeing Adam and Eve in the Garden of Eden.
3. Hammer for percussive hand-drilling by one person.
4. Steep, zigzagging roads or trails.
5. Cf. Milton's epic simile describing Satan's fall: "From morn / to noon he fell, from noon to dewy eve, / A summer's day" (*Paradise Lost* 1.742–44).

Above Pate Valley[6]

We finished clearing the last
Section of trail by noon,
High on the ridge-side
Two thousand feet above the creek
Reached the pass, went on   5
Beyond the white pine groves,
Granite shoulders, to a small
Green meadow watered by the snow,
Edged with Aspen—sun
Straight high and blazing   10
But the air was cool.
Ate a cold fried trout in the
Trembling shadows. I spied
A glitter, and found a flake
Black volcanic glass—obsidian—   15
By a flower. Hands and knees
Pushing the Bear grass, thousands
Of arrowhead leavings over a
Hundred yards. Not one good
Head, just razor flakes   20
On a hill snowed all but summer,
A land of fat summer deer,
They came to camp. On their
Own trails. I followed my own
Trail here. Picked up the cold-drill,   25
Pick, singlejack,[7] and sack
Of dynamite.
Ten thousand years.

                                                        1959

Riprap[8]

Lay down these words
Before your mind like rocks.
            placed solid, by hands
In choice of place, set
Before the body of the mind   5
            in space and time:
Solidity of bark, leaf, or wall
            riprap of things:

---

6. In Yosemite National Park.
7. Hammer for percussive hand-drilling by one person.

8. "A cobble of stone laid on steep slick rock to make a trail for horses in the mountains" [Snyder's note].

Cobble of milky way,
      straying planets,   10
These poems, people,
      lost ponies with
Dragging saddles
      and rocky sure-foot trails.
The worlds like an endless   15
      four-dimensional
Game of Go.[9]
      ants and pebbles
In the thin loam, each rock a word
      a creek-washed stone   20
Granite: ingrained
      with torment of fire and weight
Crystal and sediment linked hot
      all change, in thoughts,
As well as things.   25

1959

Burning the Small Dead

Burning the small dead
    branches
broke from beneath
    thick spreading
      whitebark pine.   5

      a hundred summers
snowmelt   rock   and air

hiss in a twisted bough.

    sierra granite;
      Mt. Ritter—[1]   10
    black rock twice as old.

Deneb, Altair[2]

windy fire

1968

---

9. Ancient Japanese game played with black and white stones, placed one after the other on a checkered board.

1. Peak south of Yosemite National Park, in California.
2. Two of the brightest stars.

The Wild Edge

Curve of the two steel spring-up prongs on
      the back of the Hermes
        typewriter—paper holders—the same
Curve as the arched wing of a gull:

       (sails through the   5
     sides of the eyes by white-stained cliffs
     car-park lots and scattered
        pop-top beer tabs in the gravel)

Birds sail away and back.

Sudden flurry and buzz of flies in the corner sun.   10
Heavy beetle drags stiff legs through moss

Caravans of ants bound for the Wall
      wandering backward—

Harsh Thrush shrieks   in the cherries.
       a murmur in the kitchen
      Kai[3] wakes and cries—   15

                         1970

The Bath

Washing Kai in the sauna,
The kerosene lantern set on a box
    outside the ground-level window,
Lights up the edge of the iron stove and the
    washtub down on the slab
Steaming air and crackle of waterdrops   5
    brushed by on the pile of rocks on top
He stands in warm water
Soap all over the smooth of his thigh and stomach
    "Gary don't soap my hair!"
    —his eye-sting fear—   10
    the soapy hand feeling
    through and around the globes and curves of his body
    up in the crotch,
And washing-tickling out the scrotum, little anus,   15
    his penis curving up and getting hard
    as I pull back skin and try to wash it
Laughing and jumping, flinging arms around,
    I squat all naked too,
              is this our body?   20

---

3. Snyder's son.

Sweating and panting in the stove-steam hot-stone
    cedar-planking wooden bucket water-splashing
    kerosene lantern-flicker wind-in-the-pines-out
    sierra forest ridges night—
Masa comes in, letting fresh cool air   25
    sweep down from the door
    a deep sweet breath
And she tips him over gripping neatly, one knee down
    her hair falling hiding one whole side of
    shoulder, breast, and belly,   30
Washes deftly Kai's head-hair
    as he gets mad and yells—
The body of my lady, the winding valley spine,
    the space between the thighs I reach through,
    cup her curving vulva arch and hold it from behind,   35
    a soapy tickle   a hand of grail
The gates of Awe
That open back a turning double-mirror world of
    wombs in wombs, in rings,
    that start in music,   40
                is this our body?

The hidden place of seed
The veins net flow across the ribs, that gathers
    milk and peaks up in a nipple—fits
    our mouth—   45
The sucking milk from this our body sends through
    jolts of light; the son, the father,
    sharing mother's joy
That brings a softness to the flower of the awesome
    open curling lotus gate I cup and kiss   50
As Kai laughs at his mother's breast he now is weaned
    from, we
    wash each other,
                this our body

Kai's little scrotum up close to his groin,   55
    the seed still tucked away, that moved from us to him
In flows that lifted with the same joys forces
    as his nursing Masa later,
    playing with her breast,
Or me within her,   60
Or him emerging,
                this is our body:

Clean, and rinsed, and sweating more, we stretch
    out on the redwood benches hearts all beating
Quiet to the simmer of the stove,   65
    the scent of cedar
And then turn over,

murmuring gossip of the grasses,
    talking firewood,
Wondering how Gen's napping, how to bring him in   70
    soon wash him too—
These boys who love their mother
    who loves men, who passes on
    her sons to other women;

The cloud across the sky. The windy pines.   75
    the trickle gurgle in the swampy meadow

    this is our body.

Fire inside and boiling water on the stove
We sigh and slide ourselves down from the benches
    wrap the babies, step outside,   80

black night & all the stars.

Pour cold water on the back and thighs
Go in the house—stand steaming by the center fire
Kai scampers on the sheepskin
Gen standing hanging on and shouting,   85

"Bao! bao! bao! bao! bao!"

This is our body. Drawn up crosslegged by the flames
    drinking icy water
    hugging babies, kissing bellies,

Laughing on the Great Earth   90

Come out from the bath.

        1972

Axe Handles

    One afternoon the last week in April
    Showing Kai how to throw a hatchet
    One-half turn and it sticks in a stump.
    He recalls the hatchet-head
    Without a handle, in the shop   5
    And go gets it, and wants it for his own.
    A broken-off axe handle behind the door
    Is long enough for a hatchet,
    We cut it to length and take it
    With the hatchet head   10
    And working hatchet, to the wood block.
    There I begin to shape the old handle

With the hatchet, and the phrase
First learned from Ezra Pound[4]
Rings in my ears!   15
"When making an axe handle
        the pattern is not far off."
And I say this to Kai
"Look: We'll shape the handle
By checking the handle   20
Of the axe we cut with—"
And he sees. And I hear it again:
It's in Lu Ji's *Wên Fu*, fourth century
A.D. "Essay on Literature"—in the
Preface: "In making the handle   25
Of an axe
By cutting wood with an axe
The model is indeed near at hand."
My teacher Shih-hsiang Chen
Translated that and taught it years ago   30
And I see: Pound was an axe,
Chen was an axe, I am an axe
And my son a handle, soon
To be shaping again, model
And tool, craft of culture,   35
How we go on.

                                                        1983

4. American poet (1885–1972).

KAMAU BRATHWAITE
b. 1930

The Barbadian poet and historian Kamau Brathwaite has sought to recover and re-value the ignored, concealed, and despised African inheritance in the Caribbean. Through most of the twentieth century, this inheritance was considered embarrassing or taboo in the English-speaking West Indies, despite the survival of African gods in West Indian religions, the sedimentation of African languages in West Indian Creole, and the persistence of African social customs and practices throughout the Caribbean. Educated as British subjects, Afro-Caribbeans, Brathwaite observes, knew more about English kings and queens than about the history of slavery that their own ancestors endured and resisted. As for landscape, they were more comfortable writing about the falling of snow—an "imported alien experience" encountered only in British poems—than about their hurricanes (*History of the Voice*). Brathwaite explores the resultant anguish of deracination and dispossession in the West Indies. "Where then is the nigger's / home?" he asks in the first part of his influential epic, *The Arrivants: A New World Trilogy* (1973), which gathers *Rights of Passage* (1967), *Masks* (1968), and *Islands* (1969). Uprooted by slavery, debased by the master, degraded by impoverishment, Africans in the New World are doomed to conspire in their own futility and despair, unless they repossess themselves by repossessing their hidden past.

For Brathwaite, what he calls "nation language," which includes West Indian Creole, is a crucial tool for recuperating Afro-Caribbean history and experience, because "nation language . . . is the *submerged* area of that dialect which is much more closely allied to the African aspect of experience in the Caribbean," saturated with African words, rhythms, even grammar (*History of the Voice*). In this regard, the Creole poet Louise Bennett is Brathwaite's most significant precursor. Brathwaite tries harder than Bennett to break the "tyranny" of British meters and of the ballad stanza, but Bennett's writing is more thoroughly creolized in diction than Brathwaite's. In Brathwaite's view, through the use of non-Standard English idioms, sounds, and syncopations poets can reclaim linguistic elements that survived the Middle Passage, the terrible voyage in slave ships across the Atlantic. Likewise, in Brathwaite's poem "Ogun," named after an African god who, like Anancy and Shango, is reborn in the New World, a craftsman who carves in nonstandard forms reconnects with ancestral Africa.

The pattern of Brathwaite's career helps explain why he became a compelling West Indian spokesman for what he calls *"the literature of reconnection"* ("The African Presence in Caribbean Literature"). He was born Lawson Edward Brathwaite on May 11, 1930, in Bridgetown, Barbados, at the eastern edge of the West Indies. (He legally changed his name in 1987, adopting the African [Kikuyu] name Kamau.) Barbados had an especially strong British colonial presence; yet as Brathwaite was fond of pointing out, it was also the Caribbean island closest to Africa. Having grown up in a middle-class family, Brathwaite went on a scholarship to Cambridge University, where he earned his B.A. in history in 1953, followed later by a D.Phil. at the University of Sussex in 1968. Like other Caribbean intellectuals, he journeyed for his education to the imperial "motherland," but in an unusual twist, he also traveled to the ancestral "mother" continent, working as an education officer for the Ministry of Education in Ghana from 1955 to 1962. After returning to the West Indies, where he was for many years a professional historian before taking a position in comparative literature at New York University in 1991, Brathwaite viewed Afro-Caribbean culture through the clarifying prism of his dual experiences in Europe and Africa—key sources of West Indian culture.

In his historical research and his poetry, Brathwaite interprets the West Indies through the powerful concept of "creolization," an idea he develops to describe the complex interchange, transformation, and resistance between the cultures of black and white, slave and master, in the Caribbean. Yet he emphasizes the African elements in this intercultural process, because of their marginality in traditional accounts of the West Indies. Analyzing one of the most important kinds of creolization, Brathwaite writes in *The Development of Creole Society in Jamaica*: "It was in language that the slave was perhaps most successfully imprisoned by his master, and it was in his (mis-) use of it that he perhaps most effectively rebelled." For Brathwaite, as for other West Indian writers, the figure of Caliban from Shakespeare's *Tempest* is the model for this transformative appropriation of the master's tools. Despite material impoverishment, the Rastafarian in "Wings of a Dove" remakes English through his distinctive diction, rhythms, and phonetics, cursing the master in a remastered version of the master's language. Translating calypso into the trochees of "Calypso" ("Steel drum steel drum / hit the hot calypso dancing"), Brathwaite syncopates literary English as a medium for West Indian identity, as the steel drummer turns the cast-off oil barrel into a Caribbean musical instrument. Like most West Indians, schooled in Standard English but speaking varieties of Creole on the street and in the yard, Brathwaite nimbly switches codes between different linguistic registers, sometimes even breaking into musical concatenations of nonsense syllables. Into this linguistic callaloo he mixes varieties of music from the African diaspora—worksongs, ska, jazz, the blues, calypso, limbo, and reggae.

Brathwaite has often been contrasted with his fellow Caribbean poet Derek Walcott.

Brathwaite works more from the oral and musical forms of the common people, Walcott from the high-literary forms of lyric and epic. Brathwaite emphasizes the African, Walcott the European ingredients in West Indian culture. Walcott accommodates the Western heritage, while Brathwaite angrily resists it. If these are useful points of departure, the contrasts nevertheless oversimplify. Walcott also searches out African survivals in the West Indies and uses Caribbean speech and song. Brathwaite is no less an inheritor of high modernist literary strategies. He has openly admitted his debt to the supremely canonical Anglo-American poet T. S. Eliot. Eliot's influence, especially when blended with that of Louise Bennett's folk-based Creole verse, helped free Brathwaite from the dead hand of Victorian colonial models. Like Eliot, Brathwaite incorporates jazz and other musical forms; shifts rapidly in tone, speaker, and cultural reference; fuses overlapping characters in overarching personae; bridges lyric despair and epic collectivity; and tries to reassemble a usable inheritance out of the shards of the cultural past. In an irony of twentieth-century literary history, a poet sometimes seen as an elitist, racist, High Church reactionary enables the career of one of the most resistant, perhaps even revolutionary poets of the African diaspora.

FROM THE ARRIVANTS

Wings of a Dove[1]

1

Brother Man the Rasta[2]
man, beard full of lichens
brain full of lice
watched the mice
come up through the floor-   5
boards of his down-
town, shanty-town kitchen,
and smiled. Blessed are the poor[3]
in health, he mumbled,
that they should inherit this   10
wealth. Blessed are the meek
hearted, he grumbled,
for theirs is this stealth.

Brother Man the Rasta
man, hair full of lichens   15
head hot as ice
watched the mice
walk into his poor
hole, reached for his peace
and the pipe of his ganja[4]   20

---

1. From *Rights of Passage* (1967), the first book of *The Arrivants* (1973).
2. Rastafarian. Rastafari, or Rastafarianism, is an Afro-Caribbean religion that posits an ultimate return to Africa and the divinity of Haile Selassie I, a former emperor of Ethiopia.

3. A revision of the beatitudes of the New Testament: "Blessed are the poor in spirit: for theirs is the kingdom of heaven" (Matthew 5.3).
4. Marijuana; used ritually and socially by Rastafarians.

and smiled how the mice
eyes, hot pumice
pieces, glowed into his room
like ruby, like rhinestone
and suddenly startled like   25
diamond.

And I
Rastafar-I
in Babylon's[5] boom
town, crazed by the moon   30
and the peace of this chalice, I
prophet and singer, scourge
of the gutter, guardian
Trench Town, the Dungle and Young's
Town,[6] rise and walk through the now silent   35
streets of affliction, hawk's eyes
hard with fear, with
affection, and hear my people
cry, my people
shout: 40

Down down
white
man, con
man, brown
man, down   45
down full
man, frown-
ing fat
man, that
white black   50
man that
lives in
the town.

Rise rise
locks-   55
man, Solo-
man[7] wise
man, rise
rise rise
leh we   60
laugh
dem, mock
dem, stop
dem, kill

5. Rastafarian term for the power structure that
has suppressed blacks for centuries; originally, an
ancient Mesopotamian city devoted to sensual and
material values.
6. Apparently, an invention, by analogy with
Trench Town (a working-class district in King-
ston). *The Dungle*: Kingston slum on a garbage
dump, demolished in the 1960s.
7. Pun on wise biblical King Solomon.

dem an' go   65
back back
to the black
man lan'
back back
to Af-   70
rica.

2

Them doan mean it, yuh know,
them cahn help it
but them clean-face browns[8] in
Babylon town is who I most fear   75

an' who fears most I.
Watch de vulture dem a-fly-
in', hear de crow a-dem crow
see what them money a-buy?

Caw caw caw caw.   80
Ol' crow, ol' crow, cruel ol'
ol' crow, that's all them got
to show.

Crow fly flip flop
hip hop   85
pun de ground; na[9]
feet feel firm

pun de firm stones; na
good pickney[1] born
from de flesh   90
o' dem bones;

naw naw naw naw.

3

So beat dem drums
dem, spread

dem wings dem,   95
watch dem fly

dem, soar dem
high dem,

---

8. Light-skinned bourgeoisie. *Cahn:* can't (Jamai-
can English).

9. Not any (Jamaican English).
1. Children.

clear in the glory of the Lord.

Watch dem ship dem   100
come to town dem

full o' silk dem
full o' food dem

an' dem 'plane dem
come to groun' dem   105

full o' flash dem
full o' cash dem

silk dem food dem
shoe dem wine dem

that dem drink dem   110
an' consume dem

praisin' the glory of the Lord.

So beat dem burn
dem, learn

dem that dem[2]   115
got dem nothin'

but dem
bright bright baubles

that will burst dem
when the flame dem   120

from on high dem
raze an' roar dem

an' de poor dem
rise an' rage dem

in de glory of the Lord.   125

                                1967

---

2. That is, teach them that they.

Calypso[3]

1

The stone had skidded arc'd and bloomed into islands:
Cuba and San Domingo
Jamaica and Puerto Rico
Grenada Guadeloupe Bonaire[4]

curved stone hissed into reef   5
wave teeth fanged into clay
white splash flashed into spray
Bathsheba Montego Bay[5]

bloom of the arcing summers . . .

2

The islands roared into green plantations   10
ruled by silver sugar cane
sweat and profit
cutlass profit
islands ruled by sugar cane

And of course it was a wonderful time   15
a profitable hospitable well-worth-your-time
when captains carried receipts for rices
letters spices wigs
opera glasses swaggering asses
debtors vices pigs   20

O it was a wonderful time
an elegant benevolent redolent time—
and young Mrs. P.'s quick irrelevant crime
at four o'clock in the morning . . .

3

But what of black Sam   25
with the big splayed toes
and the shoe black shiny skin?

He carries bucketfulls of water
'cause his Ma's just had another daughter.

And what of John with the European name   30
who went to school and dreamt of fame

3. Type of folk song originating in Trinidad, often involving commentary on current events and improvised wordplay with syncopated rhythms. This poem is from *Rights of Passage*.
4. Islands in the Caribbean. The first two stanzas refer to a creation myth in which the islands are formed in a rock-skipping game called ducks and drakes.
5. Jamaican city and tourist resort. *Bathsheba*: seaside resort in Barbados.

his boss one day called him a fool
and the boss hadn't even been to school . . .

4

Steel drum steel drum
hit the hot calypso dancing   35
hot rum hot rum
who goin' stop this bacchanalling?[6]

For we glance the banjo
dance the limbo
grow our crops by maljo[7]   40

have loose morals
gather corals
father our neighbour's quarrels

perhaps when they come
with their cameras and straw   45
hats: sacred pink tourists from the frozen Nawth

we should get down to those
white beaches
where if we don't wear breeches

it becomes an island dance   50
Some people doin' well
while others are catchin' hell

o the boss gave our Johnny the sack
though we beg him please
please to take 'im back   55

so the boy now nigratin' overseas . . .

1967

Ogun[8]

My uncle made chairs, tables, balanced doors on, dug out
coffins, smoothing the white wood out

with plane and quick sandpaper until
it shone like his short-sighted glasses.

---

6. From *Bacchanalia*: festival of Bacchus, the Roman god of wine, celebrated with song, dancing, and revelry.
7. Evil eye.

8. West African and West Indian god of iron, thunder, roads, war, creation, and destruction. The poem is from *Islands* (1969), the third and last book of *The Arrivants* (1973).

The knuckles of his hands were sil-   5
vered knobs of nails hit, hurt and flat-

tened out with blast of heavy hammer. He was knock-knee'd, flat-
footed and his clip clop sandals slapped across the concrete

flooring of his little shop where canefield mulemen and a fleet
of Bedford lorry drivers dropped in to scratch themselves and talk.   10

There was no shock of wood, no beam
of light mahogany his saw teeth couldn't handle.

When shaping squares for locks, a key hole
care tapped rat tat tat upon the handle

of his humpbacked chisel. Cold   15
world of wood caught fire as he whittled: rectangle

window frames, the intersecting x of fold-
ing chairs, triangle

trellises, the donkey
box-cart in its squeaking square.   20

But he was poor and most days he was hungry.
Imported cabinets with mirrors, formica table

tops, spine-curving chairs made up of tubes, with hollow
steel-like bird bones that sat on rubber ploughs,

thin beds, stretched not on boards, but blue high-tensioned cables,   25
were what the world preferred.

And yet he had a block of wood that would have baffled them.
With knife and gimlet care he worked away at this on Sundays,

explored its knotted hurts, cutting his way
along its yellow whorls until his hands could feel   30

how it had swelled and shivered, breathing air,
its weathered green burning to rings of time,

its contoured grain still tuned to roots and water.
And as he cut, he heard the creak of forests:

green lizard faces gulped, grey memories with moth   35
eyes watched him from their shadows, soft

liquid tendrils leaked among the flowers
and a black rigid thunder he had never heard within his hammer

came stomping up the trunks. And as he worked within his shattered
Sunday shop, the wood took shape: dry shuttered   40

eyes, slack anciently everted lips, flat
ruined face, eaten by pox, ravaged by rat

and woodworm, dry cistern mouth, cracked
gullet crying for the desert, the heavy black

enduring jaw; lost pain, lost iron;   45
emerging woodwork image of his anger.

                                                                    1969

Trane[9]

> Propped against the crowded bar
> he pours into the curved and silver horn
> his old unhappy longing for a home
>
> the dancers twist and turn
> he leans and wishes he could burn   5
> his memories to ashes like some old notorious emperor
>
> of rome. but no stars blazed across the sky when he was born
> no wise men found his hovel. this crowded bar
> where dancers twist and turn
>
> holds all the fame and recognition he will ever earn   10
> on earth or heaven. he leans against the bar
> and pours his old unhappy longing in the saxophone

                                                                    1977

Stone

(for Mikey Smith)[1]

When the stone fall that morning out of the johncrow[2] sky
it was not dark at first . that opening on to the red sea sky
but something in my mouth like feathers . blue like bubbles and light
carrying signals & planets & the sliding curve of the world like a water
    picture
in a raindrop when the pressure drop   5

---

9. Nickname of jazz saxophonist John Coltrane
(1926–1967).
1. Michael Smith (1954–1983), a charismatic
"dub," or performance, poet, was stoned to death
on Stony Hill, Jamaica, by thugs a day after he
spoke out at a political rally during Jamaican elec-
tions.
2. Turkey vulture (Jamaican English). Commonly
seen as omen of a person's imminent death.

When the stone fall that morning i
couldn't cry out because my mouth was full of beast & plunder
as if i was gnashing badwords among tombstones
as if angry water was beating up against the curbstones of the palisadoes[3]
as if that road up Stony Hill round the bend by the churchyard on the   10
   way to the

post office was a bad bad dream and the dream was on fire all the way past
   the
white houses higher up the hill and the ogogs[4] bark
ing all teeth & furnace and my mother like she upside down up a tree like
she was screaming and nobody i could hear could hear a word i shouting
even though there were so many poems left and the tape was switched   15
   on & running
and the green light was red and they was standing up everywhere in
   London
& Amsterdam & at UNESCO[5] in Paris & in West Berlin & clapping &
   clapping &
clapping & not a soul on Stony Hill to even say amen . and yet it was
   happening happening
the fences began to crack in my skull and there were loud *boodooooongs*
   like
guns going off them ole time magnums or like fireworks where I   20
   dreadlocks were in fire
and the gaps where the river coming down and the dry gully where my
   teeth used to be
smiling and my tuff gong tongue that used to press against them & parade
   pronounciation
now unannounce and like a black wick in i head & dead
and it was like a heavy heavy riddim low down in i belly bleeding dub
and there was like this heavy black dog thumping in i chest & pumping   25
   murdererrrrrrrr

and my throat like dem tie like dem tie a tight tie around it . twist
ing my neck quick crick quick crick and a never wear neck
tie yet and a laughing more blood and spittin out lawwwwwwwwwwwd
and i two eye lock to the sun and the two sun staring back bright from the
   grass and i

bline to de butterfly flittin . but i hear de tread of my heart   30
the heavy flux of the blood in my veins silver tambourines
closer & closer . st joseph[6] band crashing &
closer & bom sicai sica boom ship bell &
closer & bom sicai sica boom ship bell &
when the saints . . .   35

3. A finger of land on which Kingston's international airport is situated.
4. Wordplay on *dogs* and *Ogog* (evil power prophesied in Revelation 20 and in other Christian and Jewish apocalyptic literature).
5. United Nations Educational, Scientific and Cultural Organization, created to foster world peace through international collaboration.
6. Joseph the Patriarch, husband of the Virgin Mary; his saint's day is celebrated with parades.

•

and it was like a wave on Stony Hill caught in a crust of sunlight
and it was like a broken schooner into harbour muffled in the silence of its
    wound
and it was like the blue of peace was filling up the heavens with its
    thunder
and it was like the wind was growing skin the skin had hard hairs
    hardering
it was like Marcus Garvey[7] rising from his coin . stepping towards his   40
    people
crying dark . and every mighty word he trod the ground fell dark & hole
    behind
him like it was a scream i did not know and yet it was a scream . my ears
    were bleeding
sound. and i was quiet now because i had become that sound

the sunlit morning washed the coral limestone harsh against the soft
    volcanic ash
i was & it was slipping past me into water & it was slipping past me into   45
    root
i was & it was slipping past me into flower & it was ripping upward into shoot
while every tongue in town was lashing me with spit & cutrass[8] wit & ivy
    whip &
wrinkle jumbimum[9] . it was like warthog grunting in the ground . and
    children run
ning down the hill run right on through the splashes
that my breathing made when it was howl & red & bubble and sparrow   50

    twits pluck tic & tapeworm from the grass
as if i-man did never have no face as if i-man did never in this place

When the stone fell that morning out of the johncrow sky
i could not hold it back or black it   back or block it off or limp away
or roll it from me into memory or light or rock it steady into night be   55
cause it builds me now and fills my blood with deaf my bone with dumb &

lawwwwwwwwwwwwwwwwwwwwwwwwwwwwwwwwwwwwwwwwd

i am the stone that kills me.

1986

---

7. Jamaican national hero (1887–1940), who championed racial uplift and the return of blacks to Africa; his face appears on the Jamaican twenty-five-cent coin.
8. Pun on *cutlass* and *rass*, vulgar term for buttocks and exclamation of scorn or anger (Jamican English).
9. Author's coinage for a Caribbean plant or root with secret power. From *jumbi* (spirit) and *mum* (secret or silent, as in "mum's the word"), by analogy with West Indian words such as *jumbie-coffee* and *jumbie-chocho*.

Irae

dies irae[1] dreadful day
when the world shall pass away
so the priests & showmen say

what gaunt phantoms shall affront me
mi lai sharpville wounded knee   5
arthur[2] kissorcallatme

to what judgement meekly led
shall men gather trumpeted
by louis armstrong[3] from the dead

life & death shall here be voice   10
less rising from their moist
interment hoist

ing all their flags before them
poniard poison rocket bomb
nations of the earth shall come   15

and his record page on page
forever building he shall scan & give each age
sentences of righteous rage[4]

if the pious then shall shake me
what reply can merchants make me   20
what defences can they fake?

mighty & majestic god
head saviour of the broken herd
heal me nanny cuffee cudjoe[5]
grant me mercy at thy word   25

day of fire dreadful day
day for which all sufferers pray
grant me patience with thy plenty
grant me vengeance with thy sword

1992

---

1. Day of wrath (Latin); the opening words (and thus the title) of a thirteenth-century hymn based on Zephaniah 1.14–16. A meditation on the last judgment, once part of the liturgies of the Mass of the Dead and the Office of the Dead, it begins: "That day of wrath, that dreadful day, / shall heaven and earth in ashes lay, / as David and the Sybil say. // What horror must invade the mind / when the approaching Judge shall find / and sift the deeds of all mankind! // The mighty trumpet's wondrous tone / shall rend each tomb's sepulchral stone / and summon all before the Throne."
2. Legendary king of Britain. *Mi Lai*: Vietnamese hamlet where American soldiers massacred civilians in 1968. *Sharpville*: South African township where anti-apartheid demonstrators were shot down by the police in 1960. *Wounded Knee*: site of battle in which over two hundred Sioux men and women were massacred by U.S. troops in 1890.
3. Jazz trumpeter and vocalist (1901–1971).
4. Cf. "Dies Irae": "Then shall with universal dread / the Book of Consciences be read / to judge the lives of all the dead."
5. Three leaders of the Maroons, ex-slave rebel warriors.

CHRISTOPHER OKIGBO
1930?–1967

Born on August 16, 1930 (or 1932, according to some scholars), in Ojoto, eastern Nigeria, Christopher Okigbo was killed in the Nigerian Civil War. Before volunteering on the secessionist Biafran side in the first of many internal conflicts to tear apart postcolonial Africa, Okigbo had been a student (B.A. 1956 from the University of Ibadan), an athlete, a teacher, a librarian, a bureaucrat, and a traveling press representative. The poetry he produced in his short career influenced and impressed writers across anglophone Africa, such as fellow Nigerian Wole Soyinka, as well as Western poets, such as Geoffrey Hill and Jay Wright. Okigbo was a leading figure during the so-called golden age of postcolonial anglophone letters in Africa—the period just before and after formal independence. Resistant to the identity politics of negritude, which asserted and valued an essential blackness, he also refused the bald "platform poetry" (his phrase in a 1965 interview) practiced by many of his contemporaries, writing instead poems that are psychologically inward and insistently musical.

Indebted to W. B. Yeats, Ezra Pound, and T. S. Eliot, as well as Igbo praise songs and other oral genres, Okigbo intricately layers public and private meanings and myths in allusive, richly patterned verse. Like the modernists but in an entirely different cultural setting, Okigbo treats poetry as a literary rite. He conceives of his poetry as almost priestly: "My creative activity is in fact one way of performing those functions in a different manner. Every time I write a poem, I am in fact offering a sacrifice" (*Journal of Commonwealth Literature*, 1970). But no single code of belief structures his work. After all, he was brought up in Igbo village ritual, attended Catholic school, taught Latin and the classics, and knew intimately the modernist canon.

Okigbo's first major poetic sequence, *Heavensgate* (1962, rev. 1964), melds these disparate sources in a poetic rite of sacrifice and renewal, charted in the section titles: "The Passage," "Initiations," "Watermaid," "Lustra," and "Newcomer." In his introductory comments on the sequence, Okigbo says the poet, as an Igbo supplicant, undergoes "a complete self-surrender to the water spirit that nurtures all creation," in particular the ancestral river goddess Idoto. With one eye on another set of cultural bearings, he also says "the celebrant, a personage like Orpheus, is about to begin a journey," that is, is setting out to fashion the very poem we read. The sequence is thus both a priestly offering to a local African goddess and an Orphic exploration of poetic creativity. In one of the sequence's many intercultural ironies, the first poem also calls the poet-protagonist the biblical "prodigal" son. How does the poet return to the native religion he abandoned for Christianity? Curiously enough, by way of Christian parable. Prodigal son, Orphic poet, Igbo supplicant—the protagonist synthesizes these various paradigms. Similarly, the goddess invoked by the poet, reappearing in the guises of lioness and "watermaid," is at once Igbo river deity, muse, maternal culture, Eurydice, the beloved, and so forth. Okigbo's rich sensibility enables him to hold in solution these diverse cultural elements.

The notorious "obscurity" of Okigbo's poetry arises from its cross-cultural allusions, its compression, its psychospiritual questing, and its spare, indeterminate settings. Recycling primal images of light, water, and earth, the poet varies his simple palette with carefully paced cadences, alliterations, puns, striking images ("Rainbow . . . arched like boa bent to kill"), and surprising collocations ("armpit-dazzle"). In the late poem "Come Thunder," about the worrisome events preceding the Nigerian Civil War, Okigbo's poetic ambiguity turns nightmarish, recalling Yeats's poems nearly half a century earlier about the civil strife in Ireland. Pondering a violent but still unknowable future, Okigbo skillfully yokes precise details ("The smell of blood already floats in the lavender-mist of the afternoon") with terrifying abstractions ("a great fearful thing already tugs at the cables of the open air"). It is difficult not to see in this poem something of the power of prophecy.

FROM HEAVENSGATE

[Before You, Mother Idoto]

Before you, mother Idoto[1]
   naked I stand;
before your watery presence,
   a prodigal

leaning on an oilbean,   5
lost in your legend.

Under your power wait I
   on barefoot,
watchman for the watchword
   at *Heavensgate*;   10

out of the depths my cry:
give ear and hearken . . .

[Dark Waters of the Beginning.]

Dark waters of the beginning.

Rays, violet and short, piercing the gloom,
foreshadow the fire that is dreamed of.

Rainbow on far side, arched like boa bent to kill,
foreshadows the rain that is dreamed of.   5

Me to the orangery[2]
solitude invites,
a wagtail, to tell
the tangled-wood-tale;
a sunbird, to mourn   10
a mother on a spray.

---

1. "A village stream. The oilbean, the tortoise and the python are totems for her worship" [Okigbo's note]. The poet also writes, in his 1965 introduction to the volume: "*Heavensgate* was originally conceived as an Easter sequence. It later grew into a ceremony of innocence, something like a mass, an offering to Idoto, the village stream of which I drank, in which I washed, as a child." The first two excerpts are from a section titled "The Passage"; the next is from "Watermaid"; the last from "Newcomer," at the end of the sequence.

2. Site where orange trees are cultivated.

Rain and sun in single combat;
on one leg standing,
in silence at the passage,
the young bird at the passage.   15

[Bright]

Bright
with the armpit-dazzle of a lioness,
she answers,

wearing white light about her;

and the waves escort her,   5
my lioness,
crowned with moonlight.

So brief her presence—
match-flare in wind's breath—
so brief with mirrors around me.   10

Downward . . .
the waves distil her;
gold crop
sinking ungathered.

Watermaid of the salt-emptiness,   15
grown are the ears of the secret.

[I Am Standing above the Noontide]

I am standing above the noontide,
Above the bridgehead;

Listening to the laughter of waters
   that do not know why:

Listening to incense—   5

I am standing above the noontide
   with my head above it;

Under my feet float the waters
Tide blows them under . . .

1962, 1964

Come Thunder

Now that the triumphant march has entered the last street corners,
Remember, O dancers, the thunder among the clouds . . .

Now that laughter, broken in two, hangs tremulous between the teeth,
Remember, O dancers, the lightning beyond the earth . . .

The smell of blood already floats in the lavender-mist of the afternoon.   5
The death sentence lies in ambush along the corridors of power;
And a great fearful thing already tugs at the cables of the open air,
A nebula immense and immeasurable, a night of deep waters—
An iron dream unnamed and unprintable, a path of stone.

The drowsy heads of the pods in barren farmlands witness it,   10
The homesteads abandoned in this century's brush fire witness it:
The myriad eyes of deserted corn cobs in burning barns witness it:
Magic birds with the miracle of lightning flash on their feathers . . .

The arrows of God tremble at the gates of light,
The drums of curfew pander to a dance of death;   15

And the secret thing in its heaving
Threatens with iron mask
The last lighted torch of the century . . .

1967

TED HUGHES
1930–1998

Ted Hughes's subject matter is often violence, and his acknowledged talent in this area has evoked uneasy admiration. He was prone to depicting brutal acts, whether of classical or modern violence, as in his adaptation of Seneca's bloody version of *Oedipus* or poems such as "Out," about his father's World War I experience. When he looked at nature, he found predators and victims; when he showed nature looking at humanity, as in "Crow's First Lesson," the same dynamic appeared. The poet's imagination whirls with increasing wildness, until some readers long for modulations of this baleful glare. Such ferocity, however, is so rare in English poetry, and Hughes was so effective as its exponent, that he gripped a considerable audience. He could not have done so by subject alone: his compression, his daring vocabulary, and his jarring rhythms all contributed. In contrast to the rational lucidity and buttoned-up form of his English contemporaries in the Movement, such as Philip Larkin and Donald Davie, Hughes fashions a mythical consciousness in his poems, embodied in violent metaphors, blunt syntax, harsh alliterative clusters, bunched stresses, incantatory repetitions, insistent assonances, and a dark, brooding tone. Exemplary phrases include "sudden sharp hot stink of fox" ("The Thought-Fox") and "crackle open under a blue-black pressure"

("Thistles"). Though drawing on Shakespeare, Gerard Manley Hopkins, Wilfred Owen, D. H. Lawrence, and Robert Lowell, his primitivist vision and strenuous, muscular language are very much his own.

Such a poet might seem as far from childlike as could be, but children are fond of monstrosity, and Hughes wrote a new kind of children's poem, in which his saturnine consciousness is caught in buoyant accents. Perhaps because, as he said, he collected animals, birds, and fish as a boy, he "thinks of poems as a sort of animal" (*Poetry in the Making*). *Moortown* (1979), a notebook kept on a farm, displays an extraordinary intimacy with animals and insects. He particularly liked things that "have a vivid life of their own, outside mine." That life, as he wrote about it, is anarchic and savage. So also with human enterprises; all his lovers are demon lovers, and hatred sometimes takes over. The image of the poet that Hughes offers is in keeping with this temper of his work; in "Famous Poet," "the demeanour is of mouse, / Yet is he monster," and he speaks of "the world-shouldering, monstrous 'I' " in "The Man Seeking Experience Enquires His Way of a Drop of Water." An index to Hughes's own aspirations appears in his introduction to *A Choice of Emily Dickinson's Verse,* in which he speaks with great approval of "her frightening vision," the sense of an "icy chill," and "the conflagration within her." A blend of fire and ice is the ideal mixture sought in his poems. In Hughes's dualistic vision, darkness usually overcomes light.

Hughes was born on August 17, 1930, in Mytholmroyd, Yorkshire. His father, a carpenter, was one of a handful of survivors of a regiment that perished in the disastrous Gallipoli campaign of World War I. Hughes took a B.A. at Cambridge University, where after first studying English literature he turned to archeology and anthropology. There he met the American poet Sylvia Plath, who was on a Fulbright Scholarship. They married in 1956, at first living in the United States, then settling in England. They had two children, but their marriage was troubled, Hughes had a notorious affair, and they had separated at the time of Plath's suicide, in 1963. As poets, they both dealt in raw sensation and lacerated nerves, though Plath's work centered on the plight of the victim as her husband's centered on the consciousness of the predator. Public anger over Plath's suicide, as well as over Hughes's destruction of the journals Plath wrote when at the peak of her literary powers, followed Hughes the rest of his life; his name was repeatedly defaced from Plath's tombstone. Hughes published a series of verse letters to Plath in *The Birthday Letters* (1998), but they are slack and defensive, lacking the concentration of his earlier verse. By the time of his death, Hughes had been poet laureate of England for nearly a decade and a half (succeeding John Betjeman in 1984), a post he accepted because he thought of England, he said, as a tribe for whose chiefs he could write tribal songs.

The Horses

I climbed through woods in the hour-before-dawn dark.
Evil air, a frost-making stillness,

Not a leaf, not a bird—
A world cast in frost. I came out above the wood

Where my breath left tortuous statues in the iron light.   5
But the valleys were draining the darkness

Till the moorline—blackening dregs of the brightening grey—
Halved the sky ahead. And I saw the horses:

Huge in the dense grey—ten together—
Megalith-still.[1] They breathed, making no move,   10

With draped manes and tilted hind-hooves,
Making no sound.

I passed: not one snorted or jerked its head.
Grey silent fragments

Of a grey silent world.   15

I listened in emptiness on the moor-ridge.
The curlew's[2] tear turned its edge on the silence.

Slowly detail leafed from the darkness. Then the sun
Orange, red, red, erupted

Silently, and splitting to its core tore and flung cloud,   20
Shook the gulf open, showed blue,

And the big planets hanging.
I turned,

Stumbling in the fever of a dream, down towards
The dark woods, from the kindling tops,   25

And came to the horses.
                        There, still they stood,
But now steaming and glistening under the flow of light,

Their draped stone manes, their tilted hind-hooves
Stirring under a thaw while all around them   30

The frost showed its fires. But still they made no sound.
Not one snorted or stamped,

Their hung heads patient as the horizons,
High over valleys, in the red levelling rays—

In din of the crowded streets, going among the years, the faces,   35
May I still meet my memory in so lonely a place

Between the streams and the red clouds, hearing curlews,
Hearing the horizons endure.

                                                1957

---

1. That is, still as the great stones at, for example,   2. Migratory bird's.
Stonehenge.

The Thought-Fox

I imagine this midnight moment's forest:
Something else is alive
Beside the clock's loneliness
And this blank page where my fingers move.

Through the window I see no star: 5
Something more near
Though deeper within darkness
Is entering the loneliness:

Cold, delicately as the dark snow
A fox's nose touches twig, leaf;   10
Two eyes serve a movement, that now
And again now, and now, and now

Sets neat prints into the snow
Between trees, and warily a lame
Shadow lags by stump and in hollow   15
Of a body that is bold to come

Across clearings, an eye,
A widening deepening greenness,
Brilliantly, concentratedly,
Coming about its own business   20

Till, with a sudden sharp hot stink of fox,
It enters the dark hole of the head.
The window is starless still; the clock ticks,
The page is printed.

1957

An Otter

I

Underwater eyes, an eel's
Oil of water body, neither fish nor beast is the otter:
Four-legged yet water-gifted, to outfish fish;
With webbed feet and long ruddering tail
And a round head like an old tomcat.   5

Brings the legend of himself
From before wars or burials, in spite of hounds and vermin-poles;
Does not take root like the badger. Wanders, cries;
Gallops along land he no longer belongs to;
Re-enters the water by melting.   10

Of neither water nor land. Seeking
Some world lost when first he dived, that he cannot come at since,
Takes his changed body into the holes of lakes;
As if blind, cleaves the stream's push till he licks
The pebbles of the source; from sea   15

To sea crosses in three nights
Like a king in hiding. Crying to the old shape of the starlit land,
Over sunken farms where the bats go round,
Without answer. Till light and birdsong come
Walloping up roads with the milk wagon.   20

II

The hunt's lost him. Pads on mud,
Among sedges, nostrils a surface bead,
The otter remains, hours. The air,
Circling the globe, tainted and necessary,

Mingling tobacco-smoke, hounds and parsley,   25
Comes carefully to the sunk lungs.
So the self under the eye lies,
Attendant and withdrawn. The otter belongs

In double robbery and concealment—
From water that nourishes and drowns, and from land   30
That gave him his length and the mouth of the hound.
He keeps fat in the limpid integument[3]

Reflections live on. The heart beats thick,
Big trout muscle out of the dead cold;
Blood is the belly of logic; he will lick   35
The fishbone bare. And can take stolen hold

On a bitch otter in a field full
Of nervous horses, but linger nowhere.
Yanked above hounds, reverts to nothing at all,
To this long pelt over the back of a chair.   40

1960

Pike[4]

Pike, three inches long, perfect
Pike in all parts, green tigering the gold.
Killers from the egg: the malevolent aged grin.
They dance on the surface among the flies.

3. Surface, skin (that is, water).   4. Voracious freshwater fish.

Or move, stunned by their own grandeur   5
Over a bed of emerald, silhouette
Of submarine delicacy and horror.
A hundred feet long in their world.

In ponds, under the heat-struck lily pads—
Gloom of their stillness: 10
Logged on last year's black leaves, watching upwards.
Or hung in an amber cavern of weeds

The jaws' hooked clamp and fangs
Not to be changed at this date;
A life subdued to its instrument;   15
The gills kneading quietly, and the pectorals.

Three we kept behind glass,
Jungled in weed: three inches, four,
And four and a half: fed fry[5] to them—
Suddenly there were two. Finally one.   20

With a sag belly and the grin it was born with.
And indeed they spare nobody.
Two, six pounds each, over two feet long,
High and dry and dead in the willow-herb—

One jammed past its gills down the other's gullet: 25
The outside eye stared: as a vice locks—
The same iron in this eye
Though its film shrank in death.

A pond I fished, fifty yards across,
Whose lilies and muscular tench[6]   30
Had outlasted every visible stone
Of the monastery that planted them—

Stilled legendary depth:
It was as deep as England. It held
Pike too immense to stir, so immense and old   35
That past nightfall I dared not cast

But silently cast and fished
With the hair frozen on my head
For what might move, for what eye might move.
The still splashes on the dark pond,   40

Owls hushing the floating woods
Frail on my ear against the dream
Darkness beneath night's darkness had freed,
That rose slowly towards me, watching.

1960

---

5. Young fishes.   6. Variety of freshwater fish.

Thistles

Against the rubber tongues of cows and the hoeing hands of men
Thistles spike the summer air
Or crackle open under a blue-black pressure.

Every one a revengeful burst
Of resurrection, a grasped fistful   5
Of splintered weapons and Icelandic frost thrust up

From the underground stain of a decayed Viking.
They are like pale hair and the gutturals of dialects.
Every one manages a plume of blood.

Then they grow grey, like men.   10
Mown down, it is a feud. Their sons appear,
Stiff with weapons, fighting back over the same ground.

                                                                    1967

Second Glance at a Jaguar

Skinful of bowls, he bowls them,
The hip going in and out of joint, dropping the spine
With the urgency of his hurry
Like a cat going along under thrown stones, under cover,
Glancing sideways, running   5
Under his spine. A terrible, stump-legged waddle
Like a thick Aztec disemboweller,[7]
Club-swinging, trying to grind some square
Socket between his hind legs round,
Carrying his head like a brazier of spilling embers,   10
And the black bit of his mouth, he takes it
Between his back teeth, he has to wear his skin out,
He swipes a lap at the water-trough as he turns,
Swivelling the ball of his heel on the polished spot,
Showing his belly like a butterfly,   15
At every stride he has to turn a corner
In himself and correct it. His head
Is like the worn-down stump of another whole jaguar,
His body is just the engine shoving it forward,
Lifting the air up and shoving on under,   20
The weight of his fangs hanging the mouth open,
Bottom jaw combing the ground. A gorged look,
Gangster, club-tail lumped along behind gracelessly,
He's wearing himself to heavy ovals,

7. The Aztecs, an Indian nation of central Mexico (where the jaguar is native) at the time of the Spanish Conquest, practiced human sacrifice.

Muttering some mantra, some drum-song of murder 25
To keep his rage brightening, making his skin
Intolerable, spurred by the rosettes, the cain-brands,
Wearing the spots off from the inside,
Rounding some revenge. Going like a prayer-wheel,
The head dragging forward, the body keeping up, 30
The hind legs lagging. He coils, he flourishes
The blackjack tail as if looking for a target,
Hurrying through the underworld, soundless.

1967

Gog[8]

I woke to a shout: "I am Alpha and Omega."[9]
Rocks and a few trees trembled
Deep in their own country.
I ran and an absence bounded beside me.

The dog's god is a scrap dropped from the table. 5
The mouse's savior is a ripe wheat grain.
Hearing the Messiah cry
My mouth widens in adoration.

How fat are the lichens!
They cushion themselves on the silence. 10
The air wants for nothing.
The dust, too, is replete.

What was my error? My skull has sealed it out.
My great bones are massed in me.
They pound on the earth, my song excites them. 15
I do not look at the rocks and trees, I am frightened of what they see.

I listen to the song jarring my mouth
Where the skull-rooted teeth are in possession.
I am massive on earth. My feetbones beat on the earth
Over the sounds of motherly weeping. . . . 20

Afterwards I drink at a pool quietly.
The horizon bears the rocks and trees away into twilight.
I lie down. I become darkness.

Darkness that all night sings and circles stamping.

1967

8. Satanic spirit prophesized by the Book of Revelation.
9. The words of Jesus as reported by John in Revelation 1.8: "I am Alpha and Omega, the beginning and the ending." Alpha and omega are the first and last letters, respectively, of the Greek alphabet.

Out

1. The Dream Time

My father sat in his chair recovering
From the four-year mastication[1] by gunfire and mud,
Body buffeted wordless, estranged by long soaking
In the colors of mutilation.
                     His outer perforations 5
Were valiantly healed, but he and the hearth-fire, its blood-flicker
On biscuit-bowl and piano and table leg,
Moved into strong and stronger possession
Of minute after minute, as the clock's tiny cog
Labored and on the thread of his listening 10
Dragged him bodily from under
The mortised[2] four-year strata of dead Englishmen
He belonged with. He felt his limbs clearing
With every slight, gingerish movement. While I, small and four,
Lay on the carpet as his luckless double, 15
His memory's buried, immovable anchor,
Among jawbones and blown-off boots, tree-stumps, shell-cases and
      craters,
Under rain that goes on drumming its rods and thickening
Its kingdom, which the sun has abandoned, and where nobody
Can ever again move from shelter. 20

2

The dead man in his cave beginning to sweat;
The melting bronze visor of flesh
Of the mother in the baby-furnace—

Nobody believes, it
Could be nothing, all 25
Undergo smiling at
The lulling of blood in
Their ears, their ears, their ears, their eyes
Are only drops of water and even the dead man suddenly
Sits up and sneezes—Atishoo! 30
Then the nurse wraps him up, smiling,
And, though faintly, the mother is smiling,
And it's just another baby.

As after being blasted to bits
The reassembled infantryman 35
Tentatively totters out, gazing around with the eyes
Of an exhausted clerk.

---

1. Grinding or chewing.   2. Firmly fixed.

3. *Remembrance Day*[3]

The poppy is a wound, the poppy is the mouth
Of the grave, maybe of the womb searching—

A canvas-beauty puppet on a wire 40
Today whoring everywhere. It is years since I wore one.

It is more years
The shrapnel that shattered my father's paybook

Gripped me, and all his dead
Gripped him to a time 45

He no more than they could outgrow, but, cast into one, like iron,
Hung deeper than refreshing of ploughs

In the woe-dark under my mother's eye—
One anchor

Holding my juvenile neck bowed to the dunkings of the Atlantic. 50
So goodbye to that bloody-minded flower.

You dead bury your dead.
Goodbye to the cenotaphs[4] on my mother's breasts.

Goodbye to all the remaindered charms of my father's survival.
Let England close. Let the green sea-anemone close. 55

1967

Wodwo[5]

What am I? Nosing here, turning leaves over
Following a faint stain on the air to the river's edge
I enter water. What am I to split
The glassy grain of water looking upward I see the bed
Of the river above me upside down very clear 5
What am I doing here in mid-air? Why do I find
this frog so interesting as I inspect its most secret
interior and make it my own? Do these weeds
know me and name me to each other have they
seen me before, do I fit in their world? I seem 10

3. Holiday (November 11) commemorating sol-
diers who lost their lives in battle. The practice of
wearing red poppies in honor of lost soldiers recalls
John McCrae's poem "In Flanders Fields" (1915),
which depicts the flowers growing between the
graves on a battlefield.
4. Empty tombs.
5. Wild man of the woods, or wood demon (Mid-

dle English); from line 721 of the anonymous four-
teenth-century poem *Sir Gawain and the Green
Knight.* Hughes uses lines from this poem as the
epigraph for the book of which "Wodwo" is the title
poem: "Now with serpents he wars, now with sav-
age wolves, / Now with wild men of the woods,
that watched from the rocks" (translation by Marie
Borroff).

separate from the ground and not rooted but dropped
out of nothing casually I've no threads
fastening me to anything I can go anywhere
I seem to have been given the freedom
of this place what am I then? And picking   15
bits of bark off this rotten stump gives me
no pleasure and it's no use so why do I do it
me and doing that have coincided very queerly
But what shall I be called am I the first
have I an owner what shape am I what   20
shape am I am I huge if I go
to the end on this way past these trees and past these trees
till I get tired that's touching one wall of me
for the moment if I sit still how everything
stops to watch me I suppose I am the exact centre   25
but there's all this what is it roots
roots roots roots and here's the water
again very queer but I'll go on looking

1967

Crow's First Lesson

God tried to teach Crow how to talk.
"Love," said God. "Say, Love."
Crow gaped, and the white shark crashed into the sea
And went rolling downwards, discovering its own depth.

"No, no," said God, "Say Love. Now try it. LOVE."   5
Crow gaped, and a bluefly, a tsetse,[6] a mosquito
Zoomed out and down
To their sundry flesh-pots.

"A final try," said God. "Now, LOVE."
Crow convulsed, gaped, retched and   10
Man's bodiless prodigious head
Bulbed out onto the earth, with swiveling eyes,
Jabbering protest—

And Crow retched again, before God could stop him.
And woman's vulva dropped over man's neck and tightened.   15
The two struggled together on the grass.
God struggled to part them, cursed, wept—

Crow flew guiltily off.

1970

---

6. African fly that carries the sleeping-sickness disease.

Roe Deer[7]

In the dawn-dirty light, in the biggest snow of the year
Two blue-dark deer stood in the road, alerted.

They had happened into my dimension
The moment I was arriving just there.

They planted their two or three years of secret deerhood   5
Clear on my snow-screen vision of the abnormal

And hesitated in the all-way disintegration
And stared at me. And so for some lasting seconds

I could think the deer were waiting for me
To remember the password and sign   10

That the curtain had blown aside for a moment
And there where the trees were no longer trees, nor the road a road

The deer had come for me.

Then they ducked through the hedge, and upright they rode their legs
Away downhill over a snow-lonely field   15

Toward tree-dark—finally
Seeming to eddy and glide and fly away up

Into the boil[8] of big flakes.
The snow took them and soon their nearby hoofprints as well

Revising its dawn inspiration   20
Back to the ordinary.

                                                        1979

Orf[9]

Because his nose and face were one festering sore
That no treatment persuaded, month after month,
And his feet four sores, the same,
Which could only stand and no more,

Because his sickness was converting his growth   5
Simply to strengthening sickness

---

7. Small European and Asiatic deer, known for   8. Agitation.
their nimbleness and grace.   9. Sore mouth, a contagious disease of sheep.

While his breath wheezed through a mask of flies
No stuff could rid him of

I shot the lamb.
I shot him while he was looking the other way.   10
I shot him between the ears.

He lay down.
His machinery adjusted itself
And his blood escaped, without loyalty.

But the lamb life in my care   15
Left him where he lay, and stood up in front of me

Asking to be banished,
Asking for permission to be extinct,
For permission to wait, at least,

Inside my head   20
In the radioactive space
From which the meteorite had removed his body.

1979

From Orts[1]

17. Buzz in the Window

Buzz frantic
And prolonged. Fly down near the corner,
The cemetery den. A big bluefly
Is trying to drag a plough, too deep
In earth too stony, immovable. Then the fly   5
Buzzing its full revs forward, budges backward.
Clings. Deadlock.
The spider has gripped its anus. Slender talons
Test the blue armor gently, the head
Buried in the big game. He tugs   10
Tigerish, half the size of his prey. A pounding
Glory time for the spider. For the other
A darkening summary of some circumstances
In the window corner, with a dead bee,
Wing-petals, husks of insect-armor, a brambled[2]   15
Glade of dusty web. It buzzes less
As the drug argues deeper and deeper.
In fluttery soundless tremors it tries to keep
A hold on the air. The north sky
Slides northward. The blossom is clinging   20
To its hopes, refurnishing the constant

---

1. Leavings, scraps.   2. As if a thicket.

Of ignorant life. The bluefly,
Without changing expression, only adjusting
Its leg stance, as if to more comfort,
Undergoes ultimate ghastliness. Finally agrees to it.   25
The spider tugs, retreating. The fly
Is going to let it do everything. Something is stuck.
The fly is fouled in web. Intelligence, the spider,
Comes round to look and patiently, joyfully,
Starts cutting the mesh. Frees it. Returns   30
To the haul—homeward in that exhausted ecstasy
The loaded hunters of the Pleistocene[3]
Never recorded either.

                                                                    1979

3. The Ice Age.

OKOT P'BITEK
1931–1982

The Ugandan poet Okot p'Bitek wrote the most significant and widely read poem of anglophone East Africa, *Song of Lawino* (1966). This long poem—witty, lively, satiric—presents the boisterous voice of a traditional African woman from an Acoli village in rural Uganda. Proud of her native culture and her skills in song, dance, and cooking, Lawino furiously upbraids her husband for abandoning Acoli ways. *Song of Lawino* dramatizes as a husband-and-wife quarrel the conflicts between modernization and traditionalism, between Eurocentrism and Afrocentrism.

Although Okot drafted much of the poem in Acoli, it was first published in his English-language version, parts of which did not exist in the earlier Acoli text. African writers have hailed *Song of Lawino* as "possibly the best rounded single work of African poetry in English today," and American critics have concurred, both groups citing the poem's indigenous African imagery, rhetorical devices, and ideas; critics have often contrasted it with the more cosmopolitan work of so-called Euro-modernists such as Wole Soyinka and Christopher Okigbo. This view owes much to Lawino's energetic defense of traditional African ways. Adapting an Acoli proverb, she repeatedly warns her husband, Ocol, against uprooting the pumpkin, symbol of the household and tradition. She berates him for being intoxicated with Western clock time and ballroom dance. For her, Western cuisine seems soft and "slimy like mucus," book learning seems emasculating, Christianity seems abstract and contradictory. Worst of all, Ocol is infatuated with the Western conception of feminine beauty, as exemplified by Lawino's rival, a second wife humorously named Clementine and nicknamed Tina. Mimicking white women, Tina applies ghostly white face powder and blood-red lipstick; slims her waist like a hornet's; even fries, pulls, and stretches her hair to straighten it: "And the vigorous and healthy hair / Curly, springy and thick / That glistens in the sunshine / Is left listless and dead / Like the elephant grass / Scorched brown by the fierce / February sun. / It lies lifeless / Like the sad and dying banana leaves / On a hot and windless afternoon."

Initially engaging the reader through the dramatic tension of this triangular relationship, *Song of Lawino* sustains interest through lively imagery and figurative language that defamiliarize Western values and practices. When Lawino encounters Christian communion for the first time, she sees it as a bizarre, cannibalistic rite. For her, Western kissing is a revolting custom: "You kiss her open-sore lips / As white people do, / You suck slimy saliva / From each other's mouths / As white people do." From the face of the insistent Western clock dangles "a large single testicle," which "goes this way and that way / Like a sausage-fruit / In a windy storm." Lawino reaches for a dizzying variety of similes and metaphors to describe the unfamiliar Western world embraced by her husband. Indeed, the acuity of her figurative language disproves her husband's view of her as stupid. Okot's poem enriches anglophone verse through its figurative profusion, greatly indebted to Acoli proverbs and idioms. *Song of Lawino* is written in an emphatically Africanized English, frequently incorporating Acoli words and literally rendering Acoli phrases.

The view that *Song of Lawino* is purely "native" or "homebred" needs to be modified, however, to allow for the poem's culturally complex texture and influences. As director of the Uganda National Cultural Centre (1966–68) before being forced out for political reasons, Okot advocated a balanced cultural perspective, saying the Centre "must not be reactionary like some old men who reject all foreign art forms, nor must it reflect the bigoted ideas of some miseducated men who despise all things African" (*Africa's Cultural Revolution*). Okot repeatedly cited Longfellow's *Song of Hiawatha* and the biblical Song of Solomon among the precursor texts for *Song of Lawino*. He created something distinctive and new when he hybridized the oral traditions of Acoli song and speech with Western literary traditions, such as the long dramatic monologue.

Song of Lawino also embodies Okot's ambivalence toward the Western academic discipline of anthropology. Having gone to Britain as a member of the Uganda national soccer team that played barefoot at the Summer Olympics of 1956, Okot studied from 1960 to 1963 at Oxford University's acclaimed Institute of Social Anthropology, headed by the social anthropologist E. E. Evans-Pritchard. Plunged into British anthropology during some of its headiest days, Okot was deeply offended by its Eurocentrism and Christian bias. At Oxford, he wrote a thesis in social anthropology, "Oral Literature and Its Social Background Among the Acoli and Lang'o" (1964), which provided the basis for his books of anthropology and his collections of folk songs and folktales. He later wrote a searching critique of Western anthropology, *African Religions in Western Scholarship* (1970). In *Song of Lawino,* he implicitly contests the discipline's assumptions about voice, perspective, and power, even as he incorporates its categories of knowledge in chapters organized around time, religion, and other central Western concepts.

Okot p'Bitek was born in 1931, in Gulu, Uganda. His father was a Protestant school-teacher but also an accomplished dancer and storyteller from the Patiko chiefdom; his mother, known as Lawino among other names, was a famous composer of songs and a dancer. He attended Gulu High School, King's College, Budo, and the Mbara Teachers Training College. In 1953, he published his first book, a novel in Acoli entitled *Lak tar*, later translated as *White Teeth*; in 1956, an early Acoli version of *Wer pa Lawino* was rejected by a publisher's agent. In Britain, Okot first studied education at the University of Bristol and then received a law degree at the University of Wales, Aberystwyth, in 1960 before going on to Oxford. In the wake of Ugandan independence in 1962, Okot returned to teach in the extramural department at Makerere University in Kampala in 1963. During eleven years of enforced exile from Uganda, he taught African studies, sociology, and literature at the University of Nairobi, Kenya, with brief visiting appointments at the University of Texas and the University of Iowa's writing program. In the last few years of his life, he taught at the University of Ife, Nigeria, and at Makerere University.

From Song of Lawino

1. My Husband's Tongue Is Bitter

Husband, now you despise me
Now you treat me with spite
And say I have inherited the stupidity of my aunt;
Son of the Chief,
Now you compare me   5
With the rubbish in the rubbish pit,
You say you no longer want me
Because I am like the things left behind
In the deserted homestead.
You insult me   10
You laugh at me
You say I do not know the letter A
Because I have not been to school
And I have not been baptized

You compare me with a little dog,   15
A puppy.

My friend, age-mate of my brother,
Take care,
Take care of your tongue,
Be careful what your lips say.   20

First take a deep look, brother,
You are now a man
You are not a dead fruit!
To behave like a child does not befit you!

Listen Ocol, you are the son of a Chief,   25
Leave foolish behavior to little children,
It is not right that you should be laughed at in a song!
Songs about you should be songs of praise!

Stop despising people
As if you were a little foolish man.   30
Stop treating me like salt-less ash,[1]
Become barren of insults and stupidity;
Who has ever uprooted the Pumpkin?[2]

•

My clansmen, I cry
Listen to my voice: 35

1. "Salt is extracted from the ash of certain plants, and also from the ash of the dung of domestic animals. The ash is put in a container with small holes in its bottom, water is then poured on the ash, and the salty water is collected in another container placed below. The useless saltless ash is then thrown on the pathway and people tread on it" [Okot p'Bitek's note].
2. From Acoli proverb about the importance of preserving the household and tradition.

The insults of my man
Are painful beyond bearing.

My husband abuses me together with my parents;
He says terrible things about my mother
And I am so ashamed!   40

He abuses me in English
And he is so arrogant.

He says I am rubbish,
He no longer wants me!
In cruel jokes, he laughs at me,   45
He says I am primitive
Because I cannot play the guitar,
He says my eyes are dead
And I cannot read,
He says my ears are blocked   50
And cannot hear a single foreign word,
That I cannot count the coins.

He says I am like sheep,
The fool.

Ocol treats me   55
As if I am no longer a person,
He says I am silly
Like the *ojuu* insects that sit on the beer pot.

My husband treats me roughly.
The insults: 60
Words cut more painfully than sticks!
He says my mother is a witch,
That my clansmen are fools
Because they eat rats,
He says we are all Kaffirs.[3]   65
We do not know the ways of God,
We sit in deep darkness
And do not know the Gospel,
He says my mother hides her charms
In her necklace   70
And that we are all sorcerers.

My husband's tongue
Is bitter like the roots of the *lyonno* lily,
It is hot like the penis of the bee,
Like the sting of the *kalang*![4]   75
Ocol's tongue is fierce like the arrow of the scorpion,

---

3. Derived from the Arabic word for infidel, *Kaffir*
is both the name of the Xhosa-speaking tribes of
South Africa and a derogatory term for any black
person.
4. Large fruit bat (Acoli).

Deadly like the spear of the buffalo-hornet.
It is ferocious
Like the poison of a barren woman
And corrosive like the juice of the gourd.   80

·

My husband pours scorn
On Black People,
He behaves like a hen
That eats its own eggs
A hen that should be imprisoned under a basket.   85

His eyes grow large
Deep black eyes
Ocol's eyes resemble those of the Nile Perch!
He becomes fierce
Like a lioness with cubs,   90
He begins to behave like a mad hyena.

He says Black People are primitive
And their ways are utterly harmful,
Their dances are mortal sins
They are ignorant, poor and diseased!   95

Ocol says he is a modern man,
A progressive and civilized man,
He says he has read extensively and widely
And he can no longer live with a thing like me
Who cannot distinguish between good and bad,   100

He says I am just a village woman,
I am of the old type,
And no longer attractive.

He says I am blocking his progress,
My head, he says,   105
Is as big as that of an elephant
But it is only bones,
There is no brain in it,
He says I am only wasting his time.

2. The Woman with Whom I Share My Husband

Ocol rejects the old type.
He is in love with a modern woman,
He is in love with a beautiful girl
Who speaks English.

But only recently   5
We would sit close together, touching each other!

Only recently I would play
On my bow-harp[5]
Singing praises to my beloved.
Only recently he promised   10
That he trusted me completely.
I used to admire him speaking in English.

    •

Ocol is no longer in love with the old type.
He is in love with a modern girl;
The name of the beautiful one   15
Is Clementine.

Brother, when you see Clementine!
The beautiful one aspires
To look like a white woman;

Her lips are red-hot   20
Like glowing charcoal,
She resembles the wild cat
That has dipped its mouth in blood,
Her mouth is like raw yaws[6]
It looks like an open ulcer,   25
Like the mouth of a fiend!
Tina dusts powder on her face
And it looks so pale;
She resembles the wizard
Getting ready for the midnight dance;   30

She dusts the ash-dirt all over her face
And when little sweat
Begins to appear on her body
She looks like the guinea fowl!

The smell of carbolic soap   35
Makes me sick,
And the smell of powder
Provokes the ghosts in my head;
It is then necessary to fetch a goat
From my mother's brother.   40
The sacrifice over
The ghost-dance drum must sound
The ghost be laid
And my peace restored.

I do not like dusting myself with powder.   45
The thing is good on pink skin
Because it is already pale,
But when a black woman has used it

5. West African stringed instrument.
6. Infectious tropical disease marked by ulcerating lesions.

She looks as if she has dysentery;
Tina looks sickly   50
And she is slow moving,
She is a piteous sight.

Some medicine has eaten up Tina's face;
The skin on her face is gone
And it is all raw and red,   55
The face of the beautiful one
Is tender like the skin of a newly born baby!

And she believes
That this is beautiful
Because it resembles the face of a white woman!   60
Her body resembles
The ugly coat of the hyena;
Her neck and arms
Have real human skins!
She looks as if she has been struck   65
By lightning;
Or burnt like the kongoni[7]
In a fire hunt.

And her lips look like bleeding,
Her hair is long,   70
Her head is huge like that of the owl,
She looks like a witch,
Like someone who has lost her head
And should be taken
To the clan shrine!   75
Her neck is rope-like,
Thin, long and skinny
And her face sickly pale.

                               •

Forgive me, brother,
Do not think I am insulting   80
The woman with whom I share my husband!
Do not think my tongue
Is being sharpened by jealousy.
It is the sight of Tina
That provokes sympathy from my heart.   85

I do not deny
I am a little jealous.
It is no good lying,
We all suffer from a little jealousy.
It catches you unawares   90
Like the ghosts that bring fevers;
It surprises people

7. Large, African antelope.

Like earth tremors:
But when you see the beautiful woman
With whom I share my husband   95
You feel a little pity for her!

Her breasts are completely shrivelled up,
They are all folded dry skins,
They have made nests of cotton wool
And she folds the bits of cow-hide   100
In the nests
And call them breasts!

O! my clansmen
How aged modern women
Pretend to be young girls!   105

They mould the tips of the cotton nests
So that they are sharp
And with these they prick
The chests of their men!
And the men believe   110
They are holding the waists
Of young girls that have just shot up!
The modern type sleep with their nests
Tied firmly on their chests.

How many kids   115
Has this woman sucked?
The empty bags on her chest
Are completely flattened, dried.
Perhaps she has aborted many!
Perhaps she has thrown her twins   120
In the pit latrine!

Is it the vengeance ghosts
Of the many smashed eggs
That have captured her head?
How young is this age-mate of my mother?   125

•

The woman with whom I share my husband
Walks as if her shadow
Has been captured,
You can never hear
Her footsteps;   130

She looks as if
She has been ill for a long time!
Actually she is starving
She does not eat
She says she fears getting fat,   135
That the doctor has prevented her

From eating,
She says a beautiful woman
Must be slim like a white woman;

And when she walks   140
You hear her bones rattling,
Her waist resembles that of the hornet.
The beautiful one is dead dry
Like a stump,
She is meatless   145
Like a shell
On a dry river bed.

·

But my husband despises me,
He laughs at me,
He says he is too good   150
To be my husband.

Ocol says he is not
The age-mate of my grandfather
To live with someone like me
Who has not been to school.   155

He speaks with arrogance,
Ocol is bold;
He says these things in broad daylight.
He says there is no difference
Between me and my grandmother   160
Who covers herself with animal skins.

·

I am not unfair to my husband,
I do not complain
Because he wants another woman
Whether she is young or aged!   165
Who has ever prevented men
From wanting women?

Who has discovered the medicine for thirst?
The medicines for hunger
And anger and enmity   170
Who has discovered them?
In the dry season the sun shines
And rain falls in the wet season.
Women hunt for men
And men want women!   175

When I have another woman
With whom I share my husband,
I am glad.
A woman who is jealous

Of another, with whom she shares a man,   180
Is jealous because she is slow,
Lazy and shy,
Because she is cold, weak, clumsy!

The competition for a man's love
Is fought at the cooking place   185
When he returns from the field
Or from the hunt,

You win him with a hot bath
And sour porridge.
The wife who brings her meal first   190
Whose food is good to eat,
Whose dish is hot
Whose face is bright
And whose heart is clean
And whose eyes are not dark   195
Like the shadows:

The wife who jokes freely
Who eats in the open
Not in the bed room,
One who is not dull   200
Like stale beer,
Such is the woman who becomes
The head-dress keeper.

I do not block my husband's path
From his new wife.   205
If he likes, let him build for her
An iron roofed house on the hill!
I do not complain,
My grass thatched house is enough for me.

I am not angry   210
With the woman with whom
I share my husband,
I do not fear to compete with her.

All I ask
Is that my husband should stop the insults,   215
My husband should refrain
From heaping abuses on my head.
He should stop being half-crazy,
And saying terrible things about my mother.
Listen Ocol, my old friend,   220
The ways of your ancestors
Are good,
Their customs are solid
And not hollow
They are not thin, not easily breakable   225

They cannot be blown away
By the winds
Because their roots reach deep into the soil.

I do not understand
The ways of foreigners   230
But I do not despise their customs.
Why should you despise yours?

Listen, my husband,
You are the son of a Chief.
The pumpkin in the old homestead   235
Must not be uprooted!

1966

GEOFFREY HILL
b. 1932

Geoffrey Hill is a dominant and enigmatic presence in English poetry after World War
II. He is by nature reticent, sardonic, and unyielding, though his verse presents intense
feelings that crisscross. Everything he writes is conscious of itself and ultimately intel-
ligible, though the "drama of reason," as he puts it, is compatible with his admiration
for mystics such as Robert Southwell and St. John of the Cross. Hill's strenuously
paradoxical language evidences his religious yet skeptical sensibility. He writes short
poems and poetic sequences of compressed violence on large and painful subjects such
as Nazi concentration camps and the Wars of the Roses. He evokes the terror of night-
mare and then controls it through changes in perspective and by sporadic lyrical grace.
His poems exhibit a clenched decision to face the worst life has to offer. Though they
fix their eyes on misery, they purify it through their indignant terseness.

Many of the poems are on religious subjects, and Christianity sometimes appears,
very tentatively, as a healing presence. He asks, in the late long poem *The Triumph of
Love* (1998), "So what is faith if it is not / inescapable endurance?" In an early poem,
"Ovid in the Third Reich," the poet Ovid sings with seeming impropriety of love in a
world of murderers, yet he is no more out of place in Nazi Germany than are the damned
in the divine order. Hill's poems on the Holocaust are among the best in English.
Memorializing a victim of a Nazi concentration camp in "September Song," Hill vigi-
lantly prevents his rhetoric from drifting toward easy solace or identification. Freighting
every phrase with grim ironies or double meanings ("Undesirable you may have been,
untouchable / you were not"), he tweaks himself with constant verbal reminders of the
dead child's inaccessibility to him, despite their having been born one day apart. Even
as he elegizes the victims of genocide, Hill worries that his poetry, like other memorials,
helps make "their long death / Documented and safe" ("Two Formal Elegies"). In a
characteristic paradox, Hill wonders if memorials distance atrocity by making it ac-
cessible, by converting senseless violence into rational understanding and aesthetic
pleasure. Such ethical self-questioning is at the heart of his poetry, which is—in
the modernist tradition—densely allusive, syntactically oblique, and unapologetically
demanding.

Some of Hill's works purport to be history and biography. *Mercian Hymns,* regarded by some as his masterpiece, is written in a kind of chanting prose and returns to the eighth century, when Offa was king of Mercia—a large part of England. In describing Offa, Hill appears also to describe early national life, with some autobiographical elements. He pictures Offa as now hero, now antihero. (Seamus Heaney's poems about Sweeney have some of the same effect.) In *The Mystery of the Charity of Charles Péguy,* Hill presents as a martyr this twentieth-century poet, who died leading troops into battle at the Marne, yet he also subjects Péguy's Christianity, socialism, and other characteristics to severe criticism. Here again, Hill scrutinizes the ethics of language, asking whether a poet's metaphors risk not only figurative but worldly violence. Daring, occasionally witty, linguistically exciting, he seeks "those rare moments in which the inertia of language, which is also the coercive force of language, seems to have been overcome" ("Poetry as Menace and Atonement"). The sense of agonized struggle is inseparable from his achievement.

Hill was born on June 18, 1932, in Bromsgrove, Worcestershire, the only child of a police constable and his wife. He attended local schools and then Keble College of Oxford University. In 1952, while still an undergraduate, he published his first book of poems. He was a professor at the University of Leeds, then at Cambridge University, before moving to the United States in 1988. He teaches at Boston University.

In Memory of Jane Fraser

When snow like sheep lay in the fold[1]
And winds went begging at each door,
And the far hills were blue with cold,
And a cold shroud lay on the moor,

She kept the siege. And every day   5
We watched her brooding over death
Like a strong bird above its prey.
The room filled with the kettle's breath.

Damp curtains glued against the pane
Sealed time away. Her body froze   10
As if to freeze us all, and chain
Creation to a stunned repose.

She died before the world could stir.
In March the ice unloosed the brook
And water ruffled the sun's hair.   15
Dead cones upon the alder shook.

1959

---

1. Shelter for sheep.

Two Formal Elegies

For the Jews in Europe

1

Knowing the dead, and how some are disposed:
Subdued under rubble, water, in sand graves,
In clenched cinders not yielding their abused
Bodies and bonds to those whom war's chance saves
Without the law: we grasp, roughly, the song.   5
Arrogant acceptance from which song derives
Is bedded with their blood, makes flourish young
Roots in ashes. The wilderness revives,

Deceives with sweetness harshness. Still beneath
Live skin stone breathes, about which fires but play,   10
Fierce heart that is the iced brain's to command
To judgment—studied reflex, contained breath—
Their best of worlds since, on the ordained day,
This world went spinning from Jehovah's hand.

2

For all that must be gone through, their long death   15
Documented and safe, we have enough
Witnesses (our world being witness-proof).
The sea flickers, roars, in its wide hearth.
Here, yearly, the pushing midlanders stand
To warm themselves; men brawny with life,   20
Women who expect life. They relieve
Their thickening bodies, settle on scraped sand.

Is it good to remind them, on a brief screen,
Of what they have witnessed and not seen?
(Deaths of the city that persistently dies. . . ?)   25
To put up stones ensures some sacrifice.
Sufficient men confer, carry their weight.
(At whose door does the sacrifice stand or start?)

1959

Ovid in the Third Reich[2]

non peccat, quaecumque potest peccasse negare,
solaque famosam culpa professa facit.
　　　　　　　　　—(Amores, III, xiv)[3]

I love my work and my children. God
Is distant, difficult. Things happen.
Too near the ancient troughs of blood
Innocence is no earthly weapon.

I have learned one thing: not to look down　　　　　　5
So much upon the damned. They, in their sphere,
Harmonize strangely with the divine
Love. I, in mine, celebrate the love-choir.

　　　　　　　　　　　　　　　　　　　　　1968

September Song

born 19.6.32–deported 24.9.42

Undesirable you may have been, untouchable
you were not. Not forgotten
or passed over at the proper time.

As estimated, you died. Things marched,
sufficient, to that end.　　　　　　　　　　　5
Just so much Zyklon[4] and leather, patented
terror, so many routine cries.

(I have made
an elegy for myself it
is true)[5]　　　　　　　　　　　　　　　10

September fattens on vines. Roses
flake from the wall. The smoke
of harmless fires drifts to my eyes.

This is plenty. This is more than enough.

　　　　　　　　　　　　　　　　　　　　　1968

2. Ovid (43 B.C.E.–17 C.E.) was exiled from Rome by the Emperor Augustus, perhaps as a result of his poems about love.
3. Any woman is innocent who denies having sinned, and only a confession of guilt makes her guilty (Latin). These lines support Ovid's plea to his adulterous wife that she hide her doings and deny her guilt even if caught in the act; he promises to believe her.
4. Poisonous gas used in Nazi death camps.
5. Hill was born on June 18, 1932 (18.6.32, English style).

From Funeral Music[6]

William de la Pole, Duke of Suffolk: beheaded 1450
John Tiptoft, Earl of Worcester: beheaded 1470
Anthony Woodville, Earl Rivers: beheaded 1483[7]

6

My little son, when you could command marvels
Without mercy, outstare the wearisome
Dragon of sleep, I rejoiced above all—
A stranger well-received in your kingdom.
On those pristine fields I saw humankind   5
As it was named by the Father; fabulous
Beasts rearing in stillness to be blessed.
The world's real cries reached there, turbulence
From remote storms, rumour of solitudes,
A composed mystery. And so it ends.   10
Some parch for what they were; others are made
Blind to all but one vision, their necessity
To be reconciled. I believe in my
Abandonment, since it is what I have.

8

Not as we are but as we must appear,
Contractual ghosts of pity; not as we
Desire life but as they would have us live,
Set apart in timeless colloquy.
So it is required; so we bear witness,   5
Despite ourselves, to what is beyond us,
Each distant sphere of harmony forever
Poised, unanswerable. If it is without
Consequence when we vaunt and suffer, or
If it is not, all echoes are the same   10

6. "In this sequence I was attempting a florid grim music broken by grunts and shrieks. . . . *Funeral Music* could be called a commination [denunciation] and an alleluia [that is, song of praise] for the period popularly but inexactly known as the Wars of the Roses [1455–85, for the English throne, between the noble houses of York and Lancaster]. It is now customary to play down the violence of the Wars of the Roses and to present them as dynastic skirmishes fatal, perhaps, to the old aristocracy but generally of small concern to the common people. . . . In the accounts of the contemporary chroniclers it was a holocaust" (from Hill's essay on "Funeral Music").
7. "['Funeral Music'] bears an oblique dedication. In the case of Suffolk the word 'beheaded' is a retrospective aggrandisement; he was in fact butchered across the gunwale of a skiff. Tiptoft enjoyed a degree of ritual, commanding that he should be decapitated in three strokes 'in honour of the Trinity.' This was a nice compounding of orthodox humility and unorthodox arrogance. . . . The Woodville clan invites irritated dismissal: pushful, time-serving, it was really not its business to produce a man like Earl Rivers, who was something of a religious mystic. . . . Suffolk and Rivers were poets, though quite tame. Tiptoft, patron of humanist scholars, was known as the Butcher of England because of his pleasure in varying the accepted postures of judicial death" (from Hill's essay).

In such eternity. Then tell me, love,
How that should comfort us—or anyone
Dragged half-unnerved out of this worldly place,
Crying to the end 'I have not finished'.

1968

FROM MERCIAN HYMNS[8]

I

King of the perennial holly-groves, the riven sand-
stone: overlord of the M5:[9] architect of the his-
toric rampart and ditch, the citadel at Tamworth,
the summer hermitage in Holy Cross: guardian of
the Welsh Bridge and the Iron Bridge:[1] contractor   5
to the desirable new estates: saltmaster: money-
changer: commissioner for oaths: martyrologist:
the friend of Charlemagne.[2]

'I liked that,' said Offa, 'sing it again.'

II

A pet-name, a common name.[3] Best-selling brand, curt
graffito. A laugh; a cough. A syndicate. A specious
gift. Scoffed-at horned phonograph.[4]

The starting-cry of a race. A name to conjure with.

---

8. "The historical King Offa reigned over Mercia (and the greater part of England south of the Humber) in the years AD 757–796. During early medieval times he was already becoming a creature of legend. The Offa who figures in this sequence might perhaps most usefully be regarded as the presiding genius of the West Midlands, his dominion enduring from the middle of the eighth century until the middle of the twentieth (and possibly beyond). The indication of such a timespan will, I trust, explain and to some extent justify a number of anachronisms" [Hill's note].
9. Superhighway in Britain that runs through what was once Offa's kingdom.
1. Where the first iron bridge was built in England, in 1774. *Rampart:* broad mound of earth as a fortification. *Citadel at Tamworth:* fortress, at an ancient town where the historical Offa had a palace. *Summer hermitage:* summer retreat.
2. First-century king of the Franks (a confederation of German tribes) and later emperor of the West. *Saltmaster:* collector of duties paid for importing salt, earlier a valuable commodity. *Commissioner for oaths:* official in charge of agreements and contracts. *Martyrologist:* a specialist in or writer on the lives of the Christian martyrs.
3. "Cf. W. F. Bolton, *A History of Anglo-Latin Literature 597–1066,* Princeton (1967), I, p. 191: 'But Offa is a common name' " [Hill's note].
4. Old-fashioned phonographs had large horns to amplify the sound.

IV

I was invested in mother-earth,[5] the crypt of roots
    and endings. Child's-play. I abode there, bided my
    time: where the mole

shouldered the clogged wheel, his gold solidus; where
    dry-dust badgers thronged the Roman flues,[6] the   5
    long-unlooked-for mansions of our tribe.

V

So much for the elves' wergild,[7] the true governance
    of England, the gaunt warrior-gospel armoured in
    engraved stone. I wormed my way heavenward for
    ages amid barbaric ivy, scrollwork of fern.

Exile or pilgrim set me once more upon that ground: 5
    my rich and desolate childhood. Dreamy, smug-faced,
    sick on outings—I who was taken to be a king of
    some kind, a prodigy, a maimed one.

VI

The princes of Mercia were badger and raven. Thrall[8]
    to their freedom, I dug and hoarded. Orchards
    fruited above clefts. I drank from honeycombs of
    chill sandstone.

'A boy at odds in the house, lonely among brothers.'   5
    But I, who had none, fostered a strangeness; gave
    myself to unattainable toys.

Candles of gnarled resin, apple-branches, the tacky
    mistletoe. 'Look' they said and again 'look.' But
    I ran slowly; the landscape flowed away, back to   10
    its source.

---

5. "To the best of my recollection, the expression 'to invest in mother-earth' was the felicitous (and correct) definition of 'yird' given by Mr. Michael Hordern in the programme *Call My Bluff* televised on BBC 2 on Thursday January 29th 1970" [Hill's note]. *Yird*: a Scots word meaning, more literally, to bury in the earth.

6. Passageways for air, as in chimneys. *Solidus*: ancient gold coin.

7. " 'The price set upon a man according to his rank' (O.E.D.)" [Hill's note]; the money was paid to his family or overlord if he was slain, or exacted from him as a fine for a criminal act.

8. Slave.

In the schoolyard, in the cloakrooms, the children
    boasted their scars of dried snot; wrists and
    knees garnished with impetigo.[9]

VII

Gasholders, russet among fields. Milldams, marlpools[1]
    that lay unstirring. Eel-swarms. Coagulations of
    frogs; once, with branches and half-bricks, he
    battered a ditchful; then sidled away from the
    stillness and silence.   5

Ceolred[2] was his friend and remained so, even after
    the day of the lost fighter: a biplane, already
    obsolete and irreplaceable, two inches of heavy
    snub silver. Ceolred let it spin through a hole
    in the classroom-floorboards, softly, into the   10
    rat-droppings and coins.

After school he lured Ceolred, who was sniggering
    with fright, down to the old quarries, and flayed
    him. Then, leaving Ceolred, he journeyed for hours,
    calm and alone, in his private derelict sandlorry   15
    named *Albion*.[3]

X

He adored the desk, its brown-oak inlaid with ebony,
    assorted prize pens, the seals of gold and base
    metal into which he had sunk his name.

It was there that he drew upon grievances from the
    people; attended to signatures and retributions;   5
    forgave the death-howls of his rival. And there
    he exchanged gifts with the Muse of History.[4]

What should a man make of remorse, that it might
    profit his soul? Tell me. Tell everything to
    Mother, darling, and God bless.   10

9. Skin disease.
1. Pools in deposits of crumbling clay and chalk.
Gasholders: large metal receptacles for gas.
2. A ninth-century bishop of Leicester, but the
name is used here as a characteristic Anglo-Saxon
Mercian name.

3. Old Celtic name for England, as well as the
brand name of a famous make of British truck.
Sandlorry: sandtruck.
4. One of the nine Muses, ancient Greek god-
desses of literature and the arts.

He swayed in sunlight, in mild dreams. He tested the
little pears. He smeared catmint on his palm for
his cat Smut to lick. He wept, attempting to master
ancilla and *servus*.[5]

XI

Coins handsome as Nero's; of good substance and
weight. *Offa Rex*[6] resonant in silver, and the
names of his moneyers. They struck[7] with account-
able tact. They could alter the king's face.

Exactness of design was to deter imitation; muti-   5
lation if that failed. Exemplary metal, ripe for
commerce. Value from a sparse people, scrapers of
salt-pans and byres.[8]

Swathed bodies in the long ditch; one eye upstaring.
It is safe to presume, here, the king's anger. He   10
reigned forty years. Seasons touched and retouched
the soil.

Heathland, new-made watermeadow. Charlock, marsh-
marigold. Crepitant[9] oak forest where the boar
furrowed black mould, his snout intimate with   15
worms and leaves.

XVI

Clash of salutation. As keels thrust into shingle.[1]
Ambassadors, pilgrims. What is carried over? The
Frankish gift,[2] two-edged, regaled with slaughter.

The sword is in the king's hands; the crux[3] a crafts-
man's triumph. Metal effusing its own fragrance,   5
a variety of balm.[4] And other miracles, other
exchanges.

Shafts from the winter sun homing upon earth's rim.
Christ's mass: in the thick of a snowy forest the
flickering evergreen fissured with light.   10

5. Maidservant and manservant; also slave
(Latin).
6. King Offa (Latin). Nero was emperor of Rome
from 54 to 68 C.E.
7. Made coins, minted.
8. Stables for cows. *Salt-pans:* hollows near the
ocean where the water has evaporated, leaving salt
deposits.

9. Rattling, as of dead leaves.
1. Coarse gravel on the seashore.
2. The Franks formed the Frankish Empire in the
early Middle Ages. See also note 2 to stanza 1
above.
3. Hilt.
4. Aromatic, restorative preparation.

Attributes assumed, retribution entertained. What is
   borne amongst them? Too much or too little. In-
   dulgences of bartered acclaim; an expenditure, a
   hissing. Wine, urine and ashes.

XXV

Brooding on the eightieth letter of *Fors Clavigera*,[5]
   I speak this in memory of my grandmother, whose
   childhood and prime womanhood were spent in the
   nailer's darg.[6]

The nailshop stood back of the cottage, by the fold.   5
   It reeked stale mineral sweat. Sparks had furred
   its low roof. In dawn-light the troughed water
   floated a damson-bloom of dust—

not to be shaken by posthumous clamour. It is one
   thing to celebrate the 'quick forge', another   10
   to cradle a face hare-lipped by the searing wire.

Brooding on the eightieth letter of *Fors Clavigera*,
   I speak this in memory of my grandmother, whose
   childhood and prime womanhood were spent in the
   nailer's darg.   15

XXIX

'Not strangeness, but strange likeness. Obstinate,
   outclassed forefathers, I too concede, I am your
   staggeringly-gifted child.'

So, murmurous, he withdrew from them. Gran[7] lit the
   gas, his dice whirred in the ludo-cup,[8] he entered   5
   into the last dream of Offa the King.

XXX

And it seemed, while we waited, he began to walk to-
   wards us.   he vanished

he left behind coins, for his lodging, and traces of
   red mud.

1971

---

5. Series of "Letters to the Workmen and Labour-
ers of Great Britain" published regularly between
1871 and 1884 in which the English essayist,
critic, and reformer John Ruskin (1819–1900)
mingled personal experience, moralization, and
correspondence from his readers in a critique of
the capitalist economy.
6. A day's work. Hill's maternal grandmother
worked in the nail-making industry.
7. Grandmother (British diminutive).
8. *Ludo:* British form of the board game pachisi.

FROM THE MYSTERY OF THE CHARITY OF CHARLES PÉGUY[9]

1

Crack of a starting-pistol. Jean Jaurès[1]
dies in a wine-puddle. Who or what stares
through the café-window crêped in powder-smoke?
The bill for the new farce reads *Sleepers Awake.*[2]

History commands the stage wielding a toy gun,   5
rehearsing another scene. It has raged so before,
countless times; and will do, countless times more,
in the guise of supreme clown, dire tragedian.

In Brutus'[3] name martyr and mountebank
ghost Caesar's ghost, his wounds of air and ink   10
painlessly spouting. Jaurès' blood lies stiff
on menu-card, shirt-front and handkerchief.

Did Péguy kill Jaurès? Did he incite
the assassin? Must men stand by what they write
as by their camp-beds or their weaponry   15
or shell-shocked comrades while they sag and cry?

Would Péguy answer—stubbornly on guard
among the *Cahiers,*[4] with his army cape
and steely pince-nez and his hermit's beard,
brooding on conscience and embattled hope?   20

Truth's pedagogue, braving an entrenched class
of fools and scoundrels, children of the world,
his eyes caged and hostile behind glass—
still Péguy said that Hope is a little child.

Violent contrariety of men and days; calm   25
juddery bombardment of a silent film
showing such things: its canvas slashed with rain
and St Elmo's fire.[5] Victory of the machine!

The brisk celluloid clatters through the gate;
the cortège of the century dances in the street;   30

<hr>

9. These stanzas open a hundred-quatrain tribute to Charles Péguy (1873–1914), French poet, philosopher, and socialist killed in World War I.
1. In a biographical note at the end of the poem, Hill explains that during the Dreyfus Affair, in which France was politically divided over the case of a Jewish man falsely convicted of treason, Péguy was a great admirer of the pro-Dreyfus socialist leader Jean Jaurès (1859–1914). However, Hill notes, "by 1914 he was calling for his blood: figuratively, it must be said; though a young madman, who may or may not have been over-susceptible to

metaphor, almost immediately shot Jaurès through the head." The assassin believed that Jaurès's pacifism left France in danger of encroachment by imperial Germany.
2. Also a famous portion of J. S. Bach's Cantata 140.
3. Friend and coassassin of Julius Caesar.
4. Péguy founded the journal *Les Cahiers de la Quinzaine* in 1900.
5. Luminosity accompanying discharges of atmospheric electricity.

and over and over the jolly cartoon
armies of France go reeling towards Verdun.[6]

1983

To the High Court of Parliament

November 1994[7]

Where's probity in this—
                    the slither-frisk
to lordship of a kind
as rats to a bird-table?

England—now of genius   5
              the eidolon[8]—
unsubstantial yet voiding
substance like quicklime:[9]

privatize to the dead
her memory: 10
              let her wounds weep
into the lens of oblivion.

1997

From The Triumph of Love[1]

CXXI

So what is faith if it is not
inescapable endurance? Unrevisited, the ferns
are breast-high, head-high, the days
lustrous, with their hinterlands of thunder.
Light is this instant, far-seeing   5
into itself, its own
signature on things that recognize
salvation. I
am an old man, a child, the horizon
is Traherne's country.[2]   10

1998

---

6. Town in France where, in 1916, the longest
battle of World War I was fought.
7. Date when Tory members of Parliament alleg-
edly accepted bribes and a Westminster City
Council graveyard was sold.
8. Phantom.

9. Caustic chemical compound.
1. Also title of a 1681 French ballet.
2. Thomas Traherne (1637–1674), mystic poet
and religious writer, is the author of *The Centuries*,
considered English literature's first convincing
depiction of childhood experience.

SYLVIA PLATH
1932–1963

"Death is the mother of beauty," declares Wallace Stevens, and this certainly holds true for Sylvia Plath. She follows a long and distinguished line of poets who make luminous art out of the final darkness, from John Keats and Emily Dickinson to W. B. Yeats, T. S. Eliot, and Stevie Smith. Unavailable as a direct experience, death is for Plath a rich imaginative resource, an ultimate horizon for intensifying and defining poetic subjectivity. Her fascination with death is rooted in her father's, in 1940, when she was only eight. In her journals, Plath refers to her father as "the buried male muse and god-creator" and the "father-sea-god muse." She wrestles with this traumatic loss in poems such as "The Colossus" and "Daddy." Plath's father was a first-generation Prussian immigrant from Grabów, Poland. As an adult, he taught biology and German at Boston University and wrote a treatise on bees. A diabetic, he died after an infected toe became gangrenous and his leg had to be amputated. Through psychoanalysis, Plath became ever more aware that her feelings for her father were intensely ambivalent: "He was an autocrat," she told Nancy Hunter Steiner. "I adored and despised him, and I probably wished many times that he were dead. When he obliged me and died, I imagined that I had killed him" (*A Closer Look at Ariel*). Plath's poems about her father are the first in English to explore such explosive, suicidal grief and rage toward a dead parent, shattering the boundaries of domestic poetry.

Like Robert Lowell, Anne Sexton, and other poets of the "confessional school," Plath centers much of her poetry on intensely personal and forbidden subjects, such as death, suicide, female rage, and ambivalent mourning. "I've been very excited by what I feel is the new breakthrough that came with, say, Robert Lowell's *Life Studies*," Plath said in a 1962 interview, "this intense breakthrough into very serious, very personal, emotional experience which I feel has been partly taboo" (*The Poet Speaks*, 1966). Her poetry reaches into the recesses of unconscious feeling—hatred, desire, masochism, melancholia. Her work exemplifies the agonizing and yet creative relationship between pain and creativity. Courting emotional disaster, she discovered within herself areas of trauma, confusion, and heartbreak that she transmuted into some of the twentieth century's most distinguished works of art.

Yet Plath cautioned that her poetry isn't reducible to the personal experience that fueled it. Poets must refashion and remake private material, as she said in an interview (*The Poet Speaks*):

> I think my poems immediately come out of the sensuous and emotional experiences I have, but I must say I cannot sympathize with these cries from the heart that are informed by nothing except a needle or a knife, or whatever it is. I believe that one should be able to control and manipulate experiences, even the most terrifying, like madness, being tortured, this sort of experience, and one should be able to manipulate these experiences with an informed and an intelligent mind. I think that personal experience is very important, but certainly it shouldn't be a kind of shut box and mirror-looking, narcissistic experience. I believe it should be *relevant,* and relevant to the larger things, the bigger things such things as Hiroshima and Dachau and so on.

Plath is well aware that in representing her dead father as a "Fascist," "devil," and "vampire" in the poem "Daddy," she is mythologizing him, connecting her feelings with those of other victims of human aggression, which, for Plath, reached its most extreme form in the Nazi Holocaust. In a picture, the professor "stands at the blackboard," and

Plath represents herself as transfiguring this harmless image into a cleft-chin "devil." In juxtapositions that are deliberately jarring, she boldly interweaves this Gothic imagery with language from nursery rhyme, light verse, elegy, and love poetry.

The father in "Daddy," like the overbearing male figure in "Fever 103°" and "Lady Lazarus," is German, and Plath was uneasily conscious that her background was Germanic on both sides of her family, heightening her sense of connection with the horrific events of the Holocaust. Her mother, a second-generation Austrian immigrant, grew up speaking German at home. Plath's ambivalence toward her mother is at the center of one of her finest early poems, "The Disquieting Muses," an unnerving blend of the real and the fantastic, in which the mother floats off on a balloon of illusions while the daughter is tutored by grim, blank muses of death and oblivion.

Born on October 27, 1932, in Boston, and growing up in Winthrop, Massachusetts, Plath was already conscious at seventeen of the conflict between her powerful ambitions—"I want to be free—I want, I think, to be omniscient. . . . I think I would like to call myself 'The girl who wanted to be God' "—and the limiting expectations for postwar American women: "I am afraid of getting married. Spare me from cooking three meals a day—spare me from the relentless cage of routine and rote" (Letters Home). In the semiautobiographical figure of Esther Greenwood in the novel The Bell Jar (1963), Plath presents a young woman paralyzed between seemingly irreconcilable social roles: "a wonderful future beckoned and winked" as wife with "a happy home and children," or as "a famous poet," or as "a brilliant professor," or as "the amazing editor," and so forth.

Writing and publishing from an early age, Plath won a scholarship at Smith College and graduated summa cum laude. Among the poets she read most intently were Yeats, Dylan Thomas, and W. H. Auden. But after her junior year, having spent a month as guest college editor at Mademoiselle, Plath suffered a breakdown, attempted to kill herself, and was hospitalized at length—events fictionalized in The Bell Jar. Later, she spent two years on a Fulbright Scholarship at Cambridge University. In 1956, she married the English poet Ted Hughes. The couple lived in the United States for more than a year, and she taught at Smith, also enrolling in a poetry seminar given by Lowell at Boston University in which she befriended Sexton. But the reading of students' papers at Smith consumed all her energy, and after a short time in Boston, the couple returned to England, where Plath intended to spend the rest of her life. She published a volume of poems, The Colossus, in 1960. She and Hughes had two children, a girl in 1960 and a boy in 1962. In the summer of 1962, Plath learned that her husband was having an affair, and they separated a few months later, in October. By the end of 1962, Plath had moved back alone to London from the family home in Devon and brought the children with her.

Plath's final months were a period of extraordinary creativity, during which she wrote as many as three poems a day while contending with depression, small children, and the coldest winter in England in a century and a half. These poems were, she said in notes for a BBC program, "all written at about four in the morning—that still, blue, almost eternal hour before cockcrow, before the baby's cry, before the glassy music of the milkman, settling his bottles." On the morning of February 11, 1963, Plath laid out food and milk for her children, sealed the kitchen door, and put her head in the gas oven. This tragic life story is so affecting that it risks overshadowing the poetry. But the suicide the last poems seem to foretell was not inevitable. Plath seems to have wanted to be saved: she had tried to get herself committed to a psychiatric hospital (the beds were full), had arranged for an au pair to arrive the morning of the suicide (the door was locked), and had left a note with the doctor's name and telephone number.

Far from being mere symptoms in a personal pathology, Plath's poems are works of great aesthetic accomplishment and psychological insight. She transmutes experiences both everyday and extreme with imaginative daring. In "Cut," the mundane experience of accidentally cutting the tip of her thumb instead of an onion undergoes an astonishing series of metamorphoses. A household event becomes the occasion for an imaginative outpouring, the poem mimicking the intensified consciousness of the body in pain by leaping from one increasingly extravagant image to the next. In "The Applicant," a salesman's arrival at the door turns into a savage meditation on the objectification of women in traditional marriage. In "Fever 103°," Plath transforms a high temperature into a meditation on death, lust, fire, and imaginative liberation of the female body from dependence on men. The movement of a horse in "Ariel" becomes the ecstatic drive of the poetic "I" to fuse with the sublime "eye" of Being.

Plath's final style represents a major achievement, especially compared with the overwrought, highly formal artifice of her early poems, written in the arch, New Critical style of the 1950s. Even so, a poem such as "The Colossus" begins to hint at the eruption of something less smooth and deliberate, especially in its juxtapositions of the formal with the colloquial, the mythic with the mundane ("A blue sky out of the Oresteia" but also "pails of Lysol" and the contemptuous remark "It's worse than a barnyard"). The poems written in Plath's last year are wildly heterogeneous, yoking together extremes of Gothicism and gaiety, rage and tenderness. They leap from one metaphor to the next without explicit connections, riding the relentless velocity of short, incantatory, free verse lines. She said they were written, unlike earlier ones, "to be read aloud" (BBC interview). The persona in these poems is volcanic in energy, mercurial in affect, by turns mournful, sardonic, aggressive, visionary, and ruthlessly self-mocking.

The emotional ambivalence of Plath's poetry widened the affective range of lyric poetry in English. Here, motherhood is not all sugar and sweetness, but includes the "stink of fat and baby crap" ("Lesbos"). A grieving daughter can adore her father, but also rage at him: "Daddy, daddy, you bastard, I'm through." A husband may be a "vampire." Nor does the poet spare herself the same tumultuous mix of emotions. Plath even scorns her own supposedly confessional hawking of her inner emotional life for money: "There is a charge," proclaims Lady Lazarus, "For the eyeing of my scars."

Plath's example was not lost on a poet such as John Berryman, one of whose Dream Songs has him splitting open his father's casket and tearing apart his grave clothes. But for a host of women poets, including the Americans Sexton, Adrienne Rich, Maxine Kumin, and Sharon Olds, as well as the Irish Eavan Boland, the British Carol Ann Duffy, and the Indian Eunice de Souza, Plath's example has been fundamental, as evidenced by their poems of fury against fathers and mothers, of suicidal longing and triumphant rebirth, of ferocious self-definition and self-assertion. Plath created a style equal to her keen awareness of her psychic life. Venting repressed feeling, examining it with an icy calm, Plath delivered to us our inner tumult, conflict, but also power.

The Disquieting Muses[1]

Mother, mother, what illbred aunt
Or what disfigured and unsightly
Cousin did you so unwisely keep
Unasked to my christening,[2] that she

---

1. In a BBC radio program, Plath commented on this poem: "It borrows its title from the painting by Giorgio de Chirico—*The Disquieting Muses*. All through the poem I have in mind the enigmatic figures in this painting—three terrible faceless dressmaker's dummies in classical gowns, seated and standing in a weird, clear light that casts the long strong shadows characteristic of de Chirico's early work. The dummies suggest a twentieth-century version of other sinister trios of women—the Three Fates, the witches in *Macbeth*, [Thomas] De Quincey's sisters of madness."

2. Cf. the fairy tale of Sleeping Beauty: a fairy, angry over not being invited to the christening of the newborn princess, curses her to die on her fifteenth year, by pricking her finger on a spindle.

Sent these ladies in her stead   5
With heads like darning-eggs to nod
And nod and nod at foot and head
And at the left side of my crib?

Mother, who made to order stories
Of Mixie Blackshort the heroic bear,   10
Mother, whose witches always, always
Got baked into gingerbread, I wonder
Whether you saw them, whether you said
Words to rid me of those three ladies
Nodding by night around my bed,   15
Mouthless, eyeless, with stitched bald head.

In the hurricane, when father's twelve
Study windows bellied in
Like bubbles about to break, you fed
My brother and me cookies and Ovaltine   20
And helped the two of us to choir:
'Thor³ is angry: boom boom boom!
Thor is angry: we don't care!'
But those ladies broke the panes.

When on tiptoe the schoolgirls danced,   25
Blinking flashlights like fireflies
And singing the glowworm song, I could
Not lift a foot in the twinkle-dress
But, heavy-footed, stood aside
In the shadow cast by my dismal-headed   30
Godmothers, and you cried and cried:
And the shadow stretched, the lights went out.

Mother, you sent me to piano lessons
And praised my arabesques⁴ and trills
Although each teacher found my touch   35
Oddly wooden in spite of scales
And the hours of practicing, my ear
Tone-deaf and yes, unteachable.
I learned, I learned, I learned elsewhere,
From muses unhired by you, dear mother.   40

I woke one day to see you, mother,
Floating above me in bluest air
On a green balloon bright with a million
Flowers and bluebirds that never were
Never, never, found anywhere.   45
But the little planet bobbed away
Like a soap-bubble as you called: Come here!
And I faced my traveling companions.

---

3. Norse god of thunder.   4. Musical embellishments.

Day now, night now, at head, side, feet,
They stand their vigil in gowns of stone,　　　　　　50
Faces blank as the day I was born,
Their shadows long in the setting sun
That never brightens or goes down.
And this is the kingdom you bore me to,
Mother, mother. But no frown of mine　　　　　　55
Will betray the company I keep.

1959

Metaphors

I'm a riddle in nine syllables,
An elephant, a ponderous house,
A melon strolling on two tendrils.
O red fruit, ivory, fine timbers!
This loaf's big with its yeasty rising.　　　　　　5
Money's new-minted in this fat purse.
I'm a means, a stage, a cow in calf.
I've eaten a bag of green apples,
Boarded the train there's no getting off.

March 20, 1959　　　　　　　　　　　　　　　　　　1960

The Colossus

I shall never get you put together entirely,
Pieced, glued, and properly jointed.
Mule-bray, pig-grunt and bawdy cackles
Proceed from your great lips.
It's worse than a barnyard.　　　　　　5

Perhaps you consider yourself an oracle,
Mouthpiece of the dead, or of some god or other.
Thirty years now I have labored
To dredge the silt from your throat.
I am none the wiser.　　　　　　10

Scaling little ladders with gluepots and pails of Lysol
I crawl like an ant in mourning
Over the weedy acres of your brow
To mend the immense skull-plates and clear
The bald, white tumuli[5] of your eyes.　　　　　　15

A blue sky out of the Oresteia[6]
Arches above us. O father, all by yourself

5. Burial mounds.
6. Trilogy by Greek playwright Aeschylus (525–456 B.C.E.), in which the murder of King Agamem- non by his wife, Clytemnestra, is avenged by their children, Elektra and Orestes.

You are pithy and historical as the Roman Forum.
I open my lunch on a hill of black cypress.
Your fluted bones and acanthine[7] hair are littered   20

In their old anarchy to the horizon-line.
It would take more than a lightning-stroke
To create such a ruin.
Nights, I squat in the cornucopia
Of your left ear, out of the wind,   25

Counting the red stars and those of plum-color.
The sun rises under the pillar of your tongue.
My hours are married to shadow.
No longer do I listen for the scrape of a keel
On the blank stones of the landing.   30

                                                                    1960

Morning Song

Love set you going like a fat gold watch.
The midwife slapped your footsoles, and your bald cry
Took its place among the elements.

Our voices echo, magnifying your arrival. New statue.
In a drafty museum, your nakedness   5
Shadows our safety. We stand round blankly as walls.

I'm no more your mother
Than the cloud that distills a mirror to reflect its own slow
Effacement at the wind's hand.

All night your moth-breath   10
Flickers among the flat pink roses. I wake to listen:
A far sea moves in my ear.

One cry, and I stumble from bed, cow-heavy and floral
In my Victorian nightgown.
Your mouth opens clean as a cat's. The window square   15

Whitens and swallows its dull stars. And now you try
Your handful of notes;
The clear vowels rise like balloons.

February 19, 1961   1965

7. Like the acanthus leaf used atop ornate, Corinthian columns.

In Plaster

I shall never get out of this! There are two of me now:
This new absolutely white person and the old yellow one,
And the white person is certainly the superior one.
She doesn't need food, she is one of the real saints.
At the beginning I hated her, she had no personality—   5
She lay in bed with me like a dead body
And I was scared, because she was shaped just the way I was

Only much whiter and unbreakable and with no complaints.
I couldn't sleep for a week, she was so cold.
I blamed her for everything, but she didn't answer.   10
I couldn't understand her stupid behavior!
When I hit her she held still, like a true pacifist.
Then I realized what she wanted was for me to love her:
She began to warm up, and I saw her advantages.

Without me, she wouldn't exist, so of course she was grateful.   15
I gave her a soul, I bloomed out of her as a rose
Blooms out of a vase of not very valuable porcelain,
And it was I who attracted everybody's attention,
Not her whiteness and beauty, as I had at first supposed.
I patronized her a little, and she lapped it up—   20
You could tell almost at once she had a slave mentality.

I didn't mind her waiting on me, and she adored it.
In the morning she woke me early, reflecting the sun
From her amazingly white torso, and I couldn't help but notice
Her tidiness and her calmness and her patience: 25
She humored my weakness like the best of nurses,
Holding my bones in place so they would mend properly.
In time our relationship grew more intense.

She stopped fitting me so closely and seemed offish.
I felt her criticizing me in spite of herself,   30
As if my habits offended her in some way.
She let in the drafts and became more and more absent-minded.
And my skin itched and flaked away in soft pieces
Simply because she looked after me so badly.
Then I saw what the trouble was: she thought she was immortal.   35

She wanted to leave me, she thought she was superior,
And I'd been keeping her in the dark, and she was resentful—
Wasting her days waiting on a half-corpse!
And secretly she began to hope I'd die.
Then she could cover my mouth and eyes, cover me entirely,   40
And wear my painted face the way a mummy-case
Wears the face of a pharaoh, though it's made of mud and water.

I wasn't in any position to get rid of her.
She'd supported me for so long I was quite limp—
I had even forgotten how to walk or sit,   45
So I was careful not to upset her in any way
Or brag ahead of time how I'd avenge myself.
Living with her was like living with my own coffin:
Yet I still depended on her, though I did it regretfully.

I used to think we might make a go of it together—   50
After all, it was a kind of marriage, being so close.
Now I see it must be one or the other of us.
She may be a saint, and I may be ugly and hairy,
But she'll soon find out that that doesn't matter a bit.
I'm collecting my strength; one day I shall manage without her,   55
And she'll perish with emptiness then, and begin to miss me.

March 18, 1961   1962

Tulips

The tulips are too excitable, it is winter here.
Look how white everything is, how quiet, how snowed-in.
I am learning peacefulness, lying by myself quietly
As the light lies on these white walls, this bed, these hands.
I am nobody; I have nothing to do with explosions.   5
I have given my name and my day-clothes up to the nurses
And my history to the anesthetist and my body to surgeons.

They have propped my head between the pillow and the sheet-cuff
Like an eye between two white lids that will not shut.
Stupid pupil, it has to take everything in.   10
The nurses pass and pass, they are no trouble,
They pass the way gulls pass inland in their white caps,
Doing things with their hands, one just the same as another,
So it is impossible to tell how many there are.

My body is a pebble to them, they tend it as water   15
Tends to the pebbles it must run over, smoothing them gently.
They bring me numbness in their bright needles, they bring me sleep.
Now I have lost myself I am sick of baggage——
My patent leather overnight case like a black pillbox,
My husband and child smiling out of the family photo;   20
Their smiles catch onto my skin, little smiling hooks.

I have let things slip, a thirty-year-old cargo boat
Stubbornly hanging on to my name and address.
They have swabbed me clear of my loving associations.
Scared and bare on the green plastic-pillowed trolley   25
I watched my teaset, my bureaus of linen, my books

Sink out of sight, and the water went over my head.
I am a nun now, I have never been so pure.

I didn't want any flowers, I only wanted
To lie with my hands turned up and be utterly empty.
How free it is, you have no idea how free——   30
The peacefulness is so big it dazes you,
And it asks nothing, a name tag, a few trinkets.
It is what the dead close on, finally; I imagine them
Shutting their mouths on it, like a Communion tablet.   35

The tulips are too red in the first place, they hurt me.
Even through the gift paper I could hear them breathe
Lightly, through their white swaddling, like an awful baby.
Their redness talks to my wound, it corresponds.
They are subtle: they seem to float, though they weigh me down,   40
Upsetting me with their sudden tongues and their color,
A dozen red lead sinkers round my neck.

Nobody watched me before, now I am watched.
The tulips turn to me, and the window behind me
Where once a day the light slowly widens and slowly thins,   45
And I see myself, flat, ridiculous, a cut-paper shadow
Between the eye of the sun and the eyes of the tulips,
And I have no face, I have wanted to efface myself.
The vivid tulips eat my oxygen.

Before they came the air was calm enough,   50
Coming and going, breath by breath, without any fuss.
Then the tulips filled it up like a loud noise.
Now the air snags and eddies round them the way a river
Snags and eddies round a sunken rust-red engine.
They concentrate my attention, that was happy   55
Playing and resting without committing itself.

The walls, also, seem to be warming themselves.
The tulips should be behind bars like dangerous animals;
They are opening like the mouth of some great African cat,
And I am aware of my heart: it opens and closes   60
Its bowl of red blooms out of sheer love of me.
The water I taste is warm and salt, like the sea,
And comes from a country far away as health.

March 18, 1961   1962

Blackberrying

Nobody in the lane, and nothing, nothing but blackberries,
Blackberries on either side, though on the right mainly,
A blackberry alley, going down in hooks, and a sea
Somewhere at the end of it, heaving. Blackberries
Big as the ball of my thumb, and dumb as eyes   5
Ebon[8] in the hedges, fat
With blue-red juices. These they squander on my fingers.
I had not asked for such a blood sisterhood; they must love me.
They accommodate themselves to my milkbottle, flattening their sides.

Overhead go the choughs[9] in black, cacophonous flocks—   10
Bits of burnt paper wheeling in a blown sky.
Theirs is the only voice, protesting, protesting.
I do not think the sea will appear at all.
The high, green meadows are glowing, as if lit from within.
I come to one bush of berries so ripe it is a bush of flies,   15
Hanging their bluegreen bellies and their wing panes in a Chinese screen.
The honey-feast of the berries has stunned them; they believe in heaven.
One more hook, and the berries and bushes end.

The only thing to come now is the sea.
From between two hills a sudden wind funnels at me,   20
Slapping its phantom laundry in my face.
These hills are too green and sweet to have tasted salt.
I follow the sheep path between them. A last hook brings me
To the hills' northern face, and the face is orange rock
That looks out on nothing, nothing but a great space   25
Of white and pewter lights, and a din like silversmiths
Beating and beating at an intractable metal.

September 23, 1961   1962, 1965

Elm

For Ruth Fainlight[1]

I know the bottom, she says. I know it with my great tap root:[2]
It is what you fear.
I do not fear it: I have been there.

Is it the sea you hear in me,
Its dissatisfactions?   5
Or the voice of nothing, that was your madness?

---

8. Black.
9. Crows.
1. American poet (b. 1931), who lives in England.

2. Primary root; hence, anything that has a central
position in a line of development.

Love is a shadow.
How you lie and cry after it
Listen: these are its hooves: it has gone off, like a horse.

All night I shall gallop thus, impetuously,   10
Till your head is a stone, your pillow a little turf,
Echoing, echoing.

Or shall I bring you the sound of poisons?
This is rain now, this big hush.
And this is the fruit of it: tin-white, like arsenic.   15

I have suffered the atrocity of sunsets.
Scorched to the root
My red filaments burn and stand, a hand of wires.

Now I break up in pieces that fly about like clubs.
A wind of such violence   20
Will tolerate no bystanding: I must shriek.

The moon, also, is merciless: she would drag me
Cruelly, being barren.
Her radiance scathes me. Or perhaps I have caught her.

I let her go. I let her go   25
Diminished and flat, as after radical surgery.
How your bad dreams possess and endow me.

I am inhabited by a cry.
Nightly it flaps out
Looking, with its hooks, for something to love.   30

I am terrified by this dark thing
That sleeps in me;
All day I feel its soft, feathery turnings, its malignity.

Clouds pass and disperse.
Are those the faces of love, those pale irretrievables?   35
Is it for such I agitate my heart?

I am incapable of more knowledge.
What is this, this face
So murderous in its strangle of branches?——

Its snaky acids kiss.   40
It petrifies the will. These are the isolate, slow faults
That kill, that kill, that kill.

April 19, 1962   1963, 1965

The Arrival of the Bee Box

I ordered this, this clean wood box
Square as a chair and almost too heavy to lift.
I would say it was the coffin of a midget
Or a square baby
Were there not such a din in it.   5

The box is locked, it is dangerous.
I have to live with it overnight
And I can't keep away from it.
There are no windows, so I can't see what is in there.
There is only a little grid, no exit.   10

I put my eye to the grid.
It is dark, dark,
With the swarmy feeling of African hands
Minute and shrunk for export,
Black on black, angrily clambering.   15

How can I let them out?
It is the noise that appalls me most of all,
The unintelligible syllables.
It is like a Roman mob,
Small, taken one by one, but my god, together!   20

I lay my ear to furious Latin.
I am not a Caesar.
I have simply ordered a box of maniacs.
They can be sent back.
They can die, I need feed them nothing, I am the owner.   25

I wonder how hungry they are.
I wonder if they would forget me
If I just undid the locks and stood back and turned into a tree.
There is the laburnum,[3] its blond colonnades,
And the petticoats of the cherry.   30

They might ignore me immediately
In my moon suit and funeral veil.
I am no source of honey
So why should they turn on me?
Tomorrow I will be sweet God, I will set them free.   35

The box is only temporary.

October 4, 1962   1963

---

3. Type of tree.

The Applicant

First, are you our sort of a person?
Do you wear
A glass eye, false teeth or a crutch,
A brace or a hook,
Rubber breasts or a rubber crotch,   5

Stitches to show something's missing? No, no? Then
How can we give you a thing?
Stop crying.
Open your hand.
Empty? Empty. Here is a hand   10

To fill it and willing
To bring teacups and roll away headaches
And do whatever you tell it.
Will you marry it?
It is guaranteed   15

To thumb shut your eyes at the end
And dissolve of sorrow.
We make new stock from the salt.
I notice you are stark naked.
How about this suit——   20

Black and stiff, but not a bad fit.
Will you marry it?
It is waterproof, shatterproof, proof
Against fire and bombs through the roof.
Believe me, they'll bury you in it.   25

Now your head, excuse me, is empty.
I have the ticket for that.
Come here, sweetie, out of the closet.
Well, what do you think of *that*?
Naked as paper to start   30

But in twenty-five years she'll be silver,
In fifty, gold.
A living doll, everywhere you look.
It can sew, it can cook,
It can talk, talk, talk.   35

It works, there is nothing wrong with it.
You have a hole, it's a poultice.[4]
You have an eye, it's an image.

---

4. Cloth applied to wounds.

My boy, it's your last resort.
Will you marry it, marry it, marry it.   40

October 11, 1962   1963

Daddy

You do not do, you do not do
Any more, black shoe
In which I have lived like a foot
For thirty years, poor and white,
Barely daring to breathe or Achoo.   5

Daddy, I have had to kill you.
You died before I had time——
Marble-heavy, a bag full of God,
Ghastly statue with one grey toe
Big as a Frisco seal   10

And a head in the freakish Atlantic
Where it pours bean green over blue
In the waters off beautiful Nauset.
I used to pray to recover you.
Ach, du.[5]   15

In the German tongue, in the Polish town[6]
Scraped flat by the roller
Of wars, wars, wars.
But the name of the town is common.
My Polack friend   20

Says there are a dozen or two.
So I never could tell where you
Put your foot, your root,
I never could talk to you.
The tongue stuck in my jaw.   25

It stuck in a barb wire snare.
Ich, ich, ich, ich,[7]
I could hardly speak.
I thought every German was you.
And the language obscene   30

An engine, an engine
Chuffing me off like a Jew.
A Jew to Dachau, Auschwitz, Belsen.

---

5. Ah, you (German).
6. Perhaps modeled on Grabów, birthplace of the poet's father, Otto Plath.
7. I, I, I, I (German).

I began to talk like a Jew.
I think I may well be a Jew.   35

The snows of the Tyrol, the clear beer of Vienna
Are not very pure or true.
With my gypsy ancestress and my weird luck
And my Taroc pack and my Taroc pack
I may be a bit of a Jew.   40

I have always been scared of *you*,
With your Luftwaffe,[8] your gobbledygoo.
And your neat mustache
And your Aryan eye, bright blue.
Panzer-man, panzer-man, O You——   45

Not God but a swastika
So black no sky could squeak through.
Every woman adores a Fascist,
The boot in the face, the brute
Brute heart of a brute like you.   50

You stand at the blackboard, daddy,
In the picture I have of you,
A cleft in your chin instead of your foot
But no less a devil for that, no not
Any less the black man who   55

Bit my pretty red heart in two.
I was ten when they buried you.
At twenty I tried to die
And get back, back, back to you.
I thought even the bones would do.   60

But they pulled me out of the sack,
And they stuck me together with glue.
And then I knew what to do.
I made a model of you,
A man in black with a Meinkampf[9] look   65

And a love of the rack and the screw.
And I said I do, I do.
So daddy, I'm finally through.
The black telephone's off at the root,
The voices just can't worm through.   70

If I've killed one man, I've killed two——
The vampire who said he was you
And drank my blood for a year,

8. Air force (German).
9. *Mein Kampf* (German for "my battle"), the political autobiography of Adolf Hitler (1889–1945).

Seven years, if you want to know.
Daddy, you can lie back now.   75

There's a stake in your fat black heart
And the villagers never liked you.
They are dancing and stamping on you.
They always *knew* it was you.
Daddy, daddy, you bastard, I'm through.   80

October 12, 1962   1963

Fever 103°

Pure? What does it mean?
The tongues of hell
Are dull, dull as the triple

Tongues of dull, fat Cerberus[1]
Who wheezes at the gate. Incapable   5
Of licking clean

The aguey tendon, the sin, the sin.
The tinder cries.
The indelible smell

Of a snuffed candle!   10
Love, love, the low smokes roll
From me like Isadora's scarves, I'm in a fright

One scarf will catch and anchor in the wheel.[2]
Such yellow sullen smokes
Make their own element. They will not rise,   15

But trundle round the globe
Choking the aged and the meek,
The weak

Hothouse baby in its crib,
The ghastly orchid   20
Hanging its hanging garden in the air,

Devilish leopard!
Radiation turned it white
And killed it in an hour.

1. In Greek mythology, three-headed dog that guarded the gate of Hades.
2. Isadora Duncan (1877–1927), American danc-er, broke her neck and died when her scarf caught in the open-spoked wheel of her car.

Greasing the bodies of adulterers   25
Like Hiroshima ash and eating in.
The sin. The sin.

Darling, all night
I have been flickering, off, on, off, on.
The sheets grow heavy as a lecher's kiss.   30

Three days. Three nights.
Lemon water, chicken
Water, water make me retch.

I am too pure for you or anyone.
Your body   35
Hurts me as the world hurts God. I am a lantern——

My head a moon
Of Japanese paper, my gold beaten skin
Infinitely delicate and infinitely expensive.

Does not my heat astound you. And my light.   40
All by myself I am a huge camellia
Glowing and coming and going, flush on flush.

I think I am going up,
I think I may rise——
The beads of hot metal fly, and I, love, I   45

Am a pure acetylene
Virgin
Attended by roses,

By kisses, by cherubim,
By whatever these pink things mean.   50
Not you, nor him

Not him, nor him
(My selves dissolving, old whore petticoats)——
To Paradise.

October 20, 1962   1963, 1965

Cut

For Susan O'Neill Roe

What a thrill——
My thumb instead of an onion.
The top quite gone
Except for a sort of a hinge

Of skin,   5
A flap like a hat,
Dead white.
Then that red plush.

Little pilgrim,
The Indian's axed your scalp.   10
Your turkey wattle
Carpet rolls

Straight from the heart.
I step on it,
Clutching my bottle   15
Of pink fizz.

A celebration, this is.
Out of a gap
A million soldiers run,
Redcoats, every one.   20

Whose side are they on?
O my
Homunculus,[3] I am ill.
I have taken a pill to kill

The thin   25
Papery feeling.
Saboteur,
Kamikaze man——

The stain on your
Gauze Ku Klux Klan   30
Babushka[4]
Darkens and tarnishes and when

The balled
Pulp of your heart
Confronts its small   35
Mill of silence

How you jump——
Trepanned[5] veteran,
Dirty girl,
Thumb stump.   40

October 24, 1962   1963, 1965

3. Miniature person said to exist in the mind or in
the spermatozoon or egg.

4. Headkerchief.
5. With the skull removed.

Poppies in October

Even the sun-clouds this morning cannot manage such skirts.
Nor the woman in the ambulance
Whose red heart blooms through her coat so astoundingly——

A gift, a love gift
Utterly unasked for   5
By a sky

Palely and flamily
Igniting its carbon monoxides, by eyes
Dulled to a halt under bowlers.

O my God, what am I   10
That these late mouths should cry open
In a forest of frost, in dawn of cornflowers.

October 27, 1962   1963, 1965

Ariel[6]

Stasis in darkness.
Then the substanceless blue
Pour of tor[7] and distances.

God's lioness,
How one we grow,   5
Pivot of heels and knees!—The furrow

Splits and passes, sister to
The brown arc
Of the neck I cannot catch,

Nigger-eye   10
Berries cast dark
Hooks——

Black sweet blood mouthfuls,
Shadows.
Something else   15

Hauls me through air——
Thighs, hair;
Flakes from my heels.

6. Lion of God (Hebrew); the airy spirit in Shake-
speare's *Tempest*; also, the name of a horse Plath
used to ride.
7. High, rocky hill.

White
Godiva, I unpeel——   20
Dead hands, dead stringencies.

And now I
Foam to wheat, a glitter of seas.
The child's cry

Melts in the wall.   25
And I
Am the arrow,

The dew that flies
Suicidal, at one with the drive
Into the red   30

Eye, the cauldron of morning.

October 27, 1962   1963, 1965

Lady Lazarus[8]

I have done it again.
One year in every ten
I manage it——

A sort of walking miracle, my skin
Bright as a Nazi lampshade,[9]   5
My right foot

A paperweight,
My face a featureless, fine
Jew linen.

Peel off the napkin   10
O my enemy.
Do I terrify?——

The nose, the eye pits, the full set of teeth?
The sour breath
Will vanish in a day.   15

Soon, soon the flesh
The grave cave ate will be
At home on me

---

8. Lazarus was raised from the dead by Jesus (John 11.44).
9. The skins of some Jewish victims of the Nazis were supposedly used to make lampshades. The Nazis also stole gold fillings (line 78) from their victims' remains.

And I a smiling woman.
I am only thirty.
And like the cat I have nine times to die.   20

This is Number Three.
What a trash
To annihilate each decade.

What a million filaments.   25
The peanut-crunching crowd
Shoves in to see

Them unwrap me hand and foot——
The big strip tease.
Gentleman, ladies   30

These are my hands
My knees.
I may be skin and bone,

Nevertheless, I am the same, identical woman.
The first time it happened I was ten.   35
It was an accident.

The second time I meant
To last it out and not come back at all.
I rocked shut

As a seashell.   40
They had to call and call
And pick the worms off me like sticky pearls.

Dying
Is an art, like everything else.
I do it exceptionally well.   45

I do it so it feels like hell.
I do it so it feels real.
I guess you could say I've a call.

It's easy enough to do it in a cell.
It's easy enough to do it and stay put.   50
It's the theatrical

Comeback in broad day
To the same place, the same face, the same brute
Amused shout:

'A miracle!'   55
That knocks me out.
There is a charge

For the eyeing of my scars, there is a charge
For the hearing of my heart——
It really goes. 60

And there is a charge, a very large charge
For a word or a touch
Or a bit of blood

Or a piece of my hair or my clothes.
So, so, Herr Doktor. 65
So, Herr Enemy.

I am your opus,
I am your valuable,
The pure gold baby

That melts to a shriek. 70
I turn and burn.
Do not think I underestimate your great concern.

Ash, ash——
You poke and stir.
Flesh, bone, there is nothing there—— 75

A cake of soap,
A wedding ring,
A gold filling.

Herr God, Herr Lucifer,
Beware 80
Beware.

Out of the ash
I rise with my red hair
And I eat men like air.

October 23–29, 1962   1963

Edge

The woman is perfected.
Her dead

Body wears the smile of accomplishment,
The illusion of a Greek necessity

Flows in the scrolls of her toga, 5
Her bare

Feet seem to be saying:
We have come so far, it is over.

Each dead child coiled, a white serpent,
One at each little   10

Pitcher of milk, now empty.
She has folded

Them back into her body as petals
Of a rose close when the garden

Stiffens and odors bleed   15
From the sweet, deep throats of the night flower.

The moon has nothing to be sad about,
Staring from her hood of bone.

She is used to this sort of thing.
Her blacks crackle and drag.   20

February 5, 1963   1963

AUDRE LORDE
1934–1992

There was more than one Audre Lorde. "I am not one piece of myself," she wrote. "I cannot be simply a Black person, and not be a woman, too, nor can I be a woman without being a lesbian." Lorde contained multitudes, and these different voices survive and affirm themselves through her poetry. "When I say myself, I mean not only the Audre who inhabits my body but all those *feisty, incorrigible Black women* who insist on standing up and saying *I am,* and you can't wipe me out, no matter how irritating I am" ("My Words Will Be There").

Lorde's "biomythography," *Zami: A New Spelling of My Name,* is a fictionalized memoir of her coming-of-age as a lesbian, but it is also about the formation of her racial identity. She describes her vexed effort to learn from the example of her mother—a black woman defensively identifying with white norms. In "Hanging Fire" and other poems, Lorde explores this ambivalent relation to her mother's racial splitting. "I bear two women upon my back"—one black, the other white—says the speaker of "From the House of Yemanjá." The passions articulated in Lorde's poetry are potent and varied. She credited African writers with teaching her how to transmute rage and pain into poetry (her second book was entitled *Cables to Rage*). Love is also, she said, "very important because it is a source of tremendous power," and yet women "have not been taught to respect the erotic urge, the place that is uniquely female" ("My Words"). Describing lesbian eros, the vivid language of "Love Poem" combines vast archetypal landscapes—mountains, valleys, forests—with the particulars of the female body. "Some words," Lorde writes in "Coal," "are open like a diamond / on glass windows." Her best poetry is diamonded with such words, as when she describes being taught to swim in "A Question of Climate" ("cannons of salt   exploding / my nostrils' rage") or giving birth in "Now that I Am Forever with Child" ("My head rang like a fiery piston / My legs were towers between which / A new world was passing").

Lorde was born on February 18, 1934, to West Indian parents living in Harlem. She began writing poetry at twelve or thirteen. "I was very inarticulate as a youngster," she recalled. "I used to speak in poetry. I would read poems, and I would memorize them. People would say, well, what do you think, Audre. What happened to you yesterday? And I would recite a poem and somewhere in that poem there would be a line or a feeling I would be sharing. . . . And when I couldn't find the poems to express the things I was feeling, that's what started me writing poetry" ("My Words"). She received her B.A. from Hunter College in 1959, her Master of Library Science degree from Columbia University in 1961. She married in 1962 and divorced in 1970. Having worked as a librarian, taught school, and spent a year as poet-in-residence at Tougaloo College, in Mississippi, she taught at colleges in New York City including the John Jay College of Criminal Justice. In 1981, she became professor of English at Hunter College. In *The Cancer Journals* (1980), she described her battle with the cancer that ultimately would cause her death.

Coal

I
is the total black, being spoken
from the earth's inside.
There are many kinds of open
how a diamond comes into a knot of flame   5
how sound comes into a word, coloured
by who pays what for speaking.

Some words are open like a diamond
on glass windows
singing out within the passing crash of sun   10
Then there are words like stapled wagers
in a perforated book,—buy and sign and tear apart—
and come whatever wills all chances
the stub remains
and ill-pulled tooth with a ragged edge.   15
Some words live in my throat
breeding like adders. Others know sun
seeking like gypsies over my tongue
to explode through my lips
like young sparrows bursting from shell.   20
Some words
bedevil me.

Love is a word, another kind of open.
As the diamond comes into a knot of flame
I am Black because I come from the earth's inside   25
now take my word for jewel in the open light.

1968, 1976

Now that I Am Forever with Child

How the days went
While you were blooming within me
I remember each upon each—
The swelling changed planes of my body—
And how you first fluttered, then jumped   5
And I thought it was my heart.

How the days wound down
And the turning of winter
I recall, with you growing heavy
Against the wind. I thought   10
Now her hands
Are formed, and her hair
Has started to curl
Now her teeth are done
Now she sneezes.   15
Then the seed opened.
I bore you one morning just before spring—
My head rang like a firey piston
My legs were towers between which
A new world was passing.   20

From then
I can only distinguish
One thread within running hours
You . . . flowing through selves
Toward you.   25

1968

Love Poem

Speak earth and bless me with what is richest
make sky flow honey out of my hips
rigid as mountains
spread over a valley
carved out by the mouth of rain.   5

And I knew when I entered her I was
high wind in her forests hollow
fingers whispering sound
honey flowed
from the split cup   10
impaled on a lance of tongues
on the tips of her breasts on her navel
and my breath

howling into her entrances
through lungs of pain.   15

Greedy as herring-gulls
or a child
I swing out over the earth
over and over
again.   20

                                                      1974

From the House of Yemanjá[1]

My mother had two faces and a frying pot
where she cooked up her daughters
into girls
before she fixed our dinner.
My mother had two faces   5
and a broken pot
where she hid out a perfect daughter
who was not me
I am the sun and moon and forever hungry
for her eyes.   10

I bear two women upon my back
one dark and rich and hidden
in the ivory hungers of the other
mother
pale as a witch   15
yet steady and familiar
brings me bread and terror
in my sleep
her breasts are huge exciting anchors
in the midnight storm.   20

All this has been
before
in my mother's bed
time has no sense
I have no brothers   25
and my sisters are cruel.

Mother I need
mother I need
mother I need your blackness now
as the august earth needs rain.   30

---

1. "Mother of the other *Orisha* [gods and god-
desses of the Yoruba people, Western Nigeria],
Yemanjá is also the goddess of oceans. Rivers are
said to flow from her breasts. . . . Those who please
her are blessed with many children" (from Lorde's
glossary to her volume *The Black Unicorn*).

I am
the sun and moon and forever hungry
and sharpened edge
where day and night shall meet
and not be   35
one.

                                                          1978

Hanging Fire[2]

I am fourteen
and my skin has betrayed me
the boy I cannot live without
still sucks his thumb
in secret   5
how come my knees are
always so ashy
what if I die
before morning
and momma's in the bedroom   10
with the door closed.

I have to learn how to dance
in time for the next party
my room is too small for me
suppose I die before graduation   15
they will sing sad melodies
but finally
tell the truth about me
There is nothing I want to do
and too much   20
that has to be done
and momma's in the bedroom
with the door closed.

Nobody even stops to think
about my side of it   25
I should have been on Math Team
my marks were better than his
why do I have to be
the one
wearing braces   30
I have nothing to wear tomorrow
will I live long enough
to grow up

---

2. Hesitating, delaying.

and momma's in the bedroom
with the door closed.   35

1978

A Question of Climate

I learned to be honest
the way I learned to swim
dropped into the inevitable
my father's thumbs in my hairless armpits
about to give way   5
I am trying
to surface   carefully
remembering
the water's shadow-legged musk
cannons of salt   exploding   10
my nostrils' rage
and for years
my powerful breast stroke
was a declaration of war.

1986

Mark Strand
b. 1934

Mark Strand's poems are filled with a terrible strangeness, recorded in stunningly precise language. As in dreams, the laws that govern our waking lives no longer obtain, and the most extraordinary things happen. The speaker in Strand's poems often suffers from a psychic split, a process of self-alienation: "Wherever I am / I am what is missing" ("Keeping Things Whole"). Identity is an inscrutable "absence." Many of Strand's poems resonate with the last lines of Wallace Stevens's "The Snow Man," as well as that poem's frigid, windy setting: the listener, "nothing himself, beholds / Nothing that is not there and the nothing that is." Strand is drawn not to the sensual exuberance but to the darker, colder side of Stevens. Strand's free verse is spare and elemental, stripped down to stark reflections on the absence that is the self, the absence that surrounds the self, and the final absence that awaits the self.

Unlike surrealist paintings or writing, whose mysterious discontinuities they suggest, Strand's mature poems do not rebel against sense; they are unsettlingly clear and coherent. The poems smell of the fear of death, even when defiantly titled "Recovery" and "Not Dying," for as Strand remarks in "The Dance": "And who doesn't have one foot in the grave?" The expectation of rebirth, which figures in several poems, cannot relieve the psychic pressure of this fear, even though the poet hopes that "If a man fears death, / he shall be saved by his poems" ("The New Poetry Handbook"). For all their strangeness, then, his poems explore emotions and experiences that are widespread but rarely communicated, and one reads Strand's best work with a sense of surprised and fearful recognition. Anguished yet ascetic, mournful yet antic, Strand's poetry has the power to haunt, even as it seems haunted by the ghostly negations of language, loss, and death.

Strand was born on April 11, 1934, to American parents in Summerside, Prince Edward Island, Canada. He received his B.A. from Antioch College, then went to Yale University for a B.F.A. He studied under Donald Justice at the University of Iowa, spent a year in Italy on a Fulbright Scholarship, then completed his M.A. in 1962 and stayed on at Iowa as an instructor for three years. In 1965, he went to Rio de Janeiro as Fulbright Lecturer at the University of Brazil; since then, he has taught at a number of American universities, including Utah, Johns Hopkins, and Chicago. The author of short narratives, children's books, and art criticism, he has also edited a wide variety of anthologies, including volumes of European, Mexican, and South American writers. The winner of a MacArthur Fellowship in 1987, the Bollingen Prize in 1993, and the Pulitzer Prize in 1999, he was the U.S. poet laureate in 1990–91.

Keeping Things Whole

In a field
I am the absence
of field.
This is
always the case.   5
Wherever I am
I am what is missing.

When I walk
I part the air
and always   10
the air moves in
to fill the spaces
where my body's been.

We all have reasons
for moving.   15
I move
to keep things whole.

1964

Eating Poetry

Ink runs from the corners of my mouth.
There is no happiness like mine.
I have been eating poetry.

The librarian does not believe what she sees.
Her eyes are sad   5
and she walks with her hands in her dress.

The poems are gone.
The light is dim.
The dogs are on the basement stairs and coming up.

Their eyeballs roll,   10
their blond legs burn like brush.
The poor librarian begins to stamp her feet and weep.

She does not understand.
When I get on my knees and lick her hand,
she screams.   15

I am a new man.
I snarl at her and bark.
I romp with joy in the bookish dark.

1968

The Prediction

That night the moon drifted over the pond,
turning the water to milk, and under
the boughs of the trees, the blue trees,
a young woman walked, and for an instant

the future came to her: 5
rain falling on her husband's grave, rain falling
on the lawns of her children, her own mouth
filling with cold air, strangers moving into her house,

a man in her room writing a poem, the moon drifting into it,
a woman strolling under its trees, thinking of death,   10
thinking of him thinking of her, and the wind rising
and taking the moon and leaving the paper dark.

1970

In Celebration

You sit in a chair, touched by nothing, feeling
the old self become the older self, imagining
only the patience of water, the boredom of stone.
You think that silence is the extra page,
you think that nothing is good or bad, not even   5
the darkness that fills the house while you sit watching
it happen. You've seen it happen before. Your friends
move past the window, their faces soiled with regret.
You want to wave but cannot raise your hand.

You sit in a chair. You turn to the nightshade[1] spreading   10
a poisonous net around the house. You taste
the honey of absence. It is the same wherever
you are, the same if the voice rots before
the body, or the body rots before the voice.
You know that desire leads only to sorrow, that sorrow   15
leads to achievement which leads to emptiness.
You know that this is different, that this
is the celebration, the only celebration,
that by giving yourself over to nothing,
you shall be healed. You know there is joy in feeling   20
your lungs prepare themselves for an ashen future,
so you wait, you stare and you wait, and the dust settles
and the miraculous hours of childhood wander in darkness.

                                                            1973

FROM ELEGY FOR MY FATHER

(Robert Strand 1908–1968)

6. The New Year

It is winter and the new year.
Nobody knows you.
Away from the stars, from the rain of light,
You lie under the weather of stones.
There is no thread to lead you back.   5
Your friends doze in the dark
Of pleasure and cannot remember.
Nobody knows you. You are the neighbour of nothing.
You do not see the rain falling and the man walking away,
The soiled wind blowing its ashes across the city.   10
You do not see the sun dragging, the moon like an echo.
You do not see the bruised heart go up in flames,
The skulls of the innocent turn into smoke.
You do not see the scars of plenty, the eyes without light.
It is over. It is winter and the new year.   15
The meek are hauling their skins into heaven.
The hopeless are suffering the cold with those who have nothing to hide.
It is over and nobody knows you.
There is starlight drifting on the black water.
There are stones in the sea no one has seen.   20
There is a shore and people are waiting.
And nothing comes back.

---

1. Or deadly nightshade, a poisonous plant.

Because it is over.
Because there is silence instead of a name.
Because it is winter and the new year.   25

1973

Poor North

It is cold, the snow is deep,
the wind beats around in its cage of trees,
clouds have the look of rags torn and soiled with use,
and starlings peck at the ice.
It is north, poor north. Nothing goes right.   5

The man of the house has gone to work,
selling chairs and sofas in a failing store.
His wife stays home and stares from the window into the trees,
trying to recall the life she lost, though it wasn't much.
White flowers of frost build up on the glass.   10

It is late in the day. Brants and Canada geese are asleep
on the waters of St Margaret's Bay.
The man and his wife are out for a walk; see how they lean
into the wind; they turn up their collars
and the small puffs of their breath are carried away.   15

1978

The Idea

for Nolan Miller[2]

For us, too, there was a wish to possess
Something beyond the world we knew, beyond ourselves,
Beyond our power to imagine, something nevertheless
In which we might see ourselves; and this desire
Came always in passing, in waning light, and in such cold   5
That ice on the valley's lakes cracked and rolled,
And blowing snow covered what earth we saw,
And scenes from the past, when they surfaced again,
Looked not as they had, but ghostly and white
Among false curves and hidden erasures;   10
And never once did we feel we were close
Until the night wind said, 'Why do this,
Especially now? Go back to the place you belong';
And there appeared, with its windows glowing, small,

---

2. American editor and college professor (b. 1912), who inspired Strand to begin writing poetry.

In the distance, in the frozen reaches, a cabin;   15
And we stood before it, amazed at its being there,
And would have gone forward and opened the door,
And stepped into the glow and warmed ourselves there,
But that it was ours by not being ours,
And should remain empty. That was the idea.   20

                                                            1990

FROM DARK HARBOR

XX

Is it you standing among the olive trees
Beyond my courtyard? You in the sunlight
Waving me closer with one hand while the other

Shields your eyes from the brightness that turns
All that is not you dead white? Is it you   5
Around whom the leaves scatter like foam?

You in the murmuring night that is scented
With mint and lit by the distant wilderness
Of stars? Is it you? Is it really you

Rising from the script of waves, the length   10
Of your body casting a sudden shadow over my hand
So that I feel how cold it is as it moves

Over the page? You leaning down and putting
Your mouth against mine so I should know
That a kiss is only the beginning   15

Of what until now we could only imagine?
Is it you or the long compassionate wind
That whispers in my ear: alas, alas?

XXX

There is a road through the canyon,
A river beside the road, a forest
If there is more, I haven't seen it yet.

Still, it is possible to say this has been
An amazing century for fashion if for nothing else;   5
The way brave models held back their tears

When thinking of the millions of Jews and Serbs
That Hitler killed, and how the photographer
Steadied his hand when he considered

The Muzhiks[3] that Stalin took care of.   10
The way skirts went up and down; how breasts
Were in, then out; and the long and the short of hair.

But the road that winds through the canyon
Is covered with snow, and the river flows
Under the ice. Cross-country skiers are moving   15

Like secrets between the trees of the glassed-in forest.
The day has made a fabulous cage of cold around
My face. Whenever I take a breath I hear cracking.

                                                                        1993

---

3. Russian peasants, millions of whom died as the result of the brutal policies of Russian dictator Joseph
Stalin (1879–1953).

WOLE SOYINKA
b. 1934

Born on July 13, 1934, in Abeokuta, near Ibadan, in western Nigeria, Wole Soyinka
became in 1986 the first black African writer to receive the Nobel Prize in Literature.
His major work has been in theater, but early in his career he published two richly
textured volumes of poetry, *Idanre & Other Poems* (1967) and *The Shuttle in the Crypt*
(1972), with *Mandela's Earth* coming later (1988). Poet, playwright, director, actor,
novelist, and essayist, Soyinka has been passionate and eloquent in denouncing both
the degradations of Western imperialism and the more recent, internal colonization of
Africa by indigenous dictators and thugs. His courage has landed him repeatedly in
Nigerian jails, with periods of solitary confinement. As early as the critical moment of
Nigeria's independence celebrations, Soyinka was willing to ask skeptical questions
about the postcolonial fate of sub-Saharan Africa. His pessimism about Africa's self-
torment and carnage has deepened in recent decades.

Repressive regimes are not alone in being irked by Soyinka's independence of mind.
Among fellow African writers, he has been criticized for nearly opposite reasons. Nativ-
ists have seen him as a "cultural mulatto," overly indebted to Western models; they
remember that he was an early detractor of the Afrocentrist movement called negritude.
At the same time, Marxist and feminist critics have attacked him for, as they see it,
irresponsibly championing aesthetics over politics, as well as for celebrating a native
Yoruba culture that is said to be feudal and sexist. For many Nigerian critics, Soyinka's
writing isn't political enough, while it is often too political for metropolitan tastes. In
the West, his work, like that of other postcolonial writers, has not always been welcomed
within the traditionally Eurocentric curriculum of English departments. At Cambridge
University in 1973–74, Soyinka found himself delivering a series of lectures through
the department of anthropology instead of English, which was apparently unable to, as
he put it, "believe in any such mythical beast as 'African Literature' " (*Myth, Literature*

and the African World). Yet amid all the insults, attacks, and provocations, Soyinka has remained stubbornly, perhaps heroically faithful to his own idiom and vision.

In its citation for the Nobel Prize, the Swedish Academy observed that Soyinka "has his roots in the Yoruba people's myths, rites and cultural patterns, which in their turn have historical links to the Mediterranean region. Through his education in his native land and in Europe he has also acquired deep familiarity with western culture." Soyinka's primary achievement in poetry has been to find a compelling way of hybridizing English literary paradigms with Yoruba oral traditions. His diction and rhetorical strategies draw on Elizabethan and Jacobean dramatic models—high flown, flamboyant, and exuberant. Especially in his early work, he loads individual lines with a verbal extravagance and density that recall the language of the English Renaissance. The influence of Anglo-modernist poets can also be seen in Soyinka's deliberate opacity, gnarled compression, satiric grotesquerie, tonal instability, mythic archetypalism, and delight in incongruous, even violent juxtapositions.

But it would be wrong to see Soyinka's literary language as merely recuperating archaic English models or recapitulating Anglo-modernism. The syntactic elasticity of Yoruba exerts considerable pressure on his early English-language poetry. These are often difficult poems to puzzle out, in part because of the intercultural effect of Soyinka's hybridization of two syntactic systems. In his frequent inversions of word order, he sometimes delays the introduction of his main verb or subject, forcing English syntax to stretch beyond its normal breaking point. His energetic wordplay likewise owes much to Yoruba speech practices. He splits and extends puns until they refract a rich array of meanings. His Africanization of the English language finds its macrocosmic equivalent in Soyinka's yoking together of Yoruba cosmologies—particularly such mythological figures in the Yoruba pantheon as Ogun (god of iron, thunder, roads, war, creation, and destruction)—with the experience of modernization and Western technology.

After attending Government College and University College, in Ibadan, where the poet Christopher Okigbo was among his classmates, Soyinka continued his studies on a scholarship at the University of Leeds, in England, earning an undergraduate degree in 1958 and a doctorate in 1973. He founded a national theater in Nigeria in 1960. Having attempted to mediate between the sides in the Nigerian Civil War, Soyinka was imprisoned for two years (1967–69) for supposedly conspiring with Igbo rebels to form a new secessionist state of Biafra. Forced into exile after the war, he endured a second exile from 1994 to 1998 under the brutal dictatorship of Sani Abacha. He has taught at universities in Ibadan and Ife, as well as at Cambridge, Yale, Cornell, and Emory.

Telephone Conversation

The price seemed reasonable, location
Indifferent. The landlady swore she lived
Off premises. Nothing remained
But self-confession. 'Madam', I warned,
'I hate a wasted journey—I am African.'   5
Silence. Silenced transmission of
Pressurised good-breeding. Voice, when it came,
Lip-stick coated, long gold-rolled
Cigarette-holder pipped. Caught I was, foully.

'HOW DARK?' . . . I had not misheard . . . 'ARE YOU LIGHT   10
'OR VERY DARK?' Button B. Button A.[1] Stench
Of rancid breath of public hide-and-speak.
Red booth. Red pillar-box.[2] Red double-tiered
Omnibus[3] squelching tar. It *was* real! Shamed
By ill-mannered silence, surrender   15
Pushed dumbfoundment to beg simplification.
Considerate she was, varying the emphasis—

'ARE YOU DARK? OR VERY LIGHT?' Revelation came.
'You mean—like plain or milk chocolate?'
Her assent was clinical, crushing in its light   20
Impersonality. Rapidly, wave-length adjusted,
I chose. 'West African sepia'[4]—and as afterthought,
'Down in my passport.' Silence for spectroscopic[5]
Flight of fancy, till truthfulness clanged her accent
Hard on the mouthpiece. 'WHAT'S THAT?' conceding   25
'DON'T KNOW WHAT THAT IS.' 'Like brunette.'

'THAT'S DARK, ISN'T IT?' 'Not altogether.
'Facially, I am brunette, but madam, you should see
'The rest of me. Palm of my hand, soles of my feet
'Are a peroxide blonde. Friction, caused—   30
'Foolishly madam—by sitting down, has turned
'My bottom raven black—One moment madam'—sensing
Her receiver rearing on the thunderclap
About my ears—'Madam', I pleaded, 'Wouldn't you rather
'See for yourself?'   35

                            1960, 1962

Death in the Dawn

Driving to Lagos[6] one morning a white cockerel flew out of the dusk
and smashed itself against my windscreen. A mile further I came
across a motor accident and a freshly dead man in the smash.

Traveller, you must set out
At dawn. And wipe your feet upon
The dog-nose wetness of earth.

Let sunrise quench your lamps, and watch
Faint brush pricklings in the sky light   5
Cottoned feet to break the early earthworm
On the hoe. Now shadows stretch with sap
Not twilight's death and sad prostration

1. Buttons on old British telephones.
2. Mailbox.
3. Double-decker bus.
4. Reddish brown.
5. Related to study of the spectrum.
6. Largest city in Nigeria.

This soft kindling, soft receding breeds
Racing joys and apprehensions for   10
A naked day, burdened hulks retract,
Stoop to the mist in faceless throng
To wake the silent markets—swift, mute
Processions on grey byways. . . .

          On this   15
Counterpane, it was—
Sudden winter at the death
Of dawn's lone trumpeter, cascades
Of white feather-flakes, but it proved
A futile rite. Propitiation sped   20
Grimly on, before.

    The right foot for joy, the left, dread
    And the mother prayed, Child
    May you never walk
    When the road waits, famished.[7]   25

Traveller you must set forth
At dawn
I promise marvels of the holy hour
Presages as the white cock's flapped
Perverse impalement—as who would dare   30
The wrathful wings of man's Progression. . . .

But such another Wraith! Brother,
Silenced in the startled hug of
Your invention—is this mocked grimace
This closed contortion—I?   35

                    1967

Around Us, Dawning

Jet flight

This beast was fashioned well; it prowls
The rare selective heights
And spurns companionship with bird

Wings are tipped in sulphurs
Scouring grey recesses of the void   5
To a linear flare of dawns

Red haloes through the ports wreathe us
Passive martyrs, bound to a will of rotors

---

7. African proverb.

Yielding ours,
To the alien mote   10
The hidden ache . . . when
Death makes a swift descent

The mountains range in spire on spire
Lances at the bold carbuncle[8]
On the still night air. I am light honed   15

To a still point in the incandescent
Onrush, a fine ash in the beast's sudden
Dessication when the sun explodes.

1967

Massacre, October '66

Written in Tegel[9]

Shards of sunlight touch me here
Shredded in willows. Through stained-glass
Fragments on the lake I sought to reach
A mind at silt-bed

The lake stayed cold   5
I swam in an October flush of dying leaves
The gardener's labour flew in seasoned scrolls
Lettering the wind

Swept from painted craft
A mockery of waves remarked this idyll sham   10
I trod on acorns; each shell's detonation
Aped the skull's uniqueness.

Came sharper reckoning—
This favoured food of hogs cannot number high
As heads still harshly crop to whirlwinds   15
I have briefly fled

The oak rains a hundred more
A kind confusion to arithmetics of death:
Time to watch autumn the removal man
Dust down rare canvases   20

8. Skin inflammation.
9. Amidst the political turmoil preceding the Nigerian Civil War, thousands of members of the Igbo ethnic group were slaughtered in northern Nigeria by the Hausa army between July and October 1966. Tegel is in Germany.

To let a loud resolve of passion
Fly to a squirrel, burnished light and copper fur
A distant stance without the lake's churchwindows
And for a stranger, love.

A host of acorns fell, silent   25
As they are silenced all, whose laughter
Rose from such indifferent paths, oh God
They are not strangers all

Whose desecration mocks the word
Of peace—*salaam aleikun*[1]—not strangers any   30
Brain of thousands pressed asleep to pig fodder—
Shun pork the unholy—cries the priest.

I borrow seasons of an alien land
In brotherhood of ill, pride of race around me
Strewn in sunlit shards. I borrow alien lands   35
To stay the season of a mind.

                                                    1967

Dragonfly at My Windowpane

So when I offer me, a medium as
The windowpane, you beat upon it
Frantic wings against unyielding tolerance?

Yet did I envy this, the unambiguous pane
And thought it clarity enough. But you must   5
War upon it, wings of frosted light,

And charge in thunderclaps? Each dive
Yields proof enough; your parchment shavings read:
Even clarity masks stubborn substance.

And shall this image I present not stay   10
Its own determined shield? Much dross
Much stone, much jeweled earth and fire

Have fed the stressing of my wall of light.
Let it content you how in me
I yield a stark view of the world, and trust   15

No inner warp but smudges left
By probing hands, dust of faith-flimsy wings
Distort true vision.

---

1. Peace be with you (Arabic); a common Islamic greeting. The Hausa ethnic group is predominantly
Muslim.

When darkness gathers I may dance
The world in fey[2] reflections; or splay its truths   20
In a shadow play of doubts.

1988

2. Visionary.

AMIRI BARAKA
1934–2014

"Let my poems be a graph of me," Amiri Baraka (then LeRoi Jones) wrote in an early poem, "Balboa, the Entertainer," and his first poems find joy in the liberty of art, in the fashioning of works that make their own rules. In 1959, he wrote, in accordance with Charles Olson's concepts of projective verse and field composition, "There cannot be anything I must *fit* the poem into. Everything must be made to fit into the poem. There must not be any preconceived notion or *design* for what the poem ought to be" ("How You Sound??"). Baraka's early poems, which have affinities with Black Mountain and Beat poetry, are personal and questioning. They explore domestic tenderness and satisfaction, though the poet frequently returns to thoughts of his own death.

A transformative visit to Cuba, in 1960, led Baraka to conclude that most of American life was socially useless and that trying to create a multiracial society was pointless. He began to forsake the individualist Beat aesthetic for black nationalism. In *Blues People* (1963), a powerful book about the abiding influence of the blues and the creation of black music in white America, he describes his progressive alienation: "To understand that you are black in a society where black is an extreme liability is one thing, but to understand that it is the *society* that is lacking and impossibly deformed, and not *yourself*, isolates you even more."

Baraka condemned what he called the "superstructure of filth Americans call their way of life" and exhorted his fellow blacks to abandon the American way of life and to work to destroy it ("An Exploration of the Work"). He had once described art as the "most beautiful resolution of energies that in another context might be violent to myself or anyone else," and for a time he wrote his poems to make a life for himself within a hostile society (*San Francisco Chronicle,* August 23, 1964). From the 1960s on, he no longer sought an alternative to violence, and his social passion and his poetry fused. Yet for all the changes in Baraka's political and aesthetic philosophy, his mature poetry displays the improvisatory energy and spontaneity that jazz achieves in music. In their bold leaps of figuration, abrupt tonal shifts from the sardonic to the explosive, rapid runs of stresses, compression of high diction and the vernacular, wild scattering of lines across the page, erratic punctuation, polyphonic voicing, chants and rants and calls, his poems approach the emotional intensity, humor, and resistant anger of post-bebop jazz.

Baraka was born Leroy (later changed to Leroi) Jones on October 7, 1934, in Newark, New Jersey. He was clearly precocious and completed high school two years early. He then entered Howard University, where the poet Sterling Brown was among his teachers. After flunking out of school, he spent two years as a weatherman and gunner in the U. S. Air Force, until he was dishonorably discharged, in 1957, because of his suspected communism. "The Howard thing," Baraka said in a 1964 interview, "let me understand the Negro sickness. They teach you how to pretend to be white. But the

Air Force made me understand the white sickness. It shocked me into realizing what was happening to me and others. By oppressing Negroes, the whites have become oppressors, twisted in that sense of doing bad things to people and justifying them finally, convincing themselves they are right, as people have always convinced themselves."

In 1957, Baraka moved to New York City and joined the bohemian life of lower Manhattan, where his associates included Frank O'Hara and Allen Ginsberg, writers who shared his interest in people living on the edge of American society. An active figure in the New York literary underground, he and his first wife, the Jewish Beat writer Hettie Cohen, published *Yugen*, a poetry magazine; he was coeditor of a literary newsletter called *Floating Bear*; and in 1961, he helped found the American Theatre for Poets. He was also a brilliant and iconoclastic jazz reviewer, publishing in *Kulchur* and other magazines. Bebop was still vital in New York, but the "new music" of Ornette Coleman, John Coltrane, and other musicians was radically transforming the harmonies and rhythms of jazz. (Later, Baraka performed and recorded his poetry with leading jazz musicians.)

Baraka was searching for indigenous artistic models in African American jazz and blues, and he sharply criticized black poets who turned to Euro-American models instead of the emotionally charged music of Bessie Smith, Billie Holiday, or Ray Charles ("The Myth of a Negro Literature"). In the mid-1960s, he began to make his reputation as a dramatist. His short play *Dutchman,* an encounter in a subway between a young African American and a white woman that ends in a surprising murder, had a long run off-Broadway. In 1965, deeply disturbed by the assassination of Malcolm X, whose death is mourned in "A Poem for Black Hearts," Baraka left his mixed-race family and Greenwich Village and moved uptown to Harlem. Eager to find a focus for a black community that would use the arts, Baraka founded the Black Arts Repertory Theater/School. In 1966, he moved again, this time to the Newark slums, where he set up a community called Spirit House. In 1967, he adopted the Bantuized Muslim name Imamu ("spiritual leader") Ameer ("blessed") Baraka ("prince"), shortened and modified in the early 1970s to Amiri Baraka. During the Newark riots in the summer of 1967, Baraka was beaten by police, arrested, and charged with carrying a concealed weapon; he was convicted, and to justify the unusually heavy sentence, the judge quoted lines from the prose poem "Black People!": "We must make our own World, man, our own world, and we can not do this unless the white man is dead. Let's get together and kill him my man, let's get to gather the fruit of the sun."

Jailed for contempt, Baraka was eventually acquitted in a retrial. In 1968, he founded the Black Community Development and Defense Organization, a group then composed of a hundred men and fifty women; they wore traditional African dress, spoke Swahili as well as English, and practiced Islam. He played an increasingly important role in Newark's politics, in national black politics, and in relations between the African American community and the newly independent nations of sub-Saharan Africa. In 1974, he denounced black nationalism as racist and embraced Third World socialism. From 1979 to 1999, he taught in the Department of Africana Studies at the State University of New York, Stony Brook. He lived for the remainder of his life in Newark. Central to the Black Arts Movement of the 1960s, he continued to write fiercely witty poems, such as the epigrammatic series *Wise, Why's, Y's,* as well as increasingly elegiac and allusive jazz poems, such as "Monk's World"—a tribute to an idiosyncratic genius and to the music that inspired Baraka throughout his career.

An Agony. As Now

I am inside someone
who hates me. I look
out from his eyes. Smell
what fouled tunes come in
to his breath. Love his   5
wretched women.

Slits in the metal, for sun. Where
my eyes sit turning, at the cool air
the glance of light, or hard flesh
rubbed against me, a woman, a man,   10
without shadow, or voice, or meaning.

This is the enclosure (flesh,
where innocence is a weapon. An
abstraction. Touch. (Not mine.
Or yours, if you are the soul I had   15
and abandoned when I was blind and had
my enemies carry me as a dead man
(if he is beautiful, or pitied.

It can be pain. (As now, as all his
flesh hurts me.) It can be that. Or   20
pain. As when she ran from me into
that forest.
          Or pain, the mind
silver spiraled whirled against the
sun, higher than even old men thought   25
God would be. Or pain. And the other. The
yes. (Inside his books, his fingers. They
are withered yellow flowers and were never
beautiful.) The yes. You will, lost soul, say
'beauty.' Beauty, practiced, as the tree. The   30
slow river. A white sun in its wet sentences.

Or, the cold men in their gale. Ecstasy. Flesh
or soul. The yes. (Their robes blown. Their bowls
empty. They chant at my heels, not at yours.) Flesh
or soul, as corrupt. Where the answer moves too quickly. 35
Where the God is a self, after all.)

Cold air blown through narrow blind eyes. Flesh,
white hot metal. Glows as the day with its sun.
It is a human love, I live inside. A bony skeleton
you recognize as words or simple feeling.   40

But it has no feeling. As the metal, is hot, it is not,
given to love.

It burns the thing
inside it. And that thing
screams.   45

                                                          1964

A Poem for Speculative Hipsters

He had got, finally,
to the forest
of motives. There were no
owls, or hunters. No Connie Chatterleys[1]
resting beautifully   5
on their backs, having casually
brought socialism
to England.
              Only ideas,
and their opposites.   10
              Like,
        he was *really*
        nowhere.

                                                          1964

A Poem for Black Hearts

For Malcolm's[2] eyes, when they broke
the face of some dumb white man, For
Malcolm's hands raised to bless us
all black and strong in his image
of ourselves, For Malcolm's words   5
fire darts, the victor's tireless
thrusts, words hung above the world
change as it may, he said it, and
for this he was killed, for saying,
and feeling, and being/change, all   10
collected hot in his heart, For Malcolm's
heart, raising us above our filthy cities,
for his stride, and his beat, and his address
to the grey monsters of the world, For Malcolm's
pleas for your dignity, black men, for your life,   15
black man, for the filling of your minds
with righteousness. For all of him dead and
gone and vanished from us, and all of him which
clings to our speech black god of our time.

---

1. The heroine of *Lady Chatterley's Lover*, by the English writer D. H. Lawrence (1885–1930); married to an impotent aristocrat, she finds sexual and spiritual salvation with a working-class lover.

2. Malcolm X (1925–1965), African American leader assassinated by members of the Nation of Islam, an American Muslim organization that Malcolm X had left in 1964.

For all of him, and all of yourself, look up,   20
black man, quit stuttering and shuffling, look up,
black man, quit whining and stooping, for all of him,
For Great Malcolm a prince of the earth, let nothing in us rest
until we avenge ourselves for his death, stupid animals
that killed him, let us never breathe a pure breath if   25
we fail, and white men call us faggots till the end of
the earth.

1969

Legacy

(For Blues People)

In the south, sleeping against
the drugstore, growling under
the trucks and stoves, stumbling
through and over the cluttered eyes
of early mysterious night. Frowning   5
drunk waving moving a hand or lash.
Dancing kneeling reaching out, letting
a hand rest in shadows. Squatting
to drink or pee. Stretching to climb
pulling themselves onto horses near   10
where there was sea (the old songs
lead you to believe). Riding out
from this town, to another, where
it is also black. Down a road
where people are asleep. Towards   15
the moon or the shadows of houses.
Towards the songs' pretended sea.

1969

A New Reality Is Better Than a New Movie!

How will it go, crumbling earthquake, towering inferno, juggernaut,[3] vol-
    cano, smashup,
in reality, other than the feverish nearreal fantasy of the capitalist flunky
    film hacks
tho they sense its reality breathing a quake inferno scar on their throat
    even snorts of
100% pure cocaine cant cancel the cold cut of impending death to this
    society. On all the

---

3. Massive force or vehicle that moves forward irresistibly and crushes anything in its path. *The Towering Inferno* is Irwin Allen and John Guillermin's 1974 movie about a skyscraper on fire.

screens of america, the joint blows up every hour and a half for two dollars   5
   an fifty cents.
They have taken the niggers out to lunch, for a minute, made us partners
   (nigger charlie) or
surrogates (boss nigger) for their horror. But just as superafrikan mobutu
   cannot leopardskinhat his
way out of responsibility for lumumba's death,[4] nor even with his incred-
   ible billions rockefeller
cannot even save his pale ho's titties in the crushing weight of things as
   they really are.
How will it go, does it reach you, getting up, sitting on the side of the bed,   10
   getting ready
to go to work. Hypnotized by the machine, and the cement floor, the
   jungle treachery of trying
to survive with no money in a money world, of making the boss 100,000
   for every 200 dollars
you get, and then having his brother get you for the rent, and if you want
   to buy the car you
helped build, your downpayment paid for it, the rest goes to buy his old
   lady a foam rubber
rhinestone set of boobies for special occasions when kissinger drunkenly   15
   fumbles with
her blouse, forgetting himself.[5]
If you dont like it, what you gonna do about it. That was the question we
   asked each other, &
still right regularly need to ask. You dont like it? Whatcha gonna do, about
   it??
The real terror of nature is humanity enraged, the true technicolor spec-
   tacle that hollywood
cant record. They cant even show you how you look when you go to work,   20
   or when you come back.
They cant even show you thinking or demanding the new socialist reality,
   its the ultimate tidal
wave. When all over the planet, men and women, with heat in their hands,
   demand that society
be planned to include the lives and self determination of all the people
   ever to live. That is
the scalding scenario with a cast of just under two billion that they dare
   not even whisper.
Its called, "We Want It All . . . The Whole World!"   25

1976

---

4. Patrice Lumumba, a leader in the bloody strug-
gle for power that followed the independence of
Zaire (formerly the Belgian Congo) was murder-
ed, probably by Belgian operatives, in 1961; the
strong-arm president Sese Seko Mobutu was
placed in power by the American CIA to restore
order.
5. Henry Kissinger (b. 1923), secretary of state
under Richard Nixon, was often photographed
with attractive women.

From Wise, Why's, Y's

Wise I

> WHYS (*Nobody Knows*
> *The Trouble I Seen*)[6]
> Trad.

If you ever find
yourself, some where
lost and surrounded
by enemies
who won't let you   5
speak in your own language
who destroy your statues
& instruments, who ban
your omm bomm ba boom
then you are in trouble   10
deep trouble
they ban your
own boom ba boom
you in deep deep
trouble   15

humph!

probably take you several hundred years
to get
out!

Y The Link Will Not Always Be "Missing"
#40

> The Wise One
> Trane[7]

Think of Slavery
    as
Educational!

1995

---

6. African American spiritual.
7. John Coltrane (1926–1967), American jazz musician.

In the Funk World

If Elvis Presley/ is
    King
Who is James Brown,[8]
    God?

1996

Monk's World

'Round Midnight[9]

That street where midnight
is round, the moon flat
& blue, where fire engines solo
& cats stand around & look
is Monk's world   5

When I last saw him, turning around
high from 78 RPM,[1] growling
a landscape of spaced funk

When I last spoke to him, coming out
the Vanguard,[2] he hipped me to   10
my own secrets, like Nat[3]
he dug the numbers & letters
blowing through the grass
initials & invocations of the past

All the questions I asked Monk He   15
answered first
in a beret. Why was
a high priest[4] staring
Why were the black keys
signifying.[5] And who was   20
wrapped in common magic
like a street empty of everything
except weird birds

The last time Monk smiled I read
the piano's diary. His fingers   25
where he collected yr feelings

8. African American singer (b. 1933), sometimes called the Godfather of Soul. Elvis Presley (1935–1977), white American singer sometimes called the King of Rock and Roll.
9. Composition by American jazz composer and pianist Thelonious Monk (1917–1982).
1. Revolutions per minute, the standard record-playing speed early in Monk's career.

2. The Village Vanguard, a Manhattan jazz club.
3. According to Baraka, Nat Turner (1800–1831), American slave insurrectionist.
4. In the 1940s, Monk was called the High Priest of Bebop.
5. Boasting, playing on (African American vernacular), in addition to standard meanings.

The Bar he circled to underscore
    the anonymous laughter of smoke
    & posters.

Monk carried equations he danced at you.   30
    What's happening?" We said, as he dipped &
    spun. "What's happening?"

"Everything. All the time.
    Every googoplex[6]
    of a second."   35

Like a door, he opened, not disappearing
    but remaining a distant profile
    of intimate revelation.

Oh, man! Monk was digging Trane[7] now
    w/o a chaser[8] he drank himself   40
    in. & Trane reported from
    the 6th or 7th planet[9] deep in

    the Theloniuscape.

Where fire engines screamed the blues
    & night had a shiny mouth   45
    & scatted flying things.

        1996

---

6. An immense quantity.
7. John Coltrane (1926–1967), American jazz musician.
8. "Straight, No Chaser" is one of Monk's com-positions.
9. Five months before his death, Coltrane recorded compositions named after the planets, on *Interstellar Space*.

CHARLES WRIGHT
b. 1935

In lines from his volume *Black Zodiac* (1997), which won the Pulitzer Prize and the National Book Critics Circle Award, Charles Wright summarizes the central preoccupations of his career: death, memory, landscape, language, and God. "Out of any two thoughts I have, one is devoted to death," he declares, with perhaps some exaggeration ("Meditation on Form and Measure"). Although sly humor often deflects or mutes such thoughts, Wright broods over death, dying, and the dead almost with religious intensity. In "Homage to Paul Cézanne," he adapts the Postimpressionist painter's obsessive focus and layered images as a strategy for meditating from multiple perspectives on the omnipresent and invisible dead: "The dead are with us to stay. / Their shadows rock in the back yard, so pure, so black, / Between the oak tree and the porch." The dead are in the backyard, in the night sky, under our feet, in our clothes. "Their sighs," he writes memorably, "are gaps in the wind."

"I think of landscape incessantly," Wright announces in "Disjecta Membra," but for this landscape poet, the natural world is not a thing in itself but an epitaph of absent presences. It clamors with dead people he has known, dead poets he has read, dead selves he has been in the past, and a dead God he can neither recover nor surrender. Gazing upon the Italian, Appalachian, and Californian landscapes where he has lived, Wright is visited by the ghostly lines of earlier poets—Dante, Emily Dickinson, Gerard Manley Hopkins, Ezra Pound, and T. S. Eliot. Like the Romantics, he also sees this landscape as a tomb for his past. "Memory is a cemetery / I've visited once or twice," he notes with self-deprecating understatement ("Meditation on Form and Measure"). "Journal and landscape," he states more boldly in "Apologia Pro Vita Sua," "I tried to resuscitate both, breath and blood, / making them whole again // Through language." Making dazzling use of the pathetic fallacy and other forms of anthropomorphism and metaphor, Wright weaves together the outer world and the memory-studded river of interior consciousness. Scrutinizing the visible world for traces, signs, emblems not only of his past selves but of the God that once animated it, he writes about the withdrawal of divinity with a mixture of eschatological yearning and postreligious melancholy. If Wright's poems resemble journals, recording the quicksilver flow of his innermost thoughts, they are also what he called in a 1983 interview "little prayer wheels" and "wafers." They mournfully summon the divinity that once inhabited nature but now seems to have left it an empty husk.

Wright was born on August 25, 1935, in Pickwick Dam, Tennessee, where his father worked as a civil engineer for the Tennessee Valley Authority. Growing up in east Tennessee and west North Carolina, he attended Episcopal schools in North Carolina as a teenager, but abandoned orthodox religion after graduation. Evangelical Christianity, hymns, and country music were among his formative experiences. He graduated from Davidson College in 1957 and then served in the U.S. Army's Intelligence Service from 1957 to 1961, three years of which he spent in Verona, Italy. Reading Pound's poetry for the first time in 1959 in the context of its Italian settings inspired Wright to begin to write poetry. Pound's richly sonorous free verse, dropped lines, juxtapositions of images, East Asian interests, and lapidary compression—especially in the hauntingly elegiac *Pisan Cantos*—became abiding influences. Attending the University of Iowa's Writers' Workshop from 1961 to 1963, Wright studied with Donald Justice, befriended Mark Strand, and began to translate Italian poetry, in particular the work of Eugenio Montale. Early in his career, he was associated with the Deep Image poetry of Robert Bly, W. S. Merwin, and James Wright, and he shared the surrealist proclivity of other leading American poets born in the 1930s, including Strand and Charles Simic. After a few more years of study and teaching in Italy and Iowa, he taught at the University of California at Irvine for more than twenty years; he took a position at the University of Virginia in 1983.

Wright's work straddles the divide between the concision of haiku and the rambling openness of the long poem. It has the intensity of lyric and the unstructured freedom of a journal, the impersonality of aphorism and the inward expressiveness of a diary. Pithy, compressed, and musical, individual lines are crafted with jewel-like precision, as if to stand as nearly self-sufficient units. Though balanced and epigrammatic, they are embedded within poems that radiate outward, expanding to encompass great stretches of consciousness and observation, tonal highs and lows, and varying levels of diction, from the colloquial to the sublime. "A kind of American sprawl of a poem," Wright commented to the *Paris Review*, acknowledging his poetry's omnivorous, loose-limbed appearance, but "with a succession of sufficient checks and balances. Epiphanic and oceanic, at once. Intensive and extensive."

Since Wright eschews fixed meter and rhyme, the organizing principles behind his porous yet tightly structured poetry are not immediately self-evident. He has referred to the seven-syllable line as his "ur-line," and most of his lines have an odd number of syllables (he counts a dropped line as part of the same line). The numerological patterning of his work extends from this micro level of syllable count to the number of lines within stanzas, the number of stanzas or sections within poems, the mirror relations among poems within a volume, and even the ordering of books across the career. Thinking of each three of his books as a trilogy, which in turn becomes part of a "trilogy of trilogies," Wright adapts the inferno-purgatorio-paradiso structure of Dante's *Divine Comedy*.

Wright uses such architectonics as scaffolding. With its sensuous details, rich sonic patterning, and quick turns of phrase, his poetry is anything but a sterile exercise in numerology. His rhythms are strongly cadenced, including Hopkins-like spondees, sometimes in hyphenated compounds ("side-kick," "dream-light," "jump-start"), often followed by a rapid rush of unaccented syllables. His writing is highly metaphorical, deliberately artificial, even baroque, sublimating narrative and overt reference. His figurative language has a hallucinatory power and clarity, from his early description of twilight as flaring "like a white disease" ("Blackwater Mountain") to his later evocation of a dogwood's roots as his "mother's hair" ("Apologia Pro Vita Sua"). As if effortlessly, Wright can shift linguistic registers from biblical repetition, ecclesiastical diction, and transcendental abstraction to the down-home, deadpan, folksy interjection, and back again. "The meat of the sacrament is invisible meat and a ghostly substance. / I'll say. / Like any visible thing, / I'm always attracted downward, and soon to be killed and assimilated" ("Apologia Pro Vita Sua").

Blackwater Mountain

That time of evening, weightless and disparate,
When the loon cries, when the small bass
Jostle the lake's reflections, when
The green of the oak begins
To open its robes to the dark, the green   5
Of water to offer itself to the flames,
When lily and lily pad
Husband the last light
Which flares like a white disease, then disappears:
This is what I remember. And this: 10

The slap of the jacklight[1] on the cove;
The freeze-frame of ducks
Below us; your shots; the wounded flop
And skid of one bird to the thick brush;
The moon of your face in the fire's glow;   15
The cold; the darkness. Young,
Wanting approval, what else could I do?
And did, for two hours, waist-deep in the lake,
The thicket as black as death,
Without success or reprieve, try.   20

The stars over Blackwater Mountain
Still dangle and flash like hooks, and ducks

---

1. Light used for hunting or fishing at night.

Coast on the evening water;
The foliage is like applause.
I stand where we stood before and aim   25
My flashlight down to the lake. A black duck
Explodes to my right, hangs, and is gone.
He shows me the way to you;
He shows me the way to a different fire
Where you, black moon, warm your hands.   30

1973

Stone Canyon Nocturne

Ancient of Days, old friend, no one believes you'll come back.
No one believes in his own life anymore.

The moon, like a dead heart, cold and unstartable, hangs by a thread
At the earth's edge,
Unfaithful at last, splotching the ferns and the pink shrubs.   5

In the other world, children undo the knots in their tally strings.
They sing songs, and their fingers blear.

And here, where the swan hums in his socket, where bloodroot
And belladonna insist on our comforting,
Where the fox in the canyon wall empties our hands, ecstatic for   10
    more,

Like a bead of clear oil the Healer revolves through the night wind,
Part eye, part tear, unwilling to recognize us.

1977

Clear Night

Clear night, thumb-top of a moon, a back-lit sky.
Moon-fingers lay down their same routine
On the side deck and the threshold, the white keys and the black keys.
Bird hush and bird song. A cassia flower falls.

I want to be bruised by God.   5
I want to be strung up in a strong light and singled out.
I want to be stretched, like music wrung from a dropped seed.
I want to be entered and picked clean.

And the wind says "What?" to me.
And the castor beans, with their little earrings of death, say "What?" 10
    to me.

And the stars start out on their cold slide through the dark.
And the gears notch and the engines wheel.

1977

Homage to Paul Cézanne[2]

At night, in the fish-light of the moon, the dead wear our white shirts
To stay warm, and litter the fields.
We pick them up in the mornings, dewy pieces of paper and scraps of
    cloth.
Like us, they refract themselves. Like us,
They keep on saying the same thing, trying to get it right.   5
Like us, the water unsettles their names.

Sometimes they lie like leaves in their little arks, and curl up at the edges.
Sometimes they come inside, wearing our shoes, and walk
From mirror to mirror.
Or lie in our beds with their gloves off   10
And touch our bodies. Or talk
In a corner. Or wait like envelopes on a desk.

They reach up from the ice plant.
They shuttle their messengers through the oat grass.
Their answers rise like rust on the stalks and the spidery leaves.   15

We rub them off our hands.

•

Each year the dead grow less dead, and nudge
Close to the surface of all things.
They start to remember the silence that brought them there.
They start to recount the gain in their soiled hands.   20

Their glasses let loose, and grain by grain return to the river bank.
They point to their favorite words
Growing around them, revealed as themselves for the first time:
They stand close to the meanings and take them in.

They stand there, vague and without pain,   25
Under their fingernails an unreturnable dirt.
They stand there and it comes back,
The music of everything, syllable after syllable

---

2. French Postimpressionist painter (1839–1906).

Out of the burning chair, out of the beings of light.
It all comes back.   30
And what they repeat to themselves, and what they repeat to themselves,
Is the song that our fathers sing.

•

In steeps and sighs,
The ocean explains itself, backing and filling
What spaces it can't avoid, spaces   35
In black shoes, their hands clasped, their eyes teared at the edges:
We watch from the high hillside,
The ocean swelling and flattening, the spaces
Filling and emptying, horizon blade
Flashing the early afternoon sun.   40

The dead are constant in
The white lips of the sea.
Over and over, through clenched teeth, they tell
Their story, the story each knows by heart:
Remember me, speak my name.   45
When the moon tugs at my sleeve,
When the body of water is raised and becomes the body of light,
Remember me, speak my name.

•

The dead are a cadmium blue.[3]
We spread them with palette knives in broad blocks and planes.   50

We layer them stroke by stroke
In steps and ascending mass, in verticals raised from the earth.

We choose, and layer them in,
Blue and a blue and a breath,

Circle and smudge, cross-beak and buttonhook,   55
We layer them in. We squint hard and terrace them line by line.

And so we are come between, and cry out,
And stare up at the sky and its cloudy panes,

And finger the cypress twists.
The dead understand all this, and keep in touch,   60

Rustle of hand to hand in the lemon trees,
Flags, and the great sifts of anger

---

3. Nonexistent shade of paint; Wright's coinage, by analogy with compounds such as cadmium red and
cadmium yellow.

To powder and nothingness.
The dead are a cadmium blue, and they understand.

•

The dead are with us to stay.   65
Their shadows rock in the back yard, so pure, so black,
Between the oak tree and the porch.

Over our heads they're huge in the night sky.
In the tall grass they turn with the zodiac.
Under our feet they're white with the snows of a thousand years.   70

They carry their colored threads and baskets of silk
To mend our clothes, making us look right,
Altering, stitching, replacing a button, closing a tear.
They lie like tucks in our loose sleeves, they hold us together.

They blow the last leaves away.   75
They slide like an overflow into the river of heaven.
Everywhere they are flying.

The dead are a sleight and a fade
We fall for, like flowering plums, like white coins from the rain.
Their sighs are gaps in the wind.   80

•

The dead are waiting for us in our rooms,
Little globules of light
In one of the far corners, and close to the ceiling, hovering, thinking our
        thoughts.

Often they'll reach a hand down,
Or offer a word, and ease us out of our bodies to join them in theirs.   85
We look back at our other selves on the bed.

We look back and we don't care and we go.

And thus we become what we've longed for,
                                past tense and otherwise,
A BB, a disc of light,   90
                song without words.
And refer to ourselves
In the third person, seeing that other arm
Still raised from the bed, fingers like licks and flames in the boned air.

Only to hear that it's not time.   95
Only to hear that we must re-enter and lie still, our arms at rest at our sides,
The voices rising around us like mist

And dew, *it's all right, it's all right, it's all right . . .*

•

The dead fall around us like rain.
They come down from the last clouds in the late light for the last time   100
And slip through the sod.

They lean uphill and face north.
                                        Like grass,
They bend toward the sea, they break toward the setting sun.

We filigree[4] and we baste.   105
But what do the dead care for the fringe of words,
Safe in their suits of milk?
What do they care for the honk and flash of a new style?

And who is to say if the inch of snow in our hearts
Is rectitude enough?   110

Spring picks the locks of the wind.
High in the night sky the mirror is hauled up and unsheeted.
In it we twist like stars.

Ahead of us, through the dark, the dead
Are beating their drums and stirring the yellow leaves.   115

•

We're out here, our feet in the soil, our heads craned up at the sky,
The stars streaming and bursting behind the trees.

At dawn, as the clouds gather, we watch
The mountain glide from the east on the valley floor,
Coming together in starts and jumps.   120
Behind their curtain, the bears
Amble across the heavens, serene as black coffee . . .

Whose unction can intercede for the dead?
Whose tongue is toothless enough to speak their piece?

What we are given in dreams we write as blue paint,   125
Or messages to the clouds.
At evening we wait for the rain to fall and the sky to clear.
Our words are words for the clay, uttered in undertones,
Our gestures salve for the wind.

We sit out on the earth and stretch our limbs,   130
Hoarding the little mounds of sorrow laid up in our hearts.

                                                                    1981

4. Embellish.

Laguna Blues

It's Saturday afternoon at the edge of the world.
White pages lift in the wind and fall.
Dust threads, cut loose from the heart, float up and fall.
Something's off-key in my mind.
Whatever it is, it bothers me all the time.   5

It's hot, and the wind blows on what I have had to say.
I'm dancing a little dance.
The crows pick up a thermal that angles away from the sea.
I'm singing a little song.
Whatever it is, it bothers me all the time.   10

It's Saturday afternoon and the crows glide down,
Black pages that lift and fall.
The castor beans and the pepper plant trundle their weary heads.
Something's off-key and unkind.
Whatever it is, it bothers me all the time.   15

1981

From Apologia Pro Vita Sua[5]

I

How soon we come to road's end—
Failure, our two-dimensional side-kick, flat dream-light,
Won't jump-start or burn us in,

Dogwood insidious in its constellations of part-charred cross points,
Spring's via Dolorosa[6]   5
                      flashed out in a dread profusion,
Nowhere to go but up, nowhere to turn, dead world-weight,

They've gone and done it again,
                      dogwood,
Spring's sap-crippled, arthritic, winter-weathered, myth limb,   10
Whose roots are my mother's hair.

————————

Landscape's a lever of transcendence—
                      jack-wedge it here,
Or here, and step back,
Heave, and a light, a little light, will nimbus your going forth: 15

————

5. A defense of his life (Latin). Title of famous 1864 autobiography by theologian Cardinal John Henry Newman (1801–1890).

6. Way of suffering (Latin). Street in Jerusalem said to follow the path along which Jesus carried the cross.

The dew bead, terminal bead, opens out
                                        onto a great radiance,
Sun's square on magnolia leaf
Offers us entrance—
                    who among us will step forward,   20

Camellia brown boutonnieres
Under his feet, plum branches under his feet, white sky, white noon,
Church bells like monk's mouths tonguing the hymn?

———————

Journal and landscape
—Discredited form, discredited subject matter—   25
I tried to resuscitate both, breath and blood,
                                    making them whole again

Through language, strict attention—
Verona mi fe', disfecemi Verona,[7] the song goes.
I've hummed it, I've bridged the break   30

To no avail.
            April. The year begins beyond words,
Beyond myself and the image of myself, beyond
Moon's ice and summer's thunder. All that.

———————

The meat of the sacrament is invisible meat and a ghostly substance.   35
I'll say.
        Like any visible thing,
I'm always attracted downward, and soon to be killed and assimilated.

Vessel of life, it's said, vessel of life, brought to naught,
Then gathered back to what's visible.   40
That's it, fragrance of spring like lust in the blossom-starred orchard,

The shapeless shape of darkness starting to seep through and emerge,
The seen world starting to tilt,
Where I sit the still, unwavering point
                                under that world's waves.   45

———————

How like the past the clouds are,
Building and disappearing along the horizon,
Inflecting the mountains,
                        laying their shadows under our feet

———————

7. Verona made me, Verona undid me (Italian).
Cf. Dante's *Purgatorio* 5.133, in which two differ-
ent cities play the formative roles in the speaker's
life story: "Siena mi fe', disfecemi Maremma."

Pound's *Hugh Selwyn Mauberley* (1920) quotes
and Eliot's *Waste Land* (1922) alludes to this line
from Dante.

For us to cross over on.   50
Out of their insides fire falls, ice falls,
What we remember that still remembers us, earth and air fall.

Neither, however, can resurrect or redeem us,
Moving, as both must, ever away toward opposite corners.
Neither has been where we're going,   55
                                        bereft of an attitude.

———————

Amethyst,[8] crystal transparency,
                                        Maya and Pharaoh ring,
Malocchio, set against witchcraft,
Lightning and hailstorm, birthstone, savior from drunkenness.   60

Purple, color of insight, clear sight,
Color of memory—
                                        violet, that's for remembering,[9]
Star-crystals scattered across the penumbra,[1] hard stars.

Who can distinguish darkness from the dark, light from light,   65
Subject matter from story line,
                                        the part from the whole
When whole is part of the part and part is all of it?

———————

Lonesomeness. Morandi, Cézanne, it's all about lonesomeness.
And Rothko. Especially Rothko.[2]   70
Separation from what heals us
                                        beyond painting, beyond art.

Words and paint, black notes, white notes.
Music and landscape; music, landscape and sentences.
Gestures for which there is no balm, no intercession.   75

Two tone fields, horizon a line between abysses,
Generally white, always speechless.
Rothko could choose either one to disappear into. And did.

———————

Perch'io no spero di tornar giammai, ballatetta, in Toscana,[3]
Not as we were the first time,   80
                                        not as we'll ever be again.
Such snowflakes of memory, they fall nowhere but there.

8. Lines 57–60 describe properties and uses of amethyst, a semiprecious stone thought to ward off evil and drunkenness. *Maya:* indigenous people of southern Mexico and Central America. *Malocchio:* evil eye (Italian).
9. Cf. Ophelia's final appearance in *Hamlet* 4.5: "There's rosemary, that's for remembrance."
1. Shaded area of Earth or the moon experiencing partial phase of an eclipse.
2. Mark Rothko (1903–1970): American abstract expressionist painter noted for works consisting of large fields of color. Giorgio Morandi (1890–1964): Italian still-life painter. Paul Cézanne (1839–1906): French Postimpressionist painter.
3. Because I never hope to return, ballatetta, to Toscana (Italian); a line from the Italian poet Guido di Cavalcanti (c. 1255–1300). *Ballatetta:* small ballet. Eliot echoes this line in his "Ash Wednesday": "Because I do not hope to turn again."

Absorbed in remembering, we cannot remember—
Exile's anthem, O stiff heart,
Thingless we came into the world and thingless we leave.   85

Every important act is wordless—
                              to slip from the right way,
To fail, still accomplishes something.
Even a good thing remembered, however, is not as good as not remembering
    at all.

————————

Time is the source of all good,   90
                              time the engenderer
Of entropy and decay.
Time the destroyer, our only-begetter and advocate.

For instance, my fingernail,
                              so pink, so amplified,   95
In the half-dark, for instance,
These force-fed dogwood blossoms, green-leafed, defused,
                              limp on their long branches.

St. Stone,[4] say a little prayer for me,
                              grackles and jay in the black gum,   100
Drowse of the peony head,
Dandelion globes luminous in the last light, more work to be done . . .

                                                            1997

Stray Paragraphs in February, Year of the Rat[5]

East of town, the countryside unwrinkles and smooths out
Unctuously toward the tidewater and gruff Atlantic.
A love of landscape's a true affection for regret, I've found,
Forever joined, forever apart,
                              outside us yet ourselves.   5

Renunciation, it's hard to learn, is now our ecstasy.
However, if God were still around,
                              he'd swallow our sighs in his nothingness.

The dregs of the absolute are slow sift in my blood,
Dead branches down after high winds, dead yard grass and   10
    undergrowth—
The sure accumulation of all that's not revealed
Rises like snow in my bare places,
                              cross-whipped and openmouthed.

———————————————————————————————

4. In Matthew 16.18, Jesus gives Simon the name Peter because he will form the foundation of the Church (*petra* is Latin for stone).
5. Year of the Chinese calendar.

Our lives can't be lived in flames.
Our lives can't be lit like saints' hearts,   15
                    seared between heaven and earth.

February, old head-turner, cut us some slack, grind of bone
On bone, such melancholy music.
Lift up that far corner of landscape,
                              there, toward the west.   20
Let some of the deep light in, the arterial kind.

                                                                1998

MARY OLIVER
b. 1935

"When it's over," Mary Oliver writes, projecting from beyond the grave, "I want to say: all my life / I was a bride married to amazement. / I was the bridegroom, taking the world into my arms" ("When Death Comes"). An ecstatic admirer of nature, Oliver celebrates flora and fauna—berries and goldenrods, snakes and egrets—with the ardor of a mystic. In an age of irony, when an arch, postmodern knowingness marks much contemporary poetry, Oliver's is an earnest and impassioned voice, hymning the multiplicitous life force, "the light at the center of every cell" ("The Black Snake").

Oliver renews the Romantic and Transcendentalist impulse to inhabit nature as an invisible observer, Ralph Waldo Emerson's "transparent eyeball," or what she calls a "rich / lens of attention" ("Entering the Kingdom"). Sometimes, she seems to want to incorporate nature within her body and identity, devouring and becoming its otherness, as she devours the blackberries in the poem "August." Her reverence for nature doesn't deter her from anthropomorphism, and so a hawk becomes "an admiral, / its profile / distinguished with sideburns" ("Hawk"). Her wager is that apt metaphors for nature—the black snake as "an old bicycle tire"—renew our attention to its beauty and particularity ("The Black Snake"). Through various forms of figurative language (personification, metaphor, the pathetic fallacy), Oliver humanizes the natural and yet also animalizes the human, her poems poised on the borderline between these worlds.

Born on September 10, 1935, in Cleveland, Ohio, educated at Ohio State University and Vassar College, Oliver settled in New England, the cradle of American nature writing. She won the Pulitzer Prize in 1984 and the National Book Award in 1992. Her literary lineage can be traced back to the New England nature poetry of Robert Frost, the animal poetry of Marianne Moore and Elizabeth Bishop, the rhapsodies of Edna St. Vincent Millay and Walt Whitman, ultimately to the naive visionary stances of William Blake and William Wordsworth. Seeking immediacy, she describes nature with spare diction, free (but skillfully enjambed) verse in regular stanzas, and verbs in the present tense or present participles ("coiling and flowing"). Modulating rhythm and syntax to build to an often climactic ending, Oliver would lead us into nature's energy, cycles, and flux—human animals fused with a nonhuman world.

The Black Snake

When the black snake
flashed onto the morning road,
and the truck could not swerve—
death, that is how it happens.

Now he lies looped and useless   5
as an old bicycle tire.
I stop the car
and carry him into the bushes.

He is as cool and gleaming
as a braided whip, he is as beautiful and quiet   10
as a dead brother.
I leave him under the leaves

and drive on, thinking
about *death*: its suddenness,
its terrible weight,   15
its certain coming. Yet under

reason burns a brighter fire, which the bones
have always preferred.
It is the story of endless good fortune.
It says to oblivion: not me!   20

It is the light at the center of every cell.
It is what sent the snake coiling and flowing forward
happily all spring through the green leaves before
he came to the road.

1979

August

When the blackberries hang
swollen in the woods, in the brambles
nobody owns, I spend

all day among the high
branches, reaching   5
my ripped arms, thinking

of nothing, cramming
the black honey of summer
into my mouth; all day my body

accepts what it is. In the dark
creeks that run by there is
this thick paw of my life darting among

the black bells, the leaves; there is
this happy tongue.

1983

Hawk

This morning
   the hawk
      rose up
         out of the meadow's browse[1]

and swung over the lake—
   it settled
      on the small black dome
         of a dead pine,

alert as an admiral,
   its profile
      distinguished with sideburns
         the color of smoke,

and I said: remember
   this is not something
      of the red fire, this is
         heaven's fistful

of death and destruction,
   and the hawk hooked
      one exquisite foot
         onto a last twig

to look deeper
   into the yellow reeds
      along the edges of the water
         and I said: remember

the tree, the cave,
   the white lily of resurrection,[2]
      and that's when it simply lifted
         its golden feet and floated

---

1. Tender shoots and twigs of shrubbery that are food for animals.   2. Symbols of Jesus' crucifixion ("the tree"), burial ("the cave"), and resurrection ("the white lily").

into the wind, belly-first,
    and then it cruised along the lake—
      all the time its eyes fastened
        harder than love on some

unimportant rustling in the
    yellow reeds—and then it
      seemed to crouch high in the air, and then it
      turned into a white blade, which fell.

             30

             35

1992

MARGE PIERCY
b. 1936

Indignation and rage prompted Marge Piercy into poetry. She was a determined participant in the succession of political movements that defined her generation—the civil rights movement, the antiwar movement, and the feminist movement. For Piercy, as for many of her contemporaries, the personal and the political were inseparable. An exemplary early work, "Learning Experience," is as poetically effective as it is overtly political, recounting a teacher's observations of a boy on the verge of being drafted. Repeated words and phrases, trademark strategies of Piercy's, help create a mood of futility, boredom, and doom ("in Gary," "in Gary," "in Gary"). Characteristically vivid similes further realize the atmosphere: "in boredom thick and greasy as vegetable shortening." Her simple diction, blunt syntax, and colloquial speech ("I am supposed / to teach him to think a little on demand") draw the reader in before she whips out the poem's stinger: "tomorrow he will try and fail his license to live."

Piercy's feminism is well served by her sardonic wit. In "The Cast Off," a paean to various kinds of openings, from can-openers to zippers, Piercy humorously lists the many clothes that a Victorian lady must shed to make love, exclaiming at the end that the lady "still wants to!" Many of Piercy's poems celebrate nature and love. Like Walt Whitman, she rhapsodically hymns sexual desire and rebirth, as in such poems as "Moonburn" and "The Sky Changes." Female lust, embraced and affirmed, generates a litany of vivid images, which she has called "the rich suggestive stuff of poems." Piercy is unsentimental yet tender.

She was born on March 31, 1936, into a working-class family in Detroit. Proud of her Jewish heritage, she has written liturgy used in Reconstructionist and Reform congregations. Although she often takes an antiacademic stance, Piercy received a B.A. from the University of Michigan and an M.A. from Northwestern University, and she has held various teaching positions. In addition to numerous volumes of poetry, she has published many novels, her best-known the utopian-feminist *Woman on the Edge of Time* (1976). When she writes poetry, she has said, she feels her ordinary life fall away: "I may be dealing with my own anger, my humiliation, my passion, my pleasure; but once I am working with it in a poem, it becomes molten ore. It becomes 'not me.'" Writing poetry is, thus, "so strangely personal and so impersonal at once" (*New York Times*, December 20, 1999).

The Cyclist

Eleven-thirty and hot.
Cotton air.
Dry hands cupped.
The shadow of an empty chandelier
swings on a refrigerator door.   5
In the street a voice is screaming.
Your head scurries with ants.
Anyone's arms drip with your sweat,
anyone's pliant belly
absorbs your gymnastic thrusts   10
as your fury subsides into butter.
You are always in combat with questionnaires.
You are always boxing headless dolls
of cherry pudding.
You are the tedious marksman in a forest of thighs,   15
you with tomcat's shrapnel memory
and irritable eyes.
Tenderness is a mosquito on your arm.
Your hands are calloused with careless touch.
You believe in luck and a quick leap forward   20
that does not move you.
You rub your sore pride into moist bodies
and pedal off, slightly displeased.

                                                                  1969

Learning Experience

The boy sits in the classroom
in Gary, in the United States, in NATO, in SEATO[1]
in the thing-gorged belly of the sociobeast
in fluorescent light in slowly moving time
in boredom thick and greasy as vegetable shortening.   5
The classroom has green boards and ivory blinds,
the desks are new and the teachers not so old.
I have come out on the train from Chicago to talk
about dangling participles. I am supposed
to teach him to think a little on demand.   10
The time of tomorrow's draft exam[2] is written on the board.
The boy yawns and does not want to be in the classroom in Gary
where the furnaces that consumed his father seethe rusty smoke
and pour cascades of nerve-bright steel
while the slag goes out in little dumpcars smoking,   15

---

1. Gary, Indiana, is a large, steel-producing city; NATO and SEATO are the North Atlantic Treaty Organization and Southeast Asia Treaty Organization; the United States is a signatory to both trea- ties. SEATO was disbanded in 1977.
2. Examination that will exempt him from being drafted into the army.

but even less does he want to be in Today's Action Army
in Vietnam, in the Dominican Republic, in Guatemala,
in death that hurts.
In him are lectures on small groups, Jacksonian democracy,
French irregular verbs, the names of friends   20
around him in the classroom in Gary in the pillshaped afternoon
where tomorrow he will try and fail his license to live.

                                                                                1969

The Cast Off

This is a day to celebrate can-
openers, those lantern-jawed long-tailed
humping tools that cut through what keeps
us from what we need: a can of beans
trapped in its armor taunts the nails   5
and teeth of a hungry woman.

Today let us hear hurrahs for zippers,
those small shark teeth that part
politely to let us at what we want;
the tape on packages that unlock   10
us birthday presents; envelopes
we slit to thaw the frozen
words on the tundra[3] of paper.

Today let us praise the small
rebirths, the emerging groundhog   15
from the sodden burrow; the nut
picked from the broken fortress of walnut
shell, itself pried from the oily fruit
shaken from the high turreted
city of the tree.   20

Today let us honor the safe whose door
hangs ajar; the champagne bottle
with its cork bounced off the ceiling
and into the soup tureen; the Victorian lady
in love who has removed her hood, her cloak,   25
her laced boots, her stockings, her overdress,
her underdress, her wool petticoat, her linen
petticoats, her silk petticoats, her whalebone
corset, her bustle, her chemise, her drawers, and
who still wants to! Today let us praise the cast   30
that finally opens, slit neatly in two
like a dinosaur egg, and out at last
comes somewhat hairier, powdered in dead skin

---

3. Arctic or subarctic treeless plain.

but still beautiful, the lost for months
body of my love.   35

                                                          1980

Moonburn

I stayed under the moon too long.
I am silvered with lust.

Dreams flick like minnows through my eyes.
My voice is trees tossing in the wind.

I loose myself like a flock of blackbirds   5
storming into your face.

My lightest touch leaves blue prints,
bruises on your mind.

Desire sandpapers your skin
so thin I read the veins and arteries   10

maps of routes I will travel
till I lodge in your spine.

The night is our fur.
We curl inside it licking.

                                                          1997

LUCILLE CLIFTON
1936–2010

In her many books of poetry, essays, autobiography, and children's stories, Lucille Clifton affirms and resists. She celebrated African American culture, especially black womanhood, and she protested the injustices and degradations inflicted on it by the larger culture. As a poet, she braved the difficulties of personal loss, of racial and cultural intolerance, yet her poetry hums with prophetic assurance, vision, and candor. It is by turns humorous, angry, elegiac, and radiantly hopeful. Delighting in the wonders of everyday experience in the present, Clifton listened for the silences and absences in official chronicles of the African American past, which she assimilated to her personal, even bodily experience. "History doesn't go away," she declared in an interview with Bill Moyers. "The past isn't back there, the past is *here* too." Intensely personal and yet collectivist, Clifton's poetry bridges the gap between what is sometimes classified as "confessional poetry" (poetry of intimate disclosure) and "identity poetry" (poetry about sociocultural group experience). In poems that recall Walt Whitman in their metaphysical exuberance, Clifton embraces the interwovenness of all things, whether food, bodies, rivers, or family histories.

Like such precursors as Langston Hughes and Gwendolyn Brooks, Clifton wrote in a spare, economical style that conceals its artistry and complexity. Her colloquial language resonates with the rhetorical patterns, cadences, and diction of the Bible and those of African American speech, oratory, and song. Poems such as "at the cemetery, walnut grove plantation, south carolina, 1989" are carefully structured around a series of alternations—between shorter and longer lines, shorter and longer verse paragraphs, repeated and varied phrases—that invoke African American call and response, building cadences that sound like prayer. Clifton's figurative language is vivid and often playful, as when she apostrophizes her uterus as "my estrogen kitchen, / my black bag of desire" ("poem to my uterus"), or her menstrual period as a "hussy" in a "red dress" who has caused much trouble but seems splendid in retrospect ("to my last period"). Clifton's poetry is terse, but rich with meaning.

Thelma Lucille Sayles was born in Depew, New York, where her father worked in the steel mills and her mother in a laundry. She was educated at Howard University and Fredonia State Teachers College. She married Fred Clifton in 1958; worked as a claims clerk in Buffalo, New York; and served as a literature assistant in the U.S. Office of Education, in Washington, D.C. She published her first collection of poems in 1969. Honored as Maryland's poet laureate (1976–85), she taught at Coppin State College, in Baltimore; Columbia University; the University of California, Santa Cruz; and St. Mary's College of Maryland. In her family history, two female ancestors were of great significance to Clifton: her great-great-grandmother Caroline, a Dahomey, or west-central African, girl kidnapped by slave traders, and her great-grandmother Lucille, her namesake and the first woman legally hanged in Virginia (she had murdered the white father of her only son). Clifton wrote frankly about being an incest survivor. She raised six children, whom she credited with inspiring her books of children's stories. In 2000, she won the National Book Award for poetry.

[still]

still
it was nice
when the scissors man come round
running his wheel
rolling his wheel   5
and the sparks shooting
out in the dark
across the lot
and over to the white folks' section

still   10
it was nice
in the light of maizie's store
to watch the wheel
and catch the wheel—
fire spinning in the air   15

and our edges
and our points
sharpening good as anybody's

1969

cutting greens

curling them around
i hold their bodies in obscene embrace
thinking of everything but kinship.
collards and kale
strain against each strange other   5
away from my kissmaking hand and
the iron bedpot.
the pot is black,
the cutting board is black,
my hand,   10
and just for a minute
the greens roll black under the knife,
and the kitchen twists dark on its spine
and i taste in my natural appetite
the bond of live things everywhere.   15

1974

homage to my hips

these hips are big hips
they need space to
move around in.
they don't fit into little
petty places. these hips   5
are free hips.
they don't like to be held back.
these hips have never been enslaved,
they go where they want to go
they do what they want to do.   10
these hips are mighty hips.
these hips are magic hips.
i have known them
to put a spell on a man and
spin him like a top!   15

1980

[i am accused of tending to the past]

i am accused of tending to the past
as if i made it,
as if i sculpted it
with my own hands. i did not.
this past was waiting for me   5
when i came,
a monstrous unnamed baby,
and i with my mother's itch
took it to breast
and named it   10
History.
she is more human now,
learning language everyday,
remembering faces, names and dates.
when she is strong enough to travel   15
on her own, beware, she will.

1991

at the cemetery, walnut grove plantation, south carolina, 1989

among the rocks
at walnut grove
your silence drumming
in my bones,
tell me your names.   5

nobody mentioned slaves
and yet the curious tools
shine with your fingerprints.
nobody mentioned slaves
but somebody did this work   10
who had no guide, no stone,
who moulders under rock.

tell me your names,
tell me your bashful names
and i will testify.   15

the inventory lists ten slaves
but only men were recognized.

among the rocks
at walnut grove
some of these honored dead   20
were dark
some of these dark
were slaves
some of these slaves
were women   25
some of them did this
honored work.
tell me your names
foremothers, brothers,
tell me your dishonored names.   30
here lies
here lies
here lies
here lies
hear   35

1991

poem to my uterus

you   uterus
you have been patient
as a sock
while i have slippered into you
my dead and living children   5
now
they want to cut you out
stocking i will not need
where i am going
where am i going   10
old girl
without you
uterus
my bloody print
my estrogen kitchen   15
my black bag of desire
where can i go
barefoot
without you
where can you go   20
without me

1991

to my last period

well girl, goodbye,
after thirty-eight years.
thirty-eight years and you
never arrived
splendid in your red dress   5
without trouble for me
somewhere, somehow.

now it is done,
and i feel just like
the grandmothers who,   10
after the hussy has gone,
sit holding her photograph
and sighing, *wasn't she*
beautiful? wasn't she beautiful?

                                                              1991

cain[1]

so this is what it means
to be an old man;
every member of my body
limp and unsatisfied,
father to sons who never knew   5
my father, husband to the
sister of the east,
and all night, in the rocky
land of nod,
listening to the thunderous   10
roll of voices,
unable to tell them where
my brother is.

                                                              1993

leda[2] 3

a personal note (re: visitations)

always pyrotechnics;
stars spinning into phalluses
of light, serpents promising
sweetness, their forked tongues
thick and erect, patriarchs of bird   5

1. First son of Adam and Eve, Cain murdered his younger brother Abel and was exiled to the land of Nod (Genesis 4).

2. In Greek legend, Leda is impregnated by Zeus, who comes to her in the shape of a swan.

exposing themselves in the air.
this skin is sick with loneliness.
You want what a man wants,
next time come as a man
or don't come.   10

1993

the mississippi river empties into the gulf

and the gulf enters the sea and so forth,
none of them emptying anything,
all of them carrying yesterday
forever on their white tipped backs,
all of them dragging forward tomorrow.   5
it is the great circulation
of the earth's body, like the blood
of the gods, this river in which the past
is always flowing. every water
is the same water coming round.   10
everyday someone is standing on the edge
of this river, staring into time,
whispering mistakenly:
only here. only now.

1996

JUNE JORDAN
1936–2002

"Listen to this white man; he is so weird!" exclaims June Jordan, approving Walt Whitman's grand design for a "people's poetry" of the New World, a poetry that affirms "the pride and dignity of the common people." "I too am a descendant of Walt Whitman," she states, his voice "intimate and direct at once," and she goes on to align herself also with other New World poets, such as the Chilean poets Pablo Neruda and Gabriela Mistral and the African American poets Langston Hughes and Margaret Walker (*Passion*). In the introductory poem to *Things That I Do in the Dark,* Jordan writes that her poems are "reaching for you / whoever you are / and / are you ready?" Her lines "are desperate arms for my longing and love," and longing and love are among Jordan's primary subjects.

Jordan came out of the Black Arts Movement, which emphasized address to a black audience, nationalist self-sufficiency, and the fusion of politics and art. The women's movement of the 1960s and 1970s was another early, central influence. In some poems, Jordan is unabashedly polemical and rails against racial, gender, and other forms of oppression across the globe. In others, her approach is less direct, more humorous, though no less biting. In the dramatic monologue "Notes on the Peanut," she impersonates George Washington Carver, comically mocking his monomania through exaggeration, repetition, and the ironic intermingling of the jargons of technology, sales, art, medicine, and social theory. Jordan rejected as disempowering an exclusionary norm of Standard English, and the rhythms and rhetoric of Black English are forcefully alive in a poem such as "The Reception," which closes with the wish for "a true gut-funky blues to make her really dance." Another of Jordan's most effective strategies is the character portrait, and DeLiza, who appears in "DeLiza Spend the Day in the City," is a spunky, streetwise, comic creation: in "A Runaway Lil Bit Poem," DeLiza holds out for the "last drink to close the bars she / holler kissey lips she laugh she let / you walk yourself away." As indicated by her elegy for Buck, Jordan also delights in language's expressive sonorities—onomatopoeia ("ratatat-tat-zap"), staccato rhythms ("shrink back / jump up / cock ears / shake head"), and devices of repetition such as anaphora and rhyme.

Jordan was born on July 9, 1936, to Jamaican immigrants in New York City's Harlem. At school and at Barnard College, she said, "I diligently followed orthodox directions from *The Canterbury Tales* right through *The Waste Land*"; like Adrienne Rich, then, she began with "the poetry of the fathers" until she began to carve her own. She held teaching positions at, among other schools, Sarah Lawrence College (1969–74), the State University of New York, Stony Brook (1978–89), and, from 1989, the University of California, Berkeley. In addition to her volumes of poetry, she published fiction, plays, essays, and books for children. She died of breast cancer, after fighting it for a decade.

Notes on the Peanut

For the Poet David Henderson[1]

Hi there. My name is George
Washington
Carver.[2]
If you will bear with me
for a few minutes I
will share with you   5
a few
of the 30,117 uses to which
the lowly peanut has been put
by me
since yesterday afternoon.   10
If you will look at my feet you will notice
my sensible shoelaces made from unadulterated
peanut leaf composition that is biodegradable
in the extreme.
To your left you can observe the lovely Renoir   15
masterpiece reproduction that I have cleverly
pieced together from several million peanut
shell chips painted painstakingly so as to
accurately represent the colors of the original!   20
Overhead you will spot a squadron of Peanut B-52

---

1. American poet (b. 1942)
2. African American chemist (ca. 1864–1943), who developed over three hundred derivative products from the peanut.

Bombers flying due west.
I would extend my hands to greet you
at this time
except for the fact that I am holding a reserve   25
supply of high energy dry roasted peanuts
guaranteed to accelerate protein assimilation
precisely documented by my pocket peanut calculator;
May I ask when did you last contemplate the relationship
between the expanding peanut products' industry   30
and the development of post-Marxian economic theory
which (Let me emphasize) need not exclude moral attrition
of prepuberty
polymorphic
prehensible[3] skills within the population age sectors   35
of 8 to 15?
I hope you will excuse me if I appear to be staring at you
through these functional yet high fashion and prescriptive
peanut contact lenses providing for the most
minute observation of your physical response to all of this   40
ultimately nutritional information.
Peanut butter peanut soap peanut margarine peanut
brick houses and house and field peanuts *per se* well
illustrate the diversified
potential of this lowly leguminous[4] plant   45
to which you may correctly refer
also
as the goober the pindar the groundnut
and ground pea/let me
interrupt to take your name down on my   50
pocket peanut writing pad complete with matching
peanut pencil that only 3 or 4
chewing motions of the jaws will sharpen
into pyrotechnical utility
and no sweat.   55
Please:
Speak right into the peanut!

Your name?

     1980

July 4, 1984: For Buck

April 7, 1978–June 16, 1984

You would shrink back/jump up
cock ears/shake head
tonight
at this bloody idea of a birthday

---

3. Capable of being grasped. *Polymorphic:* able to exist in several forms without relation to sex.   4. Botanical family of peas and beans.

represented by smackajack explosions   5
of percussive lunacy and downright
(blowawayavillage) boom boom
ratatat-tat-zap

Otherwise any threat would make you stand
quivering perfect as a story   10
no amount of repetition could hope to ruin
perfect as the kangaroo boogie you concocted
with a towel in your jaws and your tail
tucked under and your paws
speeding around the ecstatic circle   15
of your refutation of the rain
outdoors

And mostly you would lunge electrical
and verge into the night
ears practically on flat alert   20
nostrils on the agitated sniff
(for falling rawhide meteors) and laugh
at compliments galore and then
teach me to love you
by hand   25
teach me to love you
by heart

as I do now

1985

DeLiza Spend the Day in the City

DeLiza drive the car to fetch Alexis
running from she building past the pickets
make she gap tooth laugh why don't
they think up something new they picket now
for three months soon it be too cold   5
to care

Opposite the Thrift Shop
Alexis ask to stop at the Botanica⁵
St. Jacques Majeur find oil to heal she
sister lying in the hospital from lymphoma⁶   10
and much western drug agenda

DeLiza stop. Alexis running back
with oil and myrrh and frankincense⁷ and coal
to burn these odors free the myrrh like rocks

---

5. Shop selling herbs and magical charms.
6. A tumor.
7. Two kinds of aromatic gum resins anciently
used in cures; the Magi brought "gold, and frank-
incense, and myrrh" as gifts to the baby Jesus (Mat-
thew 2.11).

a baby break to pieces fit inside the palm 15
of long or short lifelines

DeLiza driving and Alexis
point out Nyabinghi's African emporium
of gems and cloth and Kwanza cards and clay:
DeLiza look. 20

Alexis opening the envelope to give DeLiza
faint gray copies of she article on refugees
from Haiti and some other thing on one white
male one
David Mayer 25
sixty-six
a second world war veteran
who want America to stop atomic arms
who want America to live without the nuclear death
who want it bad enough to say he'll blow 30
the Washington
D.C. Monument into the southside of the White House
where the First White Lady counting up she
$209,000. dollar china plates and cups and bowls
but cops blow him away 35
blow him/he David Mayer
man of peace
away
Alexis saying, "Shit.
He could be Jesus. Died to save you, 40
didn't he?"
DeLiza nod she head.
God do not seem entirely to be dead.

1985

The Reception

Doretha wore the short blue lace last night
and William watched her drinking so she fight
with him in flying collar slim-jim orange
tie and alligator belt below the navel pants uptight

'I flirt. You hear me? Yes I flirt. 5
Been on my pretty knees all week
to clean the rich white downtown dirt
the greedy garbage money reek.

I flirt. Damned right. You look at me.'
But William watched her carefully 10
his mustache shaky she could see
him jealous, 'which is how he always be

at parties.' Clementine and Wilhelmina
looked at trouble in the light blue lace
and held to George while Roosevelt Senior   15
circled by the yella high and bitterly light blue face

He liked because she worked
the crowded room like clay like molding men
from dust to muscle jerked
the arms and shoulders moving when   20
she moved.

The Lord Almighty Seagrams[8]
bless
Doretha in her short blue dress
and Roosevelt waiting for his chance: 25
a true gut-funky blues to make her really dance.

                                                            1994

8. Brand of gin.

TONY HARRISON
b. 1937

Tony Harrison was born on April 30, 1937, in the large industrial city of Leeds, England. The city itself is a child of the nineteenth-century Industrial Revolution; it grew prosperous, and ugly, thanks to coal, cotton, and manufacturing of many sorts, but it has been in a state of economic decline since the Great Depression. Harrison's family was working class; his poems often recollect his mother and father (a baker) with love and with a certain remorse. They took great, often uncomprehending, pride in their poet son, who by dint of his energy and education followed a path that veered from their own. In his turn, the poet fears he has lost touch with his working-class roots, lost the regional Yorkshire dialect that he learned from his mother. Harrison's poems embody—in their rich interplay between the literary and the oral, between learned allusion and raw directness, between Standard English and working-class Yorkshire speech—the tension and yearned-for synthesis of the classically educated son and his humble origins.

A collector of languages, Harrison treasures speech, but he also treasures the silence that is the context of speech, the eloquence of the inarticulate. He knows that "Silence and poetry have their own reserves," that the "mute inglorious Miltons" sometimes achieve a force and dignity that are the special property of those for whom words are a hard-won achievement. Harrison praises James Murray, the Scottish lexicographer of rural farm origins who assembled the great *Oxford English Dictionary,* for his hospitable invitation to all words, aristocratic and low-born alike, to join his dictionary. Harrison's characteristic tone, which may have been influenced by William Empson's, is wry and self-deprecating; and sharing James Murray's benevolence toward all words regardless of their social status, delighting in their diversity, recognizing their friction, Harrison takes a similarly wry but benevolent view of human contradictions and contrasts.

Harrison's triumph has been to bring the sensual power, vigor, wit, and immediacy of working-class Yorkshire speech into an exciting amalgam with literary English. He attributes to working-class speech of the north of England a "richer engagement, a more sensual engagement, with language" (*The Economist,* January 23, 1993). Like African American poets, Latino poets, Afro-Caribbean poets, Irish poets, Scottish poets, and others, he has hybridized Standard English with nonstandard oral sounds (e.g., the "glottals" recalled in "On Not Being Milton"), as well as the diction, syntax, and grammar of his regional speech. This is not a harmonious compound but an unstable, sometimes explosive one. The deliberate tension between the sixteen-line sonnet form in the ongoing series *The School of Eloquence* and the poem's unsonnetlike language resembles the struggle between the poet and his skinhead alter ego in the powerful long poem *v.* The *v.* for *versus* signals the poem's preoccupation with oppositions of class, language, and region, but it also, through puns on *versus* and Winston Churchill's *v* sign for *victory,* suggests some hope for mediating these conflicts. One of the most significant British long poems since World War II, *v.* brought Harrison to the notice of a wider audience when a televised version of it aired in 1987, stirring public controversy and charges of obscenity. Since then, he has written on a variety of political subjects, including the Persian Gulf War.

When he was eleven, Tony Harrison was uprooted from his social origins by a scholarship that allowed him to attend the prestigious Leeds Grammar School. Told he would have to learn to speak "properly," he was forbidden, because of his working-class accent, to read his poetry aloud in the classroom. He received a B.A. in classics from the University of Leeds in 1958. After teaching in Nigeria from 1962 to 1966, he taught for a year in Czechoslovakia. In addition to poems, he has written many verse plays, among them versions of Molière's *The Misanthrope* (1973), Racine's *Phaedra Britannica* (1975), and Aeschylus's *Oresteia* (1981). At England's National Theatre, he rendered into an effective dialectal modern English the texts of a number of medieval mystery plays, as *The Mysteries* (1985). This, given what he called the "the plays' Northern character," was a task admirably suited to his genius. He has also translated opera libretti.

FROM THE SCHOOL OF ELOQUENCE[1]

'In 1799 special legislation was introduced "utterly suppressing and prohibiting" by name the London Corresponding Society and the United Englishmen.[2] Even the indefatigable conspirator, John Binns, felt that further national organization was hopeless . . . When arrested he was found in possession of a ticket which was perhaps one of the last "covers"[3] for the old LCS: *Admit for the Season to the School of Eloquence.'*
(E. P. Thompson, *The Making of the English Working Class*)

Nunc mea Pierios cupiam per pectora fontes
Irriguas torquere vias, totumque per ora
Volvere laxatum gemino de vertice rivum;
Ut, tenues oblita sonos, audacibus alis
Surgat in officium venerandi Musa parentis.
Hoc utcunque tibi gratum, pater optime, carmen
Exiguum meditatur opus, nec novimus ipsi
Aptius a nobis quae possint munera donis
Respondere tuis, quamvis nec maxima possint

---

1. A sequence of sixteen-line "sonnets," from which the rest of this volume's selections except *v.* are taken.

2. Eighteenth-century English workingmen's radical societies.
3. That is, masking device.

Respondere tuis, nedum ut par gratia donis
Esse queat, vacuis quae redditur arida verbis . . .

Si modo perpetuos sperare audebitis annos,
Et domini superesse rogo, lucemque tueri,
Nec spisso rapient oblivia nigra sub Orco,
Forsitan has laudes, decantatumque parentis
Nomen, ad exemplum, servo servabitis aevo.

(John Milton, 1637)[4]

Heredity

How you became a poet's a mystery!
Wherever did you get your talent from?
I say: I had two uncles, Joe and Harry—
one was a stammerer, the other dumb.

1981

On Not Being Milton[5]

for Sergio Vieira & Armando Guebuza (Frelimo)[6]

Read and committed to the flames, I call
these sixteen lines that go back to my roots
my *Cahier d'un retour au pays natal,*
my growing black enough to fit my boots.[7]

The stutter of the scold out of the branks   5
of condescension, class and counter-class
thickens with glottals to a lumpen mass
of Ludding morphemes[8] closing up their ranks.
Each swung cast-iron Enoch of Leeds stress[9]

4. The first eleven and the last five lines of a Latin poem, *"Ad Patrem"*—"To (My) Father"—by the seventeenth-century English poet. In Douglas Bush's translation the lines read: "Now I wish that the Pierian waters [of a spring on Mt. Olympus sacred to the Muses] would wind their refreshing way through my breast, and that the whole stream flowing from the twin peaks [of Mt. Parnassus; one sacred to Apollo, god of song, one sacred to Dionysis, god of wine and inspiration] would pour over my lips, so that my Muse, forgetting trivial strains, might rise on bold wings to pay tribute to my revered father. The poem she is meditating is a small effort, and perhaps not very pleasing to you, my dear father; yet I do not know what I can more fitly offer in return for your gifts to me, though my greatest gifts could never match yours, much less can yours be equalled by the barren gratitude expressed in mere words. . . . if only you [that is, my youthful poems] dare hope to enjoy lasting life and survive your master's pyre and see the light, and dark oblivion does not carry you down to crowded Orcus [the underworld of the dead], perhaps these praises, and the name of the father they celebrate, you will preserve as an example to a distant age" (*The Complete Poetical Works of John*

Milton, ed. Douglas Bush, 1965). In the poem, Milton first ascribes the traditional high qualities to poetry and song and then goes on to thank his father for the extensive education he provided for him.
5. See note to the Latin epigraph above.
6. Mozambique's independence party, of which both are members.
7. Cf. the proverb "He's as black as his boot." The "sixteen lines" may refer to Harrison's own attempted translation, since burned, of the sixteen Latin lines by Milton quoted in the epigraph. The French phrase means "Notebook of a return to the native country" and is the title of a work by Aimé Césaire (b. 1913), Martinican writer and a leader of Negritude, a movement asserting black identity.
8. Smallest meaningful units of language. *Branks:* that is, struttings, airs. *Glottals:* that is, glottal stops, or constrictions in the vocal cords, common to north-of-England speech. *Lumpen:* lower-class. *Ludding:* early nineteenth-century workers' protests were called "Luddite riots," after a mythical King Ludd, avenger of worker's wrongs.
9. Strong syllable in a poetic line. "[A]n 'Enoch' is an iron sledge-hammer used by the Luddites to smash the frames [used for weaving] which were

clangs a forged music on the frames of Art,   10
the looms of owned language smashed apart!

Three cheers for mute ingloriousness![1]

Articulation is the tongue-tied's fighting.
In the silence round all poetry we quote
Tidd the Cato Street conspirator who wrote: 15

Sir, I Ham a very Bad Hand at Righting.[2]

                                                              1981

Book Ends

I

Baked the day she suddenly dropped dead
we chew it slowly that last apple pie.

Shocked into sleeplessness you're scared of bed.
We never could talk much, and now don't try.

You're like book ends, the pair of you, she'd say,   5
Hog that grate, say nothing, sit, sleep, stare . . .

The 'scholar' me, you, worn out on poor pay,
only our silence made us seem a pair.

Not as good for staring in, blue gas,
too regular each bud, each yellow spike.[3]   10

A night you need my company to pass
and she not here to tell us we're alike!

Your life's all shattered into smithereens.

Back in our silences and sullen looks,
for all the Scotch we drink, what's still between 's   15
not the thirty or so years, but books, books, books.

II

The stone's too full. The wording must be terse.
There's scarcely room to carve the FLORENCE on it—

---

also made by the same Enoch Taylor of Marsden.
The cry was: 'Enoch made them, Enoch shall break
them!'" [Harrison's note].
1. Cf. "some mute inglorious Milton" in "Elegy
Written in a Country Churchyard," by English poet
Thomas Gray (1716–1771).
2. The "Cato Street conspiracy" (1820) was a

failed radical plot to kill members of the king's cab-
inet.
3. Flames from the gas fire, common in lower-
class English homes; it is often manufactured to
resemble a log, but its flames are more "regular"
than those of a real fire.

Come on, it's not as if we're wanting verse.
It's not as if we're wanting a whole sonnet!   20

After tumblers of neat *Johnny Walker*[4]
(I think that both of us we're on our third)
you said you'd always been a clumsy talker
and couldn't find another, shorter word
for 'beloved' or for 'wife' in the inscription,   25
but not too clumsy that you can't still cut:

You're supposed to be the bright boy at description
and you can't tell them what the fuck to put!

I've got to find the right words on my own.

I've got the envelope that he'd been scrawling,   30
mis-spelt, mawkish, stylistically appalling
but I can't squeeze more love into their stone.

1981

Turns

I thought it made me look more 'working class'
(as if a bit of chequered cloth could bridge that gap!)
I did a turn in it before the glass.
My mother said: *It suits you, your dad's cap.*[5]
(She preferred me to wear suits and part my hair: 5
You're every bit as good as that lot are!)

All the pension queue[6] came out to stare.
Dad was sprawled beside the postbox (still VR),[7]
his cap turned inside up beside his head,
smudged H A H in purple Indian ink   10
and Brylcreem[8] slicks displayed so folk might think
he wanted charity for dropping dead.

He never begged. For nowt![9] Death's reticence
crowns his life's, and *me*, I'm opening my trap
to busk the class that broke him for the pence   15
that splash like brackish tears into our cap.[1]

1981

---

4. Brand of Scotch whiskey.
5. Soft cloth cap with a visor, commonly worn by, as the poem says, members of the "working class."
6. Line of retired people waiting for their pension (that is, social security) checks.
7. Sidewalk mailbox dating from the time of Queen Victoria and bearing her name and Latin title, *Victoria Regina*.
8. Hair oil.
9. Nothing (northern dialect).
1. "Buskers" perform in the street, in train stations, and so on, collecting money in a cap.

Marked with D.[2]

When the chilled dough of his flesh went in an oven[3]
not unlike those he fuelled all his life,
I thought of his cataracts[4] ablaze with Heaven
and radiant with the sight of his dead wife,
light streaming from his mouth to shape her name,   5
'not Florence and not Flo but always Florrie'.
I thought how his cold tongue burst into flame
but only literally, which makes me sorry,
sorry for his sake there's no Heaven to reach.
I get it all from Earth my daily bread   10
but he hungered for release from mortal speech
that kept him down, the tongue that weighed like lead.

The baker's man that no one will see rise
and England made to feel like some dull oaf
is smoke, enough to sting one person's eyes   15
and ash (not unlike flour) for one small loaf.

                                                          1981

Timer

Gold survives the fire that's hot enough
to make you ashes in a standard urn.
An envelope of coarse official buff[5]
contains your wedding ring which wouldn't burn.

Dad told me I'd to tell them at St James's[6]   5
that the ring should go in the incinerator.
That 'eternity' inscribed with both their names is
his surety that they'd be together, 'later'.

I signed for the parcelled clothing as the son,
the cardy,[7] apron, pants, bra, dress—   10

the clerk phoned down: 6-8-8-3-1?
Has she still her ring on? (Slight pause) *Yes!*

It's on my warm palm now, your burnished ring!

2. Cf. the nursery rhyme "Pat-a-cake, pat-a-cake
baker's man, / Bake me a cake as fast as you can; /
Pat it and prick it and mark it with a D [or whatever
the baby's initial is], / And put it in the oven for
baby and me."
3. His father is being cremated.
4. Clouding of the eyes' lenses.
5. Yellowish; the color of official forms in En-
gland.
6. Presumably, the crematorium.
7. Cardigan.

I feel your ashes, head, arms, breasts, womb, legs,
sift through its circle slowly, like that thing   15
you used to let me watch to time the eggs.[8]

1981

Self Justification

Me a poet! My daughter with maimed limb
became a more than tolerable sprinter.
And Uncle Joe. Impediment spurred him,
the worst stammerer I've known, to be a printer.

He handset type much faster than he spoke.   5
Those cruel consonants, *ms*, *ps*, and *bs*
on which his jaws and spirit almost broke
flicked into order with sadistic ease.

It seems right that Uncle Joe, 'b-buckshee
from the works',[9] supplied those scribble pads   10
on which I stammered my first poetry
that made me seem a cissy[1] to the lads.

Their aggro[2] towards me, my need of them 's
what keeps my would-be mobile tongue still tied—

aggression, struggle, loss, blank printer's ems   15
by which all   eloquence   gets justified.[3]

1981

History Classes

Past scenic laybys and stag warning signs[4]
the British borderlands roll into view.

They read: *Beware of Unexploded Mines!*[5]
I tell my children that was World War II.

They want to walk or swim. We pick up speed.   5
My children boo the flash of each NO ENTRY:

8. Egg-timer that works like a miniature hour-glass.
9. That is, free from the factory.
1. Sissy.
2. Initially short for "aggravation," it now means mindless violence (British slang).
3. (1) Proven to be right; (2) printer's term: to justify is to space lines of type so that the right-hand margins are even. In handset type and linotype, a

"blank em" is a small square of metal that leaves a blank space the width of the letter *M*; here, the spaces before and after "eloquence" are "2-em spaces."
4. That is, "deer crossing" signs. *Laybys:* widenings in a highway for parking.
5. Buried underground against possible German attack.

High seas, and shooting, uniform or tweed,
Ministry of Defence, or landed gentry.[6]

Danger flags from valley mills that throve,
after a fashion, on the Empire's needs.   10

Their own clothes spun in India they wove
the Colonel's khaki and the blue blood's tweeds.

Mill angelus, and church tower twice as high.
One foundry[7] cast the work- and rest-day bells—

the same red cotton 's in the flags that fly   15
for ranges, revolutions, and rough swells.[8]

                                        1978, 1981

                        v.

'My father still reads the dictionary every day. He says your life
depends on your power to master words.'
                                        —ARTHUR SCARGILL[9]
                                The Sunday Times, 10 Jan. 1982

Next millennium you'll have to search quite hard
to find my slab behind the family dead,
butcher, publican[1] and baker, now me, bard
adding poetry to their beef, beer and bread.

With Byron three graves on I'll not go short   5
of company, and Wordsworth's[2] opposite.
That's two peers already, of a sort,
and we'll all be thrown together if the pit,

whose galleries[3] once ran beneath this plot,
causes the distinguished dead to drop   10
into the rabblement of bone and rot,
shored slack, crushed shale, smashed prop.[4]

Wordsworth built church organs, Byron tanned
luggage cowhide in the age of steam,

6. That is, "NO ENTRY" into army encampments
or private estates.
7. Metal-casting factory. *Angelus:* bell announc-
ing a Roman Catholic devotion, used here for the
mill's bell.
8. (1) Crude, pompous leaders; (2) stormy ocean.
Ranges: army firing ranges, where red flags are
used as signals.
9. Head (b. 1938) of the British National Union

of Mineworkers (N.U.M.), who led the national
miner's strike of 1984–85.
1. Keeper of a pub.
2. Here, workers (lines 13–14) with the same last
names as William Wordsworth (1770–1850) and
George Gordon, Lord Byron (1788–1824), English
poets.
3. Underground mine passages. *Pit:* mine shaft.
4. Support beam. *Slack:* small bits of coal.

and knew their place of rest before the land 15
caves in on the lowest worked-out seam.[5]

This graveyard on the brink of Beeston Hill 's
the place I may well rest if there 's a spot
under the rose roots and the daffodils
by which Dad dignified the family plot. 20

If buried ashes saw then I'd survey
the places I learned Latin, and learned Greek,
and left, the ground where Leeds United[6] play
but disappoint their fans week after week,

which makes them lose their sense of self-esteem 25
and taking a shortcut home through these graves here
they reassert the glory of their team
by spraying words on tombstones, pissed[7] on beer.

This graveyard stands above a worked-out pit.
Subsidence makes the obelisks all list. 30
One leaning left 's marked FUCK, one right 's marked SHIT
sprayed by some peeved supporter who was pissed.

Farsighted for his family's future dead,
but for his wife, this banker 's still alone
on his long obelisk, and doomed to head 35
a blackened dynasty of unclaimed stone,

now graffitied with a crude four-letter word.
His children and grandchildren went away
and never came back home to be interred
so left a lot of space for skins[8] to spray. 40

The language of this graveyard ranges from
a bit of Latin for a former mayor
or those who laid their lives down at the Somme,[9]
the hymnal fragments and the gilded prayer,

how people 'fell asleep in the Good Lord,' 45
brief chisellable bits from the good book
and rhymes whatever length they could afford
to CUNT, PISS, SHIT and (mostly) FUCK!

or, more expansively, there's LEEDS v.
the opponent of last week, this week, or next, 50
and a repertoire of blunt four-letter curses
on the team or race that makes the sprayer vexed.

---

5. Layer of coal.
6. Football (soccer) team. *Leeds:* an industrial area
in West Yorkshire, in the north of England.
7. Drunk.

8. Skinheads.
9. Site in northern France of costly battles during
World War I.

Then, rushed for time, or fleeing some observer,
dodging between tall family vaults and trees,
like his team's best-ever winger, dribbler, swerver,[1]   55
fills every space he finds with versus Vs.

Vs sprayed on the run at such a lick,
the sprayer master of his flourished tool,
get short-armed on the left like that red tick
they never marked his work much with at school.   60

Half this skinhead's age but with approval
I helped whitewash a V on a brick wall.
No one clamoured in the press for its removal
or thought the sign, in wartime, rude at all.[2]

These Vs are all the versuses of life   65
from LEEDS v. DERBY, Black/White
and (as I've known to my cost) man v. wife,
Communist v. Fascist, Left v. Right,

class v. class as bitter as before,
the unending violence of US and THEM,   70
personified in 1984
by Coal Board MacGregor[3] and the N.U.M.,

Hindu/Sikh, soul/body, heart v. mind,
East/West, male/female, and the ground
these fixtures are fought out on 's Man, resigned   75
to hope from his future what his past never found.

The prospects for the present aren't too grand
when a swastika with NF (National Front)[4] 's
sprayed on a grave, to which another hand
has added, in a reddish colour, CUNTS.   80

Which is, I grant, the word that springs to mind
when, going to clear the weeds and rubbish thrown
on the family grave by football fans, I find
UNITED graffitied on my parents' stone.

How many British graveyards now this May   85
are strewn with rubbish and choked up with weeds
since families and friends have gone away
for work or fuller lives, like me, from Leeds?

When I first came here 40 years ago
with my dad to 'see' my grandma I was 7.   90

1. Player who moves in the wing, dribbles (moves
the ball forward with short kicks), or swerves.
2. During World War II, V represented victory.
3. Sir Ian MacGregor (1912–1998), head of the
National Coal Board, which, as part of the Con-
servative government of Prime Minister Margaret
Thatcher (b. 1925), defeated an N.U.M. strike in
1984–85.
4. Fascist group.

I helped Dad with the flowers. He let me know
she'd gone to join my granddad up in Heaven.

My dad who came each week to bring fresh flowers
came home with clay stains on his trouser knees.
Since my parents' deaths I've spent 2 hours   95
made up of odd 10 minutes such as these,

Flying visits once or twice a year,
and though I'm horrified, just who's to blame
that I find instead of flowers cans of beer
and more than one grave sprayed with some skin's name?   100

Where there were flower urns and troughs of water
and mesh receptacles for withered flowers
are the HARP[5] tins of some skinhead Leeds supporter.
It isn't all his fault, though. Much is ours.

5 kids, with one in goal, play 2-a-side.   105
When the ball bangs on the hawthorn that's one post
and petals fall they hum 'Here Comes the Bride'
though not so loud they'd want to rouse a ghost.

They boot the ball on purpose at the trunk
and make the tree shed showers of shrivelled may.[6]   110
I look at this word graffitied by some drunk
and I'm in half a mind to let it stay.

(Though honesty demands that I say *if*
I'd wanted to take the necessary pains
to scrub the skin's inscription off   115
I only had an hour between trains.

So the feelings that I had as I stood gazing
and the significance I saw could be a sham,
mere excuses for not patiently erasing
the word sprayed on the grave of Dad and Mam.)   120

This pen 's all I have of magic wand.
I know this world's so torn but want no other
except for Dad who'd hoped from 'the Beyond'
a better life than this one *with* my mother.

Though I don't believe in afterlife at all   125
and know it's cheating, it's hard not to make
a sort of furtive prayer from this skin's scrawl,
his UNITED means 'in Heaven' for their sake,

an accident of meaning to redeem
an act intended as mere desecration   130

5. Brand of beer.   6. Blossoms of the hawthorn tree.

and make the thoughtless spraying of his team
apply to higher things, and to the nation.

Some, where kids use aerosols, use giant signs
to let the people know who's forged their fetters
like PRI CE O WALES above West Yorkshire mines   135
(no prizes for who nicked the missing letters!)

The big blue star for booze, tobacco ads,
the magnate's monogram, the royal crest,
insignia in neon dwarf the lads
who spray a few odd FUCKs when they're depressed.   140

Letters of transparent tubes and gas
in Dusseldorf are blue and flash out KRUPP.[7]
Arms are hoisted for the British ruling class
and clandestine, genteel aggro[8] keeps them up.

And there's HARRISON on some Leeds building sites   145
I've taken in fun as blazoning my name,
which I've also seen on books, in Broadway lights,
so why can't skins with spray cans do the same?

But why inscribe these *graves* with CUNT and SHIT?
Why choose neglected tombstones to disfigure?   150
This pitman's of last century daubed PAKI GIT,[9]
this grocer Broadbent's aerosoled with NIGGER?

They're there to shock the living, not arouse
the dead from their deep peace to lend support
for any cause skins' spray cans could espouse.   155
The dead would want their desecrators caught!

Jobless though they are how can these kids,
even though their team 's lost one more game,
believe that the 'Pakis,' 'Niggers,' even 'Yids'[1]
sprayed on the tombstones here should take the blame?   160

What is it that these crude words are revealing?
What is it that this aggro act implies?
Giving the dead their xenophobic feeling
or just a *cri-de-coeur*[2] because Man dies.

So what's a cri-de-coeur, *cunt? Can't yer speak*   165
the language that yer mam spoke? Think of 'er!
Can yer only get yer tongue round fucking Greek?
Go and fuck yerself with cri-de-coeur!

7. German company manufacturing industrial ma-
chinery. *Düsseldorf*: city in western Germany.
8. British slang for "aggravation," typically imply-
ing a threat of violence.

9. *Paki*: derogatory term for Pakistani. *Git*: worth-
less person.
1. Derogatory term for Jews.
2. Cry from the heart (French).

'She didn't talk like you do for a start!'
I shouted, turning where I thought the voice had been.   170
She didn't understand yer fucking art!
She thought yer fucking poetry obscene!

I wish on this skin's word deep aspirations,
first the prayer for my parents I can't make,
then a call to Britain and to all the nations   175
made in the name of love for peace's sake.

Aspirations, cunt! Folk on t' fucking dole[3]
'ave got about as much scope to aspire
above the shit they're dumped in, cunt, as coal
aspires to be chucked on t' fucking fire.   180

O.K., forget the aspirations! Look, I know
United's losing gets you fans incensed
and how far the HARP inside you makes you go
but all these Vs: against! against! against!

Ah'll tell yer then what really riles a bloke.   185
It's reading on their graves the jobs they did—
butcher, publican and baker. Me, I'll croak
doing t' same nowt ah do now as a kid.

'ard birth ah wor, mi mam says, almost killed 'er.
Death after life on t' dole won't seem as 'ard!   190
Look at this cunt, Wordsworth, organ builder,
this fucking 'aberdasher,[4] *Appleyard!*

If mi mam's up there, don't want to meet 'er
listening to me list mi dirty deeds
and 'ave to pipe up to St. fucking Peter[5]   195
ah've been on t' dole all mi life in fucking Leeds.

Then t' Alleluias stick in t' angels' gobs.
When dole-wallahs[6] *fuck off to the void*
what'll t' mason carve up for their jobs?
The cunts who lieth 'ere wor unemployed?   200

This lot worked at one job all life through.
Byron, 'Tanner,' Lieth 'ere interred!
They'll chisel fucking poet when they do you
and that, yer cunt, 's a crude four-letter word.

'Listen, cunt!' I said, 'before you start your jeering,   205
the reason why I want this in a book

---

3. Unemployment benefits.
4. Dealer in hats, fabrics, ribbons, and so on.
Nowt: nothing.
5. St. Peter is often represented as the holder of
the keys to the Christian Heaven.

6. People receiving unemployment. *Wallah:* British slang for person, from the Hindi suffix *wala,*
meaning "one in charge of." *Gobs:* mouths (northern English).

's to give ungrateful cunts like you a hearing!'
A book, yer stupid cunt, 's not worth a fuck!

'The only reason why I write this poem at all
on yobs[7] like you who do the dirt on death   210
's to give some higher meaning to your scrawl!'
Don't fucking bother, cunt! Don't waste your breath!

'You piss-artist skinhead cunt, you wouldn't know
and it doesn't fucking matter if you do,
the skin and poet united fucking Rimbaud[8]   215
but the *autre* that *je est* is fucking you.'

Ah've told yer, no more Greek. That's yer last warning!
Ah'll boot yer fucking balls to Kingdom Come.
They'll find yer cold on t' grave tomorrer morning.
So don't speak Greek. Don't treat me like I'm dumb.   220

'I've done my bits of mindless aggro too
not half a mile from where we're standing now.'
Yeah, ah bet yer wrote a poem, yer wanker you!
'No, shut yer gob awhile. Ah'll tell yer 'ow . . .

'Herman Darewski's[9] band played operetta   225
with a wobbly soprano warbling. Just why
I made my mind up that I'd got to get her
with the fire hose I can't say, but I'll try.

'It wasn't just the singing angered me.
At the same time half a crowd was jeering   230
as the smooth Hugh Gaitskell, our MP,[1]
made promises the other half was cheering.

'What I hated in those high soprano ranges
was uplift beyond all reason and control
and in a world where you say nothing changes   235
it seemed a sort of prick-tease of the soul.

'I tell you when I heard high notes that rose
above Hugh Gaitskell's cool electioneering
straight from the warbling throat right up my nose,
I had all your aggro in *my* jeering.   240

'And I hit the fire extinguisher ON knob
and covered orchestra and audience with spray.
I could run as fast as you then. A good job!
They yelled 'Damned vandal' after me that day . . . '

---

7. Thugs.
8. French Symbolist poet Arthur Rimbaud (1854–1891) once wrote "Je est un autre" ("I is another").
9. British band leader (1883–1947), music pub-
lisher, and composer of popular war songs.
1. Member of Parliament. Hugh Gaitskell (1906–1963), leader of the Labour Party from 1955 until his death.

And then yer saw the light and gave up 'eavy 245
And knew a man's not 'ow much 'e can sup² . . .
Yer reward for growing up's this super-bevvy,
a meths and champagne punch in t'FA Cup.³

Ah've 'eard all that from old farts past their prime.
'ow now yer live wi' all yer once detested . . . 250
Old farts wi' not much left'll give me time.
Fuckers like that get folk like me arrested.

Covet not thy neighbour's wife, thy neighbour's riches.
Vicar and cop who say, to save our souls:
Get thee behind me, Satan!⁴ drop their *breeches* 255
and get the Devil's dick right up their 'oles!

It was more a working marriage that I'd meant,
a blend of masculine and feminine.
Ignoring me, he started looking, bent
on some more aerosoling, for his tin. 260

'It was more a working marriage that I mean!'
Fuck, and save mi soul, eh? That suits me.
Then as if I'd egged him on to be obscene
he added a middle slit to one daubed V.

Don't talk to me of fucking representing 265
the class yer were born into anymore.
Yer going to get 'urt and start resenting
it's not poetry we need in this class war.

Yer've given yerself toffee, cunt. Who needs
yer fucking poufy words. Ah write mi own. 270
Ah've got mi work on show all over Leeds
like this UNITED 'ere on some sod's stone.

'O.K.!' (thinking I had him trapped). 'O.K.!'
'If you're so proud of it then sign your name
when next you're full of HARP and armed with spray, 275
next time you take this shortcut from the game.'

He took the can, contemptuous, unhurried,
and cleared the nozzle and prepared to sign
the UNITED sprayed where Mam and Dad were buried.
He aerosoled his name, and it was mine. 280

The boy footballers bawl 'Here Comes the Bride'
and drifting blossoms fall onto my head.

2. Drink. *'Eavy:* that is, heavy bitter (beer).
3. Prize awarded to the winner of the Football Association's annual Challenge Cup series. *Bevvy:* beverage. *Meths:* methylated spirits.

4. Jesus' response both to Peter's objection to the intimations of his ensuing sacrifice (Matthew 16.23, Mark 8.33) and to the temptations of the devil (Luke 4.8).

One half of me 's alive but one half died
when the skin half sprayed my name among the dead.

Half versus half, the enemies within   285
the heart that can't be whole till they unite.
As I stoop to grab the crushed HARP lager tin
the day 's already dusk, half dark, half light.

The UNITED that I'd wished onto the nation
or as reunion for dead parents soon recedes.   290
The word 's once more a mindless desecration
by some HARPoholic yob supporting Leeds.

Almost the time for ghosts. I'd better scram.
Though not give much to fears of spooky scaring
I don't fancy an encounter with mi mam   295
playing Hamlet with me for this swearing.[5]

Though I've a train to catch my step is slow.
I walk on the grass and graves with wary tread
over the subsidences, these shifts below
the life of Leeds supported by the dead.   300

Further underneath 's that cavernous hollow
that makes the gravestones lean towards the town.
A matter of mere time and it will swallow
this place of rest and all the resters down.

I tell myself I've got, say, 30 years.   305
At 75 this place will suit me fine.
I've never feared the grave but what I fear 's
that great worked-out black hollow under mine.

Not train departure time and not Town Hall
with the great white clock face I can see,   310
coal, that began, with no man here at all,
as 300-million-year-old plant debris.

5 kids still play at making blossoms fall
and humming as they do 'Here Comes the Bride.'
They never seem to tire of their ball   315
though I hear a woman's voice call one inside.

2 larking boys play bawdy bride and groom.
3 boys in Leeds strip la-la *Lohengrin.*[6]
I hear them as I go through growing gloom
still years away from being skald[7] or skin.   320

---

5. In Shakespeare's *Hamlet,* the prince is haunted
by the ghost of his father.
6. "Here Comes the Bride" comes from *Lohen-*
grin, an opera by German composer Richard Wag-
ner (1813–1883).
7. Bard.

The ground 's carpeted with petals as I throw
the aerosol, the HARP can, the cleared weeds
on top of Dad's dead daffodils, then go,
with not one glance behind away from Leeds.

The bus to the station 's still the No. 1   325
but goes by routes that I don't recognize.
I look out for known landmarks as the sun
reddens the swabs of cloud in darkening skies.

Home, home, home, to my woman as the red
darkens from a fresh blood to a dried.   330
Home, home to my woman, home to bed
where opposites are sometimes unified.

A pensioner in turban taps his stick
along the pavement past the corner shop,
that sells samosas now not beer on tick,[8]   335
to the Kashmir Muslim Club that was the Co-op.

House after house FOR SALE where we'd played cricket
with white roses[9] cut from flour sacks on our caps,
with stumps chalked on the coal grate for our wicket,
and every one bought now by 'coloured chaps,'   340

Dad's most liberal label as he felt
squeezed by the unfamiliar, and fear
of foreign food and faces, when he smelt
curry in the shop where he'd bought beer.

And growing frailer, 'wobbly on his pins,'[1]   345
the shops he felt familiar with withdrew
which meant much longer tiring treks for tins
that had a label on them that he knew.

And as the shops that stocked his favourites receded
whereas he'd fancied beans and popped next door,   350
he found that four long treks a week were needed
till he wondered what he bothered eating for.

The supermarket made him feel embarrassed.
Where people bought whole lambs for family freezers
he bought baked beans from checkout girls too harassed   355
to smile or swap a joke with sad old geezers.

But when he bought his cigs he'd have a chat,
his week's one conversation, truth to tell,
but time also came and put a stop to that
when old Wattsy got bought out by M. Patel.   360

---

8. Credit.   1. Legs.
9. The emblem of Yorkshire and its cricket team.

And there, 'Time like an ever-rolling stream' 's[2]
what I once trilled behind that boarded front.
A 1000 ages made coal-bearing seams
and even more the hand that sprayed this CUNT

on both Methodist and C of E[3] billboards   365
once divided in their fight for local souls.
Whichever house more truly was the Lord's
both's pews are filled with cut-price toilet rolls.

Home, home to my woman, never to return
till sexton or survivor has to cram   370
the bits of clinker[4] scooped out of my urn
down through the rose roots to my dad and mam.

Home, home to my woman, where the fire 's lit
these still-chilly mid-May evenings, home to you,
and perished vegetation from the pit   375
escaping insubstantial up the flue.

Listening to *Lulu*,[5] in our hearth we burn,
as we hear the high Cs rise in stereo,
what was lush swamp club moss and tree fern
at least 300 million years ago.   380

Shilbottle cobbles,[6] Alban Berg high D
lifted from a source that bears your name,
the one we hear decay, the one we see,
the fern from the foetid forest, as brief flame.

This world, with far too many people in,   385
starts on the TV logo as a taw,[7]
then ping-pong, tennis, football; then one spin
to show us all, then shots of the Gulf War.[8]

As the coal with reddish dust cools in the grate
on the late-night national news we see   390
police v. pickets at a coke[9] plant gate,
old violence and old disunity.

The map that's colour-coded Ulster/Eire[1] 's
flashed on again, as almost every night.
Behind a tiny coffin with two bearers   395
men in masks with arms show off their might.

The day's last images recede to first a glow
and then a ball that shrinks back to blank screen.

---

2. From the hymn "O God, our help in ages past."
3. Church of England.
4. Remnants of combustion.
5. Opera by avant-garde Austrian composer Alban Berg (1885–1935).
6. Coal.
7. Marble.
8. War between Iran and Iraq (1980–90).
9. Fuel made from coal.
1. Northern Ireland (Orange) and the Republic of Ireland (Green).

Turning to love, and sleep's oblivion, I know
what the UNITED that the skin sprayed *has* to mean.   400

Hanging my clothes up, from my parka hood
may and apple petals, brown and creased,
fall onto the carpet and bring back the flood
of feelings their first falling had released.

I hear like ghosts from all Leeds matches humming   405
with one concerted voice the bride, the bride
I feel united to, *my* bride is coming
into the bedroom, naked, to my side.

The ones we choose to love become our anchor
when the hawser² of the blood tie 's hacked or frays.   410
But a voice that scorns chorales is yelling: *Wanker!*
It's the aerosoling skin I met today's.

My alter ego wouldn't want to know it,
his aerosol vocab would balk at LOVE,
the skin's UNITED underwrites the poet,   415
the measures carved below the ones above.

I doubt if 30 years of bleak Leeds weather
and 30 falls of apple and of may
will erode the UNITED binding us together.
And now it's your decision. Does it stay?   420

Next millennium you'll have to search quite hard
to find out where I'm buried, but I'm near
the grave of haberdasher Appleyard,
the pile of HARPs, or some new neoned beer.

Find Byron, Wordsworth, or turn left between   425
one grave marked Broadbent, one marked Richardson.
Bring some solution with you that can clean
whatever new crude words have been sprayed on.

If love of art, or love, gives you affront
that the grave I'm in 's graffitied, then, maybe,   430
erase the more offensive FUCK and CUNT
but leave, with the worn UNITED, one small *v.*

victory? For vast, slow, coal-creating forces
that hew the body's seams to get the soul.
Will earth run out of her 'diurnal courses'³   435
before repeating her creation of black coal?

---

2. Rope used for securing a ship.
3. Cf. Wordsworth's poem "A Slumber Did My Spirit Seal," in which the speaker's spirit "neither hears nor sees; / Rolled round in earth's diurnal course, / With rocks, and stones, and trees."

> But choose a day like I chose in mid-May
> or earlier when apple and hawthorn tree,
> no matter if boys boot their ball all day,
> cling to their blossoms and won't shake them free— 440
>
> if, having come this far, somebody reads
> these verses, and he/she wants to understand,
> face this grave on Beeston Hill, your back to Leeds,
> and read the chiselled epitaph I've planned:
>
> *Beneath your feet 's a poet, then a pit.* 445
> *Poetry supporter, if you're here to find*
> *how poems can grow from* (beat you to it!) SHIT
> *find the beef, the beer, the bread, then look behind.*

1985, 1989

SUSAN HOWE
b. 1937

Susan Howe was born on June 10, 1937, in Boston. Her mother was an Irish actress and playwright, her father a law professor at Harvard with a strong interest in American colonial history. Howe remarked in a 1994 interview that her mother "had the ear as a writer," and elsewhere she has said that for her as a poet, "sound creates meaning. Sound is the core" (*The Difficulties*). Her father "was obsessed by footnotes," and Howe refers to at least one of her poems as "one huge footnote" (1994 interview). Her poetry mediates between the archival and the musical, between rigorous historicism and aesthetic abandon. It fuses the Calvinistic severity she associates with her father's New England and the verbal play and performance she associates with her mother's Ireland. After high school, Howe spent two years as an apprentice in acting at the Gate Theatre in Dublin—in her view, "an irrevocable mistake" (*The Difficulties*). Returning to the United States, she majored in painting at the School of the Museum of Fine Arts, Boston, graduating in 1961. As a visual artist, she first became interested in collage and quotation—techniques that would characterize her poetry. In the poetic series "Rückenfigur," she draws on the subgenre of paintings in which spectators are represented with their backs to the viewer. In poems such as "Thorow" (a phonetic misspelling of Thoreau), Howe makes striking use of the visual appearance of poetry on the page, printing lines at angles, upside down, or superimposed on each other. She published her first book of poetry, *Hinge Picture*, in 1974. Having worked as a radio producer and bookseller as well as an artist, she began to teach in the English Department at the State University of New York, Buffalo, in 1988.

Because of her poetry's seeming impersonality, collage-based density, and semantic and syntactic fragmentation, Howe has often been grouped with the Language poets. If poetry conventionally seeks fluent self-expression, Howe wants hers to be a poetry of stuttering, interruption, brokenness. Probing the spaces between words, the gaps between syllables, the silences surrounding lines on the page, she would recover something of what seamless language suppresses. Her poetry is a heap of broken tombstones, marking various absences and occlusions. "The moment a word is put on the page," she has said, "there's a kind of death in that." A feminist, Howe mourns the voices of women silenced by patriarchy. A revisionist, she remembers individuals and peoples marginalized or erased by traditional history. An ardent archivist, she commemorates lost or forgotten manuscripts supplanted by official texts. She mourns more personal losses as well. In the series "Rückenfigur," she obliquely elegizes her husband and companion of twenty-seven years, the sculptor David von Schlegell, who died in 1992. Responding to lost individuals, voices, histories, texts, and meanings, Howe labors to recover them and yet also to mark their ultimate irrecuperability. Without claiming that she can compensate for such losses and effacements, Howe remembers and even embodies them in her poetry's fissures, echoes, and ghostly traces.

From Thorow

Gabion
Parapet

Traverse canon night siege Constant firing
Escalade

Tranquillity of a garrison

Places to walk out to
Cove

waterbug

mud

shrub

wavelet

cusk

cedar grease chip coin

splint

drisk

The Frames should be exactly

fitted to the paper, the Margins

of which will not per[mit] of

a very deep Rabbit

Messages

The French Hatchet
neck

& singing their war song
islet

battered The War Belt

Messengers say

over the lakes

Of the far nations

canoes
wood
Fires by night
Encamp t

swamp

lily root

disc
Their plenipo
sheen

At this end of the carry

hieroglyph

Picked up arrowhead

1990

Rückenfigur[1]

Iseult stands at Tintagel[2]
on the mid stairs between
light and dark symbolism
Does she stand for phonic
human overtone for outlaw   5
love the dread pull lothly
for weariness actual brute
predestined fact for phobic
falling no one talking too
Tintagel ruin of philosophy   10
here is known change here
is come crude change wave
wave determinist caparison[3]
Your soul your separation

                        •

But the counterfeit Iseult   15
Iseult aux Blanches Mains[4]
stands by the wall to listen
Phobic thought of openness
a soul also has two faces
Iseult's mother and double   20
Iseult the Queen later in T[5]
Even Tros echoes Tristan's
infirmity through spurious
etymology the Tintagel of Fo

1. Figure seen from behind (German); translated within the poem as "retreating figure." *Rückenfigur* is also the name of a subgenre of paintings in which halted travelers have their backs to the viewer, most famously in the landscape paintings of German Romantic Caspar David Friedrich (1774–1840). In a letter to the editor of this anthology, Howe cites as sources Friedrich's paintings (e.g., *Moonrise over the Sea, Moonrise at Sea, Flatlands on the Bay of Greifswald, Woman before the Setting Sun*) and Joseph Leo Koerner's discussion of them in *Caspar David Friedrich and the Subject of Landscape* (New Haven, 1990).
2. Village south of the rocky promontory Tintagel Head, in Cornwall, England. Reputed birthplace of King Arthur and site of twelfth-century castle, where Tristan is said to have fallen in love with Iseult. *Iseult:* lover of Tristan in medieval legend of Celtic origin. Tristan is sent to Ireland to bring back Iseult to be the bride of his uncle, King Mark. But after drinking a love potion Tristan and Iseult become lovers. She dies of sorrow on learning he has died waiting for her.
3. Cloth draped over a horse's saddle; adornment.
4. Iseult of the white hands (French). According to legend, the lovers become estranged late in life and Tristan marries another woman, also named Iseult: Iseult of the White Hands.
5. *T, Tros,* and *Fo* are scholarly abbreviations for fragments of different versions of the legend.

not the dead city of night   25
Wall in the element of Logic
here is a door and beyond
here is the sail she spies

                    •

Tristran Tristan Tristrant
Tristram Trystan Trystram   30
Tristrem Tristanz Drust
Drystan[6] these names concoct
a little wreathe of victory
dreaming over the landscape
Tintagel font icon twilight   35
Grove bough dark wind cove
brine testimony Iseult salt
Iseut Isolde Ysolt Essyllt
bride of March Marc Mark in
the old French commentaries   40
your secret correspondence
Soft Iseut two Iseults one

                    •

The third of Tristan's overt
identities is a double one
his disguise as nightingale   45
in *Tros* then wild man in *Fo*
Level and beautiful La Blanche
Lande[7] of disguise episodes
the nocturnal garden of *Tros*
Fo recalls the scene in Ovid[8]   50
Orpheus grief stricken over
the loss of Eurydice sits by
the bank of a river seven days
I see Mark's shadow in water

6. The names of the main characters vary in the legend's many different versions.
7. The white moor (French).
8. Roman poet (43 B.C.E.?–17 C.E.) and author of the *Metamorphoses*, which tells the story of Orpheus's grief after losing his wife, Eurydice, in Hades.

Mark's moral right to Iseult   55

David's relationship to Saul[9]

•

Lean on handrail river below

Sense of depth focus motion

of chaos in Schlegel[1] only as

visual progress into depth its   60

harsh curb estrangement logic

Realism still exists is part

of the realist dual hypothesis

Dual on verso[2] as one who has

obeyed acceleration velocity   65

killing frost regenerative thaw

you other rowing forward face

backward Hesperides[3] messenger

into the pastness of landscape

inarticulate scrawl awash air   70

•

Insufferably pale the icy

limit pulls and pulls no

kindness free against you

Deep quietness never to be

gathered no blind threat   75

Assuredly I see division

can never be weighed once

pale anguish breathes free

to be unhallowed empty what

in thought or other sign   80

roof and lintel remember

Searching shall I know is

---

9. 1 Samuel describes David's ascension from King Saul's protégé to his successor.

1. Friedrich von Schlegel (1772–1829), German Romantic philosopher. In his book on Caspar David Friedrich's paintings, Koerner cites Schlegel's "we are potential, *chaotic* organic beings," adding that Friedrich's landscapes aspire to what Schlegel called "artful chaos" (*Kunstchaos*). Two figures at a handrail above a river can be seen in a destroyed *Rückenfigur* by Friedrich, *Augustus Bridge in Dresden* (c. 1830).

2. Left-hand page of an open book; reverse side of a coin or medal.

3. In Greek mythology, the maidens entrusted with guarding Hera's tree of golden apples.

some sense deepest moment
What is and what appears

•

The way light is broken   85
To splinter color blue
the color of day yellow
near night the color of
passion red by morning
His name of grief being   90
red sound to sense sense
in place of the slaying
Tristram must be caught
Saw the mind otherwise
in thought or other sign   95
because we are not free
Saw the mind otherwise
Two thoughts in strife

•

Separation requires an
other quest for union   100
I use a white thread
half of the same paper
and in the sun's light
I place a lens so that
the sea reflects back   105
violet and blue making
rays easily more freely
your nativity and you
of light from that of
memory when eyelids close   110
so in dream sensation
Mind's trajected light

•

It is precision we have
to deal with we can pre-

scind space from color if   115

Thomas[4] was only using a

metaphor and metaphysics

professes to be metaphor

There is a way back to the

misinterpretation of her   120

message TheseusTristan is

on the ship AegeusIseut[5]

is a land watcher she is

a mastermind her frailty

turned to the light her   125

single vision twin soul half

·

Dilemma of dead loyalty

Mark's speeches are sham

Gottfried[6] shows Tristan

only hunting for pleasure   130

Emerald jacinth sapphire

chalcedony lovely Isolt

Topaz sardonyx chrysolite

ruby[7] sir Tristan the Court

sees only the beauty of   135

their persons that they

appear to be represented

Isolt sings for your eyes

Surveillance is a constant

theme in lyric poetry   140

·

Le Page disgracié his attempt

to buy a linnet[8] for his master

from a birdcatcher he hoped

---

4. Thomas of Brittany, the author of one of the earliest *Tristan* fragments. *Prescind:* cut off.
5. *Aegeus:* king of Athens and father of the legendary hero Theseus. Wounded, Tristan waits for Iseult to come to his aid, but dies after being tricked into thinking her ship has a black, not white, sail.
6. German poet Gottfried von Strasburg, who composed his version of "Tristan und Isolt" probably around 1211.
7. *Emerald . . . chalcedony* and *Topaz . . . ruby:* precious stones.
8. Songbird. *Le Page disgracié:* title of French poet Tristan L'Hermite's (c. 1601–1655) picaresque account of his travels abroad.

to comfort him with bird song
but gambled the money away   145
and in desperation bought a
wild linnet that didn't sing
His first words occur in the
linnet episode the young master's
perplexity about the bird's   150
silence so just the linnet's
silence provokes Tristan's *je*[9]
hero his shared identity the
remarkable bird list in *L'Orphée*[1]

                    •

L'Orphée—the lanner falcon   155
takes pigeons the sparrow-
hawk sparrows the goshawk
partridge when Tristan was
young he would have watched
hawks being flown his own   160
little hunting falcon his
observation of the way in
which other birds refrain
from their characteristic
habit of "mobbing the owl"   165
Vignette of the birdcatcher
in the street that day the
linnet's mimic reputation

                    •

Parasite and liar of genius
even emptiness is something   170
not nothingness of negation
having been born Not born
wrapped in protective long
cloak power of the woodland

---

9. I (French).
1. Play and film dealing with the Orpheus myth,   by French avant-gardist Jean Cocteau (1889–1963).

No burrowing deep for warmth   175
The eagle of Prometheus[2] is a
vulture the vulture passions
go to a predator tricked up
forever unexpressed in half-
effaced ambiguous butterfly   180
disguises authentic regional
avifauna[3] an arsenal of stories

•

Ysolt that for naught might
carry them as they coasting
past strange land past haven   185
ruin garland effigy figment
sensible nature blue silver
orange yellow different lake
effect of the death-rebirth
eternal rush-return fragment   190
I cannot separate in thought
You cannot be separate from
perception everything draws
toward autumn[4] distant tumult
See that long row of folios   195
Surely Ysolt remembers Itylus[5]

•

Antigone[6] bears her secret in
her heart like an arrow she is
sent twice over into our dark
social as if real life as if real   200

---

2. In Greek mythology, Prometheus's punishment for giving humans fire is to be chained to a rock while an eagle feeds on his liver each day.
3. Birds.
4. Cf. the *Duino Elegies* (1922) of Austro-German poet Rainer Maria Rilke (1875–1926), cited in Koerner's book on Friedrich's paintings (also by Howe in a letter): "And we, spectators always, everywhere / Looking at, never out of, everything! / It fills us. We arrange it. It decays. / We re-arrange it, and decay ourselves."
5. In one story, Itylus (or Itys) is the ill-fated son of King Tereus and Procne, killed by his mother in revenge after his father rapes Philomela. In another story, Itylus is accidentally killed by his mother, Aedon, when she attempts to murder her sister-in-law's firstborn. She is changed into a nightingale, lamenting her son in song. Also the title of a poem by the English poet Algernon Charles Swinburne (1837–1909).
6. In Sophocles' tragedy of the same name, a woman who kills herself after she is imprisoned for burying her brother.

person proceeding into self-
knowledge as if there were no
proof just blind right reason
to assuage our violent earth
Ysolt's single vision of union   205
Precursor shadow self by self
in open place or on an acting
platform two personae meeting
Strophe[7] antistrophe which is
which dual unspeakable cohesion   210

•

Day binds the wide Sound
Bitter sound as truth is
silent as silent tomorrow
Motif of retreating figure
arrayed beyond expression   215
huddled unintelligible air
Theomimesis[8] divinity message
I have loved come veiling
Lyrist come veil come lure
echo remnant sentence spar   220
never never form wherefor
Wait some recognition you
Lyric over us love unclothe
Never forever whoso move

1999

---

7. Originally, in Greek choral poetry, a stanzalike series of lines forming a structure, which is then repeated in a response called an antistrophe.
8. Representation of divinity, but, according to Howe, "in relation to the viewer as halted traveler arrested by what she sees in the landscape—chaos and particularity, detail and distance" (letter to the editor). "Theomimesis" is also a chapter title of Koerner's book on Friedrich's landscape paintings.

Michael S. Harper
b. 1938

Though it was forbidden by his parents, young Michael S. Harper secretly enjoyed listening to their jazz recordings. "Jazz was my bible," he writes of his years as a college student. "How would it be to solo with that great tradition of the big bands honking you on? Could one do it in a poem?" ("Don't They Speak Jazz"). Jazz is an example of what the novelist Ralph Ellison calls "antagonistic cooperation": while the individual musician, soloist for a time, improvises, the other musicians both follow and guide him or her, and the individual must never lose touch with fellow performers. Harper's conception of the individual talent in relation to tradition also recalls T. S. Eliot's essays, another formative influence. For Harper, as for his vital precursors Sterling Brown and Langston Hughes, the blues are likewise important because they bridge poetry and music and because "they always say *yes* to life; meet life's terms but never accept them" ("Don't").

In Harper's context, "saying yes to life" is not an undiscriminating affirmation, for like the blues, his work repeatedly takes the view that life is at best a melancholy business, replete with losses and painful farewells. Drawing on the collective grief and rage at the base of jazz and the blues, Harper mourns the deaths of two infant sons in a series of tormented elegies, among the best postwar poems in the form. He fashions a strenuous style that painfully couples the emotional language of loss, guilt, and love ("We assume / you did not know we loved you") with the clinical language of the hospital ("collapsible isolette," "sterile hands," "bicarbonate," "plastic mask"). Having pursued premedical studies before being deterred by racism, Harper forces together scientific culture and black oral culture in violent collocations such as "*mamaborn, sweetsonchild / gonedowntown* into *researchtestingwarehousebatteryacid / mama-son-done-gone*" ("Nightmare Begins Responsibility"). The father's private grief is inseparable from a race-based historical experience; "Deathwatch" recalls a letter written to another mourning father, W. E. B. Du Bois, asking whether "negroes / are not able to cry." In the tensile fabric of Harper's poetry, as in that of jazz, we witness collisions and convergences between the personal and historical, blues refrains and idiosyncratic digressions, melodic cadences and "sour" notes. His lines are crowded, word pressing against word, image against image, so that each component is forced to assert its individual energies, to cooperate but with a certain antagonism.

Harper was born on March 18, 1938, in Brooklyn, New York. He went to the west coast for much of his education, attending the City College of Los Angeles and California State University at Los Angeles, where he earned a B.A. in 1961 and an M.A. in English in 1963. He also received an M.F.A. from the University of Iowa in 1963. Since 1971, he has been a professor at Brown University. In addition to publishing twelve books of his own poetry, he has edited anthologies of African American poetry and *The Collected Poems of Sterling A. Brown* (1980).

American History

Those four black girls blown up
in that Alabama church[1]
remind me of five hundred
middle passage blacks,[2]
in a net, under water   5
in Charleston harbor
so *redcoats*[3] wouldn't find them.
Can't find what you can't see
can you?

1970

We Assume: On the Death of Our Son, Reuben Masai Harper

We assume
that in twenty-eight hours,
lived in a collapsible isolette,[4]
you learned to accept pure oxygen
as the natural sky;   5
the scant shallow breaths
that filled those hours
cannot, did not make you fly—
but dreams were there
like crooked palmprints on   10
the twin-thick windows of the nursery—
in the glands of your mother.

We assume
the sterile hands
drank chemicals in and out   15
from lungs opaque with mucus,
pumped your stomach,
eeked the bicarbonate in
crooked, green-winged veins,
out in a plastic mask;   20

A woman who'd lost her first son
consoled us with an angel gone ahead
to pray for our family—
gone into that sky
seeking oxygen,   25
gone into autopsy,

1. By white racists in response to 1960s civil rights demonstrations.
2. Captured and en route from Africa to be sold as slaves.

3. That is, British soldiers patrolling the waters during an embargo.
4. Infant incubator.

a fine brown powdered sugar,
a disposable cremation:

We assume
you did not know we loved you.   30

                                                1970

Reuben, Reuben

I reach from pain
to music great enough
to bring me back,
swollenhead, madness,
lovefruit, a pickle of hate   5
so sour my mouth twicked
up and would not sing;
there's nothing in the beat
to hold it in
melody and turn human skin;   10
a brown berry gone
to rot just two days on the branch;
we've lost a son,
the music, *jazz*, comes in.

                                                1970

Deathwatch

Twitching in the cactus
hospital gown, a loon
on hairpin wings,
she tells me how
her episiotomy[5]   5
is perfectly sewn
and doesn't hurt
while she sits in a pile
of blood
which once cleaned   10
the placenta
my third son should be in.
She tells me how early
he is, and how strong,
like his father,   15
and long, like a black-

---

5. Surgical enlargement of the vulval orifice during labor.

stemmed Easter rose
in a white hand.

Just under five pounds
you lie there, a collapsed   20
balloon doll, burst in your
fifteenth hour, with the face
of your black father,
his fingers, his toes,
and eight voodoo   25
adrenalin holes in
your pinwheeled hair-lined
chest; you witness
your parents sign the autopsy
and disposal papers   30
shrunken to duplicate
in black ink
on white paper
like the country
you were born in,   35
unreal, asleep,
silent, almost alive.

This is a dedication
to our memory
of three sons—   40
two dead, one alive—
a reminder of a letter
to Du Bois[6]
from a student
at Cornell—on behalf   45
of his whole history class.
The class is confronted
with a question,
and no one—
not even the professor—   50
is sure of the answer:
"Will you please tell us
whether or not it is true
that negroes
are not able to cry?"   55

America needs a killing.
America needs a killing.
Survivors will be human.

                                               1970

---

6. W. E. B. Du Bois (1868–1963), African American educator and writer.

Dear John, Dear Coltrane

a love supreme, a love supreme[7]
a love supreme, a love supreme

Sex fingers toes
in the marketplace
near your father's church
in Hamlet, North Carolina[8]—
witness to this love   5
in this calm fallow
of these minds,
there is no substitute for pain:
genitals gone or going,
seed burned out,   10
you tuck the roots in the earth,
turn back, and move
by river through the swamps,
singing: *a love supreme, a love supreme;*
what does it all mean?   15
Loss, so great each black
woman expects your failure
in mute change, the seed gone.
You plod up into the electric city—
your song now crystal and   20
the blues. You pick up the horn
with some will and blow
into the freezing night:
a love supreme, a love supreme—

Dawn comes and you cook   25
up the thick sin 'tween
impotence and death, fuel
the tenor sax cannibal
heart, genitals, and sweat
that makes you clean—   30
a love supreme, a love supreme—

Why you so black?
cause I am
why you so funky?
cause I am   35
why you so black?
cause I am
why you so sweet?
cause I am
why you so black?   40

---

7. A phrase chanted in *A Love Supreme* (1964), a four-part composition by African American jazz saxophonist John Coltrane (1926–1967).
8. Coltrane's birthplace.

cause I am
a love supreme, a love supreme:

So sick
you couldn't play *Naima,*[9]
so flat we ached   45
for song you'd concealed
with your own blood,
your diseased liver gave
out its purity,
the inflated heart   50
pumps out, the tenor kiss,
tenor love:
a love supreme, a love supreme—
a love supreme, a love supreme—

1970

Nightmare Begins Responsibility[1]

I place these numbed wrists to the pane
watching white uniforms whisk over
him in the tube-kept
prison
fear what they will do in experiment   5
watch my gloved stickshifting gasolined hands
breathe *boxcar-information-please* infirmary tubes
distrusting white-pink mending paperthin
silkened end hairs, distrusting tubes
shrunk in his *trunk-skincapped*   10
shaven head, in thighs
distrusting-white-hands-picking-baboon-light
on his son who will not make his second night
of this wardstrewn intensive airpocket
where his father's asthmatic   15
hymns of *night-train,* train done gone
his mother can only know that he has flown
up into essential calm unseen corridor
going boxscarred home, *mamaborn, sweetsonchild*
gonedowntown into *researchtestingwarehousebatteryacid* 20
mama-son-done-gone/me telling her 'nother
train tonight, no music, no breathstroked
heartbeat in my infinite distrust of them:

and of my distrusting self
white-doctor-who-breathed-for-him-all-night   25

---

9. Coltrane composition named for his first wife.
1. Cf. the epigraph to Irish poet W. B. Yeats's *Responsibilities* (1913): "In dreams begin respon- sibilities," later used as the title to the first collec- tion published by Delmore Schwartz (1913–1966), American poet.

say it for two sons gone,
say nightmare, say it loud
panebreaking heartmadness:
nightmare begins responsibility.

1975

Double Elegy

Whatever city or country road
you two are on
there are nettles,
and the dark invisible
elements cling to your skin   5
though you do not cry
and you do not scratch
your arms at forty-five degree angles
as the landing point of a swan
in the Ohio, the Detroit River;   10

at the Paradise Theatre
you named the cellist
with the fanatical fingers
of the plumber, the exorcist,
and though the gimmickry at wrist   15
and kneecaps could lift the séance
table, your voice was real
in the gait and laughter of Uncle
Henry, who could dance on either
leg, wooden or real, to the sound   20
of the troop train, megaphone,
catching the fine pitch of a singer
on the athletic fields of Virginia.

At the Radisson Hotel,
we once took a fine angel   25
of the law to the convention center,
and put her down as an egret
in the subzero platform of a friend—
this is Minneapolis, the movies
are all of strangers, holding themselves   30
in the delicacy of treading water,
while they wait for the trumpet
of the 20th Century Limited[2]
over the bluff or cranny.
You two men like to confront   35
the craters of history and spillage,

---

2. Famous cross-country train.

our natural infections of you
innoculating blankets and fur,
ethos[3] of cadaver and sunflower.

I hold the dogwood blossom,   40
eat the pear, and watch the nettle
swim up in the pools
of the completed song
of Leadbelly and Little Crow[4]
crooning the buffalo and horse   45
to the changes and the bridge
of a twelve-string guitar,
the melody of "Irene";[5]
this is really goodbye—
I can see the precious stones   50
of embolism[6] and consumption
on the platinum wires of the mouth:
in the flowing rivers, in the public baths
of Ohio and Michigan.

1985

3. Distinguishing character.
4. Sioux Indian chief (1810–1863). *Leadbelly:* Huddie Ledbetter (1888–1949), itinerant blues singer and songwriter.

5. Leadbelly song, which became a major hit in the 1950s as "Goodnight Irene," recorded by many artists.
6. Sudden obstruction by an abnormal particle.

CHARLES SIMIC
b. 1938

After surviving the German bombing and occupation of his native Belgrade in World War II, then escaping Yugoslavia with his mother in 1948 into Austria and France, Charles Simic arrived at sixteen in the United States, haunted by memories of blasted buildings, displaced populations, and the sounds of his native Serbian. The wartime Central European experience shadows his poetry in large, black clouds of torture, dispossession, and loss. The landscape of Simic's poems is nightmarish: buildings are broken and askew, colors drab and dismal, sounds hushed and muted. Dwarfed by this gray panorama of futility are the folkloristic stick figures of the parent or grandparent, innocent child or old woman, vampire or executioner.

Yet Simic juxtaposes against this dull, ominous, vacant world images of pellucid clarity and vividness. Watches with tiny, incandescent wheels; a fly with turquoise wings; a doll's head with a painted mouth—the mind latches onto such sharp-edged details, briefly evading the vast blankness of the universe, the repressed horrors of an inconceivable past, and the sense that what really matters is always happening beyond the boundaries of consciousness. Instead of surrendering to the banalities and brutalities of history, Simic grips it with an antic humor, twisting and tweaking it in wordplay, buffoonery, offhand utterance, grotesque metaphor, and deadpan understatement. Precise amid indefiniteness, wry amid terror, Simic's poetry both acknowledges the degradations of modern history, including nationalisms and totalitarianisms of various kinds, and idiosyncratically, comically rejects them. Simic captures the wayward individuality of poetry when he outlandishly describes the "rude" propensities of his profession: "To be a poet," he says in "Assembly Required," "is to feel something like a unicyclist in a desert, a pornographic magician performing in the corner of the church during Mass, a drag queen attending night classes and blowing kisses at the teacher."

The sense of the absurd and the ridiculous, the juxtaposition of the mundane and the metaphysical, the fusion of everyday realism with folktale irrationality—these are Simic's versions of the surrealism he found in French and Latin American literature and in the Serbian poetry of Vasko Popa. In night school at the University of Chicago and afterwards, Simic also read poets such as Walt Whitman, Emily Dickinson, Hart Crane, Ezra Pound, and Theodore Roethke. He helped graft surrealism onto American poetry, along with James Tate, Mark Strand, Charles Wright, and Robert Bly. His style of grim laughter at the menace of modern life is, however, very much his own. Since his first volumes, published in the 1960s, Simic's poetry has retained its gnomic, minimalist terseness, but has loosened its plotting, expanded its range of reference, and increasingly incorporated the American urban experience.

Simic was born on May 9, 1938. Drafted into the U.S. Army in 1961, he received his B.A. from New York University in 1967 and became a U.S. citizen in 1971. In addition to many volumes of poetry, he has published books of essays, anthologies, and translations of French, Serbian, Croation, Macedonian, and Slovenian poetry. A winner of a MacArthur Fellowship in 1984 and the Pulitzer Prize in 1990, Simic has taught for several decades at the University of New Hampshire.

Fork

This strange thing must have crept
Right out of hell.
It resembles a bird's foot
Worn around the cannibal's neck.

As you hold it in your hand,   5
As you stab with it into a piece of meat,
It is possible to imagine the rest of the bird:
Its head which like your fist
Is large, bald, beakless, and blind.

1969

Watch Repair

A small wheel
Incandescent,
Shivering like
A pinned butterfly.

Hands thrown up   5
In all directions:

The crossroads
One arrives at
In a nightmare.

Higher than that   10
Number 12 presides
Like a beekeeper
Over the swarming honeycomb
Of the open watch.

Other wheels   15
That could fit
Inside a raindrop.

Tools
That must be splinters
Of arctic starlight.   20

Tiny golden mills
Grinding invisible
Coffee beans.

When the coffee's boiling
Cautiously,   25
So it doesn't burn us,
We raise it
To the lips
Of the nearest
Ear.   30

                                                  1974

A Wall

That's the only image
That turns up.

A wall all by itself,
Poorly lit, beckoning,
But no sense of the room,   5
Not even a hint
Of why it is I remember
So little and so clearly:

The fly I was watching,
The details of its wings   10
Glowing like turquoise.
Its feet, to my amusement
Following a minute crack—

An eternity
Around that simple event.   15

And nothing else; and nowhere
To go back to;
And no one else
As far as I know to verify.

1977

Prodigy

I grew up bent over
a chessboard.

I loved the word *endgame*.

All my cousins looked worried.

It was a small house   5
near a Roman graveyard.
Planes and tanks
shook its windowpanes.

A retired professor of astronomy
taught me how to play.   10

That must have been in 1944.

In the set we were using,
the paint had almost chipped off
the black pieces.

The white King was missing   15
and had to be substituted for.

I'm told but do not believe
that that summer I witnessed
men hung from telephone poles.

I remember my mother   20
blindfolding me a lot.
She had a way of tucking my head
suddenly under her overcoat.

In chess, too, the professor told me,
the masters play blindfolded,   25
the great ones on several boards
at the same time.

1980

Classic Ballroom Dances

Grandmothers who wring the necks
Of chickens; old nuns
With names like Theresa, Marianne,
Who pull schoolboys by the ear;

The intricate steps of pickpockets   5
Working the crowd of the curious
At the scene of an accident; the slow shuffle
Of the evangelist with a sandwich board;

The hesitation of the early-morning customer
Peeking through the window grille   10
Of a pawnshop; the weave of a little kid
Who is walking to school with eyes closed;

And the ancient lovers, cheek to cheek,
On the dance floor of the Union Hall,
Where they also hold charity raffles   15
On rainy Monday nights of an eternal November.

                                                                1980

Spoons with Realistic Dead Flies on Them

I cause a great many worries to my mother.
My body will run with the weeds some day.
My head will be carried by slaughterhouse ants,
The carnivorous, bloody-aproned ants.

That was never in any of your legends, O saints!   5
The years she spent working in a novelty store:
Joy buzzers, false beards, and dead flies
To talk to between the infrequent customers.

A room rented from a minor demon.
An empty bird cage and a coffee mill for company.   10
A hand-operated one for her secret guardian angel
To take a turn grinding the slow hours.

Though I'm not a believer—
Neither is she, and that's why she worries,
Looks both ways crossing the street   15
At two gusts of nothing and nothing.

                                                                1982

Eastern European Cooking

While Marquis de Sade had himself buggered[1]—
O just around the time the Turks
Were roasting my ancestors on spits,
Goethe wrote "The Sorrows of Young Werther."[2]

It was chilly, raw, down-in-the-mouth   5
We were slurping bean soup thick with smoked sausage,
On 2nd Avenue,[3] where years before I saw an old horse
Pull a wagon piled up high with flophouse mattresses.

Anyway, as I was telling my uncle Boris,
With my mouth full of pig's feet and wine: 10
"While they were holding hands and sighing under parasols,
We were being hung by our tongues."

"I make no distinction between scum,"
He said, and he meant everybody,
Us and them: A breed of murderers' helpers,   15
Evil-smelling torturers' apprentices.

                                                                      1982

Northern Exposure

When old women say, it smells of snow,
In a whisper barely audible
Which still rouses the sick man upstairs
So he opens his eyes wide and lets them fill

With the grayness of the remaining daylight.   5
When old women say, how quiet it is,
And truly today no one came to visit,
While the one they still haven't shaved

Lifts the wristwatch to his ear and listens.
In it, something small, subterranean   10
And awful in intent, chews rapidly.
When old women say, time to turn on the lights,

And not a single one gets up to do so,
For now there are loops and loose knots around their feet

1. Sodomized. Marquis de Sade (1740–1814), French nobleman whose sexually explicit novels and plays, many of which were written in prisons or asylums, gave rise to the term *sadism*.
2. Johann Wolfgang von Goethe (1749–1832), German poet, playwright, and philosopher, preeminent figure of German Romanticism, wrote the novel *The Sorrows of Young Werther* (1774), which tells the story of a hypersensitive young man led to commit suicide by his sense of alienation and disappointed love. *Turks:* Simic's native Serbia was under the Turkish Ottoman Empire from the fourteenth century until 1878.
3. In New York City; many Eastern European immigrants have lived on the Lower East Side of Manhattan.

As if someone is scribbling over them   15
With a piece of charcoal found in the cold stove.

1983

Cameo Appearance

I had a small, nonspeaking part
In a bloody epic. I was one of the
Bombed and fleeing humanity.
In the distance our great leader
Crowed like a rooster from a balcony,   5
Or was it a great actor
Impersonating our great leader?

That's me there, I said to the kiddies.
I'm squeezed between the man
With two bandaged hands raised   10
And the old woman with her mouth open
As if she were showing us a tooth

That hurts badly. The hundred times
I rewound the tape, not once
Could they catch sight of me   15
In that huge gray crowd,
That was like any other gray crowd.

Trot off to bed, I said finally.
I know I was there. One take
Is all they had time for.   20
We ran, and the planes grazed our hair,
And then they were no more
As we stood dazed in the burning city,
But, of course, they didn't film that.

1996

Head of a Doll

Whose demon are you,
Whose god? I asked
Of the painted mouth
Half buried in the sand.

A brooding gull   5
Made a brief assessment,
And tiptoed away
Nodding to himself.

At dusk a firefly or two
Dowsed its eye pits.   10
And later, toward midnight,
I even heard mice.

1999

LES MURRAY
b. 1938

Les Murray is widely acclaimed as the most versatile and verbally inventive Australian poet of his generation. Exploring his national experience, as well as the musical resources and figurative reach of the English language, Murray has been compared to two other poets at the margins of the former British Empire—Seamus Heaney and Derek Walcott. Like his Irish and Caribbean contemporaries, Murray risks metaphorical lushness and sonic opulence in his poetry, in contrast with the often minimalist models in metropolitan America and Britain. Affectionately dubbing the Australian poet "Crocodile Dandy," Walcott places the "shaggy power, grace, and mass of Les Murray's poems" in a postcolonial context. The so-called "barbarians approaching the capital," Walcott says, not only bring "the vandalization of the imperial language," but also possess "the imperial literature as if it were their own" (*The New Republic*, 1989). Murray seems intent on proving that the provincial farmer living in the imperial outpost can write poetry as learned, authoritative, and technically virtuosic as any from the metropolitan center. A poet equipped with dazzling linguistic skills and a deep knowledge of classical and modern literature, Murray nevertheless styles himself a bumbling, anti-elitist "redneck"—his ironically honorific term for working-class people from the Australian bush. A silver-tongued brawler, he wrings new sounds and sense from English.

Having grown up on a modest, family dairy farm in New South Wales, Murray returned to farming in 1985 after a number of years as translator and as writer-in-residence at various Australian universities. Many of his poems suggest the crusty Catholic conservatism and the shambling, unfashionable background of his humble rural roots. A rugged Australian ironist, Murray is suspicious of academic and city-bred pieties. But he often foregoes social satire and emphasizes compassion instead, whether sympathetically entering into the minute life of a crustacean in "Mollusc" or into the traumatic experience of a severely burned six-year-old child in "Cotton Flannelette."

Hailing the Aborigines for creating poetic forms that are keenly responsive to the Australian landscape, Murray incorporates stylistic and rhetorical strategies learned from indigenous oral poetry. In "The Buladelah-Taree Holiday Song Cycle," he borrows the lens of Aboriginal poetry to defamiliarize vacationing white Australians, revitalize the natural world, and mythologize the land. This poetic sequence formally exemplifies the intercultural process he described to an interviewer: "Every invader, every settler gradually becomes the people who are conquered. Aborigines didn't appreciate the word conquer, but in the end they will conquer us. Through all sorts of mixing and mingling and learning from each other, they won't be the same Aborigines we first encountered, and we won't be the white people that they first encountered" ("Embracing the Vernacular").

In attempting to define poetry, Murray often links it to key terms such as "presence," "interest," and "dream." He sees in poetry a "precarious fusion" of "the dreaming mind, the waking, intellectual mind, and the body." Drawing on Catholic tradition, Murray writes, "Art is a way of making a body for yourself, a body for yourself and others. A new body. You give embodiment to things" ("Embracing the Vernacular"). The balance of dream, intellect, and body has to be just right. The "linkage with dream" helps keep poetry from degenerating into what Murray disparages as "head poems" (1998 interview). Lasting poetry involves intellect but also "working always beyond // your own intelligence" ("The Instrument").

The language of Murray's poetry startles and amuses, reveling in the fecundity and elasticity of English. Murray plays energetically on verbal sonorities. He delights in the eddying reflections of homonyms and rhymes, the slapstick conjunctions of puns and onomatopoeia, in poems such as "On Removing Spiderweb." His wordplay conveys a robust pleasure in language as a tactile medium, without retreating into self-reflexive obscurity. Murray eagerly draws out the interconnections among words held together by alliteration, rhythm, rhyme, consonance, hyphenation, syntax, repetition, enjambment, and elided punctuation. By playing on these verbal resources in a poem such as "The Powerline Incarnation," he suggests a profound interconnectedness among things. Circuits of electricity override differences to fuse farms with towns, Mozart with Johnny Cash, the poet's body itself, like the body of his poetry, acting as a medium of confluence.

Metaphor, for Murray, like verbal music, serves as a connective force. In the rapid imaginative gush of some poems, such as the charmingly nostalgic "The Milk Lorry," freshly minted metaphors spill over one another in rapid succession, the poet discovering similitude between the swaying old cans in a milk truck and dancers, armed warriors, even students in "a seminar engrossed // in one swaying tradition." Weaving the world together through resemblances in sound and image, Murray's sensibility—by turns elegiac and brash, earthy and ironic—is attuned to the rich variety of human experience and to the oneness behind the many.

The Powerline Incarnation

When I ran to snatch the wires off our roof
hands bloomed teeth shouted I was almost seized
held back from this life
                O flumes   O chariot reins
you cover me with lurids deck me with gaudies feed   5
my coronal[1]   a scream sings in the air
above our dance   you slam it to me with farms
that you dark on and off numb hideous strong friend
Tooma and Geehi[2] freak and burr through me
rocks fire-trails damwalls mountain-ash trees slew   10
to darkness through me   I zap them underfoot
with the swords of my shoes
                  I am receiving mountains
piloting around me   Crackenback   Anembo
the Fiery Walls[3]   I make a hit in towns   15
I've never visited: smoke curls lightbulbs pop grey
discs hitch and slow   I plough the face of Mozart
and Johnny Cash[4]   I bury and smooth their song

---

1. Crown or garland for the head; cf. also the related word *coronary*.
2. Australian rivers.
3. Like Crackenback and Anembo, Australian mountains.
4. American country musician (b. 1932).

I crack it for copper links and fusebox spiders
I call my Friend from the circuitry of mixers   20
whipping cream for a birthday   I distract the immortal
Inhuman from hospitals
             to sustain my jazz
and here is Rigel[5] in a glove of flesh
my starry hand discloses smoke, cold Angel.   25

Vehicles that run on death come howling into
our street with lights a thousandth of my blue
arms keep my wife from my beauty   from my species
the jewels in my tips
             I would accept her in   30
blind white remarriage   cover her with wealth
to arrest the heart   we'd share Apache leaps
crying out *Disyzygy!*[6]
             shield her from me, humans
from this happiness I burn to share   this touch   35
sheet car   live ladder   wildfire garden shrub—
away off I hear the bombshell breakers thrown
diminishing me   a meaninglessness coming
over the circuits
             the god's deserting me   40
but I have dived in the mainstream   jumped the graphs
I have transited the dreams of crew-cut boys named Buzz
and the hardening music
             to the big bare place
where the strapped-down seekers, staining white clothes, come   45
to be shown the Zeitgeist[7]
             passion and death my skin
my heart all logic   I am starring there
and must soon flame out
             having seen the present god   50
It who feels nothing   It who answers prayers.

                                  1977

From The Buladelah-Taree Holiday Song Cycle[8]

3

It is good to come out after driving and walk on the bare grass;
walking out, looking all around, relearning that country.
Looking out for snakes, and looking out for rabbits as well;
going into the shade of myrtles to try their cupped climate, swinging by
     one hand around them,
in that country of the Holiday . . .   5

---

5. Star in the Orion constellation.
6. Play on *syzygy*, the alignment of three celestial
bodies (e.g., the sun, the moon, and Earth, during
an eclipse).
7. Spirit of the times (German).

8. Buladelah is a town and Taree a city in a pop-
ular tourist region in New South Wales, Australia.
The locations mentioned throughout the poem are
in this region. The poem is an imitation of Aborig-
inal song cycles.

stepping behind trees to the dam, as if you had a gun,
to that place of the Wood Duck,
to that place of the Wood Duck's Nest,
proving you can still do it; looking at the duck who hasn't seen you,
the mother duck who'd run Catch Me (broken wing) I'm Fatter (broken   10
  wing), having hissed to her children.

6

Barbecue smoke is rising at Legge's Camp; it is steaming into the midday
  air,
all around the lake shore, at the Broadwater, it is going up among the
  paperbark trees,
a heat-shimmer of sauces, rising from tripods and flat steel, at that place
  of the cone shells,
at that place of the Seagrass, and the tiny segmented things swarming in
  it, and of the Pelican.
Dogs are running around disjointedly; water escapes from their mouths,   5
confused emotions from their eyes; humans snarl at them Gwanout and
  Hereboy, not varying their tone much;
the impoverished dog people, suddenly sitting down to nuzzle themselves;
  toddlers side with them:
toddlers, running away purposefully at random, among cars, into big
  drownie water (come back, Cheryl-Ann!).
They rise up as charioteers, leaning back on the tow-bar; all their
  attributes bulge at once:
swapping swash shoulder-wings for the white-sheeted shoes that bear   10
  them,
they are skidding over the flat glitter, stiff with grace, for once not
  travelling to arrive.
From the high dunes over there, the rough blue distance, at length they
  come back behind the boats,
and behind the boats' noise, cartwheeling, or sitting down, into the lake's
  warm chair;
they wade ashore and eat with the families, putting off that uprightness,
  that assertion,
eating with the families who love equipment, and the freedom from   15
  equipment,
with the fathers who love driving, and lighting a fire between stones.

8

Forests and State Forests, all down off the steeper country; mosquitoes are
  always living in there:
they float about like dust motes and sink down, at the places of the
  Stinging Tree,[9]
and of the Staghorn Fern; the males feed on plant-stem fluid, absorbing
  that watery ichor;
the females meter the air, feeling for the warm-blooded smell, needing
  blood for their eggs.

9. Australian nettle.

They find the dingo in his sleeping-place, they find his underbelly and   5
     his anus;
they find the possum's face, they drift up the ponderous pleats of the fig
     tree, way up into its rigging,
the high camp of the fruit bats; they feed on the membranes and ears of
     bats; tired wings cuff air at them;
their eggs burning inside them, they alight on the muzzles of cattle,
the half-wild bush cattle, there at the place of the Sleeper Dump, at the
     place of the Tallowwoods.[1]
The males move about among growth tips; ingesting solutions, they   10
     crouch intently;
the females sing, needing blood to breed their young; their singing is in the
     scrub country;
their tune comes to the name-bearing humans, who dance to it and
     irritably grin at it.

12

Now the sun is an applegreen blindness through the swells, a white blast
     on the sea face, flaking and shoaling;
now it is burning off the mist; it is emptying the density of trees, it is
     spreading upriver,
hovering above the casuarina[2] needles, there at Old Bar and Manning
     Point;
flooding the island farms, it abolishes the milkers' munching breath
as they walk towards the cowyards; it stings a bucket here, a teacup there. 5
Morning steps into the world by ever more southerly gates; shadows
     weaken their north skew
on Middle Brother, on Cape Hawke, on the dune scrub toward Seal Rocks;
steadily the heat is coming on, the butter-water time, the clothes-sticking
     time;
grass covers itself with straw; abandoned things are thronged with spirits;
everywhere wood is still with strain; birds hiding down the creek   10
     galleries, and in the cockspur canes;
the cicada is hanging up her sheets; she takes wing off her music-sheets.
Cars pass with a rational zoom, panning quickly towards Wingham,
through the thronged and glittering, the shale-topped ridges, and the
     cattlecamps,
towards Wingham for the cricket, the ball knocked hard in front of smoked-
     glass ranges, and for the drinking.
In the time of heat, the time of flies around the mouth, the time of the   15
     west verandah;
looking at that umbrage along the ranges, on the New England[3] side;
clouds begin assembling vaguely, a hot soiled heaviness on the sky, away
     there towards Gloucester;
a swelling up of clouds, growing there above Mount George, and above
     Tipperary;
far away and hot with light; sometimes a storm takes root there, and fills
     the heavens rapidly;

---

1. Variety of eucalyptus tree.
2. Australian pine tree.

3. District on and around the New England Table-
land, in New South Wales.

darkening, boiling up and swaying on its stalks, pulling this way and   20
    that, blowing round by Krambach;
coming white on Bulby, it drenches down on the paddocks, and on the
    wire fences;
the paddocks are full of ghosts, and people in cornbag hoods approaching;
lights are lit in the house; the storm veers mightily on its stem, above the
    roof; the hills uphold it;
the stony hills guide its dissolution; gullies opening and crumbling down,
    wrenching tussocks and rolling them;
the storm carries a greenish-grey bag; perhaps it will find hail and send   25
    it down, starring cars, flattening tomatoes,
in the time of the Washaways,[4] of the dead trunks braiding water, and of
    the Hailstone Yarns.

1977

The Milk Lorry

Now the milk lorry is a polished submarine
that rolls up at midday, attaches a trunk and inhales
the dairy's tank to a frosty snore in minutes

but its forerunner was the high-tyred barn of crisp mornings,
reeking Diesel and mammary, hazy in its roped interior   5
as a carpet under beaters, as it crashed along potholed lanes

cooeeing at schoolgirls. Long planks like unshipped oars
butted, levelling in there, because between each farm's
stranded wharf of milk cans, the work was feverish slotting

of floors above floors, for load. It was sling out the bashed   10
paint-collared empties and waltz in the full,
stumbling on their rims under ribaldry, tilting their big gallons

then the schoolboy's calisthenic, hoisting steel men man-high
till the glancing hold was a magazine of casque armour,
a tinplate 'tween-decks,[5] a seminar engrossed   15

in one swaying tradition, behind the speeding doorways
that tempted a truant to brace and drop, short of town,
and spend the day, with book or not, down under

the bridge of a river that by dinnertime would be
tongueing like cattledogs, or down a moth-dusty reach   20
where the fish-feeding milk boat and cedar barge once floated.

1987

4. Erosion caused by flooding.
5. Area "between decks" on a sailing vessel. *Casque armour:* armor for the head.

On Removing Spiderweb

Like summer silk its denier
but stickily, oh, ickilier,
miffed bunny-blinder, silver tar,
gesticuli-gesticular,
crepe when cobbed, crap when rubbed,   5
stretchily adhere-and-there
and everyway, nap-snarled or sleek,
glibly hubbed with grots to tweak:
ehh weakly bobbined tae yer neb,
spit it Phuoc Tuy! filthy web!   10

1990

Mollusc

By its nobship sailing upside down,
by its inner sexes, by the crystalline
pimplings of its skirts, by the sucked-on
lifelong kiss of its toppling motion,
by the viscose[6] optics now extruded   5
now wizened instantaneously, by the
ridges grating up a food-path, by
the pop shell in its nick of dry,
by excretion, the earthworm coils, the glibbing,
by the gilt slipway, and by pointing   10
perhaps as far back into time as
ahead, a shore being folded interior,
by boiling on salt, by coming uncut over
a razor's edge, by hiding the Oligocene[7]
underleaf may this and every snail sense   15
itself ornament the weave of presence.

1992

Corniche[8]

I work all day and hardly drink at all.[9]
I can reach down and feel if I'm depressed.
I adore the Creator because I made myself
and a few times a week a wire jags in my chest.

The first time, I'd been coming apart all year,   5
weeping, incoherent; cigars had given me up:

6. Substance used to make rayon.
7. From the Tertiary Period (geologic).
8. Coastal road.

9. Cf. the opening of "Aubade," by the English poet Philip Larkin (1922–1985): "I work all day, and get half drunk at night."

any road round a cliff edge I'd whimper along in low gear
then: cardiac horror. Masking my pulse's calm lub-dub.

It was the victim-sickness. Adrenaline howling in my head,
the black dog was my brain. Come to drown me in my breath   10
was energy's black hole, depression, compere[1] of the predawn show
when, returned from a pee, you stew and welter in your death.

The rogue space rock is on course to snuff your world,
sure. But go acute, and its oncoming fills your day.
The brave die but once? I could go a hundred times a week,   15
clinging to my pulse with the world's edge inches away.

Laugh, who never shrank around wizened genitals there
or killed themselves to stop dying. The blow that never falls
batters you stupid. Only gradually do
you notice a slight scorn in you for what appals.   20

A self inside self, cool as conscience, one to be erased
in your final night, or faxed, still knows beneath
all the mute grand opera and uncaused effect—
that death which can be imagined is not true death.

1996

Cotton Flannelette

Shake the bed, the blackened child whimpers,
O Shake the bed! through beak lips that never
will come unwry. And wearily the iron-
framed mattress, with nodding crockery bulbs,
jinks on its way.   5
              Her brothers and sister take
shifts with the terrible glued-together baby
when their unsleeping absolute mother
reels out to snatch an hour, back to stop
the rocking and wring pale blue soap-water   10
over nude bladders and blood-webbed chars.[2]

Even their cranky evasive father
is awed to stand watches rocking the bed.
Lids frogged shut, O *please shake the bed*,
her contour whorls and braille tattoos   15
from where, in her nightdress, she flared
out of hearth-drowse to a marrow shriek
pedalling full tilt firesleeves[3] in mid-air,
              are grainier with repair
than when the doctor, crying *Dear God, woman!*   20

1. Master of ceremonies.   3. Sleeves used as insulation in engines.
2. Substances burned to carbon.

No one can save that child. Let her go!
spared her the treatments of the day.

Shake the bed. Like: count phone poles, rhyme,
classify realities, bang the head, any
iteration that will bring, in the brain's forks,   25
the melting molecules of relief,
and bring them again.
　　　　　O rock the bed!

Nibble water with bared teeth, make lymph
like arrowroot gruel, as your mother grips you   30
for weeks in the untrained perfect language,
till the doctor relents. Salves and wraps you
in dressings that will be the fire again,
ripping anguish off agony,
　　　　　　　　and will confirm   35
the ploughland ridges in your woman's skin
for the sixty more years your family weaves you
on devotion's loom, rick-racking the bed
as you yourself, six years old, instruct them.

                                                              1996

SEAMUS HEANEY
1939–2013

Rich, complex, and multifarious, Seamus Heaney's poetry yields a string of paradoxes. It is popular and accessible, with a wide readership in Ireland and across the anglophone world. Yet its lyric subtlety and rigorous technique have attracted legions of poets and academic critics. It is earthy and matter-of-fact, saturated with the physical textures, sights, smells, and sounds of farm life. Yet it is also visionary, enacting spiritual pilgrimages and tentatively crediting miracles. Heaney represented his poetic quest as digging, a grim archaeological process of recovery from dark and unknowable depths. Yet he also moved upward into the open and the glimmering light of hope, spirit, and unbridled imaginings. He wrote masterfully in meter and rhyme, revitalized meditative blank verse, and composed a number of sonnet sequences, such as his elegy for his mother, "Clearances." Yet he was also a superb poet in the looser forms of "Bog Queen" and "Punishment," his irregularly metered, short lines grouped in unrhymed quatrains. Heaney was a genial poet, brimming with wordplay and stories. Yet he was also reticent and indirect, tactfully withholding and slyly concealing.

   Many of the paradoxes of Heaney's work can be understood only in the context of his historical situation as an Irish Catholic who grew up in the predominantly Protestant North of Ireland under British rule. Heaney was a political poet, affirming his affinities with the Catholic civil rights movement, which has struggled against British and Protestant domination. Yet he refused slogans, journalistic reportage, and political pieties, instead scrutinizing the roots of communal identity and exploring his ambivalences. He was a devotedly Irish poet, who translated poetry from Gaelic; renewed Irish traditions such as the *aisling*, or vision poem; drew on the examples of W. B. Yeats, James Joyce, and Patrick Kavanagh; and strongly rejected descriptions of himself as "British." Yet he recognized his many debts to and affinities with British poets, from *Beowulf* (his prize-winning translation was published in 1999) to John Keats, William Wordsworth, Thomas Hardy, Gerard Manley Hopkins, Wilfred Owen, W. H. Auden, and Ted Hughes, and his poetry ironically uses Anglo-Saxon alliterative effects and other techniques to suggest the sounds of Irish in English. He was both a private poet—skillfully kneading his feelings of grief, love, wonder, and ambivalence into poems about his family and his humble origins—and a public poet, finding within himself the many conflicting responses of people of different views to large-scale historical events and atrocities. Eluding categories, his poetry is instantly recognizable, marked by a distinctive sensibility, grace, and sound. Some of these complexities can be explained as shifts in emphasis across his career—from the early blank verse poems of bucolic childhood to the middle free verse poems of self-questioning and guilt to later poems, written in varied forms, of mourning, vision, and spiritual quest. But any given phase in his writing life, if scrutinized, will reveal divergent propensities.

Born just two and a half months after Yeats died and widely seen as the greatest Irish poet since Yeats, Heaney responded to his major precursor with characteristic ambivalence. Reacting against "something too male and assertive" in poems such as "Under Ben Bulben," Heaney criticized Yeats for moving, by career's end, "within his mode of vision as within some invisible ring of influence and defence, some bullet-proof glass of the spirit." At the same time, he recognized in some of Yeats's late poems an introspection, a "humility," a "tenderness towards life and its uncompletedness" ("Yeats as an Example?"). The differences between Yeats and Heaney are partly explained by the discrepant affinities of a would-be aristocratic Anglo-Irish Protestant and a working-class Northern Irish Catholic. Nature for Heaney did not mean lakes, woods, and swans visible from the houses of the aristocracy. Instead, a farmer's son, Heaney describes, in "Station Island" II, the "dark-clumped grass where cows or horses dunged, / the cluck when pith-lined chestnut shells split open" (the latter a line that Hopkins would have welcomed). Heaney's nature was agricultural; it includes such farm equipment as a harrow pin, a sledge-head, a trowel. This contemporary poetry marks its difference from Yeats's by subdued rhythms, less clamant philosophy, less prophetic utterance, but Heaney's abiding respect for Yeats is evident in his rewriting of his precursor's work, as in the recasting of "The Fisherman" by "Casualty."

Irish poetry since Yeats has been at pains to purge itself of the grand manner, and Heaney austerely excluded it. His sounds are contained and clipped, "definite / as a steel nib's downstroke, quick and clean" ("Station Island" XII). Even his lyrical passages are tightly reined. He liked rugged words that sound like dialect but are respectably standard, such as *flenge* or *loaning* or *slub silk* or *scutch* or Joyce's *tundish*. Alliterations, assonances, and guttural sounds play a prominent part. Although Heaney's verse is unpretentious, this did not keep him from unearthing apt and unexpected images or from seeing the visible world as a substance compounded from materials no longer visible but still suspended in it.

The "voice of conscience and remorse" that Heaney singled out for praise in Yeats's "Man and the Echo" is a dominant aspect of Heaney's aesthetic. Out of his divided loyalties to history and art, to the dead and the living, to his rural roots and his literary gifts, Heaney crafted poems of emotional and ethical complexity. "Is it any wonder when I thought / I would have second thoughts?" he asks in "Terminus"; "I grew up in between." The political in-betweenness of a Catholic boy in the predominantly Protestant Ulster, an Irishman steeped in the English literary canon and language, a farmer's son become a rich and renowned poet are obvious. Incertus was the self-mocking pen name under which Heaney published his first poems in college. In poems about his origins, such as "Digging," "Alphabets," "The Stone Verdict," "Clearances," and "Electric Light," Heaney tries to honor his humble beginnings and ancestry while striking out on his own—"An educated man," in the words of the fisherman of "Casualty."

The voice of conscience and remorse is even stronger in Heaney's poetry about the bloody Troubles of Northern Ireland. In his essay "The Interesting Case of Nero, Chekov's Cognac and a Knocker" (1987), Heaney recalls an evening in Belfast when he and a friend decided, after explosions jolted the city, not to record songs and poems as they had planned: "to have sung and said the poems in those conditions would have been a culpable indulgence." Heaney uses this anecdote to reflect on the tension between "Song and Suffering"—song as the condition of "liberation and abundance" and suffering as the condition of the contemporary world. Even as Heaney concedes that to sing and recite after the explosions might have seemed an "affront," he questions whether he and his friend did the right thing in silencing themselves. Riddled by the inescapable contradictions between what he calls in "The Grauballe Man" "beauty and atrocity," Heaney interrogates song but refuses to be muffled by suffering. In his elegy for Francis Ledwidge, an Irishman who died fighting on behalf of the British Empire that was suppressing Irish nationalism, Heaney sees the mirror of his inner conflicts: "In you, our dead enigma, all the strains / Criss-cross in useless equilibrium."

In his first volumes of poetry, written in the early to mid-1960s, Heaney plays out his growth, guilt, and developing sexuality in the rural landscape of his childhood. But his poetry takes a darker turn after the eruption of internecine violence in Northern Ireland in 1969, which culminated in the 1972 Bloody Sunday killing of thirteen Catholic civilians by British paratroopers during a civil rights march in Derry. Across several books, but especially in *North* (1975), he wrote a series of grim "bog poems," about well-preserved Iron Age corpses discovered buried in the peat of Northern Europe and Ireland. Heaney saw the peat bog as a kind of "memory bank," or unconscious, of the landscape. These poems view contemporary violence through the lens of ancient myths, sacrifices, and feuds, an oblique approach that gives Heaney's poetry about the Troubles an unusual depth and toughness.

In the essay "Feeling into Words," Heaney describes how he discovered emblems for the violence in Northern Ireland in a book published in translation in 1969, "the year the killing started," entitled *The Bog People*: "And the unforgettable photographs of these victims blended in my mind with photographs of atrocities, past and present, in the long rites of Irish political and religious struggles." Heaney takes a serious moral risk in depicting terrorist and antiterrorist atrocities as repetitions of ancient ritual sacrifices, but while reactivating archetypal fertility myths in which ritual death assures rebirth, he aborts the usual payoff of these paradigms. The dead undergo no spiritual transcendence, but remain tenaciously material, bodies bound to the earth. At the end of "Bog Queen," he insists on bleak images of the woman's deadness—bone, skull, stitches—even as he allows her rebirth into the light and into his dramatic monologue: "and I rose from the dark, / hacked bone, skull-ware, / frayed stitches, tufts, / small gleams on the bank." In the bog poems, Heaney scrupulously inspects his own poetic art for any aestheticizing of death and murder, and the poems that result are cramped, anguished, and self-aware, among the most powerful poems about political violence written in the twentieth century.

In the late 1970s, Heaney moved away from clipped, free verse lines, emblematic for him of inwardness, to longer lines in a more conversational idiom, suggesting a more outward and social impulse. He wrote elegies for people he knew who were killed in the violence, such as his cousin Colum McCartney, elegized in "The Strand at Lough Beg," and his acquaintance Louis O'Neill, recalled in "Casualty." He returns to McCartney's death in one of his most adventurous groups of poems, "Station Island," a pilgrimage on which the poet encounters a series of familiar ghosts, who ably tell their stories to this Irish Dante in a modified terza rima and implicate him in their replies. A principal ghost is that of Joyce, who rejects the poet's pilgrimage: "Your obligation / is not discharged by any common rite." He urges Heaney instead to "keep at a tangent" and find his own "echo-soundings, searches, probes, allurements, // elver gleams in the dark of the whole sea." Heaney's subsequent volumes pursue still further the more visionary or "spiritual" temper announced in "Station Island," while also recovering some of the retrospective pastoralism of his earliest verse and the self-scrutiny of his middle work.

Heaney was born on April 13, 1939, in Mossbawn, County Derry. He was educated at a boarding school, St. Columb's College, before going on to take a First Class Honours degree in English at Queen's University, in Belfast, where he returned in 1965, after several years of schoolteaching. He also spent a year at the University of California, Berkeley (1970–71), where he read American poets such as William Carlos Williams and Robert Creeley. He moved to County Wicklow, in the Irish Republic, in 1972 and became a citizen and full-time writer, taking up residency in Dublin in 1976. From 1982 to 1996, he spent part of each year as a professor at Harvard University, which he continued to visit every other year. In 1995, he won the Nobel Prize in Literature.

Digging[1]

Between my finger and my thumb
The squat pen rests; snug as a gun.

Under my window, a clean rasping sound
When the spade sinks into gravelly ground:
My father, digging. I look down   5

Till his straining rump among the flowerbeds
Bends low, comes up twenty years away
Stooping in rhythm through potato drills[2]
Where he was digging.

The coarse boot nestled on the lug, the shaft   10
Against the inside knee was levered firmly.
He rooted out tall tops, buried the bright edge deep
To scatter new potatoes that we picked,
Loving their cool hardness in our hands.

By God, the old man could handle a spade.   15
Just like his old man.

My grandfather cut more turf[3] in a day
Than any other man on Toner's bog.
Once I carried him milk in a bottle
Corked sloppily with paper. He straightened up   20
To drink it, then fell to right away

---

1. See Heaney's account of the poem in the essay "Feeling into Words," p. 1096 in this volume.
2. Furrows in which seeds are sown.

3. Slabs of dried peat commonly used as domestic fuel in Ireland.

Nicking and slicing neatly, heaving sods
Over his shoulder, going down and down
For the good turf. Digging.

The cold smell of potato mould, the squelch and slap   25
Of soggy peat, the curt cuts of an edge
Through living roots awaken in my head.
But I've no spade to follow men like them.

Between my finger and my thumb
The squat pen rests.   30
I'll dig with it.

                                                1966

Death of a Naturalist

All year the flax-dam[4] festered in the heart
Of the townland; green and heavy headed
Flax had rotted there, weighted down by huge sods.
Daily it sweltered in the punishing sun.
Bubbles gargled delicately, bluebottles[5]   5
Wove a strong gauze of sound around the smell.
There were dragon-flies, spotted butterflies,
But best of all was the warm thick slobber
Of frogspawn that grew like clotted water
In the shade of the banks. Here, every spring   10
I would fill jampotfuls of the jellied
Specks to range on window-sills at home,
On shelves at school, and wait and watch until
The fattening dots burst into nimble-
Swimming tadpoles. Miss Walls would tell us how   15
The daddy frog was called a bullfrog
And how he croaked and how the mammy frog
Laid hundreds of little eggs and this was
Frogspawn. You could tell the weather by frogs too
For they were yellow in the sun and brown   20
In rain.

    Then one hot day when fields were rank
With cowdung in the grass the angry frogs
Invaded the flax-dam; I ducked through hedges
To a coarse croaking that I had not heard   25
Before. The air was thick with a bass chorus.
Right down the dam gross-bellied frogs were cocked
On sods; their loose necks pulsed like sails. Some hopped:
The slap and plop were obscene threats. Some sat
Poised like mud grenades, their blunt heads farting.   30

4. Dam across a stream made of flax plants and   5. That is, flies.
fibers.

I sickened, turned, and ran. The great slime kings
Were gathered there for vengeance and I knew
That if I dipped my hand the spawn would clutch it.

1966

Requiem for the Croppies[6]

The pockets of our great coats full of barley—
No kitchens on the run, no striking camp—
We moved quick and sudden in our own country.
The priest lay behind ditches with the tramp.
A people, hardly marching—on the hike—   5
We found new tactics happening each day:
We'd cut through reins and rider with the pike
And stampede cattle into infantry,
Then retreat through hedges where cavalry must be thrown.
Until, on Vinegar Hill, the fatal conclave.   10
Terraced thousands died, shaking scythes at cannon.
The hillside blushed, soaked in our broken wave.
They buried us without shroud or coffin
And in August the barley grew up out of the grave.[7]

1969

Bogland[8]

for T. P. Flanagan[9]

We have no prairies
To slice a big sun at evening—
Everywhere the eye concedes to
Encroaching horizon,

Is wooed into the cyclops' eye   5
Of a tarn.[1] Our unfenced country
Is bog that keeps crusting
Between the sights of the sun.

They've taken the skeleton
Of the Great Irish Elk[2]   10
Out of the peat, set it up
An astounding crate full of air.

6. Irish rebels of 1798, who wore their hair cut (cropped) very short in sympathy with the French Revolution.
7. See Heaney's comments on the poem in the essay "Feeling into Words," p. 1096 in this volume.
8. See the essay "Feeling into Words," p. 1096 in this volume.

9. Irish artist (b. 1929), whose 1967 painting *Boglands (for Seamus Heaney)* helped inspire the poem.
1. Mountain lake or pool; the mythical Cyclops had only one eye.
2. Extinct species of elk with huge antlers.

Butter sunk under
More than a hundred years
Was recovered salty and white.   15
The ground itself is kind, black butter

Melting and opening underfoot,
Missing its last definition
By millions of years.
They'll never dig coal here,[3]   20

Only the waterlogged trunks
Of great firs, soft as pulp.
Our pioneers[4] keep striking
Inwards and downwards,

Every layer they strip   25
Seems camped on before.
The bogholes might be Atlantic seepage.
The wet centre is bottomless.

                      1969

The Tollund Man[5]

I

Some day I will go to Aarhus
To see his peat-brown head,
The mild pods of his eyelids,
His pointed skin cap.

In the flat country nearby   5
Where they dug him out,
His last gruel of winter seeds
Caked in his stomach,

Naked except for
The cap, noose and girdle,   10
I will stand a long time.
Bridegroom to the goddess,

She tightened her torc[6] on him
And opened her fen,[7]
Those dark juices working   15
Him to a saint's kept body,

3. Because the ground is too wet for it to form.
4. Diggers or miners (archaic), implicitly contrasted with American "pioneers."
5. See Heaney's essay "Feeling into Words," in which he cites the description in P. V. Glob's *The Bog People* of the Tollund Man, whose head is preserved in a museum near Aarhus, Denmark, and who was sacrificed two thousand years ago in a fertility ritual to the Mother Goddess (p. 1096 in this volume).
6. Or *torque:* twisting force; also, necklace of precious metal, worn by ancient Gauls and Britons.
7. Lowlands covered with shallow water.

Trove of the turf-cutters'
Honeycombed workings.
Now his stained face
Reposes at Aarhus.   20

II

I could risk blasphemy,
Consecrate the cauldron bog
Our holy ground and pray
Him to make germinate

The scattered, ambushed   25
Flesh of labourers,
Stockinged corpses
Laid out in the farmyards,

Tell-tale skin and teeth
Flecking the sleepers   30
Of four young brothers, trailed
For miles along the lines.[8]

III

Something of his sad freedom
As he rode the tumbril[9]
Should come to me, driving,   35
Saying the names

Tollund, Grauballe, Nebelgard,[1]
Watching the pointing hands
Of country people,
Not knowing their tongue.   40

Out there in Jutland[2]
In the old man-killing parishes
I will feel lost,
Unhappy and at home.

1972

8. In the early 1920s, four brothers murdered by the Ulster Special Constabulary, an auxiliary police force known as the B Specials, were dragged for miles behind a train.
9. A cart used to transport condemned prisoners to their execution.
1. Cities in Denmark.
2. Projection of northern Europe forming continental Denmark and part of northwest Germany.

Bog Queen[3]

I lay waiting
between turf-face and demesne wall,[4]
between heathery levels
and glass-toothed stone.

My body was braille   5
for the creeping influences:
dawn suns groped over my head
and cooled at my feet,

through my fabrics and skins
the seeps of winter   10
digested me,
the illiterate roots

pondered and died
in the cavings
of stomach and socket.   15
I lay waiting

on the gravel bottom,
my brain darkening,
a jar of spawn
fermenting underground   20

dreams of Baltic amber.[5]
Bruised berries under my nails,
the vital hoard reducing
in the crock of the pelvis.

My diadem grew carious,[6]   25
gemstones dropped
in the peat floe[7]
like the bearings of history.

My sash was a black glacier
wrinkling, dyed weaves   30
and phoenician stitchwork
retted on my breasts'

soft moraines.[8]
I knew winter cold
like the nuzzle of fjords   35
at my thighs—

---

3. See Heaney's essay "Feeling into Words,"
p. 1096 in this volume.
4. Between the edge of the grassy turf and the wall
marking the lord's estate.
5. Yellowish fossil resin used for jewelry, from the
Baltic Sea.

6. That is, decayed.
7. Floating peat.
8. Accumulations deposited by glaciers. *Phoeni-cian:* from the ancient trading city of Phoenicia,
noted for its purple dyes. *Retted:* soaked.

the soaked fledge, the heavy
swaddle[9] of hides.
My skull hibernated
in the wet nest of my hair.   40

Which they robbed.
I was barbered
and stripped
by a turfcutter's spade

who veiled me again   45
and packed coomb softly
between the stone jambs[1]
at my head and my feet.

Till a peer's wife bribed him.[2]
The plait of my hair,
a slimy birth-cord   50
of bog, had been cut

and I rose from the dark,
hacked bone, skull-ware,
frayed stitches, tufts,   55
small gleams on the bank.

1975

The Grauballe Man[3]

As if he had been poured
in tar, he lies
on a pillow of turf
and seems to weep

the black river of himself.   5
The grain of his wrists
is like bog oak,
the ball of his heel

like a basalt egg.
His instep has shrunk   10
cold as a swan's foot
or a wet swamp root.

His hips are the ridge
and purse of a mussel,

9. That is, wrapping. *Fledge:* cloth.
1. Upright pieces at top and bottom of opening in which she was placed. *Coomb:* old word for barley stems.

2. That is, till a nobleman's wife bribed him (to cut off and give her the speaker's hair).
3. Another body exhumed from a Danish bog (see "The Tollund Man" and its note 5, above).

his spine an eel arrested   15
under a glisten of mud.

The head lifts,
the chin is a visor
raised above the vent
of his slashed throat   20

that has tanned and toughened.
The cured wound
opens inwards to a dark
elderberry place.

Who will say 'corpse'   25
to his vivid cast?
Who will say 'body'
to his opaque repose?

And his rusted hair,
a mat unlikely   30
as a foetus's.
I first saw his twisted face

in a photograph,
a head and shoulder
out of the peat,   35
bruised like a forceps baby,

but now he lies
perfected in my memory,
down to the red horn
of his nails,   40

hung in the scales
with beauty and atrocity:
with the Dying Gaul⁴
too strictly compassed

on his shield,   45
with the actual weight
of each hooded victim,
slashed and dumped.

                                          1975

4. Roman marble reproduction of a Greek bronze sculpture depicting a wounded soldier of Gaul, whose matted hair identifies him as a Celt, in Rome's Capitoline Museum.

Punishment[5]

I can feel the tug
of the halter at the nape
of her neck, the wind
on her naked front.

It blows her nipples   5
to amber beads,
it shakes the frail rigging
of her ribs.

I can see her drowned
body in the bog,   10
the weighing stone,
the floating rods and boughs.

Under which at first
she was a barked sapling
that is dug up   15
oak-bone, brain-firkin:[6]

her shaved head
like a stubble of black corn,
her blindfold a soiled bandage,
her noose a ring   20

to store
the memories of love.
Little adulteress,
before they punished you

you were flaxen-haired,   25
undernourished, and your
tar-black face was beautiful.
My poor scapegoat,

I almost love you
but would have cast, I know,   30
the stones of silence.
I am the artful voyeur

5. In 1951, the peat-stained body of a young girl who lived during the late first century C.E. was recovered from a bog in Windeby, Germany. As P. V. Glob describes her in *The Bog People*, she "lay naked in the hole in the peat, a bandage over the eyes and a collar round the neck. The band across the eyes was drawn tight and had cut into the neck and the base of the nose. We may feel sure that it had been used to close her eyes to this world. There was no mark of strangulation on the neck, so that it had not been used for that purpose." Her hair "had been shaved off with a razor on the left side of the head. . . . When the brain was removed the convolutions and folds of the surface could be clearly seen. [Glob reproduces a photograph of her brain.] . . . This girl of only fourteen had had an inadequate winter diet. . . . To keep the young body under, some birch branches and a big stone were laid upon her." According to the Roman historian Tacitus (c. 56–c. 120), the Germanic peoples punished adulterous women by shaving off their hair and scourging them out of the village or killing them.

6. *Firkin:* small cask.

of your brain's exposed
and darkened combs,[7]
your muscles' webbing   35
and all your numbered bones:

I who have stood dumb
when your betraying sisters,
cauled in tar,
wept by the railings,[8]   40

who would connive
in civilized outrage
yet understand the exact
and tribal, intimate revenge.

1975

The Strand at Lough Beg[9]

In Memory of Colum McCartney

All round this little island, on the strand
Far down below there, where the breakers strive,
Grow the tall rushes from the oozy sand.
—Dante, *Purgatorio*, 1, 100–103[1]

Leaving the white glow of filling stations
And a few lonely streetlamps among fields
You climbed the hills toward Newtownhamilton
Past the Fews Forest, out beneath the stars—
Along that road, a high, bare pilgrim's track   5
Where Sweeney fled before the bloodied heads,[2]
Goat-beards and dogs' eyes in a demon pack
Blazing out of the ground, snapping and squealing.
What blazed ahead of you? A faked road block?
The red lamp swung, the sudden brakes and stalling   10
Engine, voices, heads hooded and the cold-nosed gun?
Or in your driving mirror, tailing headlights
That pulled out suddenly and flagged you down
Where you weren't known and far from what you knew:
The lowland clays and waters of Lough Beg,   15
Church Island's[3] spire, its soft treeline of yew.

7. Valleys.
8. Women in Belfast, Northern Ireland, have sometimes been shaven, stripped, tarred, and handcuffed to railings as punishment by the Irish Republican Army for keeping company with British soldiers. *Cauled:* wrapped or enclosed; a caul is the inner fetal membrane that at birth, when it is unruptured, sometimes covers the infant's head.
9. Lake in Northern Ireland. *Strand:* beach. "Colum McCartney, a relative of the author's, was the victim of a random sectarian [that is, Catholic versus Protestant] killing in the late summer of 1975" [Heaney's note].
1. *Purgatorio*, the second part of *The Divine Comedy*, by Italian poet Dante Alighieri (1265–1321), is about the mountian of Purgatory and its various groups of repentant sinners after death.
2. "Sweeney is the hero of a Middle Irish prose and poem sequence, one part of which takes place in the Fews" [Heaney's note].
3. Island in Lough Beg on which a spire was erected in 1788 by the earl of Bristol.

There you used hear guns fired behind the house
Long before rising time, when duck shooters
Haunted the marigolds and bulrushes,
But still were scared to find spent cartridges,   20
Acrid, brassy, genital, ejected,
On your way across the strand to fetch the cows.
For you and yours and yours and mine fought shy,
Spoke an old language of conspirators
And could not crack the whip or seize the day: 25
Big-voiced scullions, herders, feelers round
Haycocks and hindquarters, talkers in byres,[4]
Slow arbitrators of the burial ground.

Across that strand of yours the cattle graze
Up to their bellies in an early mist   30
And now they turn their unbewildered gaze
To where we work our way through squeaking sedge[5]
Drowning in dew. Like a dull blade with its edge
Honed bright, Lough Beg half-shines under the haze.
I turn because the sweeping of your feet   35
Has stopped behind me, to find you on your knees
With blood and roadside muck in your hair and eyes,
Then kneel in front of you in brimming grass
And gather up cold handfuls of the dew
To wash you, cousin. I dab you clean with moss   40
Fine as the drizzle out of a low cloud.
I lift you under the arms and lay you flat.
With rushes that shoot green again, I plait
Green scapulars[6] to wear over your shroud.

                                                    1979

Casualty[7]

I

He would drink by himself
And raise a weathered thumb
Towards the high shelf,
Calling another rum
And blackcurrant, without   5
Having to raise his voice,
Or order a quick stout[8]
By a lifting of the eyes
And a discreet dumb-show
Of pulling off the top;   10
At closing time would go

---

4. Barns. *Scullions:* lowest-ranking kitchen help.
5. Coarse, grasslike plants.
6. Religious or fraternal bands of cloth worn front and back over the shoulders. *Plait:* braid.
7. An elegy for Louis O'Neill, a fisherman killed

in an Irish Republican Army bombing, after Bloody Sunday murders of Roman Catholic demonstrators.
8. Strong, dark beer.

In waders and peaked cap
Into the showery dark,
A dole-kept[9] breadwinner
But a natural for work.   15
I loved his whole manner,
Sure-footed but too sly,
His deadpan sidling tact,
His fisherman's quick eye
And turned, observant back.   20

Incomprehensible
To him, my other life.
Sometimes, on his high stool,
Too busy with his knife
At a tobacco plug   25
And not meeting my eye,
In the pause after a slug
He mentioned poetry.
We would be on our own
And, always politic   30
And shy of condescension,
I would manage by some trick
To switch the talk to eels
Or lore of the horse and cart
Or the Provisionals.[1]   35

But my tentative art
His turned back watches too:
He was blown to bits
Out drinking in a curfew
Others obeyed, three nights   40
After they shot dead
The thirteen men in Derry.
PARAS THIRTEEN, the walls said,
BOGSIDE NIL.[2] That Wednesday
Everybody held   45
Their breath and trembled.

II

It was a day of cold
Raw silence, windblown
Surplice and soutane:[3]
Rained-on, flower-laden   50
Coffin after coffin
Seemed to float from the door
Of the packed cathedral

---

9. Receiving unemployment benefits.
1. The Provisional branch of the Irish Republican Army.
2. The graffito turns into the score of a soccer match the death toll of Bloody Sunday, January 30,
1972, when the British Army Parachute Regiment shot and killed thirteen Roman Catholic demonstrators in Derry's Bogside district.
3. Vestments worn by Roman Catholic priests.

Like blossoms on slow water.
The common funeral 55
Unrolled its swaddling band,[4]
Lapping, tightening
Till we were braced and bound
Like brothers in a ring.

But he would not be held 60
At home by his own crowd
Whatever threats were phoned,
Whatever black flags waved.
I see him as he turned
In that bombed offending place, 65
Remorse fused with terror
In his still knowable face,
His cornered outfaced stare
Blinding in the flash.

He had gone miles away 70
For he drank like a fish
Nightly, naturally
Swimming towards the lure
Of warm lit-up places,
The blurred mesh and murmur 75
Drifting among glasses
In the gregarious smoke.
How culpable was he
That last night when he broke
Our tribe's complicity?[5] 80
'Now you're supposed to be
An educated man,'
I hear him say. 'Puzzle me
The right answer to that one.'

III

I missed his funeral, 85
Those quiet walkers
And sideways talkers
Shoaling out of his lane
To the respectable
Purring of the hearse . . . 90
They move in equal pace
With the habitual
Slow consolation
Of a dawdling engine,
The line lifted, hand 95
Over fist, cold sunshine
On the water, the land

4. Cloth in which babies were wrapped to restrain and warm them.

5. The Roman Catholic community's agreement to obey the curfew.

Banked under fog: that morning
When he took me in his boat,
The screw[6] purling, turning   100
Indolent fathoms white,
I tasted freedom with him.
To get out early, haul
Steadily off the bottom,
Dispraise the catch, and smile   105
As you find a rhythm
Working you, slow mile by mile,
Into your proper haunt
Somewhere, well out, beyond . . .

Dawn-sniffing revenant,[7]   110
Plodder through midnight rain,
Question me again.

                                               1979

In Memoriam Francis Ledwidge[8]

Killed in France 31 July 1917

The bronze soldier hitches a bronze cape
That crumples stiffly in imagined wind
No matter how the real winds buff and sweep
His sudden hunkering run, forever craned

Over Flanders.[9] Helmet and haversack,   5
The gun's firm slope from butt to bayonet,
The loyal, fallen names on the embossed plaque—
It all meant little to the worried pet

I was in nineteen forty-six or seven,
Gripping my Aunt Mary by the hand   10
Along the Portstewart prom, then round the crescent
To thread the Castle Walk out to the strand.[1]

The pilot from Coleraine[2] sailed to the coal-boat.
Courting couples rose out of the scooped dunes.
A farmer stripped to his studs and shiny waistcoat   15
Rolled the trousers down on his timid shins.

At night when coloured bulbs strung out the sea-front
Country voices rose from a cliff-top shelter

---

6. Propeller.
7. Ghost.
8. "Francis Ledwidge (1891–1917) was friendly with some of the leaders of the 1916 Rising [insurrection by Irish republicans] yet, like thousands of Irishmen of the time, felt himself constrained to enlist in the British Army to defend 'the rights of small nations' " [Heaney's note].
9. Area covering part of modern France and Belgium; scene of prolonged trench warfare in World War I.
1. Beach. *Prom:* promenade, paved walking path. *Crescent:* semicircular row of houses.
2. Shipping port in Northern Ireland.

With news of a great litter—'We'll pet the runt!'—
And barbed wire that had torn a friesian's elder.[3]　　　　20

Francis Ledwidge, you courted at the seaside
Beyond Drogheda one Sunday afternoon.
Literary, sweet-talking, countrified,
You pedalled out the leafy road from Slane[4]

Where you belonged, among the dolorous　　　　25
And lovely: the May altar of wild flowers,
Easter water sprinkled in outhouses,
Mass-rocks and hill-top raths and raftered byres.[5]

I think of you in your Tommy's[6] uniform,
A haunted Catholic face, pallid and brave,　　　　30
Ghosting the trenches with a bloom of hawthorn
Or silence cored from a Boyne passage-grave.[7]

It's summer, nineteen-fifteen. I see the girl
My aunt was then, herding on the long acre.
Behind a low bush in the Dardanelles[8]　　　　35
You suck stones to make your dry mouth water.

It's nineteen-seventeen. She still herds cows
But a big strafe puts the candles out in Ypres:[9]
'My soul is by the Boyne, cutting new meadows. . . .
My country wears her confirmation dress.'　　　　40

'To be called a British soldier while my country
Has no place among nations. . . .' You were rent
By shrapnel six weeks later. 'I am sorry
That party politics should divide our tents.'

In you, our dead enigma, all the strains　　　　45
Criss-cross in useless equilibrium
And as the wind tunes through this vigilant bronze
I hear again the sure confusing drum

You followed from Boyne water to the Balkans
But miss the twilit note your flute should sound.　　　　50
You were not keyed or pitched like these true-blue ones
Though all of you consort now underground.

1979

---

3. That is, an old cow.
4. Drogheda and Slane are both in northeastern Eire, Ireland.
5. Barns. *Mass-rocks:* rocks at which persecuted Roman Catholics gathered to celebrate the Mass in secret. *Raths:* circular forts built by the early Irish.
6. That is, British soldier's.

7. Subterranean burial chamber entered by means of a long tunnel or passage; the River Boyne was the scene of a battle between the Irish and the English in 1690.
8. Narrow strait between Europe and Turkey.
9. In West Flanders, the site of three heavy World War I battles; pronounced "Wipers" by British soldiers.

From Station Island[1]

VIII

Black water. White waves. Furrows snowcapped.
A magpie flew from the basilica[2]
and staggered in the granite airy space
I was staring into, on my knees
at the hard mouth of St Brigid's Bed.[3]   5
I came to and there at the bed's stone hub
was my archaeologist, very like himself,
with his scribe's face smiling its straight-lipped smile,
starting at the sight of me with the same old
pretence of amazement, so that the wing   10
of woodkerne's[4] hair fanned down over his brow.
And then as if a shower were blackening
already blackened stubble, the dark weather
of his unspoken pain came over him.
A pilgrim bent and whispering on his rounds   15
inside the bed passed between us slowly.

'Those dreamy stars that pulsed across the screen
beside you in the ward—your heartbeats, Tom, I mean—
scared me the way they stripped things naked.
My banter failed too early in that visit.   20
I could not take my eyes off the machine.
I had to head back straight away to Dublin,
guilty and empty, feeling I had said nothing
and that, as usual, I had somehow broken
covenants, and failed an obligation.   25
I half-knew we would never meet again . . .
Did our long gaze and last handshake contain
nothing to appease that recognition?'

'Nothing at all. But familiar stone
had me half-numbed to face the thing alone.   30
I loved my still-faced archaeology.
The small crab-apple physiognomies
on high crosses, carved heads in abbeys . . .
Why else dig in for years in that hard place
in a muck of bigotry under the walls   35
picking through shards and Williamite cannon balls?[5]
But all that we just turned to banter too.
I felt that I should have seen far more of you
and maybe would have—but dead at thirty-two!

---

1. "*Station Island* is a sequence of dream encounters with familiar ghosts, set on Station Island on Lough Derg in Co. Donegal. The island is also known as St Patrick's Purgatory because of a tradition that Patrick was the first to establish the penitential vigil of fasting and praying which still constitutes the basis of the three-day pilgrimage. Each unit of the contemporary pilgrim's exercises is called a 'station,' and a large part of each station involves walking barefoot and praying round the 'beds,' stone circles which are said to be the remains of early medieval monastic cells" [Heaney's note].
2. That is, old church building.
3. One of the stone circles mentioned by Heaney in note 9 above. St. Brigid (c. 450–c. 523) is, after St. Patrick, Ireland's most revered saint.
4. Irish outlaw's.
5. From the Battle of the Boyne (1690), in which William of England defeated James II of Ireland.

Ah poet, lucky poet, tell me why   40
what seemed deserved and promised passed me by?'

I could not speak. I saw a hoard of black
basalt axe heads, smooth as a beetle's back,
a cairn[6] of stone force that might detonate,
the eggs of danger. And then I saw a face   45
he had once given me, a plaster cast
of an abbess, done by the Gowran master,
mild-mouthed and cowled,[7] a character of grace.
'Your gift will be a candle in our house.'
But he had gone when I looked to meet his eyes   50
and hunkering instead there in his place
was a bleeding, pale-faced boy, plastered in mud.
'The red-hot pokers blazed a lovely red
in Jerpoint the Sunday I was murdered,'
he said quietly. 'Now do you remember?   55
You were there with poets when you got the word
and stayed there with them, while your own flesh and blood
was carted to Bellaghy from the Fews.
They showed more agitation at the news
than you did.'   60

        'But they were getting crisis
first-hand, Colum, they had happened in on
live sectarian assassination.
I was dumb, encountering what was destined.'
And so I pleaded with my second cousin.   65
'I kept seeing a grey stretch of Lough Beg
and the strand empty at daybreak.
I felt like the bottom of a dried-up lake.'

'You saw that, and you wrote that—not the fact.
You confused evasion and artistic tact.   70
The Protestant who shot me through the head
I accuse directly, but indirectly, you
who now atone perhaps upon this bed
for the way you whitewashed ugliness and drew
the lovely blinds of the *Purgatorio*   75
and saccharined my death with morning dew.'[8]

Then I seemed to waken out of sleep
among more pilgrims whom I did not know
drifting to the hostel for the night.

          XII

Like a convalescent, I took the hand
stretched down from the jetty, sensed again
an alien comfort as I stepped on ground

---

6. Heap of stones, piled as a memorial or land-
mark.
7. Hooded. *Gowran master:* that is, a master

craftsperson.
8. Cf. Heaney's "The Strand at Lough Beg,"
above.

to find the helping hand still gripping mine,
fish-cold and bony, but whether to guide   5
or to be guided I could not be certain

for the tall man in step at my side
seemed blind, though he walked straight as a rush
upon his ash plant, his eyes fixed straight ahead.[9]

Then I knew him in the flesh   10
out there on the tarmac[1] among the cars,
wintered hard and sharp as a blackthorn bush.

His voice eddying with the vowels of all rivers[2]
came back to me, though he did not speak yet,
a voice like a prosecutor's or a singer's,   15

cunning,[3] narcotic, mimic, definite
as a steel nib's downstroke, quick and clean,
and suddenly he hit a litter basket

with his stick, saying, 'Your obligation
is not discharged by any common rite.   20
What you must do must be done on your own

so get back in harness. The main thing is to write
for the joy of it. Cultivate a work-lust
that imagines its haven like your hands at night

dreaming the sun in the sunspot of a breast.   25
You are fasted now, light-headed, dangerous.
Take off from here. And don't be so earnest,

let others wear the sackcloth and the ashes.[4]
Let go, let fly, forget.
You've listened long enough. Now strike your note.'   30

It was as if I had stepped free into space
alone with nothing that I had not known
already. Raindrops blew in my face

as I came to. 'Old father, mother's son,
there is a moment in Stephen's diary   35
for April the thirteenth, a revelation

---

9. In this last section of the poem, the "familiar ghost" is James Joyce (1882–1941), Irish writer who was almost blind. *Ash plant:* walking stick made of an ash sapling; Stephen Dedalus, one of the two heroes of Joyce's *Ulysses,* carries one. Cf. the stanza form and encounter with a ghost in T. S. Eliot's "Little Gidding."
1. Surface paved with blacktop.

2. The "Anna Livia Plurabelle" section of Joyce's *Finnegans Wake* resounds with the names of many rivers.
3. "The only arms I allow myself to use—silence, exile, and cunning" (Joyce's *Portrait of the Artist as a Young Man*).
4. Traditional dress of penitents.

set among my stars—that one entry
has been a sort of password in my ears,
the collect of a new epiphany,[5]

the Feast of the Holy Tundish.'[6] 'Who cares,'   40
he jeered, 'any more? The English language
belongs to us. You are raking at dead fires,

a waste of time for somebody your age.
That subject people stuff is a cod's[7] game,
infantile, like your peasant pilgrimage.   45

You lose more of yourself than you redeem
doing the decent thing. Keep at a tangent.
When they make the circle wide, it's time to swim

out on your own and fill the element
with signatures on your own frequency,   50
echo soundings, searches, probes, allurements,

elver-gleams[8] in the dark of the whole sea.'
The shower broke in a cloudburst, the tarmac
fumed and sizzled. As he moved off quickly

the downpour loosed its screens round his straight walk.   55

1985

Alphabets

I

A shadow his father makes with joined hands
And thumbs and fingers nibbles on the wall
Like a rabbit's head. He understands
He will understand more when he goes to school.

There he draws smoke with chalk the whole first week,   5
Then draws the forked stick that they call a Y.
This is writing. A swan's neck and swan's back
Make the 2 he can see now as well as say.

Two rafters and a cross-tie on the slate[9]
Are the letter some call *ah*, some call *ay*.   10

5. Manifestations of a divine being, as of the infant Jesus to the Magi (Matthew 2); in the Christian calendar, the Feast of the Epiphany is January 6. *Collect:* short prayer assigned to a particular day. "Epiphany" was also the term Joyce used for the prose poems he wrote as a young man; it meant, he said, the "sudden revelation of the whatness of things."
6. "See the end of James Joyce's *Portrait of the Artist as a Young Man*" [Heaney's note]: "*13 April:*
That tundish [funnel] has been on my mind for a long time. I looked it up and find it English and good old blunt English too. Damn the dean of studies and his funnel! What did he come here for to teach us his own language or to learn it from us? Damn him one way or the other!"
7. Fool's. *Subject:* colonized.
8. Gleams as of young eels.
9. Small, rectangular sheet of rocklike substance, written on with chalk.

There are charts, there are headlines, there is a right
Way to hold the pen and a wrong way.

First it is 'copying out', and then 'English'
Marked correct with a little leaning hoe.
Smells of inkwells rise in the classroom hush.   15
A globe in the window tilts like a coloured O.

II

Declensions sang on air like a *hosanna*[1]
As, column after stratified column,
Book One of *Elementa Latina,*
Marbled and minatory,[2] rose up in him.   20

For he was fostered next in a stricter school
Named for the patron saint of the oak wood[3]
Where classes switched to the pealing of a bell
And he left the Latin forum for the shade

Of new calligraphy[4] that felt like home.   25
The letters of this alphabet were trees.
The capitals were orchards in full bloom,
The lines of script like briars coiled in ditches.

Here in her snooded garment and bare feet,
All ringleted in assonance and woodnotes,[5]   30
The poet's dream stole over him like sunlight
And passed into the tenebrous[6] thickets.

He learns this other writing. He is the scribe
Who drove a team of quills on his white field.
Round his cell door the blackbirds dart and dab.   35
Then self-denial, fasting, the pure cold.

By rules that hardened the farther they reached north
He bends to his desk and begins again.
Christ's sickle[7] has been in the undergrowth.
The script grows bare and Merovingian.[8]   40

III

The globe has spun. He stands in a wooden O.
He alludes to Shakespeare. He alludes to Graves.[9]

1. Cry of adoration. *Declensions:* changes in word forms according to their grammatical cases (in grammar books these are usually printed in columns).
2. Menacing. *Elementa Latina:* elements of Latin.
3. St. Louis (1214–1270), king of France, administered justice under an oak tree.
4. Elegant handwriting, as in medieval manuscripts. *Forum:* public meeting place in old Roman city. The "new calligraphy" is the Irish script. The poem moves from English through Latin to Irish.
5. Natural, artless verbal expressions. *Snooded:* with a net or cloth bag holding her hair. *Assonance:* repetition of vowels in poetry.
6. Murky.
7. In Revelation 14.14, Jesus is portrayed as having "in his hand a sharp sickle," to reap "the harvest of the earth."
8. Characteristic of the first Frankish dynasty (500–751 C.E.), in northern Europe.
9. Robert Graves (1895–1985), English poet. In *Henry V,* the theater building of Shakespeare's time is compared to a "wooden O."

Time has bulldozed the school and school window.
Balers drop bales like printouts where stooked sheaves[1]

Made lambdas on the stubble once at harvest   45
And the delta face of each potato pit
Was patted straight and moulded against frost.
All gone, with the omega that kept

Watch above each door, the good luck horse-shoe.[2]
Yet shape-note language, absolute on air   50
As Constantine's sky-lettered IN HOC SIGNO[3]
Can still command him; or the necromancer[4]

Who would hang from the domed ceiling of his house
A figure of the world with colours in it
So that the figure of the universe   55
And 'not just single things' would meet his sight

When he walked abroad. As from his small window
The astronaut sees all that he has sprung from,
The risen, aqueous, singular, lucent O
Like a magnified and buoyant ovum[5]   60

Or like my own wide pre-reflective stare
All agog at the plasterer on his ladder
Skimming our gable[6] and writing our name there
With his trowel point, letter by strange letter.

                                                                      1987

Terminus[7]

I

When I hoked[8] there, I would find
An acorn and a rusted bolt.

If I lifted my eyes, a factory chimney
And a dormant mountain.

If I listened, an engine shunting   5
And a trotting horse.

Is it any wonder when I thought
I would have second thoughts?

---

1. That is, gatherings of grain stalks and ears.
2. These images allude to the shapes of capital letters in the Greek alphabet: *lambda*: Λ; *delta*: Δ; *omega*: Ω.
3. Before a battle, according to legend, Constantine the Great (d. 337) saw a vision in the heavens of a cross and the words *In hoc signo vinces* ("in this sign you will conquer"); he won the battle and converted to Christianity.
4. One who conjures the spirits of the dead to reveal the future.
5. That is, cell (also Latin for egg). *Aqueous*: watery, *Lucent*: glowing with light.
6. That is, putting a thin layer of plaster over the triangular end of the roof.
7. Roman god who watched over boundaries.
8. Played.

II

When they spoke of the prudent squirrel's hoard
It shone like gifts at a Nativity.[9]   10

When they spoke of the mammon[1] of iniquity
The coins in my pockets reddened like stove-lids.

I was the march drain and the march drain's banks
Suffering the limit of each claim.

III

Two buckets were easier carried than one.   15
I grew up in between.

My left hand placed the standard iron weight.
My right tilted a last grain in the balance.

Baronies, parishes met where I was born.
When I stood on the central stepping stone   20

I was the last earl on horseback in midstream
Still parleying, in earshot of his peers.

1987

The Stone Verdict[2]

When he stands in the judgement place
With his stick in his hand and the broad hat
Still on his head, maimed by self-doubt
And an old disdain of sweet talk and excuses,
It will be no justice if the sentence is blabbed out.   5
He will expect more than words in the ultimate court
He relied on through a lifetime's speechlessness.

Let it be like the judgement of Hermes,[3]
God of the stone heap, where the stones were verdicts
Cast solidly at his feet, piling up around him   10
Until he stood waist-deep in the cairn[4]
Of his own absolution: maybe a gate-pillar
Or a tumbled wallstead where hogweed earths the silence
Somebody will break at last to say, 'Here
His spirit lingers,' and will have said too much.   15

1987

9. Scene depicting Jesus' birth.
1. Material wealth.
2. An anticipatory elegy for Patrick Heaney, the poet's father.
3. Greek messenger god, whose name probably derives from the word *herma*, which means "piles of stones." When Hermes killed Argos and was brought to trial by the gods, the judges made their decisions by casting voting pebbles at his feet.
4. Pyramid of stones, often a grave monument.

Clearances

in memoriam M.K.H.,[5] 1911–1984

She taught me what her uncle once taught her:
How easily the biggest coal block split
If you got the grain and hammer angled right.

The sound of that relaxed alluring blow,
Its co-opted and obliterated echo,   5
Taught me to hit, taught me to loosen,

Taught me between the hammer and the block
To face the music. Teach me now to listen,
To strike it rich behind the linear black.

I

A cobble thrown a hundred years ago   10
Keeps coming at me, the first stone
Aimed at a great-grandmother's turncoat brow.[6]
The pony jerks and the riot's on.
She's crouched low in the trap
Running the gauntlet that first Sunday   15
Down the brae[7] to Mass at a panicked gallop.
He whips on through the town to cries of 'Lundy!'[8]

Call her 'The Convert'. 'The Exogamous Bride'.
Anyhow, it is a genre piece
Inherited on my mother's side   20
And mine to dispose with now she's gone.
Instead of silver and Victorian lace,
The exonerating, exonerated stone.

II

Polished linoleum shone there. Brass taps shone.
The china cups were very white and big—   25
An unchipped set with sugar bowl and jug.
The kettle whistled. Sandwich and tea scone
Were present and correct. In case it run,
The butter must be kept out of the sun.
And don't be dropping crumbs. Don't tilt your chair.   30
Don't reach. Don't point. Don't make noise when you stir.

It is Number 5, New Row, Land of the Dead,
Where grandfather is rising from his place
With spectacles pushed back on a clean bald head

---

5. Margaret Kathleen Heaney, the poet's mother.
6. Heaney's Protestant great-grandmother married a Catholic.
7. Steep slope.

8. That is, traitor. In 1688, the Irish colonel Robert Lundy knew that Derry (or Londonderry) would be invaded by the English, but failed to prepare adequate defenses.

To welcome a bewildered homing daughter   35
Before she even knocks. 'What's this? What's this?'
And they sit down in the shining room together.

III

When all the others were away at Mass
I was all hers as we peeled potatoes.
They broke the silence, let fall one by one   40
Like solder weeping off the soldering iron:
Cold comforts set between us, things to share
Gleaming in a bucket of clean water.
And again let fall. Little pleasant splashes
From each other's work would bring us to our senses.   45

So while the parish priest at her bedside
Went hammer and tongs at the prayers for the dying
And some were responding and some crying
I remembered her head bent towards my head,
Her breath in mine, our fluent dipping knives—   50
Never closer the whole rest of our lives.

IV

Fear of affectation made her affect
Inadequacy whenever it came to
Pronouncing words 'beyond her'. *Bertold Brek.*[9]
She'd manage something hampered and askew   55
Every time, as if she might betray
The hampered and inadequate by too
Well-adjusted a vocabulary.
With more challenge than pride, she'd tell me, 'You
Know all them things.' So I governed my tongue   60
In front of her, a genuinely well-
Adjusted adequate betrayal
Of what I knew better. I'd *naw* and *aye*
And decently relapse into the wrong
Grammar which kept us allied and at bay.   65

V

The cool that came off sheets just off the line
Made me think the damp must still be in them
But when I took my corners of the linen
And pulled against her, first straight down the hem
And then diagonally, then flapped and shook   70
The fabric like a sail in a cross-wind,
They made a dried-out undulating thwack.
So we'd stretch and fold and end up hand to hand
For a split second as if nothing had happened

9. Bertolt Brecht (1898–1956), German playwright.

For nothing had that had not always happened   75
Beforehand, day by day, just touch and go,
Coming close again by holding back
In moves where I was X and she was O
Inscribed in sheets she'd sewn from ripped-out flour sacks.

VI

In the first flush of the Easter holidays   80
The ceremonies during Holy Week
Were highpoints of our *Sons and Lovers*[1] phase.
The midnight fire. The paschal candlestick.[2]
Elbow to elbow, glad to be kneeling next
To each other up there near the front   85
Of the packed church, we would follow the text
And rubrics for the blessing of the font.
As the hind longs for the streams, so my soul . . . [3]
Dippings. Towellings. The water breathed on.
The water mixed with chrism and with oil.   90
Cruet tinkle. Formal incensation
And the psalmist's outcry taken up with pride:
Day and night my tears have been my bread.[4]

VII

In the last minutes he said more to her
Almost than in all their life together.   95
'You'll be in New Row on Monday night
And I'll come up for you and you'll be glad
When I walk in the door . . . Isn't that right?'
His head was bent down to her propped-up head.
She could not hear but we were overjoyed.   100
He called her good and girl. Then she was dead,
The searching for a pulsebeat was abandoned
And we all knew one thing by being there.
The space we stood around had been emptied
Into us to keep, it penetrated   105
Clearances that suddenly stood open.
High cries were felled and a pure change happened.

VIII

I thought of walking round and round a space
Utterly empty, utterly a source
Where the decked chestnut tree had lost its place   110
In our front hedge above the wallflowers.
The white chips jumped and jumped and skited high.
I heard the hatchet's differentiated

1. Novel (1913) by English writer D. H. Lawrence (1885–1930) that largely centers on the oedipal relationship between a mother and son.
2. Large candle lit during a ceremony on the Holy
Saturday preceding Easter.
3. Psalms 42.1.
4. Psalms 42.3.

Accurate cut, the crack, the sigh
And collapse of what luxuriated   115
Through the shocked tips and wreckage of it all.
Deep-planted and long gone, my coeval[5]
Chestnut from a jam jar in a hole,
Its heft and hush become a bright nowhere,
A soul ramifying and forever   120
Silent, beyond silence listened for.

                                                                   1987

At Toombridge[6]

Where the flat water
Came pouring over the weir out of Lough Neagh
As if it had reached an edge of the flat earth
And fallen shining to the continuous
Present of the Bann.   5
                    Where the checkpoint used to be.
Where the rebel boy was hanged in '98.[7]
Where negative ions in the open air
Are poetry to me. As once before
The slime and silver of the fattened eel.   10

                                                                   2001

Electric Light

Candle-grease congealed, dark-streaked with wick-soot . . .
The smashed thumb-nail
Of that ancient mangled thumb was puckered pearl,

Rucked quartz, a littered Cumae.[8]
In the first house where I saw electric light   5
She sat with her fur-lined felt slippers unzipped,

Year in, year out, in the same chair, and whispered
In a voice that at its loudest did nothing else
But whisper. We were both desperate

The night I was left to stay, when I wept and wept   10
Under the clothes, under the waste of light
Left turned on in the bedroom. "What ails you, child,

---

5. Of the same age.
6. City in Northern Ireland where the Bann River meets Lough Neagh, the largest freshwater lake in the British Isles. Toombridge is also the home of Europe's largest eel fishery.
7. Roddy McCorley was hanged at Toombridge for his participation in the rising of 1798.

8. Ancient city near Naples, Italy, site of many archaeological finds. It was also the legendary home of the Sybil of Cumae, the female prophet who grants the hero Aeneas's wish to descend into the underworld in book 6 of the *Aeneid*, by Virgil (70–19 B.C.E.), Roman poet. Heaney's poem remembers his maternal grandmother.

What ails you, for God's sake?" Urgent, sibilant
Ails, far off and old. Scaresome cavern waters
Lapping a boatslip. Her helplessness no help.   15

•

Lisp and relapse. Eddy of sybilline[9] English.
Splashes between a ship and dock, to which,
Animula,[1] I would come alive in time

As ferries churned and turned down Belfast Lough[2]
Towards the brow-to-glass transport of a morning train,   20
The very "there-you-are-and-where-are-you?"

Of poetry itself. Backs of houses
Like the back of hers, meat-safes and mangles
In the railway-facing yards of fleeting England,

Then fields of grain like the Field of the Cloth of Gold.[3]   25
To Southwark too I came, from tube-mouth into sunlight,
Moyola-breath by Thames's "straunge stronde."[4]

•

If I stood on the bow-backed chair, I could reach
The light switch. They let me and they watched me.
A touch of the little pip would work the magic.   30

A turn of their wireless knob and light came on
In the dial. They let me and they watched me
As I roamed at will the stations of the world.

Then they were gone and Big Ben and the news
Were over. The set had been switched off,   35
All quiet behind the blackout except for

Knitting needles ticking, wind in the flue.[5]
She sat with her fur-lined felt slippers unzipped,
Electric light shone over us, I feared

The dirt-tracked flint and fissure of her nail,   40
So plectrum-hard, glit-glittery, it must still keep
Among beads and vertebrae in the Derry[6] ground.

2001

---

9. Like the strange, riddling language spoken by
the Sybil of Cumae (see preceding note).
1. Little soul (Latin).
2. Lake.
3. Place near Calais, in France, where in 1520
Henry VIII of England and Francis I of France,
with sumptuous pageantry, met to arrange an
alliance. Shakespeare describes the meeting in
Henry VIII.
4. From the "General Prologue" of *The Canter-*

bury Tales, by Geoffrey Chaucer (c. 1342–1400).
Both the Tabard Inn, where Chaucer's pilgrims
begin their trip, and the Globe Theatre, where
most of Shakespeare's plays were originally per-
formed, were located in Southwark, a borough of
London on the Thames River. *Moyola*: river in
County Derry.
5. Chimney.
6. City and district in Northern Ireland. *Plectrum*:
pick for use with stringed instruments.

FRANK BIDART
b. 1939

At a time when most of his contemporaries are writing lyrics with oblique meanings, Frank Bidart has evolved a method both old-fashioned and new. One might suppose that he is reviving the dramatic monologue, but he does so with such marked originality that it does not resemble his predecessors' use of this form. A poem about the mad dancer Vaslav Nijinsky includes imagined or recorded quotations, interfused with diary extracts, letters, and other material—a use of heterogeneous sources indebted to Ezra Pound's *Cantos*. But Bidart's effect is not miscellaneous: though his work is fragmented, sometimes almost a series of spasms, all becomes coherent in the minds of the various protagonists. He shows, as Robert Browning did in his dramatic monologues, great psychological penetration, though Bidart focuses on such subjects as guilt, obsession, or seeming grotesqueness. In "Ellen West," based on a case study by the psychiatrist Ludwig Binswanger, Bidart adopts the voice of an anorexic who responds with vexed intensity to her body and the bodies of those around her. Along with other daring and disturbing dramatic monologues, such as "Herbert White," about a necrophilic child-murderer, Bidart has written personal poems about his conflicted relationship with his parents: "the CRISES, FURIES, REFUSALS," "the ACTIONS, ANGERS, DECISIONS // that *made me* what I am" ("Confessional").

The presentation of his poems is unusual. Some phrases appear in capital letters, as if they are headlines emphasizing the most important thoughts in the poem. There are often, though not always, large spaces between lines, occasional bursts into prose, special paragraphing, dramatic uses of punctuation. Bidart boldly rewrites the biblical story of creation, and through simplification, capitalization, and pauses, he fashions a fresh and effective version. Whether lyrical or dramatic, his poems demand attention by these devices, yet on occasion their compressed language is mellifluous in a clipped way, as in the brief elegies and poems of gay experience in *Desire* (1997).

Born on May 27, 1939, in Bakersfield, California, Bidart was educated at the University of California at Riverside (B.A., 1962) and at Harvard University (M.A., 1967), where he studied with and befriended Robert Lowell, whose poetry he later edited. He teaches at Wellesley College.

Ellen West[1]

I love sweets,—
        heaven
would be dying on a bed of vanilla ice cream . . .

But my true self
is thin, all profile   5

and effortless gestures, the sort of blond
elegant girl whose
        body is the image of her soul.

---

1. Bidart's poem is based on a case study of a woman suffering from anorexia nervosa, written by Swiss existential psychiatrist Ludwig Binswanger (1881–1966).

—My doctors tell me I must give up
this ideal;
        but I
WILL NOT . . . cannot.

Only to my husband I'm not simply a "case."

But he is a fool. He married
meat, and thought it was a wife.

      •   •   •

Why am I a girl?

I ask my doctors, and they tell me they
don't know, that it is just "given."

But it has such
implications—;
             and sometimes,
I even feel like a girl.

      •   •   •

Now, at the beginning of Ellen's thirty-second year, her physical
condition has deteriorated still further. Her use of laxatives increases
beyond measure. Every evening she takes sixty to seventy tablets of a
laxative, with the result that she suffers tortured vomiting at night and
violent diarrhea by day, often accompanied by a weakness of the heart.
She has thinned down to a skeleton, and weighs only 92 pounds.

      •   •   •

About five years ago, I was in a restaurant,
eating alone
          with a book. I was
not married, and often did that . . .

—I'd turn down
dinner invitations, so I could eat alone;

I'd allow myself two pieces of bread, with
butter, at the beginning, and three scoops of
vanilla ice cream, at the end,—

                sitting there alone

with a book, both in the book
and out of it, waited on, idly
watching people,—

            when an attractive young man
and woman, both elegantly dressed,
sat next to me.
          She was beautiful—;

with sharp, clear features, a good
bone structure—;
                  if she took her make-up off
in front of you, rubbing cold cream
again and again across her skin, she still would be   50
beautiful—
            more beautiful.

And he,—
           I couldn't remember when I had seen a man
so attractive. I didn't know why. He was almost   55

a male version
             of her,—

I had the sudden, mad notion that I
wanted to be his lover . . .

—Were they married?   60
                were *they* lovers?

They didn't wear wedding rings.

Their behavior was circumspect. They discussed
politics. They didn't touch . . .

—How could I discover?   65

                  Then, when the first course
arrived, I noticed the way

each held his fork out for the other

to taste what he had ordered . . .

                  They did this   70
again and again, with pleased looks, indulgent
smiles, for each course,
               more than once for *each* dish—;
much too much for just friends . . .

—Their behavior somehow sickened me;   75

the way each *gladly*
put the *food* the other had offered *into his mouth*—;

I knew what they were. I knew they slept together.

An immense depression came over me . . .

—I knew I could never   80
with such ease allow another to put food into my mouth:

happily *myself* put food into another's mouth—;

I knew that to become a wife I would have to give up my ideal.

      •   •   •

Even as a child,
I saw that the "natural" process of aging   85

is for one's middle to thicken—
one's skin to blotch;

as happened to my mother.
And her mother.
            I loathed "Nature."   90

At twelve, pancakes
became the most terrible thought there is . . .

I shall *defeat* "Nature."

In the hospital, when they
weigh me, I wear weights secretly sewn into my belt.   95

      •   •   •

January 16. The patient is allowed to eat in her room, but comes readily
with her husband to afternoon coffee. Previously she had stoutly
resisted this on the ground that she did not really eat but devoured like
a wild animal. This she demonstrated with utmost realism . . . Her
physical examination showed nothing striking. Salivary glands are   100
markedly enlarged on both sides.
January 21. Has been reading *Faust* again. In her diary, writes that
art is the "mutual permeation" of the "world of the body" and the "world
of the spirit." Says that her own poems are "hospital poems . . . weak—
without skill or perseverance; only managing to beat their wings softly."   105
February 8. Agitation, quickly subsided again. Has attached herself
to an elegant, very thin female patient. Homo-erotic component
strikingly evident.
February 15. Vexation, and torment. Says that her mind forces her
always to think of eating. Feels herself degraded by this. Has entirely,   110
for the first time in years, stopped writing poetry.

      •   •   •

Callas[2] is my favorite singer, but I've only
seen her once—;

I've never forgotten that night . . .

—It was in *Tosca*,[3] she had long before   115
lost weight, her voice

---

2. Maria Callas (1923–1977), American opera
singer.

3. Opera by Italian composer Giacomo Puccini
(1858–1924).

had been, for years,
                        deteriorating, half itself . . .

When her career began, of course, she was fat,

enormous—; in the early photographs,   120
sometimes I almost don't recognize her . . .

The voice too then was enormous—

healthy; robust; subtle; but capable of
crude effects, even vulgar,
                        almost out of
high spirits, too much health . . .   125

But soon she felt that she must lose weight,—
that all she was trying to express

was obliterated by her body,
buried in flesh—;
                      abruptly, within   130
four months, she lost at least sixty pounds . . .

—The gossip in Milan was that Callas
had swallowed a tapeworm.

But of course she hadn't.

                      The *tapeworm*   135
was her *soul* . . .

—How her soul, uncompromising,
insatiable,
              must have loved eating the flesh from her bones,

revealing this extraordinarily   140
mercurial; fragile; masterly creature . . .

—But irresistibly, nothing
stopped there; the huge voice

also began to change: at first, it simply diminished
in volume, in size,   145
                  then the top notes became
shrill, unreliable—at last,
usually not there at all . . .

—No one knows *why*. Perhaps her mind,
ravenous, still insatiable, sensed   150

that to struggle with the *shreds* of a voice

must make her artistry subtler, more refined,
more capable of expressing humiliation,
rage, betrayal . . .

—Perhaps the opposite. Perhaps her spirit   155
loathed the unending struggle

to *embody* itself, to *manifest* itself, on a stage whose

mechanics, and suffocating customs,
seemed expressly designed to annihilate spirit . . .

—I know that in *Tosca,* in the second act,   160
when, humiliated, hounded by Scarpia,
she sang *Vissi d'arte*
                    —"I lived for art"—

and in torment, bewilderment, at the end she asks,
with a voice reaching   165
                    harrowingly for the notes,

"Art has *repaid* me LIKE THIS?"

                              I felt I was watching
autobiography—
                    an art; skill;   170
virtuosity

miles distant from the usual soprano's
athleticism,—
                    the usual musician's dream
of virtuosity *without* content . . .   175

—I wonder what she feels, now,
listening to her recordings.

For they have already, within a few years,
begun to date . . .

Whatever they express   180
they express through the style of a decade
and a half—;
                    a style *she* helped create . . .

—She must know that now
she probably would *not* do a trill in   185
exactly that way,—
                    that the whole sound, atmosphere,
dramaturgy of her recordings

have just slightly become those of the past . . .

—Is it bitter? Does her soul
tell her   190

that she was an *idiot* ever to think
anything
            material wholly could satisfy? . . .

—Perhaps it says: *The only way*   195
to escape
the History of Styles

is not to have a body.

                    •   •   •

When I open my eyes in the morning, my great
mystery   200
            stands before me . . .

—I *know* that I am intelligent; therefore

the inability not to fear food
day-and-night; this unending hunger
ten minutes after I have eaten . . .   205
                    a childish
dread of eating; hunger which can have no cause,—

half my mind says that all this
is *demeaning* . . .

                    Bread   210
for days on end
drives all real thought from my brain . . .

—Then I think, No. The ideal of being thin

conceals the ideal
not to have a body—;   215
                    which is NOT trivial . . .

This wish seems now as much a "given" of my existence

as the intolerable
fact that I am dark-complexioned; big-boned;
and once weighed   220
one hundred and sixty-five pounds . . .

—But then I think, *No.* That's too simple,—

without a body, who can
know himself at all?
                    Only by   225
acting; choosing; rejecting; have I

made myself—
          discovered who and what *Ellen* can be . . .

—But then again I think, *NO.* This *I* is anterior
to name; gender; action;
fashion;
          MATTER ITSELF,—   230

. . . trying to stop my hunger with FOOD
is like trying to appease thirst
                  with ink.   235

      •   •   •

March 30. Result of the consultation: Both gentlemen agree com-
pletely with my prognosis and doubt any therapeutic usefulness of
commitment even more emphatically than I. All three of us are agreed
that it is not a case of obsessional neurosis and not one of manic-
depressive psychosis, and that no definitely reliable therapy is possible.   240
We therefore resolved to give in to the patient's demand for discharge.

      •   •   •

The train-ride yesterday
was far *worse* than I expected . . .

                  In our compartment
were ordinary people: a student;   245
a woman; her child;—

they had ordinary bodies, pleasant faces;
                      but I thought
I was surrounded by creatures

with the pathetic, desperate   250
desire to be *not* what they were:—

the student was short,
and carried his body as if forcing
it to be taller—;

the woman showed her gums when she smiled,   255
and often held her
hand up to hide them—;

the child
seemed to cry simply because it was
small; a dwarf, and helpless . . .   260

—I was hungry. I had insisted that my husband
not bring food . . .

After about thirty minutes, the woman
peeled an orange

to quiet the child. She put a section   265
into its mouth—;
                    immediately it spit it out.

The piece fell to the floor.

—She pushed it with her foot through the dirt
toward me   270
several inches.

My husband saw me staring
down at the piece . . .

—I didn't move; how I wanted
to reach out,   275
            and as if invisible

shove it in my mouth—;

my body
became rigid. As I stared at him,
I could see him staring   280
at me,—
            then he looked at the student—; at the woman—; then
back to me . . .

I didn't move.

—At last, he bent down, and   285
casually
            threw it out the window.

He looked away.

—I got up to leave the compartment, then   290
saw his face,—

his eyes
were red;
            and I saw

—*I'm sure I saw*—

disappointment.   295

               •   •   •

On the third day of being home she is as if transformed. At breakfast
she eats butter and sugar, at noon she eats so much that—for the first
time in thirteen years!—she is satisfied by her food and gets really full.
At afternoon coffee she eats chocolate creams and Easter eggs. She
takes a walk with her husband, reads poems, listens to recordings, is   300
in a positively festive mood, and all heaviness seems to have fallen away
from her. She writes letters, the last one a letter to the fellow patient

here to whom she had become so attached. In the evening she takes a
lethal dose of poison, and on the following morning she is dead. "She
looked as she had never looked in life—calm and happy and peaceful."   305

·   ·   ·

    Dearest.—I remember how
at eighteen,
              on hikes with friends, when
they rested, sitting down to joke or talk,

    I circled   310
around them, afraid to hike ahead alone,

    yet afraid to rest
when I was not yet truly thin.

    You and, yes, my husband,—
you and he   315

have by degrees drawn me within the circle;
forced me to sit down at last on the ground.

    I am grateful.

    But something in me *refuses* it.

    —How eager I have been   320
to compromise, to kill this *refuser,*—

but each compromise, each attempt
to poison an ideal
which often seemed to *me* sterile and unreal,

heightens my hunger.   325

    I am crippled. I disappoint you.

    Will you greet with anger, or
happiness,

the news which might well reach you
before this letter?   330

    Your *Ellen.*

1977

If I Could Mourn Like a Mourning Dove

    It is what recurs that we believe,
your face not at one moment looking
sideways up at me anguished or

elate, but the old words welling up by
gravity rearranged: 5
two weeks before you died in

pain worn out, after my usual casual sign-off
with *All my love,* your simple
solemn *My love to you, Frank.*

1997

A Coin for Joe, with the Image of a Horse; c. 350–325 BC

COIN

chip of the closed,—L O S T world, toward whose unseen grasses

this long-necked emissary horse

eagerly still
stretches, to graze   5

.

World; Grass;

stretching Horse;—ripe with hunger, bright circle
of appetite, risen to feed and famish us, from exile underground . . . for

you   chip of the incommensurate
closed world   *A n g e l*   10

1997

MICHAEL LONGLEY
b. 1939

In the dozen years from the birth of Seamus Heaney, in 1939, to that of Paul Muldoon, in 1951, the ratio of outstanding poets born to the general population may be higher in Northern Ireland than anywhere else in the English-speaking world. Growing up amid the collisions of and strife between cultures, between religions, and between dialects seems to have propelled an extraordinary group of writers into poetry. Along with Heaney and Muldoon, Michael Longley, Derek Mahon, and Medbh McGuckian came to know one other during the 1960s and early 1970s, friendly competitors who swapped poems and together read the work of other writers. Born in Belfast, on July 27, 1939, a few months after Heaney, Michael Longley takes his place in this formidable company as a master of formal elegance and lyric grace. Over the years he has authored many books of poetry, and he retired in 1991 from a long career in the Arts Council of

Northern Ireland. In 2000–2001, he was triply honored when he won the Hawthornden Prize (Britain's oldest literary award), the T. S. Eliot Prize, and the Queen's Gold Medal.

In the rhymed verse characteristic of his early work (which recalls Louis MacNeice, W. H. Auden, W. B. Yeats, and Ted Hughes), Longley addresses "A Letter to Derek Mahon" to his friend and fellow Protestant, encapsulating the tension between their formalist precision and the sectarian killings of Belfast: "Two poetic conservatives / In the city of guns and long knives, / Our ears receiving then and there / The stereophonic nightmare / Of the Shankill and the Falls." Even after discarding rhyme and metaphysical conceits, Longley continued to work in polished stanzas with intricate sonic patterning, fluent meters, and sinuous syntax. Whether or not the Troubles of Northern Ireland are his explicit subject, Longley's miniaturist formal craft is, to modify Robert Frost's phrase, a delicate stay against Belfast's bloody confusion.

As a student at Trinity College, Dublin (1958–63), Longley read classics, and the example of ancient poetry's golden balance has been fruitful for him, as evidenced by his poise at the level of the line, the stanza, and the poem. Sometimes, he borrows explicitly from classical verse, as in "Ceasefire," a poem he wrote in response to the 1994 suspension of hostilities between the warring parties in Northern Ireland. He retells the story from Homer's *Iliad* of the meeting between the warrior Achilles and King Priam, father to Hector, the great Trojan warrior he has just killed. This moving poem, true both to painful family loss and to the aspiration for a peace beyond cycles of revenge, filters and thus clarifies the immediate present through an ancient paradigm. "Wounds" sees the contemporary bloodshed—a boy wanders into a home to commit sectarian murder—through a different historical parallel, that of World War I, in which Longley's father fought alongside many Ulster Protestants and other Irishmen. Like many fellow poets of Northern Ireland, Longley takes an indirect approach in his writing about atrocity. But where Heaney turns to the deflections of metaphor and of the archetypal dead, Mahon to those of rhyme and painterly texture, McGuckian to dream and figurative play, and Muldoon to irony and numerological form, Longley detours through the classics—their stories, symmetries, and universalized speakers. In lyrics such as "The Comber" and "The Beech Tree," nature's splendor also offers, in contrast to human hatred and butchery, a repose, a vital presence, an epiphanic beauty.

Casualty

Its decline was gradual,
A sequence of explorations
By other animals, each
Looking for the easiest way in—

A surgical removal of the eyes,   5
A probing of the orifices,
Bitings down through the skin,
Through tracts where the grasses melt,

And the bad air released
In a ceremonious wounding   10
So slow that more and more
I wanted to get closer to it.

A candid grin, the bones
Accumulating to a diagram

Except for the polished horns,   15
The immaculate hooves.

And this no final reduction
For the ribs began to scatter,
The wool to move outward
As though hunger still worked there,   20

As though something that had followed
Fox and crow was desperate for
A last morsel and was
Other than the wind or rain.

1973

Wounds

Here are two pictures from my father's head—
I have kept them like secrets until now:
First, the Ulster Division at the Somme[1]
Going over the top with 'Fuck the Pope!'
'No Surrender!': a boy about to die,   5
Screaming 'Give 'em one for the Shankill!'[2]
'Wilder than Gurkhas'[3] were my father's words
Of admiration and bewilderment.
Next comes the London-Scottish padre[4]
Resettling kilts with his swagger-stick,   10
With a stylish backhand and a prayer.
Over a landscape of dead buttocks
My father followed him for fifty years.
At last, a belated casualty,
He said—lead traces flaring till they hurt—   15
'I am dying for King and Country, slowly.'
I touched his hand, his thin head I touched.

Now, with military honours of a kind,
With his badges, his medals like rainbows,
His spinning compass, I bury beside him   20
Three teenage soldiers, bellies full of
Bullets and Irish beer, their flies undone.
A packet of Woodbines I throw in,
A lucifer,[5] the Sacred Heart of Jesus
Paralysed as heavy guns put out   25
The night-light in a nursery for ever;
Also a bus-conductor's uniform—
He collapsed beside his carpet-slippers

---

1. In World War I, the 36th (Ulster) Division lost
thousands of soldiers in two days of fighting at the
First Battle of the Somme, in France.
2. Protestant stronghold in Belfast.

3. Soldiers from Nepal in the British army.
4. Military chaplain.
5. Match. *Woodbines*: cigarettes commonly smoked
by soldiers in World War I.

Without a murmur, shot through the head
By a shivering boy who wandered in   30
Before they could turn the television down
Or tidy away the supper dishes.
To the children, to a bewildered wife,
I think 'Sorry Missus' was what he said.

1973

Detour

I want my funeral to include this detour
Down the single street of a small market town,
On either side of the procession such names
As Philbin, O'Malley, MacNamara, Keane.
A reverent pause to let a herd of milkers pass   5
Will bring me face to face with grubby parsnips,
Cauliflowers that glitter after a sunshower,
Then hay rakes, broom handles, gas cylinders.
Reflected in the slow sequence of shop windows
I shall be part of the action when his wife   10
Draining the potatoes into a steamy sink
Calls to the butcher to get ready for dinner
And the publican[6] descends to change a barrel.
From behind the one locked door for miles around
I shall prolong a detailed conversation   15
With the man in the concrete telephone kiosk
About where my funeral might be going next.

1991

Ceasefire[7]

I

Put in mind of his own father and moved to tears
Achilles took him by the hand and pushed the old king
Gently away, but Priam curled up at his feet and
Wept with him until their sadness filled the building.

II

Taking Hector's corpse into his own hands Achilles   5
Made sure it was washed and, for the old king's sake,

6. Republican, one who wants Northern Ireland
to be free from British rule.
7. In book 24 of Homer's *Iliad*, the Trojan king
Priam visits Achilles' camp to beg for the body of
his son, Hector, after Achilles has killed Hector
and dragged his body by chariot, in revenge for
Hector's having killed his friend Patroclus. Achil-
les receives the king graciously and gives him the
body.

Laid out in uniform, ready for Priam to carry
Wrapped like a present home to Troy at daybreak.

III

When they had eaten together, it pleased them both
To stare at each other's beauty as lovers might,   10
Achilles built like a god, Priam good-looking still
And full of conversation, who earlier had sighed:

IV

'I get down on my knees and do what must be done
And kiss Achilles' hand, the killer of my son.'

1994

The Comber

A moment before the comber turns into
A breaker—sea-spray, raggedy rainbows—
Water and sunlight contain all the colours
And suspend between Inishbofin[8] and me
The otter, and thus we meet, without my scent   5
In her nostrils, the uproar of my presence,
My unforgivable shadow on the sand—
Even if this is the only sound I make.

2000

Death of a Horse

after Keith Douglas[9]

Its expression resigned, humble even, as if it knows
And doesn't mind when the man draws the first diagonal
In white across its forehead, from ear to eyeball, then
The second, death's chalky intersection, the crossroads

Where, moments before the legs stiffen and relax and   5
The knees give way and like water from a burst drain
The blood comes jetting out, black almost, warm and thick,
The horse goes on standing still, just staring ahead.

2000

---

8. Island off the west coast of Ireland.
9. English poet (1920–1944), who wrote about and was killed in World War II.

The Beech Tree

Leaning back like a lover against this beech tree's
Two-hundred-year-old pewter trunk, I look up
Through skylights into the leafy cumulus, and join
Everybody who has teetered where these huge roots
Spread far and wide our motionless mossy dance,   5
As though I'd begun my eclogues with a beech
As Virgil[1] does, the brown envelopes unfolding
Like fans their transparent downy leaves, tassels
And prickly cups, mast, a fall of vermilion
And copper and gold, then room in the branches   10
For the full moon and her dusty lakes, winter
And the poet who recollects his younger self
And improvises a last line for the georgics
About snoozing under this beech tree's canopy.

2000

1. Roman poet (70–19 B.C.E.), author of ten eclogues, or short pastoral poems in dialogue form, as well as the *Georgics* (line 13), or poems on agricultural subjects.

MARGARET ATWOOD
b. 1939

Margaret Atwood, born November 18, 1939, published her first book just after receiving her B.A. from Victoria College, University of Toronto, in 1961. She earned an M.A. at Harvard University and later returned for doctoral research that she did not complete, publishing several volumes of verse during that time. Until 1972, she taught at Canadian universities in Montreal, Alberta, and Toronto; since then, she has been a writer-in-residence in Canada, the United States, and Wales. She has published, besides verse, acclaimed novels, stories, and critical prose. Although written with great confidence, her poems portray a quality she shares with one of her subjects, nineteenth-century Canadian writer Susanna Moodie: "the inescapable doubleness of her own vision" (*The Journals of Susanna Moodie*). Her experiences seem always to rouse cross-cutting responses: "though we knew we had never / been there before, / we knew we had been there before" ("A Morning"). Pierced by her gaze, familiar objects look different: "and you, my electric typewriter / with your cord and hungry plug / drinking a sinister transfusion / from the other side of the wall" ("Three Desk Objects").

Atwood's analysis of the Canadian experience suggests a national corollary for this divided vision: Susanna Moodie, for example, is "an ardent Canadian patriot" and yet also a "detached observer, a stranger"; "We are all immigrants to this place even if we were born here." In "Disembarking at Quebec," Atwood finds an apt metaphor for this collective sense of alienation: "I am a word / in a foreign language." Preoccupations with survival and isolation are also, in Atwood's view, among the distinguishing features of Canadian literature.

An eminent feminist, Atwood has written perceptive, surprising, and witty poems that explore the dynamics of gender relations. "How much longer can I get away / with being so fucking cute?" is the arresting question that opens "Miss July Grows Older," a poem that presents the smart, wryly self-critical voice of a woman who, hardly a passive object, has skillfully manipulated men: "It was something I did well, / like playing the flute." As she ages, Miss July transfers her psychic energies to the world outside, to sunshine and raindrops; "after a while," she explains of her feelings about sex, "these flesh arpeggios get boring." In "Manet's Olympia," Atwood describes the subject of a famous painting, another woman who refuses subordination to the male gaze, her body "unfragile, defiant." "This is no morsel," states the speaker. Blunt address, short declarative sentences, colloquial diction, precise descriptions, well-defined characters, dramatic tension, plays on clichés, and ironic inversions of the reader's expectations—these are among the strategies that help Margaret Atwood's poems command instant attention.

This Is a Photograph of Me

It was taken some time ago.
At first it seems to be
a smeared
print: blurred lines and grey flecks
blended with the paper;   5

then, as you scan
it, you see in the left-hand corner
a thing that is like a branch: part of a tree
(balsam or spruce) emerging
and, to the right, halfway up   10
what ought to be a gentle
slope, a small frame house.

In the background there is a lake,
and beyond that, some low hills.

(The photograph was taken   15
the day after I drowned.

I am in the lake, in the center
of the picture, just under the surface.

It is difficult to say where
precisely, or to say   20
how large or small I am:
the effect of water
on light is a distortion

but if you look long enough,
eventually   25
you will be able to see me.)

1966

[You Fit into Me]

you fit into me
like a hook into an eye

a fish hook
an open eye

1971

They Eat Out

In restaurants we argue
over which of us will pay for your funeral

though the real question is
whether or not I will make you immortal.

At the moment only I   5
can do it and so

I raise the magic fork
over the plate of beef fried rice

and plunge it into your heart.
There is a faint pop, a sizzle   10

and through your own split head
you rise up glowing;

the ceiling opens
a voice sings Love Is A Many

Splendoured Thing[1]   15
you hang suspended above the city

in blue tights and a red cape,
your eyes flashing in unison.

The other diners regard you
some with awe, some only with boredom: 20

they cannot decide if you are a new weapon
or only a new advertisement.

---

1. Title and theme song of a highly romantic movie of the 1950s.

As for me, I continue eating;
I liked you better the way you were,
but you were always ambitious.   25

                                                          1971

From Circe/Mud Poems[2]

[Men with the Heads of Eagles]

Men with the heads of eagles
no longer interest me
or pig-men, or those who can fly
with the aid of wax and feathers[3]

or those who take off their clothes   5
to reveal other clothes
or those with skins of blue leather[4]

or those golden and flat as a coat of arms
or those with claws, the stuffed ones
with glass eyes; or those   10
hierarchic as greaves[5] and steam-engines.

All these I could create, manufacture,
or find easily: they swoop and thunder
around this island, common as flies,
sparks flashing, bumping into each other,   15

on hot days you can watch them
as they melt, come apart,
fall into the ocean
like sick gulls, dethronements, plane crashes.

I search instead for the others,   20
the ones left over,
the ones who have escaped from these
mythologies with barely their lives;
they have real faces and hands, they think
                                of themselves as   25
wrong somehow, they would rather be trees.

                                                          1974

---

2. In Homer's *Odyssey*, Circe is the female enchanter who turns Odysseus's companions into swine; he is protected by the herb moly and thus frees his mates.
3. As did Daedalus, the legendary craftsman, and his son, Icarus, who escaped from the Cretan labyrinth on wings fashioned out of wax and feathers.
4. Probably a reference to the Picts, an early British people who painted themselves blue before going into battle.
5. Armor for the lower part of the leg.

Footnote to the Amnesty Report on Torture

The torture chamber is not like anything
you would have expected.
No opera set or sexy chains and
leather-goods from the glossy
porno magazines, no thirties horror   5
dungeon with gauzy cobwebs; nor is it
the bare cold-lighted
chrome space of the future
we think we fear.
More like one of the seedier   10
British Railways stations, with scratched green
walls and spilled tea,
crumpled papers, and a stooped man
who is always cleaning the floor.

It stinks, though; like a hospital,   15
of antiseptics and sickness,
and, on some days, blood
which smells the same anywhere,
here or at the butcher's.

The man who works here   20
is losing his sense of smell.
He's glad to have this job, because
there are few others.
He isn't a torturer, he only
cleans the floor: 25
every morning the same vomit,
the same shed teeth, the same
piss and liquid shit, the same panic.

Some have courage, others
don't; those who do what he thinks of   30
as the real work, and who are
bored, since minor bureaucrats
are always bored, tell them
it doesn't matter, who
will ever know they were brave, they might   35
as well talk now
and get it over.

Some have nothing to say, which also
doesn't matter. Their
warped bodies too, with the torn   40
fingers and ragged tongues, are thrown
over the spiked iron fence onto
the Consul's lawn, along with
the bodies of the children
burned to make their mothers talk.   45

The man who cleans the floors
is glad it isn't him.
It will be if he ever says
what he knows. He works long hours,
submits to the searches, eats   50
a meal he brings from home, which tastes
of old blood and the sawdust
he cleans the floor with. His wife
is pleased he brings her money
for the food, has been told   55
not to ask questions.

As he sweeps, he tries
not to listen; he tries
to make himself into a wall,
a thick wall, a wall   60
soft and without echoes. He thinks
of nothing but the walk back
to his hot shed of a house,
of the door
opening and his children   65
with their unmarked skin and flawless eyes
running to meet him.

He is afraid of
what he might do
if he were told to,   70
he is afraid of the door,

he is afraid, not
of the door but of the door
opening; sometimes, no matter
how hard he tries,   75
his children are not there.

                                                     1978

Miss July Grows Older

How much longer can I get away
with being so fucking cute?
Not much longer.
The shoes with bows, the cunning underwear
with slogans on the crotch—*Knock Here*,   5
and so forth—
will have to go, along with the cat suit.[6]

---

6. Tight-fitting garment from neck to feet.

After a while you forget
what you really look like.
You think your mouth is the size it was.   10
You pretend not to care.

When I was young I went with my hair
hiding one eye, thinking myself daring;
off to the movies in my jaunty pencil
skirt and elastic cinch-belt,   15
chewed gum, left lipstick
imprints the shape of grateful, rubbery
sighs on the cigarettes of men
I hardly knew and didn't want to.
Men were a skill, you had to have   20
good hands, breathe into
their nostrils, as for horses. It was something I did well,
like playing the flute, although I don't.

In the forests of grey stems there are standing pools,
tarn-coloured, choked with brown leaves.   25
Through them you can see an arm, a shoulder,
when the light is right, with the sky clouded.
The train goes past silos, through meadows,
the winter wheat on the fields like scanty fur.

I still get letters, although not many.   30
A man writes me, requesting true-life stories
about bad sex. He's doing an anthology.
He got my name off an old calendar,
the photo that's mostly bum and daisies,
back when my skin had the golden slick   35
of fresh-spread margarine.
Not rape, he says, but disappointment,
more like a defeat of expectations.
Dear Sir, I reply, I never had any.
Bad sex, that is.   40
It was never the sex, it was the other things,
the absence of flowers, the death threats,
the eating habits at breakfast.
I notice I'm using the past tense.

Though the vaporous cloud of chemicals that enveloped   45
you like a glowing eggshell, an incense,
doesn't disappear: it just gets larger
and takes in more. You grow out
of sex like a shrunk dress
into your common senses, those you share   50
with whatever's listening. The way the sun
moves through the hours becomes important,
the smeared raindrops
on the window, buds
on the roadside weeds, the sheen   55

of spilled oil on a raw ditch
filling with muddy water.

Don't get me wrong: with the lights out
I'd still take on anyone,
if I had the energy to spare.   60
But after a while these flesh arpeggios get boring,
like Bach[7] over and over;
too much of one kind of glory.

When I was all body I was lazy.
I had an easy life, and was not grateful.   65
Now there are more of me.
Don't confuse me with my hen-leg elbows:
what you get is no longer
what you see.

                                                                      1995

Manet's Olympia[8]

She reclines, more or less.
Try that posture, it's hardly languor.
Her right arm sharp angles.
With her left she conceals her ambush.
Shoes but not stockings,   5
how sinister. The flower
behind her ear is naturally
not real, of a piece
with the sofa's drapery.
The windows (if any) are shut.   10
This is indoor sin.
Above the head of the (clothed) maid
is an invisible voice balloon: *Slut.*

But. Consider the body,
unfragile, defiant, the pale nipples   15
staring you right in the bull's-eye.
Consider also the black ribbon
around the neck. What's under it?
A fine red threadline, where the head
was taken off and glued back on.   20
The body's on offer,
but the neck's as far as it goes.
This is no morsel.
Put clothes on her and you'd have a schoolteacher,
the kind with the brittle whiphand.   25

---

7. Johann Sebastian Bach (1685–1750), German
Baroque composer. *Arpeggios:* chords played rap-
idly, one note at a time.

8. Famous 1863 painting by French Impressionist
Édouard Manet (1832–1883), depicting a nude
courtesan gazing confidently at the viewer.

There's someone else in this room.
You, Monsieur Voyeur.
As for that object of yours
she's seen those before, and better.

I, the head, am the only subject   30
of this picture.
You, Sir, are furniture.
Get stuffed.

1995

Morning in the Burned House

In the burned house I am eating breakfast.
You understand there is no house, there is no breakfast,
yet here I am.

The spoon which was melted scrapes against
the bowl which was melted also.   5
No one else is around.

Where have they gone to, brother and sister,
mother and father? Off along the shore,
perhaps. Their clothes are still on the hangers,

their dishes piled beside the sink,   10
which is beside the woodstove
with its grate and sooty kettle,

every detail clear,
tin cup and rippled mirror.
The day is bright and songless,   15

the lake is blue, the forest watchful.
In the east a bank of cloud
rises up silently like dark bread.

I can see the swirls in the oilcloth,
I can see the flaws in the glass,   20
those flares where the sun hits them.

I can't see my own arms and legs
or know if this is a trap or blessing,
finding myself back here, where everything

in this house has long been over,   25
kettle and mirror, spoon and bowl,
including my own body,

including the body I had then,
including the body I have now
as I sit at this morning table, alone and happy,   30

bare child's feet on the scorched floorboards
(I can almost see)
in my burning clothes, the thin green shorts

and grubby yellow T-shirt
holding my cindery, non-existent,   35
radiant flesh. Incandescent.

                                                            1995

EUNICE DE SOUZA
b. 1940

Eunice de Souza's first collection, *Fix* (1979), was a breakthrough in Indian women's writing in English. Before this volume, Indian English women's poetry was marred by melodramatic self-dramatization and slack sentimentality. With its dry wit, spare lines, and laconic insight, *Fix* represented a new level of tonal control. A poet of cold perspicuity, de Souza satirizes the hypocrisy and self-delusion she sees in the conservative Catholic community in Goa, the former capital of Portuguese India, where she grew up. The contradictions she exposes are in part a legacy of colonialism, which remained in place in Goa even after most of India became independent.

In her free verse lyrics, de Souza often reenters the voice of a child growing up in Goa. She imports and indigenizes this strategy of American "confessional" poets of the 1960s, such as Sylvia Plath. De Souza also deploys the idiom, diction, and speech rhythms of Goan India. The speaker of "Sweet Sixteen," for example, assures another teenager that dancing can indeed cause pregnancy, rendered in the local vernacular as "getting *preggers*." While the girl's pathetic confusion is the immediate object of the poem's dramatic irony, its broader target is the Goan Catholic social code that teaches girls to repress their sexuality and ignore their bodies. The openly autobiographical poem "De Souza Prabhu" is an ironic self-portrait of the poet as a girl alienated from her own body and mind. The young de Souza places herself among the "lame ducks" because of her foreign name (part Greek, part Portuguese), her speech ("my language alien"), and her emerging sexuality. Knowing her parents would have preferred a boy, the unwanted girl tries to conceal her femininity ("I hid the bloodstains").

De Souza's understated and epigrammatic poems reveal pain, anger, and bewilderment in growing up female in middle-class Portuguese India—feelings clarified by the poetry's controlled verbal surface and descriptive precision. Humor is also present, as in "Conversation Piece," a one-joke poem about an Indian Catholic who mistakes a clay lingam, a phallic representation of the Hindu god Siva, for an ashtray. In de Souza's more recent volumes, the poetry has relaxed into a more contemplative style, though even a lyric of tender celebration, such as the nativity poem "For Rita's Daughter, Just Born," curbs sentiment with its acid final reference to "the shrill cry of kites."

Born on August 1, 1940, in Poona, India, de Souza received her B.A. from Sophia College, Bombay, in 1960; her M.A. from Marquette University, Wisconsin, in 1963; and her Ph.D. from the University of Bombay in 1988. Since 1969, she has been teaching English at St. Xavier's College, in Bombay. Along with poetry, she has published essays and children's books, while also editing volumes of fiction and poems by, and interviews with, fellow Indian writers.

Sweet Sixteen

Well, you can't say
they didn't try.
Mamas never mentioned menses.[1]
A nun screamed: you vulgar girl
don't say brassieres   5
say bracelets.
She pinned paper sleeves
onto our sleeveless dresses.
The preacher thundered:
Never go with a man alone   10
Never alone
and even if you're engaged
only passionless kisses.

At sixteen, Phoebe asked me:
Can it happen when you're in a dance hall   15
I mean, you know what,
getting *preggers*[2] and all that, when
you're dancing?
I, sixteen, assured her
you could.   20

1979

De Souza Prabhu

No, I'm not going to
delve deep down and discover
I'm really de Souza Prabhu[3]
even if Prabhu was no fool
and got the best of both worlds.   5
(Catholic Brahmin![4]
I can hear his fat chuckle still.)

No matter that
my name is Greek
my surname Portuguese   10
my language alien.

---

1. Menstruation.
2. Local idiom for *pregnant*.
3. Master; teacher; accomplished one (Sanskrit,
Hindi).
4. The priestly and highest of the four major
castes of Hinduism.

There are ways
of belonging.

I belong with the lame ducks.

I heard it said   15
my parents wanted a boy.
I've done my best to qualify.
I hid the bloodstains
on my clothes
and let my breasts sag.   20
Words the weapon
to crucify.

                                                    1979

Conversation Piece

My Portuguese-bred aunt
picked up a clay shivalingam[5]
one day and said:
Is this an ashtray?
No, said the salesman,   5
This is our god.

                                                    1979

Women in Dutch Painting

The afternoon sun is on their faces.
they are calm, not stupid,
pregnant, not bovine.
I know women like that
and not just in paintings—   5
an aunt who did not answer her husband back
not because she was plain
and Anna who writes poems
and hopes her avocado stones
will sprout in the kitchen.   10
Her voice is oatmeal and honey.

                                                    1988

For Rita's Daughter, Just Born

Luminous new leaf
May the sun rise gently
on your unfurling

5. Phallic representation of the Hindu god Siva.

in the courtyard always linger
the smell of earth after rain   5

the stone of these steps
stay cool and old

gods in the niches
old brass on the wall

never the shrill cry of kites   10

                                                              1988

Landscape

I

M. assures me she'll be back
to fling my ashes in the local creek.
(We're short on sacred rivers here).[6]

The pungent air will suit my soul:
It will find its place among   5
the plastic carrier bags and rags that float upstream
or is it downstream.
One can never tell.
The sea sends everything reeling back.
The trees go under.   10

II

We push so much under the carpet—
the carpet's now a landscape.
A worm embedded in each tuft
There's a forest moving.

Everybody smiles   15
and smiles.

III

The crows will never learn
there is garbage enough for everyone:
the mouths of the young are raw red,
soundless.   20

The egret alights on the topmost branch.
Not a leaf is disturbed.
On all sides the ocean.

---

6. Many Hindus, considering the River Ganges holy, float the bodies of the dead or spread their ashes in it.

IV

stretch marks of the city

Look the other way: 25
There are dhows[7] there
mud banks
white horses for desert kingdoms

an old monkey coughs in a tree

the young sense food   30
begin their walk up the hill
slow sure unceasing

we lock the windows
bar the doors

the sun burns through the walls   35

                                                                     1994

---

7. Sailing vessels.

ROBERT PINSKY
b. 1940

Robert Pinsky is one of the foremost contemporary poets trying to reclaim a public and discursive language for poetry. Whereas neoconfessionalists plumb the depths of psychic turmoil and anguish, and avant-gardists insist on the opacities of language, Pinsky recalls classical Roman virtues of clarity, balance, and civility. Instead of violently attacking his poetic or familial ancestors, Pinsky works in forms and patterns—measured stanzas, a rational grammar and syntax, rhetorical parallelisms and pauses—that quietly renew his inheritances. The clarity, wit, and seriousness of Pinsky's poems may be traced to the example of Yvor Winters, the poet, critic, and teacher to whom Pinsky pays tribute in his work, and whom he calls the "Old Man." But whereas Winters's poetry evinces a stoicism bolstered by reason and learning, Pinsky's is less severe and allows more for idiosyncratic feeling and contingency.

"Poetry is, among other things," says Pinsky, "a technology for remembering" (*New York Times Book Review*, September 25, 1994). In "The Uncreation," he celebrates the roots, the communal experience, and the pervasiveness of poetry, "the great excess of song that coats the world." But Pinsky's poems, if attached to past achievements, are not deaf to the contemporary. While steeped in the lyric tradition of meditations on ruins, "The Haunted Ruin" vividly describes computer technology, its internal "billion corridors / Of the semiconductor." Into somewhat elevated rhetoric and diction, Pinsky imports the new and the mundane. His poetry encompasses a wide range of experience and thought, from the imagistic ("Spraying flecks of tar and molten rock") to the abstract ("an all-but-unthinkable music"). His language is assimilative, like the historical process allegorized in the rolling hexameters of "The Figured Wheel." Solemnity and melancholy are among his moods, but so too is a gentle humor. In "ABC," the first letter of each successive word begins with the next letter of the alphabet, starting with "Any body can die, evidently."

Pinsky was born on October 20, 1940, into a Jewish family of Long Branch, New Jersey. He was educated at Rutgers University, where he received his B.A. in 1962, and at Stanford University, where he earned a Ph.D. in English in 1966. He has taught at Wellesley College (1968–80) and the University of California, Berkeley (1980–88); since 1988, he has been a professor of English and creative writing at Boston University. He has published several books of criticism on poetry and an acclaimed translation of Dante's *Inferno*. Serving from 1997 to 2000 as the U.S. poet laureate, he worked through various media to promote the reading and speaking of poetry. Presented through print, video, the Internet, and TV, his Favorite Poem Project has gathered and disseminated the diverse experiences of Americans reading and responding to their favorite poems.

The Figured[1] Wheel

The figured wheel rolls through shopping malls and prisons,
Over farms, small and immense, and the rotten little downtowns.
Covered with symbols, it mills everything alive and grinds
The remains of the dead in the cemeteries, in unmarked graves and
    oceans.

Sluiced by salt water and fresh, by pure and contaminated rivers,   5
By snow and sand, it separates and recombines all droplets and grains,
Even the infinite sub-atomic particles crushed under the illustrated,
Varying treads of its wide circumferential track.

Spraying flecks of tar and molten rock it rumbles
Through the Antarctic station of American sailors and technicians,   10
And shakes the floors and windows of whorehouses for diggers and
    smelters
From Bethany, Pennsylvania to a practically nameless, semi-penal New
    Town

In the mineral-rich tundra[2] of the Soviet northernmost settlements.
Artists illuminate it with pictures and incised mottoes
Taken from the Ten-Thousand Stories and the Register of True Dramas. 15
They hang it with colored ribbons and with bells of many pitches.

With paints and chisels and moving lights they record
On its rotating surface the elegant and terrifying doings
Of the inhabitants of the Hundred Pantheons of major Gods
Disposed in iconographic stations at hub, spoke and concentric bands,   20

And also the grotesque demi-Gods, Hopi gargoyles and Ibo dryads.[3]
They cover it with wind-chimes and electronic instruments

1. Inscribed, decorated, or prophesied.
2. Arctic or subarctic treeless plain.
3. That is, carved grotesques of the plain-dwelling Native Americans and tree nymphs of the West African Igbo.

That vibrate as it rolls to make an all-but-unthinkable music,
So that the wheel hums and rings as it turns through the births of stars

And through the dead-world of bomb, fireblast and fallout   25
Where only a few doomed races of insects fumble in the smoking grasses.
It is Jesus oblivious to hurt turning to give words to the unrighteous,
And is also Gogol's feeding pig that without knowing it eats a baby chick

And goes on feeding.[4] It is the empty armor of My Cid, clattering
Into the arrows of the credulous unbelievers, a metal suit   30
Like the lost astronaut revolving with his useless umbilicus.[5]
Through the cold streams, neither energy nor matter, that agitate

The cold, cyclical dark, turning and returning.
Even in the scorched and frozen world of the dead after the holocaust
The wheel as it turns goes on accreting ornaments.   35
Scientists and artists festoon it from the grave with brilliant

Toys and messages, jokes and zodiacs, tragedies conceived
From among the dreams of the unemployed and the pampered,
The listless and the tortured. It is hung with devices
By dead masters who have survived by reducing themselves magically   40

To tiny organisms, to wisps of matter, crumbs of soil,
Bits of dry skin, microscopic flakes, which is why they are called "great,"
In their humility that goes on celebrating the turning
Of the wheel as it rolls unrelentingly over

A cow plodding through car-traffic on a street in Iasi[6]   45
And over the haunts of Robert Pinsky's mother and father
And wife and children and his sweet self
Which he hereby unwillingly and inexpertly gives up, because it is

There, figured and pre-figured in the nothing-transfiguring wheel.

                                                                          1987

The Questions

What about the people who came to my father's office
For hearing aids and glasses—chatting with him sometimes

A few extra minutes while I swept up in the back,
Addressed packages, cleaned the machines; if he was busy

---

4. "There was also a sow with her family; as she scraped in a heap of garbage the sow in passing swallowed a chicken and, without even noticing it, continued unconcernedly to gobble up the watermelon rinds" (from Nikolai Gogol's 1842 novel *Dead Souls*, tr. George Reavey, part 1, chapter 3).
5. Navel; the astronaut's now useless "lifeline" is compared to the human umbilical cord as in a scene in Stanley Kubrick's movie *2001: A Space Odyssey* (1968). *My Cid:* El Cid, eleventh-century Spanish military leader; after he died, his followers dressed his corpse in his armor and tied it to a horse, so that he could still lead them into battle.
6. City in Romania.

I might sell them batteries, or tend to their questions: 5
The tall overloud old man with a tilted, ironic smirk

To cover the gaps in his hearing; a woman who hummed one
Prolonged note constantly, we called her "the hummer"—how

Could her white fat husband (he looked like Rev. Peale)[7]
Bear hearing it day and night? And others: a coquettish old lady   10

In a bandeau,[8] a European. She worked for refugees who ran
Gift shops or booths on the boardwalk in the summer;

She must have lived in winter on Social Security. One man
Always greeted my father in Masonic gestures and codes.[9]

Why do I want them to be treated tenderly by the world, now   15
Long after they must have slipped from it one way or another,

While I was dawdling through school at that moment—or driving,
Reading, talking to Ellen. Why this new superfluous caring?

I want for them not to have died in awful pain, friendless.
Though many of the living are starving, I still pray for these,   20

Dead, mostly anonymous (but Mr. Monk, Mrs. Rose Vogel)
And barely remembered: that they had a little extra, something

For pleasure, a good meal, a book or a decent television set.
Of whom do I pray this rubbery, low-class charity? I saw

An expert today, a nun—wearing a regular skirt and blouse,   25
But the hood or headdress navy and white around her plain

Probably Irish face, older than me by five or ten years.
The Post Office clerk told her he couldn't break a twenty

So she got change next door and came back to send her package.
As I came out she was driving off—with an air, it seemed to me,   30

Of annoying, demure good cheer, as if the reasonableness
Of change, mail, cars, clothes was a pleasure in itself: veiled

And dumb like the girls I thought enjoyed the rules too much
In grade school. She might have been a grade school teacher;

But she reminded me of being there, aside from that—as a name   35
And person there, a Mary or John who learns that the janitor

---

7. Norman Vincent Peale (1898–1993), influen-
tial clergyman.

8. Hairband.
9. Of the Order of Freemasons, a secret society.

Is Mr. Woodhouse; the principal is Mr. Ringleven; the secretary
In the office is Mrs. Apostolacos; the bus driver is Ray.

1987

The Uncreation

The crowd at the ballpark sing, the cantor sings
Kol Nidre,[1] and the equipment in our cars
Fills them with singing voices while we drive.

When the warlord hears his enemy is dead,
He sings his praises. The old men sang a song   5
And we protesters sang a song against them,

Like teams of children in a singing game;
And at the great convention all they did
They punctuated with a song: our breath

Which is an element and so a quarter   10
Of all creation, heated and thrown out
With all the body's force to shake our ears.

Everything said has its little secret song,
Strained higher and lower as talking we sing all day,
The sentences turned and tinted by the body: 15

A tune of certain pitch for questions, a tune
For *that was not a question,* a tune for *was it,*
The little tunes of begging, of coolness, of scolding.

The Mudheads[2] dance in their adobe masks
From house to house, and sing at each the misdeeds   20
Of the small children inside. And we must take you,

They sing, Now we must take you, Now we must take
You back to the house of Mud. But then the parents
With presents for the Mudheads in their arms

Come singing each child's name, and buy them back: 25
Forgive him, give her back, we'll give you presents.
And the prancing Mudheads take the bribes, and sing.

I make a feeble song up while I work,
And sometimes even machines may chant or jingle
Some lyrical accident that takes its place   30

1. Prayer led by the cantor of a Jewish synagogue
on the eve of Yom Kippur.

2. Ceremonial masked dancers who represent
Native American kachinas, or ancestral spirits.

In the great excess of song that coats the world.
But after the flood the bland Immortals will come
As holy tourists to our sunken world,

To slide like sunbeams down shimmering layers of blue:
Artemis, Gog, Priapus, Jehovah and Baal,[3]   35
With faces calmer than when we gave them names,

Walking our underwater streets where bones
And houses bloom fantastic spurts of coral,
Until they find our books. The pages softened

To a dense immobile pulp between the covers   40
Will rise at their touch in swelling plumes like smoke,
With a faint black gas of ink among the swirls,

And the golden beings shaping their mouths like bells
Will impel their breath against the weight of ocean
To sing us into the cold regard of water.   45

A girl sang dancing once, and shook her hair.
A young man fasting to have a powerful dream
Sang as he cut his body, to please a spirit.

But the Gods will sing entirely, the towering spumes
Dissolving around their faces will be the incense   50
Of their old anonymity restored

In a choral blast audible in the clouds,
An immense vibration that presses the very fish,
So through her mighty grin the whale will sing

To keep from bursting, and the tingling krill   55
Will sing in her jaws, the whole cold salty world
Humming oblation to what our mouths once made.

                                                                            1990

ABC

Any body can die, evidently. Few
Go happily, irradiating joy,

Knowledge, love. Many
Need oblivion, painkillers,
Quickest respite.   5

3. Fertility god worshipped by the Canaanites. *Artemis:* Greek goddess of fertility, chastity, and the hunt. *Gog:* in the Bible, a hostile spirit sup- posed to appear just before the end of the world. *Priapus:* Greek fertility god. *Jehovah:* Judeo- Christian name for God.

Sweet time unafflicted,
Various world:

X = your zenith.

2000

The Haunted Ruin

Even your computer is a haunted ruin, as your
Blood leaves something of itself, warming
The tool in your hand.

From far off, down the billion corridors
Of the semiconductor, military   5
Pipes grieve at the junctures.

This too smells of the body, its heated
Polymers smell of breast milk
And worry-sweat.

Hum of so many cycles in current, voltage   10
Of the past. Sing, wires. Feel, hand. Eyes,
Watch and form

Legs and bellies of characters:
Beak and eye of A. Serpentine hiss
S of the foregoers, claw-tines   15

Of E and of the claw hammer
You bought yesterday, its head
Tasting of light oil, the juice

Of dead striving—the haft
Of ash, for all its urethane varnish, is   20
Polished by body salts.

Pull, clawhead. Hold, shaft. Steel face,
Strike and relieve me. Voice
Of the maker locked in the baritone

Whine of the handsaw working.   25
Lost, lingerer like the dead souls of
Vilna, revenant.[4] Machine-soul.

2000

---

4. Ghost. *Vilna:* now Vilnius, capital of Lithuania; a center of Jewish culture until the German extermination of its Jewish population in World War II.

ROBERT HASS
b. 1941

Robert Hass, the U.S. poet laureate from 1995 through 1997 and, since 1989, a Berkeley professor, is a poet of presence and absence, plenitude and loss. Born on March 1, 1941, in San Francisco, he attended private Catholic schools. In 1963, he received his B.A. from St. Mary's College of California, where he taught beginning in 1971. In 1976, he received his Ph.D. from Stanford University. He won a MacArthur Fellowship in 1984 and the National Book Critics Circle Award in 1996.

In California, Hass came under the influence of the Beats and of west coast poets such as Gary Snyder and Kenneth Rexroth. Like them, he steeped himself in Buddhism and other aspects of East Asian culture. Many of his poems suggest the compression, meditativeness, and alertness to detail of the haiku, a form he has ably translated, in addition to translating the Polish poetry of Nobel Prize–winner Czeslaw Milosz. Hass strives to recover the naked immediacy, the radiant being of nature, objects, people, and emotions. As he says of a lover in "Meditation at Lagunitas," "I felt a wonder at her presence / like a thirst for salt." Yet Hass is no less aware of what Wordsworth called "Fallings from us, vanishings" ("Ode: Intimations of Immortality"). He concedes that, as he puts it in the same poem, "a word is elegy to what it signifies" and "desire is full / of endless distances." As desire in language, poetry is doomed to inscribe absences, to mark losses, even as it seeks to record the full sensual, vital presence of reality. Hass's poetry delights in the primal poetic activity of recovering the world through naming, and yet it is shadowed throughout by emptiness, failure, melancholy longing.

This generative tension is already evident in the early poem "Song." A father returns to an empty house "yelling, 'Hey, I'm home!' " only to encounter the ghost of his desire for physical and emotional contact, for a family "to throw their bodies on the Papa-body, / I-am-loved." To counterbalance this disappointing absence, the poem turns to the gleaming presence of the object-world, "slices of green pepper / on a bone-white dish." One of Hass's fine poems about love relationships, "Privilege of Being," sees anew the mingling of bodies in sex from the astonished perspective of angels. But the poem's celebration of physical immediacy quickly turns into a meditation on separateness and loneliness, one lover hungrily bidding the other: *"look at me."*

Hass's work exhibits mastery of tone, subtly mixing wonder and melancholy, amazement and longing, assertion and vulnerability. In poems such as "Song" and "Sonnet," the natural world evokes moods or inner feelings, as in the haiku. Spliced into the interior ruminations of other poems are quoted snatches of conversation, often in female voices. Combining conversational utterances and rhythms with elevated rhetorical structures, such as formal diction and parallel or hypotactic syntax, the poems ambitiously fuse theoretical speculation with lyrical intensity.

Song

> Afternoon cooking in the fall sun—
> who is more naked
>   than the man
> yelling, "Hey, I'm home!"

                          to an empty house?   5
            thinking because the bay is clear,
            the hills in yellow heat,
            & scrub oak red in gullies
                     that great crowds of family
            should tumble from the rooms   10
                      to throw their bodies on the Papa-body,
                          I-am-loved.

            Cat sleeps in the windowgleam,
                          dust motes.
                 On the oak table   15
                 filets of sole
            stewing in the juice of tangerines,
                 slices of green pepper
                      on a bone-white dish.

                                                                  1973

Meditation at Lagunitas[1]

All the new thinking is about loss.
In this it resembles all the old thinking.
The idea, for example, that each particular erases
the luminous clarity of a general idea. That the clown-
faced woodpecker probing the dead sculpted trunk   5
of that black birch is, by his presence,
some tragic falling off from a first world
of undivided light. Or the other notion that,
because there is in this world no one thing
to which the bramble of *blackberry* corresponds,   10
a word is elegy to what it signifies.
We talked about it late last night and in the voice
of my friend, there was a thin wire of grief, a tone
almost querulous: After a while I understood that,
talking this way, everything dissolves: *justice,*   15
pine, hair, woman, you and *I.* There was a woman
I made love to and I remembered how, holding
her small shoulders in my hands sometimes,
I felt a violent wonder at her presence
like a thirst for salt, for my childhood river   20
with its island willows, silly music from the pleasure boat,
muddy places where we caught the little orange-silver fish
called *pumpkinseed.* It hardly had to do with her.
Longing, we say, because desire is full
of endless distances. I must have been the same to her.   25
But I remember so much, the way her hands dismantled bread,
the thing her father said that hurt her, what

---

1. Small town near San Francisco.

she dreamed. There are moments when the body is as numinous
as words, days that are the good flesh continuing.
Such tenderness, those afternoons and evenings,   30
saying *blackberry, blackberry, blackberry.*

1979

Privilege of Being

Many are making love. Up above, the angels
in the unshaken ether and crystal of human longing
are braiding one another's hair, which is strawberry blond
and the texture of cold rivers. They glance
down from time to time at the awkward ecstasy—   5
it must look to them like featherless birds
splashing in the spring puddle of a bed—
and then one woman, she is about to come,
peels back the man's shut eyelids and says,
look at me, and he does. Or is it the man   10
tugging the curtain rope in that dark theater?
Anyway, they do, they look at each other;
two beings with evolved eyes, rapacious,
startled, connected at the belly in an unbelievably sweet
lubricious glue, stare at each other,   15
and the angels are desolate. They hate it. They shudder pathetically
like lithographs of Victorian beggars
with perfect features and alabaster skin hawking rags
in the lewd alleys of the novel.
All of creation is offended by this distress.   20
It is like the keening sound the moon makes sometimes,
rising. The lovers especially cannot bear it,
it fills them with unspeakable sadness, so that
they close their eyes again and hold each other, each
feeling the mortal singularity of the body   25
they have enchanted out of death for an hour or so,
and one day, running at sunset, the woman says to the man,
I woke up feeling so sad this morning because I realized
that you could not, as much as I love you,
dear heart, cure my loneliness,   30
wherewith she touched his cheek to reassure him
that she did not mean to hurt him with this truth.
And the man is not hurt exactly,
he understands that life has limits, that people
die young, fail at love,   35
fail of their ambitions. He runs beside her, he thinks
of the sadness they have gasped and crooned their way out of
coming, clutching each other with old, invented
forms of grace and clumsy gratitude, ready
to be alone again, or dissatisfied, or merely   40
companionable like the couples on the summer beach

reading magazine articles about intimacy between the sexes
to themselves, and to each other,
and to the immense, illiterate, consoling angels.

1989

Forty Something

She says to him, musing, "If you ever leave me,
and marry a younger woman and have another baby,
I'll put a knife in your heart." They are in bed,
so she climbs onto his chest, and looks directly
down into his eyes. "You understand? Your heart."   5

1996

Sonnet

A man talking to his ex-wife on the phone.
He has loved her voice and listens with attention
to every modulation of its tone. Knowing
it intimately. Not knowing what he wants
from the sound of it, from the tendered civility.   5
He studies, out the window, the seed shapes
of the broken pods of ornamental trees.
The kind that grow in everyone's garden, that no one
but horticulturists can name. Four arched chambers
of pale green, tiny vegetal proscenium arches,   10
a pair of black tapering seeds bedded in each chamber.
A wish geometry, miniature, Indian or Persian,
lovers or gods in their apartments. Outside, white,
patient animals, and tangled vines, and rain.

1996

LYN HEJINIAN
b. 1941

"The language of poetry," writes Lyn Hejinian, "is a language of inquiry." A leading
Language poet, Hejinian refuses to segregate poetry from theory. But neither are her
poems—shuttling between linguistic self-scrutiny and lyrical reminiscence—sterile
tracts on language. In *My Life* (1980, rev. and exp. 1987), a long, semiparodic, semi-
autobiographical prose poem, she recalls a typical American girlhood in the 1950s,
complete with family vacations, big cars, airports, middle-class homes, pampered
babies, and distant war. She records sensual and emotional details, such as fear of an

"uncle with the wart on his nose." Yet Hejinian's poetry resists the illusion of transparent access to a coherent past self. "Maybe writing begins not in the self but in language," she remarked in an interview, "which is far larger than the self, and prior to it. So writing, like reading, begins at a point which is 'not-I' " ("Roughly Stapled").

Seeing the personal life as at least partly constructed by language, Hejinian draws attention to this process in a number of ways. She lets the seams show between sentences. Narrative is discernible but riddled with holes. Pronoun reference is ambiguous and unstable. Like John Ashbery, Hejinian often imitates the form of a thought but twists its content, as in the seeming aphorism "Pretty is as pretty does." Like other Language poets, Hejinian was influenced by the Russian Formalist Victor Shklovsky's theory that art involves a "making strange" or "defamiliarization." With her slightly skewed generalizations, mixed genres, shifting leitmotifs, discontinuous narratives, paratactic sentences, and decentered "I," Hejinian both stimulates and frustrates our desire to construct coherence. She defamiliarizes the meaning-making process of language itself.

"Language is nothing but meanings," writes Hejinian, "and meanings are nothing but a flow of contexts. Such contexts rarely coalesce into images, rarely come to terms. They are transitions, transmutations, the endless radiating of denotation into relation" (*The Language of Inquiry*). Playing on "orb" and "orbit" in *Oxota*, "eye" and "I" in *The Cell*, "hap" and "happy" in *Happily,* and many other such homonyms and verbal cousins, Hejinian emphasizes how words generate related yet distinct words, as do sounds, phrases, and grammars. Indebted to Gertrude Stein's view that, as Hejinian puts it, "language is an order of reality itself and not a mere mediating medium," Hejinian discerns in her precursor many of the devices she also uses to accentuate language, "such as rhyming, punning, pairing, parallelisms, and running strings of changes within either vowel or consonant frames. It is the difference between rod and red and rid that makes them mean. Wordplay, in this sense, foregrounds the relationships between words."

Hejinian was born on May 17, 1941, in Alameda, California, into an academic family. In 1968, she graduated from Harvard University. After she returned to California, she eventually settled in the San Francisco Bay area. She founded Tuumba Press in 1976, was its editor until 1984, and has been coeditor, with Barrett Watten, of *Poetics Journal*. With her second husband, Larry Ochs, avant-garde jazz saxophonist and composer in the Rova Saxophone Quartet, Hejinian traveled to Russia, forming long-term intellectual friendships that have influenced her work. She has taught at several universities and colleges, including the New College of California, the University of California, Berkeley, and Iowa University.

FROM MY LIFE[1]

A pause, a rose,
something on paper
A moment yellow, just as four years later, when my father returned home from the war, the moment of greeting him, as he stood at the bottom of the stairs, younger, thinner than when he had left, was purple—though moments are no longer so colored. Somewhere, in the background, rooms share a pattern of small roses. Pretty is as pretty does. In certain families, the meaning of necessity is at one with the sentiment of

---

1. This semiautobiographical work was originally published in 1980 in thirty-seven sections, each containing thirty-seven sentences (Hejinian was thirty-seven at the time of writing). In 1987, at forty-five, Hejinian expanded the work to forty-five sections of forty-five sentences each. This excerpt is from the beginning of the 1987 version.

prenecessity. The better things were gathered in a pen. The windows were narrowed by white gauze curtains which were never loosened. Here I refer to irrelevance, that rigidity which never intrudes. Hence, repetitions, free from all ambition. The shadow of the redwood trees, she said, was oppressive. The plush must be worn away. On her walks she stepped into people's gardens to pinch off cuttings from their geraniums and succulents. An occasional sunset is reflected on the windows. A little puddle is overcast. If only you could touch, or, even, catch those gray great creatures. I was afraid of my uncle with the wart on his nose, or of his jokes at our expense which were beyond me, and I was shy of my aunt's deafness who was his sister-in-law and who had years earlier fallen into the habit of nodding, agreeably. Wool station. See lightning, wait for thunder. Quite mistakenly, as it happened. Long time lines trail behind every idea, object, person, pet, vehicle, and event. The afternoon happens, crowded and therefore endless. Thicker, she agreed. It was a tic, she had the habit, and now she bobbed like my toy plastic bird on the edge of its glass, dipping into and recoiling from the water. But a word is a bottomless pit. It became magically pregnant and one day split open, giving birth to a stone egg, about as big as a football. In May when the lizards emerge from the stones, the stones turn gray, from green. When daylight moves, we delight in distance. The waves rolled over our stomachs, like spring rain over an orchard slope. Rubber bumpers on rubber cars. The resistance on sleeping to being asleep. In every country is a word which attempts the sound of cats, to match an insolable[2] portrait in the clouds to a din in the air. But the constant noise is not an omen of music to come. "Everything is a question of sleep," says Cocteau,[3] but he forgets the shark, which does not. Anxiety is vigilant. Perhaps initially, even before one can talk, restlessness is already conventional, establishing the incoherent border which will later separate events from experience. Find a drawer that's not filled up. That we sleep plunges our work into the dark. The ball was lost in a bank of myrtle. I was in a room with the particulars of which a later nostalgia might be formed, an indulged childhood. They are sitting in wicker chairs, the legs of which have sunk unevenly into the ground, so that each is sitting slightly tilted and their postures make adjustment for that. The cows warm their own barn. I look at them fast and it gives the illusion that they're moving. An "oral history" on paper. *That* morning this morning. I say it about the psyche because it is not optional. The overtones are a denser shadow in the room characterized by its habitual readiness, a form of charged waiting, a perpetual attendance, of which I was thinking when I began the paragraph, "So much of childhood is spent in a manner of waiting."

As for we who "love to be astonished" You spill the sugar when you lift the spoon. My father had filled an old apothecary jar with what he called "sea glass," bits of old bottles rounded and textured by the sea, so abundant on beaches. There is no solitude. It buries itself in veracity. It is as if one splashed in the water lost by one's tears. My mother had climbed into the garbage can in order to stamp down the accumulated trash, but the can was knocked off balance, and when she fell she broke her arm. She could only give a little shrug. The

---

2. Incapable of being isolated.
3. Jean Cocteau (1889–1963), French avant-garde writer, artist, and filmmaker.

family had little money but plenty of food. At the circus only the elephants were greater than anything I could have imagined. The egg of Columbus,[4] landscape and grammar. She wanted one where the playground was dirt, with grass, shaded by a tree, from which would hang a rubber tire as a swing, and when she found it she sent me. These creatures are compound and nothing they do should surprise us. I don't mind, or I won't mind, where the verb "to care" might multiply. The pilot of the little airplane had forgotten to notify the airport of his approach, so that when the lights of the plane in the night were first spotted, the air raid sirens went off, and the entire city on that coast went dark. He was taking a drink of water and the light was growing dim. My mother stood at the window watching the only lights that were visible, circling over the darkened city in search of the hidden airport. Unhappily, time seems more normative than place. Whether breathing or holding the breath, it was the same thing, driving through the tunnel from one sun to the next under a hot brown hill. She sunned the baby for sixty seconds, leaving him naked except for a blue cotton sunbonnet. At night, to close off the windows from view of the street, my grandmother pulled down the window shades, never loosening the curtains, a gauze starched too stiff to hang properly down. I sat on the windowsill singing sunny lunny teena, ding-dang-dong. Out there is an aging magician who needs a tray of ice in order to turn his bristling breath into steam. He broke the radio silence. Why would anyone find astrology interesting when it is possible to learn about astronomy. What one passes in the Plymouth.[5] It is the wind slamming the doors. All that is nearly incommunicable to my friends. Velocity and throat verisimilitude. Were we seeing a pattern or merely an appearance of small white sailboats on the bay, floating at such a distance from the hill that they appeared to be making no progress. And for once to a country that did not speak another language. To follow the progress of ideas, or that particular line of reasoning, so full of surprises and unexpected correlations, was somehow to take a vacation. Still, you had to wonder where they had gone, since you could speak of reappearance. A blue room is always dark. Everything on the boardwalk was shooting toward the sky. It was not specific to any year, but very early. A German goldsmith covered a bit of metal with cloth in the 14th century and gave mankind its first button. It was hard to know this as politics, because it plays like the work of one person, but nothing is isolated in history—certain humans are situations. Are your fingers in the margin. Their random procedures make monuments to fate. There is something still surprising when the green emerges. The blue fox has ducked its head. The front rhyme of harmless with harmony. Where is my honey running. You cannot linger "on the lamb." You cannot determine the nature of progress until you assemble all of the relatives.

It seemed that we had hardly begun and we were already there

We see only the leaves and branches of the trees close in around the house. Those submissive games were sensual. I was no more than three or four years old, but when crossed I would hold my breath, not from rage but from stubbornness, until I lost consciousness. The shadows one day deeper. Every family has its own collection of stories, but not every

---

4. Puzzle in which the pieces initially form the shape of an egg and can be rearranged into other forms.
5. American brand of automobile.

family has someone to tell them. In a small studio in an old farmhouse, it is the musical expression of a glowing optimism. A bird would reach but be secret. Absence of allusion: once, and ring alone. The downstairs telephone was in a little room as dark as a closet. It made a difference between the immediate and the sudden in a theater filled with transitions. Without what can a person function as the sea functions without me. A typical set of errands. My mother stood between us and held our hands as we waded into the gray-blue water, lecturing us on the undertow, more to add to the thrill of the approaching water than to warn us of any real danger, since she would continue to grip us by the hand when the wave came in and we tried to jump over it. The curve of the rain, more, comes over more often. Four seasons circle a square year. A mirror set in the crotch of the tree was like a hole in the out-of-doors. I could have ridden in the car forever, or so it seemed, watching the scenery go by, alert as to the circumstances of a dream, and that peaceful. Roller coast. The fog lifts a late sunrise. There are floral twigs in position on it. The roots of the locust tree were lifting the corner of the little cabin. Our unease grows before the newly restless. There you are, and you know it's good, and all you have to do is make it better. He sailed to the war. A life no more free than the life of a lost puppy. It became popular and then we were inundated with imitations. My old aunt entertained us with her lie, a story about an event in her girlhood, a catastrophe in a sailboat that never occurred, but she was blameless, unaccountable, since, in the course of the telling, she had come to believe the lie herself. A kind of burbling in the waters of inspiration. Because of their recurrence, what had originally seemed merely details of atmosphere became, in time, thematic. As if sky plus sun *must* make leaves. A snapdragon volunteering in the garden among the cineraria gapes its maw between the fingers, and we pinched the buds of the fuchsia[6] to make them pop. Is that willful. Inclines. They have big calves because of those hills. Flip over small stones, dried mud. We thought that the mica might be gold. A pause, a rose, something on paper, in a nature scrapbook. What follows a strict chronology has no memory. For me, they must exist, the contents of that absent reality, the objects and occasions which now I reconsidered. The smells of the house were thus a peculiar mix of heavy interior air and the air from outdoors lingering over the rose bushes, the camellias, the hydrangeas, the rhododendron and azalea bushes. Hard to distinguish hunger from wanting to eat. My grandmother was in the kitchen, her hands on her hips, wearing what she called a "washdress," watching a line of ants cross behind the faucets of the sink, and she said to us, "Now *I* am waging war." There are strings in the terrible distance. They are against the blue. The trees are continually receiving their own shadows.

1980, 1987

---

6. Flowering shrub. *Cineraria:* garden plants with heart-shaped flowers.

From Oxota: A Short Russian Novel[7]

Chapter Seven

One person believes in nothing and another dislikes poetry
They don't present equal dangers to society
The lowness of the light stole the field from its shadows
An old babushka[8] on the ice atop the ridge of snow packed beside the
    street
In deed and word   5
She was hissing
And a pedestrian screaming, what are you doing up there, you stupid old
    woman.
The shouting samaritan[9] jerked the granny to safety
She was hissing like a street cat, not snakily
An engine, an omen of weddings   10
An habitual association with daily aesthetic impressions
An omen of the love of art and its social functioning
An orb standing for an orbit
The old woman still standing in the street

Chapter 203

A chipped flange on the dangling pipe bringing in our cooking gas
It's in a prepositional state—for, not for, off, on
What can we say of individualism? of cells?
That is just my way
A woman had been struck in a zebra[1] and killed   5
The driver clung
She was nowhere—how could I stop
Traffic lights broken, ice on the street
He's technically guilty unless she was drunk
It's five, seven years, after such an event   10
And events happen, but this doesn't have to mean that another event has
    happened before
Habits before—the favorite cup
Horses that have freed themselves
I think I should get up and chase them

1991

---

7. The fourteen-line stanza Hejinian uses for each chapter of *Oxota: A Short Russian Novel* is an adaptation of the form used by the Russian writer Aleksandr Pushkin (1799–1837) in his verse novel, *Eugene Onegin* (1823–31).

8. Russian slang for old woman.
9. In Luke 10.30–37, Jesus tells the parable of the Samaritan who demonstrates his generosity by stopping to help a man attacked by thieves.
1. Crosswalk.

FROM THE CELL

[It Is the Writer's Object]

It is the writer's object
    to supply the hollow green
    and yellow life of the
    human I
It rains with rains supplied   5
    before I learned to type
    along the sides who when
    asked what we have in
    common with nature replied opportunity
    and size   10
Readers of the practical help
They then reside
And resistance is accurate—it
    rocks and rides the momentum
Words are emitted by the   15
    rocks to the eye
Motes, parts, genders, sights collide
There are concavities
It is not imperfect to
    have died   20

October 6, 1986   1992

[Yesterday I Saw the Sun]

Yesterday I saw the sun
    sagging with assent—fat, yellow-green
    and pink
The live body in its
    spectrum   5
The guts to be sufficiently
    mental
We gawk at a brutality
And self-consciousness is the situation
    (stasis) of objection   10
She assigned herself 20 pages
    a day
Throbbing sticks, the installments stuck
    on them, the sunlight swelling
Any person who agrees will   15
    increase

So I am going, like
    a proper editor, to introduce
    the reader

Because culture does not fall   20
    into the arms of the
    first comer
The reader, with its eyes
    glued to the slits and
    its heart going out to   25
    me, surveys my efforts
The question is framed in
    something like words: "What is
    that on your mouth?"

She lowered her head and   30
    saw the grass, which had
    been almost under her feet,
    growing far below her—clearly
    reflected in it
I.e., introspected on subjective grounds,   35
    not just by being near
Subjectivity is not a misuse
    of substitution
Objectivity is not a misunderstanding
    of sex
                                            40
May 5, 1988   1992

FROM HAPPILY[2]

Constantly I write this happily
Hazards that hope may break open my lips
What I feel is taking place, a large context, long yielding, and to doubt it
    would be a crime against it
I sense that in stating "this is happening"
Waiting for us?
It has existence in fact without that   5
We came when it arrived
Here I write with inexact straightness but into a place in place immediately
    passing between phrases of the imagination
Flowers optimistically going to seed, fluttering candles lapping the air,
    persevering saws swimming into boards, buckets taking dents, and the
    hands on the clock turning—*they* aren't melancholy
Whether or not the future looks back to trigger a longing for conso-   10
    nance grieving over brevity living is "unfinished work" to remember to
    locate something in times to come
Sure a terrible thing whistling at the end of the rope is a poor way of
    laughing
And okay in the dim natural daylight producing it in fragments to the
    skeptic to take it is recognizable
Only the dull make no response

---

2. This excerpt is from the beginning of the poem.

Each reality needs to be affirmed
Several reasons can be linked to all that we ascribe to that   15
And whether or not a dog sees a rainbow as mere scratches suspending
    judgment, all gesture invisibly as we all think what we think to form a
    promising mode of communication bobbing something

The day is promising
Along comes something—launched in context
In context to pass it the flow of humanity divides and on the other side
    unites
All gazing at the stars bound in a black bow   20
I am among them thinking thought through the thinking thought to no
    conclusion
Context is the chance that time takes
Our names tossed into the air scraped in the grass before having formed
    any opinion leaving people to say only that there was a man who
    happened on a cart and crossed a gnarled field and there was a
    woman who happened on a cart and crossed a gnarled field too
Is happiness the name for our (involuntary) complicity with chance?
Anything could happen   25
A boy in the sun drives nails into a fruit a sign (cloud) in the wind swings
A woman descends a ladder into mud it gives way
But today's thought is different
Better to presuppose late
We eat with relief from our formlessness   30
Each day is drawn to its scene or scene to its day the image already under
    way and formed to proceed
Perhaps happiness is what we volunteer
A cormorant appears in the sun flashing exact notes, a phenomenon of a
    foggy day stretching its wings
Madame Cézanne[3] offers herself in homage with its various uses with its
    curve and blank stare
It resembles an apple   35
And the most unexpected aspect of this activity dependent on nothing
    personal is that it consists of praise coming by chance, viz., happiness,
    into the frame of the world

It is midday a sentence its context—history with a future
The blue is sky at all high points and the shadow underfoot moves at zero
    point
Someone speaks it within reason
The one occupied by something launched without endpoint   40
Flaubert[4] said he wanted his sentences *erect while running—almost an
    impossibility*
Nonetheless, though its punctuation is half hoping for failure, the
    sentence makes an irrevocable address to life
And though the parrot speaks but says nothing this has the impact of an
    aphorism

---

3. Wife of French Postimpressionist painter Paul
Cézanne (1839–1906). Madame Cézanne was the
subject of the painter's famous *La Femme à
l'éventail,* a portrait that became an important
influence on the method of composition developed
by the American writer Gertrude Stein (1874–
1946) and adapted by Hejinian in *Happily.*
4. Gustave Flaubert (1821–1880), French novel-
ist.

Are you there?
I'm here   45
Is that a *yes* or a *no?*

The writer over the page is driven down but like a robin by a worm
The visible world is drawn
Sentence meaning reason
Without that nothing recurs   50
Joy—a remnant of an original craziness we can hardly remember—it exists,
    everything does, without us
There is music recognizing recognition we know about boundaries and
    boundaries wound up
No straight line the riddle set I am tempted to say rough circles hazards
    lips that only things can differ
It's not not me I'm afraid saying *this* is *thus*
A name by chance for anything on which we have no claim   55
Everything for the magician is accidental
All that could possibly happen to the magical prop becomes intrinsic to it
    and knowing "all that" (could possibly happen) is what constitutes a
    magician's knowledge which is changed by the stopping of the
    thought just as such an aphorism is formed as the one that observes
    an event emerging just where time is becoming attracted to a
    particular thing (say, a branch hanging over a river) in a particular
    situation (say, mirrored in hilarity)
The event is the adventure of that moment
Then seven more days of heavy rain, one drop after another a relay that is
    all in the passing by that is inside it (the bypassing, all washed away)
If I were a fictional character thinking back she might be weeping in a   60
    hundred bedrooms tonight wanting to be good long after this
    depiction of wanting to have been good
But what is it that Plotinus[5] says—the "good" will not be something
    brought in from the outside?
Is it then a pleasure covered in all seasons out of bounds beyond the
    interior chain around the vernacular meant to bring us in, you know
    what I mean, I see what you're saying, and so on
The good is the chance with things that happen that inside and out time
    takes

It's midday a sentence, then night another
The sentence arachnid, a so-called "riddle figure"   65
Sense for its own sake saying at the same time something and its meaning
    "only the gust outside crossed the slate," "only the shale span caught
    at the consciousness that makes even sleep delicious"
Susceptible to happiness I was thinking of nothing
Thinking thing linking that to which thought goes back, the thing arrives
Tightly the hands of the clock turn but other elements also must conduct
    logic
The good of it be it love or touchiness in idleness sunk in proximity   70

                        *   *   *

                                                                        2000

5. Neoplatonic philosopher (c. 205–270 C.E.).

DEREK MAHON
b. 1941

Derek Mahon is, like Seamus Heaney, one of the gifted poets from Northern Ireland to become prominent in the late 1960s and early 1970s. Not that the Ulster poets are a homogeneous group. Born in Belfast a couple of years after Heaney, on November 23, 1941, Mahon studied French at a traditionally Protestant institution, Trinity College, Dublin, and belonged ambivalently to the Protestant community. By contrast, Heaney's early affiliations with the Northern Irish Catholic community, though equivocal, were strong. Heaney scrabbled in the farms and bogs of County Derry; Mahon was raised in the urban roar of Belfast. Heaney's earthy language is often tinged with the sonorities of Irish Gaelic; Mahon's writing evokes a cross-national metropolitanism—from Belfast to London, New York, even Paris. Irishness is central to Heaney's poetry; Mahon, whose relation to Irish national identity and native cultural traditions is greatly complicated by his Protestant background and who worked for many years as a reviewer, editor, and translator in London and New York, represents himself as a displaced cosmopolitan, unsure "what is meant by home" ("Afterlives").

Even so, many commonalities exist between the two poets. The tension between civilization and violence, between beauty and suffering, recurs in their work. Avoiding journalistic patter, both poets take an oblique approach to the Troubles in Northern Ireland. Like a French Impressionist painter, Mahon is drawn to beautiful atmospheric effects—falling snow, moonlit waves, sunlit puddles, an urban dawn after rainfall. But tucked into his poems are jarring references to war, genocide, torture, guns, bombs, and executions. The undercurrent of brutality is all the more affecting, because of its implicit contrast with the poetry's literary learning, its gauzy, delicate, languid patterns. Mahon allegorizes the suffering of the Irish, as of other suppressed and even forgotten peoples, in his most famous poem, "A Disused Shed in Co. Wexford." Here, as in poems such as "The Snow Party," "Afterlives," and "The Last of the Fire Kings," history is a nightmare, civilization an ineffective tonic. The suffering and brutality exist in ironic counterpoint to the quiet beauty of Mahon's rhymes and half-rhymes ("forms" / "worms"), consonances ("barrels" / "burials"), stately stanzas, elegant syntax, and plangent meters.

A skilled craftsman, Mahon exhibits a literary sensibility that is rich, restrained, and humanistic. In tonally complex verse, he layers irony and self-irony on melancholy, humor on pathos, hope on skepticism. Always the outsider among the living, he finds genial company among dead poetic forebears, among them Charles Baudelaire, Louis MacNeice, and W. H. Auden. Solitary figures, such as the speaker in "The Last of the Fire Kings" and the bittern in "An Bonnán Buí," evoke his estrangement. "An Bonnán Buí" instances the loosening in Mahon's style during the 1990s, when he adopted a more conversational voice and relinquished honed stanzas for a single, expansive verse paragraph. But even here, Mahon is no less allusive, literary, or elegiac than he was at the beginning of his career. In our age of psychiatric therapy and group-think, when "the odd learn to renounce / their singularity for a more communal faith" (as he wrote in an early version of the poem), he continues to defend poetry as a space for human idiosyncrasy, irresolvable ambivalence, and difficult introspection.

Afterlives

for James Simmons[1]

1

I wake in a dark flat
To the soft roar of the world.
Pigeons neck on the white
Roofs as I draw the curtains
And look out over London   5
Rain-fresh in the morning light.

This is our element, the bright
Reason on which we rely
For the long-term solutions.
The orators yap, and guns   10
Go off in a back street;
But the faith does not die

That in our time these things
Will amaze the literate children
In their non-sectarian schools   15
And the dark places be
Ablaze with love and poetry
When the power of good prevails.

What middle-class twits we are
To imagine for one second   20
That our privileged ideals
Are divine wisdom, and the dim
Forms that kneel at noon
In the city not ourselves.

2

I am going home by sea   25
For the first time in years.
Somebody thumbs a guitar
On the dark deck, while a gull
Dreams at the mast-head,
The moon-splashed waves exult.   30

At dawn the ship trembles, turns
In a wide arc to back
Shuddering up the grey lough[2]
Past lightship and buoy,
Slipway and dry dock   35
Where a naked bulb burns;

1. Poet and songwriter (b. 1933) from Northern Ireland.
2. Lake or sea.

And I step ashore in a fine rain
To a city so changed
By five years of war
I scarcely recognize   40
The places I grew up in,
The faces that try to explain.

But the hills are still the same
Grey-blue above Belfast.
Perhaps if I'd stayed behind   45
And lived it bomb by bomb
I might have grown up at last
And learnt what is meant by home.

                                        1975, 1991

The Snow Party

(for Louis Asekoff)[3]

Bashō, coming
To the city of Nagoya,
Is asked to a snow party.

There is a tinkling of china
And tea into china;   5
There are introductions.

Then everyone
Crowds to the window
To watch the falling snow.

Snow is falling on Nagoya   10
And farther south
On the tiles of Kyōto.

Eastward, beyond Irago,
It is falling
Like leaves on the cold sea.   15

Elsewhere they are burning
Witches and heretics
In the boiling squares,

Thousands have died since dawn
In the service   20
Of barbarous kings;

---

3. American poet (b. 1939). The Japanese poet Bashō (1644–1694) mentions the snow-watching party, a traditional social gathering, in *The Records of a Weather-Exposed Skeleton*.

But there is silence
In the houses of Nagoya
And the hills of Ise.

1975, 1979

The Last of the Fire Kings[4]

I want to be
Like the man who descends
At two milk churns

With a bulging
String bag and vanishes   5
Where the lane turns,

Or the man
Who drops at night
From a moving train

And strikes out over the fields   10
Where fireflies glow;
Not knowing a word of the language.

Either way, I am
Through with history—
Who lives by the sword   15

Dies by the sword.[5]
Last of the fire kings, I shall
Break with tradition and

Die by my own hand
Rather than perpetuate   20
The barbarous cycle.

Five years I have reigned
During which time
I have lain awake each night

And prowled by day   25
In the sacred grove
For fear of the usurper,

4. In *The Golden Bough*, the Cambridge anthropologist James Frazer (1854–1941) describes the Fire King as living in isolation in parts of Cambodia. Supposed to have supernatural powers, he must not die a natural death; when he becomes seriously ill, he is stabbed to death by local elders.
5. A seventeenth-century proverb. Cf. Matthew 26.52: "All they that take the sword shall perish with the sword."

Perfecting my cold dream
Of a place out of time,
A palace of porcelain   30

Where the frugivorous[6]
Inheritors recline
In their rich fabrics
Far from the sea.

But the fire-loving   35
People, rightly perhaps,
Will not countenance this,

Demanding that I inhabit,
Like them, a world of
Sirens, bin-lids   40
And bricked-up windows—

Not to release them
From the ancient curse
But to die their creature and be thankful.

1975

A Disused Shed in Co. Wexford[7]

> Let them not forget us, the weak souls among the asphodels.
> —Seferis, *Mythistorema*, tr. Keeley and Sherrard

(for J. G. Farrell)[8]

Even now there are places where a thought might grow—
Peruvian mines, worked out and abandoned
To a slow clock of condensation,
An echo trapped for ever, and a flutter
Of wild-flowers in the lift-shaft,   5
Indian compounds where the wind dances
And a door bangs with diminished confidence,
Lime crevices behind rippling rain-barrels,
Dog corners for bone burials;
And in a disused shed in Co. Wexford,   10

Deep in the grounds of a burnt-out hotel,
Among the bathtubs and the washbasins
A thousand mushrooms crowd to a keyhole.
This is the one star in their firmament
Or frames a star within a star.   15
What should they do there but desire?

6. Fruit-eating.
7. County in southeast Ireland.

8. Historical novelist (1935–1979) and friend of Mahon's.

So many days beyond the rhododendrons
With the world waltzing in its bowl of cloud,
They have learnt patience and silence
Listening to the rooks querulous in the high wood.   20

They have been waiting for us in a foetor[9]
Of vegetable sweat since civil war days,
Since the gravel-crunching, interminable departure
Of the expropriated mycologist.[1]
He never came back, and light since then   25
Is a keyhole rusting gently after rain.
Spiders have spun, flies dusted to mildew
And once a day, perhaps, they have heard something—
A trickle of masonry, a shout from the blue
Or a lorry changing gear at the end of the lane.   30

There have been deaths, the pale flesh flaking
Into the earth that nourished it;
And nightmares, born of these and the grim
Dominion of stale air and rank moisture.
Those nearest the door grow strong—   35
'Elbow room! Elbow room!'
The rest, dim in a twilight of crumbling
Utensils and broken pitchers, groaning
For their deliverance, have been so long
Expectant that there is left only the posture.   40

A half century, without visitors, in the dark—
Poor preparation for the cracking lock
And creak of hinges. Magi, moonmen,
Powdery prisoners of the old regime,
Web-throated, stalked like triffids,[2] racked by drought   45
And insomnia, only the ghost of a scream
At the flash-bulb firing-squad we wake them with
Shows there is life yet in their feverish forms.
Grown beyond nature now, soft food for worms,
They lift frail heads in gravity and good faith.   50

They are begging us, you see, in their wordless way,
To do something, to speak on their behalf
Or at least not to close the door again.
Lost people of Treblinka and Pompeii![3]
'Save us, save us,' they seem to say,   55
'Let the god not abandon us
Who have come so far in darkness and in pain.
We too had our lives to live.

---

9. Offensive smell.
1. One who studies mushrooms and other fungi.
2. Fictional plants with poisonous stingers that attack humanity in John Wyndham's science fiction novel *The Day of the Triffids* (1951) and the 1962 movie based on it.
3. Ancient Italian city destroyed by the eruption of Mt. Vesuvius in 79 c.e. *Treblinka*: site of a Nazi extermination camp.

You with your light meter and relaxed itinerary,
Let not our naive labours have been in vain!'   60

                                                    1975, 1991

An Bonnán Buí[4]

A heron-like species, rare visitors, most recent records
referring to winter months . . . very active at dusk.
                              —Guide to Irish Birds

A sobering thought, the idea of you stretched there,
bittern, under a dark sky, your exposed bones
yellow too in a ditch among cold stones,
ice glittering everywhere on bog and river,
the whole unfortunate country frozen over   5
and your voice stilled by enforced sobriety—
a thought more wrenching than the fall of Troy
because more intimate; for we'd hear your shout
of delight from a pale patch of watery sunlight
out on the mud there as you took your first   10
drink of the day and now, destroyed by thirst,
you lie in brambles while the rats rotate.
I'd've broken the ice for you, given an inkling;
now, had I known it, we might both be drinking
and singing too; for ours is the same story.   15
Others have perished—heron, blackbird, thrushes—
and lie shivering like you under whin-bushes;[5]
but I mourn only the bittern, withdrawn and solitary,
who used to carouse alone among the rushes
and sleep rough in the star-glimmering bog-drain.   20
It used to be, with characters like us,
they'd let us wander the roads in wind and rain
or lock us up and throw away the key—
but now they have a cure for these psychoses
as indeed they do for most social diseases   25
and, rich at last, we can forget our pain.
She says I'm done for if I drink again;
so now, relieved of dangerous stimuli,
at peace with my plastic bottle of H_2O
and the slack strings of insouciance, I sit   30
with bronze Kavanagh on his canal-bank seat,
not in 'the tremendous silence of mid-July'[6]
but the fast bright zing of a winter afternoon

4. Irish name for the yellow bittern, a bird popu-
larly believed to die from thirst and elegized in an
eighteenth-century Irish drinking song by Cathal
Buí Mac Giolla Ghunna (c. 1680–1756).
5. Whin: swampy meadow.
6. A bronze statue of the Irish poet Patrick Kavan-
agh (1904–1967) sits on a bench on the banks of
the Grand Canal in Dublin. The quotation is from
Kavanagh's sonnet "Lines Written on a Seat on the
Grand Canal, Dublin," which begins, "O com-
memorate me where there is water." Cf. also his
"Canal Bank Walk," which records his passive sur-
render to flux.

dizzy with head-set, flash-bulb and digifone,
to learn the *tao*[7] he once claimed as his own   35
and share with him the moor-hen and the swan,
the thoughtless lyric of a cloud in the sky
and the play of light and shadow on the slow
commemorative waters; relax, go with the flow.

1997, 1999

A Swim in Co. Wicklow

The only reality is the perpetual flow of vital energy.
—Montale[8]

Spindrift,[9] crustacean patience
and a gust of ozone,
you come back once more
to this dazzling shore,
its warm uterine rinse,   5
heart-racing heave and groan.

A quick gasp as you slip
into the hissing wash,
star cluster, dulse[1] and kelp,
slick algae, spittle, froth,   10
the intimate slash and dash,
hard-packed in the seething broth.

Soft water-lip, soft hand,
close tug of origin,
the sensual writhe and snore   15
of maidenhair and frond,
you swim here once more
smart as a rogue gene.

Spirits of lake, river
and woodland pond preside   20
mildly in water never
troubled by wind or tide;
and the quiet suburban pool
is only for the fearful—

no wind-wave energies   25
where no sea briar grips
and no freak breaker with
the violence of the ages

7. Belief that the process of change in nature is to be followed for a life of harmony. *Digifone:* Irish mobile phone.
8. Eugenio Montale (1896–1981), Italian poet, critic, and translator.
9. Sea spray.
1. Coarse red seaweed.

comes foaming at the mouth
to drown you in its depths.   30

Among pebbles a white conch
worn by the suck and crunch,
a sandy chamber old
as the centuries, in cold
and solitude reclines   35
where the moon-magnet shines;

but today you swirl and spin
in sea water as if,
creatures of salt and slime
and naked under the sun,   40
life were a waking dream
and this the only life.

                                                    1999

SHARON OLDS
b. 1942

Sharon Olds is perhaps the most prominent beneficiary of the confessional poets' "breakthrough back into life," in Robert Lowell's phrase. But if personal experience remains highly mediated in the poetry of such first-generation confessionals as Lowell and Sylvia Plath, Olds unveils her emotional and sensual life with arresting candor. Her poems are grounded in human drives, longings, and traumas. Their eroticism is unrestrained, their immediacy almost glaring. In a number of her poems, Olds penetrates all outward show to reveal what is for her the ultimate truth within the body. Looking at a 1921 photograph of a starving Russian girl, Olds surmises: "Deep in her body / the ovaries let out her first eggs, / golden as drops of grain" ("Photograph of the Girl"). Similarly, in Olds's most notoriously provocative poem, the Pope is imagined in terms of the irrepressible reproductive drive hidden within his robes ("The Pope's Penis"). In lyrics that frequently return to sex, birth, and family relationships, Olds embraces without shame or prurience the propulsive force of desire. Like Walt Whitman, she celebrates the human body with an almost religious zeal. Even when she meditates on the dead, it is their physical reality that she most memorably describes. Devoting an entire volume of poems, *The Father* (1992), to an account of her father's death, Olds conveys excruciating pain, ambivalence, and tenderness in her unsparing chronicle of his physical deterioration.

For all their intimacy, Olds's poems are far from artless. Heavily enjambed, they convey the rush of sensation and emotion in their sinuous movement from one line to the next. Meaning spills forward, carried along the arteries of a fluent syntax. Clauses are spun tightly or loosely to modulate pacing. Bold bodily images are at the center of Olds's art, often graphic, occasionally lurid. Sometimes her language, though accessible and direct, becomes richly metaphorical. Whether describing the moment of giving birth or her daughter's peeling of an orange, Olds layers her poetry with evocative sensual images. Each poem focuses on a single event, sight, or feeling, which exfoliates in an unbroken verse paragraph. Although her speakers are usually recognizable as Olds, not all of her poems are written in *propria persona*. In one poem, for example, she assumes the voice of her cremated father, who "Speaks to Me from the Dead."

Olds was born on November 19, 1942, in San Francisco, and was raised, in her words, as a "hellfire Calvinist." She completed her undergraduate education at Stanford University in 1964 and her Ph.D. at Columbia University in 1972. Since the publication of her first volume of poetry, *Satan Says* (1980), Olds has won the Lamont Poetry Selection and the National Book Critics Circle Award. She teaches poetry workshops at New York University's Graduate Creative Writing Program, while also helping run the New York University workshop program at Goldwater Hospital, on New York's Roosevelt Island. She was the New York State poet laureate for 1998–2000.

Photograph of the Girl

The girl sits on the hard ground,
the dry pan of Russia, in the drought
of 1921,[1] stunned,
eyes closed, mouth open,
raw hot wind blowing   5
sand in her face. Hunger and puberty are
taking her together. She leans on a sack,
layers of clothes fluttering in the heat,
the new radius of her arm curved.
She cannot be not beautiful, but she is   10
starving. Each day she grows thinner, and her bones
grow longer, porous. The caption says
she is going to starve to death that winter
with millions of others. Deep in her body
the ovaries let out her first eggs,   15
golden as drops of grain.

        1984

The Pope's Penis

It hangs deep in his robes, a delicate
clapper at the center of a bell.
It moves when he moves, a ghostly fish in a
halo of silver seaweed, the hair
swaying in the dark and the heat—and at night,   5
while his eyes sleep, it stands up
in praise of God.

        1987

1. An estimated five million people died in the Russian drought and famine of 1921.

The Moment the Two Worlds Meet

That's the moment I always think of—when the
slick, whole body comes out of me,
when they pull it out, not pull it but steady it
as it pushes forth, not catch it but keep their
hands under it as it pulses out,   5
they are the first to touch it,
and it shines, it glistens with the thick liquid on it.
That's the moment, while it's sliding, the limbs
compressed close to the body, the arms
bent like a crab's rosy legs, the   10
thighs closely packed plums in heavy syrup, the
legs folded like the white wings of a chicken—
that is the center of life, that moment when the
juiced bluish sphere of the baby is
sliding between the two worlds,   15
wet, like sex, it *is* sex,
it is my life opening back and back
as you'd strip the reed from the bud, not strip it but
watch it thrust so it peels itself and the
flower is there, severely folded, and   20
then it begins to open and dry
but by then the moment is over,
they wipe off the grease and wrap the child in a blanket and
hand it to you entirely in this world.

1987

The Exact Moment of His Death

When he breathed his last breath, it was he,
my father, although he was so transformed
no one who had not been with him
for the last hour would know him—the skin
now physical as animal fat,   5
the eyes cast halfway back into his head,
the nose thinned, the mouth racked open,
with that tongue in it like the fact of the mortal,
a tongue so dried, scalloped, darkened
and material. We could see the fluid   10
risen into the back of his mouth
but it was he, the huge, slack arms,
the spots of blood under the skin
black and precise, we had come this far with him
step by step, it was he, his last   15
breath was his, not taken with desire
but his, light as a milkweed seed,
coming out of his mouth and floating across the room.

And when the nurse listened for his heart,
and his stomach was silvery, it was his stomach,   20
when she did not shake her head but stood and
nodded at me, for a moment it was fully
he, my father, dead but completely
himself, a man with an open mouth and
black spots on his arms. He looked like   25
someone killed in a bloodless struggle—
the strain in his neck and the base of his head,
as if he were violently pulling back.
He seemed to be holding still, then the skin
tightened slightly around his whole body   30
as if the purely physical were claiming him,
and then it was not my father,
it was not a man, it was not an animal,
I ran my hand slowly through the hair,
lifted my fingers up through the grey   35
waves of it, the unliving glistening
matter of this world.

                                                       1992

My Father Speaks to Me from the Dead

I seem to have woken up in a pot-shed,
on clay, on shards, the bright paths
of slugs kiss-crossing my body. I don't know
where to start, with this grime on me.
I take the spider glue-net, plug   5
of the dead, out of my mouth, let's see
if where I have been I can do this.
I love your feet. I love your knees,
I love your our my legs, they are so
long because they are yours and mine   10
both. I love your—what can I call it,
between your legs, we never named it, the
glint and purity of its curls. I love
your rear end, I changed you once,
washed the detritus off your tiny   15
bottom, with my finger rubbed
the oil on you; when I touched your little
anus I crossed wires with God for a moment.
I never hated your shit—that was
your mother. I love your navel, thistle   20
seed fossil, even though
it's her print on you. Of course I love
your breasts—did you see me looking up
from within your daughter's face, as she nursed?
I love your bony shoulders and you know I   25
love your hair, thick and live

as earth. And I never hated your face,
I hated its eruptions. You know what I love?
I love your brain, its halves and silvery
folds, like a woman's labia.   30
I love in you
even what comes
from deep in your mother—your heart, that hard worker,
and your womb, it is a heaven to me,
I lie on its soft hills and gaze up   35
at its rosy vault.
I have been in a body without breath,
I have been in the morgue, in fire, in the slagged
chimney, in the air over the earth,
and buried in the earth, and pulled down   40
into the ocean—where I have been
I understand this life, I am matter,
your father, I made you, when I say now that I love you
I mean look down at your hand, move it,
that action is matter's love, for human   45
love go elsewhere.

                                                          1992

Once

I saw my father naked, once, I
opened the blue bathroom's door
which he always locked—if it opened, it was empty—
and there, surrounded by glistening turquoise
tile, sitting on the toilet, was my father,   5
all of him, and all of him
was skin. In an instant, my gaze ran
in a single, swerving, unimpeded
swoop, up: toe, ankle,
knee, hip, rib, nape,   10
shoulder, elbow, wrist, knuckle,
my father. He looked so unprotected,
so seamless, and shy, like a girl on a toilet,
and even though I knew he was sitting
to shit, there was no shame in that   15
but even a human peace. He looked up,
I said Sorry, backed out, shut the door
but I'd seen him, my father a shorn lamb,
my father a cloud in the blue sky
of the blue bathroom, my eye had driven   20
up the hairpin mountain road of the
naked male, I had turned a corner
and found his flank unguarded—gentle
bulge of the hip-joint, border of the pelvic cradle.

                                                          1999

MARILYN HACKER
b. 1942

"I do like words," Marilyn Hacker admits in the poem "Feeling and Form," and few contemporary poets are as dexterous in their use. She likes organizing words within elaborate literary grids, such as the fixed forms of the rondeau, the villanelle, the sestina, and the sonnet. She is one of the most accomplished of the New Formalists—poets committed to the revival of rhymed and metered verse—though she was belatedly included in the group and was publishing before its formation in the 1980s. Her formalism is flexible, allowing for the insertion of colloquialisms and confessional details into inherited structures, which are loosened and renewed by the liberties she takes with slant rhymes, skewed meters, coiled syntax, and wrenching enjambments. Although the New Formalism is sometimes assumed to be politically—as well as poetically—conservative, Hacker couples traditional forms with "nontraditional" content: feminist outrage, lesbian desire, and mourning across an extended family of women. "Traditional forms, or for that matter, invented forms," she said in a 1980 interview, "aren't in any way inimical to women's poetry, feminist poetry." Hacker knits together form and content to powerful effect. In the "braided" form and echoic language of "Year's End," love poetry is intertwined with elegy, erotic pleasure with grief for the bodies of lovers lost to breast cancer.

Often addressed to specific lovers, friends, and family members, Hacker's poems usually emerge from fresh joy, anger, grief, and disappointment. With her mother and her daughter, she composes a generational triad that forms, breaks apart, and reforms. She has written sonnet sequences about the end of her relationship with her daughter's father, about a love affair and its eventual unhappy conclusion, and about her struggle with breast cancer. The sonnets commemorate her grief and fear, but they also testify, with humor, to her bravery and spirit.

Hacker was born on November 27, 1942, to Jewish immigrants in New York City. She was educated at the Bronx High School of Science, New York University, and the Art Students League. She has been an antiquarian bookseller and a teacher, and she has done editorial work for books and magazines. In 1975, she won the National Book Award; in 1995, she won the Lenore Marshall Prize. She has one daughter and lives part of each year in France.

Rondeau[1] after a Transatlantic Telephone Call

Love, it was good to talk to you tonight.
You lather me like summer though. I light
up, sip smoke. Insistent through walls comes
the downstairs neighbor's double-bass. It thrums
like toothache. I will shower away the sweat,   5

smoke, summer, sound. Slick, soapy, dripping wet,
I scrub the sharp edge off my appetite.
I want: crisp toast, cold wine prickling my gums,
love. It was good

---

1. Strictly, a poem with two rhyme sounds, thirteen lines, and three stanzas, in which the refrain of the last two stanzas echoes the first line of the poem.

imagining around your voice, you, late-   10
awake there. (It isn't midnight yet
here.) This last glass washes down the crumbs.
I wish that I could lie down in your arms
and, turned toward sleep there (later), say, "Goodnight,
love. It was good."   15

                                                        1980

From Taking Notice

13

No better lost than any other woman
turned resolutely from the common pool
of our erased, emended history,
I think of water, in this book-strewn room. In
another room, my daughter, home from school,   5
audibly murmurs "spanking, stupid, angry
voice"—a closet drama where I am
played second-hand to unresisting doll
daughters. Mother and daughter both, I see
myself, the furious and unforgiven;   10
myself, the terrified and terrible;
the child punished into autonomy;
the unhealed woman hearing her own voice damn
her to the nightmares of the brooding girl.

                                                        1980

Almost Aubade[2]

The little hours: two lovers herd upstairs
two children, one of whom is one of theirs.
Past them, two of the other sex lope down,
dressed for mid-winter cruising bars in brown
bomber-jackets—their lives as uncluttered   5
as their pink shaven cheeks, one of us muttered,
fumbling with keys. Yes, they did look alike.
Hooking their scarves and parkas on the bike,
the seven-year-old women shuck a heap
of velvet jeans and Mary Janes.[3] They sleep   10
diagonal, instantly, across the top
bunk, while their exhausted elders drop,
not to the bliss breasts melt to against breasts
yet, but to kitchen chairs. One interests
herself in omelets, listening anyhow.   15
It's certain that fine women pick at food.

---

2. Morning love song.   3. Young girls' patent-leather shoes.

A loaf of bread, a jug of wine, and thou[4]
shalt piecemeal total both, gripped in that mood
whose hunger makes a contrapuntal[5] stutter
across connectives. Unwrap cheese, find butter,   20
dip bread crusts in a bowl of pasta sauce
saved from the children's supper. Tired because
of all we should stay up to say, we keep
awake together often as we sleep
together. I'll clear the plates. Leave your cup.   25
Lie in my arms until the kids get up.

1985

Year's End

for Audre Lorde and Sonny Wainwright[6]

Twice in my quickly disappearing forties
someone called while someone I loved and I were
making love to tell me another woman
had died of cancer.

Seven years apart, and two different lovers: 5
underneath the numbers, how lives are braided,
how those women's deaths and lives, lived and died, were
interleaved also.

Does lip touch on lip a memento mori?[7]
Does the blood-thrust nipple against its eager   10
mate recall, through lust, a breast's transformations
sometimes are lethal?

Now or later, what's the enormous difference?
If one day is good, is a day sufficient?
Is it fear of death with which I'm so eager   15
to live my life out

now and in its possible permutations
with the one I love? (Only four days later,
she was on a plane headed west across the
Atlantic, work-bound.)   20

Men and women, mortally wounded where we
love and nourish, dying at thirty, forty,
fifty, not on barricades, but in beds of
unfulfilled promise:

4. Slightly altered from "A Jug of Wine, a Loaf of
Bread—and Thou," Edward FitzGerald's "Rubaí-
yát of Omar Khayyám" (1859, 1889), line 46.
5. That is, complementing and contrasting.
6. Audre Lorde (1934–1992) and Sonny Wain-
wright (1930–1985), American writers, also les-
bian, who died of cancer.
7. Reminder of death (Latin); symbol reminding
the viewer of mortality.

tell me, senators, what you call abnormal?   25
Each day's obits read as if there's a war on.
Fifty-eight-year-old poet dead of cancer:
warrior woman[8]

laid down with the other warrior women.
Both times when the telephone rang, I answered,   30
wanting not to, knowing I had to answer,
go from two bodies'

infinite approach to a crest of pleasure
through the disembodied voice from a distance
saying one loved body was clay, one wave of   35
mind burst and broken.

Each time we went back to each other's hands and
mouths as to a requiem where the chorus
sings death with irrelevant and amazing
bodily music.   40

                                                                                1994

Twelfth Floor West

Brandy, who got it from a blood transfusion,
was in for MAC, with a decubitus
ulcer[9] festering. Baffled and generous,
her Baptist sisters brought each day's illusion
that she'd look back at them, that her confusion   5
would focus into words. They swabbed the pus,
they cleaned the shit, they wiped away the crust
of morning on her lids. The new bruise on
her thigh was baffling. They left an armchair
facing the window: an unspoken goal.   10
They'd come next morning, find her sitting there
with juice and coffee and a buttered roll.
The day she was released to hospice care
they came to meet her. They held her thin cold
hands on the gurney in the corridor.   15
The ambulance stood in the bay downstairs.

                                                                                2000

---

8. Toward the end of her life, Lorde adopted the African name Gamba Adisa (Warrior, She Who Makes Her Meaning Known).

9. Bedsore. MAC: Mycobacterium Avium Complex, a disease commonly afflicting people in the later stages of AIDS.

DAVE SMITH
b. 1942

Dave Smith insists on his nickname, and such informality helps prepare the reader for an unusual poet. He writes powerfully, using rough words as he inexhaustibly collates jarring bits of the local scene. His mostly outdoor world is full of objects waiting for him to assemble them: blowfish, fiddler crabs, goshawks, antelopes, sharks, sawmills, boats. He occasionally provides hints of literary tradition: Gerard Manley Hopkins has obviously had some effect on him, as have Robert Penn Warren, James Dickey, and Robert Lowell. Yet Smith scorns obviously melodic cadences; his sonorities are thickly clustered. His near-sonnets are muscular and compressed, knit with tension. Other poems present unusual epithets: "the arthritic orchard" ("Winesaps"), "the shocking gray face of the sea" ("Near the Docks"), "night leaking" ("How to Get to Green Springs"), "the beautiful last erosions" ("Messenger"). Smith's poetry accumulates odd details, brought urgently together at moments of crisis. He conveys, as he says, a sense of responsibility in situations of stress: "poetry emerges from the individual spirit in crisis. Poetry is the death-wrestler" (*Contemporary Poets*, 1991).

Memory plays a large part in his consciousness. As for many southern writers, the Civil War is a haunting transgenerational memory ("Leafless Trees, Chickahominy Swamp"). An air of doomed nostalgia hangs over his poems, with hints of violence, fear, and the grotesque. Whether in poems about an encounter with a wrecked car in the woods or with fiddler crabs on the shore, Smith's details pulsate with a kind of bleak vitalism and provide a defense against dissolution. Smith has said that his poems are "attempts to conflate the lyric and the narrative" (*Contemporary*).

Smith was born on December 19, 1942, in Portsmouth, Virginia. He graduated in 1965 from the University of Virginia, served in the air force during the Vietnam War (1969–72), and received graduate degrees from Southern Illinois University (M.A., 1969) and Ohio University (Ph.D., 1976). Among his many teaching posts have been Virginia Commonwealth University and, since 1990, Louisiana State University. In addition to his books of poetry, he has published fiction and essays and is coeditor of *The Southern Review*.

Leafless Trees, Chickahominy Swamp[1]

Humorless, hundreds of trunks, gray in the blue expanse
where dusk leaves them hacked like a breastwork,[2]
stripped like pikes planted to impale, the knots
of vines at each groin appearing placed by makers
schooled in grotesque campaigns. Mathew Brady's[3]   5
plates show them as they are, the ageless stumps,
timed-sanded solitaries, some clumped in squads
we might imagine veterans, except they're only wood,
and nothing in the world seems more dead than these.

---

1. In Virginia; Confederate staging area for Civil War battles, now a nesting spot for bald eagles.
2. Temporary fortification, a few feet high, for defense against an enemy.
3. American photographer (1823–1896), famous for his documentation of the Civil War.

Stopped by the lanes filled with homebound taillights,   10
we haven't seen the rumored Eagle we hoped to watch,
only a clutch of buzzards ferrying sticks for a nest.
Is this history, that we want the unchanged, useless
spines out there to thrust in our faces the human
qualities we covet? We read this place like generals   15
whose promised recruits don't show, who can't press on:
we feel the languor of battle, troops unable to tell
themselves from the enemy, and a file-hard fear gone

indifferent in the mortaring sun that will leave all
night after night standing in the same cold planes   20
of water. It never blooms or greens. It merely stinks.
Why can't we admit this is death's gift, the scummy
scene of our pride, blown brainpans of a century ago?
Why do we sit and sniff the rank hours inside words
blunt as ground that only stares off our question: what   25
happened? Leaf-light in our heads, don't we mean why
these grisly emblems, the slime that won't swell to hope?

The rapacious odor of swamps all over the earth bubbles
sometimes to mist, fetid flesh we can't see but know,
just cells composing, decomposing, a heart's illusions.   30
God knows what we'd do in there, we say, easing back
on the blacktop. Once we heard a whistling. Harmonicas?
But who'd listen? Surely all was green once, fragile
as a truce, words braiding sun and water, as on a lake
where families sang. What else would we hope for, do   35
in the dead miles nothing explains or changes or relieves?

1984

Fiddlers

Black mudbank pushes them out like hotel fire.
Some at water's edge seem to wait for transport.
Others sweat, pale, scattered on the shining beach.
All keep closed the mighty arms of God's damage,
waving at shadows and movements made by the sun.   5
Desire, the dragging arm, sifts, picks, tastes, untastes
endlessly the civic occasions the tide brings in.
Surely floods, cold fronts, embolisms[4] of dreams
drive them in where the earth's brain hums. They
clasp, breed. They glare upward in rooms where the moon   10
slips its question. Daylong they spout, fume, command.
Biblical as kinsmen with a son they must kill.
Nouns, verbs couple like years. Water comes, listens.

1996

4. Obstructions in blood vessels.

Wreck in the Woods

Under that embrace of wild saplings held fast,
surrounded by troops of white mushrooms, by wrens
visiting like news-burdened ministers known
only to some dim life inside, this Model
A Ford like my grandfather's entered the earth.   5
What were fenders, hood, doors, no one washed, polished,
grazed with a tip of finger, or boyhood dream.
I stood where silky blue above went wind-rent,
pines, oaks, dogwood ticking, pushing as if grief
called families to see what none understood. What   10
plot of words, what heart-shudder of men, women
here ended so hard the green world must hide it?
Headlights, large, round. Two pieces of shattered glass.

1996

Blowfish and Mudtoad[5]

Held the wrong way either will take the finger
that clamps the casual pen, changing your words,
its rows of teeth like a serrated bread knife.
Moss-covered as bottom rock, wearing the brown
scum of salt water settlers, current-fluttered   5
flags of weed, eyes like glass pitted by age,
each reads steadily the downdrifted offerings
its tongue ticks for: crawlers, wings, limbs, all
the great current gathers to sweep away at last.
Our line sinkered into that steep wants a sleek   10
one to claim us—big Blue, Striper, Thor-like[6] Drum.
Not these nibbling small-town preachers, Mudtoad's
black ambush, or Blowfish, resurrection and rage.

1996

Black Silhouettes of Shrimpers

Grand Isle, Louisiana

Along the flat sand the cupped torsos of trash fish
arch to seek the sun, but the eyes
glaze with thick gray, death's touch
already drifting these jeweled darters.

---

5. Oyster toadfish. Blowfish inflate themselves and are often poisonous.
6. *Thor*: Viking thunder god.

Back and forth against the horizon slow trawlers   5
gulp in their bags whatever rises
here with the shrimp they come for.
Boys on deck shovel the fish off

like the clothes of their fathers out of attics.
Who knows what tides beached them,   10
what lives were lived to arrive just here?
I walk without stepping on any

dead, though it is hard, the sun's many blazes
spattering and blinding the way ahead
where the wildness of water coils   15
dark in small swamps and smells fiercely of flesh.

If a cloud shadows everything for a moment, cool,
welcome, there is still no end in sight,
body after body, stench, jewels
nothing will wear, roar and fade of engines.   20

2000

Louise Glück
b. 1943

One's first impression of Louise Glück's work is its sensitivity; the second is its economy. Her minimalist poems generally begin with sharp, unrelieved feelings about love, death, and loss; these are expressed in short lines as if to cut deeper into consciousness. "Desire, loneliness, wind in the flowering almond—/ surely these are the great, the inexhaustible subjects" of lyric poetry, she writes in "Summer Night." A number of her early poems are about a sister who died as an infant before Glück was born. In these dreamlike poems, Glück, like such "confessional" poets as Sylvia Plath, Anne Sexton, and Robert Lowell, returns to childhood perception and feeling. More generally, her poems echo Sexton's adaptation of fairy tale, H. D.'s mythic minimalism, and George Oppen's use of silence and negative space. In the confessional vein, many of her later poems are about the gradual disintegration of a marriage. Family members, marriages, natural beauty—"All, all / can be lost," she writes in "The White Lilies."

But Glück's treatment of personal feeling, though stripped-down and direct, is measured and controlled. Often, she frames autobiographical experience with myths and fables. The dissolution of a marriage is told in *Meadowlands* (1996) through the Homeric story of Penelope and Odysseus. A gardener-poet, flowers, and a god speak the extended poetic sequence that makes up *The Wild Iris* (1992). The situations of her poetry—daughters and a mother in grief, a mother holding a sick child—are archetypal, embedding minute perceptions within larger contexts. She entitled one poem "Mythic Fragment," and her work is composed of fragments and sequences.

Glück insists in "Marathon" that "nakedness in woman is always a pose," and she is never unaware of the dress of formal pattern: "Then what began as love for you / became a hunger for structure" ("The Beginning"). Glück counterbalances dejection and despair with a stark, lucid language and with understatement. "You see," begins "The Drowned Children," "they have no judgment. / So it is natural that they should drown." The colloquial address, the offhand tone, the seeming acceptance ("it is natural") contrast with the horrific drowning of children in winter ponds. Similarly, Glück's cool, modulated rhythms help distill feeling, often with a ghostly echo of formal meters. Her spartan images, though they appear natural, are unexpected and glide easily from momentary perception to an abstraction. Her abstractions and occasional aphorisms ("whatever / returns from oblivion returns / to find a voice" in "The Wild Iris") filter the particular through the general. By screening personal experience through various forms of artifice, Glück's poetry succeeds in bringing us close to piercing feelings of anguish, isolation, and loss.

Glück was born on April 22, 1943, in New York City. She attended Sarah Lawrence College and Columbia University. She has taught at Williams College since 1984. In 1985, she won the National Book Critics Circle Award for *The Triumph of Achilles*; in 1993, the Pulitzer Prize for *The Wild Iris*; and in 2001, the Bollingen Prize for *Vita Nova*.

The School Children

The children go forward with their little satchels.
And all morning the mothers have labored
to gather the late apples, red and gold,
like words of another language.

And on the other shore   5
are those who wait behind great desks
to receive these offerings.

How orderly they are—the nails
on which the children hang
their overcoats of blue or yellow wool.   10

And the teachers shall instruct them in silence
and the mothers shall scour the orchards for a way out,
drawing to themselves the gray limbs of the fruit trees
bearing so little ammunition.

                                                                     1975

The Drowned Children

You see, they have no judgment.
So it is natural that they should drown,
first the ice taking them in
and then, all winter, their wool scarves
floating behind them as they sink   5
until at last they are quiet.
And the pond lifts them in its manifold dark arms.

But death must come to them differently,
so close to the beginning.
As though they had always been   10
blind and weightless. Therefore
the rest is dreamed, the lamp,
the good white cloth that covered the table,
their bodies.

And yet they hear the names they used   15
like lures slipping over the pond:
What are you waiting for
come home, come home, lost
in the waters, blue and permanent.

1980

Descending Figure

1. The Wanderer

At twilight I went into the street.
The sun hung low in the iron sky,
ringed with cold plumage.
If I could write to you
about this emptiness—   5
Along the curb, groups of children
were playing in the dry leaves.
Long ago, at this hour, my mother stood
at the lawn's edge, holding my little sister.
Everyone was gone; I was playing   10
in the dark street with my other sister,
whom death had made so lonely.
Night after night we watched the screened porch
filling with a gold, magnetic light.
Why was she never called?   15
Often I would let my own name glide past me
though I craved its protection.

2. The Sick Child

—Rijksmuseum[1]

A small child
is ill, has wakened.
It is winter, past midnight   20
in Antwerp.[2] Above a wooden chest,
the stars shine.
And the child
relaxes in her mother's arms.

1. Dutch state museum, in Amsterdam. *The Sick Child* is a painting of a mother holding her sick child at night, by Flemish painter Gabriel Metsu (1629–1667).
2. Belgian city.

The mother does not sleep; 25
she stares
fixedly into the bright museum.
By spring the child will die.
Then it is wrong, wrong
to hold her— 30
Let her be alone,
without memory, as the others wake
terrified, scraping the dark
paint from their faces.

3. *For My Sister*

Far away my sister is moving in her crib. 35
The dead ones are like that,
always the last to quiet.

Because, however long they lie in the earth,
they will not learn to speak
but remain uncertainly pressing against the wooden bars, 40
so small the leaves hold them down.

Now, if she had a voice,
the cries of hunger would be beginning.
I should go to her;
perhaps if I sang very softly, 45
her skin so white,
her head covered with black feathers. . . .

1980

Mock Orange[3]

It is not the moon, I tell you.
It is these flowers
lighting the yard.

I hate them.
I hate them as I hate sex, 5
the man's mouth
sealing my mouth, the man's
paralyzing body—

and the cry that always escapes,
the low, humiliating 10
premise of union—

In my mind tonight
I hear the question and pursuing answer

3. Shrub with showy, fragrant white flowers.

fused in one sound
that mounts and mounts and then   15
is split into the old selves,
the tired antagonisms. Do you see?
We were made fools of.
And the scent of mock orange
drifts through the window.   20

How can I rest?
How can I be content
when there is still
that odor in the world?

                                                        1985

A Fantasy

I'll tell you something: every day
people are dying. And that's just the beginning.
Every day, in funeral homes, new widows are born,
new orphans. They sit with their hands folded,
trying to decide about this new life.   5

Then they're in the cemetery, some of them
for the first time. They're frightened of crying,
sometimes of not crying. Someone leans over,
tells them what to do next, which might mean
saying a few words, sometimes   10
throwing dirt in the open grave.

And after that, everyone goes back to the house,
which is suddenly full of visitors.
The widow sits on the couch, very stately,
so people line up to approach her,   15
sometimes take her hand, sometimes embrace her.
She finds something to say to everybody,
thanks them, thanks them for coming.

In her heart, she wants them to go away.
She wants to be back in the cemetery,   20
back in the sickroom, the hospital. She knows
it isn't possible. But it's her only hope,
the wish to move backward. And just a little,
not so far as the marriage, the first kiss.

                                                        1990

The Wild Iris

At the end of my suffering
there was a door.

Hear me out: that which you call death
I remember.

Overhead, noises, branches of the pine shifting.   5
Then nothing. The weak sun
flickered over the dry surface.

It is terrible to survive
as consciousness
buried in the dark earth.   10

Then it was over: that which you fear, being
a soul and unable
to speak, ending abruptly, the stiff earth
bending a little. And what I took to be
birds darting in low shrubs.   15

You who do not remember
passage from the other world
I tell you I could speak again: whatever
returns from oblivion returns
to find a voice: 20

from the center of my life came
a great fountain, deep blue
shadows on azure seawater.

1992

Penelope's Song[4]

Little soul, little perpetually undressed one,
do now as I bid you, climb
the shelf-like branches of the spruce tree;
wait at the top, attentive, like
a sentry or look-out. He will be home soon;   5
it behooves you to be
generous. You have not been completely
perfect either; with your troublesome body
you have done things you shouldn't
discuss in poems. Therefore   10
call out to him over the open water, over the bright water

---

4. In Homer's *Odyssey*, Odysseus's wife, Penelope, waits for him while he journeys home.

with your dark song, with your grasping,
unnatural song—passionate,
like Maria Callas.[5] Who
wouldn't want you? Whose most demonic appetite   15
could you possibly fail to answer? Soon
he will return from wherever he goes in the meantime,
suntanned from his time away, wanting
his grilled chicken. Ah, you must greet him,
you must shake the boughs of the tree   20
to get his attention,
but carefully, carefully, lest
his beautiful face be marred
by too many falling needles.

1996

Quiet Evening

You take my hand; then we're alone
in the life-threatening forest. Almost immediately

we're in a house; Noah's[6]
grown and moved away; the clematis after ten years
suddenly flowers white.   5

More than anything in the world
I love these evenings when we're together,
the quiet evenings in summer, the sky still light at this hour.

So Penelope took the hand of Odysseus,[7]
not to hold him back but to impress
this peace on his memory: 10

from this point on, the silence through which you move
is my voice pursuing you.

1996

Vita Nova[8]

You saved me, you should remember me.

The spring of the year; young men buying tickets for the ferryboats.
Laughter, because the air is full of apple blossoms.

When I woke up, I realized I was capable of the same feeling.

---

5. American operatic soprano (1923–1977).
6. The poet's son.
7. See note 4 above.
8. New life (Latin). *La Vita Nova* (c. 1292) was the first major work of Italian poet Dante Alighieri (1265–1321); it describes his idealistic love for Beatrice.

I remember sounds like that from my childhood,   5
laughter for no cause, simply because the world is beautiful,
something like that.

Lugano.[9] Tables under the apple trees.
Deckhands raising and lowering the colored flags.
And by the lake's edge, a young man throws his hat into the water;   10
perhaps his sweetheart has accepted him.

Crucial
sounds or gestures like
a track laid down before the larger themes

and then unused, buried.   15

Islands in the distance. My mother
holding out a plate of little cakes—

as far as I remember, changed
in no detail, the moment
vivid, intact, having never been   20
exposed to light, so that I woke elated, at my age
hungry for life, utterly confident—

By the tables, patches of new grass, the pale green
pieced into the dark existing ground.

Surely spring has been returned to me, this time   25
not as a lover but a messenger of death, yet
it is still spring, it is still meant tenderly.

                                                              1999

Earthly Love

　　　Conventions of the time
　　　held them together.
　　　It was a period
　　　(very long) in which
　　　the heart once given freely   5
　　　was required, as a formal gesture,
　　　to forfeit liberty: a consecration
　　　at once moving and hopelessly doomed.

　　　As to ourselves:
　　　fortunately we diverged   10
　　　from these requirements,
　　　as I reminded myself

---

9. Lake on the border between Italy and Switzerland.

when my life shattered.
So that what we had for so long
was, more or less,   15
voluntary, alive.
And only long afterward
did I begin to think otherwise.

We are all human—
we protect ourselves   20
as well as we can
even to the point of denying
clarity, the point
of self-deception. As in
the consecration to which I alluded.   25

And yet, within this deception,
true happiness occurred.
So that I believe I would
repeat these errors exactly.
Nor does it seem to me   30
crucial to know
whether or not such happiness
is built on illusion:
it has its own reality.
And in either case, it will end.   35

1999

MICHAEL PALMER
b. 1943

Michael Palmer's poetry is abstract and yet affective. It bridges the divide between the rigors of postmodern suspicion and the pleasures of sonorous lyricism. Often associated with the Language poets, influenced by Louis Zukofsky and other late modernists, well-versed in the theories of Jacques Derrida, Roland Barthes, and other poststructuralists, Palmer writes poems that are fragmentary, self-reflexive, and nonsequential. Like other experimental writers, he questions the fiction of a unitary self that confesses its inner experience in a poem. "Various *selves*," he says of the process of composition, "aspects of a heightened attention, did it in a certain way, but not your *self*" ("A Conversation," 1986). Calling attention to the creative role of the reader, Palmer dramatizes the complex interactions among reader, writer, speaker, and text in his poem "Song of the Round Man," which is reminiscent of Wallace Stevens's self-reflexive meditations. "Poetry seems often a talking to self as well as other as well as self as other, a simultaneity that recognizes the elusive multiplicity of what is called 'identity' " ("Autobiography, Memory and Mechanisms of Concealment").

Hardly a mirror to the soul, the poem is, for Palmer, a verbal artifact that spotlights its own words. Palmer continually reminds us of the materiality of language—syllables, grammatical and syntactic structures, even the differences among words separated by a mere letter. "A word may be shaped like a fig or a pig, an effigy or an egg," he writes in "Sun." Syntactic parallelism, evident in this line as throughout much of his poetry, is insistent and yet defamiliarized. Similarly, Palmer often repeats an initial word or phrase, only to set up through such anaphora a false parallel that makes us scrutinize the logic of analogy. Pages of poetry—not being transparent windows onto experiences or things "out there"—are physical realities in themselves, "pages which sit up," as he puts it in "Sun," "Pages torn from their spines." Resisting the linear flow of narrative, Palmer may allow one line to pivot back on what preceded it, as in the nonsequiturs of "This Time": "Once I fell in the ocean when / I didn't know I fell in the ocean // Then Momma got me out / This isn't true // only something I remember." While this poem raises central poststructuralist questions about the complexity of knowledge, truth, memory, and identity, it also evinces the lyric's traditionally lucid imagery ("I turned blue all over // then got clear as glass") and sensual sound. Palmer's poetry is replete with assonance, consonance, alliteration, occasional rhyme, echoic rhythms, refrains, and other forms of verbal repetition. "Sun" recalls phrases and musical cadences from T. S. Eliot's *Waste Land*. The strength of Palmer's work is that, like Eliot's masterpiece, it effectively combines fluency with syntactical dislocation, violent disjunctiveness with an eerie calm.

Palmer was born on May 11, 1943, into a middle-class Italian American family in New York City, his father the manager of a small hotel. A French major at Harvard University, he received a B.A. in 1965 and an M.A. in comparative literature two years later. Along with poetry and translations, his works include various collaborations with painters and dancers. He has spent most of his life in the San Francisco area.

Song of the Round Man

(for Sarah when she's older)

The round and sad-eyed man puffed cigars as if
he were alive. Gillyflowers
to the left of the apple, purple bells to the right

and a grass-covered hill behind.
I am sad today said the sad-eyed man   5
for I have locked my head in a Japanese box

and lost the key.
I am sad today he told me
for there are gillyflowers by the apple

and purple bells I cannot see.   10
Will you look at them for me
he asked, and tell me what you find?

I cannot I replied
for my eyes have grown sugary and dim
from reading too long by candlelight.   15

Tell me what you've read then
said the round and sad-eyed man.
I cannot I replied

for my memory has grown tired and dim
from looking at things that can't be seen   20
by any kind of light

and I've locked my head in a Japanese box
and thrown away the key.
Then I am you and you are me

said the sad-eyed man as if alive.   25
I'll write you in where I should be
between the gillyflowers and the purple bells

and the apple and the hill
and we'll puff cigars from noon till night
as if we were alive.   30

1981

This Time

(another for Sarah)

Once I fell in the ocean when
I didn't know I fell in the ocean

Then Momma got me out
This isn't true

only something I remember   5
Once in the park I broke in half

and lost one half
which half I don't remember

Once I was in a room
It grew larger and larger   10

why I don't remember
One time I turned blue all over

then got clear as glass
This really happened

but not to me   15
Once I couldn't see

for a while
so I listened lying down

Another time I looked out the window
and saw myself at the window   20

across the street
This time it was me

1984

Sun

Write this. We have burned all their villages

Write this. We have burned all the villages and the people in them

Write this. We have adopted their customs and their manner of dress

Write this. A word may be shaped like a bed, a basket of tears or an X

In the notebook it says, It is the time of mutations, laughter at jokes,   5
secrets beyond the boundaries of speech

I now turn to my use of suffixes and punctuation, closing Mr. Circle with a
single stroke, tearing the canvas from its wall, joined to her, experiencing
the same thoughts at the same moment, inscribing them on a loquat[1] leaf

Write this. We have begun to have bodies, a now here and a now gone,   10
a past long ago and one still to come

Let go of me for I have died and am in a novel and was a lyric poet,
certainly, who attracted crowds to mountaintops. For a nickel I will appear
from this box. For a dollar I will have text with you and answer three
questions   15

First question. We entered the forest, followed its winding paths, and
emerged blind

Second question. My townhouse, of the Jugendstil, lies by Darmstadt[2]

Third question. He knows he will wake from this dream, conducted in the
mother-tongue   20

Third question. He knows his breathing organs are manipulated by God, so
that he is compelled to scream

1. Fruitbearing tree native to Japan and China;
interlingual pun on unrelated Latin word for "to
talk," as in *loquacious.*
2. Industrial city in central Germany devastated
by bombings during World War II. *Jugendstil:*
German name of Art Nouveau, a late nineteenth-
century design movement that emphasized the
decorative arts, ornamentation, and exotic forms.

Third question. I will converse with no one on those days of the week
which end in *y*

Write this. There is pleasure and pain and there are marks and signs.   25
A word may be shaped like a fig or a pig, an effigy or an egg
                                       but
there is only time for fasting and desire, device and design, there is
only time to swerve without limbs, organs or face into a
                                        scientific   30
silence, pinhole of light

Say this. I was born on an island among the dead. I learned language on
this island but did not speak on this island. I am writing to you from this
island. I am writing to the dancers from this island. The writers do not
dance on this island   35

Say this. There is a sentence in my mouth, there is a chariot in my mouth.
There is a ladder. There is a lamp whose light fills empty space and a space
which swallows light

A word is beside itself. Here the poem is called What Speaking Means to
Say   40
    though I have no memory of my name

Here the poem is called Theory of the Real, its name is Let's Call This,
and its name is called A Wooden Stick. It goes yes-yes, no-no. It goes one
and one

I have been writing a book, not in my native language, about violins and   45
smoke, lines and dots, free to speak and become the things we speak,
pages which sit up, look around and row resolutely toward the setting sun

Pages torn from their spines and added to the pyre, so that they will
resemble thought.

Pages which accept no ink   50

Pages we've never seen—first called Narrow Street, then Half a Fragment,
Plain of Jars or Plain of Reeds,[3] taking each syllable into her mouth,
shifting position and passing it to him

---

3. Region of marshland west of Saigon that was a
stronghold for Communist guerillas during the
Vietnam War. *Plain of Jars:* region of Laos dotted
with large stone "jars" produced—probably as bur-
ial urns—nearly two thousand years ago. The plain
was the site of prolonged battles during the Viet-
nam War and was heavily bombed by U.S. forces.

Let me say this. Neak Luong[4] is a blur. It is Tuesday in the hardwood
forest. I am a visitor here, with a notebook   55

The notebook lists My New Words and Flag above White. It claims to have
no inside
            only characters like A-against-Herself, B, C, L and
N, Sam, Hans Magnus, T. Sphere, all speaking in the dark with their
hands   60
            G for Gramsci or Goebbels,[5] blue hills, cities, cities with hills,
modern and at the edge of time
                        F for alphabet, Z for A, an H in an arbor,
shadow, silent wreckage, W or M among stars

What last. Lapwing. Tesseract.[6] X perhaps for X. The villages are known   65
as These Letters—humid, sunless. The writing occurs on their walls

                                                                                    1988

4. Cambodian city bombed by the United States
during the Vietnam War despite Cambodia's offi-
cial neutrality. Palmer took this sentence from the
headline of a newspaper story about an American
soldier returning to the city years later.
5. Joseph Goebbels (1897–1945), Nazi propa-
ganda minister. *Hans Magnus:* Hans Magnus
Enzenberger (b. 1929), German political poet and
critic. *T. Sphere:* Thelonious Sphere Monk (1917–
1982), jazz pianist and composer. *Gramsci:* Anto-
nio Gramsci (1891–1937), Italian communist phi-
losopher.
6. A four-dimensional cube (the fourth dimension
being time). *Lapwing:* species of bird named for its
slow wing-beat.

MICHAEL ONDAATJE
b. 1943

Frequently riven by internecine violence, formerly subjected to European colonial rule,
Sri Lanka (previously Ceylon) is a large, pear-shaped island just off the southern tip of
India, its landscape variegated with mountains and jungles, and its tropical vegetation
of a wild and dreamlike richness. Michael Ondaatje's family has been in Sri Lanka since
1600. Culturally, they are a mixture of the Sinhalese, the indigenous inhabitants; the
Tamils, dark-skinned emigrants from India; and the Dutch, who came to Sri Lanka in
search of spices in the seventeenth century. English, Sinhalese, and Tamil were the
languages that surrounded Ondaatje when he was growing up. He spent the first eleven
years of his life in Sri Lanka, as recalled in his 1982 memoir, *Running in the Family.*
By way of England, he eventually settled in Canada when he was nineteen. His later
trips to Sri Lanka are reflected in his poetry collection *Handwriting* (1999) and in his
novel *Anil's Ghost* (2000).

  Widely known as the author of *The English Patient* (1992), a best-seller that became
an award-winning film and the first Canadian novel to win the Booker Prize, Ondaatje
reminds interviewers that he "began as a poet and that has influenced all my writing"
and insists that poetry is "the most precise writing" (*The Observer,* November 1, 1998;
Maclean's, December 18, 2000). Earlier, Ondaatje published book-length narratives
that combine poems with highly charged prose: *The Collected Works of Billy the Kid*

(1970, 1974) and *Coming through Slaughter* (1976), the latter based on the life of a jazz cornettist who went mad. Some of Ondaatje's shorter poems are surrealistic snapshots of domestic life, such as "Biography," in which a family dog runs in her sleep and dreams of killing. Whether writing about his parents or his grown daughter, Ondaatje inspects human situations in search of the erotic, the ironic, and the humanly pathetic. These poems suggest the influence of Robert Lowell, whereas his later poetry about Sri Lankan violence, religion, and culture fuses William Carlos Williams's short-lined free verse with spare, imagistic South Asian models (classical Tamil and Sanskrit). Cryptic and fragmentary, these poems are built around haunting visual images. Ondaatje's poetry blends the dreamlike with the lucid, the offhand with the formal, as suggested in the *ars poetica* of the early poem " 'The Gate in His Head' ": "And that is all this writing should be then. / The beautiful formed things caught at the wrong moment / so they are shapeless, awkward / moving to the clear."

Ondaatje was born on September 12, 1943. After his departure from Sri Lanka (prompted by his parents' divorce), he was educated at Dulwich College, London; Bishop's University, Quebec; the University of Toronto; and Queen's University, Kingston, Ontario. From 1961 to 1971, he taught English at the University of Western Ontario, in London; beginning in 1971, at Glendon College, York University, in Toronto. He has won several awards, including the Governor-General's Award for Literature—roughly equivalent to the Pulitzer Prize. In addition to writing poems and anthologies, Ondaatje has directed several films.

Biography

The dog scatters her body in sleep,
paws, finding no ground, whip at air,
the unseen eyeballs reel deep, within.
And waking—crouches,
tacked to humility all day,   5
children ride her, stretch,
display the black purple lips,
pull hind legs to dance;
unaware that she
tore bulls apart, loosed   10
heads of partridges,
dreamt blood.

1979

Letters & Other Worlds

"for there was no more darkness for him and, no doubt
like Adam before the fall, he could see in the dark"

My father's body was a globe of fear
His body was a town we never knew
He hid that he had been where we were going
His letters were a room he seldom lived in
In them the logic of his love could grow   5

My father's body was a town of fear
He was the only witness to its fear dance
He hid where he had been that we might lose him
His letters were a room his body scared

He came to death with his mind drowning.   10
On the last day he enclosed himself
in a room with two bottles of gin, later
fell the length of his body
so that brain blood moved
to new compartments   15
that never knew the wash of fluid
and he died in minutes of a new equilibrium.

His early life was a terrifying comedy
and my mother divorced him again and again
he would rush into tunnels magnetized   20
by the white eye of trains
and once, gaining instant fame,
managed to stop a Perahara[1] in Ceylon
—the whole procession of elephants dancers
local dignitaries—by falling   25
dead drunk onto the street.

As a semi-official, and semi-white at that,
the act was seen as a crucial
turning point in the Home Rule Movement
and led to Ceylon's independence in 1948.   30

(My mother had done her share too—
her driving so bad
she was stoned by villagers
whenever her car was recognized)

For 14 years of marriage   35
each of them claimed he or she
was the injured party.
Once on the Colombo[2] docks
saying goodbye to a recently married couple
my father, jealous   40
at my mother's articulate emotion,
dove into the waters of the harbour
and swam after the ship waving farewell.
My mother pretending no affiliation
mingled with the crowd back to the hotel.   45

Once again he made the papers
though this time my mother

---

1. Or Anuradhapura Perahara, an annual religious festival of Sri Lanka (formerly Ceylon) commemorating the birth of Vishnu, one of the three primary Hindu gods. On its final night, the festival culminates in processions, the elephants carrying shrines and relics.
2. Seaport city, capital of Sri Lanka.

with a note to the editor
corrected the report—saying he was drunk
rather than broken hearted at the parting of friends.   50
The married couple received both editions
of *The Ceylon Times* when their ship reached Aden.[3]

And then in his last years
he was the silent drinker,
the man who once a week   55
disappeared into his room with bottles
and stayed there until he was drunk
and until he was sober.

There speeches, head dreams, apologies,
the gentle letters, were composed.   60
With the clarity of architects
he would write of the row of blue flowers
his new wife had planted,
the plans for electricity in the house,
how my half-sister fell near a snake   65
and it had awakened and not touched her.
Letters in a clear hand of the most complete empathy
his heart widening and widening and widening
to all manner of change in his children and friends
while he himself edged   70
into the terrible acute hatred
of his own privacy
till he balanced and fell
the length of his body
the blood screaming in   75
the empty reservoir of bones
the blood searching in his head without metaphor

                                                                    1979

(Inner Tube)[4]

On the warm July river
head back

upside down river
for a roof

slowly paddling   5
towards an estuary between trees

there's a dog
learning to swim near me
friends on shore

---

3. The Port of Aden, on the southern coast of the
Arabian peninsula, in South Yemen; then a British
colony.
4. Airtight tube often used by children as a float.

my head   10
dips
back to the eyebrow
I'm the prow
on an ancient vessel,
this afternoon   15
I'm going down to Peru
soul between my teeth

a blue heron
with its awkward
broken backed flap   20
upside down

one of us is wrong

he
in his blue grey thud
thinking he knows   25
the blue way
out of here

or me

                                                1984

Driving with Dominic in the Southern Province We See Hints of the Circus

    The tattered Hungarian tent

    A man washing a trumpet
    at a roadside tap

    Children in the trees,

    one falling   5
    into the grip of another

                                                1999

From Buried

To be buried in times of war,
in harsh weather, in the monsoon
of knives and stakes.

The stone and bronze gods carried
during a night rest of battle   5

between the sleeping camps
floated in catamarans[5] down the coast
past Kalutara.[6]
           To be buried
for safety.   10

To bury, surrounded by flares,
large stone heads
during floods in the night.
Dragged from a temple
by one's own priests,   15
lifted onto palanquins,[7]
covered with mud and straw.
Giving up the sacred
among themselves,
carrying the faith of a temple   20
during political crisis
away in their arms.
              Hiding
the gestures of the Buddha.

Above ground, massacre and race.   25
A heart silenced.
The tongue removed.
The human body merged into burning tire.
Mud glaring back
into a stare.   30

                                       1999

From Buried 2

vii

The heat of explosions
sterilized all metal.

Ball bearings and nails
in the arms, in the head.
Shrapnel in the feet.   5

Ear channels
deformed by shockwaves.
Men without balance
surrounding the dead President
on Armour Street.[8]   10

5. Rafts made of logs tied together.
6. Fishing and trade center in southwestern Sri
Lanka.
7. Conveyances in which one person is carried by
four or six people by means of poles projecting
from a large box.
8. President Ranasinghe Premadasa (1924–1993)
and sixteen others were killed by a suicide bomber
on Armour Street in Colombo, the capital of Sri
Lanka, on May 1, 1993.

Those whose bodies
could not be found.

1999

JAMES TATE
b. 1943

James Tate describes himself as writing in the "tradition of the Impurists," and he mentions in particular the poetry of Walt Whitman, William Carlos Williams, and Pablo Neruda (*Contemporary Authors,* 1969). Poetry, for Tate, is a form of protest, as well as celebration, protest not against political situations but against the difficulty of connecting deeply with one another and with the natural world that surrounds us. The dazzling surrealist world of the poem "The Wheelchair Butterfly" is both a heaven and a hell; the delight here cannot exist without destruction: "Today a butterfly froze / in midair; and was plucked like a grape / by a child who swore he could take care / of it." Presumably identifying with the child, the poet speaks of his desire to "order the world for a moment, freeze it, understand it."

Sometimes, Tate's poems seem to coast on their own zany rhetoric, propelled by the energies of the language and by the clash of images. Playful, clever, ever quirky, Tate effects his transformations with the speed and efficiency of a first-rate magician. Yet beneath the often giddy and campy surfaces of Tate's poems lurks pain and disappointment. As his former teacher Donald Justice said on the publication of *The Lost Pilot* (1967), "Once despair can be taken for granted, gaiety becomes a possibility, almost a necessity." Tate often dreams a world where an armistice will be declared in the warfare of contraries between old and young, men and women. But only the blue boobies of the Galápagos—who contrive to be at once sad, funny, and beautiful—have found a haven beyond conflict; they exemplify Tate's dictum: "The poem is man's noblest effort because it is utterly useless" (*Contemporary Poets of the English Language,* ed. R. Murphy, 1971).

Tate was born in Kansas City, Missouri, on December 8, 1943, the year his pilot father was reported missing in Germany during World War II. He received his B.A. from Kansas State College in 1965, after two years at the University of Missouri. He then went to the University of Iowa, from which he received an M.F.A. and where he taught creative writing for a year. He has since taught at the University of California, Berkeley, at Columbia University, and, since 1971, at the University of Massachusetts at Amherst. A prolific and honored poet, he was, at twenty-three, the youngest poet chosen for the Yale Series of Younger Poets (1967), and he subsequently garnered the Pulitzer Prize (1992), the National Book Award (1994), and the Tanning Prize (1995).

Stray Animals

This is the beauty of being alone
toward the end of summer:
a dozen stray animals asleep on the porch

in the shade of my feet,
and the smell of leaves burning   5
in another neighborhood.
It is late morning,
and my forehead is alive with shadows,
some bats rock back and forth
to the rhythm of my humming,   10
the mimosa[1] flutters with bees.
This is a house of unwritten poems,
this is where I am unborn.

1968

The Blue Booby

The blue booby lives
on the bare rocks
of Galápagos[2]
and fears nothing.
It is a simple life: 5
they live on fish,
and there are few predators.
Also, the males do not
make fools of themselves
chasing after the young   10
ladies. Rather,
they gather the blue
objects of the world
and construct from them

a nest—an occasional   15
Gaulois[3] package,
a string of beads,
a piece of cloth from
a sailor's suit. This
replaces the need for   20
dazzling plumage;
in fact, in the past
fifty million years
the male has grown
considerably duller,   25
nor can he sing well.
The female, though,

asks little of him—
the blue satisfies her
completely, has   30

1. Tropical tree or shrub.
2. Pacific islands famous for their unique species
of animals and birds.

3. A French brand of cigarettes with a distinctive
blue package.

a magical effect
on her. When she returns
from her day of
gossip and shopping,
she sees he has found her   35
a new shred of blue foil:
for this she rewards him
with her dark body,
the stars turn slowly
in the blue foil beside them   40
like the eyes of a mild savior.

                                                1969

The Wheelchair Butterfly

O sleepy city of reeling wheelchairs
where a mouse can commit suicide if he can

concentrate long enough
on the history book of rodents
in his underground town   5

of electrical wheelchairs!
The girl who is always pregnant and bruised
like a pear

rides her many-stickered bicycle
backward up the staircase   10
of the abandoned trolleybarn.

Yesterday was warm. Today a butterfly froze
in midair; and was plucked like a grape
by a child who swore he could take care

of it. O confident city where   15
the seeds of poppies pass for carfare,

where the ordinary hornets in a human's heart
may slumber and snore, where bifocals bulge

in an orange garage of daydreams,
we wait in our loose attics for a new season   20

as if for an ice-cream truck.
An Indian pony crosses the plains

whispering Sanskrit prayers to a crater of fleas.
Honeysuckle says: I thought I could swim.

The Mayor is urinating on the wrong side   25
of the street! A dandelion sends off sparks:
beware your hair is locked!

Beware the trumpet wants a glass of water!
Beware a velvet tabernacle!

Beware the Warden of Light has married   30
an old piece of string!

1969

The Lost Pilot

for my father, 1922–1944

Your face did not rot
like the others—the co-pilot,
for example, I saw him

yesterday. His face is corn-
mush: his wife and daughter,   5
the poor ignorant people, stare

as if he will compose soon.
He was more wronged than Job.[4]
But your face did not rot

like the others—it grew dark,   10
and hard like ebony;
the features progressed in their

distinction. If I could cajole
you to come back for an evening,
down from your compulsive   15

orbiting, I would touch you,
read your face as Dallas,
your hoodlum gunner, now,

with the blistered eyes, reads
his braille editions. I would   20
touch your face as a disinterested

scholar touches an original page.
However frightening, I would
discover you, and I would not

4. Hebrew Bible patriarch severely afflicted by God to test his faith.

turn you in; I would not make   25
you face your wife, or Dallas,
or the co-pilot, Jim. You

could return to your crazy
orbiting, and I would not try
to fully understand what   30

it means to you. All I know
is this: when I see you,
as I have seen you at least

once every year of my life,
spin across the wilds of the sky   35
like a tiny, African god,

I feel dead. I feel as if I were
the residue of a stranger's life,
that I should pursue you.

My head cocked toward the sky,   40
I cannot get off the ground,
and, you, passing over again,

fast, perfect, and unwilling
to tell me that you are doing
well, or that it was mistake   45

that placed you in that world,
and me in this; or that misfortune
placed these worlds in us.

                                                 1978

The Motorcyclists

My cuticles are a mess. Oh honey, by the way,
did you like my new negligee? It's a replica
of one Kim Novak[5] wore in some movie or other.
I wish I had a foot-long chili dog right now.
Do you like fireworks, I mean not just on the 4th   5
of July, but fireworks any time? There are people
like that, you know. They're like people who like
orchestra music, listen to it any time of day.
Lopsided people, that's what my father calls them.
Me, I'm easy to please. I like ping-pong and bobcats,   10
shatterproof drinking glasses, the smell of kerosene,

---

5. American actor (b. 1933).

the crunch of carrots. I like caterpillars and
whirlpools, too. What I hate most is being the first
one at the scene of a bad accident.

Do I smell like garlic? Are we still in Kansas?   15
I once had a chiropractor make a pass at me,
did I ever tell you that? He said that your spine
is happiest when you're snuggling. Sounds kind
of sweet now when I tell you, but he was a creep.
Do you know that I have never understood what they meant   20
by "grassy knoll."[6] It sounds so idyllic, a place to go
to dream your life away, not kill somebody. They
should have called it something like "the grudging notch."
But I guess that's life. What is it they always say?
"It's always the sweetest ones that break your heart."   25
You getting hungry yet, hon? I am. When I was seven
I sat in our field and ate an entire eggplant
right off the vine. Dad loves to tell that story,

but I still can't eat eggplant. He says I'll be the first
woman President, it'd be a waste since I talk so much.   30
Which do you think the fixtures are in the bathroom
at the White House, gold or brass? It'd be okay with me
if they were just brass. Honey, can we stop soon?
I really hate to say it but I need a lady's room.

                                                            1983

Poem

The angel kissed my alphabet,
it tingled like a cobweb in starlight.
A few letters detached themselves
and drifted in shadows, a loneliness
they carry like infinitesimal coffins   5
on their heads.

She kisses my alphabet
and a door opens: blackbirds roosting
on far ridges. A windowpeeper
under an umbrella watches   10
a funeral service. Blinkered horses
drum the cobblestones.

She kisses: Plunderers gather
in a lackluster ballroom
to display their booty. Mice   15

6. After the assassination of President John F.
Kennedy, in 1963, witnesses said that shots were
fired from a "grassy knoll," a phrase that became
associated with various conspiracy theories about
the murder.

testify against one another
in dank rodent courtrooms.

The angel kisses my alphabet,
she squeezes and bites,
and the last lights flutter,   20
and the violins are demented.
Moisture spreads across my pillow,
a chunk of quartz thirsts
to abandon my brain trust.

1990

Where Babies Come From

Many are from the Maldives,[7]
southwest of India, and must begin
collecting shells almost immediately.
The larger ones may prefer coconuts.
Survivors move from island to island   5
hopping over one another and never
looking back. After the typhoons
have had their pick, and the birds of prey
have finished with theirs, the remaining few
must build boats, and in this, of course,   10
they can have no experience, they build
their boats of palm leaves and vines.
Once the work is completed, they lie down,
thoroughly exhausted and confused,
and a huge wave washes them out to sea.   15
And that is the last they see of one another.
In their dreams Mama and Papa
are standing on the shore
for what seems like an eternity,
and it is almost always the wrong shore.   20

1997

7. Nation of islands in the Indian Ocean.

Eavan Boland
b. 1944

The great puzzle of Eavan Boland's career has been how to embrace Irish identity while rejecting certain male-centered assumptions that have long dominated Irish literary culture. For Boland, as a young woman writer, the frozen, mythical images of the Irish nation as an idealized woman—Mother Ireland, Dark Rosaleen, Cathleen Ni Houlihan—were inhibiting and insufficient. While her early verse reflects W. B. Yeats's strong influence, Boland came to decry the inadequacy of what she called "the Mimic Muse" of Irish tradition, charging that it falsified women's lives and prettified bloodshed in service to the nation. Such poetry was insensitive to the "human truths of survival and humiliation" (*A Kind of Scar*), deaf to "The scream of beaten women, / The crime of babies battered" ("Tirade for the Mimic Muse"). Irish poetry had to break with rhetorical cosmetics and masculinist iconography if it was to recover Irish women's historical experiences, including domestic labor, motherhood, famine, mortal fever, prostitution, and emigration.

Yet to slough off the encumbrances of Irish aesthetics, Boland ironically had to deploy other aesthetic strategies, including some inherited from Yeats, James Joyce, and other Irish men. Boland's declarations of freedom from the past recall Yeats's narratives of self-remaking: she promises to descend down poetic ladders into what Yeats calls the "foul rag and bone shop of the heart" ("The Circus Animals' Desertion"), to surrender the embroidery of old mythologies and walk "naked" (a word shared by Yeats's "A Coat" and Boland's "Tirade for the Mimic Muse"). At times, Boland intimates an awareness that her narratives of liberation are inevitably bound up with the Irish poetry from which she seeks liberation. "I won't go back to it," she proclaims at the start of "Mise Eire," willing her independence from traditional Irish poetry; but she later concedes the inevitability of going back when she repeats, "No. I won't go back."

Boland's break with the Irish male tradition also required an affiliation with an alternative tradition—in particular, that of American women's confessional verse. In the writing of Sylvia Plath and Adrienne Rich, Boland—caught up in the 1970s women's movement in Ireland—discovered powerful assertions of female rage and desire, as well as acid, self-mocking candor and explorations of a specifically female experience of the body. Boland's harrowing dramatic monologue "Anorexic," with its hypnotic repetitions of "I," echoes Plath's "Lady Lazarus" ("I may be skin and bone" becomes "I am skin and bone"). Her attempts to identify herself with a collective female experience, as represented at the end of "Mise Eire" by a garrisoned prostitute and an Irish emigrant holding a half-dead baby, are indebted to Rich's poetry. Boland's efforts to merge the personal with broader female history began with the collections *In Her Own Image* (1980) and *Night Feed* (1982), when she broke with her earlier, more formal, less gender-specific poetry.

In Boland's most striking poetry, form mirrors content. The body of the poem "Anorexic," for example—with its clipped, often end-stopped lines—is desiccated. Similarly, the winding syntax, obsessive anaphora, and paratactic connections of "Fever" create a linguistic fever, in Boland's gripping lament for a grandmother and others who died in a fever ward. In poems such as "Fond Memory," the long line serves Boland's retrospective meditation.

Boland was born on September 24, 1944, in Dublin. Her acute sensitivity to language owes something to her experience of growing up in between varieties of the English language. As recalled in "Fond Memory" and other poems, she was displaced as a six-year-old from Ireland to London, and then to New York, before finally returning to Ireland in adolescence. She attended convent schools in these various locations; her father was Ireland's ambassador to England and then the United Nations, her mother a painter. Educated at Trinity College, Dublin, Boland returned to teach there and has also taught at University College, the University of Iowa, and Stanford University.

Anorexic

Flesh is heretic.
My body is a witch.
I am burning it.

Yes I am torching
her curves and paps and wiles.   5
They scorch in my self-denials.

How she meshed my head
in the half-truths
of her fevers till I renounced
milk and honey   10
and the taste of lunch.

I vomited
her hungers.
Now the bitch is burning.

I am starved and curveless.   15
I am skin and bone.
She has learned her lesson.

Thin as a rib
I turn in sleep.
My dreams probe   20

a claustrophobia
a sensuous enclosure.
How warm it was and wide

once by a warm drum,
once by the song of his breath   25
and in his sleeping side.

Only a little more,
only a few more days
sinless, foodless.

I will slip   30
back into him again
as if I have never been away.

Caged so
I will grow
angular and holy   35

past pain
keeping his heart
such company

as will make me forget
in a small space   40
the fall

into forked dark,
into python needs
heaving to hips and breasts
and lips and heat   45
and sweat and fat and greed.

1980

From DOMESTIC INTERIOR

1. Night Feed

This is dawn.
Believe me
This is your season, little daughter.
The moment daisies open,
The hour mercurial rainwater   5
Makes a mirror for sparrows.
It's time we drowned our sorrows.

I tiptoe in.
I lift you up
Wriggling   10
In your rosy, zipped sleeper.
Yes, this is the hour
For the early bird and me
When finder is keeper.

I crook the bottle.   15
How you suckle!
This is the best I can be,
Housewife
To this nursery
Where you hold on,   20
Dear life.

A silt of milk.
The last suck.
And now your eyes are open,
Birth-colored and offended.   25
Earth wakes.
You go back to sleep.
The feed is ended.

Worms turn.
Stars go in.   30
Even the moon is losing face.
Poplars stilt for dawn
And we begin
The long fall from grace.
I tuck you in.   35

1982

Mise Eire[1]

I won't go back to it—

my nation displaced
into old dactyls,[2]
oaths made
by the animal tallows   5
of the candle—

land of the Gulf Stream,
the small farm,
the scalded memory,
the songs   10
that bandage up the history,
the words
that make a rhythm of the crime

where time is time past.
A palsy of regrets.   15
No. I won't go back.
My roots are brutal:

I am the woman—
a sloven's mix
of silk at the wrists,
a sort of dove-strut   20
in the precincts of the garrison—

who practices
the quick frictions,
the rictus of delight
and gets cambric[3] for it,   25
rice-colored silks.

I am the woman
in the gansy-coat[4]

---

1. I am Ireland (Irish Gaelic); the title of an earlier
poem by Irish nationalist Pádraic Pearse (1879–
1916) that continues a long tradition of personi-
fying Ireland as a woman.

2. Poetic feet of one stressed syllable followed by
two unstressed.
3. Fine linen fabric. *Rictus*: gaping mouth.
4. Woolen sweater.

on board the *Mary Belle,*   30
in the huddling cold,

holding her half-dead baby to her
as the wind shifts East
and North over the dirty
water of the wharf   35

mingling the immigrant
guttural with the vowels
of homesickness who neither
knows nor cares that

a new language   40
is a kind of scar
and heals after a while
into a passable imitation
of what went before.

                                                          1987

Fever

is what remained or what they thought
remained after the ague and the sweats
were over and the shock of wild flowers
at the bedside had been taken away;

is what they tried to shake out of   5
the crush and dimple of cotton,
the shy dust of a bridal skirt;
is what they beat, lashed, hurt like

flesh as if it were a lack of virtue
in a young girl sobbing her heart out   10
in a small town for having been seen
kissing by the river; is what they burned

alive in their own back gardens
as if it were a witch and not the full-
length winter gaberdine and breathed again   15
when the fires went out in charred dew.

My grandmother died in a fever ward,
younger than I am and far from
the sweet chills of a Louth⁵ spring—
its sprigged light and its wild flowers—   20

---

5. County on the east coast of Ireland.

with five orphan daughters to her name.
Names, shadows, visitations, hints
and a half-sense of half-lives remain.
And nothing else, nothing more unless

I re-construct the soaked-through midnights;   25
vigils; the histories I never learned
to predict the lyric of; and re-construct
risk; as if silence could become rage,

as if what we lost is a contagion
that breaks out in what cannot be   30
shaken out from words or beaten out
from meaning and survives to weaken

what is given, what is certain
and burns away everything but this
exact moment of delirium when   35
someone cries out someone's name.

                                                 1987

The Women

This is the hour I love: the in-between,
neither here-nor-there hour of evening.
The air is tea-colored in the garden.
The briar rose is spilled crepe-de-Chine.[6]

This is the time I do my work best,   5
going up the stairs in two minds,
in two worlds, carrying cloth or glass,
leaving something behind, bringing
something with me I should have left behind.

The hour of change, of metamorphosis,   10
of shape-shifting instabilities.
My time of sixth sense and second sight
when in the words I choose, the lines I write,
they rise like visions and appear to me:

women of work, of leisure, of the night,   15
in stove-colored silks, in lace, in nothing,
with crewel needles, with books, with wide open legs

who fled the hot breath of the god pursuing,
who ran from the split hoof and the thick lips
and fell and grieved and healed into myth,   20

---

6. Fine silk.

into me in the evening at my desk
testing the water with a sweet quartet,
the physical force of a dissonance—

the fission of music into syllabic heat—
and getting sick of it and standing up   25
and going downstairs in the last brightness

into a landscape without emphasis,
light, linear, precisely planned,
a hemisphere of tiered, aired cotton,

a hot terrain of linen from the iron,   30
folded in and over, stacked high,
neatened flat, stoving heat and white.

1987

Fond Memory

It was a school where all the children wore darned worsted;[7]
where they cried—or almost all—when the Reverend Mother
announced at lunch-time that the King[8] had died

peacefully in his sleep. I dressed in wool as well,
ate rationed food, played English games and learned   5
how wise the Magna Carta was, how hard the Hanoverians[9]

had tried, the measure and complexity of verse,
the hum and score of the whole orchestra.
At three-o-clock I caught two buses home

where sometimes in the late afternoon   10
at a piano pushed into a corner of the playroom
my father would sit down and play the slow

lilts of Tom Moore[1] while I stood there trying
not to weep at the cigarette smoke stinging up
from between his fingers and—as much as I could think—   15

I thought this is my country, was, will be again,
this upward-straining song made to be
our safe inventory of pain. And I was wrong.

1987

---

7. Woolen fabric.
8. King George VI of the United Kingdom died in
1952. Boland's father was a diplomat, and she
spent much of her childhood in London.

9. Family of English monarchs who controlled the
throne from 1714 to 1901. *Magna Carta*: charter
of English liberties granted by King John in 1215.
1. Irish poet and singer (1779–1852).

The Pomegranate

The only legend I have ever loved is
The story of a daughter lost in hell.
And found and rescued there.
Love and blackmail are the gist of it.
Ceres and Persephone[2] the names.   5
And the best thing about the legend is
I can enter it anywhere. And have.
As a child in exile in
A city of fogs and strange consonants,
I read it first and at first I was   10
An exiled child in the crackling dusk of
The underworld, the stars blighted. Later
I walked out in a summer twilight
Searching for my daughter at bedtime.
When she came running I was ready   15
To make any bargain to keep her.
I carried her back past whitebeams.
And wasps and honey-scented buddleias.[3]
But I was Ceres then and I knew
Winter was in store for every leaf   20
On every tree on that road.
Was inescapable for each one we passed.
And for me.
It is winter
And the stars are hidden.   25
I climb the stairs and stand where I can see
My child asleep beside her teen magazines,
Her can of Coke, her plate of uncut fruit.
The pomegranate! How did I forget it?
She could have come home and been safe   30
And ended the story and all
Our heartbroken searching but she reached
Out a hand and plucked a pomegranate.
She put out her hand and pulled down
The French sound for apple and   35
The noise of stone and the proof
That even in the place of death,
At the heart of legend, in the midst
Of rocks full of unshed tears
Ready to be diamonds by the time   40
The story was told, a child can be
Hungry. I could warn her. There is still a chance.
The rain is cold. The road is flint-coloured.
The suburb has cars and cable television.

2. In Greek myth, Persephone, the daughter of Zeus and Demeter (Roman, Ceres) is abducted by Hades and taken to the underworld. Although Hades is commanded to set her free, she is condemned to spend a portion of each year with him after eating a pomegranate seed.
3. Like whitebeams, flowering trees.

The veiled stars are above ground.   45
It is another world. But what else
Can a mother give her daughter but such
Beautiful rifts in time?
If I defer the grief I will diminish the gift.
The legend must be hers as well as mine.   50
She will enter it. As I have.
She will wake up. She will hold
The papery, flushed skin in her hand.
And to her lips. I will say nothing.

                                                      1994

CRAIG RAINE
b. 1944

In the late 1970s, Craig Raine began his literary career as one of the postwar English poets attempting a radical reconsideration of poetic subjects and attitudes. At first, his verse appears opaque and riddling, but gradually, as one reads him, his method becomes clearer. His strange images and metaphors let us see our lives in a new way, by a process that the Russian critic Victor Shklovsky calls "defamiliarization." Raine made this especially clear by the title poem of his second book, "A Martian Sends a Postcard Home." He describes this world as if from outer space. The result is a surrealistic surface. A number of poets—James Fenton and Christopher Reid, for example—flocked to Raine's banner and were promptly labeled "the Martian school." As James Fenton said, Raine "taught us to become strangers in our familiar world, to release the faculty of perception and allow it to graze at liberty in the field of experience" (quoted in Anthony Thwaite, *Poetry Today*, 1985).

Though Raine has been criticized for merely heaping up weird data, his work is tightly organized. Even the Martian postcard seems to proceed logically from external subjects (books, mist, rain) to internal ("everyone's pain has a different smell"). In later volumes, Raine has written not as someone from outer space, but as father, lover, office worker. The poet amuses and is amused by the sight of "the pagoda / of dirty dinner plates" ("A Free Translation") and is delighted by the way children see the world. One poem wittily portrays the city in metaphors of the country ("City Gent"). Raine's pleasure in unexpected juxtapositions, in a comedy of displacement, in the recognition of everyday absurdity, is contagious.

Raine was born on December 3, 1944, in Bishop Auckland, County Durham, England. He was educated at Oxford University, later returning as lecturer (1971–79) and, since 1991, as fellow. He also served in an editorial capacity on several magazines. From 1981 to 1991, he occupied a post formerly held by T. S. Eliot, as poetry editor at the publishing house of Faber & Faber Ltd. He has written essays and an opera libretto, and he applied Martian principles to epic poetry in *History: The Home Movie* (1994).

The Onion, Memory

Divorced, but friends again at last,
we walk old ground together
in bright blue uncomplicated weather.
We laugh and pause
to hack to bits these tiny dinosaurs,   5
prehistoric, crenellated, cast
between the tractor ruts in mud.

On the green, a junior Douglas Fairbanks,[1]
swinging on the chestnut's unlit chandelier,
defies the corporation spears—   10
a single rank around the bole,[2]
rusty with blood.
Green, tacky phalluses curve up, romance.
A gust—the old flag blazes on its pole.

In the village bakery   15
the pasty babies pass
from milky slump to crusty cadaver,
from crib to coffin—without palaver.
All's over in a flash,
too silently . . .   20

Tonight the arum lilies fold
back napkins monogrammed in gold,
crisp and laundered fresh.
Those crustaceous gladioli, on the sly,
reveal the crimson flower-flesh   25
inside their emerald armour plate.
The uncooked herrings blink a tearful eye.
The candles palpitate.
The Oistrakhs bow and scrape
in evening dress, on Emi-tape.[3]   30

Outside the trees are bending over backwards
to please the wind : the shining sword
grass flattens on its belly.
The white-thorn's frillies[4] offer no resistance.
In the fridge, a heart-shaped jelly   35
strives to keep a sense of balance.

I slice up the onions. You sew up a dress.
This is the quiet echo—flesh—
white muscle on white muscle,

---

1. American actor (1883–1939), famous for
swashbuckling daredevil movie roles of the 1920s
and 1930s. *Crenellated:* having battlements.
2. Tree trunk. *Corporation spears:* spiked fence
put up by the town corporation.

3. A popular British brand of audiotape. David
Oistrakh (1908–1974) and his son Igor (b. 1931),
celebrated Russian violinists.
4. Frilled undergarments (British colloquialism).

intimately folded skin,   40
finished with a satin rustle.
One button only to undo, sewn up with shabby thread.
It is the onion, memory,
that makes me cry.

Because there's everything and nothing to be said,   45
the clock with hands held up before its face,
stammers softly on, trying to complete a phrase—
while we, together and apart,
repeat unfinished gestures got by heart.

And afterwards, I blunder with the washing on the line—   50
headless torsos, faceless lovers, friends of mine.

                                                        1978

A Martian Sends a Postcard Home

Caxtons[5] are mechanical birds with many wings
and some are treasured for their markings—

they cause the eyes to melt
or the body to shriek without pain.[6]

I have never seen one fly, but   5
sometimes they perch on the hand.

Mist is when the sky is tired of flight
and rests its soft machine on ground:

then the world is dim and bookish
like engravings under tissue paper.   10

Rain is when the earth is television.
It has the property of making colours darker.

Model T[7] is a room with the lock inside—
a key is turned to free the world

for movement, so quick there is a film   15
to watch for anything missed.

But time is tied to the wrist
or kept in a box, ticking with impatience.

In homes, a haunted apparatus sleeps,
that snores when you pick it up.   20

---

5. That is, books, which William Caxton (c. 1422–
1491) was the first to print in English.
6. The Martian does not know the words for cry
or laugh.
7. An old-fashioned type of automobile; the "key"
(next line) is the ignition key.

If the ghost cries, they carry it
to their lips and soothe it to sleep

with sounds. And yet, they wake it up
deliberately, by tickling with a finger.

Only the young are allowed to suffer   25
openly. Adults go to a punishment room

with water but nothing to eat.
They lock the door and suffer the noises

alone. No one is exempt
and everyone's pain has a different smell.   30

At night, when all the colours die,
they hide in pairs

and read about themselves—
in colour, with their eyelids shut.

1979

NORMAN DUBIE
b. 1945

In a period when narrative verse about specific times and places tends to be rare,
Norman Dubie is known for evoking historical and biographical scenes, though he also
composes lyric poems. When he writes about a personage such as Czar Nicholas II or
Madame Blavatsky, Dubie comments through a reflective observer or a persona, yet he
presents his subjects as if he were intimately involved in them all. Many of his lyric
poems concern death and grief: "Any simple loss," he remarks, "is like the loss of all of
us" ("Sun and Moon Flowers: Paul Klee, 1879–1940").

Dubie has a keen eye for detail, and his diction renders realistic images—an old
Studebaker, a thermos, a box of pills—startlingly clear and yet strange. Dubie does not,
however, offer slices of externality, for everything is on the verge of being internalized:
"Just beyond two hills in the winter air, and / Somewhere inside the mind" ("The City
of the Olesha Fruit"). In "The Funeral," the speaker remembers minnows nibbling at
the toes of an aunt the year before, and after her death, this image becomes prescient:
"Uncle Peter, in a low voice, said / The cancer ate her like horse piss eats deep snow."
Many poems are built around vivid contrasts, the beautiful and the ugly bizarrely min-
gling. In a poem about Queen Elizabeth I, images of violence (the bloody carnage of
bearbaiting and a beheading) and of seeming purity (white dress, snow, and bone)
converge and clash in disturbing combinations. Despite his use of historical materials,
Dubie's poetry is oblique, between realism and surrealism. It is like a series of parables
in which the meaning must be kept implicit and somewhat indistinct.

Dubie was born on April 10, 1945, in Barre, Vermont. He was educated at Goddard
College, in Vermont (B.A., 1969), and the University of Iowa (M.F.A., 1971). Since
1975, he has taught at Arizona State University.

Elizabeth's War with the Christmas Bear

The bears are kept by hundreds within fences, are fed cracked
Eggs; the weakest are
Slaughtered and fed to the others after being scented
With the blood of deer brought to the pastures by Elizabeth's
Men—the blood spills from deep pails with bottoms of slate.   5

The balding Queen[1] had bear gardens in London and in the country.
The bear is baited:[2] the nostrils
Are blown full with pepper, the Irish wolf dogs
Are starved, then, emptied, made crazy with fermented barley:

And the bear's hind leg is chained to a stake, the bear   10
Is blinded and whipped, kneeling in his own blood and slaver, he is
Almost instantly worried by the dogs. At the very moment that
Elizabeth took Essex's head,[3] a giant brown bear
Stood in the gardens with dogs hanging from his fur . . .
He took away the sun, took   15
A wolfhound in his mouth, and tossed it into
The white lap of Elizabeth I—arrows and staves[4] rained

On his chest, and standing, he, then, stood even taller, seeing
Into the Queen's private boxes—he grinned
Into her battered eggshell face.   20
Another volley of arrows and poles, and opening his mouth
He showered
Blood all over Elizabeth and her Privy Council.[5]

The next evening, a cool evening, the Queen demanded
13 bears and the justice of 113 dogs: She slept   25

All that Sunday night and much of the next morning.
Some said she was guilty of *this* and *that*.
The Protestant Queen gave the defeated bear
A grave in a Catholic cemetery. The marker said:
Peter, a Solstice Bear, a gift of the Tsarevitch[6] to Elizabeth.   30

After a long winter she had the grave opened. The bear's skeleton
Was cleared with lye, she placed it at her bedside,
Put a candle inside behind the sockets of the eyes, and, then,
She spoke to it:

You were a Christmas bear—behind your eyes   35
I see the walls of a snow cave where you are a cub still smelling
Of your mother's blood which has dried in your hair; you have

---

1. Queen Elizabeth I (1553–1603).
2. Tied to a stake and attacked by dogs, as described below. Bearbaiting was a popular spectator sport in Elizabethan England.
3. In 1601, the earl of Essex, who had earlier been

Elizabeth's favorite, was executed for treason.
4. Narrow strips of wood.
5. That is, her advisory council.
6. The tsar's (or czar's) son. *Solstice:* in celebration of the winter solstice, December 22.

Troubled a Queen who was afraid
When seated in *shade* which, standing,
You had created! A Queen who often wakes with a dream   40
Of you at night—
Now, you'll stand by my bed in your long white bones; alone, you
Will frighten away at night all visions of bear, and all day
You will be in this cold room—your constant grin,
You'll stand in the long, white prodigy of your bones, and you are,   45

Every inch of you, a terrible vision, not bear, but virgin![7]

1979

The Funeral

It felt like the zero in brook ice.
She was my youngest aunt, the summer before
We had stood naked
While she stiffened and giggled, letting the minnows
Nibble at her toes. I was almost four—   5
That evening she took me
To the springhouse where on the scoured planks
There were rows of butter in small bricks, a mold
Like ermine on the cheese,
And cut onions to rinse the air   10
Of the black, sickly-sweet meats of rotting pecans.

She said butter was colored with marigolds
Plucked down by the marsh
With its tall grass and miner's-candles.
We once carried the offal's pail[8] beyond the barn   15
To where the fox could be caught in meditation.
Her bed linen smelled of camphor. We went

In late March for her burial. I heard the men talk.
I saw the minnows nibble at her toe.
And Uncle Peter, in a low voice, said   20
The cancer ate her like horse piss eats deep snow.

1986

Last Poem, Snow Tree

after Rafael Alberti[9]

Call a ruined shoe, the sandal—
White, the cow's blood
Forever drained from it.

---

7. Elizabeth I was known as the Virgin Queen because she never married.

8. Pail containing animal viscera after butchering.
9. Spanish poet and painter (1902–1999).

Where are the happy integers of inventory?

Call the one sandal, abstract and nostalgic: 5
Glove of the first baseman, it folds like night

Or night's daring bird feeding on amber insects.

The circulations of blood in the snow tree
Remind me of the woman we lost.
The sea rises behind us, at our backs.   10
Mr. Enos Slaughter[1] didn't die

In Nebraska, of drink. In the snow tree a sick,
Whiter angel picks its teeth.
Errors of snow in water, our names . . .
You were wrong, Rafael. The stars,   15
Violent at their tea,

Were the last children to learn the arithmetic
Of memory.

                                                              2001

---

1. Baseball player (b. 1916).

YUSEF KOMUNYAKAA
b. 1947

Yuesf Komunyakaa wrote the most acclaimed book of American poetry about the Vietnam War, *Dien Cai Dau* (1988), the title meaning "crazy" in Vietnamese. Having served in Vietnam in 1969–70 as a reporter for and editor of the military newspaper *The Southern Cross*, Komunyakaa, decorated with the Bronze Star, allowed the war to settle in memory for fourteen years. At this distance, he could distill the complexities of America's most controversial war—American indifference and empathy for the Vietnamese, cross-racial tension and camaraderie between whites and African Americans. Like Wilfred Owen and other modern war poets, Komunyakaa is attentive to inner experience and to shared political history. "My belief is that you have to have both," he remarked in an interview, "the odyssey outward as well as inward" (*Callaloo,* 1990).

Like the speaker who peers through a nightscope at eerily ghostlike figures in "Starlight Scope Myopia," Komunyakaa sees the war as distant and yet insistently present in the minds of the war's participants and observers. Touching a name carved on the Vietnam Veterans Memorial triggers a sudden memory in "Facing It": "I see the booby trap's white flash." On the wall's mirrorlike surface, memory bumps up against sight, the dead invade the present, and the self is interpenetrated by the surrounding world. The poem, like the wall, crosses and blurs lines of historical, racial, and political division. Time and space are similarly layered in Komunyakaa's poems inspired by jazz, such as "February in Sydney," in which the past erupts from beneath the protective sheen of the present.

Komunyakaa's poetry also cuts across different levels of diction, from biblical idiom to journalistic reportage, African American vernacular to high-art lyricism. Komunyakaa's remark in *Callaloo* about Melvin Tolson applies with equal force to his own work: "he brings together the street as well as the highly literary into a single poetic context in ways where the two don't even seem to exhibit division—it's all one and the same." Syncopating short, jagged lines, enjambing and coiling syntax, building musical resonances through assonance and alliteration, Komunyakaa crafts poems that have surprisingly quick turns of sound and sense. He mimics the sudden riffs, twists, and mannered elaborations of jazz improvisation, in the long tradition of African American poets who have mined jazz and the blues for poetry, from Langston Hughes and Sterling Brown to Gwendolyn Brooks and Robert Hayden, Amiri Baraka and Michael S. Harper.

Komunyakaa was born James Willie Brown Jr., on April 29, 1947, in Bogalusa, Louisiana, not far from New Orleans. He changed his name for religious reasons, adopting Komunyakaa from a grandfather smuggled, according to family legend, on a banana boat from Trinidad. His father was an illiterate carpenter, remembered with anger and affection in "My Father's Love Letters." After returning from Vietnam, Komunyakaa received his B.A. from the University of Colorado in 1975, his M.A. from Colorado State University in 1979, and his M.F.A. from the University of California, Irvine, in 1980. He has coedited anthologies of "jazz poetry" (1991, 1996) and published a volume of essays and interviews. He won the Pulitzer Prize in 1994 for *Neon Vernacular: New and Selected Poems* and, in 2001, published *Pleasure Dome: New and Collected Poems.* He teaches at Princeton University.

Starlight Scope Myopia[1]

Gray-blue shadows lift
shadows onto an oxcart.

Making night work for us,
the starlight scope brings
men into killing range.   5

The river under Vi Bridge
takes the heart away

like the Water God
riding his dragon.
Smoke-colored   10

Viet Cong[2]
move under our eyelids,

lords over loneliness
winding like coral vine through
sandalwood & lotus,   15

---

1. Nearsightedness. *Starlight scope:* electrical instrument that uses light from the night sky to improve nocturnal vision.
2. Shortened name of the Viet Nam Cong San, the Communist military forces supported by North Vietnam against South Vietnam and the United States in the Vietnam War (1955–75).

inside our lowered heads
years after this scene

ends. The brain closes
down. What looks like
one step into the trees,   20

they're lifting crates of ammo
& sacks of rice, swaying

under their shared weight.
Caught in the infrared,
what are they saying?   25

Are they talking about women
or calling the Americans

beaucoup dien cai dau?[3]
One of them is laughing.
You want to place a finger   30

to his lips & say "shhhh."
You try reading ghost talk

on their lips. They say
"up-up we go," lifting as one.
This one, old, bowlegged,   35

you feel you could reach out
& take him into your arms. You

peer down the sights of your M-16,
seeing the full moon
loaded on an oxcart.   40

1988

Tu Do Street[4]

Music divides the evening.
I close my eyes & can see
men drawing lines in the dust.
American pushes through the membrane
of mist & smoke, & I'm a small boy   5
again in Bogalusa: *White Only*
signs & Hank Snow.[5] But tonight

3. Very crazy. The phrase, used often to describe
the American soldiers, is a combination of Viet-
namese (*dien cai dau*) and French (*beaucoup*).
France had a long colonial presence in Vietnam
until 1954.
4. Street bustling with bars and brothels in Sai-

gon, the capital of South Vietnam and site of the
U.S. Army headquarters during the Vietnam War.
5. American country singer (1914–1999). *Boga-
lusa:* town in Louisiana where Komunyakaa spent
his childhood.

I walk into a place where bar girls
fade like tropical birds. When
I order a beer, the mama-san   10
behind the counter acts as if she
can't understand, while her eyes
skirt each white face, as Hank Williams[6]
calls from the psychedelic jukebox.
We have played Judas[7] where   15
only machine-gun fire brings us
together. Down the street
black GIs hold to their turf also.
An off-limits sign pulls me
deeper into alleys, as I look   20
for a softness behind these voices
wounded by their beauty & war.
Back in the bush at Dak To
& Khe Sanh,[8] we fought
the brothers of these women   25
we now run to hold in our arms.
There's more than a nation
inside us, as black & white
soldiers touch the same lovers
minutes apart, tasting   30
each other's breath,
without knowing these rooms
run into each other like tunnels
leading to the underworld.

                                                           1988

Facing It

My black face fades,
hiding inside the black granite.
I said I wouldn't,
dammit: No tears.
I'm stone. I'm flesh.   5
My clouded reflection eyes me
like a bird of prey, the profile of night
slanted against morning. I turn
this way—the stone lets me go.
I turn that way—I'm inside   10
the Vietnam Veterans Memorial
again, depending on the light
to make a difference.
I go down the 58,022 names,
half-expecting to find   15

6. American country singer and composer (1923–1953).
7. One of the twelve disciples, Judas betrayed Jesus for thirty pieces of silver.
8. Site of U.S. Marine base in South Vietnam kept under siege by the North Vietnamese army for several months in 1968. *Dak To*: city in northwest South Vietnam that, in 1967, was the site of one of the war's most violent battles.

my own in letters like smoke.
I touch the name Andrew Johnson;
I see the booby trap's white flash.
Names shimmer on a woman's blouse
but when she walks away   20
the names stay on the wall.
Brushstrokes flash, a red bird's
wings cutting across my stare.
The sky. A plane in the sky.
A white vet's image floats   25
closer to me, then his pale eyes
look through mine. I'm a window.
He's lost his right arm
inside the stone. In the black mirror
a woman's trying to erase names: 30
No, she's brushing a boy's hair.

                                                        1988

February in Sydney

Dexter Gordon's tenor sax
plays "April in Paris"
inside my head all the way back
on the bus from Double Bay.
Round Midnight,[9] the '50s,   5
cool cobblestone streets
resound footsteps of Bebop[1]
musicians with whiskey-laced voices
from a boundless dream in French.
Bud, Prez, Webster, & The Hawk,[2]   10
their names run together riffs.
Painful gods jive talk through
bloodstained reeds & shiny brass
where music is an anesthetic.
Unreadable faces from the human void   15
float like torn pages across the bus
windows. An old anger drips into my throat,
& I try thinking something good,
letting the precious bad
settle to the salty bottom.   20
Another scene keeps repeating itself:
I emerge from the dark theatre,

9. Bertrand Tavernier's 1986 movie about expatriate jazz musicians in 1950s Paris, starring jazz saxophonist Dexter Gordon (1923–1990) and named after a composition by jazz pianist Thelonious Monk (1917–1982). "April in Paris": jazz standard. Double Bay: neighborhood in Sydney, Australia.
1. Style of modern jazz developed in the 1940s and 1950s, characterized by harmonic exploration and fast-paced flurries of notes drawn from the chromatic scale.
2. 'Round Midnight was loosely based on the tragic lives of pianist Bud Powell (1924–1966) and saxophonist Lester "Prez" Young (1909–1959), who worked in Europe late in their careers, like influential saxophonists Ben Webster (1909–1973) and Coleman "The Hawk" Hawkins (1904–1969).

passing a woman who grabs her red purse
& hugs it to her like a heart attack.
Tremolo.[3] Dexter comes back to rest 25
behind my eyelids. A loneliness
lingers like a silver needle
under my black skin,
as I try to feel how it is
to scream for help through a horn. 30

1989

My Father's Love Letters

On Fridays he'd open a can of Jax[4]
After coming home from the mill,
& ask me to write a letter to my mother
Who sent postcards of desert flowers
Taller than men. He would beg, 5
Promising to never beat her
Again. Somehow I was happy
She had gone, & sometimes wanted
To slip in a reminder, how Mary Lou
Williams' "Polka Dots & Moonbeams"[5] 10
Never made the swelling go down.
His carpenter's apron always bulged
With old nails, a claw hammer
Looped at his side & extension cords
Coiled around his feet. 15
Words rolled from under the pressure
Of my ballpoint: Love,
Baby, Honey, Please.
We sat in the quiet brutality
Of voltage meters & pipe threaders, 20
Lost between sentences . . .
The gleam of a five-pound wedge
On the concrete floor
Pulled a sunset
Through the doorway of his toolshed. 25
I wondered if she laughed
& held them over a gas burner.
My father could only sign
His name, but he'd look at blueprints
& say how many bricks 30
Formed each wall. This man,
Who stole roses & hyacinth
For his yard, would stand there
With eyes closed & fists balled,

3. Rapid alternation between two or more notes.
4. Beer brewed by the Jackson Brewing Company, in New Orleans.

5. Recording by jazz pianist and composer Mary Lou Williams (1910–1981).

Laboring over a simple word, almost   35
Redeemed by what he tried to say.

                                                    1992

LORNA GOODISON
b. 1947

Lorna Goodison is one of the most gifted heirs of the pioneering West Indian poets
Derek Walcott, Kamau Brathwaite, and fellow Jamaican Louise Bennett, dubbed by
her the "mother of the Jamaican language." Born a generation later, Goodison writes
poetry that straddles the divide between Creole verse, as exemplified by Bennett's quar-
relsome street vendor in "South Parade Peddler," and visionary rhetoric, as in Walcott's
"Season of Phantasmal Peace." All such idioms are possible for Goodison, none of them
alien. In her poetry, the liquid turns between Standard English and Creole are supple,
quick, barely visible. Fluent in different linguistic and rhetorical registers, she inter-
weaves the discourses that a colonial education rigidly segregates.

Goodison, who recalls a colonial childhood in which she "spoke two languages," one
at home and one at school, one from the colonizer and one from the colonized, is
unassuming in her explanation of her facility in composing code-switching poetry.
"Some things I think of in standard English and some in Creole," she explained to an
interviewer; she is neither afraid of literary English nor ashamed of Creole and thus
refuses to be "contained" by "just one language." Forced to recite Wordsworth's "Daf-
fodils" even though she "had never seen one," she nevertheless credits Wordsworth,
along with other British writers, with helping to open her "inward," imaginative eye.

For Goodison, Jamaica's cultural heterogeneity is recorded most obviously in its mul-
tifarious place names: "There is everywhere here," she quips in the poem "To Us, All
Flowers Are Roses": along with the Ashanti name Accompong and the Amerindian
Arawak, "there is Alps and Lapland and Berlin / Armagh, Carrick Fergus, Malvern /
Rhine and Calabar, Askenish." Likewise, Goodison's poetry freely embraces a range of
cultural and linguistic inheritances, whether European, Caribbean, or African.

Goodison describes her own ancestry as mixed, declaring, "It all belongs to me": "my
great grandfather was a man called Aberdeen, who obviously came from Scotland. And
my great grandmother came from Guinea, and because they had a mating and produced
my grandmother, who looked like an American Indian—I have relatives who look like
Egyptians and my son is an African prince—all of it belongs to me" (1988 interview).
In some of her poems, Goodison has self-mockingly adopted the persona of the
"mulatta," but with an intercultural delight that stands in marked contrast to the inner
torment of "mulatto" poems such as Walcott's "A Far Cry from Africa."

Goodison sees her personal history of racial and cultural hybridity as exemplifying a
broader experience. Her poems about the genesis of her "family's history," she says of
works such as "Guinea Woman," suggest "everybody's family history in the colonial
experience, a Jamaican experience." Goodison thinks back through the lives of women
in particular, reclaiming aspects of past experience that have traditionally been margin-
alized, including the lives of Afro-Caribbean slaves and domestic servants. The char-
acter portrait is often Goodison's imaginative vehicle for individualizing and reentering
history, as in "Annie Pengelly" and "Turn Thanks to Miss Mirry." She denounces spe-
cific injustices of Jamaican colonial history—enslavement, rape, torture, incarceration—
yet offers a nuanced treatment of, for example, the white mistress of the slave girl Annie

Pengelly, exploring the parallels between racial and gender oppression. Sometimes, she bestows a voice upon a legendary historical figure, such as a great Jamaican Maroon leader and warrior in the poem "Nanny," who surrenders sexual dependency to become mother to a nation. If Goodison's poetry fearlessly crosses boundaries between languages and cultures, some of her poems explore life in the interstices between genders. In "On Becoming a Mermaid," she returns to a Western archetype and imagines the metamorphosis of woman into water nymph, a change that liberates her from sexual boundaries, yet confines her within her own body.

Goodison's poetry engages a rich field of sensual experience. An accomplished painter, she melds colors with taste in poems such as "Hungry Belly Kill Daley." Delighting in what she calls, in the title of a poem, "The Mango of Poetry," she connects the pleasures of art and poetry with the pleasures of food. Her poetry is highly musical in its cadences, sometimes shifting tempo with the speed of jazz improvisation, from staccato to langor to chanted exuberance. Mercurial shifts in voice, person, and diction help sustain the propulsive momentum. In the complex inner life of a poem such as "Bam Chi Chi Lala," disparate aspects of the poet's experience flow together—a cold North American autumn with West Indian hurricanes, monastic prayer with Caribbean superstition, even Mary, Queen of Scots with reggae and Sufism.

Goodison was born on August 1, 1947, in Kingston, Jamaica, to a lower-middle-class family, her father a telephone line worker, her mother a seamstress. Congested city life marked her youth, but trips to the Jamaican countryside fired her imagination. From her schooldays, she names *The Oxford Book of Modern Verse*, edited by W. B. Yeats, and Walcott's *In a Green Night* as formative influences. After school, she studied art both in Jamaica (1967–68) and in New York (1968–69). In Jamaica, she worked as an illustrator, artist, teacher, and cultural administrator. In 1986–87, she was a fellow at the Bunting Institute at Radcliffe College, and since 1991, she has taught creative writing both in the United States, at the University of Michigan, and in Canada, at the University of Toronto. Among other awards, she has won a Commonwealth Poetry Prize (1986) and the Musgrave Gold Medal from the Institute of Jamaica (1999).

On Becoming a Mermaid

Watching the underlife idle by
you think drowning must be easy death
just let go and let the water carry you
away and under
the current pulls your bathing-plaits loose 5
your hair floats out straightened by the water
your legs close together fuse all the length down
your feet now one broad foot
the toes spread into
a fish-tail, fan-like, 10
your sex locked under
mother-of-pearl scales
you're a nixie[1] now, a mermaid
a green-tinged fish/fleshed woman/thing
who swims with thrashing movements 15
and stands upended on the sea floor

1. Water nymph.

breasts full and floating buoyed by the salt
and the space between your arms now always
filled and your sex sealed forever under
mother-of-pearl scale/locks closes finally   20
on itself like some close-mouthed oyster.

1986

Guinea Woman[2]

Great grandmother
was a guinea woman
wide eyes turning
the corners of her face
could see behind her,   5
her cheeks dusted with
a fine rash of jet-bead warts
that itched when the rain set up.

Great grandmother's waistline
the span of a headman's hand,   10
slender and tall like a cane stalk
with a guinea woman's antelope-quick walk
and when she paused,
her gaze would look to sea
her profile fine like some obverse impression   15
on a guinea coin from royal memory.

It seems her fate was anchored
in the unfathomable sea
for great grandmother caught the eye of a sailor
whose ship sailed without him from Lucea[3] harbor.   20
Great grandmother's royal scent of
cinnamon and scallions
drew the sailor up the straits of Africa,
the evidence my blue-eyed grandmother
the first Mulatta,   25
taken into backra's[4] household
and covered with his name.
They forbade great grandmother's
guinea woman presence.
They washed away her scent of   30
cinnamon and scallions,
controlled the child's antelope walk,
and called her uprisings rebellions.

But, great grandmother,
I see your features blood dark   35

2. Woman born in Africa.
3. Town on western coast of Jamaica.

4. Master's (Jamaican English). *Mulatta:* a woman
with one black parent and one white parent.

appearing
in the children of each new
breeding.
The high yellow brown
is darkening down.   40
Listen, children,
it's great grandmother's turn.

                                                1986

Nanny[5]

My womb was sealed
with molten wax
of killer bees
for nothing should enter
nothing should leave   5
the state of perpetual siege
the condition of the warrior.

From then my whole body would quicken
at the birth of every one of my people's children.
I was schooled in the green-giving ways   10
of the roots and vines
made accomplice to the healing acts
of Chainey root, fever grass & vervain.[6]

My breasts flattened
settled unmoving against my chest   15
my movements ran equal
to the rhythms of the forest.

I could sense and sift
the footfall of men
from the animals   20
and smell danger
death's odor
in the wind's shift.

When my eyes rendered
light from the dark   25
my battle song opened
into a solitaire's moan
I became most knowing
and forever alone.

5. Warrior and Jamaican national hero who helped lead the Maroons, a society of fugitive slaves, in battles against the British in the eigh-teenth century.
6. Three plants used in Jamaica for their medicinal properties.

And when my training was over   30
they circled my waist with pumpkin seeds
and dried okra, a traveler's jigida,[7]
and sold me to the traders
all my weapons within me.
I was sent, tell that to history.   35

When your sorrow obscures the skies
other women like me will rise.

1986

Annie Pengelly

I come to represent the case
of one Annie Pengelly,
maidservant, late of the San Fleming Estate
situated in the westerly parish of Hanover.

Hanover, where that masif   5
mountain range
assumes the shape of a Dolphin's head
rearing up in the blue expanse overhead
restless white clouds round it foaming.

Those at sea would look up   10
and behold, mirrored, a seascape in the sky.

It is this need to recreate,
to run 'gainst things, that cause
all this confusion.

The same need that made men   15
leave one side of the world
to journey in long, mawed ships,
to drogue[8] millions of souls
to a world
that they call the new one   20
in competition with the original act
the creation of the old one.

So now you are telling me to proceed
and proceed swiftly.
Why have I come here representing Annie?   25

Well this is the first thing she asked me to say,
that Annie is not even her real name.
A name is the first thing we own in this world.

---

7. String of beads worn around the waist.
8. That is, drag; from nautical term for hooped canvas bag towed at boat's stern.

We lay claim to a group of sounds
which rise up and down and mark out our space   30
in the air around us.
We become owners of a harmony of vowels and consonants
singing a specific meaning.

Her real name was given to her
at the pastoral ceremony of her outdooring.[9]   35
Its outer meaning was, "she who is precious to us."

It had too a hidden part, a kept secret.
A meaning known only to those within
the circle of her family.

For sale Bidderman, one small girl,   40
one small African girl answering now
to the name of Annie.

Oh Missus my dear, when you write Lady Nugent[1]
to tell her of your splendid birthday
of the ivory moire[2] gown you wore   45
that you send clear to London for.

You can tell her too how you had built for you
a pair of soft, supple leather riding boots
fashioned from your own last
by George O'Brian Wilson   50
late of Aberdeen
now Shoemaker and Sadler of Lucea, Hanover[3]
late occupation,
bruk[4] Sailor.

One pair of tortoiseshell combs,   55
one scrolled silver backed mirror,
one dinner party where they killed
one whole cow
with oaken casks of Madeira wine
to wash it down.   60

And don't forget, one small African girl,
answering now to the name of Annie.

With all that birthday show of affection
Massa never sleep with missus.
But I am not here to talk about that,   65
that is backra[5] business.

I am really here just representing Annie Pengelly.

9. Ghanaian naming ceremony in which a new-
born is introduced to the community.
1. Wife of George Nugent, lieutenant governor of
Jamaica in the early nineteenth century.
2. Textile with a watered or clouded appearance.

3. Lucea is the capital of the parish of Hanover in
western Jamaica. *Aberdeen:* seaport in northeast
Scotland.
4. Broke (Jamaican English).
5. White people's (Jamaican English).

For Missus began to make Annie
sleep across her feet
come December when northers began to blow.   70

Northers being the chill wheeling tail end
of the winter breezes
dropping off their cold what lef' in Jamaica
to confuse the transplanted Planter.

Causing them to remember words like "hoarfrost" and "moors"   75
from a frozen vocabulary they no longer
had use for.

When this false winter breeze would
career across canefields
Missus would make Annie lie draped,   80
heaped across her feet
a human blanket
nothing covering her as she gave
her warmth to Missus.

So I come to say that History owes Annie   85
the brightest woolen blanket.
She is owed too, at least twelve years of sleep
stretched out,
free to assume the stage of sleep
flat on her back,   90
or profiled like the characters
in an Egyptian frieze.

Most nights though, Missus don't sleep.
And as Annie was subject to Missus will,
Annie was not to sleep as long   95
as Missus kept her open-eyed vigil.

Sometimes Missus sit up
sipping wine from a cut glass goblet.
Talking, talking.

Sometimes Missus dance and sing   100
like she was on a stage,
sad cantatrice⁶ solo
on a stage performing.

At the end of her performance
she would demand that Annie clap   105
clap loud and shout "encore."

Encouraged by this she would sing
and dance on,
her half-crazed torch song of rejection.

6. Female opera singer.

Sometimes Annie nod off. 110
Missus jook[7] her with a pearl-tipped pin.
Sometimes Annie tumble off the chair
felled by sleep.
Missus slap her awake again.
Then in order to keep her alert, awake 115
she devised the paper torture.

One pile of newspapers
a sharp pair of scissors later,
Annie learned about
the cruel make-work task 120
that is the *cut-up*
to *throw-away* of old newspaper.

For if Missus could not sleep
Annie gal you don't sleep that night,
and poor Missus enslaved by love 125
fighting her servitude with spite.

So I say history owes Annie
thousands of nights
of sleep upon a feather bed.
Soft feathers from the breast of 130
a free, soaring bird,
one bright blanket,
and her name returned,
she who is precious to us.

Annie Pengelly O. 135
I say, History owe you.

1995

Turn[8] Thanks to Miss Mirry

Turn thanks to Miss Mirry
ill-tempered domestic helper who hated me.
She said that she had passed through hell bareheaded
and that a whitening ash from hell's furnace

had sifted down upon her and that is why she gray early. 5
Called me "Nana." Nanny's name I have come to love.
She twisted her surname Henry into Endry
in her railing against the graceless state of her days.

She was the repository of 400 years of resentment
for being uprooted and transplanted, condemned 10
to being a stranger on this side of a world
where most words would not obey her tongue.

7. Pricked (Jamaican English).   8. Return.

She said that she came from "Ullava"
in the parallel universe of Old Harbor.
She could not read or write a word in English   15
but took every vowel and consonant of it

and rung it around, like the articulated neck
of our Sunday dinner sacrificial fowl.
In her anger she stabbed at English, walked it out,
abandoned it in favor of a long kiss teeth,   20

a furious fanning of her shift tail, a series of hawks
at the back of her throat, a long extended elastic sigh,
a severing cut eye, or a melancholy wordless moaning
as she squatted over her wooden washtub soaping

our dirty clothes with a brown wedge of hard key soap.   25
To Miss Mirry who subverted the English language
calling Barbara, Baba; my father, Tata; who desiled her mind
that I was boofuttoo, a baffan and too rampify.[9]

Who said pussbrukokonatinnadalikklegalnanayeye.[1]
Miss Mirry versus English against the west   30
once assured me that for every sickness
there exists a cure growing in the bush.

I thank her for giving me a bath in her washtub
which she had filled with water heated
in a kerosene tin and in it she had strewed   35
the fringed leaves of the emancipation tamarind.[2]

I turn thanks for the calming bath
that she gave to me which quelled effectively
the red itching measles prickling my skin.
As she sluiced the astringent waters over me   40

she was speak-singing in a language
familiar to her tongue which rose unfettered
up and down in tumbling cadences, ululations
in time with the swift sopping motion of her hands,

becoming her true self   45
in that ritual bathing, that song.
Turn thanks now to Miss Mirry
African bush healing woman.

                                                        1999

9. I was awkward, a clumsy and useless person, and too playful (Jamaican English; -ify: Creole suffix akin to -ied, as in prettified).
1. Jamaican proverb meaning "you're disrespect-
ful" (the cat has broken a coconut in that little girl Nana's eye).
2. Tree with an acidic fruit.

Hungry Belly Kill Daley[3]

I fancied that I could paint
a still life with food,
and my rendering of victuals
would be so good
that I could reach into the canvas   5
and eat and fill my belly.

Cadmium yellow could spread
butter impasto[4] over white lead
or a brown loaf baked of sienna.
Scarlet and vermilion, the wine   10
would flow, otaheiti apple
is a deep, dark, rose madder.[5]

If I could fill my hungry belly
with painted wine and bread
but they shock my visions from my head   15
at Bellevue, where Louis Q. Bowerbank[6]
sends madmen or black men mad enough
to think that we could be artists, in 1940.

                                                                  1999

Bam Chi Chi Lala[7]

It is fall again, October rains
and red trees signal you
are entering change season.
Your guinea blood courses fierce
and you think to drink gold leaf[8]   5
in a camel bid to store sun.
See how your small boy
has become a fine man.

You cross the street to bless brides
and cross yourself as ambulances shriek by.   10
This morning you woke at five and kept
company with the monk of Gethsemane,[9]

3. Henry Daley (1918?–1950?), talented but ill-fated Jamaican painter of symbolic self-portraits and trees. Starving, suffering from tuberculosis, he died at Kingston Public Hospital. *Hungry Belly:* personified companion of Henry Daley in an elegy by Jamaican poet Philip Sherlock, "Trees His Testament: A Goodbye for Daley" (1957).
4. Thick application of paint.
5. Shade of deep red paint. *Otaheiti apple:* Jamaican fruit.
6. Chief of the Kingston magistry in the nineteenth century. His statue stands inside Kingston's Bellevue hospital, a mental asylum. Bowerbank helped sentence Jamaican popular leader George William Gordon to death for the political agitation he organized in his campaign for the rights of poverty-stricken black Jamaicans.
7. Refrain of a Jamaican folk song.
8. Extremely thin sheet of gold used to gild books, paintings, and so on. *Guinea:* African.
9. Thomas Merton (1915–1968), poet and Trappist monk.

lauds and aubades. In Hanover[1] your people's
river swells because the hurricanes
have wept and flashed their epileptic   15
selves across the West Indies.

How do wild spirits gain entrance
into humans?
Do they make their way through body
orifices as we sleep?   20
If that is so then it is best to say
the sealing prayer before slumber.
"Lord, please keep all demons away
from the nine gates of my body."

Or better still, forsake shuteye,   25
join the night watch and patrol
the border country between
the worlds of sleep and wake.

Do small deeds of love for the world.
Remove traps and tripping stones   30
set by the wicked for the weak.
With the aid of clean mirrors
bring the lost from behind themselves.
And then pass silent by graveyards
taverns and public cotton trees where   35
the ambitious hold duppy[2] conventions.

Aye, earth's garments wear so heavy.
See how much the queen's robe sags,
trimmed as it is with feathers of the vain,
sleek ermine and jewels of bright ambition.   40
Be wary miss monarch of the ones who come
ostensibly to admire the intricate inlaid
workmanship of your throne, for they
may be measuring your neck's length like

Queen Mary[3] the pretender, whom some   45
toasted with wine glass on top of glass of water
because they said the real monarch lived over
the ocean. No one crowned her that is true,
she is a pretender just like you, save for this
one thing. The first word   50
you read spelled your vocation, Singer.[4]

If they knew how all ambition
should come to this, autonomy
autonomy over the me myself.

1. In Jamaica. *Aubades*: poems or songs of dawn.
2. Spirit; ghost (Jamaican English).
3. Mary, Queen of Scots (1542–1587), believed by Catholics to be the rightful queen of England, was executed by her cousin Elizabeth I.
4. Brand name of sewing machine used by the poet's mother, a seamstress.

Sovereign over self kingdom 55
feel free whomsoever to fight over
the cold food Babylon[5] has left over.
Bam chi chi lala
angels dance rocksteady[6]
on the head of a common pin. 60

Softly now
our Beloved[7]
is convening
pleasant Sunday evening.

2001

5. Ancient, wealthy Mesopotamian city; symbol of decadent materialism for Rastafarians.
6. Musical precursor to reggae.

7. In the literature of Sufism, a mystical branch of Islam, the individual is often the "lover" seeking union with the divine, or the "Beloved."

AI

1947–2010

In many of Ai's poems, writes the poet Carolyn Forché in a foreword, "there are knives, axes, blades, or pitchforks, splitting skulls, slicing off pieces of flesh, jabbing the sun." What might in another writer's hands seem like sensational violence becomes, in hers, a scalpel, an "instrument for penetrating a social order which has become anesthetized to human agony." The violence is not observed dispassionately from without, but experienced by the poems' speakers, for most of Ai's poems are dramatic monologues. In her first book, *Cruelty* (1973), the personae—anonymous, dispossessed—frequently speak at a moment of sexual desire: "I'll pull, you push, we'll tear each other in half" ("Twenty-Year Marriage"). The desire is often painful, often fatalistically felt, and the poems are brief—as brief, perhaps, as the moments themselves, stabs of energy in otherwise dreary lives.

The monologues of her subsequent books are longer. Their speakers are more rooted in a specific time or place; some are historical figures, such as Marilyn Monroe, J. Edgar Hoover, or Leon Trotsky, the Russian Communist leader ousted by Joseph Stalin. We hear Trotsky on three different occasions in "Killing Floor," at each of which his assassination comes closer. "I find it very exciting to become other people," Ai said, insisting that her adopted voices were not masks for herself (*Radcliffe Quarterly*, Spring 2000). Distinct as we read the poems, the voices—stylized, undifferentiated by diction—blend in recollection to become a chorus. They explore such lurid subjects as necrophilia, mass murder, sexual abuse, and torture. Whether from the perspective of victim or victimizer, Ai presents with vigor, bluntness, and glaring immediacy moments in which the boundaries of the body and psyche are broken. Her acts of ventriloquism counter anesthesia and cruelty by reasserting an articulate humanity and a robust interior life.

Ai used only her given middle name, which means "love" in Japanese. She was born on October 21, 1947, in Albany, Texas, to a Japanese father and a mother of African American, Native American, and European descent. Growing up in the American southwest, she attended Catholic schools until the seventh grade. She held a B.A. in Japanese from the University of Arizona and an M.F.A. from the University of California, Irvine. She taught or was writer-in-residence at a variety of institutions, including Oklahoma State University. She received the Lamont Poetry Prize in 1978 and the National Book Award in 1999.

Twenty-Year Marriage

You keep me waiting in a truck
with its one good wheel stuck in the ditch,
while you piss against the south side of a tree.
Hurry. I've got nothing on under my skirt tonight.
That still excites you, but this pickup has no windows   5
and the seat, one fake leather thigh,
pressed close to mine is cold.
I'm the same size, shape, make as twenty years ago,
but get inside me, start the engine;
you'll have the strength, the will to move.   10
I'll pull, you push, we'll tear each other in half.
Come on, baby, lay me down on my back.
Pretend you don't owe me a thing
and maybe we'll roll out of here,
leaving the past stacked up behind us;   15
old newspapers nobody's ever got to read again.

1973

Killing Floor

1. Russia, 1927

On the day the sienna-skinned man
held my shoulders between his spade-shaped hands,
easing me down into the azure water of Jordan,[1]
I woke ninety-three million miles from myself,
Lev Davidovich Bronstein,[2]   5
shoulder-deep in the Volga,
while the cheap dye of my black silk shirt darkened the water.

My head wet, water caught in my lashes.
Am I blind?
I rub my eyes, then wade back to shore,   10
undress and lie down,
until Stalin comes from his place beneath the birch tree.
He folds my clothes
and I button myself in my marmot[3] coat,

1. River that flows through what was ancient Palestine; its waters were reputedly holy.
2. Original name of the Russian revolutionist (1879–1940) who was a leader in postrevolutionary Russia until Lenin's death, in 1924, when he lost the struggle for leadership to Joseph Stalin (1879–1953). He was expelled from the Communist Party in 1927. The Volga (below) is Russia's chief river.
3. A cheap fur.

and together we start the long walk back to Moscow.   15
He doesn't ask, *what did you see in the river?,*
but I hear the hosts of a man drowning in water and holiness,
the castrati voices[4] I can't recognize,
skating on knives, from trees, from air
on the thin ice of my last night in Russia.   20
Leon Trotsky. Bread.
I want to scream, but silence holds my tongue
with small spade-shaped hands
and only this comes, so quietly
Stalin has to press his ear to my mouth: 25
I have only myself. Put me on the train.
I won't look back.

2. *Mexico, 1940*

At noon today, I woke from a nightmare:
my friend Jacques ran toward me with an ax,
as I stepped from the train in Alma-Ata.[5]   30
He was dressed in yellow satin pants and shirt.
A marigold in winter.
When I held out my arms to embrace him,
he raised the ax and struck me at the neck,
my head fell to one side, hanging only by skin.   35
A river of sighs poured from the cut.

3. *Mexico, August 20, 1940*[6]

The machine-gun bullets
hit my wife in the legs,
then zigzagged up her body.
I took the shears, cut open her gown   40
and lay on top of her for hours.
Blood soaked through my clothes
and when I tried to rise, I couldn't.

I wake then. Another nightmare.
I rise from my desk, walk to the bedroom   45
and sit down at my wife's mirrored vanity.
I rouge my cheeks and lips,
stare at my bone-white, speckled egg of a face:
lined and empty.
I lean forward and see Jacques's reflection.   50
I half-turn, smile, then turn back to the mirror.
He moves from the doorway,
lifts the pickax
and strikes the top of my head.

---

4. That is, high voices; castrati were male singers castrated in boyhood to preserve their soprano voices.
5. City in Kazakhstan. Trotsky was assassinated by the Spanish Communist Ramón Mercader, who also used the aliases Jacques van den Dreschd and Frank Jacson. He was a pretended friend of Trotsky's in Mexico, where Trotsky eventually settled after being exiled from Russia. An earlier attempt on Trotsky's life, by machine gun (lines 38–44), was led by the Mexican Communist painter David Siqueiros.
6. The date of Trotsky's assassination.

My brain splits.   55
The pickax keeps going
and when it hits the tile floor,
it flies from his hands,
a black dove on whose back I ride,
two men, one cursing,   60
the other blessing all things:
Lev Davidovich Bronstein,
I step from Jordan without you.

                                                                    1979

Sleeping Beauty

A Fiction

for the comatose patient raped by an aide

You steal into my room,
between darkness and noon
to doff the disguise as nurse's aide
and parade before me as you really are,
a man for whom time is deranged   5
and consists of your furtive visits to me,
while all the rest is just a gloomy reprieve
from your nothingness.
For me time is arranged without the past
or the future,   10
without tenses to suture me to my days and nights.
For me, there is only now,
when you are certain you won't be disturbed,
spread my legs apart
and break through the red door to my chamber.   15
After you've finished,
you use a clean, white towel
to wipe away the evidence
of how you mingled your life
with what is left of mine.   20
You think your crime won't be discovered
but the evidence survives
to dine on the flow of fluid
dripping into me,
as though I were merely a conduit   25
for the baby who knows me
only as its host
and never will as Mother
and you will never be Father,
baby never see,   30
you, who in a fever came to me.
I was "comma tose" as my mother calls it.
She hoped for a miracle,
but when it came, it was not the one she wanted,

when she prayed to Saint Jude,   35
patron saint of lost causes
and laid my photo on the altar
she'd erected in the living room,
beside a rose in a crystal vase.
My face almost glowed in the dark,   40
as if the spark of consciousness
leaped from me into the image
of what I was before I was swept away from myself,
only to return as someone else,
for whom language is silence,   45
language is thirst
that is not slaked.
Monster, you took all that was left of my body,
but could not break my body's vow
of renunciation of itself.   50
My eyes were open,
while you violated me.
All at once
you raised your hand and closed them,
but I could see   55
beyond the veil of your deceit.
At first, I thought you'd come to my rescue,
but instead of waking me with a kiss,
you pricked me with the thorn of violence
and I did not rise from my bed   60
to wed the handsome prince
as in the fairy tale
my mother once read to me,
when *forever* did not mean eternity.

1999

LESLIE MARMON SILKO
b. 1948

As early as the nineteenth century, the Laguna Pueblo was hospitable to mixed marriages and the children of these marriages. Leslie Marmon Silko is of mixed European and Native American heritage, and she builds a bridge between her native Laguna Pueblo culture, orally transmitted generally by storytelling older women, and readers of poetry in English. But she positions herself with the Native Americans in their mostly losing struggle with the murderous white invaders. One of her poems, beginning "Long time ago," imagines a world in which there were "no white people . . . / there was nothing European." The witches of many tribes gather for a contest as to who can cause the most mischief, and an unknown witch wins when she describes a people who live far away: "*When they look / they see only objects. / The world is a dead thing for them / the trees and rivers are not alive / the mountains and stones are not alive. / The deer and bear are objects / They see no life.*" Appalled, the other witches plead with the strange witch to take the story back, but that cannot be done: *"It's already coming."* A gifted storyteller, Silko condenses the past, present, and future, inverts the dominant Euro-American perspective on history, and effectively combines a rhetoric of repetition (*"Killing killing killing killing"*) with vivid details (*"covered with festered sores / shitting blood / vomiting blood"*). Yet angry lament is not Silko's only note. "Prayer to the Pacific" dissolves temporal boundaries to represent a powerfully animistic and prophetic encounter with the natural world. Instancing her skill as an ironist, "Toe'osh: A Laguna Coyote Story" begins by relating traditional Native American trickster stories, but then shifts to modern examples of how Coyote continues to survive. Episodic in structure, compressed in timing, the poem fuses bleak realism and mischievous humor in describing encounters between whites and Native peoples.

Silko was born on March 5, 1948, in Albuquerque, New Mexico, and grew up in Laguna Pueblo, forty miles to the west. She was educated at the University of New Mexico, where she has also taught; since 1978, she has held a position at the University of Arizona. In addition to her poems, she has written short stories and novels, including *Ceremony* (1977). In 1981, she received a MacArthur Fellowship.

[Long Time Ago]

Long time ago
in the beginning
there were no white people in this world
there was nothing European.
And this world might have gone on like that   5
except for one thing:
witchery.
This world was already complete
even without white people.
There was everything   10
including witchery.

Then it happened.
These witch people got together.
Some came from far far away
across oceans   15
across mountains.
Some had slanty eyes
others had black skin.
They all got together for a contest
the way people have baseball tournaments nowadays   20
except this was a contest
in dark things.

So anyway
they all got together
witch people from all directions   25
witches from all the Pueblos
and all the tribes.
They had Navajo witches there,

some from Hopi, and a few from Zuni.[1]
They were having a witches' conference,
    that's what it was   30
Way up in the lava rock hills
    north of Cañoncito[2]
    they got together
    to fool around in caves   35
    with their animal skins.
Fox, badger, bobcat, and wolf
    they circled the fire
    and on the fourth time
they jumped into that animal's skin.   40

But this time it wasn't enough
    and one of them
maybe a Sioux[3] or some Eskimos
    started showing off.
    "That wasn't anything,   45
    watch this."

The contest started like that.
Then some of them lifted the lids
    on their big cooking pots,
    calling the rest of them over   50
    to take a look:
dead babies simmering in blood
    circles of skull cut away
    all the brains sucked out.
    Witch medicine   55
to dry and grind into powder
    for new victims.

Others untied skin bundles of disgusting objects:
dark flints, cinders from burned hogans[4] where the
    dead lay   60
    Whorls of skin
    cut from fingertips
sliced from the penis end and clitoris tip.

Finally there was only one
who hadn't shown off charms or powers.   65
The witch stood in the shadows beyond the fire
and no one ever knew where this witch came from
    which tribe
    or if it was a woman or a man.
    But the important thing was   70
this witch didn't show off any dark thunder charcoals

1. Native American peoples of, respectively, northern New Mexico and Arizona, northeastern Arizona, and western New Mexico.
2. That is, Cañon City, in southern Colorado.
3. Native American people of the northern Mississippi Valley.
4. Navajo dwellings.

or red ant-hill beads.
This one just told them to listen:
"What I have is a story."

At first they all laughed   75
but this witch said
Okay
go ahead
laugh if you want to
but as I tell the story   80
it will begin to happen.

Set in motion now
set in motion by our witchery
to work for us.

Caves across the ocean   85
in caves of dark hills
white skin people
like the belly of a fish
covered with hair.

Then they grow away from the earth   90
then they grow away from the sun
then they grow away from the plants and animals.
They see no life
When they look
they see only objects.   95
The world is a dead thing for them
the trees and rivers are not alive
the mountains and stones are not alive.
The deer and bear are objects
They see no life.   100

They fear
They fear the world.
They destroy what they fear.
They fear themselves.

The wind will blow them across the ocean   105
thousands of them in giant boats
swarming like larva
out of a crushed ant hill.

They will carry objects
which can shoot death   110
faster than the eye can see.

They will kill the things they fear
all the animals
the people will starve.

They will poison the water   115
they will spin the water away
and there will be drought
the people will starve.

They will fear what they find
They will fear the people   120
They kill what they fear.

Entire villages will be wiped out
They will slaughter whole tribes.

Corpses for us
Blood for us   125
Killing killing killing killing.

And those they do not kill
will die anyway
at the destruction they see
at the loss   130
at the loss of the children
the loss will destroy the rest.

Stolen rivers and mountains
the stolen land will eat their hearts
and jerk their mouths from the Mother.[5]   135
The people will starve.

They will bring terrible diseases
the people have never known.
Entire tribes will die out
covered with festered sores   140
shitting blood
vomiting blood.
Corpses for our work

Set in motion now
set in motion by our witchery   145
set in motion
to work for us.

They will take this world from ocean to ocean
they will turn on each other
they will destroy each other   150
Up here
in these hills
they will find the rocks,
rocks with veins of green and yellow and black.
They will lay the final pattern with these rocks   155
they will lay it across the world
and explode everything.

5. That is, the earth.

Set in motion now
set in motion
To destroy   160
To kill
Objects to work for us
objects to act for us
Performing the witchery
for suffering   165
for torment
for the stillborn
the deformed
the sterile
the dead.   170

Whirling
Whirling
Whirling
Whirling
set into motion now   175
set into motion.

So the other witches said
"Okay you win; you take the prize,
but what you said just now—
it isn't so funny   180
It doesn't sound so good.
We are doing okay without it
we can get along without that kind of thing.
Take it back.
Call that story back."   185

But the witch just shook its head
at the others in their stinking animal skins, fur
and feathers.
It's already turned loose.
It's already coming.   190
It can't be called back.

1981

Prayer to the Pacific

I traveled to the ocean
distant
from my southwest land of sandrock
to the moving blue water
Big as the myth of origin.   5

Pale
pale water in the yellow-white light of

sun   floating west
> to China
> where ocean herself was born.   10
Clouds that blow across the sand are wet.

Squat in the wet sand and speak to the Ocean:
> I return to you   turquoise   the red coral you sent us,
> > sister spirit of Earth.
Four round stones in my pocket   I carry back the ocean   15
> to suck and to taste.

Thirty thousand years ago
> Indians came riding across the ocean
> carried by giant sea turtles.

Waves were high that day   20
> great sea turtles waded   slowly out
> > from the gray sundown sea.
Grandfather Turtle rolled in the sand   four times
> and disappeared
> > swimming into the sun.   25

And so   from that time
> immemorial,
> > as the old people say,
rain clouds drift from the west
> gift from the ocean.   30

Green leaves in the wind
Wet earth on my feet
> swallowing raindrops
> > clear from China.

1981

Toe'osh: A Laguna Coyote Story

for Simon Ortiz,[6] July 1973

In the wintertime
at night
we tell coyote stories
> and drink Spañada[7] by the stove.
How coyote got his   5
ratty old fur coat
> bits of old fur
> the sparrows stuck on him
> with dabs of pitch.
That was after he lost his proud original one in a poker game.   10

---

6. Native American poet (b. 1941).   7. Spanish wine.

anyhow, things like that
are always happening to him,
that's what he said, anyway.

And it happened to him at Laguna
and Chinle   15
and Lukachukai[8] too, because coyote got too smart for his own good.

But the Navajos say he won a contest once.
It was to see who could sleep out in a
snowstorm the longest
and coyote waited until chipmunk badger and skunk were all   20
curled up under the snow
and then he uncovered himself and slept all night
inside
and before morning he got up and went out again
and waited until the others got up before he came   25
in to take the prize.

Some white men came to Acoma[9] and Laguna a hundred years ago
and they fought over Acoma land and Laguna women, and even now
some of their descendants are howling in
the hills southeast of Laguna.   30

Charlie Coyote wanted to be governor
and he said that when he got elected
he would run the other men off
the reservation
and keep all the women for himself.   35

One year
the politicians got fancy
at Laguna.
They went door to door with hams and turkeys
and they gave them to anyone who promised   40
to vote for them.
On election day all the people
stayed home and ate turkey
and laughed.

The Trans-Western pipeline vice president came   45
to discuss right-of-way.
The Lagunas let him wait all day long
because he is a busy and important man.
And late in the afternoon they told him
to come back again tomorrow.   50

They were after the picnic food
that the special dancers left
down below the cliff.

8. Pueblos (Native American villages).   9. Pueblo in west central New Mexico.

And Toe'osh and his cousins hung themselves
down over the cliff   55
holding each other's tail in their mouth making a coyote chain
until someone in the middle farted
and the guy behind him opened his
mouth to say "What stinks?" and they
all went tumbling down, like that.   60

Howling and roaring
Toe'osh scattered white people
out of bars all over Wisconsin.
He bumped into them at the door
until they said   65
   "Excuse me"
And the way Simon meant it
was for 300 or maybe 400 years.

          1981

AGHA SHAHID ALI
1949–2001

Agha Shahid Ali was born in New Delhi, India, on February 4, 1949, just a year and a half after the triumphant "birth" and traumatic partition of India. He was the leading anglophone Indian poet of the generation born after independence. Like his peer in the earlier generation, A. K. Ramanujan, Ali enriched English-language poetry by hybridizing it with South Asian traditions. But whereas Ramanujan belonged to the majority Hindu population, Ali came from the Shi'a Muslim minority. And whereas Ramanujan's poetry draws on literature in south Indian languages (Tamil and Kannada), Ali brings into English-language poetry "the music of Urdu," the north Indian language spoken by most Muslims of the Indian subcontinent. Indebted to T. S. Eliot's sharply etched, dreamlike, fragmentary lines, he synthesizes this Western modernist influence with the ornate forms, rhetorical patterning, and melancholy tonality of Urdu poetry.

Ali considered himself a "Kashmiri-American" and yet a "triple exile" from Kashmir, India, and the United States. He spent a few years as a teenager in the United States, but otherwise he grew up in Srinagar, Kashmir, and the violence and instability of his disputed homeland haunted his imagination. By internalizing this violence, he conjured it powerfully in nightmarish images of homes, religious sites, artifacts, and human lives devastated by conflict. As in the poetry of his Urdu precursors, the political and the personal are inseparable in Ali's work, though his poetry eschews polemics, favoring the emotionally inscribed landscape, the unpredictably visualized image.

One prominent example of the political realities that mark Ali's work is an event mourned in the title poem of *The Country without a Post Office* (1997): a catastrophic fire, in 1995, in the picturesque, twenty-thousand-person Kashmiri town of Chrar-e-Sharif. In this poem, written in a mirrorlike rhyme scheme (ABCDDCBA), Ali imaginatively returns to the displaced and the dead, to walls of flame, to houses burning like leaves, to a broken and buried minaret, ultimately to a country reduced to ash. Yet he acknowledges the impossibility of his reentering the scene of destruction or poetically rehabilitating it, dwelling on images of undeliverable "dead letters" with "vanished envelopes" and "blank stamps." As in much of Ali's work, the poet's remembrance of ruin and loss is vivified, not trivialized, by his personal anguish over his own limitations as poet and exile.

The imaginative yet incomplete return to a remembered landscape is often the psychic impetus of Ali's poetry. In "Postcard from Kashmir," the postcolonial poet conjures his native landscape, yet implicitly mocks his own retrospective reconstruction. Like a postcard, he acknowledges, the poetry of the postcolonial émigré risks miniaturizing, idealizing, and reducing his native place. In "The Dacca Gauzes," his poetry implicitly aspires to the condition of the dewlike muslins woven by earlier generations of Bengalis, before their brutal suppression by the British (their hands were mutilated), though this poem acknowledges, again, its language's incapacity to resurrect fully the lost art it memorializes.

The deliberate self-consciousness of Ali's poetry owes much to that modernist tradition in which poets allegorize the work of shoring fragments against personal and cultural ruins. It also owes something to the self-mirroring artifice of James Merrill's poetry, which influenced Ali's shift from his early free verse to rhymed and metered forms, including the sestina and the canzone. But it is especially evident in his use of a non-Western form—the ghazal (pronounced gha*zal* in Persian, *ghuz*zle in Urdu), the last lines of which typically include a reference to the poet by name, such as the poignant ending of the ghazal reprinted here: "And I, Shahid, only am escaped to tell thee—/ God sobs in my arms. Call me Ishmael tonight." Indeed, Ali became the most visible spokesman for this form borrowed from medieval Persian and Arabic. Because the last line of each couplet rhymes ("tell" and the earlier "farewell") and ends in the same word ("tonight"), the ghazal builds a hypnotic momentum, also evident in Ali's many other ghazal-inflected poems, such as "The Country without a Post Office" and "Lenox Hill." But because a ghazal's couplets are strung together without regard to thematic or narrative unity, each standing on its own without enjambments between couplets, they also enable the poet to jump across the disjunctures and incoherences of contemporary life. For Ali, as for poets as divergent as Adrienne Rich, Galway Kinnell, John Hollander, and Paul Muldoon, the ghazal becomes a tool for inscribing the obsessions and the gaps of modernity.

Absence, loss, exile—these are the fruitful obsessions of Ali's poetry. Responding to "the death of tribes, the death of landscapes and the death of a language," he said in 1998, "I see everything in a very elegiac way. It's not something morbid, but it's part of my emotional coloring." Imbued with a sense of national dislocation and grief over the horrors of Kashmir, Ali also writes effectively about other histories of loss and destruction. In "Leaving Sonora," he remembers the unexplained fifteenth-century disappearance of the Hohokam (said to mean "those who have vanished") from their homes in Arizona. The atrocities and disappearances under Chilean dictator Pinochet and other South American autocrats are surreally compressed as an absent visual presence in "I See Chile in My Rearview Mirror." In these poems, the speaker is driving or flying, his mobility exemplifying contemporary migrancy, one diaspora or violent displacement becoming superimposed upon another as in the works' palimpsestic allusions and cross-cultural textures.

Ali studied literature at the University of Kashmir, Srinagar (B.A., 1968), and at the University of Delhi (M.A., 1970) before earning a Ph.D. in English at Pennsylvania State University (1984) and an M.F.A. at the University of Arizona (1985). He taught creative writing at various American universities, including the University of Arizona, Hamilton College, the University of Massachusetts, Amherst, and the University of Utah. When his mother died of brain cancer, he mourned her death in the elegy "Lenox Hill," one of the crowning achievements of his career. Not long after, he was killed by the same disease.

Postcard from Kashmir[1]

Kashmir shrinks into my mailbox,
my home a neat four by six inches.

I always loved neatness. Now I hold
the half-inch Himalayas in my hand.

This is home. And this the closest   5
I'll ever be to home. When I return,
the colors won't be so brilliant,
the Jhelum's[2] waters so clean,
so ultramarine. My love
so overexposed.   10

And my memory will be a little
out of focus, in it
a giant negative, black
and white, still undeveloped.

                 (for Pavan Sahgal)

                                                      1987

The Dacca Gauzes

          . . . for a whole year he sought
          to accumulate the most exquisite
          Dacca gauzes.
          —Oscar Wilde / *The Picture of*
                              Dorian Gray

Those transparent Dacca gauzes[3]
known as woven air, running
water, evening dew:

a dead art now, dead over
a hundred years. "No one   5
now knows," my grandmother says,

"what it was to wear
or touch that cloth." She wore
it once, an heirloom sari from

---

1. Mountainous northwestern region of the Indian subcontinent subject to tense border disputes and armed conflict between India and Pakistan since 1947.
2. River running through Kashmir and the Punjab region of Pakistan.

3. Finely woven and exceptionally soft muslins once produced in the city of Dacca, now the capital of Bangladesh. The first stanza of the poem continues the quotation from *The Picture of Dorian Gray.*

her mother's dowry, proved 10
genuine when it was pulled, all
six yards, through a ring.

Years later when it tore,
many handkerchiefs embroidered
with gold-thread paisleys 15

were distributed among
the nieces and daughters-in-law.
Those too now lost.

In history we learned: the hands
of weavers were amputated, 20
the looms of Bengal silenced,

and the cotton shipped raw
by the British to England.[4]
History of little use to her,

my grandmother just says 25
how the muslins of today
seem so coarse and that only

in autumn, should one wake up
at dawn to pray, can one
feel that same texture again. 30

One morning, she says, the air
was dew-starched: she pulled
it absently through her ring.

1987

Leaving Sonora[5]

> living in the desert
> has taught me to go inside myself
> for shade
> —Richard Shelton[6]

Certain landscapes insist on fidelity.
Why else would a poet of this desert
go deep inside himself for shade?
Only there do the perished tribes live.

4. In the early nineteenth century, the British decided that the Indian muslins were threatening the sales of British fabrics in India and, consequently, cut off the thumbs of the muslin weavers so they could no longer produce the fabric or pass on the skills to their children.
5. State in northwestern Mexico.
6. American poet (b. 1933). The epigraph comes from Shelton's "Notes toward an Autobiography."

The desert insists, always: Be faithful,   5
even to those who no longer exist.

The Hohokam[7] lived here for 1500 years.
In his shade, the poet sees one of their women,
beautiful, her voice low as summer thunder.
Each night she saw, among the culinary ashes,   10
what the earth does only through a terrible pressure—
the fire, in minutes, transforming the coal into diamonds.

I left the desert at night—to return
to the East. From the plane I saw Tucson's lights
shatter into blue diamonds. My eyes dazzled   15
as we climbed higher: below a thin cloud,
and only for a moment, I saw those blue lights fade
into the outlines of a vanished village.

                                                                              1991

I See Chile in My Rearview Mirror

> By dark the world is once again intact
> Or so the mirrors, wiped clean, try to reason . . .
> —James Merrill[8]

This dream of water—what does it harbor?
I see Argentina and Paraguay
under a curfew of glass, their colors
breaking, like oil. The night in Uruguay

is black salt. I'm driving toward Utah,   5
keeping the entire hemisphere in view—
Colombia vermilion, Brazil blue tar,
some countries wiped clean of color: Peru

is titanium white. And always oceans
that hide in mirrors: when beveled edges   10
arrest tides or this world's destinations
forsake ships. There's Sedona, Nogales[9]

far behind. Once I went through a mirror—
from there too the world, so intact, resembled
only itself. When I returned I tore   15
the skin off the glass. The sea was unsealed

---

7. Said to mean "those who have vanished"; Native American tribe that flourished between the fourth and fifteenth centuries in what is now Arizona before disappearing for unknown reasons.

8. American poet (1926–1995). The epigraph comes from Merrill's "Amsterdam."
9. Cities in Arizona.

by dark, and I saw ships sink off the coast
of a wounded republic. Now from a blur
of tanks in Santiago,[1] a white horse
gallops, riderless, chased by drunk soldiers   20

in a jeep; they're firing into the moon.
And as I keep driving in the desert,
someone is running to catch the last bus, men
hanging on to its sides. And he's missed it.

He is running again; crescents of steel   25
fall from the sky. And here the rocks
are under fog, the cedars a temple,
Sedona carved by the wind into gods—

each shadow their worshiper. The siren
empties Santiago; he watches   30
—from a hush of windows—blindfolded men
blurred in gleaming vans. The horse vanishes

into a dream. I'm passing skeletal
figures carved in 700 B.C.
Whoever deciphers these canyon walls   35
remains forsaken, alone with history,

no harbor for his dream. And what else will
this mirror now reason, filled with water?
I see Peru without rain, Brazil
without forests—and here in Utah a dagger   40

of sunlight: it's splitting—it's the summer
solstice—the quartz center of a spiral.
Did the Anasazi[2] know the darker
answer also—given now in crystal

by the mirrored continent? The solstice,   45
but of winter? A beam stabs the window,
diamonds him, a funeral in his eyes.
In the lit stadium of Santiago,

this is the shortest day. He's taken there.
Those about to die are looking at him,   50
his eyes the ledger of the disappeared.
What will the mirror try now? I'm driving,

still north, always followed by that country,
its floors ice, its citizens so lovesick

---

1. Capital of Chile. Between 1973 and 1990, the government of Chile was controlled by a military junta led by Agusto Pinochet (b. 1915) and responsible for over three thousand deaths or disappearances.

2. Native American civilization dating back to c. 100 C.E. in what is today the southwestern United States and famous for the dwellings it built into the sides of cliffs and canyon walls.

that the ground—sheer glass—of every city   55
is torn up. They demand the republic

give back, jeweled, their every reflection.
They dig till dawn but find only corpses.
He has returned to this dream for his bones.
The waters darken. The continent vanishes.   60

                                                    1991

Ghazal[3]

> Pale hands I loved beside the Shalimar
> —Laurence Hope[4]

Where are you now? Who lies beneath your spell tonight
before you agonize him in farewell tonight?

Pale hands that once loved me beside the Shalimar:
Whom else from rapture's road will you expel tonight?

Those "Fabrics of Cashmere—" "to make Me beautiful—"   5
"Trinket"—to gem—"Me to adorn—How—tell"—tonight?[5]

I beg for haven: Prisons, let open your gates—
A refugee from Belief seeks a cell tonight.

Executioners near the woman at the window.
Damn you, Elijah, I'll bless Jezebel[6] tonight.   10

Lord, cried out the idols, *Don't let us be broken;*
Only we can convert the infidel tonight.

Has God's vintage loneliness turned to vinegar?
He's poured rust into the Sacred Well tonight.

In the heart's veined temple all statues have been smashed. 15
No priest in saffron's left to toll its knell tonight.

He's freed some fire from ice, in pity for Heaven;
he's left open—for God—the doors of Hell tonight.

---

3. A poetic form with a long history in Urdu, Persian, and Arabic dating back to the seventh century. In the classical version, the thematically discontinuous couplets of the ghazal have a rhyme scheme (called *qafia*) and refrain (called *radif*), and the last couplet includes the poet's name.
4. Pseudonym of English poet Violet Nicolson (1865–1904). The epigraph as well as the language of the first two stanzas of Ali's poem is taken from her "Kashmiri Song." The Shalimar Gardens of Lahore, in present-day Pakistan, were designed in the seventeenth century.
5. The third stanza is borrowed from Emily Dickinson's "I am ashamed—I hide" (#473).
6. 1 Kings 16–22 describes the Hebrew prophet Elijah's confrontation with Queen Jezebel, who introduced the cult of Baal into Israel.

And I, Shahid, only am escaped to tell thee—
God sobs in my arms. Call me Ishmael[7] tonight.   20

                                                                    1997

The Country without a Post Office[8]

> . . . letters sent
> To dearest him that lives alas! away.
> —Gerard Manley Hopkins[9]

1

Again I've returned to this country
where a minaret[1] has been entombed.
Someone soaks the wicks of clay lamps
in mustard oil, each night climbs its steps
to read messages scratched on planets.   5
His fingerprints cancel blank stamps
in that archive for letters with doomed
addresses, each house buried or empty.

Empty? Because so many fled, ran away,
and became refugees there, in the plains,   10
where they must now will a final dewfall
to turn the mountains to glass. They'll see
us through them—see us frantically bury
houses to save them from fire that, like a wall,
caves in. The soldiers light it, hone the flames,   15
burn our world to sudden papier-mâché

inlaid with gold, then ash. When the muezzin[2]
died, the city was robbed of every Call.
The houses were swept about like leaves
for burning. Now every night we bury   20
our houses—and theirs, the ones left empty.
We are faithful. On their doors we hang wreaths.
More faithful each night fire again is a wall
and we look for the dark as it caves in.

7. Son of Abraham and Hagar and, according to legend, the ancestor to whom the origin of the Arab people can be traced. "Call me Ishmael" is the first sentence of Herman Melville's *Moby-Dick* (1851). "I only am escaped alone to tell thee" is a refrain spoken by Job in response to his calamities (Job 1). 8. This poem mourns the 1995 destruction by fire of one of Kashmir's most important Muslim shrines, the mausoleum of Kashmir's patron saint Sheikh Noor-ud-Din (1377?–1438?), and the surrounding town of Chrar-e-Sharif in the Indian-governed region of Kashmir. The blaze was the culmination of a two-month standoff between the Indian army and a group of 150 Muslim militants. Each side blamed the other for the conflagration. 9. English poet (1844–1889). The epigraph is from the poem beginning "I wake and feel the fell of dark, not day." 1. Tall tower of a mosque, from which worshipers are called to prayer. 2. The official who proclaims the call to prayer in Islam.

2

"We're inside the fire, looking for the dark,"   25
one card lying on the street says. "I want
to be he who pours blood. To soak your hands.
Or I'll leave mine in the cold till the rain
is ink, and my fingers, at the edge of pain,
are seals all night to cancel the stamps."   30
The mad guide! The lost speak like this. They haunt
a country when it is ash. Phantom heart,

pray he's alive. I have returned in rain
to find him, to learn why he never wrote.
I've brought cash, a currency of paisleys   35
to buy the new stamps, rare already, blank,
no nation named on them. Without a lamp
I look for him in houses buried, empty—
He may be alive, opening doors of smoke,
breathing in the dark his ash-refrain: 40

"Everything is finished, nothing remains."
I must force silence to be a mirror
to see his voice again for directions.
Fire runs in waves. Should I cross that river?
Each post office is boarded up. Who will deliver   45
parchment cut in paisleys, my news to prisons?
Only silence can now trace my letters
to him. Or in a dead office the dark panes.

3

"The entire map of the lost will be candled.
I'm keeper of the minaret since the muezzin died.   50
Come soon, I'm alive. There's almost a paisley
against the light, sometimes white, then black.
The glutinous wash is wet on its back
as it blossoms into autumn's final country—
Buy it, I issue it only once, at night.   55
Come before I'm killed, my voice canceled."

In this dark rain, be faithful, Phantom heart,
this is your pain. Feel it. You must feel it.
"Nothing will remain, everything's finished,"
I see his voice again: "This is a shrine   60
of words. You'll find your letters to me. And mine
to you. Come soon and tear open these vanished
envelopes." And I reach the minaret:
I'm inside the fire. I have found the dark.

This is your pain. You must feel it. Feel it,   65
Heart, be faithful to his mad refrain—
For he soaked the wicks of clay lamps,

lit them each night as he climbed these steps
to read messages scratched on planets.
His hands were seals to cancel the stamps.   70
This is an archive. I've found the remains
of his voice, that map of longings with no limit.

4

I read them, letters of lovers, the mad ones,
and mine to him from whom no answers came.
I light lamps, send my answers, Calls to Prayer   75
to deaf worlds across continents. And my lament
is cries countless, cries like dead letters sent
to this world whose end was near, always near.
My words go out in huge packages of rain,
go there, to addresses, across the oceans.   80

It's raining as I write this. I have no prayer.
It's just a shout, held in, It's Us! It's Us!
whose letters are cries that break like bodies
in prisons. Now each night in the minaret
I guide myself up the steps. Mad silhouette,   85
I throw paisleys to clouds. The lost are like this:
They bribe the air for dawn, this their dark purpose.
But there's no sun here. There is no sun here.

Then be pitiless you whom I could not save—
Send your cries to me, if only in this way: 90
I've found a prisoner's letters to a lover—
One begins: "These words may never reach you."
Another ends: "The skin dissolves in dew
without your touch." And I want to answer:
I want to live forever. What else can I say?   95
It rains as I write this. Mad heart, be brave.

(for James Merrill)   1997

Lenox Hill

(In Lenox Hill Hospital,[3] after surgery, my mother said the sirens
sounded like the elephants of Mihiragula when his men drove them
off cliffs in the Pir Panjal Range.)[4]

The Hun so loved the cry, one falling elephant's,
he wished to hear it again. At dawn, my mother
heard, in her hospital-dream of elephants,

3. In New York City. This poem is in the form of
a canzone.
4. Part of the western Himalayas in northwestern
India. Mihiragula (or Mihirakula) was a sixth-

century Hun (or Central Asian) king in India.
Known for his cruelty, he amused himself by roll-
ing elephants off precipices to watch their suffer-
ing, according to Buddhist legend.

sirens wail through Manhattan like elephants
forced off Pir Panjal's rock cliffs in Kashmir: 5
the soldiers, so ruled, had rushed the elephant,
The greatest of all footprints is the elephant's,
said the Buddha. But not lifted from the universe,
those prints vanished forever into the universe,
though nomads still break news of those elephants   10
as if it were just yesterday the air spread the dye
("War's annals will fade into night / Ere their story die"),[5]

the punishing khaki whereby the world sees us die
out, mourning you, O massacred elephants!
Months later, in Amherst,[6] she dreamt: She was, with dia-   15
monds, being stoned to death. I prayed: If she must die,
let it only be some dream. But there were times, Mother,
while you slept, that I prayed, "Saints, let her die."
Not, I swear by you, that I wished you to die
but to save you as you were, young, in song in Kashmir,   20
and I, one festival, crowned Krishna[7] by you, Kashmir
listening to my flute. You never let gods die.
Thus I swear, here and now, not to forgive the universe
that would let me get used to a universe

without you. She, she alone, was the universe   25
as she earned, like a galaxy, her right not to die,
defying the Merciful of the Universe,
Master of Disease, "in the circle of her traverse"[8]
of drug-bound time. And where was the god of elephants,
plump with Fate, when tusk to tusk, the universe,   30
dyed green, became ivory? Then let the universe,
like Paradise, be considered a tomb. Mother,
they asked me, *So how's the writing?* I answered *My mother
is my poem.* What did they expect? For no verse
sufficed except the promise, fading, of Kashmir   35
and the cries that reached you from the cliffs of Kashmir

(across fifteen centuries) in the hospital. *Kashmir,
she's dying!* How her breathing drowns out the universe
as she sleeps in Amherst. Windows open on Kashmir:
There, the fragile wood-shrines—so far away—of Kashmir!   40
O Destroyer, let her return there, if just to die.
Save the right she gave its earth to cover her, Kashmir
has no rights. When the windows close on Kashmir,
I see the blizzard-fall of ghost-elephants.
I hold back—she couldn't bear it—one elephant's   45
story: his return (in a country far from Kashmir)
to the jungle where each year, on the day his mother
died, he touches with his trunk the bones of his mother.

---

5. From Thomas Hardy's "In Time of the 'The Breaking of Nations.' "
6. Town in Massachusetts.
7. Indian god; his cult explores analogies between divine and human love.
8. From Wallace Stevens's "The Paltry Nude Starts on a Spring Voyage." The next line refers to the elephant-headed Hindu god Ganesh.

"As you sit here by me, you're just like my mother,"
she tells me. I imagine her: a bride in Kashmir,   50
she's watching, at the Regal, her first film with Father.
If only I could gather you in my arms, Mother,
I'd save you—now my daughter—from God. The universe
opens its ledger. I write: How helpless was God's mother!
Each page is turned to enter grief's accounts. Mother,   55
I see a hand. *Tell me it's not God's.* Let it die.
I see it. It's filling with diamonds. Please let it die.
Are you somewhere alive, somewhere alive, Mother?
Do you hear what I once held back: in one elephant's
cry, by his mother's bones, the cries of those elephants   60

that stunned the abyss? Ivory blots out the elephants.
I enter this: *The Belovéd leaves one behind to die.*
For compared to my grief for you, what are those of Kashmir,
and what (I close the ledger) are the griefs of the universe
when I remember you—beyond all accounting—O my mother?   65

2001

JAMES FENTON
b. 1949

Although James Fenton gave the Martian poets their name, on the basis of a poem by Craig Raine, and was considered a central member of that movement, he strikes a note of his own. His experiences as a journalist in Southeast Asia and in Germany have provided him with a first-hand understanding of suffering. He feels particularly for those people, especially children, whom "geography condemns to war" ("Children in Exile"). In "A German Requiem," a series of negative images sparsely recalls widescale destruction. The simplicity of grief is heightened by sardonic details, such as "Professor Sargnagel was buried with four degrees, two associate memberships." Fenton is at his best in confronting horror with humor, not to mitigate but to enhance it. His title "Dead Soldiers" refers to both consumed bottles of Napoleon brandy and actual dead men; in the poem, the wild party at the beginning gives way to the barbarous civil war at the end. The jocularity heightens the pity.

Fenton has written few poems and reprinted even fewer; those that survive his winnowing are strong and individual. Suffering appears to be immemorial; no wonder he finds the Deity, in "God, a Poem," anything but beneficent. Yet if Fenton has no confidence in redemption, he has some trust in human wit and fantasy. Like W. H. Auden, his major precursor, Fenton adapts a variety of poetic forms and ranges tonally from light humor and satire to the didactic, the sardonic, and the elegiac. His use of rhetorical and sonic repetition is especially effective, whether for mocking naive belief or, in poems such as "For Andrew Wood" and "A German Requiem," for mourning the dead.

Fenton was born on April 25, 1949, in Lincoln, England. He was educated at Oxford University and won the Newdigate Prize for poetry there. In the 1970s, he wrote for the *New Statesman* and the *Guardian*, working abroad as well as in London. He has been a principal reviewer of books for the *Sunday Times* and the *New York Review of Books*. He has written about theater and art as well as poetry.

A German Requiem[1]

(To T. J. G.-A.)

> For as at a great distance of place, that which wee look at, appears
> dimme, and without distinction of the smaller parts; and as Voyces
> grow weak, and inarticulate: so also after great distance of time,
> our imagination of the Past is weak; and wee lose (for example) of
> Cities wee have seen, many particular Streets; and of Actions, many
> particular Circumstances. This *decaying sense,* when wee would
> express the thing it self, (I mean *fancy* it selfe,) wee call *Imagination,*
> as I said before: But when we would express the *decay,* and signifie
> that the Sense is fading, old, and past, it is called Memory. So that
> *Imagination* and *Memory* are but one thing . . .
> —Hobbes, *Leviathan*[2]

It is not what they built. It is what they knocked down.
It is not the houses. It is the spaces between the houses.
It is not the streets that exist. It is the streets that no longer exist.
It is not your memories which haunt you.
It is not what you have written down. 5
It is what you have forgotten, what you must forget.
What you must go on forgetting all your life.
And with any luck oblivion should discover a ritual.
You will find out that you are not alone in the enterprise.
Yesterday the very furniture seemed to reproach you. 10
Today you take your place in the Widow's Shuttle.[3]

·

The bus is waiting at the southern gate
To take you to the city of your ancestors
Which stands on the hill opposite, with gleaming pediments,[4]
As vivid as this charming square, your home. 15
Are you shy? You should be. It is almost like a wedding,
The way you clasp your flowers and give a little tug at your veil. Oh,
The hideous bridesmaids, it is natural that you should resent them
Just a little, on this first day.
But that will pass, and the cemetery is not far. 20
Here comes the driver, flicking a toothpick into the gutter,
His tongue still searching between his teeth.
See, he has not noticed you. No one has noticed you.
It will pass, young lady, it will pass.

·

How comforting it is, once or twice a year, 25
To get together and forget the old times.
As on those special days, ladies and gentlemen,
When the boiled shirts[5] gather at the graveside

---

1. Mass or chant for the dead. Also, the title of a
requiem by the German composer Johannes
Brahms (1833–1897).
2. *Leviathan, or the Matter, Form, and Power of a
Commonwealth, Ecclesiastical and Civil* (1651), by
the English philosopher Thomas Hobbes (1588–
1679).
3. Popular name for bus going to cemetery.
4. Triangular shapes above doors or windows.
5. (Men wearing) dress shirts with starched fronts.

And a leering waistcoat approaches the rostrum.
It is like a solemn pact between the survivors.   30
The mayor has signed it on behalf of the freemasonry.[6]
The priest has sealed it on behalf of all the rest.
Nothing more need be said, and it is better that way—

                                        •

The better for the widow, that she should not live in fear of surprise,
The better for the young man, that he should move at liberty between   35
      the armchairs,
The better that these bent figures who flutter among the graves
Tending the nightlights and replacing the chrysanthemums
Are not ghosts,
That they shall go home.
The bus is waiting, and on the upper terraces   40
The workmen are dismantling the houses of the dead.

                                        •

But when so many had died, so many and at such speed,
There were no cities waiting for the victims.
They unscrewed the name-plates from the shattered doorways
And carried them away with the coffins.   45
So the squares and parks were filled with the eloquence of young
      cemeteries:
The smell of fresh earth, the improvised crosses
And all the impossible directions in brass and enamel.

                                        •

'Doctor Gliedschirm, skin specialist, surgeries 14–16 hours or by
      appointment.'
Professor Sargnagel was buried with four degrees, two associate   50
      memberships
And instructions to tradesmen to use the back entrance.
Your uncle's grave informed you that he lived on the third floor, left.
You were asked please to ring, and he would come down in the lift[7]
To which one needed a key . . .

                                        •

Would come down, would ever come down   55
With a smile like thin gruel, and never too much to say.
How he shrank through the years.
How you towered over him in the narrow cage.[8]
How he shrinks now . . .

                                        •

But come. Grief must have its term? Guilt too, then.   60
And it seems there is no limit to the resourcefulness of recollection.
So that a man might say and think:
When the world was at its darkest,

---

6. Secret society for mutual help, called Free and   7. Elevator (British usage).
Accepted Order of Masons.   8. Of the wire-screened elevator.

When the black wings passed over the rooftops[9]
(And who can divine His purposes?) even then   65
There was always, always a fire in this hearth.
You see this cupboard? A priest-hole![1]
And in that lumber-room whole generations have been housed and fed.
Oh, if I were to begin, if I were to begin to tell you
The half, the quarter, a mere smattering of what we went through!   70

•

His wife nods, and a secret smile,
Like a breeze with enough strength to carry one dry leaf
Over two pavingstones, passes from chair to chair.
Even the enquirer is charmed.
He forgets to pursue the point.   75
It is not what he wants to know.
It is what he wants not to know.
It is not what they say.
It is what they do not say.

                                                                1981

Dead Soldiers

When His Excellency Prince Norodom Chantaraingsey[2]
Invited me to lunch on the battlefield
I was glad of my white suit for the first time that day.
They lived well, the mad Norodoms, they had style.
The brandy and the soda arrived in crates.   5
Bricks of ice, tied around with raffia,[3]
Dripped from the orderlies' handlebars.

And I remember the dazzling tablecloth
As the APCs[4] fanned out along the road,
The dishes piled high with frogs' legs,
Pregnant turtles, their eggs boiled in the carapace,   10
Marsh irises in fish sauce
And inflorescence[5] of a banana salad.

On every bottle, Napoleon Bonaparte
Pleaded for the authenticity of the spirit.
They called the empties Dead Soldiers   15
And rejoiced to see them pile up at our feet.

Each diner was attended by one of the other ranks
Whirling a table-napkin to keep off the flies.

---

9. Cf. Exodus 12.27: "It is the sacrifice of the Lord's passover, who passed over the houses of the children of Israel in Egypt, when he smote the Egyptians, and delivered our houses."
1. Originally, a hiding place for a Roman Catholic priest during periods of persecution.
2. Uncle of Prince Norodom Sihanouk, former ruler of Cambodia. Fenton was a war correspondent in Vietnam and Cambodia.
3. Palm fibers.
4. Armored personnel carriers.
5. That is, cluster (of bananas in salad). *Carapace:* shell. *Marsh irises:* that is, water plants.

It was like eating between rows of morris[6] dancers— 20
Only they didn't kick.

On my left sat the prince;
On my right, his drunken aide.
The frogs' thighs leapt into the sad purple face
Like fish to the sound of a Chinese flute. 25
I wanted to talk to the prince. I wish now
I had collared his aide, who was Saloth Sar's brother.
We treated him as the club bore. He was always
Boasting of his connections, boasting with a head-shake
Or by pronouncing of some doubtful phrase. 30
And well might he boast. Saloth Sar, for instance,
Was Pol Pot's[7] real name. The APCs
Fired into the sugar palms but met no resistance.

In a diary, I refer to Pol Pot's brother as the Jockey Cap.
A few weeks later, I find him 'in good form 35
And very skeptical about Chantaraingsey.'
'But one eats well there,' I remark.
'So one should,' says the Jockey Cap:
'The tiger always eats well,
It eats the raw flesh of the deer, 40
And Chantaraingsey was born in the year of the tiger.
So, did they show you the things they do
With the young refugee girls?'

And he tells me how he will one day give me the gen.[8]
He will tell me how the prince financed the casino 45
And how the casino brought Lon Nol[9] to power.
He will tell me this.
He will tell me all these things.
All I must do is drink and listen.

In those days, I thought that when the game was up 50
The prince would be far, far away—
In a limestone faubourg, on the promenade at Nice,[1]
Reduced in circumstances but well enough provided for.
In Paris, he would hardly require his private army.
The Jockey Cap might suffice for café warfare, 55
And matchboxes for APCs.

But we were always wrong in these predictions.
It was a family war. Whatever happened,
The principals were obliged to attend its issue.

---

6. Vigorous English folk dance.
7. Leader of Cambodian Communist guerilla force Khmer Rouge, who in 1976 ousted Lon Nol (line 46, note 9), proclaimed the new state of Kampuchea, and instituted a reign of terror.
8. General information (British slang).

9. Corrupt military leader of Cambodia, who in 1970 overthrew the government of Prince Norodom Sihanouk.
1. French resort city on the Mediterranean. *Faubourg*: suburb of a French city.

A few were cajoled into leaving, a few were expelled,   60
And there were villains enough, but none of them
Slipped away with the swag.

For the prince was fighting Sihanouk, his nephew,
And the Jockey Cap was ranged against his brother
Of whom I remember nothing more   65
Than an obscure reputation for virtue.
I have been told that the prince is still fighting
Somewhere in the Cardamoms or the Elephant Mountains.
But I doubt that the Jockey Cap would have survived his good
     connections.
I think the lunches would have done for him—   70
Either the lunches or the dead soldiers.

                                                     1981

God, a Poem

A nasty surprise in a sandwich,
A drawing-pin caught in your sock,
The limpest of shakes from a hand which
You'd thought would be firm as a rock,

A serious mistake in a nightie,   5
A grave disappointment all round
Is all that you'll get from th'Almighty,
Is all that you'll get underground.

Oh he *said:* 'If you lay off the crumpet
I'll see you alright[2] in the end.   10
Just hang on until the last trumpet.[3]
Have faith in me, chum—I'm your friend.'

But if you remind him, he'll tell you:
'I'm sorry, I must have been pissed[4]—
Though your name rings a sort of a bell. You   15
Should have guessed that I do not exist.

'I didn't exist at Creation,
I didn't exist at the Flood,
And I won't be around for Salvation
To sort out the sheep from the cud—   20

'Or whatever the phrase is. The fact is
In soteriological[5] terms

2. That is, I'll take care of you (British). *Crumpet:*   4. Drunk (British slang).
here, British for girls.   5. Concerning salvation.
3. That is, Judgment Day.

I'm a crude existential malpractice
And you are a diet of worms.[6]

'You're a nasty surprise in a sandwich.   25
You're a drawing-pin caught in my sock.
You're the limpest of shakes from a hand which
I'd have thought would be firm as a rock,

'You're a serious mistake in a nightie,
You're a grave disappointment all round—   30
That's all that you are,' says th'Almighty,
'And that's all that you'll be underground.'

                                                          1983

For Andrew Wood

What would the dead want from us
Watching from their cave?
Would they have us forever howling?
Would they have us rave
Or disfigure ourselves, or be strangled   5
Like some ancient emperor's slave?[7]

None of my dead friends were emperors
With such exorbitant tastes
And none of them were so vengeful
As to have all their friends waste   10
Waste quite away in sorrow
Disfigured and defaced.

I think the dead would want us
To weep for what *they* have lost.
I think that our luck in continuing   15
Is what would affect them most.
But time would find them generous
And less self-engrossed.

And time would find them generous
As they used to be   20
And what else would they want from us
But an honoured place in our memory,
A favourite room, a hallowed chair,
Privilege and celebrity?

---

6. (1) Food for worms (after death); (2) confer-
ence (or "Diet") held at Worms, Germany, in 1521,
to dissuade Martin Luther from his agitations for
reform. *Existential malpractice:* that is, empirical
mistake.
7. In ancient Babylonian and Sumerian civiliza-
tions, servants were killed and buried with their
rulers to serve them in the afterlife.

And so the dead might cease to grieve   25
And we might make amends
And there might be a pact between
Dead friends and living friends.
What our dead friends would want from us
Would be such living friends.   30

1993

GRACE NICHOLS
b. 1950

Grace Nichols is, along with poets such as Linton Kwesi Johnson, David Dabydeen, and Fred D'Aguiar, one of the foremost "black British" poets. She was born on January 18, 1950, in Guyana, then a British colony. Educated in the English literary tradition, she became a freelance journalist after receiving a diploma in communications from the University of Guyana. In 1977, she and her companion, the poet John Agard, left Guyana for England.

As "a Caribbean person," Nichols emphasizes that "the Caribbean embraces so much": "The mixture of races and cultures, American-Indian, Asian, European, African. If you are Caribbean, you are a citizen of the world" (*Guardian*, 1991). The geographical vectors of Nichols's poetry point in multiple directions: Africa is "a kind of spiritual homeland" that she imaginatively reclaims; the Caribbean is a much-missed topography of vibrant color, heat, and lush vegetation; and chilly, gray, rain-spattered England is her current home. But Nichols is not only nostalgic; sometimes she celebrates, like Louise Bennett, the reverse colonization of England. In the poem "Wherever I Hang," she ironically inverts the schizophrenic agonies of Derek Walcott's early poetry and the agonized homelessness of Kamau Brathwaite's: "Yes, divided to de ocean / Divided to de bone // Wherever I hang me knickers—that's my home."

Culturally mixed, Nichols writes poetry that is also melded linguistically. Her enslaved ancestors were transported from African to the West Indies, she remembers in "Epilogue," and there a new tongue grew "from the root of the old one." The mixture of English with African and European languages became the Creole—"vibrant, exciting and alive"—that is often the medium of her poetry, as it is for such West Indian poets as Bennett and Brathwaite (*Guardian*, 1991). Like her Afro-Caribbean contemporary Lorna Goodison, Nichols writes in a language that moves across varieties of English: "I myself like working in both standard English and Creole, and tend to want to fuse the two tongues because I come from a background where the two were constantly interacting" ("The Battle with Language"). Celebrating the once despised Creole, Nichols likewise revalorizes the black female body. In *The Fat Black Woman's Poems* (1984) and elsewhere, she appropriates and reverses negative cultural and gender stereotypes, affirming, with infectious glee and sass, the "fat black woman's" size and erotic energy. "Poetry thankfully is a radical synthesizing force," she has written. "The erotic isn't separated from the political or spiritual" ("Battle").

Epilogue

I have crossed an ocean
I have lost my tongue
from the root of the old one
a new one has sprung

1983, 1984

Invitation

1

If my fat
was too much for me
I would have told you
I would have lost a stone[1]
or two   5

I would have gone jogging
even when it was fogging
I would have weighed in
sitting the bathroom scale
with my tail tucked in   10

I would have dieted
more care than a diabetic

But as it is
I'm feeling fine
feel no need   15
to change my lines
when I move I'm target light

Come up and see me sometime[2]

2

Come up and see me sometime
Come up and see me sometime   20

My breasts are huge exciting
amnions[3] of watermelon
          your hands can't cup

---

1. British term of weight, equivalent to fourteen pounds.
2. A line attributed to Mae West (1893–1980), bawdy, wisecracking American actor.
3. Membranes enclosing sacs.

my thighs are twin seals
                    fat slick pups   25
there's a purple cherry
below the blues
                    of my black seabelly
there's a mole that gets a ride
each time I shift the heritage   30
of my behind

Come up and see me sometime

                                                            1984

Tropical Death

The fat black woman want
a brilliant tropical death
not a cold sojourn
in some North Europe far/forlorn

The fat black woman want   5
some heat/hibiscus at her feet
blue sea dress
to wrap her neat

The fat black woman want
some bawl   10
no quiet jerk tear wiping
a polite hearse withdrawal

The fat black woman want
all her dead rights
first night   15
third night
nine night
all the sleepless droning
red-eyed wake nights

In the heart   20
of her mother's sweetbreast
In the shade
of the sun leaf's cool bless
In the bloom
of her people's bloodrest   25

the fat black woman want
a brilliant tropical death yes

                                                            1984

Wherever I Hang

I leave me people, me land, me home
For reasons, I not too sure
I forsake de sun
And de humming-bird splendour
Had big rats in de floorboard   5
So I pick up me new-world-self
And come, to this place call England
At first I feeling like I in dream—
De misty greyness
I touching de walls to see if they real   10
They solid to de seam
And de people pouring from de underground system
Like beans
And when I look up to de sky
I see Lord Nelson[4] high—too high to lie   15

And is so I sending home photos of myself
Among de pigeons and de snow
and is so I warding off de cold
And is so, little by little
I begin to change my calypso ways   20
Never visiting nobody
Before giving them clear warning
And waiting me turn in queue[5]
Now, after all this time
I get accustom to de English life   25
But I still miss back-home side
To tell you de truth
I don't know really where I belaang

     Yes, divided to de ocean
     Divided to de bone   30

Wherever I hang me knickers—that's my home.

1989

---

4. British naval hero (1758–1805), whose statue is atop a tall column in Trafalgar Square, London. There are also many monuments to him in the Caribbean, where he spent much of his career.
5. Line.

CHARLES BERNSTEIN
b. 1950

Charles Bernstein was born on April 4, 1950, in New York City, his father the head of a dressmaking company. From 1968 to 1972, he attended Harvard University, where he studied philosophy and was active in the antiwar movement. After college, while producing and promoting experimental writing, he worked, for nearly twenty years, as a commercial writer and editor for the healthcare industry. In 1978, together with Bruce Andrews, he founded $L=A=N=G=U=A=G=E$ magazine, the name of which became associated with a now-famous group of avant-garde writers. Leftist in politics and post-structuralist in theoretical outlook, the Language poets foregrounded the materiality and constitutive power of language. They extended and radicalized the language-centered poetics of the modernists Gertrude Stein and James Joyce, the Objectivists Louis Zukofsky and Charles Reznikoff, and the New York school of John Ashbery and Frank O'Hara. After teaching at several universities, Bernstein was appointed in 1990 the David Gray Professor of Poetry and Letters at the State University of New York at Buffalo, where he has been a central organizer, proponent, and catalyst for avant-garde poetry in the United States.

In his critical prose and his poetry, Bernstein states unambiguously what he is against. He is a fierce—if tongue-in-cheek—opponent of what he debunks as "official verse culture." In his view, the leading poetry publishers, reviewers, institutions, and M.F.A. programs sanction poetry of, as he put it in 1983, "restricted vocabulary, neutral and univocal tone in the guise of voice or persona, grammar-book syntax, received conceits, static and unitary form." Despite its pretense of diversity, "mainstream poetry" assumes a restrictive norm in which a single voice expresses personal feeling. Bernstein proposes instead a poetry of multiple voices and discourses, ruptured grammar and syntax, and blurred generic boundaries. He aims not for a completely abstract or nonreferential language but for what he called in a 1999 interview "polyreferential" language, "in that the poems do not necessarily mean one fixed, definable, paraphrasable thing" (see also the essay "Semblance"). In lieu of appealing to personal or divine authority to ground the meaning of his texts, he riotously plays with the textures and structures of language that create meaning. "Against the priestly function of the poet or of poetry," he writes, "I propose the comic and bathetic, the awkward and railing: to be grounded horizontally in the social and not vertically in the ethers" ("Poetry and/or the Sacred").

Aware of their textual reality, many of Bernstein's poems offer—directly or obliquely—an imbedded self-description, or *ars poetica*. In a poem humorously cast in the fourteen-line sonnet form, "The Kiwi Bird in the Kiwi Tree," he writes, "I want no paradise," such as that of normative lyric transcendence, "only to be / drenched in the downpour of words, fecund / with tropicality." His joyfully irreverent poems are drenched in different kinds of words taken from a variety of contexts. Like a frenetic ventriloquist or stand-up comic, he forces together the discourses of TV, movies, business, computers, nursery rhyme, and canonical literature. The incongruities of this verbal collage defamiliarize and satirize each dialect. As the rhetorical posture of the poetry continually shifts, clichés, imperatives, near-proverbs, witty epigrams, and jingles jostle side by side. Although Bernstein seeks to avoid the grace and mellifluousness of traditional lyric, he insistently rhymes, chimes, puns, and otherwise plays on verbal euphonies. Hoping to resist the easy absorption or commodification of language, he writes a difficult, recalcitrant poetry not of grace, clarity, and self-expression but of—as he told an interviewer in 1999—"confusion, anger, ambiguity, distress, fumbling, awkwardness."

Autonomy Is Jeopardy

I hate artifice. All these
contraptions so many barriers
against what otherwise can't
be contested, so much seeming
sameness in a jello of   5
squirms. Poetry scares me. I
mean its virtual (or ventriloquized)
anonymity—no protection, no
bulwark to accompany its pervasive
purposivelessness,[1] its accretive   10
acceleration into what may or
may not swell. Eyes demand
counting, the nowhere seen everywhere
behaved voicelessness everyone is clawing
to get a piece of. Shudder   15
all you want it won't
make it come any faster
last any longer: the pump
that cannot be dumped.

                                                                   1990

The Kiwi Bird[2] in the Kiwi Tree

I want no paradise only to be
drenched in the downpour of words, fecund
with tropicality. Fundament be-
yond relation, less 'real' than made, as arms
surround a baby's gurgling: encir-   5
cling mesh pronounces its promise (not bars
that pinion, notes that ply). The tailor tells
of other tolls, the seam that binds, the trim,
the waste. & having spelled these names, move on
to toys or talcums, skates & scores. Only   10
the imaginary is real—not trumps
beclouding the mind's acrobatic vers-
ions. The first fact is the social body,
one from another, nor needs no other.

                                                                   1991

---

1. Translation of German term used by philosopher Immanuel Kant (1724–1804) in defining the nonutility and autonomy of the aesthetic object.
2. Small, flightless bird native to New Zealand.

From The Lives of the Toll Takers

* * *

Our new

service orientation   280

mea

nt

not only changing the way we wrote poems but also diversifying

into new poetry services. Poetic

opportunities   285

,

however, do not fall into your lap, at least not

very often. You've got to seek them out, and when you find them

you've got to have the knowhow to take advantage

of them.   290

Keeping up with the new aesthetic environment is an ongoing

process: you can't stand still. Besides, our current fees

barely cover our expenses; any deviation from these levels

would

mean working for nothing. Poetry services provide cost savings   295

to readers, such

as avoiding hospitalizations (you're less likely

to get in an accident if you're home reading poems), minimizing

wasted time (*condensare*),[3] and reducing

adverse idea interactions   300

---

3. To condense (Latin). For Ezra Pound, condensation was the essence of poetry, as also for later, Objectivist poets Louis Zukofsky and Lorine Niedecker.

(studies show higher levels of resistance to double-bind
political programming among those who read 7.7 poems or
more each week

).

Poets deserve compensation   305

for such services.

For readers unwilling to pay the price

we need to refuse to provide such

service as alliteration,
        internal rhymes,   310
        exogamic[4] structure, and
        unusual vocabulary.

    Sharp edges which become shady groves,

mosaic walkways, emphatic asymptotes[5] (asthmatic microtolls).

The hidden language of the Jews: self-reproach, laden with   315
ambivalence, not this or this either, seeing five sides to
every issue, the old *pilpul*[6] song and dance, obfuscation
clowning as ingratiation, whose only motivation is never
offend, criticize only with a discountable barb: Genocide
is made of words like these, Pound laughing (with Nietzsche's   320
gay laughter) all the way to the canon's bank spewing forth
about the concrete value of gold, the "plain sense of the
word", a people rooted in the land they sow, and cashing
in on such verbal usury (language held hostage: year one
thousand nine hundred eighty seven).[7]   325

    There is no plain sense of the word,

nothing is straightforward,

        description a lie behind a lie:

    but truths can still be told.

---

4. Literally, having to do with intertribal or inter-group marriage.
5. Geometric curves.
6. From the Hebrew for pepper; a method of Talmudic study based on comparing opposing arguments.
7. Ezra Pound (1885–1972), poet, anti-Semite, and supporter of Italian Fascism, believed usury was corrupting and destroying modern civilization (cf. Canto 45). In a wartime radio broadcast from Fascist Italy on April 20, 1943, he reaffirmed the Imagist principle of "the plain sense of the word," amid attacks on capitalism, communism, Jews, British prime minister Winston Churchill, and so forth. *Nietzsche:* Friedrich Nietzsche (1844–1900), German philosopher, who in his book *The Gay Science* (1882) proposed an alliance of laughter and wisdom. The Nazis appropriated his ideas for their Fascist program.

These are the sounds of science (whoosh, blat, 330
flipahineyhoo), brought to
you by DuPont,[8] *a broadly diversified company dedicated to*
exploitation through science and industry.

Take this harrow off

my chest, I don't feel it anymore 335

it's getting stark, too stark

to see, feel I'm barking at Hell's spores.[9]

The new sentience.[1]

As if Harvard Law School

was not a re-education camp. 340

I had decided to go back

to school after fifteen years in

community poetry because I felt

I did not know enough to navigate

through the rocky waters that 345

lie ahead for all of us in this field.

How had Homer done it, what might Milton

teach? Business training turned

out to be just what I most needed.

Most importantly, I learned that 350

for a business to be successful, it

needs to be different, to stand out

from the competition. In poetry,

---

8. Chemical company. *The sounds of science*: allusion to "The Sound of Silence," a 1965 song by folk-rock musicians Paul Simon and Art Garfunkel.
9. Cf. the first verse of "Knockin' on Heaven's Door," by the American singer-songwriter Bob Dylan (b. 1941): "Mama, take this badge off of me / I can't use it anymore. / It's gettin' dark, too dark for me to see / I feel like I'm knockin' on heaven's door."
1. Pun on fellow Language poet Ron Silliman's concept of "The New Sentence," the building block of a disjunctive, avant-garde poetics.

this differentiation is best

achieved through the kind of form   355

we present.

Seduced by its own critique, the heady operative with twin
peaks and a nose for a brain, remodeled the envelope she
was pushing only to find there was nobody home and no
time when they were expected. Water in the brain,   360
telescopic Malthusian[2] dumbwaiter, what time will the train
arrive?, I feel weird but then I'm on assignment, a plain blue
wrapper with the taps torn, sultan of my erogenous bull's
eyes, nothing gratis except the tall tales of the Mughali
terraces, decked like plates into the Orangerie's[3] glacial   365
presentiment . . .

    No,

only that the distinction

    between nature and

        culture may obs   370

            cure

the

    b

      odily

gumption of language.   375

*   *   *

1994

Have Pen, Will Travel

It's not my

business to describe

anything. The only

report is the

---

2. Thomas Robert Malthus (1766–1857), English
economist who warned of unchecked population
growth.

3. Museum in Paris. *Mughali*: referring to the
Mughal Empire in India (1526–1857), known for
its opulence.

discharge of   5

words called

to account for

their slurs.

A seance of sorts—

or transport into   10

that nether that

refuses measure.

1995

CAROLYN FORCHÉ
b. 1950

A quotation from Stéphane Mallarmé serves as an epigraph for Carolyn Forché's "Reunion": "Just as he changes himself, in the end eternity changes him." The remark could be a motto for most of her poems. She has cultivated a sense of the past, her own past that has been increasingly impinged on by the forces of power and cruelty that rule much of the world and by the speechless victims of these forces. In "Taking Off My Clothes," exemplary of her poetry of psychological and sexual experience, the poet discovers that her relationship with her male lover is essentially false and conveys this lack in dry, clipped declarative sentences. In "Reunion," by contrast, the poet remembers an early lover from whom she learned "how much tenderness we could / wedge between a stairwell/ and a police lock." But Forché is best known for the poetry that came out of her work as a human rights advocate and journalist in Central America, writing that bridges the distance between verse and journalism, lyric and politics. These poems, perhaps the most gruesome and memorable of which is the prose poem "The Colonel," render vividly the suffering and humiliation of the people of El Salvador. They show a powerful sympathetic identification and sometimes a poignant humor. "The Memory of Elena," another of Forché's best-known poems, is at once delicate and horrifying. The voice is that of the poet, who, by her friendship with an Argentinian woman, participates in the historic cruelty that has been visited on that country. Eating becomes a kind of cannibalism, and the flowers on the husband's grave remind Forché of the impotent silence of the victims.

Forché was born on April 28, 1950, in Detroit, Michigan. She was educated at Michigan State University, receiving a B.A. in international relations and creative writing in 1972 (prefiguring her lasting concern with poetry and international politics), and at Bowling Green State University, where she received an M.F.A. in 1975. She has taught creative writing at a variety of colleges and universities, since 1988 at George Mason University. She worked for Amnesty International in El Salvador from 1978 to 1980 and as the Beirut correspondent for National Public Radio's "All Things Considered" in 1983. Her first collection of poems, *Gathering the Tribes* (1976), was chosen for the Yale Series of Younger Poets, and the second, *The Country between Us* (1981), won the Lamont Poetry Selection Award. She has since published translations, volumes of poetry about global atrocities and suffering, and the anthology *Against Forgetting: Twentieth-Century Poetry of Witness* (1993).

Taking Off My Clothes

I take off my shirt, I show you.
I shaved the hair out under my arms.
I roll up my pants, I scraped off the hair
on my legs with a knife, getting white.

My hair is the color of chopped maples.   5
My eyes dark as beans cooked in the south.
(Coal fields in the moon on torn-up hills)

Skin polished as a Ming bowl[1]
showing its blood cracks, its age, I have hundreds
of names for the snow, for this, all of them quiet.   10

In the night I come to you and it seems a shame
to waste my deepest shudders on a wall of a man.

You recognize strangers,
think you lived through destruction.
You can't explain this night, my face, your memory.   15

You want to know what I know?
Your own hands are lying.

1976

The Memory of Elena[2]

We spend our morning
in the flower stalls counting
the dark tongues of bells
that hang from ropes waiting
for the silence of an hour.   5
We find a table, ask for *paella*,[3]
cold soup and wine, where a calm
light trembles years behind us.

---

1. Bowl created during the peak of Chinese ceramic-making.
2. This poem is part of a group titled "In Salvador"; Forché spent some time in the Central American country El Salvador while it was under a military dictatorship.
3. Spanish and Latin American dish containing rice, meat, seafood, and vegetables.

In Buenos Aires[4] only three
years ago, it was the last time his hand   10
slipped into her dress, with pearls
cooling her throat and bells like
these, chipping at the night—

As she talks, the hollow
clopping of a horse, the sound   15
of bones touched together.
The *paella* comes, a bed of rice
and *camarones*,[5] fingers and shells,
the lips of those whose lips
have been removed, mussels   20
the soft blue of a leg socket.

This is not *paella*, this is what
has become of those who remained
in Buenos Aires. This is the ring
of a rifle report on the stones,   25
her hand over her mouth,
her husband falling against her.

These are the flowers we bought
this morning, the dahlias tossed
on his grave and bells   30
waiting with their tongues cut out
for this particular silence.

1977   1981

Reunion

Just as he changes himself, in the end eternity changes him.
—Mallarmé[6]

On the phonograph, the voice
of a woman already dead for three
decades, singing of a man
who could make her do anything.
On the table, two fragile   5
glasses of black wine,
a bottle wrapped in its towel.
It is that room, the one
we took in every city, it is
as I remember: the bed, a block   10
of moonlight and pillows.

4. Capital of Argentina.
5. Shrimp.

6. First line of "Le Tombeau d'Edgar Poe," by
French poet Stéphane Mallarmé (1842–1898).

My fingernails, pecks of light
on your thighs.
The stink of the fire escape.
The wet butts of cigarettes   15
you crushed one after another.
How I watched the morning come
as you slept, more my son
than a man ten years older.
How my breasts feel, years   20
later, the tongues swishing
in my dress, some yours, some
left by other men.
Since then, I have always
wakened first, I have learned   25
to leave a bed without being
seen and have stood
at the washbasins, wiping oil
and salt from my skin,
staring at the cupped water   30
in my two hands.
I have kept everything
you whispered to me then.
I can remember it now as I see you
again, how much tenderness we could   35
wedge between a stairwell
and a police lock,[7] or as it was,
as it still is, in the voice
of a woman singing of a man
who could make her do anything.   40

1981

The Colonel

What you have heard is true. I was in his house. His wife carried a tray
of coffee and sugar. His daughter filed her nails, his son went out for the
night. There were daily papers, pet dogs, a pistol on the cushion beside
him. The moon swung bare on its black cord over the house. On the
television was a cop show. It was in English. Broken bottles were   5
embedded in the walls around the house to scoop the kneecaps from a
man's legs or cut his hands to lace. On the windows there were gratings
like those in liquor stores. We had dinner, rack of lamb, good wine, a gold
bell was on the table for calling the maid. The maid brought green
mangoes, salt, a type of bread. I was asked how I enjoyed the country.   10
There was a brief commercial in Spanish. His wife took everything away.
There was some talk then of how difficult it had become to govern. The
parrot said hello on the terrace. The colonel told it to shut up, and pushed
himself from the table. My friend said to me with his eyes: say nothing.

7. Lock with a heavy iron rod in the floor that prevents an apartment door from being forcibly open-
ed; common in high-crime neighborhoods.

The colonel returned with a sack used to bring groceries home. He spilled 15
many human ears on the table. They were like dried peach halves. There
is no other way to say this. He took one of them in his hands, shook it in
our faces, dropped it into a water glass. It came alive there. I am tired of
fooling around he said. As for the rights of anyone, tell your people they
can go fuck themselves. He swept the ears to the floor with his arm and 20
held the last of his wine in the air. Something for your poetry, no? he said.
Some of the ears on the floor caught this scrap of his voice. Some of the
ears on the floor were pressed to the ground.

May 1978   1981

JORIE GRAHAM
b. 1950

Jorie Graham is a poet of large ideas. Her philosophical bent owes something to her
polyglot background. Born on May 9, 1950, in New York, to an Irish American father
and a Jewish American mother, she grew up with one ear to American speech. Raised
in Italy and attending French schools, she had another ear to European languages and
culture. As a child, Graham "was taught three/names for the tree facing" her window:
"*Castagno . . . Chassagne . . . chestnut*" ("I Was Taught Three"). It was not until this
trilingual poet was in her twenties that, after studying at the Sorbonne in Paris, she
moved to the United States as a film student at New York University—an influence
apparent in the cinematic techniques and rhetoric of her poetry. Seeing the world
through the prism of three languages, Graham early on experienced the relation
between word and world as complex and contingent.

Her European affiliations, her philosophical questioning of the relation between
mind and reality, and her fascination with the visual arts recall her precursors, the
Francophile modernists Wallace Stevens and T. S. Eliot. In an interview with the *Den-
ver Quarterly*, Graham remarked, "I think many poets writing today realize we need to
recover a high level of ambition, a rage, if you will—the big hunger." She is at the
forefront of contemporary poets working to recover this "big hunger," the large philo-
sophical and formal ambition of modernist poetry.

Graham has this hunger, but also distrusts it. She longs for an ethical, philosophical,
or scientific system that would heal the split between thing and representation and also
make sense of our place in the world, of personal experience within the context of
public atrocities—the Holocaust, imperialism, assassination, and so forth. She calls
this, in the title of one of her most ambitious poems, "The Dream of the Unified Field."
She thus compares large events with small, deliberately forces analogies between the
personal and the historical, and braids together intimate disclosure with metaphysics.
She also juxtaposes different modes of representation from art, film, history, and poetry.
Yet Graham fiercely questions her own impulse toward philosophical systematization.
She explodes her analogies as she crafts them. She undermines the myth of continuous
subjectivity even as she relies on personal memory. And she views her own poetic lan-
guage with corrosive suspicion.

Her poems typically take personal moments of crisis or revelation as their points of
departure, such as hearing about the shooting of President Kennedy in a movie theater
or bringing her daughter a leotard. She slows down and reenters the moment to ask
about its meaning in collective history, about the relation between inner experience and

external reality, and about the ethics of representation. The psychic structure of her poetry is daringly associative, leaping from one image to another and thus compelling the reader to puzzle out the resemblances and differences—in "The Dream of the Unified Field," for example, between the mind and a pocket; between starlings, a crow, and a Russian ballet teacher; between the poet's ambitions for her daughter and Columbus's colonization of the New World.

Graham has criticized the generation after the modernists for being limited "by the strictly secular sense of reality (domestic, confessional), as well as their unquestioned relationship to the act of representation." But her own work bears fruitful comparison with that of Robert Lowell, Sylvia Plath, and other "confessionalists," who often examined their personal experience within broader historical and cultural contexts. At the same time, her poetry can also be compared with that of anticonfessional poets, such as Susan Howe, Lyn Hejinian, Michael Palmer, and Charles Bernstein: her poems, too, interrogate subjectivity, resist closure, and fracture time, space, and the speaking voice. Although Graham relies less on pastiche and collage than do these experimentalists, her anxieties about the ethical implications of form—narrative as complicit in imperialism, language as a kind of violence, closure as commodification—dovetail with their concerns.

The texture of Graham's poems has changed dramatically over the course of her career. "At Luca Signorelli's Resurrection of the Body," like many of Graham's early poems an example of *ekphrasis*, a poem about a visual artifact, is written in regular stanzas with alternate lines indented. By the time of "Fission," the indentations remain, but the strophes have become irregular, the lines have lengthened, and ellipses, dashes, and parentheses have fissured the syntax. The stilled, balanced ekphrastic poem has been abandoned for the hurried, disjunctive, jump-cut cinematic poem. She is seeking, as she put it, "new strategies by which to postpone closure," to resist its "suction," new "forms of delay, digression, side-motions." With her book *Materialism* (1993), the spatial organization of the poem on the page becomes still more sprawling, with large blocks of type and more dropped lines, her syntax and semantics become increasingly fragmented, frenzied, and opaque. "For me," Graham says, "each book is a critique of the previous," and so she has challenged herself to begin again with each new volume.

After receiving her M.F.A. in 1978 from the University of Iowa Writers' Workshop, Graham taught briefly at several universities before returning to Iowa, as a teacher, in 1983. In 1999, she succeeded Seamus Heaney as Boylston Professor of Rhetoric and Oratory at Harvard University. She was honored with a MacArthur Fellowship in 1990 and the Pulitzer Prize in 1996 for *The Dream of the Unified Field: Selected Poems, 1974–1994*.

At Luca Signorelli's Resurrection of the Body[1]

> See how they hurry
>   to enter
>   their bodies,
>   these spirits.
> Is it better, flesh,   5
>   that they

1. Renaissance painter Luca Signorelli (c. 1445–1523) was famous for the anatomical precision and musculature of his human figures. The poem considers his *Resurrection of the Body* (c. 1500), part of a series of frescoes in the cathedral at Orvieto, in central Italy.

should hurry so?
From above
the green-winged angels
blare down
trumpets and light. But
they don't care,

they hurry to congregate,
they hurry
into speech, until
it's a marketplace,
it is humanity. But still
we wonder

in the chancel
of the dark cathedral,
is it better, back?
The artist
has tried to make it so: each tendon
they press

to re-enter
is perfect. But is it
perfection
they're after,
pulling themselves up
through the soil

into the weightedness, the color,
into the eye
of the painter? Outside
it is 1500,
all round the cathedral
streets hurry to open

through the wild
silver grasses. . . .
The men and women
on the cathedral wall
do not know how,
having come this far,

to stop their
hurrying. They amble off
in groups, in
couples. Soon
some are clothed, there is
distance, there is

perspective. Standing below them
in the church
in Orvieto, how can we

10

15

20

25

30

35

40

45

50

tell them
to be stern and brazen
and slow,

that there is no   55
entrance,
only entering. They keep on
arriving,
wanting names,
wanting   60

happiness. In his studio
Luca Signorelli
in the name of God
and Science
and the believable   65
broke into the body

studying arrival.
But the wall
of the flesh
opens endlessly,   70
its vanishing point so deep
and receding

we have yet to find it,
to have it
stop us. So he cut   75
deeper,
graduating slowly
from the symbolic

to the beautiful. How far
is true?   80
When his one son
died violently,[2]
he had the body brought to him
and laid it

on the drawing-table,   85
and stood
at a certain distance
awaiting the best
possible light, the best depth
of day,   90

then with beauty and care
and technique

---

2. According to an anecdote recorded by Italian painter and biographer Giorgio Vasari (1511–1574), after Signorelli's son was killed the painter had his body brought to him so that he could study it and preserve it in his drawings.

and judgment, cut into
    shadow, cut
into bone and sinew and every   95
    pocket

in which the cold light
    pooled.
It took him days,
    that deep   100
caress, cutting,
    unfastening,

until his mind
    could climb into
the open flesh and   105
    mend itself.

                1983

Fission

The real electric lights light upon the full-sized
screen
    on which the greater-than-life-size girl appears,
almost nude on the lawn—sprinklers on—
    voice-over her mother calling her name out—loud—[3]   5
camera angle giving her lowered lids their full
    expanse—a desert—as they rise

out of the shabby annihilation,
    out of the possibility of never-having-been-seen,
and rise,
    till the glance is let loose into the auditorium,   10
and the man who has just stopped in his tracks
    looks down
for the first

    time. Tick tock. It's the birth of the mercantile   15
dream (he looks down). It's the birth of
    the dream called
new world (looks down). She lies there. A corridor of light
                filled with dust
flows down from the booth to the screen.   20
Everyone in here wants to be taken off

    somebody's list, wants to be placed on
somebody else's list.

---

3. The scene described is from Stanley Kubrick's 1962 movie *Lolita*, an adaptation of the 1955 novel by Vladimir Nabokov. In the scene, the middle-aged Humbert (James Mason) first sees Lolita (Sue Lyon), the adolescent girl who becomes the object of his obsession.

Tick. It is 1963. The idea of history is being   25
outmaneuvered.
    So that as the houselights come on—midscene—
not quite killing the picture which keeps flowing beneath,

        a man comes running down the aisle
asking for our attention—
        Ladies and Gentlemen.   30
I watch the houselights lap against the other light—the tunnel
        of image-making dots licking the white sheet awake—
a man, a girl, her desperate mother—daisies growing in the
                                        corner—

        I watch the light from our real place   35
suck the arm of screen-building light into itself
        until the gesture of the magic forearm frays,
and the story up there grays, pales—them almost lepers now,
                                        saints, such

white on their flesh in   40
        patches—her thighs like receipts slapped down on a
                                        slim silver tray,

her eyes as she lowers the heart-shaped shades,
        as the glance glides over what used to be the open,
the free,   45
        as the glance moves, pianissimo, over the glint of day,
over the sprinkler, the mother's voice shrieking like a grappling
        hook
the grass blades aflame with being-seen, here on the out-

skirts. . . . You can almost hear the click at the heart of   50
                                        the silence
where the turnstile shuts and he's *in*—our hero—
        the moment spoked,
our gaze on her fifteen-foot eyes,
        the man hoarse now as he waves his arms,   55
as he screams to the booth to cut it, cut the sound,
        and the sound is cut,
and her sun-barred shoulders are left to turn

soundless as they accompany
        her neck, her face, the   60
looking-up.
        Now the theater's skylight is opened and noon slides in.
I watch as it overpowers the electric lights,
        whiting the story out one layer further

till it's just a smoldering of whites   65
        where she sits up, and her stretch of flesh
is just a roiling up of graynesses,
        vague stutterings of
light with motion in them, bits of moving zeros

in the infinite virtuality of light,   70
    some *likeness* in it but not particulate,
a grave of possible shapes called *likeness*—see it?—something
    scrawling up there that could be skin or daylight or even

the expressway now that he's gotten her to leave with him—
    (it happened rather fast) (do you recall)—   75

the man up front screaming the President's been shot,[4] waving
    his hat, slamming one hand flat
over the open
    to somehow get
our attention,   80

in Dallas, behind him the scorcher—whites, grays,
    laying themselves across his face—
him like a beggar in front of us, holding his hat—
    I don't recall what I did,
I don't recall what the right thing to do would be,   85
    I wanted someone to love. . . .

    There is a way she lay down on that lawn
to begin with,
    in the heart of the sprinklers,
before the mother's call,   90
    before the man's shadow laid itself down,

there is a way to not yet be wanted,

    there is a way to lie there at twenty-four frames
per second—no faster—
    not at the speed of plot,   95
not at the speed of desire—
    the road out—expressway—hotels—motels—
no telling what we'll have to see next,
    no telling what all we'll have to want next,
(right past the stunned rows of houses),   100
    no telling what on earth we'll have to marry marry marry. . . .

Where the three lights merged:
    where the image licked my small body from the front, the story
                                                    playing
all over my face my   105
    forwardness,
where the electric lights took up the back and sides,
    the unwavering houselights,
seasonless,

    where the long thin arm of day came in from the top   110
to touch my head,

4. President John F. Kennedy was assassinated in Dallas, Texas, on November 22, 1963.

reaching down along my staring face—
where they flared up around my body unable to

merge into each other
        over my likeness,   115
slamming down one side of me, unquenchable—here static

        there flaming—
sifting grays into other grays—
        mixing the split second into the long haul—
flanking me—undressing something there where my   120
        body is
though not my body—
        where they play on the field of my willingness,

where they kiss and brood, filtering each other to no avail,
        all over my solo   125
appearance,
        bits smoldering under the shadows I make—
and aimlessly—what we call *free*—there

the immobilism sets in,
        the being-in-place more alive than the being,   130
my father sobbing beside me, the man on the stage
        screaming, the woman behind us starting to
pray,
        the immobilism, the being-in-place more alive than

the being,   135
        the squad car now faintly visible on the screen
starting the chase up,
        all over my countenance,
the velvet armrest at my fingers, the dollar bill

in my hand,   140
        choice the thing that wrecks the sensuous here the glorious
                                        here—
that wrecks the beauty,
        choice the move that rips the wrappings of light, the
                        ever-tighter wrappings   145

of the layers of the
        real: what is, what also is, what might be that is,
what could have been that is, what
        might have been that is, what I say that is,
what the words say that is,   150
        what you imagine the words say that is—Don't move, don't

wreck the shroud, don't move—

                                                                1991

The Dream of the Unified Field[5]

1

On my way to bringing you the leotard
you forgot to include in your overnight bag,
the snow started coming down harder.
I watched each gathering of leafy flakes
melt round my footfall.   5
I looked up into it—late afternoon but bright.
Nothing true or false in itself. Just motion. Many strips of
motion. Filaments of falling marked by the tiny certainties
of flakes. Never blurring yet themselves a cloud. Me in it
                and yet   10
moving easily through it, black Lycra leotard balled into
              my pocket,
your tiny dream in it, my left hand on it or in it
          to keep
warm. Praise this. Praise that. Flash a glance up and try   15
         to see
the arabesques and runnels,[6] gathering and loosening, as they
define, as a voice would, the passaging through from
         the-other-than-
human. Gone as they hit the earth. But embellishing.   20
Flourishing. The road with me on it going on through. In-
scribed with the present. As if it really
were possible to exist, and exist, never to be pulled back
in, given and given never to be received. The music
of the footfalls doesn't stop, doesn't   25
mean. *Here are your things*, I said.

2

Starting home I heard—bothering, lifting, then
         bothering again—
the huge flock of starlings massed over our
         neighborhood   30
these days; heard them lift and
swim overhead through the falling snow
as though the austerity of a true, cold thing, a verity,
the black bits of their thousands of bodies swarming
         then settling   35
overhead. I stopped. All up and down the empty oak
they stilled. Every limb sprouting. Every leafy backlit
         body
filling its part of the empty crown. I tried to count—
then tried to estimate—   40
but the leaves of this wet black tree at the heart of
         the storm—shiny—

5. In particle physics, unified field theory repre-
sents an attempt to account for the interaction of
all forces and particles under a single explanatory
framework.

6. Small streams. *Arabesques:* ballet position; also,
flowing lines.

river through limbs, back onto limbs,
scatter, blow away, scatter, recollect—
undoing again and again the tree without it ever ceasing to be   45
                                      full.

Foliage of the tree of the world's waiting.
Of having waited a long time and
                still having
to wait. Of trailing and screaming.   50
Of engulfed readjustments. Of blackness redisappearing
                                  into
downdrafts of snow. Of indifference. Of indifferent
                          reappearings.
                I think of you   55
back of me now in the bright house of
          your friend
twirling in the living room in the shiny leotard
                    you love.
I had looked—as I was leaving—through the window   60

to see you, slick in your magic,
pulling away from the wall—

I watch the head explode then recollect, explode, recollect.

                         3

Then I heard it, inside the swarm, the single cry

of the crow. One syllable—one—inside the screeching and the   65
                                skittering,
inside the constant repatterning of a thing not nervous yet
                        not ever
still—but not uncertain—without obedience
yet not without law—one syllable—   70
black, shiny, twirling on its single stem,
rooting, one foot on the earth,
twisting and twisting—

and then again—a little further off this time—*down the*
ravine, voice inside a head, filling a head. . . .   75

See, my pocket is empty now. I let my hand
open and shut in there. I do it again. Two now, skull and
                           pocket
with their terrified inhabitants.

    You turn the music up. The window nothing to you, liquid, dark,   80
where now your mother has come back to watch.

                         4

Closeup, he's blue—streaked iris blue, india-ink blue—and
black—an oily, fiery set of blacks—none of them

true—as where hate and order touch—something that cannot
become known. Stages of black but without   85
graduation. So there is no direction.
All of this happened, yes. Then disappeared
into the body of the crow, chorus of meanings,
layers of blacks, then just the crow, plain, big,
lifting his claws to walk thrustingly   90
forward and back—indigo, cyanine, beryl, grape, steel. . . . Then suddenly he
wings and—braking as he lifts
the chest in which an eye-sized heart now beats—
—he's up—a blunt clean stroke—
one ink-streak on the early evening snowlit scene—   95
See the gesture of the painter?—Recall the
crow?—Place him quickly on his limb as he comes sheering in,
close to the trunk, to land—Is he now
disappeared again?

5

. . . . *long neck, up, up with the head,*   100
eyes on the fingertips, bent leg, shift of
the weight—*turn*—No, no, begin again . . .
What had she seen, Madame Sakaroff, at Stalingrad,[7] now in
her room of mirrors tapping her cane
as the piano player begins the interrupted Minuet again   105
and we line up right foot extended, right
                        hand extended, the Bach mid-phrase—
Europe? The dream of Europe?—midwinter afternoon,
rain at the windowpane, ceilings at thirty feet and coffered
floating over the wide interior spaces . . .   110
No one must believe in God again I heard her say
one time when I had come to class too soon
and had been sent to change. The visitor had left,
kissing her hand, small bow, and I had seen her (from the curtain)
(having forgotten I was there)   115
turn from the huge pearl-inlaid doors she had just closed,
one hand still on the massive, gold, bird-headed knob,
and see—a hundred feet away—herself—a woman in black in
                        a mirrored room—
saw her not shift her gaze but bring her pallid tensile hand—   120
as if it were not part of her—slowly down from
the ridged, cold, feathered knob and, recollected, fixed upon
                        that other woman, emigrée,
begin to move in stiffly towards her . . . You out there
                        now,   125
you in here with me—I watched the two of them,
black and black, in the gigantic light,
glide at each other, heads raised, necks long—
me wanting to cry out—where were the others?—wasn't it late?
the two of her like huge black hands—   130
clap once and once only and the signal is given—

7. Former name of Volgograd, city in southwestern Russia.

but to what?—regarding what?—till closer-in I saw
                    more suddenly
how her eyes eyed themselves: no wavering:
like a vast silver page burning: the black hole   135
                expanding:
like a meaning coming up quick from inside that page—
coming up quick to seize the reading face—
each face wanting the other to *take* it—
but where? and *from* where?—I was eight—   140
I saw the different weights of things,
saw the vivid performance of the present,
saw the light rippling almost shuddering where her body finally
                    touched
the image, the silver film between them like something that would have 145
                shed itself in nature now
but wouldn't, couldn't, here, on tight,
between, not thinning, not slipping off to let some
                  seed-down[8]
through, no signal in it, no information . . . Child,   150
              what should I know
to save you that I do not know, hands on this windowpane?—

6

The storm: I close my eyes and,
standing in it, try to make it *mine*. An inside
thing. Once I was. . . . once, once.   155
It settles, in my head, the wavering white
sleep, the instances—they stick, accrue,
grip up, connect, they do not melt,
I will not let them melt, they build, cloud and cloud,
I feel myself weak, I feel the thinking muscle-up—   160
outside, the talk-talk of the birds—outside,
strings and their roots, leaves inside the limbs,
in some spots the skin breaking—
but inside, no more exploding, no more smoldering, no more,
inside, a splinter colony, new world, possession   165
gripping down to form,
wilderness brought deep into my clearing,
out of the ooze of night,
limbed, shouldered, necked, visaged, the white—
now the clouds coming in (don't look up),   170
now the Age behind the clouds, The Great Heights,
all in there, reclining, eyes closed, huge,
centuries and centuries long and wide,
and underneath, barely attached but attached,
like a runner, my body, my tiny piece of   175
the century—minutes, houses going by—The Great
                Heights—
anchored by these footsteps, now and now,

---

8. The soft hairs on seeds, such as cotton.

the footstepping—now and now—carrying its vast
white sleeping geography—mapped—   180
not a lease—*possession*—"At the hour of vespers
in a sudden blinding snow,
they entered the harbor and he named it Puerto de

7

San Nicolas[9] and at its entrance he imagined he
                         could see   185
its beauty and goodness, *sand right up to the land
where you can put the side of a ship.* He thought
                     he saw
Indians fleeing through the white before
the ship . . . As for him, he did not believe what his   190
                          crew
told him, nor did he understand them well, nor they
him. In the white swirl, he placed a large cross
                 at the western side of
the harbor, on a conspicuous height,   195
as a sign that Your Highness claim the land as
Your own. After the cross was set up,
three sailors went into the bush (immediately erased
from sight by the fast snow) to see what kinds of
trees. They captured three very black Indian   200
women—one who was young and pretty.
The Admiral ordered her clothed and returned to
                          her land
courteously. There her people told
that she had not wanted to leave the ship,   205
but wished to stay on it. The snow was wild.
Inside it, though, you could see
this woman was wearing a little piece of
gold on her nose, which was a sign there was
                          gold   210
on that land"—

1993

The Surface

It has a hole in it. Not only where I
                 concentrate.
The river still ribboning, twisting up,
            into its re-
arrangements, chill enlightenments, tight-knotted   5
                 quickenings

---

9. The quotation is adapted from the diary of
Christopher Columbus's first voyage to the New
World. Graham adds to the passage the snow
and the adjective "black" describing the Indian
women.

and loosenings—whispered messages dissolving
                    the messengers—
the river still glinting-up into its handfuls, heapings,
                              glassy   10
forgettings under the river of
my attention—
and the river of my attention laying itself down—
                         bending,
reassembling—over the quick leaving-offs and windy   15
                         obstacles—
and the surface rippling under the wind's attention—
rippling over the accumulations, the slowed-down drifting
                         permanences
of the cold   20
bed.
I say *iridescent* and I look down.
The leaves very still as they are carried.

                                                            1993

The Swarm

(Todi,[1] 1996)

I wanted you to listen to the bells,
holding the phone out the one small window
to where I thought
the ringing was—

Vespers[2] scavenging the evening air,   5
headset fisted against the huge dissolving

where I stare at the tiny holes in the receiver's transatlantic opening
to see evening-light and then churchbells

send their regrets, slithering, in—
in there a white flame charged with duplication—.   10
I had you try to listen, bending down into the mouthpiece to whisper,
     hard,

can you hear them (two petals fall and then the   is wholly
changed) (yes) (and then another yes like a vertebrate enchaining)
yes yes yes yes

We were somebody. A boat stills on a harbor and for a while no one   15
appears,
not on deck, not on shore,
only a few birds glancing round,

1. Town in central Italy.
2. Bells rung at the hour of the Roman Catholic evening prayers.

then—before a single face appears—something
          announces itself   20
like a piece of the whole blueness broken off and thrown down,
a roughness inserted,

yes,
the infinite variety of *having once been,*
of being, of *coming to life,* right there in the thin air, a debris re-   25
assembling, a blue transparent bit of paper flapping in also-blue air,

boundaries being squeezed out of the blue, out of the inside of the blue,
human eyes
held shut,

and then the whisking-open of the lash—the *be thou, be thou*—   30

—*a boat stills in a harbor and for a while no one*
appears—a sunny day, a crisp Aegean blue,
easy things—a keel, a sail—

why should you fear?—
me holding my arm out into the crisp December air—   35
beige cord and then the plastic parenthetical opening wherein I

have you—you without eyes or arms or body now—listen to

the long ocean between us

—the plastic cooling now—this tiny geometric swarm of
openings sending to you   40

no parts of me you've touched, no places where you've

gone—

Two petals fall—hear it?—moon, are you not coming soon?—two fall

             2000

ANNE CARSON
b. 1950

In much of her poetry, Anne Carson evocatively juxtaposes the modern and the classical, the personal and the literary. She writes about recent love relationships, contemporary video and TV, twentieth-century writers such as Virginia Woolf, Antonin Artaud, and Sylvia Plath. But she sandwiches these references with older texts, whether writings by the Brontë sisters ("The Glass Essay"), stories from the Bible ("Lazarus Standup: Shoot-ing Script"), or ancient Greek poetry by Homer, Sappho, and Stesichorus.

    Like the incongruous equations in metaphor, these rich connections make the familiar strange. As Carson writes: "metaphor causes the mind to experience itself // in the act of making a mistake"; but "from the true mistakes of metaphor a lesson can be learned. . . . / Metaphors teach the mind // to enjoy error / and to learn / from the juxtaposition of *what is* and *what is not* the case" ("Essay on What I Think about Most"). Spanning vast distances in time and space, Carson's poetry shimmers in the gap between her own emotional life and the rediscovered past, between the contemporary media and ancient forms. She renews the modernist promise to "make it new," in Ezra Pound's slogan, by rereading the contemporary in the light of the classical and vice versa.

Formally inventive, Carson braids together the ruminative texture of the essay, the narrative propulsion of the novel, the self-analysis of autobiography, and the lapidary compression of lyric. In "The Glass Essay," she vividly describes the end of a love affair with a man named Law, a visit with a difficult mother, the degeneration of a father with Alzheimer's in a nursing home, and walks on a bleak Canadian moor. Into this semiautobiographical mix, she weaves commentary on the writings of the Brontë sisters, whose works function—like the classical texts she often incorporates into her poetry—as oblique and remote points of comparison for the poet's personal experience.

Carson casts the net of her poetry around philosophical speculation, epigrammatic insight, personal drama, and literary-critical analysis. Tightly wound with crisp diction, studded with striking metaphors, her poems are lucid in feeling and intense in thought. They are at one and the same time intellectually crystalline and emotionally volcanic.

Carson was born on June 21, 1950, in Toronto, Canada, and grew up in Ontario. From the University of Toronto she received both her B.A. (1974) and her Ph.D. (1981). The recipient of a MacArthur Fellowship in 2000, she teaches classics at McGill University, in Montreal, and earlier held positions at the University of Calgary (1979), Princeton University (1980–87), and Emory University (1987). Along with lyric poetry, she has published books of criticism on classical literature, books that include both poetry and criticism, and a novel-in-verse, *Autobiography of Red* (1998).

From The Glass Essay

*   *   *

Well there are many ways of being held prisoner,
I am thinking as I stride over the moor.   160
As a rule after lunch mother has a nap

and I go out to walk.
The bare blue trees and bleached wooden sky of April
carve into me with knives of light.

Something inside it reminds me of childhood—   165
it is the light of the stalled time after lunch
when clocks tick

and hearts shut
and fathers leave to go back to work
and mothers stand at the kitchen sink pondering   170

something they never tell.
You remember too much,
my mother said to me recently.

Why hold onto all that? And I said,
Where can I put it down?   175
She shifted to a question about airports.

Crops of ice are changing to mud all around me
as I push on across the moor
warmed by drifts from the pale blue sun.

On the edge of the moor our pines   180
dip and coast in breezes
from somewhere else.

Perhaps the hardest thing about losing a lover is
to watch the year repeat its days.
It is as if I could dip my hand down   185

into time and scoop up
blue and green lozenges[1] of April heat
a year ago in another country.

I can feel that other day running underneath this one
like an old videotape—here we go fast around the last corner   190
up the hill to his house, shadows

of limes and roses blowing in the car window
and music spraying from the radio and him
singing and touching my left hand to his lips.

Law[2] lived in a high blue room from which he could see the sea.   195
Time in its transparent loops as it passes beneath me now
still carries the sound of the telephone in that room

and traffic far off and doves under the window
chuckling coolly and his voice saying,
You beauty. I can feel that beauty's   200

heart beating inside mine as she presses into his arms in the high blue
        room—
No, I say aloud. I force my arms down
through air which is suddenly cold and heavy as water

and the videotape jerks to a halt
like a glass slide under a drop of blood.   205
I stop and turn and stand into the wind,

1. Diamond-shaped figures.   2. The speaker's lover.

936 / Anne Carson

which now plunges towards me over the moor.
When Law left I felt so bad I thought I would die.
This is not uncommon.

I took up the practice of meditation.   210
Each morning I sat on the floor in front of my sofa
and chanted bits of old Latin prayers.

De profundis clamavi ad te Domine.[3]
Each morning a vision came to me.
Gradually I understood that these were naked glimpses of my soul.   215

I called them Nudes.
Nude #1. Woman alone on a hill.
She stands into the wind.

It is a hard wind slanting from the north.
Long flaps and shreds of flesh rip off the woman's body and lift   220
and blow away on the wind, leaving

an exposed column of nerve and blood and muscle
calling mutely through lipless mouth.
It pains me to record this,

I am not a melodramatic person.   225
But soul is "hewn in a wild workshop"
as Charlotte Brontë says of *Wuthering Heights.*[4]

Charlotte's preface to *Wuthering Heights* is a publicist's masterpiece.
Like someone carefully not looking at a scorpion
crouched on the arm of the sofa Charlotte   230

talks firmly and calmly
about the other furniture of Emily's workshop—about
the inexorable spirit ("stronger than a man, simpler than a child"),

the cruel illness ("pain no words can render"),
the autonomous end ("she sank rapidly, she made haste to leave us")   235
and about Emily's total subjection

to a creative project she could neither understand nor control,
and for which she deserves no more praise nor blame
than if she had opened her mouth

"to breathe lightning." The scorpion is inching down   240
the arm of the sofa while Charlotte
continues to speak helpfully about lightning

---

3. Psalm 130: Out of the depths I have called unto thee, O Lord (Latin).
4. Novel by English writer Emily Brontë (1818–1848). Her sister Charlotte (1816–1855) wrote an introduction for the 1850 edition, attempting to explain how a novel of such extreme passion, imagination, and apparent "coarseness" could have been produced by a woman with such a reserved life. Throughout "The Glass Essay," the poet compares her own life with Emily Brontë's.

and other weather we may expect to experience
when we enter Emily's electrical atmosphere.
It is "a horror of great darkness" that awaits us there   245

but Emily is not responsible. Emily was in the grip.
"Having formed these beings she did not know what she had done,"
says Charlotte (of Heathcliff and Earnshaw and Catherine).[5]

Well there are many ways of being held prisoner.
The scorpion takes a light spring and lands on our left knee   250
as Charlotte concludes, "On herself she had no pity."

Pitiless too are the Heights, which Emily called Wuthering
because of their "bracing ventilation"
and "a north wind over the edge."

Whaching[6] a north wind grind the moor   255
that surrounded her father's house on every side,
formed of a kind of rock called millstone grit,

taught Emily all she knew about love and its necessities—
an angry education that shapes the way her characters
use one another. "My love for Heathcliff," says Catherine,   260

"resembles the eternal rocks beneath—
a source of little visible delight, but necessary."
Necessary? I notice the sun has dimmed

and the afternoon air sharpening.
I turn and start to recross the moor towards home.   265
What are the imperatives

that hold people like Catherine and Heathcliff
together and apart, like pores blown into hot rock
and then stranded out of reach

of one another when it hardens? What kind of necessity is that?   270
The last time I saw Law was a black night in September.
Autumn had begun,

my knees were cold inside my clothes.
A chill fragment of moon rose.
He stood in my living room and spoke   275

without looking at me. Not enough spin on it,
he said of our five years of love.
Inside my chest I felt my heart snap into two pieces

5. Three characters from the novel.
6. Earlier in the poem, Carson explains that *whacher* is Brontë's idiosyncratic spelling of *watcher*. This excerpt is from the poem's fourth section, "Whacher."

which floated apart. By now I was so cold
it was like burning. I put out my hand   280
to touch his. He moved back.

I don't want to be sexual with you, he said. Everything gets crazy.
But now he was looking at me.
Yes, I said as I began to remove my clothes.

Everything gets crazy. When nude   285
I turned my back because he likes the back.
He moved onto me.

Everything I know about love and its necessities
I learned in that one moment
when I found myself   290

thrusting my little burning red backside like a baboon
at a man who no longer cherished me.
There was no area of my mind

not appalled by this action, no part of my body
that could have done otherwise.   295
But to talk of mind and body begs the question.

Soul is the place,
stretched like a surface of millstone grit between body and mind,
where such necessity grinds itself out.

Soul is what I kept watch on all that night.   300
Law stayed with me.
We lay on top of the covers as if it weren't really a night of sleep and time,

caressing and singing to one another in our made-up language
like the children we used to be.
That was a night that centred Heaven and Hell,   305

as Emily would say. We tried to fuck
but he remained limp, although happy. I came
again and again, each time accumulating lucidity,

until at last I was floating high up near the ceiling looking down
on the two souls clasped there on the bed   310
with their mortal boundaries

visible around them like lines on a map.
I saw the lines harden.
He left in the morning.

It is very cold   315
walking into the long scraped April wind.
At this time of year there is no sunset
just some movements inside the light and then a sinking away.

1995

From TV Men

XI

TV is presocial, like Man.

On the last day of the Death Valley shoot
driving through huge slow brown streaks of mountain
towards the light-hole,

Hektor[7] feels his pits go dry.   5

Clouds drop their lines down the faces of the rock
as if marking out a hunting ground.
Hektor, whose heart

walked ahead of him always,

ran ahead like a drunk creature   10
to lick salt particles off the low bushes
as if they were butter or silver honey,
whose heart Homer compared to a lion

turning in a net of dogs and men and
whichever way the lion lunges the men and dogs give way   15
yet the net keeps contracting—

Hektor trembles.

The human way includes two kinds of knowledge.
Fire and Night. Hektor has been to the Fire
in conditions of experimental purity.   20

It is 6:53 A.M. when his Night unhoods itself.

Hektor sees that he is living at the centre of a vast metal disc.
A dawn clot of moon dangles oddly above
and this realization comes coldly through him:

the disc is tilting.   25

Very slowly the disc attains an angle of thirty degrees.
Dark blue signal is flowing steadily
from the centre to the edge

as Hektor starts to slide.

It takes but an instant to realize you are mortal.   30
Troy reared up on its hind legs
and a darkness of life flowed through the town

---

7. In Homer's *Iliad*, the chief warrior of the Trojan army.

from purple cup to purple cup.

Toes to the line please, says the assistant camera man,
slapping two pieces of yellow tape   35
on the surface of the disc

just in front of Hektor's feet.

Dashing back to the camera he raises his slate.
Places everyone, calls the director as a thousand wasps
come stinging out of the arc lamp   40

and the camera is pouring its black butter,

its bitter honey,
straight into Hektor's eye.
Hektor steps to the line.

War has always interested me, he begins.   45

1995

Epitaph: Zion[8]

Murderous little world once our objects had gazes. Our lives
    Were fragile, the wind
Could dash them away. Here lies the refugee breather
    Who drank a bowl of elsewhere.

2000

Lazarus[9] Standup: Shooting Script

How does a body do in the ground?

Clouds look like matted white fur.
Which are the animals? He has forgotten the difference
between near and far.
Round pink ones come at him.   5
From the pinks shoot fluids
some dark (from eyes) some loud (from mouth).

His bones are moving like a mist in him

---

8. In the Hebrew Bible, the eastern hill of Jeru-
salem. In Judaism, it came to symbolize a promised
homeland; in Christianity, a heavenly or ideal city
of faith.
9. A man brought back to life by Jesus after being
dead four days (John 11).

all blown to the surface then sideways.
I do not want to see,   10
he thinks in pain
as a darkish clump
cuts across his field of vision,
and some
strange   15

silver milk
is filling the space,
gets caught in the mist,
twists all his bones to the outside where they ignite in air.
The burning   20
of his bones

lets Lazarus know where each bone is.

And so
shifted forward into solidity—
although he pulls against it and groans to turn away—   25
Lazarus locks on
with a whistling sound behind him
as panels slide shut

and his soul congeals on his back in chrysolite[1] drops

which almost at once evaporate.   30
Lazarus
(someone is calling his name)—his name!
And at the name (which he knew)
not just a roar of darkness
the whole skeletal freight   35

of him
took pressure,
crushing him backward into the rut where he lay
like a damp
petal   40
under a pile of furniture.

And the second fact of his humanity began.

For the furniture shrank upon him as a bonework of
not just volume but
secret volume—   45
where fingers go probing
into drawers
and under
pried-up boxlids,

---

1. Pale yellow-green gemstone.

go rifling mute garments of white   50

and memories are streaming from his mind to his heart—
of someone standing at the door.
Of white breath in frozen air.
Mary. Martha.[2]   55
Linen of the same silence.
Lazarus! (again the voice)
and why not

climb the voice

where it goes spiralling upward
lacing him on a glow point   60
into the nocturnal motions of the world so that he is
standing now
propped on a cage of hot pushes of other people's air
and he feels more than hears
her voice (again)   65

like a salt rubbed whole into raw surface—

Lazarus!
A froth of fire is upon his mind.
It crawls to the back of his tongue,
struggles a bit,   70
cracking the shell
and pushes out a bluish cry that passes at once to the soul.
Martha!

he cries, making a little scalded place

on the billows of tomb that lap our faces as we watch.   75
We know the difference now
(life or death).
For an instant it parts our hearts.
Someone take the linen napkin off his face,
says the director quietly.   80

2000

Stanzas, Sexes, Seductions

It's good to be neuter.
I want to have meaningless legs.
There are things unbearable.
One can evade them a long time.
Then you die.   5

2. Sisters of Lazarus.

The oceans remind me
of your green room.
There are things unbearable.
Scorn, princes, this little size
of dying.   10

My personal poetry is a failure.
I do not want to be a person.
I want to be unbearable.
Lover to lover, the greenness of love.
Cool, cooling.   15

Earth bears no such plant.
Who does not end up
a female impersonator?
Drink all the sex there is.
Still die.   20

I tempt you.
I blush.
There are things unbearable.
Legs, alas.
Legs die.   25

Rocking themselves down,
crazy slow,
some ballet term for it—
fragment of foil, little
spin, little drunk, little do, little oh, alas.   30

2001

MEDBH MCGUCKIAN
b. 1950

Not since the early W. B. Yeats has there been an Irish poet more preoccupied
with the dimly lit interior world, hidden from rational consciousness, than Medbh
McGuckian (her first name an Irish rendering of Maeve). She has said that her poetry's
"territory is the feminine subconscious, or semi-conscious," that she seeks "to tap the
sensual realms of dream or daydream for their spiritual value" (*Contemporary Poets*,
1996). Born on August 12, 1950, in Belfast, Northern Ireland, McGuckian studied,
like fellow Ulster poet Seamus Heaney, at Queen's University, Belfast, where Heaney
was among her teachers. She shares Heaney's Catholic background and his poetry's
lush organicism and musicality, but McGuckian, who continues to live in Belfast, is a
still more intensely private, enigmatic, and subjective poet than Heaney or, for that
matter, Yeats. "I forfeit the world outside / For the sake of my own inwardness," she
writes ("Sky Writing"). McGuckian's dream-tipped lyrics set her apart, contrasting

sharply, for example, with the declarative, public poetry of her Irish contemporary Eavan Boland.

McGuckian has averred, "I believe wholly in the beauty and power of language, the music of words, the intensity of images to shadow-paint the inner life of the soul" (*Contemporary Poets*). She is less interested in the paraphrasable content of words than in their connotations, resonances, and associations. In "Slips" and "The Dream-Language of Fergus," she represents language as layered, bound together by complex psychological, etymological, and sonic interconnections. These self-describing poems form a kind of *ars poetica*, or theory of poetry within poetry, according to which poetry is predicated on verbal slips, misconnections, and misreadings that reveal the nether reaches of our minds. Not that her poems are devoid of people. "The Dream-Language of Fergus" features her son Fergus; "The War Ending" alludes to the birth of a child; and "Captain Lavender" elegizes her father. And yet as a "threader / of double-stranded words" ("The Dream-Language of Fergus"), McGuckian elaborates and embroiders the significance of these human figures.

McGuckian's interest in evading the dictates of rationality for a poetics of ambiguity, music, and suggestiveness may be partly indebted to her sense of English as an imperial tongue that displaced the native Gaelic of Ireland. She makes something rich and strange from the bones of an imposed language. Her poetry can be baffling because its language is released from many of its usual moorings in the everyday world. Action is absent or undefined. Pronouns appear without referents. People, objects, and ideas dissolve into one another. Long, nonlinear sentences syntactically defer meaning. Instead, McGuckian's oblique poems unfold through metaphorical chains of evocation. Eschewing direct statement, they have a figurative and sonic texture that is sumptuous and involuted. Pushing the bounds of sense, sensorily and emotionally charged, they tease the reader with meanings just beyond the reach of understanding.

Slips

The studied poverty of a moon roof,
the earthenware of dairies cooled by apple trees,
the apple tree that makes the whitest wash . . .

But I forget names, remembering them wrongly
where they touch upon another name,   5
a town in France like a woman's Christian name.

My childhood is preserved as a nation's history,
my favorite fairytales the shells
leased by the hermit crab.

I see my grandmother's death as a piece of ice,   10
my mother's slimness restored to her,
my own key slotted in your door—

tricks you might guess from this unfastened button,
a pen mislaid, a word misread,
my hair coming down in the middle of a conversation.   15

1982

The Dream-Language of Fergus[1]

1

Your tongue has spent the night
in its dim sack as the shape of your foot
in its cave. Not the rudiment
of half a vanquished sound,
the excommunicated shadow of a name,   5
has rumpled the sheets of your mouth.

2

So Latin sleeps, they say, in Russian speech,
so one river inserted into another
becomes a leaping, glistening, splashed
and scattered alphabet   10
jutting out from the voice,
till what began as a dog's bark
ends with bronze, what began
with honey ends with ice;
as if an aeroplane in full flight   15
launched a second plane,
the sky is stabbed by their exits
and the mistaken meaning of each.

3

Conversation is as necessary
among these familiar campus trees   20
as the apartness of torches;
and if I am a threader
of double-stranded words, whose
Quando[2] has grown into now,
no text can return the honey   25
in its path of light from a jar,
only a seed-fund, a pendulum,
pressing out the diasporic snow.

1988

---

1. Much of the language of this poem is borrowed
from the essays of Russian poet and critic Osip
Mandelstam (1891–1938), especially "Conversa-
tion with Dante," "About the Nature of the Word,"
and "Notes about Poetry." Fergus is McGuckian's
son.
2. When (Italian).

The War Ending

In the still world
between the covers of a book,
silk glides through your name
like a bee sleeping in a flower
or a seal that turns its head to look   5
at a boy rowing a boat.

The fluttering motion of your hands
down your body presses into my thoughts
as an enormous broken wave,
a rainbow or a painting being torn   10
within me. I remove the hand
and order it to leave.

Your passion for light
is so exactly placed,
I read them as eyes, mouth, nostrils,   15
disappearing back into their mystery
like the war that has gone
into us ending,

there you have my head,
a meeting of Irish eyes   20
with something English:
and now,
today,
it bursts.

                                        1991

Captain Lavender

Night-hours. The edge of a fuller moon
waits among the interlocking patterns
of a flier's sky.

Sperm names, ovum names, push inside
each other. We are half-taught   5
our real names, from other lives.

Emphasise your eyes. Be my flare-
path, my uncold begetter,[3]
my air-minded bird-sense.

                                        1995

3. Cf. "onlie begetter," in the dedication to Shakespeare's sonnets.

Mantilla[4]

for Shane Murphy

My resurrective verses shed people
and reinforced each summer.
I saw their time as my own time,
I said, this day will penetrate
those other days, using a thorn   5
to remove a thorn in the harness
of my mind where anyone's touch
stemmed my dreams.
            From below
to above all decay I stated   10
my contentless name and held
the taste as though it were dying
all over true in the one day light.

My sound world was a vassal state,
a tightly bonded lattice of water   15
sealed with cunning to rear
the bridge of breathing.
            And my raw
mouth a non-key of spring, a cousin
sometimes source, my signature   20
vibrational as parish flowers.

1998

4. Large veil or cape worn over the head and covering the shoulders.

JOY HARJO
b. 1951

The sacred, the mythical, and the natural are central to Joy Harjo's poetry, which draws on and celebrates the oral narratives and the images of her Muskogee Creek heritage. By means of symbolic and densely figurative language, incantatory rhythms, and nativist allusions, Harjo infuses the polluted cities, sordid bars, and other mundane realities of contemporary life with a visionary texture and consciousness. Like Sherman Alexie, who cites her as an influence, Harjo works out of a profound awareness of the colonial devastation of native cultures, though Alexie's poems are like acerbic jokes and hers are more like prayers or chants.

Harjo's blending of the everyday with archetypal stories and symbols is evident in the prose poem (her characteristic medium) "Deer Dancer," in which the dancer fuses a mythical deer with a female stripper. Despite the dancer's "stained red dress" and "tape on her heels," remarks the speaker, "She was the myth slipped down through dream-time." Clock time is juxtaposed with dreamtime; the stripper's magical transformation occurs side by side with a degraded reality—a drunk "passed out, his head by the toilet."

Harjo grimly observes the taped heels, drunks, failed lives, and—in the prose poems "Insomnia and the Seven Steps to Grace" and "The Path to the Milky Way Leads through Los Angeles"—night skies wiped out by glare, "lit by chemical yellow." But Harjo's language hovers between such bleak realism and a dreamlike lyricism, which seeks to recover suppressed cultural and psychic truths. Her mythopoeic work reclaims such native presences as the shape-shifting panther and the trickster crow. The elemental world—stars, flowers, trees, the sky—radiates. Dislocations of normal speech through symbol and metaphor ("The way back is deer breath on icy windows") hint at mystical experiences just beyond the reach of colloquial English. "How do I say it?" asks the speaker of "Deer Dancer," "In this language there are no words for how the real world collapses."

In making reality as defined by the culture of "the colonizer" seem strange, not ineluctable, Harjo recalls Native American writers such as Leslie Marmon Silko, as well as global postcolonial influences such as the Ugandan poet Okot p'Bitek. The example of feminist autobiographical verse and of African American poetry, as practiced by poets such as Audre Lorde and Gwendolyn Brooks, has also been important.

Harjo was born on May 9, 1951, in Tulsa, Oklahoma, and the typical landscapes and cityscapes of her poetry are of the American southwest and west. She was a painter early on and later embraced music, playing the saxophone in her group Poetic Justice. She received her B.A. from the University of New Mexico in 1976, her M.F.A. from the University of Iowa in 1978. She has taught at Arizona State University, the University of Colorado, the University of Arizona, and the University of New Mexico.

Deer Dancer

Nearly everyone had left that bar in the middle of winter except the
hardcore. It was the coldest night of the year, every place shut down,
but not us. Of course we noticed when she came in. We were Indian
ruins. She was the end of beauty. No one knew her, the stranger whose
tribe we recognized, her family related to deer, if that's who she was, a   5
people accustomed to hearing songs in pine trees, and making them
hearts.

The woman inside the woman who was to dance naked in the bar of
misfits blew deer magic. Henry Jack, who could not survive a sober day,
thought she was Buffalo Calf Woman come back, passed out, his head   10
by the toilet. All night he dreamed a dream he could not say. The next
day he borrowed money, went home, and sent back the money I lent.
Now that's a miracle. Some people see vision in a burned tortilla, some
in the face of a woman.

This is the bar of broken survivors, the club of shotgun, knife wound, of   15
poison by culture. We who were taught not to stare drank our beer. The
players gossiped down their cues. Someone put a quarter in the jukebox
to relive despair. Richard's wife dove to kill her. We had to hold her
back, empty her pockets of knives and diaper pins, buy her two beers to
keep her still, while Richard secretly bought the beauty a drink.   20

How do I say it? In this language there are no words for how the real
world collapses. I could say it in my own and the sacred mounds would

come into focus, but I couldn't take it in this dingy envelope. So I look
at the stars in this strange city, frozen to the back of the sky, the only
promises that ever make sense.   25

My brother-in-law hung out with white people, went to law school with
a perfect record, quit. Says you can keep your laws, your words. And
practiced law on the street with his hands. He jimmied to the proverbial
dream girl, the face of the moon, while the players racked a new game.
He bragged to us, he told her magic words and that's when she broke,   30
    became human.
But we all heard his bar voice crack:

What's a girl like you doing in a place like this?

That's what I'd like to know, what are we all doing in a place like this?

You would know she could hear only what she wanted to; don't we all?
Left the drink of betrayal Richard bought her, at the bar. What was she   35
on? We all wanted some. Put a quarter in the juke. We all take risks
stepping into thin air. Our ceremonies didn't predict this. Or we
expected more.

I had to tell you this, for the baby inside the girl sealed up with a lick of
hope and swimming into praise of nations. This is not a rooming house,   40
but a dream of winter falls and the deer who portrayed the relatives of
strangers. The way back is deer breath on icy windows.

The next dance none of us predicted. She borrowed a chair for the
stairway to heaven and stood on a table of names. And danced in the
room of children without shoes.   45

You picked a fine time to leave me, Lucille.
With four hungry children and a crop in the field.[1]

And then she took off her clothes. She shook loose memory, waltzed
with the empty lover we'd all become.

She was the myth slipped down through dreamtime. The promise of   50
feast we all knew was coming. The deer who crossed through knots of a
curse to find us. She was no slouch, and neither were we, watching.

The music ended. And so does the story. I wasn't there. But I imagined
her like this, not a stained red dress with tape on her heels but the deer
who entered our dream in white dawn, breathed mist into pine trees,   55
her fawn a blessing of meat, the ancestors who never left.

1990

---

1. First two lines from the chorus of the 1970s hit song "Lucille," by the American country-pop performer
Kenny Rogers (b. 1938).

Mourning Song[2]

It's early evening here in the small world, where gods gamble for good
weather as the sky turns red. Oh grief rattling around in the bowl of my
skeleton. How I'd like to spit you out, turn you into another human, or
remake the little dog spirit who walked out of our house without its skin
toward an unseen land. We were left behind to figure it out during a   5
harvest turned to ashes. I need to mourn with the night, turn to the
gleaming house of bones under your familiar brown skin. The hot stone of
our hearts will make a fire. If we cry more tears we will ruin the land with
salt; instead let's praise that which would distract us with despair. Make a
song for death, a song with yellow teeth and bad breath. For loneliness,   10
the house guest who eats everything and refuses to leave. A song for bad
weather so we can stand together under our leaking roof, and make a
terrible music with our wise and ragged bones.

                                                                    1994

Insomnia and the Seven Steps to Grace[3]

At dawn the panther of the heavens peers over the edge of the world.
She hears the stars gossip with the sun, sees the moon washing her lean
darkness with water electrified by prayers. All over the world there are
those who can't sleep, those who never awaken.

My granddaughter sleeps on the breast of her mother with milk on   5
her mouth. A fly contemplates the sweetness of lactose.

Her father is wrapped in the blanket of nightmares. For safety he
approaches the red hills near Thoreau.[4] They recognize him and sing for
him.

Her mother has business in the house of chaos. She is a prophet dis-   10
guised as a young mother who is looking for a job. She appears at the
door of my dreams and we put the house back together.

Panther watches as human and animal souls are lifted to the heavens by
rain clouds to partake of songs of beautiful thunder.

Others are led by deer and antelope in the wistful hours to the vil-   15
lages of their ancestors. There they eat cornmeal cooked with berries
that stain their lips with purple while the tree of life flickers in the sun.

2. In commentary following this poem, Harjo
writes that she was once shocked to realize that a
"filthy" homeless man, "his hair thick with lice,"
was her "old friend, a tall good-looking Navajo."
3. "I think of Bell's theorem which states that all
actions have a ripple effect in this world. We could
name this theorem for any tribe in this country as
tribal peoples knew this long before we knew
English or the scientific method" [Harjo's com-
ments]. Bell's theorem was proposed by physicist
John Stuart Bell (1928–1990).
4. New Mexico town locally believed to be named
after Henry David Thoreau (1817–1862), Ameri-
can writer.

It's October, though the season before dawn is always winter. On the
city streets of this desert town lit by chemical yellow travelers
search for home.   20

Some have been drinking and intimate with strangers. Others are
escapees from the night shift, sip lukewarm coffee, shift gears to the
other side of darkness.

One woman stops at a red light, turns over a worn tape to the last
chorus of a whispery blues. She has decided to live another day.   25

The stars take notice, as do the half-asleep flowers, prickly pear and
chinaberry tree who drink exhaust into their roots, into the earth.

She guns the light to home where her children are asleep and may
never know she ever left. That their fate took a turn in the land of
nightmares toward the sun may be untouchable knowledge.   30

It is a sweet sound.

The panther relative yawns and puts her head between her paws.
She dreams of the house of panthers and the seven steps to grace.

                                                                    1994

The Path to the Milky Way Leads through Los Angeles

There are strangers above me, below me and all around me and we are all
strange in this place of recent invention.
This city named for angels appears naked and stripped of anything
        resembling
the shaking of turtle shells, the songs of human voices on a summer night
outside Okmulgee.[5]   5
Yet, it's perpetually summer here, and beautiful. The shimmer of gods is
        easier
to perceive at sunrise or dusk,
when those who remember us here in the illusion of the marketplace
turn toward the changing of the sun and say our names.
We matter to somebody,   10
We must matter to the strange god who imagines us as we revolve together
        in
the dark sky on the path to the Milky Way.
We can't easily see that starry road from the perspective of the crossing of
boulevards, can't hear it in the whine of civilization or taste the minerals of
planets in hamburgers.   15
But we can buy a map here of the stars' homes, dial a tone for dangerous
        love,

---

5. City and county in central Oklahoma.

choose from several brands of water or a hiss of oxygen for gentle
    rejuvenation.
Everyone knows you can't buy love but you can still sell your soul for less
    than a song to a stranger who will sell it to someone else for a profit
until you're owned by a company of strangers
in the city of the strange and getting stranger.   20
I'd rather understand how to sing from a crow
who was never good at singing or much of anything
but finding gold in the trash of humans.
So what are we doing here I ask the crow parading on the ledge of falling
    that
hangs over this precarious city?   25
Crow[6] just laughs and says *wait, wait and see* and I am waiting and not
    seeing
anything, not just yet.
But like crow I collect the shine of anything beautiful I can find.

2000

6. Trickster character in many Native American stories and myths.

PAUL MULDOON
b. 1951

Paul Muldoon has much in common with the hedgehog he writes about in one of his early poems: "Shares its secret with no one. / We say, *Hedgehog, come out / Of yourself and we will love you.* // *We mean no harm. We want / Only to listen to what / You have to say.*" Muldoon does not easily yield up his feelings or his meanings; nor are we likely to fall in love with him on first reading. In the context of the violent internecine Troubles and long colonial history of his native Northern Ireland, this ironic secretiveness, this postmodern play of disguises and masks, takes on a special significance. *"We mean no harm,"* we may protest, but the hedgehog knows better. Though Muldoon's tone is typically arch and his cleverness can be forbidding, his poems dazzle with their lexical exuberance, formal engineering, and wry allusiveness. For sheer wit and structural inventiveness, few contemporary poets rival him.

    Like all contemporary Irish poets, Muldoon must contend with the long shadow cast by W. B. Yeats. In this, as in much else, Muldoon combines seriousness of purpose with irreverence. Yeats is tormented by guilt in his great, late poem "Man and the Echo," and he asks whether his art helped inspire the Easter Rising of 1916, which ended in the execution by the British of its poet-leaders: "Did that play of mine send out / Certain men the English shot?" Adopting the voice of his fellow ironist W. H. Auden, Muldoon answers with a quip in "7, Middagh Street": " 'Certainly not'. // If Yeats had saved his pencil-lead / would certain men have stayed in bed?" Whereas Yeats saw art as a force that could create nations and alter the course of history, Muldoon is more circumspect about the relation between art and politics. Even so, in poems such as "Lunch with Pancho Villa," "Meeting the British," and "Aftermath," he offers oblique parables or verbal puzzles about the violence of history. Like his major immediate predecessor, Seamus Heaney—his tutor at Queen's University, Belfast—Muldoon mistrusts journalistic directness in approaching the Troubles. But whereas Heaney is indirect, Muldoon is doubly so; Heaney worries that "song" may betray "suffering," and Muldoon is still more unsure of language's ability to be faithful to a reality outside itself. In contrast to Heaney's rooted sense of self, history, and Irishness, Muldoon's is transnational, fractured, and decentered. Muldoon writes about Heaney, with characteristic slyness and playfulness, in "The Briefcase," among other poems.

In "7, Middagh Street," Muldoon explores various views on the relation of art and politics through imaginary monologues by such literary and artistic figures as Auden, Salvador Dalí, and Louis MacNeice. This is one of a number of long poems and poetry cycles that Muldoon has written, including "Madoc: A Mystery," the autobiographical "Yarrow" and "Sleeve Notes," and "Immram," which laconically tells of a hero's nightmarish search for his father, a demented recluse who lives in squalor at the top of a luxury hotel and cries out for Baskin-Robbins banana-nut ice cream. In his long poems and in the carefully arranged sequences of his books, Muldoon invites his readers to see interconnections. He says: "I've become very interested in structures that can be fixed like mirrors at angles to each other . . . so that new images can emerge from the setting up of the poems in relationship to each other" (*Viewpoints: Poets in Conversation with John Haffenden,* 1981). Muldoon takes pleasure in his skills and in the amiable surprises and tricks he arranges for us, even as he explores such grim matters as mortality, urban warfare, and our generally futile attempts to recover the past. A poem such as the skewed sonnet "Quoof," in which the speaker goes to bed with a non-English-speaking woman in New York, offers off-kilter but searching reflections on sex, language, and colonization. In "The Grand Conversation," as elsewhere, he turns his mixed marriage to American Jewish writer Jean Korelitz into a densely specific yet allegorical poem about identity and intercultural experience. Other poems on the commerce between love and sex are sometimes delicately graphic. "Alternate worlds"—Auden's phrase for works of art and what they offer us—are what we find in the situations Muldoon invents for his readers.

Muldoon was born on June 20, 1951, in County Armagh, Northern Ireland, where his mother was a schoolteacher and his father, a frequent subject of his poems, a produce gardener and farm laborer with Republican sympathies. Muldoon was educated at St. Patrick's College, Armagh, and Queen's University, Belfast, where he came to know such poets as Medbh McGuckian and Michael Longley. Recognition came early, with the publication of his first book of poems at twenty-one. For more than ten years he worked as a producer, first in radio and then in television for the British Broadcasting Corporation in Belfast. In 1986, he left to devote himself to writing and to teaching, and since 1990, he has taught at Princeton University. In addition to books of poetry, he has published opera libretti, anthologies, and translations from poetry in Irish.

Hedgehog

The snail moves like a
Hovercraft,[1] held up by a
Rubber cushion of itself,
Sharing its secret

---

1. Vehicle that moves over land or water, supported by a cushion of air provided by downward-directed fans.

With the hedgehog. The hedgehog 5
Shares its secret with no one.
We say, *Hedgehog, come out*
Of yourself and we will love you.

We mean no harm. We want
Only to listen to what 10
You have to say. We want
Your answers to our questions.

The hedgehog gives nothing
Away, keeping itself to itself.
We wonder what a hedgehog 15
Has to hide, why it so distrusts.

We forget the god
Under this crown of thorns.[2]
We forget that never again
Will a god trust in the world. 20

1973

Lunch with Pancho Villa[3]

I

'Is it really a revolution, though?'
I reached across the wicker table
With another $10,000 question.
My celebrated pamphleteer,
Co-author of such volumes 5
As *Blood on the Rose*,
The Dream and the Drums,
And *How It Happened Here*,
Would pour some untroubled Muscatel[4]
And settle back in his cane chair. 10

'Look, son. Just look around you.
People are getting themselves killed
Left, right and centre
While you do what? Write rondeaux?[5]
There's more to living in this country 15
Than stars and horses, pigs and trees,
Not that you'd guess it from your poems.

---

2. Like the one Jesus was crowned with at his crucifixion (Matthew 27.29).
3. Francisco Villa (1878–1923), Mexican revolutionary and guerrilla leader who fought in the Mexican Revolution (1910–20).
4. Sweet wine made from the muscat grape.
5. Poetic and musical forms in which a main theme returns several times.

Do you never listen to the news?
You want to get down to something true,
Something a little nearer home.'   20

I called again later that afternoon,
A quiet suburban street.
'You want to stand back a little
When the world's at your feet.'
I'd have liked to have heard some more   25
Of his famous revolution.
I rang the bell, and knocked hard
On what I remembered as his front door,
That opened then, as such doors do,
Directly on to a back yard.   30

II

Not any back yard, I'm bound to say,
And not a thousand miles away
From here. No one's taken in, I'm sure,
By such a mild invention.
But where (I wonder myself) do I stand,   35
In relation to a table and chair,
The quince-tree I forgot to mention,
That suburban street, the door, the yard—
All made up as I went along
As things that people live among.   40

And such a person as lived there!
My celebrated pamphleteer!
Of course, I gave it all away
With those preposterous titles.
The Bloody Rose? The Dream and the Drums?   45
The three-day-wonder of the flowering plum!
Or was I desperately wishing
To have been their other co-author,
Or, at least, to own a first edition
Of *The Boot Boys and Other Battles?*   50

'When are you going to tell the truth?'
For there's no such book, so far as I know,
As *How it Happened Here*,
Though there may be. There may.
What should I say to this callow youth   55
Who learned to write last winter—
One of those correspondence courses—
And who's coming to lunch today?
He'll be rambling on, no doubt,
About pigs and trees, stars and horses.   60

1977

Anseo

When the Master was calling the roll
At the primary school in Collegelands,
You were meant to call back *Anseo*
And raise your hand
As your name occurred.   5
Anseo, meaning here, here and now,
All present and correct,
Was the first word of Irish I spoke.
The last name on the ledger
Belonged to Joseph Mary Plunkett Ward   10
And was followed, as often as not,
By silence, knowing looks,
A nod and a wink, the Master's droll
'And where's our little Ward-of-court?'

I remember the first time he came back   15
The Master had sent him out
Along the hedges
To weigh up for himself and cut
A stick with which he would be beaten.
After a while, nothing was spoken;   20
He would arrive as a matter of course
With an ash-plant, a salley-rod.[6]
Or, finally, the hazel-wand
He had whittled down to a whip-lash,
Its twist of red and yellow lacquers   25
Sanded and polished,
And altogether so delicately wrought
That he had engraved his initials on it.

I last met Joseph Mary Plunkett Ward
In a pub just over the Irish border.   30
He was living in the open,
In a secret camp
On the other side of the mountain.
He was fighting for Ireland,
Making things happen.   35
And he told me, Joe Ward,
Of how he had risen through the ranks
To Quartermaster, Commandant:
How every morning at parade
His volunteers would call back *Anseo*   40
And raise their hands
As their names occurred.

1980

---

6. Stick made from a willow tree. *Ash-plant:* stick or whip made from a sapling of the ash tree.

Why Brownlee Left

Why Brownlee left, and where he went,
Is a mystery even now.
For if a man should have been content
It was him; two acres of barley,
One of potatoes, four bullocks,   5
A milker, a slated farmhouse.
He was last seen going out to plough
On a March morning, bright and early.

By noon Brownlee was famous;
They had found all abandoned, with   10
The last rig[7] unbroken, his pair of black
Horses, like man and wife,
Shifting their weight from foot to
Foot, and gazing into the future.

                                      1980

Quoof

How often have I carried our family word
for the hot water bottle
to a strange bed,
as my father would juggle a red-hot half-brick
in an old sock   5
to his childhood settle.[8]
I have taken it into so many lovely heads
or laid it between us like a sword.

An hotel room in New York City
with a girl who spoke hardly any English,   10
my hand on her breast
like the smouldering one-off spoor of the yeti[9]
or some other shy beast
that has yet to enter the language.

                                      1983

Meeting the British

We met the British in the dead of winter.
The sky was lavender

and the snow lavender-blue.
I could hear, far below,

---

7. Ridge between a pair of plough furrows.
8. Wooden bed that can also be used as a bench.

9. Hypothetical apelike creature of the Himalayas; the "abominable snowman." *Spoor:* footprint.

the sound of two streams coming together   5
(both were frozen over)

and, no less strange,
myself calling out in French

across that forest-
clearing. Neither General Jeffrey Amherst[1]   10

nor Colonel Henry Bouquet
could stomach our willow-tobacco.

As for the unusual
scent when the Colonel shook out his hand-

kerchief: *C'est la lavande,*   15
une fleur mauve comme le ciel.[2]

They gave us six fishhooks
and two blankets embroidered with smallpox.

                                                           1987

From 7, MIDDAGH STREET[3]

Wystan

Quinquereme of Nineveh from distant Ophir;[4]
a blizzard off the Newfoundland[5] coast
had, as we slept, metamorphosed

the *Champlain*'s decks
to a wedding cake,   5
on whose uppermost tier stood Christopher

1. Commander-in-chief of British forces in the French and Indian War (1754–63); fought against France and its Native American allies. During Pontiac's Rebellion (1763–64), led by Ottawa chief Pontiac in the Great Lakes region, Amherst wrote to the British officer Colonel Bouquet, "Could it not be contrived to Send the *Small Pox* among those Disaffected Tribes of Indians?" Bouquet replied, "I will try to inocculate the Indians by means of Blanketts that may fall in their hands, taking care however not to get the disease myself," to which Amherst responded, "You will Do well to try to Innoculate the Indians by means of Blanketts, as well as to try Every other method that can serve to Extirpate this Execreble Race." Apparently as a result of this and similar plans of other British officers, many Native Americans in the area, never having been exposed to smallpox, were killed by the disease in 1763–64. Pontiac concluded a peace treaty with the British in July 1766.
2. It is lavender, a flower purple as the sky (French).
3. Address of the building in Brooklyn Heights in which the poet W[ystan] H[ugh] Auden (1907–

1973) lived at one time or another—along with an impressive list of bohemian housemates including the poet Louis MacNeice (1907–1973), novelists Carson McCullers (1917–1967) and Anaïs Nin (1903–1977), and the famous striptease artist Gypsy Rose Lee (1914–1970)—during the early years of World War II. In the sections of the poem printed here, Muldoon speaks in the voices of Auden and surrealist painter Salvador Dalí (1904–1989), who was also in exile in New York at this time.
4. Muldoon borrows this line from "Cargoes" (1902), by American poet John Masefield (1878–1967). *Quinquereme:* ship with five banks or oars. *Nineveh:* ancient city of the Assyrian Empire on the east bank of the Tigris River. *Ophir:* in the Bible, a region from which Solomon's ships brought large quantities of exquisite gold.
5. Island and province on the eastern coast of Canada. On January 26, 1939, Auden and the author Christopher Isherwood (1904–1986) arrived aboard the French liner *Champlain* in New York, where they eventually decided to immigrate from Great Britain.

and I like a diminutive bride and groom.
A heavy-skirted Liberty[6] would lunge
with her ice-cream
at two small, anxious   10

boys, and Erika[7] so grimly wave
from the quarantine-launch
she might as truly have been my wife
as, later that day, Barcelona was Franco's.

———

There was a time when I thought it mattered   15
what happened in Madrid

or Seville
and, in a sense, I haven't changed
my mind; the forces of Good and Evil
were indeed ranged   20

against each other, though not unambiguously.
I went there on the off-chance
they'd let me try
my hand at driving an ambulance;

there turned out to be some bureau-   25
cratic hitch.[8]
When I set out for the front on a black burro
it promptly threw me in the ditch.

I lay there for a year, disillusioned, dirty,
until a firing-party   30

of Chinese soldiers[9]
came by, leading dishevelled ponies.
They arranged a few sedimentary boulders
over the body of a Japanese

spy they'd shot   35
but weren't inclined to bury,
so that one of his feet stuck out.
When a brindled pariah[1]

6. Isherwood later recalled that the Statue of Liberty seemed intimidating rather than welcoming as they arrived in New York during a snowstorm.

7. Auden and Isherwood were met at the quarantine launch by their friends Klaus and Erika Mann, the eldest children of German-born novelist Thomas Mann. Auden and Erika, both homosexuals, had entered into a marriage of convenience in 1936 so that Erika could become a British citizen and escape Nazi Germany. Earlier on the day of Auden and Isherwood's arrival, Barcelona had fallen to the Fascist army of Francisco Franco (1892–1975), signifying that the Spanish Republicans had in effect lost the Spanish Civil War (1936–39).

8. In 1937, Auden traveled to Spain to volunteer as an ambulance driver for the Spanish Republican army. For reasons that remain unclear, the Spanish Medical Aid Committee turned him down. Instead, British Communists apparently arranged for Auden to travel to the front and write articles supporting the Republican side. According to a possibly apocryphal story, Auden refused a car and rode a mule, making it six miles from Valencia before being bucked by the mule and returning to take the car.

9. In 1938, Auden and Isherwood traveled through China as correspondents observing the war between the Japanese and Chinese.

1. A striped, "tabby" dog.

began to gnaw
on it, I recognized the markings of the pup   40
whose abscessed paw
my father had lanced on our limestone doorstep.

———

Those crucial years he tended
the British wounded

in Egypt, Gallipoli   45
and France,[2] I learned to play

Isolde to my mother's Tristan.[3]
Are they now tempted to rechristen

their youngest son
who turned his back on Albion   50

a Quisling?[4]
Would their *chaise-longue*[5]

philosophers have me somehow inflate
myself and float

above their factories and pylons   55
like a flat-footed barrage-balloon?

———

For though I would gladly return to Eden
as that ambulance-driver
or air-raid warden
I will never again ford the river   60
to parley with the mugwumps[6]
and fob them off with monocles and mumps;
I will not go back as *Auden.*

———

And were Yeats living at this hour
it should be in some ruined tower   65

not malachited Ballylee[7]
where he paid out to those below

2. Auden's father, George Auden, left his family to work as a doctor for the Royal Army Medical Corps during World War I, serving in Egypt, France, and Gallipoli, a Turkish seaport. In "Letter to Lord Byron" (1936), Auden claims this sight of surgery on a dog was his "earliest recollection."
3. *Tristan* and *Isolde*: central characters from a famous medieval romance. The young man Tristan was sent as a messenger to arrange for the Princess Isolde to be married to his uncle. However, after drinking a love potion, Tristan and Isolde became inseparable lovers involved in numerous adventures. Auden, the youngest of three children, once sang Isolde's role while his mother, at the piano, played Tristan.
4. Traitor, after Vidkun Quisling (1887–1945), a Norwegian officer who collaborated with the Germans during their World War II occupation of Norway. *Albion:* the earliest known name for Britain.
5. Sofa.
6. People who assume a superior lack of interest in politics or other affairs.
7. The castle that Irish poet W. B. Yeats (1865–1939) renovated and lived in. *Malachite:* an ornate, green mineral.

one gilt-edged scroll from his pencil
as though he were part-Rapunzel

and partly Delphic oracle.[8]   70
As for his crass, rhetorical

posturing, 'Did that play of mine
send out certain men (*certain* men?)

the English shot . . . ?'[9]   75
the answer is 'Certainly not'.

If Yeats had saved his pencil-lead
would certain men have stayed in bed?

For history's a twisted root
with art its small, translucent fruit

and never the other way round.   80
The roots by which we were once bound

are severed here, in any case,
and we are all now dispossessed;

prince, poet, construction worker,
salesman, soda fountain jerker—   85

all equally isolated.
Each loads flour, sugar and salted

beef into a covered wagon
and strikes out for his Oregon,

each straining for the ghostly axe   90
of a huge, blond-haired lumberjack.

———

'If you want me look for me under your boot-soles';[1]
when I visited him in a New Hampshire hospital
where he had almost gone for a Burton
with peritonitis   95
Louis[2] propped himself up on an ottoman
and read aloud the ode to Whitman
from *Poeta en Nueva York*[3]

8. In ancient Greece, a cave and shrine on the slope of Mt. Parnassus where questioners received a god's riddling answers. *Rapunzel:* fairy-tale character imprisoned in a tall tower who lowers her exceptionally long hair for her rescuer to climb.
9. From Yeats's late poem "Man and the Echo" (1939), in which he worries that his nationalist play *Cathleen ni Houlihan* (1902) helped inspire the violence associated with the Easter 1916 uprising.

1. From "Song of Myself," by American poet Walt Whitman (1819–1892).
2. Anglo-Irish poet Louis MacNeice (1907–1963), who suffered from a near-fatal case of peritonitis, an inflammation of the membrane lining the abdominal wall, during his visit to the United States in 1939.
3. *Poet in New York:* 1940 collection by Spanish poet Federico García Lorca (1898–1936).

The impossible Eleanor Clark[4]
had smuggled in a pail of oysters and clams   100
and a fifth column
of Armagnac.[5]
Carson McCullers extemporized a blues harmonica
on urinous pipkins and pannikins
that would have flummoxed Benjamin Franklin.[6]   105
I left them, so, to the reign
of the ear of corn
and the journey-work of the grass-leaf
and found my way next morning to Bread Loaf
and the diamond-shaped clearing in the forest   110
where I learned to play softball with Robert Frost.[7]

————

For I have leapt with Kierkegaard
out of the realm of Brunel and Arkwright[8]

with its mills, canals and railway-bridges
into this great void   115
where Chester[9] and I exchanged love-pledges
and vowed
our marriage-vows. As he lay asleep
last night the bronze of his exposed left leg
made me want nothing so much as to weep.   120
I thought of the terrier, of plague,
of Aschenbach at the Lido.[1]
Here was my historical
Mr W. H., my 'onlie begetter' and fair lady;
for nothing this wide universe I call . . . [2]   125

Salvador[3]

This lobster's not a lobster but the telephone
that rang for Neville Chamberlain.[4]

4. American writer (b. 1913) and wife of poet Robert Penn Warren (1905–1989). While MacNeice was in the United States, she had an affair with him. Her book *The Oysters of Locmariaquer* won the National Book Award in 1965.
5. That is, a bottle of French brandy. A "column" is a vessel used to distill spirits; "fifth column" means, loosely, traitor or spy.
6. One of Benjamin Franklin's many inventions was the glass harmonica, a musical instrument made of a series of bowls that vibrate (like the mouth of a wine glass) when rubbed with wetted fingers. Carson McCullers (1917–1967): American novelist. *Pipkins*: small pots or pans. *Pannikins*: small, metal drinking cups.
7. American poet (1874–1963), who helped found the Breadloaf School of English, in Vermont. Auden played softball with Frost at Breadloaf in August 1940. While teaching summers at Breadloaf, Muldoon lived in Frost's old home.
8. Sir Richard Arkwright (1732–1792): British industrialist, who opened mills in Auden's native Midlands. Søren Kierkegaard (1813–1855): Danish philosopher, whose blend of Christianity and

proto-existentialism required a profound leap of faith. Sir Marc Brunel (1769–1849): French-born British engineer, who designed the shielding used to build the Thames Tunnel in 1843. His son Isambard was also a famous engineer.
9. American poet and librettist Chester Kallman (1921–1975), Auden's lover.
1. Italian seaside resort where, in Thomas Mann's *Death in Venice* (1912), the writer Aschenbach falls in love with a young boy.
2. From Shakespeare's Sonnet 109: "For nothing this wide universe I call, / Save thou, my rose; in it thou art my all." Shakespeare's dedication of his sonnets, "To the onlie begetter . . . Mr. W. H.," possibly includes a misprint of his own initials, but has generated speculation about the young man who might be the inspiration for many of the poems. "W. H." were also the initials Auden used instead of a spelled-out first name.
3. Spanish surrealist painter Salvador Dalí (1904–1989).
4. British politician (1869–1940), greatly criticized for the strategy of "appeasement" he adopted toward Adolf Hitler in the years preceding World

It droops from a bare branch
above a plate, on which the remains of lunch

include a snapshot of Hitler   5
and some boiled beans left over

from *Soft Construction: A Premonition
of Civil War.*[5] When Breton

hauled me before his kangaroo-court
I quoted the Manifesto;[6] we must disregard   10

moral and aesthetic considerations
for the integrity of our dream-visions.

What if I dreamed of Hitler as a masochist
who raises his fist

only to be beaten?   15
I might have dreamed of fucking André Breton

he so pooh-poohed my *Enigma of William Tell.*
There I have Lenin kneel

with one massive elongated buttock
and the elongated peak   20

of his cap supported by two forked sticks.
This time there's a raw beef-steak

on the son's head. My father croons a lullaby.
Is it that to refer, however obliquely,

is to refer? In October 1934,   25
I left Barcelona by the back door

with a portfolio of work
for my first one-man show in New York.

A starry night. The howling of dogs.
The Anarchist taxi-driver carried two flags,   30

War II. He was forced to step down as prime min-
ister in 1940. *The Lobster Telephone* (1936) is an
example of Dalí's surrealist assemblages.
5. *Soft Construction with Boiled Beans: A Premo-
nition of Civil War:* 1934 Dalí painting depicting
giant body parts on a desolate plain.
6. André Breton (1896–1966): French poet and
critic whose *Surrealist Manifesto* (1924) helped
found the surrealist movement, which was dedi-
cated to exploring the creative power of the uncon-
scious with dreamlike imagery and unexpected
juxtapositions. In the mid-1930s, Dalí's relation-
ship with the other surrealists was becoming

strained, largely because of his growing interest in
Hitler, who, according to Dalí, exhibited a gratui-
tous masochism that made him a surrealist icon.
After Breton and the others saw Dalí's *Enigma of
William Tell* (1933), which seemed to insult com-
munism by putting the face of Russian revolution-
ary V. I. Lenin (1870–1924) on a highly distorted
and sexualized body, the surrealists convened a
meeting to confront Dalí about his fascination with
fascism. Dalí's immediate response was to suggest
that he would dream about having sex with Breton
and then paint the encounter when he awoke.

Spanish and Catalan. Which side was I on?
Not one, or both, or none.

I who had knelt with Lenin in Breton's court
and sworn allegiance to the proletariat

had seen the chasm   35
between myself and surrealism

begin as a hair-crack on a tile.
In *Soft Construction* I painted a giant troll

tearing itself apart limb
by outlandish limb.   40

Among the broken statues of Valladolid[7]
there's one whose foot's still welded

to the granite plinth[8]
from which, like us, it draws its strength.

From that, and from those few boiled beans.   45
We cannot gormandize upon

the flesh of Cain and Abel[9]
without some melancholic vegetable

bringing us back to earth, to the boudoir
in the abattoir.[1]   50

Our civil wars, the crumbling of empires,
the starry nights without number

safely under our belts,
have only slightly modified the tilt

of the acanthus[2] leaf,   55
its spiky puce-and-alabaster an end in itself.

                                                                      1987

The Briefcase

for Seamus Heaney[3]

I held the briefcase at arms's length from me;
the oxblood or liver

---

7. City and province of northwestern Spain.
8. Blocklike base for a statue.
9. Cain's murder of his brother Abel is told in Genesis 4.

1. Slaughterhouse. *Boudoir:* private bedroom.
2. Prickly Mediterranean plant, whose image is often carved into classical moldings or plinths.
3. Irish poet (b. 1939).

eelskin with which it was covered
had suddenly grown supple.

I'd been waiting in line for the cross-town   5
bus when an almighty cloudburst
left the sidewalk a raging torrent.

And though it contained only the first
inkling of this poem, I knew I daren't
set the briefcase down   10
to slap my pockets for an obol[4]—

for fear it might slink into a culvert
and strike out along the East River
for the sea. By which I mean the 'open' sea.

1990

Cauliflowers

Plants that glow in the dark have been developed through gene-
splicing, in which light-producing bacteria from the mouths of fish
are introduced to cabbage, carrots and potatoes.
—*The National Enquirer*

More often than not he stops at the headrig[5] to light
his pipe
and try to regain
his composure. The price of cauliflowers
his gone down   5
two weeks in a row on the Belfast market.

From here we can just make out
a platoon of Light
Infantry going down
the road to the accompaniment of a pipe-   10
band. The sun glints on their silver-
buttoned jerkins.

My uncle, Patrick Regan,
has been leaning against the mud-guard
of the lorry. He levers   15
open the bonnet and tinkers with a light
wrench at the hose-pipe
that's always going down.

Then he himself goes down
to bleed oil into a jerry-can.   20

4. Small coin.
5. A sawmill, specifically its principal machine and carriage.

My father slips the pipe
into his scorch-marked
breast pocket and again makes light
of the trepanned[6] cauliflowers.

All this as I listened to lovers   25
repeatedly going down
on each other in the next room . . . 'light
of my life . . . ' in a motel in Oregon.
All this. Magritte's
pipe[7]   30

and the pipe-
bomb. White Annetts. Gillyflowers.
Margaret,
are you grieving?[8] My father going down
the primrose path with Patrick Regan.   35
All gone out of the world of light.

All gone down
the original pipe. And the cauliflowers
in an unmarked pit, that were harvested by their own light.

                                                           1990

The Sonogram

Only a few weeks ago, the sonogram of Jean's womb
resembled nothing so much
as a satellite-map of Ireland:

now the image
is so well-defined we can make out not only a hand   5
but a thumb;

on the road to Spiddal,[9] a woman hitching a ride;
a gladiator in his net, passing judgement on the crowd.

                                                           1994

6. Cored.
7. One of the most famous paintings by Belgian surrealist René Magritte (1898–1967) depicts a pipe, beneath which a caption reads in French "This is not a pipe."
8. The opening line of "Spring and Fall," by English poet Gerard Manley Hopkins (1844–1889). Line 36 below recalls "They are all gone into the world of light!", the first line of a poem by English religious poet Henry Vaughan (1621 or 1622–1695).
9. Town in County Galway, in western Ireland.

Aftermath

I

"Let us now drink," I imagine patriot cry to patriot
after they've shot
a neighbor in his own aftermath, who hangs still between two sheaves
like Christ between two tousle-headed thieves,
his body wired up to the moon, as like as not.   5

II

To the memory of another left to rot
near some remote beauty spot,
the skin of his right arm rolled up like a shirtsleeve,
let us now drink.

III

Only a few nights ago, it seems, they set fire to a big house and it   10
    got so preternaturally hot
we knew there would be no reprieve
till the swallows' nests under the eaves
had been baked into these exquisitely glazed little pots
from which, my love, let us now drink.

1998

The Grand Conversation

She. My people came from Korelitz,[1]
where they grew yellow cucumbers
and studied the Talmud.[2]
He. Mine pored over the mud
of mangold- and potato-pits   5
of flicked through kale plants from Comber[3]
as bibliomancers of old
went a-flicking through deckle-mold.[4]

She. Mine would lie low in the shtetl[5]
when they heard the distant thunder   10
stolen by the Cossacks.[6]

1. Town now in Belarus, once famous for its cucumbers. During World War II, the Nazis largely massacred its population.
2. Collection of writings that constitutes the Jewish civil and religious law.
3. Village in Northern Ireland. *Mangold:* a beet.
4. Rough edges of pages before they are trimmed.

Bibliomancers: people who predicted the future from the text in a book opened at random.
5. Former Jewish village-communities of Eastern Europe.
6. A Polish people known for their horsemanship, they massacred hundreds of thousands of Polish Jews in 1648–49.

He. It was potato sacks
lumped together on a settle[7]
mine found themselves lying under,
the Peep O'Day Boys from Loughgall   15
making Defenders[8] of us all.

She. Mine once controlled the sugar trade
from the islets of Langerhans[9]
and were granted the deed
to Charlottesville. *He.* Indeed?   20
My people called a spade a spade
and were admitted to the hanse[1]
of pike- and pickax-men, shovels
leaning to their lean-to hovels.

She. Mine were trained to make a suture   25
after the bomb and the bombast
have done their very worst.
He. Between *fearsad* and *verst*[2]
we may yet construct our future
as we've reconstructed our past   30
and cry out, my love, each to each
from his or her own quicken-queach.[3]

She. Each from his stand of mountain-ash
will cry out over valley farms
spotlit with pear-blossom.   35
He. There some young Absalom[4]
picks his way through cache after cache
of ammunition and small arms
hidden in grain wells, while his nag
tugs at a rein caught on a snag.   40

2002

---

7. Long wooden bed or bench.
8. Eighteenth-century Catholic group in Ireland that fought Protestants who called themselves the Peep O'Day Boys. *Loughgall:* village where Protestants formed a larger coalition, the Orange Order, at the beginning of the nineteenth century.
9. The groups of cells in the pancreas that produce the hormone insulin, which regulates the sugar level in the bloodstream.
1. Merchant guild.

2. Russian land measure, roughly two-thirds of a mile. *Fearsad:* sandbank (Irish).
3. *Queach:* dense growth of bushes. Cf. T. S. Eliot's "Love Song of J. Alfred Prufrock": "Do I dare to eat a peach? / . . . . I have heard the mermaids singing, each to each."
4. King David's son, killed leading a rebellion against his father (2 Samuel). Riding his mule, he was accidentally hung up on a low branch and was thus made vulnerable to enemy spears.

GARY SOTO
b. 1952

In 1848, at the end of the Mexican-American War, Mexico ceded its territory above the Rio Grande River to the United States. The Mexicans who lived there became American citizens and yet maintained their language and traditions, while other Mexicans, dreaming of becoming rich Americans, also came to the southwest. Whether native or immigrant, Mexican Americans found themselves defined as outsiders, second-class citizens who were segregated into barrios—essentially, Spanish-speaking ghettos. Over time, literary stirrings and a growing group consciousness began within the Chicano community, but not until the late 1960s could leaders such as César Chávez make *La Causa* a nationalistic Chicano movement. *La Causa* produced a protest literature; it also made way for other Chicano writers, including Gary Soto, to become visible.

Soto both emerged from this cultural moment and felt distinct from it; "the work I was trying to do," he has said, even at this "nationalistic" time, "was so private—talking about loss, death" (*The Boston Globe*, October 18, 1998). Soto's first two books—*The Element of San Joaquin* (1977) and *The Tale of Sunlight* (1978)—describe private experience, but they do so within the contexts of the ugly urban life of Fresno, California, the migration of the hungry poor out of Mexico, and the dreary toil of farmwork in the San Joaquin Valley—toil that Soto had experienced firsthand. In a grim Fresno poem, "After Tonight," violent death and injury are a constant threat. Grief is everywhere: the tavern keeper Manuel, of "The Manuel Zaragoza Poems," is plunged into mourning when his wife's birthing goes awry ("Graciela").

In later books, Soto enlarges his repertoire. With a keen memory for the atmosphere and feelings of childhood, he recalls some charming moments of relief amid the culture of poverty. "Oranges" touchingly relates a boy's first date, with only a nickel and two oranges in his pockets, and his redemption by a kindly salesperson. In "Practicing Eulogies," the young Soto and his brother turn a rooster's claws into toys that grasp things. "Sensitive me," concludes the poet self-mockingly, "I went for the box of Kleenex, / Tendons closing and tissues jerking up like ghosts." Evincing poverty as it impinges on the lives of individuals, Soto uses fresh and vivid figurative language and conjures physical sensations with immediacy.

Soto was born on April 12, 1952, in Fresno. In 1974, he earned a B.A. at California State University, Fresno, where he studied with a master poet of working-class life, Philip Levine; in 1976, he earned an M.F.A. at the University of California, Irvine. He has also written several books of autobiographical prose, including books for children and young adults. From 1979 to 1996, he taught Chicano studies and English at the University of California, Berkeley.

After Tonight

Because there are avenues
Of traffic lights, a phone book
Of brothers and lawyers,
Why should you think your purse
Will not be tugged from your arm   5
Or the screen door
Will remain latched

Against the man
Who hugs and kisses
His pillow   10
In the corridor of loneliness?

There is a window of light
A sprinkler turning
As the earth turns,
And you do not think of the hills   15
And of the splintered wrists it takes
To give you
The heat rising toward the ceiling.

You expect your daughter
To be at the door any moment   20
And your husband to arrive
With the night
That is suddenly all around.
You expect the stove to burst
A collar of fire   25
When you want it,
The siamese cats
To move against your legs, purring.

But remember this:
Because blood revolves from one lung to the next,   30
Why think it will
After tonight?

1977

The Drought

The clouds shouldered a path up the mountains
East of Ocampo,[1] and then descended,
Scraping their bellies gray on the cracked shingles of slate.

They entered the valley, and passed the roads that went
Trackless, the houses blown open, their cellars creaking   5
And lined with the bottles that held their breath for years.

They passed the fields where the trees dried thin as hat racks
And the plow's tooth bit the earth for what endured.
But what continued were the wind that plucked the birds spineless

And the young who left with a few seeds in each pocket,   10
Their belts tightened on the fifth notch of hunger—
Under the sky that deafened from listening for rain.

1978

---

1. Town in Mexico.

Graciela[2]

Wedding night
Graciela bled lightly—
But enough to stain his thighs—
And left an alphabet
Of teeth marks on his arm.   5
At this, he was happy.
They drank mescal[3]
In bed like the rich
And smoked cigarettes.
She asleep   10
And the bottle empty, he hid
A few coins in her left shoe,
Earrings in the right.
They worked long hours
Hoeing crooked rows of maize.   15
Evenings she wove rugs
And embroidered curtains
To market in Taxco.[4]
In short they lived well.
However in the seventh month   20
With child, her belly
Rising like a portion of the sun,
Something knotted inside her.
The ribs ached. A fever climbed.
Manuel summoned the Partera[5]   25
And though she burned pepper,
And tied belts around
The stretched belly,
The child did not ease out.
Days later she turned   30
Onto her belly
And between her legs
Unraveled a spine of blood.

                                      1978

Oranges

The first time I walked
With a girl, I was twelve,
Cold, and weighted down
With two oranges in my jacket.
December. Frost cracking   5
Beneath my steps, my breath
Before me, then gone,

---

2. One of the first poems in "The Manuel Zara-
goza Poems," a section of the book *The Tale of
Sunlight*.

3. Mexican liquor.
4. Town in central Mexico.
5. Midwife.

As I walked toward
Her house, the one whose
Porch light burned yellow   10
Night and day, in any weather.
A dog barked at me, until
She came out pulling
At her gloves, face bright
With rouge. I smiled,   15
Touched her shoulder, and led
Her down the street, across
A used car lot and a line
Of newly planted trees,
Until we were breathing   20
Before a drugstore. We
Entered, the tiny bell
Bringing a saleslady
Down a narrow aisle of goods.
I turned to the candies   25
Tiered like bleachers,
And asked what she wanted—
Light in her eyes, a smile
Starting at the corners
Of her mouth. I fingered   30
A nickel in my pocket,
And when she lifted a chocolate
That cost a dime,
I didn't say anything.
I took the nickel from   35
My pocket, then an orange,
And set them quietly on
The counter. When I looked up,
The lady's eyes met mine,
And held them, knowing   40
Very well what it was all
About.

    Outside,
A few cars hissing past,
Fog hanging like old   45
Coats between the trees.
I took my girl's hand
In mine for two blocks,
Then released it to let
Her unwrap the chocolate.   50
I peeled my orange
That was so bright against
The gray of December
That, from some distance,
Someone might have thought   55
I was making a fire in my hands.

1985

How Things Work

Today it's going to cost us twenty dollars
To live. Five for a softball. Four for a book,
A handful of ones for coffee and two sweet rolls,
Bus fare, rosin for your mother's violin.
We're completing our task. The tip I left   5
For the waitress filters down
Like rain, wetting the new roots of a child
Perhaps, a belligerent cat that won't let go
Of a balled sock until there's chicken to eat.
As far as I can tell, daughter, it works like this: 10
You buy bread from a grocery, a bag of apples
From a fruit stand, and what coins
Are passed on helps others buy pencils, glue,
Tickets to a movie in which laughter
Is thrown into their faces.   15
If we buy a goldfish, someone tries on a hat.
If we buy crayons, someone walks home with a broom.
A tip, a small purchase here and there,
And things just keep going. I guess.

1985

Practicing Eulogies

Momma cat died in the weeds,
A stink swirling in my nostrils
Until the flat hand of slapping rain
Leveled its odor. Then a neighbor died,
The one who said, Look, I got my wife's cancer—   5
His bony hands transparent as paper.
That was more than I needed
—mortal cat and mortal, old man—
And walked to the courthouse to sit by a pond,
Sickly fish gasping, their gills like razor slits.   10
Turd-coiled toads lay on the bottom, not daring to come up.
I was stirring the surface with a finger
When a suicidal cricket leaped into the pond.
Honest-to-God, I tried to save that armored insect—
My hand scooped and scooped   15
Like a pelican. The fish,
Sick as they were, ate antenna and spindly legs.
On the way home, I petted a stray dog,
Stared at a bird's egg cracked like a crown,
And wondered about death,   20
That flea-juice under my fingernail.
I grew scared. In the kitchen,
The neighbor's rooster was on the stove,

Boiling among diced celery and coins of carrots.
Do saints ever sleep? I asked my mom,   25
And she said, Put out the big spoons.
We ate that rooster,
Tastier than store-bought chicken.
After dinner I got Frankie's left claw
And my brother got the right claw.   30
We worked the tendons like pulleys
As the claws opened and closed on things—
My laughing brother picked up pencils and erasers.
Sensitive me, I went for the box of Kleenex,
Tendons closing and tissues jerking up like ghosts.   35

                                                           1999

RITA DOVE
b. 1952

Appealing to our common humanity, Rita Dove's poems may be enjoyed by both the mind and the senses. Made out of intricate associative puzzles, they tell stories in miniature. Their language is musically pitched and cadenced but restrained, richly textured but taut. Like Robert Hayden and Gwendolyn Brooks, Dove is a poet of understatement who gives by holding back, demanding that we attend as much to what is unsaid as to what is said. Although much of her work is autobiographical, she distills this emotional material through crystalline phrasing, chiseled lines, precise diction and similes, careful rhythms, and sonic patterning. Whether she writes about the sensual body or historical atrocity, Dove approaches her subject with a sympathetic but cool eye. Her early series "Adolescence" recalls emerging sexuality, endowing this experience with curiosity, fearfulness, and pleasure. A later poem, "After Reading *Mickey in the Night Kitchen* for the Third Time before Bed," describes with frankness and yet considerable grace and humor a mother and daughter sharing the secrets of their bodies: "That we're in the pink / and the pink's in us."

Many of Dove's poems are written out of her sense of history and its injustices. Inventing some incidents (e.g., "The House Slave"), she also makes poems out of the lives of historical men and women whom she, like Odysseus on his visit to the underworld, restores to life long enough for them to speak to us and thus endure. In "Claudette Colvin Goes to Work," she imagines the inner life of the young, African American woman who helped precipitate the Montgomery bus boycott. In this poem, as elsewhere, Dove finds within her character not the straightforward emotions one might expect of a "role model," but more ambiguous feelings. Dove's historical poems witness injustice without falsifying the variety of emotions roused by it, from pain and anger to guilt, resignation, and ambivalence.

Dove's Pulitzer Prize–winning sequence, *Thomas and Beulah*, recounts the inner lives of her grandparents, reflecting in microcosm the movements and social history of African Americans in the first sixty years of the twentieth century. The sequence encapsulates two lifetimes, told in a series of short poems. Dove celebrates the lives of her grandparents, and the work shines with gratitude and joy. Part of her purpose was also to combat the assumption that the inner lives of the poor and unlettered are less complex than the lives of those who are on easier terms with society. Thomas is haunted by guilt over his friend's accidental death, as recounted in "The Incident." Beulah, hidden from the white customers of the dress shop, ironing the sweaty dress of a white woman while reflecting on the spoiled darlings of the French courts, is complex and heroic. Using free, indirect discourse to mirror the inner world of her grandparents, Dove employs both colloquial and elevated diction, rhetoric, and figurative language, creating a fascinating convergence between the minds of the poet and her characters.

What to make of a mixed cultural inheritance—black and white, African American and European? This central question confronts Dove as it did such predecessors as Melvin Tolson, Brooks, and Hayden. In contrast to African American poets inspired by the cultural nationalism of the Black Arts Movement, such as Amiri Baraka and June Jordan, Dove wants less to separate the African American aesthetic from other cultural traditions than to offer a synthesis. The myth of Demeter and Persephone is not off limits because of its European origins, but a powerful archetype for interpreting her experience as a mother, in *Mother Love* (1995). So too with poetic forms. For her brilliant poem "Parsley," about how the Dominican dictator Rafael Trujillo slaughtered twenty thousand blacks who spoke Haitian Creole, she loosely adapts the villanelle (in the first part) and the sestina (in the second). She has explained that the "obsessiveness of the sestina, the repeated words, was something I wanted to get at—that driven quality" (*Black American Literature Forum*, Fall 1986). Dove ironically adapts European poetic forms to retell the story of one of the twentieth century's most horrific and gratuitous atrocities against New World blacks, promulgated by a dictator who insisted on a European norm of speech. Like Claude McKay with the sonnet, Tolson with the Pindaric ode, or Derek Walcott with Homeric epic, Dove wrests European forms from those who enslaved her ancestors to recount vividly a crime against men and women of the African diaspora. Dove is no less bold about imaginatively entering the mind of the murderous dictator, as she explained in an interview: "It was important to me to try to understand that arbitrary quality of his cruelty. And I'm not afraid of making him too human. I don't believe anyone's going to like him after reading my poem. Making us get into his head may shock us all into seeing what the human being is capable of, and what in fact we're capable of, because if we can go that far into his head we're halfway there ourselves" (*Black American*). Recovering the ethical and experiential messiness of history, Dove risks implicating herself (and us as readers) in the fate not only of the slaughtered Haitians, but also of the cruel dictator, who is as obsessed as any poet by the sound and power of words.

In another of her most powerful poems, "Agosta the Winged Man and Rasha the Black Dove," Dove reflects on a 1929 German painting of two sideshow performers, one afflicted with a bone disease that made him almost seem to have wings, another a Madagascan woman whose only oddity was her blackness. In this disturbing meditation on art, race, and spectatorship, Dove's identification is again mixed: she shares some kinship not only with the objectified black woman or "Dove," but also perhaps with the objectifying gaze of the painter, who uses "classical drapery" and makes art out of the people he portrays. Similarly, in a poem about slavery, "The House Slave," the poet wonders whether she (and the reader) have more in common with the sister whipped in the field or with the house slave who, racked with guilt, stays in the house and overhears her sister's cries at a distance. Dove's poems explore such difficult questions about art and suffering with courage, subtlety, and rigor.

Dove was born on August 28, 1952, in Akron, Ohio, where her father was a chemist. She was educated at Miami University in Oxford, Ohio, traveled to Tübingen University in Germany as a Fulbright fellow (1974–75), and received her M.F.A. from the University of Iowa (1977). She has taught creative writing at Arizona State University (1981–89) and, since 1989, at the University of Virginia. Besides her books of poetry, she has published short stories, a play, and a novel. Winner of the 1987 Pulitzer Prize and many other awards, she was the first African American poet laureate of the United States (1993–95).

Geometry

I prove a theorem and the house expands:
the windows jerk free to hover near the ceiling,
the ceiling floats away with a sigh.

As the walls clear themselves of everything
but transparency, the scent of carnations   5
leaves with them. I am out in the open

and above the windows have hinged into butterflies,
sunlight glinting where they've intersected.
They are going to some point true and unproven.

                                                                    1980

The House Slave

The first horn lifts its arm over the dew-lit grass
and in the slave quarters there is a rustling—
children are bundled into aprons, cornbread

and water gourds grabbed, a salt pork breakfast taken.
I watch them driven into the vague before-dawn   5
while their mistress sleeps like an ivory toothpick

and Massa dreams of asses, rum and slave-funk.
I cannot fall asleep again. At the second horn,
the whip curls across the backs of the laggards—

sometimes my sister's voice, unmistaken, among them.   10
"Oh! pray," she cries. "Oh! pray!" Those days
I lie on my cot, shivering in the early heat,

and as the fields unfold to whiteness,
and they spill like bees among the fat flowers,
I weep. It is not yet daylight.   15

                                                                    1980

Adolescence—II

Although it is night, I sit in the bathroom, waiting.
Sweat prickles behind my knees, the baby-breasts are alert.
Venetian blinds slice up the moon; the tiles quiver in pale strips.

Then they come, the three seal men with eyes as round
As dinner plates and eyelashes like sharpened tines.   5
They bring the scent of licorice. One sits in the washbowl,

One on the bathtub edge; one leans against the door.
"Can you feel it yet?" they whisper.
I don't know what to say, again. They chuckle,

Patting their sleek bodies with their hands.   10
"Well, maybe next time." And they rise,
Glittering like pools of ink under moonlight,

And vanish. I clutch at the ragged holes
They leave behind, here at the edge of darkness.
Night rests like a ball of fur on my tongue.   15

                                                    1980

Agosta the Winged Man and Rasha the Black Dove[1]

    Schad paced the length of his studio
    and stopped at the wall,
                staring
    at a blank space. Behind him
    the clang and hum of Hardenbergstrasse,[2] its   5
    automobiles and organ grinders.
                      Quarter to five.
    His eyes traveled
    to the plaster scrollwork
    on the ceiling. Did *that*   10
              hold back heaven?
    He could not leave his skin—once
    he'd painted himself in a new one,
    silk green, worn
    like a shirt.   15
          He thought
    of Rasha, so far from Madagascar,
    turning slowly in place as
    the boa constrictor
    coiled counterwise its   20
            heavy love. How
    the spectators gawked, exhaling
    beer and sour herring sighs.
    When the tent lights dimmed,
    Rasha went back to her trailer and plucked   25

1. Title of a 1929 painting by German painter Christian Schad (1894–1982), depicting two Berlin sideshow performers. Agosta had a bone disease that caused his ribs and shoulder blades to jut out of his body like wings. Rasha was a Madagascan woman whose title, "the Black Dove," recalls the emblem of the serpent and the dove, since she performed with a boa constrictor twined around her (though not in Schad's painting).
2. Street in Berlin.

a chicken for dinner.
                    The canvas,

not his eye, was merciless.
He remembered Katja the Russian
aristocrat, late   30
for every sitting,
                    still fleeing
the October Revolution[3]—
how she clutched her sides
and said not   35
                    one word. Whereas Agosta
(the doorbell rang)
was always on time, lip curled
as he spoke in wonder of women
                              trailing   40
backstage to offer him
the consummate bloom of their lust.

Schad would place him
on a throne, a white sheet tucked
over his loins, the black suit jacket   45
thrown off like a cloak.
Agosta had told him
                    of the medical students
at the Charité,[4]
that chill arena   50
                    where he perched on
a cot, his torso
exposed, its crests and fins
a colony of birds, trying
to get out . . .   55
                    and the students,
lumps caught
in their throats, taking notes.

Ah, Rasha's
          foot on the stair.   60
She moved slowly, as if she carried
the snake around her body
always.

          Once
she brought fresh eggs into   65
the studio, flecked and
warm as breath.
                    Agosta in
classical drapery, then,
and Rasha at his feet.   70
Without passion. Not

---

         the canvas
                  but their gaze,
                  so calm,
         was merciless.   75

                                                              1983

Parsley[5]

1. The Cane Fields[6]

There is a parrot imitating spring
in the palace, its feathers parsley green.
Out of the swamp the cane appears

to haunt us, and we cut it down. El General
searches for a word; he is all the world   5
there is. Like a parrot imitating spring,

we lie down screaming as rain punches through
and we come up green. We cannot speak an R—
out of the swamp, the cane appears

and then the mountain we call in whispers *Katalina*.[7]   10
The children gnaw their teeth to arrowheads.
There is a parrot imitating spring.

El General has found his word: *perejil*.
Who says it, lives. He laughs, teeth shining
out of the swamp. The cane appears   15

in our dreams, lashed by wind and streaming.
And we lie down. For every drop of blood
there is a parrot imitating spring.
Out of the swamp the cane appears.

2. The Palace

The word the general's chosen is parsley.   20
It is fall, when thoughts turn
to love and death; the general thinks
of his mother, how she died in the fall
and he planted her walking cane at the grave
and it flowered, each spring stolidly forming   25
four-star blossoms. The general

---

5. "On October 2, 1937, Rafael Trujillo (1891–
1961), dictator of the Dominican Republic,
ordered 20,000 blacks to be killed because they
could not pronounce the letter 'r' in *perejil*, the
Spanish word for parsley" [Dove's note].

6. This first section is in the form of a (nonrhym-
ing) villanelle. *Cane*: sugar cane.
7. That is, Katarina (since "we cannot speak an
R").

pulls on his boots, he stomps to
her room in the palace, the one without
curtains, the one with a parrot
in a brass ring. As he paces he wonders   30
Who can I kill today. And for a moment
the little knot of screams
is still. The parrot, who has traveled

all the way from Australia in an ivory
cage, is, coy as a widow, practising   35
spring. Ever since the morning
his mother collapsed in the kitchen
while baking skull-shaped candies
for the Day of the Dead,[8] the general   40
has hated sweets. He orders pastries
brought up for the bird; they arrive

dusted with sugar on a bed of lace.
The knot in his throat starts to twitch;
he sees his boots the first day in battle
splashed with mud and urine   45
as a soldier falls at his feet amazed—
how stupid he looked!— at the sound
of artillery. *I never thought it would sing*
the soldier said, and died. Now

the general sees the fields of sugar   50
cane, lashed by rain and streaming.
He sees his mother's smile, the teeth
gnawed into arrowheads. He hears
the Haitians sing without R's
as they swing the great machetes: 55
Katalina, they sing, *Katalina*,

mi madle, mi amol en muelte.[9] God knows
his mother was no stupid woman; she
could roll an R like a queen. Even
a parrot can roll an R! In the bare room   60
the bright feathers arch in a parody
of greenery, as the last pale crumbs
disappear under the blackened tongue. Someone

calls out his name in a voice
so like his mother's, a startled tear   65
splashes the tip of his right boot.
My mother, my love in death.
The general remembers the tiny green sprigs
men of his village wore in their capes

8. Roman Catholic celebration honoring the souls
of the dead.

9. That is, *mi madre, mi amor en muerte:* "my
mother, my love in death."

to honor the birth of a son. He will   70
order many, this time, to be killed

for a single, beautiful word.

1983

FROM THOMAS AND BEULAH[1]

The Event

Ever since they'd left the Tennessee ridge
with nothing to boast of
but good looks and a mandolin,

the two Negroes leaning
on the rail of a riverboat   5
were inseparable: Lem plucked

to Thomas' silver falsetto.
But the night was hot and they were drunk.
They spat where the wheel

churned mud and moonlight,   10
they called to the tarantulas
down among the bananas

to come out and dance.
You're so fine and mighty; let's see
what you can do, said Thomas, pointing   15

to a tree-capped island.
Lem stripped, spoke easy: *Them's chestnuts,*
I believe. Dove

quick as a gasp. Thomas, dry
on deck, saw the green crown shake   20
as the island slipped

under, dissolved
in the thickening stream.
At his feet

1. "These poems tell two sides of a story and are meant to be read in sequence" [Dove's introduction]. *Thomas and Beulah* was inspired by incidents in the lives of Dove's grandparents in Akron, Ohio, and begun after she heard this story from her grandmother: Dove's grandfather dared a friend "to jump off the boat and swim to an island and to pick some chestnuts and the friend died in the river."

a stinking circle of rags,   25
the half-shell mandolin.
Where the wheel turned the water

gently shirred.[2]

Dusting

Every day a wilderness—no
shade in sight. Beulah[3]
patient among knicknacks,
the solarium a rage
of light, a grainstorm   5
as her gray cloth brings
dark wood to life.

Under her hand scrolls
and crests gleam
darker still. What   10
was his name, that
silly boy at the fair with
the rifle booth? And his kiss and
the clear bowl with one bright
fish, rippling   15
wound!

Not Michael—
something finer. Each dust
stroke a deep breath and
the canary in bloom.   20
Wavery memory: home
from a dance, the front door
blown open and the parlor
in snow, she rushed
the bowl to the stove, watched   25
as the locket of ice
dissolved and he
swam free.

That was years before
Father gave her up   30
with her name, years before
her name grew to mean
Promise, then
Desert-in-Peace.

2. Drew together.
3. Hebrew for married; used in the Bible to refer to the promised land.

Long before the shadow and
sun's accomplice, the tree.   35

Maurice.

Weathering Out

She liked mornings the best—Thomas gone
to look for work, her coffee flushed with milk,

outside autumn trees blowsy and dripping.
Past the seventh month she couldn't see her feet

so she floated from room to room, houseshoes flapping,   5
navigating corners in wonder. When she leaned

against a door jamb to yawn, she disappeared entirely.

Last week they had taken a bus at dawn
to the new airdock. The hangar slid open in segments

and the zeppelin nosed forward in its silver envelope.   10
The man walked it out gingerly, like a poodle,

then tied it to a mast and went back inside.
Beulah felt just that large and placid, a lake;

she glistened from cocoa butter smoothed in
when Thomas returned every evening nearly   15

in tears. He'd lean an ear on her belly
and say: *Little fellow's really talking,*

though to her it was more the *pok-pok-pok*
of a fingernail tapping a thick cream lampshade.

Sometimes during the night she woke and found him   20
asleep there and the child sleeping, too.

The coffee was good but too little. Outside
everything shivered in tinfoil—only the clover

between the cobblestones hung stubbornly on,
green as an afterthought. . . .   25

The Great Palaces of Versailles[4]

Nothing nastier than a white person!
She mutters as she irons alterations
in the backroom of Charlotte's Dress Shoppe.
The steam rising from a cranberry wool
comes alive with perspiration[5]   5
and stale Evening of Paris.
Swamp she born from, swamp
she swallow, swamp she got to sink again.

The iron shoves gently
into a gusset,[6] waits until   10
the puckers bloom away. Beyond
the curtain, the white girls are all
wearing shoulder pads to make their faces
delicate. That laugh would be Autumn,
tossing her hair in imitation of Bacall.[7]   15

Beulah had read in the library
how French ladies at court would tuck
their fans in a sleeve
and walk in the gardens for air. Swaying
among lilies, lifting shy layers of silk,   20
they dropped excrement as daintily
as handkerchieves. Against all rules

she had saved the lining from a botched coat
to face last year's gray skirt. She knows
whenever she lifts a knee   25
she flashes crimson. That seems legitimate;
but in the book she had read
how the *cavaliere*[8] amused themselves
wearing powder and perfume and spraying
yellow borders knee-high on the stucco   30
of the *Orangerie*.[9]

A hanger clatters
in the front of the shoppe.
Beulah remembers how
even Autumn could lean into a settee   35
with her ankles crossed, sighing
I need a man who'll protect me
while smoking her cigarette down to the very end.

---

4. The magnificent complex of palaces built principally by Louis XIV (1638–1715) of France.
5. Beulah "can smell the perspiration. In that poem, it's one of those rare moments where, with her rage, she even allows it to come to the surface in terms of response. It's a political situation, actually, in the dress shop, because white girls can sell the dresses in the front of the shop and she, as the black help, gets to iron in the back room" [Dove's comments].
6. Insert in the seam of a garment.
7. Lauren Bacall (b. 1924), American actor.
8. Lovers, gallants.
9. Building housing orange trees at Versailles.

Wingfoot Lake[1]

(Independence Day, 1964)

On her 36th birthday, Thomas had shown her
her first swimming pool. It had been
his favorite color, exactly—just
so much of it, the swimmers' white arms jutting
into the chevrons[2] of high society.   5
She had rolled up her window
and told him to drive on, fast.

Now this *act of mercy*: four daughters
dragging her to their husbands' company picnic,
white families on one side and them   10
on the other, unpacking the same
squeeze bottles of Heinz, the same
waxy beef patties and Salem potato chip bags.
So he was dead for the first time
on Fourth of July—ten years ago   15

had been harder, waiting for something to happen,
and ten years before that, the girls
like young horses eying the track.
Last August she stood alone for hours
in front of the T.V. set   20
as a crow's wing moved slowly through
the white streets of government.
That brave swimming

scared her, like Joanna saying
Mother, we're Afro-Americans now!   25
What did she know about Africa?
Were there lakes like this one
with a rowboat pushed under the pier?
Or Thomas' Great Mississippi
with its sullen silks? (There was   30
the Nile but the Nile belonged
to God.) Where she came from
was the past, 12 miles into town
where nobody had locked their back door,
and Goodyear hadn't begun to dream of a park   35
under the company symbol, a white foot
sprouting two small wings.

                                        1986

---

1. Lake and park owned by the Goodyear Tire &
Rubber Company, for whom the poet's grandfather
worked in Akron, Ohio.

2. V shapes; badges of honor or rank worn on the
sleeve.

After Reading *Mickey in the Night Kitchen*[3] for the Third Time before Bed

I'm in the milk and the milk's in me! . . . I'm Mickey!

My daughter spreads her legs
to find her vagina:
hairless, this mistaken
bit of nomenclature
is what a stranger cannot touch   5
without her yelling. She demands
to see mine and momentarily
we're a lopsided star
among the spilled toys,
my prodigious scallops   10
exposed to her neat cameo.

And yet the same glazed
tunnel, layered sequences.
She is three; that makes this
innocent. *We're pink!*   15
she shrieks, and bounds off.

Every month she wants
to know where it hurts
and what the wrinkled string means
between my legs. *This is good blood*   20
I say, but that's wrong, too.
How to tell her that it's what makes us—
black mother, cream child.
That we're in the pink
and the pink's in us.   25

                                    1987

Claudette Colvin Goes to Work[4]

Another Negro woman has been arrested and thrown into jail
because she refused to get up out of her seat on the bus and give
it to a white person. This is the second time since the Claudette
Colbert [sic] case. . . . This must be stopped.
                              —Boycott Flier, December 5, 1955

Menial twilight sweeps the storefronts along Lexington[5]
as the shadows arrive to take their places
among the scourge of the earth. Here and there

---

3. *In the Night Kitchen* (1970): children's book by
Maurice Sendak and Dena Wallenstein Neusner.
4. Claudette Colvin, an African American woman,
was fifteen when she was arrested in Montgomery,
Alabama, for refusing to give up her seat on a bus
to a white person. Her example helped start the

Montgomery bus boycott of 1955. The author of
the flier in the epigraph mixes up Colvin's name
with that of Claudette Colbert (1903–1996),
French-born American actor.
5. Avenue running through Harlem in New York
City.

a fickle brilliance—lightbulbs coming on
in each narrow residence, the golden wattage   5
of bleak interiors announcing *Anyone home?*
or *I'm beat, bring me a beer.*

Mostly I say to myself *Still here.* Lay
my keys on the table, pack the perishables away
before flipping the switch. I like the sugary   10
look of things in bad light—one drop of sweat
is all it would take to dissolve an armchair pillow
into brocade residue. Sometimes I wait until
it's dark enough for my body to disappear;

then I know it's time to start out for work.   15
Along the Avenue, the cabs start up, heading
toward midtown; neon stutters into ecstasy
as the male integers light up their smokes and let loose
a stream of brave talk: "Hey Mama" souring quickly to
"Your Mama" when there's no answer—as if   20
the most injury they can do is insult the reason

you're here at all, walking in your whites
down to the stop so you can make a living.
So ugly, so fat, so dumb, so greasy—
What do we have to do to make God love us?   25
Mama was a maid; my daddy mowed lawns like a boy,
and I'm the crazy girl off the bus, the one
who wrote in class she was going to be President.

I take the Number 6 bus to the Lex Ave train
and then I'm there all night, adjusting the sheets,   30
emptying the pans. And I don't curse or spit
or kick and scratch like they say I did then.
I help those who can't help themselves,
I do what needs to be done . . . and I sleep
whenever sleep comes down on me.   35

1999

ALBERTO RÍOS
b. 1952

"You see, there are in our countries rivers which have no names, trees which nobody
knows, and birds which nobody has described. . . . Our duty, then, as we understand
it, is to express what is unheard of." Alberto Ríos used this remark—made by the Chi-
lean poet Pablo Neruda—as the epigraph for his first book, *Whispering to Fool the Wind*
(1981), and he perhaps has adopted it as his own program. Ríos quietly makes his
readers accept, understand, and take pleasure in his fanciful, "unheard-of" characters.
The "old Russian" in "A Man Then Suddenly Stops Moving" is merely "surprised" when,

out of a plum he has thrown to the ground, emerges his "younger self," which he simply puts "on the shelf / with the pictures." When the priest Anselmo Luna dies on a ladder, as recounted in the later collection *Teodora Luna's Two Kisses* (1990), his "muscular" soul is said to leap "from his ribs / As he had stepped / On the rungs of the ladder." Blurring boundaries between the actual and the mysterious, Ríos tells such miniaturized stories in a matter-of-fact tone, his insouciance disarming the reader's skepticism.

One of Ríos's finest grotesques is "Madre Sofía," the fat, old gypsy fortune-teller his mother takes him to when he is ten, "because she couldn't / wait the second ten years to know" her son's future. We see Madre Sofía through the child's eyes, and with him we are bewildered and terrified by her. In this poem, as in Ríos's short story about the same visit, "Eyes Like They Say the Devil Has," vivid details haunt the speaker: the "unfamiliar poppies" growing out of Sofía's head, her breasts like "horse nuzzles" or "like the quarter-arms of the amputee Joaquín," and the final prediction, which dissolves fear: *The future will make you tall.* In such poems, Ríos embodies the mixture of fantasy and realism—the "magical realism"—of Latin American writers such as Gabriel García Márquez. Unlike Gary Soto, a contemporary and fellow Chicano poet who also pays homage to Márquez, but who is typically more realistic in his textured evocations of the culture of Mexican American poverty, Ríos hybridizes English-language poetry with both Latin American tradition and the rhetoric and rhythms of Latino English. His poetic language indirectly but beautifully recalls the Spanish he was forced to give up in junior high school.

Ríos was born on September 18, 1952, in Nogales, Arizona, on the border of Mexico. "My father, born in southern Mexico, and my mother, born in England, gave me a language-rich, story-fat upbringing," he has said. He earned B.A.s in English and psychology at the University of Arizona (1974, 1975). After a brief stint at law school, which he left to pursue writing, he earned an M.F.A. at the University of Arizona (1979). In addition to poetry and prose fiction, he has published a memoir. Since 1982, he has taught creative writing at Arizona State University.

Madre Sofía[1]

My mother took me because she couldn't
wait the second ten years to know.
This was the lady rumored to have been
responsible for the box-wrapped baby
among the presents at that wedding,   5
but we went in, anyway, through the curtains.
Loose jar-top, half turned
and not caught properly in the threads
her head sat mimicking its original intention
like the smile of a child hitting himself.   10
Central in that head grew unfamiliar poppies
from a face mahogany, eyes half yellow
half gray at the same time, goat and fog,
slit eyes of the devil, his tweed suit, red
lips, and she smelled of smoke, cigarettes,   15

---

1. Mother Sofía (Spanish); "Sofía" derives from the Greek word meaning wisdom.

but a diamond smoke, somehow; I inhaled
sparkles, I could feel them, throat, stomach.
She did not speak, and as a child
I could only answer, so that together
we were silent, cold and wet, dry and hard: 20
from behind my mother pushed me forward.
The lady put her hand on the face
of a thin animal wrap, tossing that head
behind her to be pressured incredibly
as she sat back in the huge chair and leaned.   25
And then I saw the breasts as large as her
head, folded together, coming out of her dress
as if it didn't fit, not like my mother's.
I could see them, how she kept them
penned up, leisurely, in maroon feed bags,   30
horse nuzzles of her wide body,
but exquisitely penned up
circled by pearl reins and red scarves.
She lifted her arm, but only with the tips
of her fingers motioned me to sit opposite.   35
She looked at me but spoke to my mother
words dark, smoky like the small room,
words coming like red ants stepping occasionally
from a hole on a summer day in the valley,
red ants from her mouth, her nose, her ears,   40
tears from the corners of her cinched eyes.
And suddenly she put her hand full on my head
pinching tight again with those finger tips
like a television healer, young Oral Roberts
half standing, quickly, half leaning   45
those breasts swinging toward me
so that I reach with both my hands to my lap
protecting instinctively whatever it is
that needs protection when a baseball is thrown
and you're not looking but someone yells,   50
the hand, then those breasts coming toward me
like the quarter-arms of the amputee Joaquín
who came back from the war to sit
in the park, reaching always for children
until one day he had to be held back.   55
I sat there, no breath, and could see only
hair around her left nipple, like a man.
Her clothes were old.
Accented, in a language whose spine had been
snapped, she whispered the words of a city   60
witch, and made me happy, alive like a man:
The future will make you tall.

1982

Mi Abuelo[2]

Where my grandfather is is in the ground
where you can hear the future
like an Indian with his ear at the tracks.
A pipe leads down to him so that sometimes
he whispers what will happen to a man   5
in town or how he will meet the best
dressed woman tomorrow and how the best
man at her wedding will chew the ground
next to her. Mi abuelo is the man
who speaks through all the mouths in my house.   10
An echo of me hitting the pipe sometimes
to stop him from saying *my hair is a*
sieve is the only other sound. It is a phrase
that among all others is the best,
he says, and *my hair is a sieve* is sometimes   15
repeated for hours out of the ground
when I let him, which is not often.
An abuelo should be much more than a man
like you! He stops then, and speaks: *I am a man*
who has served ants with the attitude   20
of a waiter, who has made each smile as only
an ant who is fat can, and they liked me best,
but there is nothing left. Yet I know he ground
green coffee beans as a child, and sometimes
he will talk about his wife, and sometimes   25
about when he was deaf and a man
cured him by mail and he heard groundhogs
talking, or about how he walked with a cane
he chewed on when he got hungry.
At best, mi abuelo is a liar.   30
I see an old picture of him at nani's[3] with an
off-white yellow center mustache and sometimes
that's all I know for sure. He talks best
about these hills, *slowest waves,* and where this man
is going, and I'm convinced his hair is a sieve,   35
that his fever is cooled now underground.
Mi abuelo is an ordinary man.
I look down the pipe, sometimes, and see a
ripple-topped stream in its best suit, in the ground.

1982

---

2. My grandfather (Spanish).   3. Grandma's (informal Spanish).

A Man Then Suddenly Stops Moving

The old Russian spits up a plum
fruit of the rasping sound
he has stored in his throat
all these lonely years

made in fact lonely by his wife   5
who left him, God knows
without knowing how to cook for himself.

He examines the plum
notes its purplish consistency
almost the color and shape of her buttocks   10
whose circulation was bad

which is why he himself wears a beret:
black, good wool, certainly warm enough
the times he remembers.

He shoots the plum   15
to the ground like a child
whose confidence is a game of marbles

whose flick of a thumb
is a smile inside his mouth
knowing what he knows will happen.   20

But his wife, Marthe
does not spill out
when the plum breaks open.

Instead, it is a younger self
alive and waving   25
just the size he remembers
himself to have been.

The old Russian puts him onto his finger
like a parakeet
and sits him on the shelf   30
with the pictures.

For the rest of his days
he nags himself constantly
into a half-sleep
surprised by this turn of events.   35

1985

Anselmo's Moment with God[4]

Anselmo in a fit of pique
Over a spatula he could not find
As the eggs were burning
And as he did not yet have the services
Of the housekeeper Mrs. M.   5
He would have in later years,
Renounced his love of God
And of the world, right there.

He threw the drawer of utensils to the ground
And let the eggs burn dry   10
Until they gave texture to
And became part of the black iron pan itself.
Every day for the rest of his life
He remembered himself that moment—
Himself but not the event: 15
His spatula became through the years
The Hand of God.

Of God's smell
He could not be certain:
Only that the burning of candles   20
Had for him a certain urgency.

                                                        1990

The Death of Anselmo Luna

Since he was the priest,
No one could say for certain about Anselmo Luna.
What began as a lark
One slow afternoon of interminable chores
Regarding candles and residue on the walls,   5
Became his drawings:
First of the saints,
Then the twelve Stations of the Cross,[5]
The sketches of simpler remembrances.
All of these chiaroscuros[6] he made   10
In and from the soot on the walls of this church,
A work that moved into years
And which finally filled his life.
What began as a lark became the seed

4. This poem and "The Death of Anselmo Luna" are taken from Ríos's *Teodoro Luna's Two Kisses*, a book of poems detailing the history of the fictitious Luna family. Anselmo is a priest and the brother of Teodoro.

5. A series of images depicting the final events in the life of Jesus.
6. Technique of painting with dramatic contrasts between light and dark.

Of his miracle, a simple   15
Moving of a finger along a pillar
Just to see, was there enough
To require cleansing,
This test also used on parked cars,
A line spelling *wash me* in the soil of a window.   20
He died while perched on a ladder
High behind the altar, underneath
The fine woodwork: that moment
As he fell, and as he made a mark
Not unlike a moustache   25
Where none should have been,
He died already partway
Toward heaven. It was said
His soul took the advantage,
Leaping out from his body   30
Right there, stepping from his ribs
As he had stepped
On the rungs of the ladder.
It was a strong soul, muscular,
On account of his years of devoted effort,   35
And it knew like an animal what to do
When the moment came.

1990

Mark Doty
b. 1953

Mark Doty quotes W. H. Auden's remarks that a poem should be "a verbal earthly paradise, a timeless world of pure play, which gives us delight precisely because of its contrast to our historical existence with all its insoluble problems and inescapable suffering"; and yet "a poet cannot bring us any truth without introducing into his poetry the problematic, the painful, the disorderly, the ugly" ("Here in Hell"). Doty tries to meet the demands of both delight and truth in his poetry of shimmering surfaces and numb grief, of exultant play and mortal pain. His work displays, as he has suggested, something of the drag queen's pleasure in ravishing texture and spectacle, but it also employs something of the mortician's cold stare at the grim inevitabilities of loss and death.

A poem such as "A Green Crab's Shell" is indeed an earthly paradise. The poem takes us inside a small crab's shell with its "shocking, Giotto blue" and "lavish lining," and it evokes the glory of a life "surrounded by / the brilliant rinse / of summer's firmament." Characteristically sensuous and painterly, Doty re-creates this magnificent and yet minute "chamber" in the artfully constructed chambers of his poem. But the shell that offers a fantastical escape into beauty reminds us also of death's inevitability.

Doty works in the tradition of American autobiographical poetry that extends from Walt Whitman to Elizabeth Bishop and Robert Lowell. The propulsive cadences and rhetorical patterns of "Homo Will Not Inherit," a charged repudiation of homophobia, echo Whitman. Here Doty also appropriates but transfigures biblical rhetoric in his sacramental descriptions of gay sex ("I've seen flame flicker around the edges of the body, / pentecostal") and of the soiled beauty of the homoerotic city: "This city's inescapable, // gorgeous, and on fire. I have my kingdom." The opening of "A Green Crab's Shell" may remind us of Bishop's penchant for exactly calibrated descriptions of nature's details ("Not, exactly, green: / closer to bronze / preserved in kind brine") and of Lowell's capacity for uncovering stress and violence in seeming calm ("something retrieved / from a Greco-Roman wreck, / patinated and oddly // muscular"). But for all his interest in gorgeous surfaces and lavish language, Doty can also write in a plain style. His austere AIDS elegy "The Embrace" largely withholds description, until the "physical fact" of the dead man's face—"smooth-shaven, loving, alert"—emerges with luminous power, only to be eclipsed by the quiet severity of the final line: "without thinking you were alive again."

Doty was born on August 10, 1953, in Maryville, Tennessee. His father was an army engineer whose work required frequent moves in the suburban American south and west. Doty married early, but divorced after receiving his B.A. from Drake University in Iowa. While working toward his M.F.A. from Goddard College, in Vermont, he met his partner, Wally Roberts, whose illness and death (in 1994, from AIDS) Doty has memorialized in prose as well as verse. Doty has taught creative writing at the Universities of Utah, Iowa, and Houston, Columbia University, and Sarah Lawrence College. He has received, among other prizes, the National Book Critics Circle Award in 1994 and the T. S. Eliot Prize in 1995.

A Green Crab's Shell

Not, exactly, green:
closer to bronze
preserved in kind brine,

something retrieved
from a Greco-Roman wreck,   5
patinated and oddly

muscular. We cannot
know what his fantastic
legs were like—

though evidence   10
suggests eight
complexly folded

scuttling works
of armament, crowned
by the foreclaws'   15

gesture of menace
and power. A gull's
gobbled the center,

leaving this chamber
—size of a demitasse— 20
open to reveal

a shocking, Giotto[1] blue.
Though it smells
of seaweed and ruin,

this little traveling case 25
comes with such lavish lining!
Imagine breathing

surrounded by
the brilliant rinse
of summer's firmament. 30

What color is
the underside of skin?
Not so bad, to die,

if we could be opened
into *this*— 35
if the smallest chambers

of ourselves,
similarly,
revealed some sky.

1995

Homo Will Not Inherit[2]

Downtown anywhere and between the roil
of bathhouse steam—up there the linens of joy
and shame must be laundered again and again,

all night—downtown anywhere
and between the column of feathering steam 5
unknotting itself thirty feet above the avenue's

shimmered azaleas of gasoline,
between the steam and the ruin
of the Cinema Paree (marquee advertising

its own milky vacancy, broken showcases sealed, 10
ticketbooth a hostage wrapped in tape
and black plastic, captive in this zone

---

1. Giotto di Bondone (c. 1266–1337), Italian artist. *Demitasse:* small cup.
2. "For Michael Carter" [Doty's note].

of blackfronted bars and bookstores
where there's nothing to read
but longing's repetitive texts,   15

where desire's unpoliced, or nearly so)
someone's posted a xeroxed headshot
of Jesus: permed, blonde, blurred at the edges

as though photographed through a greasy lens,
and inked beside him, in marker strokes: 20
HOMO WILL NOT INHERIT. *Repent & be saved.*[3]

I'll tell you what I'll inherit: the margins
which have always been mine, downtown after hours
when there's nothing left to buy,

the dreaming shops turned in on themselves,   25
seamless, intent on the perfection of display,
the bodegas[4] and offices lined up, impenetrable:

edges no one wants, no one's watching. Though
the borders of this shadow-zone (mirror and dream
of the shattered streets around it) are chartered   30

by the police, and they are required,
some nights, to redefine them. But not now, at twilight,
permission's descending hour, early winter darkness

pillared by smoldering plumes. The public city's
ledgered and locked, but the secret city's boundless;   35
from which do these tumbling towers arise?

I'll tell you what I'll inherit: steam,
and the blinding symmetry of some towering man,
fifteen minutes of forgetfulness incarnate.

I've seen flame flicker around the edges of the body,   40
pentecostal,[5] evidence of inhabitation.
And I have been possessed of the god myself,

I have been the temporary apparition
salving another, I have been his visitation, I say it
without arrogance, I have been an angel   45

for minutes at a time, and I have for hours
believed—without judgment, without condemnation—
that in each body, however obscured or recast,

---

3. "Be not deceived: neither fornicators, nor idol-
aters, nor adulterers, nor effeminate, nor abusers
of themselves with mankind, nor thieves, nor cov-
etous, nor drunkards, nor revilers, nor extortioners,
shall inherit the kingdom of God" (1 Corinthians
6.9–10).
4. Shops selling groceries and wine (Spanish).
5. During Pentecost, the Holy Spirit descended in
the form of fire onto the disciples, causing them to
speak in tongues (Acts 2.1–4).

is the divine body—common, habitable—
the way in a field of sunflowers   50
you can see every bloom's

the multiple expression
of a single shining idea,
which is the face hammered into joy.

I'll tell you what I'll inherit: 55
stupidity, erasure, exile
inside the chalked lines of the police,

who must resemble what they punish,
the exile you require of me,
you who's posted this invitation   60

to a heaven nobody wants.
You who must be patrolled,
who adore constraint, I'll tell you

what I'll inherit, not your pallid temple
but a real palace, the anticipated   65
and actual memory, the moment flooded

by skin and the knowledge of it,
the gesture and its description
—do I need to say it?—

the flesh *and* the word. And I'll tell you,   70
you who can't wait to abandon your body,
what you want me to, maybe something

like you've imagined, a dirty story:
Years ago, in the baths,
a man walked into the steam,   75

the gorgeous deep indigo of him gleaming,
solid tight flanks, the intricately ridged abdomen—
and after he invited me to his room,

nudging his key toward me,
as if perhaps I spoke another tongue   80
and required the plainest of gestures,

after we'd been, you understand,
worshipping a while in his church,
he said to me, *I'm going to punish your mouth.*

I can't tell you what that did to me.   85
My shame was redeemed then;
I won't need to burn in the afterlife.

It wasn't that he hurt me,
more than that: the spirit's transactions
are enacted now, here—no one needs   90

your eternity. This failing city's
radiant as any we'll ever know,
paved with oily rainbow, charred gates

jeweled with tags, swoops of letters
over letters, indecipherable as anything   95
written by desire. I'm not ashamed

to love Babylon's scrawl.⁶ How could I be?
It's written on my face as much as on
these walls. This city's inescapable,

gorgeous, and on fire. I have my kingdom.   100

                                                                    1995

The Embrace

You weren't well or really ill yet either;
just a little tired, your handsomeness
tinged by grief or anticipation, which brought
to your face a thoughtful, deepening grace.

I didn't for a moment doubt you were dead.   5
I knew that to be true still, even in the dream.
You'd been out—at work maybe?—
having a good day, almost energetic.

We seemed to be moving from some old house
where we'd lived, boxes everywhere, things   10
in disarray: that was the *story* of my dream,
but even asleep I was shocked out of narrative

by your face, the physical fact of your face:
inches from mine, smooth-shaven, loving, alert.
Why so difficult, remembering the actual look   15
of you? Without a photograph, without strain?

So when I saw your unguarded, reliable face,
your unmistakable gaze opening all the warmth
and clarity of you—warm brown tea—we held
each other for the time the dream allowed.   20

---

6. Daniel 5 describes the writing that appeared on a palace wall and that Daniel interpreted as a condemnation of Belshazzar, the king of Babylon.

Bless you. You came back, so I could see you
once more, plainly, so I could rest against you
without thinking this happiness lessened anything,
without thinking you were alive again.

1998

THYLIAS MOSS
b. 1954

The subject matter of Thylias Moss's poetry is often emotionally disturbing, even explosive. "Lunchcounter Freedom" recalls African American sit-ins during the civil rights movement. "Crystals" chronicles a nineteenth-century doctor's experimental operations on a slave's vagina. Historical injustices toward African American women, the contradictions of motherhood, and questions of sexuality, rapture, death, and God—Moss does not shy away from such charged issues. But her approach to this weighty material is oblique, riddling, and gnomic. "Only what seems extraordinary compels me to write," she remarks, and her poetry conveys by its strangeness some of the oddity and wonder of undomesticated human experiences ("The Extraordinary Hoof"). In Moss's hands, even an encounter as routine as rereading Robert Frost's "Stopping by Woods on a Snowy Evening" is defamiliarized, the poet rethinking the lyric through the lens of racial binarism ("Interpretation of a Poem by Frost").

Moss says she avoids "imposing certain agendas" on her poems, such as those of "identity" politics. Instead, she lets her poems ramble associatively, and their turns—imbedded in syntactic sprawl—are often surprising. "I prefer that unanticipated discovery lead me to and through a poem," she comments ("The Extraordinary Hoof"). Digressive, elliptical, allusive, her poems nevertheless tend to return to their central themes. Moss credits as a strong influence Sunday sermons in which the preacher makes "text," and her work recalls this model in its impassioned, if indirect, explorations of themes such as joy and infanticide. In the poem "The Rapture of Dry Ice Burning off Skin as the Moment of the Soul's Apotheosis," Moss meditates on the meanings of joy, performing extravagant metaphorical leaps from buffalo-stomach hair to Tiffany-lamp fringes and from needle tracks on the arms of drug addicts to umbrellas (that is, the veins of addicts are compared to the "metal veins" of a collapsed umbrella). Shifting gears in her figurative language, Moss may also suddenly change tone, from arch knowingness to the earnestness of prayer, from acid bleakness to the fierce confidence of prophecy. Though her poems are loosely jointed, their stunningly climactic endings are anything but haphazard. In the last lines of "After Reading *Beloved*," she compares the nails that held Jesus on the cross to the Virgin Mary's nipples. "Crystals" closes with an image of the doctor's hand remaining inside the slave's vagina.

Strange juxtapositions were part of Moss's childhood. Born on February 27, 1954, to a working-class family in Cleveland, Ohio, Moss grew up in circumstances that combined nightmare and "paradise" (her word). In her 1998 memoir, *Tale of a Sky-Blue Dress*, she describes her parents as lavishing care and affection on her as an only child, yet for several years she was also cruelly abused by a babysitter, only later rediscovering happiness in her own family. She began her undergraduate work at Syracuse University, but received her B.A. from Oberlin College (1981) and her M.A. from the University of New Hampshire (1983), where she studied with Charles Simic. A 1996

MacArthur Fellow, she has taught at Phillips Academy (1984–92) and, since 1993, at the University of Michigan.

Lunchcounter Freedom[1]

I once wanted a white man's eyes upon
me, my beauty riveting him to my slum
color. Forgetting his hands are made for my
curves, he would raise them to shield his eyes
and they would fly to my breasts with gentleness   5
stolen from doves.

I've made up my mind not to order a sandwich on
light bread if the waitress approaches me
with a pencil. My hat is the one I wear
the Sundays my choir doesn't sing. A dark   10
bird on it darkly sways to the gospel music,
trying to pull nectar from a cloth flower.
Psalms are mice in my mind, nibbling,
gnawing, tearing up my thoughts.
White men are the walls. I can't tell anyone   15
how badly I want water. In the mirage that
follows, the doves unfold into hammers.
They still fly to my breasts.

Because I'm nonviolent I don't act or
react. When knocked from the stool   20
my body takes its shape from what
it falls into. The white man cradles
his tar baby. Each magus[2] in turn.
He fathered it, it looks just like him,
the spitting image. He can't let go of   25
his future. The menu offers tuna fish,
grits, beef in a sauce like desire.
He is free to choose from available
choices. An asterisk marks the special.

1990

---

1. The sit-ins of the black civil rights movement began in the early 1960s, when college students staged a sit-in at a lunchcounter in Greensboro, North Carolina.
2. One of the three wise men traditionally believed to have paid homage to the infant Jesus. *Tar baby*: sticky black doll used as a trap in many African-derived folktales and made famous in the stories of the American writer Joel Chandler Harris (1848–1908).

Interpretation of a Poem by Frost[3]

A young black girl stopped by the woods,
so young she knew only one man: Jim Crow[4]
but she wasn't allowed to call him Mister.
The woods were his and she respected his boundaries
even in the absence of fence.   5
Of course she delighted in the filling up
of his woods, she so accustomed to emptiness,
to being taken at face value.
This face, her face eternally the brown
of declining autumn, watches snow inter the grass,   10
cling to bark making it seem indecisive
about race preference, a fast-to-melt idealism.
With the grass covered, black and white are the only options,
polarity is the only reality; corners aren't neutral
but are on edge.   15
She shakes off snow, defiance wasted
on the limited audience of horse.
The snow does not hypnotize her as it wants to,
as the blond sun does in making too many prefer daylight.
She has promises to keep,   20
the promise that she bear Jim no bastards,
the promise that she ride the horse only as long
as it is willing to accept riders,
the promise that she bear Jim no bastards,
the promise to her face that it not be mistaken as shadow,   25
and miles to go, more than the distance from Africa to Andover,[5]
more than the distance from black to white
before she sleeps with Jim.

                                                                1991

The Rapture of Dry Ice Burning off Skin as the Moment of the Soul's Apotheosis[6]

How will we get used to joy
if we won't hold onto it?

Not even extinction stops me; when
I've sufficient craving, I follow the buffalo,
their hair hanging below their stomachs like   5
fringes on Tiffany lampshades,[7] they can be turned on
so can I by a stampede, footsteps whose sound

---

3. "Stopping by Woods on a Snowy Evening," by
the American poet Robert Frost (1874–1963).
4. Jim Crow laws enforced racial segregation in
southern U.S. states between the 1880s and
1950s; originally, name of a character in a black-
face-minstrel song-and-dance act.
5. Town in Massachusetts.
6. Glorification; transformation into a god.
7. Decorated, stained-glass lampshades.

is my heart souped up, doctored, ninety pounds
running off a semi's invincible engine. Buffalo
heaven is Niagara Falls. There their spirit   10
gushes. There they still stampede and power
the generators that operate the Tiffany lamps
that let us see in some of the dark. Snow
inundates the city bearing their name; buffalo
spirit chips later melt to feed the underground,   15
the politically dredlocked tendrils of roots. And this
has no place in reality, is trivial juxtaposed with

the faces of addicts, their eyes practically as sunken
as extinction, gray ripples like hurdlers' track lanes
under them, pupils like just more needle sites.   20
And their arms: flesh trying for a moon apprenticeship,
a celestial antibody. Every time I use it
the umbrella is turned inside out,
metal veins, totally hardened arteries and survival
without anything flowing within, nothing saying   25
life came from the sea, from anywhere but coincidence
or God's ulcer, revealed. Yet also, inside out
the umbrella tries to be a bouquet, or at least
the rugged wrapping for one that must endure much,
without dispensing coherent parcels of scent,   30
before the refuge of vase in a room already accustomed
to withering mind and retreating skin. But the smell
of the flowers lifts the corners of the mouth as if
the man at the center of this remorse has lifted her
in a waltz. This is as true as sickness. The Jehovah's   35

Witness will come to my door any minute with tracts, an
inflexible agenda and I won't let him in because
I'm painting a rosy picture with only blue and
yellow (sadness and cowardice).
I'm something of an alchemist. Extinct.   40
He would tell me time is running out.
I would correct him: time *ran* out; that's why
history repeats itself, why we can't advance.
What joy will come has to be here right now: Cheer
to wash the dirt away, Twenty Mule Team Borax and   45
Arm & Hammer to magnify Cheer's power, lemon-scented
bleach and ammonia to trick the nose, improved—changed—
Tide, almost all-purpose starch that cures any limpness
except impotence. Celebrate that there's *Master*card
to rule us, bring us to our knees, the protocol we follow   50
in the presence of the head of our state of ruin, the
official with us all the time, not inaccessible in
palaces or White Houses or Kremlins. Besides every
ritual is stylized, has patterns and repetitions
suitable for adaptation to dance. Here come toe shoes,   55
brushstrokes, oxymorons. Joy

is at our tongue tips: Let the great thirsts and hungers
of the world be the *marvelous* thirsts, *glorious* hungers.
Let heartbreak be alternative to coffeebreak, five
midmorning minutes devoted to emotion.   60

1991

Crystals

In 1845 Dr. James Marion Sims[8] had seen it many times,
vesico-vaginal fistula, abnormal passageway
between bladder and vagina through which urine leaks
almost constantly if the fistula is large

as it tends to become after those pregnancies   5
not quite a year apart in Anarcha and her slave
friends Lucy, Betsey. *If you can just fix this*
the girl said, probably pregnant again, her vulva inflamed,
her thighs caked with urinary salts; from the beginning
he saw his future in those crystals.   10

Society women sometimes had this too, a remaking of the vulva,
more color, pustules like decorations of which women
were already fond; beads, cultured pearls of pus, status.
Perhaps the design improves in its greater challenger to love
and fondle even in the dark except that there is pain,   15
inability to hold water.

He tried to help Anarcha first, drawing on what
he was inventing: frontier ingenuity and gynecology,
and operated thirty times, using a pewter teaspoon
that he reshaped, bent and hammered for each surgery,   20
no sterilant but spit, while she watched; it became
his famous duck-bill speculum too large and sharp
to be respectful, yet it let him look.

Such excoriation, such stretching of the vaginal walls, tunnel
into room; such remembrance of Jericho, prophecy of Berlin[9]   25
when his mind was to have been on her comfort and healing.

Through the vulva was the way most tried to access her
yet they did not come close. Using

8. American doctor (1813–1883), considered the
"father of modern gynecology." Sims began his sur-
gical career by conducting experiments on slave
women such as the seventeen-year-old Anarcha,
who underwent over thirty such operations with-
out anesthesia. "Although in 'Crystals,' the impli-
cation is that Anarcha, her actual name, was or had
been pregnant, there is not yet evidence of her
pregnancies, suggesting that her fistula had some

other cause, such as horseback riding. However,
among those multiparas [women who have given
birth more than once], especially enslaved multi-
paras, who develop these fistulas, repeated child-
birth is often the cause" [Moss's note].
9. The Berlin Wall, separating East and West Ber-
lin, was taken down in 1989. The walls of Jericho
were destroyed by Joshua and the Israelites (Joshua
6).

a half-dollar he formed the wire suture that closed
Anarcha's fistula on the thirtieth, it bears repeating, thirtieth   30
attempt.

For the rest of her life she slept in the Sims position:
on her left side, right knee brought to her chest; she so long,
four years, on his table came to find it comfortable, came to find
no other way to lose herself, relieve her mind,   35
ignore Sims' rising glory, his bragging in the journals
that he had seen the fistula *as no man had ever seen it before.*
Now they all can.

Anarcha who still does not know anesthesia except
for her willed loss of awareness went on peeing as she'd   40
always done, just not so frequently and in reduced
volume, hardly enough for a tea cup, but whenever
necessary, the doctor poked, prodded, practiced

then, successful, went gloved and shaven to help ladies
on whom white cloths were draped; divinity   45
on the table to indulge his tastefulness.

It should be noted
that Anarcha's fistula closed well,
sealed in infection, scarred
thickly   50

as if his hand remained.

1998

LOUISE ERDRICH
b. 1954

"My characters choose me and once they do it's like standing in a field and hearing echoes," Louise Erdrich said in a 1986 interview. "All I can do is trace their passage." She was speaking of the people in one of her acclaimed novels, *The Beet Queen* (1986), but the remark applies as well to the personae of the many remarkable dramatic monologues in her first book of poems, *Jacklight* (1984), named after a light used for hunting or fishing at night. Among them are unidealized portraits of the Native Americans with whom she grew up near North Dakota's Turtle Mountain Reservation, such as Debby, who speaks in "Family Reunion" of Ray, her beer-drinking uncle. They also include historical figures, such as Mary Rowlandson, the seventeenth-century author of a famous narrative about her "captivity" by the Wampanoag Indians; once restored to her family, bewildered by the change, she can "see no truth in things." Erdrich never judges the speakers in her poems; she quietly observes the details of their lives in the strong yet sympathetic ray of her jacklight.

Erdrich wrote many poems in her second collection, *Baptism of Desire* (1989), according to a note, "between the hours of two and four in the morning, a period of insomnia brought on by pregnancy." The circumstance of the poems' composition is sometimes reflected in their subject matter. "The Fence" is a beautiful lyric about pregnancy, interweaving images of the poet ("My body is a golden armor around my unborn child's body") and growth in her garden ("the young plant trembles on its stalk"). But Erdrich knows that what is a miracle to one person can become a nightmare for someone else, and she also included a bleak narrative poem about an unwanted pregnancy and infanticide ("Poor Clare"). Mediating between gritty narrative realism and personal lyricism, between Christian and Native American lore, Erdrich's poetry is marked by luminous revelations of character, resiliently unsentimental language, and vivid storytelling.

Erdrich was born on June 7, 1954, in Minnesota, and she grew up in a small town in North Dakota near the Turtle Mountain Reservation, where her grandparents lived and her grandfather served as tribal chairman. Her French Ojibwa (Chippewa) mother and her German-born father both worked at a Bureau of Indian Affairs boarding school. She spent several years at a Catholic school, but began writing at Dartmouth College, from which she received her B.A. (1976); she also has an M.A. (1979) from the Writing Seminars at Johns Hopkins University, then directed by Richard Howard, another contemporary master of the dramatic monologue.

Family Reunion

Ray's third new car in half as many years.
Full cooler in the trunk, Ray sogging[1] the beer
as I solemnly chauffeur us through the bush
and up the backroads, hardly cowpaths and hub-deep in mud.
All day the sky lowers, clears, lowers again.   5
Somewhere in the bush near Saint John
there are uncles, a family, one mysterious brother
who stayed on the land when Ray left for the cities.
One week Ray is crocked. We've been through this before.
Even, as a little girl, hands in my dress,   10
Ah punka, you's my Debby, come and ki me.

Then the road ends in a yard full of dogs.
Them's Indian dogs, Ray says, lookit how they know me.
And they do seem to know him, like I do. His odor—
rank beef of fierce turtle pulled dripping from Metagoshe,[2]   15
and the inflammable mansmell: hair tonic, ashes, alcohol.
Ray dances an old woman up in his arms.
Fiddles reel in the phonograph and I sink apart
in a corner, start knocking the Blue Ribbons[3] down.
Four generations of people live here.   20
No one remembers Raymond Twobears.

So what. The walls shiver, the old house caulked with mud
sails back into the middle of Metagoshe.

1. Soaking.   3. That is, beers.
2. Lake Metagoshe, in North Dakota.

A three-foot-long snapper is hooked on a troutline,
so mean that we do not dare wrestle him in   25
but tow him to shore, heavy as an old engine.
Then somehow Ray pries the beak open and shoves
down a cherry bomb. Lights the string tongue.

Headless and clenched in its armor, the snapper
is lugged home in the trunk for tomorrow's soup.   30
Ray rolls it beneath a bush in the backyard and goes in
to sleep his own head off. Tomorrow I find
that the animal has dragged itself someplace.
I follow torn tracks up a slight hill and over
into a small stream that deepens and widens into a marsh.   35

Ray finds his way back through the room into his arms.
When the phonograph stops, he slumps hard in his hands
and the boys and their old man fold him into the car
where he curls around his bad heart, hearing how it knocks
and rattles at the bars of his ribs to break out.   40

Somehow we find our way back. Uncle Ray
sings an old song to the body that pulls him
toward home. The gray fins that his hands have become
screw their bones in the dashboard. His face
has the odd, calm patience of a child who has always   45
let bad wounds alone, or a creature that has lived
for a long time underwater. And the angels come
lowering their slings and litters.

                                                                 1984

Captivity

> He (my captor) gave me a bisquit, which I put in my pocket, and
> not daring to eat it, buried it under a log, fearing he had put
> something in it to make me love him.
> —from the narrative of the captivity of Mrs. Mary Rowlandson,
> who was taken prisoner by the Wampanoag when Lancaster,
> Massachusetts, was destroyed, in the year 1676

The stream was swift, and so cold
I thought I would be sliced in two.
But he dragged me from the flood
by the ends of my hair.
I had grown to recognize his face.   5
I could distinguish it from the others.
There were times I feared I understood
his language, which was not human,
and I knelt to pray for strength.

We were pursued! By God's agents   10
or pitch⁴ devils I did not know.
Only that we must march.
Their guns were loaded with swan shot.⁵
I could not suckle and my child's wail
put them in danger.   15
He had a woman
with teeth black and glittering.
She fed the child milk of acorns.
The forest closed, the light deepened.

I told myself that I would starve   20
before I took food from his hands
but I did not starve.
One night
he killed a deer with a young one in her
and gave me to eat of the fawn.   25
It was so tender,
the bones like the stems of flowers,
that I followed where he took me.
The night was thick. He cut the cord
that bound me to the tree.   30

After that the birds mocked.
Shadows gaped and roared
and the trees flung down
their sharpened lashes.
He did not notice God's wrath.   35
God blasted fire from half-buried stumps.
I hid my face in my dress, fearing He would burn us all
but this, too, passed.

Rescued, I see no truth in things.
My husband drives a thick wedge   40
through the earth, still it shuts
to him year after year.
My child is fed of the first wheat.
I lay myself to sleep
on a Holland-laced pillowbeer.⁶   45
I lay to sleep.
And in the dark I see myself
as I was outside their circle.

They knelt on deerskins, some with sticks,
and he led his company in the noise   50
until I could no longer bear
the thought of how I was.
I stripped a branch

---

4. That is, pitch-black.   6. Pillowcases with lace made in the Netherlands.
5. A large size of shot used in hunting wildfowl.

and struck the earth,
in time, begging it to open   55
to admit me
as he was
and feed me honey from the rock.[7]

1984

Windigo

For Angela

The Windigo is a flesh-eating, wintry demon with a man buried deep inside of it. In some Chippewa stories, a young girl vanquishes this monster by forcing boiling lard down its throat, thereby releasing the human at the core of ice.

You knew I was coming for you, little one,
when the kettle jumped into the fire.
Towels flapped on the hooks,
and the dog crept off, groaning,
to the deepest part of the woods.   5

In the hackles of dry brush a thin laughter started up.
Mother scolded the food warm and smooth in the pot
and called you to eat.
But I spoke in the cold trees:
New one, I have come for you, child hide and lie still.   10

The sumac pushed sour red cones through the air.
Copper burned in the raw wood.
You saw me drag toward you.
Oh touch me, I murmured, and licked the soles of your feet.
You dug your hands into my pale, melting fur.   15

I stole you off, a huge thing in my bristling armor.
Steam rolled from my wintry arms, each leaf shivered
from the bushes we passed
until they stood, naked, spread like the cleaned spines of fish.

Then your warm hands hummed over and shoveled themselves full   20
of the ice and the snow. I would darken and spill
all night running, until at last morning broke the cold earth
and I carried you home,
a river shaking in the sun.

1984

7. Cf. Psalm 81.16: "But you would be fed with the finest of wheat; with honey from the rock I would satisfy you."

The Fence

Then one day the gray rags vanish
and the sweet wind rattles her sash.
Her secrets bloom hot. I'm wild for everything.
My body is a golden armor around my unborn child's body,
and I'll die happy, here on the ground.   5
I bend to the mixture of dirt, chopped hay,
grindings of coffee from our dark winter breakfasts.
I spoon the rich substance around the acid-loving shrubs.
I tear down last year's drunken vines,
pull the black rug off the bed of asparagus   10
and lie there, knowing by June I'll push the baby out
as easily as seed wings fold back from the cotyledon.[8]
I see the first leaf already, the veined tongue
rigid between the thighs of the runner beans.
I know how the shoot will complicate itself   15
as roots fill the trench.
Here is the link fence, the stem doubling toward it,
and something I've never witnessed.
One moment the young plant trembles on its stalk.
The next, it has already gripped the wire.   20
Now it will continue to climb, dragging rude blossoms
to the other side
until in summer fruit like green scimitars,
the frieze of vines, and then the small body
spread before me in need   25
drinking light from the shifting wall of my body,
and the fingers, tiny stems wavering to mine,
flexing for the ascent.

1989

8. Seed leaf in a seed's embryo.

LORNA DEE CERVANTES
b. 1954

Em-plu-ma-do *v.m.*, feathered; in plumage, as after molting
plu-ma-da *n.f.*, pen flourish

Lorna Dee Cervantes used these definitions as the epigraph to her first book of poems
(1981). She entitled the book *Emplumada*, combining the two Spanish words, so that
feathers, wings, birds become fused with writing, a neologism that suggests visionary
hope for the power of poetry. As this playful use of Spanish suggests, both the language
and Mexican American culture have been important resources for her poetry. Even so,

Cervantes grew up speaking English primarily, because Spanish was forbidden to her. "I'm orphaned from my Spanish name," she writes in "Refugee Ship," an early poem. "The words are foreign, stumbling / on my tongue." And yet, though she feels "a captive / aboard the refugee ship" of English, she reclaims her ancestral and cultural language in the hybrid language of her poetry. Perhaps her work's most striking feature is its bilingual texture, its sinuous integration of Spanish words and phrases, rhetorical structure and oral rhythms, into contemporary English. Both of and distanced from that culture, Cervantes voices in richly imagistic free verse a range of feelings, from fierce optimism and love ("The Body as Braille") to anger and grief over the debilitating social circumstances and grim history of Mexican Americans ("Cannery Town in August," "Poema para los Californios Muertos").

Cervantes was born into a working-class family in San Francisco, California, on August 6, 1954. That year, the word *Chicano* first became an individualizing name for Mexican Americans; Mexican American women adopted the label *Chicana* in 1967. Of Mexican and Native American ancestry, Cervantes grew up in San José, reading Shakespeare and the English Romantic poets in the houses cleaned by her mother. She was educated at San José City College, San José State University (B.A., 1984), and the University of California, Santa Cruz (1985–88). Long active in Chicano/a community and literary affairs, she founded a small press, Mango Publications, in 1976. She teaches creative writing at the University of Colorado, Boulder.

Cannery Town in August

All night it humps the air.
Speechless, the steam rises
from the cannery columns. I hear
the night bird rave about work
or lunch, or sing the swing shift[1]   5
home. I listen, while bodyless
uniforms and spinach specked shoes
drift in monochrome down the dark
moon-possessed streets. Women
who smell of whiskey and tomatoes,   10
peach fuzz reddening their lips and eyes—
I imagine them not speaking, dumbed
by the can's clamor and drop
to the trucks that wait, grunting
in their headlights below.   15
They spotlight those who walk
like a dream, with no one
waiting in the shadows
to palm them back to living.

                                                                       1981

---

1. Work shift between day and night shifts.

The Body as Braille

He tells me, "Your back
is so beautiful." He traces
my spine with his hand.

I'm burning like the white ring
around the moon. "A witch's moon,"   5
dijo mi abuela.[2] The schools call it

"a reflection of ice crystals."
It's a storm brewing in the cauldron
of the sky. I'm in love

but won't tell him   10
if it's omens
or ice.

                                                      1981

Refugee Ship

Like wet cornstarch, I slide
past my grandmother's eyes. Bible
at her side, she removes her glasses.
The pudding thickens.

Mama raised me without language.   5
I'm orphaned from my Spanish name.
The words are foreign, stumbling
on my tongue. I see in the mirror
my reflection: bronzed skin, black hair.

I feel I am a captive   10
aboard the refugee ship.
The ship that will never dock.
El barco que nunca atraca.[3]

                                                      1981

---

2. Said my grandmother (Spanish).   3. Spanish translation of above line.

Poema para los Californios Muertos[4]

Once a refuge for Mexican Californios . . .
—plaque outside a restaurant
in Los Altos, California, 1974.

These older towns die
into stretches of freeway.
The high scaffolding cuts a clean cesarean
across belly valleys and fertile dust.
What a bastard child, this city   5
lost in the soft
llorando de las madres.[5]
Californios moan like husbands of the raped,
husbands de la tierra,
tierra la madre.[6]   10

I run my fingers
across this brass plaque.
Its cold stirs in me a memory
of silver buckles and spent bullets,
of embroidered shawls and dark rebozos.[7]   15
Yo recuerdo los antepasados muertos.
Los recuerdo en la sangre,
la sangre fértil.[8]

What refuge did you find here,
ancient Californios?   20
Now at this restaurant nothing remains
but this old oak and an ill-placed plaque.
Is it true that you still live here
in the shadows of these white, high-class houses?
Soy la hija pobrecita   25
pero puedo maldecir estas fantasmas blancas.
Las fantasmas tuyas deben aquí quedarse,
solas las tuyas.[9]

In this place I see nothing but strangers.
On the shelves there are bitter antiques,   30
yanqui[1] remnants
y estos no de los Californios.[2]
A blue jay shrieks
above the pungent odor of crushed
eucalyptus and the pure scent   35
of rage.

1981

---

4. Poem for dead Californios (Spanish).
5. Crying of mothers.
6. Husbands of the earth, mother earth.
7. Shawls.
8. I remember dead ancestors. I remember them
in the blood, the fertile blood.

9. I am the poor daughter, but I can curse these
white ghosts. Your ghosts must remain here, only
yours.
1. American.
2. And these not pertaining to the Californios.

MARILYN CHIN
b. 1955

"I am a Chinese American poet," Marilyn Chin wrote to the American Poetry Society, "born in Hong Kong and raised in Portland, Oregon. My poetry both laments and celebrates my 'hyphenated' identity." In an interview published in 1995, Chin explained that, as "a Pacific Rim person," she does not "believe in static identities" but sees them as "forever changing." While she fears losing her Chinese heritage and language, she feels strongly that one "can't recapture the past." Chin defines and redefines herself in her poetry, her biting irony and unvarnished language suggesting the contingency of her acts of self-definition. Her hyphenated identity finds expression in the hybridization of East and West, whether in poetic forms, as when she combines Chinese quatrains with the confessional lyric, or in imagery and allusion, as when she refers to chop suey and bamboo shoots while citing William Carlos Williams and John Berryman.

Chin finds in her name itself a potent emblem of her hybrid identity. "I am Marilyn Mei Ling Chin," she declares with mock solemnity at the start of "How I Got That Name"; she goes on to explain that her father, "obsessed with a bombshell blonde / transliterated 'Mei Ling' to 'Marilyn.' " Her father later abandoned his Chinese family for a white woman, and the emotional scars of this desertion are evident in the anti-patriarchal anger of her poetry. In voicing such anger despite cultural and gender stereotypes of silent submission, and in seeking to create a poetic voice that at once is personal and has a broader political significance, Chin follows the example of such American women poets as Sylvia Plath, Adrienne Rich, and June Jordan.

Chin rejects both her father's assimilationist denial of his cultural background and the effort to reify and idealize Chinese culture. A poem such as "Altar" has the trappings of an immigrant writer's nostalgic reverie—an armchair, the morning sun, a moth— and yet is characteristically bracing and acerbic about ancestor worship. Nor does Chin spare herself her mocking tongue. Her tone is bold, wry, and irreverent. In "How I Got That Name," she remembers her father describing her as " 'not quite boiled, not quite cooked,' " and her poetic style is indeed somewhat raw and deliberately jarring. Its sharp edges contrast with the smoothly contoured and mellifluous poetry of her Asian American contemporaries Cathy Song and Li-Young Lee. Along with cultural boundaries, Chin crosses lines between elevated diction and chatty colloquialism, between the essay and the poem, between lyricism and parody.

Chin was born on January 14, 1955. She received her B.A. in 1977 from the University of Massachusetts at Amherst, her M.F.A. in 1981 from the University of Iowa. She teaches at San Diego State University.

How I Got That Name

An Essay on Assimilation

I am Marilyn Mei Ling Chin.
Oh, how I love the resoluteness
of that first person singular
followed by that stalwart indicative
of "be," without the uncertain i-n-g
of "becoming." Of course,
the name had been changed

5

somewhere between Angel Island and the sea,
when my father the paperson[1]
in the late 1950s   10
obsessed with a bombshell blonde[2]
transliterated "Mei Ling" to "Marilyn."
And nobody dared question
his initial impulse—for we all know
lust drove men to greatness,   15
not goodness, not decency.
And there I was, a wayward pink baby,
named after some tragic white woman
swollen with gin and Nembutal.
My mother couldn't pronounce the "r."   20
She dubbed me "Numba one female offshoot"
for brevity: henceforth, she will live and die
in sublime ignorance, flanked
by loving children and the "kitchen deity."
While my father dithers,   25
a tomcat in Hong Kong trash—
a gambler, a petty thug,
who bought a chain of chopsuey joints
in Piss River, Oregon,
with bootlegged Gucci cash.   30
Nobody dared question his integrity given
his nice, devout daughters
and his bright, industrious sons
as if filial piety were the standard
by which all earthly men were measured.   35

•

Oh, how trustworthy our daughters,
how thrifty our sons!
How we've managed to fool the experts
in education, statistics and demography—
We're not very creative but not averse to rote-learning.   40
Indeed, they can *use* us.
But the "Model Minority" is a tease.
We know you are watching now,
so we refuse to give you any!
Oh, bamboo shoots, bamboo shoots!   45
The further west we go, we'll hit east;
the deeper down we dig, we'll find China.
History has turned its stomach
on a black polluted beach—
where life doesn't hinge   50
on that red, red wheelbarrow,[3]

1. Many Chinese immigrants became *paper sons* or *daughters*, overcoming U.S. exclusionary laws and gaining admission into the country by purchasing paperwork claiming they had American parents. *Angel Island:* island off the coast of San Francisco that served as an immigration station and detention center during the first half of the twentieth century.
2. Marilyn Monroe (1926–1962), American actor, who died of an overdose of the barbiturate Nembutal (line 19).
3. Cf. William Carlos Williams's "The Red Wheelbarrow."

but whether or not our new lover
in the final episode of "Santa Barbara"[4]
will lean over a scented candle
and call us a "bitch."   55
Oh God, where have we gone wrong?
We have no inner resources![5]

Then, one redolent spring morning
the Great Patriarch Chin
peered down from his kiosk in heaven   60
and saw that his descendants were ugly.[6]
One had a squarish head and a nose without a bridge.
Another's profile—long and knobbed as a gourd.
A third, the sad, brutish one
may never, never marry.   65
And I, his least favorite—
"not quite boiled, not quite cooked,"
a plump pomfret[7] simmering in my juices—
too listless to fight for my people's destiny.
"To kill without resistance is not slaughter"   70
says the proverb. So, I wait for imminent death.
The fact that this death is also metaphorical
is testament to my lethargy.

So here lies Marilyn Mei Ling Chin,
married once, twice to so-and-so, a Lee and a Wong,   75
granddaughter of Jack "the patriarch"
and the brooding Suilin Fong,
daughter of the virtuous Yuet Kuen Wong
and G. G. Chin the infamous,
sister of a dozen, cousin of a million,   80
survived by everybody and forgotten by all.
She was neither black nor white,
neither cherished nor vanquished,
just another squatter in her own bamboo grove
minding her poetry—   85
when one day heaven was unmerciful,
and a chasm opened where she stood.
Like the jowls of a mighty white whale,
or the jaws of a metaphysical Godzilla,
it swallowed her whole.   90
She did not flinch nor writhe,
nor fret about the afterlife,
but stayed! Solid as wood, happily
a little gnawed, tattered, mesmerized

---

4. American soap opera.
5. Cf. John Berryman's Dream Song 14: "I con-
clude now I have no / inner resources."

6. Cf. Genesis 1.
7. Type of fish.

by all that was lavished upon her   95
and all that was taken away!

                                                            1994

Altar

I tell her she has outlived her usefulness.
I point to the corner where dust gathers,
where light has never touched. But there she sits,
a thousand years, hands folded, in a tattered armchair,
with yesterday's news, "the Golden Mountain Edition."   5
The morning sun slants down the broken eaves,
shading half of her sallow face.

On the upper northwest corner (I'd consulted a geomancer),[8]
a deathtrap shines on the dying bougainvillea.
The carcass of a goatmoth hangs upsidedown,   10
hollowed out. The only evidence
of her seasonal life is a dash
of shimmery powder, a last cry.

She, who was attracted to that bare bulb,
who danced around that immigrant dream,   15
will find her end here, this corner,
this solemn altar.

                                                            1994

Autumn Leaves

The dead piled up, thick, fragrant, on the fire escape.
My mother ordered me again, and again, to sweep it clean.
All that blooms must fall. I learned this not from the Tao,[9]
    but from high school biology.

Oh, the contradictions of having a broom and not a dustpan! 5
I swept the leaves down, down through the iron grille
and let the dead rain over the Wong family's patio.

And it was Achilles[1] Wong who completed the task.
    We called her:
The-one-who-cleared-away-another-family's-autumn.   10
She blossomed, tall, benevolent, notwithstanding.

                                                            1994

---

8. One who divines special information from geo-
graphical features.
9. The *Tao-te Ching*, the fundamental text of Tao-

ism, teaches that one should abjure from all striv-
ing.
1. Greek hero of the Trojan War.

Chinese Quatrains (The Woman in Tomb 44)[2]

The aeroplane is shaped like a bird
Or a giant mechanical penis
My father escorts my mother
From girlhood to unhappiness

A dragonfly has iridescent wings   5
Shorn, it's a lowly pismire
Plucked of arms and legs
A throbbing red pepperpod[3]

Baby, she's a girl
Pinkly propped as a doll   10
Baby, she's a pearl
An ulcer in the oyster of God

Cry little baby clam cry
The steam has opened your eyes
Your secret darkly hidden   15
The razor is sharpening the knife

Abandoned taro-leaf[4] boat
Its lonely black sail broken
The corpses are fat and bejeweled
The hull is thoroughly rotten   20

The worm has entered the ear
And out the nose of my father
Cleaned the pelvis of my mother
And ringed around her fingerbone

One child beats a bedpan   25
One beats a fishhook out of wire
One beats his half sister on the head
Oh, teach us to fish and love

Don't say her boudoir[5] is too narrow
She could sleep but in one cold bed   30
Don't say you own many horses
We escaped on her skinny mare's back

Man is good said Meng-Tzu
We must cultivate their natures

---

2. "Adapted from *jue-ju*, literally 'cut verse,' four-line poems, usually seven characters per line" [Chin's note].
3. Cf. a story of the Japanese poet Bashō (1644–1694), a master of the haiku verse form. His student proposed as an idea for a poem, "Pull the wings off a dragonfly and look—you get a red pep-perpod." Bashō replied that more appropriate to the spirit of haiku would be, "Add wings to a pep-perpod and look—you get a red dragonfly." *Pismire*: ant.
4. A plant.
5. Bedroom.

Man is evil said Hsun-Tzu[6]   35
There's a worm in the human heart

He gleaned a beaded purse from Hong Kong
He procured an oval fan from Taiwan
She married him for a green card
He abandoned her for a blonde   40

My grandmother is calling her goslings
My mother is summoning her hens
The sun has vanished into the ocean
The moon has drowned in the fen

Discs of jade for her eyelids   45
A lozenge of pearl for her throat
Lapis and kudzu in her nostrils
They will rob her again and again

2002

6. Chinese Confucian philosopher (c. 300–c. 230 B.C.E.). *Meng-Tzu*: Chinese Confucian philosopher (c. 371–c. 289 B.C.E.), known in the West as Mencius.

CATHY SONG
b. 1955

In 1982, the poet Richard Hugo, then judge of the Yale Series of Younger Poets, chose as the winning manuscript Cathy Song's *Picture Bride*, praising its "strength of quiet resolve." Song's paternal grandmother came from Korea, the poet tells us in that first collection's title poem; she went to Hawaii as a "picture bride" (a mail-order bride), like many other Korean and Japanese women. Trying to reconstruct what she can of her ancestral Asia from the perspective of contemporary Hawaii, Song often explores the gains and losses of her grandmother's move from the Old World to the New, without idealizing either world. However beautiful and gauzy the texture of her poetry, Song does not miss the harsh reality of the traps that family and society set for women. She writes, in "Beauty and Sadness," of the Japanese printmaker Kitagawa Utamaro's "floating world" of "teahouse waitresses, actresses, / geishas, courtesans and maids." In "Lost Sister," the sister has escaped Chinese norms of female immobility and foot-binding, but she discovers that the New World imposes its own constraints—"the possibilities, / the loneliness, / can strangulate like jungle vines."

In her later books, Song extends her exploration of the family heritage to include her own children. She continues to reconstruct memories of her childhood, which she reproduces with singular transparency. In "Sunworshippers," the mother teaches her daughter that Americans are grotesquely self-indulgent, their "bodies glazed and glistening like raw fish in the market," and this revulsion later contributes to the college-age daughter's anorexia. As this and other poems demonstrate, Song's carefully structured poetry works through vivid imagery and implication. Astutely exploring intercultural perception, the poem "Ghost" offers an extended play on the Chinese for white person—which can be translated as "white ghost." The speaker's mother sees whites as ghostly, as well as noisy, hairy, smelly, and round eyed, but the speaker also sees herself as a ghost to white schoolchildren for whom she, too, is alien. Precise and economical, Song's poetry is also distinguished by its delicate sensibility and artful framing. "What frames the view," she commented in a letter, "is the mind in the diamond pinpoint light of concentration tunneling into memory, released by the imagination. Out of that depth, squares of light form, like windows you pass at night, like photographs developing in the dark."

Cathy-Lynn Song was born on August 20, 1955, in Honolulu, Hawaii, to a Chinese American mother and a Korean American father. She attended the University of Hawaii at Manoa for two years, then went to Wellesley College for her B.A. (1977) and to Boston University for her M.F.A. (1981). Since 1987, she has taught in Hawaii's Teacher in the Schools program. She lives and writes in Honolulu.

Beauty and Sadness

for Kitagawa Utamaro[1]

He drew hundreds of women
in studies unfolding
like flowers from a fan.
Teahouse waitresses, actresses,
geishas,[2] courtesans and maids.   5
They arranged themselves
before this quick, nimble man
whose invisible presence
one feels in these prints
is as delicate   10
as the skinlike paper
he used to transfer
and retain their fleeting loveliness.

Crouching like cats,
they purred amid the layers of kimono[3]   15
swirling around them
as though they were bathing
in a mountain pool with irises
growing in the silken sunlit water.
Or poised like porcelain vases,   20
slender, erect and tall; their heavy
brocaded hair was piled high
with sandalwood combs and blossom sprigs
poking out like antennae.
They resembled beautiful iridescent insects,   25
creatures from a floating world.[4]

1. Japanese artist (1753–1806), who specialized in studies of sensuous and beautiful women.
2. Women trained to provide entertaining, light-hearted company for men.
3. Traditional Japanese robe with long sleeves.
4. The pictures "were called 'pictures of the floating world' because of their preoccupation with the pleasures of the moment" [Song's glossary].

Utamaro absorbed these women of Edo[5]
in their moments of melancholy
as well as of beauty.
He captured the wisp of shadows,   30
the half-draped body
emerging from a bath; whatever
skin was exposed
was powdered white as snow.
A private space disclosed.   35
Portraying another girl
catching a glimpse of her own vulnerable
face in the mirror, he transposed
the trembling plum lips
like a drop of blood   40
soaking up the white expanse of paper.

At times, indifferent to his inconsolable
eye, the women drifted
through the soft gray feathered light,
maintaining stillness, the moments in between.   45
Like the dusty ash-winged moths
that cling to the screens in summer
and that the Japanese venerate
as ancestors reincarnated;
Utamaro graced these women with immortality   50
in the thousand sheaves of prints
fluttering into the reverent hands of keepers:
the dwarfed and bespectacled painter
holding up to a square of sunlight
what he had carried home beneath his coat   55
one afternoon in winter.

                                                                    1983

Lost Sister

1

In China,
even the peasants
named their first daughters
Jade—
the stone that in the far fields   5
could moisten the dry season,
could make men move mountains
for the healing green of the inner hills
glistening like slices of winter melon.

And the daughters were grateful: 10
They never left home.

---

5. "Present-day Tokyo" [Song's glossary].

To move freely was a luxury
stolen from them at birth.
Instead, they gathered patience,
learning to walk in shoes   15
the size of teacups,
without breaking—
the arc of their movements
as dormant as the rooted willow,
as redundant as the farmyard hens.   20
But they traveled far
in surviving,
learning to stretch the family rice,
to quiet the demons,
the noisy stomachs.   25

2

There is a sister
across the ocean,
who relinquished her name,
diluting jade green
with the blue of the Pacific.   30
Rising with a tide of locusts,
she swarmed with others
to inundate another shore.
In America,
there are many roads   35
and women can stride along with men.

But in another wilderness,
the possibilities,
the loneliness,
can strangulate like jungle vines.   40
The meager provisions and sentiments
of once belonging—
fermented roots, Mah-Jong[6] tiles and firecrackers—
set but a flimsy household
in a forest of nightless cities.   45
A giant snake rattles above,
spewing black clouds into your kitchen.
Dough-faced landlords
slip in and out of your keyholes,
making claims you don't understand,   50
tapping into your communication systems
of laundry lines and restaurant chains.

You find you need China:
your one fragile identification,
a jade link   55
handcuffed to your wrist.

6. Chinese game.

You remember your mother
who walked for centuries,
footless—
and like her,   60
you have left no footprints,
but only because
there is an ocean in between,
the unremitting space of your rebellion.

                                                                        1983

Sunworshippers

"Look how they love themselves,"
my mother would lecture as we drove through
the ironwoods, the park on one side,
the beach on the other, where sunworshippers,
splayed upon towels, appeared sacrificial,   5
bodies glazed and glistening like raw fish in the market.
There was folly and irreverence to such exposure,
something only people with dirty feet did.
Who will marry you
if your skin is sunbaked and dried up like beef jerky?   10
We put on our hats and gloves
whenever we went for a drive.
When the sun broke through clouds,
my mother sprouted her umbrella.
The body is a temple we worship   15
secretly in the traveling revivalist tent of our clothes.
The body, hidden, banished to acceptable
rooms of the house, had only a mouth
for eating and a hole for eliminating
what the body rejected: the lower forms of life.   20
Caramel-colored stools, coiled heavily
like a sleeping python, were a sign
we were living right.
But to erect a statue of the body
and how the body, insolent and defiant   25
in a bikini, looked was self-indulgent, sun-
worshipping, fad diets and weight-lifting proof
you loved yourself too much.
We were not allowed to love ourselves too much.
So I ate less, and less, and less,   30
nibbling my way out of meals—
the less I ate, the less
there was of me to love.
I liked it best when standing before the mirror,
I seemed to be disappearing into myself,   35
breasts sunken into the cavity of my bird-cage chest,
air my true element which fed
in those days of college, snow and brick bound,

the coal fire in my eyes.
No one knew how I truly felt about myself.   40
Fueled by my own impending disappearance,
I neither slept nor ate, but devoured radiance,
essential as chlorophyll,
the apple's heated core.
Undetected, I slipped in and out of books,   45
passages of music, brightly painted rooms
where, woven into the signature of voluptuous vines,
was the one who flew one day out the window,
leaving behind an arrangement of cakes and ornamental flowers;
to weave one's self, one's breath, ropes of it, whole   50
and fully formed, was a way of shining
out of this world.

                                                            1994

Ghost

1

Yellow ghost,
I flutter like a moth
invisible to these
children of soldiers,
dusting camphor wings,   5
pollen from the ancient pages

of poems, texts
that have no meaning
to the alley maps
of fast food and hard   10

cash, trash on the heels
of their need to go fast—

so very fast,
I am a blur to them,

without scent, a ghost   15
they rush right through

the light
I am so confident
I shed.

Who called the ghost white?   20

Yellow face of the oppressor—
one of a long line of Asian
schoolteachers who have stood before them,

yardstick in hand to measure
how far   25
they fail to measure up.

I say I am different.
I offer them
a jeweled seeded fruit,
a poem I pare and peel   30
that has no flesh.
It tastes like nothing
they want to eat.

2

Bok gwai,
my mother called   35
the round eye,
persons of a certain
body odor—
a pungent offense
to the delicate flower of her nostrils.   40

Bok gwai filled flesh
more than any ghost
I could conjure,
noisy and hairy,
they moved visibly   45
with authority
in the world they were
so sure
belonged to them.

Bok gwai, white ghost,   50
she chose to call them.
By choosing, she chose
not to see
them
as she so surely saw   55
she was not seen.

Eyes sunken into
the bone hood of their skulls,
how could they possibly see?

But I saw,   60
and I liked
what I saw,
the round-eyed men
with golden fur on their arms.
They moved like soldiers   65
who on leave toss a confetti
of coins and candy

and cigarettes
to the waving sea of the weak,
the conquered, the invisible.   70

When I caught and brought
a round eye home,
my mother recoiled
at the sharp
scent of his skin.   75
It was the odor
of a meat eater,
unwashed flesh
she shrank from.
He had an earnest appetite   80
and good horse teeth.
His bite was strong.
He got under her yellow skin.
She invited him back again.
She said she liked the way   85
he chewed his bone.

2001

CAROL ANN DUFFY
b. 1955

Widely acclaimed for her deft dramatic monologues, Carol Ann Duffy gained international notoriety as a leading contender for the post of British poet laureate after the death of Ted Hughes. She was seen as the anti-establishment candidate. The lesbian partner of "black British" poet Jackie Kay, she was born on December 23, 1955, in Glasgow, Scotland, to an Irish mother in a left-wing, working-class, Catholic family, and she graduated from a non-Oxbridge institution (the University of Liverpool). After a period of intense public speculation, she was not chosen.

Like other contemporary masters of the dramatic monologue (e.g., Frank Bidart, Ai, Richard Howard, Louise Bennett, Okot p'Bitek), Duffy is an expert ventriloquist. Because she moved to Stafford, England, as a child, her skill may owe something to having grown up amid Scottish, English, and Irish accents. In "Medusa," "Mrs Lazarus," and other poems, she assumes the voice of a mythological, historical, or fictive female character. She invites us, as did Robert Browning, to enter into the mind of a character distant from ourselves historically, culturally, or morally, exploiting the tension between our identification and our alienation. Dramatic monologue is especially suited to Duffy's feminist revisions of myth and history: it enables her to dramatize a silenced or marginalized female perspective, wittily playing on the ironic contrast between the traditional version of the story and her own.

Lazarus's resurrection, for example, looks different from the perspective of his imaginary wife. After successive stages of mourning (she "howled, shrieked, clawed"), when her dead husband has become mere "legend, language," no more than "memory," Mrs. Lazarus falls in love with a schoolteacher. For her, Lazarus's resurrection is not only miraculous but shattering and repulsive: "I breathed / his stench," she says. Brilliantly reimagined, the story is propelled to its climax by Duffy's gift for narrative. Likewise, Medusa's frightening ability to petrify becomes—in Duffy's vivid, compact account—a delightful game of transformation, like the quick turns afforded by Duffy's own poetic metaphors: "I looked at a snuffling pig, / a boulder rolled / in a heap of shit."

The author of love poetry and political satire as well as dramatic monologues, Duffy has a sharp eye for detail. She encapsulates the intensity of erotic desire in the contrast and interchange between pearls and skin, heat and coolness in "Warming Her Pearls." Another poem about longing adopts a child's perspective on her "good teachers": they "swish down the corridor in long, brown skirts." Working in well-constructed stanzas, carefully pacing her rhythms, playing on half-rhymes, effectively conjuring the senses of touch, smell, and sight, Duffy mobilizes the resources of traditional lyric, turning them to contemporary ends. Economical and witty, sensual and exuberant, Duffy's best work displays the ongoing potential of broadly accessible poetry.

Warming Her Pearls

for Judith Radstone[1]

Next to my own skin, her pearls. My mistress
bids me wear them, warm then, until evening
when I'll brush her hair. At six, I place them
round her cool, white throat. All day I think of her,

resting in the Yellow Room, contemplating silk   5
or taffeta, which gown tonight? She fans herself
whilst I work willingly, my slow heat entering
each pearl. Slack on my neck, her rope.

She's beautiful. I dream about her
in my attic bed; picture her dancing   10
with tall men, puzzled by my faint, persistent scent
beneath her French perfume, her milky stones.

I dust her shoulders with a rabbit's foot,
watch the soft blush seep through her skin
like an indolent sigh. In her looking-glass   15
my red lips part as though I want to speak.

Full moon. Her carriage brings her home. I see
her every movement in my head . . . Undressing,
taking off her jewels, her slim hand reaching
for the case, slipping naked into bed, the way   20

1. British political activist and bookseller (1925– 2001). According to Radstone's obituary in *The Guardian,* the poem was inspired by a conversation with Radstone about the practice of ladies' maids increasing the luster of their mistresses' pearls by wearing them beneath their clothes.

she always does . . . And I lie here awake,
knowing the pearls are cooling even now
in the room where my mistress sleeps. All night
I feel their absence and I burn.

1987

The Good Teachers

You run round the back to be in it again.
No bigger than your thumbs, those virtuous women
size you up from the front row. Soon now,
Miss Ross will take you for double History.
You breathe on the glass, making a ghost of her, say   5
South Sea Bubble Defenestration of Prague.[2]

You love Miss Pirie. So much, you are top
of her class. So much, you need two of you
to stare out from the year, serious, passionate.
The River's Tale by Rudyard Kipling[3] by heart.   10
Her kind intelligent green eye. Her cruel blue one.
You are making a poem up for her in your head.

But not Miss Sheridan. Comment vous appelez.[4]
But not Miss Appleby. Equal to the square
of the other two sides. Never Miss Webb.   15
Dar es Salaam. Kilimanjaro.[5] Look. The good teachers
swish down the corridor in long, brown skirts,
snobbish and proud and clean and qualified.

And they've got your number. You roll the waistband
of your skirt over and over, all leg, all   20
dumb insolence, smoke-rings. You won't pass.
You could do better. But there's the wall you climb
into dancing, lovebites, marriage, the Cheltenham
and Gloucester,[6] today. The day you'll be sorry one day.

1993

---

2. *Defenestration of Prague:* incident in 1618 in
which two imperial agents were thrown from the
window of Prague Castle by a group of dissenting
Bohemian Protestants. *South Sea Bubble:* first
major stock market crash in England, in 1720.
3. British author (1865–1936) famous for his
treatment of colonialism.

4. What is your name (French).
5. Tanzanian mountain. *Dar es Salaam:* capital of
Tanzania.
6. British mortgage and investment bank, named
after two cities (and districts) in Gloucestershire,
England.

Medusa[7]

A suspicion, a doubt, a jealousy
grew in my mind,
which turned the hairs on my head to filthy snakes,
as though my thoughts
hissed and spat on my scalp.   5

My bride's breath soured, stank
in the grey bags of my lungs.
I'm foul mouthed now, foul tongued,
yellow fanged.
There are bullet tears in my eyes.   10
Are you terrified?[8]

Be terrified.
It's you I love,
perfect man, Greek God, my own;
but I know you'll go, betray me, stray   15
from home.
So better by far for me if you were stone.

I glanced at a buzzing bee,
a dull grey pebble fell
to the ground.   20
I glanced at a singing bird,
a handful of dusty gravel
spattered down.

I looked at a ginger cat,
a housebrick   25
shattered a bowl of milk.
I looked at a snuffling pig,
a boulder rolled
in a heap of shit.

I stared in the mirror.   30
Love gone bad
showed me a Gorgon.
I stared at a dragon.
Fire spewed
from the mouth of a mountain.   35

And here you come
with a shield for a heart
and a sword for a tongue
and your girls, your girls.

---

7. In Greek mythology, the mortal, snake-haired gorgon with the power to turn anyone who gazed upon her into stone. Looking at her reflection in a shield given him by Athena, Perseus cut off Medusa's head as she slept.
8. Cf. Sylvia Plath's "Lady Lazarus": "Do I terrify?—."

Wasn't I beautiful?   40
Wasn't I fragrant and young?

Look at me now.

1999

Mrs Lazarus[9]

I had grieved. I had wept for a night and a day
over my loss, ripped the cloth I was married in
from my breasts, howled, shrieked, clawed
at the burial stones till my hands bled, retched
his name over and over again, dead, dead.   5

Gone home. Gutted the place. Slept in a single cot,
widow, one empty glove, white femur
in the dust, half. Stuffed dark suits
into black bags, shuffled in a dead man's shoes,
noosed the double knot of a tie round my bare neck,   10

gaunt nun in the mirror, touching herself. I learnt
the Stations of Bereavement,[1] the icon of my face
in each bleak frame; but all those months
he was going away from me, dwindling
to the shrunk size of a snapshot, going,   15

going. Till his name was no longer a certain spell
for his face. The last hair on his head
floated out from a book. His scent went from the house.
The will was read. See, he was vanishing
to the small zero held by the gold of my ring.   20

Then he was gone. Then he was legend, language;
my arm on the arm of the schoolteacher—the shock
of a man's strength under the sleeve of his coat—
along the hedgerows. But I was faithful
for as long as it took. Until he was memory.   25

So I could stand that evening in the field
in a shawl of fine air, healed, able
to watch the edge of the moon occur to the sky
and a hare thump from a hedge; then notice
the village men running towards me, shouting,   30

behind them the women and children, barking dogs,
and I knew. I knew by the sly light

9. Lazarus was the man raised from the dead by
Jesus (John 11).
1. Allusion to the Stations of the Cross, a series of
fourteen icons (pictures or carvings) correspond-
ing to the stages of Jesus' crucifixion and over each
of which a prayer is said.

on the blacksmith's face, the shrill eyes
of the barmaid, the sudden hands bearing me
into the hot tang of the crowd parting before me.   35

He lived. I saw the horror on his face.
I heard his mother's crazy song. I breathed
his stench; my bridegroom in his rotting shroud,
moist and dishevelled from the grave's slack chew,
croaking his cuckold name, disinherited, out of his time.   40

1999

DIONISIO D. MARTÍNEZ
b. 1956

Dionisio D. Martínez grew up speaking Spanish, but his poetry has wrung new possibilities from English. Born on April 7, 1956, in Cuba, he was three at the start of Fidel Castro's revolution and remembers the confiscation of his family's home and personal property—even his toys. He and his family went into exile in 1965, first living in northern Spain; but he grew up in Glendale, California. In 1972, his sophomore year in high school, his family moved to Tampa, Florida, which has since been his home. In high school, he was inspired by reading T. S. Eliot, Archibald MacLeish, and the Spanish poet Federico García Lorca.

Martínez's poetry is offbeat and radially allusive, assimilating diverse ingredients from the cultures of the Americas and of Europe, painting and music, the highbrow and the lowbrow—composer Niccolò Paganini and painter Jackson Pollock but also the White Sox and advertising. A poem such as "Hysteria," like the map and the newspaper it invokes, folds over and over. The half-humorous, half-panicked recycling of images from various sources—TV and the paper, history and poetry—releases new and unexpected connective energies among them. "The Prodigal Son in His Own Words: Bees" also manically recirculates images, alternating between a decaying house and bee hives, as if to give this prose poem the vertiginous circularity of such fixed forms as the sestina and the villanelle.

Martínez is a poet of gaps, losses, and interstices. While we find no paeans to Cuban American identity in his poetry, we can perhaps infer an indirect expression of his divided cultural experience in his preoccupation with displacement and disorientation, with orphans, exiles, and abandoned houses. "I want to learn / to think in American," says the speaker of "Hysteria," but a skewed relation to the dominant culture helps Martínez see that culture afresh, as if always through the lens of metaphor. "No matter where I go," he writes in "Temporary Losses," "I carry foreign currency." In "Moto Perpetuo," the poet's comments about Pollock's art also describe his own poetics: "how important / the gaps and absences were to him; // how crucial the distances, the gulfs." Martínez's poetry of juxtaposition owes something to surrealist technique and moves with the velocity of cinematic montage. It also recalls the seemingly logical illogic and elusiveness of John Ashbery's poetry. In tone, it is, like the work of the New York school, both zany and insistent, colloquial and authoritative. Its cultural and psychological kaleidoscope of images, puzzling and humorous, has the strange forcefulness of dream.

Hysteria

It only takes one night with the wind on its knees
to imagine Carl Sandburg unfolding
a map of Chicago,[1] puzzled, then walking the wrong way.

The lines on his face are hard to read. I alternate
between the tv, where a plastic surgeon is claiming   5
that every facial expression causes wrinkles, and

the newspaper. I picture the surgeon reading the lines
on Sandburg's face, lines that would've made more sense
if the poet had been, say, a tree growing

in a wind orchard. Maybe he simply smiled too much.   10
I'm reading about the All-Star game, thinking
that maybe Sandburg saw the White Sox of 1919.[2]

· · ·

I love American newspapers, the way each section
is folded independently and believes it owns
the world. There's this brief item in the inter-   15

national pages: the Chinese government has posted
signs in Tiananmen Square,[3] forbidding laughter.
I'm sure the plastic surgeon would approve, he'd say

the Chinese will look young much longer, their faces
unnaturally smooth, but what I see (although   20
no photograph accompanies the story) is laughter

bursting inside them. I go back to the sports section
and a closeup of a rookie in mid-swing, his face
keeping all the wrong emotions in check.

· · ·

When I read I bite my lower lip, a habit   25
the plastic surgeon would probably call
cosmetic heresy because it accelerates the aging

process. I think of Carl Sandburg and the White Sox;
I think of wind in Tiananmen Square, how a country
deprived of laughter ages invisibly; I think   30

1. American poet Carl Sandburg (1878–1967)
published *Chicago Poems* in 1916.
2. The 1919 World Series resulted in a front-page
news story when eight players from the Chicago
White Sox were accused of a crime: throwing the
series against the Cincinnati Reds. The players
were legally acquitted but permanently banned
from professional baseball.
3. Public square in the center of Beijing where
pro-reform demonstrators were massacred by the
government in 1989.

of the Great Walls of North America, each of them
a grip on some outfield like a rookie's hands
around a bat when the wind is against him; I bite

my lower lip again; I want to learn
to think in American, to believe that a headline   35
is a fact and all stories are suspect.

For Ana Menéndez

1995

Temporary Losses

Now that I know where circus children
go when they run away, I have no desire to move.
I load the moving van and tell the driver
to go until he runs out of road or out of gas or
out of towns that refuse his worthless cargo.   5

To define what remains, we speak the language of
the invisible man who argues with the doctors long
after the amputation, tells them
that he still walks with a phantom limb. Literally.

I begin to count the change in my pocket   10
and think of Thoreau[4] living on 27 cents a week,
walking too much, becoming accustomed
to the calluses from the ax, the strained
muscles and all that winter rising from the pond.

When I lay the change on the floor I find   15
a penny rubbed since 1944 by fingers not unlike
my own. I rub it too. For luck,
I think. All my superstitions are hand-me-downs.
What do I know about luck? What do I care if
the face of Lincoln rubs off on my fingers?   20

The oldest train route on the island began
a block from home. We laid coins
on the tracks and moved out of the way quickly,
remembering the kid who'd been half blinded.
I still wonder if a man with a glass eye   25
sees half of everything—half of the road, half
of the woman who will not tell him all the truth,
always a half moon regardless of the tides.

You want me to believe in everything, but there's
something to be said for knowing that a house   30

---

4. Henry David Thoreau (1817–1862), American author famous for the experiment in simple, self-sufficient living recorded in *Walden* (1854).

is not the world, that we can live without
the wicker furniture that made our house as tangible
as a father's arms. After all, sooner
or later they'll stop calling us orphans.

I hold my life savings in this hand.   35
No matter where I go, I carry foreign currency.

For María Menéndez

1995

Moto Perpetuo[5]

1

I've been walking in circles for what seems like days.
They've been playing Paganini, but you know

how intermittent the conscious ear
can be. How selective. Walking has nothing to do

with distance as clearly as Paganini   5
has nothing to do with the violin that plays him hard.

2

How it hurt Jackson Pollock,[6] during his black
and white period, to hear the critics say

that he was painting black *on* white; how important
the gaps and absences were to him;   10

how crucial the distances, the gulfs; how
critical each emptiness to each composition.

3

There is that moment in, say, the finale of Beethoven's
Fifth,[7] when you hear nothing between the various

false endings, so you make your own music,   15
a bridge of silence from one illusion

to the next. A deeper and more refined
ear—Beethoven's ear—takes care of this.

1995

5. Perpetual motion (Italian); title of a composi-
tion by Italian composer Niccolò Paganini (1782–
1840).
6. American abstract expressionist painter (1912–
1956), famous for his action paintings made by

dripping paint onto canvas.
7. *Symphony No. 5 in C minor* by Ludwig van Bee-
thoven (1770–1827), German composer who con-
tinued to write music even after going deaf in his
later years.

The Prodigal Son in His Own Words: Bees

There is a mathematical illusion that, if performed correctly, makes two
halves mirror one another. We've seen enough disparities within the
whole to know better. Some female bees mate only once. Carrying
enough sperm for a lifetime, they continue to reproduce without further
need for the male. Don't let the well-stocked shelves of the hardware   5
store fool you: the part you need is never available. This is why the
house deteriorates: hairline cracks appear, compromising the integrity
of the structure, and your solution is another coat of paint. Door frames
buckle and the doors never shut comfortably again. In one species of
the mining bee, some females are never inseminated because their work   10
is more valuable than any possible offspring. Pipes burst, filling the
basement with water, and you can't find the right joint. I visit an
excavation of my paternal ancestors' dwellings, built maybe three
thousand years ago. Seen from higher ground, the community is an
enormous honeycomb, the walls for the most part still standing solidly   15
against the elements. My father's own house, by contrast, is barely
habitable after only two centuries. Where I sleep, I do so with the
uneasy feeling that I'll wake in a field, the house gone and the
millennium gone with the house. Mason bees secrete their own cement.
Though it may be rebuilt ad nauseam, the first house falls only once.   20

2001

Henri Cole
b. 1956

Beset with contradictions between his homosexuality and his Catholicism, his mind at
war with itself, Henri Cole writes poems that are taut with an inner violence. Sinewy,
tense, conflicted, they yoke together love of God with desire for the bodies of men.
Through their controlled linguistic surfaces and muscular compression, they contain
the immense pressure of these and other irreconcilable longings. To hold in suspension
his profoundly antithetical feelings, Cole has often turned to the sonnet, ratcheting up
the emotional intensity of this inherited form.

Having visited the Vatican, the poet opens the sonnet "White Spine" with a harsh
question: "Liar, I thought, kneeling with the others, / how can He love me and hate
what I am?" Cole's anger and self-reviling find no relief in the course of the poem. In
another sonnet, "Childlessness," he confronts the clash between two desires: to fuse
with his dead mother and to hold at bay her overbearing presence. Severe and unspar-
ingly honest, Cole's poetry renews the tradition of Elizabeth Bishop, Robert Lowell,
and James Merrill, affording psychic self-examination without self-pity, self-disclosure
without bathos. The power of his verse arises from its inner affective tension, its blunt
and authoritative tone, and its luminous figurative language.

Metaphor can be a language of miniaturized tension, holding together the like and
the unlike, and Cole's gift for figuration is unmistakable. In "White Spine," Cole writes,
"The dome of St. Peter's shone yellowish / gold, like butter and eggs." In "Folly," swans

tearing up weeds in a decadent Roman garden are seen as "dripping like a chandelier." In the double sonnet "Buddha and the Seven Tiger Cubs," a male erotic dancer slings his leg over the bar rail for tips, and the speaker, unabashed about his sexual longing, remarks: "He's a black swan straining its elastic / neck to eat bread crumbs and nourish itself."

Cole's early poetry is overtly formal, relying on patterned meter, rhyme, and off-rhyme. But he opens his 1998 collection *The Visible Man* by recanting "description & rhyme, / which had nursed and embalmed me at once" ("Arte Povera"). When in *Life Studies* (1959) Lowell broke with formal prosody, its ghost remained an animating presence within his free verse. Cole likewise transfers the formal impulse from end rhyme to a forceful syntax, focused tone, and potent verbs. In "Folly," the nutrea "eradicating" a garden are said to "root" along ditches, "to hunt . . . and gut" cygnet eggs.

Born to a military family on May 9, 1956, in Fukuoka, Japan, Cole has written sadly about his imposing mother, his largely absent father, and his shabby circumstances as a child. Violence, he has said, regularly erupted in the household. But he eventually found solace in poetry, especially that of Hart Crane, who, he states, "gave the young homosexual I was a model, an inflected language, an ecstatic voice, to begin to write about the social and domestic life I wanted to reveal secretly in art" ("First Loves"). Cole was educated at the College of William and Mary (B.A., 1978), the University of Wisconsin at Milwaukee (M.A., 1980), and Columbia University (M.F.A., 1982). He has taught at various universities and colleges, including Columbia, Reed, Yale, Maryland, Harvard, Brandeis, and Smith.

Harvard Classics[1]

It is the hour of lamps.
On our knees my mother
and I, still young, color
with crayons threadbare nap

on the livingroom rug.   5
Though there is no money,
no one seems to care. We
are self-possessed as bugs

waving their antennae
through cracks in the kitchen's   10
linoleum floor. When
Father begins to read

from the red gilt volume
in his lap, a circle
of light encapsulates   15
us like hearts in a womb.

Except their marriage is
already dead. I know

---

1. A series of fifty works of world literature chosen in 1908 by Harvard University president Charles Eliot (1834–1926) to represent a compact liberal arts education.

this though I'm only six.
So we visit Pharoahs,   20

a boatman on the Nile,
Crusaders[2] eating grapes
on a beach. Life escapes
with all its sadness while

two tragic Greek poets   25
inhabit Father's voice.
Who'd know I'm just a boy
when he begins a stoic

moral tale concerning
a dull provincial doctor's   30
young French wife.[3] If Mother,
in French, begins to sing

to herself, I know she's
had enough. Crayon stubs
litter the crumbling rug.   35
Our prostrate cat sneezes

at the dust in her fur.
And cries from a swallow
remind us one swallow
doesn't make a summer.   40

                                                    1995

Buddha and the Seven Tiger Cubs[4]

Holding a varnished paper parasol,
the gardener—a shy man-off-the-street—
ripple-rakes the white sand, despite rainfall,
into a pattern effortlessly neat,
meant to suggest, only abstractly, the sea,   5
as eight weathered stones are meant to depict
Buddha and the hungry cubs he knows he
must sacrifice himself to feed. I sit
in a little red gazebo and think—
as the Zen monks[5] do—about what love means,   10

---

2. Christian participants in medieval military ex-
peditions against Muslim powers.
3. *Madame Bovary* (1857), by French novelist
Gustave Flaubert (1821–1880), tells of the adul-
tery committed by the wife of a country doctor.
4. According to legend, upon finding seven starv-
ing tiger cubs abandoned by their mother, the Bud-
dha decided to offer himself as food so the animals

might survive.
5. Practitioners of the Zen branch of Buddhism,
which emphasizes the importance of meditation
and breaking out of ordinary modes of thinking to
achieve enlightenment. The speaker of the poem
is located in the Japanese Gardens in Portland,
Oregon. Stark Street is another Portland locale.

unashamed to have known it as something
tawdry and elusive from watching lean
erotic dancers in one of the dives
on Stark Street, where I go some lovesick nights.

Even in costume they look underage,   15
despite hard physiques and frozen glances
perfected for the ugly, floodlit stage,
where they are stranded like fish. What enhances
their act is that we're an obedient crowd,
rheumy with liquor; our stinginess   20
is broken. When one slings his leg proudly
across the bar rail where I sit, I kiss
a five dollar bill and tuck it in his belt.
He's a black swan straining its elastic
neck to eat bread crumbs and nourish itself.   25
My heart is not alert; I am transfixed,
loving him as tiger cubs love their
mother who abandons them forever.

                                                          1995

White Spine

Liar, I thought, kneeling with the others,
how can He love me and hate what I am?
The dome of St. Peter's[6] shone yellowish
gold, like butter and eggs. *My God*, I prayed
anyhow, as if made in the image   5
and likeness of Him. Nearby, a handsome
priest looked at me like a stone; I looked back,
not desiring to go it alone.
The college of cardinals[7] wore punitive red.
The white spine waved to me from his white throne.[8]   10
Being in a place not my own, much less
myself, I climbed out, a beast in a crib.
Somewhere a terrorist rolled a cigarette.
Reason, not faith, would change him.

                                                          1998

---

6. St. Peter's Basilica at the Vatican, in Rome.
7. The members of the Sacred College of Cardinals act as the pope's main counselors and wear distinctive red dress.

8. The silk-covered armchair (*sedia gestatoria*) on which the pope ("white spine") sits during solemn ceremonies.

Folly

In the Doria Pamphili garden,[9]
most of the granite niches are empty,
the male gods have lost their genitals,
and the Great Mother, Hera,[1] has no head.

Something has gone awry   5
in the artificial lake.
Burrowing deep into the black banks
enclosed by wire mesh,
families of nutria[2] are eradicating—
with webbed hind feet,   10
blunt muzzled heads
and long orange incisors—
Pope Innocent X's pleasure garden's
eco-system.

      Gothic as the unconscious,
the heavy tapered bodies   15
root along the irrigation ditches,
making their way in a criminal trot
toward the swans, whose handsome,
ecclesiastical wings open out
obliviously.   20

Each day I come back.
The sky is Della Robbia blue.[3]
As I rise to my feet,
a swan—immaculate
and self-possessed as the ambulance   25
bearing my half-dead Mother—
grasps into the depths
and tears a weed up,
dripping like a chandelier,
while paddling behind are the derelict rodents,   30
hankering—with big sleepy eyes,
suggesting something like matrimonial bliss,
and plush gray fur,
undulating like the coat my mother wore—
to hunt the grass-shrouded   35
cygnet eggs and gut
their bloody embryos.

1998

9. Roman garden commissioned in the mid-seventeenth century by Pope Innocent X and now part of Rome's largest public park.
1. In Greek mythology, wife of Zeus and queen of the gods.
2. Aquatic rodent native to South America and considered a pest in parts of North America and Europe.
3. Color associated with the glaze Florentine sculptor Luca Della Robbia (c. 1400–1482) invented and applied to his terra cotta sculptures.

Childlessness

For many years I wanted a child
though I knew it would only illuminate life
for a time, like a star on a tree; I believed
that happiness would at last assert itself,
like a bird in a dirty cage, calling me,   5
ambassador of flesh, out of the rough
locked ward of sex.

          Outstretched on my spool-bed,[4]
I am like a groom, alternately seeking fusion
with another and resisting engulfment by it.
A son's love for his mother is like a river   10
dividing the continent to reach the sea:
I believed that once. When you died, Mother,
I was alone at last. And then you came back,
dismal and greedy like the sea, to reclaim me.

          1998

4. Style of bed with ribbed bedposts.

LI-YOUNG LEE
b. 1957

Born on August 19, 1957, to Chinese parents in Jakarta, Indonesia, Li-Young Lee is one of the preeminent poets of the East Asian diaspora in the United States. His father had been a personal physician to Communist leader Mao Tse-tung in China, before moving with his family to Indonesia, Hong Kong, Macao, and Japan, finally settling, in 1964, in a small town in western Pennsylvania, where he became a Presbyterian minister. Li-Young Lee said in an interview published in 1995 that his family's migrant experience, though "an outward manifestation of a homelessness that people in general feel," is responsible for his intense "feeling of disconnection and dislocation." As a child, Lee learned from his father Chinese poetry of the Tang Dynasty, as well as psalms and proverbs in the King James Bible. Having grown up between Mandarin Chinese and English, Lee explores through his poetry the tensions and ambiguities of his biculturalism: "You live / a while in two worlds / at once" ("My Indigo").

The painful experience of being in between languages as an immigrant child is the subject of one of Lee's best-known poems. "Persimmons" tells the story of a young Chinese immigrant slapped by a schoolteacher for being unable to differentiate the sounds of "persimmon" and "precision." Imperfectly grounded in English as a child, the adult speaker, likewise unable to remember some Chinese words, is completely at home in neither language. Lee's early sense of linguistic estrangement can be seen, paradoxically, in his powerful attachment to the sounds and textures of English words. His poetic language is richly sensuous. Lee savors the phonemic resources of English, almost eroticizing words and their relationships. In an exemplary line, Lee revels in assonance and alliteration: a hornet in a rotten pear "spun crazily, glazed in slow, glistening juice" ("Eating Alone"). Studding his poems with pellucid visual images (a splinter is "a silver tear, a tiny flame" in "The Gift"), Lee evokes the smell, the feel, and the taste of an often ethnically specific experience (the steamed trout with ginger in "Eating Together").

Although Lee's work bears the imprint of his Chinese background, it should not be exoticized. It descends from the American confessional poetry of Theodore Roethke and Sylvia Plath, and from the Deep Image poetry of James Wright and Philip Levine. It is written in free—if strongly cadenced—verse, sometimes cleverly enjambed ("How to choose//persimmons. This is precision"). Emotionally charged, rooted in childhood experience, the poems narrate simple stories. Lee's father plays the dominant role as figure of ambivalence, associated in "The Gift" and other poems with tenderness and love, and yet with discipline and pain. Squarely in the Romantic tradition, many of the poems drink at the well of early memory, relying on images and dreams to recover feelings from the past. John Keats, Walt Whitman, and Rainer Maria Rilke are among Lee's formative influences.

Lee was educated at the Universities of Pittsburgh (B.A., 1979) and Arizona (1979–80) and the State University of New York College at Brockport (1980–81). He has taught at various universities, including Northwestern University and the University of Iowa. He lives with his family in Chicago.

The Gift

To pull the metal splinter from my palm
my father recited a story in a low voice.
I watched his lovely face and not the blade.
Before the story ended, he'd removed
the iron sliver I thought I'd die from.   5

I can't remember the tale,
but hear his voice still, a well
of dark water, a prayer.
And I recall his hands,
two measures of tenderness   10
he laid against my face,
the flames of discipline
he raised above my head.

Had you entered that afternoon
you would have thought you saw a man   15
planting something in a boy's palm,
a silver tear, a tiny flame.
Had you followed that boy
you would have arrived here,
where I bend over my wife's right hand.   20

Look how I shave her thumbnail down
so carefully she feels no pain.
Watch as I lift the splinter out.
I was seven when my father
took my hand like this,   25

and I did not hold that shard
between my fingers and think,
Metal that will bury me,
christen it Little Assassin,
Ore Going Deep for My Heart.   30
And I did not lift up my wound and cry,
Death visited here!
I did what a child does
when he's given something to keep.
I kissed my father.   35

                                        1986

Persimmons

In sixth grade Mrs. Walker
slapped the back of my head
and made me stand in the corner
for not knowing the difference
between *persimmon* and *precision*.   5
How to choose

persimmons. This is precision.
Ripe ones are soft and brown-spotted.
Sniff the bottoms. The sweet one
will be fragrant. How to eat: 10
put the knife away, lay down newspaper.
Peel the skin tenderly, not to tear the meat.
Chew the skin, suck it,
and swallow. Now, eat
the meat of the fruit,   15
so sweet,
all of it, to the heart.

Donna undresses, her stomach is white.
In the yard, dewy and shivering
with crickets, we lie naked,   20
face-up, face-down.
I teach her Chinese.
Crickets: *chiu chiu.* Dew: I've forgotten.
Naked: I've forgotten.
Ni, wo: you and me.   25
I part her legs,
remember to tell her
she is beautiful as the moon.

Other words
that got me into trouble were   30
fight and *fright, wren* and *yarn.*
Fight was what I did when I was frightened,
fright was what I felt when I was fighting.

Wrens are small, plain birds,
yarn is what one knits with.   35
Wrens are soft as yarn.
My mother made birds out of yarn.
I loved to watch her tie the stuff;
a bird, a rabbit, a wee man.

Mrs. Walker brought a persimmon to class   40
and cut it up
so everyone could taste
a *Chinese apple*. Knowing
it wasn't ripe or sweet, I didn't eat
but watched the other faces.   45

My mother said every persimmon has a sun
inside, something golden, glowing,
warm as my face.

Once, in the cellar, I found two wrapped in newspaper,
forgotten and not yet ripe.   50
I took them and set both on my bedroom windowsill,
where each morning a cardinal
sang, *The sun, the sun.*

Finally understanding
he was going blind,   55
my father sat up all one night
waiting for a song, a ghost.
I gave him the persimmons,
swelled, heavy as sadness,
and sweet as love.   60

This year, in the muddy lighting
of my parents' cellar, I rummage, looking
for something I lost.
My father sits on the tired, wooden stairs,
black cane between his knees,   65
hand over hand, gripping the handle.

He's so happy that I've come home.
I ask how his eyes are, a stupid question.
All gone, he answers.

Under some blankets, I find a box.   70
Inside the box I find three scrolls.
I sit beside him and untie
three paintings by my father:
Hibiscus leaf and a white flower.
Two cats preening.   75
Two persimmons, so full they want to drop from the cloth.

He raises both hands to touch the cloth,
asks, *Which is this?*

This is persimmons, Father.

Oh, the feel of the wolftail on the silk,[1]   80
the strength, the tense
precision in the wrist.
I painted them hundreds of times
eyes closed. These I painted blind.
Some things never leave a person: 85
scent of the hair of one you love,
the texture of persimmons,
in your palm, the ripe weight.

                                                                    1986

Eating Alone

I've pulled the last of the year's young onions.
The garden is bare now. The ground is cold,
brown and old. What is left of the day flames
in the maples at the corner of my
eye. I turn, a cardinal vanishes.   5
By the cellar door, I wash the onions,
then drink from the icy metal spigot.

Once, years back, I walked beside my father
among the windfall pears. I can't recall
our words. We may have strolled in silence. But   10
I still see him bend that way—left hand braced
on knee, creaky—to lift and hold to my
eye a rotten pear. In it, a hornet
spun crazily, glazed in slow, glistening juice.

It was my father I saw this morning   15
waving to me from the trees. I almost
called to him, until I came close enough
to see the shovel, leaning where I had
left it, in the flickering, deep green shade.

White rice steaming, almost done. Sweet green peas   20
fried in onions. Shrimp braised in sesame
oil and garlic. And my own loneliness.
What more could I, a young man, want.

                                                                    1986

1. Materials used in Chinese calligraphy.

Eating Together

In the steamer is the trout
seasoned with slivers of ginger,
two sprigs of green onion, and sesame oil.
We shall eat it with rice for lunch,
brothers, sister, my mother who will   5
taste the sweetest meat of the head,
holding it between her fingers
deftly, the way my father did
weeks ago. Then he lay down
to sleep like a snow-covered road   10
winding through pines older than him,
without any travelers, and lonely for no one.

1986

Pillow

There's nothing I can't find under there.
Voices in the trees, the missing pages
of the sea.

Everything but sleep.

And night is a river bridging   5
the speaking and the listening banks,

a fortress, undefended and inviolate.

There's nothing that won't fit under it:
fountains clogged with mud and leaves,
the houses of my childhood.   10

And night begins when my mother's fingers
let go of the thread
they've been tying and untying
to touch toward our fraying story's hem.

Night is the shadow of my father's hands   15
setting the clock for resurrection.

Or is it the clock unraveled, the numbers flown?

There's nothing that hasn't found home there:
discarded wings, lost shoes, a broken alphabet.

Everything but sleep. And night begins   20

with the first beheading
of the jasmine, its captive fragrance
rid at last of burial clothes.

2001

SHERMAN ALEXIE
b. 1966

Though widely known as a gifted novelist and screenwriter, Sherman Alexie began his literary career as a poet and has regularly published volumes of poetry. A "registered" (in the bureaucratic jargon) Spokane/Coeur d'Alene Indian, Alexie is a master of the trickster aesthetic. Wily and poker-faced, he dons rhetorical guises with cunning force. Occasionally a clenched fist is visible behind his characteristic curtain of irony. The Native American speaker in the poem "On the Amtrak from Boston to New York City" listens and nods cordially to a well-meaning white woman, as she, smiling, reads the landscape outside in terms of a "history" that is exclusively white, effacing thousands of years of Native American experience. Never revealed to his fellow passenger, the anger is all the more effectively presented in the poem, as in "Evolution" and "How to Write the Great American Indian Novel," smoldering behind a facade of agreeable good cheer.

Many of Alexie's poems explore the collision and tension between the perspectives of Native and white Americans. Tricksters must know the dominant as well as their own culture if they are to manipulate appearances effectively. "[I]t's hard to live in both worlds," Alexie remarked in a 1998 interview. "But I'm always doing it, it's part of who I am. It's actually a strength. . . . I know a lot more about white people than white people know about Indians." In the surreal world of "Tourists," Alexie imaginatively juxtaposes popular American cultural icons with reservation life. As he put it in another 1998 interview, his poetry is "always about the image, and about the connection, often, of very disparate, contradictory images."

If the ironic conjunction of antagonistic cultural perspectives is one of the key features of Alexie's work, another is narrative momentum. Alexie repeatedly refers to the "strong narrative drive" in his poetry. He shows little interest in lyric density or syntactic and lexical complexity. But his ear for colloquial speech, his feel for incremental repetition, and his eye for telling incongruity help him build narrative tension toward an ultimate climax. His brilliance as a storyteller has helped Alexie repeatedly win poetry slams, such as the Taos Poetry Circus World Heavyweight Championship in 1998, 1999, and 2000.

Born on October 7, 1966, Alexie grew up in Wellpinit, a town in a Spokane reservation in eastern Washington. Diagnosed with hydrocephalus, a large amount of cerebrospinal fluid in the cranial cavity, he was expected to die or at least to suffer from severe mental retardation after brain surgery at six months. Teased as "The Globe" for his enlarged skull in childhood, he retreated to the library, where he devoured books. He was educated at Gonzaga University in Spokane (1985–87) and Washington State University in Pullman (B.A., 1991). He lives in Seattle.

Evolution

Buffalo Bill[1] opens a pawn shop on the reservation
right across the border from the liquor store
and he stays open 24 hours a day, 7 days a week

and the Indians come running in with jewelry
television sets, a VCR, a full-length beaded buckskin outfit   5
it took Inez Muse 12 years to finish. Buffalo Bill

takes everything the Indians have to offer, keeps it
all catalogued and filed in a storage room. The Indians
pawn their hands, saving the thumbs for last, they pawn

their skeletons, falling endlessly from the skin   10
and when the last Indian has pawned everything
but his heart, Buffalo Bill takes that for twenty bucks

closes up the pawn shop, paints a new sign over the old
calls his venture THE MUSEUM OF NATIVE AMERICAN CULTURES
charges the Indians five bucks a head to enter.   15

                                                                      1991

On the Amtrak from Boston to New York City

The white woman across the aisle from me says, "Look,
look at all the history, that house
on the hill there is over two hundred years old,"
as she points out the window past me

into what she has been taught. I have learned   5
little more about American history during my few days
back East than what I expected and far less
of what we should all know of the tribal stories

whose architecture is 15,000 years older
than the corners of the house that sits   10
museumed on the hill. "Walden Pond,"[2]
the woman on the train asks, "Did you see Walden Pond?"

and I don't have a cruel enough heart to break
her own by telling her there are five Walden Ponds
on my little reservation out West   15
and at least a hundred more surrounding Spokane,

---

1. William F. Cody (1846–1917), whose life was mythologized in a series of dime novels and theatrical productions celebrating his bravery and skill as a cavalry scout and buffalo hunter.
2. Small lake just south of Concord, Massachu-setts, where American Transcendentalist Henry David Thoreau (1817–1862) tried to live simply and self-reliantly in a small cabin for two years, as described in his *Walden* (1854).

the city I pretend to call my home. "Listen,"
I could have told her. "I don't give a shit
about Walden. I know the Indians were living stories
around that pond before Walden's grandparents were born   20

and before his grandparents' grandparents were born.
I'm tired of hearing about Don-fucking-Henley[3] saving it, too,
because that's redundant. If Don Henley's brothers and sisters
and mothers and fathers hadn't come here in the first place

then nothing would need to be saved."   25
But I didn't say a word to the woman about Walden
Pond because she smiled so much and seemed delighted
that I thought to bring her an orange juice

back from the food car. I respect elders
of every color. All I really did was eat   30
my tasteless sandwich, drink my Diet Pepsi
and nod my head whenever the woman pointed out

another little piece of her country's history
while I, as all Indians have done
since this war began, made plans   35
for what I would do and say the next time

somebody from the enemy thought I was one of their own.

                                                    1993

Tourists

1. James Dean[4]

walks everywhere now. He's afraid of fast cars
and has walked this far, arriving
suddenly on the reservation, in search
of the Indian woman of his dreams.
He wants an Indian woman who could pass   5
for Natalie Wood.[5] He wants an Indian woman
who looks like the Natalie Wood
who was kidnapped by Indians
in John Ford's classic movie, "The Searchers."
James Dean wants to rescue somebody beautiful.   10
He still wears that red jacket,
you know the one. It's the color of a powwow[6] fire.

---

3. American rock musician Don Henley (b. 1947) helped start the Walden Woods Project in 1990 to preserve the woodlands surrounding the pond from encroaching commercial development.
4. American actor (1931–1955), most famous for his role in the film *Rebel without a Cause* (1955); his early death in a car accident helped contribute to his status as a tragic symbol of misunderstood youth in the 1950s.
5. American actor (1938–1981), who starred in such films as *Rebel without a Cause* (opposite Dean) and *The Searchers* (1956), a western directed by American filmmaker John Ford (1894–1973).
6. Tribal or intertribal event featuring dancing, singing, prayers, and speeches.

James Dean has never seen
a powwow, but he joins right in, dancing
like a crazy man, like a profane clown.   15
James Dean cannot contain himself.
He dances in the wrong direction. He tears
at his hair. He sings in wild syllables
and does not care. The Indian dancers stop
and stare like James Dean was lightning   20
or thunder, like he was bad weather.
But he keeps dancing, bumps into a man
and knocks loose an eagle feather.
The feather falls, drums stop.
This is the kind of silence   25
that frightens white men. James Dean
looks down at the feather
and knows that something has gone wrong.
He looks into the faces of the Indians.
He wants them to finish the song.   30

2. Janis Joplin[7]

sits by the jukebox in the Powwow Tavern,
talking with a few drunk Indians
about redemption. She promises each of them
she can punch in the numbers
for the song that will save their lives.   35
All she needs is a few quarters, a beer,
and their own true stories. The Indians
are as traditional as drunk Indians can be
and don't believe in autobiography,
so they lie to Janis Joplin about their lives.   40
One Indian is an astronaut, another killed JFK,
while the third played first base
for the New York Yankees. Janis Joplin knows
the Indians are lying. She's a smart woman
but she listens anyway, plays them each a song,   45
and sings along off key.

3. Marilyn Monroe[8]

drives herself to the reservation. Tired and cold,
she asks the Indian women for help.
Marilyn cannot explain what she needs
but the Indian women notice the needle tracks
on her arms and lead her to the sweat lodge[9]   50
where every woman, young and old, disrobes
and leaves her clothes behind
when she enters the dark of the lodge.

7. Rock vocalist (1943–1970), renowned for her raucous, bluesy voice and early death, of a heroin overdose.
8. American actor and Hollywood sex symbol (1926–1962), who died of an overdose of sleeping pills.
9. Small building that, when filled with steam, is used for purification and healing.

Marilyn's prayers may or may not be answered here   55
but they are kept sacred by Indian women.
Cold water is splashed on hot rocks
and steam fills the lodge. There is no place like this.
At first, Marilyn is self-conscious, aware
of her body and face, the tremendous heat, her thirst,   60
and the brown bodies circled around her.
But the Indian women do not stare. It is dark
inside the lodge. The hot rocks glow red
and the songs begin. Marilyn has never heard
these songs before, but she soon sings along.   65
Marilyn is not Indian, Marilyn will never be Indian
but the Indian women sing about her courage.
The Indian women sing for her health.
The Indian women sing for Marilyn.
Finally, she is no more naked than anyone else.   70

1996

How to Write the Great American Indian Novel

All of the Indians must have tragic features: tragic noses, eyes, and arms.
Their hands and fingers must be tragic when they reach for tragic food.

The hero must be a half-breed, half white and half Indian, preferably
from a horse culture. He should often weep alone. That is mandatory.

If the hero is an Indian woman, she is beautiful. She must be slender   5
and in love with a white man. But if she loves an Indian man

then he must be a half-breed, preferably from a horse culture.
If the Indian woman loves a white man, then he has to be so white

that we can see the blue veins running through his skin like rivers.
When the Indian woman steps out of her dress, the white man gasps   10

at the endless beauty of her brown skin. She should be compared to
    nature:
brown hills, mountains, fertile valleys, dewy grass, wind, and clear water.

If she is compared to murky water, however, then she must have a secret.
Indians always have secrets, which are carefully and slowly revealed.

Yet Indian secrets can be disclosed suddenly, like a storm.   15
Indian men, of course, are storms. They should destroy the lives

of any white women who choose to love them. All white women love
Indian men. That is always the case. White women feign disgust

at the savage in blue jeans and T-shirt, but secretly lust after him.
White women dream about half-breed Indian men from horse cultures.   20

Indian men are horses, smelling wild and gamey. When the Indian man
unbuttons his pants, the white woman should think of topsoil.

There must be one murder, one suicide, one attempted rape.
Alcohol should be consumed. Cars must be driven at high speeds.

Indians must see visions. White people can have the same visions   25
if they are in love with Indians. If a white person loves an Indian

then the white person is Indian by proximity. White people must carry
an Indian deep inside themselves. Those interior Indians are half-breed

and obviously from horse cultures. If the interior Indian is male
then he must be a warrior, especially if he is inside a white man.   30

If the interior Indian is female, then she must be a healer, especially if she
    is inside
a white woman. Sometimes there are complications.

An Indian man can be hidden inside a white woman. An Indian woman
can be hidden inside a white man. In these rare instances,

everybody is a half-breed struggling to learn more about his or her horse 35
    culture.
There must be redemption, of course, and sins must be forgiven.

For this, we need children. A white child and an Indian child, gender
not important, should express deep affection in a childlike way.

In the Great American Indian novel, when it is finally written,
all of the white people will be Indians and all of the Indians will be ghosts. 40

1996

Crow Testament

1

Cain lifts Crow, that heavy black bird
and strikes down Abel.[1]

Damn, says Crow, I guess
this is just the beginning.

---

1. According to Genesis 4, Cain is history's first murderer, slaying his younger brother in a fit of jealousy. The Crow is a prominent trickster figure in the mythologies of many Native American tribes.

2

The white man, disguised   5
as a falcon, swoops in
and yet again steals a salmon
from Crow's talons.

Damn, says Crow, if I could swim
I would have fled this country years ago.   10

3

The Crow God as depicted
in all of the reliable Crow bibles
looks exactly like a Crow.

Damn, says Crow, this makes it
so much easier to worship myself.   15

4

Among the ashes of Jericho,[2]
Crow sacrifices his firstborn son.

Damn, says Crow, a million nests
are soaked with blood.

5

When Crows fight Crows   20
the sky fills with beaks and talons.

Damn, says Crow, it's raining feathers.

6

Crow flies around the reservation
and collects empty beer bottles

but they are so heavy   25
he can carry only one at a time.

So, one by one, he returns them
but gets only five cents a bottle.

Damn, says Crow, redemption
is not easy.   30

---

2. Town on the west side of the Jordan River Valley famous in biblical history for its destruction under the attack of Joshua and the Israelites after God caused its walls to tumble (Joshua 6).

7

Crow rides a pale horse
into a crowded powwow
but none of the Indians panic.

Damn, says Crow, I guess
they already live near the end of the world.   35

2000

Poetics

PROJECTIVE VERSE

In the post–World War II period, this landmark essay by Charles Olson, leader of the Black Mountain school, which also included Robert Creeley, Robert Duncan, and Denise Levertov, has been a major catalyst of poetic innovation. Published at a time when the so-called closed forms of New Criticism and T. S. Eliot's version of modernism predominated, Olson's essay inspired many poets to experiment with open forms. In contrast to the concept of poetry as the well-wrought urn, static and timeless, Olson proposes a model of poetry as the dynamic transfer and discharge of energy. Grounded in the poet's body and breath, the poem should convey the spontaneity, the process, the excitement of composition. Propounding what he calls "objectism," Olson urges poets to reach beyond their individual egos and open themselves to the larger forces of nature. He breaks with some literary precedents, but adapts others, such as Romantic ideas of inspiration, organicism, and responsiveness to nature, as well as the modernist ideas and practices of Ezra Pound and William Carlos Williams. First published in *Poetry New York*, No. 3 (1950), the essay has been reprinted from *Collected Prose* (1997).

CHARLES OLSON

Projective / Verse

(projectile   (percussive   (prospective[1]

vs.

The NON-Projective

(or what a French critic calls "closed" verse, that verse which print bred and which is pretty much what we have had, in English & American, and have still got, despite the work of Pound & Williams:

it led Keats, already a hundred years ago, to see it (Wordsworth's, Milton's) in the light of "the Egotistical Sublime";[2] and it persists, at this latter day, as what you might call the private-soul-at-any-public-wall)

---

1. Throughout his writing, Olson used unclosed parentheses to signify birth and a receptive consciousness.
2. English Romantic poet John Keats (1795–1821) contrasted the "[W]ordsworthian or egotis-

tical sublime," the poet's habit of focusing attention on his or her own mind, with his own poetic strategies, including "negative capability," the poet's tolerance of uncertainty and sympathetic identification with nature.

Verse now, 1950, if it is to go ahead, if it is to be of *essential* use, must, I take it, catch up and put into itself certain laws and possibilities of the breath, of the breathing of the man who writes as well as of his listenings. (The revolution of the ear, 1910, the trochee's heave, asks it of the younger poets.)[3]

I want to do two things: first, try to show what projective or OPEN verse is, what it involves, in its act of composition, how, in distinction from the non-projective, it is accomplished; and II, suggest a few ideas about what stance toward reality brings such verse into being, what that stance does, both to the poet and to his reader. (The stance involves, for example, a change beyond, and larger than, the technical, and may, the way things look, lead to new poetics and to new concepts from which some sort of drama, say, or of epic, perhaps, may emerge.)

I

First, some simplicities that a man learns, if he works in OPEN, or what can also be called COMPOSITION BY FIELD, as opposed to inherited line, stanza, over-all form, what is the "old" base of the non-projective.

(1) the *kinetics* of the thing. A poem is energy transferred from where the poet got it (he will have some several causations), by way of the poem itself to, all the way over to, the reader. Okay. Then the poem itself must, at all points, be a high energy-construct and, at all points, an energy-discharge. So: how is the poet to accomplish same energy, how is he, what is the process by which a poet gets in, at all points energy at least the equivalent of the energy which propelled him in the first place, yet an energy which is peculiar to verse alone and which will be, obviously, also different from the energy which the reader, because he is a third term, will take away?

This is the problem which any poet who departs from closed form is specially confronted by. And it involves a whole series of new recognitions. From the moment he ventures into FIELD COMPOSITION—puts himself in the open—he can go by no track other than the one the poem under hand declares, for itself. Thus he has to behave, and be, instant by instant, aware of some several forces just now beginning to be examined. (It is much more, for example, this push, than simply such a one as Pound put, so wisely, to get us started: "the musical phrase," go by it, boys, rather than by, the metronome.)[4]

(2) is the *principle*, the law which presides conspicuously over such composition, and, when obeyed, is the reason why a projective poem can come into being. It is this: FORM IS NEVER MORE THAN AN EXTENSION OF CONTENT. (Or so it got phrased by one, R. Creeley,[5] and it makes absolute sense to me, with this possible corollary, that right form, in any given poem, is the only and exclusively possible extension of content under hand.) There it is, brothers, sitting there, for USE.

Now (3) the *process* of the thing, how the principle can be made so to shape the energies that the form is accomplished. And I think it can be boiled down to one statement (first pounded into my head by Edward Dahlberg[6]):

---

3. Cf. Canto 81, by Ezra Pound (1885–1972): "To break the pentameter, that was the first heave."
4. The third principle of Imagism: "As regarding rhythm: to compose in the sequence of the musical phrase, not in sequence of a metronome" (Pound,

"A Retrospect," vol. 1 of this anthology).
5. Robert Creeley (b. 1926), fellow poet of the Black Mountain school.
6. American poet and novelist (1900–1977).

ONE PERCEPTION MUST IMMEDIATELY AND DIRECTLY LEAD TO
A FURTHER PERCEPTION. It means exactly what it says, is a matter of,
at *all* points (even, I should say, of our management of daily reality as of the
daily work) get on with it, keep moving, keep in, speed, the nerves, their
speed, the perceptions, theirs, the acts, the split second acts, the whole busi-
ness, keep it moving as fast as you can, citizen. And if you also set up as a
poet, USE USE USE the process at all points, in any given poem always,
always one perception must must must MOVE, INSTANTER, ON
ANOTHER!

So there we are, fast, there's the dogma. And its excuse, its usableness, in
practice. Which gets us, it ought to get us, inside the machinery, now, 1950,
of how projective verse is made.

If I hammer, if I recall in, and keep calling in, the breath, the breathing
as distinguished from the hearing, it is for cause, it is to insist upon a part
that breath plays in verse which has not (due, I think, to the smothering of
the power of the line by too set a concept of foot) has not been sufficiently
observed or practiced, but which has to be if verse is to advance to its proper
force and place in the day, now, and ahead. I take it that PROJECTIVE
VERSE teaches, is, this lesson, that that verse will only do in which a poet
manages to register both the acquisitions of his ear *and* the pressures of his
breath.

Let's start from the smallest particle of all, the syllable. It is the king and
pin of versification, what rules and holds together the lines, the larger forms,
of a poem. I would suggest that verse here and in England dropped this secret
from the late Elizabethans to Ezra Pound, lost it, in the sweetness of meter
and rime, in a honey-head.[7] (The syllable is one way to distinguish the orig-
inal success of blank verse, and its falling off, with Milton.)

It is by their syllables that words juxtapose in beauty, by these particles of
sound as clearly as by the sense of the words which they compose. In any
given instance, because there is a choice of words, the choice, if a man is in
there, will be, spontaneously, the obedience of his ear to the syllables. The
fineness, and the practice, lie here, at the minimum and source of speech.

> O western wynd, when wilt thou blow
> And the small rain down shall rain
> O Christ that my love were in my arms
> And I in my bed again[8]

It would do no harm, as an act of correction to both prose and verse as
now written, if both rime and meter, and, in the quantity words, both sense
and sound, were less in the forefront of the mind than the syllable, if the
syllable, that fine creature, were more allowed to lead the harmony on. With
this warning, to those who would try: to step back here to this place of the
elements and minims of language, is to engage speech where it is least care-
less—and least logical. Listening for the syllables must be so constant and
so scrupulous, the exaction must be so complete, that the assurance of the

---

7. Cf. the end of chapter 78 of Herman Melville's
(1819–1891) novel *Moby-Dick* (1851), in which
the narrator compares falling into the oil from a
whale's head or into a honey tree with falling into
the idealism of ancient Greek philosopher Plato:

"How many, think ye, have likewise fallen into
Plato's honey head, and sweetly perished there?"
8. Anonymous English lyric from the late fifteenth
or early sixteenth century.

ear is purchased at the highest—40 hours a day—price. For from the root out, from all over the place, the syllable comes, the figures of, the dance:

> "Is" comes from the Aryan root, *as*, to breathe. The English "not" equals the Sanscrit *na*, which may come from the root *na*, to be lost, to perish. "Be" is from *bhu*, to grow.

I say the syllable, king, and that it is spontaneous, this way: the ear, the ear which has collected, which has listened, the ear, which is so close to the mind that it is the mind's, that it has the mind's speed . . .

it is close, another way: the mind is brother to this sister and is, because it is so close, is the drying force, the incest, the sharpener . . .

it is from the union of the mind and the ear that the syllable is born.

But the syllable is only the first child of the incest of verse (always, that Egyptian thing, it produces twins!). The other child is the LINE. And together, these two, the syllable *and* the line, they make a poem, they make that thing, the—what shall we call it, the Boss of all, the "Single Intelligence." And the line comes (I swear it) from the breath, from the breathing of the man who writes, at the moment that he writes, and thus is, it is here that, the daily work, the WORK, gets in, for only he, the man who writes, can declare, at every moment, the line its metric and its ending—where its breathing, shall come to, termination.

The trouble with most work, to my taking, since the breaking away from traditional lines and stanzas, and from such wholes as, say, Chaucer's *Troilus* or S's *Lear*, is: contemporary workers go lazy RIGHT HERE WHERE THE LINE IS BORN.

Let me put it baldly. The two halves are:

the HEAD, by way of the EAR, to the SYLLABLE

the HEART, by way of the BREATH, to the LINE

And the joker? that it is in the 1st half of the proposition that, in composing, one lets-it-rip; and that it is in the 2nd half, surprise, it is the LINE that's the baby that gets, as the poem is getting made, the attention, the control, that it is right here, in the line, that the shaping takes place, each moment of the going.

I am dogmatic, that the head shows in the syllable. The dance of the intellect[9] is there, among them, prose or verse. Consider the best minds you know in this here business: where does the head show, is it not, precise, here, in the swift currents of the syllable? can't you tell a brain when you see what it does, just there? It is true, what the master says he picked up from Confusion:[1] all the thots men are capable of can be entered on the back of a postage stamp. So, is it not the PLAY of a mind we are after, is not that that shows whether a mind is there at all?

And the threshing floor for the dance? Is it anything but the LINE? And when the line has, is, a deadness, is it not a heart which has gone lazy, is it not, suddenly, slow things, similes, say, adjectives, or such, that we are bored by?

For there is a whole flock of rhetorical devices which have now to be brought under a new bead, now that we sight with the line. Simile is only one bird who comes down, too easily. The descriptive functions generally

---

9. From Pound's definition of logopoeia: "the dance of the intellect among words" (Pound, *How to Read*, vol. 1 of this anthology).

1. Wordplay on Confucius (551–479 B.C.E.), Chinese philosopher.

have to be watched, every second, in projective verse, because of their easiness, and thus their drain on the energy which composition by field allows into a poem. *Any* slackness takes off attention, that crucial thing, from the job in hand, from the *push* of the line under hand at the moment, under the reader's eye, in his moment. Observation of any kind is, like argument in prose, properly previous to the act of the poem, and, if allowed in, must be so juxtaposed, apposed, set in, that it does not, for an instant, sap the going energy of the content toward its form.

It comes to this, this whole aspect of the newer problems. (We now enter, actually, the large area of the whole poem, into the FIELD, if you like, where all the syllables and all the lines must be managed in their relations to each other.) It is a matter, finally, of OBJECTS, what they are, what they are inside a poem, how they got there, and, once there, how they are to be used. This is something I want to get to in another way in Part II, but, for the moment, let me indicate this, that every element in an open poem (the syllable, the line, as well as the image, the sound, the sense) must be taken up as participants in the kinetic of the poem just as solidly as we are accustomed to take what we call the objects of reality; and that these elements are to be seen as creating the tensions of a poem just as totally as do those other objects create what we know as the world.

The objects which occur at every given moment of composition (of recognition, we can call it) are, can be, must be treated exactly as they do occur therein and not by any ideas or preconceptions from outside the poem, must be handled as a series of objects in field in such a way that a series of tensions (which they also are) are made to *hold*, and to hold exactly inside the content and the context of the poem which has forced itself, through the poet and them, into being.

Because breath allows *all* the speech-force of language back in (speech is the "solid" of verse, is the secret of a poem's energy), because, now, a poem has, by speech, solidity, everything in it can now be treated as solids, objects, things; and, though insisting upon the absolute difference of the reality of verse from that other dispersed and distributed thing, yet each of these elements of a poem can be allowed to have the play of their separate energies and can be allowed, once the poem is well composed, to keep, as those other objects do, their proper confusions.

Which brings us up, immediately, bang, against tenses, in fact against syntax, in fact against grammar generally, that is, as we have inherited it. Do not tenses, must they not also be kicked around anew, in order that time, that other governing absolute may be kept, as must the space-tensions of a poem, immediate, contemporary to the acting-on-you of the poem? I would argue that here, too, the LAW OF THE LINE, which projective verse creates, must be hewn to, obeyed, and that the conventions which logic has forced on syntax must be broken open as quietly as must the too set feet of the old line. But an analysis of how far a new poet can stretch the very conventions on which communication by language rests, is too big for these notes, which are meant, I hope it is obvious, merely to get things started.

Let me just throw in this. It is my impression that *all* parts of speech suddenly, in composition by field, are fresh for both sound and percussive use, spring up like unknown, unnamed vegetables in the patch, when you work it, come spring. Now take Hart Crane.[2] What strikes me in him is the singleness of the push to the nominative, his push along that one arc of

2. American poet (1899–1932).

freshness, the attempt to get back to word as handle. (If logos is word as thought, what is word as noun, as, pass me that, as Newman Shea used to ask, at the galley table, put a jib on the blood, will ya.) But there is a loss in Crane of what Fenollosa[3] is so right about, in syntax, the sentence as first act of nature, as lightning, as passage of force from subject to object, quick, in this case, from Hart to me, in every case, from me to you, the VERB, between two nouns. Does not Hart miss the advantages, by such an isolated push, miss the point of the whole front of syllable, line, field, and what happened to all language, and to the poem, as a result?

I return you now to London, to beginnings, to the syllable, for the pleasures of it, to intermit;

> If music be the food of love, play on,
> give me excess of it, that, surfeiting,
> the appetite may sicken, and so die.
> That strain again. It had a dying fall,
> o, it came over my ear like the sweet sound
> that breathes upon a bank of violets,
> stealing and giving odour.[4]

What we have suffered from, is manuscript, press, the removal of verse from its producer and its reproducer, the voice, a removal by one, by two removes from its place of origin *and* its destination. For the breath has a double meaning which latin had not yet lost.[5]

The irony is, from the machine has come one gain not yet sufficiently observed or used, but which leads directly on toward projective verse and its consequences. It is the advantage of the typewriter that, due to its rigidity and its space precisions, it can, for a poet, indicate exactly the breath, the pauses, the suspensions even of syllables, the juxtapositions even of parts of phrases, which he intends. For the first time the poet has the stave and the bar a musician has had. For the first time he can, without the convention of rime and meter, record the listening he has done to his own speech and by that one act indicate how he would want any reader, silently or otherwise, to voice his work.

It is time we picked the fruits of the experiments of Cummings, Pound, Williams,[6] each of whom has, after his way, already used the machine as a scoring to his composing, as a script to its vocalization. It is now only a matter of the recognition of the conventions of composition by field for us to bring into being an open verse as formal as the closed, with all its traditional advantages.

If a contemporary poet leaves a space as long as the phrase before it, he means that space to be held, by the breath, an equal length of time. If he suspends a word or syllable at the end of a line (this was most Cummings' addition) he means that time to pass that it takes the eye—that hair of time suspended—to pick up the next line. If he wishes a pause so light it hardly separates the words, yet does not want a comma—which is an interruption of the meaning rather than the sounding of the line—follow him when he uses a symbol the typewriter has ready to hand:

3. Ernest Fenollosa (1853–1908), American scholar whose work on Chinese and Japanese literature greatly influenced Pound, emphasized the importance of action and verbs. *Newman Shea*: sailor on a ship Olson worked on one summer. "Put a jib on the blood" was Shea's way of saying "pass the ketchup."
4. Beginning of Shakespeare's *Twelfth Night*.
5. In Latin, *spiritus*: breath; soul or life.
6. William Carlos Williams (1883–1963) and E. E. Cummings (1894–1962), American poets.

What does not change / is the will to change[7]

Observe him, when he takes advantage of the machine's multiple margins, to juxtapose:

Sd he:
 to dream takes no effort
  to think is easy
   to act is more difficult
    but for a man to act after he has taken thought, this!
  is the most difficult thing of all[8]

Each of these lines is a progressing of both the meaning and the breathing forward, and then a backing up, without a progress or any kind of movement outside the unit of time local to the idea.

There is more to be said in order that this convention be recognized, especially in order that the revolution out of which it came may be so forwarded that work will get published to offset the reaction now afoot to return verse to inherited forms of cadence and rime. But what I want to emphasize here, by this emphasis on the typewriter as the personal and instantaneous recorder of the poet's work, is the already projective nature of verse as the sons of Pound and Williams are practicing it. Already they are composing as though verse was to have the reading its writing involved, as though not the eye but the ear was to be its measurer, as though the intervals of its composition could be so carefully put down as to be precisely the intervals of its registration. For the ear, which once had the burden of memory to quicken it (rime & regular cadence were its aids and have merely lived on in print after the oral necessities were ended) can now again, that the poet has his means, be the threshold of projective verse.

II

Which gets us to what I promised, the degree to which the projective involves a stance toward reality outside a poem as well as a new stance towards the reality of a poem itself. It is a matter of content, the content of Homer or of Euripides or of Seami[9] as distinct from that which I might call the more "literary" masters. From the moment the projective purpose of the act of verse is recognized, the content does—it will—change. If the beginning and the end is breath, voice in its largest sense, then the material of verse shifts. It has to. It starts with the composer. The dimension of his line itself changes, not to speak of the change in his conceiving, of the matter he will turn to, of the scale in which he imagines that matter's use. I myself would pose the difference by a physical image. It is no accident that Pound and Williams both were involved variously in a movement which got called "objectivism."[1] But that word was then used in some sort of a necessary quarrel, I take it, with "subjectivism." It is now too late to be bothered with the latter. It has excellently done itself to death, even though we are all caught in its dying.

---

7. From Olson's "The Kingfishers" (1950).
8. From Olson's "The Praises" (1950).
9. Japanese Noh playwright (1363–1443). Euripides (c. 484–406 B.C.E.), Greek dramatist.
1. In the 1930s, the Objectivists, inspired by Pound and Williams, emphasized composition

uncloaded by authorial sentiment and the poem as material object. Among those affiliated with the group were American poets Louis Zukofsky, Charles Reznikoff, George Oppen, and Lorine Niedecker and British poet Basil Bunting.

What seems to me a more valid formulation for present use is "objectism," a word to be taken to stand for the kind of relation of man to experience which a poet might state as the necessity of a line or a work to be as wood is, to be as clean as wood is as it issues from the hand of nature, to be as shaped as wood can be when a man has had his hand to it. Objectism is the getting rid of the lyrical interference of the individual as ego, of the "subject" and his soul, that peculiar presumption by which western man has interposed himself between what he is as a creature of nature (with certain instructions to carry out) and those other creations of nature which we may, with no derogation, call objects. For a man is himself an object, whatever he may take to be his advantages, the more likely to recognize himself as such the greater his advantages, particularly at that moment that he achieves an humilitas sufficient to make him of use.

It comes to this: the use of a man, by himself and thus by others, lies in how he conceives his relation to nature, that force to which he owes his somewhat small existence. If he sprawl, he shall find little to sing but himself, and shall sing, nature has such paradoxical ways, by way of artificial forms outside himself. But if he stays inside himself, if he is contained within his nature as he is participant in the larger force, he will be able to listen, and his hearing through himself will give him secrets objects share. And by an inverse law his shapes will make their own way. It is in this sense that the projective act, which is the artist's act in the larger field of objects, leads to dimensions larger than the man. For a man's problem, the moment he takes speech up in all its fullness, is to give his work his seriousness, a seriousness sufficient to cause the thing he makes to try to take its place alongside the things of nature. This is not easy. Nature works from reverence, even in her destructions (species go down with a crash). But breath is man's special qualification as animal. Sound is a dimension he has extended. Language is one of his proudest acts. And when a poet rests in these as they are in himself (in his physiology, if you like, but the life in him, for all that) then he, if he chooses to speak from these roots, works in that area where nature has given him size, projective size.

It is projective size that the play, *The Trojan Women*,[2] possesses, for it is able to stand, is it not, as its people do, beside the Aegean—and neither Andromache or the sea suffer diminution. In a less "heroic" but equally "natural" dimension Seami causes the Fisherman and the Angel to stand clear in *Hagoromo*.[3] And Homer, who is such an unexamined cliché that I do not think I need to press home in what scale Nausicaa's girls wash their clothes.[4]

Such works, I should argue—and I use them simply because their equivalents are yet to be done—could not issue from men who conceived verse without the full relevance of human voice, without reference to where lines come from, in the individual who writes. Nor do I think it accident that, at this end point of the argument, I should use, for examples, two dramatists and an epic poet. For I would hazard the guess that, if projective verse is practiced long enough, is driven ahead hard enough along the course I think

---

2. Greek tragedy (c. 415 B.C.E.) by Euripedes about the aftermath of the Trojan War. Andromache, Hector's loyal wife, is forced to marry the son of her husband's killer, Achilles.
3. The Noh play by Seami (trans. Arthur Waley in 1922) in which a fisherman steals an angel's cloak

and prevents her from returning to Heaven.
4. Cf. book 6 of Homer's *Odyssey*, in which the Phaeacian princess Nausicaa encounters the shipwrecked Odysseus as she and her maids wash clothes on the shore.

it dictates, verse again can carry much larger material than it has carried in our language since the Elizabethans. But it can't be jumped. We are only at its beginnings, and if I think that the *Cantos* make more "dramatic" sense than do the plays of Mr. Eliot,[5] it is not because I think they have solved the problem but because the methodology of the verse in them points a way by which, one day, the problem of larger content and of larger forms may be solved. Eliot is, in fact, a proof of a present danger, of "too easy" a going on the practice of verse as it has been, rather than as it must be, practiced. There is no question, for example, that Eliot's line, from "Prufrock" on down, has speech-force, is "dramatic," is, in fact, one of the most notable lines since Dryden. I suppose it stemmed immediately to him from Browning,[6] as did so many of Pound's early things. In any case Eliot's line has obvious relations backward to the Elizabethans, especially to the soliloquy. Yet O. M. Eliot is *not* projective. It could even be argued (and I say this carefully, as I have said all things about the non-projective, having considered how each of us must save himself after his own fashion and how much, for that matter, each of us owes to the non-projective, and will continue to owe, as both go alongside each other) but it could be argued that it is because Eliot has stayed inside the non-projective that he fails as a dramatist—that his root is the mind alone, and a scholastic mind at that (no high *intelletto*[7] despite his apparent clarities)—and that, in his listenings he has stayed there where the ear and the mind are, has only gone from his fine ear outward rather than, as I say a projective poet will, down through the workings of his own throat to that place where breath comes from, where breath has its beginnings, where drama has to come from, where, the coincidence is, all act springs.

1950

5. American-born poet and dramatist T. S. Eliot (1888–1965), who became a British citizen in 1927. "O. M.," below, refers to the British Order of Merit.

6. Robert Browning (1812–1889), English poet famous for his dramatic monologues.
7. Intellect (Italian).

POETIC MANIFESTO

In the summer of 1951, a student writing a thesis on Dylan Thomas asked the poet five questions. Though not intended for publication, Thomas's response is one of the most cogent and evocative postwar statements on the verbal craft of poetry. It appeared after his death under the title "Poetic Manifesto," initially as a reproduction of the hand-written text. In his response, Thomas defines poetry as an art celebrating language, humanity, and God. For him, the love not of ideas but of language itself—rhythm, rhyme, assonance, metaphor, and all other elements of verbal magic—is the fundamental basis of poetry. He reports being smitten as a child by "the shape and shade and size and noise of the words." Although he dutifully responds to questions about influences and movements, Thomas writes exuberantly on behalf of the pleasure of verbal artifice, the poet's joy in "twistings and convolutions of words." Originally reproduced in *Texas Quarterly* 4.4 (Winter 1961), the manifesto has been reprinted from *Early Prose Writings* (1971), ed. Walford Davies.

DYLAN THOMAS

Poetic Manifesto

You want to know why and how I first began to write poetry, and which poets or kind of poetry I was first moved and influenced by.

To answer the first part of this question, I should say I wanted to write poetry in the beginning because I had fallen in love with words. The first poems I knew were nursery rhymes, and before I could read them for myself I had come to love just the words of them, the words alone. What the words stood for, symbolised, or meant, was of very secondary importance; what mattered was the *sound* of them as I heard them for the first time on the lips of the remote and incomprehensible grown-ups who seemed, for some reason, to be living in my world. And these words were, to me, as the notes of bells, the sounds of musical instruments, the noises of wind, sea, and rain, the rattle of milk-carts, the clopping of hooves on cobbles, the fingering of branches on a window pane, might be to someone, deaf from birth, who has miraculously found his hearing. I did not care what the words said, overmuch, nor what happened to Jack & Jill & the Mother Goose rest of them; I cared for the shapes of sound that their names, and the words describing their actions, made in my ears; I cared for the colours the words cast on my eyes. I realise that I may be, as I think back all that way, romanticising my reactions to the simple and beautiful words of those pure poems; but that is all I can honestly remember, however much time might have falsified my memory. I fell in love—that is the only expression I can think of—at once, and am still at the mercy of words, though sometimes now, knowing a little of their behaviour very well, I think I can influence them slightly and have even learned to beat them now and then, which they appear to enjoy. I tumbled for words at once. And, when I began to read the nursery rhymes for myself, and, later, to read other verses and ballads, I knew that I had discovered the most important things, to me, that could be ever. There they were, seemingly lifeless, made only of black and white, but out of them, out of their own being, came love and terror and pity and pain and wonder and all the other vague abstractions that make our ephemeral lives dangerous, great, and bearable. Out of them came the gusts and grunts and hiccups and heehaws of the common fun of the earth; and though what the words meant was, in its own way, often deliciously funny enough, so much funnier seemed to me, at that almost forgotten time, the shape and shade and size and noise of the words as they hummed, strummed, jigged and galloped along. That was the time of innocence; words burst upon me, unencumbered by trivial or portentous association; words were their spring-like selves, fresh with Eden's dew, as they flew out of the air. They made their own original associations as they sprang and shone. The words, 'Ride a cock-horse to Banbury Cross', were as haunting to me, who did not know then what a cock-horse was nor cared a damn where Banbury Cross might be, as, much later, were such lines as John Donne's, 'Go and catch a falling star, Get with child a mandrake root',[1] which also I could not understand when I first read them. And as I read more and

---

1. From "Go and Catch a Falling Star," by English poet John Donne (1572–1631).

more, and it was not all verse, by any means, my love for the real life of words increased until I knew that I must live *with* them and *in* them, always. I knew, in fact, that I must be a writer of words, and nothing else. The first thing was to feel and know their sound and substance; what I was going to do with those words, what use I was going to make of them, what I was going to *say* through them, would come later. I knew I had to know them most intimately in all their forms and moods, their ups and downs, their chops and changes, their needs and demands. (Here, I am afraid, I am beginning to talk too vaguely. I do not like writing *about* words, because then I often use bad and wrong and stale and woolly words. What I like to do is to treat words as a craftsman does his wood or stone or what-have-you, to hew, carve, mould, coil, polish and plane them into patterns, sequences, sculptures, fugues of sound expressing some lyrical impulse, some spiritual doubt or conviction, some dimly-realised truth I must try to reach and realise.) It was when I was very young, and just at school, that, in my father's study, before homework that was never done, I began to know one kind of writing from another, one kind of goodness, one kind of badness. My first, and greatest, liberty was that of being able to read everything and anything I cared to. I read indiscriminately, and with my eyes hanging out. I could never have dreamt that there were such goings-on in the world between the covers of books, such sand-storms and ice-blasts of words, such slashing of humbug,[2] and humbug too, such staggering peace, such enormous laughter, such and so many blinding bright lights breaking across the just-awaking wits and splashing all over the pages in a million bits and pieces all of which were words, words, words, and each of which was alive forever in its own delight and glory and oddity and light. (I must try not to make these supposedly helpful notes as confusing as my poems themselves.) I wrote endless imitations, though I never thought them to be imitations but, rather, wonderfully original things, like eggs laid by tigers. They were imitations of anything I happened to be reading at the time: Sir Thomas Browne, de Quincey, Henry Newbolt, the Ballads, Blake, Baroness Orczy, Marlowe, Chums, the Imagists, the Bible, Poe, Keats, Lawrence, Anon., and Shakespeare.[3] A mixed lot, as you see, and randomly remembered. I tried my callow hand at almost every poetical form. How could I learn the tricks of a trade unless I tried to do them myself? I learned that the bad tricks come easily; and the good ones, which help you to say what you think you wish to say in the most meaningful, moving way, I am still learning. (But in earnest company you must call these tricks by other names, such as technical devices, prosodic experiments, etc.)

The writers, then, who influenced my earliest poems and stories were, quite simply and truthfully, all the writers I was reading at the time, and, as you see from a specimen list higher up the page, they ranged from writers of school-boy adventure yarns to incomparable and inimitable masters like Blake. That is, when I began, bad writing had as much influence on my stuff as good. The bad influences I tried to remove and renounce bit by bit, shadow

---

2. Empty or misleading talk.
3. Sir Thomas Browne (1605–1682): English writer and physician. Thomas De Quincey (1785–1859): English writer famous for his *Confessions of an English Opium-Eater*. Henry Newbolt (1862–1938): English lawyer and writer of nautical poetry. William Blake (1757–1827): English poet and printer. Baroness Orczy (1865–1947): Hungarian-born author of *The Scarlet Pimpernel* (1905). Christopher Marlowe (1564–1593): English dramatist. Imagists: early twentieth-century poets who wrote in direct, clear, image-based free verse, as proposed by Ezra Pound (1885–1972) and others. Edgar Allan Poe (1809–1849): American poet and fiction writer. John Keats (1795–1821): English Romantic poet. D. H. Lawrence (1885–1930): English poet and novelist.

by shadow, echo by echo, through trial and error, through delight and disgust and misgiving, as I came to love words more and to hate the heavy hands that knocked them about, the thick tongues that had no feel for their multitudinous tastes, the dull and botching hacks who flattened them out into a colourless and insipid paste, the pedants who made them moribund and pompous as themselves. Let me say that the things that first made me love language and want to work *in* it and *for* it were nursery rhymes and folk tales, the Scottish Ballads, a few lines of hymns, the most famous Bible stories and the rhythms of the Bible, Blake's *Songs of Innocence,* and the quite incomprehensible magical majesty and nonsense of Shakespeare heard, read, and near-murdered in the first forms[4] of my school.

You ask me, next, if it is true that three of the dominant influences on my published prose and poetry are Joyce, the Bible, and Freud.[5] (I purposely say my 'published' prose and poetry, as in the preceding pages I have been talking about the primary influences upon my very first and forever unpublishable juvenilia.) I cannot say that I have been 'influenced' by Joyce, whom I enormously admire and whose *Ulysses,* and earlier stories I have read a great deal. I think this Joyce question arose because somebody once, in print, remarked on the closeness of the title of my book of short stories, *Portrait of the Artist As a Young Dog* to Joyce's title, *Portrait of the Artist as a Young Man.* As you know, the name given to innumerable portrait paintings by their artists is, 'Portrait of the Artist as a Young Man'—a perfectly straightforward title. Joyce used the painting title for the first time as the title of a literary work. I myself made a bit of doggish fun of the *painting*-title and, of course, intended no possible reference to Joyce. I do not think that Joyce has had any hand at all in my writing; certainly his *Ulysses* has not. On the other hand, I cannot deny that the shaping of some of my *Portrait* stories might owe something to Joyce's stories in the volume, *Dubliners.* But then *Dubliners* was a pioneering work in the world of the short story, and no good storywriter since can have failed, in some way, however little, to have benefited by it.

The Bible, I have referred to in attempting to answer your first question. Its great stories of Noah, Jonah, Lot, Moses, Jacob, David, Solomon and a thousand more, I had, of course, known from very early youth; the great rhythms had rolled over me from the Welsh pulpits; and I read, for myself, from Job and Ecclesiastes; and the story of the New Testament is part of my life. But I have never sat down and studied the Bible, never consciously echoed its language, and am, in reality, as ignorant of it as most brought-up Christians. All of the Bible that I use in my work is remembered from childhood, and is the common property of all who were brought up in English-speaking communities. Nowhere, indeed, in all my writing, do I use any knowledge which is not commonplace to any literate person. I *have* used a few difficult words in early poems, but they are easily looked-up and were, in any case, thrown into the poems in a kind of adolescent showing-off which I hope I have now discarded.

And that leads me to the third 'dominant influence': Sigmund Freud. My only acquaintance with the theories and discoveries of Dr Freud has been through the work of novelists who have been excited by his case-book his-

---

4. Grades (British).
5. Sigmund Freud (1856–1939): Austrian found-er of psychoanalysis. James Joyce (1882–1941): Irish novelist.

tories, of popular newspaper scientific-potboilers who have, I imagine, vul-
garised his work beyond recognition, and of a few modern poets, including
Auden,[6] who have attempted to use psychoanalytical phraseology and theory
in some of their poems. I have read only one book of Freud's, *The Interpre-
tation of Dreams,* and do not recall having been influenced by it in any way.
Again, no honest writer today can possibly avoid being influenced by Freud
through his pioneering work into the Unconscious and by the influence of
those discoveries on the scientific, philosophical, and artistic work of his con-
temporaries: but not, by any means, necessarily through Freud's own writing.

To your third question—Do I deliberately utilise devices of rhyme, rhythm,
and word-formation in my writing—I must, of course, answer with an imme-
diate, Yes. I am a painstaking, conscientious, involved and devious craftsman
in words, however unsuccessful the result so often appears, and to whatever
wrong uses I may apply my technical paraphernalia, I use everything and
anything to make my poems work and move in the directions I want them
to: old tricks, new tricks, puns, portmanteau-words, paradox, allusion, par-
anomasia, paragram, catachresis, slang, assonantal rhymes, vowel rhymes,
sprung rhythm.[7] Every device there is in language is there to be used if you
will. Poets have got to enjoy themselves sometimes, and the twistings and
convolutions of words, the inventions and contrivances, are all part of the
joy that is part of the painful, voluntary work.

Your next question asks whether my use of combinations of words to create
something new, 'in the Surrealist way', is according to a set formula or is
spontaneous.
There is a confusion here, for the Surrealists' set formula was to juxtapose
the unpremeditated.
Let me make it clearer if I can. The Surrealists—(that is, super-realists,
or those who work *above* realism)—were a coterie of painters and writers in
Paris, in the nineteen twenties, who did not believe in the conscious selection
of images. To put it in another way: They were artists who were dissatisfied
with both the realists—(roughly speaking, those who tried to put down in
paint and words an actual representation of what they imagined to be the
real world in which they lived)—and the impressionists who, roughly speak-
ing again, were those who tried to give an impression of what they imagined
to be the real world. The Surrealists wanted to dive into the subconscious
mind, the mind below the conscious surface, and dig up their images from
there without the aid of logic or reason, and put them down, illogically and
unreasonably, in paint and words. The Surrealists affirmed that, as three
quarters of the mind was submerged, it was the function of the artist to
gather his material from the greatest, submerged mass of the mind rather
than from that quarter of the mind which, like the tip of an iceberg, pro-
truded from the subconscious sea. One method the Surrealists used in their
poetry was to juxtapose words and images that had no rational relationship;
and out of this they hoped to achieve a kind of subconscious, or dream,
poetry that would be truer to the real, imaginative world of the mind, mostly

---

6. W. H. Auden (1907–1973): Anglo-American
poet.
7. Metrical system using a variable number of syl-
lables per foot, devised by English poet Gerard
Manley Hopkins (1844–1889). *Portmanteau-*

words: words made from the blending of two words.
Paranomasia: pun. *Paragram:* wordplay involving
alteration of letters. *Catachresis:* intentional mis-
use of a word or figure, as in a strained or mixed
metaphor.

submerged, than is the poetry of the conscious mind that relies upon the rational and logical relationship of ideas, objects, and images.

This is, very crudely, the credo of the Surrealists, and one with which I profoundly disagree. I do not mind from where the images of a poem are dragged up: drag them up, if you like, from the nethermost sea of the hidden self; but before they reach paper, they must go through all the rational processes of the intellect. The Surrealists, on the other hand, put their words down together on paper exactly as they emerge from chaos; they do not shape these words or put them in order; to them, chaos is the shape and order. This seems to me to be exceedingly presumptuous; the Surrealists imagine that whatever they dredge from their subconscious selves and put down in paint or in words must, essentially, be of some interest or value. I deny this. One of the arts of the poet is to make comprehensible and articulate what might emerge from subconscious sources; one of the great main uses of the intellect is to *select,* from the amorphous mass of subconscious images, those that will best further his imaginative purpose, which is to write the best poem he can.

And question five is, God help us, what is my definition of Poetry?

I, myself, do not read poetry for anything but pleasure. I read only the poems I like. This means, of course, that I have to read a lot of poems I don't like before I find the ones I do, but, when I *do* find the ones I do, then all I can say is, 'Here they are', and read them to myself for pleasure.

Read the poems you like reading. Don't bother whether they're 'important', or if they'll live. What does it matter what poetry *is,* after all? If you want a definition of poetry, say: 'Poetry is what makes me laugh or cry or yawn, what makes my toenails twinkle, what makes me want to do this or that or nothing', and let it go at that. All that matters about poetry is the enjoyment of it, however tragic it may be. All that matters is the eternal movement behind it, the vast undercurrent of human grief, folly, pretension, exaltation, or ignorance, however unlofty the intention of the poem.

You can tear a poem apart to see what makes it technically tick, and say to yourself, when the works are laid out before you, the vowels, the consonants, the rhymes or rhythms, 'Yes, this is *it.* This is why the poem moves me so. It is because of the craftsmanship.' But you're back again where you began.

You're back with the mystery of having been moved by words. The best craftsmanship always leaves holes and gaps in the works of the poem so that something that is *not* in the poem can creep, crawl, flash, or thunder in.

The joy and function of poetry is, and was, the celebration of man, which is also the celebration of God.

1951   1961

THE PLEASURE PRINCIPLE

In this essay, the English poet Philip Larkin argues for a reclamation of pleasure as the chief end of poetry. Poetry must return to its primary function of capturing an emotional experience and communicating it to the reader if it is to regain an audience wider than academic critics, scholars, and their students. Larkin worries that "once the other end of the rope is dropped" between poet and general reader, poetry becomes self-involved and obscure, because untested by the challenge of communicating to a reader with a different education or experience. "Hence, no pleasure. Hence, no poetry." First printed in *Listen* 2.3 (1957), the essay has been reprinted from *Required Writing* (1984).

PHILIP LARKIN

The Pleasure Principle

It is sometimes useful to remind ourselves of the simpler aspects of things normally regarded as complicated. Take, for instance, the writing of a poem. It consists of three stages: the first is when a man becomes obsessed with an emotional concept to such a degree that he is compelled to do something about it. What he does is the second stage, namely, construct a verbal device that will reproduce this emotional concept in anyone who cares to read it, anywhere, any time. The third stage is the recurrent situation of people in different times and places setting off the device and re-creating in themselves what the poet felt when he wrote it. The stages are interdependent and all necessary. If there has been no preliminary feeling, the device has nothing to reproduce and the reader will experience nothing. If the second stage has not been well done, the device will not deliver the goods, or will deliver only a few goods to a few people, or will stop delivering them after an absurdly short while. And if there is no third stage, no successful reading, the poem can hardly be said to exist in a practical sense at all.

What a description of this basic tripartite structure shows is that poetry is emotional in nature and theatrical in operation, a skilled re-creation of emotion in other people, and that, conversely, a bad poem is one that never succeeds in doing this. All modes of critical derogation are no more than different ways of saying this, whatever literary, philosophical or moral terminology they employ, and it would not be necessary to point out anything so obvious if present-day poetry did not suggest that it had been forgotten. We seem to be producing a new kind of bad poetry, not the old kind that tries to move the reader and fails, but one that does not even try. Repeatedly he is confronted with pieces that cannot be understood without reference beyond their own limits or whose contented insipidity argues that their authors are merely reminding themselves of what they know already, rather than re-creating it for a third party. The reader, in fact, seems no longer present in the poet's mind as he used to be, as someone who must understand and enjoy the finished product if it is to be a success at all; the assumption now is that no one will read it, and wouldn't understand or enjoy it if they did. Why should this be so? It is not sufficient to say that poetry has lost its audience, and so need no longer consider it: lots of people still read and even buy poetry. More accurately, poetry has lost its old audience, and gained a new one. This has been caused by the consequences of a cunning merger between poet, literary critic and academic critic (three classes now notoriously indistinguishable): it is hardly an exaggeration to say that the poet has gained the happy position wherein he can praise his own poetry in the press and explain it in the class-room, and the reader has been bullied into giving up the consumer's power to say 'I don't like this, bring me something different.' Let him now so much as breathe a word about not liking a poem, and he is in the dock before he can say Edwin Arlington Robinson.[1] And the charge is a grave one: flabby sensibility, insufficient or inadequate critical tools, and inability to meet new verbal and emotional situations. Verdict: guilty, plus a few riders on the prisoner's mental upbringing, addiction to mass amusements, and enfeebled responses. It is time some of you playboys realized, says the judge, that reading a poem is hard work. Fourteen days in stir. Next case.

The cash customers of poetry, therefore, who used to put down their money in the sure and certain hope of enjoyment as if at a theatre or concert hall, were quick to move elsewhere. Poetry was no longer a pleasure. They have been replaced by a humbler squad, whose aim is not pleasure but self-improvement, and who have uncritically accepted the contention that they cannot appreciate poetry without preliminary investment in the intellectual equipment which, by the merest chance, their tutor happens to have about him. In short, the modern poetic audience, when it is not taking in its own washing, is a *student* audience, pure and simple. At first sight this may not seem a bad thing. The poet has at last a moral ascendancy, and his new clientele not only pay for the poetry but pay to have it explained afterwards. Again, if the poet has only himself to please, he is no longer handicapped by the limitations of his audience. And in any case nobody nowadays believes that a worthwhile artist can rely on anything but his own judgement: public taste is always twenty-five years behind, and picks up a style only when it is exploited by the second-rate. All this is true enough. But at bottom poetry, like all art, is inextricably bound up with giving pleasure, and if a poet loses his pleasure-seeking audience he has lost the only audience worth having, for which the dutiful mob that signs on every September is no substitute. And the effect will be felt throughout his work. He will forget that even if he finds what he has to say interesting, others may not. He will concentrate on moral worth or semantic intricacy. Worst of all, his poems will no longer be born of the tension between what be non-verbally feels and what can be got over in common word-usage to someone who hasn't had his experience or education or travel grant, and once the other end of the rope is dropped what results will not be so much obscure or piffling (though it may be both) as an unrealized, 'undramatized' slackness, because he will have lost the habit of testing what he writes by this particular standard. Hence, no pleasure. Hence, no poetry.

What can be done about this? Who wants anything done about it? Certainly not the poet, who is in the unprecedented position of peddling both his work and the standard by which it is judged. Certainly not the new reader, who, like a partner of some unconsummated marriage, has no idea of any-

1. American poet (1869–1935).

thing better. Certainly not the old reader, who has simply replaced one pleasure with another. Only the romantic loiterer who recalls the days when poetry was condemned as sinful might wish things different. But if the medium is in fact to be rescued from among our duties and restored to our pleasures, I can only think that a large-scale revulsion has got to set in against present notions, and that it will have to start with poetry readers asking themselves more frequently whether they do in fact enjoy what they read, and, if not, what the point is of carrying on. And I use 'enjoy' in the commonest of senses, the sense in which we leave a radio on or off. Those interested might like to read David Daiches's essay 'The New Criticism: Some Qualifications' (in *Literary Essays*, 1956); in the meantime, the following note by Samuel Butler may reawaken a furtive itch for freedom: 'I should like to like Schumann's music better than I do; I dare say I could make myself like it better if I tried; but I do not like having to try to make myself like things; I like things that make me like them at once and no trying at all' (*Notebooks*, 1919).

1957

INTRODUCTION TO *ALL WHAT JAZZ*

Leading the charge against modernist difficulty in poetry, Philip Larkin offered perhaps his most cogent remarks on the subject in relation to another art form—jazz. A longtime follower of the traditional jazz style rooted in New Orleans, Larkin was unhappy that the music was becoming increasingly harsh, edgy, and inaccessible, ever since saxophonist Charlie Parker, a major innovator of the bebop revolution in the 1940s and 1950s, abandoned traditional melodies to experiment with complicated rhythms and harmonies. In this excerpt from Larkin's introduction to *All What Jazz* (1970), a collection of his 1960s jazz criticism, he proposes that jazz history parallels the history of art in general: like modern painting and poetry, modern jazz—from bebop to free jazz and other avant-garde styles—neglects the audience and becomes preoccupied with its own material. In all the arts, this narcissistic modernism is elitist and exclusionary. Music, like poetry, should instead reaffirm the human values that give art its value. This excerpt has been taken from *Required Writing* (1984).

PHILIP LARKIN

From Introduction to *All What Jazz*

*   *   *

And yet again, there was something about the books [of jazz criticism] I was now reading that seemed oddly familiar. This *development*, this *progress*, this *new language* that was more *difficult*, more *complex*, that required you to *work hard at appreciating it*, that you *couldn't expect to understand first go,* that needed *technical and professional knowledge* to evaluate it *at all levels,* this *revolutionary explosion* that *spoke for our time* while at the same time being *traditional* in the *fullest,* the *deepest.* . . . Of course! This was the language of criticism of modern painting, modern poetry, modern music. *Of course!* How glibly I had talked of modern jazz, without realizing the force of the adjective: this was *modern* jazz, and Parker was a modern jazz player just as Picasso was a modern painter and Pound a modern poet. I hadn't realized that jazz had gone from Lascaux to Jackson Pollock[1] in fifty years, but now I realized it relief came flooding in upon me after nearly two years' despondency. I went back to my books: 'After Parker, you had to be something of a musician to follow the best jazz of the day.'[2] Of course! After Picasso! After Pound! There could hardly have been a conciser summary of what I don't believe about art.

The reader may here have the sense of having strayed into a private argument. All I am saying is that the term 'modern', when applied to art, has a more than chronological meaning: it denotes a quality of irresponsibility peculiar to this century, known sometimes as modernism, and once I had classified modern jazz under this heading I knew where I was. I am sure there are books in which the genesis of modernism is set out in full. My own theory is that it is related to an imbalance between the two tensions from which art springs: these are the tension between the artist and his material, and between the artist and his audience, and that in the last seventy-five years or so the second of these has slackened or even perished. In consequence the artist has become over-concerned with his material (hence an age of technical experiment), and, in isolation, has busied himself with the two principal themes of modernism, mystification and outrage. Piqued at being neglected, he has painted portraits with both eyes on the same side of the nose, or smothered a model with paint and rolled her over a blank canvas. He has designed a dwelling-house to be built underground. He has written poems resembling the kind of pictures typists make with their machines during the coffee break, or a novel in gibberish, or a play in which the characters sit in dustbins. He has made a six-hour film of someone asleep. He has carved human figures with large holes in them. And parallel to this activity ("every idiom has its idiot," as an American novelist has written) there has grown up a kind of critical journalism designed to put it over. The terms and the arguments vary with circumstances, but basically the message is: Don't trust your eyes, or ears, or understanding. They'll tell you this is ridiculous, or ugly, or meaningless. Don't believe them. You've got to work at this: after all, you don't expect to understand anything as important as art straight off, do you? I mean, this is pretty complex stuff: if you want to know how complex, I'm giving a course of ninety-six lectures at the local college, starting next week, and you'd be more than welcome. The whole thing's on the rates, you won't have to pay. After all, think what asses people have made of themselves in the past by not understanding art—you don't want to be like that, do you? And so on, and so forth. Keep the suckers spending.

The tension between artist and audience in jazz slackened when the Negro stopped wanting to entertain the white man, and when the audience as a whole, with the end of the Japanese war and the beginning of television,

---

1. American abstract expressionist painter (1912–1956). Charlie Parker (1920–1955): bebop jazz saxophonist. Pablo Picasso (1881–1973): Spanish expatriate painter. *Lascaux:* site of prehistoric cave paintings in France.
2. "Benny Green, *The Reluctant Art* (1962), pp. 182–3' [Larkin's note].

didn't in any case particularly want to be entertained in that way any longer. The jazz band in the night club declined just as my old interest, the dance band, had declined in the restaurant and hotel: jazz moved, ominously, into the culture belt, the concert halls, university recital rooms and summer schools where the kind of criticism I have outlined has freer play. This was bound to make the re-establishment of any artist–audience nexus more difficult, for universities have long been the accepted stamping ground for the subsidized acceptance of art rather than the real purchase of it—and so, of course, for this kind of criticism, designed as it is to prevent people using their eyes and ears and understandings to report pleasure and discomfort. In such conditions modernism is bound to flourish.

I don't know whether it is worth pursuing my identification of modern jazz with other branches of modern art any further: if I say I dislike both in what seems to me the same way I have made my point. * * *

* * *

* * * To say I don't like modern jazz because it's modernist art simply raises the question of why I don't like modernist art: I have a suspicion that many readers will welcome my grouping of Parker with Picasso and Pound as one of the nicest things I could say about him. Well, to do so settles at least one question: as long as it was only Parker I didn't like, I might believe that my ears had shut up about the age of twenty-five and that jazz had left me behind. My dislike of Pound and Picasso, both of whom pre-date me by a considerable margin, can't be explained in this way. The same can be said of Henry Moore and James Joyce[3] (a textbook case of declension from talent to absurdity). No, I dislike such things not because they are new, but because they are irresponsible exploitations of technique in contradiction of human life as we know it. This is my essential criticism of modernism, whether perpetrated by Parker, Pound or Picasso:[4] it helps us neither to enjoy nor endure. It will divert us as long as we are prepared to be mystified or outraged, but maintains its hold only by being more mystifying and more outrageous: it has no lasting power. Hence the compulsion on every modernist to wade deeper and deeper into violence and obscenity: hence the succession of Parker by Rollins and Coltrane, and of Rollins and Coltrane by Coleman, Ayler and Shepp.[5] In a way, it's a relief: if jazz records are to be one long screech, if painting is to be a blank canvas, if a play is to be two hours of sexual intercourse performed *coram populo*,[6] then let's get it over, the sooner the better, in the hope that human values will then be free to reassert themselves.

* * *

1970

3. Irish novelist (1882–1941). Henry Moore (1898–1986): English abstract sculptor.
4. "The reader will have guessed by now that I am using these pleasantly alliterative names to represent not only their rightful owners but every practitioner who might be said to have succeeded them" [Larkin's note].
5. All jazz saxophonists. Sonny Rollins (b. 1930) and John Coltrane (1926–1967) extended Parker's experimentation with complicated harmonies. Ornette Coleman (b. 1930), Albert Ayler (1936–1970), and Archie Shepp (b. 1937) helped develop free jazz, abandoning to an even greater degree traditional melody and structure.
6. Before the public (Latin).

PERSONISM: A MANIFESTO

In his 1959 essay, Frank O'Hara parodically deflates the pretensions of other poetic manifestos proliferating at the time and yet offers a valuable point of entry into his poetry and the work of the New York school (which also includes John Ashbery and Kenneth Koch). In contrast to the prophetic exhortations and moralistic tone of many manifesto writers, O'Hara humorously concedes that a manifesto is unlikely to make people who dislike poetry read it and that discussions of formal structures often stray from the essential energy at the heart of good poetry—"You just go on your nerve." But O'Hara also outlines a poetics, and if his implied claims were recast in the standard rhetoric of manifestos, they might read thus: the poet must be witty, never boring; the poet must communicate the spontaneity of imaginative creation; the poet must be effortlessly allusive (this essay nimbly leaps from Romantic poets to surrealist painters to the French New Novel); and the poet must convey a robust sense of personal immediacy and yet not be dully confessional. O'Hara encapsulates this last idea in his self-mocking rubric of "personism," hinting at the strange combination of almost erotically charged intimacy and depersonalized abstraction that characterizes his poetry. Composed on September 3 for Donald Allen's *New American Poetry*, but turned down as too frivolous, the manifesto first appeared in *Yugen*, No. 7 (1961) and has been reprinted from *The Selected Poems of Frank O'Hara* (1972).

FRANK O'HARA

Personism: A Manifesto

Everything is in the poems, but at the risk of sounding like the poor wealthy man's Allen Ginsberg[1] I will write to you because I just heard that one of my fellow poets thinks that a poem of mine that can't be got at one reading is because I was confused too. Now, come on. I don't believe in god, so I don't have to make elaborately sounded structures. I hate Vachel Lindsay,[2] always have; I don't even like rhythm, assonance, all that stuff. You just go on your nerve. If someone's chasing you down the street with a knife you just run, you don't turn around and shout, "Give it up! I was a track star for Mineola Prep."

That's for the writing poems part. As for their reception, suppose you're in love and someone's mistreating (*mal aimé*)[3] you, you don't say, "Hey, you can't hurt me this way, I care!" you just let all the different bodies fall where they may, and they always do may after a few months. But that's not why you fell in love in the first place, just to hang onto life, so you have to take

---

1. American poet (1926–1997). In "Abstraction in Poetry," *It Is*, No. 3 (1959), Ginsberg had argued that O'Hara's work was developing an abstraction similar to that of painting.
2. American poet (1879–1931), who employed powerful rhythms and emphasized poetry's oral

character.
3. Poorly loved (French). Cf. "La Chanson du Mal Aimé" (1913), by Guillaume Apollinaire (1880–1918), French avant-garde and early surrealist poet.

your chances and try to avoid being logical. Pain always produces logic, which is very bad for you.

I'm not saying that I don't have practically the most lofty ideas of anyone writing today, but what difference does that make? They're just ideas. The only good thing about it is that when I get lofty enough I've stopped thinking and that's when refreshment arrives.

But how can you really care if anybody gets it, or gets what it means, or if it improves them. Improves them for what? For death? Why hurry them along? Too many poets act like a middle-aged mother trying to get her kids to eat too much cooked meat, and potatoes with drippings (tears). I don't give a damn whether they eat or not. Forced feeding leads to excessive thinness (effete). Nobody should experience anything they don't need to, if they don't need poetry bully for them. I like the movies too. And after all, only Whitman and Crane and Williams,[4] of the American poets, are better than the movies. As for measure and other technical apparatus, that's just common sense: if you're going to buy a pair of pants you want them to be tight enough so everyone will want to go to bed with you. There's nothing metaphysical about it. Unless, of course, you flatter yourself into thinking that what you're experiencing is "yearning."

Abstraction in poetry, which Allen [Ginsberg] recently commented on in *It Is,* is intriguing. I think it appears mostly in the minute particulars where decision is necessary. Abstraction (in poetry, not in painting) involves personal removal by the poet. For instance, the decision involved in the choice between "the nostalgia *of* the infinite"[5] and "the nostalgia *for* the infinite" defines an attitude towards degree of abstraction. The nostalgia *of* the infinite representing the greater degree of abstraction, removal, and negative capability (as in Keats and Mallarmé).[6] Personism, a movement which I recently founded and which nobody knows about, interests me a great deal, being so totally opposed to this kind of abstract removal that it is verging on a true abstraction for the first time, really, in the history of poetry. Personism is to Wallace Stevens what *la poésie pure* was to Béranger.[7] Personism has nothing to do with philosophy, it's all art. It does not have to do with personality or intimacy, far from it! But to give you a vague idea, one of its minimal aspects is to address itself to one person (other than the poet himself), thus evoking overtones of love without destroying love's life-giving vulgarity, and sustaining the poet's feelings towards the poem while preventing love from distracting him into feeling about the person. That's part of Personism. It was founded by me after lunch with LeRoi Jones[8] on August 27, 1959, a day in which I was in love with someone (not Roi, by the way, a blond). I went back to work and wrote a poem for this person. While I was writing it I was realizing that if I wanted to I could use the telephone instead of writing the poem, and so Personism was born. It's a very exciting movement which will undoubtedly have lots of adherents. It puts the poem squarely between the

4. Walt Whitman (1819–1892), Hart Crane (1899–1932), and William Carlos Williams (1883–1963), American poets.
5. Title of painting by Italian surrealist Giorgio di Chirico (1888–1978).
6. Stéphane Mallarmé (1842–1898): French Symbolist poet. British Romantic poet John Keats (1795–1821) identified his own creative talent as negative capability, the ability to tolerate uncertainty and identify with other people and things.

7. Pierre-Jean de Béranger (1780–1857), French political and satirical poet, whose work is contrasted here with *la poésie pur,* Symbolist doctrine according to which poetry is, like music, patterns of sound. Similarly, the poetry of Wallace Stevens (1879–1955) is contrasted with O'Hara's personism.
8. American poet and playwright (b. 1934); now Amiri Baraka.

poet and the person, Lucky Pierre[9] style, and the poem is correspondingly gratified. The poem is at last between two persons instead of two pages. In all modesty, I confess that it may be the death of literature as we know it. While I have certain regrets, I am still glad I got there before Alain Robbe-Grillet[1] did. Poetry being quicker and surer than prose, it is only just that poetry finish literature off. For a time people thought that Artaud[2] was going to accomplish this, but actually, for all their magnificence, his polemical writings are not more outside literature than Bear Mountain is outside New York State. His relation is no more astounding than Debuffet's[3] to painting.

What can we expect of Personism? (This is getting good, isn't it?) Everything, but we won't get it. It is too new, too vital a movement to promise anything. But it, like Africa, is on the way. The recent propagandists for technique on the one hand, and for content on the other, had better watch out.

September 3, 1959   1961

---

9. Having sexual intercourse with two other people simultaneously.
1. Experimental French writer (b. 1922) and theorist of the *nouveau roman* (new novel).
2. Antonin Artaud (1896–1948), French writer associated with the experimental "theatre of cruelty."
3. Jean Dubuffet (1901–1985), French painter associated with *art brut* (raw art).

Notes Written on Finally Recording *Howl*

In this essay, a version of which appeared as a liner note to the 1959 recording of *"Howl" and Other Poems*, Allen Ginsberg, the central figure of the Beat movement, explains the poetic innovations, such as "wild phrasing" and "rhythmic buildup," of "Howl"—an important long poem that combined the use of breath units with oracular proclamations and exceptionally long lines. Tracing his development, Ginsberg credits William Carlos Williams' measures based on units of breath and American speech patterns with inspiring him, as did the cadences, tonalities, and visions of William Blake, Walt Whitman, and Jack Kerouac. He also finds sources for "Howl," "Kaddish," "Sunflower Sutra," "America," and other poems in such heterogeneous sources as drug use, a madhouse wail, the Hebrew prophets, and the haiku. Ginsberg emphasizes the rapidity, associative psychology, and Romantic spontaneity of his initial outpourings, which—particularly in such long poems as "Howl" and "Kaddish"—he reshaped and carefully edited before publication. First published in *Evergreen Review* 3.10 (1959), the essay has been reprinted from *Deliberate Prose: Selected Essays 1952–1995* (2000), ed. Bill Morgan.

ALLEN GINSBERG

Notes Written on Finally Recording *Howl*

By 1955 I wrote poetry adapted from prose seeds, journals, scratchings, arranged by phrasing or breath groups into little short-line patterns according to ideas of measure of American speech I'd picked up from William Carlos Williams' imagist[1] preoccupations. I suddenly turned aside in San Francisco, unemployment compensation leisure, to follow my romantic inspiration—Hebraic-Melvillean[2] bardic breath. I thought I wouldn't write a *poem*, but just write what I wanted to without fear, let my imagination go, open secrecy, and scribble magic lines from my real mind—sum up my life—something I wouldn't be able to show anybody, writ for my own soul's ear and a few other golden ears. So the first line of *Howl*, "I saw the best minds etc.," the whole first section typed out madly in one afternoon, a tragic custard-pie comedy of wild phrasing, meaningless images for the beauty of abstract poetry of mind running along making awkward combinations like Charlie Chaplin's walk, long saxophone-like chorus lines I knew Kerouac[3] would hear *sound* of—taking off from his own inspired prose line really a new poetry.

I depended on the word "who" to keep the beat, a base to keep measure, return to and take off from again onto another streak of invention: "who lit cigarettes in boxcars boxcars boxcars," continuing to prophesy what I really knew despite the drear consciousness of the world: "who were visionary Indian angels." Have I really been attacked for this sort of joy? So the poem got awesome, I went on to what my imagination believed true to eternity (for I'd had a beatific illumination years before during which I'd heard Blake's[4] ancient voice and saw the universe unfold in my brain), and what my memory could reconstitute of the data of celestial experiences.

But how sustain a long line in poetry (lest it lapse into prosaic)? It's natural inspiration of the moment that keeps it moving, disparate thinks put down together, shorthand notations of visual imagery, juxtapositions of hydrogen jukebox—abstract *haikus* sustain the mystery and put iron poetry back into the line: the last line of *Sunflower Sutra* is the extreme, one stream of single word associations, summing up. Mind is shapely, art is shapely. Meaning mind practiced in spontaneity invents forms in its own image and gets to last thoughts. Loose ghosts wailing for body try to invade the bodies of living men. I hear ghostly academies in limbo screeching about form.

Ideally each line of *Howl* is a single breath unit. My breath is long—that's the measure, one physical-mental inspiration of thought contained in the elastic of a breath. It probably bugs Williams now, but it's a natural consequence, my own heightened conversation, not cooler average-daily-talk short breath. I get to mouth more madly this way.

---

1. In the early twentieth century, Imagism emphasized cadenced free verse and direct language. William Carlos Williams (1883–1963), American poet.
2. Herman Melville (1819–1891), American poet, novelist, and author of *Moby-Dick* (1851). *Hebraic:* here, recalling the Hebrew prophets.
3. Jack Kerouac (1922–1969): American novelist

and spokesman for the Beat movement. Charlie Chaplin (1889–1977): English actor and film producer, famous for his "tramp" character.
4. William Blake (1757–1827), English visionary, poet, and printmaker. Ginsberg reported having heard in 1948 William Blake's voice reciting "Ah Sun-Flower" and "The Sick Rose."

So these poems are a series of experiments with the formal organization of the long line. Explanations follow. I realized at the time that Whitman's[5] form had rarely been further explored (improved on even) in the U.S.— Whitman always a mountain too vast to be seen. Everybody assumes (with Pound?) (except [Robinson] Jeffers)[6] that his line is a big freakish uncontrollable necessary prosaic goof. No attempt's been made to use it in the light of early twentieth century organization of new speech-rhythm prosody to *build up* large organic structures.

I had an apartment on Nob Hill, got high on peyote, and saw an image of the robot skullface of Moloch[7] in the upper stories of a big hotel glaring into my window; got high weeks later again, the visage was still there in red smoky downtown metropolis, I wandered down Powell street muttering, "Moloch Moloch" all night and wrote *Howl II* nearly intact in cafeteria at foot of Drake Hotel, deep in the hellish vale. Here the long line is used as a stanza form broken into exclamatory units punctuated by a base repetition, Moloch.

The rhythmic paradigm for Part III was conceived and half-written same day as the beginning of *Howl*, I went back later and filled it out. Part I, a lament for the Lamb in America with instances of remarkable lamblike youths; Part II names the monster of mental consciousness that preys on the Lamb; Part III a litany of affirmation of the Lamb in its glory: "O starry spangled shock of Mercy." The structure of Part III, pyramidal, with a graduated longer response to the fixed base.

I remembered the archetypal rhythm of Holy Holy Holy weeping in a bus on Kearny Street, and wrote most of it down in notebook there. That exhausted this set of experiments with a fixed base. I set it as *Footnote to Howl* because it was an extra variation of the form of Part II. (Several variations on these forms, including stanzas of graduated litanies followed by fugues, will be seen in *Kaddish.*)

A lot of these forms developed out of an extreme rhapsodic wail I once heard in a madhouse. Later I wondered if short quiet lyrical poems could be written using the long line. *A Strange New Cottage in Berkeley* and *A Supermarket in California* (written same day) fell in place later that year. Not purposely, I simply followed my angel in the course of compositions.

What if I just simply wrote, in long units and broken short lines, spontaneously noting prosaic realities mixed with emotional upsurges, solitaries? *Transcription of Organ Music* (sensual data), strange writing which passes from prose to poetry and back, like the mind.

What about poem with rhythmic buildup power equal to *Howl* without use of repetitive base to sustain it? *The Sunflower Sutra* (composition time 20 minutes, me at desk scribbling, Kerouac at cottage door waiting for me to finish so we could go off somewhere party) did that, it surprised me, one long who.

Next what happens if you mix long and short lines, single breath remaining the rule of measure? I didn't trust free flight yet, so went back to fixed base to sustain the flow, *America*. After that, a regular formal type long poem in parts, short and long breaths mixed at random, no fixed base, sum of earlier experiments—*In the Baggage Room at Greyhound*. *In Back of the Real* shows what I was doing with short lines (see sentence above) before I accidentally wrote *Howl*.

---

5. Walt Whitman (1819–1892), American poet, who sometimes wrote in long, paratactic, free verse lines.
6. Robinson Jeffers (1887–1962) and Ezra Pound

(1885–1972), American poets.
7. Deity to which children were sacrificed in ancient Middle Eastern cultures. *Nob Hill:* in San Francisco.

Later I tried for a strong rhythm built up using free short syncopated lines, *Europe! Europe!* a prophecy written in Paris.

Last, the Proem to *Kaddish* (NY 1959 work)—finally, completely free composition, the long line breaking up within itself into short staccato breath units—notations of one spontaneous phrase after another linked within the line by dashes mostly: the long line now perhaps a variable stanzaic unit, measuring groups of related ideas, grouping them—a method of notation. Ending with a hymn in rhythm similar to the synagogue death lament. Passing into dactylic? says Williams? Perhaps not: at least the ear hears itself in Promethean[8] natural measure, not in mechanical count of accent.

All these poems are recorded now as best I can, though with scared love, imperfect to an angelic trumpet in mind. I have quit reading in front of live audiences for a while. I began in obscurity to communicate a live poetry, it's become more a trap and duty than the spontaneous ball it was first.

A word on the Academies: poetry has been attacked by an ignorant and frightened bunch of bores who don't understand how it's made, and the trouble with these creeps is they wouldn't know poetry if it came up and buggered them in broad daylight.

A word on the Politicians: my poetry is angelic ravings, and has nothing to do with dull materialistic vagaries about who should shoot who. The secrets of individual imagination—which are transconceptual and non-verbal—I mean unconditioned spirit—are not for sale to this consciousness, are no use to this world, except perhaps to make it shut its trap and listen to the music of the spheres. Who denies the music of the spheres denies poetry, denies man, and spits on Blake, Shelley,[9] Christ, and Buddha. Meanwhile have a ball. The universe is a new flower. America will be discovered. Who wants a war against roses will have it. Fate tells big lies, and the gay creator dances on his own body in eternity.[1]

July 4, 1959   1959

8. Life-giving, courageously original; in Greek myth, Prometheus stole fire from Olympus for humankind and was severely punished for it.
9. Percy Bysshe Shelley (1792–1822), English Romantic poet.
1. "Need comment on end—This provocative even inflammatory peroration seems to have offended a number of straight poets, and was oft quoted, a declaration of absolute poetic purpose

that the critic Richard Howard [b. 1929] still remembered decades later, taking exception to my insistence of 'unconditioned Spirit.' This aggression may have exacerbated the Battle of Anthologies between Open Form and Closed Form poets. An incendiary tract, aimed at both Marxist and CIA Capitalist (*Encounter*) Critics, as well as bourgeois judgmental sociologists, Norman Podhoretz probably in mind" [Ginsberg's note].

THE MYTH OF A NEGRO LITERATURE

A leader of the Black Arts Movement, Amiri Baraka delivered this essay as an address to the American Society for African Culture on March 14, 1962, before he changed his name from LeRoi Jones and at a time when he was in between his early Beat aesthetic and his later black nationalism. Baraka attacks as derivative those writers who produce a "Negro literature" according to Euro-American models for the approval of middle-class white society. Instead, black artists should follow the models in African American music, particularly jazz and the blues, which best exemplify how African traditions can be forged into African American art. From slave songs to avant-garde jazz, black music is rooted in African traditions "translated and transmuted" in America. Black music shows poets the way forward, because it is true to the African American experience of pain, hybridization, and survival—an experience estranged from and invisible to mainstream American culture, yet absolutely central to it. Originally published in the *Saturday Review* 46 (April 20, 1963), the essay has been reprinted from *Home: Social Essays* (1966).

AMIRI BARAKA

From The Myth of a "Negro Literature"

* * *

American Negro music from its inception moved logically and powerfully out of a fusion between African musical tradition and the American experience. It was, and continues to be, a natural, yet highly stylized and personal version of the Negro's life in America. It is, indeed, a chronicler of the Negro's movement, from African slave to American slave, from Freedman to Citizen. And the literature of the blues is a much more profound contribution to Western culture than any other literary contribution made by American Negroes. * * *

* * *

The development of the Negro's music was, as I said, direct and instinctive. It was the one vector out of African culture impossible to eradicate completely. The appearance of blues as a native *American* music signified in many ways the appearance of American Negroes where once there were African Negroes. The emotional fabric of the music was colored by the emergence of an American Negro culture. It signified that culture's strength and vitality. In the evolution of form in Negro music it is possible to see not only the evolution of the Negro as a cultural and social element of American culture, but also the evolution of that culture itself. The "Coon Shout" proposed one version of the American Negro—and of America; Ornette Coleman[1] proposes another. But the point is that both these versions are accurate and informed with a legitimacy of emotional concern nowhere available in what is called "Negro Literature," and certainly not in the middlebrow literature of the white American.

The artifacts of African art and sculpture were consciously eradicated by slavery. Any African art that based its validity on the production of an artifact, *i.e.,* some *material* manifestation such as a wooden statue or a woven cloth, had little chance of survival. It was only the more "abstract" aspects of African culture that could continue to exist in slave America. Africanisms still persist in the music, religion, and popular cultural traditions of American Negroes. However, it is not an African art American Negroes are responsible for, but an American one. The traditions of Africa must be utilized within the culture of the American Negro where they *actually* exist, and not because

---

1. American jazz musician (b. 1930), who helped pioneer free jazz.

of a defensive rationalization about the *worth* of one's ancestors or an attempt to capitalize on the recent eminence of the "new" African nations. African-isms do exist in Negro culture, but they have been so translated and trans-muted by the American experience that they have become integral parts of that experience.

The American Negro has a definable and legitimate historical tradition, no matter how painful, in America, but it is the only place such a tradition exists, simply because America is the only place the American Negro exists. He is, as William Carlos Williams said, "A pure product of America."[2] [The paradox of the Negro experience in America is that it is a separate experience, but inseparable from the complete fabric of American life.] The history of Western culture begins for the Negro with the importation of the slaves. It is almost as if all Western history before that must be strictly a learned concept. It is only the American experience that can be a persistent cultural catalyst for the Negro. In a sense, history for the Negro, before America, must remain an emotional abstraction. The cultural memory of Africa informs the Negro's life in America, but it is impossible to separate it from its American transformation. Thus, the Negro writer if he wanted to tap his legitimate cultural tradition should have done it by utilizing the entire spec-trum of the American experience from the point of view of the emotional history of the black man in this country: as its victim and its chronicler. The soul of such a man, as it exists outside the boundaries of commercial diver-sion or artificial social pretense. But without a deep commitment to cultural relevance and intellectual purity this was impossible. The Negro as a writer, was always a social object, whether glorifying the concept of white superi-ority, as a great many early Negro writers did, or in crying out against it, as exemplified by the stock "protest" literature of the thirties. He never moved into the position where he could propose his own symbols, erect his own personal myths, as any great literature must. Negro writing was always "after the fact," *i.e.*, based on known social concepts within the structure of bour-geois idealistic projections of "their America," and an emotional climate that never really existed.

The most successful fiction of most Negro writing is in its emotional con-tent. The Negro protest novelist postures, and invents a protest quite ame-nable with the tradition of bourgeois American life. He never reaches the central core of the America which *can* cause such protest. The intellectual traditions of the white middle class prevent such exposure of reality, and the black imitators reflect this. The Negro writer on Negro life in America pos-tures, and invents a Negro life, and an America to contain it. And even most of those who tried to rebel against that *invented* America were trapped because they had lost all touch with the reality of their experience within the *real* America, either because of the hidden emotional allegiance to the white middle class, or because they did not realize where the reality of their experience lay. When the serious Negro writer disdained the "middlebrow" model, as is the case with a few contemporary black American writers, he usually rushed headlong into the groves of the Academy, perhaps the most insidious and clever dispenser of middlebrow standards of excellence under the guise of "recognizable tradition." That such recognizable tradition is nec-essary goes without saying, but even from the great philosophies of Europe a contemporary usage must be established. No poetry has come out of

---

2. From Williams's poem "To Elsie" (1923).

England of major importance for forty years, yet there are would-be Negro poets who reject the gaudy excellence of 20th century American poetry in favor of disembowelled Academic models of second-rate English poetry, with the notion that somehow it is the only way poetry should be written. It would be better if such a poet listened to Bessie Smith sing *Gimme A Pigfoot,* or listened to the tragic verse of a Billie Holiday,[3] than be content to imperfectly imitate the bad poetry of the ruined minds of Europe. And again, it is this striving for respectability that has it so. For an American, black or white, to say that some hideous imitation of Alexander Pope means more to him, emotionally, than the blues of Ray Charles or Lightnin' Hopkins,[4] it would be required for him to have completely disappeared into the American Academy's vision of a Europeanized and colonial American culture, or to be lying. In the end, the same emotional sterility results. It is somehow much more tragic for the black man.

A Negro literature, to be a legitimate product of the Negro experience in America, must get at that experience in exactly the terms America has proposed for it, in its most ruthless identity. Negro reaction to America is as deep a part of America as the root causes of that reaction, and it is impossible to accurately describe that reaction in terms of the American middle class; because for them, the Negro has never really existed, never been glimpsed in anything even approaching the complete reality of his humanity. The Negro writer has to go from where he actually is, completely outside of that conscious white myopia. That the Negro does exist is the point, and as an element of American culture he is completely misunderstood by Americans. The middlebrow, commercial Negro writer assures the white American that, in fact, he doesn't exist, and that if he does, he does so within the perfectly predictable fingerpainting of white bourgeois sentiment and understanding. Nothing could be further from the truth. The Creoles of New Orleans resisted "Negro" music for a time as raw and raucous, because they thought they had found a place within the white society which would preclude their being Negroes. But they were unsuccessful in their attempts to "disappear" because the whites themselves reminded them that they were still, for all their assimilation, "just coons." And this seems to me an extremely important idea, since it is precisely this bitter insistence that has kept what can be called "Negro Culture" a brilliant amalgam of diverse influences. There was always a border beyond which the Negro could not go, whether musically or socially. There was always a possible limitation to any dilution or excess of cultural or spiritual reference. The Negro could not ever become white and that was his strength; at some point, always, he could not participate in the dominant tenor of the white man's culture, yet he came to understand that culture as well as the white man. It was at this juncture that he had to make use of other resources, whether African, sub-cultural, or hermetic. And it was this boundary, this no-man's-land, that provided the logic and beauty of his music. And this is the only way for the Negro artist to provide his version of America—from that no-man's-land outside the mainstream. A no-man's-land, a black country, completely invisible to white America, but so essentially part of it as to stain its whole being an ominous gray. Were there really

3. Jazz singer (1915–1959). Bessie Smith (1894 or 1898–1937): blues singer.
4. Sam "Lightnin' " Hopkins (1912–1982): blues singer and guitarist. Alexander Pope (1688–1744): English Augustan poet. Ray Charles (b. 1930): jazz, blues, and soul singer.

a Negro literature, now it could flower. At this point when the whole of Western society might go up in flames, the Negro remains an integral part of that society, but continually outside it, a figure like Melville's Bartleby.[5] He is an American, capable of identifying emotionally with the fantastic cultural ingredients of this society, but he is also, forever, outside that culture, an invisible strength within it, an observer. If there is ever a Negro literature, it must disengage itself from the weak, heinous elements of the culture that spawned it, and use its very existence as evidence of a more profound America. But as long as the Negro writer contents himself with the imitation of the useless ugly inelegance of the stunted middle-class mind, academic or popular, and refuses to look around him and "tell it like it is"— preferring the false prestige of the black bourgeoisie or the deceitful "acceptance" of *buy and sell* America, something never included in the legitimate cultural tradition of "his people"—he will be a failure, and what is worse, not even a significant failure. Just another dead American.

1962   1963

---

5. Extraordinarily passive protagonist of "Bartleby, the Scrivener," an 1853 short story by Herman Melville (1819–1891).

SOME NOTES ON ORGANIC FORM

In the 1950s and 1960s, Anglo-American poet Denise Levertov tried to find new ways of talking about open form, as did other poets associated with the Black Mountain school, such as Charles Olson and Robert Creeley. In her view, poetry should discover the inner distinctiveness of an experience—what the English poet Gerard Manley Hopkins termed *inscape*—instead of imposing on it a preconceived form. Adapting a semi-religious, semi-Romantic vocabulary, Levertov says that poetic inspiration begins in a moment of awed contemplation in "the temple of life." The poet then assembles words in patterns of rhythm, sonority, and recurrent imagery, all in close harmony with the intrinsic nature of the experience. The organic poem—as distinct from either the fixed forms of closed verse, or the shapelessness of some free verse—emerges as a whole, coherent both within itself and in relation to the dictates of the experience. Adapting Creeley's maxim, she insists: "Form is never more than a *revelation* of content." Originally published in *Poetry* 106.6 (September 1965), the piece has been reprinted from *New & Selected Essays* (1992).

DENISE LEVERTOV

Some Notes on Organic Form

For me, back of the idea of organic form is the concept that there is a form in all things (and in our experience) which the poet can discover and reveal. There are no doubt temperamental differences between poets who use prescribed forms and those who look for new ones—people who need a tight schedule to get anything done, and people who have to have a free hand—but the difference in their conception of "content" or "reality" is functionally more important. On the one hand is the idea that content, reality, experience, is essentially fluid and must be given form; on the other, this sense of seeking out inherent, though not immediately apparent, form. Gerard Manley Hopkins[1] invented the word "inscape" to denote intrinsic form, the pattern of essential characteristics both in single objects and (what is more interesting) in objects in a state of relation to each other, and the word "instress" to denote the experiencing of the perception of inscape, the apperception of inscape. In thinking of the process of poetry as I know it, I extend the use of these words, which he seems to have used mainly in reference to sensory phenomena, to include intellectual and emotional experience as well; I would speak of the inscape of an experience (which might be composed of any and all of these elements, including the sensory) or of the inscape of a sequence or constellation of experiences.

A partial definition, then, of organic poetry might be that it is a method of apperception, i.e., of recognizing what we perceive, and is based on an intuition of an order, a form beyond forms, in which forms partake, and of which man's creative works are analogies, resemblances, natural allegories. Such poetry is exploratory.

How does one go about such a poetry? I think it's like this: first there must be an experience, a sequence or constellation of perceptions of sufficient interest, felt by the poet intensely enough to demand of him their equivalence in words: he is *brought to speech*. Suppose there's the sight of the sky through a dusty window, birds and clouds and bits of paper flying through the sky, the sound of music from his radio, feelings of anger and love and amusement roused by a letter just received, the memory of some long-past thought or event associated with what's seen or heard or felt, and an idea, a concept, he has been pondering, each qualifying the other; together with what he knows about history; and what he has been dreaming—whether or not he remembers it—working in him. This is only a rough outline of a possible moment in a life. But the condition of being a poet is that periodically such a cross section, or constellation, of experiences (in which one or another element may predominate) demands, or wakes in him this demand: the poem. The beginning of the fulfillment of this demand is to contemplate, to meditate; words which connote a state in which the heat of feeling warms the intellect. To contemplate comes from "*templum*, temple, a place, a space for observation, marked out by the augur." It means, not simply to observe, to regard, but to do these things in the presence of a god. And to meditate is "to keep the mind in a state of contemplation"; its synonym is "to muse,"

---

1. English poet (1844–1889).

and to muse comes from a word meaning "to stand with open mouth"—not so comical if we think of "inspiration"—to breathe in.

So—as the poet stands open-mouthed in the temple of life, contemplating his experience, there come to him the first words of the poem: the words which are to be his way in to the poem, if there is to be a poem. The pressure of demand and the meditation on its elements culminate in a moment of vision, of crystallization, in which some inkling of the correspondence between those elements occurs; and it occurs as words. If he forces a beginning before this point, it won't work. These words sometimes remain the first, sometimes in the completed poem their eventual place may be elsewhere, or they may turn out to have been only forerunners, which fulfilled their function in bringing him to the words which are the actual beginning of the poem. It is faithful attention to the experience from the first moment of crystallization that allows those first or those forerunning words to rise to the surface: and with that same fidelity of attention the poet, from that moment of being let in to the possibility of the poem, must follow through, letting the experience lead him through the world of the poem, its unique inscape revealing itself as he goes.

During the writing of a poem the various elements of the poet's being are in communion with each other, and heightened. Ear and eye, intellect and passion, interrelate more subtly than at other times; and the "checking for accuracy," for precision of language, that must take place throughout the writing is not a matter of one element supervising the others but of intuitive interaction between all the elements involved.

In the same way, content and form are in a state of dynamic interaction; the understanding of whether an experience is a linear sequence or a constellation raying out from and into a central focus or axis, for instance, is discoverable only in the work, not before it.

Rhyme, chime, echo, reiteration: they not only serve to knit the elements of an experience but often are the very means, the sole means, by which the density of texture and the returning or circling of perception can be transmuted into language, apperceived. A may lead to E directly through B, C, and D: but if then there is the sharp remembrance or revisioning of A, this return must find its metric counterpart. It could do so by actual repetition of the words that spoke of A the first time (and if this return occurs more than once, one finds oneself with a refrain—not put there because one decided to write something with a refrain at the end of each stanza, but directly because of the demand of the content). Or it may be that since the return to A is now conditioned by the journey through B, C, and D, its words will not be a simple repetition but a variation . . . Again, if B and D are of a complementary nature, then their thought- or feeling-rhyme may find its corresponding word-rhyme. Corresponding images are a kind of nonaural rhyme. It usually happens that within the whole, that is between the point of crystallization that marks the beginning or onset of a poem and the point at which the intensity of contemplation has ceased, there are distinct units of awareness; and it is—for me anyway—these that indicate the duration of stanzas. Sometimes these units are of such equal duration that one gets a whole poem of, say, three-line stanzas, a regularity of pattern that looks, but is not, predetermined.

When my son was eight or nine I watched him make a crayon drawing of a tournament. He was not interested in the forms as such, but was grappling with the need to speak in graphic terms, to say, "And a great crowd of people were watching the jousting knights." There was a need to show the tiers of seats, all those people sitting in them. And out of the need arose a formal design that was beautiful—composed of the rows of shoulders and heads. It is in very much the same way that there can arise, out of fidelity to instress, a design that is the form of the poem—both its total form, its length and pace and tone, and the form of its parts (e.g., the rhythmic relationships of syllables within the line, and of line to line; the sonic relationships of vowels and consonants; the recurrence of images, the play of associations, etc.). "Form follows function" (Louis Sullivan).

Frank Lloyd Wright[2] in his autobiography wrote that the idea of organic architecture is that "the reality of the building lies in the space within it, to be lived in." And he quotes Coleridge: "Such as the life is, such is the form." (Emerson says in his essay "Poetry and Imagination," "Ask the fact for the form.") The *Oxford English Dictionary* quotes Huxley (Thomas, presumably)[3] as stating that he used the word organic "almost as an equivalent for the word 'living.' "

In organic poetry the metric movement, the measure, is the direct expression of the movement of perception. And the sounds, acting together with the measure, are a kind of extended onomatopoeia—i.e., they imitate not the sounds of an experience (which may well be soundless, or to which sounds contribute only incidentally), but the feeling of an experience, its emotional tone, its texture. The varying speed and gait of different strands of perception within an experience (I think of strands of seaweed moving within a wave) result in counterpointed measures.

Thinking about how organic poetry differs from free verse, I wrote that "most free verse is failed organic poetry, that is, organic poetry from which the attention of the writer had been switched off too soon, before the intrinsic form of the experience had been revealed." But Robert Duncan[4] pointed out to me that there is a "free verse" of which this is not true, because it is written not with any desire to seek a form, indeed perhaps with the longing to avoid form (if that were possible) and to express inchoate emotion as purely as possible.[5] There is a contradiction here, however, because if, as I suppose, there is an inscape of emotion, of feeling, it is impossible to avoid presenting something of it if the rhythm or tone of the feeling is given voice in the poem. But perhaps the difference is this: that free verse isolates the "rightness" of each line or cadence—if it seems expressive, then never mind the relation of it to the next; while in organic poetry the peculiar rhythms of the parts are in some degree modified, if necessary, in order to discover the rhythm of the whole.

But doesn't the character of the whole depend on, arise out of, the character of the parts? It does; but it is like painting from nature: suppose you absolutely imitate, on the palette, the separate colors of the various objects you are going to paint; yet when they are closely juxtaposed in the actual painting, you may have to lighten, darken, cloud, or sharpen each color in order to produce an effect equivalent to what you see in nature. Air, light, dust, shadow, and distance have to be taken into account.

2. American architect (1867–1959), like Louis Sullivan (1856–1924).
3. Thomas Huxley (1825–1895): English biologist. Samuel Taylor Coleridge (1772–1834): English Romantic poet. Ralph Waldo Emerson (1803–1882): American poet, essayist, and Transcendentalist.

4. American poet (1919–1988).
5. "See for instance, some of the forgotten poets of the early 20s—also, some of Amy Lowell [1874–1925]—[Carl] Sandburg [1878–1967]—John Gould Fletcher [1886–1950]. Some Imagist poems were written in 'free verse' in this sense, but by no means all" [Levertov's note].

Or one could put it this way: in organic poetry the form sense or "traffic sense," as Stefan Wolpe[6] speaks of it, is ever present along with (yes, paradoxically) fidelity to the revelations of meditation. The form sense is a sort of Stanislavsky[7] of the imagination: putting a chair two feet downstage there, thickening a knot of bystanders upstage left, getting this actor to raise his voice a little and that actress to enter more slowly; all in the interest of a total form he intuits. Or it is a sort of helicopter scout flying over the field of the poem, taking aerial photos and reporting on the state of the forest and its creatures—or over the sea to watch for the schools of herring and direct the fishing fleet toward them.

A manifestation of form sense is the sense the poet's ear has of some rhythmic norm peculiar to a particular poem, from which the individual lines depart and to which they return. I heard Henry Cowell tell that the drone in Indian music is known as the horizon note. Al Kresch,[8] the painter, sent me a quotation from Emerson: "The health of the eye demands a horizon." This sense of the beat or pulse underlying the whole I think of as the horizon note of the poem. It interacts with the nuances or forces of feeling which determine emphasis on one word or another, and decides to a great extent what belongs to a given line. It relates the needs of that feeling-force which dominates the cadence to the needs of the surrounding parts and so to the whole.

Duncan also pointed to what is perhaps a variety of organic poetry: the poetry of linguistic impulse. It seems to me that the absorption in language itself, the awareness of the world of multiple meaning revealed in sound, word, syntax, and the entering into this world in the poem, is as much an experience or constellation of perceptions as the instress of nonverbal sensuous and psychic events. What might make the poet of linguistic impetus appear to be on another tack entirely is that the demands of his realization may seem in opposition to truth as we think of it; that is, in terms of sensual logic. But the apparent distortion of experience in such a poem for the sake of verbal effects is actually a precise adherence to truth, since the experience itself was a verbal one.

Form is never more than a *revelation* of content.[9]

"The law—one perception must immediately and directly lead to a further perception" (Edward Dahlberg,[1] as quoted by Charles Olson in "Projective Verse," *Selected Writings*). I've always taken this to mean, "no loading of the rifts with ore,"[2] because there are to be no rifts. Yet alongside this truth is another truth (that I've learned from Duncan more than from anyone else)— that there must be a place in the poem for rifts too—(never to be stuffed with imported ore). Great gaps between perception and perception which must be leapt across if they are to be crossed at all.

The X-factor, the magic, is when we come to those rifts and make those leaps. A religious devotion to the truth, to the splendor of the authentic,

6. German-born composer (1902–1972) and director of music at Black Mountain College from 1952 to 1956. His music, structured in nonlinear, or "organic," modes, allowed for the unplanned element of ambient noise.
7. Konstantin Stanislavsky (1863–1938): Russian theater director associated with "method" acting, in which the actor makes use of personal memory and emotion to create a believable character.
8. Albert Kresch (b. 1922): American figurative painter. Henry Cowell: American composer (1897–1965).

9. Cf. Robert Creeley's (b. 1926) statement "Form is never more than an extension of content," cited by fellow Black Mountain poet Charles Olson (1910–1970) in his essay "Projective Verse," reprinted above.
1. American poet (1900–1977).
2. Cf. the English Romantic poet John Keats's suggestion in a letter of August 16, 1820, to fellow poet Percy Bysshe Shelley: "be more of an artist, and 'load every rift' of your subject with ore" (echoing English Renaissance poet Edmund Spenser's *Faerie Queene* 2.7.28.5).

involves the writer in a process rewarding in itself; but when that devotion brings us to undreamed abysses and we find ourselves sailing slowly over them and landing on the other side—that's ecstasy.

1965

WHEN WE DEAD AWAKEN

One of the preeminent literary figures who helped shape the women's movement of the 1960s and 1970s, Adrienne Rich writes in this essay about her "awakening conscious-ness" as a woman writer. She uses her own poetic development as an example of a more general trend away from self-effacing formalism toward a feminist poetics. Grounding her insights in her self-transformation as a poet, she fuses social commentary, literary criticism, and personal exploration and thus resists the polarities of the personal and the political. Enacting interpretive "re-vision"—in her view, not a luxury but a survival tool for women—she analyzes disempowering images of femininity in earlier literature. She traces a path from alienation and inert impersonality, through rage at social and cultural victimization, to a poetics of integrated self-expression and liberation. Origi-nally delivered as part of a panel on "The Woman Writer in the Twentieth Century" at the Modern Language Association in 1971 and printed in *College English* 34.1 (October 1972), the essay has been reprinted from the revised version, with introductory para-graphs, in Rich's *On Lies, Secrets, and Silence: Selected Prose, 1966–1978* (1979).

ADRIENNE RICH

When We Dead Awaken: Writing as Re-Vision

The Modern Language Association[1] is both marketplace and funeral parlor for the professional study of Western literature in North America. Like all gatherings of the professions, it has been and remains a "procession of the sons of educated men" (Virginia Woolf):[2] a congeries of old-boys' networks, academicians rehearsing their numb canons in sessions dedicated to the literature of white males, junior scholars under the lash of "publish or perish" delivering papers in the bizarrely lit drawing-rooms of immense hotels: a ritual competition veering between cynicism and desperation.

However, in the interstices of these gentlemanly rites (or, in Mary Daly's words, on the boundaries of this patriarchal space),[3] some feminist scholars, teachers, and graduate students, joined by feminist writers, editors, and pub-lishers, have for a decade been creating more subversive occasions, chal-lenging the sacredness of the gentlemanly canon, sharing the rediscovery of buried works by women, asking women's questions, bringing literary history

---

1. Association of scholars, critics, and teachers of language and literature.
2. English novelist (1882–1941).
3. "Mary Daly, *Beyond God the Father* (Boston: Beacon, 1971), pp. 40–41" [Rich's note]. Mary Daly (b. 1928): American feminist philosopher and theologian.

and criticism back to life in both senses. The Commission on the Status of Women in the Profession was formed in 1969, and held its first public event in 1970. In 1971 the Commission asked Ellen Peck Killoh, Tillie Olsen, Elaine Reuben, and myself, with Elaine Hedges as moderator, to talk on "The Woman Writer in the Twentieth Century."[4] The essay that follows was written for that forum, and later published, along with the other papers from the forum and workshops, in an issue of *College English* edited by Elaine Hedges ("Women Writing and Teaching," vol. 34, no. 1, October 1972.) With a few revisions, mainly updating, it was reprinted in *American Poets in 1976*, edited by William Heyen (New York: Bobbs-Merrill, 1976). That later text is the one published here.

The challenge flung by feminists at the accepted literary canon, at the methods of teaching it, and at the biased and astigmatic view of male "literary scholarship," has not diminished in the decade since the first Women's Forum; it has become broadened and intensified more recently by the challenges of black and lesbian feminists pointing out that feminist literary criticism itself has overlooked or held back from examining the work of black women and lesbians. The dynamic between a political vision and the demand for a fresh vision of literature is clear: without a growing feminist movement, the first inroads of feminist scholarship could not have been made; without the sharpening of a black feminist consciousness, black women's writing would have been left in limbo between misogynist black male critics and white feminists still struggling to unearth a white women's tradition; without an articulate lesbian/feminist movement, lesbian writing would still be lying in that closet where many of us used to sit reading forbidden books "in a bad light."

Much, much more is yet to be done; and university curricula have of course changed very little as a result of all this. What *is* changing is the availability of knowledge, of vital texts, the visible effects on women's lives of seeing, hearing our wordless or negated experience affirmed and pursued further in language.

Ibsen's[5] *When We Dead Awaken* is a play about the use that the male artist and thinker—in the process of creating culture as we know it—has made of women, in his life and in his work; and about a woman's slow struggling awakening to the use to which her life has been put. Bernard Shaw wrote in 1900 of this play:

> [Ibsen] shows us that no degradation ever devized or permitted is as disastrous as this degradation; that through it women can die into luxuries for men and yet can kill them; that men and women are becoming conscious of this; and that what remains to be seen as perhaps the most interesting of all imminent social developments is what will happen "when we dead awaken."[6]

It's exhilarating to be alive in a time of awakening consciousness; it can also be confusing, disorienting, and painful. This awakening of dead or sleeping consciousness has already affected the lives of millions of women, even

---

4. The panelists are writers and teachers. Tillie Olsen (b. c. 1913) is a prominent Jewish American fiction writer.
5. Henrik Ibsen (1828–1906), Norwegian playwright and poet.

6. "G. B. Shaw, The Quintessence of Ibsenism (New York: Hill & Wang, 1922), p. 139" [Rich's note]. George Bernard Shaw (1856–1950), Irish playwright and critic.

those who don't know it yet. It is also affecting the lives of men, even those who deny its claims upon them. The argument will go on whether an oppressive economic class system is responsible for the oppressive nature of male/ female relations, or whether, in fact, patriarchy—the domination of males— is the original model of oppression on which all others are based. But in the last few years the women's movement has drawn inescapable and illuminating connections between our sexual lives and our political institutions. The sleepwalkers are coming awake, and for the first time this awakening has a collective reality; it is no longer such a lonely thing to open one's eyes.

Re-vision—the act of looking back, of seeing with fresh eyes, of entering an old text from a new critical direction—is for women more than a chapter in cultural history: it is an act of survival. Until we can understand the assumptions in which we are drenched we cannot know ourselves. And this drive to self-knowledge, for women, is more than a search for identity: it is part of our refusal of the self-destructiveness of male-dominated society. A radical critique of literature, feminist in its impulse, would take the work first of all as a clue to how we live, how we have been living, how we have been led to imagine ourselves, how our language has trapped as well as liberated us, how the very act of naming has been till now a male prerogative, and how we can begin to see and name—and therefore live—afresh. A change in the concept of sexual identity is essential if we are not going to see the old political order reassert itself in every new revolution. We need to know the writing of the past, and know it differently than we have ever known it; not to pass on a tradition but to break its hold over us.

For writers, and at this moment for women writers in particular, there is the challenge and promise of a whole new psychic geography to be explored. But there is also a difficult and dangerous walking on the ice, as we try to find language and images for a consciousness we are just coming into, and with little in the past to support us. I want to talk about some aspects of this difficulty and this danger.

Jane Harrison, the great classical anthropologist, wrote in 1914 in a letter to her friend Gilbert Murray:

> By the by, about "Women," it has bothered me often—why do women never want to write poetry about Man as a sex—why is Woman a dream and a terror to man and not the other way around? . . . Is it mere convention and propriety, or something deeper?[7]

I think Jane Harrison's question cuts deep into the myth-making tradition, the romantic tradition; deep into what women and men have been to each other; and deep into the psyche of the woman writer. Thinking about that question, I began thinking of the work of two twentieth-century women poets, Sylvia Plath and Diane Wakoski. It strikes me that in the work of both Man appears as, if not a dream, a fascination and a terror; and that the source of the fascination and the terror is, simply, Man's power—to dominate, tyrannize, choose, or reject the woman. The charisma of Man seems to come purely from his power over her and his control of the world by force, not from anything fertile or life-giving in him. And, in the work of both these poets, it is finally the woman's sense of *herself*—embattled, possessed—that gives the poetry its dynamic charge, its rhythms of struggle, need, will, and

---

7. "J. G. Stewart, *Jane Ellen Harrison: A Portrait from Letters* (London: Merlin, 1959), p. 140" [Rich's note]. Jane Harrison (1850–1928): English archeologist. Gilbert Murray (1866–1957): English classicist.

female energy. Until recently this female anger and this furious awareness of the Man's power over her were not available materials to the female poet, who tended to write of Love as the source of her suffering, and to view that victimization by Love as an almost inevitable fate. Or, like Marianne Moore and Elizabeth Bishop,[8] she kept sexuality at a measured and chiseled distance in her poems.

One answer to Jane Harrison's question has to be that historically men and women have played very different parts in each others' lives. Where woman has been a luxury for man, and has served as the painter's model and the poet's muse, but also as comforter, nurse, cook, bearer of his seed, secretarial assistant, and copyist of manuscripts, man has played a quite different role for the female artist. Henry James repeats an incident which the writer Prosper Mérimée described, of how, while he was living with George Sand,

> he once opened his eyes, in the raw winter dawn, to see his companion, in a dressing-gown, on her knees before the domestic hearth, a candle-stick beside her and a red *madras* round her head, making bravely, with her own hands the fire that was to enable her to sit down betimes to urgent pen and paper. The story represents him as having felt that the spectacle chilled his ardor and tried his taste; her appearance was unfortunate, her occupation an inconsequence, and her industry a reproof—the result of all which was a lively irritation and an early rupture.[9]

The specter of this kind of male judgment, along with the misnaming and thwarting of her needs by a culture controlled by males, has created problems for the woman writer: problems of contact with herself, problems of language and style, problems of energy and survival.

In rereading Virginia Woolf's *A Room of One's Own* (1929) for the first time in some years, I was astonished at the sense of effort, of pains taken, of dogged tentativeness, in the tone of that essay. And I recognized that tone. I had heard it often enough, in myself and in other women. It is the tone of a woman almost in touch with her anger, who is determined not to appear angry, who is *willing* herself to be calm, detached, and even charming in a roomful of men where things have been said which are attacks on her very integrity. Virginia Woolf is addressing an audience of women, but she is acutely conscious—as she always was—of being overheard by men: by Morgan and Lytton and Maynard Keynes and for that matter by her father, Leslie Stephen.[1] She drew the language out into an exacerbated thread in her determination to have her own sensibility yet protect it from those masculine presences. Only at rare moments in that essay do you hear the passion in her voice; she was trying to sound as cool as Jane Austen,[2] as Olympian as

8. American poets from earlier generations.
9. "Henry James, 'Notes on Novelists,' in *Selected Literary Criticism of Henry James*, Morris Shapira, ed. (London: Heinemann, 1963), pp. 157–58" [Rich's note]. Prosper Mérimée (1803–1870): French Romantic author. George Sand (1804–1876): male pseudonym of French novelist Armandine-Aurore-Lucie (or Lucile) Dupin. *Madras*: brightly colored handkerchief worn on the head.
1. "A. R., 1978: This intuition of mine was corroborated when, early in 1978, I read the correspondence between Woolf and Dame Ethel Smyth (Henry W. and Albert A. Berg Collection, The New

York Public Library, Astor, Lenox and Tilden Foundations); in a letter dated June 8, 1933, Woolf speaks of having kept her own personality out of *A Room of One's Own* lest she not be taken seriously: '. . . how personal, so will they say, rubbing their hands with glee, women always are; *I even hear them as I write*.' (Italics mine.)" [Rich's note]. Edward Morgan (E. M.) Forster (1879–1970): English novelist. Lytton Strachey (1880–1932): English biographer. John Maynard Keynes (1883–1946): English economist. Leslie Stephen (1832–1904): English critic.
2. English novelist (1775–1817).

Shakespeare, because that is the way the men of the culture thought a writer should sound.

No male writer has written primarily or even largely for women, or with the sense of women's criticism as a consideration when he chooses his materials, his theme, his language. But to a lesser or greater extent, every woman writer has written for men even when, like Virginia Woolf, she was supposed to be addressing women. If we have come to the point when this balance might begin to change, when women can stop being haunted, not only by "convention and propriety" but by internalized fears of being and saying themselves, then it is an extraordinary moment for the woman writer—and reader.

I have hesitated to do what I am going to do now, which is to use myself as an illustration. For one thing, it's a lot easier and less dangerous to talk about other women writers. But there is something else. Like Virginia Woolf, I am aware of the women who are not with us here because they are washing the dishes and looking after the children. Nearly fifty years after she spoke, the fact remains largely unchanged. And I am thinking also of women whom she left out of the picture altogether—women who are washing other people's dishes and caring for other people's children, not to mention women who went on the streets last night in order to feed their children. We seem to be special women here, we have liked to think of ourselves as special, and we have known that men would tolerate, even romanticize us as special, as long as our words and actions didn't threaten their privilege of tolerating or rejecting us and our work according to *their* ideas of what a special woman ought to be. An important insight of the radical women's movement has been how divisive and how ultimately destructive is this myth of the special woman, who is also the token woman. Every one of us here in this room has had great luck—we are teachers, writers, academicians; our own gifts could not have been enough, for we all know women whose gifts are buried or aborted. Our struggles can have meaning and our privileges—however precarious under patriarchy—can be justified only if they can help to change the lives of women whose gifts—and whose very being—continue to be thwarted and silenced.

My own luck was being born white and middle-class into a house full of books, with a father who encouraged me to read and write. So for about twenty years I wrote for a particular man, who criticized and praised me and made me feel I was indeed "special." The obverse side of this, of course, was that I tried for a long time to please him, or rather, not to displease him. And then of course there were other men—writers, teachers—the Man, who was not a terror or a dream but a literary master and a master in other ways less easy to acknowledge. And there were all those poems about women, written by men: it seemed to be a given that men wrote poems and women frequently inhabited them. These women were almost always beautiful, but threatened with the loss of beauty, the loss of youth—the fate worse than death. Or, they were beautiful and died young, like Lucy and Lenore. Or, the woman was like Maud Gonne,[3] cruel and disastrously mistaken, and the poem reproached her because she had refused to become a luxury for the poet.

A lot is being said today about the influence that the myths and images of women have on all of us who are products of culture. I think it has been a

---

3. Irish patriot (1865–1953), memorialized in the poetry of her refused suitor W. B. Yeats (1865–1939). *Lucy and Lenore*: tragic female figures from the poetry of William Wordsworth (1770–1850) and Edgar Allan Poe (1809–1849), respectively.

peculiar confusion to the girl or woman who tries to write because she is peculiarly susceptible to language. She goes to poetry or fiction looking for *her* way of being in the world, since she too has been putting words and images together; she is looking eagerly for guides, maps, possibilities; and over and over in the "words' masculine persuasive force" of literature she comes up against something that negates everything she is about: she meets the image of Woman in books written by men. She finds a terror and a dream, she finds a beautiful pale face, she finds La Belle Dame Sans Merci, she finds Juliet or Tess or Salomé,[4] but precisely what she does not find is that absorbed, drudging, puzzled, sometimes inspired creature, herself, who sits at a desk trying to put words together.

So what does she do? What did I do? I read the older women poets with their peculiar keenness and ambivalence: Sappho, Christina Rossetti, Emily Dickinson, Elinor Wylie, Edna Millay, H. D.[5] I discovered that the woman poet most admired at the time (by men) was Marianne Moore, who was maidenly, elegant, intellectual, discreet. But even in reading these women I was looking in them for the same things I had found in the poetry of men, because I wanted women poets to be the equals of men, and to be equal was still confused with sounding the same.

I know that my style was formed first by male poets: by the men I was reading as an undergraduate—Frost, Dylan Thomas, Donne, Auden, MacNiece, Stevens, Yeats. What I chiefly learned from them was craft.[6] But poems are like dreams: in them you put what you don't know you know. Looking back at poems I wrote before I was twenty-one, I'm startled because beneath the conscious craft are glimpses of the split I even then experienced between the girl who wrote poems, who defined herself in writing poems, and the girl who was to define herself by her relationships with men. "Aunt Jennifer's Tigers" (1951), written while I was a student, looks with deliberate detachment at this split.[7] In writing this poem, composed and apparently cool as it is, I thought I was creating a portrait of an imaginary woman. But this woman suffers from the opposition of her imagination, worked out in tapestry, and her life-style, "ringed with ordeals she was mastered by." It was important to me that Aunt Jennifer was a person as distinct from myself as possible—distanced by the formalism of the poem, by its objective, observant tone—even by putting the woman in a different generation.

In those years formalism was part of the strategy—like asbestos gloves, it allowed me to handle materials I couldn't pick up bare-handed. A later strategy was to use the persona of a man, as I did in "The Loser" (1958):

---

4. In the Bible, a woman who beguiled King Herod into beheading John the Baptist. *La Belle Dame Sans Merci*: woman whose lover dies after she refuses him, in French poem by Alain Chartier (c. 1385–c. 1433), and who seduces a knight, in a ballad by John Keats (1795–1821). *Juliet*: female protagonist of Shakespeare's *Romeo and Juliet*. *Tess*: tragic heroine of the novel *Tess of the d'Urbervilles*, by Thomas Hardy (1840–1928).
5. American poet (1886–1961), like Emily Dickinson (1830–1886), Elinor Wylie (1885–1928), and Edna St. Vincent Millay (1892–1950). Sappho (c. 610–c. 580 B.C.E.): Greek lyric poet. Christina Rossetti (1830–1894): English poet.
6. "*A. R., 1978:* Yet I spent months, at sixteen,

memorizing and writing imitations of Millay's sonnets; and in notebooks of that period I find what are obviously attempts to imitate Dickinson's metrics and verbal compression. I knew H. D. only through anthologized lyrics; her epic poetry was not then available to me" [Rich's note]. Robert Frost (1874–1963): American poet. Dylan Thomas (1914–1953): Welsh poet. John Donne (1572–1631): English poet. W. H. Auden (1907–1973): Anglo-American poet. Wallace Stevens (1879–1955): American poet. Louis MacNeice (1907–1963): Anglo-Irish poet.
7. The original essay reprinted "Aunt Jennifer's Tigers," on p. 459 of this volume.

A man thinks of the woman he once loved: first, after her wedding, and then nearly a decade later.

I

I kissed you, bride and lost, and went
home from that bourgeois sacrament,
your cheek still tasting cold upon
my lips that gave you benison[8]
with all the swagger that they knew—
as losers somehow learn to do.

Your wedding made my eyes ache; soon
the world would be worse off for one
more golden apple dropped to ground
without the least protesting sound,
and you would windfall lie, and we
forget your shimmer on the tree.

Beauty is always wasted: if
not Mignon's song sung to the deaf,
at all events to the unmoved.
A face like yours cannot be loved
long or seriously enough.
Almost, we seem to hold it off.

II

Well, you are tougher than I thought.
Now when the wash with ice hangs taut
this morning of St. Valentine,
I see you strip the squeaking line,
your body weighed against the load,
and all my groans can do no good.

Because you are still beautiful,
though squared and stiffened by the pull
of what nine windy years have done.
You have three daughters, lost a son.
I see all your intelligence
flung into that unwearied stance.

My envy is of no avail.
I turn my head and wish him well
who chafed your beauty into use
and lives forever in a house
lit by the friction of your mind.
You stagger in against the wind.

I finished college, published my first book by a fluke, as it seemed to me, and broke off a love affair. I took a job, lived alone, went on writing, fell in love. I was young, full of energy, and the book seemed to mean that others

8. Blessing.

agreed I was a poet. Because I was also determined to prove that as a woman poet I could also have what was then defined as a "full" woman's life, I plunged in my early twenties into marriage and had three children before I was thirty. There was nothing overt in the environment to warn me: these were the fifties, and in reaction to the earlier wave of feminism, middle-class women were making careers of domestic perfection, working to send their husbands through professional schools, then retiring to raise large families. People were moving out to the suburbs, technology was going to be the answer to everything, even sex; the family was in its glory. Life was extremely private; women were isolated from each other by the loyalties of marriage. I have a sense that women didn't talk to each other much in the fifties—not about their secret emptinesses, their frustrations. I went on trying to write; my second book and first child appeared in the same month. But by the time that book came out I was already dissatisfied with those poems, which seemed to me mere exercises for poems I hadn't written. The book was praised, however, for its "gracefulness"; I had a marriage and a child. If there were doubts, if there were periods of null depression or active despairing, these could only mean that I was ungrateful, insatiable, perhaps a monster.

About the time my third child was born, I felt that I had either to consider myself a failed woman and a failed poet, or to try to find some synthesis by which to understand what was happening to me. What frightened me most was the sense of drift, of being pulled along on a current which called itself my destiny, but in which I seemed to be losing touch with whoever I had been, with the girl who had experienced her own will and energy almost ecstatically at times, walking around a city or riding a train at night or typing in a student room. In a poem about my grandmother I wrote (of myself): "A young girl, thought sleeping, is certified dead" ("Halfway").[9] I was writing very little, partly from fatigue, that female fatigue of suppressed anger and loss of contact with my own being; partly from the discontinuity of female life with its attention to small chores, errands, work that others constantly undo, small children's constant needs. What I did write was unconvincing to me; my anger and frustration were hard to acknowledge in or out of poems because in fact I cared a great deal about my husband and my children. Trying to look back and understand that time I have tried to analyze the real nature of the conflict. Most, if not all, human lives are full of fantasy—passive day-dreaming which need not be acted on. But to write poetry or fiction, or even to think well, is not to fantasize, or to put fantasies on paper. For a poem to coalesce, for a character or an action to take shape, there has to be an imaginative transformation of reality which is in no way passive. And a certain freedom of the mind is needed—freedom to press on, to enter the currents of your thought like a glider pilot, knowing that your motion can be sustained, that the buoyancy of your attention will not be suddenly snatched away. Moreover, if the imagination is to transcend and transform experience it has to question, to challenge, to conceive of alternatives, perhaps to the very life you are living at that moment. You have to be free to play around with the notion that day might be night, love might be hate; nothing can be too sacred for the imagination to turn into its opposite or to call experimentally by another name. For writing is re-naming. Now, to be maternally with small children all day in the old way, to be with a man in the old way of marriage, requires a holding-back, a putting-aside of that imaginative activity, and

9. See Rich's *The Fact of a Doorframe: Poems Selected and New 1950–1984* (1984), p. 73.

demands instead a kind of conservatism. I want to make it clear that I am *not* saying that in order to write well, or think well, it is necessary to become unavailable to others, or to become a devouring ego. This has been the myth of the masculine artist and thinker; and I do not accept it. But to be a female human being trying to fulfill traditional female functions in a traditional way *is* in direct conflict with the subversive function of the imagination. The word traditional is important here. There must be ways, and we will be finding out more and more about them, in which the energy of creation and the energy of relation can be united. But in those years I always felt the conflict as a failure of love in myself. I had thought I was choosing a full life: the life available to most men, in which sexuality, work, and parenthood could coexist. But I felt, at twenty-nine, guilt toward the people closest to me, and guilty toward my own being.

I wanted, then, more than anything, the one thing of which there was never enough: time to think, time to write. The fifties and early sixties were years of rapid revelations: the sit-ins and marches in the South, the Bay of Pigs,[1] the early antiwar movement, raised large questions—questions for which the masculine world of the academy around me seemed to have expert and fluent answers. But I needed to think for myself—about pacifism and dissent and violence, about poetry and society, and about my own relationship to all these things. For about ten years I was reading in fierce snatches, scribbling in notebooks, writing poetry in fragments; I was looking desperately for clues, because if there were no clues then I thought I might be insane. I wrote in a notebook about this time:

> Paralyzed by the sense that there exists a mesh of relationships—e.g., between my anger at the children, my sensual life, pacifism, sex (I mean sex in its broadest significance, not merely sexual desire)—an interconnectedness which, if I could see it, make it valid, would give me back myself, make it possible to function lucidly and passionately. Yet I grope in and out among these dark webs.

I think I began at this point to feel that politics was not something "out there" but something "in here" and of the essence of my condition.

In the late fifties I was able to write, for the first time, directly about experiencing myself as a woman. The poem was jotted in fragments during children's naps, brief hours in a library, or at 3:00 A.M. after rising with a wakeful child. I despaired of doing any continuous work at this time. Yet I began to feel that my fragments and scraps had a common consciousness and a common theme, one which I would have been very unwilling to put on paper at an earlier time because I had been taught that poetry should be "universal," which meant, of course, nonfemale. Until then I had tried very much *not* to identify myself as a female poet. Over two years I wrote a ten-part poem called "Snapshots of a Daughter-in-Law" (1958–1960), in a longer looser mode than I'd ever trusted myself with before. It was an extraordinary relief to write that poem. It strikes me now as too literary, too dependent on allusion; I hadn't found the courage yet to do without authorities, or even to use the pronoun "I"—the woman in the poem is always "she." One section of it, No. 2, concerns a woman who thinks she is going mad; she is haunted

---

1. Failed attempt by U.S.-financed Cuban exiles to overthrow Fidel Castro (b. 1926/27) on April 17, 1961.

by voices telling her to resist and rebel, voices which she can hear but not obey.[2]

The poem "Orion," written five years later, is a poem of reconnection with a part of myself I had felt I was losing—the active principle, the energetic imagination, the "half-brother" whom I projected, as I had for many years, into the constellation Orion. It's no accident that the words "cold and egotistical" appear in this poem, and are applied to myself.[3] The choice still seemed to be between "love"—womanly, maternal love, altruistic love—a love defined and ruled by the weight of an entire culture; and egotism—a force directed by men into creation, achievement, ambition, often at the expense of others, but justifiably so. For weren't they men, and wasn't that their destiny as womanly, selfless love was ours? We know now that the alternatives are false ones—that the word "love" is itself in need of re-vision.

There is a companion poem to "Orion," written three years later, in which at last the woman in the poem and the woman writing the poem become the same person. It is called "Planetarium," and it was written after a visit to a real planetarium, where I read an account of the work of Caroline Herschel, the astronomer, who worked with her brother William, but whose name remained obscure, as his did not.[4]

In closing I want to tell you about a dream I had last summer. I dreamed I was asked to read my poetry at a mass women's meeting, but when I began to read, what came out were the lyrics of a blues song. I share this dream with you because it seemed to me to say something about the problems and the future of the woman writer, and probably of women in general. The awakening of consciousness is not like the crossing of a frontier—one step and you are in another country. Much of woman's poetry has been of the nature of the blues song: a cry of pain, of victimization, or a lyric of seduction.[5] And today, much poetry by women—and prose for that matter—is charged with anger. I think we need to go through that anger, and we will betray our own reality if we try, as Virginia Woolf was trying, for an objectivity, a detachment, that would make us sound more like Jane Austen or Shakespeare. We know more than Jane Austen or Shakespeare knew: more than Jane Austen because our lives are more complex, more than Shakespeare because we know more about the lives of women—Jane Austen and Virginia Woolf included.

Both the victimization and the anger experienced by women are real, and have real sources, everywhere in the environment, built into society, language, the structures of thought. They will go on being tapped and explored by poets, among others. We can neither deny them, nor will we rest there. A new generation of women poets is already working out of the psychic energy released when women begin to move out towards what the feminist philosopher Mary Daly has described as the "new space" on the boundaries of patriarchy.[6] Women are speaking to and of women in these poems, out of

---

2. The original essay quoted section 2 of "Snapshots of a Daughter-in-Law," on p. 459 of this volume.
3. The original essay reprinted "Orion," on p. 464 of this volume.
4. The original essay reprinted "Planetarium," on p. 465 of this volume. Caroline Herschel (1750–1848), German-born British astronomer and brother of Sir William Herschel (1738–1822).

5. "A. R., 1978: When I dreamed that dream, was I wholly ignorant of the tradition of Bessie Smith [1894 or 1898–1937] and other women's blues lyrics which transcended victimization to sing of resistance and independence?" [Rich's note].
6. "Mary Daly, *Beyond God the Father: Towards a Philosophy of Women's Liberation* (Boston: Beacon, 1973)" [Rich's note].

a newly released courage to name, to love each other, to share risk and grief and celebration.

To the eye of a feminist, the work of Western male poets now writing reveals a deep, fatalistic pessimism as to the possibilities of change, whether societal or personal, along with a familiar and threadbare use of women (and nature) as redemptive on the one hand, threatening on the other; and a new tide of phallocentric sadism and overt woman-hating which matches the sexual brutality of recent films. "Political" poetry by men remains stranded amid the struggles for power among male groups; in condemning U.S. imperialism or the Chilean junta the poet can claim to speak for the oppressed while remaining, as male, part of a system of sexual oppression. The enemy is always outside the self, the struggle somewhere else. The mood of isolation, self-pity, and self-imitation that pervades "nonpolitical" poetry suggests that a profound change in masculine consciousness will have to precede any new male poetic—or other—inspiration. The creative energy of patriarchy is fast running out; what remains is its self-generating energy for destruction. As women, we have our work cut out for us.

1971   1972, 1979

FEELING INTO WORDS

The Irish poet and Nobel laureate Seamus Heaney conceived of poetry as being at once public and personal, political and autobiographical. In this early essay, originally delivered as a lecture at London's Royal Society of Literature in 1974, he explores the poet's multifaceted vocation. Poetry, in Heaney's view, plumbs the depths of experience, giving shape and heft to what would otherwise remain hidden and inarticulate. Using his own work as an example, Heaney argues that a successful poem bears the watermark of the poet's voice and that its technique, beyond craft, reveals a unique relationship to the world. Heaney also describes how the eruption of tensions between Protestants and Catholics in Northern Ireland affected his work in the late 1960s and early 1970s. "From that moment," he explains, "the problems of poetry moved from being simply a matter of achieving the satisfactory verbal icon to being a search for images and symbols adequate to our predicament." In the shadow of the violent Troubles, Heaney wrote his famous "bog poems," which he describes as exploring analogies between the contemporary bloodshed and ancient sacrificial rites. The essay was originally published in the journal *Essays by Diverse Hands*, New Series 40 (1979) and has been reprinted from the slightly revised version in *Preoccupations: Selected Prose, 1968–1978* (1980).

SEAMUS HEANEY

Feeling into Words

I intend to retrace some paths into what William Wordsworth called in *The Prelude*[1] 'the hiding places'.

> The hiding places of my power
> Seem open; I approach, and then they close;
> I see by glimpses now; when age comes on,
> May scarcely see at all, and I would give,
> While yet we may, as far as words can give,
> A substance and a life to what I feel:
> I would enshrine the spirit of the past
> For future restoration.

Implicit in those lines is a view of poetry which I think is implicit in the few poems I have written that give me any right to speak: poetry as divination, poetry as revelation of the self to the self, as restoration of the culture to itself; poems as elements of continuity, with the aura and authenticity of archaeological finds, where the buried shard has an importance that is not diminished by the importance of the buried city; poetry as a dig, a dig for finds that end up being plants.

'Digging', in fact, was the name of the first poem I wrote where I thought my feelings had got into words, or to put it more accurately, where I thought my *feel* had got into words. Its rhythms and noises still please me, although there are a couple of lines in it that have more of the theatricality of the gunslinger than the self-absorption of the digger. I wrote it in the summer of 1964, almost two years after I had begun to 'dabble in verses'. This was the first place where I felt I had done more than make an arrangement of words: I felt that I had let down a shaft into real life. The facts and surfaces of the thing were true, but more important, the excitement that came from naming them gave me a kind of insouciance and a kind of confidence. I didn't care who thought what about it: somehow, it had surprised me by coming out with a stance and an idea that I would stand over[.][2]

As I say, I wrote it down years ago; yet perhaps I should say that I dug it up, because I have come to realize that it was laid down in me years before that even. The pen/spade analogy was the simple heart of the matter and *that* was simply a matter of almost proverbial common sense. As a child on the road to and from school, people used to ask you what class you were in and how many slaps you'd got that day and invariably they ended up with an exhortation to keep studying because 'learning's easy carried' and 'the pen's lighter than the spade'. And the poem does no more than allow that bud of wisdom to exfoliate, although the significant point in this context is that at the time of writing I was not aware of the proverbial structure at the back of my mind. Nor was I aware that the poem was an enactment of yet another digging metaphor that came back to me years later. This was the rhyme we

---

1. Autobiographical epic (1850) by the English Romantic poet (1770–1850).

2. The original essay reprinted lines 25–31 of "Digging," on p. 723 of this volume.

used to chant on the road to school, though, as I have said before, we were not fully aware of what we were dealing with:

> 'Are your praties[3] dry
> And are they fit for digging?'
> 'Put in your spade and try,'
> Says Dirty-Faced McGuigan.

There digging becomes a sexual metaphor, an emblem of initiation, like putting your hand into the bush or robbing the nest, one of the various natural analogies for uncovering and touching the hidden thing. I now believe that the 'Digging' poem had for me the force of an initiation: the confidence I mentioned arose from a sense that perhaps I could do this poetry thing too, and having experienced the excitement and release of it once, I was doomed to look for it again and again.

I don't want to overload 'Digging' with too much significance. It is a big coarse-grained navvy of a poem, but it is interesting as an example—and not just as an example of what one reviewer called 'mud-caked fingers in Russell Square',[4] for I don't think that the subject-matter has any particular virtue in itself—it is interesting as an example of what we call 'finding a voice'.

Finding a voice means that you can get your own feeling into your own words and that your words have the feel of you about them; and I believe that it may not even be a metaphor, for a poetic voice is probably very intimately connected with the poet's natural voice, the voice that he hears as the ideal speaker of the lines he is making up.

In his novel *The First Circle*, Solzhenitzyn[5] sets the action in a prison camp on the outskirts of Moscow where the inmates are all highly skilled technicians forced to labour at projects dreamed up by Stalin. The most important of these is an attempt to devise a mechanism to bug a phone. But what is to be special about this particular bugging device is that it will not simply record the voice and the message but that it will identify the essential sound patterns of the speaker's voice; it will discover, in the words of the narrative, 'what it is that makes every human voice unique', so that no matter how the speaker disguises his accent or changes his language, the fundamental structure of his voice will be caught. The idea was that a voice is like a fingerprint, possessing a constant and unique signature that can, like a fingerprint, be recorded and employed for identification.

Now one of the purposes of a literary education as I experienced it was to turn the student's ear into a poetic bugging device, so that a piece of verse denuded of name and date could be identified by its diction, tropes and cadences. And this secret policing of English verse was also based on the idea of a style as a signature. But what I wish to suggest is that there is a connection between the core of a poet's speaking voice and the core of his poetic voice, between his original accent and his discovered style. I think that the discovery of a way of writing that is natural and adequate to your sensibility depends on the recovery of that essential quick which Solzhenitzyn's technicians were trying to pin down. This is the absolute register to which your proper music has to be tuned.

How, then, do you find it? In practice, you hear it coming from somebody

---

3. Potatoes (Irish).
4. In London. *Navvy*: unskilled laborer (British).
5. Aleksandr Solzhenitsyn (b. 1918), Russian nov-

elist who drew on his own experiences in the Soviet prisons of Joseph Stalin (1879–1953) in the late 1940s for *The First Circle*.

else, you hear something in another writer's sounds that flows in through your ear and enters the echo-chamber of your head and delights your whole nervous system in such a way that your reaction will be, 'Ah, I wish I had said that, in that particular way'. This other writer, in fact, has spoken something essential to you, something you recognize instinctively as a true sounding of aspects of yourself and your experience. And your first steps as a writer will be to imitate, consciously or unconsciously, those sounds that flowed in, that in-fluence.

One of the writers who influenced me in this way was Gerard Manley Hopkins.[6] The result of reading Hopkins at school was the desire to write, and when I first put pen to paper at university, what flowed out was what had flowed in, the bumpy alliterating music, the reporting sounds and ricochetting consonants typical of Hopkins's verse. I remember lines from a piece called 'October Thought' in which some frail bucolic images foundered under the chainmail of the pastiche:

> Starling thatch-watches, and sudden swallow
> Straight breaks to mud-nest, home-rest rafter
> Up past dry dust-drunk cobwebs, like laughter
> Ghosting the roof of bog-oak, turf-sod and rods of willow . . .

and then there was 'heaven-hue, plum-blue and gorse-pricked with gold' and 'a trickling tinkle of bells well in the fold'.

Looking back on it, I believe there was a connection, not obvious at the time but, on reflection, real enough, between the heavily accented consonantal noise of Hopkins's poetic voice, and the peculiar regional characteristics of a Northern Ireland accent. The late W. R. Rodgers,[7] another poet much lured by alliteration, said in his poem 'The Character of Ireland' that the people from his (and my) part of the world were

> an abrupt people
> who like the spiky consonants of speech
> and think the soft ones cissy; who dig
> the k and t in orchestra, detect sin
> in sinfonia, get a kick out of
> tin-cans, fricatives, fornication, staccato talk,
> anything that gives or takes attack
> like Micks, Teagues, tinker's gets, Vatican.

It is true that the Ulster[8] accent is generally a staccato consonantal one. Our tongue strikes the tangent of the consonant rather more than it rolls the circle of the vowel—Rodgers also spoke of 'the round gift of the gab in southern mouths'. It is energetic, angular, hard-edged, and it may be because of this affinity between my dialect and Hopkins's oddity that those first verses turned out as they did.

I couldn't say, of course, that I had found a voice but I had found a game. I knew the thing was only word-play, and I hadn't even the guts to put my name to it. I called myself *Incertus,* uncertain, a shy soul fretting and all that. I was in love with words themselves, but had no sense of a poem as a whole structure and no experience of how the successful achievement of a poem could be a stepping stone in your life. Those verses were what we might

6. English poet (1844–1889).
7. Irish poet (1909–1969).

8. Northern Irish.

call 'trial-pieces', little stiff inept designs in imitation of the master's fluent interlacing patterns, heavy-handed clues to the whole craft.

I was getting my first sense of crafting words and for one reason or another, words as bearers of history and mystery began to invite me. Maybe it began very early when my mother used to recite lists of affixes and suffixes, and Latin roots, with their English meanings, rhymes that formed part of her schooling in the early part of the century. Maybe it began with the exotic listing on the wireless dial: Stuttgart, Leipzig, Oslo, Hilversum.[9] Maybe it was stirred by the beautiful sprung rhythms of the old BBC weather forecast: Dogger, Rockall, Malin, Shetland, Faroes, Finisterre;[1] or with the gorgeous and inane phraseology of the catechism; or with the litany of the Blessed Virgin that was part of the enforced poetry in our household: Tower of Gold, Ark of the Covenant, Gate of Heaven, Morning Star, Health of the Sick, Refuge of Sinners, Comforter of the Afflicted. None of these things were consciously savoured at the time but I think the fact that I still recall them with ease, and can delight in them as verbal music, means that they were bedding the ear with a kind of linguistic hardcore that could be built on some day.

That was the unconscious bedding, but poetry involves a conscious savouring of words also. This came by way of reading poetry itself, and being required to learn pieces by heart, phrases even, like Keats's,[2] from 'Lamia':

> and his vessel now
> Grated the quaystone with her brazen prow,

or Wordsworth's:

> All shod with steel,
> We hiss'd along the polished ice,[3]

or Tennyson's:

> Old yew, which graspest at the stones
> That name the underlying dead,
> Thy fibres net the dreamless head,
> Thy roots are wrapped about the bones.[4]

These were picked up in my last years at school, touchstones of sorts, where the language could give you a kind of aural gooseflesh. At the university I was delighted in the first weeks to meet the moody energies of John Webster—'I'll make Italian cut-works in their guts / If ever I return'[5]—and later on to encounter the pointed masonry of Anglo-Saxon verse and to learn about the rich stratifications of the English language itself. Words alone were certain good.[6] I even went so far as to write these 'Lines to myself':

> In poetry I wish you would
> Avoid the lilting platitude.
> Give us poems humped and strong,
> Laced tight with thongs of song,

9. Suburb of Amsterdam, Holland. *Stuttgart* and *Leipzig*: cities in Germany. *Oslo*: capital of Norway.
1. Lighthouses by the seas surrounding Great Britain and Ireland, mentioned in the shipping forecast broadcast on BBC radio. *Sprung rhythm*: metrical system with a variable number of syllables per foot, developed by Gerard Manley Hopkins.
2. John Keats (1795–1821), English Romantic poet.
3. *The Prelude* 1.433–34.
4. *In Memoriam* 2.1–4, by English poet Alfred, Lord Tennyson (1809–1892).
5. From *The White Devil*, by English dramatist John Webster (c. 1580–1632).
6. Line 10 of Irish poet W. B. Yeats's "Song of the Happy Shepherd."

Poems that explode in silence
Without forcing, without violence.
Whose music is strong and clear and good
Like a saw zooming in seasoned wood.
You should attempt concrete expression,
Half-guessing, half-expression.

Ah well. Behind that was 'Ars Poetica', MacLeish's and Verlaine's, Eliot's 'objective correlative'[7] (half understood) and several critical essays (by myself and others) about 'concrete realization'. At the university I kept the whole thing at arm's length, read poetry for the noise and wrote about half a dozen pieces for the literary magazine. But nothing happened inside me. No experience. No epiphany. All craft—and not much of that—and no technique.

I think technique is different from craft. Craft is what you can learn from other verse. Craft is the skill of making. It wins competitions in the *Irish Times* or the *New Statesman*. It can be deployed without reference to the feelings or the self. It knows how to keep up a capable verbal athletic display; it can be content to be *vox et praeterea nihil*—all voice and nothing else— but not voice as in 'finding a voice'. Learning the craft is learning to turn the windlass at the well of poetry. Usually you begin by dropping the bucket halfway down the shaft and winding up a taking of air. You are miming the real thing until one day the chain draws unexpectedly tight and you have dipped into waters that will continue to entice you back. You'll have broken the skin on the pool of yourself. Your praties will be 'fit for digging'.

At that point it becomes appropriate to speak of technique rather than craft. Technique, as I would define it, involves not only a poet's way with words, his management of metre, rhythm and verbal texture; it involves also a definition of his stance towards life, a definition of his own reality. It involves the discovery of ways to go out of his normal cognitive bounds and raid the inarticulate: a dynamic alertness that mediates between the origins of feeling in memory and experience and the formal ploys that express these in a work of art. Technique entails the watermarking of your essential patterns of perception, voice and thought into the touch and texture of your lines; it is that whole creative effort of the mind's and body's resources to bring the meaning of experience within the jurisdiction of form. Technique is what turns, in Yeats's phrase, 'the bundle of accident and incoherence that sits down to breakfast' into 'an idea, something intended, complete'.[8]

It is indeed conceivable that a poet could have a real technique and a wobbly craft—I think this was true of Alun Lewis and Patrick Kavanagh[9]— but more often it is a case of a sure enough craft and a failure of technique. And if I were asked for a figure who represents pure technique, I would say a water diviner. You can't learn the craft of dowsing or divining[1]—it is a gift for being in touch with what is there, hidden and real, a gift for mediating between the latent resource and the community that wants it current and released. As Sir Philip Sidney[2] notes in his *Apologie for Poetry*: 'Among the Romans a Poet was called *Vates*, which is as much as a Diviner . . .'

---

7. Term coined by T. S. Eliot for a feature of a literary work designed to elicit specific emotional responses. *Ars Poetica*: the art of poetry (Latin); title of poems about poetry by American poet Archibald MacLeish (1892–1982) and French poet Paul Verlaine (1844–1896), and originally the title of a work by Latin poet Horace (65 B.C.E.–8 B.C.E.).

8. Phrases from Yeats's 1937 introduction to a proposed edition of his collected works, in vol. 1 of this anthology.

9. Irish poet (1904–1967). Alun Lewis (1915–1944), Welsh poet.

1. Using a divining rod, or dowsing rod, to search for underground water.

2. English poet and statesman (1554–1586).

The poem was written simply to allay an excitement and to name an experience, and at the same time to give the excitement and the experience a small *perpetuum mobile*[3] in language itself. I quote it here, not for its own technique but for the image of technique contained in it. The diviner resembles the poet in his function of making contact with what lies hidden, and in his ability to make palpable what was sensed or raised.

The Diviner

Cut from the green hedge a forked hazel stick
That he held tight by the arms of the V:
Circling the terrain, hunting the pluck
Of water, nervous, but professionally

Unfussed. The pluck came sharp as a sting.
The rod jerked with precise convulsions,
Spring water suddenly broadcasting
Through a green hazel its secret stations.

The bystanders would ask to have a try.
He handed them the rod without a word.
It lay dead in their grasp till nonchalantly
He gripped expectant wrists. The hazel stirred.

What I had taken as matter of fact as a youngster became a matter of wonder in memory. When I look at the thing now I am pleased that it ends with a verb, 'stirred', the heart of the mystery; and I am glad that 'stirred' chimes with 'word', bringing the two functions of *vates* into the one sound.

Technique is what allows that first stirring of the mind round a word or an image or a memory to grow towards articulation: articulation not necessarily in terms of argument or explication but in terms of its own potential for harmonious self-reproduction. The seminal excitement has to be granted conditions in which, in Hopkins's words, it 'selves, goes itself . . . crying / What I do is me, for that I came'.[4] Technique ensures that the first gleam attains its proper effulgence. And I don't just mean a felicity in the choice of words to flesh the theme—that is a problem also but it is not so critical. A poem can survive stylistic blemishes but it cannot survive a still-birth. The crucial action is pre-verbal, to be able to allow the first alertness or come-hither, sensed in a blurred or incomplete way, to dilate and approach as a thought or a theme or a phrase. Robert Frost[5] put it this way: 'a poem begins as a lump in the throat, a homesickness, a lovesickness. It finds the thought and the thought finds the words'. As far as I am concerned, technique is more vitally and sensitively connected with that first activity where the 'lump in the throat' finds 'the thought' than with 'the thought' finding 'the words'. That first emergence involves the divining, vatic, oracular function; the second, the making function. To say, as Auden did,[6] that a poem is a 'verbal contraption' is to keep one or two tricks up your sleeve.

Traditionally an oracle speaks in riddles, yielding its truths in disguise, offering its insights cunningly. And in the practice of poetry, there is a cor-

---

3. Perpetual motion (Latin).
4. From the poem beginning "As kingfishers catch fire, dragonflies draw flame."
5. American poet (1874–1963), quoted from a letter to Louis Untermeyer (1885–1977), American

editor.
6. W. H. Auden (1907–1973), Anglo-American poet, quoted from the essay "Making, Knowing and Judging."

responding occasion of disguise, a protean, chameleon moment when the lump in the throat takes protective colouring in the new element of thought. One of the best documented occasions in the canon of English poetry, as far as this process is concerned, is a poem that survived in spite of its blemish. In fact, the blemish has earned it a peculiar fame:

> High on a mountain's highest ridge,
> Where oft the stormy winter gale
> Cuts like a scythe, while through the clouds
> It sweeps from vale to vale;
> Not five yards from the mountain path,
> This thorn you on your left espy;
> And to the left, three yards beyond,
> You see a little muddy pond
> Of water never dry;
> I've measured it from side to side:
> 'Tis three feet long and two feet wide.

Those two final lines were probably more ridiculed than any other lines in *The Lyrical Ballads* yet Wordsworth maintained 'they ought to be liked'. That was in 1815, seventeen years after the poem had been composed; but five years later he changed them to 'Though but of compass small, and bare / To thirsting suns and parching air'. Craft, in more senses than one.

Yet far more important than the revision, for the purposes of this discussion, is Wordsworth's account of the poem's genesis. " 'The Thorn' ", he told Isabella Fenwick in 1843,

> arose out of my observing on the ridge of Quantock Hills, on a stormy day, a thorn which I had often passed in calm and bright weather without noticing it. I said to myself, 'Cannot I by some invention do as much to make this thorn permanently an impressive object, as the storm has made it to my eyes at this moment?' I began the poem accordingly, and composed it with great rapidity.

The storm, in other words, was nature's technique for granting the thorn-tree its epiphany, awakening in Wordsworth that engendering, heightened state which he describes at the beginning of *The Prelude*—again in relation to the inspiring influence of wind:

> For I, methought, while the sweet breath of Heaven
> Was blowing on my body, felt within
> A corresponding, mild, creative breeze,
> A vital breeze which travell'd gently on
> O'er things which it had made, and is become
> A tempest, a redundant energy
> Vexing its own creation.

This is exactly the kind of mood in which he would have 'composed with great rapidity'; the measured recollection of the letter where he makes the poem sound as if it were written to the thesis propounded (retrospectively) in the Preface of 1800—'cannot I by some invention make this thorn permanently an impressive object?'—probably tones down an instinctive, instantaneous recognition into a rational procedure. The technical triumph was to discover a means of allowing his slightly abnormal, slightly numinous vision of the thorn to 'deal out its being'.

What he did to turn 'the bundle of accident and incoherence' of that moment into 'something intended, complete' was to find, in Yeats's language, a mask. The poem as we have it is a ballad in which the speaker is a garrulous superstitious man, a sea captain, according to Wordsworth, who connects the thorn with murder and distress. For Wordsworth's own apprehension of the tree, he instinctively recognized, was basically superstitious: it was a standing over, a survival in his own sensibility of a magical way of responding to the natural world, of reading phenomena as signs, occurrences requiring divination. And in order to dramatize this, to transpose the awakened appetites in his consciousness into the satisfactions of a finished thing, he needed his 'objective correlative'. To make the thorn 'permanently an impressive object', images and ideas from different parts of his conscious and unconscious mind were attracted by almost magnetic power. The thorn in its new, wind-tossed aspect had become a field of force.

Into this field were drawn memories of what the ballads call 'the cruel mother' who murders her own baby:

> She leaned her back against a thorn
> All around the loney-o
> And there her little babe was born
> Down by the greenwood side-o

is how a surviving version runs in Ireland. But there have always been variations on this pattern of the woman who kills her baby and buries it. And the ballads are also full of briars and roses and thorns growing out of graves in symbolic token of the life and death of the buried one. So in Wordsworth's imagination the thorn grew into a symbol of tragic, feverish death, and to voice this the ballad mode came naturally; he donned the traditional mask of the tale-teller, legitimately credulous, entering and enacting a convention. The poem itself is a rapid and strange foray where Wordsworth discovered a way of turning the 'lump in the throat' into a 'thought', discovered a set of images, cadences and sounds that amplified his original visionary excitement into 'a redundant energy / Vexing its own creation':

> And some had sworn an oath that she
> Should be to public justice brought;
> And for the little infant's bones
> With spades they would have sought.
> But then the beauteous hill of moss
> Before their eyes began to stir;
> And for full fifty yards around
> The grass it shook upon the ground.

'The Thorn' is a nicely documented example of feeling getting into words, in ways that paralleled much in my own experience; although I must say that it is hard to discriminate between feeling getting into words and words turning into feeling, and it is only on posthumous occasions like this that the distinction arises. Moreover, it is dangerous for a writer to become too self-conscious about his own processes: to name them too definitively may have the effect of confining them to what is named. A poem always has elements of accident about it, which can be made the subject of inquest afterwards, but there is always a risk in conducting your own inquest: you might begin to believe the coroner in yourself rather than put your trust in the man in you who is capable of the accident. Robert Graves's[7] 'Dance of Words' puts this delightfully:

> To make them move, you should start from lightning
> And not forecast the rhythm: rely on chance
> Or so-called chance for its bright emergence
> Once lightning interpenetrates the dance.
>
> Grant them their own traditional steps and postures
> But see they dance it out again and again
> Until only lightning is left to puzzle over—
> The choreography plain and the theme plain.

What we are engaged upon here is a way of seeing that turns the lightning into 'the visible discharge of electricity between cloud and cloud or between cloud and ground' rather than its own puzzling, brilliant self. There is nearly always an element of the bolt from the blue about a poem's origin.

When I called my second book *Door into the Dark* I intended to gesture towards this idea of poetry as a point of entry into the buried life of the feelings or as a point of exit for it. Words themselves are doors; Janus[8] is to a certain extent their deity, looking back to a ramification of roots and associations and forward to a clarification of sense and meaning. And just as Wordsworth sensed a secret asking for release in the thorn, so in *Door into the Dark* there are a number of poems that arise out of the almost unnameable energies that, for me, hovered over certain bits of language and landscape.

The poem 'Undine', for example. It was the dark pool of the sound of the word that first took me: if our auditory imaginations were sufficiently attuned to plumb and sound a vowel, to unite the most primitive and civilized associations, the word 'undine' would probably suffice as a poem in itself. *Unda,* a wave, *undine,* a water-woman—a litany of undines would have ebb and flow, water and woman, wave and tide, fulfilment and exhaustion in its very rhythms. But, old two-faced vocable that it is, I discovered a more precise definition once, by accident, in a dictionary. An undine is a water-sprite who has to marry a human being and have a child by him before she can become human. With that definition, the lump in the throat, or rather the thump in the ear, *undine,* became a thought, a field of force that called up other images. One of these was an orphaned memory, without a context, obviously a very early one, of watching a man clearing out an old spongy growth from a drain between two fields, focusing in particular on the way the water, in the cleared-out place, as soon as the shovelfuls of sludge had been removed, the way the water began to run free, rinse itself clean of the soluble mud and make its own little channels and currents. And this image was gathered into a more conscious reading of the myth as being about the liberating, humanizing effect of sexual encounter. Undine was a cold girl who got what the dictionary called a soul through the experience of physical love. So the poem uttered itself out of that nexus—more short-winded than 'The Thorn', with less redundant energy, but still escaping, I hope, from my incoherence into the voice of the undine herself:

---

7. English poet (1895–1985).
8. Double-faced Roman god of doorways and bridges.

He slashed the briars, shovelled up grey silt
To give me right of way in my own drains
And I ran quick for him, cleaned out my rust.

He halted, saw me finally disrobed,
Running clear, with apparent unconcern.
Then he walked by me. I rippled and I churned

Where ditches intersected near the river
Until he dug a spade deep in my flank
And took me to him. I swallowed his trench

Gratefully, dispersing myself for love
Down in his roots, climbing his brassy grain—
But once he knew my welcome, I alone

Could give him subtle increase and reflection.
He explored me so completely, each limb
Lost its cold freedom. Human, warmed to him.

I once said it was a myth about agriculture, about the way water is tamed
and humanized when streams become irrigation canals, when water becomes
involved with seed. And maybe that is as good an explanation as any. The
paraphrasable extensions of a poem can be as protean as possible as long as
its elements remain firm. Words can allow you that two-faced approach also.
They stand smiling at the audience's way of reading them and winking back
at the poet's way of using them.

Behind this, of course, there is a good bit of symbolist theory. Yet in prac-
tice, you proceed by your own experience of what it is to write what you
consider a successful poem. You survive in your own esteem not by the
corroboration of theory but by the trust in certain moments of satisfaction
which you know intuitively to be moments of extension. You are confirmed
by the visitation of the last poem and threatened by the elusiveness of the
next one, and the best moments are those when your mind seems to implode
and words and images rush of their own accord into the vortex. Which hap-
pened to me once when the line 'We have no prairies' drifted into my head
at bedtime, and loosened a fall of images that constitute the poem 'Bogland',
the last one in *Door into the Dark*.

I had been vaguely wishing to write a poem about bogland, chiefly because
it is a landscape that has a strange assuaging effect on me, one with asso-
ciations reaching back into early childhood. We used to hear about bog-
butter, butter kept fresh for a great number of years under the peat. Then
when I was at school the skeleton of an elk had been taken out of a bog
nearby and a few of our neighbours had got their photographs in the paper,
peering out across its antlers. So I began to get an idea of bog as the memory
of the landscape, or as a landscape that remembered everything that hap-
pened in and to it. In fact, if you go round the National Museum in Dublin,
you will realize that a great proportion of the most cherished material heri-
tage of Ireland was 'found in a bog'. Moreover, since memory was the faculty
that supplied me with the first quickening of my own poetry, I had a tentative
unrealized need to make a congruence between memory and bogland and,

for the want of a better word, our national consciousness. And it all released itself after 'We have no prairies . . . '—but we have bogs.

At that time I was teaching modern literature in Queen's University, Belfast, and had been reading about the frontier and the west as an important myth in the American consciousness, so I set up—or rather, laid down—the bog as an answering Irish myth. I wrote it quickly the next morning, having slept on my excitement, and revised it on the hoof, from line to line, as it came[.][9] Again, as in the case of 'Digging', the seminal impulse had been unconscious. What generated the poem about memory was something lying beneath the very floor of memory, something I only connected with the poem months after it was written, which was a warning that older people would give us about going into the bog. They were afraid we might fall into the pools in the old workings so they put it about (and we believed them) that *there was no bottom* in the bog-holes. Little did they—or I—know that I would filch it for the last line of a book.

There was also in that book a poem called 'Requiem for the Croppies' which was written in 1966 when most poets in Ireland were straining to celebrate the anniversary of the 1916 Rising.[1] That rising was the harvest of seeds sown in 1798, when revolutionary republican ideals and national feeling coalesced in the doctrines of Irish republicanism and in the rebellion of 1798 itself—unsuccessful and savagely put down. The poem was born of and ended with an image of resurrection based on the fact that some time after the rebels were buried in common graves, these graves began to sprout with young barley, growing up from barley corn which the 'croppies' had carried in their pockets to eat while on the march. The oblique implication was that the seeds of violent resistance sowed in the Year of Liberty had flowered in what Yeats called 'the right rose tree' of 1916.[2] I did not realize at the time that the original heraldic murderous encounter between Protestant yeoman and Catholic rebel was to be initiated again in the summer of 1969, in Belfast, two months after the book was published.[3]

From that moment the problems of poetry moved from being simply a matter of achieving the satisfactory verbal icon to being a search for images and symbols adequate to our predicament. I do not mean liberal lamentation that citizens should feel compelled to murder one another or deploy their different military arms over the matter of nomenclatures such as British or Irish. I do not mean public celebrations or execrations of resistance or atrocity—although there is nothing necessarily unpoetic about such celebration, if one thinks of Yeats's 'Easter 1916'. I mean that I felt it imperative to discover a field of force in which, without abandoning fidelity to the processes and experience of poetry as I have outlined them, it would be possible to encompass the perspectives of a humane reason and at the same time to grant the religious intensity of the violence its deplorable authenticity and

9. The original essay reprinted "Bogland," on p. 725 of this volume.
1. In the week of Easter, 1916, Irish Republican nationalists in Dublin staged a revolt against British rule. Although the rising was technically a failure, the leaders of the rebellion became martyrs when executed by the British, further fueling Irish anger against British authorities. The rising of 1798, in which Irish Roman Catholics rose up against the Protestant British government, is often viewed as the inaugural moment of Irish republi-

canism.
2. In "The Rose Tree."
3. The devastating sectarian violence in Northern Ireland developed from the tensions between the Catholic minority and the Protestant majority. In 1969, unrest generated by the Catholic civil rights movement was countered by police action, and in the early 1970s, British troops entered Northern Ireland. Acts of violence were perpetrated by both sides and hundreds of civilians had been killed at the time that Heaney delivered his lecture.

complexity. And when I say religious, I am not thinking simply of the sectarian division. To some extent the enmity can be viewed as a struggle between the cults and devotees of a god and a goddess. There is an indigenous territorial numen, a tutelar of the whole island, call her Mother Ireland, Kathleen Ni Houlihan, the poor old woman, the Shan Van Vocht,[4] whatever; and her sovereignty has been temporarily usurped or infringed by a new male cult whose founding fathers were Cromwell, William of Orange and Edward Carson,[5] and whose godhead is incarnate in a rex or caesar resident in a palace in London. What we have is the tail-end of a struggle in a province between territorial piety and imperial power.

Now I realize that this idiom is remote from the agnostic world of economic interest whose iron hand operates in the velvet glove of 'talks between elected representatives', and remote from the political manoeuvres of power-sharing; but it is not remote from the psychology of the Irishmen and Ulstermen who do the killing, and not remote from the bankrupt psychology and mythologies implicit in the terms Irish Catholic and Ulster Protestant. The question, as ever, is 'How with this rage shall beauty hold a plea?' And my answer is, by offering 'befitting emblems of adversity'.[6]

Some of these emblems I found in a book that was published in English translation, appositely, the year the killing started, in 1969. And again appositely, it was entitled *The Bog People*. It was chiefly concerned with preserved bodies of men and women found in the bogs of Jutland, naked, strangled or with their throats cut, disposed under the peat since early Iron Age times. The author, P. V. Glob, argues convincingly that a number of these, and in particular the Tollund Man, whose head is now preserved near Aarhus in the museum at Silkeburg,[7] were ritual sacrifices to the Mother Goddess, the goddess of the ground who needed new bridegrooms each winter to bed with her in her sacred place, in the bog, to ensure the renewal and fertility of the territory in the spring. Taken in relation to the tradition of Irish political martyrdom for that cause whose icon is Kathleen Ni Houlihan, this is more than an archaic barbarous rite: it is an archetypal pattern. And the unforgettable photographs of these victims blended in my mind with photographs of atrocities, past and present, in the long rites of Irish political and religious struggles. When I wrote this poem, I had a completely new sensation, one of fear. It was a vow to go on pilgrimage and I felt as it came to me—and again it came quickly—that unless I was deeply in earnest about what I was saying, I was simply invoking dangers for myself. It is called 'The Tollund Man'[.][8]

And just how persistent the barbaric attitudes are, not only in the slaughter but in the psyche, I discovered, again when the *frisson* of the poem itself had passed, and indeed after I had fulfilled the vow and gone to Jutland, 'the holy blisful martyr for to seke'.[9] I read the following in a chapter on 'The Religion of the Pagan Celts' by the Celtic scholar, Anne Ross:

4. Popular figures personifying Ireland as a woman.
5. Northern Irish politician (1854–1935), who led the Protestant anti–Home Rule movement, which helped ensure that Northern Ireland did not become part of the Irish Republic. Oliver Cromwell (1599–1658): English soldier, who in the wake of the English Civil War acted as lord protector of England, Scotland, and Ireland from 1653–58 and brutally suppressed an Irish rebellion in 1649. William of Orange (1650–1702): Protestant King William III of Great Britain, who defeated the Catholic King James II.
6. The first quotation is from Shakespeare's Sonnet 65; the second, from Yeats's "Meditations in Time of Civil War."
7. Like Aarhus, a city in the eastern Jutland region of Denmark.
8. The original essay quoted "The Tollund Man," on p. 726 of this volume.
9. From the "General Prologue" to the *Canterbury Tales,* by Geoffrey Chaucer (c. 1342/43–1400).

Moving from sanctuaries and shrines . . . we come now to consider the nature of the actual deities. . . . But before going on to look at the nature of some of the individual deities and their cults, one can perhaps bridge the gap as it were by considering a symbol which, in its way, sums up the whole of Celtic pagan religion and is as representative of it as is, for example, the sign of the cross in Christian contexts. This is the symbol of the severed human head; in all its various modes of iconographic representation and verbal presentation, one may find the hard core of Celtic religion. It is indeed . . . a kind of shorthand symbol for the entire religious outlook for the pagan Celts.[1]

My sense of occasion and almost awe as I vowed to go to pray to the Tollund Man and assist at his enshrined head had a longer ancestry than I had at the time realized.

I began by suggesting that my point of view involved poetry as divination, as a restoration of the culture to itself. In Ireland in this century it has involved for Yeats and many others an attempt to define and interpret the present by bringing it into significant relationship with the past, and I believe that effort in our present circumstances has to be urgently renewed. But here we stray from the realm of technique into the realm of tradition; to forge a poem is one thing, to forge the uncreated conscience of the race, as Stephen Dedalus[2] put it, is quite another and places daunting pressures and responsibilities on anyone who would risk the name of poet.

1974   1979, 1980

---

1. From Ross's *Pagan Celtic Britain: Studies in Iconography and Tradition* (1967).
2. Protagonist of *A Portrait of the Artist as a Young Man* (1916), by Irish novelist James Joyce (1882–

1941); at the conclusion of that work, Stephen Dedalus vows "to forge in the smithy of my soul the uncreated conscience of my race."

JAMAICA LANGUAGE

The poet Louise Bennett, who has been called "the mother of the Jamaican language," or Creole, wittily mocks the idea that Standard English is the only worthy variety of the English language. In this radio monologue, one of many broadcast between 1966 and 1982 as part of Bennett's program "Miss Lou's Views," Bennett, through her popular persona as Aunty Roachy, ridicules the view that Jamaican Creole is a corruption of "Standard English," which is itself derived from other languages and constantly evolving. Ever since slavery, speakers of Jamaican English, which combines African languages with English, have been able to "meck it soun like it no got no English at all eena it," strategically thwarting outsiders from understanding. For all the influences on Jamaican Creole, it is a distinctive product of an Afro-Caribbean people's historical experience and remains vibrant and richly expressive today. Originally broadcast in 1979–81, the monologue has been reprinted from *Aunty Roachy Seh* (1993), ed. Mervyn Morris.

LOUISE BENNETT

Jamaica Language

Listen, na!
My Aunty Roachy seh dat it bwile[1] her temper an really bex[2] her fi true anytime she hear anybody a style we Jamaican dialec as "corruption of the English language." For if dat be de case, den dem shoulda call English Language corruption of Norman French an Latin an all dem tarra[3] language what dem seh dat English is derived from.

Oonoo[4] hear de wud? "Derived." English is a derivation but Jamaica Dialec is corruption! What a unfairity!

Aunty Roachy seh dat if Jamaican Dialec is corruption of de English Language, den it is also a corruption of de African Twi Language to, a oh!

For Jamaican Dialec did start when we English forefahders did start mus-an-boun[5] we African ancestors fi stop talk fi-dem African Language altogedder an learn fi talk so-so[6] English, because we English forefahders couldn understan what we African ancestors-dem wasa seh to dem one anodder when dem wasa talk eena dem African Language to dem one annodder!

But we African ancestors-dem pop[7] we English forefahders-dem. Yes! Pop dem an disguise up de English Language fi projec fi-dem African Language in such a way dat we English forefahders-dem still couldn understan what we African ancestors-dem wasa talk bout when dem wasa talk to dem one annodder!

Yes, bwoy!

So till now, aldoah plenty a we Jamaica Dialec wuds-dem come from English wuds, yet, still an for all, de talkin is so-so Jamaican, an when we ready we can meck it soun like it no got no English at all eena it! An no so-so English-talkin smaddy[8] cyaan[9] understan weh we a seh if we doan want dem to understan weh we a seh, a oh!

An we fix up we dialec wud fi soun like whatsoever we a talk bout, look like! For instance, when we seh sinting "kooroo-kooroo"[1] up, yuh know seh dat it mark-up mark-up. An if we seh one house "rookoo-rookoo"[2] up, it is plain to see dat it ole an shaky-shaky. An when we seh smaddy "boogoo-yagga", everybody know seh dat him outa-order; an if we seh dem "boonoo-noonoos",[3] yuh know seh dat dem nice an we like dem. Mmmm.

Aunty Roachy seh dat Jamaica Dialec is more direc an to de point dan English. For all like how English smaddy would seh "Go away", Jamaican jus seh "Gweh!" An de only time we use more wuds dan English is when we want fi meck someting soun strong: like when dem seh sinting "batter-batter" up, it soun more expressive dan if yuh seh "it is battered." But most of all

1. Boils.
2. Vexes.
3. Other.
4. You (plural).
5. Compel.
6. Only.
7. Outwitted.

8. People.
9. Can't.
1. Rough; rocky. *Sinting*: something.
2. Unsteady.
3. Beautiful; wonderful (term of endearment). *Boogoo-yagga*: ill-mannered.

we fling weh all de bangarang an trimmins[4] dem an only lef what wantin, an dat's why when English smaddy seh "I got stuck by a prickle" Jamaican jus seh "Macca[5] jook me"!

So fi-we Jamaica Language is not no English Language corruption at all, a oh! An we no haffi shame a it, like one gal who did go a Englan go represent we Jamaican folk-song "One shif me got" as "De sole underwear garment I possess", and go sing "Mumma, Mumma, dem ketch Puppa" as "Mother, Mother, they apprehended Father"!

Ay ya yie!

1979–81   1993

---

4. Miscellaneous trash and trimmings.
5. A prickly plant.

SEMBLANCE

This essay exemplifies the fusion of philosophy and linguistic experimentation that marks both the poetry and the prose of Charles Bernstein, a central contemporary exponent and practitioner of avant-garde poetry. Composed for the symposium "Death of the Referent?" and published while Bernstein was coediting $L=A=N=G=U=A=G=E$ magazine with Bruce Andrews, "Semblance" distills the postmodernist tenets of Language poetry and explains Bernstein's own practice as a poet. By freeing language from normative rules of syntax and grammar, reference and narrative, Bernstein hopes to achieve in his poetry a new level of musical, sensory, associative, and conceptual fecundity. Drawing on structuralist and poststructuralist philosophies of language, as well as such poetic precursors as the Russian Futurist Velimir Khlebnikov and projectivist Charles Olson, Bernstein emphasizes that words are enmeshed in complicated relationships with one another, in contrast to a correspondence theory of language, in which each word's primary relationship is to the named object. The poet's task, he argues, is neither to submit to nor to deny the referentiality of language, but to electrify it by removing the constraints of conventional structures of meaning. Originally printed in *Reality Studios* 2.4 (1980), the essay has been reprinted from *Content's Dream: Essays 1975–1984* (1986, 2001).

CHARLES BERNSTEIN

Semblance

> It's as if each of these things has a life of its own. You can stretch
> them, deform them and even break them apart, and they still have
> an inner cohesion that keeps them together.

Not "death" of the referent—rather a recharged use of the multivalent referential vectors that any word has, how words in combination tone and modify the associations made for each of them, how 'reference' then is not a one-on-one relation to an 'object' but a perceptual dimension that closes in to pinpoint, nail down (*this* word), sputters omnitropically[1] (the in in the which of who where what wells), refuses the build up of image track/projection while, pointillistically,[2] fixing a reference at each turn (fills vats ago lodges spire), or, that much rarer case (Peter Inman's *Platin* and David Melnick's *Pcoet* two recent examples) of "zaum"[3] (so-called transrational, pervasively neologistic)—"ig ok aberflappi"—in which reference, deprived of its automatic reflex reaction of word/stimulus image/response roams over the range of associations suggested by the word, word shooting off referential vectors like the energy field in a Kirillian photograph.[4]

All of which are ways of releasing the energy inherent in the referential dimension of language, that these dimensions are the material of which the writing is made, define its medium. Making the structures of meaning in language more tangible and in that way allowing for the maximum resonance for the medium—the traditional power that writing has always had to make experience palpable not by simply pointing to it but by (re)creating its conditions.[5]

Point then, at first instance, to see the medium of writing—our area of operation—as maximally open in vocabulary, forms, shapes, phoneme/morpheme/word/phrase/sentence[6] order, etc., so that possible areas covered, ranges of things depicted, suggested, critiqued, considered, etc., have an outer limit (asymptotic[7]) of what can be thought, what can (might) be. But then, taking that as zero degree, not to gesturalize the possibility of poetry to operate in this 'hyperspace', but to create works (poems) within it.

---

1. In all figures of speech.
2. Pointillism is a Postimpressionist style of painting in which small dots of color seem to fuse when seen from afar.
3. Term associated with the Russian Futurist Velimir Khlebnikov (1885–1922), who treated words as things in attempting to develop a transrational language.
4. Colorful image that displays the aura surrounding an object.
5. "Alan Davies has objected that language and experience are separate realms and that the separation should be maximized in writing, in this way questioning the value of using language to make experience palpable.—But I don't mean 'experience' in the sense of a picture/image/representation that is calling back to an already constituted experience. Rather, language itself constitutes experience at every moment (in reading and otherwise). Experience, then, is not tied into representation exclusively but is a separate 'perception'-like

category. (& perception not necessarily as in perception onto a physical/preconstituted world, as "eyes" in the [Charles] Olson sense, that is, not just onto a matrix-qua-the world but as operating/projecting/composing activity.) The point is, then, that experience is a dimension necessarily built into language—that far from being avoidable, or a choice, it is a property. So this view attempts to rethink representational or pictorial or behaviorist notions of what 'experience' is, i.e., experience is not inextricably linked to representation, normative syntax, images, but rather, the other way around, is a synthetic, generative activity—"in the beginning was the word" & so on, or that's our 'limit' of beginnings" [Bernstein's note].
6. *Phoneme*: smallest unit of speech distinguishing one word (or part of a word) from another. *Morpheme*: smallest grammatical unit of speech.
7. In math, an asymptote is a straight line approaching but never reaching a curve.

The order of the words, the syntax, creates possibilities for images, pictures, representations, descriptions, invocation, ideation, critique, relation, projection, etc. Sentences that follow standard grammatical patterns allow the accumulating references to enthrall the reader by diminishing diversions from a constructed representation. In this way, each word's references work in harmony by reinforcing a spatiotemporal order conventionalized by the bulk of writing practice that creates the 'standard'. "The lamp sits atop the table in the study"—each word narrowing down the possibilities of each other, limiting the interpretation of each word's meaning by creating an ever more specific context. In a similar way, associations with sentences are narrowed down by conventional expository or narrational paragraph structure, which directs attention away from the sentence as meaning generating event and onto the 'content' depicted. By shifting the contexts in which even a fairly 'standard' sentence finds itself, as in some of the prose-format work of Barrett Watten,[8] the seriality of the ordering of sentences within a paragraph displaces from its habitual surrounding the projected representational fixation that the sentence conveys. "Words elect us. The lamp sits atop the table in the study. The tower is burnt orange. . . ." By rotating sentences within a paragraph (a process analogous to jump cutting in film) according to principles generated by and unfolding in the work (rather than in accordance with representational construction patterns) a perceptual vividness is intensified for each sentence since the abruptness of the cuts induces a greater desire to savor the tangibility of each sentence before it is lost to the next, determinately other, sentence. Juxtapositions not only suggest unsuspected relations but induce reading along ectoskeletal and citational lines. As a result, the operant mechanisms of meaning are multiplied and patterns of projection in reading are less restricted. The patterns of projection are not, however, undetermined. The text operates at a level that not only provokes projections by each sentence but by the sequencing of the sentences suggests lines or paths for them to proceed along. At the same time, circumspection about the nature and meaning of the projections is called forth. The result is both a self-reflectiveness and an intensification of the items/conventions of the social world projected/suggested/provoked. A similar process can also take place within sentences and phrases and not only intersententially. Syntactic patterns are composed which allow for this combination of projection and reflection in the movement from word to word. "For as much as, within the because, tools their annoyance, tip to toward."—But, again, to acknowledge this as the space of the text, and still to leave open what is to be said, what projections desire these reflections.

The sense of music in poetry: the music of meaning—emerging, fogging, contrasting, etc. Tune attunement in understanding—the meaning sounds. It's impossible to separate prosody from the structure (the form and content seen as an interlocking figure) of a given poem. You can talk about strategies of meaning generation, shape, the kinds of sounds accented, the varieties of measurement (of scale, of number, of line length, of syllable order, of word length, of phrase length, or measure as punctuation, of punctuation as metrics). But no one has primacy—the music is the orchestrating these into the poem, the angles one plays against another, the shading. In much of my own work: working at angles to the strong tidal pull of an expected sequence of

---

8. Language poet, critic, and professor (b. 1948).

a sentence—or by cutting off a sentence or phrase midway and counting on the mind to complete where the poem goes off in another direction, giving two vectors at once—the anticipated projection underneath and the actual wording above.

My interest in not conceptualizing the field of the poem as a unitary plane, and so also not using overall structural programs: that any prior principle of composition violates the priority I want to give to the inherence of surface, to the total necessity in the durational space of the poem for every moment to *count*. The moment not subsumed into a schematic structure, hence instance of it, but at every juncture creating (synthesizing) the structure. So not to have the work resolve at the level of the "field" if this is to mean a uniplanar surface within which the poem operates. Structure that can't be separated from decisions made within it, constantly poking through the expected parameters. Rather than having a single form or shape or idea of the work pop out as you read, the structure itself is pulled into a moebius-like[9] twisting momentum. In this process, the language takes on a centrifugal force that seems to trip it out of the poem, turn it out from itself, exteriorizing it. Textures, vocabularies, discourses, constructivist modes of radically different character are not integrated into a field as part of a predetermined planar architecture; the gaps and jumps compose a space within shifting parameters, types and styles of discourse constantly crisscrossing, interacting, creating new gels. (Intertextual, interstructural . . .) (Bruce Andrews[1] has suggested the image of a relief map for the varying kinds of referential vectors—reference to different domains of discourse, references made by different processes—in some of his work in which words and phrases are visually spaced out over the surface of the page. However, the structural dissonance in these works is counterbalanced by the perspicacious poise of the overall design, which tends to even-out the surface tension.)

Writing as a process of pushing whatever way, or making the piece cohere as far as can: stretching my mind—to where I know it makes sense but not quite why—suspecting relations that I understand, that make the sense of the ready-to-hand—i.e. pushing the composition to the very limits of sense, meaning, to that razor's edge where judgment/aesthetic sense is all I can go on (know-how). (Maybe what's to get beyond in Olson's field theory[2] is just the idea of form as a single web, a unified field, one matrix, with its implicit idea of 'perception' onto a given world rather than, as well, onto the language through which the world is constituted.) So that the form, the structure, that, finally, is the poem, has emerged, is come upon, is made.

1980

---

9. That is, like a Möbius strip.
1. Language poet (b. 1948).
2. For Charles Olson's theory of "field composi-

tion," in which the poet "puts himself in the open," see his essay "Projective Verse," reprinted above.

Where Mirrors Are Windows

The distinguished Indian poet A. K. Ramanujan was also an award-winning translator and scholar of South Asian languages and literatures. In this essay on the reflexivity and continuity of Indian poetry, he proposes an indigenous Indian model of literary inheritance. Revising T. S. Eliot's Europe-centered "Tradition and the Individual Talent," he argues that the literatures of the world are "indissolubly plural" and interact in complex intertextual networks. He traces the intricate web of relationships connecting Indian poetry in myriad languages from various traditions. Indian poems are, in his view, internally self-reflexive and also "reflect, invert, and subvert" one another: "Every poem resonates with the absent presence of others that sound with it, like the unstruck strings of a sitar." Ramanujan's analysis also bears indirectly on the work of many postwar anglophone poets of South Asia, including his own. Writing poetry in English, as well as Kannada and Tamil, he cites such Western poets as W. B. Yeats and Wallace Stevens alongside such Sanskrit epics as the *Rāmāyaṇa*. The essay has been excerpted from the journal *History of Religions* 28.3 (1989).

A. K. RAMANUJAN

From Where Mirrors Are Windows: Toward an Anthology of Reflections

* * *

One way of defining diversity for India is to say what the Irishman is said to have said about trousers. When asked whether trousers were singular or plural, he said, "Singular at the top and plural at the bottom." This is the view espoused by people who believe that Indian traditions are organized as a pan-Indian Sanskritic Great Tradition (in the singular) and many local Little Traditions (in the plural). Older Indian notions of *mārga* and *deśi*[1] and modern Indian politicians' rhetoric about unity in diversity fall in line with the same position. The official Indian literary academy, the Sahitya Akademi, has the motto, "Indian literature is one but written in many languages." I, for one, would prefer the plural, "Indian literatures," and would wonder if something would remain the same if it is written in several languages, knowing as I do that even in the same language, "a change of style is a change of subject," as Wallace Stevens[2] would say.

Another way of talking about a culture like the Indian is through the analogy of a hologram[3]—that is, to say that any section is a cross-section, any piece of it is a true representation of the whole, as any cell of the body is

---

1. *Mārga* and *deśi*: ancient Sanskrit distinction between classical, learned (*mārga*) and local, folk (*deśi*) forms of culture.
2. American poet (1879–1955), quoted from his *Adagia*, vol. 1 of this anthology.
3. Which achieves its three-dimensional appearance by encoding, in each portion of the object, information about the whole.

supposed to be a true sample of the whole body. Linguists and anthropologists, especially structuralists in general, have operated on this assumption for a while. To them, any native speaker contains the whole of his language; any informant, any myth or ritual, contains the whole of the culture. To study his or its grammar is to study the grammar of the whole language or culture. Such a holographic view implies uniform texture, the replication of one structure in all systems of a culture, without negations, warps, or discontinuities and with no pockets in space or time. It is a very attractive view, especially to people in a hurry, and I have myself held it for many years, though somewhat uneasily. In this view, the classics of Indian civilization, the *Mahābhārata*, the *Rāmāyaṇa*, and the *Purāṇas*,[4] as well as the folklore, the so-called Little (or as we say in India, the "little little") Traditions, are all of one piece. At worst, the latter are garbled versions of the former, simplified for or by the little man. The Great Traditions for the elite, and the little Little Traditions for the little little folks, that is, semi- or illiterate, rural, regional people who are competent only in a mother tongue—but basically there is no difference in kind, only in quality. At its best, it is a form of monism; at its worst, it is a form of cultural imperialism, an upstairs/downstairs view of India.

I would like to suggest the obvious: that cultural traditions in India are indissolubly plural and often conflicting but are organized through at least two principles, (*a*) context-sensitivity and (*b*) reflexivity of various sorts, both of which constantly generate new forms out of the old ones. What we call Brahminism, Bhakti traditions, Buddhism, Jainism, Tantra,[5] tribal traditions and folklore, and lastly, modernity itself, are the most prominent of these systems. They are responses to previous and surrounding traditions; they invert, subvert, and convert their neighbors. Furthermore, each of these terms, like what we call India itself, is "a verbal tent with three-ring circuses" going on inside them. Further dialogic divisions are continuously in progress. They look like single entities, like neat little tents, only from a distance.

Reflexivity takes many forms: awareness of self and other, mirroring, distorted mirroring, parody, family resemblances and rebels, dialectic, antistructure, utopias and dystopias, the many ironies connected with these responses, and so on. In this paper on Indian literary texts and their relations to each other ("intertextuality," if you will), I will concentrate on three related kinds of reflexivity. I shall call them (1) *responsive*, where text A responds to text B in ways that define both A and B; (2) *reflexive*, where text A reflects on text B, relates itself to it directly or inversely; (3) *self-reflexive*, where a text reflects on itself or its kind. The parts or texts in relation 1 may be called co-texts, in 2, countertexts, and in 3, metatexts. We could also speak of pretexts, intertexts, subtexts, and so on. The vast variety of Indian literature, oral and written, over the centuries, in hundreds of languages and dialects, offers an intricate but open network of such relations, producing families of texts as well as texts that are utterly individual in their effect, detail, and temporal/regional niches. But these relations are perceived by native commentators and by readers. To them, texts do not come in historical stages

---

4. Collection of ancient Hindu tales. *Mahābhārata* and *Rāmāyaṇa*: the two major Sanskrit epics.
5. Tradition of esoteric texts and practices within some Hindu, Buddhist, and Jaina sects. *Brahminism*: an orthodox Hinduism emphasizing the pantheism of the Vedas (ancient sacred writings),

family ceremonies, and ritual sacrifices. *Bhakti*: devotional movement of Hinduism emphasizing the emotional relation between a devotee and a personal god. *Jainism*: Indian religion emphasizing enlightenment through *ahimsa*, or nonviolence to all living things.

but form "a simultaneous order," where every new text within a series confirms yet alters the whole order ever so slightly, and not always so slightly. T. S. Eliot spoke of a simultaneous order for European literature, but the phrase applies even more strongly to Indian literary traditions, especially until the nineteenth century.[6] Modernity disrupted the whole tradition of reflexivity with new notions of originality and the autonomy of single works. Among other things, the printing press radically altered the relation of audience to author and of author to work, and it bifurcated the present and the past so that the pastness of the past is more keenly felt than the presence of the past. Reflexive elements may occur in various sizes: one part of the text may reflect on another part; one text may reflect on another; a whole tradition may invert, negate, rework, and revalue another. Where cultures (like the "Indian") are stratified yet interconnected, where the different communities communicate but do not commune, the texts of one stratum tend to reflect on those of another: encompassment, mimicry, criticism and conflict, and other power relations are expressed by such reflexivities. Self-conscious contrasts and reversals also mark off and individuate the groups—especially if they are closely related, like twins. Closely related sects, like the *teṅkalai* (Southern) and *vaṭakalai* (Northern) sects of Tamil Śrī Vaiṣnavism, serve even food in different orders, and self-consciously list "eighteen differences."[7]

The rather grossly conceived Great Tradition and Little Traditions are only two such moieties:[8] as suggested earlier, Bhakti, Tantra, and other countertraditions, as well as Buddhism, Jainism, and, for later times, Islam and Christianity, should be included in this web of intertextuality. I shall draw here only on earlier Indian literatures for my instances. Stereotypes, foreign views, and native self-images on the part of some groups all tend to regard one part (say, the Brahminical texts[9] or folklore) as the original, and the rest as variations, derivatives, aberrations, so we tend to get monolithic conceptions. But the civilization, if it can be described at all, has to be described in terms of all these dynamic interrelations between different traditions, their texts, ideologies, social arrangements, and so forth. Reflexivities are crucial to the understanding of both the order and diversity, the openness and the closures, of this civilization. One may sometimes feel that "mirror on mirror mirrored is all the show."[1] Such an anthology can be made about other aspects of the culture, like ritual, philosophy, food, and sociolinguistic patterns, or across them.[2] * * *

* * *

Furthermore, in such traditions, poems do not come singly, but in sequences often arranged in tens, hundreds, sometimes thousands: sharing motifs, images, structures, yet playing variations that individuate each poem. Every poem resonates with the absent presence of others that sound with it,

6. From "Tradition and the Individual Talent," by T. S. Eliot (1880–1965), vol. 1 of this anthology.
7. "A. Govindacarya, ' "The Aṣṭadaśa-bhedas," or the Eighteen Points of Doctrinal Differences between the Tengalais (Southerners) and the Vadagalais (Northerners) of the Visistadvaita Vaisnava School, South India,' " *Journal of the Royal Asiatic Society* (1910), p. 1103–12" [Ramanujan's note]. *Tamil:* south Indian and Sri Lankan language and people. *Śrī Vaiṣnavism:* major south Indian sect

of Hinduism dedicated to the worship of Vishnu.
8. Parts, components.
9. Early Sanskrit texts such as the Vedas and the Upanishads.
1. From "The Statues," by Irish poet W. B. Yeats (1865–1939).
2. "See A. K. Ramanujan, 'Food for Thought: Towards an Anthology of Hindu Food Images'" [Ramanujan's note], reprinted in his *Collected Essays* (1999).

like the unstruck strings of a sitar. So we respond to a system of presences and absences; our reading then is not linear but what has been called "radial."[3] Every poem is part of a large self-reflexive paradigm; it relates to all others in absentia, gathers ironies, allusions; one text becomes the context of others. Each is precisely foregrounded against a background of all the others.

Once such genres are established, they not only classify, they generate. The settled conventions make possible, indeed cry out for, another kind of reflexivity. Poems beget metapoems that reflect on themselves or their kind, make the audience conscious of the genre and its limits. Genres give rise to antigenres and metagenres that still use all the properties of the genre they are parodying or reflecting on. * * *

* * *

What is merely suggested in one poem may become central in a "repetition" or an "imitation" of it. Mimesis is never only mimesis, for it evokes the earlier image in order to play with it and make it mean other things. When the "same" Indian poem appears in different ages and bodies of poetry, we cannot dismiss them as interlopers and anachronisms, for they become signifiers in a new system: mirrors again that become windows.

I have suggested above, and elsewhere, that in traditions like the Indian, different genres (and generic texts like these epics) specialize in different "provinces of reality."[4] What one does, another does not. The realities of the civilization are expressed in a spectrum of forms, where one complements, contradicts, reflects, and refracts another—we have to take them together to make sense of the civilization and catch a glimpse of the complex whole. Each has to be read in the light of others, as each is defined by the presence of others in the memory of both poet and audience—like the Mahādēvi poem in the light of texts that speak of *māyā*, the three *guṇas*, *vāsanas*,[5] and so on or the Bengali love-death poem in the context of the Vedic hymn about death.

Contradictions, inversions, multiple views, multiforms affecting and animating one another, expressing conflict and dissent through the same repertoire of forms—all these are ways the traditions relate to each other. Reflexivity binds them together and gives them a common yet creative language for dissent. Without the other, there is no language for the self.

Among Western thinkers, Bakhtin's dialogism seems to anticipate some of these thoughts. Speaking of Dostoevsky's heroes, he says, "Every thought . . . senses itself to be from the very beginning a rejoinder in an unfinished dialogue. Such thought is not impelled towards a well-rounded, finalized, systematically monologic whole. It lives a tense life on the borders of someone else's consciousness."[6]

* * *

3. "Jerome J. McGann, 'Theory of Texts,' *London Review of Books* (February 18, 1988), p. 21" [Ramanujan's note].
4. "A. K. Ramanujan, 'Two Realms of Kannada Folklore,' in *Another Harmony: New Essays in South Asian Folklore*, ed. Stuart Blackburn and A. K. Ramanujan (Berkeley and Los Angeles: University of California Press, 1986), pp. 41–75" [Ramanujan's note].
5. Unconscious areas from which psychic energies develop. *Mahādēvi*: great goddess, wife of Siva.

Māyā: creative energy. *Guṇas*: the three qualities— *sattva* (purity), *rajas* (energy), and *tamas* (inertia)— from which all things are created.
6. "Quoted in Katarina Clark and Michael Holquist, *Mikhail Bakhtin* (Cambridge, Mass.: Harvard University Press, Belknap, 1984), p. 242" [Ramanujan's note]. Mikhail Bakhtin (1895– 1975), Russian critic who developed his theories about dialogic and polyphonic languages in his readings of the work of the Russian novelist Fyodor Dostoyevsky (1821–1881).

Mirror on mirror. Doubles, shadow worlds, upside-down reflections, are common in Indian myth and story. When Viśvāmitra the sage sent his protégé Triśaṅku to heaven and the gods would not accept him and threw him down, the sage held him midair with his powers. And, piqued by his own failure to send Triśaṅku to heaven, he decided to make a second world exclusively for him, a world like the first but a bit botched: it is said that the buffalo is Viśvāmitra's version of the cow, the donkey his version of the horse, and so on.

The creation of doubles is a favorite literary device. In some Rāmāyaṇas, the chaste Sītā is not abducted at all, only a shadow double suffers all the hardships. Seducers in Indian texts appear as replicas of the husband. When Śiva creates, he creates clones of himself. As with DNA, to create is to project one's copies onto the world. * * *

* * *

1989

THE ANTILLES: FRAGMENTS OF EPIC MEMORY

In this lecture, delivered on the occasion of his acceptance of the 1992 Nobel Prize in Literature, Derek Walcott celebrates the cultural and linguistic hybridity and heterogeneity of the Antillean islands of the Caribbean, where peoples from around the world live side by side, creating new identities and fresh imaginative possibilities. Walcott recognizes the continuities with the Old World while rejecting the idea that the art and culture of the islands are mere imitations of African, Asian, or European originals. He also acknowledges the pain and horror of Caribbean history—the massacre and destruction of Amerindian peoples, the enslavement and importation of African slaves, and the indentured servitude of East Indians—but insists that the West Indian poet transfigure such inheritances in an art of awe, wonder, even ecstasy before the splendor of the New World. First published as Walcott's *Nobel Lecture* (December 7, 1992), the piece has been reprinted from *What the Twilight Says* (1998).

DEREK WALCOTT

The Antilles: Fragments of Epic Memory

Felicity is a village in Trinidad on the edge of the Caroni plain, the wide central plain that still grows sugar and to which indentured cane cutters were brought after emancipation,[1] so the small population of Felicity is East Indian, and on the afternoon that I visited it with friends from America, all the faces along its road were Indian, which, as I hope to show, was a moving, beautiful thing, because this Saturday afternoon *Ramleela,* the epic dramatization of the Hindu epic the *Ramayana,*[2] was going to be performed, and the costumed actors from the village were assembling on a field strung with different-coloured flags, like a new gas station, and beautiful Indian boys in red and black were aiming arrows haphazardly into the afternoon light. Low blue mountains on the horizon, bright grass, clouds that would gather colour before the light went. Felicity! What a gentle Anglo-Saxon name for an epical memory.

Under an open shed on the edge of the field, there were two huge armatures of bamboo that looked like immense cages. They were parts of the body of a god, his calves or thighs, which, fitted and reared, would make a gigantic effigy. This effigy would be burnt as a conclusion to the epic. The cane structures flashed a predictable parallel: Shelley's sonnet on the fallen statue of Ozymandias[3] and his empire, that "colossal wreck" in its empty desert.

Drummers had lit a fire in the shed and they eased the skins of their tablas[4] nearer the flames to tighten them. The saffron flames, the bright grass, and the hand-woven armatures of the fragmented god who would be burnt were not in any desert where imperial power had finally toppled but were part of a ritual, evergreen season that, like the cane-burning harvest, is annually repeated, the point of such sacrifice being its repetition, the point of the destruction being renewal through fire.

Deities were entering the field. What we generally call "Indian music" was blaring from the open platformed shed from which the epic would be narrated. Costumed actors were arriving. Princes and gods, I supposed. What an unfortunate confession! "Gods, I suppose" is the shrug that embodies our African and Asian diasporas. I had often thought of but never seen *Ramleela,* and had never seen this theatre, an open field, with village children as warriors, princes, and gods. I had no idea what the epic story was, who its hero was, what enemies he fought, yet I had recently adapted the *Odyssey* for a theatre in England, presuming that the audience knew the trials of Odysseus, hero of another Asia Minor epic, while nobody in Trinidad knew any more than I did about Rama, Kali, Shiva, Vishnu,[5] apart from the Indians, a phrase I use perversely because that is the kind of remark you can still hear in Trinidad: "apart from the Indians."

It was as if, on the edge of the Central Plain, there was another plateau, a raft on which the *Ramayana* would be poorly performed in this ocean of

---

1. In the 1830s, slavery was abolished in the British West Indies.
2. One of the two major epics—along with the *Mahabharata*—of Hinduism, the *Ramayana* tells the story of Rama, whose heroic deeds are enacted annually in performances of the *Ramaleela,* or the

play of Rama.
3. "Ozymandias," by English poet Percy Bysshe Shelley (1792–1822), describes the desert ruins of an inscribed statue of an ancient king.
4. Small drums prominent in much Indian music.
5. Important deities appearing in the *Ramayana.*

cane, but that was my writer's view of things, and it is wrong. I was seeing the *Ramleela* at Felicity as theatre when it was faith.

Multiply that moment of self-conviction when an actor, made-up and costumed, nods to his mirror before stopping on stage in the belief that he is a reality entering an illusion and you would have what I presumed was happening to the actors of this epic. But they were not actors. They had been chosen; or they themselves had chosen their roles in this sacred story that would go on for nine afternoons over a two-hour period till the sun set. They were not amateurs but believers. There was no theatrical term to define them. They did not have to psych themselves up to play their roles. Their acting would probably be as buoyant and as natural as those bamboo arrows crisscrossing the afternoon pasture. They believed in what they were playing, in the sacredness of the text, the validity of India, while I, out of the writer's habit, searched for some sense of elegy, of loss, even of degenerative mimicry in the happy faces of the boy-warriors or the heraldic profiles of the village princes. I was polluting the afternoon with doubt and with the patronage of admiration. I misread the event through a visual echo of History—the cane fields, indenture, the evocation of vanished armies, temples, and trumpeting elephants—when all around me there was quite the opposite: elation, delight in the boys' screams, in the sweets-stalls, in more and more costumed characters appearing; a delight of conviction, not loss. The name Felicity made sense.

Consider the scale of Asia reduced to these fragments: the small white exclamations of minarets or the stone balls of temples in the cane fields, and one can understand the self-mockery and embarrassment of those who see these rites as parodic, even degenerate. These purists look on such ceremonies as grammarians look at a dialect, as cities look on provinces and empires on their colonies. Memory that yearns to join the centre, a limb remembering the body from which it has been severed, like those bamboo thighs of the god. In other words, the way that the Caribbean is still looked at, illegitimate, rootless, mongrelized. "No people there," to quote Froude, "in the true sense of the word."[6] No people. Fragments and echoes of real people, unoriginal and broken.

The performance was like a dialect, a branch of its original language, an abridgement of it, but not a distortion or even a reduction of its epic scale. Here in Trinidad I had discovered that one of the greatest epics of the world was seasonally performed, not with that desperate resignation of preserving a culture, but with an openness of belief that was as steady as the wind bending the cane lances of the Caroni plain. We had to leave before the play began to go through the creeks of the Caroni Swamp, to catch the scarlet ibises coming home at dusk. In a performance as natural as those of the actors of the *Ramleela,* we watched the flocks come in as bright as the scarlet of the boy archers, as the red flags, and cover an islet until it turned into a flowering tree, an anchored immortelle. The sigh of History meant nothing here. These two visions, the *Ramleela* and the arrowing flocks of scarlet ibises, blent into a single gasp of gratitude. Visual surprise is natural in the Caribbean; it comes with the landscape, and faced with its beauty, the sigh of History dissolves.

We make too much of that long groan which underlines the past. I felt privileged to discover the ibises as well as the scarlet archers of Felicity.

6. From *The English in the West Indies; or, The Bow of Ulysses* (1888), by James Anthony Froude (1818–1894), English historian.

The sigh of History rises over ruins, not over landscapes, and in the Antilles there are few ruins to sigh over, apart from the ruins of sugar estates and abandoned forts. Looking around slowly, as a camera would, taking in the low blue hills over Port of Spain,[7] the village road and houses, the warrior-archers, the god-actors and their handlers, and music already on the sound track, I wanted to make a film that would be a long-drawn sigh over Felicity. I was filtering the afternoon with evocations of a lost India, but why "evocations"? Why not "celebrations of a real presence"? Why should India be "lost" when none of these villagers ever really knew it, and why not "continuing," why not the perpetuation of joy in Felicity and in all the other nouns of the Central Plain: Couva, Chaguanas, Charley Village? Why was I not letting my pleasure open its windows wide? I was entitled like any Trinidadian to the ecstasies of their claim, because ecstasy was the pitch of the sinuous drumming in the loudspeakers. I was entitled to the feast of Husein,[8] to the mirrors and crêpe-paper temples of the Muslim epic, to the Chinese Dragon Dance, to the rites of that Sephardic Jewish[9] synagogue that was once on Something Street. I am only one-eighth the writer I might have been had I contained all the fragmented languages of Trinidad.

Break a vase, and the love that reassembles the fragments is stronger than that love which took its symmetry for granted when it was whole. The glue that fits the pieces is the sealing of its original shape. It is such a love that reassembles our African and Asiatic fragments, the cracked heirlooms whose restoration shows its white scars. This gathering of broken pieces is the care and pain of the Antilles, and if the pieces are disparate, ill-fitting, they contain more pain than their original sculpture, those icons and sacred vessels taken for granted in their ancestral places. Antillean art is this restoration of our shattered histories, our shards of vocabulary, our archipelago becoming a synonym for pieces broken off from the original continent.

And this is the exact process of the making of poetry, or what should be called not its "making" but its remaking, the fragmented memory, the armature that frames the god, even the rite that surrenders it to a final pyre; the god assembled cane by cane, reed by weaving reed, line by plaited line, as the artisans of Felicity would erect his holy echo.

Poetry, which is perfection's sweat but which must seem as fresh as the raindrops on a statue's brow, combines the natural and the marmoreal; it conjugates both tenses simultaneously: the past and the present, if the past is the sculpture and the present the beads of dew or rain on the forehead of the past. There is the buried language and there is the individual vocabulary, and the process of poetry is one of excavation and of self-discovery. Tonally the individual voice is a dialect; it shapes its own accent, its own vocabulary and melody in defiance of an imperial concept of language, the language of Ozymandias, libraries and dictionaries, law courts and critics, and churches, universities, political dogma, the diction of institutions. Poetry is an island that breaks away from the main. The dialects of my archipelago seem as fresh to me as those raindrops on the statue's forehead, not the sweat made

7. Capital of Trinidad, where Walcott directed the Trinidad Theatre Workshop from 1958 to 1976.
8. Shi'a Muslim festival commemorating the martyrdom of Muhammad's grandson. Indo-Trinidadians have culturally adapted and carnivalized the event, including in it colorful street theater, dancing, drinking, and nighttime processions with floats that represent Husein's tomb.
9. Sephardic Jews trace their ancestors back to Spain and Portugal, from which they were expelled in the fifteenth century.

from the classic exertion of frowning marble, but the condensations of a refreshing element, rain and salt.

Deprived of their original language, the captured and indentured tribes create their own, accreting and secreting fragments of an old, an epic vocabulary, from Asia and from Africa, but to an ancestral, an ecstatic rhythm in the blood that cannot be subdued by slavery or indenture, while nouns are renamed and the given names of places accepted like Felicity village or Choiseul.[1] The original language dissolves from the exhaustion of distance like fog trying to cross an ocean, but this process of renaming, of finding new metaphors, is the same process that the poet faces every morning of his working day, making his own tools like Crusoe,[2] assembling nouns from necessity, from Felicity, even renaming himself. The stripped man is driven back to that self-astonishing, elemental force, his mind. That is the basis of the Antillean experience, this shipwreck of fragments, these echoes, these shards of a huge tribal vocabulary, these partially remembered customs, and they are not decayed but strong. They survived the Middle Passage and the *Fatel Rozack,* the ship that carried the first indentured Indians from the port of Madras[3] to the cane fields of Felicity, that carried the chained Cromwellian convict[4] and the Sephardic Jew, the Chinese grocer and the Lebanese merchant selling cloth samples on his bicycle.

And here they are, all in a single Caribbean city, Port of Spain, the sum of history, Trollope's[5] "non-people." A downtown babel of shop signs and streets, mongrelized, polyglot, a ferment without a history, like heaven. Because that is what such a city is, in the New World, a writer's heaven.

A culture, we all know, is made by its cities.

Another first morning home, impatient for the sunrise—a broken sleep. Darkness at five, and the drapes not worth opening; then, in the sudden light, a cream-walled, brown-roofed police station bordered with short royal palms, in the colonial style, back of it frothing trees and taller palms, a pigeon fluttering into the cover of an eave, a rain-stained block of once-modern apartments, the morning side road into the station without traffic. All part of a surprising peace. This quiet happens with every visit to a city that has deepened itself in me. The flowers and the hills are easy, affection for them predictable; it is the architecture that, for the first morning, disorients. A return from American seductions used to make the traveller feel that something was missing, something was trying to complete itself, like the stained concrete apartments. Pan left along the window and the excrescences rear— a city trying to soar, trying to be brutal, like an American city in silhouette, stamped from the same mould as Columbus or Des Moines. An assertion of power, its decor bland, its air conditioning pitched to the point where its secretarial and executive staff sport competing cardigans; the colder the offices the more important, an imitation of another climate. A longing, even an envy of feeling cold.

In serious cities, in grey, militant winter with its short afternoons, the days

1. Old village on the southwest coast of Saint Lucia, near which live the island's small remaining population of Caribs—an Amerindian people largely killed off after the European conquest.
2. Shipwrecked protagonist of the novel *Robinson Crusoe,* by English writer Daniel Defoe (1660–1731), and in Walcott's work, a frequent figure for the Caribbean poet.
3. South Indian city where the British established a trading post in the seventeenth century. *Middle*

Passage: transatlantic journey of slaves, transported from Africa to the Americas in morbidly overcrowded ships.
4. During the rule of Oliver Cromwell (1599–1658), who served as lord protector of England after the Civil War, the Caribbean was used as an English penal colony.
5. Anthony Trollope (1815–1882), English novelist; his travel books include *The West Indies and the Spanish Main* (1859).

seem to pass by in buttoned overcoats, every building appears as a barracks with lights on in its windows, and when snow comes, one has the illusion of living in a Russian novel, in the nineteenth century, because of the literature of winter. So visitors to the Caribbean must feel that they are inhabiting a succession of postcards. Both climates are shaped by what we have read of them. For tourists, the sunshine cannot be serious. Winter adds depth and darkness to life as well as to literature, and in the unending summer of the tropics not even poverty or poetry (in the Antilles poverty is poetry with a V, *une vie*,[6] a condition of life as well as of imagination) seems capable of being profound because the nature around it is so exultant, so resolutely ecstatic, like its music. A culture based on joy is bound to be shallow. Sadly, to sell itself, the Caribbean encourages the delights of mindlessness, of brilliant vacuity, as a place to flee not only winter but that seriousness that comes only out of culture with four seasons. So how can there be a people there, in the true sense of the word?

They know nothing about seasons in which leaves let go of the year, in which spires fade in blizzards and streets whiten, of the erasures of whole cities by fog, of reflection in fireplaces; instead, they inhabit a geography whose rhythm, like their music, is limited to two stresses: hot and wet, sun and rain, light and shadow, day and night, the limitations of an incomplete metre, and are therefore a people incapable of the subtleties of contradiction, of imaginative complexity. So be it. We cannot change contempt.

Ours are not cities in the accepted sense, but no one wants them to be. They dictate their own proportions, their own definitions in particular places and in a prose equal to that of their detractors, so that now it is not just St. James but the streets and yards that Naipaul[7] commemorates, its lanes as short and brilliant as his sentences; not just the noise and jostle of Tunapuna but the origins of C. L. R. James's *Beyond a Boundary*,[8] not just Felicity village on the Caroni plain, but Selvon[9] Country, and that is the way it goes up the islands now: the old Dominica of Jean Rhys[1] still very much the way she wrote of it; and the Martinique of the early Césaire; Perse's[2] Guadeloupe, even without the pith helmets and the mules; and what delight and privilege there was in watching a literature—one literature in several imperial languages, French, English, Spanish—bud and open island after island in the early morning of a culture, not timid, not derivative, any more than the hard white petals of the frangipani[3] are derivative and timid. This is not a belligerent boast but a simple celebration of inevitability: and this flowering had to come.

On a heat-stoned afternoon in Port of Spain, some alley white with glare, with love vine spilling over a fence, palms and a hazed mountain appear around a corner to the evocation of Vaughn or Herbert's "that shady city of palm-trees,"[4] or to the memory of a Hammond organ from a wooden chapel

6. A life (French); *V* was also the symbol for Allied victory in World War II.
7. V. S. Naipaul (b. 1932), Trinidad-born writer, who in his fiction and travel writing describes St. James, a region of Port of Spain, Trinidad, with a large Indian population.
8. In this work, C. L. R. James (1901–1989), historian and political activist born in Tunapuna, Trinidad, explores the sport of cricket as a metaphor for Britain and the West Indies.
9. Samuel Selvon (1923–1994), West Indian writer born in Trinidad.

1. Novelist Jean Rhys (1890–1979) spent her childhood on the small West Indian island of Dominica, the setting of part of her novel *Wide Sargasso Sea* (1966).
2. Saint-John Perse (1887–1975): French poet born in the Guadeloupe islands of the French Antilles. Aimé Césaire (b. 1913): poet and cofounder of the Negritude movement, born on the French Antillean island of Martinique.
3. Flowering tropical tree or shrub.
4. From line 25 of "The Retreate," by English religious poet Henry Vaughan (1621 or 1622–1695).

in Castries,[5] where the congregation sang "Jerusalem, the Golden." It is hard for me to see such emptiness as desolation. It is that patience that is the width of Antillean life, and the secret is not to ask the wrong thing of it, not to demand of it an ambition it has no interest in. The traveller reads this as lethargy, as torpor.

Here there are not enough books, one says, no theatres, no museums, simply not enough to do. Yet, deprived of books, a man must fall back on thought, and out of thought, if he can learn to order it, will come the urge to record, and in extremity, if he has no means of recording, recitation, the ordering of memory which leads to metre, to commemoration. There can be virtues in deprivation, and certainly one virtue is salvation from a cascade of high mediocrity, since books are now not so much created as remade. Cities create a culture, and all we have are these magnified market towns, so what are the proportions of the ideal Caribbean city? A surrounding, accessible countryside with leafy suburbs, and if the city is lucky, behind it, spacious plains. Behind it, fine mountains; before it, an indigo sea. Spires would pin its centre and around them would be leafy, shadowy parks. Pigeons would cross its sky in alphabetic patterns, carrying with them memories of a belief in augury,[6] and at the heart of the city there would be horses, yes, horses, those animals last seen at the end of the nineteenth century drawing broughams[7] and carriages with top-hatted citizens, horses that live in the present tense without elegiac echoes from their hooves, emerging from paddocks at the Queen's Park Savannah[8] at sunrise, when mist is unthreading from the cool mountains above the roofs, and at the centre of the city seasonally there would be races, so that citizens could roar at the speed and grace of these nineteenth-century animals. Its docks, not obscured by smoke or deafened by too much machinery, and above all, it would be so racially various that the cultures of the world—the Asiatic, the Mediterranean, the European, the African—would be represented in it, its humane variety more exciting than Joyce's Dublin.[9] Its citizens would intermarry as they chose, from instinct, not tradition, until their children find it increasingly futile to trace their genealogy. It would not have too many avenues difficult or dangerous for pedestrians, its mercantile area would be a cacophony of accents, fragments of the old language that would be silenced immediately at five o'clock, its docks resolutely vacant on Sundays.

This is Port of Spain to me, a city ideal in its commercial and human proportions, where a citizen is a walker and not a pedestrian, and this is how Athens may have been before it became a cultural echo.

The finest silhouettes of Port of Spain are idealizations of the craftsman's handiwork, not of concrete and glass, but of baroque woodwork, each fantasy looking more like an involved drawing of itself than the actual building. Behind the city is the Caroni plain, with its villages, Indian prayer flags, and fruit vendors' stalls along the highway over which ibises come like floating flags. Photogenic poverty! Postcard sadnesses! I am not recreating Eden; I mean, by "the Antilles," the reality of light, of work, of survival. I mean a house on the side of a country road, I mean the Caribbean Sea, whose smell is the smell of refreshing possibility as well as survival. Survival is the triumph of stubbornness, and spiritual stubbornness, a sublime stupidity, is what

---

George Herbert (1593–1633), English religious poet of the same period.
5. Capital of Saint Lucia.
6. Practice of divining the future from the flight of birds.

7. One-horse carriages.
8. Large park in Port of Spain, Trinidad.
9. Irish writer James Joyce (1882–1941), whose novel *Ulysses* (1922) details minutely a day's life in Dublin.

makes the occupation of poetry endure, when there are so many things that should make it futile. Those things added together can go under one collective noun: "the world."

This is the visible poetry of the Antilles, then. Survival.

If you wish to understand that consoling pity with which the islands were regarded, look at the tinted engravings of Antillean forests, with their proper palm trees, ferns, and waterfalls. They have a civilizing decency, like Botanical Gardens, as if the sky were a glass ceiling under which a colonized vegetation is arranged for quiet walks and carriage rides. Those views are incised with a pathos that guides the engraver's tool and the topographer's pencil, and it is this pathos which, tenderly ironic, gave villages names like Felicity. A century looked at a landscape furious with vegetation in the wrong light and with the wrong eye. It is such pictures that are saddening rather than the tropics itself. These delicate engravings of sugar mills and harbours, of native women in costume, are seen as a part of History, that History which looked over the shoulder of the engraver and, later, the photographer. History can alter the eye and the moving hand to conform a view of itself; it can rename places for the nostalgia in an echo; it can temper the glare of tropical light to elegiac monotony in prose, the tone of judgement in Conrad,[1] in the travel journals of Trollope.

These travellers carried with them the infection of their own malaise, and their prose reduced even the landscape to melancholia and self-contempt. Every endeavor is belittled as imitation, from architecture to music. There was this conviction in Froude that since History is based on achievement, and since the history of the Antilles was so genetically corrupt, so depressing in its cycles of massacres, slavery, and indenture, a culture was inconceivable and nothing could ever be created in those ramshackle ports, those monotonously feudal sugar estates. Not only the light and salt of Antillean mountains defied this, but the demotic vigour and variety of their inhabitants. Stand close to a waterfall and you will stop hearing its roar. To be still in the nineteenth century, like horses, as Brodsky[2] has written, may not be such a bad deal, and much of our life in the Antilles still seems to be in the rhythm of the last century, like the West Indian novel.

By writers even as refreshing as Graham Greene,[3] the Caribbean is looked at with elegiac pathos, a prolonged sadness to which Lévi-Strauss has supplied an epigraph: *Tristes Tropiques*. Their *tristesse*[4] derives from an attitude to the Caribbean dusk, to rain, to uncontrollable vegetation, to the provincial ambition of Caribbean cities where brutal replicas of modern architecture dwarf the small houses and streets. The mood is understandable, the melancholy as contagious as the fever of a sunset, like the gold fronds of diseased coconut palms, but there is something alien and ultimately wrong in the way such a sadness, even a morbidity, is described by English, French, or some of our exiled writers. It relates to a misunderstanding of the light and the people on whom the light falls.

These writers describe the ambitions of our unfinished cities, their unrealized, homiletic[5] conclusion, but the Caribbean city may conclude just at that

---

1. Polish-born English novelist Joseph Conrad (1857–1924); his fiction reflects his experience as a young man of working on ships in the West Indies.
2. Joseph Brodsky (1940–1996), Russian-born American poet and 1987 Nobel laureate.

3. British novelist (1904–1991).
4. Sadness (French). French (Belgian-born) structural anthropologist Claude Lévi-Strauss (b. 1908) titled his memoir *Tristes Tropiques* (melancholy tropics).
5. Sermonlike.

point where it is satisfied with its own scale, just as Caribbean culture is not evolving but already shaped. Its proportions are not to be measured by the traveller or the exile, but by its own citizenry and architecture. To be told you are not yet a city or a culture requires this response. I am not your city or your culture. There might be less of *Tristes Tropiques* after that.

Here, on the raft of this dais, there is the sound of the applauding surf: our landscape, our history recognized, "at last." *At Last* is one of the first Caribbean books. It was written by the Victorian traveller Charles Kingsley.[6] It is one of the early books to admit the Antillean landscape and its figures into English literature. I have never read it but gather that its tone is benign. The Antillean archipelago was there to be written about, not to write itself, by Trollope, by Patrick Leigh-Fermor,[7] in the very tone in which I almost wrote about the village spectacle at Felicity, as a compassionate and beguiled outsider, distancing myself from Felicity village even while I was enjoying it. What is hidden cannot be loved. The traveller cannot love, since love is stasis and travel is motion. If he returns to what he loved in a landscape and stays there, he is no longer a traveller but in stasis and concentration, the lover of that particular part of earth, a native. So many people say they "love the Caribbean," meaning that someday they plan to return for a visit but could never live there, the usual benign insult of the traveller, the tourist. These travellers, at their kindest, were devoted to the same patronage, the islands passing in profile, their vegetal luxury, their backwardness and poverty. Victorian prose dignified them. They passed by in beautiful profiles and were forgotten, like a vacation.

Alexis Saint-Léger Léger, whose writer's name is St.-John Perse, was the first Antillean to win this prize for poetry. He was born in Guadeloupe and wrote in French, but before him, there was nothing as fresh and clear in feeling as those poems of his childhood, that of a privileged white child on an Antillean plantation, *"Pour fêter une enfance," "Eloges,"* and later *"Images à Crusoe."*[8] At last, the first breeze on the page, salt-edged and self-renewing as the trade winds, the sound of pages and palm trees turning as "the odour of coffee ascends the stairs."

Caribbean genius is condemned to contradict itself. To celebrate Perse, we might be told, is to celebrate the old plantation system, to celebrate the *bequé*[9] or plantation rider, verandahs and mulatto servants, a white French language in a white pith helmet, to celebrate a rhetoric of patronage and hauteur; and even if Perse denied his origins, great writers often have this folly of trying to smother their source, we cannot deny him any more than we can the African Aimé Césaire. This is not accommodation, this is the ironic republic that is poetry, since, when I see cabbage palms moving their fronds at sunrise, I think they are reciting Perse.

The fragrant and privileged poetry that Perse composed to celebrate his white childhood and the recorded Indian music behind the brown young archers of Felicity, with the same cabbage palms against the same Antillean sky, pierce me equally. I feel the same poignancy of pride in the poems as in the faces. Why, given the history of the Antilles, should this be remarkable? The history of the world, by which of course we mean Europe, is a record of intertribal lacerations, of ethnic cleansings. At last, islands not

---

6. English clergyman and writer (1819–1875).
7. English travel writer (b. 1915).
8. To celebrate a childhood, eulogies, images of Crusoe (French).
9. White person (French Creole).

written about but writing themselves! The palms and the Muslim minarets are Antillean exclamations. At last! the royal palms of Guadeloupe recite *"Eloges"* by heart.

Later, in *Anabase,* Perse assembled fragments of an imaginary epic, with the clicking teeth of frontier gates, barren wadis with the froth of poisonous lakes, horsemen burnoosed[1] in sandstorms, the opposite of cool Caribbean mornings, yet not necessarily a contrast any more than some young brown archer at Felicity, hearing the sacred text blared across the flagged field, with its battles and elephants and monkey-gods, in a contrast to the white child in Guadeloupe assembling fragments of his own epic from the lances of the cane fields, the estate carts and oxens, and the calligraphy of bamboo leaves from the ancient languages, Hindi, Chinese, and Arabic, on the Antillean sky. From the *Ramayana* to Anabasis, from Guadeloupe to Trinidad, all that archaeology of fragments lying around, from the broken African kingdoms, from the crevasses of Canton, from Syria and Lebanon, vibrating not under the earth but in our raucous, demotic streets.

A boy with weak eyes skims a flat stone across the flat water of an Aegean inlet, and that ordinary action with the scything elbow contains the skipping lines of the *Iliad* and the *Odyssey,* and another child aims a bamboo arrow at a village festival, and another hears the rustling march of cabbage palms in a Caribbean sunrise, and from that sound, with its fragments of tribal myth, the compact expedition of Perse's epic is launched, centuries and archipelagos apart. For every poet it is always morning in the world. History a forgotten, insomniac night; History and elemental awe are always our early beginning, because the fate of poetry is to fall in love with the world, in spite of History.

There is a force of exultation, a celebration of luck, when a writer finds himself a witness to the early morning of a culture that is defining itself, branch by branch, leaf by leaf, in that self-defining dawn, which is why, especially at the edge of the sea, it is good to make a ritual of the sunrise. Then the noun, the "Antilles" ripples like brightening water, and the sounds of leaves, palm fronds, and birds are the sounds of fresh dialect, the native tongue. The personal vocabulary, the individual melody whose metre is one's biography, joins in that sound, with any luck, and the body moves like a walking, a waking island.

This is the benediction that is celebrated, a fresh language and a fresh people, and this is the frightening duty owed.

I stand here in their name, if not their image—but also in the name of the dialect they exchange like the leaves of the trees whose names are suppler, greener, more morning-stirred than English—*laurier canelles, bois-flot, bois-canot*—or the valleys the trees mention—*Fond St. Jacques, Mabonya, Forestièr, Roseau, Mahaut*—or the empty beaches—*L'Anse Ivrogne, Case en Bas, Paradis*—all songs and histories in themselves, pronounced not in French—but in patois.[2]

One rose hearing two languages, one of the trees, one of schoolchildren reciting in English:

> *I am monarch of all I survey,*
> *My right there is none to dispute;*

---

1. A burnoose is a long cloak with a hood, worn by Arabs. *Wadis:* valleys or ravines dry except during the rainy season (from Arabic).

2. French Creole, borne of a fusion of French with African and European languages; the everyday language of Walcott's native Saint Lucia.

> *From the centre all round to the sea*
> *I am lord of the fowl and the brute.*
> *Oh, solitude! where are the charms*
> *That sages have seen in thy face?*
> *Better dwell in the midst of alarms,*
> *Than reign in this horrible place . . .* [3]

While in the country to the same metre, but to organic instruments, hand-made violin, chac-chac,[4] *and goatskin drum, a girl named Sensenne singing:*

> *Si mwen di 'ous' ça fait mwen la peine*
> *'Ous kai dire ça vrai.*
> > *(If I told you that caused me pain*
> > *You'll say, "It's true.")*
> *Si mwen di 'ous ça pentetrait mwen*
> *'Ous peut dire ça vrai.*
> > *(If I told you you pierced my heart*
> > *You'd say, "It's true.")*
> *Ces mamailles actuellement*
> *Pas ka faire l'amour z'autres pour un rien.*
> > *(Children nowadays*
> > *Don't make love for nothing.)*

It is not that History is obliterated by this sunrise. It is there in Antillean geography, in the vegetation itself. The sea sighs with the drowned from the Middle Passage, the butchery of its aborigines, Carib and Aruac and Taino,[5] bleeds in the scarlet of the immortelle, and even the actions of surf on sand cannot erase the African memory, or the lances of cane as a green prison where indentured Asians, the ancestors of Felicity, are still serving time.

That is what I have read around me from boyhood, from the beginnings of poetry, the grace of effort. In the hard mahogany of woodcutters: faces, resinous men, charcoal burners; in a man with a cutlass cradled across his forearm, who stands on the verge with the usual anonymous khaki dog; in the extra clothes he put on this morning, when it was cold when he rose in the thinning dark to go and make his garden in the heights—the heights, the garden, being miles away from his house, but that is where he has his land—not to mention the fishermen, the footmen on trucks, groaning up mornes,[6] all fragments of Africa originally but shaped and hardened and rooted now in the island's life, illiterate in the way leaves are illiterate; they do not read, they are there to be read, and if they are properly read, they create their own literature.

But in our tourist brochures the Caribbean is a blue pool into which the republic dangles the extended foot of Florida as inflated rubber islands bob and drinks with umbrellas float towards her on a raft. This is how the islands from the shame of necessity sell themselves; this is the seasonal erosion of their identity, that high-pitched repetition of the same images of service that cannot distinguish one island from the other, with a future of polluted marinas, land deals negotiated by ministers, and all of this conducted to the music of Happy Hour and the rictus[7] of a smile. What is the earthly paradise for

---

3. From William Cowper's (1731–1800) poem written in the voice of Alexander Selkirk (1676–1721), the Scottish sailor after whom Robinson Crusoe was modeled.
4. Maracalike instrument.

5. Peoples native to the Antilles at the time of the Spanish conquest.
6. Small, independent mountains (French Creole).
7. Mouth.

our visitors? Two weeks without rain and a mahogany tan, and, at sunset, local troubadours in straw hats and floral shirts beating "Yellow Bird" and "Banana Boat Song"[8] to death. There is a territory wider than this—wider than the limits made by the map of an island—which is the illimitable sea and what it remembers.

All of the Antilles, every island, is an effort of memory; every mind, every racial biography culminating in amnesia and fog. Pieces of sunlight through the fog and sudden rainbows, *arcs-en-ciel*.[9] That is the effort, the labour of the Antillean imagination, rebuilding its gods from bamboo frames, phrase by phrase.

Decimation from the Aruac downwards is the blasted root of Antillean history, and the benign blight that is tourism can infect all of those island nations, not gradually, but with imperceptible speed, until each rock is whitened by the guano of white-winged hotels, the arc and descent of progress.

Before it is all gone, before only a few valleys are left, pockets of an older life, before development turns every artist into an anthropologist or folklorist, there are still cherishable places, little valleys that do not echo with ideas, a simplicity of rebeginnings, not yet corrupted by the dangers of change. Not nostalgic sites but occluded sanctities as common and simple as their sunlight. Places as threatened by this prose as a headland is by the bulldozer or a sea almond grove by the surveyor's string, or from blight, the mountain laurel.

One last epiphany: A basic stone church in a thick valley outside Soufrière,[1] the hills almost shoving the houses around into a brown river, a sunlight that looks oily on the leaves, a backward place, unimportant, and one now being corrupted into significance by this prose. The idea is not to hallow or invest the place with anything, not even memory. African children in Sunday frocks come down the ordinary concrete steps into the church, banana leaves hang and glisten, a truck is parked in a yard, and old women totter towards the entrance. Here is where a real fresco should be painted, one without importance, but one with real faith, mapless, Historyless.

How quickly it could all disappear! And how it is beginning to drive us further into where we hope are impenetrable places, green secrets at the end of bad roads, headlands where the next view is not of a hotel but of some long beach without a figure and the hanging question of some fisherman's smoke at its far end. The Caribbean is not an idyll, not to its natives. They draw their working strength from it organically, like trees, like the sea almond or the spice laurel of the heights. Its peasantry and its fishermen are not there to be loved or even photographed; they are trees who sweat, and whose bark is filmed with salt, but every day on some island, rootless trees in suits are signing favourable tax breaks with entrepreneurs, poisoning the sea almond and the spice laurel of the mountains to their roots. A morning could come in which governments might ask what happened not merely to the forests and the bays but to a whole people.

They are here again, they recur, the faces, corruptible angels, smooth black skins and white eyes huge with an alarming joy, like those of the Asian children of Felicity at *Ramleela*; two different religions, two different continents, both filling the heart with the pain that is joy.

---

8. Popular 1950s song by American singer and actor Harry Belafonte (b. 1927). "Yellow Bird" is an anonymous song.
9. Rainbows (French).

1. Town on west coast of Saint Lucia; nearby are the tourist attractions of an active volcano and the island's twin peaks, the Pitons.

But what is joy without fear? The fear of selfishness that, here on this podium with the world paying attention not to them but to me, I should like to keep these simple joys inviolate, not because they are innocent, but because they are true. They are as true as when, in the grace of this gift, Perse heard the fragments of his own epic of Asia Minor in the rustling of cabbage palms, that inner Asia of the soul through which imagination wanders, if there is such a thing as imagination as opposed to the collective memory of our entire race, as true as the delight of that warrior-child who flew a bamboo arrow over the flags in the field at Felicity; and now as grateful a joy and a blessed fear as when a boy opened an exercise book and, within the discipline of its margins, framed stanzas that might contain the light of the hills on an island blest by obscurity, cherishing our insignificance.

1992

Selected Bibliographies

African Poetry

Book-length studies of African poetry include Jonathan Kariara and Ellen Kitonga's *An Introduction to East African Poetry* (1976); Romanus Egudu's *Four Modern West African Poets* (1977) and *Modern African Poetry and the African Predicament* (1978); K. L. Goodwin's *Understanding African Poetry* (1982); Tayo Olafioye's *Politics in African Poetry* (1982); Jacques Alvarez-Pereyre's *The Poetry of Commitment in South Africa* (1984); Robert Fraser's *West African Poetry: A Critical History* (1986); *Oral and Written Poetry in African Literature Today* (1988), ed. Eldred D. Jones; Emmanuel Ngara's *Ideology and Form in African Poetry* (1990); Adrian Roscoe's *The Quiet Chameleon: Modern Poetry from Central Africa* (1992); Tanure Ojaide's *Poetic Imagination in Black Africa* (1996); and Charles Bodunde's *Oral Traditions and Aesthetic Transfer: Creativity and Social Vision in Contemporary Black Poetry* (2001). Other works dealing with African literature include Adrian Roscoe's *Mother Is Gold: A Study of West African Literature* (1971); Nadine Gordimer's *The Black Interpreters* (1973); O. R. Dathorne's *The Black Mind: A History of African Literature* (1974); Kofi Awoonor's *The Breast of the Earth: A Survey of the History, Culture, and Literature of Africa South of the Sahara* (1975); Gerald Moore's *Twelve African Writers* (1980); Chinweizu, Onwuchekwa Jemie, and Ihechukwu Madubuike's *Toward the Decolonization of African Literature* (1983); and Ursula A. Barnett's *A Vision of Order: A Study of Black South African Literature in English, 1914–1980* (1983).

Anthologies of African poetry written in English include *West African Verse* (1967), ed. Donatus Ibe Nwoga; *Poems from East Africa* (1971), ed. David Cook and David Rubadiri; *The Word Is Here: Poetry from Modern Africa* (1973), ed. Keroapetse Kgositsile; *Poems of Black Africa* (1975), ed. Wole Soyinka; *The Return of the Amasi Bird: Black South African Poetry, 1891–1981* (1982), ed. Tim Couzens and Essop Patel; *A New Book of African Verse* (1984), ed. John Reed and Clive Wake; *The Penguin Book of Modern African Poetry* (1984), ed. Gerald Moore and Ulli Beier; *The Heritage of African Poetry* (1985), ed. Isidore Okpewho; *When My Brothers Come Home: Poems from Central and Southern Africa* (1985), ed. Frank Chipasula; *The Fate of Vultures: New Poetry of Africa* (1989), ed. Kofi Anyidoho, Peter Porter, and Musaemura Zimunya; *The Heinemann Book of African Women's Poetry* (1995), ed. Stella Chipasula; and *The New African Poetry* (1999), ed. Tanure Ojaide. See also **Christopher Okigbo, Okot p'Bitek, Wole Soyinka.**

American Poetry

Critical works especially helpful for the study of contemporary American poetry include Richard Howard's *Alone with America* (1969, 1980), Harold Bloom's *Ringers in the Tower* (1971) and *Figures of Capable Imagination* (1976), Robert Pinsky's *The Situation of Poetry* (1976), David Kalstone's *Five Temperaments* (1977), Helen Vendler's *Part of Nature, Part of Us* (1980), Cary Nelson's *Our Last First Poets* (1981), Marjorie Perloff's *The Poetics of Indeterminacy* (1981), James E. B. Breslin's *From Modern to Contemporary: American Poetry, 1945–1965* (1984), Charles Altieri's *Self and Sensibility in Contemporary American Poetry* (1984), Robert von Hallberg's *American Poetry and Culture, 1945–1980* (1985), Andrew Ross's *The Failure of Modernism: Symptoms of American Poetry* (1986), Paul Breslin's *The Psycho-Political Muse* (1987), Lynn Keller's *Re-Making It New* (1987), J. D. McClatchy's *White Paper* (1989), Willard Spiegelman's *The Didactic Muse* (1989), Perloff's *Radical Artifice* (1991), Vernon Shetley's *After the Death of Poetry* (1993), Vendler's *The Given and the Made* (1995) and *Soul Says* (1995), James Longenbach's *Modern Poetry after Modernism* (1997), Peter Stitt's *Uncertainty and Plenitude* (1997), Perloff's *Poetry on and off the Page* (1998), and Thomas Gardner's *Regions of Unlikeness* (1999). An excellent compendium is *Encyclopedia of American Poetry: The Twentieth Century* (2001), ed. Eric L. Haralson. The Academy of American Poets maintains a useful website, www.poets.org, with an audio component and links to other sites on contemporary poetry.

Asian American Poetry

Studies of Asian American poetry and literature include *Asian-American Authors* (1972), ed. Kai-yu Hsu and Helen Palubinskas; Elaine H. Kim's *Asian American Literature: An Introduction to the Writings and Their Social Context* (1982); Stephen Sumida's *And the View from the Shore: Literary Traditions of Hawaii* (1991); *Reading the Literatures of Asian America* (1992), ed. Shirley Geok-lin Lim and Amy Ling; Sau-ling Cynthia Wong's *Reading Asian American Literature: From Necessity to Extravagance* (1993); Esther Mikyung Ghymn's *Images of Asian American Women by Asian American Women Writers* (1995); Lisa Lowe's *Immigrant Acts: On Asian American Cultural Politics* (1996); *Asian American Women Writers* (1997), ed. Harold Bloom; *An Interethnic Companion to Asian American Literature* (1997), ed. King-Kok Cheung; Eileen Tabios's *Black Lightning: Poetry-in-Progress* (1998); Jinqi Ling's *Narrating Nationalism: Ideology and Form in Asian American Literature* (1998); *Words Matter: Conversations with Asian American Writers* (2000), ed. King-Kok Cheung; and Anne Anlin Cheng's *The Melancholy of Race* (2001). Bibliographic information is available in *Asian American Literature: An Annotated Bibliography* (1988), ed. Cheung and Stan Yogi.

Anthologies of Asian American literature include *Aiiieeeee!: An Anthology of Asian-American Writers* (1974), ed. Frank Chin, Jeffery Paul Chan, Lawson Fusao Inada, and Shawn Hsu Wong; *The Forbidden Stitch: An Asian American Women's Anthology* (1989), ed. Shirley Geok-lin Lim, Mayumi Tsutakawa, and Margaret Donnelly; *The Big Aiiieeeee!: An Anthology of Chinese American and Japanese American Literature* (1991), ed. Chan et al.; *Asian American Literature: A Brief Introduction and Anthology* (1996), ed. Shawn Wong; *Quiet Fire: A Historical Anthology of Asian American Poetry* (1996), ed. Juliana Chang; *Making More Waves: New Writing by Asian American Women* (1997), ed. Elaine H. Kim, Lilia V. Villanueva, and Asian Women United of California; and *Bold Words: A Century of Asian American Writing* (2001), ed. Rajini Srikanth and Esther Y. Iwanaga. See also **Marilyn Chin, Li-Young Lee, Cathy Song.**

Australian Poetry

For studies of Australian poetry, see Judith Wright's *Preoccupations in Australian Poetry* (1965); Brian Elliott's *The Landscape of Australian Poetry* (1967); Vincent Buckley's *Essays in Poetry, Mainly Australian* (1969); James Phillip McAuley's *A Map of Australian Verse: The Twentieth Century* (1975); Andrew Taylor's *Reading Australian Poetry* (1987); *Poetry and Gender: Statements and Essays in Australian Women's Poetry and Poetics* (1989), ed. David Brooks and Brenda Walker; *Australian Poetry in the Twentieth Century* (1991), ed. Robert Gray and Geof-

frey Lehmann; Bruce Dawe's *Tributary Streams: Some Sources of Social and Political Concerns in Modern Australian Poetry* (1992); R. P. Rama's *Dialogues with Australian Poets* (1993); and Paul Kane's *Australian Poetry: Romanticism and Negativity* (1996).

Anthologies include *The Penguin Book of Modern Australian Verse* (1972), ed. Harry P. Heseltine; *The New Australian Poetry* (1979), ed. John Tranter; *The Collins Book of Australian Poetry* (1981), ed. R. Hall; *The New Oxford Book of Australian Verse* (1986), ed. Les Murray; *The Penguin Book of Australian Women Poets* (1986), ed. Susan Hampton and K. Llewellyn; *Contemporary Australian Poetry: An Anthology* (1990), ed. John Leonard; and *The Penguin Book of Modern Australian Poetry* (1991), ed. Tranter. See also **Les Murray, Judith Wright;** in volume 1, **A. D. Hope.**

Beat Movement

For discussions of the Beat movement, see Lawrence Ferlinghetti and Nancy J. Peters's *Literary San Francisco* (1980); Michael Davidson's *The San Francisco Renaissance: Poetics and Community at Mid-Century* (1989); John Arthur Maynard's *Venice West: The Beat Generation in Southern California* (1991); Ann Charters's "Beat Poetry and the San Francisco Poetry Renaissance," *Columbia History of American Poetry* (1993), ed. Jay Parini and Brett C. Millier; Pierre Delattre's *Episodes* (1993); Steven Watson's *The Birth of the Beat Generation* (1995); David Sterritt's *Mad to Be Saved: The Beats, The Fifties, and Film* (1998); *The Beat Writers at Work: Paris Review Interviews* (1999), ed. George Plimpton; Ronna C. Johnson and Maria Damon's "Recapturing the Skipped Beats: Women and Minorities in the Beat Generation," *Chronicle of Higher Education* (1 October 1999); James Campbell's *This Is the Beat Generation: New York, San Francisco, Paris* (1999); Neeli Cherkovski's *Whitman's Wild Children* (1999); Barry Miles's *The Beat Hotel* (2000); and David Meltzer's *San Francisco Beats: Talking with the Poets* (2001). See also **Amiri Baraka, Lawrence Ferlinghetti, Allen Ginsberg, Gary Snyder, San Francisco Renaissance.**

Black Arts Movement

For Black Arts Movement anthologies, see Amiri Baraka and Larry Neal's *Black Fire* (1968); Toni Cade Bambara's *The Black Woman* (1970); Addison Gayle's *The Black Aesthetic* (1971); Abraham Chapman's *New Black Voices* (1972); Stephen Henderson's *Understanding the New Black Poetry* (1972); Eugene Redmond's *Drumvoices, The Mission of Afro-American Poetry: A Critical History* (1976); and Neal's *Visions of a Liberated Future* (1989). Discussions of the Black Arts Movement include *The LeRoi Jones/*

Amiri Baraka Reader (1991, 2000), ed. William J. Harris; William Cook's "The Black Arts Poets," *Columbia History of American Poetry* (1993), ed. Jay Parini and Brett C. Millier; and Kalamu ya Salaam's "Black Arts Movement," *Oxford Companion to African American Literature* (1997), ed. William L. Andrews, Frances Smith Foster, and Trudier Harris. See also **Amiri Baraka, Lucille Clifton, June Jordan, Audre Lorde.**

Black Mountain School

For discussion of the Black Mountain school, see Martin Duberman's *Black Mountain: An Exploration in Community* (1972); Sherman Paul's *Olson's Push: Origin, Black Mountain, and Recent American Poetry* (1978); Paul Christensen's *Charles Olson: Call Him Ishmael* (1979); Charles Altieri's *Self and Sensibility in Contemporary American Poetry* (1984); Mary Emma Harris's *The Arts at Black Mountain College* (1987); Willard Fox's *Robert Creeley, Edward Dorn, and Robert Duncan: A Reference Guide* (1989); *Black Mountain College: Sprouted Seeds: An Anthology of Personal Accounts* (1990), ed. Mervin Lane; Brian Conniff's "Reconsidering Black Mountain: The Poetry of Hilda Morley," *American Literature* 65.1 (1993); Edward Halsey Foster's *Understanding the Black Mountain Poets* (1995); Marjorie Perloff's "Whose New American Poetry? Anthologizing the Nineties," *Diacritics* 26.3–4 (1996); and Paul Breslin's "Black Mountain Reunion," *Poetry* 176.3 (2000). See also **Robert Creeley, Robert Duncan, Denise Levertov, Charles Olson.**

British Poetry

Works especially helpful for the study of contemporary British poetry include *British Poetry since 1960* (1972), ed. Michael Schmidt and Grevel Lindop; Calvin Bedient's *Eight Contemporary Poets* (1974); Anthony Thwaite's *Twentieth-Century English Poetry: An Introduction* (1978); Blake Morrison's *The Movement: English Poetry and Fiction of the 1950s* (1980); John Haffenden's *Viewpoints: Poets in Conversation with John Haffenden* (1981); Bruce K. Martin's *British Poetry since 1939* (1985); *Poets of Great Britain and Ireland since 1960* (1985), ed. Vincent B. Sherry Jr.; John Lucas's *Modern English Poetry—From Hardy to Hughes* (1986); Edna Longley's *Poetry in the Wars* (1986); Alan Robinson's *Instabilities in Contemporary British Poetry* (1988); Donald Davie's *Under Brigg flatts: A History of Poetry in Great Britain, 1960–1988* (1989); Ian Gregson's *Contemporary Poetry and Postmodernism: Dialogue and Estrangement* (1996); Keith Tuma's *Fishing by Obstinate Isles: Modern and Postmodern British Poetry and American Readers* (1998); and Dillon Johnston's

The Poetic Economies of England and Ireland, 1912–2000 (2001).

Canadian Poetry

For more information on Canadian poetry in English, see *The Making of Modern Poetry in Canada* (1967), ed. Louis Dudek and Michael Gnarowski; *Canadian Poetry* (1982), ed. Jack David and Robert Lecker; George Bowering's *A Way with Words* (1982); Frank Davey's *Reading Canadian Reading* (1988); Caroline Bayard's *The New Poetics in Canada and Quebec: From Concretism to Postmodernism* (1989); *Beyond Tish* (1991), ed. Douglas Barbour; Warren Tallman's *In the Midst: Writings 1962–1992* (1992); and George Woodcock's *George Woodcock's Introduction to Canadian Poetry* (1993). Other works on Canadian literature include Douglas G. Jones's *Butterfly on Rock* (1970), Northrop Frye's *The Bush Garden* (1971), Margaret Atwood's *Survival: A Thematic Guide to Canadian Literature* (1972), and E. D. Blodgett's *Configuration: Essays in the Canadian Literatures* (1982).

Anthologies include *The New Oxford Book of Canadian Verse in English* (1982), ed. Margaret Atwood, and *The New Canadian Poets* (1985), ed. Dennis Lee. See also **Margaret Atwood, Anne Carson, Michael Ondaatje, P. K. Page.**

Caribbean Poetry

Studies of Caribbean poetry include *West Indian Literature* (1979), ed. Bruce King; *Fifty Caribbean Writers: A Bio-Bibliographical Critical Sourcebook* (1986), ed. Daryl Cumber Dance; Edward Kamau Brathwaite's *Roots* (1986); Frank Birbalsingh's *Passion and Exile: Essays in Caribbean Literature* (1988); *New World Adams: Conversations with Contemporary West Indian Writers* (1992), ed. Dance; Gordon Rohlehr's *My Strangled City* (1992) and *The Shape of That Hurt* (1992); Antonio Benítez Rojo's *The Repeating Island: The Caribbean and the Postmodern Perspective* (1992), tr. James Maraniss; J. Edward Chamberlin's *Come Back to Me My Language: Poetry and the West Indies* (1993); Birbalsingh's *Frontiers of Caribbean Literature* (1996); Silvio Torres-Saillant's *Caribbean Poetics: Toward an Aesthetics of West Indian Literature* (1997); Laurence A. Breiner's *An Introduction to West Indian Poetry* (1998); J. Michael Dash's *The Other America: Caribbean Literature in a New World Context* (1998); Louis James's *Caribbean Literature in English* (1999); and *Talk Yuh Talk: Interviews with Anglophone Caribbean Poets* (2001), ed. Kwame Senu Neville Dawes.

Anthologies include *The Penguin Book of Caribbean Verse in English* (1986), ed. Paula Burnett; *Hinterland: Caribbean Poetry from the West Indies and Britain* (1989), ed. E. A. Markham; *Voiceprint: An Anthology of Oral and*

Related Poetry from the Caribbean (1989), ed. Stewart Brown and Mervyn Morris; and *The Heinemann Book of Caribbean Poetry* (1992), ed. Ian McDonald and Stewart Brown. See also **Louise Bennett, Kamau Brathwaite, Lorna Goodison, Grace Nichols, Derek Walcott.**

Confessional Poetry

For more on confessional poetry, see Robert S. Phillips's *The Confessional Poets* (1973); Ralph J. Mills's *Cry of the Human* (1975); David Perkins's *A History of Modern Poetry: The Eighteen-Nineties to the High Modernist Mode* (1976); Charles Molesworth's *The Fierce Embrace* (1979); James E. B. Breslin's *From Modern to Contemporary* (1984); Paul Breslin's *The Psycho-Political Muse* (1987); Jeffrey Meyers's *Manic Power: Robert Lowell and His Circle* (1987); Diane Wood Middlebrook's "What Was Confessional Poetry?" *Columbia History of American Poetry* (1993), ed. Jay Parini and Brett C. Millier; Marjorie Perloff's "Realism and the Confessional Mode of Robert Lowell," *The Critical Response to Robert Lowell* (1999), ed. Steven Gould Axelrod; and Lucy Collins's "Confessionalism," *A Companion to Twentieth-Century Poetry* (2001), ed. Neil Roberts. See also **John Berryman, Robert Lowell, Sylvia Plath, Adrienne Rich, Anne Sexton, W. D. Snodgrass.**

Cross-National Studies

David Perkins's *A History of Modern Poetry: Modernism and After* (1987) is an indispensable guide for British, Irish, and American poetry. Other helpful cross-national studies include M. L. Rosenthal's *The New Poets: American and British Poetry since World War II* (1967); *50 Modern American and British Poets, 1920–1970* (1973), ed. Louis Untermeyer; Louis Simpson's *A Revolution of Taste* (1978); *Modern Poetry* (1979), ed. Charles Altieri; Helen Vendler's *The Music of What Happens* (1988); Jahan Ramazani's *Poetry of Mourning* (1994); Vendler's *The Breaking of Style* (1995); David Bromwich's *Skeptical Music: Essays on Modern Poetry* (2001); and Ramazani's *The Hybrid Muse* (2001). Valuable critical and biographical material can also be found in *The Oxford Companion to Twentieth-Century Poetry* (1996), ed. Ian Hamilton; the essay collection *A Companion to Twentieth-Century Poetry* (2001), ed. Neil Roberts; and the volumes (many now available online) of *Contemporary Poets* and *The Dictionary of Literary Biography*.

Deep Image Poetry

For more on Deep Image poetry, see Robert Kelly's "Notes on the Poetry of the Deep Image," *Trobar* (1961); James E. B. Breslin's *From Modern to Contemporary* (1984); Kevin Power's "Robert Bly," *American Poetry Observed: Poets on Their Work* (1984), ed. Joe D. Bellamy; Robert Bly's *American Poetry: Wildness and Domesticity* (1990); Paul Christensen's *Minding the Underworld: Clayton Eshleman and Late Postmodernism* (1991); Cramer R. Cauthen's "Deep Image and the Poetics of Oppen's 'Of Being Numerous,' " *Sagetrieb* 13.3 (1994); and Nick Halpern's " 'Coming Back Here How Many Years Now': August Kleinzahler and James Wright's *Shall We Gather at the River*," *Contemporary Literature* 42.2 (2001). See also **Robert Bly, W. S. Merwin, James Wright.**

Gay and Lesbian Poetry

Studies dealing with gay and lesbian poetry include Robert K. Martin's *The Homosexual Tradition in Modern Poetry* (1979, 1998), Judy Grahn's *The Highest Apple: Sappho and the Lesbian Poetic Tradition* (1985), and Gregory Woods's *Articulate Flesh: Male Homo-Eroticism and Modern Poetry* (1987). Anthologies include *The Male Muse: A Gay Anthology* (1973), ed. Ian Young; *Angels of the Lyre: A Gay Poetry Anthology* (1975), ed. Winston Leyland; *The Penguin Book of Homosexual Verse* (1983), ed. Stephen Coote; *Beautiful Barbarians: Lesbian Feminist Poetry* (1986), ed. Lilian Mohin; *Gay and Lesbian Poetry in Our Time* (1988), ed. Carl Morse and Joan Larkin; *Naming the Waves: Contemporary Lesbian Poetry* (1988), ed. Christian McEwen; *The World in Us: Lesbian and Gay Poetry of the Next Wave* (2000), ed. Michael Lassell; and *Love Speaks Its Name: Gay and Lesbian Love Poems* (2001), ed. J. D. McClatchy.

Indian Poetry

For studies of Indian poetry in English, see *Contemporary Indian English Verse* (1980), ed. Chirantan Kulshrestha; M. K. Naik's *Perspectives on Indian Poetry in English* (1984); Bruce King's *Modern Indian Poetry in English* (1987); Makarand Paranjape's *Mysticism in Indian English Poetry* (1988); *Living Indian English Poets* (1989), ed. Madhusudan Prasad; D. S. Mishra's *Contemporary Indian English Poetry: A Revaluation* (1990); Lakshmi Raghunandan's *Contemporary Indian Poetry in English* (1990); P. K. J. Kurup's *Contemporary Indian Poetry in English* (1991); King's *Three Indian Poets* (1991); Vinay Dharwadker's "Some Contexts of Modern Indian Poetry," *Chicago Review* 38.1–2 (1992); *Indian Poetry in English* (1993), ed. Paranjape; John Oliver Perry's "Contemporary Indian Poetry in English," *World Literature Today* 68.2 (1994); G. J. V. Prasad's *Continuities in Indian English Poetry: Nation Language Form* (1999); and Eunice de Souza's *Talking Poems: Conversations with Poets* (1999).

Anthologies include *India: An Anthology of Contemporary Writing* (1983), ed. David Ray and Amritjit Singh; *Another India* (1990), ed. Nissim Ezekiel and Meenakshi Mukherjee; and

The Oxford Anthology of Modern Indian Poetry (1994), ed. Vinay Dharwadker and A. K. Ramanujan. See also **Agha Shahid Ali, Eunice de Souza, A. K. Ramanujan.**

Irish Poetry

For studies of contemporary Irish poetry, see Terence Brown's *Northern Voices: Poets from Ulster* (1975); A. Norman Jeffares's *Anglo-Irish Literature* (1982); Seamus Deane's *Celtic Revivals: Essays in Modern Irish Literature 1880–1980* (1985); Robert F. Garratt's *Modern Irish Poetry: Tradition and Continuity from Yeats to Heaney* (1986); Edna Longley's *Poetry in the Wars* (1987); *The Chosen Ground: Essays on the Contemporary Poetry of Northern Ireland* (1992), ed. Neil Corcoran; *Contemporary Irish Poetry: A Collection of Critical Essays* (1992), ed. Elmer Andrews; Clair Wills's *Improprieties: Politics and Sexuality in Northern Irish Poetry* (1993); Theo Dorgan's *Irish Poetry since Kavanagh* (1995); Michael Kenneally's *Poetry in Contemporary Irish Literature* (1995); Patricia Boyle Haberstroh's *Women Creating Women* (1996); Steven Matthews's *Irish Poetry: Politics, History, Negotiation: The Evolving Debate, 1969 to the Present* (1997); Peter McDonald's *Mistaken Identities: Poetry and Northern Ireland* (1997); *Contemporary Irish Women Poets: Some Male Perspectives* (1999), ed. Alexander G. Gonzalez; Eamon Grennan's *Facing the Music: Irish Poetry in the Twentieth Century* (1999); Neil Corcoran's *Poets of Modern Ireland: Text, Context, Intertext* (1999); Jonathan Hufstader's *Tongue of Water, Teeth of Stones: Northern Irish Poetry and Social Violence* (1999); John Goodby's *From Stillness into History: Irish Poetry since 1950* (2000); Fran Brearton's *The Great War in Irish Poetry: W. B. Yeats to Michael Longley* (2000); Frank Sewell's *Modern Irish Poetry: A New Alhambra* (2000); Patrick Grant's *Literature, Rhetoric, and Violence in Northern Ireland, 1968–98* (2001); and *My Self, My Muse: Irish Women Poets Reflect on Life and Art* (2001), ed. Haberstroh.

Anthologies include *Contemporary Irish Poetry* (1980, 1988), ed. Anthony Bradley; *The Faber Book of Contemporary Irish Poetry* (1986), ed. Paul Muldoon; *The New Oxford Book of Irish Verse* (1986), ed. Thomas Kinsella; and *The Penguin Book of Contemporary Irish Poetry* (1990), ed. Peter Fallon and Derek Mahon. See also **Eavan Boland, Seamus Heaney, Thomas Kinsella, Michael Longley, Derek Mahon, Medbh McGuckian, Paul Muldoon.**

Language Poetry

For works associated with Language poetry, see Bruce Andrews and Charles Bernstein's *The L=A=N=G=U=A=G=E Book* (1984); Barrett Watten's *Total Syntax* (1984); Bob Perelman's *Writing/Talks* (1985); Ron Silliman's *The New Sentence* (1987); Bernstein's *The Politics of Poetic Form* (1990); and Lyn Hejinian's "The Rejection of Closure," reprinted in *The Language of Inquiry* (2000). *In the American Tree* (1986), ed. Silliman, is a representative anthology. For critical discussions, see Jerome McGann's "Contemporary Poetry, Alternate Routes," *Critical Inquiry* 13.3 (Spring 1987); George Hartley's *Textual Politics and the Language Poets* (1989); Marjorie Perloff's *Radical Artifice* (1991); Linda Reinfeld's *Language Poetry: Writing as Rescue* (1992); Perelman's *The Marginalization of Poetry: Language Writing and Literary History* (1996); Perloff's *Poetry on and off the Page* (1998); and Simon Perril's entry in *A Companion to Twentieth-Century Poetry* (2001), ed. Neil Roberts. See also **Charles Bernstein, Lyn Hejinian, Susan Howe, Michael Palmer.**

Latino Poetry

For studies of Latino poetry, see Américo Paredes's "The Folk Base of Chicano Literature," *Modern Chicano Writers: A Collection of Critical Essays* (1979), ed. Joseph Sommers and Tomás Ybarro-Frausto; Bruce-Novoa's *Chicano Poetry: A Response to Chaos* (1982); Marta Ester Sánchez's *Contemporary Chicana Poetry* (1985); *Partial Autobiographies: Interviews with Twenty Chicano Poets* (1985), ed. Wolfgang Binder; Cordelia Candelaria's *Chicano Poetry: A Critical Introduction* (1986); Bruce-Novoa's *RetroSpace: Collected Essays on Chicano Literature, Theory, and History* (1990); José Eduardo Límon's *Mexican Ballads, Chicano Poems: History and Influence in Mexican-American Social Poetry* (1992); Rafael Pérez-Torres's *Movements in Chicano Poetry: Against Myths, Against Margins* (1995); Alfred Arteaga's *Chicano Poetics: Heterotexts and Hybridities* (1997); and Teresa McKenna's *Migrant Song: Politics and Process in Contemporary Chicano Literature* (1997).

Anthologies include *Fiesta in Aztlan* (1982), ed. Toni Empringham; *Contemporary Chicano Poetry* (1986), ed. Wolfgang Binder; *Touching the Fire: Fifteen Poets of Today's Latino Renaissance* (1998), ed. Ray González. See also **Lorna Dee Cervantes, Dionisio D. Martínez, Alberto Ríos, Gary Soto.**

The Movement

New Lines (1956), ed. Robert Conquest, is the anthology that first attracted attention to the Movement. A fine book-length study is Blake Morrison's *The Movement: English Poetry and Fiction of the 1950s* (1980). For other discussions, see William Van O'Connor's *The New University Wits and the End of Modernism* (1963); Kenneth Allsop's *The Angry Decade* (1964); Anthony Saroop's "The Anti-Aestheticism of the British Movement Poets," *Studies in English Literature* 54 (1977); Florence Elon's "The Movement against Itself: British Poetry of the 1950s," *Southern Review* 19.1 (1983); Andrew Crozier's "Thrills and Frills: Poetry as Figures of Empirical Lyricism," *Society and Literature, 1945–1970* (1983), ed. Alan Sinfield; Michael Dirda's "The Movement," *Grand Street* 6.3 (1987); Hans Osterwalder's *British Poetry between the Movement and Modernism: Anthony Thwaite and Philip Larkin* (1991); and Stephen Regan's "The Movement," *A Companion to Twentieth-Century Poetry* (2001), ed. Neil Roberts. See also **Kingsley Amis, Donald Davie, Thom Gunn, Philip Larkin.**

Native American Poetry

For discussions of Native American poetry, see John Milton's *The American Indian Speaks* (1969); Kenneth Roemer's "Bear and Elk: The Nature(s) of Contemporary Indian Poetry," *Journal of Ethnic Studies* 5.2 (1977); J. Rupert's "The Uses of Oral Tradition in Six Contemporary Native American Poets," *American Indian Culture and Research Journal* 4 (1980); Anne Bromley's "Renegade Wants the Word: Contemporary Native American Poetry," *Literary Review* 23.3 (1980); Kenneth Lincoln's *Native American Renaissance* (1983); Duane Niatum's "History in the Colors of Song: A Few Words on Contemporary Native American Poetry," *Coyote Was Here: Essays on Contemporary Native American Literary and Political Mobilization* (1984), ed. Bo Schöler; Andrew Wiget's "Sending a Voice: The Emergence of Contemporary Native American Poetry," *College English* 46.6 (1984); Andrew Wiget's *Native American Literature* (1985); Joseph Bruchach's "Many Tongues: Native American Poetry Today," *North Dakota Quarterly* 55.4 (1987) and *Survival This Way: Interviews with American Indian Poets* (1987); Laura Coltelli's *Winged Words: American Indian Writers Speak* (1990); Robin Riley Fast's "Borderland Voice in Contemporary Native American Poetry," *Contemporary Literature* 36.3 (1995); Janet McAdams's "We, I, 'Voice,' and Voices: Reading Contemporary Native American Poetry," *Studies in American Indian Literatures* 7.3 (1995); Kathleen M. Donovan's *Feminist Readings of Native American Literature* (1998); *Native American Writers* (1998), ed. Harold Bloom; Fast's *The Heart as a Drum: Continuance and Resistance in American Indian Poetry* (1999); Lincoln's *Sing with the Heart of a Bear: Fusions of Native and American Poetry, 1890–1999* (2000); and Norma Wilson's *The Nature of Native American Poetry* (2001).

Anthologies include *The Remembered Earth: An Anthology of Contemporary Native American Literature* (1979, 1981), ed. Geary Hobson; *Harper's Anthology of 20th Century Native American Poetry* (1988), ed. Duane Niatum; *Durable Breath: Contemporary Native American Poetry* (1994), ed. John E. Smelcer; *Reinventing the Enemy's Language: Contemporary Native Women's Writings of North America* (1997), ed. Joy Harjo; and *Native American Women's Writing c. 1800–1924* (2000), ed. Karen Kilcup. See also **Sherman Alexie, Louise Erdrich, Joy Harjo, Leslie Marmon Silko.**

The New Criticism and Poetry

For the original critical works in which the tenets of the New Criticism were worked out, see Laura Riding and Robert Graves's *A Survey of Modernist Poetry* (1927); John Crowe Ransom's *The New Criticism* (1941); Cleanth Brooks's *The Well Wrought Urn* (1947) and his anthology *Understanding Poetry* (with Robert Penn Warren, 1938); William Empson's *Seven Types of Ambiguity* (1947); W. K. Wimsatt and Monroe C. Beardsley's *The Verbal Icon* (1954), especially their essay on "The Intentional Fallacy"; and Murray Krieger's *The New Apologists for Poetry* (1956). For critical discussions of the movement, see J. N. Patnaik's *The Aesthetics of the New Criticism* (1982); James E. B. Breslin's *From Modern to Contemporary* (1984); J. Timothy Bagwell's *American Formalism and the Problem of Interpretation* (1986); Mark Doty's "The 'Forbidden Planet' of Character: The Revolutions of the 1950s," *A Profile of Twentieth-Century American Poetry* (1991), ed. Jack Myers, David Wojahn, and Ed Folsom; Robert Bechtold's *The Southern Connection* (1991); Mark Jancovich's *Cultural Politics of the New Criticism* (1993); Mark Royden Winchell's *Cleanth Brooks and the Rise of Modern Criticism* (1996); and Stephen Burt and Jennifer Lewin's "Poetry and the New Criticism," *A Companion to Twentieth-Century Poetry* (2001).

New Formalism

For critical discussions of New Formalism, see Diane Wakoski's "The New Conservatism in American Poetry," *American Book Review* 7.4 (1986); *Expansive Poetry: Essays on the New Narrative and the New Formalism* (1989), ed. Frederick Feirstein; Robert McPhillips's "Reading the New Formalists," *Sewanee Review* 47.1 (1989); Wyatt Prunty's *"Fallen from the Symboled World": Precedents for the New Formalism* (1990); Ira Sadoff's "Neo-Formalism: A Dangerous Nostalgia," *American Poetry Review* 19.1 (1990); Lewis Turco's "New-Formalism in Contemporary American Poetry," *Poet* 2.3 (1990); Vernon Shetley's *After the Death of Poetry* (1993); *After New Formalism: Poets on Form, Narrative, and Tradition* (1999), ed. Annie Finch. Two anthologies associated with the movement are *Strong Measures: Contemporary American Poetry in Traditional Forms* (1986), ed. Philip Dacey and David Jauss; and *Rebel Angels: 25 Poets of the New Formalism* (1996), ed. Mark Jarman and David Mason. See also **Marilyn Hacker.**

New York School

Works dealing with the New York school include Geoffrey Ward's *Statutes of Liberty: The New York School of Poets* (1993); David Lehman's *The Last Avant-Garde: The Making of the New York School of Poets* (1998); John Simon's "Partying on Parnassus: The New York School Poets," *New Criterion* 17.2 (1998); William Watkin's *In the Process of Poetry: The New York School and the Avant-Garde* (2001); Terence Diggory and Stephen Paul Miller's *The Scene of My Selves : New Work on New York School Poets* (2001); and Paul Hoover's "Fables of Representation: Poetry of The New York School," *American Poetry Review* 31.4 (2002). The early anthologies *The Poets of the New York School* (1969), ed. John Bernard Myers, and *An Anthology of New York School Poets* (1970), ed. Ron Padgett and David Shapiro, helped institutionalize the poets as a school. See also **John Ashbery, Kenneth Koch, Frank O'Hara.**

San Francisco Renaissance

For more on the San Francisco Renaissance, see Daniel Aaron's *Writers on the Left: Episodes in American Literary Communism* (1961); Kenneth Rexroth's *American Poetry in the Twentieth Century* (1971); *The Poetics of the New American Poetry* (1973), ed. Donald Allen and Warren Tallman; William Everson's *Archetype West: The Pacific Coast as a Literary Region* (1976); *Towards a New American Poetics* (1978), ed. Ekbert Faas; Lawrence Ferlinghetti and Nancy J. Peters's *Literary San Francisco* (1980); Michael McClure's *Scratching the Beat Surface* (1982); *The Literary Review* (San Francisco Renaissance issue, Fall 1988); Michael Davidson's *The San Francisco Renaissance: Poetics and Community at Mid-Century* (1989); Lee Bartlett's *The Sun Is but a Morning Star: Studies in West Coast Poetry and Poetics* (1989); and Linda Hamalian's "Regionalism Makes Good: The San Francisco Renaissance," *Reading the West: New Essays on the Literature of the American West* (1996), ed. Michael Kowalewski. See also **Beat Poetry, Robert Duncan, Lawrence Ferlinghetti, Gary Snyder; in volume 1, Kenneth Rexroth.**

Ai

Ai's volumes of poetry include *Cruelty* (1973), *Killing Floor* (1979), *Sin* (1986), *Fate* (1991), *Greed* (1993), and *Vice: New and Selected Poems* (1999). She is also the author of a novel, *Black Blood* (1997). Selected periodical publications include "On Being ½ Japanese, ⅛ Choctaw, ¼ Black, and 1/16 Irish," *Ms.* 6 (June 1974); and "Movies, Mom, Poetry, Sex and

Death: A Self-Interview," *Onthebus* 3–4 (1991). Interviews include Lawrence Kearney and Michael Cuddihy's in *Ironwood* 12 (1978) and Lisa Erb's in *Manoa: A Pacific Journal of International Writing* 2 (1990).

Critical articles include Rob Wilson's "The Will to Transcendence in Contemporary American Poet, Ai," *Canadian Review of American Studies* 17.4 (1986); Susannah B. Mintz's " 'A Descent into the Unknown' in the Poetry of Ai," *Sage* 9.2 (1995); Jeanne Heuving's "Divesting Social Registers: Ai's Sensational Portraiture of the Renowned and the Infamous," *Critical Survey* 9.2 (1997); Claudia Ingram's "Writing the Crises: The Deployment of Abjection in Ai's Dramatic Monologues," *Lit: Literature Interpretation Theory* 8.2 (1997); and Karen L. Kilcup's "Dialogues of the Self: Toward a Theory of (Re)Reading Ai," *Journal of Gender Studies* 7.1 (1998).

Sherman Alexie

Alexie's books of poetry include *The Business of Fancydancing* (1992), *I Would Steal Horses* (1992), *First Indian on the Moon* (1993), *Old Shirts & New Skins* (1993), *Seven Mourning Songs for the Cedar Flute I Have Yet to Learn to Play* (1994), *Water Flowing Home* (1994), *The Summer of Black Widows* (1996), *The Man Who Loves Salmon* (1998), and *One Stick Song* (2000). Alexie has also published fiction, including the novels *Reservation Blues* (1995) and *Indian Killer* (1996), and short-story collections, *The Lone Ranger and Tonto Fistfight in Heaven* (1993) and *The Toughest Indian in the World* (2000). He also wrote the screenplays for the films *Smoke Signals* (1998) and *The Business of Fancydancing* (2002), which he also directed. Interviews include John and Carl Bellante's in *Bloomsbury Review* 14 (1994); Mark Weber's in *Chiron Review* (1995); and Kelly Myers's in *Tonic* 1 (1995).

Discussions of Alexie's work include Jennifer Gillan's "Reservation Home Movies: Sherman Alexie's Poetry," *American Literature* 68.1 (1996); Ron McFarland's "Another Kind of Violence: Sherman Alexie's Poetry," *American Indian Quarterly* 21 (1997); "Sherman Alexie," *Studies in American Indian Literatures* 9.4 (1997); Lynne Cline's "About Sherman Alexie," *Ploughshares* 26.4 (2000–2001); Kenneth Lincoln's *Sing with the Heart of a Bear: Fusions of Native and American Poetry, 1890–1999* (2000); John Newton's "Sherman Alexie's Autoethnography," *Contemporary Literature* 42.2 (2001); and Carrie Etter's "Dialectic to Dialogic: Negotiating Bicultural Heritage in Sherman Alexie's Sonnets," *Telling the Stories: Essays on American Literatures and Cultures* (2001), ed. Elizabeth Hoffman Nelson. See also **Native American Poetry.**

Agha Shahid Ali

Ali's volumes of poetry include *Bone Sculpture* (1972), *"In Memory of Begum Akhtar" and Other Poems* (1979), *The Half-Inch Himalayas* (1987), *A Walk through the Yellow Pages* (1987), *A Nostalgist's Map of America* (1991), *The Beloved Witness: Selected Poems* (1992), *The Country without a Post Office* (1997), and *Rooms Are Never Finished* (2001). He also edited a volume of ghazals, *Ravishing Disunities: Real Ghazals in English* (2000), translated the poetry of Faiz Ahmed Faiz in *The Rebel's Silhouette: Selected Poems* (1992), and wrote a scholarly study of T. S. Eliot, *T. S. Eliot as Editor* (1986).

Critical essays on his work include the review in *Indian Literature* 145.5 (1991); Neile Graham's in *Poet Lore* 87.1 (1992); Sudeep Sen's in *Poetry Review* 83.1 (1993); Lawrence Needham's "The Sorrows of a Broken Time," *Reworlding: Writers of the Indian Diaspora* (1992), ed. Emmanuel Nelson, and also Needham's "In Pursuit of Evanescence: Agha Shahid Ali's *A Nostalgist's Map of America*," *Kunapipi* 15.2 (1993); Ketu H. Katrak's "South Asian American Literature," *An Interethnic Companion to Asian American Literature* (1996), ed. King-Kok Cheung; Rajeev S. Patke's "Translation as Metaphor: The Poetry of Agha Shahid Ali," *Metamorphoses: Journal of the Five-College Seminar on Literary Translation* 8.2 (2000); and Amitav Ghosh's " 'The Ghat of the Only World': Agha Shahid Ali in Brooklyn," *Nation* (11 February 2002). See also **Indian Poetry**.

Kingsley Amis

Amis's *Collected Poems, 1944–1979* was published in 1979. Most famous for his many novels—notably *Lucky Jim* (1954)—Amis also wrote short stories, essays, science fiction, scripts for radio and television, and *The King's English: A Guide to Modern Usage* (1998). Zachary Leader edited *The Letters of Kingsley Amis* in 2000. Recent biographies are Eric Jacobs's *Kingsley Amis* (1995) and Richard Bradford's *Lucky Him: The Life of Kingsley Amis* (2001).

Book-length studies include Philip Gardner's *Kingsley Amis* (1981) and Paul Fussell's *The Anti-Egotist* (1994). Collections of essays include *Kingsley Amis in Life and Letters* (1990), ed. Dale Salwak; and *Critical Essays on Kingsley Amis* (1998), ed. Robert H. Bell. Other critical discussions include William Van O'Connor's *The New University Wits and the End of Modernism* (1963); John Press's *Rule and Energy: British Poetry since the Second World War* (1963); Blake Morrison's *The Movement: English Poetry and Fiction of the 1950s* (1980); Florence Elon's "The Movement Against Itself: British Poetry of the 1950s," *Southern Review* 19.1 (1983); and Edward Lobb's "The Dead Father: Notes on Literary Influence," *Studies in the Humanities* 13.2 (1986). Two bibliographies are Jack Benoit Gohn's *Kingsley Amis: A Checklist* (1976) and Salwak's *Kingsley Amis: A Reference Guide* (1978). See also **The Movement**.

A. R. Ammons

Collections of Ammons's poetry include *Collected Poems, 1951–1971* (1972), *Selected Longer Poems* (1980), *Selected Poems: Expanded Edition* (1986), and the *Really Short Poems of A. R. Ammons* (1990). Other volumes include *Sphere: The Form of Motion* (1974), *Diversifications* (1975), *Highgate Rode* (1977), *The Snow Poems* (1977), *A Coast of Trees* (1981), *Worldly Hopes* (1982), *Lake Effect Country* (1983), *Sumerian Vista* (1987), *Garbage* (1993), *Brink Road* (1996), *Glare* (1997), and *Strip* (1997). *Set in Motion* (1996) is a collection of essays and interviews.

Book-length studies of his work include Alan Holder's *A. R. Ammons* (1978) and Steven P. Schneider's *A. R. Ammons and the Poetics of Widening Scope* (1994). Other discussions of his work are included in Richard Howard's *Alone with America* (1969, 1980); Harold Bloom's *The Ringers in the Tower* (1971); Helen Vendler's *The Music of What Happens* (1988); Mary Kinzie's *The Cure of Poetry in an Age of Prose* (1993); Stephen Cushman's *Fictions of Form in American Poetry* (1993); Robert Kirschten's *Approaching Prayer: Ritual and the Shape of Myth in A. R. Ammons and James Dickey* (1998); Leonard M. Scigaj's *Sustainable Poetry: Four American Ecopoets* (1999); and Bonnie Costello's "Ammons: Pilgrim, Sage, Ordinary Man," *Raritan* (Winter 2002). There are numerous useful critical essays in the collections *A. R. Ammons* (1986), ed. Harold Bloom; *Critical Essays on A. R. Ammons* (1997), ed. Kirschten; and *Complexities of Motion: New Essays on A. R. Ammons's Long Poems* (1999), ed. Steven P. Schneider. Two special journal issues dedicated to Ammons are *Diacritics* 3 (Winter 1973) and *Pembroke Magazine* 18 (1986). Stuart Wright's *A. R. Ammons: A Bibliography, 1954–1979* was published in 1980.

John Ashbery

Ashbery's volumes of poetry include *Some Trees* (1956), *The Tennis Court Oath* (1962), *Rivers and Mountains* (1966), *The Double Dream of Spring* (1970), *Three Poems* (1972), *Self-Portrait in a Convex Mirror* (1975), *The Vermont Notebook* (with Joe Brainard, 1975); *Houseboat Days* (1977), *As We Know* (1979), *Shadow Train* (1981), *A Wave* (1984), *Selected Poems* (1985); *April Galleons* (1987); *Flow Chart* (1991); *Hotel Lautréamont* (1992), *Three Books* (1993), *And the Stars Were Shining* (1994), *Can You Hear, Bird* (1995); *The Mooring of Starting Out: The First Five Books of Poetry* (1997), *Wakefulness* (1998), *Girls on the Run* (1999), and *Your Name*

Here (2000). He is also the author of plays and the collaborative novel *A Nest of Ninnies* (with James Schuyler, 1969). His art criticism is collected in *Reported Sightings* (1989) and his series of lectures on neglected modern poets in *Other Traditions* (2000). Interviews include Janet Bloom and Robert Losada's in *The Craft of Poetry: Interviews from "The New York Quarterly"* (1974), ed. William Packard; A. Poulin's in *Michigan Quarterly Review* 20 (1981); John Koethe's in *Sub/Stance* 37/38 (1983); and David Herd's in *Pn Review* 21.1 (1994).

John Shoptaw's *On The Outside Looking Out* (1994) is an especially useful study of Ashbery's books from *Some Trees* to *Flow Chart*. Other studies include David Shapiro's *John Ashbery: An Introduction to the Poetry* (1979) and David Herd's *John Ashbery and American Poetry* (2000). Important discussions of his work include David Kalstone's *Five Temperaments* (1977); Charles Altieri's *Self and Sensibility in Contemporary American Poetry* (1984); Andrew Ross's *The Failure of Modernism: Symptoms of American Poetry* (1986); Lee Edelman's "The Pose of Imposture: Ashbery's 'Self-Portrait in a Convex Mirror,'" *Twentieth Century Literature* 32.1 (1986); Geoff Ward's "Ashbery and Influence," *Statutes of Liberty: The New York School of Poets* (1993, 2001); Catherine Imbriglio's "'Our Days Put on Such Reticence': The Rhetoric of the Closet in John Ashbery's *Some Trees*," *Contemporary Literature* 36.2 (1995); James Longenbach's "John Ashbery's Individual Talent," *Modern Poetry After Modernism* (1997); Peter Stitt's *Uncertainty and Plenitude* (1997); Thomas Gardner's "John Ashbery's New Voice," *Regions of Unlikeness* (1999); and Peter Nicholls's "Ashbery and Language Poetry," *Poetry and the Sense of Panic: Critical Essays on Elizabeth Bishop and John Ashbery* (2000), ed. Lionel Kelly. David Lehman's *The Last Avant-Garde: The Making of the New York School of Poets* (1998) combines biographical information with critical analysis of Ashbery and his fellow New York school poets. Many important essays are included in the collections *Beyond Amazement: New Essays on John Ashbery* (1980), ed. David Lehman; *John Ashbery* (1985), ed. Harold Bloom; and *The Tribe of John: Ashbery and Contemporary Poetry* (1995), ed. Susan M. Schultz. David K. Kermani's *John Ashbery: A Comprehensive Bibliography* appeared in 1976. See also **New York School.**

Margaret Atwood

Atwood's most recent collection of selected poetry is *Eating Fire: Selected Poems 1965–1995* (1998). Other volumes include *Double Persephone* (1961), *Kaleidoscopes: Baroque* (1965), *Talismans for Children* (1965), *The Circle Game* (1966), *Expeditions* (1966), *Speeches for Doctor Frankenstein* (1966), *The Animals in*

That Country (1968), *The Journals of Susanna Moodie* (1970), *Procedures for the Underground* (1970), *Power Politics* (1971), *You Are Happy* (1974), *Selected Poems* (1976), *Marsh, Hawk* (1977), *Two-Headed Poems* (1978), *Notes Towards a Poem That Can Never Be Written* (1981), *True Stories* (1981), *Snake Poems* (1983), *Interlunar* (1984), *Selected Poems II: Poems Selected and New 1976–1986* (1986), and *Morning in the Burned House* (1995). She is also the author of numerous novels, including *The Edible Woman* (1969), *The Handmaid's Tale* (1985), and *Cat's Eye* (1988), as well as short stories and children's fiction. Some of her criticism can be found in *Second Words: Selected Critical Prose* (1984), and interviews in *Margaret Atwood: Conversations* (1990), ed. Earl Ingersoll. She has also written a book on writing, *Negotiating with the Dead* (2002), and a guide to Canadian literature, *Survival* (1972), and edited *The New Oxford Book of Canadian Verse in English* (1982).

Collections of critical essays include *Margaret Atwood: A Symposium* (1977), ed. Linda Sandler; *The Art of Margaret Atwood: Essays in Criticism* (1981), ed. Arnold E. and Cathy N. Davidson; *Margaret Atwood: Language, Text, and System* (1983), ed. Grace and Lorraine Weir; *Critical Essays on Margaret Atwood* (1988), ed. Judith McCombs; *Margaret Atwood* (2000), ed. Harold Bloom; and *Margaret Atwood: Works and Impact* (2000), ed. Reingard M. Nischik. Other studies include Frank Davey's *Margaret Atwood: A Feminist Poetics* (1984) and Karen Stein's *Margaret Atwood Revisited* (1999). Alan J. Horne has compiled bibliographies of Atwood's poetry and prose in *The Annotated Bibliography of Canada's Major Authors 1–2* (1979–1980), ed. Robert Lecker and Jack David. See also **Canadian Poetry.**

Amiri Baraka

Baraka's *Selected Poetry* was published in 1979. Other volumes include *Preface to a Twenty Volume Suicide Note* (1961), *The Dead Lecturer* (1964), *Black Art* (1966), *Black Magic: Collected Poetry, 1961–1967* (1969), *It's Nation Time* (1970), *Spirit Reach* (1972), *Afrikan Revolution* (1973), *Hard Facts* (1976), *AM/TRAK* (1979), *Reggae or Not!* (1981); *Wise, Why's Y's* (1995), *Eulogies* (1996), and *Funk Lore: New Poems, 1984–1995* (1996). His dramatic and prose works have been collected in *Selected Plays and Prose* (1979) and, with selected poetry, in the *LeRoi Jones/Amiri Baraka Reader* (1991, 2000), ed. William J. Harris. Some of his most important plays can be found in *Dutchman and the Slave* (1964) and *Four Black Revolutionary Plays* (1969). Prose writings include *Blues People* (1963), *Home: Social Essays* (1966), *Raise Race Rays Raze* (1972), *The Autobiography of LeRoi Jones* (1984), *Daggers and Javelins: Essays,*

1974–1979 (1984), and *The Music: Reflections on Jazz and Blues* (1987). Charlie Reilly edited a book of interviews, *Conversations with Amiri Baraka*, in 1994. Baraka performed his poetry to jazz accompaniment on audio recordings such as *New Music—New Poetry* (1981), with David Murray and Steve McCall.

Imamu Amiri Baraka (1978), ed. Kimberly W. Benston, is a collection of critical essays. Other useful studies include Werner Sollors's *Amiri Baraka/LeRoi Jones: The Quest for a "Populist Modernism"* (1978); Lloyd Brown's *Amiri Baraka* (1980); William J. Harris's *Poetry and Poetics of Amiri Baraka: The Jazz Aesthetic* (1985); Komozi Woodard's *A Nation within a Nation: Amiri Baraka (LeRoi Jones) and Black Power Politics* (1999); and Jerry Gafio Watts's *Amiri Baraka: The Politics and Art of a Black Intellectual* (2001). Theodore R. Hudson's *A LeRoi Jones (Amiri Baraka) Bibliography* (1971) and Letitia Dace's *LeRoi Jones (Imamu Amiri Baraka): A Checklist of Works by and about Him* (1971), provide reference information on primary and secondary materials. Some individual articles about Baraka's work are W. D. E. Andrews's "'All Is Permitted': The Poetry of LeRoi Jones/Amiri Baraka," *Southwest Review* 67.2 (1982); David Smith's "Amiri Baraka and the Black Arts of Black Art" in *Boundary 2* 15.1–2 (1986–87); and Fred Moten's "Tragedy Elegy Improvisation: Voices of Baraka, II" in *Semiotics 1994* (1995), ed. C. W. Spinks and John Deely. See also **Beat Movement, Black Arts Movement.**

Louise Bennett

Bennett's *Selected Poems* (1982, 1983) was edited by Mervyn Morris and contains his excellent introduction and notes; an earlier edited selection, also important, is *Jamaica Labrish* (1966), edited by Rex Nettleford. Other volumes of poetry, folktales, and stories include *Jamaica Dialect Verses* (1942), compiled by George R. Bowen; *Anancy Stories and Poems in Dialect* (1944); *Jamaican Dialect Poems* (1949); *Anancy Stories and Dialect Verse* (with others, 1950, 1957); *Laugh with Louise: A Pot-Pourri of Jamaican Folklore, Stories, Songs, Verses* (with Lois Kelle-Barrow) (1961); and *Anancy and Miss Lou* (1979). *Aunty Roachy Seh* (1993), ed. Mervyn Morris, is a collection of monologues from Bennett's popular radio broadcasts. Her brilliant performances of her poetry can be heard on recordings such as *Yes M'Dear: Miss Lou Live!* (1983).

Discussions of Bennett's works can be found in Rex Nettleford's introduction to Bennett's *Jamaica Labrish* (1966); Lloyd W. Brown, *West Indian Poetry* (1978); Morris's "Louise Bennett in Print," *Caribbean Quarterly* 28.1–2 (1982); Edward Kamau Brathwaite's *History of the Voice: The Development of Nation Language in*

Anglophone Caribbean Poetry (1984); Carolyn Cooper's *Noises in the Blood: Orality, Gender and the "Vulgar" Body of Jamaican Popular Culture* (1993); Eric Doumerc's "Louise Bennett and the Mento Tradition," *Ariel* 31.4 (2000); and Jahan Ramazani's *The Hybrid Muse* (2001). See also **Caribbean Poetry.**

Charles Bernstein

An extensive collection of Bernstein's poetry is *Republics of Reality: 1975–1995* (2000). Other volumes include *Asylums* (1975), *Parsing* (1976), *Shade* (1978), *Poetic Justice* (1979), *Senses of Responsibility* (1979), *Controlling Interests* (1980), *Legend* (with others, 1980), *The Occurrence of Tune* (photographs by Susan Bee Laufer, 1980), *Disfrutes* (1981), *Stigma* (1981), *Islets/Irritations* (1983), *Resistance* (1983), *Amblyopia* (1985), *The Sophist* (1987), *Veil* (1987), *Four Poems* (1988), *The Nude Formalism* (1989), *The Absent Father in Dumbo* (1990), *Fool's Gold* (with Laufer, 1990), *Rough Trades* (1990), *Dark City* (1994), *Little Orphan Anagram* (with Laufer, 1997), *Log Rhythms* (with Laufer, 1998), *My Way: Speeches and Poems* (1999), and *With Strings* (2001). Bernstein's critical and theoretical contributions include *Content's Dream: Essays* (1986, 2001), *The Politics of Poetic Farm: Poetry and Public Policy* (1990), and *A Poetics* (1992). Bernstein has also written libretti for operas such as *The Blind Witness News* (1990) and *The Lenny Paschen Show* (1992). Along with Bruce Andrews, Bernstein edited L=A=N=G=U=A=G=E, the journal at the center of the Language poetry movement, from 1978 to 1981.

Critical discussions of Bernstein's work can be found in *The Difficulties* 2 (1982), ed. Tom Beckett; Marjorie Perloff's *The Dance of the Intellect: Studies in the Poetry of the Pound Tradition* (1985); Linda Reinfeld's *Language Poetry: Writing as Rescue* (1992); Jerome McGann's *Black Riders: The Visible Language of Modernism* (1993); Hank Lazer's "Charles Bernstein's Dark City: Polis, Policy, and the Policing of Poetry," *American Poetry Review* 24.5 (1995); Paul Naylor's "(Mis)Characterizing Charlie: Language and the Self in the Poetry and Poetics of Charles Bernstein," *Sagetrieb* 14.3 (1995); and Charles Altieri's "Some Problems about Agency in the Theories of Radical Poetics," *Contemporary Literature* 37.2 (1996). Among other interviews is Loss Pequeño Glazier's "An Autobiographical Interview with Charles Bernstein," *Boundary 2* 23.3 (1996). A bibliography appears in *The Difficulties* 2 (1982). See also **Language Poetry.**

John Berryman

Collections of Berryman's poetry include *Collected Poems, 1937–1971* (1989), ed. Charles Thornbury, and *Selected Poems, 1938–1968*

(1972). *77 Dream Songs* (1964) and *His Toy, His Dream, His Rest* (1968) were published together as *The Dream Songs* in 1969. Berryman also wrote a novel, *Recovery* (1973), a biography of Stephen Crane (1950), and Shakespeare criticism, published posthumously as *Berryman's Shakespeare* (1999). *The Freedom of the Poet* (1976) includes prose, short fiction, and interviews. Biographies include Paul Mariani's *Dream Song: The Life of John Berryman* (1982), John Haffenden's *The Life of John Berryman* (1990), and Eileen Simpson's memoir, *Poets in Their Youth* (1982).

Collections of critical essays include *Berryman's Understanding* (1988), ed. Harry Thomas; *John Berryman* (1989), ed. Harold Bloom; and *Recovering Berryman* (1993), ed. Richard J. Kelly and Alan K. Lathrop. Other useful studies include J. M. Linebarger's *John Berryman* (1974); Joel Conarroe's *John Berryman: An Introduction to the Poetry* (1977); Haffenden's *John Berryman: A Critical Commentary* (1980); Bruce Bawer's *The Middle Generation* (1986); Stephen Matterson's *Berryman and Lowell: The Art of Losing* (1988); Helen Vendler's *The Given and the Made* (1995); and Thomas Travisano's *Midcentury Quartet: Bishop, Lowell, Jarrell, Berryman, and the Making of a Postmodern Aesthetic* (1999). Bibliographies include Richard J. Kelly's *John Berryman: A Checklist* (1972); Ernest C. Stefanik Jr.'s *John Berryman: A Descriptive Bibliography* (1974); and Gary Q. Arpin's *John Berryman: A Reference Guide* (1976). See also **Confessional Poetry.**

Frank Bidart

In the Western Night: Collected Poems, 1965–90 was published in 1990. Subsequent volumes are *Desire* (1997) and *Music Like Dirt* (2002). Interviews include Mark Halliday's in *Ploughshares* 9.1 (1983), Tim Liu's in *Lambda Book Report: A Review of Gay and Lesbian Literature* 6.9 (1998), and Andrew Rathmann and Danielle Allen's in *Chicago Review* 47.3 (2001).

Discussions of his work can be found in Robert Pinsky's *The Situation of Poetry* (1976), Louise Glück's *Proofs and Theories: Essays on Poetry* (1994), and Anne Ferry's *The Title to the Poem* (1996). Relevant essays include Alan Nadel's "Wellesley Poets: The Works of Robert Pinsky and Frank Bidart," *New England Review & Bread Loaf Quarterly* 4.2 (1981); Brad Crenshaw's "The Sin of the Body: Frank Bidart's Human Bondage," *Chicago Review* 33.4 (1983); David Young's "Out beyond Rhetoric: Four Poets and One Critic," *Field: Contemporary Poetry & Poetics* 30 (1984); Seamus Heaney's "Frank Bidart: A Salute," *Agni* 36 (1992); Jeffrey Gray's " 'Necessary Thought': Frank Bidart and the Postconfessional," *Contemporary Literature* 34.4 (1993); Justin Quinn's "Frank Bidart and the Fate of the Lyric," *Pn Review* 27 (July–

August 2001); and Ann Keniston's " 'The Fluidity of Damaged Form': Apostrophe and Desire in Nineties Lyric," *Contemporary Literature* 42.2 (2001).

Elizabeth Bishop

Bishop's collected poetry is available in *The Complete Poems, 1927–1979* (1983). Stories, memoirs, and other prose works can be found in *The Collected Prose* (1984). Bishop also published travel writing, *Brazil* (1962); translated Portuguese literature; and edited collections of poetry such as *An Anthology of Twentieth-Century Brazilian Poetry* (with Emanuel Brasil, 1972). *Conversations with Elizabeth Bishop* (1996), ed. George Monteiro, is a collection of interviews; *One Art* (1994), ed. Robert Giroux, is a collection of letters; and the standard biography is Brett C. Millier's *Elizabeth Bishop: Life and the Memory of It* (1993).

Book-length studies of Bishop's work include Thomas Travisano's *Elizabeth Bishop: Her Artistic Development* (1988), Robert Dale Parker's *The Unbeliever: The Poetry of Elizabeth Bishop* (1988), David Kalstone's *Becoming a Poet: Elizabeth Bishop with Marianne Moore and Robert Lowell* (1989), Bonnie Costello's *Elizabeth Bishop: Questions of Mastery* (1991), Lorrie Goldensohn's *Elizabeth Bishop: The Biography of a Poetry* (1992), Victoria Harrison's *Elizabeth Bishop's Poetics of Intimacy* (1993), Carole Doreski's *Elizabeth Bishop: The Restraints of Language* (1993), Susan McCabe's *Elizabeth Bishop: Her Poetics of Loss* (1994), Marilyn May Lombardi's *The Body and the Song: Elizabeth Bishop's Poetics* (1995), Anne Colwell's *Inscrutable Houses: Metaphors of the Body in the Poems of Elizabeth Bishop* (1997), and Anne Stevenson's *Five Looks at Elizabeth Bishop* (1998). Other illuminating discussions of her work can be found in Helen Vendler's *Part of Nature, Part of Us* (1980), Susan Schweik's *A Gulf So Deeply Cut* (1991), James Longenbach's *Modern Poetry after Modernism* (1997), and Thomas Gardner's *Regions of Unlikeness* (1999). Collections of essays on Bishop include *Elizabeth Bishop and Her Art* (1983), ed. Lloyd Schwartz and Sybil P. Estess; *Elizabeth Bishop* (1985), ed. Harold Bloom; and *Elizabeth Bishop: The Geography of Gender* (1993), ed. Lombardi. A bibliography by Candace W. MacMahon appeared in 1980.

Robert Bly

Bly's most recent collection of selected poems is *Eating the Honey of Words: New and Selected Poems* (1999). Other volumes include *The Lion's Tail and Eyes: Poems Written out of Laziness and Silence* (with James Wright and William Duffy, 1962), *Silence in the Snowy Fields* (1962), *Chrysanthemums* (1967), *The Light Around the Body* (1967), *Ducks* (1968), *The Morning Glory* (1969, 1975), *The Shadow-Mothers* (1970), *The*

Teeth-Mother Naked at Last (1970), *Poems for Tennessee* (with William Stafford and William Matthews, 1971), *Christmas Eve Service at Midnight at St. Michael's* (1972), *Jumping out of Bed* (1972), *Water under the Earth* (1972), *The Dead Seal Near McClure's Beach* (1973), *Sleepers Joining Hands* (1973), *The Hockey Poem* (1974), *Point Reyes Poems* (1974), *Leaping Poetry* (1975), *Old Man Rubbing His Eyes* (1975), *The Loon* (1977), *This Body Is Made of Camphor and Gopherwood* (1977), *This Tree Will Be Here for a Thousand Years* (1979), *"Visiting Emily Dickinson's Grave" and Other Poems* (1979), *Finding an Old Ant Mansion* (1981), *The Man in the Black Coat Turns* (1981), *The Eight Stages of Translation* (1983), *Four Ramages* (1983), *"Out of the Rolling Ocean" and Other Love Poems* (1984), *Loving a Woman in Two Worlds* (1985), *Selected Poems* (1986), *The Moon on a Fencepost* (1988), *The Apple Found in the Plowing* (1989), *What Have I Ever Lost by Dying?: Collected Prose Poems* (1992), *Gratitude to Old Teachers* (1993), *Meditations on the Insatiable Soul* (1994), *Holes the Crickets Have Eaten in Blankets* (1997), *Morning Poems* (1997), and *The Night Abraham Called to the Stars* (2001). He has also translated extensively from the work of poets such as Georg Trakl, Pablo Neruda, and Rainer Maria Rilke, and written a book on masculinity, *Iron John* (1990). A book of interviews is *Talking All Morning* (1979). An interview also appears in Bill Moyers's *The Language of Life* (1995).

Critical discussions of his work can be found in Ingegerd Friberg's *Moving Inward: A Study of Robert Bly's Poetry* (1977); *Of Solitude and Silence: Writings on Robert Bly* (1981), ed. Kate Daniels and Richard Jones; James E. B. Breslin's *From Modern to Contemporary: American Poetry, 1945–1965* (1984); Howard Nelson's *Robert Bly: An Introduction to the Poetry* (1984); Richard P. Sugg's *Robert Bly* (1986); *Critical Essays on Robert Bly* (1992), ed. William V. Davis; Victoria Harris's *The Incorporative Consciousness of Robert Bly* (1992); and Davis's *Robert Bly: The Poet and His Critics* (1994). A bibliography is William H. Roberson's *Robert Bly: A Primary and Secondary Bibliography* (1986). See also **Deep Image Poetry.**

Eavan Boland

An Origin Like Water: Collected Poems, 1967–1987 appeared in 1996. Subsequent volumes of poetry include *Outside History* (1990), *In a Time of Violence* (1994), *Night Feed* (1994), *Collected Poems* (1995), *The Lost Land* (1998), *Against Love Poetry* (2001), and *Code* (2001). Her essay *A Kind of Scar: The Woman Poet in a National Tradition* (1989) offers essential insight into her work, as does *Object Lessons: The Life of the Woman and the Poet in Our Time* (1995). She has also coedited *The Making of a Poem: A Nor-*

ton Anthology of Poetic Forms (2000). Interviews include Amy Klauke's in *Northwest Review* 25.1 (1987), Marilyn Reizbaum's in *Contemporary Literature* 30.4 (1989), Patty O'Connell's in *Poets & Writers* 22.6 (1994), and Margaret Mills Harper's in *Five Points* 1.2 (1997).

Studies of her work include Patricia L. Hagen and Thomas W. Zelman's " 'We Were Never on the Scene of the Crime': Eavan Boland's Repossession of History," *Twentieth Century Literature* 37.4 (1991); Ellen M. Mahon's "Eavan Boland's Journey with the Muse," *Learning the Trade: Essays on W. B. Yeats and Contemporary Poetry* (1993), ed. Deborah Fleming; Jody Allen-Randolph's "Finding a Voice Where She Found a Vision," *Pn Review* 21.1 (1994); Kerry E. Robertson's "Anxiety, Influence, Tradition, and Subversion in the Poetry of Eavan Boland," *Colby Quarterly* 30.4 (1994); Patricia Boyle Habberstroh's *Women Creating Women: Contemporary Women Irish Poets* (1996); David C. Ward's "Eavan Boland: Mazing Her Way," *Sewanee Review* 106.2 (1998); Katie Conboy's essay in *Border Crossings: Irish Women Writers and National Identities* (2000), ed. Kathryn Kirkpatrick; *Critical Ireland: New Essays in Literature and Culture* (2001), ed. Alan A. Gillis and Aaron Kelly; and Richard Rankin Russell's "W. B. Yeats and Eavan Boland: Postcolonial Poets?" in *W. B. Yeats and Postcolonialism* (2001), ed. Deborah Fleming. *Irish University Review* (Spring/Summer 1993) and *Colby Quarterly* 35.4 (1999) are special issues dedicated to Boland. See also **Irish Poetry.**

Kamau Brathwaite

Brathwaite's volumes of poetry are *The Arrivants: A New World Trilogy* (1973), which includes *Rights of Passage* (1967), *Masks* (1968), and *Islands* (1969); *Days and Nights* (1975); *Other Exiles* (1975); *Black + Blues* (1976); *Mother Poem* (1977); *Soweto* (1979); *Word Making Man: A Poem for Nicólas Guillén* (1979); *Sun Poem* (1982); *Third World Poems* (1983); *Jah Music* (1986); *X/Self* (1987); *Sappho Sakyi's Meditations* (1989); *Middle Passages* (1992); *Shar/Hurricane Poem* (1992); *Trench Town Rock* (1994); *Words Need Love Too* (2000); and *Ancestors: A Reinvention of Mother Poem, Sun Poem, and X/Self* (2001). Brathwaite has also written plays, including *Four Plays for Primary Schools* (1964) and *Odale's Voice* (1967). A revised edition of his *Roots: Essays in Caribbean Literature* (1986) appeared in 1993. He has also written important works of nonfiction, *The Development of Creole Society in Jamaica, 1770–1820* (1971) and *History of the Voice: The Development of Nation Language in Anglophone Caribbean Poetry* (1984), and edited collections of literature, *Iouanaloa: Recent Writing from St. Lucia* (1963) and *New Poets from Jamaica* (1979).

Collections of essays include *The Art of Kamau Brathwaite* (1995), ed. Stewart Brown; a special issue of *World Literature Today* 68.4 (1994); and *For the Geography of a Soul: Emerging Perspectives on Kamau Brathwaite*, ed. Timothy J. Reiss (2001). Other relevant discussions include Gordon Rohlehr's *Pathfinder: Black Awakening in* The Arrivants *of Edward Kamau Brathwaite* (1981); Maureen Warner Lewis's *E. Kamau Brathwaite's Masks: Essays and Annotations* (1992); Elaine Savory's "The Word Becomes *Nam*: Self and Community in the Poetry of Kamau Brathwaite and Its Relation to Caribbean Culture and Postmodern Theory," *Writing the Nation: Self and Country in the Post-Colonial Imagination* (1996), ed. John C. Hawley; Silvio Torres-Saillant's *Caribbean Poetics: Toward an Aesthetic of West Indian Literature* (1997); June D. Bobb's *Beating a Restless Drum: The Poetics of Kamau Brathwaite and Derek Walcott* (1998); and Paul Naylor's *Poetic Investigations: Singing the Holes in History* (1999). See also **Caribbean Poetry**.

Gwendolyn Brooks

Brooks's volumes of poetry include *A Street in Bronzeville* (1945), *Annie Allen* (1949), *Bronzeville Boys and Girls* (1956), *The Bean Eaters* (1960), *Selected Poems* (1963, 1999), *In the Mecca* (1968), *Riot* (1969), *Family Pictures* (1970), *Aloneness* (1971), *Beckonings* (1975), *To Disembark* (1981), *"The Near-Johannesburg Boy" and Other Poems* (1986, 1991), *Winnie* (1988), and *Children Coming Home* (1991). Poetry and prose are collected in *The World of Gwendolyn Brooks* (1971) and *Blacks* (1987, 1991). Other prose works include the novel *Maud Martha* (1953, 1974) and the autobiographical *Report from Part One* (1972) and *Report from Part Two* (1996). She also edited *A Broadside Treasury* (1971), *Jump Bad: A New Chicago Anthology* (1971), and *A Capsule Course in Black Poetry Writing* (1975). George E. Kent published the biography *A Life of Gwendolyn Brooks* in 1990.

Collections of essays on her work include Maria K. Mootry and Gary Smith's *A Life Distilled: Gwendolyn Brooks, Her Poetry and Fiction* (1987); *Say That the River Turns: The Impact of Gwendolyn Brooks* (1987), ed. Haki R. Madhubuti; *On Gwendolyn Brooks: Reliant Contemplation* (1996), ed. Stephen Caldwell Wright; and *Gwendolyn Brooks*, ed. Harold Bloom (2000). Other studies include Harry B. Shaw's *Gwendolyn Brooks* (1980); D. H. Melhem's *Gwendolyn Brooks: Poetry and the Heroic Voice* (1987); and B. J. Bolden's *Urban Rage in Bronzeville: Social Commentary in the Poetry of Gwendolyn Brooks* (1999). Also of interest is Melhem's "Cultural Challenge, Heroic Response: Gwendolyn Brooks and the New Black Poetry," *Perspectives of Black Popular Culture* (1990), ed.

Harry Shaw; Susan Schweik's chapter on Brooks in *A Gulf So Deeply Cut* (1991); Kathryne Lindberg's "Whose Canon? Gwendolyn Brooks: Founder at the Center of the 'Margins,'" *Gendered Modernisms* (1996), ed. Margaret Dickie and Thomas Travisano; and essays and an interview in *The Furious Flowering of African American Poetry*, ed. Joanne V. Gabbin (1999). Bibliographic information can be found in R. Baxter Miller's *Langston Hughes and Gwendolyn Brooks: A Reference Guide* (1978).

Anne Carson

Poetry and prose are often combined in Carson's books, which include *Short Talks* (1992), *Plainwater* (1995), *Glass, Irony, and God* (1995), *Autobiography of Red* (1998), *Men in the Off Hours* (2000), and *The Beauty of the Husband: A Fictional Essay in 29 Tangos* (2001). Other works include her classical study *Eros the Bittersweet* (1986) and *Economy of the Unlost: Reading Simonides of Keos with Paul Celan* (1999). John D'Agata has interviewed Carson in *Iowa Review* 27.2 (1997) and *Brick* 57 (1997).

Guy Davenport introduces Carson's *Glass, Irony, and God*. Other relevant essays include Jorie Graham's "An Introduction to Anne Carson," *Brick* 57 (1997); Paula Melton's "Essays at Anne Carson's *Glass, Irony and God*," *Iowa Review* 27.1 (1997); Jeff Hamilton's "This Cold Hectic Dawn and I," *Denver Quarterly* 32.1–2 (1997); Mark Halliday's "Carson: Mind and Heart," *Chicago Review* 45.2 (1999); Sharon Wahl's "Erotic Sufferings: *Autobiography of Red* and Other Anthropologies," *Iowa Review* 29.1 (1999); Kevin McNeilly's "Home Economics" and Ian Rae's "'Dazzling Hybrids': The Poetry of Anne Carson," both in *Canadian Literature* 166 (2000); Melanie Rehak's "Things Fall Together," *New York Times Magazine* (26 March 2000); David C. Ward's "Anne Carson: Addressing the Wound," *Pn Review* 27.5 (2001); Chris Jennings's "The Erotic Poetics of Anne Carson," *University of Toronto Quarterly* 70.4 (2001); and Harriet Zinnes's "What Is Time Made Of? The Poetry of Anne Carson," *Hollins Critic* 38.1 (2001). See also **Canadian Poetry**.

Lorna Dee Cervantes

Cervantes's volumes of poetry are *Emplumada* (1981) and *From the Cables of Genocide: Poems of Love and Hunger* (1991). Interviews include Bernadette Monda's in *Third Woman* 2.1 (1984), Ray Gonzalez's in *Bloomsbury Review* 17.5 (1997), and one in Karin Ikas's *Chicana Ways: Conversations with Ten Chicana Writers* (2001).

Marta Ester Sánchez's *Contemporary Chicana Poetry: A Critical Approach to an Emerging Literature* (1985) and Deborah L. Madsen's *Understanding Contemporary Chicana Literature* (2000) offer discussions of Cervantes in the larger context of Chicana literature. Critical essays include Bárbara Brinson-Curiel's "Our Own Words: *Emplumada*," *Tecolote* 3 (1982); Lynette Seator, "*Emplumada*: Chicana Rites-of-Passages," *MELUS* 11.2 (1984); Tey Diana Rebolledo's "Soothing Restless Serpents: The Dreaded Creation and Other Inspirations in Chicana Poetry," *Third Woman* 2.1 (1984); John F. Crawford's "Notes toward a New Multicultural Criticism: Three Works by Women of Color," *A Gift of Tongues: Critical Challenges in Contemporary American Poetry* (1987), ed. Marie Harris and Kathleen Aguero; Yvonne Yarbro-Bejarano's "Chicana Literature from a Chicana Feminist Perspective," *Chicana Creativity and Criticism: Charting New Frontiers in American Literature* (1988, 1996), ed. María Herrera-Sobek and Helena María Viramontes; Patricia Wallace's "Divided Loyalties: Literal and Literary in the Poetry of Lorna Dee Cervantes, Cathy Song and Rita Dove," *MELUS* 18.3 (1993); and Ada Savin's "Bilingualism and Dialogism: Another Reading of Lorna Dee Cervantes's Poetry," *An Other Tongue: Nation and Ethnicity in the Linguistic Borderlands* (1994), ed. Alfred Arteaga. See also **Latino Poetry.**

Marilyn Chin

Chin's volumes of poetry include *Dwarf Bamboo* (1987), *The Phoenix Gone, The Terrace Empty* (1994), and *Rhapsody in Plain Yellow* (2002). She has also translated Gozo Yoshimasu's *Devil Wind: A Thousand Steps or More* (1980) and *Selected Poems of Ai Qing* (with Peng Wenlan and Eugene Eoyang, 1982), as well as the work of various contemporary Chinese poets. In addition, she coedited *Dissident Song: A Contemporary Asian American Anthology* (with David Wong Louie, 1991).

Discussions of Chin's work can be found in *Reading the Literatures of Asian America* (1992), ed. Shirley Geok-lin Lim and Amy Ling; Anne-Elizabeth Green's entry on Chin in *Contemporary Women Poets* (1998), ed. Pamela L. Shelton; Adrienne McCormick's "'Being Without': Marilyn Chin's Poems as Feminist Acts of Theorizing," *Hitting Critical Mass* 6.2 (2000); Mary Slowik's "Beyond Lot's Wife: The Immigration Poems of Marilyn Chin, Garrett Hongo, Li-Young Lee, and David Mura," *MELUS* 25.3–4 (2000); and John Gery's "'Mocking My Own Happiness': Authenticity, Heritage, and Self-Erasure in the Poetry of Marilyn Chin," *Lit: Literature Interpretation Theory* 12.1 (2001). See also **Asian American Poetry.**

Amy Clampitt

The Collected Poems of Amy Clampitt appeared in 1997, with a useful introduction by Mary Jo Salter. *Predecessors, Et Cetera* (1991) is a collection of Clampitt's essays. Clampitt also edited *The Essential Donne* (1988). An interview with

Laura Fairchild appears in *The American Poetry Review* 16.4 (1987), and one with Jan Huesgen and Robert W. Lewis in *North Dakota Quarterly* 58.1 (1990).

Discussions of Clampitt's work can be found in Peter Sacks's *The English Elegy* (1985), Helen Vendler's *The Music of What Happens* (1976, 1988) and *Soul Says* (1995), J. D. McClatchy's *White Paper: On Contemporary American Poetry* (1989), Jahan Ramazani's *Poetry of Mourning* (1994), and James Longenbach's *Modern Poetry After Modernism* (1997). Other essays and reviews include Edmund White's "Poetry as Alchemy," *Nation* 236 (16 April 1983); Robert E. Hosmer Jr.'s "Amy Clampitt: The Art of Poetry," *Paris Review* 126 (1993); a special issue of *Verse* 10.3 (1993), ed. Bonnie Costello; and Willard Spiegelman's "What to Make of an Augmented Thing," *Kenyon Review* 21.1 (1999).

Lucille Clifton

Clifton's volumes of poetry include *Good Times* (1969), *Good News about the Earth* (1972), *An Ordinary Woman* (1974), *Two-Headed Woman* (1980), *Good Woman: Poems and a Memoir, 1969–1980* (1987), *Next* (1987), *Ten Oxherding Pictures* (1988), *Quilting* (1991), *The Book of Light* (1993), *Terrible Stories* (1996), *Selected Poems* (1996), and *Blessing the Boats: New and Selected Poems, 1988–2000* (2000). She also wrote a family memoir, *Generations* (1976), and many books for children, including the *Everett Anderson* series. An interview appears in Bill Moyers's *The Language of Life* (1995).

Several discussions of Clifton's work can be found in *Black Women Writers (1950–1980): A Critical Evaluation* (1984), ed. Mari Evans: Clifton's own "A Simple Language," Haki Madhubuti's "Lucille Clifton: Warm Water, Greased Legs, and Dangerous Poetry," and Audrey T. McCluskey's "Tell the Good News: A View of the Works of Lucille Clifton." Other studies include Andrea Benton Rushing's "Lucille Clifton: A Changing Voice for Changing Times," *Coming to Light: American Women Poets in the Twentieth Century* (1985), ed. Diane Wood Middlebrook and Marilyn Yalom; Alicia Ostriker's "Kin and Kind: The Poetry of Lucille Clifton," *American Poetry Review* 22.6 (1993); Akasha Hull's "In Her Own Images: Lucille Clifton and the Bible," *Dwelling in Possibility: Women Poets and Critics on Poetry* (1997), ed. Yopie Prins and Maeera Shreiber; Hillary Holladay's "Songs of Herself: Lucille Clifton's Poems about Womanhood," *The Furious Flowering of African American Poetry* (1999), ed. Joanne V. Gabbin; and Ajuan Maria Mance's "Re-Locating the Black Female Subject: The Landscape of the Body in the Poems of Lucille Clifton," *Recovering the Black Female Body: Self-Representations by African American Women* (2001), ed. Michael Bennett and Vanessa D. Dickerson. See also **Black Arts Movement.**

Henri Cole

Cole's volumes of poetry are *The Marble Queen* (1986), *The Zoo Wheel of Knowledge* (1989), *The Look of Things* (1995), and *The Visible Man* (1998). He appears in *Under 35: The New Generation of American Poets* (1989), ed. Nicholas Christopher. A brief section of his journal appears in *The Writer's Journal* (1997), ed. Sheila Bender. He has interviewed Helen Vendler in *Paris Review* 38.141 (1996) and Seamus Heaney in *Paris Review* 39.144 (1997), and Vendler discusses his work in *Soul Says: On Recent Poetry* (1995). Reviews include Wayne Koestenbaum's in *New Yorker* 71.10 (1 May 1995), Richard Holinger's in *Midwest Quarterly* 37.3 (1996), Timothy Liu's in *Lambda Book Report* 7.4 (1998), Tim Gavin's in *Library Journal* 123.16 (1998), Phoebe Pettingell's "Poetry Read in Canoes," *New Leader* 82.1 (1999), and John Taylor's in *Antioch Review* 58.1 (2000).

Robert Creeley

The Collected Poems of Robert Creeley, 1945–1975 was published in 1982. Other volumes include *Away* (1976), *Presences* (1976), *Myself* (1977), *Thanks* (1977), *The Children* (1978), *Desultory Days* (1978), *Later* (1979), *Corn Close* (1980), *Mother's Voice* (1981), *Mirrors* (1983), *A Calendar* (1984), *Four Poems* (1984), *Memories* (1984), *Memory Gardens* (1986), *The Company* (1988), *7and6* (with Robert Therrien and Michel Butor, 1988), *Dreams* (1989), *It* (with Francesco Clemente, 1989), *Places* (1990), *Windows* (1990), *Selected Poems, 1945–1990* (1991), *Gnomic Verses* (1991), *The Old Days* (1991), *Echoes* (1994), *Loops* (1995), *Life and Death* (with Clemente, 1998), *So There: Poems 1976–1983* (1998), *En Famille* (1999), *For Friends* (2000), and *Just in Time: Poems, 1984–1994* (2001). Prose writings can be found in *The Collected Prose* (1984) and *The Collected Essays* (1989). Creeley has also written fiction, including *The Gold Diggers* (1954) and *The Island* (1963). Interviews have been collected in *Contexts of Poetry: Interviews, 1961–1971* (1973), ed. Donald Allen; and *Tales out of School* (1993). *Charles Olson and Robert Creeley: The Complete Correspondence* (1980), ed. George Butterick, publishes the letters between these two poets.

Critical discussions of Creeley's work include Arthur Ford's *Robert Creeley* (1978), Cynthia Dubin Edelberg's *Robert Creeley's Poetry: A Critical Introduction* (1978), Charles Altieri's *Self and Sensibility in Contemporary American Poetry* (1984), Robert von Hallberg's *American Poetry and Culture, 1945–1980* (1985), Brian Conniff's *The Lyric and Modern Poetry: Olson, Creeley, Bunting* (1988), and Tom Clark's *Robert Creeley and the Genius of the American Common Place* (1993). Numerous useful essays can be found in the special Creeley issue of *Sagetrieb* 2.1 (1982) and in the collections *Robert Creeley: The Poet's Workshop* (1984), ed. Carroll Terrell, and *Robert Creeley's Life and Work: A Sense of Increment* (1987), ed. John Wilson. Bibliographies are Mary Novik's *Robert Creeley: An Inventory, 1945–1970* (1973) and Willard Fox's *Robert Creeley, Edward Dorn, and Robert Duncan: A Reference Guide* (1989). See also **Black Mountain School.**

Donald Davie

Davie's complete *Collected Poems*, ed. Neil Powell, was published in 2002. Among Davie's many works of criticism are *Purity of Diction in English Verse* (1952); *Articulate Energy* (1955); *Ezra Pound: Poet as Sculptor* (1964); *The Poet in the Imaginary Museum* (1977), ed. Barry Alpert; *Dissentient Voice* (1982); and *With the Grain: Essays on Thomas Hardy and Modern British Poetry* (1998).

A book-length study is Martin Dodsworth's *Donald Davie* (1976), and a collection of essays is *Donald Davie and the Responsibilities of Literature* (1983), ed. George Dekker. *On Modern Poetry: Essays Presented to Donald Davie*, ed. Vereen Bell and Laurence Lerner, was published in 1988. *Agenda* 14.2 (1976) is a special issue on Davie. Critical essays include Bernard Bergonzi's "The Poetry of Donald Davie," *Critical Quarterly* 4 (1962); Calvin Bedient's "On Donald Davie," *Iowa Review* 2.2 (1971); William H. Pritchard's "In the British Looking-Glass," *Parnassus* 4.2 (1976); Robert von Hallberg's "Two Poet-Critics: Donald Davie's *The Poet in the Imaginary Museum* and Robert Pinsky's *The Situation of Poetry*," *Chicago Review* 30.1 (1978); Kieran Quinlan's "Donald Davie: The Irish Years," *Southern Review* 20.1 (1984); Andrew Shelley's "Donald Davie and the Canon," *Essays in Criticism* 42.1 (1992); and Michael Grant's "Donald Davie and the Concept of Time," *Pn Review* 23.1 (1996). Bibliographic information is available in Stuart T. Wright's *Donald Davie: A Checklist of his Writings, 1946–1988* (1991). See also **The Movement.**

Eunice de Souza

De Souza's volumes of poetry include *Fix* (1979), *Women in Dutch Painting* (1988), *Ways of Belonging: Selected Poems* (1990), and *Selected and New Poems* (1994). She also edited *Statements: An Anthology of Indian Prose in English* (with Adil Jussawalla, 1976) and *Nine Indian Women Poets: An Anthology* (1997). *Talking Poems: Conversations with Poets* appeared in 1999. She has also published literature for children.

Discussions of her work can be found in Kersey Katrak's "Three Poets Come of Age," *Sunday Observer* (Bombay, 12 December 1982); Bruce King's *Modern Indian Poetry in English* (1987); and Veronica Brady's " 'One Long Cry in the Dark'?: The Poetry of Eunice de Souza," *Literature and Theology* 5.1 (1991). See also **Indian Poetry**.

James Dickey

Dickey's *The Whole Motion: Collected Poems, 1945–1992* appeared in 1992, and *James Dickey: The Selected Poems* in 1998. He also published novels, *Deliverance* (1970), *Alnilam* (1987), and *To the White Sea* (1993). Autobiographical and critical prose includes *The Suspect in Poetry* (1964), *Babel to Byzantium* (1968), *Self-Interviews* (1970), *Sorties: Journals and New Essays* (1971), and *The Poet Turns on Himself* (1982). A book of interviews is *The Voiced Connections of James Dickey* (1984), ed. Ronald Baughman. *Striking In* (1996) is a selection from Dickey's early notebooks. *Crux: The Letters of James Dickey* was published in 1999. Two biographies are Neal Bowers's *James Dickey: The Poet as Pitchman* (1985) and Henry Hart's *James Dickey: The World as a Lie* (2000).

Collections of essays on his work include *The Expansive Imagination* (1973), ed. Richard J. Calhoun; *The Imagination as Glory* (1984), ed. Bruce Weigl and T. R. Hummer; *James Dickey* (1987), ed. Harold Bloom; and *Critical Essays on James Dickey* (1994), ed. Robert Kirschten. Other studies include Gordon Van Ness's *Outbelieving Existence: The Measured Motion of James Dickey* (1992); Ernest Suarez's *James Dickey and the Politics of Canon* (1993); and Kirschten's *Struggling for Wings* (1997) and *Approaching Prayer: Ritual and the Shape of Myth in the Poetry of A. R. Ammons and James Dickey* (1998). Bibliographies include Jim Elledge's *James Dickey: A Bibliography, 1947–1974* (1979) and Matthew Joseph Bruccoli's *James Dickey: A Descriptive Bibliography* (1990).

Mark Doty

Doty's volumes of poetry include *Turtle, Swan* (1987), *Bethlehem in Broad Daylight* (1991), *My Alexandria* (1993), *Atlantis* (1995), *Sweet Machine* (1998), *Murano* (2000), *Turtle, Swan & Bethlehem in Broad Daylight* (2000), *Source* (2001), and *Still Life with Oysters and Lemon* (2001). He has also written memoirs, including *Heaven's Coast* (1996) and *Firebird* (1999). Interviews appear in *New Statesman* 126.4336 (1997); *Atlantic* (10 November 1999); and *Writer's Digest* 79.11 (1999).

Discussions of his work include Deborah Landau's " 'How to Live. What to Do': The Poetics and Politics of AIDS," *American Literature* 68.1 (1996); Helen Vendler's "The Poetry of August Kleinzahler and Mark Doty," *New Yorker* (8 April 1996); David R. Jarraway's " 'Creatures of the Rainbow': Wallace Stevens, Mark Doty, and the Poetics of Androgyny," *Mosaic* 30.3 (1997); William Joseph Reichard's "Mercurial and Rhapsodic: Manifestations of the Gay Male Body in the Poetry of Mark Doty and Wayne Koestenbaum," *Humanities and Social Sciences* 58.4 (1997); Mark Wunderlich's "About Mark Doty," *Ploughshares* 25.1 (1999); Yaakov Perry's "The Homecoming Queen: The Reconstruction of Home in Queer Life-Narratives," *A/B: Auto/Biography Studies* 15.2 (2000); and Hugh Dunkerley's "Unnatural Relations?: Language and Nature in the Poetry of Mark Doty and Les Murray," *Isle: Interdisciplinary Studies in Literature and Environment* 8.1 (2001).

Rita Dove

Dove's volumes of poetry include *Ten Poems* (1977), *The Yellow House on the Corner* (1980), *Museum* (1983), *Thomas and Beulah* (1986), *Grace Notes* (1989), *Selected Poems* (1993), *Mother Love* (1995), *On the Bus with Rosa Parks* (1999), and *Domestic Work* (2000). She has also written a collection of stories, *Fifth Sunday* (1985), and a novel, *Through the Ivory Gate* (1992). Other work includes a play, *The Darker Face of the Earth* (1994), and a collection of essays, *The Poet's World* (1995). Interviews include "A Conversation with Rita Dove" in *Black American Literature Forum* 20.3 (1986); Steven Schneider's in *Iowa Review* 19.3 (1989); Mohammed B. Taleb-Khyar's in *Callaloo* 14.2 (1991); William Walsh's in *Kenyon Review* 16.3 (1994); Grace Cavalieri's in *American Poetry Review* 24.2 (1995); Bill Moyers's in *The Language of Life* (1995); and Malin Pereira's in *Contemporary Literature* 40.2 (1999).

A book-length study is Therese Steffen's *Crossing Color: Transcultural Space and Place in Rita Dove's Poetry, Fiction, and Drama* (2001). Other discussions of Dove's work include Arnold Rampersad's "The Poems of Rita Dove," *Callaloo* 9.1 (1986); Robert McDowell's "The Assembling Vision of Rita Dove," *Conversant Essays: Contemporary Poets on Poetry* (1990), ed. James McCorkle; Bonnie Costello's "Scars and Wings: Rita Dove's *Grace Notes*," *Callaloo* 14.2 (1991); Kirkland C. Jones's "Folk Idiom in the Literary Expression of Two African American Authors: Rita Dove and Yusef Komunyakaa," *Language and Literature in the African American Imagination* (1992), ed. Carol Aisha Blackshire-Belay; Patricia Wallace's "Divided Loyalties: Literal and Literary in the Poetry of Lorna Dee Cervantes, Cathy Song, and Rita Dove," *MELUS* 18.3 (1993); Helen Vendler's *The Given and the Made* (1995) and *Soul Says* (1995); Lynn Keller's *Forms of Expansion: Recent Long Poems by Women* (1997); and Susan Van Dyne's "Siting the Poet: Rita Dove's Refiguring of Traditions," *Women Poets of the Americas: Toward a Pan-American Gathering*

(1999), ed. Jacqueline Vaught Brogan and Cordelia Candelaria. Articles on Dove's work by numerous critics appear in *Callaloo* 19.1 (1996).

Norman Dubie

The Mercy Seat: Collected and New Poems, 1967–2001 was published in 2001. Interviews include Julie Fay and David Wojahn's in *American Poetry Review* 7.4 (1978) and James Green's in *American Poetry Review* 18.6 (1989).

Discussions of Dubie's work include Richard Howard's introduction to *The Illustrations* (1977); John Weston's "Norman Dubie: The Vision of Astonishment," *Gramercy Review* 11.3 (1978); Greg Simon's "We Live for Cries: On Norman Dubie," *Sonora Review* 1 (1980); Frederick Garber's "On Dubie and Seidel," *American Poetry Review* 11.3 (1982); John Bensko's "Reflexive Narration in Contemporary American Poetry," *Journal of Narrative Technique* 16.2 (1986); David St. John's "A Generous Salvation: The Poetry of Norman Dubie," *Conversant Essays: Contemporary Poets on Poetry* (1990), ed. James McCorkle; and William Slattery's "My Dubious Calculus," *Antioch Review* 52.1 (1994).

Carol Ann Duffy

Duffy's volumes of poetry include *"Fleshweathercock" and Other Poems* (1973), *Fifth Last Song* (1982), *Standing Female Nude* (1985), *Thrown Voices* (1986), *Selling Manhattan* (1987), *The Other Country* (1990), *Mean Time* (1993), *Selected Poems* (1994), and *The World's Wife: Poems* (2000). She has also written plays, including *Loss* (1986), and a book for younger readers, *The Oldest Girl in the World* (2000). Collections edited by Duffy include *I Wouldn't Thank You for a Valentine: Poems for Young Feminists* (illustrated by Trisha Rafferty, 1992) and *Stopping for Death: Poems of Death and Loss* (illustrated by Rafferty, 1996). Interviews include Andrew McAllister's in *Bete Noir* 6 (1988). In 1999, when she appeared to be a leading candidate for British poet laureate, a number of profiles and interviews appeared in the *Guardian, The Independent*, and other British newspapers.

A book-length study is Dervyn Rees-Jones's *Carol Ann Duffy* (1999). Other discussions of Duffy include Jane E. Thomas's " 'The Intolerable Wrestle with Words': The Poetry of Carol Ann Duffy," *Bete Noir* 6 (1988); Eavan Boland's "Making the Difference: Eroticism and Ageing in the Work of the Woman Poet," *Pn Review* 20.4 (1994); *Four Women Poets* (1995), ed. Judith Baxter; Istvan Racz's "Carol Ann Duffy's Poetry," *B.A.S.: British and American Studies* 1.1 (1996); Danette DiMarco's "Exposing Nude Art: Carol Ann Duffy's Response to Robert Browning," *Mosaic* 31.3 (1998); Angelica Mich-

elis's "The Pleasure of Saying It: Images of Sexuality and Desire in Contemporary Women's Poetry," *Seeing and Saying: Self-Referentiality in British and American Literature* (1998), ed. Detlev Gohrbandt; Elzbieta Wojcik-Leese's " 'Her Language Is Simple': The Poetry of Carol Ann Duffy" and Susanne Schmid's "Realities Within Reality—The Poetry of Carol Ann Duffy," both in *Poetry Now: Contemporary British and Irish Poetry in the Making* (1999), ed. Holger Klein, Sabine Coelsch-Foisner, and Wolfgang Gortschacher; Eleanor Porter's " 'What Like Is It?' Landscape and Language in Carol Ann Duffy's Love Poetry," *Neohelicon* 26.1 (1999); Linda A. Kinnahan's " 'Now I Am Alien': Immigration and the Discourse of Nation in the Poetry of Carol Ann Duffy," *Contemporary Women's Poetry: Reading, Writing, Practice* (2000), ed. Alison Mark and Rees-Jones; and Antony Rowland's "Love and Masculinity in the Poetry of Carol Ann Duffy," *English* 50.198 (2001).

Alan Dugan

Dugan's *Poems Seven: New and Complete* was published in 2001. Interviews include Michael Ryan's in *Iowa Review* 4.3 (1973), Donald Heines's in *Massachusetts Review* 22 (1981), and Keith Althaus's in *Northwest Review* 20.1 (1982).

Discussions of his work include Robert Boyers's "Alan Dugan: The Poetry of Survival" in his *Contemporary Poetry in America: Essays and Interviews* (1974); Wayne McGinnis's "Christian Symbology in Alan Dugan's 'Morning Song,' " *Nassau Review* 3.3 (1977); David Wojahn's "Recent Poetry," *Western Humanities Review* 38.3 (1984); John Gery's " 'Pieces of Harmony': The Quiet Politics of Alan Dugan's Poetry," *Politics and the Muse: Studies in the Politics of Recent American Literature* (1989), ed. Adam J. Sorkin.

Robert Duncan

Volumes of Duncan's selected work include *Selected Poems* (1959), *The Years as Catches; First Poems, 1939–1941* (1966), *The First Decade: Selected Poems, Vol. 1* (1968), *Derivations: Selected Poems, 1950–1956* (1968), *Ground Work: Before the War* (1984); *Ground Work II: In the Dark* (1987), and *Selected Poems* (1993). Other volumes include *The Opening of the Field* (1960), *Roots and Branches* (1964), and *Bending the Bow* (1968). Prose work can be found in *Fictive Certainties* (1985) and *A Selected Prose* (1995), ed. Robert J. Bertholf, which contains Duncan's important essay "The Homosexual in Society." Duncan's correspondence with H. D. has been published as *A Great Admiration* (1992), ed. Bertholf.

Robert Duncan: Scales of the Marvelous (1979), ed. Bertholf and Ian Reid, is a collection of essays on Duncan's work. Other studies include Ekbert Faas's *Robert Duncan: Portrait of the Poet as Homosexual in Society* (1983); Mark Andrew Johnson's *Robert Duncan* (1988); and Michael Davidson's *The San Francisco Renaissance: Poetics and Community at Mid-Century* (1989). Useful critical essays include Charles Altieri's "The Book of the World: Robert Duncan's Poetics of Presence," *Sun and Moon* 1 (1976); Geoffrey Thurley's "Robert Duncan: The Myth of Open Form," *The American Moment: American Poetry in Mid-Century* (1977); and Wendy McIntyre's "Psyche, Christ, and the Poem," *Ironwood* 11.2 (1983). Several journals have dedicated special issues to Duncan: *Boundary* 28.2 (1980); *Ironwood* 22 (1983); and *Sagetrieb* 4.2–3 (1985). Bertholf published *Robert Duncan: A Descriptive Bibliography* in 1986. See also **Black Mountain School, San Francisco Renaissance.**

Louise Erdrich

Erdrich's volumes of poetry are *Jacklight* (1984) and *Baptism of Desire* (1989). She has also written acclaimed novels, including *Love Medicine* (1984) and *The Antelope Wife* (1998), and collections of short stories, *The Bingo Palace* (1994) and *Tales of Burning Love* (1996). Interviews appear in Laura Coltelli's *Winged Word: American Indian Writers Speak* (1990) and *Conversations with Louise Erdrich and Michael Dorris* (1994), ed. Allan Chavkin and Nancy Feyl Chavkin.

Studies of her work include Daniela Daniele's "Transactions in a Native Land: Mixed-Blood Identity and Indian Legacy in Louise Erdrich's Writing," *RSA Journal* 3 (1992); Jeannie Ludlow's "Working (in) the In-Between: Poetry, Criticism, Interrogation, and Interruption," *Studies in American Indian Literatures* 6.1 (1994); Jane P. Hafen's "Sacramental Language: Ritual in the Poetry of Louise Erdrich," *Great Plains Quarterly* 16.3 (1996); Hans Bak's "Circles Blaze in Ordinary Days: Louise Erdrich's *Jacklight*," *Native American Women in Literature and Culture* (1997), ed. Susan Castillo and Victor Da Rosa; Alan Shucard's entry in *Contemporary Women Poets* (1998), ed. Pamela L. Shelton; and Sheila Hassell Hughes's "Falls of Desire/Leaps of Faith: Religious Syncretism in Louise Erdrich's and Joy Harjo's 'Mixed-Blood' Poetry," *Religion and Literature* 33.2 (2001). See also **Native American Poetry.**

James Fenton

Fenton's volumes of poetry include *Our Western Furniture* (1968), *Put Thou Thy Tears into My Bottle* (1969), *Terminal Moraine* (1972), *A Vacant Possession* (1978), *The Memory of War: Poems, 1968–1982* (1982), *Children in Exile: Poems 1968–1984* (1984), *Partingtime Hall* (1987), *Manila Envelope* (1989), and *Out of Danger* (1993). Fenton's critical works include *Leonardo's Nephew: Essays on Art and Artists* (1998), *The Strength of Poetry* (2001), and *An Introduction to English Poetry* (2002). Fenton has also published travel literature, including *All the Wrong Places: Adrift in the Politics of the Pacific Rim* (1988). Interviews include Manuel Gómez Lara's in *Revista Canaria de Estudios Ingleses* 12 (1986) and Bruce Meyer's in *Eclectic Literary Forum* 8.3–4 (1998).

Discussions of Fenton's poetry include Michael Hulse's "The Poetry of James Fenton," *Antigonish Review* 58 (1984); Alan Robinson's "James Fenton's 'Narratives': Some Reflections on Postmodernism," *Critical Quarterly* 29.1 (1987); Ellen Krieger Stark's "An American Confession: On Reading James Fenton's 'Out of Danger,'" *Critical Quarterly* 36.2 (1994); Ian Parker's "Auden's Heir," *New Yorker* (25 July 1994); Douglas Kerr's "Orientations: James Fenton and Indochina," *Contemporary Literature* 35.3 (1994); and Dana Gioia's "The Rise of James Fenton," *Dark Horse* 8 (1999) and 9–10 (2000).

Lawrence Ferlinghetti

Ferlinghetti's volumes of poetry include *Pictures of the Gone World* (1955, 1995), *A Coney Island of the Mind* (1958), *Tentative Description of a Dinner Given to Promote the Impeachment of President Eisenhower* (1958), *Berlin* (1961), *One Thousand Fearful Words for Fidel Castro* (1961), *Starting from San Francisco* (1961, 1967), *Penguin Modern Poets* 5 (with Gregory Corso and Allen Ginsberg, 1963), *Thoughts of a Concerto of Telemann* (1963), *Christ Climbed Down* (1965), *To Fuck Is to Love Again, Kyrie Eleison Kerista; or, The Situation in the West, Followed by a Holy Proposal* (1965), *Where Is Vietnam?* (1965), *After the Cries of the Birds* (1967), *An Eye on the World: Selected Poems* (1967), *Moscow in the Wilderness, Segovia in the Snow* (1967), *Fuclock* (1968), *Reverie Smoking Grass* (1968), *The Secret Meaning of Things* (1969), *Tyrannus Nix?* (1969), *Back Roads to Far Places* (1971), *The Illustrated Wilfred Funk* (1971), *Love Is No Stone on the Moon* (1971), *Open Eye, Open Heart* (1973), *Director of Alienation* (1976), *Who Are We Now?* (1976), *Landscapes of Living and Dying* (1979), *Mule Mountain Dreams* (1980), *A Trip to Italy and France* (1980), *Endless Life: Selected Poems* (1981), *Over All the Obscene Boundaries: European Poems and Transitions* (1984), *Inside the Trojan Horse* (1987), *Wild Dreams of a New Beginning* (1988), *When I Look at Pictures* (1990), *These Are My Rivers: New & Selected Poems, 1955–1993* (1993), *Ends and Beginnings* (1994), *A Far Rockaway of the Heart* (1997), and *How to Paint Sunlight: Lyric Poems*

& Others (1997–2000) (2001). He has also published novels, including *Her* (1960) and *Love in the Days of Rage* (1988), plays, and works of journalism, including *Howl of the Censor* (1961), ed. J. W. Ehrlich; *Literary San Francisco* (with Nancy J. Peters, 1980), and *Seven Days in Nicaragua Libre* (1984). *The Cool Eye* (1993) is a book-length interview with Alexis Lykiard. Biographies include Neeli Cherkovski's *Ferlinghetti: A Biography* (1979) and Larry Smith's *Lawrence Ferlinghetti: Poet-at-Large* (1983).

Book-length studies include Michael Skau's *"Constantly Risking Absurdity": The Writings of Lawrence Ferlinghetti* (1989) and Barry Silesky's *Ferlinghetti: The Artist in His Time* (1990). Other discussions of his work include David Kherdian's *Six Poets of the San Francisco Renaissance* (1967); *The San Francisco Poets* (1971), ed. David Meltzer; Samuel Barclay Charters's *Some Poems/Poets: Studies in American Underground Poetry since 1945* (1971); Crale D. Hopkins's "The Poetry of Lawrence Ferlinghetti: A Reconsideration," *Italian Americana* 1.1 (1974); and Tony Curtis's "A Hundred Harms: Poetry and the Gulf War—Ferlinghetti at Laugharne," *Poetry Review* 82.2 (1992). Bill Morgan published an updated bibliography on Ferlinghetti in *The Bulletin of Bibliography* 51.2 (1994). See also **Beat Movement, San Francisco Renaissance.**

Carolyn Forché

Forché's volumes of poetry are *Gathering the Tribes* (1976), *The Country between Us* (1981), and *The Angel of History* (1994). She has also written journalism and nonfiction on El Salvador, such as the *History and Motivations of U.S. Involvement and Control of the Peasant Movement in El Salvador: The Role of the AIFLD in the Agrarian Reform Process, 1970–1980* (with Philip Wheaton, 1980), and composed the text for *El Salvador: The Work of Thirty Photographers* (1983), ed. Harry Mattison, Susan Meiselas, and Fae Rubenstein. In addition, she has published translations of Spanish and French poetry and edited the anthology *Against Forgetting: Twentieth-Century Poetry of Witness* (1993). An interview appears in Bill Moyers's *The Language of Life* (1995). Other interviews include David Montenegro's in *American Poetry Review* 17.6 (1988) and Jill Taft-Kaufman's in *Text and Performance Quarterly* 10.1 (1990).

Studies of Forché's work include Imogen Forster's "Constructing Central America," *Red Letters: A Journal of Cultural Politics* 16 (1984); John Mann's "Carolyn Forché: Poetry and Survival," *American Poetry* 3.3 (1986); Michael Greer's "Politicizing the Modern: Carolyn Forché in El Salvador and America," *Centennial Review* 30.2 (1986); Paul Rea's "The Poet as Witness: Carolyn Forché's Powerful Pleas from El Salvador," *Confluencia* 2.2 (1987); Leonora

Smith's "Carolyn Forché: Poet as Witness," *Still the Frame Holds: Essays of Women Poets and Writers* (1993), ed. Sheila Roberts and Yvonne Pacheco Tevis, Peter Balakian's "Carolyn Forché and the Poetry of Witness: Another View," *Agni* 40 (1994); Nora Mitchell and Emily Skoler's "History, Death, Politics, Despair," *New England Review* 17.2 (1995; and Anita Helle's "Elegy as History: Three Women Poets 'By the Century's Deathbed,'" *South Atlantic Review* 61.2 (1996).

Allen Ginsberg

Collections of Ginsberg's poetry include *Collected Poems, 1947–1980* (1984), *White Shroud: Poems, 1980–1985* (1986), *Selected Poems 1947–1995* (1996), and *Death and Fame: Poems, 1993–1997* (1999). Ginsberg's essays are collected in *Deliberate Prose: Selected Essays, 1952–1995* (2000), ed. Bill Morgan. A collection of lectures is *Allen Verbatim* (1974) and a book of correspondence is *Journals: Early Fifties, Early Sixties* (1977). *Howl: Original Draft Facsimile, Transcript, and Variant Versions, Fully Annotated by Author, with Contemporaneous Correspondence, Account of First Public Reading, Legal Skirmishes, Precursor Texts, and Bibliography* (1986), ed. Barry Miles, supplies illuminating material for the study of Ginsberg's most famous poem. Interviews include those in *Spontaneous Mind: Selected Interviews, 1958–1996* (2001), ed. David Carter, *Composed on the Tongue* (1980), ed. Donald Allen; and the *Paris Review* dialogue in Tom Clarkin's *Writers at Work*, Third Series (1967). Two biographies are Barry Miles's *Ginsberg* (1989) and Michael Schumacher's *Dharma Lion* (1992).

A collection of essays on his work is *On the Poetry of Allen Ginsberg* (1984), ed. Lewis Hyde. Other discussions of his work include Leslie Fiedler's *Waiting for the End* (1964); Jane Kramer's *Allen Ginsberg in America* (1969); Eric Mottram's *Allen Ginsberg in the Sixties* (1972); Paul Portugés's *The Visionary Poetics of Allen Ginsberg* (1978); Robert K. Martin's *The Homosexual Tradition in American Poetry* (1979, 1998); Richard Howard's *Alone with America* (1980); James E. B. Breslin's *From Modern to Contemporary* (1984); Paul Breslin's *The Psycho-Political Muse* (1987); Helen Vender's *The Music of What Happens* (1988); Michael Davidson's *The San Francisco Renaissance* (1989); Marjorie Perloff's *Poetic License* (1990); John Tytell's *Naked Angels* (1991); Alicia Ostriker's "'Howl' Revisited: The Poet as Jew," *American Poetry Review* 26 (1997); and Edward Sanders's *The Poetry and Life of Allen Ginsberg* (2000). Bibliographies include George Dowden and Lawrence McGilvery's *A Bibliography of Works by Allen Ginsberg, October, 1943–July 1, 1967* (1971); Michelle P. Kraus's *Allen Ginsberg: An Annotated Bibliography, 1969–1977* (1980);

and Bill Morgan's *The Response to Allen Ginsberg, 1926–1994* (1996). See also **Beat Movement**.

Louise Glück

Glück's poetry from 1969 to 1985 is available as *The First Four Books of Poems* (1995). Subsequent volumes include *Ararat* (1990), *The Wild Iris* (1992), *Meadowlands* (1996), *Vita Nova* (1999), and *The Seven Ages* (2001). A collection of her essays is *Proofs and Theories* (1994).

Critical discussions of her work are found in Helen Vendler's *The Music of What Happens* (1988) and Elizabeth Dodd's *The Veiled Mirror and the Woman Poet: H. D., Louise Bogan, Elizabeth Bishop and Louise Glück* (1992). Other studies include Lynn Keller's " 'Free / of Blossom and Subterfuge': Louise Glück and the Language of Renunciation," *World, Self, Poem: Essays on Contemporary Poetry from the "Jubilation of Poets"* (1990), ed. Leonard M. Trawick; Lynne McMahon's "The Sexual Swamp: Female Erotics and the Masculine Art," *Southern Review* 28.2 (1992); Suzanne Matson's "Without Relation: Family and Freedom in the Poetry of Louise Glück," *Mid-America Review* 14.2 (1994); and Lee Upton's *The Muse of Abandonment: Origins, Identity, Mastery in Five American Poets* (1998).

Lorna Goodison

Goodison's volumes of poetry include *Tamarind Season* (1980), *I Am Becoming My Mother* (1986), *Heartease* (1988), *Selected Poems* (1992), *To Us, All Flowers Are Roses* (1995), *Turn Thanks* (1999), *Guinea Woman: New and Selected Poems* (2000), and *Travelling Mercies* (2001). *Baby Mother and the King of Swords* (1990) is a collection of short stories. Along with Kamau Brathwaite and Mervyn Morris, Goodison is included in *Three Caribbean Poets on Their Work* (1993), ed. Victor L. Chang. Interviews appear in *Wasafiri* 11 (1990); *Commonwealth Essays and Studies* 13.2 (1991); and *Talk Yuh Talk: Interviews with Anglophone Caribbean Poets* (2001), ed. Kwame Dawes.

Critical discussions of Goodison's work can be found in Edward Baugh's "Goodison on the Road to Heartease," *Journal of West Indian Literature* 1.1 (1986) and his "Lorna Goodison in the Context of Feminist Criticism," *Journal of West Indian Literature* 4.1 (1990); *Caribbean Women Writers: Essays from the First International Conference* (1990), ed. Selwyn R. Cudjoe; Susheila Nasta's *Motherlands* (1991); Denise deCaires Narain's "Body Language in the Work of Four Caribbean Poets," *Wasafiri* 16 (1992); J. Edward Chamberlin's *Come Back to Me My Language: Poetry and the West Indies* (1993); Velma Pollard's *Dread Talk: The Language of Rastafari* (1994); Christine Pagnoulle's "Pilgrimage Out of Dispossession," *Commonwealth*

Essays and Studies 17.1 (1994); *Frontiers of Caribbean Literature in English* (1996), ed. Frank Birbalsingh; Gudrun Webhofer's *Identity in the Poetry of Grace Nichols and Lorna Goodison* (1996); Elaine Campbell and Pierrette M. Frickey's *The Whistling Bird* (1998); and Dannabang Kuwabong's "The Mother as Archetype of Self: A Poetics of Matrilineage in the Poetry of Claire Harris and Lorna Goodison," *Ariel* 30.1 (1999). See also **Caribbean Poetry**.

Jorie Graham

Graham's volumes of poetry are *Hybrids of Plants and of Ghosts* (1980), *Erosion* (1983), *The End of Beauty* (1987), *Region of Unlikeness* (1991), *Materialism* (1993), *The Dream of the Unified Field: Selected Poems, 1974–1994* (1995), *The Errancy* (1997), *Swarm* (2000), and *Never* (2002). Thomas Gardner's interview in his *Regions of Unlikeness: Explaining Contemporary Poetry* (1999) is an especially illuminating look at Graham's poetics.

Critical work on Graham includes Charles Altieri's "Jorie Graham and Ann Lauterbach: Towards a Contemporary Poetry of Eloquence," *Cream City Review* 12 (1988); Bonnie Costello's "Jorie Graham: Art and Erosion," *Contemporary Literature* 33.2 (1992); James Longenbach's "Jorie Graham's Big Hunger," *Modern Poetry after Modernism* (1997); Calvin Bedient's "Like a Chafing of the Visible" and Willard Spiegelman's "Jorie Graham's 'New Way of Looking,' " both in *Salmagundi* 120 (1998); Gudrun Grabher's "Epistemological Empathy: A. R. Ammons and Jorie Graham," *Strategies of Difference* (1998), ed. Pierre Lagayette; Eric Murphy Selinger's "In Each Other's Arms, or No, Not Really," *Parnassus* (1999); and Gardner's "Jorie Graham's Incandescence," *Regions of Unlikeness* (1999). Helen Vendler discusses Graham in *The Breaking of Style* (1995), *The Given and the Made* (1995), and *Soul Says* (1995).

Thom Gunn

Thom Gunn's *Collected Poems* appeared in 1993. Subsequent volumes include *Boss Cupid* (2000). *The Occasions of Poetry* (1982, 1985) and *Shelf Life* (1993) are collections of essays and autobiographical writings. Interviews appear in *Talking Poetry* (1987), ed. Lee Bartlett; *Critical Survey* 2.2 (1990); *Agni* 36.2 (1992); *Paris Review* (Summer 1995); and *Gay and Lesbian Review Worldwide* 7.3 (2000).

Work on Gunn includes Alan Norman Bold's *Thom Gunn and Ted Hughes* (1976); *Three Contemporary Poets: Thom Gunn, Ted Hughes, and R. S. Thomas: A Casebook* (1990), ed. A. E. Dyson; Bruce Woodcock's " 'But Oh Not Loose': Form and Sexuality in Thom Gunn's Poetry," *Critical Quarterly* 35 (1993); and Tyler Hoffman's "Representing AIDS: Thom Gunn and the

Modalities of Verse," *South Atlantic Review* 65.2 (2000). Jack W. C. Hagstrom and George Bixby's *Thom Gunn: A Bibliography, 1940–1978* (1979) was last updated in *Bulletin of Bibliography* 51. 1 (1994). See also **The Movement.**

Marilyn Hacker

Hacker's volumes of poetry include *The Terrible Children* (1967), *Quark* (1970), *Presentation Piece* (1974), *Separations* (1976), *Taking Notice* (1980), *Assumptions* (1985), *Love, Death, and the Changing of the Seasons* (1986), *Going Back to the River* (1990), *The Hang-Glider's Daughter: New and Selected Poems* (1990), *Selected Poems 1965–1990* (1994), *Winter Numbers* (1994), and *Squares and Courtyards* (2000). She has also published translations, including Claire Malroux's *A Long-Gone Sun* (2000) and Vénus Khoury-Ghata's *Here There Was Once a Country* (2001), and edited *Woman Poet: The East* (1982). Interviews include Karla Hammond's in *Frontiers: A Journal of Woman's Studies* 5.3 (1980), Judith Johnson's in *13th Moon* 9.1–2 (1991); and Annie Finch's in *American Poetry Review* 25.3 (1996). A conversation between Hacker and Richard Howard appears in *Antioch Review* (Summer 2000).

Critical discussions of Hacker's work include Suzanne Gardinier's "Marilyn Hacker," *Lesbian Writers of the United States: A Bio-Bibliographical Critical Sourcebook* (1993), ed. Sandra Pollack and Denise D. Knight; Lynn Keller's "Measured Feet 'in Gender-Bender Shoes': The Politics of Form in Marilyn Hacker's *Love, Death, and the Changing of the Seasons*," *Feminist Measures: Soundings in Poetry and Theory* (1994), ed. Keller and Cristanne Miller; Rafael Campo's "About Marilyn Hacker," *Ploughshares* (Spring 1996); and Nancy Honicker's "Marilyn Hacker's *Love, Death, and the Changing of the Seasons*: Writing/Living within Formal Constraints," *Freedom and Form: Essays in Contemporary American Poetry* (1998), ed. Esther Giger and Agnieszka Salska. See also **New Formalism.**

Joy Harjo

Harjo's collections of poetry include *The Last Song* (1975), *What Moon Drove Me to This?* (1979), *She Had Some Horses* (1983, 1997), *In Mad Love and War* (1990), *The Woman Who Fell from the Sky* (1994), *A Map to the Next World* (2000), and *How We Became Human: New and Selected Poems: 1975–2001* (2002). *Secrets from the Center of the World* (1989) is a collaboration with the photographer Steven Strom. She has also written children's literature, *The Good Luck Cat* (2000); and short stories, in *Talking Leaves: Contemporary Native American Short Stories* (1991), ed. Carig Lesley; and she edited an anthology, *Reinventing the Enemy's Language: Contemporary Native Women's Writing of North America* (1997). *Letter from the End of the Twentieth Century* (1997) is a CD of her poetry backed by the music of Poetic Justice, in which she also played saxophone. Her essay "Oklahoma: The Prairie of Words" is included in *The Remembered Earth: An Anthology of Contemporary Native-American Literature* (1979), ed. Geary Hobson. *The Spiral of Memory* (1996), ed. Laura Coltelli, is a collection of interviews.

Critical studies include Paula Gunn Allen's *The Sacred Hoop: Recovering the Feminine in American Indian Traditions* (1986); John Scarry's "Representing Real Worlds: The Evolving Poetry of Joy Harjo," *World Literature Today* 66.2 (1992); Elaine A. Jahner's "Knowing All the Way Down to Fire," *Feminist Measures: Soundings in Poetry and Theory* (1994), ed. Lynn Keller and Cristanne Miller; Norma C. Wilson's "Joy Harjo," *Native American Writers of the United States* (1997), ed. Kenneth M. Roemer; Rhonda Pettit's *Joy Harjo* (1998); and Kenneth Lincoln's *Sing with the Heart of a Bear: Fusions of Native and American Poetry, 1890–1999* (2000). See also **Native American Poetry.**

Michael S. Harper

Harper's volumes of poetry include *Dear John, Dear Coltrane* (1970), *History Is Your Own Heartbeat* (1971), *Photographs: Negatives: History as Apple Tree* (1972); *Song: I Want a Witness* (1972); *Debridement* (1973); *Nightmare Begins Responsibility* (1974); *Images of Kin: New and Selected Poems* (1977); *Rhode Island* (1981); *Healing Song for the Inner Ear* (1985); *Songlines: Mosaics* (1991); *Honorable Amendments* (1995); and *Songlines in Michaeltree: New and Collected Poems* (2000). Harper also edited *The Collected Poems of Sterling A. Brown* (1980) and coedited various anthologies, including *Chant of Saints: A Gathering of Afro-American Literature, Art and Scholarship* (with Robert B. Stepto, 1979) and *Every Shut Eye Ain't Asleep: An Anthology of Poetry by Americans since 1945* (with Anthony Walton, 1994). An interview appears in Bill Moyers's *The Language of Life* (1995). Other interviews include James Randall's in *Ploughshares* 7.1 (1981) and David Lloyd's in *TriQuarterly* (1986).

Critical discussions of Harper's work can be found in Joseph A. Brown's " 'Their Long Scars Touch Ours': A Reflection on the Poetry of Michael Harper," *Callaloo* 9.1 (1986); John F. Callahan's " 'Close Roads': The Friendship Songs of Michael Harper" and Niccolo N. Donzella's "The Rage of Michael Harper," both in *Callaloo* 13.4 (1990); Jahan Ramazani's *Poetry of Mourning* (1994); Xavier Nicholas's "Robert Hayden and Michael Harper: A Literary Friendship," *Callaloo* 17.4 (1994); Laurence Lieberman's *Beyond the Muse of Memory* (1995);

Michael Bibby's *Hearts and Minds: Bodies, Poetry, and Resistance in the Vietnam Era* (1996); and Elizabeth Dodd's "Another Version: Michael S. Harper, William Clark, and the Problem of Historical Blindness," *Western American Literature* 33.1 (1998). *Callaloo* 13.4 (1990) is a special issue dedicated to Harper.

Tony Harrison

Harrison's volumes of poetry include *Earthworks* (1964), *Newcastle Is Peru* (1969), *The Loiners* (1970), *From "The School of Eloquence" and Other Poems* (1978), *Continuous: Fifty Sonnets from "The School of Eloquence"* (1981), *A Kumquat for John Keats* (1981), *U.S. Martial* (1981), *Selected Poems* (1984, 1987), *The Mysteries* (1985), *"V." and Other Poems* (1990), *A Cold Coming: Gulf War Poems* (1991), *The Gaze of the Gorgon* (1992), *Permanently Bard* (1995), and *"The Shadow of Hiroshima" and Other Film/Poems* (1995). Among his collections of dramatic verse are *Theatre Works: 1973–1985* (1986) and *Plays Three* (1996), *Plays Two* (2002), and *Plays Four* (2002). He also wrote and directed a movie, *Prometheus* (1998), and wrote the screenplay for a short television production, *Crossings* (2002). Biographical information can be found in Joe Kelleher's *Tony Harrison* (1996).

Bloodaxe Critical Anthologies 1: Tony Harrison (1991), ed. Neil Astley, and *Tony Harrison: Loiner* (1997), ed. Sandie Byrne, are collections of essays. Other criticism of his work includes Luke Spencer's *The Poetry of Tony Harrison* (1994); Raymond Hargreaves's "Tony Harrison and the Poetry of Leeds," *Poetry in the British Isles: Non-Metropolitan Perspectives* (1995), ed. Hans-Werner Ludwig and Lothar Fietz; Byrne's *H, v. & O: The Poetry of Tony Harrison* (1998); and Antony Rowland's *Tony Harrison and the Holocaust* (2001). John R. Kaiser's *Tony Harrison: A Bibliography, 1957–1987* was published in 1989.

Robert Hass

Hass's volumes of poetry include *Field Guide* (1973), *Praise* (1979), *Human Wishes* (1989), and *Sun under Wood* (1996). Interviews appear in Bill Moyers's *The Language of Life* (1995) and Thomas Gardner's *Regions of Unlikeness: Explaining Contemporary Poetry* (1999).

Discussions of his work include Alan Shapiro's "'And There Will Always Be Melons': Some Thoughts on Robert Hass," *Chicago Review* 33.3 (1983) and his "Some Thoughts on Robert Hass," *In Praise of the Impure* (1993); Charles Altieri's *Self and Sensibility in Contemporary American Poetry* (1984); Charles Berger's "Poetry Chronicle: Dan Pagis and Robert Hass," *Raritan* 10.1 (1990); Calvin Bedient's "Man Is Altogether Desire?" *Salmagundi* 90–91 (1991); Terrence Doody's "From Image to Sentence: The Spiritual Development of Robert

Hass," *American Poetry Review* 26.2 (1997); and Gardner's *Regions of Unlikeness* (1999).

Robert Hayden

Robert Hayden: Collected Poems, ed. Frederick Glaysher, appeared in 1985 and his *Collected Prose*, also edited by Glaysher, in 1984. Hayden edited several anthologies, including *Kaleidoscope: Poems of American Negro Poets* (1967); *Afro-American Literature: An Introduction* (with David J. Burrows and Frederick Lapides, 1971); and *The Human Condition: Literature Written in the English Language* (1974). Hayden also published "A Portfolio of Recent American Poems," *World Order* 5 (1971), and "Recent American Poetry—Portfolio II," *World Order* 9 (1975), and wrote the preface to the 1968 edition of Alain Locke's *The New Negro*. A biography is Fred M. Fetrow's *Robert Hayden* (1984).

Book-length studies include John Hatcher's *From the Auroral Darkness: The Life and Poetry of Robert Hayden* (1984); and Pontheolla T. Williams's *Robert Hayden: A Critical Analysis of His Poetry* (1987). *Robert Hayden: Essays on the Poetry* (2001), ed. Laurence Goldstein, is a collection of essays. Other discussions of Hayden include Vera M. Kutzinski's "Changing Permanences: Historical and Literary Revisionism in Robert Hayden's 'Middle Passage,'" *Callaloo* 9.1 (1986); Fetrow's "Minority Reporting and Psychic Distancing in the Poetry of Robert Hayden," *CLA Journal* 33 (1989); Alan Shapiro's "In Praise of the Impure: Narrative Consciousness in Poetry," *TriQuarterly* 81 (1991); Michael Collins's "On the Track of the Universal: 'Middle Passage' and America," *Parnassus* 17 (1992); Xavier Nicholas's "Robert Hayden: Some Introductory Notes," *Michigan Quarterly Review* 31 (1992); Nicholas's "Robert Hayden and Michael Harper: A Literary Friendship," *Callaloo* 17.4 (1994); Benjamin Friedlander's "Robert Hayden's Epic of Community," *MELUS* 23.3 (1998); Brian Conniff's "Answering 'The Waste Land': Robert Hayden and the Rise of the African American Poetic Sequence," *African American Review* 33.3 (1999); and Jon Woodson's "Consciousness, Myth, and Transcendence: Symbolic Action in Three Poems on the Slave Trade," *The Furious Flowering of African American Poetry* (1999), ed. Joanne V. Gabbin.

Seamus Heaney

Heaney's volumes of poetry include *Death of a Naturalist* (1966), *Door into the Dark* (1969), *Wintering Out* (1972), *North* (1975), *Field Work* (1979), *Sweeney Astray* (1983), *Station Island* (1984), *The Haw Lantern* (1987), *Seeing Things* (1991), *The Spirit Level* (1996), *Open Ground: Selected Poems, 1966–1996* (1998), and *Electric Light* (2001). His translation of *Beowulf* was published in 1999. Collections of essays are *Preoccupations: Selected Prose, 1968–1978* (1980), *The Government of the Tongue*

(1988), *The Redress of Poetry: Oxford Lectures* (1995), and *Finders Keepers: Selected Prose, 1971–2001* (2002). A biography is Michael Parker's *Seamus Heaney: The Making of the Poet* (1993).

Essay collections on Heaney's work include *The Art of Seamus Heaney* (1982), ed. Tony Curtis; *Seamus Heaney* (1988), ed. Harold Bloom; *Seamus Heaney: A Collection of Critical Essays* (1992), ed. Elmer Andrews; and *Critical Essays on Seamus Heaney* (1995), ed. Robert F. Garratt. Other critical studies include Blake Morrison's *Seamus Heaney* (1982); Neil Corcoran's *Seamus Heaney: A Faber Study Guide* (1986); Andrews's *The Poetry of Seamus Heaney: All the Realms of Whisper* (1988); Thomas C. Foster's *Seamus Heaney* (1989); Henry Hart's *Seamus Heaney: Poet of Contrary Progressions* (1992); Bernard O'Donoghue's *Seamus Heaney* (1994); J. W. Foster's *The Achievement of Seamus Heaney* (1995); and Helen Vendler's *Seamus Heaney* (1998). Bibliographical information can be found in Michael J. Durkan and Rand Brandes's *Seamus Heaney: A Reference Guide* (1996). See also **Irish Poetry.**

Anthony Hecht

Hecht's volumes of poetry include *A Summoning of Stones* (1954), *The Hard Hours* (1967), *Millions of Strange Shadows* (1977), *The Venetian Vespers* (1979), *Collected Earlier Poems* (1990), *The Transparent Man* (1990), *Flight among the Tombs* (1996), and *The Darkness and the Light* (2001). Works of criticism include *Obbligati: Essays in Criticism* (1986), *The Hidden Law: The Poetry of W. H. Auden* (1993), and *On the Laws of the Poetic Art* (1995). He has also published translations from Latin and French and edited Jonathan Aaron's *Second Sight* (1982), Susan Donnelly's *Eve Names the Animals* (1985), *The Essential Herbert* (1987), and an edition of Shakespeare's sonnets (1996).

The Burdens of Formality (1989), ed. Sydney Lea, is a collection of essays on Hecht's work. Other relevant studies include Richard Howard's *Alone with America: Essays on the Art of Poetry in the United States since 1950* (1969, 1980); Norman German's *Anthony Hecht* (1989); J. D. McClatchy's *White Paper: On Contemporary American Poetry* (1989); Geoffrey Lindsay's " 'Laws That Stand for Other Laws': Anthony Hecht's Dramatic Strategy," *Essays in Literature* 21.2 (1994); John Hollander's "On Anthony Hecht," *Raritan* 17 (1997); and A. Alvarez's "A Light Black World," *New York Review of Books* (May 9, 2002). A recent interview by Daniel Anderson is published in *Bomb* 62 (1998).

Lyn Hejinian

Hejinian's books include *A Thought Is the Bride of What Thinking* (1976), *A Mask of Motion* (1977), *Gesualdo* (1978), *Writing Is an Aid to Memory* (1978), *My Life* (1980, 1987), *Redo* (1984), *Individuals* (with Kit Robinson, 1988), *Oxota: A Short Russian Novel* (1991), *The Cell* (1992), *The Cold of Poetry* (1994), *Guide, Grammar, Watch, and the Thirty Nights* (1996), *The Little Book of a Thousand Eyes* (1996), *Wicker: A Collaborative Poem* (with Jack Collom, 1996), *Hearing* (with Leslie Scalapino, 1998), *The Traveler and the Hill; and, The Hill* (1998), *Sight* (with Scalapino, 1999), *Chartings* (with Ray DiPalma, 2000), *Happily* (2000), *A Border Comedy* (2001), and *The Lake* (with Emilie Clark, 2001). A selection of Hejinian's criticism, including her essay "The Rejection of Closure," as well as poetry, appears in *The Language of Inquiry* (2000).

Marjorie Perloff has written about Hejinian in various places, including *The Dance of the Intellect* (1985), *Radical Artifice* (1991), and *Poetry on and off the Page* (1998). Other studies include Hilary Clark's "The Mnemonics of Autobiography: Lyn Hejinian's *My Life*," *Biography* 14.4 (1991); David Jarraway's "*My Life* through the Eighties," *Contemporary Literature* 33.2 (1992); Juliana Spahr's "Resignifying Autobiography: Lyn Hejinian's *My Life*," *American Literature* 68 (1996); Christopher Beach's "Poetic Positionings: Stephen Dobyns and Lyn Hejinian in Cultural Context," *Contemporary Literature* 38.1 (1997); and Charles Altieri's "Lyn Hejinian and the Possibilities of Postmodernism in Poetry," *Women Poets of the Americas* (1999), ed. Jaqueline Brogan and Cordelia Candelaria. See also **Language Poetry.**

Geoffrey Hill

Hill's *New and Collected Poems, 1952–1992* was published in 1994. Subsequent volumes include *Canaan* (1997), *The Triumph of Love* (1998), *Speech! Speech!* (2000), and *The Orchards of Syon* (2002). Prose works include *The Lords of Limit: Essays on Literature and Ideas* (1984) and *Illuminating Shadow: The Mythic Power of Film* (1992). An interview appears in *Viewpoints: Poets in Conversation with John Haffenden* (1981).

Two collections of criticism are *Geoffrey Hill: Essays on His Work* (1985), ed. Peter Robinson, and *Geoffrey Hill* (1986), ed. Harold Bloom. Book-length studies include Christopher Ricks's *Geoffrey Hill and "The Tongue's Atrocities"* (1978); Henry Hart's *The Poetry of Geoffrey Hill* (1986); Vincent Sherry's *The Uncommon Tongue: The Poetry and Criticism of Geoffrey Hill* (1987); and E. M. Knottenbelt's *Passionate Intelligence: The Poetry of Geoffrey Hill* (1990). *Agenda* 17.1 (1979) and 23 (1985–86) are special issues dedicated to Hill. Other critical discussions can be found in John Silkin's chapter in *British Poetry since 1960* (1972), ed. Michael Schmidt and Grevel Lindop; Seamus Heaney's "Now and in England," *Critical Inquiry* 3 (1977); Calvin Bedient's "On Geoffrey Hill,"

Critical Quarterly 23.2 (1981); Thomas H. Getz's "Geoffrey Hill: History as Poetry, Poetry as Salutation," *Contemporary Poetry* 4.3 (1982); Stephen T. Glynn's "'Biting Nothings to the Bone': The Exemplary Failure of Geoffrey Hill," *English* 36.156 (1987); Michael North's "The Word as Bond: Money and Performative Language in Hill's *Mercian Hymns*," *ELH* 54.2 (1987); William Logan's "The Absolute Unreasonableness of Geoffrey Hill," *Conversant Essays: Contemporary Poets on Poetry* (1990), ed. James McCorkle; Jeffrey Donaldson's "Must Men Stand by What They Write?," *Partisan Review* 58.3 (1991); Eleanor J. McNees's *Eucharistic Poetry: The Search for Presence in the Writings of John Donne, Gerard Manley Hopkins, Dylan Thomas, and Geoffrey Hill* (1992); and Karen A. Weisman's "Romantic Constructions and Epic Subversions in Geoffrey Hill's *Mercian Hymns*," *Modern Language Quarterly* 57.1 (March 1996).

John Hollander

Hollander's volumes of poetry include *A Crackling of Thorns* (1958), *A Beach Vision* (1962), *"Movie Going" and Other Poems* (1962), *Visions from the Ramble* (1965), *Philomel* (1968), *Types of Shape* (1969, 1991), *The Night Mirror* (1971), *Town and Country Matters* (1972), *Selected Poems* (1972), *The Head of the Bed* (1974), *Tales Told of the Fathers* (1975), *Reflections on Espionage* (1976), *In Place* (1978), *Spectral Emanations: New and Selected Poems* (1978), *Blue Wine and Other Poems* (1979), *Looking Ahead* (1982), *Powers of Thirteen* (1983), *A Hollander Garland* (1985), *In Time and Place* (1986), *Harp Lake* (1988), *Some Fugitives Take Cover* (1988), *Selected Poetry* (1993), *"Tesserae" and Other Poems* (1993), *The Gazer's Spirit: Poems Speaking to Silent Works of Art* (1995), *The Poetry of Everyday Life* (1998), and *"Figurehead" & Other Poems* (1999). Hollander's *Rhyme's Reason: A Guide to English Verse* (1981, 2001) is a helpful and amusing guide to poetic forms. Other works of criticism include *Modern Poetry: Modern Essays in Criticism* (1968) and *Melodious Guile: Fictive Pattern in Poetic Language* (1988). He also coedited *The Oxford Anthology of English Literature* (1973) and edited *American Poetry: The Nineteenth Century* (1994). Interviews include Wesley Wark's in *Queen's Quarterly* 100.2 (1993) and Langdon Hammer's in *Southwest Review* 80 (1995).

Studies dealing with Hollander's work include Richard Howard's *Alone with America* (1969, 1980); Helen Vendler's "A Quarter of Poetry," *New York Times Book Review* (6 April 1975); J. D. McClatchy's "Speaking of Hollander," *The American Poetry Review* 11.5 (1982); and David Lehman's "The Sound and Sense of the Sleight-of-Hand Man," *Parnassus* 12.1 (1984); Rosanna Warren's "Night Thoughts and a Figurehead,"

and Kenneth Gross's "John Hollander's Game of Patience," both in *Raritan* 20.2 (2000); and Ernest Suarez's "John Hollander," *Five Points* 6.1 (2001).

Richard Howard

Howard's volumes of poetry include *Quantities* (1962), *The Damages* (1967), *Untitled Subjects* (1969), *Findings* (1971), *Two-Part Inventions* (1974), *Fellow Feelings* (1976), *Misgivings* (1979), *Lining Up* (1984), *Quantities/Damages: Early Poems* (contains *Quantities* and *The Damages*, 1984), *No Traveller* (1989), *Selected Poems* (1991), *Like Most Revelations* (1994), *If I Dream I Have You, I Have You* (1997), and *Trappings* (1999). Howard is also an extremely prolific translator, translating a wide range of French works from Baudelaire to Roland Barthes. His *Alone with America* (1969, 1980) is an important work of criticism on American poetry after 1960. Interviews appear in *Shenandoah* 24.1 (1973) and *Ohio Review* 16.1 (1974). A conversation with Marilyn Hacker appears in *Antioch Review* 58.3 (Summer 2000).

Discussions of Howard's work include Christopher Ricks's "Conspicuous Consumption," *Parnassus* 3.1 (1974); Robert K. Martin's "The Unconsummated Word," *Parnassus* 4.1 (1975); Henry Sloss's "Cleaving and Burning: An Essay on Richard Howard's Poetry," *Shenandoah* 29.1 (1977); Michael Lynch's "The Life below the Life," *The Gay Academic* (1978), ed. Louie Crew; and James Longenbach's "Richard Howard's Modern World," *Modern Poetry after Modernism* (1997).

Susan Howe

Howe's volumes of poetry—which often also incorporate other genres—include *Hinge Picture* (1974), *Chanting at the Crystal Sea* (1975), *The Western Borders* (1976), *Secret History of the Dividing Line* (1978), *Cabbage Gardens* (1979), *Deep in a Forest of Herods* (1979), *The Liberties* (1980), *Pythagorean Silence* (1982), *Defenestration of Prague* (1983), *Articulation of Sound Forms in Time* (1987), *A Bibliography of the King's Book; or, Eikon Basilike* (1989), *The Europe of Trusts* (1990), *Singularities* (1990), *The Nonconformist's Memorial* (illustrations by Robert Mangold, 1992), *Frame Structures: Early Poems, 1974–1979* (1996), *Pierce-Arrow* (1999), and *Bed Hangings* (pictures by Susan Bee, 2001). Her *My Emily Dickinson* (1985) is an important contribution to Dickinson criticism. Other critical works include *Incloser* (1992) and *The Birth-Mark: Unsettling the Wilderness in American Literary History* (1993). An interview with Lynn Keller appears in *Contemporary Literature* 36.1 (1995).

Critical studies dealing with Howe's work include *The Difficulties* 3.2 (1989); *Talisman* 4 (1990); Rachel Blau DuPlessis's *The Pink Gui-*

tar (1990); Marjorie Perloff's *Poetic License* (1990); Peter Middleton's "On Ice: Julia Kristeva, Susan Howe, and Avant-Garde Poetics," *Contemporary Poetry Meets Modern Theory* (1991), ed. Anthony Easthope and John O. Thompson; Peter Quartermain's *Disjunctive Poetics: From Gertrude Stein and Louis Zukofsky to Susan Howe* (1992); Linda Reinfeld's *Language Poetry: Writing as Rescue* (1992); Mingqian Ma's "Articulating the Inarticulate: Singularities and the Counter-Method in Susan Howe," *Contemporary Literature* 36.3 (1995); Peter Nicholls's "Unsettling the Wilderness: Susan Howe and American History," *Contemporary Literature* 37.4 (1996); Geoffrey O'Brien's *Bardic Deadlines: Reviewing Poetry 1984–1995* (1998); and Paul Naylor's *Poetic Investigations: Singing the Holes in History* (1999). See also **Language Poetry.**

Ted Hughes

Hughes's volumes of poetry include *The Hawk in the Rain* (1957), *Lupercal* (1960), *Wodwo* (1967), *Crow* (1970, 1972), *Season Songs* (1975), *Gaudete* (1977), *Cave Birds* (1978), *Moortown* (1979), *Remains of Elmet* (1979), *River* (1983), *Flowers and Insects* (1986), *Wolf-watching* (1989), *Cappriccio* (1990), *"Rain-Charm for the Duchy" and Other Laureate Poems* (1992), *New Selected Poems 1957–1994* (1995), *Difficulties of a Bridegroom* (1995), *Tales from Ovid* (1997), and *Birthday Letters* (1998). Works of prose include *Poetry in the Making* (1969), *Shakespeare and the Goddess of Complete Being* (1992), and *Winter Pollen: Occasional Prose* (1994). His translations include Seneca's *Oedipus* (1969) and Jean Racine's *Phedre* (1998). He also published children's literature and edited collections of Shakespeare, Coleridge, Dickinson, Keith Douglas, and Sylvia Plath. A biography is Elaine Feinstein's *Ted Hughes: The Life of a Poet* (2001).

Collections of essays include *The Achievement of Ted Hughes* (1983), ed. Keith Sagar; *Critical Essays on Ted Hughes* (1992), ed. Leonard M. Scigaj; and *The Epic Poise: A Celebration of Ted Hughes* (1999), ed. Nick Gammage. Book-length studies include Sagar's *The Art of Ted Hughes* (1978), Terry Gifford and Neil Roberts's *Ted Hughes: A Critical Study* (1981), Thomas West's *Ted Hughes* (1985), Dennis Walder's *Ted Hughes* (1987), Craig Robinson's *Ted Hughes as Shepherd of Being* (1989), Nick Bishop's *Re-Making Poetry: Ted Hughes and a New Critical Psychology* (1991), Ann Skea's *Ted Hughes: The Poetic Quest* (1994), and Paul Bentley's *The Poetry of Ted Hughes: Language, Illusion, and Beyond* (1998). Discussions of Hughes and Plath include Janet Malcolm's *The Silent Woman: Sylvia Plath and Ted Hughes* (1993), Erica Wagner's *Ariel's Gift* (2000), and Lynda K. Bundtzen's *The Other Ariel* (2001).

Bibliographical information is available in Keith Sagar and Stephen Tabor's *Ted Hughes: A Bibliography, 1946–1980* (1983).

Richard Hugo

Making Certain It Goes On: The Collected Poems of Richard Hugo was published in 1984. Other works include *The Triggering Town: Lectures and Essays on Poetry and Writing* (1979) and the novel *Death and The Good Life* (1981). Hugo's *The Real West Marginal Way: A Poet's Autobiography*, ed. Ripley S. Hugo, Louis M. Welch, and James Welch, was published in 1986. Interviews include David Dillon's in *Southwest Review* 62 (Spring 1977), Michael S. Allen's in *Ohio Review* 19 (Winter 1978), and Thomas Gardner's in *Contemporary Literature* 22 (Spring 1981). A conversation between Hugo and William Stafford appears in *Northwest Review* 13 (March 1974).

Book-length studies of Hugo include Michael S. Allen's *We Are Called Human: The Poetry of Richard Hugo* (1982) and Donna Gerstenberger's *Richard Hugo* (1983). *A Trout in the Milk* (1982), ed. Jack Myers, is a collection of essays on Hugo. *Slackwater Review* produced a special Hugo issue in 1978. Other critical discussions of Hugo include Dave Smith's "Getting Right: Richard Hugo's *Selected Poems* and *The Triggering Town*," *American Poetry Review* 10.5 (September–October 1981); Hank Lazer's "The Letter Poem," *Northwest Review* 19.1–2 (1981); Paul Lindholdt's "Richard Hugo's Language: The Poem as 'Obsessive Musical Deed,' " *Contemporary Poetry* 16.2 (Fall 1983); Julian Gitzen's " 'What We Want to Save': The Odyssey of Richard Hugo," *Northwest Review* 24.2 (1986); Sanford Pinsker's *Three Pacific Northwest Poets* (1987); Larry Levinger's "Poet Richard Hugo: The Open Field Beyond," *Ploughshares* 18.1 (1992); and Jonathan Holden's "West Marginal Way: Richard Hugo's Poetry as Self-Psychoanalysis," *Mid-American Review* 16.1 (1995). Bibliographies include Allen's in *A Trout in the Milk* and James Bense's in *Bulletin of Bibliography* 40.3 (September 1983).

Randall Jarrell

Jarrell's *Complete Poems* appeared in 1969 and a *Selected Poems*, ed. William H. Pritchard, in 1990. Jarrell also wrote children's literature and adult fiction, including *Pictures from an Institution: A Comedy* (1954), and translated from German. Jarrell's criticism can be found in *The Poetry of the Age* (1953, expanded in a 2001 edition), *The Third Book of Criticism* (1969), and *No Other Book: Selected Essays* (1999). Pritchard's *Randall Jarrell: A Literary Life* (1990) is a fine biography. Mary Jarrell edited *Randall Jarrell's Letters* (1985).

Collections of essays on Jarrell include *Rand-*

all Jarrell, 1914–1965, a memorial volume edited by Robert Lowell, Peter Taylor, and Robert Penn Warren in 1967, and *Critical Essays on Randall Jarrell* (1983), ed. Suzanne Ferguson. Other discussions of Jarrell's work can be found in Ferguson's *The Poetry of Randall Jarrell* (1971), M. L. Rosenthal's *Randall Jarrell* (1972), J. A. Bryant Jr.'s *Understanding Randall Jarrell* (1986), Richard Flynn's *Randall Jarrell and the Lost World of Childhood* (1990), James Longenbach's *Modern Poetry after Modernism* (1997), and Thomas Travisano's *Midcentury Quartet* (1999). A bibliography is Stuart T. Wright's *Randall Jarrell: A Descriptive Bibliography: 1929–1983* (1986).

June Jordan

Jordan's volumes of poetry include *Who Look at Me* (1969), *Some Changes* (1971), *New Days: Poems of Exile and Return* (1974), *Things That I Do in the Dark: Selected Poetry* (1977, 1981), *Passion* (1980), *Living Room* (1985), *Lyrical Campaigns: Selected Poems* (1989), *Naming Our Destiny: New and Selected Poems* (1989), *Haruko/Love Poetry: New and Selected Love Poems* (1994), and *Kissing God Goodbye: Poems, 1991–1997* (1997). Collections of essays are *Civil Wars* (1981), *On Call: Political Essays* (1985), *Technical Difficulties: African American Notes on the State of the Union* (1992), and *Affirmative Acts: Political Essays* (1998). She has published many books for children and edited *Soulscript: Afro-American Poetry* (1970) and *The Voice of the Children* (with Terri Bush, 1970). She wrote plays, *In the Spirit of Sojourner Truth* (1979) and *The Issue* (1985), and the libretto for *I Was Looking at the Ceiling and Then I Saw the Sky: Earthquake/Romance* (1995), an opera composed by John Adams. In 2000, Jordan published the autobiographical *Soldier: A Poet's Childhood*. An interview with June Jordan appears in *High Plains Literary Review* 3.2 (1988) and one with Peter Erickson in *Transition* 63 (1994).

A collection of essays on Jordan's work is *June Jordan's Poetry for the People: A Revolutionary Blueprint* (1995), ed. Lauren Muller and the Poetry for the People Collective. Other discussions of Jordan's work can be found in Erickson's "The Love Poetry of June Jordan," *Callaloo* 9.1 (1986); *Diverse Voices: Essays on Twentieth-Century Women Writers in English* (1991), ed. Harriet Devine Jump; Jacqueline Vaught Brogan's "From Warrior to Womanist: The Development of June Jordan's Poetry," *Speaking the Other Self: American Women Writers* (1997), ed. Jeanne Campbell Reesman; Scott MacPhail's "June Jordan and the New Black Intellectuals," *African American Review* 33.1 (1999); and AnaLouise Keating's "The Intimate Distance of Desire: June Jordan's Bisexual Inflec-

tions," *Journal of Lesbian Studies* 4.2 (2000). See also **Black Arts Movement**.

Donald Justice

Justice's volumes of poetry include *The Summer Anniversaries* (1960), *A Local Storm* (1963), *Night Light* (1967), *Sixteen Poems* (1970), *From a Notebook* (1972), *Departures* (1973), *Selected Poems* (1979), *Tremayne* (1984), *New and Selected Poems* (1995), and *Orpheus Hesitated Beside the Black River: Poems 1952–1997* (1998). *The Sunset Maker* (1987) includes stories and a memoir as well as verse. *The Donald Justice Reader* (1991) collects poetry and prose. *Oblivion* (1998) contains essays on writers and writing. Other works include the play *The Death of Lincoln* (1988) and translations, including Eugène Guillevic's *The Man Closing Up* (1973). Justice also edited *The Collected Poems of Weldon Kees* (1960) and Joe Bolton's *The Last Nostalgia: Poems, 1982–1990* (1999). An interview appears in *American Poetry Review* 25.1 (1996).

Donald Justice in Conversation with Philip Hoy (2001) contains a long interview and an overview of Justice's work and critical reception. A collection of critical essays is *Certain Solitudes: On the Poetry of Donald Justice* (1997), ed. Dana Gioia and William Logan. Other discussions include Mark Jarman's "Ironic Elegies: The Poetry of Donald Justice," *Pequod* 16/17 (1984); Michael Ryan's "Flaubert in Florida," *New England Review and Breadloaf Quarterly* 7.2 (1984); Gioia's "A Poet's Poet," *New Criterion* (May 1992); Lewis Turco's "The Progress of Donald Justice," *Hollins Critic* 29.4 (1992); Clive Watkin's "Some Reflections on Donald Justice's Poem 'After a Phrase Abandoned by Wallace Stevens,'" *Wallace Stevens Journal* 17.2 (1993); Charles Wright's "Homage to the Thin Man," *Southern Review* 30.4 (1994); Carol Frost's "The Poet's Tact, and a Necessary Tactlessness," *New England Review* 20.3 (1999).

Galway Kinnell

Kinnell's volumes of poetry include *What a Kingdom It Was* (1960), *Flower Herding on Mount Monadnock* (1964), *Body Rags* (1968), *Poems of Night* (1968), *The Hen Flower* (1969), *First Poems: 1946–1954* (1970), *The Book of Nightmares* (1971), *The Shoes of Wandering* (1971), *The Avenue Bearing the Initial of Christ into the New World: Poems 1946–1964* (1974), *Mortal Acts, Mortal Words* (1980), *Selected Poems* (1982), *The Past* (1985), *When One Has Lived a Long Time Alone* (1990), *Three Books* (includes *Body Rags; Mortal Acts, Mortal Words;* and *The Past*, 1993), *Imperfect Thirst* (1994), and *A New Selected Poems* (2000). He has also published translations, including *The Poems of François Villon* (1977) and *The Essential Rilke* (with Hannah Liebmann, 1999), children's literature, and a novel, *Black Light* (1966). *Walking Down the Stairs* (1978) is a selection of interviews.

Book-length studies of Kinnell include Lee Zimmerman's *Intricate and Simple Things: The Poetry of Galway Kinnell* (1987) and Richard J. Calhoun's *Galway Kinnell* (1992). Collections of essays on his work include *On the Poetry of Galway Kinnell: The Wages of Dying* (1987), ed. Howard Nelson, and *Critical Essays on Galway Kinnell* (1996), ed. Nancy L. Tuten. Other helpful discussions can be found in Richard Howard's *Alone with America* (1969, 1980), Ralph Mills's *Cry of the Human* (1975), and Cary Nelson's *Our Last First Poets* (1981). A bibliography is *Galway Kinnell: A Bibliography and Index of His Published Works and Criticism of Them* (1968).

Thomas Kinsella

Kinsella's *The Collected Poems 1956–2001* was published in 2001. Works of criticism include *Davis, Mangan, Ferguson?: Tradition and the Irish Writer* (with writings by W. B. Yeats, 1970) and *The Dual Tradition: An Essay on Poetry and Politics in Ireland* (1995). He has also published translations of literature in Irish.

Book-length considerations of Kinsella's work include Maurice Harmon's *The Poetry of Thomas Kinsella: "With Darkness for a Nest"* (1974), Thomas H. Jackson's *The Whole Matter: The Poetic Evolution of Thomas Kinsella* (1995), Donatella Abbate Badin's *Thomas Kinsella* (1996), and Brian John's *Reading the Ground: The Poetry of Thomas Kinsella* (1996). Critical essays include Floyd Skloot's "The Evolving Poetry of Thomas Kinsella," *New England Review* 18.4 (1997); Taffy Martin's "Thomas Kinsella and the Poetry of Irish Difference," *Strategies of Difference in Modern Poetry: Case Studies in Poetic Composition* (1998), ed. Pierre Lagayette; and Daniel T. O'Hara's "The Pen Shop of Thomas Kinsella," *Boundary 2* 28.2 (2001). *The Hollins Critic* published a special issue on Kinsella in 1968. J. Chris Westgate's bibliography appears in *Bulletin of Bibliography* 56.3 (1999). See also **Irish Poetry.**

Kenneth Koch

Koch's volumes of poetry include *Poems* (1953), *Ko; or A Season on Earth* (1959), *Permanently* (1960), *"Thank You" and Other Poems* (1962), *Poems from 1952 and 1953* (1968), *The "Pleasures of Peace" and Other Poems* (1969), *Sleeping with Women* (1969), *When the Sun Tries to Go On* (1969), *The Art of Love* (1975), *The Duplications* (1977), *The Burning Mystery of Anna in 1951* (1979), *From the Air* (1979), *Days and Nights* (1982), *Selected Poems, 1950–1982* (1985), *On the Edge* (1986), *Seasons on Earth* (1987), *Selected Poems* (1991), *One Train*

(1994), *On the Great Atlantic Rainway: Selected Poems, 1950–1988* (1994), *Straits* (1998), and *New Addresses* (2000). *The Art of Poetry* (1996) is a collection of poems, interviews, essays, and other writings. Koch published short stories, including *"Hotel Lambosa" and Other Stories* (1993); a novel, *The Red Robins* (1975); and many plays, including those collected in *Gold Standard* (1996). He also published extensively on questions of pedagogy: *Wishes, Lies, and Dreams: Teaching Children to Write Poetry* (1970), *Rose, Where did You Get That Red?: Teaching Great Poetry to Children* (1973), and *I Never Told Anybody: Teaching Poetry Writing in a Nursing Home* (1977). His *Making Your Own Days* (1998) is a delightful introduction to reading and writing poetry that includes a small anthology of poems. Interviews include John Tranter's in *Scripsi* 4.2 (1986), David Herd's in *Pn Review* 22 (1995), and Jordan Davis's in *American Poetry Review* 25.6 (1996).

Discussions of Koch's work can be found in David Spurr's "Beyond Irony," *American Poetry Review* 12.2 (1983); Philip Auslander's *The New York School Poets as Playwrights* (1989); John Paul Tassoni's "Play and Co-Option in Kenneth Koch's *Ko; or, A Season on Earth*: 'Freedom and the Realizable World!'" *Sagetrieb* 10.1–2 (1991); David Lehman's "Dr. Fun," *American Poetry Review* 24.6 (1995); Mark Halliday's "Koch and Sense," *Michigan Quarterly Review* 36.1 (1997); Lehman's *The Last Avant-Garde* (1998); and Paul Hoover's "Fables of Representation: Poetry of The New York School," *American Poetry Review* 31.4 (2002). *The Scene of My Selves: New Work on the New York School Poets* (2001), ed. Terrence Diggory and Stephen Paul Miller, contains three essays on Koch: David Chinitz's "'Arm the Paper Arm': Kenneth Koch's Postmodern Comedy," Theodore Pelton's "Kenneth Koch's Poetics of Pleasure," and David Spurr's "Kenneth Koch's 'Serious Moment.'" See also **New York School.**

Yusef Komunyakaa

Komunyakaa's poetry is collected in *Pleasure Dome: New and Collected Poems* (2001). *Blue Notes* (2000) is a collection of essays, interviews, and other writings. Komunyakaa also coedited the two-volume *Jazz Poetry Anthology* (1991, 1996) with Sascha Feinstein. Interviews include Vincente F. Gotera's in *Callaloo* 13.2 (1990); Robert Kelley's "Jazz and Poetry," *Georgia Review* 46.4 (1992); Muna Asali's in *New England Review* 16.1 (1994); Thomas C. Johnson's in *Worcester Review* 19.1–2 (1998); and Ernest Suarez's in *Five Points* (1999).

For discussions of Komunyakaa's work, see Vincente F. Gotera's "'Depending on the Light': Yusef Komunyakaa's *Dien Cai Dau*," *America Rediscovered: Critical Essays on Literature and*

Film of the Vietnam War (1990), ed. Owen W. Gilman Jr. and Lorrie Smith; Kirkland C. Jones's "Folk Idiom in the Literary Expression of Two African American Authors: Rita Dove and Yusef Komunyakaa," *Language and Literature in the African American Imagination* (1992), ed. Carol Aisha Blackshire-Belay; Don Ringnalda's "Rejecting 'Sweet Geometry': Komunyakaa's Duende," *Journal of American Culture* 16.3 (1993); Michael Collins's "Staying Human," *Parnassus* 18–19 (1993); Stuart Friebert's "The Truth of the Matter," *Field* 48 (1993); Alvin Aubert's "Yusef Komunyakaa: The Unified Vision—Canonization and Humanity," *African American Review* 27.1 (1993); Kevin Stein's "Vietnam and the 'Voice Within': Public and Private History in Yusef Komunyakaa's *Dien Cai Dau*," *Massachusetts Review* 36.4 (1995–96); Ernest Suarez's "Yusef Komunyakaa," *Five Points* 4.1 (1999); and Angela M. Salas's "'Flashbacks through the Heart': Yusef Komunyakaa and the Poetry of Self-Assertion," *The Furious Flowering of African American Poetry* (1999), ed. Joanne V. Gabbin.

Maxine Kumin

Kumin's volumes of poetry include *Halfway* (1961), *The Privilege* (1965), *The Nightmare Factory* (1970), *Up Country: Poems of New England, New and Selected* (illustrated by Barbara Swan, 1972), *House, Bridge, Fountain, Gate* (1975), *The Retrieval System* (1978), *Our Ground Time Here Will Be Brief: New and Selected Poems* (1982), *Closing the Ring: Selected Poems* (1984), *The Long Approach* (1985), *Nurture* (1989), *Looking for Luck* (1992), *Connecting the Dots* (1996), *Selected Poems, 1960–1990* (1997), and *The Long Marriage* (2001). She also wrote novels, including *The Designated Heir* (1974), short stories, and children's literature. *To Make a Prairie: Essays on Poets, Poetry, and Country Living* (1979) and *Always Beginning: Essays on a Life in Poetry* (2000) offer a selection of memoirs, essays, and criticism. In her memoir *Inside the Halo and Beyond* (2000), Kumin discusses her recovery from a serious injury. Interviews include Enid Shomer's in *Massachusetts Review* 37.4 (1996–97), Steve Kronen's in *Shenandoah* 48.4 (1998), and Jeffrey S. Cramer's in *New Letters* 66.3 (2000). A conversation between Kumin, Elaine Showalter, Carol Smith, and Anne Sexton appears in *Women's Studies* 4 (1976).

Many critical essays can be found in the collection *Telling the Barn Swallow: Poets on the Poetry of Maxine Kumin* (1997), ed. Emily Grosholz. Other discussions of Kumin's work include Sybil P. Estess's "Past Halfway: The *Retrieval System*, by Maxine Kumin," *Iowa Review* 10.4 (1979); Diane Wood Middlebrook's "Housewife into Poet: The Apprenticeship of Anne Sexton," *New England Quarterly* 56.4

(1983); Jean B. Gearhart's "Courage to Survive: Maxine Kumin," *Pembroke Magazine* 20 (1988); Diana Hume George's "'Keeping Our Working Distance': Maxine Kumin's Poetry of Loss and Survival," *Aging and Gender in Literature* (1993), ed. Anne M. Wyatt-Brown and Janice Rossen; and Ben Howard's "Review of Selected Poems, 1960–1990," *Poetry* 172.3 (1998).

Philip Larkin

Larkin's *Collected Poems*, ed. Anthony Thwaite, was published in 1988. Thwaite also edited *Selected Letters of Philip Larkin, 1940–1985* (1992) and *Further Requirements: Interviews, Broadcasts, Statements, and Book Reviews* (2001). Other works include Larkin's novels *Jill* (1946) and *A Girl in Winter* (1947); a collection of music reviews, *All What Jazz: A Record Diary, 1961–1971* (1985); and *The Oxford Book of Twentieth-Century English Verse* (1973), which Larkin edited. Previously unpublished material has recently been published in two posthumous collections: fiction in *"Trouble at Willow Gables" and Other Fictions* (2002), ed. James Booth, and jazz writings in *Larkin's Jazz: Essays and Reviews, 1940–84* (2001), ed. Richard Palmer and John White. *Required Writing: Miscellaneous Pieces, 1955–1982* (1983) contains much of Larkin's important prose. The standard biography is Andrew Motion's *Philip Larkin: A Writer's Life* (1993). An additional interview appears in *Viewpoints: Poets in Conversation with John Haffenden* (1981).

Book-length studies include David Timms's *Philip Larkin* (1973), Bruce K. Martin's *Philip Larkin* (1978), Motion's *Philip Larkin* (1982), Terrence Whalen's *Philip Larkin and English Poetry* (1986), Salem K. Hassan's *Philip Larkin and His Contemporaries: An Air of Authenticity* (1988), Janice Rossen's *Philip Larkin: His Life's Work* (1989), Stephen Regan's *Philip Larkin* (1992), James Booth's *Philip Larkin: Writer* (1992), Andrew Swarbrick's *Out of Reach: The Poetry of Philip Larkin* (1995), and A. T. Tolley's *Larkin at Work: A Study of Larkin's Mode of Composition as Seen in His Workbooks* (1997). Collections of essays include *Larkin at Sixty* (1982), ed. Thwaite; *Critical Essays on Philip Larkin: The Poems* (1989), ed. Linda Cookson and Bryan Loughrey; *Philip Larkin: The Man and His Work* (1989), ed. Dale Salwak; *Philip Larkin* (1997), ed. Regan; and *New Larkins for Old: Critical Essays* (2000), ed. James Booth. *Phoenix* 11–12 (1973–74) is a special Larkin issue. B. C. Bloomfield's bibliography was first published in 1979 and expanded in 2002. See also **The Movement.**

Li-Young Lee

Lee's volumes of poetry include *Rose* (1986), *The City in Which I Love You* (1990), and *Book of My Nights* (2001). His autobiography, *The Winged Seed*, was published in 1995. Gerald Stern's foreword to *Rose* provides a useful introduction. A helpful interview is found in Bill Moyers's *The Language of Life* (1995). Other interviews include James Kyung-Jin Lee's in *Words Matter: Conversations with Asian American Writers* (2000), ed. King-Kok Cheung, and Tod Marshall's "To Witness the Invisible: A Talk with Li-Young Lee," *Kenyon Review* 22.1 (2000).

Critical studies include Zhou Xiaojing's "Inheritance and Invention in Li-Young Lee's Poetry," *MELUS* 21.1 (1996); Walter A. Hesford's "The City in Which I Love You: Li-Young Lee's Excellent Song," *Christianity and Literature* 46.1 (1996); Tim Engles's "Lee's 'Persimmons,'" *Explicator* 54.3 (1996); Mary Slowik's "Beyond Lot's Wife: The Immigration Poems of Marilyn Chin, Garrett Hongo, Li-Young Lee, and David Mura," *MELUS* 25.3–4 (2000); Timothy Yu's "Form and Identity in Language Poetry and Asian American Poetry," *Contemporary Literature* 41.1 (2000); and Steven G. Yao's "The Precision of Persimmons: Hybridity, Grafting and the Case of Li-Young Lee," *Lit: Literature Interpretation Theory* 12.1 (2001). See also **Asian American Poetry.**

Denise Levertov

Collections of Levertov's poems include *Collected Earlier Poems, 1940–1960* (1979), *Poems, 1960–1967* (1983), *Selected Poems* (1986), *Poems 1968–1972* (1987), and *Poems 1972–1982* (2001). Two thematic selections are *The Stream and the Sapphire: Selected Poems on Religious Themes* and *The Life around Us: Selected Poems on Nature*, both published in 1997. Uncollected individual volumes include *Oblique Prayers* (1984), *Breathing the Water* (1987), *A Door in the Hive* (1989), *Evening Train* (1992), *Sands of the Well* (1996), and *This Great Unknowing: Last Poems* (1999). Other helpful texts include her *New and Selected Essays* (1992); a collection of autobiographical writings, *Tesserae: Memories and Supposition* (1995); and the interviews in *Conversations with Denise Levertov* (1998), ed. Jewel Spears Brooker. She also published short stories, *In the Night* (1966); translated French and Bengali poetry; and edited *Out of the War Shadow: An Anthology of Current Poetry* (1967). *The Letters of Denise Levertov and William Carlos Williams*, ed. Christopher MacGowan, was published in 1998.

Important critical studies include Linda Wagner-Martin's *Denise Levertov* (1967); Harry Marten's *Understanding Denise Levertov* (1988); Audrey T. Rodgers's *Denise Levertov: The Poetry of Engagement* (1993); and Linda A. Kinnahan's *Poetics of the Feminine: Authority and Literary Tradition in William Carlos Williams, Mina Loy,*

Denise Levertov, and Kathleen Fraser (1994). Many useful essays are included in the collections *Critical Essays on Denise Levertov* (1990), ed. Wagner-Martin; *Denise Levertov: Selected Criticism* (1993), ed. Albert Gelpi; and *Denise Levertov: New Perspectives* (2000), ed. Anne C. Little and Susie Paul. *Twentieth Century Literature* 38.3 (1992) and *Renascence* 50.1–2 (1997–98) are special issues dedicated to Levertov. Liana Sakelliou-Schultz's *Denise Levertov: An Annotated Primary and Secondary Bibliography* appeared in 1988. See also **Black Mountain School.**

Philip Levine

Volumes of Levine's poetry include *On the Edge* (1963), *Not This Pig* (1968), *Red Dust* (1971), *They Feed They Lion* (1972), *1933* (1974), *The Names of the Lost* (1976), *7 Years from Somewhere* (1979), *Ashes: Poems New and Old* (1979), *One for the Rose* (1981), *Selected Poems* (1984), *Sweet Will* (1985), *A Walk with Tom Jefferson* (1988), *New Selected Poems* (1991), *What Work Is* (1991), *The Simple Truth* (1994), *Unselected Poems* (1997), and *The Mercy* (1999). His memoir, *The Bread of Time*, was published in 1994, and a collection of interviews, *Don't Ask*, in 1981. He has also translated *Tarumba: The Selected Poems of Jaime Sabines* (with Ernest Trejo, 1979) and *Off the Map: Selected Writings of Gloria Fuertes* (with Ada Long, 1984).

Essays on Levine's work can be found in *Parnassus* (Fall–Winter 1977); *American Poetry Review* (November–December 1979); and *On the Poetry of Philip Levine: Stranger to Nothing* (1991), ed. Christopher Buckley. Other studies include Edward Hirsch's "The Visionary Poetics of Philip Levine and Charles Wright," *The Columbia History of American Poetry* (1993), ed. Jay Parini and Brett C. Millier; Ernest Suarez's "Philip Levine," *Five Points* 3.2 (1999); Gary Pacernick's "Staying Power: A Lifetime in Poetry," *Kenyon Review* 21.2 (1999); and Peter Hitchcock's "They Must Be Represented? Problems in Theories of Working-Class Representation," *PMLA* 115.1 (2000).

Michael Longley

Longley's volumes of poetry include *Ten Poems* (1965), *Room to Rhyme* (with Seamus Heaney and David Hammond, 1968), *Secret Marriages* (1968), *Three Regional Voices* (with Barry Tebb and Iain Crichton Smith, 1968), *No Continuing City: Poems, 1963–1968* (1969), *Lares* (1972), *An Exploded View: Poems 1968–72* (1973), *Fishing in the Sky: Love Poems* (1975), *Man Lying on a Wall* (1976), *The Echo Gate* (1979), *Selected Poems, 1963–1980* (1981), *Patchwork* (drawings by Jim Allen, 1981), *Poems, 1963–1983* (1985), *Gorse Fires* (1991), *The Ghost Orchid* (1995), *The Ship of the Wind* (1997),

Broken Dishes (1998), *Selected Poems* (1998), *Out of the Cold: Drawings & Poems for Christmas* (with Sarah Longley, 1999), and *The Weather in Japan* (2000). He has also published *Tuppenny Stung: Autobiographical Chapters* (1994) and edited *Causeway: The Arts of Ulster* (1971), *Under the Moon, Over the Stars: Young People's Writing from Ulster* (1971), Louis MacNeice's *Selected Poems* (1988), *Poems by W. R. Rodgers* (1993), *Louis MacNeice: Poems* (2001), and *20th Century Irish Poems* (2002). Interviews appear in *Pn Review* 20 (1994), *Southern Review* 31.3 (1995), and *Irish Studies Review* 18 (1997).

Critical discussions of Longley's work include Michael Allen's "Options: The Poetry of Michael Longley," *Eire-Ireland* 10.4 (1975); John Mole's "A Question of Balance," *Times Literary Supplement* (8 February 1980); Harry Marten's " 'Singing the Darkness into the Light': Reflections on Recent Irish Poetry," *New England Review* 3 (1980); D. E. S. Maxwell's "Semantic Scruples: A Rhetoric for Politics in the North," *Literature and the Changing Ireland* (1982), ed. Peter Connelly; Charles O'Neill's "Three Irish Voices," *Spirit* (Fall–Winter 1989); Brian McIlroy's "Poetry Imagery as Political Fetishism," *Canadian Journal of Irish Studies* 16.1 (1990); Peter McDonald's "Michael Longley's Homes," *The Chosen Ground: Essays on the Contemporary Poetry of Northern Ireland* (1992), ed. Neil Corcoran; John Lyon's "Michael Longley's List," *English* 45.183 (1996); and Victor Luftig's "Poetry, Causality, and an Irish Ceasefire," *Peace Review* (June 2001). See also **Irish Poetry.**

Audre Lorde

The Collected Poems of Audre Lorde appeared in 1997. Lorde also published a biographical novel, *Zami: A New Spelling of My Name* (1982), and a meditation on her experience with cancer, *The Cancer Journals* (1980). Two collections of essays and speeches are *Sister Outsider* (1984) and *A Burst of Light* (1988). Interviews appear in *Black Women Writers at Work* (1983), ed. Claudia Tate, and *Callaloo* 23.1 (2000).

Essays on Lorde appear in *Black Women Writers (1950–1980): A Critical Evaluation* (1983), ed. Mari Evans, and *Black Feminist Criticism: Perspectives on Black Women Writers* (1985, 1997), ed. Barbara Christian. Other critical studies include Mary DeShazer's *Inspiring Women: Reimagining the Muse* (1986); Gloria T. Hull's "Living on the Line: Audre Lorde and Our Dead behind Us," *Changing Our Own Words* (1989), ed. Cheryl A. Wall; AnaLouise Keating's *Women Reading Women Writing: Self-Invention in Paula Gunn Allen, Gloria Anzaldúa, and Audre Lorde* (1996); Carmen Birkle's *Women's Stories of the Looking Glass: Autobiographical Reflections and Self-Representations in the Poetry of Sylvia Plath,*

Adrienne Rich, and Audre Lorde (1996); Alexis De Veaux's "Searching for Audre Lorde," *Callaloo* 23.1 (2000); and Cassie Premo Steele's *We Heal from Memory: Sexton, Lorde, Anzaldúa, and the Poetry of Witness* (2000). See also **Black Arts Movement.**

Robert Lowell

Lowell's volumes of poetry include *Lord Weary's Castle* (1946), *The Mills of the Kavanaughs* (1951), *Life Studies* (1959), *Imitations* (1961), *For the Union Dead* (1964), *Near the Ocean* (1967), *Notebook 1967–68* (1969, 1979), *The Dolphin* (1973), *For Lizzie and Harriet* (1973), *History* (1973), *Selected Poems* (1976, 1977), and *Day by Day* (1977). His *Collected Prose*, ed. Robert Giroux, appeared in 1987. Lowell adapted works for the stage, including Racine's *Phaedra* (1961); Melville and Hawthorne stories in *The Old Glory* (1965); and Aeschylus's *Prometheus Unbound* (1969). An important interview appears in *Robert Lowell: A Collection of Critical Essays* (1968), ed. Thomas Parkinson. Other interviews can be found in *Robert Lowell, Interviews and Memoirs* (1988), ed. Jeffrey Meyers. Ian Hamilton's *Robert Lowell* (1982) and Paul Mariani's *The Lost Puritan* (1994) are helpful biographies.

Important critical works include Hugh B. Staples's *Robert Lowell: The First Twenty Years* (1962), Jerome Mazzaro's *The Poetic Themes of Robert Lowell* (1965), Philip Cooper's *The Autobiographical Myth of Robert Lowell* (1970), Marjorie Perloff's *The Poetic Art of Robert Lowell* (1973), Alan Williamson's *Pity the Monsters: The Political Vision of Robert Lowell* (1974), Stephen Yenser's *Circle to Circle* (1975), Steven Gould Axelrod's *Robert Lowell: Life and Art* (1978), Vereen Bell's *Robert Lowell, Nihilist as Hero* (1983), Jeffrey Meyers's *Manic Power: Robert Lowell and His Circle* (1987), Katharine Wallingford's *Robert Lowell's Language of the Self* (1988), Helen Vendler's *The Given and the Made* (1995), Richard Tillinghast's *Robert Lowell's Life and Work: Damaged Grandeur* (1995), Henry Hart's *Robert Lowell and the Sublime* (1995), Thomas Travisano's *Midcentury Quartet* (1999), and William Doreski's *Robert Lowell's Shifting Colors* (1999). Other collections of essays on Lowell include *Robert Lowell: Essays on the Poetry* (1986), ed. Axelrod and Helen Deese, and *The Critical Response to Robert Lowell* (1999), ed. Axelrod. Axelrod and Deese also compiled *Robert Lowell: A Reference Guide* (1982). See also **Confessional Poetry.**

Derek Mahon

Mahon's *Collected Poems* was published in 1999. *Journalism: Selected Prose 1970–1995* was published in 1996. His translations include Nerval's *The Chimeras* (1982) and Jean Racine's *Phaedra* (1996). Among his plays are adaptations of Molière's *High Time* (1985) and *The*

School for Wives (1986) and an adaptation of Euripides' *The Bacchae* (1991). He edited the collections *Modern Irish Poetry* (1972) and *The Penguin Book of Contemporary Irish Poetry* (with Peter Fallon, 1990). Interviews appear in *Irish Literary Supplement* 10 (1991) and *Poetry Review* 81.2 (1991).

Critical discussions of Mahon's work include Brian Donnelly's "The Poetry of Derek Mahon," *English Studies* 60 (1979); Dillon Johnston's "Unaccommodated Mahon: An Ulster Poet," *Hollins Critic* 17.5 (1980); Andrew Waterman's "Somewhere, out There, Beyond: The Poetry of Seamus Heaney and Derek Mahon," *Pn Review* 8.1 (1981); Eamon Grennan's " 'To the Point of Speech': The Poetry of Derek Mahon," *Contemporary Irish Writing* (1983), ed. James D. Brophy and Raymond J. Porter; Conor Johnston's "Poetry and Politics: Responses to the Northern Ireland Crisis in the Poetry of John Montague, Derek Mahon, and Seamus Heaney," *Poesis* 5.4 (1984); David E. William's "The Poetry of Derek Mahon," *Journal of Irish Literature* 13.3 (1984); John M. Byrne's *The Significance of Landscape and History in the Poetry of Seamus Heaney, Derek Mahon, and John Montague* (1984); John Constable's "Derek Mahon's Development," *Agenda* 22.3–4 (1984–85); Robert Taylor's "Derek Mahon: The Lute and the Stars," *Massachusetts Review* 28.3 (1987); Bill Tinley's "International Perspectives in the Poetry of Derek Mahon," *Irish University Review* 21.1 (1991); Hugh Houghton's " 'Even Now There Are Places Where a Thought Might Grow': Place and Displacement in the Poetry of Derek Mahon," *The Chosen Ground: Essays on the Contemporary Poetry of Northern Ireland* (1992), ed. Neil Corcoran; David G. Williams's " 'A Decadent Who Lived to Tell the Story': Derek Mahon's *The Yellow Book*," *Journal of Modern Literature* 23.1 (1999); and Richard Tillinghast's "Derek Mahon: Exile and Stranger," *New Criterion* 18.1 (1999). *Irish University Review* 24.1 (1994) is a special issue dedicated to Mahon and includes Jody Allen-Randolph's bibliography. See also **Irish Poetry.**

Dionisio D. Martínez

Martínez's books of poetry include *Dancing at the Chelsea* (1992), *History as a Second Language* (1993), *Bad Alchemy* (1995), and *Climbing Back* (2001).

Discussions of his poetry include Carolyne Wright's "On Agosín and Martínez," *Iowa Review* 25.1 (1995) and Bill Christophersen's review of *Climbing Back* in *Poetry* 179.4 (2002). A number of useful journalistic profiles have appeared in *The St. Petersburg Times* and *The Tampa Tribune*. See also **Latino Poetry.**

Medbh McGuckian

McGuckian's volumes of poetry include *Portrait of Joanna* (1980), *Single Ladies* (1980), *The Flower Master* (1982), *Venus and the Rain* (1984), *On Ballycastle Beach* (1988), *Two Women, Two Shores: Poems by Medbh McGuckian and Nuala Archer* (1989), *Marconi's Cottage* (1991), *"The Flower Master" and Other Poems* (1993), *Captain Lavender* (1995), *Selected Poems 1978–1994* (1997), *Shelmalier* (1998), and *Drawing Ballerinas* (2001). With Eiléan Ní Chuilleanáin she translated the poems in Nuala Ní Dhomhnaill's *The Water Horse* (1999). She has also written a study of the automobile in Seamus Heaney's poetry, *Horsepower Pass By!* (1999). Interviews include Rebecca Wilson's in *Cencrastus* (Spring 1988), Kathleen McCracken's in *Irish Literary Supplement* 9.2 (1990), Laura O'Connor's in *Southern Review* 28.1 (1995), and Sawnie Morris's in *Kenyon Review* 23.3–4 (2001).

Clair Wills's *Improprieties: Politics and Sexuality in Northern Irish Poetry* (1993) and Patricia Boyle Haberstroh's *Women Creating Women: Contemporary Irish Women Poets* (1996) offer extensive examinations of McGuckian's work. Other critical discussions include Ann Beer's "Medbh McGuckian's Poetry: Maternal Thinking and a Politics of Peace," *Canadian Journal of Irish Studies* 18.1 (1992); Thomas Docherty's "Initiations, Tempers, Seductions: Postmodern McGuckian," *The Chosen Ground: Essays on the Contemporary Poetry of Northern Ireland* (1992), ed. Neil Corcoran; Susan Porter's "The 'Imaginative Space' of Medbh McGuckian," *International Women's Writing: New Landscapes of Identity* (1995), ed. Anne E. Brown and Marjanne E. Gooze; Mary O'Connor's " 'Rising Out': Medbh McGuckian's Destabilizing Poetics," *Eire-Ireland* 30.4 (1996); Shane Murphy's "Obliquity in the Poetry of Paul Muldoon and Medbh McGuckian," *Eire-Ireland* 31.3–4 (1996) and " 'You Took Away My Biography': The Poetry of Medbh McGuckian," *Irish University Review* 28.1 (1998); *Gender and Sexuality in Modern Ireland* (1997), ed. Anthony Bradley and Maryann Gialanella; and *Border Crossings: Irish Women Writers and National Identities* (2000), ed. Kathryn Kirkpatrick. See also **Irish Poetry.**

William Meredith

Meredith's volumes of poetry include *Love Letter from an Impossible Land* (1944), *Ships and Other Figures* (1948), *"The Open Sea" and Other Poems* (1957), *Winter Verse* (1964), *"The Wreck of the Thresher" and Other Poems* (1964), *Year End Accounts* (1965), *Two Pages from a Colorado Journal* (1967), *Earth Walk: New and Selected Poems* (1970), *Hazard, the Painter* (1975), *The Cheer* (1980), *Partial Accounts: New and Selected Poems* (1987), and *Effort at Speech: New and Selected Poems* (1997). Two collections of his criticism, lectures, and prose are the two-lecture volume, *Reasons for Poetry; and, The Reason for Criticism* (1982) and *Poems*

Are Hard to Read (1991). He published numerous translations, including Guillaume Apollinaire's *Alcools: Poems, 1898–1913* (1964), and wrote the libretto for *The Bottle Imp* (1958), an opera composed by Peter Whiton. Interviews appear in *Southwest Review* 57 (1972) and *Plum Review* 4 (1992).

Critical discussions of Meredith can be found in James Dickey's "Orientations," *American Scholar* 34 (1965); Raymond Roselip's "From Woodcarver to Wordcarver," *Poetry* 107 (1966); Richard Howard's *Alone with America* (1969, 1980); Jeremy Robson's *Corgi Modern Poets in Focus 2* (1971); Henry Taylor's "In Charge of Morale in a Morbid Time: The Poetry of William Meredith," *Hollins Critic* 16.1 (1979); Neva Herrington's "The Language of the Tribe: William Meredith's Poetry," *Southwest Review* 67.1 (1982); Guy Rotella's *Three Contemporary Poets of New England* (1983); and Michael Collier's foreword to *Effort at Speech* (1997) and "An Exact Ratio," *Passing the Word: Writers on Their Mentors* (2001), ed. Jeffrey Skinner and Lee Martin.

James Merrill

The Collected Poems of James Merrill, ed. J. D. McClatchy and Stephen Yenser, was published in 2001. His prose is collected in *Recitative* (1986), and his autobiography is *A Different Person* (1993). Merrill also wrote two novels, *The Seraglio* (1957) and *The (Diblos) Notebook* (1965). Biographical information can be found in Alison Lurie's *Familiar Spirits: A Memoir of James Merrill and David Jackson* (2001). Ross Labrie's *James Merrill at Home* (1982) is a helpful book-length interview. Stephen Yenser's *The Consuming Myth: The Work of James Merrill* (1987) is an important book-length study. Other useful studies include Labrie's *James Merrill* (1982), Judith Moffett's *James Merrill, an Introduction to the Poetry* (1984), Don Adams's *James Merrill's Poetic Quest* (1997), and Timothy Materer's *James Merrill's Apocalypse* (2000). Robert Polito's *A Reader's Guide to James Merrill's The Changing Light at Sandover* (1994) offers assistance for the study of Merrill's trilogy. Other helpful discussions of his work can be found in David Kalstone's *Five Temperaments* (1977), Helen Vendler's *Part of Nature, Part of Us* (1980), Robert von Hallberg's *American Poetry and Culture, 1945–1980* (1985), Vernon Shetley's *After the Death of Poetry* (1993), Mutlu Konuk Blasing's *Politics and Form in Postmodern Poetry* (1995), and Rachel Hadas's *Merrill, Cavafy, Poems, and Dreams* (2000). Collections of critical essays include *James Merrill: Essays in Criticism* (1983), ed. David Lehman and Charles Berger; *James Merrill* (1985), ed. Harold Bloom; and *Critical Essays on James Merrill* (1996), ed. Guy L. Rotella.

W. S. Merwin

Merwin's early volumes have been collected as *The First Four Books of Poems* (1975), *The Second Four Books of Poems* (1993), and *Flower and Hand: Poems, 1977–1983* (1997). Uncollected later volumes include *The Rain in the Trees* (1988), *Selected Poems* (1988), *The Vixen* (1996), *The Folding Cliffs: A Narrative* (1998), *The River Sound* (1999), and *The Pupil* (2001). Among his many translations are *East Window: The Asian Translations* (1998), Dante's *Purgatorio* (2000), and *Gawain and the Green Knight* (2002). He has also published television scripts and plays, including *Darkling Child* (1956) and *Favor Island* (1957). *The Miner's Pale Children* (1970) and *Houses and Travellers* (1977) are collections of short fiction. Two collections of essays and memoirs are *Unframed Original* (1982) and *Regions of Memory* (1987), ed. Ed Folsom and Cary Nelson.

Collections of essays on Merwin include *W. S. Merwin: Essays on the Poetry* (1987), ed. Cary Nelson and Ed Folsom, and *Many Mountains Moving* (2001), ed. Mark Irwin. Other work on Merwin includes Cheri Davis's *W. S. Merwin* (1981), Mark Christhilf's *W. S. Merwin: The Myth Maker* (1986), Thomas B. Byers's *What I Cannot Say: Self, Word, and World in Whitman, Stevens, and Merwin* (1989), Edward J. Brunner's *Poetry as Labor and Privilege* (1991), Edward Haworth Hoeppner's *Echoes and Moving Fields: Structure and Subjectivity in the Poetry of W. S. Merwin and John Ashbery* (1994), H. L. Hix's *Understanding W. S. Merwin* (1997), Jane Frazier's *From Origin to Ecology: Nature and the Poetry of W. S. Merwin* (1999), and Leonard M. Scigaj's *Sustainable Poetry: Four American Ecopoets* (1999). See also **Deep Image Poetry.**

Thylias Moss

Moss's volumes of poetry include *Hosiery Seams on a Bowlegged Woman* (1983), *Pyramid of Bone* (1989), *At Redbones* (1990), *Rainbow Remnants in Rock Bottom Ghetto Sky* (1991), *Small Congregations: New and Selected Poems* (1993), and *Last Chance for the Tarzan Holler* (1998). Moss's memoir, *Tale of a Sky-Blue Dress*, appeared in 1998. She has also written children's literature and two plays, *Talking to Myself* (1984) and *The Dolls in the Basement* (1984). Interviews appear in *Onthebus* 4–5 (1992) and *Fourth Genre* 1.2 (1999).

Critical discussions of Moss include Rafael Campo's "Sturdy Boxcars and Exploding Pickle Jars," *Parnassus* 21.1–2 (1995), and Eric Murphy Selinger's "This Personal Maze Is Not the Prize," *Parnassus* 24.2 (2000).

Paul Muldoon

Muldoon's collected *Poems, 1968–1998* appeared in 2001. He has also published translations, including Nuala Ní Dhomhnaill's *The Astrakhan Cloak* (1993) and Aristophanes' *The Birds* (with Richard Martin, 1999), and edited collections of poetry, including *The Faber Book of Contemporary Irish Poetry* (1986). His lectures on Irish literature, *To Ireland, I*, were published in 2000. He has also written libretti, including the one for *Bandanna* (1999), an opera composed by Daron Hagen. An important early interview appeared in *Viewpoints: Poets in Conversation with John Haffenden* (1981); more recent interviews appear in *Contemporary Literature* 35.1 (1994), *Bomb* 65 (1998), and *Michigan Quarterly Review* 37.1 (1998).

Two book-length studies are Tim Kendall's *Paul Muldoon* (1996) and Clair Wills's *Reading Paul Muldoon* (1998). Other critical works include Wills's "The Lie of the Land: Language, Imperialism, and Trade in Paul Muldoon's 'Meeting the British,' " *The Chosen Ground: Essays on the Contemporary Poetry of Northern Ireland* (1992), ed. Neil Corcoran; Wills's *Improprieties: Politics and Sexuality in Northern Irish Poetry* (1993); David Wheatley's "An Irish Poet in America," *Raritan* 18.4 (1999); Sven Birkerts's "About Paul Muldoon," *Ploughshares* 26.1 (2000); Andrew Osborn's "Skirmishes on the Border: The Evolution and Function of Paul Muldoon's Fuzzy Rhyme," *Contemporary Literature* 41.2 (2000); and Rachael Buxton's " 'Structure and Serendipity': The Influence of Robert Frost on Paul Muldoon," *Critical Ireland: New Essays in Literature and Culture* (2001), ed. Alan A. Gillis and Aaron Kelly. See also **Irish Poetry**.

Les Murray

Murray's *Collected Poems* were published in 1994. Subsequent volumes of poetry include *Subhuman Redneck Poems* (1996), *Collected Poems* (1998), *New Selected Poems* (1998), *Conscious and Verbal* (1999), *Fredy Neptune: A Novel in Verse* (1999), *Learning Human: Selected Poems* (2000), and *Poems the Size of Photographs* (2002). Prose collections include *The Paperbark Tree* (1992) and *A Working Forest* (1997). He edited *The New Oxford Book of Australian Verse* (1986, 1991) and the *Anthology of Australian Religious Poetry* (1986, 1991). Peter F. Alexander's biography, *Les Murray: A Life in Progress*, appeared in 2000.

Collections of essays on Murray include *Counterbalancing Light: Essays on Les Murray* (1997), ed. Carmel Gaffney; *Poetry of Les Murray: Critical Essays* (2001), ed. Laurie Hergenhan and Bruce Clunies Ross; and *Les Murray and Australian Poetry*, ed. Angela Smith (2002). Other critical studies include Lawrence Bourke's *A Vivid Steady State: Les Murray and Australian Poetry* (1992) and Steven Matthews's *Les Murray* (2001). *Australian Literary Studies* 20.2 (2001) is a special issue dedicated to Mur-

ray and contains Carol Hetherington's bibliographical "Les Murray: A Selective Checklist." See also **Australian Poetry**.

Howard Nemerov

Nemerov's *The Collected Poems* appeared in 1977. Subsequent volumes include *By Al Lebowitz's Pool* (1979), *Sentences* (1980), *Inside the Onion* (1984), *War Stories: Poems about Long Ago and Now* (1987), *Trying Conclusions: New and Selected Poems 1961–1991* (1991), and *A Howard Nemerov Reader* (1991), which includes prose. Essays are collected in *Reflections on Poetry and Poetics* (1972), *Figures of Thought* (1978), and *New and Selected Essays* (1985). In addition, Nemerov published novels, including *The Homecoming Game* (1957); short stories, including *Stories, Fables, and Other Diversions* (1971); and plays. An interview appears in *Massachusetts Review* 22.1.

Critical work on Nemerov's poetry include Peter Meinke's *Howard Nemerov* (1968), Julia Bartholomay's *The Shield of Perseus* (1972), William Mills's *The Stillness in Moving Things* (1975), Ross Labrie's *Howard Nemerov* (1980), and Rodney Edgecombe's *A Reader's Guide to the Poetry of Howard Nemerov* (1999). Bibliographic information can be found in *The Critical Reception of Howard Nemerov: A Selection of Howard Nemerov and a Bibliography* (1971) and Diane E. Wyllie's *Elizabeth Bishop and Howard Nemerov: A Reference Guide* (1983).

Grace Nichols

Nichols's volumes of poetry include *I Is a Long-Memoried Woman* (1983), *The Fat Black Woman's Poems* (1984), *"Lazy Thoughts of a Lazy Woman" and Other Poems* (1989), and *Sunris* (1996). She has also written numerous books for children and edited anthologies, including *Black Poetry* (1988) and *Can I Buy a Slice of Sky?* (1991). Her novel, *Whole of a Morning Sky*, was published in 1986. An interview appears in *Wasafiri* 8 (1988). Prose statements by Nichols include "The Battle with Language," *Caribbean Women Writers: Essays from the First International Conference* (1990), ed. Selwyn Cudjoe, and "Grace Nichols," *Let It Be Told: Black Women Writers in Britain* (1988), ed. Lauretta Ngcobo.

Critical studies of Nichols's work include Peter Fraser's "I Is a Long-Memoried Woman," *Let It Be Told: Black Women Writers in Britain* (1988); Patrick Williams's "Difficult Subjects: Black British Women's Poetry," in *Literary Theory and Poetry: Extending the Canon* (1989), ed. David Murray; Gabriele Griffin's "Writing the Body: Reading Joan Riley, Grace Nichols and Ntozake Shange" and Bruce Woodcock's "Long Memoried Women: Caribbean Women Poets," both in *Black Women's Writing* (1993), ed. Gina Wisker; Elfi Bettinger's "Grace Nichols' 'Sugar

Cane': A Post-Colonial and Feminist Perspective," *Anglistik und Englischunterrischt* 53 (1994); Alison Easton's "The Body as History and 'Writing the Body': The Example of Grace Nichols," *Journal of Gender Studies* 3.1 (1994); Gudrun Webhofer's *Identity in the Poetry of Grace Nichols and Lorna Goodison* (1996); Mara Scanlon's "The Divine Body in Grace Nichols's The Fat Black Women's Poems," *World Literature Today* 72.1 (1998); Aleid Fokkema's "On the (False) Idea of Exile: Derek Walcott and Grace Nichols," *(Un)Writing Empire* (1999), ed. Theo D'haen. See also **Caribbean Poetry.**

Frank O'Hara

The Collected Poems of Frank O'Hara, ed. Donald Allen, appeared in 1971. Allen also edited two subsequent volumes, *Early Writings* (1977) and *Poems Retrieved* (1977). O'Hara's art criticism can be found in *Jackson Pollock* (1959), *Art Chronicles, 1954–1966* (1975), and *What's with Modern Art?* (1999), and other essays in *Standing Still and Walking in New York* (1975). He also wrote numerous plays and collaborated with visual artists such as Joe Brainard and Larry Rivers. Brad Gooch's biography, *City Poet: The Life and Times of Frank O'Hara,* was published in 1993. Memoirs, anecdotes, and essays about O'Hara have been collected in *Homage to Frank O'Hara* (1978), ed. Bill Berkson and Joe Le-Sueur. *In Memory of My Feelings* (1967), ed. Berkson, is a memorial volume of O'Hara's poems accompanied by paintings.

A new edition of Marjorie Perloff's important study, *Frank O'Hara: A Poet among Painters* (1977), was published with a new introduction in 1998. Also helpful are the essays by various critics collected in *Frank O'Hara: To Be True to a City* (1990), ed. Jim Elledge. Other helpful books on O'Hara include Alan Feldman's *Frank O'Hara* (1979), Russell Ferguson's *In Memory of My Feelings: Frank O'Hara and American Art* (1999), and Hazel Smith's *Hyperscapes in the Poetry of Frank O'Hara: Difference, Homosexuality, Topography* (2000). Important chapters and essays include Bruce Boone's "Gay Language as Political Praxis: The Poetry of Frank O'Hara," *Social Text* 1.1 (1982); James E. B. Breslin's chapter in *From Modern to Contemporary* (1984); Andrew Ross's "The Death of Lady Day," *Poetics Journal* 8 (June 1989); John Lowney's "The 'Post-Anti-Esthetic' Poetics of Frank O'Hara," *Contemporary Literature* 32.2 (1991); Geoff Ward's "Frank O'Hara: Accident and Design," *Statutes of Liberty* (1993, 2001); Timothy Gray's "Semiotic Shepherds: Gary Snyder, Frank O'Hara, and the Embodiment of an Urban Pastoral," *Contemporary Literature* 39.4 (1998); Mark Goble's " 'Our Country's Black and White Past': Film and the Figures of History in Frank O'Hara," *American Literature* 71.1 (1999); David L. Sweet's "Parodic Nostalgia for

Aesthetic Machismo: Frank O'Hara and Jackson Pollock," *Journal of Modern Literature* 23.3–4 (2000); Michael Magee's "Tribes of New York: Frank O'Hara, Amiri Baraka, and the Poetics of the Five Spot," *Contemporary Literature* 42.4 (2001); and Terrell Scott Herring's "Frank O'Hara's Open Closet," *PMLA* 117.3 (2002). David Lehman's *The Last Avant-Garde* (1998) combines critical analysis with biographical information on O'Hara and his companions in the New York school. Alexander Smith's comprehensive bibliography appeared in 1979. See also **New York School.**

Christopher Okigbo

Okigbo's *Collected Poems* was published in 1986. Other writings include "Dance of the Painted Maidens," *Verse & Voice: A Festival of Poetry* (1965), ed. Douglas Cleverdon; "In Lament of Masks," *W. B. Yeats, 1865–1965: Centenary Essays on the Art of W. B. Yeats* (1965), ed. D. E. S. Maxwell and Suheil B. Bushrui; and "Lament of the Deer," in Chinua Achebe and John Iroaganachi's *How the Leopard Got His Claws* (1972). Achebe and Dubem Okafor edited *Don't Let Him Die: An Anthology of Memorial Poems for Christopher Okigbo (1932–1967)* (1978). Interviews appear in *Journal of Commonwealth Literature* 9 (1970) and *African Writers Talking* (1972), ed. Dennis Duerden and Cosmo Pieterse.

Collections of essays on his work include *Critical Perspectives on Christopher Okigbo* (1984), ed. Donatus Ibe Nwoga, and *Critical Essays on Christopher Okigbo* (2000), ed. Uzoma Esonwanne. Other critical studies include Gerald Moore's *The Chosen Tongue* (1969), Ali A. Mazrui's *The Trial of Christopher Okigbo* (1971), Sunday O. Anozie's *Christopher Okigbo: Creative Rhetoric* (1972), Nyong J. Udoeyop's *Three Nigerian Poets* (1973), Romanus N. Egudu's *Four Modern West African Poets* (1977) and *Modern African Poetry and the African Predicament* (1978), K. L. Goodwin's *Understanding African Poetry: A Study of Ten Poets* (1982), Robert Fraser's *West African Poetry* (1986), James Wieland's *The Ensphering Mind* (1988), and Dubem Okafor's *The Dance of Death: Nigerian History and Christopher Okigbo's Poetry* (1998). Joseph C. Anafulu's bio-bibliography and Bernth Lindfors's addenda are included in *Critical Perspectives on Christopher Okigbo* (1984), ed. Nwoga. See also **African Poetry.**

Okot p'Bitek

Okot's books of poetry include *Song of Lawino* (1966), *Song of Ocol* (1967), *Song of Malaya* (1971), and *Song of a Prisoner* (1971). He also published important books of and about anthropology and African culture, including *African Religions in Western Scholarship* (1970) and *Africa's Cultural Revolution* (1973), and translations of folk literature, including *The Horn of My Love* (1974), *Hare and Hornbill* (1978), and *Acholi Proverbs* (1985). Interviews appear in *Kunapipi* 1.1 (1979); *World Literature Written in English* 16 (1977); and *Conversations with African Writers* (1981), ed. Lee Nichols. A biographical sketch by Lubwa p'Chong appears in Okot's *Artist, the Ruler* (1986).

Book-length studies include G. A. Heron's *The Poetry of Okot p'Bitek* (1976) and Monica Nalyaka Wanambisi's *Thought and Technique in the Poetry of Okot p'Bitek* (1984). Other critical studies include Michael R. Ward's "Okot p'Bitek and the Rise of East African Writing," *A Celebration of Black and African Writing* (1975), ed. Bruce King and Kolawole Ogungbesan; Gerald Moore's "The Horn of the Grasslands," *Twelve African Writers* (1980); Bernth Lindfors's "The Songs of Okot p'Bitek," *The Writing of East and Central Africa* (1984), ed. G. D. Killam; G. A. Heron's introduction to Okot's "*Song of Lawino*" *and* "*Song of Ocol*" (1984); Ogo A. Ofuani's "Digression as Discourse Strategy in Okot p'Bitek's Dramatic Monologue Texts," *Research in African Literatures* 19.3 (1988); Charles Okumu's "The Form of Okot p'Bitek's Poetry: Literary Borrowing from Acoli Oral Traditions," *Research in African Literatures* 23.3 (1992); Nkem Okoh's "Writing African Oral Literature: A Reading of Okot p'Bitek's *Song of Lawino*," *Bridges* 5.2 (1993); and Jahan Ramazani's *The Hybrid Muse* (2001). See also **African Poetry.**

Sharon Olds

Olds's volumes of poetry include *Satan Says* (1980), *The Dead and the Living* (1984), *The Gold Cell* (1987), *The Matter of This World: New and Selected Poems* (1987), *The Sign of Saturn* (1991), *The Father* (1992), *The Wellspring* (1996), *Blood, Tin, Straw* (1999), and *The Unswept Room* (2002). Interviews include Laurel Blossom's in *Poets & Writers Magazine* 21.5 (1993) and Esta Spalding's in *Brick* 67 (2001).

Critical essays on Olds include Roland Flint's "A Way of Knowing," *Poet Lore* 83.1 (1988); Suzanne Matson's "Talking to Our Father: The Political and Mythical Appropriation of Adrienne Rich and Sharon Olds," *The American Poetry Review* 18.6 (1989); Jonathan Holden's "American Poetry: 1970–1990," *A Profile of Twentieth-Century American Poetry* (1991), ed. Jack Myers and David Wojahn; Terri Brown-Davidson's "The Belabored Scene, The Subtlest Detail: How Craft Affects Heat in the Poetry of Sharon Olds and Sandra McPherson," *Hollins Critic* 29.1 (1992); Brian Dillon's " 'Never Having Had You, I Cannot Let You Go': Sharon Olds's Poems of a Father-Daughter Relationship," *The Literary Review: An International Journal of Contemporary Writing* 37.1 (1993); Calvin Bedient's "Sentencing Eros," *Salma-*

gundi 97 (1993); Alicia Ostriker's "I Am (Not) This: Erotic Discourse in Bishop, Olds, and Stevens," *Wallace Stevens Journal* 19.2 (1995); Laura E. Tanner's "Death-Watch: Terminal Illness and the Gaze in Sharon Olds's *The Father*," *Mosaic* 29.1 (1996); James Sutherland-Smith's "Death and the Unmaidenly: An Exploration of Sharon Olds' *The Wellspring* with Reference to George Bataille," *Pn Review* 24.4 (1998); and Kenneth Lincoln's *Sing with the Heart of a Bear: Fusions of Native and American Poetry 1890–1999* (2000).

Mary Oliver

Oliver's volumes of poetry include "*No Voyage*" *and Other Poems* (1963, 1965), "*The River Styx, Ohio*," *and Other Poems* (1972), *Twelve Moons* (1979), *American Primitive* (1983), *Dream Work* (1986), *House of Light* (1990), *New and Selected Poems* (1992), *White Pine* (1994), *West Wind* (1997), *The Leaf and the Cloud* (2000), and *What Do We Know* (2002). Her essays have been collected in *Blue Pastures* (1995) and *Winter Hours* (1999), which also contains poetry. She has also published two poetry handbooks, *A Poetry Handbook* (1994) and *Rules for the Dance: A Handbook for Writing and Reading Metrical Verse* (1998). An interview appears in *Bloomsbury Review* 10.3 (1990).

Critical essays on Oliver's work include Janet McNew's "Mary Oliver and the Tradition of Romantic Nature Poetry," *Contemporary Literature* 30.1 (1989); Robin Riley Fast's "The Native American Presence in Mary Oliver's Poetry," *Kentucky Review* 12.1–2 (1993) and "Moore, Bishop, and Oliver: Thinking Back, Re-Seeing the Sea," *Twentieth Century Literature* 39.3 (1993); Vicki Graham's " 'Into the Body of Another': Mary Oliver and the Poetics of Becoming Other," *Papers on Language and Literature* 30.4 (1994); and Sue Russell's "Mary Oliver: The Poet and the Persona," *The Harvard Gay & Lesbian Review* 4.4 (1997).

Charles Olson

The Collected Poems of Charles Olson, ed. George F. Butterick, was published in 1987. This collection excludes *The Maximus Poems*, a complete edition of which, also edited by Butterick, appeared in 1983. *The Selected Writings of Charles Olson* (1966), ed. Robert Creeley, offers a good overview of the poet's thought. *The Collected Prose* (1997) was edited by Donald Allen, Benjamin Friedlander, and Creeley. Olson published a study of Melville, *Call Me Ishmael* (1947); and *Mathologos* (1976–79), ed. Butterick, is a collection of lectures and interviews. A *Selected Letters*, ed. Ralph Maud, appeared in 2000, in addition to which the seven volumes of Butterick's *Charles Olson and Robert Creeley: The Complete Correspondence* (1980–86) are illuminating. Biographical information can be found in Tom Clark's *Charles Olson: The Allegory of a Poet's Life* (1991), Maud's *Charles Olson's Reading* (1996), and Olson's autobiographical *The Post Office* (1975).

Among the useful critical discussions of Olson's work are Ed Dorn's *What I See in the Maximus Poems* (1960), Robert von Hallberg's *Charles Olson: The Scholar's Art* (1978), Butterick's *A Guide to the Maximus Poems of Charles Olson* (1978), Sherman Paul's *Olson's Push* (1978), Paul Christensen's *Charles Olson: Call Him Ishmael* (1979), Thomas F. Merrill's *The Poetry of Charles Olson: A Primer* (1982), Andrew Ross's *The Failure of Modernism* (1986), Eniko Bollobás's *Charles Olson* (1992), Stephen Fredman's *The Grounding of American Poetry: Charles Olson and the Emersonian Tradition* (1993), and Libbie Rifkin's *Career Moves: Olson, Creeley, Zukofsky, Berrigan, and the American Avant-Garde* (2000). A bibliography compiled by Butterick and Albert Glover appeared in 1967. See also **Black Mountain School.**

Michael Ondaatje

Ondaatje's volumes of poetry include *The Dainty Monsters* (1967), *The Man with Seven Toes* (1969), *The Collected Works of Billy the Kid: Left Handed Poems* (1970), *Rat Jelly* (1973), *Elimination Dance* (1978), *There's a Trick with a Knife I'm Learning to Do: Poems, 1963–1978* (1979), *Secular Love* (1985), *All along the Mazinaw: Two Poems* (1986), *The Cinnamon Peeler: Selected Poems* (1989), and *Handwriting* (1998). His novels include *Coming through Slaughter* (1976), *In the Skin of a Lion* (1987), *The English Patient* (1992), and *Anil's Ghost* (2000). His memoir, *Running in the Family*, appeared in 1982. He has also edited several anthologies, including the collection of animal verse *The Broken Ark* (1971) and *The Faber Book of Contemporary Canadian Short Stories* (1990). Interviews appear in *Manna* 1 (March 1972); *Rune* 2 (Spring 1975); *Twelve Voices: Interviews with Canadian Poets* (1980), ed. Jon Pearce; *Revista Espanola de Estudios Canadienses* 3.1 (1996); and *Wasafiri* 32 (2000).

A collection of essays on his work is *Spider Blues* (1985), ed. Sam Solecki. *Canadian Review of Comparative Literature* 22.1 (1995) is a special issue dedicated to Ondaatje. Other critical studies include Solecki's "Nets and Chaos," *Studies in Canadian Literature* 2 (Winter 1977), and "Michael Ondaatje," *Descant* 42 (Autumn 1983); Lynette Hunter's "Form and Energy in the Poetry of Michael Ondaatje," *Journal of Canadian Poetry* 1.1 (1978); Stephen Scobie's "His Legend a Jungle Sleep," *Canadian Literature* 76 (Spring 1978); Leslie Mundwiler's *Michael Ondaatje: Word, Image, Imagination* (1984); Arun P. Mukherjee's "The Poetry of Michael Ondaatje and Cyril Dabydeen: Two

Responses to Otherness," *Journal of Commonwealth Literature* 20.1 (1985); Steven Heighton's "Approaching 'That Perfect Edge': Kinetic Techniques in the Poetry and Fiction of Michael Ondaatje," *Studies in Canadian Literature* 13.2 (1988); Lorraine Mary York's *The Other Side of Dailiness: Photography in the Works of Alice Munro, Timothy Findley, Michael Ondaatje, and Margaret Laurence* (1988); Ajay Heble's "Michael Ondaatje and the Problem of History," *Clio* 19.2 (1990); Douglas Barbour's *Michael Ondaatje* (1993); Ed Jewinski's *Michael Ondaatje: Express Yourself Beautifully* (1994); John Cooke's *The Influence of Painting on Five Canadian Writers* (1996); and Geert Lernout's "Multicultural Canada: The Case of Michael Ondaatje," *Union in Partition: Essays in Honour of Jeanne Delbaere* (1997), ed. Gilbert Debusscher, Jeanne Delbaere, and Marc Maufort. Judith Brady's annotated bibliography appears in *The Annotated Bibliography of Canada's Major Authors* (1985), ed. Robert Lecker and Jack David. See also **Canadian Poetry.**

P. K. Page

Page's *The Hidden Room: Collected Poems* was published in 1997. Other works include the story collections *"The Sun and the Moon" and Other Fictions* (1973), *Unless the Eye Catch Fire* (1994), and *A Kind of Fiction* (2001); the libretto for the opera *The Travelling Musicians* (1994), composed by Ruth Watson Henderson; children's literature; and *Brazilian Journal* (1987), a work of travel writing and autobiography. She also edited *To Say the Least: Canadian Poets from A to Z* (1979).

A book-length study is John Orange's *P. K. Page and Her Work* (1989). A collection of essays is *P. K. Page: Essays on her Works* (2001), ed. Linda Rogers and Barbara Colebrook Peace. Other critical discussions include John Sutherland's "The Poetry of P. K. Page," *Northern Review* 1 (1946–47); A. J. M. Smith's "The Poetry of P. K. Page," *Canadian Literature* 50 (1971); Constance Rooke's "P. K. Page: The Chameleon and the Centre," *Malahat Review* 45 (1978); Rosemary Sullivan's "A Size Larger than Seeing," *Canadian Literature* 79 (1978); Diane Schoemperlen's "Four Themes in the Poetry of P. K. Page," *English Quarterly* 12 (1979); Jean Mallinson's "Retrospect and Prospect," *West Coast Review* 13 (1979); Douglas Freake's "The Multiple Self in the Poetry of P. K. Page," *Studies in Canadian Literature* 19.1 (1994); Diana Relke's "Tracing a Terrestrial Vision in the Early Work of P. K. Page," *Canadian Poetry* 35 (1994); Brian Bartlett's "For Sure the Kittiwake: Naming, Nature, and P. K. Page," *Canadian Literature* 155 (1997); and Sara Jamieson's " 'Now That I Am Dead': P. K. Page and the Self-Elegy," *Canadian Literature* 166 (2000). *Malahat Review* 117 (Winter 1996) is a special issue dedicated to Page. John Orange's bibliography appears in *The Annotated Bibliography of Canada's Major Authors* (1985), ed. Robert Lecker and Jack David. See also **Canadian Poetry**.

Michael Palmer

Palmer's volumes of poetry include *Plan of the City of O* (1971), *Blake's Newton* (1972), *C's Songs* (1973), *Six Poems* (1973), *The Circular Gates* (1974), *Without Music* (1977), *Alogon* (1980), *Notes for Echo Lake* (1981), *First Figure* (1984), *For a Reading: A Selection of Poems* (1988), *Sun* (1988), *An Alphabet Underground/Underjordisk Alfabet* (with Danish translations by Poul Borum and illustrations by Jens Birkemose, 1993), *At Passages* (1995), *The Lion Bridge: Selected Poems, 1972–1995* (1998), *The Promises of Glass* (2000), and *Codes Appearing: Poems, 1979–1988* (2001). He also wrote plays; published translations, including *Sky-Eclipse* (2000); and edited a collection of essays on poetics, *Code of Signals* (1983). Interviews appear in *Acts* 2.1 (1986); *Talking Poetry* (1987), ed. Lee Bartlett; *Contemporary Literature* 30.1 (1989); *Sagetrieb* 12.3 (1993); and Thomas Gardner's *Regions of Unlikeness* (1999).

Critical discussions of Palmer's work include Steve McCaffery's "Michael Palmer's LANGUAGE of Language," *North of Intention* (1986); Norman Finkelstein's "The Case of Michael Palmer," *Contemporary Literature* 29.4 (1988); Linda Reinfeld's *Language Poetry: Writing as Rescue* (1992); Eric Murphy Selinger's "Important Pleasures and Others: Michael Palmer, Ronald Johnson," *Postmodern Culture* 4.3 (1994); David Clippinger's "Making the Dust Rise: Michael Palmer's Interrogation into Being," *Salt Hill Journal* 2 (1996); Gardner's *Regions of Unlikeness* (1999); and Calvin Bedient's "Breath and Blister: The Word-Burns of Michael Palmer and Leslie Scalapino," *Parnassus* 24.2 (2000). *Occident* 103.1 (1990) is a special issue with essays on Palmer, including Bruce Campbell's "'A Body Disappears into Itself': Michael Palmer's *Sun*." See also **Language Poetry**.

Marge Piercy

Piercy's volumes of poetry include *Breaking Camp* (1968), *Hard Loving* (1969), *To Be of Use* (1973), *Living in the Open* (1976), *The Twelve-Spoked Wheel Flashing* (1978), *The Moon Is Always Female* (1980), *Circles on the Water: Selected Poems* (1982), *Stone, Paper, Knife* (1983), *My Mother's Body* (1985), *Available Light* (1988), *The Earth Shines Secretly: A Book of Days* (with Nell Blaine, 1990), *Mars and Her Children* (1992), *What Are Big Girls Made Of?* (1997), *Written in Bone: The Early Poems of Marge Piercy* (1998), *The Art of Blessing the Day:* *Poems with a Jewish Theme* (1999), and *Early Grrrl: The Early Poems of Marge Piercy* (1999). She has also published many novels, including *Women on the Edge of Time* (1976). *Parti-Colored Blocks for a Quilt* (1982) is a collection of her criticism and interviews. She also edited *Early Ripening: American Women's Poetry* (1987). *Sleeping with Cats*, a memoir, appeared in 2002. An interview appears in Gary Pacernick's *Meaning and Memory: Interviews with Fourteen Jewish Poets* (2001).

A collection of essays on Piercy's work is *Ways of Knowing* (1991), ed. Sue Walker and Eugenie Hamner. Other critical work on Piercy's poetry includes Victor Contoski's "Marge Piercy: A Vision of the Peaceable Kingdom" and Jean Rosenbaum's "You Are Your Own Magician: A Vision of Integrity in the Poetry of Marge Piercy," both in *Modern Poetry Studies* 8 (1977); Edith Wynne's "Imagery of Association in the Poetry of Marge Piercy," *Publications of the Missouri Philological Association* 10 (1985); Felicia Mitchell's "Marge Piercy's *The Moon Is Always Female*: Feminist Text, Great Books Context," *Virginia English Bulletin* 40.2 (1990); and Naomi Guttman's "'Rooms without Walls': Marge Piercy's Ecofeminist Garden Poetry," *Proteus* 15.2 (1998). Patricia Doherty's *Marge Piercy: An Annotated Bibliography* appeared in 1997.

Robert Pinsky

The Figured Wheel: New and Collected Poems, 1966–1996 appeared in 1996. A subsequent volume, *Jersey Rain*, was published in 2000. Pinsky has also published translations, including Dante's *Inferno* (1994) and, with Robert Hass, Czeslaw Milosz's *The Separate Notebooks* (1984). Pinsky's important books of criticism include *The Situation of Poetry* (1976), *Poetry and the World* (1988), and *The Sounds of Poetry: A Brief Guide* (1998). Interviews appear in *Ploughshares* 6.2 (1980), *TriQuarterly* (1992), *New Letters* 64.4 (1998), *Pembroke Magazine* 31 (1991), and *Bomb* 68 (1999).

Critical work on Pinsky includes Charles Molesworth's "Proving Irony by Compassion: The Poetry of Robert Pinksy," *Hollins Critic* 21.5 (1984); Robert Richman's "At the Intersection of Art and Life," *The New Criterion* 7.10 (1989); Willard Spiegelman's *The Didactic Muse* (1989); Calvin Bedient's "'Man Is Altogether Desire'?" *Salmagundi* 90–91 (1991); Peter Sacks's "'Also This, Also That': Robert Pinsky's Poetics of Inclusion," *Agni* 36 (1992); Timothy Erwin's "The Extraordinary Language of Robert Pinsky," *Halcyon* 16 (1994); Louise Glück's "Story Tellers," *American Poetry Review* 26.4 (1997); James Longenbach's *Modern Poetry after Modernism* (1997); Tony Whedon's "The Transfiguration of Pinsky," *Agni* 49 (1999) and his "Public Pinksy," *Northwest Review* 38.3

(2000); and Jonathan Freedman's "How Now, Middlebrow?" *Raritan* 20.3 (2001).

Sylvia Plath

Plath's *Collected Poems*, ed. Ted Hughes, appeared in 1981, and a *Selected Poems*, also ed. Hughes, in 1985. *Above the Oxbow: Selected Writings* (1985) includes poetry and prose. She also wrote children's literature and a major novel, *The Bell Jar* (1963). Correspondence is available in *Letters Home: Correspondence, 1950–1963* (1975). *The Journals of Sylvia Plath*, ed. Hughes and Frances McCullough, was published in 1982, and *The Unabridged Journals of Sylvia Plath, 1950–1962*, ed. Karen V. Kukil, in 2000. Biographies include Linda Wagner-Martin's *Sylvia Plath: A Biography* (1987), Anne Stevenson's *Bitter Fame* (1989), Paul Alexander's *This Rough Magic* (1991), Janet Malcolm's *The Silent Woman: Sylvia Plath and Ted Hughes* (1994), and Wagner-Martin's *Sylvia Plath: A Literary Life* (1999).

Important critical studies include Caroline King Barnard Hall's *Sylvia Plath* (1978, 1998), Margaret Dickie's *Sylvia Plath and Ted Hughes* (1979), Jon Rosenblatt's *Sylvia Plath: The Poetry of Initiation* (1979), Pamela J. Annas's *A Disturbance in Mirrors* (1988), Steven Gould Axelrod's *Sylvia Plath: The Wound and the Cure of Words* (1990), Jacqueline Rose's *The Haunting of Sylvia Plath* (1992), Susan R. Van Dyne's *Revising Life: Sylvia Plath's Ariel Poems* (1993), Christina Bitzolakis's *Sylvia Plath and the Theatre of Mourning* (1999), Tim Kendall's *Sylvia Plath: A Critical Study* (2000), and Lynda K. Bundtzen's *The Other Ariel* (2001). Collections of essays include *The Art of Sylvia Plath* (1970), ed. Charles Newman; *Critical Essays on Sylvia Plath* (1984), ed. Linda Wagner; *Ariel Ascending* (1985), ed. Paul Alexander; and *The Poetry of Sylvia Plath* (2001), ed. Claire Brennan. Other discussions of her work can be found in Paul Breslin's *The Psycho-Political Muse* (1987); Kathleen Margaret Lant's "The Big Strip Tease: Female Bodies and Male Power in the Poetry of Sylvia Plath," *Contemporary Literature* 34.4 (1993); Jahan Ramazani's *Poetry of Mourning* (1994); and Cynthia Sugar's "Sylvia Plath as Fantasy Space; or, The Return of the Living Dead," *Literature and Psychology* 45.3 (1999). Bibliographies include Gary Lane's (1978) and Sheryl L. Meyering's (1990). See also **Confessional Poetry**.

Craig Raine

Raine's *Collected Poems, 1978–1999* appeared in 2000. Selections of his essays and criticism are available in *Haydn and the Valve Trumpet* (1990) and *In Defense of T. S. Eliot* (2000). He has also written libretti for opera, including the *Electrification of the Soviet Union* (1986), based on a novella by Boris Pasternak, with music by

Nigel Osborne. An interview appears in John Haffenden's *Viewpoints* (1981).

Ploughshares 13.4, ed. Bill Knott, is a special issue containing an interview and several articles on Raine. Other critical discussions of Raine's work include John Osborne's "The Incredulous Eye: Craig Raine and Postmodernist Aesthetics," *Stone Ferry Review* 2 (1978); Michael Hulse's "Alms for Every Beggared Sense: Craig Raine's Aesthetic in Context," *Critical Quarterly* 23.4 (1981); Hulse's "The Dialectic of the Image: Notes on the Poetry of Craig Raine and Christopher Reid," *Malahat Review* 64 (1983); A. D. Moody's "Telling It Like It's Not: Ted Hughes and Craig Raine," *Yearbook of English Studies* 17 (1987); Ian Gregson's " 'But Who Is Speaking?': 'Novelisation' in the Poetry of Craig Raine," *English* 41.170 (1992); and David G. Williams's "Elizabeth Bishop and the 'Martian' Poetry of Craig Raine and Christopher Reid," *English Studies* 78.5 (1997).

A. K. Ramanujan

The Collected Poems of A. K. Ramanujan was published in 1995, and *The Collected Essays* in 1999. A volume of *Uncollected Poems and Prose* was published in 2001. Ramanujan published many important translations from Tamil and Kannada, including *The Interior Landscape: Love Poems from a Classical Tamil Anthology* (1967), *Speaking of Siva* (1973), and *Hymns for the Drowning* (1983).

A. N. Dwivedi has published two book-length studies of Ramanujan: *A. K. Ramanujan and His Poetry* (1983) and *The Poetic Art of A. K. Ramanujan* (1995). Other discussions of Ramanujan's poetry include R. Parthasarathy, "How It Strikes a Contemporary: The Poetry of A. K. Ramanujan," *Literary Criterion* 12.2–3 (1976); Emmanuel Narendra Lall's *The Poetry of Encounter* (1983); M. K. Naik's "A. K. Ramanujan and the Search for Roots," *Living Indian English Poets*, ed. Madhusudan Prasad; Bruce King's *Three Indian Poets: Nissim Ezekiel, A. K. Ramanujan, Dom Moraes* (1991); Vinay Dharwadker's introduction to the *Collected Poems*; Shirish Chindhade's *Five Indian Poets* (1996); Rajeev S. Patke's "The Ambivalence of Poetic Self-Exile: The Case of A. K. Ramanujan," *Jouvert* 5.2 (2001); and Jahan Ramazani's *The Hybrid Muse* (2001). See also **Indian Poetry**.

Adrienne Rich

Rich's *The Fact of a Doorframe: Poems 1950–2000* was published in 2002. *Collected Early Poems* (1993) includes Rich's poetry from 1950 to 1970. Later works include *Diving into the Wreck* (1973), *Poems Selected and New* (1975), *Twenty-One Love Poems* (1976), *The Dream of a Common Language* (1978), *A Wild Patience Has Taken Me This Far* (1981), *Sources* (1983),

The Fact of a Doorframe: Poems Selected and New, 1950–1984 (1984), Your Native Land, Your Life (1986), Time's Power (1989), An Atlas of the Difficult World (1991), Dark Fields of the Republic (1995), Midnight Salvage (1999), and Fox (2001). Adrienne Rich's Poetry and Prose (1993), ed. Barbara Charlesworth Gelpi and Albert Gelpi, contains, in addition to selections of Rich's own work, selected essays and reviews by critics and scholars. Other prose works include Of Woman Born: Motherhood as Experience and Institution (1976), On Lies, Secrets, and Silence: Selected Prose, 1966–1978 (1979), Blood, Bread, and Poetry: Selected Prose, 1979–1985 (1986), and What Is Found There: Notebooks on Poetry and Politics (1993). Interviews and other major essays are collected in Arts of the Possible (2001). Another interview appears in Bill Moyers's The Language of Life (1995). Rich has also published translations and edited The Best American Poetry 1996 (1996).

Book-length studies of her work include Claire Keyes's The Aesthetics of Power (1986), Craig Werner's Adrienne Rich: The Poet and Her Critics (1988), Alice Templeton's The Dream and the Dialogue: Adrienne Rich's Feminist Poetics (1994), and Liz Yorke's Adrienne Rich: Passion, Politics, and the Body (1997). Reading Adrienne Rich (1984), ed. Jane Roberta Cooper, is a collection of essays on her work. Other important discussions include Rachel Blau DuPlessis's "The Critique of Consciousness and Myth in Levertov, Rich, and Rukeyser," Shakespeare's Sisters: Feminist Essays on Women Poets (1979), ed. Sandra M. Gilbert and Susan Gubar; Alicia Ostriker's "Her Cargo: Adrienne Rich and the Common Language" in her Writing Like a Woman (1983); Wendy Martin's An American Triptych: Anne Bradstreet, Emily Dickinson, Adrienne Rich (1984); Susan Stanford Friedman's " 'I Go Where I Love': An Intertextual Study of H. D. and Adrienne Rich," Coming to Light: American Women Poets of the Twentieth Century (1985), ed. Diane Wood Middlebrook and Marilyn Yalom; Mary Hussmann's "On Adrienne Rich," Iowa Review 22.1 (1992); Kim Whitehead's The Feminist Poetry Movement (1996); Barbara L. Estrin's "Re-Versing the Past: Adrienne Rich's Postmodern Inquietude," Tulsa Studies in Women's Literature 16.2 (1997); Margaret Dickie's Stein, Bishop, and Rich: Lyrics of Love, War, and Place (1997); and Maeera Shreiber's " 'Where Are We Moored?' Adrienne Rich, Women's Mourning, and the Limits of Lament," Dwelling in Possibility: Women Poets and Critics on Poetry (1997), ed. Shreiber and Yopie Prins.

Alberto Ríos

Ríos's volumes of poetry include Whispering to Fool the Wind (1982), Five Indiscretions (1985), The Lime Orchard Woman (1988), Teodora

Luna's Two Kisses (1990), and The Smallest Muscle in the Human Body (2002). Ríos's fiction includes The Iguana Killer (1984), "Pig Cookies" and Other Stories (1995), and The Curtain of Trees (1999). His autobiographical Capirotada: A Nogales Memoir was published in 1999. Interviews include Leslie Wootten's in Bloomsbury Review 16.1 (1996) and William Barillas's in Americas Review 24.3–4 (1996).

Critical discussions of Ríos's work can be found in José David Saldívar's "The Real and the Marvelous in Nogales, Arizona," Denver Quarterly 17.2 (1982); Cordelia Candelaria's Chicano Poetry: A Critical Introduction (1986); Saldívar's "Towards a Chicano Poetics: The Making of the Chicano Subject, 1969–1982," Confluencia 1.2 (1985); Renato Rosaldo's "Fables of the Fallen Guy," Criticism in the Borderlands: Studies in Chicano Literature, Culture, and Ideology (1991), ed. Hector Calderon and Saldívar; Deneen Jenks's "The Breathless Patience of Alberto Ríos," Hayden's Ferry Review 11 (1992); and Joseph Deters's "Fireworks on the Borderlands: A Blending of Cultures in the Poetry of Alberto Ríos," Confluencia 15.2 (2000). See also **Latino Poetry.**

Muriel Rukeyser

The Collected Poems of Muriel Rukeyser was published in 1978. A Muriel Rukeyser Reader (1994), ed. Jan Heller Levi with an introduction by Adrienne Rich, offers a good selection of her work. The Life of Poetry, originally published in 1949, provides essential insight into Rukeyser's politics and poetics. She also published translations, including Octavio Paz's Sun Stone (1963) and Gunnar Ekelöf's Three Poems (1967). She wrote biographies of Willard Gibbs (1942), Wendell Willkie (1957), and Thomas Harriet (1971). She also wrote plays, including Houdini (1973), and fiction, More Night (1981). Collections of letters include Bubbles (1967) and Mazes (1970).

How Shall We Tell Each Other of the Poet?: The Life and Writing of Muriel Rukeyser (1999), ed. Anne F. Herzog and Janet E. Kaufman, is a helpful collection of essays. A good book-length study is Louise Kertesz's The Poetic Vision of Muriel Rukeyser (1980). Other critical work on Rukeyser includes Walter Kalaidjian's American Culture between the Wars (1993); Kim Whitehead's The Feminist Poetry Movement (1996); Thomas Travisano's "Muriel Rukeyser and Her Literary Critics," and Kate Daniels's " 'The Buried Life and the Body of Waking': Muriel Rukeyser and the Politics of Literary History," both in Gendered Modernisms (1996), ed. Margaret Dickie and Travisano; Michael Davidson's Ghostlier Demarcations: Modern Poetry and the Material World (1997); David Kadlec's "X-Ray Testimonials in Muriel Rukeyser," Modernism/Modernity 5 (1998); Michael Thurston's "Documentary Modernism as Popular Front Poetics: Muriel Rukeyser's 'Book of the Dead,' " *Modern Language Quarterly* 60.1 (1999); Robert Shulman's *The Power of Political Art: The 1930s Literary Left Reconsidered* (2000); and Adrienne Rich's "Muriel Rukeyser: Her Vision" in her *Arts of the Possible* (2001).

Delmore Schwartz

Schwartz's volumes of poetry include *In Dreams Begin Responsibilities* (1938), *Genesis: Book One* (1943), *"Vaudeville for a Princess" and Other Poems* (1950), *Summer Knowledge: New and Selected Poems, 1938–1958* (1959); and *Last and Lost Poems of Delmore Schwartz* (1979), ed. Robert Phillips. Schwartz also wrote a play, *Shenandoah* (1940), and fiction, including *The World Is a Wedding* (1948) and *"Successful Love" and Other Stories* (1961). His *Selected Essays*, ed. Donald A. Dike and David H. Zucker, was published in 1970, and *Portrait of Delmore: Journals and Notes of Delmore Schwartz, 1939–1959*, ed. Elizabeth Pollet, appeared in 1986. He also translated Arthur Rimbaud's *A Season in Hell* (1939, 1940). Karl Shapiro and Robert Phillips edited the *Letters of Delmore Schwartz* (1984), and Phillips edited *Delmore Schwartz and James Laughlin: Selected Letters* (1993). The standard biography is James Atlas's *Delmore Schwartz: The Life of an American Poet* (1977); also useful is Eileen Simpson's *Poets in Their Youth* (1982).

Important studies include Richard McDougall's *Delmore Schwartz* (1974) and Bruce Bawer's *The Middle Generation: The Lives and Poetry of Delmore Schwartz, Randall Jarrell, John Berryman, and Robert Lowell* (1986). Other discussions of his work include William Barrett's "The Truants: *Partisan Review* in the Forties," *Commentary* 49 (June 1974); Douglas Dunn's introduction to Schwartz's *What Is to Be Given* (1976); Phillips's introduction to *Last and Lost Poems of Delmore Schwartz* (1979); David Zucker's " 'Alien to Myself': Jewishness in the Poetry of Delmore Schwartz," *Studies in American Jewish Literature* 9.2 (1990); and Raymond J. Wilson's "Delmore Schwartz and Purgatory," *Partisan Review* 57.3 (1990).

Anne Sexton

Sexton's *Complete Poems* were published in 1981; a *Selected Poems*, ed. Diane Wood Middlebrook and Diane Hume George, in 1988. *No Evil Star* (1985), ed. Steven E. Colburn, is a collection of essays and interviews, and *Anne Sexton: A Self-Portrait in Letters* (1977), ed. Linda Gray Sexton and Lois Ames, is a selection of letters. Sexton also cowrote children's books with Maxine Kumin. The standard biography is Middlebrook's *Anne Sexton* (1991). Sexton's daughter, Linda Gray Sexton, published a memoir, *Searching for Mercy Street: My Journey Back to*

My Mother, Anne Sexton, in 1994, and Arthur Furst's *Anne Sexton: The Last Summer* (2000) contains photographic portraits of the poet, as well as correspondence.

Collections of essays on Sexton include *Anne Sexton: The Artist and Her Critics* (1978), ed. J. D. McClatchy; *Anne Sexton: Telling the Tale* (1988), ed. Steven E. Colburn; *Sexton: Selected Criticism* (1988), ed. Diana Hume George; *Critical Essays on Anne Sexton* (1989), ed. Linda Wagner-Martin; and *Original Essays on the Poetry of Anne Sexton* (1998), ed. Frances Bixler. Useful book-length studies are George's *Oedipus Anne: The Poetry of Anne Sexton* (1987) and Caroline King Barnard Hall's *Anne Sexton* (1989). Other critical work on Sexton includes Greg Johnson's "The Achievement of Anne Sexton," *Hollins Critic* (1984); Janice Markey's *A New Tradition?: The Poetry of Sylvia Plath, Anne Sexton, and Adrienne Rich* (1985); and Cassie Premo Steele's *We Heal from Memory: Sexton, Lorde, Anzaldúa, and the Poetry of Witness* (2000). Bibliographic information is available in Cameron Northouse and Thomas P. Walsh's *Sylvia Plath and Anne Sexton: A Reference Guide* (1974).

Karl Shapiro

Shapiro's *Collected Poems: 1948–1978* was published in 1978. Subsequent volumes include *Love and War, Art and God* (1984); *Adam and Eve* (1986), ed. John Wheatcroft; *New and Selected Poems, 1940–1986* (1987); *The Old Horsefly* (1992); and *The Wild Card: Selected Poems, Early and Late* (1998), ed. Stanley Kunitz and David Ignatow. He also wrote a novel, *Edsel* (1971). Works of Shapiro's criticism include *In Defense of Ignorance* (1960); *The Writer's Experience* (with Ralph Ellison, 1964); and *The Poetry Wreck: Selected Essays, 1950–1970* (1975). He also published *Poet: An Autobiography in Three Parts* (1988, 1990). Shapiro edited the magazine *Poetry* from 1948 to 1950. Interviews appear in *Talks with Authors* (1968), ed. Charles F. Madden; *TriQuarterly* 43 (1978); *Southern Humanities Review* 15.3 (1981); *Prairie Schooner* 55.3 (1981); and *Paris Review* 28.99 (1986).

A book-length study is Joseph Reino's *Karl Shapiro* (1981). Useful essays appear in the collection *Seriously Meeting Karl Shapiro* (1993), ed. Sue B. Walker. Other discussions of Shapiro's work include Louis D. Rubin's "The Search for Lost Innocence: Karl Shapiro's *The Bourgeois Poet*," *Hollins Critic* 1.5 (1964); Hyatt H. Waggoner's *American Poets from the Puritans to the Present* (1968); Karl Malkoff's "The Self in the Modern World: Karl Shapiro's Jewish Poems," *Contemporary American-Jewish Literature* (1973), ed. Irving Malin; Robert Phillips's "Poetry, Prosody, and Meta-Poetics: Karl Shapiro's Self-Reflexive Poetry," *Poetics in the*

Poem: Critical Essays on American Self-Reflexive Poetry (1997), ed. Dorothy Z. Baker; Diederik Oostdijk's " 'Someplace Called Poetry': Karl Shapiro, *Poetry* Magazine and Post-War American Poetry," *English Studies* 81.4 (2000); and L. D. Rubin's "Karl Shapiro (1913–2000)—He Took His Stands," *Sewanee Review* 109.1 (2001). Two bibliographies are William White's *Karl Shapiro: A Bibliography* (1960) and Lee Bartlett's *Karl Shapiro: A Descriptive Bibliography* (1979).

Leslie Marmon Silko

Silko's poetry appears in her *Laguna Woman* (1974). Her fiction includes *Ceremony* (1977), *Storyteller* (1981), *Almanac of the Dead* (1991), *Sacred Water* (1993), and *Gardens in the Dunes* (1999). A collection of essays on Native American life is *Yellow Woman and a Beauty of the Spirit* (1996). Silko has also published her correspondence with James Wright, *With the Delicacy and Strength of Lace* (1985). A collection of interviews is *Conversations with Leslie Marmon Silko* (2000), ed. Ellen L. Arnold.

A book-length study is Per Seyerstad's *Leslie Marmon Silko* (1980). A collection of essays is *Leslie Marmon Silko: A Collection of Critical Essays* (1999), ed. Louise K. Barnett and James L. Thorson. Other critical work on Silko includes E. Blicksilver's "Traditionalism vs. Modernity: Leslie Silko on American Indian Women," *Southwest Review* 64 (1979); Alan R. Velie's *Four American Indian Literary Masters* (1982); Kenneth M. Roemer's "Bear and Elk: The Nature(s) of Contemporary American Indian Poetry," *Studies in American Indian Literature: Critical Essays and Course Designs* (1983), ed. Paula Gunn Allen; Susan Perez Castillo's "Postmodernism, Native American Literature, and the Real: The Silko-Erdrich Controversy," *Massachusetts Review* 32.2 (1991); Jeanne Perreault's "New Dreaming: Joy Harjo, Wendy Rose, Leslie Marmon Silko," *Deferring a Dream: Literary Sub-Versions of the American Columbiad* (1994), ed. Gert Buelens and Ernst Rudin; Kate Adams's "Northamerican Silences: History, Identity, and Witness in the Poetry of Gloria Anzaldúa, Cherríe Moraga, and Leslie Marmon Silko," *Listening to Silences: New Essays in Feminist Criticism* (1994), ed. Elain Hedges and Shelley Fisher Fishkin; and Joni Adamson Clarke's "Toward an Ecology of Justice: Transformative Ecological Theory and Practice," *Reading the Earth: New Directions in the Study of Literature and Environment* (1998), ed. Michael P. Branch, Rochelle Johnson, Daniel Patterson, and Scott Slovic. See also **Native American Poetry**.

Charles Simic

Simic's volumes of poetry include *What the Grass Says* (1967), *Somewhere among Us a Stone Is Taking Notes* (1969), *Dismantling the Silence* (1971), *White* (1972, 1980), *Return to a Place Lit by a Glass of Milk* (1974), *Biography and a Lament* (1976), *Charon's Cosmology* (1977), *Brooms: Selected Poems* (1978), *School for Dark Thoughts* (1978), *Classic Ballroom Dances* (1980), *Austerities* (1982), *Weather Forecast for Utopia and Vicinity* (1983), *Selected Poems, 1963–1983* (1985), *Unending Blues* (1986), *Nine Poems* (1989), *The World Doesn't End* (1989), *The Book of Gods and Devils* (1990), *Hotel Insomnia* (1992), *A Wedding in Hell* (1994), *Frightening Toys* (1995), *Walking the Black Cat* (1996), *Jackstraws* (1999, 2000), *Selected Early Poems* (2000), and *Night Picnic* (2001). *Wonderful Words, Silent Truth* (1990), *The Unemployed Fortune-Teller* (1994), *Orphan Factory* (1997), and *A Fly in the Soup* (2000) are collections of essays and memoirs. A book of prose poetry/art criticism is *Dime-Store Alchemy: The Art of Joseph Cornell* (1992). *The Uncertain Certainty* (1985) contains interviews as well as essays and criticism.

An extensive collection of essays is *Charles Simic: Essays on the Poetry* (1996), ed. Bruce Weigl. Other critical studies include Victor Contoski's "Charles Simic: Language at the Stone's Heart," *Chicago Review* 28.6 (1977); Richard Jackson's "Charles Simic and Mark Strand: The Presence of Absence," *Contemporary Literature* 21 (1980); Peter Schmidt's "White: Charles Simic's Thumbnail Epic," *Contemporary Literature* 23.4 (1982); Bruce Bond's "Immanent Distance: Silence and the Poetry of Charles Simic," *Mid-American Review* 8.1 (1988); Kevin Hart's "Writing Things: Literary Property in Heidegger and Simic," *New Literary History* 21.1 (1989); Marci Janas's "The Secret World of Charles Simic," *Field* 44 (1991); Seamus Heaney's "Shorts for Simic," *Agni* 44 (1996); Daniel Morris's " 'My Shoes': Charles Simic's Self-Portraits," *A/B: Auto/Biography Studies* 11.1 (1996) and "Responsible Viewing: Charles Simic's *Dime-Store Alchemy: The Art of Joseph Cornell*," *Papers on Language & Literature* 34.4 (1998); and Peter Stitt's *Uncertainty and Plenitude* (1997). Brian C. Avery's bibliography appears in *Charles Simic: Essays on the Poetry* (1996), ed. Weigl.

Louis Simpson

Simpson's *Collected Poems* appeared in 1988. Subsequent volumes include *In the Room We Share* (1990) and *There You Are* (1995). *Selected Prose* (1989) and *Ships Going into the Blue* (1994) are collection of Simpson's essays and criticism. He also published numerous books of criticism, including *James Hogg* (1962), *Three on the Tower: The Lives and Works of Ezra Pound, T. S. Eliot, and William Carlos Williams* (1975), *A Revolution of Taste: Studies of Dylan Thomas, Allen Ginsberg, Sylvia Plath,* and Robert Lowell (1978), and *The Character of the Poet* (1986). Simpson has also written fiction, *Riverside Drive* (1962); translations, including *Modern Poets of France: A Bilingual Anthology* (1998); and plays. He coedited *New Poets of England and America* (1957) with Donald Hall and Robert Pack.

Ronald Moran's *Louis Simpson* (1972) is a book-length study. A collection of critical essays is *On Louis Simpson: Depths beyond Happiness* (1988), ed. Hank Lazer. Other critical discussions include George Lensing and Moran's *Four Poets and the Emotive Imagination* (1976); Lazer's "Louis Simpson and Walt Whitman: Destroying the Teacher," *Walt Whitman Review* 1.3 (1983); Bruce Bawer's "Louis Simpson and American Dreams," *Arizona Quarterly* 40.2 (1984); Peter Stitt's *The World's Hieroglyphic Beauty* (1985); Henry Taylor's "Great Experiments: The Poetry of Louis Simpson," *Hollins Critic* 27.3 (1990); and James M. Cox's "Reviewing Louis Simpson," *Southern Review* 31.1 (1995). Bibliographic information can be found in William H. Roberson's *Louis Simpson: A Reference Guide* (1980).

Dave Smith

Smith's volumes of poetry include *Bull Island* (1970), *Mean Rufus Throw Down* (1973), *Drunks* (1974), *The Fisherman's Whore* (1974), *Cumberland Station* (1977), *In Dark, Sudden with Light* (1977), *Goshawk, Antelope* (1979), *Apparitions* (1981), *Blue Spruce* (1981), *Dream Flights* (1981), *Homage to Edgar Allan Poe* (1981), *Gray Soldiers* (1983), *In the House of the Judge* (1983), *Southern Delights: Poems and Stories* (1984), *The Roundhouse Voices: Selected and New Poems* (1985), *Three Poems* (1988), *Cuba Night* (1990), *Night Pleasures: New and Selected Poems* (1992), *Fate's Kite: Poems, 1991–1995* (1995), *Floating on Solitude: Three Volumes of Poetry* (1996), and *The Wick of Memory: New and Selected Poems, 1974–2000* (2000). His novel *Onliness* was published in 1981, and a book of criticism on contemporary American poetry, *Local Assays*, in 1985. He is coeditor of *The Southern Review*; he has also edited *The Pure Clear Word: Essays on the Poetry of James Wright* (1982), *The Morrow Anthology of Younger American Poets* (with David Bottoms, 1985), and *The Essential Poe* (1990). An interview appears in *Contemporary Literature* 37.3 (1996).

A collection of critical essays is *The Giver of Morning: On the Poetry of Dave Smith* (1982), ed. Bruce Weigl. Other discussions can be found in Helen Vendler's *Part of Nature, Part of Us* (1980); Peter Stitt's "The Sincere, the Mythic, the Playful: Forms of Voice in Current Poetry," *Georgia Review* 34 (Spring 1980); Thom Swiss's "Unfold the Fullness: Dave Smith's Poetry and Fiction," *Sewanee Review*

(Summer 1983); and Vendler's " 'Catching a Pig on the Farm,' " *New York Review of Books* (March 8, 2001).

W. D. Snodgrass

Snodgrass's volumes of poetry include *Heart's Needle* (1959), *After Experience* (1968), *Remains* (as S. S. Gardons, 1970, 1985), *The Führer Bunker: A Cycle of Poems in Progress* (1977, 1995), *If Birds Build with Your Hair* (1979), *The Boy Made of Meat* (1983), *A Colored Poem* (1986), *The House the Poet Built* (1986), *A Locked House* (1986), *Selected Poems, 1957–1987* (1987), *W. D.'s Midnight Carnival* (with DeLoss McGraw, 1988), *To Shape a Song* (1989), *Snow Songs* (1992), *Each in His Season* (1993), and *Spring Suite* (1994). In 2001, he published *De/Compositions: 101 Good Poems Gone Wrong*, in which poems are rewritten to demonstrate how the originals work. *In Radical Pursuit* (1975) is a collection of essays and lectures. *Selected Translations* was published in 1998. Interviews appear in *Papers on Language and Literature* 13.4 (1977), *High Plains Literary Review* 8.2 (1993), and *New England Review* 21.1 (2000).

Critical studies of Snodgrass include Paul Gaston's *W. D. Snodgrass* (1978); Gertrude M. White's *To Tell the Truth: The Poems of W. D. Snodgrass* (1979); Lewis Turco's "The Poetics of W. D. Snodgrass," *Hollins Critic* 30.3 (1993); Stephen Haven's *The Poetry of W. D. Snodgrass: Everything Human* (1993); James Fenton's "W. D. Snodgrass: An Introduction," *Agenda* 34.1 (1996); and Philip Raisor's *Tuned and Under Tension: The Recent Poetry of W. D. Snodgrass* (1998). William White's bibliography appeared in 1960. See also **Confessional Poetry.**

Gary Snyder

Snyder's volumes of poetry include *Riprap* (1959), *Myths and Texts* (1960), *Riprap; and Cold Mountain Poems* (1965), *Six Sections from Mountains and Rivers without End* (1965), *A Range of Poems,* (1966), *Three Worlds, Three Realms, Six Roads* (1966), *The Back Country* (1967), *Regarding Wave* (1969, 1970), *Anasazi* (1971), *Manzanita* (1972), *Turtle Island* (1974), *Axe Handles* (1983), *Left Out in the Rain: New Poems, 1947–1985* (1986), *No Nature: New and Selected Poems* (1992), *North Pacific Lands and Waters: A Further Six Sections* (1993), and *Mountains and Rivers without End* (1996). *The Gary Snyder Reader* (1999) contains prose and translations as well as poetry. Other collections of essays include *The Practice of the Wild* (1990) and *A Place in Space: Ethics, Aesthetics, and Watersheds* (1995). *The Real Work: Interviews and Talks, 1964–1979* (1980) was edited by William Scott McLean. Snyder also coedited *The Wooden Fish: Basic Sutras and Gathas of*

Rinzai Zen (with Gutetsu Kanetsuki, 1961). Other interviews appear in *Western American Literature* 30.1 (1995); Bill Moyers's *The Language of Life* (1995); *Western American Literature* 33.3 (1998); and *The San Francisco Beat* (2001), ed. David Meltzer. Biographical information can be found in David Kherdian's *A Biographical Sketch and a Descriptive Checklist of Gary Snyder* (1965) and *Gary Snyder: Dimensions of a Life* (1991), ed. Jon Halper.

Book-length studies include Bob Steuding's *Gary Snyder* (1976), Charles Molesworth's *Gary Snyder's Vision* (1983), Tim Dean's *Gary Snyder and the American Unconscious: Inhabiting the Ground* (1991), Patrick D. Murphy's *Understanding Gary Snyder* (1992), Robert J. Schuler's *Journeys toward the Original Mind: The Long Poems of Gary Snyder* (1994), and Murphy's *A Place for Wayfaring* (2000). Murphy also edited the collection *Critical Essays on Gary Snyder* (1990) and *Studies in the Humanities* 26.1–2 (1999), a special issue on Snyder. Other critical discussions can be found in Charles Altieri's *Self and Sensibility in Contemporary American Poetry* (1984); Sherman Paul's *In Search of the Primitive* (1986); *Beneath a Single Moon: Buddhism in Contemporary American Poetry* (1991), ed. Kent Johnson and Craig Paulenich; David Robertson's "The Circumambulation of Mt. Tamalpais," *Western American Literature* 30.1 (1995); Anthony Hunt's " 'The Hump-Backed Flute Player': The Structure of Emptiness in Gary Snyder's *Mountains and Rivers without End*," *Isle: Interdisciplinary Studies in Literature and Environment* 1.2 (1993) and "Singing the Dyads: The Chinese Landscape Scroll and Gary Snyder's *Mountains and Rivers without End*," *Journal of Modern Literature* 23.1 (1999); and Leonard Scigaj's *Sustainable Poetry* (1999). Bibliographic information can be found in Katherine McNeil's *Gary Snyder: A Bibliography* (1983) and Tom Lavazzi's "Gary Snyder: An International Checklist of Criticism," *Sagetrieb* 12 (1993). See also **Beat Poetry, San Francisco Renaissance.**

Cathy Song

Song's volumes of poetry are *Picture Bride* (1983), *Frameless Windows, Squares of Light* (1988), *School Figures* (1994), and *The Land of Bliss* (2001). She also coedited *Sister Stew: Fiction and Poetry by Women* (with Juliet Kono, 1991). An interview appears in *Honolulu Weekly* 4 (15 June 1994).

Critical discussions of Song's work can be found in *Talk Story: An Anthology of Hawaii's Local Writers* (1978), ed. Eric Chock; Debbie Murakami Nomaguchi's "Cathy Song: 'I'm a Poet Who Happens to Be Asian American,' " *International Examiner* 2.11 (2 May 1984); Gayle K. Fujita-Sato's " 'Third World' as Place and Paradigm in Cathy Song's *Picture Bride*,"

MELUS 15.1 (1988); Stephen Sumida's *And the View from the Shore: Literary Traditions of Hawaii* (1991); Patricia Wallace's "Divided Loyalties: Literal and Literary in the Poetry of Lorna Dee Cervantes, Cathy Song and Rita Dove," *MELUS* 18.3 (1993); Kyhan Lee's "Korean-American Literature: The Next Generation," *Korea Journal* 34.1 (1994); Masami Usui's "Women Disclosed: Cathy Song's Poetry and Kitagawa Ukiyoe," *Studies in Culture and the Humanities* (1995); Jessica Greenbaum's "Cathy Song," *Asian American Literature: Reviews and Criticism of Works by American Writers of Asian Descent* (1995), ed. Lawrence J. Trudeau; and Zhou Xiaojing's "Breaking from Tradition: Experimental Poems by Four Contemporary Asian American Women Poets," *Revista Canaria de Estudios Ingleses* 37 (1998). See also **Asian American Poetry.**

Gary Soto

Soto's volumes of poetry include *The Elements of San Joaquin* (1977), *The Tale of Sunlight* (1978), *Where Sparrows Work Hard* (1981), *Black Hair* (1985), *A Fire in My Hands* (1990), *Who Will Know Us?* (1990), *Home Course in Religion* (1991), *Neighborhood Odes* (1992), *Canto Familiar/Familiar Song* (1995), *New and Selected Poems* (1995), *The Sparrows Move South: Early Poems* (1995), *Super-Eight Movies* (illustrated John Digby, 1996), *Junior College* (1997), *A Natural Man* (1999), and *Poetry Lover* (2001). He has published many books for children and edited *California Childhood: Recollections and Stories of the Golden State* (1988). Memoirs include *Living up the Street: Narrative Recollections* (1985), *A Summer Life* (1990), and *The Effects of Knut Hamsun on a Fresno Boy* (2000). "The Childhood Worries; or, Why I Became a Writer" appears in *Iowa Review* 25.2 (1995). Soto also edited *Four Chicano Poets* (1976) and *Pieces of the Heart: New Chicano Fiction* (1993). Interviews appear in Wolfgang Binder's *Partial Autobiographies: Interviews with Twenty Chicano Poets* (1985) and *Hayden's Ferry Review* 18 (1996).

Critical work on Soto includes Bruce-Novoa's *Chicano Poetry: A Response to Chaos* (1982); Alberto Ríos's "Chicano/Borderlands Literature and Poetry," *Contemporary Latin American Culture: Unity and Diversity* (1984), ed. C. Gail Guntermann; Patricia De La Fuente's "Entropy in the Poetry of Gary Soto: The Dialectics of Violence," *Discurso Literario: Revista de Temas Hispanicos* 5.1 (1987) and "Mutability and Stasis: Images of Time in Gary Soto's *Black Hair*," *Americas Review: A Review of Hispanic Literature and Art of the USA* 17.1 (1989); Julian Olivares's "The Streets of Gary Soto," *Latin American Literary Review* 18 (1990); Rudolf Erben's "Popular Culture, Mass Media, and Chicano Identity in Gary Soto's *Living up the*

Street and *Small Faces*," *MELUS* 17.3 (1991–92); Don Lee's "About Gary Soto," *Ploughshares* 21.1 (1995); and Michael Tomasek Manson's "Poetry and Masculinity on the Anglo/Chicano Border: Gary Soto, Robert Frost, and Robert Hass," *The Calvinist Roots of the Modern Era* (1997), ed. Aliki Barnstone, Manson, and Carol J. Singley. See also **Latino Poetry**.

Wole Soyinka

Soyinka's volumes of poetry include *"Idanre" and Other Poems* (1969), *Poems from Prison* (1969, expanded as *A Shuttle in the Crypt*, 1972), *Ogun Abibiman* (1976), *"Mandela's Earth" and Other Poems* (1988), and *Early Poems* (1998). Among Soyinka's many major plays are *Camwood on the Leaves* (1960), *The Trials of Brother Jero* (1960), *Kongi's Harvest* (1964), *Madmen and Specialists* (1970), *Jero's Metamorphosis* (1973), *Poems of Black Africa* (1975), *Death and the King's Horseman* (1976), *Opera Wonyosi* (adaptation of Brecht's *The Threepenny Opera*, 1977), *A Play of Giants* (1984), *From Zia, with Love* (1992), and *The Beatification of Area Boy* (1995). Soyinka has also published two novels, *The Interpreters* (1965) and *Season of Anomy* (1973), and written scripts for radio, television, and film. Works dealing with the politics of Nigeria include his prison diary, *The Man Died: Prison Notes* (1972), and his lectures in *The Open Sore of a Continent: A Personal Narrative of the Nigerian Crisis* (1996). Other prose works include *Myth, Literature, and the African World* (1976), the autobiographical *Aké: The Years of Childhood* (1981); *The Critic and Society* (1981); *Art, Dialogue and Outrage* (1988); the Nobel lecture, *This Past Must Address Its Present* (1988); *Ibadan—The Penkelemes Years* (1994); and *The Burden of Memory, The Muse of Forgiveness* (1999). In addition, he edited the anthology *Poems of Black Africa* (1975). Biodun Jeyifo edited a book of interviews, *Conversations with Wole Soyinka*, in 2001.

Book-length studies of Soyinka include Gerald Moore's *Wole Soyinka* (1971, 1978), Eldred D. Jones's *The Writing of Wole Soyinka* (1973, 1983), James Gibbs's *Wole Soyinka* (1986), Obi Maduakor's *Wole Soyinka: An Introduction to His Writing* (1986), Aderemi Bamikunle's *Introduction to Soyinka's Poetry: Analysis of A Shuttle in the Crypt* (1991), Akomaye Oko's *The Tragic Paradox* (1992), Derek Wright's *Wole Soyinka Revisited* (1993), Tanure Ojaide's *The Poetry of Wole Soyinka* (1994), and Tunde Adeniran's *The Politics of Wole Soyinka* (1994). Collections of essays dedicated to Soyinka include *Before Our Very Eyes: Tribute to Wole Soyinka* (1987), ed. Dapo Adelugba; *Critical Perspectives on Wole Soyinka* (1980), ed. Gibbs; *Research on Wole Soyinka* (1993), ed. Bernth Lindfors and Gibbs; *Soyinka: A Collection of Critical Essays* (1994), ed. Oyin Ogunba; and Jeyifo's *Perspec-*

tives on Wole Soyinka: Freedom and Complexity (2001). Other discussions of his work include Nyong J. Udoeyop's *Three Nigerian Poets: A Critical Study of the Poetry of Soyinka, Clark, and Okigbo* (1973), Ken Goodwin's *Understanding African Poetry* (1982), and Kole Omotoso's *Achebe or Soyinka?: A Study in Contrasts* (1996). B. M. Okpu's bibliography was published in 1984, and Gibbs's in 1986. See also **African Poetry**.

William Stafford

Stafford's volumes of poetry include *West of Your City* (1960); *Traveling through the Dark* (1962); *The Rescued Year* (1966); *Eleven Untitled Poems* (1968); *Weather* (1969); *Allegiances* (1970); *Temporary Facts* (1970); *In the Clock of Reason* (1973); *Someday, Maybe* (1973); *That Other Alone* (1973); *Going Places* (1974); *Braided Apart* (with Kim Robert Stafford, 1976); *The Design on the Oriole* (1977); *Stories That Could Be True: New and Collected Poems* (1977); *Tuft by Puff* (1978); *Sometimes Like A Legend: Puget Sound Poetry* (1981); *A Glass Face in the Rain* (1982); *Segues: A Correspondence in Poetry* (with Marvin Bell, 1983); *Roving across Fields: A Conversation and Uncollected Poems, 1942–1982* (1983), ed. Thom Tammaro; *Smoke's Way: Poems from Limited Editions, 1968–1981* (1983); *Listening Deep* (1984); *Stories and Storms and Strangers* (1984); *Brother Wind* (1986); *An Oregon Message* (1987); *Annie-Over* (with Bell, 1988); *Fin, Feather, Fur* (1989), *A Scripture of Leaves* (1989); *How to Hold Your Arms When It Rains* (1990); *History Is Loose Again* (1991); *Passwords* (1991); *The Animal That Drank Up Sound* (for children, 1992); *Holding onto the Grass* (1992); *My Name Is William Tell* (1992); *Seeking the Way* (1992); *The Darkness Around Us Is Deep: Selected Poems* (1993), ed. Robert Bly; *Who Are You Really, Wanderer?* (1993); *Learning to Live in the World: Earth Poems* (1994), ed. Jerry Watson and Linda Obbink; *The Methow River Poems* (1995); *Even in Quiet Places* (1996); and *The Way It Is: New and Selected Poems* (1998). *Down in My Heart* (1947, 1985) is a memoir, and essays and interviews are collected in *You Must Revise Your Life* (1986). *Writing the Australian Crawl* (1978) and *Crossing Unmarked Snow* (1998) are collections of "views on the writer's vocation." Other interviews appear in *Prairie Schooner* 44 (Summer 1970), *Northwest Review* 13 (1973), *Sunstone* 1 (Fall 1976), *American Poetry Review* 10.6 (1981), *Cimarron Review* 72 (July 1985), *Michigan Quarterly Review* 30.2 (1991), and *American Poetry Review* 22.3 (1993).

Book-length studies of his work include Jonathan Holden's *The Mark to Turn: A Reading of William Stafford's Poetry* (1976), David A. Carpenter's *William Stafford* (1986), Judith Kitchen's *Understanding William Stafford*

(1989), and Kitchen's *Writing the World: Understanding William Stafford* (1999). A collection of essays is *On William Stafford: The Worth of Local Things* (1993), ed. Tom Andrews. Other studies include George S. Lensing and Ronald Moran's *Four Poets and the Emotive Imagination* (1976), Peter Stitt's *The World's Hieroglyphic Beauty* (1985), and Sanford Pinsker's *Three Pacific Northwest Poets* (1987). Two bibliographies are James W. Pirie's *William Stafford: A Primary Bibliography, 1942–1982* (1983) and Lars Nordstrom's in *Studia Neophilologica* 59 (1987).

Mark Strand

Strand's volumes of poetry include *Sleeping with One Eye Open* (1964), *Reasons for Moving* (1968), *Darker* (1970), *Elegy for My Father* (1973), *The Sergeantville Notebook* (1973), *The Story of Our Lives* (1973), *The Late Hour* (1978), *Selected Poems* (1980), *The Continuous Life* (1990), *Explain That You Live* (with Karl Elder, 1992), *Dark Harbor* (1993), *A Poet's Alphabet of Influences* (1993), *A Suite of Appearances* (1993), *Blizzard of One* (1998), and *Chicken, Shadow, Moon, and More* (2000). Prose and criticism is available in *Hopper* (1994) and *Weather of Words: Poetic Invention* (2000). He has also published short stories, *"Mr. and Mrs. Baby," and Other Stories* (1985), and many translations, including Rafael Alberti's *The Owl's Insomnia* (1973) and Jorge Luis Borges's *Texas* (1975). He has also coedited *The Making of a Poem: A Norton Anthology of Poetic Forms* (2000). An interview appears in *Chicago Review* 28.4 (1977).

A book-length study of Strand's work is David Kirby's *Mark Strand and the Poet's Place in Contemporary Culture* (1990). Other critical discussions can be found in Richard Howard's *Alone with America* (1969, 1980); Harold Bloom's *Figures of Capable Imagination* (1976); Richard Jackson's "Charles Simic and Mark Strand: The Presence of Absence," *Contemporary Literature* 21.1 (1980); Linda Gregerson's "Negative Capability," *Parnassus* 9.2 (1981); Peter Stitt's "Stages of Reality: The Mind/Body Problem in Contemporary Poetry," *Georgia Review* 37.1 (1983); Harold Bloom's "Mark Strand," *Gettysburg Review* 4.2 (1991); Charles Berger's "Poetry Chronicle," *Raritan* 10.3 (1991); Jeffrey Donaldson's "The Still Life of Mark Strand's Darkening Harbor," *Dalhousie Review* 74 (1994); Sarah Manguso's "Where Is that Boy?" *Iowa Review* 29.2 (1999); and Christopher R. Miller's "Mark Strand's Inventions of Farewell," *Wallace Stevens Journal* 24.2 (2000).

May Swenson

Swenson's volumes of poetry include *Another Animal* (1954), *A Cage of Spines* (1958), *To Mix with Time: New and Selected Poems* (1963), *Half Sun, Half Sleep: New Poems* (1967), *Icono-*

graphs (1970), *New and Selected Things Taking Place* (1978), *In Other Words* (1987), *The Love Poems of May Swenson* (1991), *Nature: Poems Old and New* (1994), and *May Out West* (1996). Works of Swenson's criticism include *The Contemporary Poet as Artist and Critic* (1964) and *Made with Words* (1998). *Dear Elizabeth: Five Poems and Three Letters to Elizabeth Bishop* appeared in 2000. Swenson also participated in the translation of *Windows and Stones: Selected Poems of Tomas Tranströmer* (1972). Interviews appear in *New York Quarterly* 19 (1977); *Parnassus* 7 (1978); and *Truthtellers of the Times: Interviews with Contemporary Women Poets* (1998), ed. Janet Palmer Mullaney. A biography for young adults is R. R. Knudson's *The Wonderful Pen of May Swenson* (1993). Knudson and Suzanne Bigelow also published *May Swenson: A Poet's Life in Photos* (1996).

Critical works on Swenson include Alicia Ostriker's "May Swenson and the Shapes of Speculation," *Writing Like a Woman* (1983); Grace Schulman's "Life's Miracles: The Poetry of May Swenson," *American Poetry Review* 23.5 (1994); Sue Russell's "A Mysterious and Lavish Power: How Things Continue to Take Place in the Work of May Swenson," *Kenyon Review* 16.3 (1994); Kirstin Hotelling Zona's "A 'Dangerous Game of Change': Images of Desire in the Love Poems of May Swenson," *Twentieth Century Literature* 44.2 (1998); Mark Doty's "Queer Sweet Thrills: Reading May Swenson," *Yale Review* 88.1 (2000); and Richard Howard's "Banausics," *Parnassus* 25.1–2 (2001). Kenneth E. Gadomski's "May Swenson: A Bibliography of Primary and Secondary Sources," appeared in *Bulletin of Bibliography* 44.4 (1987).

James Tate

Tate's volumes of poetry include *Cages* (1966), *The Destination* (1967), *The Lost Pilot* (1967), *Notes of Woe* (1968), *The Torches* (1968, 1971), *Row with Your Hair* (1969), *Shepherds of the Mist* (1969), *Are You Ready, Mary Baker Eddy???* (with Bill Knott, 1970), *The Oblivion Ha-Ha* (1970, 1984), *Hints to Pilgrims* (1971, 1981), *Absences* (1972), *Viper Jazz* (1976), *Riven Doggeries* (1979), *Constant Defender* (1983), *Reckoner* (1986), *Distance from Loved Ones* (1990), *Selected Poems* (1991), *Worshipful Company of Fletchers* (1994), *Shroud of the Gnome* (1997), and *Memoir of the Hawk* (2001). He has also published a novel, *Lucky Darryl* (with Bill Knott, 1977), and collections of short stories, *Hottentot Ossuary* (1974) and *Dreams of a Robot Dancing Bee* (2002), and edited *The Best American Poetry 1997* (1997). *The Route as Briefed* (1999) contains interviews and essays. With Alberta Turner, Tate contributed "A Box for Tom" to the volume *Fifty Contemporary Poets: The Creative Process* (1977).

Denver Quarterly 33.3 (1998) is a special issue with numerous essays on Tate. Other critical work includes R. D. Rosen's "James Tate and Sidney Goldfarb and the Inexhaustible Nature of the Murmur," *American Poetry since 1960: Some Critical Perspectives* (1973), ed. Robert B. Shaw; William Logan's "Language against Fear," *Poetry* 80.4 (1977); Mark Rudman's "Private but No Less Ghostly Worlds," *American Poetry Review* 10.4 (1981); Donald Revell's "The Desperate Buck and Wing: James Tate and the Failure of Ritual," *Western Humanities Review* 38.4 (1984); *American Poetry Observed* (1984), ed. Joe David Bellamy et al.; Lee Upton's "The Masters Can Only Make Us Laugh," *South Atlantic Review* 55.4 (1990) and *The Muse of Abandonment* (1998); David Young's "Some Huge Pageant," *Field: Contemporary Poetry and Poetics* 46 (Spring 1992); and Anthony Caleshu's "What Kind of Disorganization Is This?" *Pn Review* 25 (1999).

Dylan Thomas

The Collected Poems, ed. Walford Davies and Ralf Ward, was published in 1988. *Quite Early One Morning* (1954) is a collection of short stories, essays, and other writings. Other important works include the autobiographical *Portrait of the Artist as a Young Dog* (1940); *Adventures in the Skin Trade* (1955); and the radio play *Under Milk Wood* (1954). *The Notebooks of Dylan Thomas,* ed. Ralph N. Maud, appeared in 1967, and *The Collected Letters of Dylan Thomas,* ed. Paul Ferris, in 1985. Biographies include Constantine Fitzgibbon's *The Life of Dylan Thomas* (1965), Ferris's *Dylan Thomas: A Biography* (1977, 2000), and Andrew Sinclair's *Dylan the Bard* (2000).

Helpful collections of essays on Thomas's work include *Critical Essays on Dylan Thomas* (1989), ed. Georg Gaston, and *Dylan Thomas* (2001), ed. John Goodby and Chris Wigginton. Book-length studies include David Holbrook's *Llareggub Revisited: Dylan Thomas and the State of Modern Poetry* (1962), H. H. Kleinman's *The Religious Sonnets of Dylan Thomas* (1963), Walford Davies's *Dylan Thomas* (1985), Alan Bold's *Dylan Thomas: Craft or Sullen Art* (1990), Jacob Korg's *Dylan Thomas* (1992), John Ackerman's *Dylan Thomas: His Life and Work* (1996), William York Tindall's *A Reader's Guide to Dylan Thomas* (1996), Barbara Hardy's *Dylan Thomas: An Original Language* (2000), and Eynel Wardi's *Once Below a Time: Dylan Thomas, Julia Kristeva, and Other Speaking Subjects* (2000). Bibliographic information can be found in John Ackerman's *A Dylan Thomas Companion* (1991) and James A. Davies's *A Reference Companion to Dylan Thomas* (1998).

Charles Tomlinson

Tomlinson's *Collected Poems* appeared in 1985 and was enlarged in 1987. Subsequent volumes include *The Return* (1987), *Annunciations* (1989), *Selected Poems* (1989), *The Door in the Wall* (1992), *Jubilation* (1995), *Selected Poems: 1955–1997* (1997), and *Vineyard above the Sea* (1999). A selection of prose work is available in *American Essays: Making It New* (2001). He has also published works of graphic art, including *In Black and White* (1981), and edited many collections, including *Selected Poems of William Carlos Williams* (1976) and *Poems of George Oppen, 1908–1984* (1990). *The Letters of William Carlos Williams and Charles Tomlinson* published in 1992. Interviews include Jed Rasula and Mike Erwin's in *Contemporary Literature* 16 (1975), Bruce Meyer's in *Hudson Review* 43.3 (1990), and Jordi Doce's in *Agenda* 33.2 (1995).

Book-length studies of Tomlinson include Brian John's *The World as Event* (1989); Richard Swigg's *Charles Tomlinson and the Objective Tradition* (1994); and *William Carlos Williams and Charles Tomlinson: A Transatlantic Connection* (1999), ed. Barry Magid and Hugh Witemeyer. A collection of essays is *Charles Tomlinson: Man and Artist* (1988), ed. Kathleen O'Gorman, and *Agenda* 33.2 (1995) is a special issue dedicated to Tomlinson. Other discussions can be found in Denis Donoghue's *The Ordinary Universe* (1968); Calvin Bedient's *Eight Contemporary Poets* (1974); *British Poetry since 1960: A Critical Survey* (1972), ed. Michael Schmidt and Grevel Lindop; Paul Mariani's "Tomlinson's Use of the Williams Triad," *Contemporary Literature* 18 (1977); J. Keith Hardie's "Charles Tomlinson and the Language of Silence," *Boundary* 2 15.1–2 (1986–87); Hearne Pardee's "A Distant Vision: Charles Tomlinson and American Art," *Partisan Review* 58.3 (1991); Judith P. Saunders's "Charles Tomlinson and the Automobile: Shifting Perspectives and a Moving Frame," *Sagetrieb* 14.3 (1995); Willard Spiegelman's "Just Looking," *Parnassus* 21.1–2 (1995); Michael Hennessy's "Louis Zukofsky, Charles Tomlinson, and the 'Objective Tradition,' " *Contemporary Literature* 37.2 (1996); and Swigg's "One World You Say?: Charles Tomlinson's Poetry," *Contemporary Literature* 41.2 (2000).

David Wagoner

Wagoner's *Traveling Light* (1999) contains new and collected poems. A subsequent volume, *The House of Song,* was published in 2002. He has also written many novels, including *Rock* (1958), and edited *Straw for the Fire: From the Notebooks of Theodore Roethke, 1943–63* (1972). Since 1966, he has edited the journal *Poetry Northwest.*

A book-length study is Ron McFarland's *The World of David Wagoner* (1997). Other critical works dealing with Wagoner are Sanford Pinsker's "On David Wagoner," *Salmagundi* 22–23 (1973); Robert Peters's "Thirteen Ways of Looking at David Wagoner's New Poems," *Western Humanities Review* 35.3 (1981); Sarah Mc-

Aulay's " 'Getting There' and Going Beyond: David Wagoner's Journey without Regret," *The Literary Review: An International Journal of Contemporary Writing* 28.1 (1984); Justin Askins's "Mild Delight," *Parnassus* 12.1 (1984); Pinsker's *Three Pacific Northwest Poets: William Stafford, Richard Hugo, and David Wagoner* (1987); and Laurie Ricou's "David Wagoner," *Updating the Literary West* (1997), ed. Max Westbrook.

Derek Walcott

Walcott's *Collected Poems, 1948–1984* was published in 1986. Subsequent volumes include *The Arkansas Testament* (1987), *Omeros* (1990), *The Bounty* (1997), and *Tiepolo's Hound* (2000). His many plays include *Ti-Jean and His Brothers* (1958), *Dream on Monkey Mountain* (1967), and *The Odyssey* (1993). *What the Twilight Says* (1998) offers a selection of Walcott's essays, and *Conversations with Derek Walcott* (1996), ed. William Baer, is a collection of interviews. In addition to Bruce King's biography, *Derek Walcott: A Caribbean Life* (2000), a useful introduction to Walcott's life and work is Paul Breslin's *Nobody's Nation* (2001).

An essential collection of primary and secondary materials is *Critical Perspectives on Derek Walcott* (1993), ed. Robert D. Hamner. Other collections of essays include *The Art of Derek Walcott* (1991), ed. Stewart Brown, and *Approaches to the Poetics of Derek Walcott* (2001), ed. José Luis Martínez-Dueñas Espejo and José María Pérez Fernández. *Verse* 11.2 (1994) and *South Atlantic Quarterly* 96.2 (1997) are special issues dedicated to Walcott. Other book-length studies include Edward Baugh's *Derek Walcott: Memory as Vision* (1978), Ned Thomas's *Derek Walcott: Poet of the Islands* (1980), Rei Terada's *Walcott's Poetry: American Mimicry* (1992), Hamner's *Derek Walcott* (1981, 1993) and *Epic of the Dispossessed: Derek Walcott's Omeros* (1997), John Thieme's *Derek Walcott* (1999), Paula Burnett's *Derek Walcott: Politics and Poetics* (2000), and Patricia Ismond's *Abandoning Dead Metaphors: The Caribbean Phase of Derek Walcott's Poetry* (2001). Other discussions of Walcott's poetry include Joseph Brodsky's "On Derek Walcott," *New York Review of Books* (10 November 1983); Rita Dove's " 'Either I'm Nobody, or I'm a Nation," *Parnassus* 14.1 (1987); June D. Bobb's *Beating a Restless Drum: The Poetics of Kamau Brathwaite and Derek Walcott* (1998); and Jahan Ramazani's *The Hybrid Muse* (2001). The standard bibliography is Irma E. Goldstraw's *Derek Walcott: An Annotated Bibliography of His Works* (1984). See also **Caribbean Poetry.**

Richard Wilbur

Wilbur's *New and Collected Poems* appeared in 1988. Subsequent volumes include *About Sylvia* (1996) and *Mayflies: New Poems and Transla-*

tions (2000). Wilbur has also published many translations, notably the works of Molière, including *The Misanthrope* (1955) and *Tartuffe* (1964). He has also written plays and children's literature and edited *Poe: Complete Poems* (1959). *Responses* (1976) selects prose from 1953 to 1976, and *The Catbird's Song* (1997) from 1963 to 1995. Interviews are collected in *Conversations with Richard Wilbur* (1990), ed. William Butts.

A collection of essays on Wilbur is *Richard Wilbur's Creation* (1983), ed. Wendy Salinger. Book-length studies include Donald Louis Hill's *Richard Wilbur* (1967), Paul F. Cummins's *Richard Wilbur: A Critical Essay* (1971), Bruce Michelson's *Wilbur's Poetry: Music in a Scattering Time* (1991), Rodney Stenning Edgecombe's *A Reader's Guide to the Poetry of Richard Wilbur* (1995), and John B. Hougen's *Ecstasy within Discipline: The Poetry of Richard Wilbur* (1995). Other works dealing with Wilbur include Randall Jarrell's *Poetry and the Age* (1953) and *The Third Book of Criticism* (1965); Frank Littler's "Wilbur's 'Love Calls Us to the Things of This World,' " *Explicator* 40.3 (1982); and Peter Harris's "Forty Years of Richard Wilbur: The Loving Work of an Equilibrist," *Virginia Quarterly Review* 66.3 (1990).

Charles Wright

Wright's volumes of poetry include *The Voyage* (1963), *6 Poems* (1965), *The Dream Animal* (1968), *Private Madrigals* (1969), *The Grave of the Right Hand* (1970), *The Venice Notebook* (1971), *Backwater* (1973), *Hard Freight* (1973), *Bloodlines* (1975), *China Trace* (1977), *Colophons* (1977), *Dead Color* (1980), *The Southern Cross* (1981), *Country Music: Selected Early Poems* (1982), *Four Poems of Departure* (1983), *The Other Side of the River* (1984), *Five Journals* (1986), *Zone Journals* (1988), *The World of the Ten Thousand Things* (1990), *Xionia* (1990), *Chickamauga* (1995), *Black Zodiac* (1997), *Appalachia* (1998), *Negative Blues: Selected Later Poems* (2000), and *A Short History of the Shadow* (2002). *Halflife* (1988) and *Quarter Notes* (1995) collect "improvisations and interviews." Wright has also published translations, including Eugenio Montale's *The Storm* (1978) and *Motels* (1981). Recent interviews include Willard Spiegelman's in *Literary Imagination* 2.1 (2000) and Ted Genoways's in *Southern Review* 36.2 (2000).

A collection of essays on Wright's work is *The Point Where All Things Meet: Essays on Charles Wright* (1995), ed. Tom Andrews. Other critical studies include Nance Van Winckel's "Charles Wright and the Landscape of the Lyric," *New England Review* 12.3 (1988); Helen Vendler's *The Music of What Happens* (1988); David Young's "The Blood Bees of Paradise," *Field* 44 (1991); Floyd Collins's "Metamorphosis within the Poetry of Charles Wright," *Gettysburg*

Review 4.3 (1991) and "A Poetry of Transcendence," *Gettysburg Review* 10.4 (1997); Edward Hirsch's "The Visionary Poetics of Philip Levine and Charles Wright," *Columbia History of American Poetry* (1993), ed. Jay Parini and Brett C. Millier; Peter Stitt's *Uncertainty and Plenitude* (1997); Ernest Suarez's "Charles Wright," *Five Points* 2.3 (1998); Lee Upton's *The Muse of Abandonment* (1998); David Garrison's "From Feeling to Form: Image as Translation in the Poetry of Charles Wright," *Midwest Quarterly* 4.1 (1999); and Bonnie Costello's "Charles Wright's Via Negativa: Language, Landscape, and the Idea of God," *Contemporary Literature* 36.2 (2000).

James Wright

Wright's *Above the River: The Complete Poems* was published in 1990. His *Collected Prose*, ed. Anne Wright, was published in 1983. Wright also translated German and Spanish poetry, including the work of Theodor Storm, Hermann Hesse, Georg Trakl, César Vallejo, and Pablo Neruda. Collections of letters include *With the Delicacy and Strength of Lace: Letters between Leslie Marmon Silko and James Wright* (1986), ed. Anne Wright, and *In Defense against This Exile: Letters to Wayne Burns* (1985), ed. John R. Doheny. Anne Wright also edited *A Secret Field: Selections from the Final Journals of James Wright* (1985).

Book-length studies of Wright include David C. Dougherty's *James Wright* (1987), Kevin Stein's *James Wright: The Poetry of a Grown Man* (1989), and Andrew Elkins's *The Poetry of James Wright* (1991). *The Pure Clear Word: Essays on the Poetry of James Wright* (1982), ed. Dave Smith, and *James Wright: The Heart of the Light* (1990), ed. Peter Stitt and Frank Graziano, contain many helpful essays. Other critical discussions of Wright's work can be found in Robert Hass's "James Wright," *Ironwood* 10

(1977); James E. B. Breslin's *From Modern to Contemporary* (1984); Henry Taylor's *Compulsory Figures* (1992); Nathan A. Scott Jr.'s *Visions of Presence in Modern American Poetry* (1993); and Nick Halpern's " 'Coming Back Here How Many Years Now': August Kleinzahler and James Wright's *Shall We Gather at the River*," *Contemporary Literature* 42.2 (2001). William H. Roberson's annotated bibliography was published in 1995. See also **Deep Image Poetry.**

Judith Wright

Wright's *Collected Poems, 1942–1985* was published in 1994. Collections of essays on writing, conservation, and other topics include *Born of the Conquerors* (1991) and *Going on Talking* (1992). She edited *Australian Poetry* (1948), *A Book of Australian Verse* (1956, 1968), and *New Land, New Language: An Anthology of Australian Verse* (1957). She wrote children's literature; a biographical novel, *Generations of Men* (1959, 1995); and works of history, including *The Cry for the Dead* (1981). Her study of the Australian writer Charles Harpur was published in 1963. *Half a Life* (1999) is an autobiography.

Collections of essays dealing with Wright include *Critical Essays on Judith Wright* (1968), ed. A. K. Thomson; *Judith Wright: An Appreciation* (1976), ed. Norman Simms; and *Considerations: New Essays on Kenneth Slessor, Judith Wright, and Douglas Stewart* (1977), ed. Brian Kiernan. Book-length studies include W. N. Scott's *Focus on Judith Wright* (1967); A. D. Hope's *Judith Wright* (1975); Jennifer Strauss's *Judith Wright* (1995); and four works by Shirley Walker: *The Poetry of Judith Wright: A Search for Unity* (1980), *Judith Wright* (1981), *Flame and Shadow: A Study of Judith Wright's Poetry* (1991), and *Vanishing Edens: Responses to Australia in the Works of Mary Gilmore, Judith Wright, and Dorothy Hewett* (1992). See also **Australian Poetry.**

Permissions Acknowledgments

Margaret Atwood: "Miss July Grows Older," "Manet's Olympia," and "Morning in the Burned House" from MORNING IN THE BURNED HOUSE by Margaret Atwood. Copyright © 1995 by Margaret Atwood. Used by permission of Houghton Mifflin Co. and McClelland & Stewart Ltd., The Canadian Publishers. All rights reserved. From "Circe / Mud Poems" from SELECTED POEMS 1965–1975 by Margaret Atwood. Copyright © 1976 by Margaret Atwood. Published in Canada in SELECTED POEMS 1966–1984. Copyright © 1990 Margaret Atwood. Reprinted by permission of Houghton Mifflin Co. and Oxford University Press Canada. All rights reserved. "This Is a Photograph of Me" from THE CIRCLE GAME, copyright © 1968, 1998 by Margaret Atwood. "You Fit into me" and "They Eat Out" from POWER POLITICS, copyright © 1971, 1996 by Margaret Atwood. Reprinted by permission of House of Anansi Press, Toronto. "Footnote to the Amnesty Report on Torture" is reprinted by permission of Margaret Atwood from the collection TWO HEADED POEMS, copyright © 1978 by Margaret Atwood, first published in Canada by Oxford University Press and in the US by Simon & Schuster.

Amiri Baraka: "A Poem for Black Hearts" from THE LEROI JONES / AMIRI BARAKA READER by Amiri Baraka. Copyright © 2000 by Amiri Baraka. Appears by permission of the publisher, Thunder's Mouth Press. From "The Myth of a 'Negro Literature' " by Amiri Baraka, reprinted by permission of Sterling Lord Literistic, Inc. Copyright © 1998 by Amiri Baraka. "An Agony. As Now.," "A Poem for Speculative Hipsters, "Legacy," "Wise I," "Y The Link Will Not Always Be 'Missing' #40," and "A New Reality Is Better Than a New Movie" are reprinted by permission of Sterling Lord Literistic, Inc. Copyright by Amiri Baraka. "In the Funk World" and "Monk's World" are reprinted by permission of Sterling Lord Literistic, Inc. Copyright © 1995 by Amiri Baraka.

Louise Bennett: From LOUISE BENNETT: SELECTED POEMS edited by Mervyn Morris. First published in 1982 by Sangster's Book Stores Ltd. (Kingston, Jamaica). Copyright © by the Ministry of Education. "Jamaica Language" from AUNT ROACHY SEH by Louise Bennett, edited by Mervyn Morris. First published in 1993 by Sangster's Book Stores Ltd. (Kingston, Jamaica). Copyright © by the Ministry of Education.

Charles Bernstein: "The Kiwi Bird in the Kiwi Tree" from ROUGH TRADES (Los Angeles: Sun & Moon, 1991), p. 11. Copyright © 1991 by Charles Bernstein. "Autonomy Is Jeopardy" and "Have Pen Will Travel" from REPUBLICS OF REALITY 1975–1995 (Los Angeles: Sun & Moon, 1991), pp. 307 and 359. Copyright © 2000 by Charles Bernstein. "Lives of the Toll Takers (excerpt) from DARK CITY (Los Angeles: Sun & Moon, 1994), pp. 22–26. Copyright © 1994 by Charles Bernstein. "Semblance" from CONTENT'S DREAM: ESSAYS 1975–1984 (Los Angeles: Sun & Moon Press, 1986), pp. 34–39. Reprinted with the permission of the publisher.

John Berryman: "Henry's Understanding" from DELUSIONS, ETC. by John Berryman. Copyright © 1972 by the Estate of John Berryman. Dream Songs # 1, #4, #14, #29, #37, #76, #145, #149, #153, #219, #312 and #384 from THE DREAM SONGS by John Berryman. Copyright © 1969 by John Berryman. Copyright renewed 1997 by Kate Donahue Berryman. Reprinted by permission of Farrar, Straus and Giroux, LLC.

Frank Bidart: "A Coin for Joe, with the Image of a Horse: c. 350–325 BC" and "If I Could Mourn Like a Morning Dove" from DESIRE by Frank Bidart. Copyright © 1997 by Frank Bidart. "Ellen West" from IN THE WESTERN NIGHT: COLLECTED POEMS 1965–1990 by Frank Bidart. Copyright © 1990 by Frank Bidart. Reprinted by permission of Farrar, Straus and Giroux, LLC. Excerpts from "Der Fall Ellen West," tr. by Werner M. Mendel and Joseph Lyons, from EXISTENCE, ed. by Rollo May et al. Reprinted by permission of Jason Aronson, Inc.

Elizabeth Bishop: "The Map," "The Man-Moth," "The Monument," "Roosters," "The Fish," "Over 2000 Illustrations and a Complete Concordance," "At the Fishhouses," "Brazil, January 1, 1502," "The Armadillo," "Sestina," "In the Waiting Room," "Crusoe in England," "One Art," "The End of March," "North Haven," and "Poem" from THE COMPLETE POEMS 1927–1979 by Elizabeth Bishop. Copyright © 1979, 1983 by Alice Helen Methfessel. Reprinted by permission of Farrar, Straus & Giroux, LLC.

Robert Bly: "A Week after Your Death" from EATING THE HONEY OF WORDS by Robert Bly. Copyright © 1999 by Robert Bly. "Johnson's Cabinet Watched by Ants" and "The Great Society" from THE LIGHT AROUND THE BODY by Robert Bly. Copyright © 1967 by Robert Bly. Copyright renewed 1995 by Robert Bly. Reprinted by permission of HarperCollins Publishers, Inc. "My Father's Wedding" and "Kneeling Down to Look into a Culvert" from THE MAN IN THE BLACK COAT TURNS by Robert Bly, copyright © 1981 by Robert Bly. Used by permission of Doubleday, a division of Random House, Inc.

MAN by Henri Cole, copyright © 1998 by Henri Cole. Used by permission of Alfred A. Knopf, a division of Random House, Inc.

Robert Creeley: "The Door," "Naughty Boy," "A Wicker Basket," "I Know a Man, " "For Love," and "Again" from THE COLLECTED POEMS OF ROBERT CREELEY 1945–1975. Copyright © 1983 the Regents of the University of California. Reprinted by permission of the Regents of the University of California and the University of California Press. "The Long Road" and "When it Comes" from LIFE AND DEATH, copyright © 1998 by Robert Creeley. "I Keep to Myself Such Measures . . ." and "Mother's Voice" from MIRRORS, copyright © 1983 by Robert Creeley. Reprinted by permission of New Directions Publishing Corp.

Donald Davie: From COLLECTED POEMS (1990) by Donald Davie. Used by permission of the publisher, Carcanet Press Ltd.

Eunice de Souza: "Sweet Sixteen," "De Souza Prabhu," "Conversation Piece," "Women in Dutch Painting," "For Rita's Daughter, Just Born," and "Landscape" by Eunice de Souza, copyright © by Eunice de Souza. Reprinted by permission of the author.

James Dickey: "The Hospital Window," "The Heaven of Animals," "Buckdancer's Choice," and "The Sheep Child" by James Dickey from JAMES DICKEY: THE SELECTED POEMS, copyright © 1998 by Matthew J. Bruccoli, Literary Executor of the Estate of James Dickey. Reprinted by permission of Wesleyan University Press.

Mark Doty: "A Green Crab's Shell" and "Homo Will Not Inherit" from ATLANTIS by Mark Doty. Copyright © 1995 by Mark Doty. "The Embrace" from SWEET MACHINE by Mark Doty. Copyright © 1998 by Mark Doty. Reprinted by permission of HarperCollins Publishers Inc.

Rita Dove: "Geometry," "The House Slave," "Adolescence II," "Agosta the Winged Man and Rasha the Black Dove," "Parsley," "The Event," "Dusting," "Weathering Out," "The Great Palaces of Versailles," and "Wingfoot Lake" from SELECTED POEMS by Rita Dove (Pantheon Books), copyright © 1993 by Rita Dove. Reprinted by permission of the author. "Claudette Colvin Goes to Work" from ON THE BUS WITH ROSA PARKS by Rita Dove. Copyright © 1999 by Rita Dove. "After Reading *Mickey in the Night Kitchen* for the Third Time before Bed" from GRACE NOTES by Rita Dove. Copyright © 1989 by Rita Dove. Used by permission of the author and W. W. Norton & Co., Inc.

Norman Dubie: "Elizabeth's War with the Christmas Bear," "The Funeral," and "Last Poem, Snow Tree" from THE MERCY SEAT: NEW AND COLLECTED POEMS 1967–2001. Copyright © 2001 by Norman Dubie. Reprinted with the permission of Copper Canyon Press, P.O. Box 271, Port Townsend, WA 98368–0271.

Carol Ann Duffy: "Warming Her Pearls" from SELLING MANHATTAN by Carol Ann Duffy (Anvil Press 1987). "The Good Teachers" from MEAN TIME by Carol Ann Duffy (Anvil Press 1993). Reprinted by permission of Anvil Press Poetry Ltd. "Medusa" and "Mrs. Lazarus" from THE WORLD'S WIFE by Carol Ann Duffy. Reprinted by permission of the publisher, Macmilllan Publishers Ltd. (London).

Alan Dugan: "For Euthanasia and Pain Killing Drugs" from POEMS SEVEN: NEW AND COMPLETE POETRY by Alan Dugan. "Love Song: I and Thou," "Fabrication of Ancestors," "On Being a Householder," and "Internal Migration: On Being on Tour" from NEW AND COLLECTED POEMS 1961–1983 by Alan Dugan. Reprinted by permission of Seven Stories Press.

Robert Duncan: From BENDING THE BOW, copyright © 1968 by Robert Duncan. From GROUND WORK: BEFORE THE WAR, copyright © 1984 by Robert Duncan. From SELECTED POEMS, copyright © 1950 by Robert Duncan. Reprinted by permission of New Directions Publishing Corp.

Louise Erdrich: "The Fence" from BAPTISM OF DESIRE by Louise Erdrich. Copyright © 1990 by Louise Erdrich. Reprinted by permission of HarperCollins Publishers, Inc. "Family Reunion," "Captivity," and "Windigo" from JACKLIGHT by Louise Erdrich, copyright © 1984 by Louise Erdrich. Reprinted by permission of Henry Holt and Co., LLC.

James Fenton: "Dead Soldiers," "A German Requiem," and "God, a Poem" from CHILDREN IN EXILE by James Fenton. Copyright © 1985 by James Fenton. "For Andrew Wood" from OUT OF DANGER by James Fenton. Copyright © 1994 by James Fenton. Reprinted by permission of Farrar, Straus & Giroux, LLC and Sterling Lord Literistic, Inc.

Lawrence Ferlinghetti: From A CONEY ISLAND OF THE MIND, copyright © 1958 by Lawrence Ferlinghetti. From THESE ARE MY RIVERS, copyright © 1981 by Lawrence Ferlinghetti. Reprinted by permission of New Directions Publishing Corp.

Carolyn Forché: "Taking Off My Clothes" from GATHERING THEIR TRIBES by Carolyn Forché. Copyright © 1976 by Carolyn Forché. All lines from "The Memory of Elena" from THE COUNTRY BETWEEN US by Carolyn Forché. All lines from "Reunion" from THE COUNTRY BETWEEN US by Carolyn Forché. Copyright © 1978 by Carolyn Forché. All lines from "The Colonel" from THE COUNTRY BETWEEN US by Carolyn Forché. Copyright © 1981 by Carolyn Forché. Originally appeared in *Women's International Resource Exchange*. Reprinted by permission of HarperCollins Publishers Inc.

Allen Ginsberg: "Howl," "A Supermarket in California," and "Sunflower Sutra" copyright © 1955 by Allen Ginsberg. "To Aunt Rose" copyright © 1958 by Allen Ginsberg. From "Kaddish," "America," "Last Night in Calcutta," and "Mugging" from COLLECTED POEMS 1947–1980 by Allen Ginsberg. Copyright © 1984 by Allen Ginsberg. "Sphincter" and "Personals Ad" from COSMOPOLITAN GREETINGS: POEMS 1986–1992 by Allen Ginsberg. Copyright © 1994 by Allen Ginsberg. "Notes Written on Finally Recording 'Howl' " from DELIBERATE PROSE: SELECTED ESSAYS 1952–1995 by Allen Ginsberg. Copyright © 1999 by the Allen Ginsberg Trust. All selections reprinted by permission of HarperCollins Publishers, Inc.

Louise Glück: "Vita Nova" and "Earthly Love" from VITA NOVA by Louise Glück. Copyright © 1999 by Louise Glück. "Penelope's Song" and "Quiet Evening" from MEADOWLANDS by Louise Glück. Copyright © 1996 by Louise Glück. "The Wild Iris" from THE WILD IRIS by Louise Glück. Copyright © 1993 by Louise Glück. "A Fantasy" from ARARAT by Louise Glück. Copyright © 1990 by Louise Glück. "The School Children," "The Drowned Children," "Descending Figure" 1, 2, 3 and "Mock Orange" from THE FIRST FOUR BOOKS OF POEMS by Louise Glück. Copyright © 1968, 1971, 1972, 1973, 1974, 1975, 1976, 1977, 1978, 1979, 1980, 1985, 1995 by Louise Glück. Reprinted by permission of HarperCollins Publishers, Inc.

Lorna Goodison: "Bam Chi Chi Lala" from TRAVELLING MERCIES by Lorna Goodison. Used by permission of McClelland & Stewart Ltd., The Canadian Publishers. "On Becoming a Mermaid," "Guinea Woman" and "Nanny" from I AM BECOMING MY MOTHER by Lorna Goodison, published by New Beacons Books Ltd. in 1986; reprinted by permission of the publisher. "Annie Pengelly" from TO US, ALL FLOWERS ARE ROSES: POEMS. Copyright © 1995 by Lorna Goodison. "Turn Thanks to Miss Mirry" and "Hungry Belly Kill Daley" from TURN THANKS: POEMS. Copyright © 1999 by Lorna Goodison. Used with permission of the poet and the University of Illinois Press.

Jorie Graham: "At Luca Signorelli's Resurrection of the Body," "Fission," "The Dream of the Unified Field," and "The Surface" from THE DREAM OF THE UNIFIED FIELD: POEMS 1974–1994. Copyright © 1995 by Jorie Graham. "The Swarm" from SWARM by Jorie Graham. Copyright © 1999 by Jorie Graham. Reprinted by permission of HarperCollins Publishers, Inc.

Thom Gunn: "The Problem" from BOSS CUPID by Thom Gunn. Copyright © 2000 by Thom Gunn. "A Blank," "The Missing," "Moly," "My Sad Captains," and "Still Life" from COLLECTED POEMS by Thom Gunn. Copyright © 1994 by Thom Gunn. Reprinted by permission of Farrar, Straus and Giroux, LLC and Faber and Faber Ltd.

Marilyn Hacker: "Rondeau after Taking a Transatlantic Telephone Call" and from "Taking Notice" from TAKING NOTICE by Marilyn Hacker. Copyright © 1976, 1978, 1979, 1980 by Marilyn Hacker. "Almost Aubade" from ASSUMPTIONS by Marilyn Hacker. Copyright © 1980 by Marilyn Hacker. Used by permission of Frances Collin, Literary Agent. "Year's End" from WINTER NUMBERS by Marilyn Hacker. Copyright © 1994 by Marilyn Hacker. "Twelfth Floor West" from SQUARES AND COURTYARDS by Marilyn Hacker. Copyright © 2000 by Marilyn Hacker. Used by permission of the author and W. W. Norton & Co., Inc.

Joy Harjo: "Mourning Song" and "Insomnia and the Seven Steps to Grace" from THE WOMAN WHO FELL FROM THE SKY by Joy Harjo. Copyright © 1994 by Joy Harjo. "The Path to the Milky Way Leads through Los Angeles" from A MAP TO THE NEXT WORLD: POEMS AND TALES by Joy Harjo. Copyright © 2000 by Joy Harjo. Used by permission of W. W. Norton & Co., Inc. "Deer Dancer" from IN MAD LOVE AND WAR, © 1990 by Joy Harjo. Reprinted by permission of Wesleyan University Press.

Michael S. Harper: "Double Elegy" from HEALING SONG FOR THE INNER EAR: POEMS. Copyright © 1985 by Michael S. Harper. "Nightmare Begins Responsibility" from NIGHTMARE BEGINS RESPONSIBILITY: POEMS. Copyright © 1975 by Michael S. Harper. "We Assume: On the Death of Our Son, Reuben Masai Harper," "Reuben, Reuben," and "Deathwatch" from SONGLINES IN MICHAELTREE: NEW AND COLLECTED POEMS. Copyright © 2000 by Michael S. Harper. "American History" and "Dear John, Dear Coltrane" from DEAR JOHN, DEAR COLTRANE: POEMS. Copyright © 1970 by Michael S. Harper. Used with permission of the poet and the University of Illinois Press.

Tony Harrison: "Heredity," "On Not Being Milton," "Book Ends," "Turns," "Marked with D.," "Timer," "Self Justification," "History Classes," and "V." from SELECTED POEMS by Tony Harrison (Penguin 1987). Copyright © by Tony Harrison. Reprinted by permission of Gordon Dickerson on behalf of the author.

Robert Hass: "Song" from FIELD GUIDE by Robert Hass. Copyright © 1973 by Robert Hass. Reprinted by permission of the publisher, Yale University Press. "Forty Something" and "Sonnet" from SUN UNDER WOOD by Robert Hass. "Sonnet" first appeared in *The New Yorker*. Copyright © 1996 by Robert Hass. "Meditation at Lagunitas" from PRAISE by Robert Hass. Copyright © 1979 by Robert Hass. "Privilege of Being" from HUMAN WISHES by Robert Hass. Copyright © 1989 by Robert Hass. Reprinted by permission of HarperCollins Publishers Inc.

Robert Hayden: "Middle Passage," copyright © 1962, 1966 by Robert Hayden, "Homage to the Empress of the Blues," copyright © 1966 by Robert Hayden; "Mourning Poem for the Queen of Sunday," copyright © 1966 by Robert Hayden; "Witch Doctor" and "Those Winter Sundays," copyright © 1966 by Robert Hayden; "Night, Death, Mississippi" copyright © 1962, 1966 by Robert Hayden; "Bone-Flower Elegy" and "Elegies for Paradise Valley," copyright © 1978 by Robert Hayden from COLLECTED POEMS OF ROBERT HAYDEN by Robert Hayden, ed. by Frederick Glaysher. Copyright © 1985 by Emma Hayden. Used by permission of Liveright Publishing Corporation.

Seamus Heaney: "At Toomebridge" and "Electric Light" from ELECTRIC LIGHT by Seamus Heaney. Copyright © 2001 by Seamus Heaney. "In Memoriam Francis Sedwidge" and "The Strand at Lough Beg" from FIELD WORK by Seamus Heaney. Copyright © 1987 by Seamus Heaney. "Digging," "The Tollund Man," "The Grauballe Man," "Casualty," "Terminus," "The Stone Verdict," "Clearances," from OPENED GROUND: SELECTED POEMS 1966–1996 by Seamus Heaney. Copyright © 1998 by Seamus Heaney. From STATION ISLAND by Seamus Heaney. Copyright © 1984 by Seamus Heaney. "Death of a Naturalist," "Requiem for the Croppies," "Bogland," "Bog Queen," "Punishment" from POEMS 1965–1975 by Seamus Heaney. Copyright © 1980 by Seamus Heaney. "Alphabets" from THE HAW LANTERN by Seamus Heaney. Copyright © 1987 by Seamus Heaney. "Feeling into Words" from PREOCCUPATIONS: SELECTED PROSE 1968–1978 by Seamus Heaney. Copyright © 1980 by Seamus Heaney. Reprinted by permission of Farrar, Straus and Giroux, LLC. and Faber and Faber Ltd.

Anthony Hecht: "A Hill," "Birdwatchers of America," " 'It Out-Herods Herod, Pray You, Avoid It' " and "The Deodand" from COLLECTED EARLIER POEMS by Anthony Hecht, copyright © 1990 by Anthony E. Hecht. Used by permission of Alfred A. Knopf, a division of Random House, Inc. "The Book of Yolek" from THE TRANSPARENT MAN by Anthony Hecht, copyright © 1990 by Anthony E. Hecht. Used by permission of Alfred A. Knopf, a division of Random House, Inc.

Lyn Hejinian: From OXOTA: A SHORT RUSSIAN NOVEL by Lyn Hejinian. Copyright © 1991 by Lyn Hejinian. Reprinted by permission of The Figures and the author. From "Happily" from THE LANGUAGE OF INQUIRY by Lyn Hejinian. Copyright © 2000 The Regents of the University of California. Reprinted by permission of the Regents of the University of California and the University of California Press. From MY LIFE (Los Angeles: Sun & Moon, 1987), pp. 7–13. Copyright © 1980, 1987 by Lyn Hejinian. Reprinted with the permission of the publisher. From THE CELL (Los

Angeles: Sun & Moon, 1992), pp. 7, 143–44. Copyright © 1992 by Lyn Hejinian. Reprinted with the permission of the publisher.

Geoffrey Hill: "CXXI" from THE TRIUMPH OF LOVE by Geoffrey Hill. Copyright © 1998 by Geoffrey Hill. Reprinted by permission of Houghton Mifflin Co. All rights reserved. "Funeral Music" #s 6 and #8, "Mercian Hymns" I, II, IV, V, VI, VII, X, XI, XVI, XXV, XXIX, XXX, "The Mystery of Charles Péguy" #1, "In Memory of Jane Fraser," "Two Formal Elegies," "Ovid in the Third Reich," and "September Song" from NEW AND COLLECTED POEMS, 1952–1994 by Geoffrey Hill. Published in Great Britain in GEOFFREY HILL: COLLECTED POEMS. Reprinted by permission of Houghton Mifflin Co. and Penguin Books Ltd. All rights reserved. "To the High Court of Parliament" from CANAAN by Geoffrey Hill. Copyright © 1996 by Geoffrey Hill. Reprinted by permission of Houghton Mifflin Co. and Penguin Books Ltd. All rights reserved.

John Hollander: "By Heart" by John Hollander was first published in *The New Yorker*. Reprinted by permission of the author. "Under Cancer," "Back to Town," and "Adam's Task" from SELECTED POETRY by John Hollander, copyright © 1993 by John Hollander. "Variations on a Fragment by Trumbull Stickney" from TESSERAE AND OTHER POEMS by John Hollander, copyright © 1993 by John Hollander. Used by permission of Alfred A. Knopf, a division of Random House, Inc.

Richard Howard: "My Last Hustler" from TRAPPINGS by Richard Howard. Copyright © 1999 by Richard Howard. Reprinted by permission of Turtle Point Press. " 'Man Who Beat Up Homosexuals Reported to Have AIDS Virus' " from LIKE MOST REVELATIONS by Richard Howard, copyright © 1994 by Richard Howard. Used by permission of Pantheon Books, a division of Random House, Inc., and the author.

Susan Howe: From "Thorow" in SINGULARITIES by Susan Howe. Copyright © 1990 by Susan Howe and reprinted by permission of Wesleyan University Press. "Rückenfigur" from PIERCE-ARROW, copyright © 1999 by Susan Howe. Reprinted by permission of New Directions Publishing Corp.

Ted Hughes: From NEW AND SELECTED POEMS and from MOORTOWN by Ted Hughes. Reprinted by permission of the publisher Faber and Faber Ltd.

Richard Hugo: "White Center" and "The Lady in Kicking Horse Reservoir," copyright © 1973 by Richard Hugo. "Degrees of Gray in Phillipsburg," copyright © 1973 by Richard Hugo from MAKING CERTAIN IT GOES ON: COLLECTED POEMS OF RICHARD HUGO by Richard Hugo. Copyright © 1984 by The Estate of Richard Hugo. Used by permission of W. W. Norton & Co., Inc.

Randall Jarrell: "The Death of the Ball Turret Gunner," "Eighth Air Force," "Next Day," "90 North" and "Thinking of the Lost World" from THE COMPLETE POEMS by Randall Jarrell. Copyright © 1969, renewed 1997 by Mary von S. Jarrell. Reprinted by permission of Farrar, Straus & Giroux, LLC.

June Jordan: "Notes on the Peanut" from PASSION by June Jordan is reprinted by permission of the June M. Jordan Trust. "July 4, 1964: For Buck" and "DeLiza Spend the Day in the City" from LIVING ROOM by June Jordan. Copyright © 1985 by June Jordan. "The Reception" from NAMING OUR DESTINY: NEW AND SELECTED POEMS by June Jordan. Copyright © 1989 by June Jordan. Appears by permission of the publisher, Thunder's Mouth Press.

Donald Justice: "After a Phrase Abandoned by Wallace Stevens" from A DONALD JUSTICE READER, copyright © 1991 by Donald Justice, reprinted with permission of University Press of New England. All other poems from NEW AND SELECTED POEMS by Donald Justice, copyright © 1995 by Donald Justice. Used by permission of Alfred A. Knopf, a division of Random House, Inc.

Galway Kinnell: "First Song" from WHAT A KINGDOM IT WAS by Galway Kinnell. Copyright © 1960, renewed 1988 by Galway Kinnell. "Sheffield Ghazal 4: Driving West" from IMPERFECT THIRST by Galway Kinnell. Copyright © 1994 by Galway Kinnell. Reprinted by permission of Houghton Mifflin Co. All rights reserved. "After Making Love We Hear Footsteps" from MORTAL ACTS, MORTAL WORDS by Galway Kinnell. Copyright © 1980 by Galway Kinnell. "On the Oregon Coast" from THE PAST by Galway Kinnell. Copyright © 1985 by Galway Kinnell. Reprinted by permission of Houghton Mifflin Co. All rights reserved.

Index